Alcohol and Temperance in Modern History

An International Encyclopedia

Advisory Board

Alcohol and Temperance in Modern History

An International Encyclopedia

Volume 1: A–L

Jack S. Blocker, Jr., David M. Fahey, and Ian R. Tyrrell, Editors

ABC CLIO

Santa Barbara, California   Denver, Colorado   Oxford, England

Library of Congress Cataloging-in-Publication Data
Blocker, Jack S.
Alcohol and temperance in modern history : an international encyclopedia / Jack S. Blocker, Jr., David M. Fahey, and Ian R. Tyrrell.
p. cm.
Includes bibliographical references and index.
ISBN 1-57607-833-7 (hardcover : alk. paper) — ISBN 1-57607-834-5 (e-book)
1. Alcohol—Encyclopedias. 2. Drinking of alcoholic beverages—Encyclopedias. 3. Alcoholism—Encyclopedias. 4. Temperance—Encyclopedias. 5. Alcoholic beverage industry—Encyclopedias. I. Fahey, David M. II. Tyrrell, Ian R. II. Title.
HV5017.B56 2003
362.292'03—dc21
8679
06 05 04 03 0 9 8 7 6 5 4 3 2 1

This book is also available on the World Wide Web as an e-book. Visit abc-clio.com for details.

ABC-CLIO, Inc.
130 Cremona Drive, P.O. Box 1911
Santa Barbara, California 93116-1911

This book is printed on acid-free paper ♾.

Manufactured in the United States of America

Contents

Alcohol and Temperance in Modern History

Volume I

D

E

F

G

H

Volume II

Contributors and Their Entries

Kathryn A. Abbott
Western Kentucky University
Handsome Lake (Ga-nya-di-yoh) (ca. 1735–1815)
Native Americans: Drinking Patterns and Temperance Reform

Ernest Abel
Wayne State University
Fetal Alcohol Syndrome (FAS)

Daryl Adair
University of Canberra
Loyal Orange Institution (Ireland and Britain)
St. Patrick's Day

Jo Aitken
Monash University
Home Protection

Allaman Allamani
Centro Alcologico Integrato, Firenze, Italy
Italy

Charles Ambler
University of Texas, El Paso
Africa, Southern
Shebeens (Southern Africa)
South African Breweries (SAB)

Lisa Andersen
University of Chicago
Hunt, Mary Hannah Hanchett (1830–1906)
Intercollegiate Prohibition Association (IPA)
Temperance Commission of the Federal Council of Churches

Raymond Gale Anderson
Brewery History Society, UK
Allied Breweries
Allsopps
Beer
Beer Orders (United Kingdom)
Carlsberg
Courage Brewery
Institute and Guild of Brewing
Maltsters' Association of Great Britain (MAGB)
Watneys
Whitbread

Nigel Ansell-Roberts
Cheshire, UK
Working-Class Social Clubs (United Kingdom)

Thomas H. Appleton, Jr.
Eastern Kentucky University
Gough, John Bartholomew (1817–1886)
Haggard, Howard Wilcox (1891–1959)

Andrew Barr
London, UK
Licensing Hours (United Kingdom)
Toasts

Margaret Barrow
University of Manchester Institute of Science and Technology
Band of Hope
British Women's Temperance Association (BWTA)
Carlile, Ann Jane (1775–1864)
Carlisle, Countess of (Rosalind Howard) (1845–1921)
Lucas, Margaret Bright (1818–1890)
National British Women's Temperance Association (NBWTA)
Nonconformists (United Kingdom)
Parker, Margaret Eleanor (1828–1896)
Slack, Agnes Elizabeth (1857–1946)
Somerset, Isabella Caroline (Lady Henry Somerset) (1851–1921)
Women's Total Abstinence Union (WTAU)

Jim Baumohl
Bryn Mawr College
Treatment Institutions
Washingtonians

Cynthia Belaskie-Simeon
Nipissing University
Bible Wine
Lewis, Elizabeth Ann (1849–1924)
Ottawa Home for Friendless Women

Brian Robert Bennison
Corbridge, UK
Scottish & Newcastle Breweries Limited
Working Men's Clubs Breweries (United Kingdom)

Anna Blainey
East Melbourne, Australia
Australia
Woman's Christian Temperance Union (WCTU) (Australia)

Jack S. Blocker, Jr.
Huron University College
University of Western Ontario
Alcohol and Temperance History Group (ATHG)
Prohibition Party (United States)
State Prohibition (United States)

I. M. B. Bongers
University of Tilburg
The Netherlands

Iris Borowy
University of Rostock
League of Nations Health Organisation (LNHO)

Thomas Brennan
U.S. Naval Academy
France, Production and Consumption of Alcohol in

Asa (Lord) Briggs
Ringmer, East Sussex, UK
Victoria Wine Company

Sally Brown
United Church of Christ, Palo Alto, CA
Mann, Marty (1904–1980)

Jana Brubaker
Northern Illinois University
Foster, Judith Ellen Horton (1840–1910)
Stevens, Lillian Marion Norton Ames (1844–1914)

Dominic Bryan
Queen's University, Belfast
Loyal Orange Institution (Ireland and Britain)

John C. Burnham
Ohio State University
Clark, Norman Harold (1925–)

Stephen Byers
Milwaukee, WI
Home, as Drinking Site
Home Brewing
Saloons and Taverns (United States)

Shawn Cafferky
University of Victoria
Alcohol, Consumption of, per Capita (Canada)
Licensing (Canada)
Saloons, Taverns, Pubs, and Beerhouses (Canada)

Robert A. Campbell
Capilano College
Provincial Liquor Boards (Canada)
Provincial Stores (Canada)

Antoine Capet
University of Rouen
Churchill, Winston (1874–1965)

Catherine Carstairs
University of British Columbia
Mothers Against Drunk Driving (MADD)
Sporting Events, as Drinking Sites
Students Against Destructive Decisions (SADD)

Malcolm Chase
University of Leeds
Chartism

Yuet Wah Cheung
The Chinese University of Hong Kong
China

Mary A. Conley
Marquette University
Robinson, Sarah (1834–1921)
Weston, Agnes (1840–1918)

Sharon Anne Cook
University of Ottawa
Woman's Christian Temperance Union (WCTU) (Dominion of Canada)
Wright, Bertha (1863–1949)
Youmans, Letitia (1827–1896)

Matthew Copping
University of Kent
Arsenic-in-Beer Scare
Pure Beer Movement (United Kingdom)

Michael Cronin
De Monfort University
Loyal Orange Institution (Ireland and Britain)
St. Patrick's Day

Cynthia Curran
St. John's University
Impey, Catherine (1847–1923)
Labour Party (United Kingdom)

Bertrand Dargelos
Sorbonne University
Cabaret (France)
Ligue Nationale contre l'Alcoolisme
Pernod-Ricard Group

Andrew Davison
English Heritage
Campaign for Real Ale (CAMRA)

Michael Dawson
Portland State University
Gusfield, Joseph R. (1923–)
Presidential Commission on Drunk Driving
Sociological Theories of Drinking and Temperance

Theresa W. Devasahayam
National University of Singapore
Islam as Cultural Influence

Kristin Doern
Bath Spa University College
Salvation Army

Ian Donnachie
The Open University in Scotland
Brewers' Association of Scotland (BAS)
Brewers' Company
Brewers' Society (BS)
McEwan, William (1827–1913)
Tennent, Hugh (1863–1890)

Laurie Meijer Drees
Malaspina University College
First Nations, the Indian Act, and Prohibition (Canada)

Stephen C. Due
Geelong, Australia
Rechabite Friendly Society

Irmgard Eisenbach-Stangl
Institute for Addiction Research, Vienna, Austria
Austria

Ruth C. Engs
Indiana University
Committee of Fifty
Fisher, Irving (1867–1947)
Reformed Men's Clubs
Scientific Temperance Federation
Stoddard, Cora Frances (1872–1936)

Sidsel Eriksen
University of Copenhagen
Denmark
Sweden

C. Wyatt Evans
Drew University
Congressional Temperance Society (CTS)
Methodist Board of Temperance, Prohibition, and Public Morals (MBPT)

David M. Fahey
Miami University
Allied Brewery Traders' Association (ABTA)
British Temperance League (BTL)
Buckingham, James Silk (1787–1855)
Burns, (James) Dawson (1828–1909)
Caine, William Sproston (1842–1903)
Central Sunday Closing Association
Chamberlain, Joseph (1836–1914)
Conservative Party (United Kingdom)
Gladstone, William Ewart (1809–1898)
Good Templars (IOGT)
Harcourt, Sir William (1827–1904)
Horsley, Sir Victor (1857–1916)
Liberal Party (United Kingdom)
National Temperance League (NTL)
National Trade Defence Association (NTDA)
Pope, Samuel (1826–1901)
Rae, John Turner (1851–1929)
Raper, James Hayes (1820–1897)
Rutherford, Derek (1939–)
Standard Encyclopedia of the Alcohol Problem
Stuart, Wilson (1873–1934)
Temperance Standard Bearers
Whittaker, Thomas (1813–1899)
Winskill, Peter Turner (1834–1912)

Luciano R. A. Figueiredo
Universidad Federal Fluminense
Colonization, European, and Drinking Behavior among Indigenous Peoples (Portuguese America)

Kieran Foley
Essex University
Licensed Victuallers' National Defence League (LVNDL)
Licensed Victuallers' Protection Society of London
Publicans (England)

John W. Frick
University of Virginia
Drama, Representations of Temperance in

Nancy G. Garner
Wright State University
Loyal Temperance Legion (LTL)

H. F. L. Garretsen
University of Tilburg
The Netherlands

Geoffrey J. Giles
University of Florida
Germany (translator)

Kevin Grace
University of Cincinnati
Juke Joints
Sunday, William Ashley (1862–1935)

John Greenaway
University of East Anglia
Astor, Lord Waldorf (1879–1952)
Carter, Henry (1874–1951)
Central Policy Review Staff (CPRS) Report (United Kingdom)
D'Abernon, Lord (Sir Edgar Vincent) (1857–1941)
Drunk Driving Laws (United Kingdom)
Erroll and Clayson Committees (United Kingdom)
Harrison, Brian (1937–)
Jones, Leif (1862–1939)
Lawson, Sir Wilfrid (1829–1906)
National Temperance Federation (NTF)
Rowntree, Joseph (1836–1925)
United Kingdom Alliance (UKA)
Whittaker, Thomas (1813–1899)

James Gregory
University of Southampton
Barker, Thomas Halliday (1818–1889)
Hills, Arnold Frank (1857–1927)
Hoyle, William (1832–1886)
Lees, Frederic Richard (1815–1897)
Vegetarianism and the Anti-Tobacco Movement (United Kingdom)

David W. Gutzke
Southwest Missouri State University
Beer Orders (United Kingdom)
Gothenburg Schemes/Disinterested Management
Pubs and Beerhouses (United Kingdom)

W. Scott Haine
University of Maryland University College
Drinking Establishments (France)

Richard F. Hamm
State University of New York at Albany
Federal Regulation of Alcohol before 1920 (United States)

Robert L. Hampel
University of Delaware
Fifteen Gallon Law
Massachusetts Society for the Suppression of Intemperance (MSSI)

Kevin Hardman
Bury, UK
Temperance Bars in East Lancashire

Sara Harrington
Rutgers University
Art, Representations of Drinking in

Jennifer Harrison
College of William & Mary
American Temperance Society (ATS)
Edwards, Justin (1787–1853)

Dwight B. Heath
Brown University
Caribbean
Central America
South America

Robert A. Hohner
University of Western Ontario
Cannon, James, Jr. (1864–1944)
Cherrington, Ernest Hurst (1877–1950)

Shane Homan
University of Newcastle, Australia
Drinking Sites and Culture (Australia)
Liquor Licensing (Australia)

Andrew Horrall
National Archives of Canada
Music Halls

John P. Hundley
Chicago, IL
Leavitt, Mary Greenleaf Clement (1830–1912)
New Year's Eve
Roadhouses

David J. Ingle
Framingham, MA
English Songs, Representations of Drinking in (1600–1900)

James D. Ivy
San Antonio, TX
Bryan, William Jennings (1860–1925)
Local Option
Nation, Carry Amelia Moore (1846–1911)
Sheppard, John Morris (1875–1941)
Sinclair, Upton (1878–1962)
Sons of Temperance
United States Brewers' Association (USBA)
Wittenmeyer, Annie Turner (1827–1900)
Woman's Christian Temperance Union (WCTU) (United States)

Deborah James
University of Glamorgan
Wales

Janice E. Jones
University of Wisconsin–Milwaukee
Drunk Driving Laws (United States)

Bradley Kadel
University of Wisconsin–Madison
Shebeens

Thomas Karlsson
STAKES, Helsinki, Finland
Belgium
Greece
Portugal

K. Austin Kerr
Ohio State University
Anti-Saloon League of America (ASLA)
Baker, Purley Albert (1858–1924)
Non-Partisan Woman's Christian Temperance Union
Russell, Howard Hyde (1855–1946)
Wheeler, Wayne Bidwell (1869–1927)

Diane Kirkby
La Trobe University
Barmaids (Australia)

Susan M. Kling
San Mateo, CA
Pubs and Beerhouses (United Kingdom)

William Kostlevy
Asbury Theological Seminary
Crafts, Wilbur Fisk (1850–1922)
International Reform Federation, Inc.

Ivan A. Krasnov
The Eco Chronicle Magazine, St. Petersburg
Alcohol, Consumption of (Russia)

Kathryn Kueny
Lawrence University
Islamic World

Ernest Kurtz
University of Michigan
Alcoholics Anonymous (AA)
Smith, Robert Holbrook (1879–1950)
Wilson, William Griffith (1895–1971)

David E. Kyvig
Northern Illinois University
Association Against the Prohibition Amendment (AAPA)
Raskob, John Jakob (1879–1950)
Sabin, Pauline Morton (1887–1955)
Stayton, William H. (1861–1942)
Voluntary Committee of Lawyers (VCL)
Women's Organization for National Prohibition Reform (WONPR)

Yves Laberge
Institut Québécois des Hautes Études Internationales
Film, Representations of Drinking and Temperance in
Music, Popular, Representations of Drinking in

William Lahey
Dalhousie Law School
Canada Temperance Act
Provincial Prohibition (Canada)
Provincial Regulation (Canada)

Isaac Land
Texas A & M University
Trotter, Thomas (1760–1832)

Dorothy A. Lander
St. Francis Xavier University
Appendix B: Internet Resources
Art as Temperance Activism
Cyclopædia of Temperance and Prohibition

Michael Patrick Leach
Deakins University
Lane, William (1861–1917)

Milton James Lewis
University of Sydney
Inebriate Institutions (Australia)
Physicians and Alcohol (Australia)

Lori Loeb
University of Toronto
Patent Medicines

Charlotte J. Macdonald
University of Wellington
New Zealand
Sheppard, Catherine ("Kate") Wilson (1847–1934)

Elizabeth Malcolm
University of Melbourne
Ireland
Mathew, Father Theobald (1790–1856)

Dan Malleck
Brock University
Addiction Research Foundation of Ontario (ARF)
American Association for the Study and Cure of Inebriety (AASCI)
Bronfman Family
Busch Family
Crothers, Thomas Davison (1842–1918)
Federal Prohibition (Canada)
Kerr, Norman Shanks (1834–1899)
Laurier, Sir Wilfrid (1841–1919)
Royal Commission on the Liquor Traffic (Canada)
Seagram
Society for the Study of Addiction
Tequila
Whiskies

Padma Manian
San Jose City College
Barmaids (England)

Mac Marshall
University of Iowa
Anthropological Theories of Drinking and Temperance
Kava
Pacific Islands

Scott C. Martin
Bowling Green State University
Daughters of Temperance
Martha Washington Societies
Moral Suasion

Irene Elizabeth Maver
University of Glasgow
Dunlop, John (1789–1868)
Scotland

James R. McIntosh
Lehigh University
Alcoholism
Gin Craze

Matthew McKean
Queen's University, Kingston, Ontario, Canada
Christian Socialism
Evangelical Temperance (United Kingdom)
Hayler, Guy (1850–1943)
World Prohibition Federation

Jon Miller
University of Akron
Literature, Representations of Drinking in
Literature, Representations of Temperance in

Wilbur R. Miller
State University of New York at Stony Brook
Moonshine

Stephanie Mitchell
Oxford University
Comité Nacional de Lucha contra el Alcoholismo
Dirección Anti-Alcohólica
Franco, Ing. *Luis G. (fl. 1930s)*
Portes Gil, Emilio (1891–1978)

Amy Mittelman
Amherst, MA
Anheuser-Busch
Bureau of Alcohol, Tobacco, and Firearms (BATF)
Cirrhosis of the Liver
Labor in the U.S. Liquor Industry
Lauer, Frederick (1810–1883)
Microbreweries (United States, United Kingdom, and Canada)
Taxation of Liquor (United States)

Kenneth Owen (Lord) Morgan
The Queen's College, Oxford
Lloyd George, David (1863–1945)

Jacek Moskalewicz
Institute of Psychiatry and Neurology, Warsaw, Poland
Poland

Willliam H. Mulligan, Jr.
Murray State University
Coors, Adolph, Brewing Company
Du Pont, Pierre Samuel (1870–1954)
Miller Brewing Company
Olympia Brewing Company
Pabst Brewing Company
Stroh Brewing Company

Kenneth M. Murchison
Louisiana State University
Prohibition Bureau

Guillermina Natera
Instituto Nacional de Psiquiatría Ramón de la Fuente Muñoz
Mexico

Katherine Nelson
American University
Knights of Father Mathew

Caryn E. Neumann
Ohio State University
Cider
Hiram Walker
Knights of Labor
Murphy, Francis (1836–1907)

Jan Noel
University of Toronto
Chiniquy, Father Charles Paschal Telesphore (1809–1899)
Dougall, John (1808–1886)
Mailloux, Father Alexis (1801–1877)

Thierry Nootens
Université de Québec à Montréal
Interdiction and Curatorship

Sturla Nordlund
Norwegian Institute for Alcohol and Drug Research
Norway

Fusako Ogata
Tezukayama University
Microbreweries (Japan)

Jennifer Oldstone-Moore
Wittenberg University
Buddhism
Confucianism
Daoism

Gerald Wayne Olsen
Nipissing University
Christian Socialism
Church of England Temperance Society (CETS)
Church of England Temperance Society (CETS) Inebriate Homes
Church of England Temperance Society (CETS) Police Court Mission
Close, Francis (1797–1882)
Davidson, Randall (1848–1930)
Ellison, Henry (1813–1899)
Evangelical Temperance (United Kingdom)
Gore, Charles (1853–1932)
Green, T. H. (1836–1882)
Maguire, Robert (1826–1890)
Moule, Handley Carr Glyn (1841–1920)
Temple, Frederick (1831–1902)
Wightman, Julia Bainbrigge (1817–1890)
Wilberforce, Basil (1841–1916) and Wilberforce, Ernest (1840–1907)

Stephanie Olsen
McGill University
Church of England Temperance Society (CETS) Police Court Mission
Close, Francis (1797–1882)
Cruikshank, George (1792–1878)
Gore, Charles (1853–1932)
Green, T. H. (1836–1882)
Maguire, Robert (1826–1890)
Moule, Handley Carr Glyn (1841–1920)
Wilberforce, Basil (1841–1916) and Wilberforce, Ernest (1840–1907)

Lisa L. Ossian
Southwestern Community College
Anderson, William Hamilton (1874–1959)
Brookhart, Smith Wildman (1869–1944)
Jones, Wesley Livsey (1863–1932)

Esa Österberg
STAKES, Helsinki, Finland
Belgium
Finland
Greece
Portugal

Joshua Paddison
University of California Los Angeles
Dashaway Association
Marsh, John (1788–1868)
National Temperance Society and Publication House (NTSPH)

Penny B. Page
Rutgers University
Jellinek, Elvin Morton (1890–1963)
Journal of Studies on Alcohol
Keller, Mark (1907–1995)
Rutgers Center of Alcohol Studies
Yale Center of Alcohol Studies

Elaine Parsons
Duquesne University
Civil Damage Laws
Personal Liberty League

Kenneth Pearl
Queensborough Community College
British Medical Temperance Association (BMTA)
Malins, Joseph (1844–1926)
Strength of Britain

Thomas R. Pegram
Loyola College in Maryland
Democratic Party (United States)
Hoover, Herbert Clark (1874–1964)
National Prohibition (United States)
Republican Party (United States)
Smith, Alfred Emanuel (1873–1944)

Glen C. Phillips
University of Edinburgh
Carling, Sir John (1828–1911)
Carling Brewery
Corby Distilleries Limited
Gooderham and Worts Distillery
Labatt Brewing Company Limited
Mackenzie, Alexander (1822–1892)
Molson Incorporated
O'Keefe Brewery
Shea's Winnipeg Brewery Limited
Wiser Distillery

Rod Phillips
Carleton University
Absinthe
Gallo
Gin
Wine

Sylvain B. Poosson
Hampton University
Chafetz, Morris Edward (1924–)

Patricia E. Prestwich
University of Alberta
France, Temperance in

Paul E. Priester
University of Wisconsin–Milwaukee
Rand Report
Server Responsibility Laws (United States)
Synanon

John F. Quinn
Salve Regina University
Manning, Henry Edward (1808–1892)
Nugent, James (1822–1905)

Dr. Rajshekhar
Jawaharlal Nehru University
Gandhi, Mohandas Karamchand (1869–1947)

Jessy Randall
Colorado College
Drinking Songs (United States)
"Girl" Drinks

John David Rausch, Jr.
West Texas A & M University
Foster's
State Stores (United States)

Jonathan Reinarz
University of Birmingham
Advertising (United Kingdom)
Labor and the Brewing Industry (United Kingdom)

Frank Robson
Edinburgh, Scotland
Distillers Company Limited (DCL)
Malt Distillers' Association of Scotland (MDA)

Paul Roman
University of Georgia
Bacon, Selden Daskam (1909–1992)
Employee Assistance Programs (EAPs)
National Institute on Alcohol Abuse and Alcoholism (NIAAA)

William J. Rorabaugh
University of Washington
Alcohol, Consumption of, by Indices (United States)
Alcohol, Consumption of, per Capita (United States)

Derek Rutherford
Institute of Alcohol Studies, London, UK
Davies, Arthur C. (1909–1992)
Hall, W. Glenvil (1887–1962)
Hayler, Mark (1887–1986)
Heath, H. Cecil (1898–1972)
Hudson, James H. (1881–1962)
Institute of Alcohol Studies (IAS)
IOGT International
Temperance Council of the Christian Churches (TCCC)
United Kingdom Temperance Alliance (UKTA)
Wilson, George Bailey (1863–1952)
Wilson Black, Robert (1871–1951)
Winterton, Ernest (1873–1942) and Winterton, Wilfrid (1885–1976)

Margaret Sankey
Auburn University
Astor, Lady Nancy Wicher Langhorne (1879–1964)
Oglethorpe, James Edward (1696–1785)
Tenskwatawa (1775–1826)

Carol A. Scally-Grigas
Washington State University
Spain

Jeff R. Shutts
Georgetown University and University of British Columbia
Soft Drinks

Robert F. Skilnik
Plainfield, IL
Heileman, G., Brewing Company
Schlitz, Joseph, Brewing Company

Reginald Smart
Centre for Addiction and Mental Health, Toronto
Psychological Theories of Drinking

Frederick H. Smith
Western Michigan University
Archaeological Approaches to Drinking and Temperance
Rum

Mark C. Smith
University of Texas at Austin
Kolb, Lawrence (1881–1972)
Turner, Joseph Edward (1822–1889)

Stephen R. Smith
Wittenberg University
Japan
Sake

Megan Smitley
University of Glasgow
Blaikie, Margaret Catherine (1823–1915)
Honeyman, Tom (1858–1934)
Scottish Christian Union (SCU)
Scottish Temperance League (STL)
Scrymgeour, Edwin (1866–1947)
White, Mary (1827–1903)

George E. Snow
Shippensburg University of Pennsylvania
International Congresses on Alcoholism
Russia, Imperial, Temperance in
Vodka

T. Jason Soderstrum
Iowa State University
Beecher, Lyman (1775–1863)
Boole, Ella Alexander (1858–1952)
Delavan, Edward Cornelius (1793–1871)
Dow, Neal (1804–1897)
Gordon, Anna Adams (1853–1931)
Hobson, Richmond Pearson (1870–1937)
Johnson, William Eugene "Pussyfoot" (1862–1945)
McBride, Francis Scott (1872–1955)
McCarthy, Raymond Gerald (1901–1964)
Rush, Benjamin (1746–1813)
Tilley, Samuel Leonard (1818–1896)

Mark G. Spencer
St. Catharines, Ontario
Whiskey Rebellion

Hasso Spode
Freie Universität Berlin
Berlin, Germany
Forel, Auguste (1848–1931) (translated by Jennifer Hosek)
Germany (translated by Geoffrey Giles)
World Health Organization (WHO) (translated by Jennifer Hosek)

Margaret A. Spratt
California University of Pennsylvania
Young Women's Christian Association (YWCA)

Martin Stack
Rockhurst University
Interbrew

Peter Stanley
Australian War Memorial
Army Temperance Association

Michelle J. Stecker
University of Toledo
Women's Temperance Crusade

Jon Sterngass
Saratoga Springs, NY
Maine Law
Resorts

Veronica Strong-Boag
University of British Columbia
McClung, Nellie Letitia (1873–1951)

Grazyna Swiatkiewicz
Institute of Psychiatry and Neurology, Warsaw, Poland
Poland

Kenneth Thomas
University of the West of England
Courage Family
Simonds Family

Paul Townend
University of North Carolina
Guinness Brewery
Haughton, James (1795–1873)
Pioneer Total Abstinence Association of the Sacred Heart

Kate Transchel
California State University
Soviet Union and Russia since 1917, Alcohol and Temperance in

Aidan Turner-Bishop
University of Central Lancashire
Livesey, Joseph (1794–1884)

Alex Tyrrell
La Trobe University
Preston Teetotal Monument

Ian R. Tyrrell
University of New South Wales
India
Willard, Frances Elizabeth Caroline (1839–1898)
World League Against Alcoholism (WLAA)
World's Woman's Christian Temperance Union (WWCTU)

Mariana Valverde
University of Toronto
Degeneration Theories

L. A. M. van de Goor
University of Tilburg
The Netherlands

Renato P. Venâncio
Universidade Federal de Ouro Prieto
Colonization, European, and Drinking Behavior among Indigenous Peoples (Portuguese America)

Cheryl Krasnick Warsh
Malaspina University College
Advertising Regulations (Canada)
Dominion Alliance for the Total Suppression of the Liquor Traffic
Homewood Retreat
Keeley, Leslie Enraught (1832–1900)
Keeley Institutes
Lett, Stephen (1847–1905)
Medicine, Alcohol as
Spence, Francis Stephens (1850–1917)

R. B. Weir
University of York
Cumming, Sir Ronald Stuart (1900–1982)
Hayman, Sir (Cecil George) Graham (1893–1966)
Ross, Sir Henry (James) (1893–1973)

William White
Chestnut Health Systems, Bloomington, IL
Alcoholic Mutual Aid Groups (United States)
Alcoholics Anonymous (AA)
Christopher D. Smithers Foundation
Hazelden Foundation
Hughes, Harold Everett (1922–1996)
National Council on Alcoholism and Drug Dependence (NCADD)
Treatment Institutions

Justin Willis
University of Durham
Africa, Central
Banana Wine
Brussels Act and Conventions, 1890–1912
Carlisle, Countess of (Rosalind Howard) (1845–1921)
Indigenous Peoples and the Liquor Traffic Controversy
Palm Wine
Processed Sugar Ferments
St. Germain en Laye Convention, 1919

Catharine Anne Wilson
University of Guelph
Bees

Richard G. Wilson
University of East Anglia
Greene, Edward (1815–1891)
Guinness, Edward Cecil, First Earl of Iveagh (1847–1927)

Clare Wright
University of Melbourne
Women Publicans (Australia)

Rumi Yasutake
Konan University
Woman's Christian Temperance Union (WCTU) (Japan)

Timothy Yates
University of California, Davis
Blue Ribbon Movement
Research Council on Problems of Alcohol (RCPA)

Preface

Drinking, drinking problems, and social responses to drinking and drinking problems are significant contemporary concerns as well as being deeply rooted in the past. In the twenty-first century, producers of alcoholic beverages continue to manufacture and sell their products, governments regulate them, drinkers consume them, and an array of public and private organizations attempt to understand and cope with the results. Historical perspective is useful, indeed necessary, to comprehend how the modern configurations of human behavior associated with beverage alcohol came about, but reference works capable of providing such perspective are few. No other reference work attempts to present the history of beverage alcohol as a commercial product, cultural icon, behavioral solvent, object of medicosociological research, and political issue. *Alcohol and Temperance in Modern History* has been designed to fulfill this multifaceted purpose.

The editors define alcohol use broadly to include: the production of alcoholic beverages, whether carried out by individuals or families in their homes or by major corporations; cultural perceptions of alcohol, as reflected in music, literature, drama, and film; sites and occasions of drinking, from the least to the most formal; advertising and marketing; patterns of consumption; and diseases associated with alcohol use. The rubric "temperance" covers attempts to define and to resolve problems attributed to alcohol use, which include not only formally organized temperance movements, but also scientific research, government commissions, treatment institutions, and legal frameworks.

We bring to this work the premise that neither the history of alcohol nor the history of temperance can be properly understood in isolation from the other. In the modern world, alcohol production, marketing, sale, and consumption all take place within frameworks created and maintained by governments. Although commonly concerned with the revenue that can be generated by alcohol taxation, governments also act in accordance with attitudes toward alcohol that have been shaped by many years of temperance reform. Temperance activism has taken on a multitude of guises, including voluntaristic self-help societies, political movements, and scientific research. Although cultural, religious, economic, and other factors have motivated temperance reformers, so too has alcohol use. Thus are the histories of alcohol use and temperance reform intertwined and conjoined.

If the histories of drinking and temperance within a particular society are interrelated, so too are the histories of temperance across societies. Globalization is nothing new for temperance reform, which has been an international movement for well over a hundred years. First through various temperance societies that crossed national boundaries in the English-speaking world, then through the World's Woman's Christian Temperance Union (WWCTU) after 1884, and then in a series of alcoholism congresses in the early twentieth century, temperance reform became international. Governments paid attention to the forms of alcohol control tried by other governments, and, beginning in the late nineteenth century, governments agreed to cooperate in placing some controls on the liquor trade internationally. If temperance is international, temperance history must be as well.

Another reason for a cross-national focus in both alcohol and temperance history is the potential scope for comparison. As will be seen in the articles in this encyclopedia on various nations, each society has its own pattern of alcohol use. How those patterns arose and evolved is a fascinating question, but it is one that can usefully be framed only with an awareness of modes of alcohol use in other societies, whether they are similar or divergent. The same goes for the forms of social response to alcohol use, which our contributors reveal to have varied widely as well. Only through comparison can the uniqueness of a given society's models of alcohol use and its social response be established, and only through comparison can similarities among societies be identified. Both tasks form a necessary prelude to explanation.

The preceding considerations have led us to construct this project as an international examination of alcohol and temperance. Within this broad scope, we have attempted to give equal attention to social elites—who are involved in every aspect, from liquor production, advertising, marketing, sale, and consumption, through formulation of government policy, to temperance movements—and to "the rest of us"—who are involved as workers, sellers, drinkers, victims, reformers, and researchers. Our articles follow the course of multinational corporations engaged in worldwide mergers and sales campaigns, but also portray the mundane drinking sites where drinker and bottle meet. We describe the theories through which social scientists attempt to grasp the contours and causes of drinking, and, as well, depict the institutions in which therapists try to ameliorate the human damage that excessive consumption can produce. In sum, we have sought to provide material for a social history of alcohol, one that can encompass not only variation and change among societies, but also differences within them.

The social history of alcohol also incorporates more than stories of drink and temperance. Both drinking and its social response are shaped by the context in which they appear. The story of alcoholic beverages both is influenced by and influences more commonly studied stories such as "modernization," industrialization, urbanization, and imperialism. Religious thought and practice, gender roles and relations, and communications media too influence drinking and temperance, and are in turn affected by alcohol use and temperance reform. At every point, the story of drink and sobriety rubs shoulders with innumerable other stories.

In its chronological reach, this encyclopedia spans the period from ancient times to the present, but it focuses on the period from the eighteenth century to the present. This choice reflects both the pace of historical change and the state of modern scholarship. Certainly, both drinking and efforts to control it were features of the premodern world, but both seem to have changed most rapidly since the coming of distilled spirits and the adoption of modern methods of production and distribution. Furthermore, the recent history of drinking and its social response are most directly relevant to understanding contemporary societies' experiences with alcohol.

Alcohol and Temperance in Modern History contains three types of articles, distinguished by breadth of focus. First, *international* articles deal with beverages in use across many societies, the international liquor trade, temperance movements and leaders whose work spanned a significant number of societies, major disease and treatment concepts and institutions, the principal theories that guide research, and the rare attempts at international regulation of the liquor trade. Second, *national/regional* articles focus on particular societies or world regions distinguished by geographic or cultural commonality. These identify favorite national beverages; national alcohol producers and sellers or retail systems; national or regional drinking patterns according to sex, age, social class, race, and ethnicity; major temperance organizations and leaders; principal alcohol research organizations; and patterns of regulation. Third, *specific* articles focus on each of the categories listed above in the English-speaking world (the United Kingdom, United States, Canada, Australia, and New Zealand), where alcohol and temperance historical scholarship is most fully developed. A guide to the encyclopedia's contents according to geographic area is included to assist those interested in pursuing place-specific information.

Alcohol and Temperance in Modern History refracts the findings of scholarship on alcohol and its social response in societies around the world. Where gaps in its coverage appear (and there are some), we have tried to ensure that these are the result of lacunae in scholarship, rather than lack of effort on our part in seeking out qualified authors. By presenting the results of current scholarship, the encyclopedia demonstrates the variety of forms taken both by patterns of alcohol use and regulation around the world, and by the temperance impulse, which is usually and mistakenly identified with its U.S. variant. The work is conceived as both a reflection of existing scholarship and a stimulus to future research.

Acknowledgments

Jack S. Blocker wishes to thank research assistants Matthew McKean, David Blocker, Katie Norton, and Kirsteen Ritchie for their diligent and efficient help with this project. He also thanks Patricia Fulton, Dean of Arts and Social Science, Huron University College, for authorizing secretarial support, and Maryanne Harkins and Brenda Sefeldas for providing it with care and skill.

David M. Fahey wishes to thank his wife, Mary Fuller, and his daughter, Juliana Fuller, for their help and support.

Ian R. Tyrrell wishes to thank all of the people who have so generously contributed their ideas in the form of articles for this work, and also Jack and David for advice and support at critical times in the process. I especially thank my colleague Max Harcourt for his assistance in research on the India entry.

Entries by Geographic Area

Asia

Buddhism
China
Confucianism
Daoism
Gandhi, Mohandas Karamchand (1869–1947)
India
Japan
Microbreweries (Japan)
Sake
Woman's Christian Temperance Union (WCTU) (Japan)

Australia and New Zealand

Australia
Barmaids (Australia)
Drinking Sites and Culture (Australia)
Inebriate Institutions (Australia)
Lane, William (1861–1917)
Liquor Licensing (Australia)
New Zealand
Physicians and Alcohol (Australia)
Sheppard, Catherine ("Kate") Wilson (1847–1934)
Woman's Christian Temperance Union (WCTU) (Australia)
Women Publicans (Australia)

British Isles

Advertising (United Kingdom)
Alcohol, Consumption of (United Kingdom)
Allied Breweries
Allied Brewery Traders' Association (ABTA)
Allsopps
Army Temperance Association
Arsenic-in-Beer Scare
Astor, Lady Nancy Wicher Langhorne (1879–1964)
Astor, Lord Waldorf (1879–1952)
Band of Hope
Barker, Thomas Halliday (1818–1889)
Barmaids (England)
Bass
Beer Orders (United Kingdom)
Bible Wine
Blaikie, Margaret Catherine (1823–1915)
Brewers' Association of Scotland (BAS)
Brewers' Company
Brewers' Society (BS)
British Medical Temperance Association (BMTA)
British Temperance League (BTL)
British Women's Temperance Association (BWTA)
Buckingham, James Silk (1787–1855)
Burns, (James) Dawson (1828–1909)
Caine, William Sproston (1842–1903)
Campaign for Real Ale (CAMRA)
Carlile, Ann Jane (1775–1864)
Carlisle, Countess of (Rosalind Howard) (1845–1921)
Carlisle System
Carter, Henry (1874–1951)
Central Policy Review Staff (CPRS) Report (United Kingdom)
Central Sunday Closing Association
Chamberlain, Joseph (1836–1914)
Chartism
Christian Socialism
Church of England Temperance Society (CETS)
Church of England Temperance Society (CETS) Inebriate Homes
Church of England Temperance Society (CETS) Police Court Mission
Churchill, Winston (1874–1965)
Close, Francis (1797–1882)
Conservative Party (United Kingdom)
Courage Brewery
Courage Family
Cruikshank, George (1792–1878)
Cumming, Sir Ronald Stuart (1900–1982)
D'Abernon, Lord (Sir Edgar Vincent) (1857–1941)
Davidson, Randall (1848–1930)
Davies, Arthur C. (1909–1992)
Distillers Company Limited (DCL)
Drunk Driving Laws (United Kingdom)
Dunlop, John (1789–1868)
Ellison, Henry (1813–1899)
English Songs, Representations of Drinking in (1600–1900)
Erroll and Clayson Committees (United Kingdom)
Evangelical Temperance (United Kingdom)
Gin Craze
Gladstone, William Ewart (1809–1898)
Gore, Charles (1853–1932)
Gothenburg Schemes/Disinterested Management
Green, T. H. (1836–1882)

Canada

Europe

International

Hiram Walker
Home Protection
Indigenous Peoples and the Liquor Traffic Controversy
Interbrew
International Congresses on Alcoholism
International Reform Federation, Inc.
IOGT International
Islam as Cultural Influence
Journal of Studies on Alcohol
Kava
Keeley, Leslie Enraught (1832–1900)
Keeley Institutes
League of Nations Health Organisation (LNHO)
Leavitt, Mary Greenleaf Clement (1830–1912)
Literature, Representations of Drinking in
Literature, Representations of Temperance in
Loyal Temperance Legion (LTL)
Malins, Joseph (1844–1926)
Medicine, Alcohol as
Moonshine
Murphy, Francis (1836–1907)
Music, Popular, Representations of Drinking in
New Year's Eve
Palm Wine
Patent Medicines
Pernod-Ricard Group
Processed Sugar Ferments
Psychological Theories of Drinking
Rum
Sake
Salvation Army
Seagram
Sociological Theories of Drinking and Temperance
Soft Drinks
Somerset, Isabella Caroline (Lady Henry Somerset) (1851–1921)
South African Breweries (SAB)
Sporting Events, as Drinking Sites
St. Germain en Laye Convention, 1919
Standard Encyclopedia of the Alcohol Problem
Tequila
Toasts
Treatment Institutions
Vodka
Whiskies
Willard, Frances Elizabeth Caroline (1839–1898)
Wine
World Health Organization (WHO)
World League Against Alcoholism (WLAA)
World Prohibition Federation
World's Woman's Christian Temperance Union (WWCTU)
Young Women's Christian Association (YWCA)

Mexico
Comité Nacional de Lucha contra el Alcoholismo
Dirección Anti-Alcohólica
Franco, *Ing.* Luis G. (fl. 1930s)
Mexico
Portes Gil, Emilio (1891–1978)

Regions and Groupings
Africa, Central
Africa, Southern
Caribbean
Central America
Islamic World
Pacific Islands
South America

United States of America
Alcohol, Consumption of, by Indices (United States)
Alcohol, Consumption of, per Capita (United States)
Alcoholic Mutual Aid Groups (United States)
American Association for the Study and Cure of Inebriety (AASCI)
American Temperance Society (ATS)
Anderson, William Hamilton (1874–1959)
Anheuser-Busch
Anti-Saloon League of America (ASLA)
Association Against the Prohibition Amendment (AAPA)
Bacon, Selden Daskam (1909–1992)
Baker, Purley Albert (1858–1924)
Beecher, Lyman (1775–1863)
Boole, Ella Alexander (1858–1952)
Brookhart, Smith Wildman (1869–1944)
Bryan, William Jennings (1860–1925)
Bureau of Alcohol, Tobacco, and Firearms (BATF)
Busch Family
Cannon, James, Jr. (1864–1944)
Chafetz, Morris Edward (1924–)
Cherrington, Ernest Hurst (1877–1950)
Christopher D. Smithers Foundation
Civil Damage Laws
Clark, Norman Harold (1925–)
Committee of Fifty
Congressional Temperance Society (CTS)
Coors, Adolph, Brewing Company
Dashaway Association
Daughters of Temperance
Delavan, Edward Cornelius (1793–1871)
Democratic Party (United States)
Dow, Neal (1804–1897)
Drinking Songs (United States)
Drunk Driving Laws (United States)
Du Pont, Pierre Samuel (1870–1954)

Woman's Christian Temperance Union (WCTU) (United States)
Women's Organization for National Prohibition Reform (WONPR)
Women's Temperance Crusade
Yale Center of Alcohol Studies

Other Countries and Regions

Colonization, European, and Drinking Behavior among Indigenous Peoples (Portuguese America)
Shebeens (Southern Africa)

Chronology

1494–1495 The earliest evidence of Scotch whiskey appears in the Scottish Exchequer Roll.

1516 Bavaria adopts the Reinheitsgebot to guarantee the purity of beer: Only barley, hops, and water could be used in brewing. Later, yeast is added.

1644 The Scottish Parliament imposes the first excise tax on spirits.

1661 The English impose the first tax on Irish whiskey, establishing two other notable Irish institutions: the Excise Office in Dublin and illicit distillation across the country.

1703 The English government concludes a treaty according to which Portuguese wines are to be admitted into England on more favorable terms than French and German wines.

1720s Inexpensive brown beer brewed in London acquires name of porter.

1721 Controversy begins about gin drinking by working-class Londoners. Controversy ends with legislation in 1751.

1756 A prohibition of production of spirits in Denmark is introduced by the country's leaders in order to protect the Danish merchants' monopoly on spirits imports.

1784 Philadelphia physician, signer of the Declaration of Independence, and Revolutionary War surgeon-general Benjamin Rush publishes *An Inquiry into the Effects of Spirituous Liquors on the Human Body and the Mind,* a classic text of American temperance.

1785 English immigrant John Molson buys the Montreal brewery he joined as a partner three years before. In 1786, he will produce his first batch of beer, which will set his company on the road to national, and eventually international, prominence.

1790–1791 British East India Company (EIC) introduces excise on alcohol in areas under British control. Supposedly intended to suppress illegal distilleries and restrict consumption, this policy bore heavily upon poor, low-caste, and tribal communities who had hitherto distilled their own alcohol.

1791 The U.S. Congress levies an excise tax on domestic whiskey distillers.

1794 Western farmers revolt against the distilling tax, but the Whiskey Rebellion ends when federal troops are sent in against the rebels.

1799 The Seneca, Handsome Lake, experiences a vision, which leads him to advocate a reform program, including temperance, for the Iroquois people.

1802 The U.S. Congress passes the first of many laws seeking to prohibit the sale of liquor to Native Americans.

1813 Massachusetts Society for the Suppression of Intemperance (MSSI) is founded in Boston. The society campaigns against use of ardent spirits among church members and in the wider community.

1819–1826 The first Russian alcohol monopoly is introduced, producing, intially, a decline in alcohol consumption.

1823 The British Parliament passes the Act to Eliminate Illicit Distilling, which mandates significant changes in the structure of and procedures for taxation of the whiskey industry.

1826 Reformers found the American Society for Promotion of Temperance, with Justin Edwards as corresponding secretary.

1828 Douglas Jerrold, an English journalist, reformer, and dramatist, writes *Fifteen Years of a*

Drunkard's Life, the prototype temperance drama.

1829 First antispirits temperance societies appear in Britain (in the west of Scotland).

1830 British Parliament adopts the Beer Act, a free-trade approach to retail licensing.

1831 Aeneas Coffey modifies the patent or column still, invented during the 1820s by Robert Stein, allowing distillation to produce a lighter form of Scotch whiskey.

1831–1835 Temperance reformers in the United States adopt teetotal pledge.

1832 Reformers organize what reputedly is the first temperance society in Australia, at Hobart, Tasmania.

1833 Joseph Livesey and the Seven Men of Preston organize the first teetotal society in England. Members are from the working class.

Teetotalers organize a national society, British Association for the Promotion of Temperance. Its headquarters are in northern England.

American reformers found the Congressional Temperance Society.

1835 English teetotalers organize a fraternal insurance society, the Independent Order of Rechabites, Salford Unity, mostly working-class in membership.

mid-1800s Mild and pale ales displace porter as the beer preferred in England. The Irish remain loyal to porter into the mid-1900s.

1836 Reformers found the short-lived United States Temperance Society.

1837 Reformers organize the American Temperance Union as a replacement for the American Temperance Society (ATS) and the United States Temperance Society. The new society requires a teetotal pledge. The Reverend John Marsh edits the *Journal of the American Temperance Union* in support of prohibition. The organization continues until 1865.

1838 The Massachusetts legislature restricts the sale of spirits more severely than any state had ever done: No licensed inn holder, retailer, or grocer could sell distilled liquor in quantities under fifteen gallons. The law will be repealed in 1840.

late 1830s Father Theobald Mathew leads a temperance campaign among Irish Catholics. It fades in the mid-1840s.

1839 English teetotalers organize the New British and Foreign Temperance Society and British and Foreign Society for the Suppression of Intemperance. They disagree about the nature of the teetotal pledge, whether teetotalers must promise not to serve other people alcoholic drink.

1840 Reformed drunkards form the Washingtonian Total Abstinence Society in Baltimore on a teetotal-pledge basis. The movement spreads nationwide in the 1840s.

1840–1850 Local-option no-license campaign spreads in Massachusetts.

1842 Washingtonians in New York City found the Sons of Temperance, spreading nationwide by 1845. By the end of the decade, it becomes one of the largest temperance societies in the United States and will play a key role in launching the movement for prohibition.

English moral suasion teetotalers organize the National Temperance Society, with headquarters in London.

A Bavarian-born brewer produces a straw-colored lager in Pilsen (now in the Czech Republic).

1843 Thomas Carling sets up a brewery in London, Ontario, that will become the foundation for a major Canadian and eventually international brewing company.

1844 The classic American temperance drama *The Drunkard* is first presented, in Boston, Massachusetts.

Priests from the Silesian town of Piekary Slaskie form a temperance society, which immediately attracts tens of thousands of adherents. As the movement spreads across Poland, alcohol consumption drops sharply.

Middle-class teetotalers organize the Scottish Temperance League.

1845 The partnership Gooderham and Worts (G&W) is formed, based on a distillery founded in Toronto during the previous decade by English immigrants.

1847 The Rechabites temperance organization arrives in Australia.

Irish immigrant John Kinder Labatt and a partner buy a brewery in London, Ontario, Canada, and begin an expansion program that will make it first a regional, then a national brewer.

Advocates of temperance societies for children start the Band of Hope movement in the United Kingdom.

1848 Father Charles Chiniquy begins a temperance crusade that over the following three years will elicit temperance pledges from 400,000 people in Canada East (Quebec).

Women in New York organize the Daughters of Temperance.

1849–1851 Father Theobald Mathew intermittently visits the United States. As a result, Father Mathew Societies spread in the United States and Canada.

1850 Milwaukee saloonkeeper and brewer Georg Krug hires Joseph Schlitz as his bookkeeper. Six years later, Schlitz will take over the business after Krug's death and begin a process of expansion that, under the leadership of Schlitz's successor as bookkeeper, August Uihlein, and Uihlein's brothers, will make the Joseph Schlitz Brewing Company a major national, then international brewer.

1851 As a result of a campaign led by Portland mayor Neal Dow, Maine enacts the first statewide prohibition law. By 1855, prohibition laws modeled on Maine's are enacted in twelve states and territories.

1852 Teetotalers in New York State organize the Independent Order of Good Templars (IOGT), a fraternal temperance society that accepts women as well as men into membership. The IOGT soon commits itself to prohibition. In the early twenty-first century, IOGT stands for the International Organization of Good Templars.

Female temperance reformers (including Susan B. Anthony and Amelia Bloomer) organize the Women's New York Temperance Society.

1853 Advocates of prohibition organize the United Kingdom Alliance (UKA). Shortly afterward, the alliance shifts from national prohibition to local-option prohibition by referendum.

The British Parliament establishes statutory Sunday closing for Scotland. Parliament repeals this legislation in 1976.

1854 The British Association for Promotion of Temperance changes its name to the British Temperance League (BTL).

1855 German immigrant Frederick J. Miller purchases the Plank Road Brewery in Milwaukee, which, as the Miller Brewing Company, he will turn into a major national brewing company.

1855–1856 American states repeal Maine Laws for prohibition.

1856 English moral suasion teetotalers dissolve the National Temperance Society and another London organization, and create the National Temperance League (NTL).

1858 Julia Wightman, wife of an Anglican vicar, publishes *Haste to the Rescue,* an influential book calling for teetotalism.

Tasmania introduces Sunday closing; other Australian colonies follow by 1880s.

1859 Teetotalers in Preston in northern England erect Temperance Monument.

Asbjørn Kloster, a Quaker, founds the first teetotaler association in Norway, thus beginning one of the greatest grassroots movements in the country's history.

1860 The British Parliament passes the Spirits Act, which for the first time recognizes the practice of blending whiskies.

Eberhard Anheuser invests in the Saint Louis brewery Hammer and Urban, which he will later turn into Anheuser-Busch.

1862 The U.S. Congress launches the modern system of alcohol taxation with a set of excise taxes and license fees justified as a means of funding the Civil War. The taxes, however, will not be repealed at the war's end.

The United States Brewers' Association is founded in response to the imposition of federal taxes on beer.

1863 Captain Frederick Pabst enters a partnership with Milwaukee brewer Philip Best. Two years later, he will buy out Best and begin turning the company into a major shipping brewer, marketing its product across the United States.

Phylloxera vastatrix begins to devastate French vineyards. In 1876, phylloxera-resistant American vines are grafted with French vines.

Imperial Russia introduces excise system.

1865 The Victoria Wine Company opens its first retail store in London.

The city of Gothenburg (Göteborg) in Sweden creates a monopoly for noncommercial sale of aquavit (spirits) for on-premises consumption. This experiment attracts international attention, especially in the 1890s and early 1900s.

1866 English Sabbatarians organize the Central Association for Stopping the Sale of Intoxicating Liquors.

1868 Good Templars claim a half million members in North America.

Working-class teetotalers organize the first English lodge of the Good Templar fraternal temperance society. Joseph Malins heads the Grand Lodge of England from its organization in 1870 until his retirement in 1914.

1869 Public houses and beerhouses reach their largest number in England and Wales at 120,000.

Prohibitionist activists meet in Chicago to launch the Prohibition Party.

1870 The American Association for the Study and Cure of Inebriety (AASCI) is founded.

The American Association for the Cure of Inebriates is founded.

1871 France's first antialcoholism organization, *Société française contre l'abus des boissons alcooliques,* is founded in Paris by the *Académie de médecine.*

The local merchants in Kristiansand join forces and create the first cooperative spirits trade in Norway. In succeeding years, the idea will spread to many other Norwegian communities.

The Liberal government proposes an ambitious licensing bill for England and Wales, which, among other things, would have reduced the number of licensed premises and allowed ratepayers a voice in deciding how many pubs there would be in their local district. The bill, however, is not enacted.

1872 The British Parliament adopts a more limited Liberal-sponsored licensing bill that restricts hours of sale in England and Wales.

English publicans organize the Licensed Victuallers' National Defence League, with its strength outside metropolitan London.

1873 Anglicans organize the Church of England Temperance Society (CETS). In a compromise, the society includes both a section for abstainers, mostly working-class, and for moderate drinkers, mostly middle-class. The CETS replaces an earlier Anglican teetotal society.

Adolph Coors and Jacob Schuler establish the Adolph Coors Brewing Company in Golden, Colorado.

Irish immigrant Francis Murphy founds the Gospel Temperance movement in the United States.

Women in Fredonia, New York, march on the saloons of their town, beginning the Women's Temperance Crusade of 1873–1874. Before it ends, tens of thousands of women in towns and cities across the Northeast and Midwest will join in a range of actions aimed at reducing drinking.

First teaching and research institution for brewing opens in Germany.

1874 Delegates from sixteen states meet in Cleveland, Ohio, to found the Woman's Christian Temperance Union (WCTU), electing Annie Wittenmeyer as the organization's first president.

1875 The Yokohama Japanese Temperance Society is founded, the first temperance group in Japan for Japanese.

1876 Per capita beer consumption reaches its peak in the United Kingdom at 42.2 imperial gallons (50.68 U.S. gallons).

Women teetotalers, mostly English Nonconformists, organize the British Women's Temperance Association (BWTA).

Women teetotalers organize the Scottish Christian Union (SCU).

Teetotal physicians organize the British Medical Temperance Association (BMTA).

The Dominion of Canada enacts the Indian Act, prohibiting sale of intoxicants to Native people.

President U. S. Grant appoints Green B. Raum as commissioner of Internal Revenue. Raum launches an all-out campaign against southern moonshining. The campaign is largely successful.

First International Women's Temperance Convention takes place in Philadelphia in conjunction with United States Centennial Exhibition.

1877 Six Lowland distilleries merge to form the Distillers Company Limited (DCL), which quickly becomes one of the largest distillers of Scotch whiskey.

Joseph Chamberlain introduces a parliamentary bill for a Gothenburg experiment in Birmingham. He hopes that noncommercial management of the retail drink trade will reduce heavy drinking in big cities.

Gospel temperance (also known as the Blue Ribbon Army) comes from the United States to England.

1878 The Dominion of Canada adopts the Canada Temperance Act (also known as the Scott Act), creating the framework for local option.

French novelist Émile Zola's naturalistic novel of slum life, *L'Assommoir,* is adapted for the stage with a temperance message added.

The British Parliament enacts legislation for Sunday closing in Ireland except in the largest cities. This legislation is extended to Belfast in 1921 after Irish partition. Sunday closing will be repealed in the Irish republic in 1960 and in Northern Ireland in 1987.

The American brewer Anheuser-Busch introduces refrigerated railway cars for transporting beer.

1879 Dr. Leslie E. Keeley establishes a treatment institute for alcoholism in Dwight, Illinois, which during the 1890s will become the model for more than 100 franchised treatment centers in 6 countries and will make Keeley a millionaire.

Frances Elizabeth Caroline Willard is elected as president of the Woman's Christian Temperance Union (WCTU) and proceeds to reshape it into a dynamic, wide-ranging national women's organization, whose multifaceted activism will revitalize the American temperance and prohibition movements.

1880s "Running ales" (related to bitter) become the preference of English beer drinkers.

1881 Hiram Walker distillery introduces a new brand of whiskey called Three Star Club, which, after subsequent name changes to "Club" and "Canada Club," in 1893 will become the hugely successful brand Canadian Club.

Parliament enacts legislation for Sunday closing in Wales. Parliament changes mandatory Sunday closing in 1961 to allow local option. In

1996, the last Sunday "dry" district votes to allow sale of alcoholic beverages.

New Zealand Licensing Act introduces the requirement that anyone selling alcohol have a license and imposes a strict limit on the number of licenses; a restriction on selling hours, places, and conditions; and a close regulation of the trade.

1882 Richard Booth and William Noble introduce the Blue Ribbon temperance reform movement to Australia.

1883 The British House of Commons passes a resolution in favor of the principle of local option.

England's "advanced" temperance reformers organize the National Temperance Federation.

Emil Christian Hansen of the Carlsberg brewery in Denmark develops a pure yeast culture for brewing.

Joseph E. Seagram buys a distillery in Waterloo, Ontario, Canada, which under his leadership (and after 1928, that of the Bronfman family) will become a major national and international distiller.

Reformers in Finland organize the Friends of Temperance.

1884 British physicians and moral reformers found the Society for the Study and Cure of Inebriety to study addiction and influence legislation. Changing its name after World War II to the Society for the Study of Addiction, it will last into the twenty-first century.

New York City brewery workers organize the first brewery workers' union, a local of the Knights of Labor.

Frances Elizabeth Caroline Willard and other leaders of the American Woman's Christian Temperance Union (WCTU) organize the World's Woman's Christian Temperance Union (WWCTU), which will become one of the most significant international women's organizations of the late nineteenth and early twentieth centuries, and a forerunner of many transnational organizations interested in social justice, peace, and global governance as well as the narrower concerns of prohibition and Protestant morality.

World's Woman's Christian Temperance Union (WWCTU) round-the-world missionary Mary Greenleaf Clement Leavitt departs San Francisco bound for Honolulu to begin what will be nearly a decade of continuous travel, proselytizing for the WWCTU and its message. She will organize eighty-six international WCTU chapters and twenty-one men's temperance societies in over forty countries.

1885 Frances Elizabeth Caroline Willard starts the polyglot petition of women against alcohol and other drugs. Over the next ten years, 7 million "signatures" are obtained worldwide (many of them by "attestation" through the leaders of large religious and temperance organizations).

Mary Greenleaf Clement Leavitt founds first Woman's Christian Temperance Union (WCTU) in New Zealand.

The first international congress against alcoholism, called the Antwerp Meeting against the Abuse of Alcoholic Beverages, is held in Belgium.

late 1800s English breweries reach the peak of their prosperity. Major breweries incorporate as limited companies and purchase licensed property to create "tied houses."

1886 Coca-Cola is introduced as a temperance drink.

World's Woman's Christian Temperance Union (WWTCU) missionary Mary Greenleaf Clement Leavitt arrives in Japan to found Japanese branches of the organization.

Brewery workers from five U.S. cities meet to launch the National Union of United Brewery Workmen. As one of the nation's first industrial unions, it aims to enlist all brewery workers regardless of skill level.

Reformers organize the New Zealand Alliance for the Suppression and Prohibition of the Liquor Traffic (NZA) and begin an influential paper, *The Prohibitionist.*

1887 William Manning Foster and Ralph Rose Foster, two brothers from New York, establish the Foster's Brewing Company in Melbourne, Australia's first commercial lager brewery.

1888 The Conservative government of the United Kingdom introduces a bill that would have provided a statutory right to compensation for licensed premises denied license renewal despite not having violated any rules. Conservatives introduce a similar bill in 1890. Neither bill becomes law.

English brewers organize the National Trade Defence Fund (renamed National Trade Defence Association in 1890).

Guinness, the Irish brewing firm, incorporates as a limited company, selling shares to the public.

W. S. Caine, member of Parliament (M.P.) founds the Anglo-Indian Temperance Association. Though based in London, by the 1920s, the association had 195 affiliates in India with a membership mainly of Indians. The association publishes a London journal called *Abkari.*

1889 Allsopps, the Burton brewing firm, incorporates as a limited company, selling shares to the public. It is the first large English brewery to incorporate.

1890 Brussels Conference agrees to restrictions on the supply of spirits to Africa as part of an overall anti–slave trade program. The conference bans the import or manufacture of spirits for African consumption in any area of Africa between the latitudes of 20° north and 22° south in which "the use of distilled liquors does not exist or has not been developed." Further conferences (to 1912) debate and tighten restrictions.

1891 The Hotel and Restaurant Employees and Bartenders Union is founded in the United States.

Women reformers create the Australasian Woman's Christian Temperance Union (WCTU), with Jessie Ackermann as first president (1891–1894).

1892 At a convention in Cincinnati, college students, supported by the Prohibition Party, found the Intercollegiate Prohibition Association (IPA), which within a year will have branches on 146 U.S. campuses.

The Liberal government of the United Kingdom introduces a bill for prohibition by local option. It introduces a similar bill in 1895, but the government fails to bring either bill to a final House of Commons vote.

1893 The Ohio Anti-Saloon League is founded in Oberlin, Ohio. Two years later, it will lead in founding the Anti-Saloon League of America (ASLA).

The U.S. federal government proceeds under the Sherman Anti-Trust Act to investigate the "Whiskey Trust" (actually the Distillers' and Cattle Feeders' Trust, of Peoria, Illinois).

The British Women's Temperance Association (BWTA) breaks up. Supporters of Lady Henry Somerset organize the National British Women's Temperance Association (NBWTA), and her opponents organize the Women's Total Abstinence Union. The organizations reunite in 1926 as the National British Women's Total Abstinence Union (now called the White Ribbon Association).

The New Zealand Woman's Christian Temperance Union (WCTU), under leadership of Kate Sheppard, leads the successful agitation to have women granted suffrage in New Zealand.

Dispensary system in South Carolina, involving state liquor-shops monopoly, raises specter of government ownership of liquor trade throughout the United States.

1896 Wracked by internal dissension, the Prohibition Party splits into two parties.

English supporters of noncommercial management of the retail drink trade organize the People's Refreshment House Association.

1898 A national referendum in Canada endorses prohibition, but the federal government of Sir Wilfrid Laurier refuses to enact a prohibitory law.

Roman Catholic teetotalers organize the Pioneer Total Abstinence Association of the Sacred Heart in Ireland.

Frances Elizabeth Caroline Willard, preeminent American women's temperance leader, and World's Woman's Christian Temperance Union (WCTU) president, dies.

1899 Lord Peel's Royal Commission on Liquor Licensing Laws issues majority and minority reports. The temperance movement largely supports the minority report; a minority of United Kingdom prohibitionists reject it.

Joseph Rowntree and Arthur Sherwell publish *The Temperance Problem and Social Reform,* in favor of noncommercial management of British public houses and opposed to prohibition.

Temperance reformers estimate that there are 3 million adult teetotalers in the United Kingdom.

early 1900s British beer production stagnates.

1900 The Tokyo Temperance Union (later the Japan Temperance Union [JTU]) is founded.

Carry A. Nation, who during the previous year has led attacks on other Kansas saloons (all saloons are illegal under the state's prohibition law) brings national attention to herself by smashing the furnishings of the bar of the Hotel Carey in Wichita.

1901 English supporters of noncommercial management of the retail drink trade organize the Central Public House Trust Association.

1902 The G. Heileman Brewing Company, founded in 1858, introduces Old Style, which will become its flagship product.

1903 France's leading antialcoholism organizations, the Société française de temperance and the Union française antialcoolique, join to form the Ligue nationale contre l'alcoolisme.

1904 English brewers organize the Brewers' Society (BS), which ceased to exist under this name in 1994.

The Unionist government (predominantly Conservative) of the United Kingdom enacts a Licensing Act that affords the drink trade in England and Wales relative security for license renewal at a considerable financial price. The act brings about a slow but eventually considerable reduction in the number of pubs.

1907 The first known traffic accident in Finland involving a motor car occurs when a drunken driver in Helsinki runs into a lamppost in the Railway Station Square.

1908 The Liberal government of the United Kingdom introduces a licensing bill that the Conservative-dominated House of Lords rejects.

"Durban System" gives local governments in South Africa monopolies over brewing grain beer and selling it through municipal beer halls.

1909 Anglo-American prohibitionists organize the International Prohibition Confederation. It is renamed the World Prohibition Federation in 1919 and apparently ceased to exist in 1968.

1912 Iceland introduces prohibition.

1913 The U.S. Congress passes the Webb-Kenyon Act, banning the shipment of liquor into a state if state law forbids such imports.

The British Parliament enacts legislation that allows voters in Scottish districts to vote for prohibition. The legislation goes into effect in 1920.

1914 In August, the French government bans the sale of absinthe and all similar beverages, and in the following January prohibits all domestic commerce in absinthe. When Parliament confirms the policy in March 1915, the measure is portrayed as an integral part of national defense during the war against Germany.

As a wartime mobilization measure, the Russian government introduces Prohibition, but bootlegging grows. Prohibition continues under Bolshevik rule until 1925.

1915 Parliament creates the Central Control Board (CCB, Liquor Traffic), which imposes restrictions on British beer production and sales, including hours of operation.

Led by the Wesleyan Methodists, British churches organize the Temperance Council of the Christian Churches.

1916 The Central Control Board (CCB, Liquor Traffic) begins the Carlisle experiment in state management of retail and wholesale trade in northern England that will last until 1971.

The Strength of Britain movement calls for wartime prohibition.

The wartime coalition government of the United Kingdom considers state purchase of the alcoholic drink trade; it does so again in 1917, but again it rejects the idea.

Four of the six Australian states introduce six o'clock closing as a partial prohibition measure. The temperance "alliances" of the various states form a national body, the Australian Alliance Prohibition Council.

1917 The U.S. Congress passes the Lever Act, banning distilling and limiting beer production as a war measure. Later in the year, Congress passes a constitutional amendment that will become the Eighteenth (National Prohibition) Amendment and sends it to the states for possible ratification.

Bratt system of rationing alcoholic beverages begins in Sweden. It continues until 1955.

1918 The U.S. Congress adopts wartime Prohibition after the first world war has ended.

The Association Against the Prohibition Amendment (AAPA) is founded.

Belgium adopts a short-lived law prohibiting sale of distilled spirits.

The Canadian federal government passes an Order-in-Council imposing Prohibition to reinforce prohibition laws in force in all provinces. A wartime measure, federal Prohibition is to end one year after the termination of the war.

1919 On 16 January, the Eighteenth Amendment to the U.S. Constitution is declared adopted, after the thirty-sixth state legislature ratifies it. Ultimately, forty-six state legislatures will ratify the amendment.

The U.S. Congress passes the National Prohibition Act (the Volstead Act) to implement the Eighteenth Amendment, over President Woodrow Wilson's veto.

Finland adopts a Prohibition Act that will last until 1932.

Norway adopts a partial prohibition law that will last until 1927.

Shortly after regaining its independence, Poland introduces a partial government monopoly on spirits distillation and provides for local option on liquor sales.

Prohibitionists establish the World League against Alcoholism, with Ernest Hurst Cherrington as general secretary.

After starting in 1917 as a wartime measure, 6 o'clock closing becomes permanent in New Zealand from 1918 to 1967. This early closing led to the so-called 6 o'clock swill, which made hotels standing-room only places for as much beer to be drunk in as short a time as possible.

New Zealand's popular vote for prohibition rises above 55 percent for the second time (the previous referendum was in 1911), but falls short by just over 3,000 votes of the 60 percent majority vote required by law. The votes of soldiers in Europe, awaiting return to New Zealand at the conclusion of World War I, made the difference, ensuring defeat. Thereafter, support for prohibition faded, gradually dropping to 30 percent in a 1935 vote.

The Convention signed at Saint Germain en Laye as part of the World War I peace settlement gives new direction to the attempts by European colonial powers to control the supply of distilled liquor to Africans. The League of Nations thus required the "Mandatory" powers that had taken over the former German colonies to "exercise a strict control" over the supply of spirituous liquors in these territories. This requirement is only loosely enforced, but lasts until around 1950.

1920 On 16 January, one year after its ratification, the Eighteenth Amendment goes into effect.

1921 The postwar coalition government of the United Kingdom enacts a Licensing Act that consolidates many wartime reforms, including a prohibition on pub sales in the mid-afternoon.

The Indian National Congress endorses M. K. Gandhi's campaign to picket liquor shops as part of the nonresistance campaign aimed at achieving Indian independence.

1921–1925 The Soviet government gradually ends Prohibition and reintroduces the state liquor monopoly.

1922 Edwin Scrymgeour, "Prohibition Labour" candidate, defeats Winston Churchill for a parliamentary seat at Dundee, Scotland.

Referendum for prohibition fails in Sweden.

1924 The National Distillers Products Corporation is formed, a lineal descendant of the Distillers' and Cattle Feeders' Trust of the 1890s. Over the years before 1933, it will buy up the stocks of defunct bourbon distilleries, leaving it, at the repeal of National Prohibition, with control over more than half the aged whiskey in the United States.

1925 The Anti-Saloon League of America (ASLA) publishes the first volume of the *Standard Encyclopedia of the Alcohol Problem;* the sixth and final volume appears in 1930.

1927 Distillers Company Limited (DCL) completes a series of mergers with the five other largest distillers of Scotch whiskey.

Guinness begins the "Guinness is Good For You" advertising campaign in Scotland; it later appears in the rest of Britain.

1928 After a U.S. presidential campaign focused on the prohibition issue, antiprohibitionist Democratic candidate Alfred Emanuel Smith loses to Republican Herbert Hoover.

1929 Pauline Morton Sabin and twenty-three other women form the Women's Organization for National Prohibition Reform. Over the next four years, the organization's rapid growth will destroy the widespread belief that women support National Prohibition.

1930 Voters defeat prohibitionist drive in Australia. A referendum in the Australian state of Victoria is the last attempt to introduce prohibition.

1930s Mild ale and bitter become the preference of English beer drinkers.

British beer consumption falls sharply, the result of increased taxes and widespread unemployment.

1932 Paul Ricard begins to market a pastis liqueur from his own recipe, which will quickly come to dominate the French market and eventually form the basis for the Pernod-Ricard Group, an international liquor producer and marketer.

The Finnish Parliament creates a state alcohol monopoly.

1933 Following the election of the antiprohibition candidate, Franklin D. Roosevelt, in the previous fall's presidential election, the U.S. Congress submits to the states a constitutional amendment repealing the Eighteenth Amendment. The amendment will be ratified and become the Twenty-First Amendment by December. Congress also amends the Volstead Act to permit beer up to 3.2 percent alcohol by volume.

Their cause victorious, the Association Against the Prohibition Amendment (AAPA) and the Women's Organization for National Prohibition Reform disband.

English brewers begin the "Beer is Best" advertising campaign.

1935 Alcoholics Anonymous (AA) begins with a chance meeting in Akron, Ohio, between two habitual drunkards, William Griffith Wilson ("Bill W.") and Dr. Robert Holbrook Smith ("Dr. Bob").

Pabst Brewery in the United States introduces the beer can.

1936 The Federal Alcohol Administration Act is passed, creating the framework for federal regulation of alcoholic beverages after repeal of National Prohibition.

1939 Alcoholics Anonymous (AA) publishes the first edition of its "Big Book" (*Alcoholics Anonymous: The Story of How More than One Hundred Men and Women Have Recovered from Alcoholism*).

1940 The first number of the *Quarterly Journal of Studies on Alcohol* (later the *Journal of Studies on Alcohol*) is published by Dr. Howard G. Haggard, director of the Laboratory of Applied Physiology (LAP) at Yale University.

The first Alcoholics Anonymous (AA) chapter in Mexico is founded. By 1997, Mexican chapters of AA will number 13,200 and will be the world's second most numerous.

1942 To ensure adequate supplies of grain during wartime, the British government forbids distilling.

The United Kingdom Alliance (UKA) organizes the nonpolitical United Kingdom Temperance Alliance (UKTA) to avoid heavy wartime taxation. In 2003 the UKTA becomes the Alliance House Foundation.

1943 The Yale Center of Alcohol Studies, led by E. M. Jellinek, establishes two institutions critical in spreading new thinking about alcoholism: Yale Plan Clinics, dedicated to outpatient treatment of alcoholics, training for social service workers, and a research base for clinical studies; and the Yale School of Alcohol Studies, which holds its first session this summer.

1944 Marty Mann founds the National Council on Alcoholism (NCA) to publicize the disease concept of alcoholism championed by the Yale Center of Alcohol Studies and Alcoholics Anonymous (AA). Her organization will evolve into the National Council on Alcoholism and Drug Dependence (NCADD).

In accordance with its new socialist system, Poland restores the state alcohol monopoly.

1948 Prince Edward Island becomes the last Canadian province to repeal its prohibition law.

Kansas repeals its state prohibition law, which has lasted since 1881.

1949 The Addiction Research Foundation (ARF) is created by the Province of Ontario as a research, education, and treatment body.

The Hazelden Foundation is established in Center City, Minnesota, to facilitate recovery for those suffering from alcoholism and drug dependence.

The Constitution of newly independent India allows state prohibition.

1954 The Christopher D. Smithers Foundation changes its mission, taking on the task of addressing alcoholism as a public-health problem.

The Australian state of New South Wales ends six o'clock closing, effective in 1955

South Australia and Victoria follow in the 1960s (Tasmania had extended Sunday trading hours in 1932).

1955 The London brewers Barclay, Perkins and Courage merge under the latter name.

1958 Watneys purchases another large brewing firm and is renamed Watney Mann, one of the "Big Six" brewing firms into which the British brewing trade soon consolidates (together with Allied, Bass, Courage, Scottish & Newcastle (S&N), and Whitbread).

1960s Lager begins to be popular in Britain (and becomes dominant in the 1990s).

1960 A merger of brewing firms in Scotland and northern England creates Scottish & Newcastle Breweries (S&N).

E. M. Jellinek publishes his classic work, *The Disease Concept of Alcoholism.*

1961 Tetley Walker and Ansells merge with Ind Coope to form the largest brewer in the United Kingdom; the firm becomes Allied Breweries in 1963. The firm sold its breweries in 1993 and 1997 and its pubs in 1999.

1963 The All Nippon Sobriety Association (Danshukai) is formed, an umbrella organization for groups based on the Alcoholics Anonymous (AA) model, but modified to suit Japanese culture.

Major Irish distillers Jameson, Power and Cork Distilleries combine to form the United Distillers of Ireland (later the Irish Distillers Group).

1966 Mississippi becomes the last U.S. state to repeal its prohibition law.

1967 The British Parliament enacts an alcohol breath test for motorists.

1970 In *R. vs. Drybones,* the Supreme Court of Canada strikes down the part of the Indian Act (1876) regulating the sale of intoxicants to Native people as incompatible with the Charter of Rights and Freedoms, returning control over liquor to individual tribes.

The U.S. Congress passes the Comprehensive Alcoholism Treatment and Prevention Act (the "Hughes Act"), which establishes the National Institute on Alcohol Abuse and Alcoholism (NIAAA), the first nationally funded agency for alcoholism research.

1971 English critics of bland keg beers organize the Campaign for Real Ale (CAMRA) and target Red Barrel, brewed by Watneys.

Grand Metropolitan Hotels purchase Truman's brewery in England (and in the following year acquire Watneys).

Brian Harrison publishes *Drink and the Victorians,* which establishes the importance of alcoholic drink and the temperance movement in modern English history.

1972 The Bureau of Alcohol, Tobacco, and Firearms is created by U.S. federal legislation.

1973 Fetal alcohol syndrome (FAS) is first identified as a distinct clinical entity.

1976 The Rand Corporation issues the first of two studies of alcoholism treatment (the second appeared in 1981) commissioned by the National Institute on Alcohol Abuse and Alcoholism (NIAAA). The studies provoke controversy by questioning the disease concept of alcoholism.

The British Parliament liberalizes Scottish licensing laws.

1977 Australian national per capita consumption of beer peaks at 134.8 liters (35.6 U.S. gallons), declining to 95 liters (25.1 U.S. gallons) in 1999. Conversely, per capita wine consumption over a longer period had more than doubled, from 8.9 liters (2.4 U.S. gallons) in 1969, to 19.7 liters (5.2 U.S. gallons) in 1999.

1978–1990 Australian states introduces a legal blood-alcohol limit of 0.08; they then reduce this to 0.05. Compulsory roadside Breathalyzer testing follows soon after.

1979 The U.S. Congress passes the Cranston Act, which allows adults to brew at home up to 100 gallons of beer.

1980 Candy Lightner founds Mothers Against Drunk Driving (MADD) in Sacramento, California, after a drunk driver kills her thirteen-year-old daughter.

1981 High-school hockey coach Robert Anastas and his students create Students against Driving Drunk—later to change its name to Students against Destructive Decisions—in Wayland, Massachusetts, after two of the school's players died in separate car crashes in less than a week.

1982 Enthusiasts of brewing history found the Scottish Brewing Archive.

1983 The United Kingdom Temperance Alliance (UKTA) establishes the Institute of Alcohol Studies.

1984 The Canada Temperance Act is repealed.

1985 In one of the largest takeovers in the history of the liquor industry, Guinness Brewery acquires Distillers Company Limited (DCL).

New leader of the Soviet Union, Mikhail Gorbachev, takes up the issue of alcoholism as a high priority for his administration. State and party officials issue a series of decrees restricting the amount of alcohol that can be bought, the hours it can be sold, and the places it can be drunk. In September 1985, officials establish an All-Union Voluntary Society for the Struggle for Temperance.

1987 The major international brewing company Interbrew is formed through a merger of two leading Belgian breweries, Brasseries Artois and Brasseries Piedboeuf.

Parliament permits sales at licensed premises in England and Wales on weekdays without the previously required mid-afternoon "gap."

1989 Beer Orders discourages tie between brewing and control of pubs in England and Wales. As a result, many large firms sell their breweries or their pubs, or both, in the 1990s.

1990s Liberalization of trading laws in Australian states allow longer, and in some cases twenty-four-hour, hotel liquor trading. Pubs, feeling competition from restaurants and licensed clubs (and with beer drinking declining), successfully lobby for introduction of poker machines as supplementary sources of revenue.

1994 In anticipation of its upcoming membership in the European Union (EU), Finland ends its partial state monopoly on alcohol production and sale, which has endured since the end of prohibition in 1932.

1995 Scottish & Newcastle (S&N) purchases Courage. The company becomes known as Scottish Courage.

Parliament permits sales at licensed premises in England and Wales on Sundays without the previously required mid-afternoon "gap."

1997 Grand Metropolitan sells its pubs (most of them formerly Watneys) to the Japanese banking group Nomura.

Grand Metropolitan merges with Diageo, another British-based firm, under the latter's name.

Diageo purchases Guinness.

ca. 2000 Anheuser-Busch, Miller, and Coors hold 80 percent of the U.S. market.

2000 The U.S. Congress sets a blood-alcohol concentration (BAC) of 0.08 (80 milligrams of alcohol in 100 milliliters of blood) as the national standard for defining drunk driving.

2002 South African Breweries (SAB) merges with the American brewer Miller to form the world's second largest brewer.

2003 National Brewing Library at Oxford Brookes University in England opens to researchers.

The British Labour government ends most restrictions on opening hours for pubs in England and Wales.

China brews more beer than any other country, although its per capita consumption is less than one-tenth of that in the Czech Republic (which has the highest per capita consumption).

A

Absinthe

Absinthe has the distinction of having been the single most widely banned alcoholic beverage in Western society. Its production and sale were first forbidden in Belgium and Switzerland in 1906, and within ten years many other countries, including the United States and France, followed suit. Before long, there was an almost universal prohibition on absinthe, and only in the 1990s were these bans relaxed so as to permit variants of absinthe to be manufactured.

Absinthe and Its Effects

What distinguished absinthe from other alcoholic beverages is that its active ingredient is not only alcohol but also thujone, an oil derived from the wormwood from which absinthe is made. There is much scientific uncertainty about the properties of thujone and the effects of its consumption. In the mid-1850s, at the time when alcoholism was beginning to be described as a medical condition, doctors also identified "absinthism" as a separate category. The symptoms, which included hallucinations and addiction to the beverage, were similar to the symptoms attributed to alcoholism, but absinthism was regarded as an even more serious form of disease because of apparently stronger links to severe health and social dangers.

There is some question whether the effects of consuming absinthe were much, if at all, different from consuming other alcoholic beverages. Depending on the relative levels of alcohol and thujone, it is likely that absinthe consumers became intoxicated by the alcohol before they experienced significant effects from the thujone. There is evidence that the anxiety that led to the widespread ban on absinthe had as much to do with its many negative associations in the mind of the public and with moral panics about the broader effects of intoxicants on health and social order as it did with the properties and effects of the beverage itself.

Growing Popularity

Absinthe became a popular drink in France in the 1880s when a shortage of wine, resulting from the *Phylloxera vastatrix* epidemic, led consumers to find alternative beverages. Until that time, absinthe had been quite expensive and was consumed mainly by the middle classes and in certain artistic circles.

Artists and intellectuals are said to have appreciated its apparently hallucinatory effects, and there is widespread speculation about the role of absinthe in much of the artistic production of the nineteenth and early twentieth centuries, especially in France but also in other countries. Prominent artists like van Gogh and Picasso and writers like Verlaine and Rimbaud regularly consumed absinthe. Absinthe was celebrated in many of the café and brothel scenes painted by Toulouse-Lautrec, and in 1914 (as absinthe was being banned), Picasso designed a bronze sculpture called *Glass of Absinthe.* And while Paris might have been the center of artistic absinthe consumption, other centers included New Orleans in the United States.

As demand for aperitifs grew beyond the middle classes and artistic milieux, absinthe manufacturers responded by producing alcohol from less expensive material, notably sugar beets. Consumption rates began to rise steadily, particularly among urban workers. Drinking absinthe was institutionalized in *l'heure verte* (the green hour), when the green liquid was consumed before the evening meal. Drinking absinthe was a ritual that involved pouring water over a sugar cube, held in a slotted spoon over a glass of absinthe, and watching the sugar dissolve and the absinthe turn from green to a cloudy white color. (Yellow anise-flavored drinks such as Pernod and Pastis are similar to absinthe in this respect, although consumers do not add sugar to them.)

Descriptions of the effects of drinking absinthe vary. Some describe the effects as similar to intoxication from alcohol, but others describe the effects as more like those produced by opium. Setting the specific effects of thujone aside, most absinthe was extremely high in alcohol (55 to 75 degrees), and this alone made the drink an extremely powerful intoxicant. When it was consumed on an empty stomach, as during l'heure verte, its effects were more rapid and potent.

Development of Anti-Absinthe Sentiments

Absinthe quickly caught the attention of the French medical establishment, and in 1890, absinthism was recognized as a disease. By 1903, the national Academy of Medicine had declared absinthe to be the most dangerous of all substances. Medical observation had linked absinthe consumption to a wide range of pathological conditions, including hallucinations, convulsions, and a violent type of insanity. Doctors and social scientists drew up catalogs of violent crimes and homicides apparently committed under the influence of absinthe.

Absinthe was also linked to the supposed physical, intellectual, and moral decline of French workers in the decades before World War I. During this period, belief in the degeneration of people was not confined to France, but theories of physical and national decline had particular resonance in that country after its defeat in the 1870–1871 Franco-Prussian War. As middle-class commentators looked for explanations, they understandably identified absinthe, which was growing in popularity among classes they regarded as dangerous and immoral to begin with, as a prime culprit.

What became in some quarters an obsession against absinthe coincided with the rise of the temperance movements in France and elsewhere. In France, most temperance advocates focused on distilled or "industrial" spirits to the exclusion of wine. Indeed, some French temperance supporters encouraged the consumption of wine as a healthy alternative to liquor. But if wine was thought healthy, absinthe was considered the most dangerous of all beverages. Even temperance campaigners, who sought the suppression of all forms of distilled alcohol, were prepared to focus on absinthe first and to use its suppression as a precedent for banning a wider range of alcoholic beverages.

Many socialists, believing that absinthe was partly responsible for perpetuating the poverty of the working classes, allied with the anti-absinthe lobby. The socialist newspaper *L'Humanité* came out against absinthe, and one socialist representative declared in the Chamber of Deputies, "The worker who spends his salary on aperitifs isn't just a bad father, a bad worker, but also a detestable comrade who lets down the entire working class."

Against the accusations of the anti-absinthe lobby, absinthe supporters (led by manufacturers) argued in favor of its beneficial properties. They classified absinthe as a natural beverage, a category that had particular force in the contemporary French debate on alcohol, where beverages such as wine were considered natural, while distilled liquor and aperitifs were considered industrial.

Absinthe supporters insisted that, rather than causing insanity and physical harm, absinthe was actually good for its consumers and promoted intellectual growth. Moreover, there was no evidence of higher rates of illness or insanity in those areas of France where absinthe consumption was concentrated: large urban industrial centers like Paris, Rouen, Lyon, and Marseilles.

Legislative Campaigns

Uncertainty over the effects of consuming absinthe ensured that the road to banning it in France was long and hard. Legislative campaigns were mounted in the 1880s, but although they succeeded in having regulations placed on the consumption of absinthe, and although taxes on the beverage were raised in the hope of depressing demand, successive administrations were reluctant to ban it outright. One of the principal reasons was that the state raised considerable sums from the taxes imposed on absinthe production and sales. In 1907, absinthe contributed 60 million francs a year in taxes, compared to 10 million francs from other aperitifs and 5 million from wine. No French government of the time, facing rising tensions in Europe and considering the need to increase military spending, could easily contemplate the loss of such revenues.

Against these fiscal considerations, the opponents of absinthe raised the specter of national decline, social disruption, and spreading crime and insanity. In 1907, a petition calling for a ban on absinthe garnered 400,000 signatures. Although that represented only a small percentage of the French population, the percentage was far bigger than on any preceding petition. Even so, in 1907, a government commission once again decided to raise the taxes on absinthe instead of banning it. This strategy could be portrayed as an attempt to deal with the problem without adopting the draconian measure of prohibition, while at the same time ensuring that the state benefited fiscally from the measure.

In 1911, the French government commission adopted another way of avoiding prohibition. Having identified thujone as the dangerous substance in absinthe, it proposed banning any beverage in which thujone was an ingredient. That proposal had not been adopted by the time World War I broke out in 1914.

Impact of World War I

Once the war was under way, the French government, like others in Europe, quickly enacted legislation that it had been unwilling to act on during peacetime. In August 1914, within a month of war having been declared, the government banned the sale of absinthe and all similar beverages, and in the following January all domestic commerce in absinthe was prohibited. Confirmed by a vote in Parliament in March 1915, the measure was portrayed as an integral part of national defense. It would protect the French against the effects of absinthe, even if they were not clear, and promote discipline and efficiency within the military and civilian populations. Measures to ban, restrict, or dilute alcoholic beverages were adopted in other belligerent countries at about the same time and for similar reasons.

The ban on absinthe was maintained in France and other European jurisdictions throughout the twentieth century. A concession was made in 1922, however, when beverages similar to absinthe but made without thujone were legalized once again. This opened the way for the production of anise-flavored drinks such as the Ricard and Pernod brands.

The history of absinthe in France was paralleled to some extent in other countries, although not all countries waited for war to provide the political conditions that would permit the government to ban absinthe. It was banned in the United States in 1912, when most states had already enacted forms of prohibition with respect to alcohol generally. But as in France, absinthe was singled out in the United States as a peculiarly pernicious beverage. A member of the U.S. Pure Food Board described absinthe as "one of the worst enemies of man" and declared that "if we can keep the people of the United States from becoming a slave to this demon, we will do it."

In other countries, specific circumstances led to the prohibition on absinthe. In Switzerland, for example, absinthe was implicated when a man murdered his wife and two daughters in 1905. Although the evidence showed that the culprit had consumed only a small amount of absinthe (two ounces) but large quantities of wine and cordials in the ten hours before the murders, absinthe became the focus of national attention. Reaction was such that the Swiss government was able to ban its production and sale in 1906.

Like the gin craze in England in the first half of the eighteenth century, the campaign against absinthe alerts us to historical tendencies to focus on alcohol or particular alcohols as apparent causes of complex social conditions that are of concern to specific interest groups.

Rod Phillips

See also: Degeneration Theories; Drinking Establishments (France); Forel, Auguste; France, Temperance in; Gin; Wine

References

Conrad, Barnaby, III. *Absinthe: History in a Bottle.* San Francisco: Chronicle, 1988.

Haine, W. Scott. *The World of the Paris Café: Sociability among the French Working Class, 1789–1914.* Baltimore: Johns Hopkins University Press, 1996.

Lanier, Doris. *Absinthe: The Cocaine of the Nineteenth Century.* Jefferson, NC: McFarland, 1995.

Prestwich, Patricia E. *Drink and the Politics of Social Reform: Antialcoholism in France since 1870.* Palo Alto: Society for the Promotion of Science and Scholarship, 1988.

Addiction Research Foundation of Ontario (ARF)

The Addiction Research Foundation (ARF) was a research, education, and treatment body founded in 1949 by the provincial government of Ontario, Canada. The ARF became important in the provincial, federal, and international addiction treatment and policy arena before being folded into a larger organization in 1998.

The ARF was founded by the Ontario government on the recommendation of H. David Archibald, a lecturer at the University of Toronto who had researched Alcoholics Anonymous and studied at the School of Alcohol Studies at Yale University. Archibald had been hired as director of research by the Liquor Control Board of Ontario in 1949 and given a mandate to identify the size of the alcoholism problem in Ontario and develop a system of research grants to universities. When the ARF was founded later that year, Archibald became the executive director, remaining in that post until 1976.

The ARF's initial work was in outpatient alcoholism treatment in Toronto. In 1951, it established headquarters on Avenue Road in Toronto, turned the Brookside Hospital west of Toronto into its first alcoholic convalescent treatment unit, set up an outpatient clinic, and arranged for acute treatment beds in two Toronto general hospitals. Shortly afterward, it sold the Brookside Hospital and established a fifteen-bed treatment unit, outpatient clinic, and research unit on Bedford Road.

The foundation's work quickly expanded. In 1953, it initiated education and training activities for treatment staff in the province. In 1954, it began establishing throughout the province branch offices that engaged in outpatient services, community relations, and education, depending on the needs of the individual communities. Initially, the ARF awarded grants to universities and hospitals for specific research, but in 1954 it set up an in-house formal research department. By the late 1950s, the ARF carried out social, biological, and clinical research.

In 1961, concerns over new psychoactive drugs led the foundation to enlarge its mandate to include drug addiction, and it became the Alcoholism and Drug Addiction Research Foundation (still the "ARF"). In 1971, the ARF further expanded its work, adding a 100-bed clinical facility with formal teaching-hospital status, the Clinical Institute (later the Clinical Research and Treatment Institute—CRTI), and consolidating most of its activities in a pair of buildings at 33 Russell Avenue in Toronto, adjacent to the University of Toronto. In 1978, the ARF opened its School for Addiction Studies in Toronto.

The ARF also worked beyond provincial and national borders. Its research agreement, introduced in the 1950s, with the Finnish Foundation for Alcoholism Studies became a model for similar agreements between research institutions in the alcohol field. By the 1970s, the ARF played an important international role in policy development. Archibald took a key role in the landmark 1973 World Health Organization (WHO) Expert Committee on Drug Dependence. In 1977, the ARF was designated the first WHO Collaborating Centre and a Centre of Excellence for Research and Training. In 1976–1977, the WHO asked Archibald to help Thailand develop an opium crop substitution program. By the 1980s, the ARF was collaborating on programs and research linked to Caribbean and Latin American countries, including programs such as the Caribbean Institute on Alcoholism and Other Drug Problems, which the ARF helped to establish. In the 1980s, its School for Addiction Studies was the site for training professionals from Thailand.

The ARF's international activity was reciprocal. ARF researchers introduced European ideas that challenged conventional North American thought on drug policies. The most notable challenge involved research that contradicted the "disease concept" of alcoholism—the idea that alcoholism was an individual condition that had little to do with alcohol availability. Building upon seminal work such as French researcher Sully Ledermann's work in alcohol epidemiology, ARF researchers demonstrated how a reduction in alcohol availability could reduce the incidence of alcoholism. Other new approaches the ARF endorsed included the Nordic tradition of policy impact studies, controversial harm-reduction ideas on drug policy, and challenges to public-health thinking on nicotine policy. It also developed strong research in cognitive behavioral therapy.

In its prime, the ARF was a center of research and treatment unparalleled in Canada. It established a tradition of research autonomy. It protected researchers from controversies over nonabstinence approaches to addiction treatment. Research autonomy was possible because the ARF researchers were salaried, rather than relying upon external grant funding. Whereas grants require researchers to tailor work to the interests of funding bodies, the salaried researchers at ARF were free to pursue the research they considered necessary and important to their field.

By the early 1980s, the ARF had grown to over 700 staff members engaged in a wide array of activities. The CRTI had expanded to include radiology, an emergency room, a toxicology laboratory, and a liver clinic. The ARF housed a bookstore, a publishing division, and an audiovisual department. It had programs in 38 communities throughout the province, coordinated through its community programs offices.

The recession that followed 1991 brought a series of cutbacks and mergers in drug and alcohol research, and the ARF bore the brunt of these changes. Its funding was reduced by one-third, more than the cutbacks at most provincial social services. In response, the ARF continued to innovate: It developed treatment models that de-emphasized medical treatment except for methadone therapy, shifted its work to outpatient modalities except for its detoxication facility, disseminated knowledge-based treatment modalities, and turned the dissemination process itself into a topic of research. In 1998, the ARF merged with the Queen Street Mental Health Centre, The Donwood Institute, and the Clark Institute of Psychiatry to form the Centre for Addiction and Mental Health. Within this new organizational framework, the ARF's broad-based approach to addiction treatment—taking a biological as well as a mental-health approach—and research on biological, social, and epidemiological bases was subsumed under a predominantly mental-health oriented management.

Dan Malleck

See also: Alcoholics Anonymous (AA); Alcoholism; World Health Organization (WHO); Yale Center of Alcohol Studies

References

Anonymous. *The First Twenty Years.* Toronto: Addiction Research Foundation, ca. 1972.

Archibald, H. David. *The Addiction Research Foundation: A Voyage of Discovery.* Toronto: The Addiction Research Foundation, 1990.

Fisher, Honey R. *From Vision to Legacy.* Toronto: Centre for Addiction and Mental Health, 2000.

Room, Robin. "The End of a Unique Institution" in *Addiction.* 94, no. 12 (1998): 1781–1783.

Advertising (United Kingdom)

According to historians of the drink trades, there was very little deliberate sales-promotion of products during the eighteenth century. Conspicuous is the absence of brand names. Manufacturers of alcoholic beverages were more concerned with producing products of consistent quality. Rather than consciously capturing specific markets, drink manufacturers originally concentrated on securing sites of distribution such as public houses. Advertising initially grew from these retail outlets, starting with the pub sign.

Producers of alcohol ordinarily generated limited publicity as soon as a supply of alcohol could be offered publicly. For example, after completing winter brewing, most brewers announced sales in newspapers. Firms also had trade cards and placed insignia, if not simply their names, on casks and even wagons. Generally, London brewers and the largest Scottish and provincial firms advertised widely, usually in the provincial and Irish press, while smaller regional brewers announced the completion of each brewing season in local newspapers. In most cases, newspaper advertisements cost shillings, not pounds, and were limited to a few lines clearly indicating both products and prices. For this reason, such newspaper publicity often has been described as information rather than advertising. This kind of advertising flourished after the abolition of the advertising duty in 1853 and continued throughout the Victorian period. In general, sales developed through the use of commercial travelers and agents, who established contacts with local consumers and promoted products by word of mouth and attending events such as fairs.

Similarly, most brewers were their own best publicists. Many brewers held political office, and they exploited their contacts and social positions for publicity purposes. Occasionally, they attracted attention by hosting royal visits or obtaining a royal warrant. Many brewers promoted products by sponsoring sporting events and even agricultural fairs in the towns in which firms were based and where their products sold best. These methods are still used to this day. Publicity was also generated through benefactions to hospitals and other local charities, because donations were recorded in any associated printed materials, such as subscription lists. Rarely was this recognized as deliberate advertising at the time, however. In business records, "advertising" refers primarily to notices placed in newspapers.

Though originally restricted to a few lines in local newspapers, print advertising grew more sophisticated in the Victorian period. Advertisements began to reappear in trade directories and other periodicals and stood out through the use of trademarks. This avenue of sales promotion developed with amendments to patent law. After the passage of the Trade Marks Act (1875), most firms were granted exclusive usage of images, which reappeared on correspondence, casks, buildings, and especially on labels affixed to casks and bottles. Registration, however, did not halt trademark infringements, which plagued large manufacturers, such as Bass. Smaller manufacturers also spent fortunes protecting regional brands, funds that could have been spent on additional publicity. Though appearing primarily on bottles, trademarks adorned a variety of promotional materials designed in these years, including posters, show cards, signs, and business cards. By the late nineteenth and early twentieth centuries, trademarks appeared on presentation clocks, office calendars, diaries, and ashtrays.

The majority of early print advertisements stressed the quality and purity of alcoholic beverages. Circumstances in the brewing trade ensured that these ideals changed only slowly. Brewers used such slogans to counter beliefs that beer was being doctored using new methods as a result of the introduction of science to brewing in the second half of the nineteenth century. Temperance campaigns also inspired such mottos. An arsenic scare in the late Victorian brewing trade further encouraged brewers to stress the purity of their products.

Though tradition restricted innovations in advertising, it was recognized for its promotional value. Dressed in red caps and topcoats, brewers' draymen were regarded by brewers as mobile advertisements, as were their heavy horses, if not also their earliest motorized replacements. When motorcars became more common and lost their novelty appeal, brewers' horses again increased in promotional value, and some London firms retained horses until the middle of the twentieth century.

Changes in consumption patterns and growing competition in the late nineteenth century stimulated brewers' efforts to improve print advertisements. Companies such as Guinness—which had rejected a tied-house strategy—felt vulnerable to reduced demand in the early twentieth century and spent greater sums on advertising than did other firms. For example, in 1927, the company began to advertise in Scotland. The well-known experiment was managed by the London agency S. H. Benson, that produced the "Guinness Is Good for You" slogan that became a national campaign. As in the past, health properties of products were emphasized. Products also began to be associated with middle-class sporting activities such as golf and cricket. By 1929, Guinness spent £229,000 on advertising, and sums later increased. Companies that controlled tied estates, such as Bass, spent less on print advertising. For example, while Guinness spent £115,000 in 1933 on press advertising, Bass, the next greatest spender, paid £54,000. At all firms, however, advertising expenses began to rise, though in the 1920s and 1930s, most provincial firms spent less than a tenth of the figure that Bass spent.

With a sharp fall in consumption following increased beer duties in the 1930s, the brewing industry commenced a collective advertising campaign in 1933, orchestrated by the Brewers' Society and financed by a levy on members according to output. The scheme was executed by Major G. Harrison of the London Press Exchange and, in December 1933, resulted in the "Beer Is Best" slogan, a success from its inception until the outbreak of war. The venture, costing £139,000 per annum, was one of the largest cooperative campaigns of the day and prompted a similar campaign in the wine industry. Stressing the purity of ingredients, sports, and the role of the public house, the campaign used newspapers, posters, and even film, but depicted middle-class consumers principally. This reflected the undeveloped marketing efforts of the time, when few brewers actively investigated their consumer base. *John Bull* readership surveys of food and drink preferences in 1933 and 1938 gave brewers some idea of consumer predilections for bottled beer. Identifying thirty-nine leading brands, the survey suggested Guinness controlled a 38 percent share of brand preferences, followed by Bass with 8.2 percent, and Whitbread with 6.4 percent. The survey also revealed that the number of brands was in decline.

A 1932 Guinness advertisement from the Illustrated London News *(Hulton/Archive)*

Although collective advertising continued, the postwar period saw an increase in advertising activities by individual companies, including some use of television. Brewers' Society campaigns continued to stress the social aspect of pubs, and a 1953 campaign again emphasized the wholesomeness of beer. The majority of collective subscriptions went toward press advertising, but further levies were used to develop poster campaigns and limited radio broadcasts. Though these methods remained popular, television was first used by the society in 1959 and consumed the majority of resources after 1963. In the brewing industry alone, television publicity accounted for 30 percent of the total advertising expenditure and rose to 65 percent a decade later. The collective scheme eventually ceased because of growing segmentation of the drinks market, though public relations campaigns continued.

Spending on beer advertising in general increased from approximately £2.2 million in 1955 to £33.4 million in 1979. The fastest growth coincided with the consolidation of the major brewing companies, such as Bass Charrington, Courage, and Scottish and Newcastle. The "big seven" increased their share of total advertising expenditure from 54 percent in 1955 to 71 percent in 1965, rising to over 90 percent in the 1970s. Although it remained under 2 percent of overall advertising expenditure, beer advertising increased faster than total United Kingdom advertising, though some breweries still spent almost nothing on advertising. Stabilization came in the 1970s when the new corporate structure was established. Expenditure was also pronounced in the periods from 1955 to 1960 and from 1965 to 1970 when the new keg and lager brands were heavily promoted, as in 1960 and 1965 when Watneys promoted Red Barrel. Spending in the lager area also fluctuated, declining from 19 percent of media advertising in 1960 to 10 percent in 1965.

Market research techniques were also being adopted in the industry. As a result, advertising became more sophisticated, taking regional variations into consideration. The Brewers' Society commissioned regular studies of attitudes toward drink, most notably a series of studies by Market and Opinion Research International (MORI) in 1973 through 1981. United Breweries also commissioned studies in the early 1960s, revealing changing drinking patterns and the popularity of lager among women and the young. Consequently, early lager advertising was aimed at women and youth, leading the Advertising Standards Authority and the Independent Broadcasting Authority in 1975 to introduce codes of practice for alcohol advertising. Appeals to the young were prohibited, and advertisers were prevented from associating alcohol consumption with characteristics such as sexual prowess and physical strength. Anxiety in the industry also encouraged brewers to stabilize their real advertising expenditures. The Campaign for Real Ale (CAMRA) emerged in 1971 and began to stress the virtues of traditional mild and bitter just when consumers were turning to "upmarket" keg beers and lagers. As a result of the CAMRA, several smaller brewers in the 1970s witnessed a boost in sales, and many larger firms reintroduced local brand names, which had been phased out after a period of takeovers in the 1960s. Market segmentation, on the other hand, further encouraged brewers to appeal to a range of consumer lifestyles, though the public house remained the principal source of alcohol sales in the United Kingdom despite a continuing decline in pubs relative to other licensed premises.

Jonathan Reinarz

See also: Arsenic-in-Beer Scare; Bass; Beer; Brewers' Society (BS); Campaign for Real Ale (CAMRA); Guinness Brewery; Pubs and Beerhouses (United Kingdom); Scottish & Newcastle Breweries Limited; Victoria Wine Company; Watneys; Whitbread; Wine

References

Briggs, Asa. *Wine for Sale: Victoria Wine and the Liquor Trade, 1860–1984.* London: B. T. Batsford, 1985.

Donnachie, Ian. *A History of the Brewing Industry in Scotland.* 2d ed. Edinburgh: John Donald Publishers, 1998.

Gourvish, Terry R., and Richard G. Wilson. *The British Brewing Industry, 1830–1980.* Cambridge: Cambridge University Press, 1994.

Jones, Michael. *Time, Gentlemen, Please! Early Brewing Posters in the Public Records Office.* London: Kew, 1997.

Mathias, Peter. *The Brewing Industry in England, 1700–1830.* Cambridge: Cambridge University Press, 1959.

Weir, Ronald B. *The History of the Distillers Company, 1877–1939: Diversification and Growth in Whisky and Chemicals.* Oxford: Clarendon Press, 1995.

Wigglesworth, F. G. "The Evolution of Guinness Advertising" in *Journal of Advertising History.* 3 (1980): 14–18.

Williams, Gwylmor Prys, and George Thompson Brake. *Drink in Great Britain, 1900–1979.* London: Edsall, 1980.

Advertising Regulations (Canada)

The Canadian federal and provincial governments have attempted to control liquor consumption by limiting advertising since National Prohibition in the 1920s. Consequently, liquor advertising is far less ubiquitous in Canada than in the United States and Europe. However, the checkerboard of provincial legislation and the proximity of the U.S. border and its media to most of the Canadian population have rendered these attempts apparently ineffective. Contemporary legislation concerns lifestyle advertisements, sales to minors, and reducing drunk driving.

In 1942, Prime Minister Mackenzie King banned liquor advertising as part of the imposition of wartime temperance. Following the war, control of advertising reverted to provincial jurisdiction, although the newer media of radio and television remained under the jurisdiction of the federal Canadian Radio-Television and Telecommunications Commission (CRTC), which at first continued the ban on alcohol advertising. These regulations were relaxed in 1955, when the CRTC permitted limited radio advertising of beer and wine unless outlawed by provincial regulations. A checkerboard of regulations thus came into existence nationwide. Prince Edward Island, for instance, does not allow liquor advertising, while in 1988, Saskatchewan rescinded a fifty-eight-year ban. Ontario and Quebec have the most liberal laws; Ontario permits advertising on subway and bus-stop posters, although not on highway billboards. British Columbia's regulations have fluctuated over the course of the twentieth century, with occasionally ridiculous results. The Liquor Act of 1953 permitted newspaper advertising only, while in 1954, British Columbia bartenders were ordered to cover bottle labels as they poured drinks. During the 1950s, Montreal's Seagram's Distillers distributed free, full-colored art reproductions, which were banned, to the disgruntlement of many residents in British Columbia, as illegal advertising.

Magazine and newspaper advertising can be regulated by individual provinces, yet practically this is ineffective, since imported reading material is readily available from other jurisdictions (including the United States), as are radio and television advertisements. Studies from Manitoba, Saskatchewan, and British Columbia found such bans to have few discernible effects.

Substance abuse and media-watch agencies remain convinced that long-term exposure to liquor advertising, particularly from childhood, affects drinking behavior, and that liquor companies use indirect advertising, such as product placement and the manipulation of news stories concerning alcohol issues. In the 1970s, Ontario developed the first regulations concerning lifestyle content, such as advertisements featuring healthy, attractive drinkers or including content directed toward children. In 1994, Ontario's advertising guidelines included the "principle of responsibility," that is, that excessive or beneficial consumption should not be portrayed, nor should consumption appear as a prerequisite for social, professional, or personal achievement; athletic prowess; sexual opportunity; or enjoyment of an activity. Well-known personalities also were not to be used for endorsements. Subsequent submissions to the CRTC by media-watch groups found, however, that lifestyle advertisements continued to employ images of gratuitous sexuality, while sponsorships of sporting events continued the association of drinking with health and personal success. Liquor advertisements, particularly for beer, regularly portray teenaged situations (e.g., snowboarding, rock music), and manufacturers sponsor events, such as hockey games, that children watch. What constitutes "lifestyle" is open to interpretation and difficult to enforce. In the 1990s, bans on spirits advertising in the electronic media have not held up to constitutional court challenges. The 1996 CRTC Code for Broadcast Advertising of Alcoholic Beverages reflected the Ontario guidelines, focusing upon material and role models directed toward minors and the association of liquor with status, success, and motor vehicles. The code did not, however, address the issue of gender degradation, and it was based primarily on self-regulation by the industry.

Cheryl Krasnick Warsh

See also: Provincial Regulation (Canada)

References

Campbell, Robert A. *Demon Rum or Easy Money: Government Control of Liquor in British Columbia from Prohibition to Privatization.* Ottawa: Carleton University Press, 1991.

Canadian Radio-Television and Telecommunications Commission. *Code for Broadcast Advertising of Alcoholic Beverages.* 1 August 1996.

Smart, Reginald G., and Alan C. Ogborne. *Northern Spirits: A Social History of Alcohol in Canada.* Toronto: Addiction Research Foundation, 1996.

Africa, Central

This entry covers, roughly, the region south of the Sahara and north of the River Zambezi. The literature on this diverse region is patchy, and this account relies heavily on information from certain areas. Overall, up to the nineteenth century in this region, alcohol was consumed in the form of live fermented beverages produced on a small scale from a variety of ingredients, often on a noncommercial basis. Ideas of temperance were related to age and gender. The twentieth century saw substantial changes: the spread of a cash market for locally produced liquor; increasing challenges to established ideas of temperance, from drinkers and from Christian or Muslim advocates of new kinds of temperance; and the spread of new kinds of drink, notably bottled beer and locally produced distillates. Much of the production of liquor nonetheless remained small-scale, and former notions of temperance have persisted alongside newer ones.

Precolonial Drinking

It has been suggested that the spread of techniques of grain cultivation through sub-Saharan Africa between 3,000 and 2,000 years ago was the result of enthusiasm for the possibility of producing beer from the grain. This entertaining theory cannot be proven, but it usefully suggests the extent to which grains—both red and white sorghum and eleusine millet, and more recently maize—have entered the diet in sub-Saharan Africa as mildly alcoholic beverages. Generally served unstrained and live, these grain beers were so thick that they were often taken through straws with small filters on them to exclude larger particles; warm water was also added in some cases to make the beverages easier to drink. The germination of the grain prior to brewing improved its nutritive qualities as well as releasing sugar for fermentation, and the food value of this kind of beer was considerable.

Techniques of production varied somewhat, but it is likely that limited control over the fermentation process would have led to a significant proportion of failed brews. Generally, production relied on simple equipment available to most households (pots, baskets, and grinding stones), was small in scale, and, for beer-making, used the labor resources of only a single household.

Grain beers were by no means the only beverages available, and it can be assumed that people in central Africa had access to alcohol before the spread of grain cultivation. Like the grain beers of the region, the other alcoholic beverages were all "live" and were palatable for only a few days after they had been made. The sap of some species of palm and bamboo provided a source of fermentable sugar in areas where these grew; some fruits—notably the banana—were used for beverage alcohol production; other starch staples such as cassava or sweet potatoes could be used; and in arid areas where vegetable sources of sugar were scarce, honey provided an ingredient. Control of yeast strains was attempted through reuse of vessels and in some instances by the use of a fibrous root or fruit that was steeped in each batch of liquor, then dried and removed. Producing alcohol from these sources required no heating; in colder seasons or highland areas, fermentation might be assisted by keeping the liquor in a warm place, near a fire. The production process for these beverages was also generally small in scale, though there could be cooperation in production, with several households coming together to crush sugarcane, for example.

Grain beers, whose production was sometimes symbolically identified with sexual reproduction, and which involved considerable labor in processing grains and heating the brew, were usually made by women; in some cases, restrictions on sexual activity during the period of brewing and/or on the involvement of menstruating women underlined the association with fertility. Beverages like palm wine and bamboo wine, whose production depended on the ownership of a tree or a long-living plant, involved limited labor, and were generally produced by men. With other beverages, gender boundaries were not consistently drawn across the region.

The gendering of ideas of temperance and proper drinking was even more apparent. Concepts of temperance revolved not around limiting individual consumption, but rather around which categories of person could drink at all, and with whom they might drink. The consumption of alcohol was seen as an activity associated with the creation or display of power, and alcoholic beverages played a substantial role in ritual performances. Ritual drinking was particularly closely governed by ideas of propriety, but social drinking reflected—and invoked—the same notions of who should drink, and with whom. Across much of the region, the practice of elder men engaging in drinking was viewed as unproblematic, indeed desirable, and alcoholic drinks were supplied to elder men at weddings and funerals, in ceremonies of blessing and reconciliation, and at neighborly drinking parties. The spitting out of drinks by elder men as a form of blessing was a widespread phenomenon. By contrast, drinking by younger men or by women was seen as undesirable in many societies. Temperance was, however, debated and challenged: the assumption that all precolonial drinking was an "integrated" part of a smoothly functioning social system is mistaken. Women and younger men did drink, sometimes, as in the interlacustrine region, as part of an institutionalized and centralizing ideology of authority that challenged the claims of the gerontocracy, sometimes as a localized challenge by women or young men to the authority of elder men.

Levels of consumption in this period are impossible to estimate; impressionistic accounts from Europeans tell us more about the preconceptions of the observers than the practices of the populace. There were almost certainly significant seasonal variations: a surplus of grain just after the harvest would encourage brewing, and honey would be hard to find during a long season of rain. Partly for this reason, events that involved considerable drinking—weddings, circumcisions, and propitiatory rites—would also cluster seasonally. In some societies, drinking parties were associated with cultivation, as individual households supplied beer to work parties of neighbors.

The selling of alcoholic beverages, or their exchange by barter for other goods, was a practice well established in some areas—particularly where the effects of commercial contacts with a wider world were at their strongest—but unknown in others. Sale or exchange potentially challenged age and gender restrictions on consumption, and was resisted in societies where elder men in particular saw it as a profound moral challenge.

Distillation was not widely practiced before the colonial period. Distilled drinks were brought to the west coast of Africa in considerable quantities from the seventeenth century by European traders and to the east coast by European and Asian traders during the nineteenth century. These distilled drinks acquired a distinctive status throughout the region, sparking prolonged debates over whether they could and should be consumed in the same ways as other alcoholic beverages, and governed by the same notions of temperance.

Colonial Drinking

Colonial rule saw significant changes in drinking. These were associated with three major dynamics: the growth of central states, and of new kinds of power associated with these; the introduction of new kinds of drink and techniques of drink production; and the increasing role of money in the production and consumption of drinks—as in other aspects of human relationships.

The advance of direct European control across the region was most rapid in the later nineteenth century, at a time when debates in Europe over temperance and the role of alcohol were particularly intense. Colonial powers sought to limit African access to certain drinks of European origin, arguing that these would have a destructive effect on African morality and society. They also, however, created colonial states, which in some cases relied substantially on taxing imported alcohol, so that the aims of raising state revenue and of imposing temperance came into conflict. More generally, colonial states also sought to control African consumption of the kinds of beverage that Africans themselves made. Called "native liquor" in anglophone Africa, the term was replaced with "traditional liquor" by the end of the colonial period. There was particular concern with the imposition of new kinds of discipline of time and space on Africans; drinking had to be restricted to particular licensed spaces and to certain times when it would not interfere with the possible demands of employers who needed African labor. These restrictions on traditional liquor were initially imposed only in towns and areas of European settlement; systems of licensing then spread through rural areas, too.

Licensing was particularly aimed at the *sale* of traditional liquor. At the same time, the elaboration of the colonial state encouraged sale by producing groups of waged, mostly male employees who wanted to spend money on drink, among other things. Women generally lacked this access to wages, and turned to making liquor to sell to men. There was widespread evasion of licensing restrictions and of the hours of sale that the state sought to impose. Beyond this conflict between colonial state and African drinkers, there was a wider and more complex debate within African societies over the consequences of the sale of alcohol: Should selling be allowed at all, or was it a threat to the morality of society and the authority of elder men, who saw their position challenged by wage-earning young men and drink-selling women, who had more direct access to money than did their elders? In British-ruled parts of West Africa, chiefs and elder men encouraged the prohibition of cheaper brands of imported spirits to prevent the young from drinking these; across the whole region, elder men often sought tighter restrictions on the sale of traditional liquor. The growing influence of certain men, who gained power through the involvement in the local structures of state authority such as councils, increased the complexity of this. Some favored increased local government control of the trade as a way of funding an expansion of services; others saw this as a desirable field for private enterprise in which they and their friends might be involved.

The influence of Islam and Christianity came to be increasingly significant in determining ideas of temperance. The desirability of complete abstinence for African Christians had been suggested by the missionaries of various Protestant sects, and the importance of avoiding alcohol came to be even greater in a number of African-led churches, particularly those in which Pentecostalism and revivalism played a major part. Although the development of trade in drink had been encouraged by individual Muslims in a number of areas, Muslim clerics remained almost entirely hostile to drink. For Muslims and Christians, renouncing alcohol could be an important, public way to signal their rejection of some established patterns of authority and some obligations to neighbors, kin, and elders.

There were some experiments with central or local government control of "traditional" liquor sale, with the twin aims of reducing consumption and creating revenue. These did not, however, reach the scale attempted in parts of southern Africa, and alcoholic beverages did not become an important element in state revenue until the end of the colonial period, when the relaxation of racial restrictions on drinking and the new wealth possessed by some Africans encouraged the expansion of the brewing of bottled beer in the region.

Overall, distillates were more widely available by the end of colonial rule, in the early 1960s, than they had been in the 1890s. In British-ruled parts of West Africa, a period of prohibition on cheaper spirits had reduced imports, but this prohibition was lifted in the early 1950s. In eastern Africa, a more rigorous prohibition on (imported) spirits and bottled beer and wine had been enforced by the British; this prohibition was gradually eased from the 1950s. There was also a ban on any production of beverage spirits, which was maintained up to independence. Small amounts of imported spirits were consumed by politically prominent and wealthy Africans in eastern Africa; even smaller amounts were pilfered and smuggled by others. But across much of the region, heavy duties on imported spirits made them too expensive, even when they could be obtained, and the real innovation of the period was the spread of local, small-scale distillation as a technique. This occurred at different times across the region, but by the late 1940s small-scale illicit distillation was reported—and regarded as a problem—from Africa's west coast to the east. Distillates were a stable product, much easier to transport and sell—particularly in a hostile legal environment—than were locally made fermented liquors, and the clear association of colonial power with the spirituous liquors that the state sought particularly to control meant that distillates acquired a special status and commanded a premium price. They were in demand in particular from those Africans who had some access to cash and a degree of status through employment with the colonial state: government chiefs, minor officials, policemen, drivers, and the like.

Postcolonial Drinking

Since independence, bottled beer and spirits have maintained a special status as the drinks of the successful and modern. There has been a very considerable growth in the consumption of bottled beer—mostly lager beer—in the region and an associated growth in the local production of such beer, since breweries were among the first industrial ventures in a number of countries. Zambia's brewing industry, which grew by 27 percent each year through the 1960s, was by no means unusual. Economic protectionism was used to foster the growth of the brewing industry in the region, and the independent states of the region have all taken a considerable interest in bottled beer production, sometimes through nationalizing breweries, sometimes through forms of shared control with private capital. Everywhere, the relative ease with which tax can be collected from the bottled beer industry has made this a popular source of government revenue. The level of direct government involvement in brewing fell in the 1990s, in the period of liberalization, and at the same time the market dominance of a relatively small group of multinational brewers grew. Tax on beer nonetheless continued to be very important to state revenues.

Official encouragement for bottled beer has gone beyond economic protection. The drinking patterns of the political and economic elite, and their freely expressed attitudes, have lent weight to a consistent theme of advertising from the breweries: that their products are clean, modern, and associated with success. "Traditional" liquor, on the other hand, has been associated in official rhetoric with disease and backwardness, and is regarded with some disapproval. Nonetheless, the price of bottled beer has been kept high by taxes, and the beverage remains unaffordable on a regular basis for many people in the region. Locally made "traditional" liquor has therefore continued to account for a large part of consumption—as much as 90 percent in Uganda and Tanzania, for example. The widely used term "traditional" conceals considerable innovation: the greatly increased use of maize, rather than any other grain; the increased use of dried baker's yeast to accelerate fermentation; the use of new fruit bases (notably pineapples); and the very widespread use of processed or semiprocessed sugar to provide all or part of the fermentable base. The scale of production has remained generally small, however; experiments with the industrial production of live grain beer have been made, but only in Zambia have they achieved a success similar to that seen in southern Africa.

The production of these beverages has become an important part of the "informal economy" in many parts of the region. In many instances, this is a particularly important source of income for women. Licensing and other restrictions are poorly enforced, as the trade offers many opportunities for small-scale corruption. The production of distillates has become particularly important. There are legal beverage spirits industries in many countries, but these are even more heavily taxed than the bottled beer industry, and so illicit production thrives. Much illicit production is small-scale, relying on the use of oil drums as distilling vessels and on the labor of family or friends, but there are some larger operations. The beverage abuse of industrial alcohol has also become more common in some countries in the region.

Attitudes toward spirits consumption vary. In Ghana, distillates do not seem to be categorized differently than other products; in eastern Africa spirits tend to be drunk in less convivial, more individualistic ways, and, like bottled beer, they assert a distance from the "traditional" and an association with the "modern." Estimating the consumption of "traditional" liquor or spirits is extremely difficult, but the various attempts made all suggest that illicitly distilled spirits now make up a significant proportion of total consumption—perhaps more than 50 percent in Uganda, for example—even though most governments in the region continue to regard illicit distillation as particularly dangerous and socially problematic. This is an opinion hardened by occasional incidents of mass poisoning, usually involving the abuse of industrial alcohol.

There are continuities in ideas of temperance. Complaints about the moral threat posed by the drinking of young men and women are routinely heard, and across the region many social events still involve patterns of alcohol giving that stress the propriety and desirability of drinking by elder men. There are also newer ideas about the relationship between alcohol and power, and the nature of temperance. The influence of Christianity and Islam has continued to grow, and so too has a militant abstinence that stresses individual responsibility and agency, identifying all kinds of alcoholic beverage as a challenge to the spiritual well-being of the individual. The idea—associated with the drinkers of bottled beer and bottled spirits—that it is the drinking of "traditional" liquor or illicit distillates that threatens morality is a powerful one, but so too is the converse notion that identifies the drinkers of these "modern" beverages as the corrupt representatives of oppressive and incompetent states that have lost touch with their people. It is not clear whether drinking has actually increased in the region in recent decades, though some would argue that it has. It is, however, apparent that arguments over temperance have become ever more involved and vociferous.

Justin Willis

See also: Banana Wine; Brussels Act and Conventions, 1890–1912; Indigenous Peoples and the Liquor Traffic Controversy; Islam as Cultural Influence; Islamic World; Palm Wine; Processed Sugar Ferments

References

Akyeampong, E. *Drink, Power and Cultural Change: A Social History of Alcohol in Ghana, c. 1800 to Recent Times.* Portsmouth, NH, and Oxford: Heinemann and James Currey, 1996.

Ambler, Charles. "Alcohol, Racial Segregation and Popular Politics in Northern Rhodesia" in *Journal of African History.* 31 (1990): 295–313.

———. "Drunks, Brewers and Chiefs: Alcohol Regulation in Colonial Kenya, 1900–39" in *Drinking: Behavior and Belief in Modern History,* edited by S. Barrows and R. Room, 165–183. Berkeley and Oxford: University of California Press, 1991.

Colson, Elizabeth, and Thayer Scudder. *For Prayer and Profit: The Ritual, Economic and Social Importance of Beer in the Gwembe District, Zambia, 1950–82.* Stanford: Stanford University Press, 1988.

Curto, Jose. "Alcohol in Africa: A Preliminary Compilation of the Post-1875 Literature" in *Current Bibliography on African Affairs.* 21 (1989): 3–31.

Pan, Lyn. *Alcohol in Colonial Africa.* Helsinki and Uppsala: Finnish Foundation for Alcohol Studies, 1975.

Partanen, Juha. *Sociability and Intoxication: Drinking in Kenya, Africa and the Modern World.* Helsinki: Finnish Foundation for Alcohol Studies, 1991.

Willis, Justin. *Potent Brews. A Social History of Alcohol in East Africa, 1850–1999.* Oxford and Nairobi: James Currey and the British Institute, 2002.

Africa, Southern

Alcohol has been deeply implicated in the crucial relationships between rulers and those ruled and between employers and workers throughout the entire turbulent history of southern Africa. During the last century, as the region was industrialized and white supremacist regimes were established, control over the manufacture, sale, and consumption of liquor emerged as a central battleground in the struggles for domination that played out across the subcontinent along the fault lines of race, class, and gender.

Traditional Drinking Patterns

Most of the agricultural societies of southern Africa have deep traditions of producing and consuming alcoholic beverages. These societies made use of a wide range of fruits and grains to produce fermented drinks with relatively low alcoholic content. As a rule, people regarded these grain beers as foods and invested them with positive and healthy attributes. Drinking practices were in general defined by gender and age as well as by political position. Production typically took place within households during harvest seasons, and women did most of the arduous work involved in brewing these fruit and grain beers. These drinks were often produced for the parties that were organized to reward and compensate the men who assembled to provide communal labor. Because these drinks could not be stored for more than a brief period, drinkers were usually expected to finish all of the beer provided. In the celebratory atmosphere in which such parties took place, inebriation was not necessarily discouraged, at least among older men. When early European travelers observed some of these parties, they sometimes drew inaccurate conclusions about the level of drinking in these societies and the potency of the drinks.

Whereas ordinary people drank infrequently, men in positions of power had greater access to alcohol; the courts of some southern African leaders were awash in grain beer. These leaders could command the labor and grain reserves necessary to ensure regular supplies of liquor, or they were in a position to demand tribute from their subjects. Much of the anthropological scholarship on "traditional" drinking has argued that alcohol consumption in these kinds of societies was "constructive" in the sense that it took place within the context of and reinforced existing social, economic, and political structures. Certainly, the penetration of imperial power into the region and the advance of market forces transformed drinking practices and promoted alcohol abuse, but even in precolonial societies the power that some individuals possessed to command labor for alcohol production exacerbated social and gender inequalities and promoted hunger and impoverishment.

European Colonization and African Resistance

The establishment of the Dutch East India Company station at the Cape of Good Hope in 1652 and the subsequent if sporadic and uneven expansion of European power into the interior dramatically altered patterns of alcohol use and production. Moreover, the concomitant creation of settler political economies in South Africa—and later in the rest of southern Africa—made control over the production and distribution of drink crucial elements in the structures of domination that were gradually constructed across these territories. The Europeans who built the station and surrounding settlements at the future Cape Town brought with them the wine and other alcoholic drinks that they, not unlike the indigenous populations of South Africa, regarded as necessary parts of their diets. The ships that arrived from Europe, however, carried with them distilled drinks such as brandy, which were at that time still unknown in Africa, but which could be stored for long periods and transported over great distances. Brandy and other liquors quickly became essential commodities in commercial contacts with local people. In contrast to the vast majority of people across southern Africa, the hunting and herding populations living in the zone near Cape Town had no tradition of producing alcoholic drinks, and as a consequence were tragically susceptible to the effects of the drinks that the European settlers quickly introduced into trade. Alcohol also became a crucial ingredient in the recruitment and control of labor. Within a few years of the establishment of the company settlement, officials were paying wages in brandy, the beginning of the notorious *dop* system that has persisted to the present day in the agricultural districts of the Cape.

The Cape of Good Hope settlement was founded as a supply station to service the Dutch trade between Europe and the Indies. The company officials who encouraged the development of a local agricultural economy to provide supplies to ships soon realized that the Cape climate was well suited to viniculture, and a wine industry emerged. The cheap, low-quality wine that was produced supplied ships and a rising local demand. By the late 1600s, wine was being distilled to make the Cape brandy that became known by the name "Cape smoke." Wine and brandy were soon widely available in local canteens and in the bars in Cape Town, which helped earn the port city the nickname "tavern of the seas." The establishment of British control of the Cape Colony around 1800 opened new markets to Cape wine producers through the system of imperial tariff preference. Wine production rose sharply over the next three decades, until by the 1820s fully one-third of the Cape labor force (most of whom were slaves) were engaged in the wine industry. The end of imperial preference in 1830 cut off the growth of wine growing, and during the remainder of the century many growers moved out of the wine industry. The abolition of slavery after 1834, however, made white rural employers increasingly dependent on the dop or wine ration as a weapon of labor control. Agricultural workers were routinely provided wine several times a day and were issued bottles of cheap wine for weekends.

Political and religious leaders made periodic efforts to limit alcohol consumption, especially among the African population. During the midcentury, branches of British temperance organizations established themselves among whites in the Cape and among educated and Christian Africans, but the political power of the wine growers defeated any serious efforts to restrict the alcohol trade in the Cape region. Beginning in the 1830s, white settlers and traders moved into the interior of South Africa, accelerating a process of expansion that would culminate at the end of the century in the subjugation of all the independent African states in the region. Alcohol formed a key element of the trade that accompanied this expansion. Some African leaders attempted to resist the introduction of distilled spirits into their territories. In 1854, for example, the founder king of Lesotho, Moshweshwe, attempted to ban all such drinks. Drawing a clear distinction with traditional grain beers that he regarded as healthful and nutritious, the king declared that "the spirituous liquors of the white are nothing else than fire" (Thompson 1975:

199). Moshweshwe was just the first in a series of southern African "temperance kings" who would attempt, and ultimately fail, to limit the spread of liquor into their territories. The Tswana leader, Khama, actually carried his campaign directly to England in the 1890s, where he was celebrated by the temperance and humanitarian forces that had already succeeded in securing international agreements to limit the production and trade of spirits in sub-Saharan Africa. Those treaties, however, specifically excluded South Africa, leaving the territory open for the expansion of its domestic distilling industry.

The possibility for such growth arose with the mineral revolution that began with the discovery of diamonds and then gold in the interior in the second half of the nineteenth century. The creation of a major gold-mining industry in the Witwatersrand region created a huge market for cheap African labor and spawned a substantial urban center surrounding Johannesburg. Many of the new workers migrated to the gold region from the neighboring Portuguese territory of Mozambique, where a substantial cane liquor industry provided cheap spirits to the African population. The South African Breweries (SAB) was formed at this time to provide British-style beer to a white clientele, but the sale of spirits was in the hands of a monopoly granted to a single company by the Afrikaner government. The Hatherley distillery rapidly expanded production to meet the new demand from the African workforce. By 1897, the facility was producing 1,000 gallons of spirits per day, and there were more than 500 canteens where workers could buy Hatherley's products—some of which were adulterated with questionable substances. Initially, the mining companies, like their counterpart farmers in the Cape, saw liquor as a tool to recruit workers and retain them.

As consumption shot up, however, employers became increasingly concerned about raucous drunkenness, crime, and especially absenteeism. The Chamber of Mines began to pressure the authorities for limits on liquor, but they met strong opposition from the Afrikaner farmers who supplied grain to the distillery and to the many whites who profited from the trade. But support for restriction grew, and in 1897 a new law came into force imposing prohibition on Africans. An illicit trade continued, but the new British administration imposed after the South African War (1899–1902) reaffirmed prohibition, actively prosecuted illegal dealers, and closed down the distillery. Notwithstanding these measures, a substantial illicit trade persisted and grew, sustained by criminal gangs and small-scale producers, most of whom were women. In Mozambique and Angola, international regulation forced the closing of the domestic distilleries, but cheap alcohol, much of which was imported from Portugal, continued to be widely available.

Twentieth-Century Patterns

During the first half of the twentieth century, the development of alcohol production and patterns of consumption varied substantially by region. Within South Africa itself, the Cape wine and brandy producers, beginning in 1916, established a cooperative association that managed to control production and maintain relatively stable prices. Quality-control regulations led to improvements in South African wines, and in the mid-1920s Commonwealth tariff preferences gave South African vintners access to British markets. The political influence of the wine interests meant that alcohol remained relatively freely available in the Cape Province, while in the remainder of the country, as in colonial Zimbabwe, Zambia, and Malawi, African production and consumption of liquor were sharply restricted.

Commercial brewing in southern Africa dates to the nineteenth century, when the precursor company to the SAB was first established. The brewing industry expanded rapidly in scope and scale with the mineral discoveries and the subsequent development of the Witwatersrand. During the twentieth century, brewing, like distilling, steadily consolidated toward the monopolistic configurations that dominate the South African liquor industry today. Breweries were also established relatively early in other British territories, and there, as in South Africa, European-style bottled beer tended to be defined as a drink reserved for white consumption. For the most part, Africans were prevented from buying or consuming such beers as well as distilled spirits. Blacks had access to wine and brandy in the Cape region, and alcohol abuse was certainly an element of the impoverishment of the "Coloured" population there. The mythologies surrounding this abuse were often appropriated by white officials to justify restrictive alcohol regulation elsewhere in southern Africa. In general, white authorities regarded access to alcohol as a crucial element in maintaining the boundaries of racial distinction, and African drinking represented a threat to workforce discipline and to the rituals of obeisance that were so important to the structure and culture of white supremacy.

The authorities tended to turn a blind eye to the persistence of traditional patterns of brewing in the rural areas, although even there the commercial availability of the raw materials for brewing transformed both production and consumption. Brewing increasingly became a source of scarce cash for women in communities that the migratory labor system left largely devoid of men. Growing numbers of women followed male workers into the urban areas and established brewing and drinking establishments on the fringes of towns or in the heart of black residential areas. The struggle of these women brewers to provide for themselves in the face of draconian liquor regulations and continual police harassment is among the epic stories of black resistance to increasingly repressive regimes in twentieth-century southern Africa. In the South African province of Natal, officials in the major port city of Durban determined to stamp out African involvement in brewing and to control African drinking tightly. By 1907, there were more than 100 illegal drinking establishments in Durban, and the city fathers became increasingly agitated by the effects of rampant drinking on the workforce, as well as on the alternative sources of income that African-controlled enterprises represented.

In 1908, the "Durban System" was imposed, which gave local governments monopolies over brewing grain beer and selling it through municipal beer halls. The substantial profits derived from these enterprises were then plowed into the development of strictly segregated African residential ghettos known euphemistically as townships. Not surprisingly, elements of this system were widely adopted in the east, central, and southern African British dependencies, creating a strong fiscal dependency on alcohol. In the 1930s, even the Witwatersrand abandoned its prohibition policies in favor of the beer hall system. African consumers were less attracted to the beer halls, and they referred to the experience of visiting these establishments as "drinking in a cage." In time, however, urban residents even managed to put their cultural stamp on these large-scale and impersonal establishments, and they became important elements in vibrant urban cultures, even as they resonated with alcohol abuse and despair.

In the years after the second world war, increasingly intrusive state forces clashed continually with Africans attempting to produce and consume beer outside the law. In South Africa and the British territories, a growing population of relatively well-educated and affluent Africans demanded the right to drink European beers, wines, and spirits in more decorous surroundings than those provided by beer halls. At the same time, the mostly female legion of illicit brewers resisted police as they sought to protect one of the few opportunities for women to earn cash in urban areas. Beginning in the 1920s and climaxing in the large-scale demonstrations in Cato Manor near Durban in 1959, the brewers fought aggressively to protect their interests. The illegal shebeens that sprang up in South Africa's urban areas not only provided the chance for people to drink beyond the scrutiny of the state, but also helped to sustain a vibrant subculture that emerged in the shadow of the establishment of apartheid. The glamour of high-class shebeens contrasted sharply, however, with the misery caused by police repression and alcohol abuse. The number of convictions for liquor offenses exceeded 200,000 annually during the 1950s in South Africa. And while many Africans fought to abolish racially defined alcohol regulations, many others, especially active Christians, abstained from alcohol and pressed for even stricter control. Some of that fervor fired the demonstrators who ignited the Soweto rebellion in 1976. There and in the protests that spread across urban South Africa, state-owned liquor stores were among the initial targets of attack.

In the 1960s, the South African state reformed alcohol regulations, making bottled beer and wine available to Africans while keeping the alcohol commerce firmly in the hands of white businessmen and municipalities. The independence of the former British dependencies brought an end to racial discrimination in alcohol regulation, but across the region the state revenues derived from liquor sales became increasingly important. Not surprisingly, these changes did not benefit the women who had dominated the illicit trade. Businessmen gained control over legal distribution and the bar trade.

Across southern Africa, production and consumption grew very rapidly after the 1960s, and the signs of alcohol abuse became more visible; but efforts aimed at restricting consumption threatened critical commercial interests and vital state revenue sources. Before the 1960s, disease models of alcoholism found considerable favor in the treatment of excessive drinking in the white population. In contrast, social-service providers tended to define alcohol abuse among blacks in collective, racialized terms, as a proclivity or as a symptom of the stresses associated with modernization. South African efforts to address alcohol abuse problems among the majority black population were inevitably compromised by the racial assumptions that shaped many policies and by the very nature of the regime that promoted them. With the gradual decolonization of health services, limitations on resources meant that there would be fewer funds to support prevention or treatment programs. Across the region, as economic decline cuts into consumption levels, historically formed patterns of excessive drinking reinforce a range of social and health problems, including domestic violence and HIV/AIDS.

Charles H. Ambler

See also: Shebeens (Southern Africa); South African Breweries (SAB)

References

Colson, E., and T. Scudder. *For Prayer and Profit: The Ritual, Economic and Social Importance of Beer in the Gwembe District, Zambia, 1950–82.* Stanford, CA: Stanford University Press, 1988.

Crush, Jonathan, and Charles Ambler, eds. *Liquor and Labor in Southern Africa.* Athens: Ohio University Press; Pietermaritzburg, South Africa: Natal University Press, 1992.

Frifjhon, Michael, and Andy Murray. *Conspiracy of Giants: The South African Liquor Industry.* Johannesburg: Divaris Stein, 1986.

La Hausse, Paul. *Brewers, Beerhalls and Boycotts: A History of Liquor in South Africa.* History Workshop Booklet. Johannesburg: Ravan Press, 1988.

Mager, A. "The First Decade of 'European Beer' in Apartheid South Africa: The State, the Brewers and the Drinking Public, 1962–72" in *Journal of African History.* 40 (1999): 367–388.

Parry, Charles D. H., and Anna L. Bennetts. *Alcohol Policy and Public Health in South Africa.* Cape Town: Oxford University Press, 1998.

Thompson, Leonard M. *Survival in Two Worlds: Moshoeshoe of Lesotho, 1786–1870.* Oxford: Clarendon Press, 1975.

West, Michael. "Liquor and Libido: 'Joint Drinking' and the Politics of Sexual Control in Colonial Zimbabwe, 1920s–1950s" in *Journal of Social History.* 31 (1997): 645–667.

Alcohol, Consumption of (Russia)

Reliable data on alcohol consumption in Russia are available from the late eighteenth century; the rate of drinking of Russians in the earlier periods can only be estimated. Up to the late

1850s and early 1860s, the Russian government had a very vague notion of the amount of alcohol sales in the country, as the official data in many cases were compiled from the reports sent in by *otkupshchiki* (private concessionaires running the alcohol trade before 1863), who were not interested in showing real incomes from the alcohol trade.

Late Eighteenth and Early Nineteenth Centuries

According to the unreliable data provided by these reports, in the late eighteenth and early nineteenth centuries the average level of alcohol consumption in Russia was 5 liters of pure alcohol per year, in vodka only (1 U.S. gallon is equivalent to 3.785 liters). Consumption of other alcoholic drinks in most of the provinces up to the Soviet period was very low and did not significantly influence the general drinking situation in Russia. Between 1819 and 1826, when the first Russian alcohol monopoly was introduced, there was an insignificant decrease in consumption. After the abolition of the monopoly, the rate of consumption returned to the previous level.

Around this time, the rate of alcohol consumption in the St. Petersburg and Moscow areas (the so-called capital provinces) was higher than in other Great Russian provinces. Thus, in the St. Petersburg province in 1837 the average per capita consumption of vodka was estimated at 33.5 liters (approximately 13.4 liters of pure alcohol) per year, and consumption of various liqueurs was 1.85 liters; of brandies, 1.28 liters; and of beer, 1.78 liters. In the Moscow province, the per capita consumption of vodka was 13.9 liters (5.56 liters of pure alcohol), of liqueurs, 0.47 liter; of brandies, 0.41 liter; and of beer, 3.13 liters. For comparison, in Voronezh province per capita consumption of vodka was 4.92 liters (1.97 liters of pure alcohol); of liqueurs, 0.05 liter; of brandies, 0.03 liter; and of beer, 0.3 liter.

In provinces and areas annexed to Russia in the seventeenth and eighteenth centuries, the level of alcohol consumption up to the 1860s was traditionally also higher than in Great Russia on average. This fact is usually explained by the more severe fiscal control of the alcohol production and trade in the Great Russian provinces at that time. Just before the introduction of the excise system of alcohol trade in 1863, the average annual per capita alcohol consumption in the Russian Empire was estimated at 4.31 liters of pure alcohol, in vodka only. In Great Russian provinces, average consumption was 2.83 liters; in the Don area, 4.55 liters; in the Baltic provinces, 5.53 liters; in Ukrainian, Belorussian, and Novorussian provinces (so-called former privileged provinces) and in Polish provinces, 7.38 liters. In Sibir the alcohol consumption was very low—2.34 liters of pure alcohol in vodka.

Consumption after 1863 under the Excise

In 1863, the first year of the excise system, there was registered for the Russian Empire a very high rate of average vodka consumption—6.05 liters of pure alcohol per capita annually. In 1864, per capita vodka consumption decreased to 4.33 liters, and it stayed at around that level for the next fifteen years, gradually decreasing to 3.25 liters in 1884. This decrease, which continued into the 1890s, was the most noticeable in western, formerly privileged provinces; alcohol consumption in the Great Russian provinces was growing, though not considerably, until the mid-1870s. In the 1880s, a decrease was observed in the Great Russian provinces, too. During the period 1885–1891, per capita vodka consumption in Russia decreased noticeably, from 3 to 2.41 liters of pure alcohol per capita annually. This was the low point in alcohol consumption in prerevolutionary Russia. In the following years, consumption remained at this low level, with increases noted in 1905–1907 (up to 3.10 liters of pure alcohol annually in 1907) and in 1912–1913 (up to 3.05 liters). The difference between the average levels of annual per capita vodka consumption in the Russian Empire as a whole and its European provinces before the revolution fluctuated from between 0.05 and 0.3 liter more in the former. Values of per capita vodka consumption in Russian provinces in 1913 ranged from 1.65 to 8.15 liters of pure alcohol. The first third of this range (1.65 to 3.82 liters) covered thirty-seven provinces (the Polish provinces excluded); the second third (3.83 to 5.99 liters) covered twelve provinces—Don Region and Vladimir, Kherson, Kaluga, Smolensk, Kharkov, Liflandia, Yaroslavl, Arkhangelsk, Tula, Estlandia, and Ekaterinoslav provinces; and only the two capital provinces were found in the third segment (6 to 8.17 liters). The gap in the alcohol consumption values for the provinces of Moscow and Ekaterinoslav was as large as 2.95 liters, whereas in the first two segments the gaps in the values between any two provinces next to one another in the list was not more than 0.35 liter.

In beer, Russians in 1900 consumed approximately 0.17 liter of pure alcohol per capita (given the average strength of beer, which was 4 percent), with this value growing to 0.3 liter by 1913. The precise data on beer consumption in various regions are not available for that period because the fiscal competence of the Russian Finance Ministry did not cover this sphere. The main centers of beer production were St. Petersburg, Moscow, Vilna, Kovno, Grodno, and Kazan provinces. Per capita consumption of pure alcohol in wines, brandies, and liqueurs before the Bolshevik Revolution averaged approximately 0.2 liter.

In several regions, homemade alcoholic drinks were traditionally consumed in large amounts (homemade beer was widely spread in rural areas, first of all in the west and south; homemade wine was used in Moldavia, Caucasus, and Novorussia; milk-based mash *kumys* was popular among the minor nations of the Volga, South Ural, and Kazakhstan regions; as was grain mash *kumyshka* among national minorities of the Ural region. Consumption of these beverages has never been estimated.

Urban Alcohol Consumption

Alcohol consumption among the urban population in the late nineteenth and early twentieth centuries surpassed dramatically the general level of consumption in the Russian Empire. The highest level of alcohol consumption was reported in the towns of Kostroma (17.9 liters of pure alcohol, in vodka only), Arkhangelsk (17.45 liters), Novgorod provinces (16.2 liters), and Estlandia (16.2 liters). The lowest level was observed in the western areas—including the Kovno (3.4 liters), Grodno (4.6 liters), and Bessarabia (now Moldavia) provinces (4.7 liters). Consumption in the biggest cities of the Russian Empire—Moscow (population 1.5 million) and St. Petersburg (population 2 million)—did not differ much from that in other Russian cities and towns: 9.05 liters of pure alcohol per capita in St. Petersburg and 9.40 liters in Moscow. Some prerevolutionary researchers estimated that average vodka consumption was 3.4 times higher in urban areas than among peasants.

Alcohol consumption in Russia during the decades before the revolution was more regular in urban areas than in rural parts of the country. Russian peasants drank mainly in religious festivals, at weddings, and at funeral repasts. During Lent, alcohol consumption in the rural areas decreased 60 to 80 percent, whereas consumption in towns and cities only rarely fell by more than 50 percent. The diversity of alcoholic beverages in urban areas was by far greater than in rural areas. Peasants usually consumed only vodka, except for homemade drinks. In contrast, 50–60 liters of beer was consumed per capita in St. Petersburg in the early twentieth century, a very high rate for the Russian Empire.

Social Groups and Classes

According to studies on the budgets of peasants (Shcherbina 1900) and workers (Prokopovich 1909), both the most and the least prosperous groups in these classes featured higher alcohol consumption than the medium stratum did. The statistical data of St. Petersburg clinics for 1886–1897 collected by N. I. Grigoryev (1900) indicate that the biggest susceptibility to alcoholism among people of various professions was observed among clerks and draughtsmen (297 alcoholics per 10,000), bricklayers (236.2 per 10,000), and workers engaged in the construction and maintenance of the waterways and in the shipping trade (197.4 per 10,000). Factory workers accounted for only 76.4 alcoholics per 10,000. Among women, the professions where drinking was most prevalent were laundresses (260.6 per 10,000) and factory workers (93.2 per 10,000). The districts in such big cities as St. Petersburg and Moscow subject to the most alcohol abuse were areas inhabited by craftsmen, street-mongers, odd-job workers, and outcasts.

Women accounted for approximately 25 percent of the alcohol-caused chronic diseases in this period, which could be regarded as circumstantial evidence that they consumed the same share of the alcohol sold in Russia as men. Among 2,970 alcoholics treated in Moscow in the early twentieth century, 1.7 percent had begun drinking vodka before they were five years old; 8 percent began at ages six to ten; 25 percent began before they were fifteen years old; 47 percent began at sixteen to twenty; and only 4.2 percent began at an age above twenty-five. The number of abstainers among Russian Orthodox people did not exceed 5–7 percent. Several religious and ethnic groups of the Russian Empire were considered to be abstainers (Muslims, Old Believers, and some sectarians) or very temperate drinkers (Jews). According to official data, the number of Muslims, Old Believers, and Jews in prerevolutionary Russia did not exceed 20 percent of the Russian population, although several prerevolutionary publications made unsubstantiated claims that 40 percent of Russians were abstainers.

The Soviet Era

Tsarist Russia imposed a Dry Law in 1914 as part of the mobilization of the troops and to improve the social and moral condition of the populace during the war. The law, which remained in effect until the Stalin era, prohibited the sale of alcohol, including vodka, except in clubs, assemblies, and certain other drinking establishments (which, after the Bolshevik Revolution, of course, were scarce). It also prohibited the sale of wine that was more than 15 percent alcohol and beer that was more than 3.7 percent alcohol. The punishments for violations, and for public drunkenness, were made considerably more severe.

It is difficult to assess the effects of this law in the history of alcohol consumption in Russia. Officially, there was almost no alcohol on sale, except in first-class restaurants and clubs. At the same time, the use of various substitutes for alcohol increased markedly. After the reestablishment of a state alcohol monopoly under the Soviets in 1925, the level of alcohol consumption was incredibly low: 0.88 liter of pure alcohol per capita, in vodka only, in 1925; 1.04 liters in 1932; 1.9 liters in 1940; and 1.85 liters in 1950. This low level of consumption could be explained by continued use of alcohol substitutes or homemade drinks, by the very scanty purchasing capacity of the broad masses of the population, and by "paramilitary" discipline on the Soviet collective farms and industrial enterprises.

From the 1950s to the 1970s, per capita consumption in the USSR grew steadily: to 4.82 liters of pure alcohol in various drinks in 1960, 9.22 liters in 1970, 9.9 liters in 1975, and 10.5 liters in 1980. The structure of alcohol consumption changed as compared with the prerevolutionary period. Apart from vodka, Soviet people drank cheap cognacs and dry and fortified wines. For example, in 1980 Soviets consumed 2,072 million liters of vodka and liqueurs, 2,747 million liters of wine, 76 million liters of champagne, 52 million liters of cognac, and 3,346 million liters of beer. The difference between rural and urban consumption smoothed out, with alcohol abuse in villages in many cases being even more considerable than in towns. The share of abstainers for religious reasons decreased, represented mostly by traditionally minded people in the Middle Asia and Caucasus regions. Consumption of alcohol by women grew significantly and was only slightly below men's consumption. At the same time, alcoholism was uncharacteristic of young people, especially in urban areas. As shown by a study carried out by sociologists at the Russian Academy of Science in the early 1980s, 32 percent of senior pupils at schools and 30 percent of students at professional and technical colleges had never tried alcoholic drinks.

After 1985, the level of reported alcohol consumption per capita decreased to 4 liters of pure alcohol in 1987 due to Mikhail Gorbachev's antialcohol campaigning. At the same time, the use of homemade alcoholic drinks and substitutes was growing. Information on alcohol consumption in the early 1990s is especially unreliable, since on the eve of—and after—the collapse of the USSR there emerged a huge black (and gray) market for alcohol. These years featured a very high mortality rate related to the use of poor-quality alcohol. In 1990, official statistics reported the level of per capita consumption at 5.6 liters of pure alcohol; in 1991, 5.6 liters; in 1992, 5 liters; and in 1993, 6 liters. When in the mid-1990s the state control of the alcohol trade was toughened, the official index of per capita alcohol consumption stabilized at the level of 10 liters of pure alcohol, in various drinks, per capita. Some experts who tried to estimate the consumption rate of homemade alcoholic drinks and substitutes in late-Soviet and post-Soviet Russia (A. V. Nemtsov and V. Treml, for example) claim that the total amount of per capita consumption did not fall below 10 liters of pure alcohol even in Gorbachev's period and reached 14 liters in several years of the 1980s and early 1990s.

Ivan Krasnov

See also: Russia, Imperial, Temperance in; Soviet Union and Russia since 1917, Alcohol and Temperance in; Vodka

References

Dmitriyev, V. K. *Kriticheskiye issledovaniya o potreblenii alkogolya v Rossii* (Critical studies of alcohol consumption in Russia). Moscow: 1911.

Grigoryev, N. I. *Alkogolizm i prestupleniya v Sankt-Peterburge* (Alcoholism and crime in St. Petersburg). St. Petersburg: 1900.

Kratkoye obozreniye piteynykh sborov s 1831 po 1835 v 28 Velikorossiyskikh guberniyakh i Kavkazskoi oblasti (The concise review of the drinking duties from 1831 to 1835 in 28 provinces of Great Russia and the Caucasus Region). St. Petersburg: Finance Ministry of the Russian Empire, 1835.

Kratkoye obozreniye piteynykh sborov s 1839 po 1843 . . . (The concise review of drinking duties from 1839 to 1843 . . .). St. Petersburg: Finance Ministry of the Russian Empire, 1843.

Narodnoye Khozaistvo SSSR (National economics of the USSR). Various years.

Nemtsov, A. V. "Alcohol Consumption, Alcohol-Related Consequences and Alcohol Policy in Russia (1945–1996)" in *Alcologia.* 11 (1999): 57–61.

———. *Alkogolnaya smertnost' v Rossii* (Alcohol-caused mortality in Russia). Moscow: 2001.

Otchyoty Departamenta/Glavnogo upravleniya neokladnykh sborov (Reports of the Department for Non-Tax Duties). St. Petersburg and Moscow: various years.

Pervushin, S. A. *Opyt teorii massovogo alkogolizma v sviazi s teoriyei potrbnostei* (An attempt to make a theory of mass alcoholism in relation to the theory of necessities). Moscow: Moscow University, 1912.

Prokopovich, S. N. "*Budgety peterburgskikh rabochikh*" (The budgets of St. Petersburg workers) in *Poznaniye Rossii* (Cognition of Russia), Book II, *1909,* 42–76.

Rossiya v Tsifrakh (Russia in figures). Various years.

Rossiyskiy Statisticheskiy Yezhegodnik (Russian statistical yearbook). Various years.

Shcherbina, F. A. *Krestyanskiye budzhety* (The peasants' budgets). Voronezh: 1900.

Sikorsky, I. A. *O vliyanii spirtnykh napitkov na zdorov'ye i nravstvennost' naseleniya Rossii* (Of the influence of alcoholic beverages on public health and morals in Russia). Kiev: 1899.

Simpura, J., B. M. Levin, and H. Mustonen. "Russian Drinking in the 1990s: Patterns and Trends in International Comparison" in *Demystifying Russian Drinking,* edited by J. Simpura and B. M. Levin, 7–30. Research Report 85. Helsinki: National Research and Development Centre for Welfare and Health (STAKES), 1997.

SSSR v tsifrakh (USSR in figures). Various years.

Statisticheskiy Yezhegodnik Rossiyskoy Imperii (Annual statistical yearbook of the Russian Empire). Various years.

Svedeniya o piteinykh sborakh v Rossii (Materials on the alcohol taxes in Russia). Parts 1–5. Edition of the State Chancellery, 1860.

Tersky, N. S. *Piteynyye sbory i aktsiznaya sistema v Rossii* (Drinking fees and the excise system in Russia). St. Petersburg: 1890.

Treml, V. "Soviet and Russian Statistics on Alcohol Consumption and Abuse" in *Premature Death in the New Independent States,* edited by J. L. Bobadilla, C. A. Costello, and F. Mitchell, 220–238. Washington, DC: National Academy Press.

Yezhegodnik Ministerstva Finansov (Yearbooks of the Russian Finance Ministry). Various years.

Zohoori, N., K. Gleiter, and B. M. Popkin. *Monitoring Health Conditions in the Russian Federation: The Russian Longitudinal Monitoring Survey, 1992–1996.* Report submitted to the U.S. Agency for International Development. Chapel Hill: Carolina Population Center, University of North Carolina, 2002.

Alcohol, Consumption of (United Kingdom)

In modern times, a majority of the adult British population has drunk beer of one kind or another or, less often, other alcoholic beverages. Working-class males drink more than most other people, with the peak in beer drinking taking place in the 1870s. In recent decades, there has been a dramatic change in what drinkers consume, notably, the new popularity of lager beer.

Statistics and Their Problems

Statistical comparisons between the United States and the United Kingdom must take into account different meanings for the same terms. The British drinks statistician George B. Wilson noted that "the American gallon is only 0.833 of our imperial gallon, and as the percentage of alcohol in our proof spirit is higher, 137 American proof gallons only equal 100 British proof gallons." An imperial pint contains 20 fluid ounces, in contrast to the U.S. pint's 16 ounces, so an imperial pint is equivalent to 1.201 U.S. pints. Effective in 1980, what now is called the European Union established new criteria for measuring alcoholic content. For Britain, this meant replacing the old system of degrees of proof for spirits, liqueurs, and fortified wines with new definitions by volume and mass.

The central government has taxed alcoholic beverages heavily. As a result, the statistics for alcoholic drink are mostly tax records that describe production and so, indirectly, consumption. Although flawed, such statistics indicate broad trends. For instance, since the 1870s, per capita beer consumption has declined, although not consistently.

Alcoholic content matters more than liquid volume. Consequently, it is important to take into account that during the twentieth century the alcoholic content of most beer declined from nineteenth-century standards, a decline especially sharp during the world wars. For instance, the alcohol content of beer in 1919 was only 58 percent what it had been in 1914. It also matters whether drinkers consumed small amounts at various times, for instance, at meals, or concentrated their drinking at a single time. Here, the only official statistical guide is arrests for public drunkenness that ignore private intoxication, reflect binge drinking and not total consumption, and depend on police discretion. For instance, in 1870, prosecutions for drunkenness in Liverpool were almost ten times higher than those in Birmingham, a discrepancy that suggests local policy mattered more than local drunkenness in producing the statistics. Most prosecutions for drunkenness have been against men.

For most of the nineteenth century, there is only anecdotal evidence about who drank more or less than the statistical norm. Since the end of the nineteenth century, however, sociological studies exist. For instance, in 1899, Joseph Rowntree and Arthur Sherwell published *The Temperance Problem and Social Reform.* This influential book estimated that, at that time, there were at least 3 million adult teetotalers in the United Kingdom.

Nobody challenges the broad outlines of the orthodox view: the working class drank more than other classes, men drank more than women, and thus working-class men drank the most. The concentration of pubs in working-class neighborhoods, particularly in the Victorian era, supports the thesis about disproportionate working-class drinking. Early studies of the household budgets of the poor show heavy expenditures on alcohol. It was widely believed that the fluctuation in alcohol consumption in the nineteenth century was directly related to working-class income. Good times and regular wages meant more money spent on beer. The urban population was more likely to drink than the rural population; laborers doing heavy work (such as dockers) were more likely to drink than, say, textile operatives; and young men were more likely to drink than older men. The Irish and the Scots were especially heavy drinkers, and working-class Irish and Scots were much more likely to drink whiskey than their English and Welsh counterparts. (Whisky is the British spelling.) Heavy drinking and a vigorous temperance movement could exist side by side, as they did in Scotland.

Beer

Beer was the national drink in England and Wales. The historians Terry R. Gourvish and Richard G. Wilson have criticized and revised the pioneering interpretation by the statistician George B. Wilson. The per capita consumption of beer in England and Wales from 1800 to 1804 averaged 33.9 imperial gallons (40.71 U.S. gallons). Consumption generally declined because of a bad economy until the Beer Act of 1830 almost doubled the number of drink sellers for on-premises consumption by creating beerhouses that did not need a license from the justices of the peace. Consumption surged, peaking at 37 gallons (44.4 U.S.) per capita in 1836. After a period of decline, consumption increased in the 1860s and 1870s, reaching a peak of 42.2 gallons (50.68 U.S.) in 1876. Afterwards, consumption declined. For instance, in 1913, it was 28.7 gallons (34.47 U.S.) per capita, perhaps a sign that the working class had developed alternative ways of spending money. New consumer goods and leisure activities competed with drink for working-class wages. In addition, beer had become expensive compared with foodstuffs, the prices of which had fallen considerably.

There was a sharp decline in proceedings for drunkenness, which decreased from 108.4 per 10,000 population in 1891 to 8.4 per 10,000 population in 1931 in mining districts. Although figures for other districts are not as dramatic, in all instances those for 1891 are much higher than for 1931. Of course, 1931 was a year of economic depression.

The social investigators Joseph Rowntree and Arthur Sherwell calculated that in 1899 the average adult male drank 76 gallons (91.27 U.S.) of beer, 2.57 gallons (3.09 U.S.) of spirits, and 0.96 gallon (1.15 U.S.) of wine, while the average adult woman allegedly drank half these amounts. In the nineteenth and early twentieth centuries, the working class spent more on beer than on bread or meat.

During the interwar years, beer consumption declined, affected by high unemployment. The available figures are for the United Kingdom and thus are depressed by including Scotland and Northern Ireland, where many drinkers preferred whiskey to beer. The lowest per capita beer consumption occurred in 1932, when consumption dropped to 10.73 gallons (12.89 U.S.). Beer consumption grew during the second world war, declined during the early years of peacetime, and then increased from the late 1950s through the late 1970s (with wine, cider, and spirit consumption growing at even faster rates). According to the historian John Burnett, the peak year for postwar United Kingdom per capita beer consumption was 1979, when it reached 27.1 gallons (32.55 U.S.). By 1995, it had fallen to 21.9 gallons (26.3 U.S.).

Wine, Cider, and Spirits

Per capita wine consumption can be calculated through the statistics for imports. Few British people drank wine until recently. According to Burnett, as recently as 1950, almost 95 percent of men and women over age sixteen never drank wine. Beginning in the 1960s, wine consumption grew significantly. For instance, in 1960, the annual per capita wine consumption was 3.6 imperial pints (4.32 U.S. pints), while by 1995, it had grown to 32.1 pints (38.55 U.S.).

Cider consumption grew at a faster rate than any other alcoholic beverage. According to Burnett, cider "consumption rose from 18 million gallons [21.62 million U.S.] in 1963 to . . . 123 million [147.7 million U.S.] in 1995," or 20 pints (24.02 U.S.) a year per capita for persons over age fifteen. Women are a slight majority among cider drinkers. Since the 1990s, grocers catering to the luxury trade have sold "champagne cider," refermented in the bottle.

For the United Kingdom as a whole, consumption of whiskey and other spirits declined after the first world war. For instance, it has been estimated that in 1948 only 9.6 percent of the United Kingdom population were "regular" drinkers of spirits, defined as consuming spirits at least once each week. This soon changed. Burnett points out that spirit consumption tripled between 1953 and 1990, with the increase especially rapid in the 1970s, reaching a peak consumption of 7.36 pints (8.84 U.S.) per capita in 1979. By the mid-1990s, spirit consumption once again declined: 5.3 pints (6.37 U.S.) per capita in 1996. The type of spirits drunk has changed as well. Whiskey remained the favorite "strong drink," but vodka became more popular than gin.

Early Twenty-First Century

At the beginning of the twenty-first century, consumption of alcoholic beverages has stabilized at levels higher than during the interwar period, apparently with youthful drinkers consuming alcoholic drink disproportionately. The alcoholic beverages drunk often differ from those consumed in the nineteenth century or even in the years immediately after the second world war. The drinks specialist Andrew Barr notes the new taste for cold drinks: for instance, "chilled, light white wine," the "rise of lager," and "the popularity of white spirits [such as vodka] as a mixer in long, cold, fruity drinks." In the first years of the twenty-first century, compared with the other countries of the world, the United Kingdom ranks fifteenth in per capita retail beer sales (46.2 liters [43.7 U.S. quarts]) and twentieth in per capita retail wine sales (10.2 liters [9.7 U.S. quarts]).

In a more prosperous society, alcoholic drink now bulks less prominently in household budgets than the sixth or more of earnings that the working class had spent at the end of the nineteenth century. The 4.3 percent of income in the mid-1990s as an average for families of all socioeconomic classes seems a relatively manageable expenditure. Yet figures available for 2002 indicate that the people of the United Kingdom spent more on alcoholic beverages, including taxes, than their counterparts in all but four other countries.

David M. Fahey

See also: Alcohol Consumption of (Russia); Alcohol, Consumption of, by Indices (United States); Alcohol, Consumption of, per Capita (Canada); Alcohol, Consumption of, per Capita (United States); Beer; Cider; France, Production and Consumption of Alcohol in; Gin; Pubs and Beerhouses (United Kingdom); Vodka; Whiskies; Wine

References

Barr, Andrew. Review of *Liquid Pleasures,* by John Burnett, in *Social History of Alcohol Review.* 16, nos. 1–2 (Fall/Winter 2001): 55–62.

Burnett, John. *Liquid Pleasures: A Social History of Drinks in Modern Britain.* London and New York: Routledge, 1999.

Dingle, A. E. "Drink and Working Class Living Standards in Britain, 1870–1914" in *Economic History Review.* 2d series, 25 (1972): 608–622.

Gourvish, Terry R., and Richard G. Wilson. *The British Brewing Industry, 1830–1980.* Cambridge: Cambridge University Press, 1994.

Gutzke, David W. "Consumption Trends and Advertising" in *Alcohol in the British Isles from Roman Times to 1996: An Annotated Bibliography,* compiled by David W. Gutzke, 13–18. Westport and London: Greenwood, 1996.

Long Term Drink Trends: An Analysis of Trends in Alcoholic Drinks Consumption in the UK, Covering the Years 1700–2000. Henley-on-Thames: NTC, 2000.

Rowntree, Joseph, and Arthur Sherwell. *The Temperance Problem and Social Reform.* London: Hodder and Stoughton, 1899.

Williams, Gwylmor Prys, and George Thompson Brake. *Drink in Great Britain, 1900–1979.* London: Edsall, 1980.

Wilson, George B. *Alcohol and the Nation: A Contribution to the Study of the Liquor Problem in the United Kingdom from 1800 to 1935.* London: Nicolson and Watson, 1940.

Alcohol, Consumption of, by Indices (United States)

In the United States, as in most other complex societies, both the amounts of alcohol consumed and the patterns of use have varied widely by age, sex, class, race, and ethnicity. In general, Americans in their twenties are the heartiest drinkers, and consumption gradually declines with age. Men drink more than women do. Class differences are relatively unimportant concerning quantity of consumption, but they are very important concerning styles of drinking. White Americans have been heavier consumers of alcohol than have African Americans, Hispanics, or Asian Americans. Large numbers of Native Americans have had drinking problems. Among white ethnic groups, practices have varied.

Age

High alcohol consumption among adolescents and young adults has both physiological and social roots. Although alcohol acts as a depressant, it also reduces inhibitions before the onset of depression. Many young people have questions about identity, personal relationships, and careers. It is an anxious stage of life, and one characteristic of alcohol is that it reduces anxiety. Alcohol affects different people in different ways. For some drinkers, liquor calms nerves and breaks down barriers, especially socially instilled sexual taboos. For other drinkers, alcohol produces anger and violence. Alcohol can be frightening, and its unpredictability explains why it is normally taken in a group. This pattern of use is related to alcohol's ability to reduce inhibitions and thereby to help integrate the individual drinker into the group. Young people often feel a need to act together.

As adults age, they tend to lose their anxieties, and they tend to leave groups to marry, have children, and form families. Alcohol does little to promote family life, and under these circumstances, consumption usually declines. In addition, aging changes the body's ability to handle alcohol in two distinct ways. The body processes alcohol at a slower rate, so that pleasing effects occur more slowly. This fact discourages consumption. At the same time, constant use reduces the stimulative effect of a particular amount of alcohol on the body. Therefore, a larger amount is needed to achieve the same result that was produced at an earlier age. As Americans get older, they typically decrease intake; by age sixty-five, a majority are abstainers. In contrast, a few drinkers increase their intake over time, even though larger amounts may no longer bring the joy felt when they were young. Such persons risk becoming abusers of alcohol.

Gender and Class

American men, like men in most societies, drink more than women. Men account for 70 percent of alcohol consumed. There are many explanations for this difference, including greater female abstinence. Of women, 49 percent abstain; 27 percent of men do. Another reason men drink more is that they are usually larger than women, and body weight plays an important role in the body's ability to absorb alcohol. Larger persons can process a given quantity faster, so that a large person can drink a large amount and remain sober, while a small person consuming the same amount becomes intoxicated. Women's bodies typically have more body fat and less water than men's bodies, and therefore absorb alcohol faster. In addition, ovulation can cause blood alcohol to increase more rapidly. Compared to men of the same size who drink the same amount, women report greater intoxication.

In American society, male drinking has also been associated with manhood. Going to a bar to take one's first drink has been a rite of passage for many young males. Participation in bar culture confirms manhood, and conversation about sports, women, or politics reinforces the "manliness" of the setting. Talk is about victory or conquest, real or imagined. Although drinking does not itself constitute a form of power, the use of alcohol can be a substitute for power. Drinking often occurs in proximity to power. Important business or political deals are sealed with drinks, and success is celebrated with toasts or with champagne poured over athletes' heads. Drinking is closely related to male success in socially prescribed ways, or drinking can be a way to handle failure. Thus, both success and failure encourage male drinking. In contrast, women, as a group, typically handle these matters in very different, abstinent ways.

Americans of all classes drink. Although consumption rates do not vary much by class, the wealthy do drink the most, and the poor the least. The ability to drink is partly a function of being able to afford alcohol. In terms of occupations, doctors are generally the heaviest drinkers; they also lead in income. Lawyers are second in both categories. Drinking styles, however, differ by class. Upper-class drinking, like other aspects of life among the wealthy, is often hidden from view, and a rich man who gets drunk at his club can afford to have someone else drive him home. In a society where as many as 88 percent of Americans have called themselves middle-class, middle-class drinking habits are defined as the norm. Restrained use is the approved pattern, but a member of the middle class who is arrested for drunk driving will hire an attorney to challenge the charge. Lower-class drinking produces the most criticism because it tends to violate middle-class norms. It is usually a poor person, commonly male and often nonwhite, who is arrested for reeling down the street drunk.

Minority Patterns

Drinking attitudes and habits are a part of culture that changes only slowly, over generations. Americans of European ancestry brought their thirst for alcohol across the Atlantic, and white Americans remain the country's heaviest drinkers. In contrast, consumption among African Americans has always been low. Whereas 55 percent of blacks abstain, only 36 percent of whites do, and black drinkers consume slightly less per person than do white drinkers. Among African Americans, women are likely to abstain, and youths start drinking at a later age than white youths. Whereas white consumption peaks during the twenties, black use does so in the thirties. Low consumption by African Americans probably can be traced to Africa, a continent where alcohol is used infrequently. In addition, American slaves drank sparingly. Slaveholders opposed the practice, except during limited periods when drunkenness was approved. After the end of slavery, poverty kept African Americans from buying much alcohol. Further, many African Americans live in the South, where religious opposition to liquor is strong. African Americans who live in northern cities drink more than those in the South. Among black drinkers, both men and women have more alcohol problems than whites do.

Hispanics have a mixed cultural heritage that is heavily Native American. Distillation was unknown in the Americas prior to European contact, although some Native American tribes brewed beer, often for limited ceremonial use. In some Spanish-controlled areas, however, distilled spirits gained popularity, and the West Indies became famous for its rum. Patterns of alcohol use by Hispanics depend upon a person's country of origin. Puerto Ricans tend to be heavy drinkers, while Central Americans are not. Of all U.S. Hispanics, 49 percent abstain. In all Hispanic groups, most women do not drink, and very few women have alcohol problems. Mexican Americans drink a considerable amount of beer, but their overall consumption of alcohol is below that of native-born whites. There are also geographical variations. Texans of Mexican heritage are likely to abstain or to drink minimally, mirroring the drinking patterns of the state's Anglos. Similarly, the consumption rate of Californians of Mexican heritage mirrors the patterns of that state's Anglo population. Like Anglos, Mexican American men who drink often do so heavily in their twenties, but unlike Anglos, many continue heavy drinking into their thirties and thereby have greater risk for alcohol problems.

Although both beer and distilled spirits have long been known in Asia, 62 percent of Asian Americans are abstainers, and most Asians who drink have been light drinkers. Patterns, however, vary by group and by locale. Studies are insufficient to provide detailed information.

Native Americans present a special case. Alcohol was not part of everyday life until white contact. Europeans found that rum and other distilled spirits made excellent trade goods to obtain furs or other valuable commodities from Native Americans. Because Native American cultures did not have social mechanisms for handling alcohol, liquor proved destructive both to individuals and to tribal society. Generations later, many Native Americans have serious problems with alcohol. Although 53 percent are abstainers, those who do drink have often done so in destructive ways. There are, however, tribal variations. Many Native American women are heavy users, and fetal alcohol syndrome is a problem. Native American youths begin drinking at a young age, and Native Americans have high death rates from cirrhosis of the liver and from alcohol-related accidents, homicides, and suicides.

European Immigrants

As much as possible, European immigrants to the United States tried to retain Old World drinking customs. Those who arrived after 1840 often found it difficult to fit into a culture that was increasingly split between a middle-class temperance movement that emphasized abstinence as proof of respectability and a drinking culture that traditionally emphasized heavy whiskey drinking. Irish Americans, mostly Catholics who had little use for Protestant appeals to abstain, opened saloons in America's cities. These saloons served as community centers, labor markets, loan offices, and political headquarters. Plentiful, cheap whiskey in the United States encouraged heavy consumption among the Irish. So did loneliness for single males who came to America in search of work. Cultural disorientation in a strange, hostile society also spurred drinking.

German immigrants who arrived in large numbers in the 1840s and 1850s brewed and drank German-style beer, which was more flavorful than the English-style beer that Americans had drunk previously. German Americans also opened family-oriented beer gardens. At first, there was considerable antagonism between the antiliquor movement and German Americans, especially over the practice of serving beer to families in suburban beer gardens on Sundays. Native-born Protestants held that Sunday should be a day of rest, with all businesses closed. During the Civil War, when one-quarter of the soldiers in the Union army were immigrants, mostly from Ireland and Germany, the army distributed beer to troops. After the war, German immigration continued, and beer sales rose. Beer gardens lasted until World War II, when Americans of German ancestry tended to drop customs that had set them apart.

Italian immigrants, as well as those from other wine-drinking cultures, found it difficult to continue their traditional patterns of alcohol consumption in the United States. Italians considered wine to be a food and consumed it in large quantities with meals. They seldom drank other alcoholic beverages. Italian immigrants tried to maintain their customs, but they often found that their practices clashed with the norms of American culture. Wine was often not available. Italian Americans in California planted vineyards and maintained their customs better than in many other places. Over time, Old World practices died out. After World War II, third-generation Italian Americans no longer thought of wine as a food, and they no longer took wine with every meal, but they were still more likely than other Americans to drink wine, and they were less likely to drink other alcoholic beverages.

Jewish immigrants came from a culture that emphasized self-restraint in general and particularly with respect to alcohol. Wine played an important role in Jewish religious observances, where small amounts were used in rituals that included participation by children, and that fact may explain how and why Jewish Americans were able to pass an unusually restrained drinking style to their children. Although third-generation Jewish Americans assimilated to American culture, they continued to restrict drinking. For example, a Jewish American hostess was likely to provide a before-dinner cocktail, but, in a pattern that showed restraint, a second cocktail was not necessarily offered. Few Jews are abstainers, but few have had alcohol problems.

W. J. Rorabaugh

See also: Alcohol, Consumption of, per Capita (United States); Anthropological Theories of Drinking and Temperance; Psychological Theories of Drinking; Sociological Theories of Drinking and Temperance

References

Austin, Gregory A., and Ron Roizen. *Alcohol Consumption among Youth: Current Trends and Research Findings.* Washington, DC: U.S. Department of Education, Office of Educational Research and Improvement, Educational Resources Information Center, 1993. Fiche ED380737.

Barrows, Susanna, and Robin Room, eds. *Drinking: Behavior and Belief in Modern History.* Berkeley: University of California Press, 1991.

Kissin, Benjamin, and Henri Begleiter, eds. *The Biology of Alcoholism.* 7 vols. New York: Plenum, 1971–1983.

MacAndrew, Craig, and Robert B. Edgerton. *Drunken Comportment: A Social Explanation.* Chicago: Aldine, 1969.

U.S. Department of Health and Human Services, National Institute on Alcohol Abuse and Alcoholism. *Alcohol Use among U.S. Ethnic Minorities.* Rockville, MD: National Institute on Alcohol Abuse and Alcoholism, 1989.

———. *Women and Alcohol Use.* Washington: U.S. Department of Health and Human Services, 1988.

Alcohol, Consumption of, per Capita (Canada)

Canadians have had a reputation of being heavy imbibers, and statistics bear that out. During the colonial period, per capita consumption peaked at anywhere from 5 to 7 gallons per person fifteen years of age and older. By the mid-nineteenth century, liquor intake had dropped to approximately 4 imperial gallons (3.3 U.S. gallons), due in part to the rise of temperance societies. By the time Prohibition was introduced during the first world war, annual consumption had fallen to 0.6 imperial gallon (0.5 U.S.) of absolute alcohol. Consumption increased dramatically following the second world war, and reached 11.14 liters (2.9 U.S. gallons) of absolute alcohol by the late 1970s. Since 1981, per capita consumption has declined, and by 1996, the national average had reached 7.62 liters (or roughly 2.0 U.S. gallons) of absolute alcohol.

Early Years

Alcohol has been an important component of Canada's cultural landscape since the first settlers arrived in the 1600s. The experiences of the early settlers who came to New France mirrored those who came to what is now the United States, since all brought along their own beer and wine. In an age when alcohol was considered safer than water, settlers believed that they would encounter the same conditions upon their arrival in New France and secured their own supply. Equally important, alcohol was believed to be a restorative with medicinal benefits that lessened the pain of childbirth and fevers, among other maladies. Also, alcohol was believed to have nutritional value and was seen as a source of energy, which was particularly important for laborers and farmers. Not surprisingly, alcohol was part of everyday life during the colonial period in Canada's history.

Colonial tastes mirrored those found back home in Europe. For example, the English preferred dark beer, which at first was imported from England. Later, settlers made their own. Cider was also popular, as was a wide variety of fruit and vegetable wines produced locally for personal consumption. Imported beer was reserved for those who could afford it. Other popular drinks included imported rum and whiskey, both of which were cheap and traveled better than beer.

Our knowledge about per capita consumption prior to 1851 is fragmentary at best. Anecdotal evidence from the period suggests, however, that Canadians were heavy drinkers. Drinking took place year-round, but was particularly heavy from May through November, when colonists assembled at pioneer bees. Bees brought members of the community together to complete large projects such as raising barns, building houses and fences, and logging and clearing the land, all work that primarily involved men. According to Edwin C. Guillet, it was customary to provide a gallon of whiskey for each family at the bee. In some cases, there was an unlimited supply of alcohol. Alcohol was readily available at all manner of functions, including dances, festivals, militia parades, elections, and in the taverns, which promoted heavy drinking. Men of prestige were also heavy drinkers and could be frequently seen stumbling out of the local tavern. Magistrates holding court sessions in taverns frequently drank during the proceedings.

W. J. Rorabaugh observed that in the United States in the 1820s, per capita consumption of distilled spirits for the population fifteen years and older was approximately 4.7 U.S. gallons, and that overall consumption peaked in 1825 at about 7 U.S. gallons. There is every reason to believe that Canadian per capita consumption figures matched those of the Americans. William Proudfoot reported in his unpublished diary that there were few men who drank less than 4 glasses of whiskey per day (Guillet 1964). Some historians have suggested that drinking was pervasive, crossing regional, gender, age, and class lines, while others believe that many Canadians abstained from drinking. In modern times, recent evidence has shown that those who reside in rural settings are more likely to abstain from drinking. Since 85 percent of the population in 1851 lived in rural areas, it is reasonable to assume that a significant percentage of the populace did not drink. Also, children could probably be listed among the abstainers, and because of large families and shorter average life span, children comprised approximately 65 percent of the total population. F. L. Barron has argued that because the proportion of children was higher in the 1850s, and because Canadians stepped forward in droves to take the pledge to abstain from drinking, per capita consumption of absolute alcohol by those who did drink was perhaps 25–30 percent higher than today's figures for per capita consumption.

A number of factors, including psychological, cultural, and economic factors, accounted for high per capita consumption rates in Canada. Perhaps the most important factor was that work during the preindustrial period was task oriented rather than time oriented. Work, for men at least, involved short bursts of energy at certain times of the year, followed by extended periods of inactivity. Men who were employed in heavy extractive industries such as logging and mining had a reputation for being heavy drinkers, as did sailors, those in the militia, and those who worked on the docks in Canada's port cities.

Nevertheless, by the 1850s the temperance movement had made inroads into Canadians' drinking habits, and per capita consumption began to drop as more and more Canadians joined the movement, which identified drinking with sin. Alcohol was blamed for everything from crime to poverty, wife beating, prostitution, and poor health. Two other factors also account for the drop in consumption, namely the appearance of new technologies in the workplace that required a sober labor force, and changes in leisure activities and the rise of organized sports. Finally, higher taxes on alcohol also contributed to the drop in consumption. An imperial gallon of whiskey that cost roughly two shillings (fifty-two cents Canadian) in 1840 cost three shillings (seventy-five cents Canadian) by 1851. By 1867, taxes alone on a gallon of whiskey totaled sixty cents.

By 1871, per capita consumption rates in the Maritimes, specifically Nova Scotia and Prince Edward Island, were the lowest in the country. By 1880, they stood at 0.273 and 0.278 imperial gallon (about 0.22 U.S.) of absolute alcohol per capita respectively. This downward trend reflected the national trend. That said, there were exceptions such as British Columbia, a province known for its heavy drinkers, where per capita consumption had increased to an average of 0.759 imperial gallon (0.6 U.S.). Canadian per capita sales of alcohol were also dropping in the post-Confederation period (after 1867) from approximately 5.5 liters (1.4 U.S. gallons) of absolute alcohol in 1871 to about 3.5 liters (0.9 U.S. gallon) by the time Prohibition was invoked during the first world war.

The Twentieth Century

Little is known about per capita consumption rates in Canada in the period from 1896 to 1924. We do know, however, that public drunkenness had become socially unacceptable. Moreover, by the 1880s, any public (or private) drinking had become unacceptable for respectable women. Nevertheless, by the turn of the century, drinking among women was on the increase. We also know that beer consumption stood at 5.25 imperial gallons (4.4 U.S.) per capita in 1890 and had risen to 6.54 imperial gallons (5.45 U.S.) by 1921. Far less is known about per capita consumption during Prohibition—which ran approximately from 1914 until 1924—because alcohol was strictly regulated.

Although people could still purchase liquor, Prohibition very nearly eliminated its legal private sale. James H. Gray has suggested that on the prairies, consumption dropped as much as 80 to 90 percent. Nevertheless, Canadians continued to drink, and the temperance movement ultimately failed in its bid to rid Canadian society of alcohol. The various temperance societies did, however, succeed in changing drinking habits and were responsible for a drop in overall consumption.

A few short years after Prohibition ended, the country plunged into an economic depression that lasted a decade, from 1929 until 1939. Not surprisingly, widespread poverty during the depression—approximately one in four Canadians was unemployed—discouraged use. Per capita consumption rose sharply during and following the second world war and peaked in 1981. Per capita sales of alcohol rose from approximately 3.75 liters (1.0 U.S. gallon) of absolute alcohol in 1941 to about 5.5 liters (1.4 U.S. gallons) in 1946 and continued to increase until 1981, when per capita sales of liquor reached 11.5 liters (3.0 U.S. gallons) of absolute alcohol.

The liberalization of licensing laws as a result of changing attitudes toward drink, starting in the 1960s, was partially responsible for this increase in per capita consumption. In 1974–1975, per capita consumption among those fifteen years and older reached 11.14 liters (2.9 U.S. gallons) of absolute alcohol, with only British Columbia, Yukon, and the Northwest Territories above the national average. In the period from 1970 to 1974, per capita consumption for beer alone stood at 21.7 U.S. gallons, and consumption of wine was 1.4 U.S. gallons. The postwar generation had a marked preference for beer and wine, and this was reflected in the changing consumption patterns of Canadians. By 1980–1981, Canadians were averaging 12.4 drinks per week among those fifteen years of age and older. Again, British Columbians were above the national average at 14.8 drinks per week. Thereafter, the national average began to drop, and by 1990–1991, it had fallen to 10 drinks per week among those fifteen years of age and older (a 1989 survey placed the national average for the population as a whole at 3.7 drinks per week).

By the mid-1990s, per capita consumption in Canada stood at 7.52 liters (2.0 U.S. gallons) of pure alcohol for the population fifteen years of age and older (based on 1996 figures). Although some western European countries had higher per capita consumption levels, based upon cultural, economic, and social differences, the data suggest a marked reduction in world alcohol consumption levels since the mid-1980s. In North America, and specifically Canada, several factors may explain that trend: the educational efforts of groups such as Mothers Against Drunk Driving (MADD), roadside drunk driving counterattack programs run by police forces across the country, and declining real per capita income. One other factor may account for the decline in per capita consumption, namely, the fact that the average Canadian is working twenty hours more per week than he or she did in the 1960s. Despite the tendency of per capita consumption to be higher in economically developed countries, it seems likely that per capita consumption rates in Canada will continue to drop, reflecting the wider trend found around the world.

Shawn Cafferky

See also: Bees; Federal Prohibition (Canada); Mothers Against Drunk Driving (MADD); Provincial Prohibition (Canada); Saloons, Taverns, Pubs, and Beerhouses (Canada)

References

Barron, F. L. "The Genesis of Temperance in Ontario, 1828–1850" (Ph.D. dissertation, University of Guelph, 1976).

Gray, James H. *Booze: The Impact of Whiskey on the Prairie West.* Toronto: Macmillan, 1972.

Guillet, Edwin Clarence. *Pioneer Days in Upper Canada.* Toronto: University of Toronto Press, 1964.

———. *Pioneer Inns and Taverns.* Toronto: Ontario Publishing Company, 1964.

Rorabaugh, W. J. *The Alcoholic Republic: An American Tradition.* New York: Oxford University Press, 1979.

Smart, Reginald G., and Alan C. Ogborne. *Northern Spirits: A Social History of Alcohol in Canada.* Toronto: Addiction Research Foundation, 1996.

Warsh, Cheryl Krasnick, ed. *Drink in Canada: Historical Essays.* Montreal and Kingston: McGill-Queen's University Press, 1993.

Alcohol, Consumption of, per Capita (United States)

Americans have been hard drinkers since the beginning of European settlement. Around 1825, annual consumption of alcohol, mostly from whiskey, peaked at about 7 gallons for each American of drinking age, defined as fifteen or older. Due to the temperance movement, use dropped by more than two-thirds by 1850. After the Civil War, overall alcohol consumption remained steady at around 2 gallons, but beer gradually displaced whiskey. National Prohibition (1917–1933) caused annual consumption to fall by more than half, to less than 1 gallon, but consumption rebounded after 1933, increased sharply during World War II, and rose to a high of 2.8 gallons in 1980. Since 1981, alcohol use has declined. In 1998, consumption was close to the long-term average at 2.2 gallons per drinking-aged American.

Early colonists brought with them from Europe a thirst for alcohol. During the 1700s, rum importation and distilling imported molasses into rum became major businesses. Rum was widely drunk. It was also important in trade with Native Americans. Farmers pressed apples into alcoholic cider, which kept all winter long. In apple-growing areas, cider consumption ran as high as a pint a day. Housewives routinely brewed mild beer for home use. Its low percentage of alcohol caused it to spoil in a few days. Although annual per capita alcohol consumption among drinking-aged colonists may have reached 6 gallons, precise amounts cannot be measured.

During the American Revolution, the British cut off rum and molasses, and Americans distilled whiskey from cheap, plentiful corn and rye. By 1790, whiskey was heralded as a patriotic drink. Settlement of the Midwest produced a corn glut, and whiskey became, at five cents for a fifth of a gallon, the cheapest beverage. Consumption grew rapidly until the 1820s, when the amount of alcohol in all forms that each drinking-aged American took annually peaked at a rate that came close to the maximum amount that a body can metabolize. In addition to whiskey, which was close to 60 percent of the total alcohol consumed, Americans continued to drink cider, but home brewing declined and only a few wealthy people used wine, which remained rare, expensive, and imported. Alcohol from wine represented less than 2 percent of the total alcohol consumed.

The temperance movement (1825–1850) was a backlash against whiskey. Evangelical Protestants, especially women, led this crusade and identified drinking with sin. Liquor was blamed for crime, poverty, and wife beating. In the new industrial age, factory owners were alarmed by drunken workers who wrecked expensive equipment. Doctors concluded that alcohol ruined health. In New York State, 80 percent of the Protestant ministers and half the doctors stopped drinking by 1840. Ten years later, half of Americans, especially those living in rural areas and small towns, were abstainers. Farmers quit making cider and cut down orchards.

After 1840, massive immigration from European countries with hearty drinking traditions challenged the antiliquor campaign. The Irish opened saloons, and Germans brought beer to the booming cities of the United States. During the Civil War, the United States government taxed alcohol heavily. After the war, taxes remained high on whiskey and other distilled spirits, but taxes on beer were low. Drinkers gradually switched to beer because it was less expensive. By 1890, Americans got as much alcohol from beer as from whiskey. Wine consumption remained tiny, representing only about 5 percent of all alcohol consumption, except in California, where Italian and French immigrants established wineries. After 1900, whiskey consumption was flat, but beer consumption continued to rise as saloons owned or controlled by brewers became important community centers for immigrants in cities. Around 1910, alcohol consumption peaked at 2.6 gallons per drinking-aged person.

In 1917, the United States entered World War I and prohibited alcohol as a wartime measure both to guarantee sober soldiers and to overcome grain shortages. In 1920, Prohibition was continued by constitutional amendment. During the 1920s, alcohol consumption dropped by more than half. Beer, the favorite beverage, was bulky and hard to hide, so it tended to be replaced by bathtub gin or illegally imported Canadian whiskey. Although many Americans stopped drinking out of respect for law or out of fear of being poisoned, millions continued to drink.

In 1933, Prohibition ended. Beer production began immediately, and so did legal importation of Canadian liquor, but American whiskey took several years to be aged properly. In the 1930s, annual per capita alcohol consumption remained at around 1.5 gallons, well below the pre-Prohibition level. Poverty during the depression discouraged use, and the generation that came of age in the 1920s tended not to drink. World War II brought prosperity, tension, and increased drinking. By 1945, consumption reached 2.3 gallons per drinking-aged American. More than half of the alcohol came from beer.

In the 1950s and 1960s, beer sales were flat despite massive television advertising. Per capita hard liquor sales rose to a level not seen since 1880, as vodka, Scotch whiskey, and specialty products outpaced old-line whiskey. In the 1970s, consumption patterns changed as numerous baby boomers entered their twenties, the age group with the highest alcohol consumption. Boomers favored beer and wine over hard liquor. Forgoing their parents' predinner cocktails for wine, they set off an explosion in the number of high-quality American wineries. For the first time, as much as 12 percent of alcohol consumption came from wine.

After 1981, alcohol consumption dropped. Declining real per capita income played a role, and so did the aging of the baby boomers. Other factors included raising the drinking age to twenty-one, aggressive campaigns against drunk driving, increasing legal liabilities for bars and restaurants whose customers became intoxicated, growing awareness that alcohol damaged fetuses, and employer urine tests that detected alcohol as well as drugs. Per capita beer consumption peaked in 1981 and then dropped 10 percent over two decades. This decline tracked the aging of the population. During the same period, wine was also off 10 percent, hard liquor 40 percent. However, imported beers, specialty brands, and brew pubs thrived. Expensive, high-quality wines sold well, as did wine coolers and other newly devised sweet beverage concoctions. These manufactured nectars partly displaced home-mixed drinks made with hard liquor.

W. J. Rorabaugh

See also: Alcohol, Consumption of, by Indices (United States); Beer; Cider; National Prohibition (United States); Rum; Whiskies; Wine

References

Blocker, Jack S., Jr. *American Temperance Movements: Cycles of Reform.* Boston: Twayne, 1989.

Rorabaugh, W. J. *The Alcoholic Republic.* New York: Oxford University Press, 1979.

U.S. Department of Health and Human Services, National Institute on Alcohol Abuse and Alcoholism. "Apparent per Capita Alcohol Consumption: National, State, and Regional Trends, 1977–98." http:/www.niaaa.gov/publications/Cons98.pdf [15 December 2001].

Alcohol and Temperance History Group (ATHG)

The Alcohol and Temperance History Group (ATHG) is the only academic society devoted to the history of the beverage use of alcohol and its social response. Founded in 1979, it has sponsored an international conference as well as sessions at various scholarly meetings, including the annual meeting of the American Historical Association (AHA), of which the ATHG is an affiliated society. The society publishes a journal, *The Social History of Alcohol Review,* and maintains an electronic discussion list (listserv) and website. The editors of this encyclopedia and many of the contributors are drawn from the ranks of the society's membership.

The ATHG was founded on the crest of a wavelet of newly published books on U.S. drinking and temperance reform. Its five founders—U.S. historians Jack S. Blocker Jr. (a Canadian), Jed Dannenbaum, Susan Dye Lee, Amy Mittelman, and Jay Rubin—organized the society in New York City at the AHA's annual meeting. For the society's first five years, it accomplished little besides occasionally publishing a mimeographed newsletter. An organizational structure including a constitution and elected officers was created in 1984 as a by-product of the first international conference on the social history of alcohol, organized in Berkeley, California, by the Alcohol Research Group associated with the University of California. The moving force behind reorganization was British historian David Fahey (an American). Fahey also transformed the newsletter into a scholarly journal, which published bibliographies, news of members and the organization, and book reviews. Affiliation with the AHA followed in 1986. From its early days, the ATHG attracted support from sociologists and anthropologists as well as historians; more recently, literary scholars have joined. The geographical scope of its interests has always been international, although the membership is predominantly based in the United States, and most of the scholarship within its purview deals with the English-speaking world.

In 1993, the ATHG sponsored an International Congress on the Social History of Alcohol, held at Huron University College, London, Ontario, Canada. The conference included a business meeting and a keynote address by historian Ian Tyrrell. Tyrrell's address urged scholars in the field to extend the international reach of their research. Selected papers from this meeting were published in several scholarly journals and collected in a book.

Jack S. Blocker Jr.

References

Alcohol and Temperance History Group website. http://www.athg.org.

Blocker, Jack S., Jr., and Cheryl Krasnick Warsh, eds. *The Changing Face of Drink: Substance, Imagery, and Behaviour.* Ottawa, Canada: Les Publications Histoire Sociale (Social History), 1997.

Contemporary Drug Problems. 21, nos. 3–4 (1994).

The Social History of Alcohol Review (formerly *Alcohol in History*). 1979–present.

Alcoholic Mutual Aid Groups (United States)

Abstinence-based mutual aid societies, organized by and for those experiencing severe alcohol-related problems, have a long and rich history in the United States. The first of these societies arose in two cultural contexts: within Native American tribes in the eighteenth century and then within Euro-American communities in the mid-nineteenth century. The impetus for these societies was the rise of alcohol problems among Native peoples and a threefold rise in annual per capita alcohol consumption

Alcoholic Mutual Aid Groups: A Chronology

Native Recovery "Circles" (1737–1750)
Handsome Lake Religion (1799)
Washingtonians (1840)
Fraternal Temperance Societies

- Sons of Temperance (1842)
- Independent Order of Good Samaritans and Daughters of Samaria (1847)
- Order of Good Templars (1851)

The Dashaway Association (1859)
The Ollapod Club (1868)
Ribbon Reform Clubs (1870s)

- Royal Ribbon Reform Club (1871)
- Blue Ribbon Reform Club (1871)
- Red Ribbon Reform Club (1874)

The Drunkard's Club (ca. 1871)
The Godwin Association (1872)
Peyotism (1870s)/The American Indian Church (1918)
Business Men's Moderation Society (1879)
The Indian Shaker Church (1882)
The Keeley Leagues (1891)
Jacoby Club (1910)
United Order of Ex-Boozers (1914)
Alcoholics Anonymous (AA) (1935)
Calix Society (1947)
Narcotics Anonymous (1947, 1953)
Alcoholics Victorious (AV) (1948)
Potsmokers Anonymous (1968)
Pills Anonymous (1975)
Women For Sobriety (WFS) (1975)
Overcomers Outreach (1977)
Jewish Alcoholics, Chemically Dependent People and Significant Others (JACS) (1979)
Liontamers Anonymous (1980)
Cocaine Anonymous (1982)
Secular Organization for Sobriety (SOS) (1985)
Rational Recovery (RR) (1986)
Moderation Management (MM) (1994)
Self Management And Recovery Training (SMART) (1994)
One Church–One Addict (1994)
LifeRing Secular Recovery (1999)
Teen-Anon (1999)

and related personal and social problems within the new American republic.

Native leaders, including Papounhan, Wagomend, Neolin (the Delaware prophet), Tenskwatawa (the Shawnee prophet), Handsome Lake, and Kennekuk (the Kickapoo prophet), introduced nativist religious and cultural revitalization movements that called for the rejection of alcohol and a return to Native traditions. The mid-eighteenth-century recovery "circles" among the Delaware Indians constitute the earliest geographically decentralized, sobriety-based support structures in the United States. Native religious and cultural revitalization movements, created by messianic leaders who themselves had suffered from alcoholism, emerged at a time when alcohol was being used as a tool of economic, political, and sexual exploitation of Native peoples. These early movements were followed by "Indian Preachers" in recovery from alcoholism (Samson Occom, William Apess) who provided a Christian framework of recovery from alcoholism, and late-nineteenth-century abstinence movements that blended both Native and Christian beliefs and rituals (e.g., The Indian Shaker Church and the Native American Church).

Sobriety as a Cultural Phenomenon

By the 1830s, Americans suffering from what was about to be newly christened as "alcoholism" sought shelter within a rising temperance movement. It was within the local temperance societies that the drunkard would find a mechanism to stop drinking (signing the pledge), a forum for public confession and commitment, sober fellowship, and support for keeping the pledge. Between 1840 and 1875, recently sobered drunkards began to organize their own temperance societies that were focused more on personal reformation than public education and political reform. The first society founded exclusively for the purpose of such reformation was the Washingtonian Total Abstinence Society, organized in April 1840 in Baltimore, Maryland.

The Washingtonian Society emphasized the importance of public confession, pledge signing, mentorship of new members, continued sharing in the Washingtonian meetings, sober fellowship, and service to other "hard cases." The society experienced explosive growth, quickly rising to a membership of more than 500,000, and rapid geographical dispersion that was due, in part, to the leadership of men like John Hawkins and John Bartholomew Gough, two of the most effective and widely traveled temperance lecturers of the nineteenth century. In spite of this dramatic increase in membership and public visibility, most Washingtonian groups collapsed within a few years due to the loss of their closed ("drunkards only") meeting structure, internal dissension over political and religious issues, damaged public credibility, and cooptation by more powerful temperance organizations.

Following the collapse of the Washingtonians, fraternal temperance societies filled the void of mutual support for "reformed men" seeking to be shielded from the temptations of drink. Among the more prominent societies were the Sons of Temperance, the Order of Good Templars, the Independent Order of Rechabites, the Order of the Friends of Temperance, and the Independent Order of Good Samaritans. The membership of some of these societies was made up almost exclusively of reformed men. The emphasis on sober fellowship and economic assistance eventually widened the doors of membership to include anyone willing to sign the pledge and meet other requirements for membership. Membership in these societies declined as conflict arose over whether their focus should be on the personal reformation of the drunkard exclusively or whether it should include the legal prohibition of alcohol.

Another genre of alcoholic mutual aid society, the Ribbon Reform Clubs, emerged in the 1870s under the leadership of men such as J. K. Osgood, Dr. Henry Reynolds, and Francis Murphy. The Ribbon Clubs drew their name from the practice of members wearing a ribbon on their clothing, both to convey publicly the hope of reform for the drunkard and to recognize one another as they traveled. The purple, blue, and red ribbons became visible symbols of personal recovery in the closing decades of the nineteenth century. The Ribbon Reform Clubs emphasized pledge signing, regular meetings for mutual support, rescue work with other drunkards, and a prohibition against political discussions at their sponsored events.

These early alcoholic mutual aid societies inspired calls for the creation of special institutions to care for the inebriate. Several hundred inebriate homes, medically directed inebriate asylums, and proprietary addiction-cure institutes opened in the last half of the nineteenth century. These institutions spawned patient-led organizations that provided mutual support both during and following treatment. Among the more prominent of these societies were the Ollapod Club (New York Inebriate Asylum), the Godwin Association (Franklin Reformatory Home for Inebriates), the Dashaway Association (The San Francisco Home for the Care of the Inebriate) and the Keeley Leagues (Keeley Institutes). The Keeley Leagues were the largest of these institutional aftercare groups, with more than 370 chapters and 30,000 members during the mid-1890s.

Another type of alcoholic mutual aid society emerged from the work of Jerry McAuley. McAuley, an alcoholic ex-convict, achieved sobriety through religious conversion and went on to open the Water Street Mission in New York City in 1872. This marks the beginning of the urban mission movement in the United States, out of which also grew the alcoholism programs of the Salvation Army and rural religious inebriate colonies such as Keswick Colony of Mercy, founded by William Raws in 1889. Mutual aid groups such as The Drunkard's Club, founded by Orville "Awful" Gardner in New York City, were the earliest precursors to modern religiously oriented alcoholism recovery support groups such as the United Order of Ex-Boozers, Alcoholics Victorious, Alcoholics for Christ, Mountain Movers, Liontamers Anonymous, High Ground, and Overcomers Outreach. There is a more recent trend toward offering recovery support groups within the framework of a larger addiction ministry, such as the One Church–One Addict program founded by Father George Clements of Chicago.

Groups such as the Business Men's Moderation Society, founded in 1879, marked the beginning of mutual aid societies that were neither abstinence based nor religiously oriented. The moderation societies pledged themselves to limit the frequency and volume of alcohol consumption and to avoid practices such as "treating" that encouraged drunkenness.

Collapse and Rebirth

Most of the alcoholic mutual aid societies and alcoholism treatment institutions founded in the nineteenth century collapsed during the first two decades of the twentieth century. One attempt to revive this type of support was Boston's Jacoby Club, founded in 1910 by Ernest Jacoby as a club for alcoholic men to "help themselves by helping others." The Jacoby Club was created as an appendage to the Emmanuel Clinic, which sought to combine religion, psychology, and medicine in the treatment of alcoholism.

This dearth of mutual aid resources changed in 1935 when the meeting of two alcoholics, William Griffith Wilson and Dr. Robert Holbrook Smith, reaching out for mutual support, marked the founding of Alcoholics Anonymous (AA). AA grew slowly, extracting its Twelve Steps and Twelve Traditions from the experiences of its early members and groups. It stood alone as the dominant sobriety-based support structure from its founding into the mid-1970s. There were adaptations of AA to alcoholism (Alcoholics Victorious) and eleventh-step adaptations of AA for AA members of particular religious faiths (e.g., Calix Society for Catholic AA members), but virtually no major competing groups. AA's survival as an organization and its continuing growth mark it as the yardstick by which all other such societies are measured.

AA's sole cultural ownership of alcoholism mutual aid was challenged in the mid-1970s and 1980s with the founding of new alcoholic mutual aid societies. This began with the founding by Dr. Jean Kirkpatrick of Women For Sobriety (WFS), which was later followed by another women-focused alternative to AA, Charlotte Kasl's sixteen-step empowerment program. Secular alternatives to AA were also emerging: the Secular Organization for Sobriety (SOS), founded by James Christopher, and Rational Recovery (RR), founded by Jack Trimpey. Schisms within SOS and RR spawned other abstinence-based secular organizations—LifeRing Secular Recovery and the Alcohol and Drug Abuse Self-Help Network, the latter evolving into Self Management And Recovery Training (SMART). The 1980s also witnessed the rebirth of moderation-oriented mutual support groups such as Moderation Management (MM), founded by Audrey Kishline. MM provides a nine-step framework that includes a brief, thirty-day period of abstinence, a self-analysis of life priorities and drinking patterns, drinking within prescribed limits, and mutual support in face-to-face and on-line support groups.

The other modern trend is the adaptation of AA's twelve-step program for those experiencing problems with drugs other than alcohol. The most significant of these are Narcotics Anonymous, Cocaine Anonymous, Pills Anonymous, and Potsmokers Anonymous. Although the support group movement has expanded far beyond AA to encompass an ever-widening circle of problems, nearly three-fourths of all support meetings attended in the United States are meetings for the resolution of alcohol- and/or other drug-related problems.

The modern story of mutual aid groups is clearly one of expansion and specialization. In spite of their many differences, there are common threads within all of the mutual aid societies discussed here. Each provided or continues to provide a framework for acknowledging and defining the nature of an alcohol or other drug problem, and initiating and sustaining changes in alcohol and drug consumption. They also provide a means of reconstructing personal identity and interpersonal relationships and clarifying one's personal goals and values. What distinguishes them from professionally directed addiction treatment is that such change occurs in the context of relationships that are nonhierarchical, noncommercialized, reciprocal, and often long lasting.

William L. White

See also: Alcoholics Anonymous (AA); Good Templars (IOGT); Handsome Lake (Ga-nya-di-yoh); Keeley Institutes; Murphy, Francis; Native Americans: Drinking Patterns and Temperance Reform; Rechabite Friendly Society; Reformed Men's Clubs; Salvation Army; Sons of Temperance; Tenskwatawa; Treatment Institutions; Washingtonians

References

Kessler, Ronald C., Kristin D. Mickelson, and Shanyang Zhao. "Patterns and Correlates of Self-Help Group Membership in the United States" in *Social Policy.* 27 (1997): 27–45.

Volpicelli, Joseph, and Maia Szalavitz. *Recovery Options.* New York: John Wiley and Sons, 2000.

White, William L. "Pre-A.A. Alcoholic Mutual Aid Societies" in *Alcoholism Treatment Quarterly.* 19, no. 2 (2001): 1–21.

———. *Slaying the Dragon: The History of Addiction Treatment and Recovery in America.* Bloomington, IL: Chestnut Health Systems, 1998.

Alcoholics Anonymous (AA)

According to the presentation of itself read at the beginning of most meetings of Alcoholics Anonymous:

> Alcoholics Anonymous is a fellowship of men and women who share their experience, strength and hope with each other that they may solve their common problem and help others to recover from alcoholism.
>
> The only requirement for membership is a desire to stop drinking. There are no dues or fees for AA membership; we are self-supporting through our own contributions.
>
> AA is not allied with any sect, denomination, politics, organization or institution; does not wish to engage in any controversy, neither endorses nor opposes any causes.
>
> Our primary purpose is to stay sober and to help other alcoholics to achieve sobriety.

Beginnings: 1935–1950

Alcoholics Anonymous (AA) began on 12 May 1935, when a recently sobered broker's representative from New York, while visiting Akron, Ohio, experienced a craving for alcoholic refreshment and, to stave it off, sought out an alcoholic local surgeon. The visiting New Yorker was William Griffith Wilson; the surgeon was Dr. Robert Holbrook Smith. Eventually, they would be known as "Bill W." and "Dr. Bob," cofounders of Alcoholics Anonymous.

But not immediately, for Dr. Smith, attending a medical convention in Atlantic City, New Jersey, went on "one last toot." Dr. Bob's sobriety date is usually given as 10 June 1935, which has become known in AA as "Founders' Day," despite recent evidence that Dr. Smith took his last drink on 17 June 1935. The exact date makes little difference. What was important about the first meeting between Wilson and Smith were three discoveries made by the two men in the course of that meeting.

First, they discovered the role of "the spiritual." Bill Wilson located Dr. Bob Smith through a "spiritual" connection. Wilson was introduced to Smith by Henrietta Seiberling, a member of the Oxford Group. Seiberling's name had been given him by an Oxford Group–oriented minister. Bill had joined the group after his own "spiritual experience" while sobering up in Towns Hospital in New York City in December 1934. The message underlying that experience originated with Dr. Carl Gustav Jung's observation that those in the second half of life could recover from alcoholism only through some kind of "spiritual conversion." The Oxford Group was the leading vehicle for such conversion among middle-class Americans in the 1930s. Although much extended in meaning, the centrality of "the spiritual" has always characterized Alcoholics Anonymous.

The second discovery was the need to "carry the message." Wilson had tried to carry the message to other drunks in New York, but he found no one interested. His meeting with Dr. Smith, soon reinforced by their approach to "AA #3," Bill D., was different because in these cases they made the approach for their own sakes, not primarily to help the person they approached. The only way to keep their own sobriety, they discovered, was to give it away.

The third discovery was the importance of identification by way of story. Just before Wilson left for Akron, his physician, Dr. William Duncan Silkworth, cautioned him to stop emphasizing his "spiritual experience" when he approached other drunks. Silkworth, who viewed alcoholism as an allergy, urged Bill to "Give them the medical business." "Fine idea," Bill thought some weeks later in Akron, but how could he teach medicine to a physician? So Wilson fell back on telling his own story—the story of his life as it was affected by alcohol and the story of his recovery without alcohol. And Dr. Bob Smith identified; he recognized his own experience in Bill's autobiographical tale. The only way an alcoholic could get through to another alcoholic was by identification, and the only way to achieve that was by the mutual sharing of stories.

The Writing of the AA Big Book

Although the Oxford Group was the womb within which Alcoholics Anonymous came into being, AA left those auspices in 1937 in New York and in 1939 in Akron. The departure came mainly because of the Oxford Group's intrusive spirituality in such practices as group "guidance," and the group's focus on "the four absolutes" of honesty, unselfishness, purity, and love. Those virtues, Wilson later wrote, "are sought and practiced by members of Alcoholics Anonymous as much as by any other people, but if you put the word 'absolute' in front of them, alcoholics just couldn't stand the pace [and got drunk again]." In New York, those who left began to refer to themselves as "a nameless bunch of drunks"—a term that would be transmuted into "Alcoholics Anonymous" as the group later sought a title for its book.

In the early enthusiasm of their separate existence, some members proposed large projects such as hospitals. Largely due to Dr. Smith's urging to "Keep it simple," all designs other than writing a book detailing their method were discarded. Wilson began drafting what would become the book *Alcoholics Anonymous,* and the "alcoholic squadron" of the Oxford Group in Akron and the newly dry who met weekly at the Wilson residence in Brooklyn offered comments and suggestions. When published, the tome became known as the "Big Book" because the New Yorkers urged their printer to use the thickest paper available for the first edition so that it would seem worth the price to the generally impecunious alcoholics at whom it was targeted.

No groundswell of welcome greeted the publication of AA's book. Medical journals panned it. Attempts at publicity, such as a massive mailing of postcards to physicians, fell flat. But slowly, through newspaper coverage, most importantly through a 1941 article by investigative reporter Jack Alexander in *The Saturday Evening Post,* the public—and especially some drinking alcoholics—heard of AA. Some of those who heard contacted the listed New York office to purchase copies of the book.

Early Outcomes

The members' original intention was that individual alcoholics would read the book, "make surrender," and carry the message to other alcoholics. Meetings were for newcomers: "We meet frequently so that newcomers may find the fellowship they seek." Another purpose of the weekly meetings, now in Cleveland as well as in New York and Akron, was to provide a forum for answering the questions of newcomers. Alcoholism was a puzzling malady to those who suffered it. Their earlier attempts at sobriety had failed. Why did AA work? And what about . . . whatever? But meetings did not become question-and-answer sessions—most of the early sober alcoholics were acutely aware that they had no "answers." There developed, rather, a practice that would be enshrined in the Preamble as "sharing their experience, strength and hope." Questions were answered by someone who identified with the questioner; the "answer" consisted of telling how a similar situation had worked out in his life. ("His" is used here because at this point, there was only one female member each in New York, Washington, and Chicago.)

Meanwhile, another need surfaced—the need for detoxification rather than what would later be termed "treatment." Alcoholics who could get to Akron were hospitalized for detoxification under the care of Dr. Smith. But not all drunks could go to Akron. Some few did not require large medical intervention, but most who approached Alcoholics Anonymous in those early years had severely damaged their health during their drinking. These people obviously needed hospitalization, but in those days, most hospitals did not admit alcoholics, mainly because they rarely paid their bills. This was how the practice of "sponsorship" began within Alcoholics Anonymous, first in Cleveland, then more widely. The "sponsor" was someone who promised to pay the detoxification hospital bill if the new recruit failed to do so. Sponsorship soon evolved into a more comprehensive concern for the individual newcomer's sobriety.

Following the example of the program devised by Dr. Smith and Sister Ignatia at Saint Thomas Hospital in Akron, a five-day hospital program opened at Knickerbocker Hospital in New York City by 1945. After the war, this type of program became available in other cities as well. Usually, a local physician, impressed with the success at sobriety of former patients, helped them set up an "AA ward" in the hospital. The medical care consisted of detoxification and nutritional buildup, and the usual program ran five days. During that time, the patient was allowed no outside distractions but was visited virtually around the clock by members of AA. Early on, a truism was discovered: "AA is for those who want it, not those who need it." Many who patently needed AA did not want it, and so did not get it. This observation led some Philadelphia physicians to begin keeping track of AA success. In 1937, Dr. Silkworth and Bill Wilson had both expressed the opinion that AA was unlikely to work for more than "about half" of what were then generally termed "chronic inebriates." The Philadelphia study suggested that AA was actually more successful. Among "those who really tried," it was found, about 50 percent achieved dryness almost at once, within a period of about 90 days, while another 25 percent did so after going out and drinking again but then coming back to AA. The final 25 percent seemed beyond AA's help.

These are important figures. In later years, when the popularity of "treatment" and the practice of employer coercion and court mandates forced more individuals to attend AA meetings, it appeared that less than 5 percent of those who attended an AA meeting got sober. What had been forgotten was the "really tried" part. Although never spelled out in detail, "really trying" was generally understood to consist of at least 90 days of fairly regular attendance at AA meetings, getting a sponsor, reading the literature, and attempting to work the Twelve Steps. Of that population, the 50–25–25 ratio first found in Philadelphia in 1946 still holds true in the opening years of the twenty-first century.

The End of the Beginning

The World War II years saw the debut of AA's "unofficial" but significant publication, *The AA Grapevine.* Begun in June 1944 as a means of keeping in touch "with our boys in the armed forces," this journal has to this day continued monthly publication of members' sharing of their "experience, strength and hope." The magazine soon began to serve another purpose in the great postwar expansion into sprawling new suburbs and a vibrant new consumer economy. From the beginning, given its Akron and New York City origins, a keynote of Alcoholics Anonymous was *variety.* As meetings developed more widely, they took on different formats: speaker, several speakers, one-topic discussion, open discussion, and so forth. Similarly, the attitudes of groups and members toward such topics as "the spiritual" and "other drugs" varied. *The AA Grapevine* offered a forum in which these various approaches could be presented and discussed. The *AA Grapevine*'s welcoming of such diversities marked the culmination of AA's first decade of existence. Between 1935 and 1945, the fellowship grew from 2 members to 12,986 members, organized into 556 local groups.

The trial-and-error development that took place in each new location led to a desire to learn from the experience of other groups. An attempt to produce a general handbook failed in the mid-1940s, though many locations developed their own guides, setting forth the practices of the locality for the edification of new groups. By the late 1940s, Bill Wilson began to review the growing correspondence in which members told of what worked and what did not work in their situations. When some wrote asking advice on a matter, Wilson and others in what became AA's General Service Office developed a practice of telling what had happened in similar circumstances in other settings. There thus emerged the "Twelve Traditions of Alcoholics Anonymous," first promulgated in 1950 at the fellowship's first international convention held at Cleveland, Ohio. The traditions emerged during a period of explosive growth for AA: by 1950, membership exceeded 96,000 and local groups numbered more than 3,500. Though this would not become apparent until much later, AA's Twelve Traditions became to the existence of the fellowship what the Twelve Steps are to the sobriety of its individual members.

Coming of Age: 1951–1970

The promulgation of its Twelve Traditions in 1950 marked the beginning of AA's "Coming of Age," though that would not be formally celebrated until its 1955 Saint Louis convention. The 1950 convention marked Dr. Bob Smith's last public appearance before his death in November of that year. Two significant developments marked the early 1950s, developments that would continue to unfold in the following two decades. The first was the large social acceptance bestowed on Alcoholics Anonymous in the United States. Second, during this half-decade, Bill Wilson produced a book, *Twelve Steps and Twelve Traditions,* that guided many members' understanding of "the spiritual" during the changing times of the 1960s and 1970s.

From its earliest days, Alcoholics Anonymous had won support from many physicians and members of the clergy. The medical and religious professions generally welcomed the new fellowship and its program, which honored their contributions and even claimed a kind of joint origin from them. The Eisenhower decade of the 1950s proved an ideal setting for "the spiritual rather than religious" program of Alcoholics Anonymous to attain wide acceptance. Practically as well as symbolically, that acceptance came less with AA's winning of the 1951 Lasker Award or the congratulatory telegram President Dwight Eisenhower sent AA on the occasion of its twentieth-year "Coming of Age" convention than in the regular recommendation of the fellowship by advice columnists Ann Landers and Dear Abby. Reinforcing this acceptance were the movies *Smash-Up* and *The Lost Weekend,* eventually followed by *Days of Wine and Roses* and references that, though less focused on Alcoholics Anonymous, by that very fact attested to the broad basis of its cultural acceptance.

Throughout this period, AA's Twelve Traditions offered guidance that helped the fellowship resolve many troublesome issues, though not always unanimously. The establishment of "a desire to stop drinking" as "the only requirement for membership," the exclusion of "outside issues," the "one primary purpose" of carrying the AA message "to the alcoholic who still suffers"—each in time would be challenged, and following the principle of "group autonomy," some groups would opt for broad interpretation. But at least until the impact of commercialized "treatment," AA remained not only recognizably but unambiguously the AA that had been founded in 1935.

As the 1960s progressed, AA cofounder William Griffith Wilson suffered increasing health problems, especially emphysema. Wilson's last public appearance was at the Alcoholics Anonymous thirty-fifth annual convention at Miami Beach in 1970, where he had to be physically propped up to appear momentarily before the cheering throng. He died on 24 January 1971. At his death, there were more than 16,000 local AA groups and more than 310,000 members.

Few organizations led for so long by a charismatic leader survive his or her demise. Alcoholics Anonymous both refuted and bore out this generalization. AA refuted it in that, given its reverse-pyramidal, bottom-up structure, the individual groups and most members kept on functioning as they always had: carrying the message, living out the Twelve Steps of their program. Few people dropping into an AA meeting in the mid-1970s heard mention of Bill Wilson. But on a deeper level, the vacuum of leadership occurred at the dawning edge of a monumental change in cultural attitudes toward alcoholism, a change for which AA was partially responsible.

The Treatment Era: 1970–2000

From their beginnings, local AA groups carried their message of hope to alcoholics in missions, general and psychiatric hospitals, prisons, halfway houses, sanatoria, and various "drying out" facilities. During the middle decades of the twentieth century, AA members created sober sanctuaries ("AA farms," "AA retreats," "Twelve Step houses") in communities where institutional support for recovery was lacking. AA members—as individuals, not as representatives of AA—were also heavily represented among the leaders of newly forming alcoholism councils, who advocated the establishment of local alcoholism information and referral centers, detoxification facilities, and rehabilitation programs. Under the leadership of the National Council on Alcoholism (NCA), this sustained advocacy campaign culminated in passage of the 1970 Comprehensive Alcoholism Prevention and Treatment Act, the landmark legislation that launched the modern alcoholism treatment field. With this infusion of federal funding, alcoholism treatment facilities in the United States grew in number from less than 200 in 1970 to 4,200 in 1980, to more than 9,000 in 1990.

Directly, this new social development had nothing to do with AA, but many AA members played roles—as alcoholism counselors, nurses, physicians, and administrators—in the emergence and evolution of modern alcoholism treatment. Most of these new institutions also incorporated AA's Twelve Steps into their treatment philosophies and recommended that their clients affiliate with AA during and following their professional treatment. This incorporation of AA philosophy was particularly pronounced in the "Minnesota Model"—a style of chemical dependency treatment that became the dominant approach to the treatment of addiction in the United States. By the mid-1970s, professional concern was voiced about the inordinate influence AA was exerting on alcoholism treatment in the United States. Within a decade, there were equal concerns about the influence the treatment field was exerting on AA.

For as the treatment field grew into a treatment industry, it came to exert considerable influence on AA. The most immediate effect was growth. Between 1970 and 1980, AA membership rose from 311,450 to 907,575, and the number of local AA groups jumped from 16,459 to 42,105. By 1990, AA membership had further increased to 2,047,469 (93,914 groups). This dramatic growth was accompanied by the adaptation of AA's Twelve Steps to every imaginable problem. "Recovery" became something of a cultural phenomenon as the concept of "addiction" became applied to processes as well as to substances, and twelve-step groups were inundated by people bearing an endless list of unmet needs. This popular invasion created a transience in AA that was masked within the raw growth figures.

The growing percentage of people who entered AA while in treatment and the growing number of external bodies coercing people into AA combined to raise serious concerns within the organization. The fellowship did not remain passive in the face of such impacts. It reasserted the importance of its traditions on everything from anonymity to nonaffiliation; it issued guidelines for AA members working in the alcoholism field; and it published literature seeking to distinguish AA from treatment and to define the relationship between AA and treatment. These efforts, however, did little to stem the growing concern that AA's spiritual program of recovery was, through the influence of treatment and the criminal justice system, being watered down by "New Age" pop psychology at the same time it was taking on a coercive dimension. Many longtime AA members began to lament the secularization of AA, and several serious students of Alcoholics Anonymous began to distinguish between the elements of a "real" AA, characterized by the language of spirituality enshrined in the Twelve Steps, and an ersatz "twelve-step movement" employing the vocabulary of therapy, which—however helpful to some—marked an abandonment of the classic Alcoholics Anonymous insight and approach. There also developed a growing fundamentalist movement within AA itself, one that sought to regain the practices of AA's earliest generations, though often at the cost of confusing Alcoholics Anonymous itself with its Oxford Group parent. The effort to distinguish between AA and outside enterprises that in one way or another attempted to clothe themselves in its reputation became increasingly important as the alcoholism treatment industry experienced both ideological and financial backlash during the late 1980s and 1990s. All this led not only to visibility but also to a new vulnerability for Alcoholics Anonymous. By the early 1990s, more than 3,000 books and articles had been written about this "simple" program of recovery. But heightened visibility invited public and professional criticism.

AA Critics

Serious criticism of AA began with a 1964 magazine article by psychologist Arthur Cain and accelerated rapidly during the 1980s and 1990s. Such criticisms were often entwined with broader attacks on the disease concept of alcoholism (often erroneously attributed to AA) and the alcoholism treatment industry. Critics included philosophers, psychologists, and sociologists, as well as groups advocating alternative alcoholism recovery approaches. The latter included the first nationally visible alternatives to Alcoholics Anonymous: Women For Sobriety (WFS), Secular Organization for Sobriety (SOS), Rational Recovery (RR), and Moderation Management (MM). By the mid-1980s, extremist critics of AA coalesced into something of a countermovement with their own publishing genre, star speakers, and Internet websites. The growing acrimony toward AA was revealed in such book titles as *Alcoholics Anonymous: Cult or Cure?*, *How Alcoholics Anonymous Failed Me*, and *Twelve-Step Horror Stories*, as well as Internet websites bearing such names as AA Kills, AA Deprogramming, and Recovery Liberation.

The critics of AA argued that: (1) AA is not effective or (more conservatively) its effectiveness has not been scientifically established, (2) AA works only with particular types of alcoholics and may be harmful to other types, (3) AA's religious ideas and language discourage many alcoholics from seeking help, (4) AA is just a substitute dependence, and (5) AA has discouraged the scientific advancement of alcoholism treatment.

Helpfully, some researchers began to test scientifically the propositions within this debate. Keith Humphreys, for one early example, tested the proposition that AA was ineffective for women, people of color, and persons experiencing co-occurring psychiatric illness. Humphreys found that individuals from these groups affiliated with and successfully recovered within AA at rates comparable to white males.

Varieties of AA Experience

A trend within AA as important as AA's dramatic growth and its public attention is the continuing and growing variety of AA experience. Such variety is not new, as anyone familiar with the differences between New York and Akron AA in the 1930s realizes. Much of the quiet humor within Alcoholics Anonymous is rooted in the realization that no one will ever lead alcoholics very far in any direction—an alcoholic is by definition one who cannot be led. And so, not only is AA membership diverse but so are AA rituals, meeting practices, formats, outside-of-meeting events, and understandings of anonymity. Such diversity is an enduring phenomenon in AA, and this theme of diversity continues to be reflected in AA membership, in the growing propensity of local AA meetings to be organized around special populations or needs, and in the wide range of styles through which people "work" the AA program.

Membership surveys portray this: the 1996 and 1998 surveys reveal a membership increasingly diverse in age, gender (34 percent women), racial composition (12–14 percent nonwhite), and occupational background. Most AA members attend more than two meetings a week and more than 70 percent have been sober more than a year, with nearly half having been sober more than five years. The major factors bringing people to AA are self-motivation and contact with another AA member, closely followed by referral by a treatment or counseling agency, or by court order. Surveys cannot fully convey the diversity of AA experience, but local meeting lists reflect the growing specialization of the process of member-to-member identification within AA, including meetings by gender (women only), age (young people, "old-timers"), language (Spanish, no profanity), sexual orientation (gay, lesbian, bisexual, transgender), relationship status (singles, couples), co-occurring problems (HIV/AIDS, psychiatric illness), and smoking status (nonsmoking), to name a few of the most common demarcations. But even these categories do not fully express the multidimensional character of AA groups—groups that differ dramatically in their degree and type of religious orientation (from Christian to nonbelievers), their meeting styles, their pre- and postmeeting rituals, their degree of emphasis on the steps and traditions, and their approach to service work. What this means is that AA in the opening years of the twenty-first century offers more potential varieties of recovery experiences than at any time in its history. All future efforts to summarize or categorize AA will need to address this enormous diversification of AA style and experience.

The Present and Future: 2001 and Beyond

Alcoholics Anonymous has become a worldwide phenomenon currently embracing more than 2.1 million members and 100,766 groups in approximately 150 countries. About 60 percent of AA's current groups and members are located outside the United States. Its literature is published in 39 languages, and more than a million copies of its basic text, *Alcoholics Anonymous,* are sold each year. AA's success can be attributed to many things, but the unique organizational structure and the operating principles set forth in the Twelve Traditions certainly top the list of contending factors. The latter have protected AA from many of the pitfalls that proved fatal to its myriad of predecessors.

AA's greatest historical significance may rest in its having found a way to convey an experience of community in societies where the connecting tissue of authentic personal relationships seems in danger of disappearing. AA is the core of a growing phenomenon of recovery communities: people across the world who have created sober sanctuaries of mutual support, the personal meaning of which far transcends that of alcoholism recovery. These communities that defy boundaries of geography, age, gender, ethnicity, and political or religious affiliation may be one of AA's subtle but most important legacies.

Ernest Kurtz and William L. White

See also: Alcoholic Mutual Aid Groups (United States); Alcoholism; Employee Assistance Programs (EAPs); National Council on Alcoholism and Drug Dependence (NCADD); Smith, Robert Holbrook; Wilson, William Griffith

References

Anonymous. *Alcoholics Anonymous.* New York: AAWS, 1976 [1939].

Anonymous. *Alcoholics Anonymous Comes of Age.* New York: AAWS, 1957.

Anonymous. *Pass It On.* New York: AAWS, 1984.

Bufe, Charles. *Alcoholics Anonymous: Cult or Cure?* San Francisco: See Sharp Press, 1991.

Humphreys, K., and M. Woods. "Researching Mutual Help Group Affiliation in a Segregated Society" in *Journal of Applied Behavioral Science.* 29 (1993): 181–201.

Kurtz, Ernest. "Alcoholics Anonymous and the Disease Concept of Alcoholism." http://www.bhrm.org/papers/AAand%20DiseaseConcept.pdf.

———. *Not-God: A History of Alcoholics Anonymous.* rev. ed. Center City, MN: Hazelden, 1991.

White, William L. *Slaying the Dragon.* Bloomington, IL: Lighthouse, 1998.

Alcoholism

Alcoholism refers to the pathological use of alcohol. This disease model of drinking behavior is a relatively new concept—one still evolving in its meaning. It remains controversial and hotly debated in some quarters. Often used as a synonym for addiction, alcoholism is seen as the disease of those who are intemperate in their consumption of any form of alcohol. There is no one definition of the concept alcoholism; it has many different meanings, often dependent upon who is using it. As a result, it is commonly asserted that there are many different "alcoholisms." In the United States, despite widespread acceptance of alcoholism as a disease, strong resistance nonetheless remains because the notion that alcoholism is the result of volitional conduct is deeply imbedded in American culture. The disease model of alcoholism is a work in progress. Alcohol professionals in other parts of the world have been slower to accept the disease model than their counterparts in the United States.

Dr. Benjamin Rush, a signer of the Declaration of Independence and surgeon general for the Continental army in the late eighteenth century, argued that those who could not control their use of alcohol were addicted to it. Often called the father of the American temperance movement, Rush was opposed only to "ardent spirits" or hard liquor. In contrast, he regarded beer, wine, and hard cider in moderation as acceptable. He argued that the development of the addiction to spirits was progressive, and that such drunkenness was a threat to one's health. He called for the establishment of sober houses where drunks could receive treatment. This was a position contrary to existing popular belief. Rush had been exposed to these ideas at the medical school at the University of Edinburgh. Not only did Rush challenge the notion that alcohol was good for you, but he laid the groundwork for the development of the disease model. Temperance advocates welcomed this position and utilized it in their propaganda. The Washingtonian Total Abstinence Society, founded in Baltimore in 1840, was an organization with a goal of helping drunks to reform. For over a decade, this precursor of Alcoholics Anonymous enjoyed phenomenal support.

By the middle of the nineteenth century, alcoholism had been introduced to the English language. In 1849, a Swedish physician, Magnus Huss, used the term to describe excessive alcohol consumption. In 1866, M. Gabriel, a French doctoral student, used the term in its modern sense and called alcoholism a disease—a disease in which people could not control their drinking. Alcoholics were powerless to stop their excesses. Physicians and some of the temperance movement people saw the need for inebriate asylums where treatment could be provided for the drunkard. These efforts produced a few state-run asylums, many more private ones, and inventive cures; some, like the "Keeley Cure," became quite popular. The successes of these efforts were varied, short-term, and in many cases unknown. Nonetheless, they did help publicize the idea of alcoholism as a disease.

Alcoholics Anonymous

In 1935, Alcoholics Anonymous (AA) was created by William Griffith Wilson and Dr. Robert Holbrook Smith, later to be called Bill W. and Dr. Bob. This self-help organization maintained the disease model as a central tenet. Although never formally defining it, AA regarded alcoholism as "an obsession of the mind and an allergy of the body," a description provided by Dr. William Duncan Silkworth, the head of a New York hospital that offered treatment to drunks. Alcoholics were powerless to control their drinking, so their only way to handle the disease was abstinence. The AA General Service Office reports most of its members regard alcoholism as an illness, but this belief is not a prerequisite for membership. Only the desire to stop drinking is expected from a member.

Alcoholism as a concept in general parlance received a tremendous boost from the rapid growth and acceptance of AA. Among other things, AA taught that some people are susceptible to the disease, while others are not. This put Alcoholics Anonymous in the position of not being opposed to alcohol per se, but convinced that some people should never drink. It also meant that an alcoholic was not a bad person, a sinner, or simply a lout with deviant propensities.

In keeping with its emphasis on anonymity, AA keeps no membership lists, so reports of the number of members and success rates in treating the disease of alcoholism are estimates based on various sources. Affiliated chapters may submit a report on the number of attendees, and the AA General Service Office conducts surveys of its membership. However, because members are self-identified, the validity of such data is a moot point. Currently, the General Service Office reports membership at more than 2 million people in 150 countries. It states that 47 percent of its members report being sober for more than five years, 26 percent have not had a drink in between one and five years, and 27 percent have abstained for less than a year. The General Service Office calculates the average number of years of sobriety for AA members is seven.

The effectiveness of the organization is a matter of some debate. The question of how a nonmedical group of people can bring about a cure is not an issue because AA maintains that there is no cure other than abstinence. A major tenet of the organization is the belief that once a person is an alcoholic, he or she is always an alcoholic, although remission is possible. The goal of AA, similar to that of the Washingtonians of the 1840s, is to assist alcoholics in pursuit of a nondrinking life. Help takes the form of fellowship, a new lifestyle, and understanding of the properties of alcohol from the group's point of view. Hope for a future without alcohol is the prescription of AA.

Elvin Morton Jellinek

In 1943, the Yale Summer School of Alcohol Studies was created by Elvin Morton Jellinek, a professor of applied physiology at Yale, along with other faculty members. The school's avowed purpose was defining the problem of alcoholism in the broadest sense. Jellinek's research would contribute to the widespread acceptance of alcoholism being defined as a disease. He developed a typology of alcoholics and offered a phase model of alcoholism. His typology called attention to the idea that there was more than one type of alcoholic, and his phase model stressed the progressive nature of the disease.

Jellinek used Greek letters to differentiate between types or species of alcoholics. An alpha alcoholic was psychologically dependent upon alcohol, using it to escape stress or loosen inhibitions. An alpha was not physically dependent on alcohol, but some alphas would become addicted. Beta drinkers were alcoholics who developed serious medical problems related to their drinking. He regarded betas as not physically dependent upon alcohol, but beta alcoholics drank for social reasons despite the aggravating medical problems. The gamma type was the most commonly found type of alcoholic, an alcoholic who had a drinking career reflecting the progressive development of social and physical problems related to excessive consumption. Jellinek called this species the prototype of AA members, one whose drinking career could have started as alpha. The delta alcoholic is a maintenance drinker, one who drinks all day. Deltas rarely lose control as they pace their consumption and have built up tolerance to alcohol. They have a physical dependence on alcohol but are unaware of it until denied access to it. Finally, Jellinek spoke of the epsilon alcoholic, one who is inclined to episodic drinking, going on binges or sprees of consumption, but who in between may abstain from tippling.

Jellinek concluded from his research that the three most commonly shared behaviors among alcoholics were blackouts, losing control over drinking, and going on benders. Although his typology is not mutually exclusive nor is it exhaustive, Jellinek's interpretation of his data underscores the complexity of defining alcoholism. It calls into question the popular conception of alcoholics as drunken bums or members of bottle gangs passing around a brown bag on a street corner. The common belief that alcoholism is the fault of a weak person, perhaps even a sinner, is challenged by the typology offered by Jellinek. His descriptions resonated with professionals working with alcoholics and with members of AA.

Jellinek's phase model is debated, but it remains familiar to therapists and practitioners working with alcoholics. He argued that the gamma alcoholic passed through a prealcoholic symptomatic phase to a prodromal phase, to a crucial phase, and a chronic phase. Initially, an alcoholic occasionally experiences the use of alcohol as self-medication or relief from anxiety or stress. During this phase, tolerance is being built and the consumption is fairly heavy. The prodromal or warning phase is marked by the appearance of blackouts, gulping of drinks, and drinking on the sly. The phase finds the drinker preoccupied with drinking, and the beginnings of some guilt feelings occur. The crucial phase is marked by loss of control once one starts to drink. Intoxication is the final result because stopping at a moderate level of consumption is impossible. Morning drinks occur, along with periods of remorse and abstinence. In the chronic phase, drinking dominates one's life, and intoxication is the standard. Impairment of thinking and psychomotor problems develop.

Thus, the model of progression from an occasional loss of control to a complete surrender to alcohol was the path of Jellinek's garden-variety alcoholic. Empirical support for this stage-by-stage approach to the disease of alcoholism is contradictory, but it is an avenue traveled by many alcoholics. The phases are familiar to students of alcohol behavior and counselors working with people with drinking problems. AA members share their drinking biographies at some of their meetings and often report a progressive decline into the grips of alcoholism. One way to regard the work of Jellinek is that his extensive writings and scientific reputation were a catalyst to spreading the popularity of the disease model of alcoholism. What he wrote about was familiar to the general population.

Efforts to Define and Diagnose Alcoholism

Throughout the 1950s and 1960s, various professional organizations accepted the disease model of alcoholism. In the mid-1950s, the American Medical Association and the American Hospital Association came out with policy statements calling alcoholism a disease. As its popularity increased among a wider group of practitioners and within the general population, the need for a diagnostic tool became apparent. Such a need could only be met if a definition of alcoholism could be established. The World Health Organization (WHO) declared alcoholism a disease with any or all of the following five characteristics: (1) noticeable mental disturbance, (2) interference with bodily and mental health, (3) interference with personal relations, (4) interference with smooth social and economic functioning, and (5) any symptoms of such developments due to alcohol consumption. The lack of specificity weakened the effectiveness of this diagnostic tool because many heavy drinkers never possess such characteristics and some modest consumers do.

The National Council on Alcoholism (NCA, now known as the National Council on Alcoholism and Drug Dependence or NCADD), a coalition of state and local organizations established in 1944, held the position that alcoholism was an incurable disease, but that it was treatable. The council's initial founder and leader was Marty Mann, who has been described as the first female member of Alcoholics Anonymous. In 1972, the NCA offered a tool for diagnosis of alcoholism based on extensive research into prior understandings of the disease. A committee of experts was formed, and it reviewed data ranging from physicians' medical examinations, to self-reported case histories, to various laboratory tests. From this material, two sets of signs were created for use as a diagnostic tool for doctors. One group represented the physiological and clinical data obtained from physicians, while the other was composed of behavioral, psychological, and attitudinal data gathered from the patient, family, and friends.

Within each category, a further division was made, sorting data into major and minor criteria. A one-to-three scale of importance was created for each item, with a one weighted to mean definite alcoholic, a two a probable alcoholic, and a three a possible alcoholic. For instance, a major physiological trait was the appearance of withdrawal symptoms when the drinker stopped drinking. An example of a major behavioral trait was continued drinking despite social problems. Minor criteria from the physiological side of the chart included the patient exhibiting a 0.1 blood-alcohol level at the time of an examination by the doctor. A spouse's complaints about the drinking were a behavioral minor criterion. Physicians were to consult the charts when having to decide the seriousness of a patient's drinking behavior. Although the instrument provided by the NCA was supposed to provide an objective diagnosis, it fell short of such a lofty goal. Besides being cumbersome to employ, it has been criticized for being too inclusive, thus leading to too many false positives.

The most often used definition and diagnostic tool for alcoholism is one that eschews the use of the term alcoholism. The American Psychiatric Association publishes a *Diagnostic Statistical Manual* (DSM), a standardized source for dealing with addictive and mental disorders. It was first published in 1952 and has been revised several times. It is now available as *Diagnostic Statistical Manual IV* (DSM-IV). In its early editions, it employed the concept of alcoholism to describe a personality disorder. People who consumed alcohol to the point where it impaired their social and everyday activities or their health were suffering from alcoholism. The illness was divided into three types: episodic excessive drinking, defined as becoming intoxicated four or more times a year; habitual excessive drinking, defined as being drunk more than twelve times a year or functioning under the influence of alcohol more than once a year; and alcohol addiction, where one exhibits withdrawal symptoms or cannot go one day without drinking.

Subsequent revisions have removed abnormal drinking behavior from the personality disorder area and given abnormal drinking its own section. In the DSM-III, alcohol problems stood alone as a disease that was not a symptom of a psychiatric problem. Furthermore, alcohol problems were divided into alcohol abuse and alcohol dependency, with the concept of alcoholism being replaced by dependency. Although not employing the word alcoholism, many of the characteristics that the NCA and Jellinek described as symptomatic of alcoholic drinking are found in the manual. For instance, DSM-IV describes alcohol dependence as a state when three of the following seven items have occurred in a one-year period: (1) tolerance, (2) withdrawal, (3) drinking large amounts for a longer period than intended, (4) continued unsuccessful attempts to control drinking, (5) considerable time spent drinking or recovering from drinking, (6) giving up or reducing important activities because of drinking, and (7) continued drinking despite known medical consequences. Alcohol abuse occurs when one or more of four behavioral criteria are met as a result of drinking over a one-year period: (1) failure to fulfill major role obligations at work, school, or home; (2) driving or engaging in other risky recreational activities while drinking; (3) alcohol-related legal problems; and (4) continued drinking in the face of persistent social and interpersonal problems because of that drinking.

The DSM-IV, along with the WHO's *International Statistical Classification of Diseases,* tenth revision, are two primary diagnostic tools that avoid the use of the concept alcoholism and offer a split view of the disease: alcohol dependency and alcohol abuse. Both suggest alcohol dependence is a more severe condition, and both are fairly compatible in defining this syndrome. However, the area of alcohol abuse remains controversial, with subjectivity being a difficult issue to settle. One argument has been that alcohol abuse is simply a preliminary stage of alcohol dependency, reflecting the belief in the progressive theory of the disease alcoholism. The debate over what alcoholism is and how to recognize it continues to evolve.

Criticism of the Disease Model

The disease model of alcoholism has never been without critics. From the time of its introduction into the lexicon, resistance to the idea has come from a variety of sources. Puritan clergy regarded habitual drunkenness as a sin, punishable in the afterlife. Most colonials agreed with that position or defined the choice of drunkenness as a result of the pleasure one received from it. In the early decades of the nineteenth century, many temperance enthusiasts believed alcohol was addictive and had the ability to enslave people. This was particularly the case for believers in the heredity character of the disease. Until near the end of the nineteenth century, temperance advocates called for sympathy for the drunk and hostility for the drink.

After the Civil War, a change in attitude toward drunks began to guide the temperance movement. Prohibition became the goal, and as this policy was promoted, data were used to demonstrate a multitude of serious problems related to drunken behavior. The saloon was a source of crime and corruption, and was destroying families. As industrial accidents and loss of worker efficiency due to alcohol were publicized, the liquor industry was portrayed as undermining the nation's economy. The drunk became a problem, a menace to society, and was represented by the image of a skid row bum—not a sick person, but a lazy, evil deviant choosing to ignore society's expectations. This view of alcoholism as the behavior of the morally weak—that it is a bad habit that a person could stop—has a variety of supporters. Some academics, conservative clergy, elected officials, and a minority of the general public reject the disease model and argue the volitional perspective. There is a suggestion in some of these volitional arguments that the disease model excuses the alcoholic's behavior. The residue of these attitudes continues to factor into the debate over how to define alcoholism.

Additional disagreements with the disease model are offered by a variety of scholars and practitioners favoring a perspective that regards alcoholism as volitional behavior. One of their themes is that there is no medical basis for the disease model because no virus or germs can be detected that would account for excessive drinking. There is no known biological factor that explains the alcoholic's behavior. According to critics of the disease model, the problem of delineating heavy drinkers from alcoholics remains unresolved. Finally, critics often claim that alcoholism is a symptom of another disease, and that asserting that one's uncontrollable drinking is a sickness means the underlying cause is ignored.

The responses to these and other criticisms are part of the evolving disease model for understanding alcoholism. Proponents of the medical approach for defining alcoholism counter various complaints by extending the analysis of alcoholism. Comparisons are made with other diseases that lack the usual medical factors and involve considerable self-imposed behavior. Certain types of chronic heart disease and hypertension are similar to alcoholism in that they lack the common components of other diseases. They are related to behaviors that are under considerable self-control, such as diet or exercise. No one would deny that clogged arteries or high blood pressure are diseases, despite the influence of self-controlled behaviors like eating habits, smoking, a sedentary lifestyle, or overuse of salt. Differentiating heavy drinkers from alcoholics poses a problem only if one perceives alcoholism as a unitary concept. The distinction between primary and secondary alcoholism was introduced to resolve controversy over alcoholism being a condition stemming from another disease.

In an effort to develop coherency and consistency in the disease model of alcoholism, the NCADD and the American Society of Addiction Medicine created a panel of experts with the mission of defining alcoholism. The results of the panel's work were published in 1992 in the *Journal of the American Medical Association.* The key components of the changing concept of alcoholism are spelled out in the panel's definition. These components also represent areas of research that are ongoing as the effort to elaborate on the disease model continues.

The panel claims that alcoholism is a primary disease that stands alone or predates or stems from other medical disorders. Even if alcoholism is the result of self-medicating activity to overcome depression or a nonmental ailment, it can become a disease separate from the catalyst. It is a disease caused by multiple factors—biological, sociological, and psychological. Many research projects seeking an understanding of alcoholism have supported the ideas of multiple types of alcoholism and the melding of different influences in the production of the disease. It is often progressive, and because of resulting medical problems or trauma events such as an automobile accident, it can be fatal. Impaired control is associated with alcoholism (implying total loss of control may or may not be appropriate). In some contexts, alcoholics may drink moderately. It is noted that alcoholism leads to a preoccupation with drinking. Examples of this are seeking and ensuring drinking opportunities, becoming aware of the dominant place that drinking assumes in one's thoughts, and the limiting of one's drinking repertoire (the narrowing or limiting of one's choice of drink). Continuing to drink abnormally in face of "adverse consequences" such as loss of health, job, or spouse, or interference in carrying out responsibilities are behaviors displayed by people suffering from alcoholism. Finally, the definition includes a statement about denial. Denial is a complex psychological mechanism that in its simplest form prevents one from acknowledging the reality of the situation.

The sociopolitical debate over the disease model of alcoholism expands as scientists, philosophers, practitioners, and policymakers participate. The legal system's refusal to allow a person to employ the disease as a defense illustrates the ambivalent status of alcoholism. Nor has there been a conclusive ruling that grants alcoholism legal status as a disease.

James R. McIntosh

See also: Alcoholics Anonymous (AA); Degeneration Theories; Jellinek, Elvin Morton; Keeley Institutes; Mann, Marty; National Council on Alcoholism and Drug Dependence (NCADD); National Institute on Alcohol Abuse and Alcoholism (NIAAA); Psychological Theories of Drinking; Sociological Theories of Drinking and Temperance; Washingtonians; World Health Organization (WHO)

References

Alcoholics Anonymous website. http://www.alcoholics-anonymous.org/

American Psychiatric Association. *Diagnostic and Statistical Manual of Mental Disorders.* 4th ed. Washington, DC: American Psychiatric Association, 1996.

Blocker, Jack S., Jr. *American Temperance Movements.* Boston: Twayne, 1989.

Fingarette, Herbert. "Alcoholism: the Mythical Disease" in *Society, Culture, and Drinking Patterns Reexamined,* edited by David J. Pittman and Helene Raskin White, 417–438. New Brunswick, NJ: Rutgers Center of Alcohol Studies, 1991.

Flavin, Daniel K., and Robert M. Morse. "What Is Alcoholism? Current Definitions and Diagnostic Criteria and Their Implications for Treatment" in *Alcohol World Health and Research.* 15, no. 4 (1991): 266–271.

Keller, Mark, and John Doria. "On Defining Alcoholism" in *Alcohol World Health and Research.* 15, no. 4 (1991): 253–259.

Kinney, Jean. *Loosening the Grip.* 6th ed. Boston: McGraw-Hill Education, 2000.

Lender, Mark Edward, and James Kirby Martin. *Drinking in America.* rev. ed. New York: Free Press, 1987.

Levine, Harry G. "The Discovery of Addiction: Changing Conceptions of Habitual Drunkenness in America" in *Journal of Studies on Alcohol.* 39, no. 1 (1978): 143–174.

Mendelson, Jack H., and Nancy K. Mello. *Alcohol.* Boston: Little, Brown, 1985.

National Council on Alcoholism and Drug Dependence website. http://www.ncadd.org/

Vaillant, George E. *The Natural History of Alcoholism Revisited.* Cambridge, MA: Harvard University Press, 1995.

World Health Organization. *Manual of the International Statistical Compilation of Diseases, Injuries and Causes of Death.* 9th ed. Geneva, Switzerland: World Health Organization, 1977.

Allied Breweries

In 1961, in a move that brought together three of the ten largest United Kingdom brewers, Edward Thompson persuaded two strong but docile regional companies, Tetley Walker and Ansells, to join his dynamic national company, Ind Coope. The new company was by any measure easily the biggest brewer in the United Kingdom and, in terms of assets because of its considerable property holdings, the largest brewing group in the world at the time. The company, which took the name Allied Breweries in 1963, was initially successful, but after it started to diversify its activities through acquisition in the late 1960s, it lost ground as a brewer. Renamed Allied-Lyons in 1981 and Allied Domecq in 1994, the company grew ever larger as it absorbed food and drink companies both in the United Kingdom and internationally. Widely seen as unwieldy and underperforming by the end of the 1980s, the company was dismembered during the 1990s. The breweries, pubs, and many other assets were sold, and it emerged after a troubled decade as an international spirits group, a poor second to Diageo in the world rankings, generating over 90 percent of its earnings outside the United Kingdom.

Ind Coope, the oldest and largest of the three founding companies of Allied Breweries, contributing over half the assets, was founded in Romford in 1799 and opened a second brewery in Burton on Trent in 1856. In 1934, it merged with a Burton neighbor, Allsopps. After 1945, Ind Coope and Allsopps grew rapidly. By the end of the 1950s, the company had accumulated a large tied estate (about 5,200 pubs) and developed its bottled Double Diamond Pale Ale into a national brand. Tetley Walker was formed through the 1960 merger of Joshua Tetley, which began in Leeds in 1822, and Walker Cain, which started in Warrington in 1846 as Peter Walker. Ansells began malting in Birmingham in 1857 and turned to brewing in 1881. The founding firms had grown by friendly acquisition of other brewers and came together at a time when the threat of unwelcome takeover bids from perceived outsiders had prompted a surge in defensive mergers in the industry.

Edward Thompson's new company had twelve breweries, owned 11 percent of the United Kingdom's pubs, and through extensive reciprocal trading agreements and the free trade, supplied 48 percent of total outlets including hotels, clubs, and off-license establishments. This wide penetration was particularly advantageous to Double Diamond, which now blossomed after being launched as a keg beer in 1962. Allied Breweries was less fortunate with their lager brand, Skol. Although an early leader in the embryo British lager boom of the 1960s, it fell behind, hampered by lack of continental pedigree. Partly in an attempt to overcome this and with the hope of creating a wider market, a consortium was formed in 1964 to brew Skol internationally. This brave attempt was ultimately unsuccessful; at its peak, Skol was brewed in eighteen countries and never threw off its homespun image in the United Kingdom.

The key event in Allied's transformation from a brewer to a lackluster conglomerate of disparate businesses was the takeover in August 1968 of Showerings, Vine Products and Whiteway's (SVPW). Under Edward Thompson, Allied was run as a loose federation of its three founders, a "Commonwealth of brewers" as he called it, and enjoyed a degree of success with an increase in pretax profits of 22 percent in real terms in six years. Following the takeover of SVPW and the retirement of Thompson, the new chairman, Derek Pritchard, introduced a divisional structure at the end of 1969 in the wake of an aborted attempt to merge with Unilever. Centralized management, with the authority of the regional companies reduced significantly, was adopted for the beer division. The prime motivation for this change was to facilitate the growth of national beers, but the move was not a success. The division was slow to respond to market changes and demonstrated little synergy between production and sales. Allied had lost 15 percent of its share of the beer market before the policy was reversed in 1978 and a devolved, profit-centered approach was introduced. But the new management structure was to no avail, and the decline in market share continued, compounded by major brewery strikes in 1979 and 1981.

The purchase of SVPW brought with it Babycham (a sparkling perry that had enjoyed phenomenal success as the first new postwar alcoholic drink that appealed to women), Cockburn's Port, Harvey's Sherry, Whiteway's Cider, and many other brands. Adding these products to Allied's wine shipper and wholesaler Grants of Saint James and its off-license chain Victoria Wine made the company the largest wholesaler and retailer of wines and spirits in the United Kingdom. Adding four millionaire members of the Showering family to the Allied board changed the balance of power in the company. When Keith Showering became chairman in 1975, the shift from brewing gathered momentum. A crucial move was the purchase of Lyons (ice cream, tea, coffee, cakes, catering, motor vehicles, and meat products) in 1978. After Sir Keith's death in 1982, diversification continued under his like-minded successors. Particularly notable purchases among many were the Canadian distiller Hiram Walker in 1986 (undertaken when Allied was under threat of takeover from the Australian brewing company Elders IXL) and Dunkin' Donuts in 1989. These seemingly piecemeal acquisitions were not viewed well in the City and, when the company's loss of £147 million in foreign currency dealings in 1991 prompted changes at the top, rationalization became the prime objective. Cider, perry, British wines, specialty drinks, and Lyons Maid Ice Cream had all gone by February 1992. Divestment of brewing interests took a little longer. After separating the pubs from production in the wake of the Beer Orders announced in 1989, which restricted pub ownership by brewers, Allied offloaded a 50 percent stake in its breweries to Carlsberg in 1993, and the remainder in 1997. The Spanish drinks company Pedro Domecq was purchased in 1994, and following a particularly poor set of results, the pubs were sold in 1999 in a final break with Allied's brewing past.

In 2003, seventy boxes of technical books, journals, and patents at the Leeds brewery of Carlsberg-Tetley, formerly part of the research library of Allied at Burton on Trent, were transferred to the National Brewing Library at Oxford Brookes University.

Raymond G. Anderson

See also: Allsopps; Beer; Beer Orders (United Kingdom); Cider; Hiram Walker; Pubs and Beerhouses (United Kingdom); Victoria Wine Company

References

Faulkner, N. O. *Allied Breweries, A Long Life: A Directory of Ancestor Breweries.* Rochester, UK: Allied Breweries Limited History Project, 1988.

Gourvish, Terry R., and Richard G. Wilson. *The British Brewing Industry 1830–1980.* Cambridge: Cambridge University Press, 1994.

This Is Allied Lyons. London: Allied Lyons, 1984.

Thompson, Edward. *Allied Breweries and Its Place in the Brewing Industry.* [London]: Allied Breweries, 1966.

Allied Brewery Traders' Association (ABTA)

The Allied Brewery Traders' Association (ABTA), organized in 1907, brought together those who supplied English brewers with goods and services to defend the drink trade against the Liberal government then in office. Historian David W. Gutzke identifies Reginald Mortimer as having provided "the main impetus" for the formation of the ABTA (Gutzke 1989: 161). He became its secretary. Mortimer, a barrister who worked for a distributor of brewing sugar, was an honorary member of the general committee of the Brewers' Society and a former manager for the National Trade Defence Association. The ABTA included members of the malt, hop, and barley trades, as well as coopers, distillers, engineers, chemical analysts, and sugar manufacturers. Regional affiliate organizations were set up in parts of England, Wales, and Scotland. At first, the ABTA emphasized its autonomy. Independence supposedly gave it more credibility with the Liberal government and with newspapers. After 1910, the ABTA worked more openly with the brewers to put pressure on people in the ancillary trades to join. Internal conflicts made unity difficult. For instance, hop growers resented the brewers' practice of using cheaper hop substitutes in brewing beer. As a propaganda and electoral organization, the ABTA emphasized the variety of jobs and investments that Liberal licensing proposals endangered. For instance, the ABTA distributed 35,000 pamphlets to farmers in the campaign that preceded the first general election of 1910.

Under a new name, the Brewing, Food and Beverage Industry Suppliers Association, the organization still exists.

David M. Fahey

See also: Brewers' Society (BS); National Trade Defence Association (NTDA)

Reference

Gutzke, David W. *Protecting the Pub: Brewers and Publicans against Temperance.* Woodbridge, Suffolk: Boydell for the Royal Historical Society; Wolfeboro, NH: Boydell and Brewer, 1989.

Allsopps

From eighteenth-century roots, Samuel Allsopp and Sons thrived in the mid-nineteenth century through burgeoning sales of Burton-brewed India pale ale to become one of the largest brewing companies then in existence. The firm was brought low in the 1890s by the third generation of the Allsopp family in a classic case of arrogant and reckless mismanagement. After twenty troubled years, pragmatic professional management stabilized the company, allowing a mutually beneficial merger with a neighboring brewery in the 1930s.

Burton on Trent had long been noted for the keeping quality and flavor of its nut-brown ales (properties derived from the water and barley used in their production), but the geographical isolation of the town encouraged only limited distribution of the beer. The opening of the river Trent to navigation in 1712 allowed ready access to a wider market. Benjamin Wilson, a merchant-brewer who came to the town in the 1730s, was a pioneer in exploiting this new avenue for commerce and built up a considerable trade in the export of beer to the Baltic ports via Hull. In 1778, Wilson's youngest son, also named Benjamin, assumed sole control of the business, and around the year 1800, he took his nephew Samuel Allsopp into the firm. Samuel bought the brewery outright from his bachelor uncle for £7,000 in 1807. With Napoleon then in control of the Baltic ports, the export trade had collapsed, and new markets were needed. After some difficult years, the breakthrough came in 1822 when the brewery successfully copied the India pale ale of the London brewer Mark Hodgson. Burton water was particularly suited to the production of this pale, bright, sparkling beer, which had found favor among the British in India. Allsopps had built up a major stake in the Indian export trade by the time Samuel died in 1838. In the following year, the railway reached Burton, allowing efficient and cheap inland distribution of beer. This was backed by what was soon a highly developed countrywide sales organization of travelers and agents who pushed the virtues of the superior Burton India Pale Ale. From around 15,000 hectoliters (396,000 U.S. gallons) in 1830, Allsopps produced 1.25 million hectoliters (33 million U.S. gallons) in 1876, putting them briefly second in the world only to Bass in terms of output.

Henry Allsopp, Samuel's third son, presided over the massive expansion of the firm, enriching himself and his partners. Around 1860, he bought a country mansion, Hindlip Hall in Worcestershire, some eighty miles from Burton. He was elected to Parliament in 1874, received a baronetcy in 1880, and was created a baron in 1886 with the title Lord Hindlip. His sons, three of whom were also members of Parliament (M.P.s), were educated at Eton or Harrow and Trinity College, Cambridge; had their own country houses; and married into the exclusive social elite. This dedicated pursuit of political and social kudos diverted the Allsopp family from wholehearted attention to the business—with disastrous results.

In February 1887, the firm was floated on the stock market as a limited liability company with a total capitalization of £3.3 million. The share issue was enthusiastically received following the successful launch of Guinness four months earlier and was some thirty times oversubscribed. Soon, however, the shareholders showed discontent because it emerged that an artfully conceived prospectus had not revealed declining beer sales during the 1880s in the grossly overvalued company. These were difficult years for the Burton brewers, who depended heavily on the free trade and saw their vinous double-fermented "stock" pale ales being supplanted in the public taste by more readily produced "running beers" similar to the ales of today. But no company handled the situation so badly as Allsopps. The company owned no pubs in 1887 and had little invested in loans to publicans.

In an increasingly tied market, the directors had remained aloof, professing that their beer would sell regardless. The share issue itself alienated many of Allsopps customers in the trade, who were affronted not to have received an allocation and promptly closed their accounts with the company. As beer sales slid ever downward, profits and share price fell and dividends were cut. In October 1890, Samuel Charles Allsopp, chairman of the firm since 1882 and ennobled as the second Lord Hindlip on the death of his father in March 1887, resigned. An elderly banker, Henry R. Grenfell, replaced him and kept the company afloat through strict financial control. In 1895, Grenfell retired and was replaced as chairman by the thirty-three-year-old Alfred Percy Allsopp, seventh son of the first Lord Hindlip. Percy would bring the company to its knees in a dash for growth. The issue of share and loan stock financed the spending of £3.5 million on the belated purchase of public houses and in loans to publicans—a complete reversal of his elder brother's policy. In other ill-timed moves, one of the breweries was converted to lager production and an amusement park was purchased. These massive investments were not matched by the necessary increase in beer sales. By April 1900, it became clear that the profits could not cover the promised dividend, and Percy resigned. A new board was formed and the capital was eventually written down to account for a deficit of £1.43 million. But it was to no avail. Sales of the company's ales continued to slide, there was little market for its lager, and the huge investment in pubs turned out to have occurred at the height of the market. The company went into receivership in 1911.

Following a complete restructuring of capital, John Joseph Calder, an experienced brewery manager from Alloa, was appointed managing director in 1913. Calder's capable hard-faced management, helped by favorable immediate postwar conditions and the astute purchase of other breweries, restored Allsopps's profitability. In 1934, Allsopps merged with Ind Coope to form Ind Coope and Allsopp Ltd. The name Allsopp was dropped in 1959 and the firm merged with others in 1961 to form a company that by 1963 was called Allied Breweries Ltd.

Raymond G. Anderson

See also: Allied Breweries; Beer

References

Bushman, J. Stevenson. *Burton and Its Bitter Beer.* London: William S. Orr, 1853.

Gourvish, Terry R., and Richard G. Wilson. "Profitability in the Brewing Industry 1885–1914" in *Business History.* 27 (1985): 146–165.

Hawkins, Kevin H. "The Conduct and Development of the Brewing Industry in England and Wales, 1880–1938. A Study of the Role of Entrepreneurship in Determining Business Strategy, with Particular Reference to Samuel Allsopp and Sons Limited" (Ph.D. dissertation, University of Bradford, 1981).

Owen, Colin C. *The Development of Industry in Burton upon Trent.* Chichester, Sussex: Phillimore, 1978.

American Association for the Study and Cure of Inebriety (AASCI)

The American Association for the Study and Cure of Inebriety (AASCI) was a pioneering organization of physicians, reformers, and superintendents of inebriety treatment facilities created to promote the systematic and scientific study of alcohol and drug addiction. Its view of alcoholism as a medically treatable physical condition fell out of favor during its organizational lifetime, but was to gain renewed and widespread support under different auspices following the repeal of National Prohibition.

Founded in 1870 as the American Association for the Cure of Inebriates, the AASCI was initially led by several well-respected professionals in the inebriety treatment field. It was founded by Dr. Joseph Parrish, medical director and chair of the board of directors of the Pennsylvania Inebriate Asylum, in Media, Pennsylvania. Its first president was Dr. Willard Parker, the president of the board of the New York State Inebriate Asylum in Binghamton. Dr. Nathan S. Davis, who helped to found the American Medical Association and establish the Chicago Washingtonian Home, contributed a paper to the AASCI's first proceedings. Dr. Thomas Davison Crothers joined in 1873, and in 1876 he became the editor of the AASCI's journal, the *Quarterly Journal of Inebriety,* which he edited for the journal's full run, until 1914. Crothers would soon become an internationally recognized authority on inebriety treatment. George M. Beard, who coined the term neurasthenia, joined the AASCI in the mid-1870s and contributed articles to the first volumes of the journal.

The AASCI leadership declared that its principles were to expound a scientific perspective on inebriety: that inebriety was a disease and should be treated in a medical manner. The disease theory of inebriety was a relatively new perspective, and it challenged the drunkenness-as-vice view promoted by many moralists and physicians. Indeed, the disease theory was not initially agreed upon by all members of the association. The early papers published in the AASCI's proceedings demonstrated a variety of dissenting opinions from the scientific perspective, notably by individuals representing religious groups. In contrast, proponents of the disease theory of inebriety argued that inebriety was a physical weakness, often inherited, and could be treated by physical means. This conflict continued to plague the AASCI meetings and debates. Several of its founding organizations and members disagreed with the strictly physicalist perspective. Dr. Robert Harris, for example, the attending physician of the Franklin Reformatory Home for Inebriates in Philadelphia, wrote a paper in 1873 insisting that drunkenness remained a sin and a crime and that medical treatment had to be wedded to individualized moral reform. As a result, the AASCI leadership attempted to define its goals in broad enough terms so as to include people who shared Harris's perspective. Records suggest, however, that the perspective of Harris and his like-minded colleagues was ridiculed and marginalized within the organization.

This tension underlaid much of the work of the AASCI, not the least because the terminology was unclear. The term "disease" could be deployed in several ways. It could refer to a departure from the healthy condition, and therefore could apply to any person who was drunk. Others used "disease" to refer to chronic conditions (the term "chronic poisoning" was often applied to opium users). The idea of alcoholism as a form of neurasthenia, or psychological taint, was also prominent. One term that came into use was "diathesis," a fluid concept with no fixed meaning. It could mean a hereditary taint, and therefore unavoidable, or a condition caused by repeated indulgence.

Notwithstanding the lack of clarity surrounding the disease theory of inebriety and the conflict over that theory within its ranks, the AASCI did much to promote a scientific approach to addiction and concomitant views that inebriety should be treated in a physical rehabilitative rather than moral reformist or punitive manner. Yet, despite the apparent scientific perspective, members of the AASCI continued to argue from a blatantly class-oriented perspective. They delineated between "more" and "less" curable inebriates. More curable inebriates did not repeat too often; usually consisted of artisans, merchants, and professionals; and could be treated adequately in private or semiprivate institutions. Less curable inebriates were generally unskilled or semiskilled workers, and were more appropriately treated in publicly financed state institutions, with less sophisticated treatment facilities and standards of care.

The AASCI was a pioneer organization in the study and cure of inebriety. It expanded rapidly during the 1870s. In 1870, it had invited all six known inebriety institutions to participate in the association. By 1878, thirty-two public and private facilities were in existence or planned in North America. Although no causative link can be drawn between the AASCI and the appearance of these new institutions, the coincidence suggests that the views of the AASCI were probably meeting a sympathetic response. The AASCI views also received exposure sufficient that the conservative Association of Medical Superintendents of American Institutions felt it necessary to attack the disease theory. Fourteen years after the AASCI's founding, the British Society for the Study of Inebriety (SSI) formed in 1884 and invited Crothers and Parrish to be international members. In 1891, Dr. Nathan S. Davis founded the American Medical Temperance Association (AMTA).

The rapid growth turned into rapid decline by the end of the century. In 1903, the AMTA's *Bulletin* was consolidated with the AASCI's *Quarterly Journal of Inebriety*, and one year later, the AASCI united with the AMTA, calling the new organization the American Medical Society for the Study of Alcohol and Other Narcotics. This consolidation may have been an indication of its growing redundancy. In 1910 and again in 1912, Crothers published editorials defending the work of the association. Yet it continued to decline. Perhaps the persistence of a strong prohibitionist sentiment within the ranks diminished its stature. In contrast, the British SSI (renamed the Society for the Study of Addiction), which also saw ongoing membership tension, rejected the prohibitionist and total-abstinence sentiment. This policy may have led to the SSI's perseverance, while the AASCI clung to sentiments that may have been considered outmoded by the twentieth century. The *Journal* folded in 1914, and soon afterward, the association fell from view. It did still exist in the 1920s, since it was mentioned in the *Standard Encyclopedia of the Alcohol Problem* as still in operation, but there is little indication that it lasted in any significant form long afterward.

Daniel J. Malleck

See also: Alcoholism; Crothers, Thomas Davison; Society for the Study of Addiction; Treatment Institutions

References

American Association for the Study and Cure of Inebriety. *Proceedings, 1870–1875.* New York: Arno Press, 1981 [reprint edition in Addiction in America series].

"American Association for the Study and Cure of Inebriety" in *Standard Encyclopedia of the Alcohol Problem,* edited by Ernest Hurst Cherrington et al. 6 vols. 1: 151–152. Westerville, OH: American Issue Press, 1924–1930.

"American Medical Society for the Study of Alcohol and Other Narcotics" in *Standard Encyclopedia of the Alcohol Problem,* edited by Ernest Hurst Cherrington et al. 6 vols. 1: 155–156. Westerville, OH: American Issue Press, 1924–1930.

Berridge, Virginia. "The Society for the Study of Addiction" in *British Journal of Addiction.* 85 (1990): 991–1070.

Blumberg, Leonard. "The American Association for the Study and Cure of Inebriety" in *Alcoholism: Clinical and Experimental Research.* 2 (July 1978): 235–240.

Jaffe, Arnold. "Reform in American Medical Science: The Inebriety Movement and the Origins of the Psychological Disease Theory of Addiction, 1870–1920" in *British Journal of Addiction.* 73 (1978): 139–147.

American Temperance Society (ATS)

The American Society for the Promotion of Temperance, more commonly known as the American Temperance Society (ATS), pledged abstinence from spirits and was the first national temperance organization in the United States. As one of the central reform movements in the antebellum United States, temperance was an effort to define and control alcohol consumption. The ultimate consequence of these attempts to control drinking would be the prohibition movement of the early twentieth century. Historian John J. Rumbarger defined temperance reform as the "kaleidoscopic patterns of a people stressed and distressed by the common drinking practices of their society" (xvii). Alcohol had been socially acceptable during the colonial era, but a shift in thinking in the early nineteenth century concentrated on the belief that drinking was no longer respectable. The per capita consumption of liquor, for example, declined from over 5.5 gallons in 1810 to 4 gallons in 1850. An early proponent of the attempt to curb alcohol consumption, Benjamin Rush, first expressed his anxiety over "intemperate" drinking in a 1772 pamphlet, *Sermons to Gentlemen upon Temperance and Exercise,* that urged moderate drinking and exercise (Rorabaugh 1979: 39). Two years later, he further expressed anxiety over intemperate drinking and expoused his belief that drinking was an obstacle to the development of liberty and commerce in the United States (Rumbarger 1989: 4).

Background of Early Temperance Agitation

The emphasis on obstacles indicated that men of power and social standing defined and controlled the temperance agenda at the outset. These men were initially drawn from the federal elite that regarded temperance reform as a necessity for control of social order. The organized campaign for temperance occurred mainly on the local level during the first ten years of the nineteenth century, until the formation of the Massachusetts Society for the Suppression of Intemperance (MSSI), which in 1813 began to focus exclusively on the temperance issue. The MSSI membership peaked in 1818, with approximately forty local auxiliaries, each with an average of a hundred members; nevertheless, it was an elitist society that enrolled men from only the highest ranks of society. Members of the MSSI appealed to local officials to arrest those who were publicly drunk, and advocated restriction of licenses for selling liquor. Licenses, they argued, could only be granted to men of character and standing. The MSSI members did not want to eliminate alcohol production, but preferred to place it under the control of a local elite. The members were mostly Federalists, in accord with much of the temperance movement membership; they refused, however, to proselytize to adopt a mass attack in order to control social behavior.

Distinguishing Features of the ATS

Conversely, the formation of the ATS represented the beginning of a new phase in the American temperance movement. Similar to the MSSI, the ATS originated in Boston, but the similarities between the two organizations ended there. The organization quickly spread after its founding, and unlike the provincial focus of the MSSI, the ATS had a mass appeal. Founded in January 1826 by Marcus Morton, a colleague of Walter Channing (the founder of the MSSI), the American Temperance Society became the vehicle for the regulation of the use of "ardent spirits." Organized from the grassroots local-organization level to the more developed national level (so that the smallest organizations could regulate their own movements), the ATS placed only minimal limits on its constituency and wanted to encourage those who were nondrinkers to advocate total abstinence from alcohol rather than trying to reform those who refused to be reformed, namely the "drunkards" and alcoholics. Despite the fact that this approach was advocated in the ATS charter, members still attempted to "save" alcoholics from ruin.

The formation of the ATS represented the centralization of temperance into a united national organization—one not limited to volunteer efforts since it had a salaried secretary, Justin Edwards. Before taking this position as ATS secretary, he had believed in total abstinence, in accord with the beliefs of the MSSI, but he had expressed some concern about the mass reform efforts for total abstinence. His temperance tracts and sermons reflected his educational background and methodical ways, and his thoughts evolved to focus more strongly on persuasion rather than coercion to attain the goal of a temperate society. He wrote in the Fourth Annual Report of the American Temperance Society, "Temperance societies took their origin in America, in the following manner: The Reverend Dr. Beecher, deeply impressed with the evils of drunkenness, attacked that vice from the pulpit with so much vigor as to engage public attention, and to lead to the formation of the Societies in many parts of the Union, for its suppression." Many among the ATS leadership were much younger than their earlier counterparts, and only half of the sixteen ATS leaders had a college education. In addition to Edwards, the executive committee of the ATS included John Tappan, philanthropist and brother of antislavery advocate Lewis Tappan; Leonard Woods, a theology professor at Andover Seminary; and George Odiorne, a wealthy Boston banker and iron manufacturer. In keeping with the wealth-based membership, many of the members were doctors and businessmen, with 80 percent of the membership from New England (all of the members were from the Northeast).

Tactics and Techniques

With its mass appeal, the ATS used propaganda and traveling agents to spread the word about the mission of temperance societies. These itinerant agents were also responsible for the establishment of various temperance tract and mission societies. This propagandization required a strong financial system; itinerant agents gathered contributions from local groups and congregations, and encouraged larger donations by making the donors honorary members of the ATS. Two-thirds of the donations came from donors who gave more than thirty dollars in the first years, but by the demise of the ATS, this dollar amount had decreased to an average of five dollars.

Rather than using speeches to raise money and gather support, the ATS also had to rely on the written word. The ATS would often pay the salary of the editor of a weekly newspaper, the *Journal of Humanity,* to circulate it for subscribers. The printed literature, financing, voluntary organizations, and paid, full-time organizers changed the character of the temperance message, even leading to an emphasis on female membership. By aiming at a young audience, including women and young adults, the ATS became one of the first American voluntary organizations to attract large numbers of female members. Women often outnumbered men in terms of membership; an 1831 tally reported twenty-four women's temperance societies. The women's temperance societies attracted women of diverse backgrounds; they were divided by social class, religious beliefs, and length of residence in an area, yet united by temperance reform. Male leaders, in one sense, may have welcomed the female membership, citing the need for women's moral influence upon the next generations. Women could not assume leadership positions, yet they organized the first women's temperance convention in Montpelier, Vermont, in 1835. Women were actively involved, mainly because the ATS strategy did not involve formal political activity; by emphasizing informal persuasion, public speaking, propagandization, and organization (activities in which women could participate) rather than the public activities, the female membership increased significantly.

The involvement of women in temperance societies mirrored their involvement in religious benevolent societies as well, since temperance reformers drew heavily on Evangelicalism. The ATS relied heavily on church involvement to advance reform efforts, particularly because distilleries were owned and operated by members of the upper social class. Since the ATS pledge included a component urging individual temperance societies to exclude those who trafficked in ardent spirits, churches became instruments of reform. Intemperance, in accord with the ideas of Justin Edwards, "blotted out man's moral sense and his rational perception of spiritual problems and thus made him indifferent to the appeals of religion" (Tyrrell 1979: 70). Edwards in particular felt that each person must avoid wrongdoing and work to eradicate evil from society. If an individual refused to assist in this effort, the sins of the failure to oppose "evil" would cause problems with prospects for salvation. Similarly, the temperance movement mirrored the asylum reform movements in the 1820s and 1830s, although temperance reformers, unlike asylum reformers, understood the root of the problem. Nonetheless, both ATS and asylum reformers agreed that pauperism threatened to burden the community.

When the ATS reached its peak, it claimed more than 1.5 million members divided between 8,000 auxiliary societies, about 12 percent of the free population at the time. By 1834, it had become clear that the churches had not made any progress against moderate drinking or liquor trafficking, so the ATS attempted to advocate state political action against the liquor traffic. Until the demise of the ATS, the propertied class had united behind the temperance cause, and this support would be carried over to its successor, the United States Temperance Union, which would push temperance reform into the political area. Nevertheless, the main key to the success of the ATS was an ability to abandon previous MSSI practices that limited membership to only one affiliate society within a community.

Jennifer Harrison

See also: Beecher, Lyman; Edwards, Justin; Massachusetts Society for the Suppression of Intemperance (MSSI); State Prohibition (United States)

References

Blocker, Jack S., Jr. *American Temperance Movements: Cycles of Reform.* Boston: Twayne Publishers, 1989.

Fourth Report of the American Temperance Society. Boston: ATS, 1831. 69.

Perrin, Steven Wayne. "Nothing but Water: The Rise of Temperance and the Emergence of the American Temperance Society" (Ph.D. dissertation, Southern Illinois University, 1990).

Rorabaugh, W. J. *The Alcoholic Republic: An American Tradition.* New York: Oxford University Press, 1979.

Rumbarger, John J. *Profits, Power, and Prohibition: Alcohol Reform and the Industrializing of America, 1800–1930.* Albany: State University of New York Press, 1989.

Tyrrell, Ian R. *Sobering Up: From Temperance to Prohibition in Antebellum America, 1800–1860.* Westport, CT: Greenwood, 1979.

Anderson, William Hamilton (1874–1959)

William Hamilton Anderson (1874–1959) was an aggressive and abrasive field organizer for the Anti-Saloon League of America (ASLA) from 1900 through 1923. His most significant assignment was as the state superintendent, or chief executive officer, of the New York Anti-Saloon League from 1914 through 1923, because New York was considered the most difficult and wettest state for the prohibitionist, or "dry," forces.

William H. Anderson was born in Carlinville, Illinois. He graduated in 1892 with a bachelor's degree from Blackburn College, a Presbyterian school in Illinois, and in 1896 with a law degree from the University of Michigan. He practiced law until becoming an Illinois Anti-Saloon League attorney in 1900, then served as Illinois superintendent until 1905, when he resigned due to intraorganizational disagreements. He transferred for a year to New York, then served in Maryland as the superintendent from 1907 to 1914, when he returned to New York.

Anderson transferred to Maryland in 1907 to rally support for an ASLA-sponsored local-option bill patterned after an Illinois measure. The bill was launched with supportive prohibitionists singing "Onward Christian Soldiers" as Anderson organized businessmen, educators, and church officials to support the local-option measure. Anderson's campaign, however, failed to gain enactment over stubborn opposition.

Anderson's New York work started on New Year's Day, 1914, and by six o'clock, he had six newspaper reporters writing about his plans. Anderson established an Anti-Saloon League office in Manhattan and reinvigorated prohibition political battles within months, earning the titles "White Hope of Temperance" and "Arch Foe of Demon Rum." Although his first local-option bill was killed, he introduced a bill requiring liquor to be labeled with a skull and crossbones. Although the introduction of the bill was no more than a publicity stunt, it angered many New Yorkers who did not support the prohibition movement, as did a later incident in 1914, in which Anderson hired a private detective to investigate Speaker Thaddeus Sweet of the New York legislature. Sweet denounced the investigation as a frame-up.

Anderson's first battle with Alfred Emanuel Smith (who, as New York governor and Democratic presidential candidate, was to become the nation's leading antiprohibitionist politician) occurred in 1918 during Smith's initial campaign for governor. The battle concerned the declaration against Prohibition in the state Democratic Party platform. In another public incident shortly thereafter, Anderson sponsored a broadside that was signed by 1,000 clergy from twenty-five denominations in 57 New York counties outside of New York City. The broadside declared New York City to be the "center of nullification and seditious activity" aimed against legal restrictions on alcohol (Coffey 1976: 14). The reference to "seditious activity" represented an attempt to appropriate for the prohibition movement the force of the post–World War I Red Scare, which was especially virulent in New York.

Many politicians recognized Anderson as an able and challenging opponent, although his vigorous methods of personal abuse and scorn toward uncooperative legislators and clergy ("using the meat axe") alienated many political opponents. Some enemies accused him of using the ASLA as an opportunity for personal advancement. Therefore, he was called many names: "pirate king," "enemy to the public good," "political blackhand," "camerlingo of the Anti-Saloon League," as well as "chaser of moonbeams." However, Anderson described the work of the ASLA as "the church in action against the saloon" and authored the league's definitive defense of this image.

Anderson's strong political skills enabled the Eighteenth Amendment to be ratified in January 1919 by New York, the forty-fourth state to do so. He also led the successful struggle for passage of the Mullan-Gage Act, New York State's enforcement law. Anderson portrayed the victories in these two campaigns as proof that rural states were not controlling the drive for National Prohibition.

After ratification of the Eighteenth Amendment, Anderson's work still continued at a rapid pace, and he angered enemies as he condemned Governor Al Smith, many Catholic leaders, various newspapers, and New York City. He even criticized his own organization's lack of established state structures in 1921, claiming: "There is not any blinking at the fact that the Anti-Saloon League is afflicted with dry rot" (Kerr 1985: 247). Several setbacks occurred, however, in 1923: New York's Mullan-Gage Act was repealed, and the New York Anti-Saloon League was required by the state court to report its campaign expenditures. Also in 1923, a complex legal imbroglio arose over Anderson's use of personal funds in Anti-Saloon League publicity campaigns. He was later indicted for larceny, extortion, and third-degree forgery because of his commission system for league fundraisers and suspected methods of campaign-fund repayments to his personal accounts. He argued that although this method of financing was perhaps informal, he had not falsified league records.

Anderson was sentenced to two years in Sing Sing Prison and served nine months. After his conviction, the league executive committee publicly stated their belief in Anderson's "integrity, ability, and efficiency," which later caused much league embarrassment. Although some of his directors and many in the church press supported him during his prison time, Anderson's indictment was considered the second greatest scandal for the Anti-Saloon League after the trials of Bishop James Cannon Jr. on various charges.

William Anderson once summed up his controversial Anti-Saloon League career in the following way: "I probably made more explosive statements . . . than any hundred others of the Anti-Saloon League fellows. It was kind of left to me to do that sort of thing because it didn't seem to bother me much" (Coffey 1976: 28).

Lisa L. Ossian

See also: Anti-Saloon League of America (ASLA); Cannon, James, Jr.; National Prohibition (United States); Smith, Alfred Emanuel

References

Behr, Edward. *Prohibition: Thirteen Years That Changed America.* New York: Arcade Publishing, 1996.

Blocker, Jack S., Jr. *Retreat from Reform: The Prohibition Movement in the United States, 1890–1913.* Westport, CT: Greenwood, 1976.

Cashman, Sean Dennis. *Prohibition: The Lie of the Land.* New York: Free Press, 1981.

Coffey, Thomas M. *The Long Thirst: Prohibition in America, 1920–1933.* London: Hamish Hamilton, 1976.

Kerr, K. Austin. *Organized for Prohibition: A New History of the Anti-Saloon League.* New Haven and London: Yale University Press, 1985.

Kobler, John. *Ardent Spirits: The Rise and Fall of Prohibition.* New York: Da Capo Press, 1993.

Kyvig, David E. *Repealing National Prohibition.* 2d ed. Kent, OH: Kent State University Press, 2000.

Merz, Charles. *The Dry Decade.* Seattle: University of Washington Press, 1970.

Odegard, Peter H. *Pressure Politics: The Story of the Anti-Saloon League.* New York: Octagon Books, 1928.

Anheuser-Busch

Anheuser-Busch is the largest brewer in both the United States and the world. The company accounts for nearly 50 percent of the U.S. domestic market and produces five of the top ten brands. By itself, Budweiser commands 18.3 percent of the market. Bud Light commands another 15 percent of the market, representing one-third of light beer sales. In 2001, Anheuser-Busch shipped over 100 million barrels to wholesalers. This was a first for the brewery, which is over 150 years old.

Anheuser-Busch Companies Inc. employs over 23,000 people and has 30 subsidiaries in areas ranging from malt to theme parks. Anheuser-Busch owns 9 theme parks, including the various Busch Gardens and Sea World locations. The company is the third largest malt producer in the United States.

Origins and Growth

The origins of the world's largest brewer are in an 1850s Saint Louis brewery, Hammer and Urban. Eberhard Anheuser, a German immigrant and soap and candle manufacturer, invested in this brewery in the 1850s and then, in 1860, became majority owner along with William O'Dench. The latter left the business in 1864. Lily Anheuser, Eberhard's daughter, married Adolphus Busch, who eventually took over the brewery. Anheuser retired in 1877, and in 1879, Busch assumed sole responsibility. At this time, the company, which had incorporated in 1875, changed its

The Anheuser-Busch brewery on the corner of Broadway and Pestalozzi in Saint Louis, Missouri (Library of Congress)

name to the Anheuser-Busch Brewery Association. The brewing industry in the 1870s was small in scale, with most breweries operating in local or regional markets. In 1877, Anheuser-Busch produced 44,961 barrels. During the next two decades, rapid technological change occurred, transforming both the brewing industry and Anheuser-Busch.

The development of pasteurization and refrigeration enabled brewers to expand their market. Anheuser-Busch was in the forefront of these changes. In 1887, the company formed a subsidiary, Manufacturer's Railway, to manufacture refrigerated cars. In the twenty-first century, this subsidiary continues to provide switching and terminal services for Anheuser-Busch.

As United States industry grew, so did advertising. Anheuser-Busch was innovative in this arena, acquiring the rights to Budweiser and then associating the product with a picture—Custer's Last Stand. Anheuser-Busch eventually distributed over 1 million prints, all imprinted with the company's name.

These marketing and technological efforts paid off; by 1895, Anheuser-Busch was the nation's second largest brewer, with a production of nearly 800,000 barrels, lagging behind only Pabst. In 1901, Busch topped 1 million barrels and vaulted into first place, a position it has held for 100 years with only one brief exception.

Adolphus Busch died in 1913, and his son, August A. Busch Sr., became the company's president. In 1919, the company acquired the name Anheuser-Busch, Inc. The great expansion that the company had experienced occurred in the context of the overall expansion of the U.S. brewing industry, which produced 66 million barrels in 1914.

Anheuser-Busch, like all brewers, faced the devastation of National Prohibition and responded by brewing "near beer" and using its grain supplies for production of cereal, soft drinks, corn syrup, and other agriculturally based products.

Since Prohibition

In 1933, immediately following the repeal of Prohibition, Anheuser-Busch reopened with Adolphus Busch III at the helm, as 311 brewers resumed operations. By 1934, 756 were in operation. In that first year, the industry produced a little more than 20 million barrels, which was less than one-third of its pre-Prohibition output.

During World War II, worried that a war might bring renewed efforts at prohibition, Anheuser-Busch worked hard to foster a patriotic image. The company halted production of Budweiser on the west coast so that its freight cars could be used for the war effort. At the same time, Anheuser-Busch continued its efforts at increasing market share. The brewery increased production significantly; in 1941, it produced 3 million barrels, increasing to almost 5 million by 1950.

Despite such spectacularly productive efforts, in 1950 Anheuser-Busch slipped from number one, as Milwaukee-based Joseph Schlitz occupied that position by producing 5,096,840 barrels of beer. That year was the only time in 100 years that Anheuser-Busch had not been the country's top brewer.

Adolphus's brother, August A. Busch Jr., took over leadership of the company in 1946 and was its chief executive until 1975. During his tenure, Anheuser-Busch produced new beers, built new production facilities, acquired established breweries, and diversified its holdings by purchasing the Saint Louis Cardinals baseball team.

In the 1950s and 1960s, Anheuser-Busch faced stiff competition from both Carling and Schlitz but still managed to retain top rank among U.S. brewers. By 1970, the company had more than doubled its production, remaining first by a margin of 7 million barrels. Schlitz remained second, while Carling slipped from fourth to eighth. At the close of the 1970s, August Busch III became chief executive officer, replacing his father.

In 1974, Anheuser-Busch faced its stiffest challenge since it slipped from first place in 1950. Miller Brewing Company, which cigarette manufacturer Philip Morris had purchased in 1970, introduced Miller Lite, the first successful reduced-calorie beer. Miller Lite was the country's number one beer for a few months, shocking Anheuser-Busch. The company responded first with Natural Light and Michelob Light, but Bud Light became its best response. Anheuser-Busch and Miller were now engaged in a fierce battle for first place, spending massive amounts on advertising. Anheuser-Busch has continued to retain its supremacy by a fairly wide margin. Its market share rose from 29 percent in 1979 to 45 percent in 1990. In 1990, Miller controlled 22 percent of the U.S. market.

In the 1980s, Anheuser-Busch continued to diversify, branching out into the food industry. The company's most notable purchase was Eagle Snacks, Inc. Although not beverages, the chips, honey roasted nuts, and other snacks produced by Eagle Snacks have a natural affinity with beer. During the decade, Anheuser-Busch also expanded its interest in theme parks by acquiring Sea World in 1989.

In 1981, Anheuser-Busch made a commitment to expanding its foreign market by creating Anheuser-Busch International. By 1993, the company commanded a 9 percent market share worldwide and over 45 percent of U.S. beer exports.

Recent Changes

The 1990s presented Anheuser-Busch with several new challenges, including the first federal tax increase since 1951 and market competition from both U.S. microbreweries and foreign imports. The company responded by creating new brands fashioned in the style of the imports and "craft" beers as well as new nonalcoholic beers. At the same time, after diversifying for forty years, Anheuser-Busch decided to concentrate more exclusively on brewing beer. In 1995, the company sold both Eagle Snacks and the Saint Louis Cardinals. Anheuser-Busch retained its theme parks.

In the new century, Anheuser-Busch remains strongly on top, producing more than its next three competitors combined.

August Busch IV is slated to become head of the company in 2003 and hopes to have a 60 percent market share by 2005.

Amy Mittelman

See also: Beer; Busch Family; Carling Brewery; Miller Brewing Company; Pabst Brewing Company; Schlitz, Joseph, Brewing Company

References

Baron, Stanley. *Brewed in America.* Boston: Little, Brown, 1962.

Downard, William. *Dictionary of the History of the American Brewing and Distilling Industries.* Westport, CT: Greenwood, 1980.

Dun and Bradstreet. *America's Corporate Families 2001.* Parsippany, NJ: Dun's Marketing Services, 2001.

Grant, Tina, ed. *International Directory of Company Histories,* vol. 12. Chicago: St. James Press, 1996.

"Here's Mud in Your Eye" in *The Economist.* 29 September 1990: 82.

Lee, Thomas. "A-B Ships Record 99.5 Million Barrels" in *St. Louis Post-Dispatch.* 9 January 2002, Wednesday Five Star Lift Edition.

Market Research Centre and the Canadian Trade Commissioner Service. "The Alcoholic Beverage Market in the United States." http://atn-riae.agr.ca/public/htmldocs/e3111.htm [March 2002].

Pederson, Jay P., ed. *International Directory of Company Histories,* vol. 34. Chicago: St. James Press, 2000.

Plavchan, Ronald J. "A History of Anheuser-Busch, 1852–1933" (Ph.D. dissertation, Saint Louis University, 1969).

"Shakeout in the Brewing Industry." American Brewery History Page. http://www.beerhistory.com/library/holdings/shaakeout.shtml [March 2002]

Taylor, Christopher. "Subsector Analysis of the United States Brewing Industry." Unpublished paper, 1999. http://www.econ.iastate.edu/classes/econ535/hayenga/protected/Brewing-Chris.pdf.

Theodore, Sarah. "Beer's on the Up and Up" in *Beverage Industry.* 94, no. 4 (2001): 18.

"Top 10 U.S. Brewers in 1997." American Brewery History Page. http://www.beerhistory.com/library/holdings/top10.shtml [March 2002].

Anthropological Theories of Drinking and Temperance

Alcohol studies is a fundamentally interdisciplinary arena, and one in which anthropology has played a relatively minor role when compared with such fields as sociology, psychology, or epidemiology. Many theories of drinking and temperance are better thought of as sociocultural theories, or as social science theories, and are somewhat difficult to identify with one *particular* discipline like anthropology. Given this state of affairs, the review below covers two sorts of theories: those put forward *by* anthropologists themselves, on the one hand, and those presented by scholars whose primary training is in a different discipline but who *use anthropological data,* on the other.

The roots of anthropological theories, so defined, reach back approximately sixty years to efforts by sociologists to mine the then-available ethnographic record on cross-cultural drinking behavior. Drawing on George Peter Murdock's newly compiled effort to catalog and categorize the world's cultures in a single large, coded database (which has since become the Human Relations Area Files [HRAF]), Donald Horton offered the first identifiably anthropological theory of drinking in 1943. Referred to as "anxiety theory," Horton's hypothesis was that alcoholic beverages primarily function to reduce anxiety for drinkers in all societies. Horton's ideas have been retested (Field 1962), summarized and critiqued (Heath 1988a; Room 1988a), and long since supplanted by more sophisticated approaches, but they remain an important pioneering effort to look at drinking behavior beyond the narrow confines of European societies and to show the potential value of the ethnographic record in understanding human interactions with alcoholic beverages. Other theories of drinking using data from the HRAF were Peter Field's "social organization theory" (1962); Margaret Bacon, Herbert Barry, and Irving Child's "dependency theory" (1965); and David McClelland et al.'s "power theory" (1972). Over the last thirty years, this mode of analysis has fallen into disfavor in anthropology, and none of these approaches plays a central role in current anthropological debates over drinking and temperance (*see* Heath 1988a and Room 1988a for summaries and reviews of these various HRAF-based theories).

Drunken Comportment

In 2001, Robin Room argued that Craig MacAndrew and Robert Edgerton's 1969 volume, *Drunken Comportment: A Social Explanation,* is a "landmark study" that has been perhaps the most influential contribution from the ethnographic literature to the wider field of alcohol research. The essence of their argument is that drunken behavior differs markedly (1) from one society to the next, (2) within a given society depending upon the context of drinking, and (3) within a society from one historical moment to another. MacAndrew and Edgerton introduced two concepts in their book that have become commonplace in subsequent sociocultural studies of alcohol: (1) that drunken comportment may be viewed as a "time out" from normal sober behavior, allowing the drinker to "get away with" otherwise unacceptable acts, and (2) that even allowing for "time out," drunken behavior always occurs "within limits," although those limits may be more relaxed than when alcohol has not been consumed. Together, the "time out" concept and the "within limits" clause help account for the frequently observed and remarked "excuse value" of drunkenness, reducing or eliminating culpability for the drunkard's bad behavior.

Room (2001) revisits *Drunken Comportment,* acknowledging its importance but also pointing out its limitations. He urges alcohologists to move beyond MacAndrew and Edgerton's focus on individual behavior to look at group behavior and to more carefully examine "the dimensions of cultural variation in drunken comportment."

Theories from the 1970s and 1980s

Hard on the heels of MacAndrew and Edgerton's book came another book that contributed importantly to anthropological theories of drinking: Jerrold E. Levy and Stephen J. Kunitz's *Indian Drinking: Navajo Practices and Anglo-American Theories* (1974). As Edwin Lemert (1964) had done for three Polynesian societies, Levy and Kunitz looked closely at and compared drinking among three Native American populations of the U.S. Southwest—the Navajo, the Hopi, and the White Mountain Apache. Joining standard ethnographic fieldwork methods to historical materials, crime statistics, and mortality and other medical data (for example, cirrhosis rates), these authors pointed the way toward a more methodologically sophisticated anthropological approach to alcohol, and they concluded their volume by challenging the definitions of alcoholism that have been used in cross-cultural studies. Their most significant contributions were (1) to emphasize the necessity for understanding the past history of alcohol use for insight into contemporary drinking patterns, (2) to suggest that colonized peoples who did not have alcoholic beverages before contact with outsiders (most indigenous peoples of Canada and the United States, and all Pacific islanders) typically copied drinking customs and attitudes from their colonizers, and (3) to document that observable drunkenness did not necessarily correlate with the amounts of alcohol typically consumed or with rates of serious physiological harm from excessive drinking.

By the 1980s, the number of anthropologists writing about alcohol began to grow, and this is reflected in various important publications that appeared during that decade. Room (1984a), a very well known sociologist of alcohol, threw down a gauntlet to his anthropological colleagues, arguing that the functionalist theory that had dominated anthropology for much of the twentieth century had led anthropologists to overlook the harms associated with drinking—an oversight he called "problem deflation." His article included commentaries by sixteen colleagues, twelve of them anthropologists. The commentators generally praised the article but found various issues to quarrel with, including Room's assumption that anthropologists were still in the thrall of functionalism. Later in 1984, Dwight Heath took strong issue with Room on a number of counts, and this led to a spirited debate over the possible biases in ethnographic research and over whether or not anthropologists should become involved in alcohol control policies and other public-health approaches (*see,* for example, Heath 1986, 1987, 1988b, 1988c; Marshall 1990; Room 1984b, 1988b).

For all its importance in focusing debate, Room's article (1984a) ignored significant developments that had already occurred in anthropological studies of alcohol, for example Levy and Kunitz's (1974) examination of harms associated with drinking among Native peoples of the Southwest. One year after Room's article appeared, Linda A. Bennett and Genevieve M. Ames (1985) published an edited collection of studies that showed the contrasting experiences and perspectives Americans have with beverage alcohol based upon ethnicity, regionalism, religious affiliation, and social class. In light of the debate generated by Room's contention of problem deflation, many contributors to this book examined alcohol-related harms, and certainly cannot be accused of problem deflation.

Allied with Dwight Heath in the debate generated by Robin Room's article (1984a), Mary Douglas edited a collection (1987a) on drinking that concentrated on the drinking of alcohol even as it went beyond this to include other psychoactive beverages such as kava and coffee. Increasingly, in subsequent years, anthropologists who study alcohol have also studied other drug substances, whether taken as beverages or by other means. In her introduction to the volume, Douglas (1987b) describes how "drinks construct the world as it is" and how the process of "drinking constructs an ideal world." Such a social constructionist position also has gained favor as a theoretical framework for anthropological analyses of alcohol in more recent years.

In 1988, Elizabeth Colson and Thayer Scudder's *For Prayer and Profit* appeared, and it set the standard for theoretically sophisticated anthropological studies of drinking. Drawing on close to thirty years of fieldwork by one or the other of the authors, the volume carefully traced the specific ways that unfolding historical events (social change) altered the production, supply, consumption, and meanings of alcoholic beverages among the Gwembe Tonga of Zambia. This volume pulled together various threads introduced here previously: It showed how alcohol use provided a "time out" that was "within limits"; it was situated historically and it attended to both the positive and the negative effects of drinking; it was neither functionalist in argument, nor did it deflate alcohol's problem side; it paid attention to the role of alcohol in religious ceremonies; and it discussed several ways that alcohol production and use "constructed" the Gwembe Tonga world.

Theories from the 1990s

In 1992, the Finnish sociologist Pertti Alasuutari published *Desire and Craving: A Cultural Theory of Alcoholism,* in which he gave primary attention to tavern drinking by Finnish blue-collar workers and to cultural explanations of heavy drinking in modern society. His book picks up Levy and Kunitz's (1974) questioning of the alcoholism concept and Douglas's (1987b) social constructionism around drink to argue that alcoholism is a culture-bound syndrome of the West. This is particularly interesting as a critique of medicalization, especially when read along with Ames (1985) and Chrisman (1985).

Echoing somewhat Colson and Scudder's longitudinal study of drinking among the Gwembe Tonga (1988), Stephen J. Kunitz and Jerrold E. Levy (1994) offered a follow-up to their earlier book on Navajo drinking. This second volume examined alcohol-related mortality in greater depth, followed Navajo "drinking careers," compared Navajo mortality with mortality rates among other regional populations, and then discussed alcohol treatment options. They documented that men who drank in an alcoholic pattern according to clinical assessment criteria often altered their drinking, or even stopped completely, as they aged. Kunitz and Levy also demonstrated that there is considerable diversity among Navajo men and women in patterns of alcohol use, drawing attention to gender differences and to intracultural diversity all at once.

Gender is the topic that most characterizes anthropological theories of drinking and temperance during the 1990s. The background to and effects of a prohibition movement led by women against men's drinking in Truk (Chuuk), Micronesia, drew on a number of the themes discussed above (Marshall and Marshall 1990). The somewhat different ways that Maya women were connected to alcoholic beverages in Chiapas, Mexico, where they also led opposition movements, were chronicled by Christine Eber in 1995. Two edited collections that spotlighted gender and drink also appeared in this decade. The first, edited by Dimitra Gefou-Madianou in 1992, contains chapters for several European societies and one for Egypt, showing how alcohol is used to define gender roles, to lubricate gender relations, and to transform identities. The second volume, edited by Maryon McDonald in 1994, casts a wider ethnographic net and—like Douglas (1987a)—includes other substances as well as alcohol (kava and tchat [qat] in this case). Both volumes contain insightful introductions by their editors that bring gender studies and feminist anthropological theory into the mix, positioned within medical anthropological theory as well.

Theory after the Millennium

In the brief period that has passed since we entered the twenty-first century, three major trends appear. First, case studies of drinking by individuals or by various social groups continue to be employed in comparative studies. This trend is illustrated by Heath (2000) who uses case studies from Spain, France, Truk (Chuuk) in Micronesia, the Navajo, the Kofyar of Nigeria, and the Camba of Bolivia to provide descriptive summaries of drinking patterns and to reach a set of ethnographic generalizations that can usefully be investigated in future work. The second major trend since 2000 is to examine alcohol problems along with related health problems. Work by Kunitz and Levy with the assistance of five other colleagues (2000) gives special attention to drinking's relationship with conduct disorder as set against a backdrop of social change among the Navajo. Marshall's involvement with a diverse disciplinary mix of international colleagues has resulted in two recent volumes that infuse an anthropological perspective on drinking and temperance into alcohol policy materials for use by public-health workers in developing societies (Riley and Marshall 1999; Room et al. 2002). The most recent trend is toward greater involvement by anthropologists in research in the United States and other Western societies in applied medical anthropological work (including public health) and in studying alcohol along with other drug substances. This work, and some of the disciplinary controversy that surrounds it, is summarized in a set of eight articles contained in a special issue of *Social Science and Medicine* (Marshall and Bennett 2001).

Mac Marshall

See also: Kava; Native Americans: Drinking Patterns and Temperance Reform; Pacific Islands

References

Alasuutari, Pertti. *Desire and Craving: A Cultural Theory of Alcoholism.* Albany: State University of New York Press, 1992.

Ames, Genevieve M. "American Beliefs about Alcoholism: Historical Perspectives on the Medical-Moral Controversy" in *The American Experience with Alcohol: Contrasting Cultural Perspectives,* edited by Linda A. Bennett and Genevieve M. Ames, 23–39. New York: Plenum Press, 1985.

Bacon, Margaret K., Herbert Barry III, and Irving L. Child. "A Cross-Cultural Study of Drinking: II. Relations to Other Features of Culture" in *Quarterly Journal of Studies on Alcohol.* Supplement. no. 3 (1965): 29–48.

Bennett, Linda A., and Genevieve M. Ames, eds. *The American Experience with Alcohol: Contrasting Cultural Perspectives.* New York: Plenum Press, 1985.

Chrisman, Noel J. "Alcoholism: Illness or Disease?" in *The American Experience with Alcohol: Contrasting Cultural Perspectives,* edited by Linda A. Bennett and Genevieve M. Ames, 7–21. New York: Plenum Press, 1985.

Colson, Elizabeth, and Thayer Scudder. *For Prayer and Profit: The Ritual, Economic, and Social Importance of Beer in Gwembe District, Zambia, 1950–1982.* Stanford, CA: Stanford University Press, 1988.

Douglas, Mary. "A Distinctive Anthropological Perspective" in *Constructive Drinking: Perspectives on Drink from Anthropology,* edited by Mary Douglas, 3–15. New York: Cambridge University Press, 1987b.

———, ed. *Constructive Drinking: Perspectives on Drink from Anthropology.* New York: Cambridge University Press, 1987a.

Eber, Christine. *Women and Alcohol in a Highland Maya Town: Water of Hope, Water of Sorrow.* Austin: University of Texas Press, 1995.

Field, Peter B. "A New Cross-Cultural Study of Drunkenness" in *Society, Culture, and Drinking Patterns,* edited by David J. Pittman and Charles R. Snyder, 48–74. New York: John Wiley and Sons, 1962.

Gefou-Madianou, Dimitra, ed. *Alcohol, Gender and Culture.* London: Routledge, 1992.

Heath, Dwight B. "Alcohol Control Policies and Drinking Patterns: An International Game of Politics against Science" in *Journal of Substance Abuse.* 1 (1988b): 109–115.

———. "Anthropology and Alcohol Studies: Current Issues" in *Annual Review of Anthropology.* 16 (1987): 99–120.

———. "CA Comment on Alcohol and Ethnography: A Case of Problem Deflation?" in *Current Anthropology.* 25 (1984): 180–181.

———. "Drinking and Drunkenness in Transcultural Perspective" in *Transcultural Psychiatric Research Review.* 23 (1986): 103–126.

———. *Drinking Occasions: Comparative Perspectives on Alcohol and Culture.* Philadelphia: Brunner/Mazel, 2000.

———. "Emerging Anthropological Theory and Models of Alcohol Use and Alcoholism" in *Theories on Alcoholism,* edited by C. Douglas Chaudron and D. Adrian Wilkinson, 353–410. Toronto: Addiction Research Foundation, 1988a.

———. "Quasi-Science and Public Policy: A Reply to Robin Room about Details and Misrepresentations in Science" in *Journal of Substance Abuse.* 1 (1988c): 121–125.

Horton, Donald. "The Functions of Alcohol in Primitive Societies: A Cross-Cultural Study" in *Quarterly Journal of Studies on Alcoho*l. 4 (1943): 199–320.

Kunitz, Stephen J., and Jerrold E. Levy. *Drinking Careers: A Twenty-Five-Year Study of Three Navajo Populations.* New Haven, CT: Yale University Press, 1994.

———. *Drinking, Conduct Disorder, and Social Change: Navajo Experiences.* New York: Oxford University Press, 2000.

Lemert, Edwin M. "Forms and Pathology of Drinking in Three Polynesian Societies" in *American Anthropologist.* 66 (1964): 361–374.

Levy, Jerrold E., and Stephen J. Kunitz. *Indian Drinking: Navajo Practices and Anglo-American Theories.* New York: John Wiley and Sons, 1974.

MacAndrew, Craig, and Robert B. Edgerton. *Drunken Comportment: A Social Explanation.* Chicago: Aldine Publishing, 1969.

Marshall, Mac. "'Problem Deflation' and the Ethnographic Record: Interpretation and Introspection in Anthropological Studies of Alcohol" in *Journal of Substance Abuse.* 2 (1990): 353–367.

Marshall, Mac, and Leslie B. Marshall. *Silent Voices Speak: Women and Prohibition in Truk.* Belmont, CA: Wadsworth Publishing, 1990.

Marshall, Mac, and Linda A. Bennett, eds. Special Issue: Anthropological Perspectives on Alcohol and Drugs at the Turn of the New Millennium. *Social Science and Medicine.* 53, no. 2 (2001): 153–262.

McClelland, David C., W. N. Davis, R. Kalin, and E. Wanner, eds. *The Drinking Man: Alcohol and Human Motivation.* New York: Free Press, 1972.

McDonald, Maryon, ed. *Gender, Drink and Drugs.* Oxford: Berg, 1994.

Riley, Leanne, and Mac Marshall, eds. *Alcohol and Public Health in Eight Developing Countries.* Geneva: World Health Organization, 1999.

Room, Robin. "Alcohol and Ethnography: A Case of Problem Deflation?" in *Current Anthropology.* 25, no. 2 (1984a): 169–191 [including commentaries].

———. "Alcohol Control and Public Health" in *Annual Review of Public Health.* 5 (1984b): 293–317.

———. "Cross-Cultural Research in Alcohol Studies: Research Traditions and Analytical Issues" in *Cultural Influences and Drinking Patterns: A Focus on Hispanic and Japanese Populations,* edited by Leland H. Towle and Thomas C. Harford, 9–40. NIAAA Research Monograph no. 19. Rockville, MD: National Institute on Alcohol Abuse and Alcoholism, 1988a.

———. "Intoxication and Bad Behaviour: Understanding Cultural Differences in the Link" in *Social Science and Medicine,* Special Issue: Anthropological Perspectives on Alcohol and Drugs at the Turn of the New Millennium, edited by Mac Marshall and Linda A. Bennett, 189–198. 53, no. 2 (2001).

———. "Science is in the Details: Towards a Nuanced View of Alcohol Control Studies" in *Journal of Substance Abuse.* 1 (1988b): 117–120.

Room, Robin, et al. *Alcohol in Developing Societies: A Public Health Approach.* Helsinki: Finnish Foundation for Alcohol Studies in collaboration with the World Health Organization, 2002.

Anti-Saloon League of America (ASLA)

The Anti-Saloon League of America (ASLA) mobilized sentiment for prohibition. Although prohibition was a decades-old reform, the ASLA successfully turned it into an issue in tune with American "Progressivism" in the early twentieth century. The league, founded in 1893, followed a nonpartisan approach and a single-minded purpose: achieving national prohibition. Inspired in part by the organizational model of the vertically integrated business firm, the league assumed the leadership of the dry cause, setting its strategy and coordinating political campaigns with other groups. Its leaders always controlled it, although interested constituencies enjoyed at least nominal representation on the board of trustees. With its success, the league created the model for the modern U.S. single-purpose pressure group. And by its very name, the league focused attention on the most prominent liquor retailers, the saloons, whose operators were often corrupt and criminal and thus widely seen as undesirable by genteel and pious Americans. This strategy for the most part united prohibition supporters in their common fight, but the league was less successful in maintaining its single-minded focus after the enactment of the Eighteenth Amendment, and ultimately, it failed to maintain support for Prohibition. Although significantly reduced in strength from its heyday, the league eventually reconstituted itself as the American Council on Alcohol Problems.

The ASLA was a relative latecomer among prohibition organizations. Prior to the 1890s, a host of organizations had formed at the local, state, and national levels, seeking prohibition laws. Although those organizations often energized large numbers of citizens and enjoyed no little success in enacting local and state laws restricting the liquor businesses, they were unable to agree on a single strategy for winning dry laws, and they often dissipated support by engaging other reform issues. The league, in contrast, defined its purpose clearly: to work on a nonpartisan basis to elect prohibition supporters and to build, however slowly, the coalitions necessary for enacting prohibition. Prohibition for the league meant outlawing the businesses that manufactured, distributed, and sold liquor. The league strategy called for a focus first on the local level, so as to expand steadily the territory in which liquor businesses were outlawed. Meanwhile building public sentiment favorable to prohibition, the league would eventually move beyond the local level to campaign for state prohibition and, eventually, an amendment to the United States Constitution. That final action, the league leaders believed, would permanently forbid the liquor trades, branding them criminal, and driving them underground. In the end, prohibition would lead to a sober society when liquor businesses were unable to use advertising and other promotions to entice drinking.

Development of the ASLA

The Anti-Saloon League began as the Ohio Anti-Saloon League in 1893. That state was closely contested between the two major political parties and was the scene of bitter fights between prohibition advocates and their opponents. For decades, large numbers of evangelical Protestants in Ohio had seen the liquor businesses as part of the "Kingdom of Evil," encouraging sinful behaviors and inhibiting individuals' ability to sustain the proper relationship with God and achieve salvation. Ohio was also home to substantial numbers who disagreed with these beliefs, viewing liquor consumption instead as an acceptable and pleasant custom. The two views were deeply held and deeply divisive. The prohibitionists were mostly Republicans, but Republican Party leaders knew that taking a dry stand would likely lead to electoral defeats; therefore, the Republicans tried to draft balanced positions, offering hope to prohibitionists without alienating those opposed to prohibition.

Howard Hyde Russell was the founder of the league. An experienced attorney, Russell had trained for a new career as a Congregational minister at Oberlin College, then a hotbed of evangelical Protestantism and reform sentiments. After five years of ministry in the stockyard districts of Kansas City and Chicago, Russell returned to Oberlin in 1893 to realize a vision he had discussed at the college: forming a new business-like organization to mount steady pressure on politicians, regardless of party affiliation, to enact legislation restricting (and eventually eliminating) the liquor businesses. Winning prohibition, he believed, required full-time work by leaders who developed real expertise in fund-raising, legal affairs, administration, and propaganda. The purpose was to persuade and organize voters at the precinct and township levels to reward dry politicians and to punish those who helped the liquor businesses. Russell obtained support in Oberlin, and the new organization established its headquarters in Columbus, the state's capital. Soon, the league energized the state's dry voters. In the meantime, Russell communicated his organizational and strategic ideas more widely among the nation's prohibitionists. At the end of 1895 at a meeting in Washington, D.C., Russell and dry leaders from fifteen states formed the American Anti-Saloon League, headquartered along with the Ohio League in Columbus. It billed itself as "the church in action" against the saloon. Its goal was to keep pressing for legislation outlawing liquor businesses in local districts, states, and, eventually, the nation.

Although some temperance leaders saw the wisdom of the league's fresh approach, the early years were a struggle for survival. In the absence of major victories, donations trickled. The league always relied on the generosity of thousands of supporters. Russell built support by scheduling special sermons in sympathetic local churches. The preceding evening, he visited local saloons to gather stories for the next day's sermon, allowing him to tell of saloon conditions that shocked his listeners. In the critical early years, Russell also persuaded the nation's wealthiest prohibitionist, John D. Rockefeller, to donate funds, donations that were timely in allowing the organization to survive. Gradually, it built its strength in its home base, Ohio, and spread elsewhere, so that by the early twentieth century, the league had organizations in every region of the country. Sometimes it built new groups, but the league also took over older state organizations and reshaped them in its image. In 1903, Purley Albert Baker replaced Russell as the head of the organization.

The league never became the omnipotent organization its opponents portrayed. Local variation in state prohibition agitation remained, as did other prohibition organizations. But the league did become the center of U.S. prohibition forces, setting the strategy for prohibition campaigns and, except for organizations that disagreed with its nonpartisan approach, coordinating attacks on the liquor trades. It raised considerable funds and dispersed them to state groups according to the national strategy. And the league produced prodigious amounts of printed matter—material that gave the movement cohesiveness while expanding its popular base.

By 1909, the league was well established. That year, it changed its name to the Anti-Saloon League of America, and moved its headquarters to Westerville, Ohio, a dry community near the state capital. That small town became the epicenter of the nation's prohibition movement. ASLA workers processed thousands of donations from supporters. The ASLA incorporated the American Issue Publishing Company, found lenders, and built a substantial printing plant, which it used to churn out pamphlets, newspapers, magazines, and broadsides. Translators developed foreign-language publications for reaching the rapidly growing immigrant population. The Westerville post office became the busiest small-town facility in the nation. And, the ASLA had begun the fight to have Congress enact a statute forbidding the shipment of liquor from wet to dry areas.

The interstate shipment statute, the Webb-Kenyon Act of 1913, was the ASLA's first significant victory in Congress; it forbade shipping liquors from wet into dry territory. The fight took years of effort. When the Republican caucus controlled the House of Representatives, the powerful speaker, Joseph Cannon of Illinois, thwarted attempts to bring the bill to the floor, preferring to bury the divisive issue. To win, the ASLA had to fight Cannon, which it did in 1908, cooperating with other frustrated reform organizations. The resulting changes in the House rules made it easier for reform legislation to reach the floor for a vote. Finally, in 1913, the Webb-Kenyon Act passed, over the veto of President William Howard Taft. The ASLA had clearly become a powerful national political organization.

Winning Prohibition

Later in 1913 at its twentieth anniversary convention in Columbus, the ASLA announced its campaign for national prohibition through a constitutional amendment. This campaign meant that the league had to reach out to other temperance and reform organizations as never before, mount a huge educational and propaganda campaign, and collect ever more substantial sums. Ernest Hurst Cherrington was the person who assumed most of the leadership functions in those tasks. Cherrington, based in Westerville, was in effect the league's business manager and its principal strategist for the campaign.

Cherrington and his colleagues believed that opportunity to win national prohibition was short-lived. They observed the great wave of immigrants entering the United States from southern and eastern Europe, and recognized that those immigrants were not persuaded by evangelical Protestantism about the wisdom of prohibition. Not only did their presence require huge propaganda efforts in many languages, but it also meant that the Prohibition amendment had to be initiated by Congress prior to the reapportionment that would follow the 1920 census, when immigrant-rich states would gain congressional representation and increase their electoral weight in presidential politics.

The ASLA thus initiated the fight by arranging for a floor debate and vote on a Prohibition amendment in the House of Representatives. That debate and vote occurred in 1914. The result was defeat, but the vote had forced representatives to take a stand on prohibition. The league set out to reward its friends and punish its enemies, regardless of party affiliation, in the 1916 elections, when it won the two-thirds support required in both houses of Congress to initiate what became the Eighteenth Amendment.

The die was cast, and in 1918, Congress initiated the amendment, with the proviso that the states must ratify it in seven years. This requirement, which prohibition opponents hoped would bury the measure, posed still another challenge for the ASLA. Again wanting to reach a conclusion before the reapportionment of state legislatures after 1920, the league successfully launched a whirlwind ratification campaign. By January 1919, two-thirds of the states had ratified the amendment, and it went into effect the following year.

The Decline of the ASLA

Ironically, the successful enactment of the Prohibition amendment led to the decline of the ASLA. The league had successfully brought together a coalition of Americans who agreed on prohibition as a reform, but who disagreed on appropriate policies to follow. And disagreement there was. It began over the enforcement statute introduced by Representative Andrew Volstead of Minnesota. One faction, led by Wayne Bidwell Wheeler, who served as the league's general counsel after 1916, wanted the statute to follow some state laws and forbid the possession of liquor. Cherrington and other leaders disagreed, however, as the prohibition campaign had focused not on the individual drinker but on the businesses that supplied drink. The law did, however, define intoxicating liquors so narrowly that it ruled out trade in any beer or wine (except for sacramental and medicinal purposes).

The ASLA also split over questions of law enforcement. Although all leaders wanted to see the law enforced, the majority of league officials thought that the organization's focus, now that the liquor trades were driven underground, should be on education and persuasion. Led by Cherrington, this faction felt that, in the absence of open retailing and liquor advertising, the churches, led by the league, had their long-sought opportunity to reach out to new generations of Americans to persuade them to lead abstemious lives. Nor should the effort stop at the nation's borders. Cherrington arranged for the ASLA to form the World League against Alcoholism, headquartered in Westerville, to promote the dry message across the globe.

A minority of ASLA leaders, however, disagreed. Led by the energetic and able Wayne Wheeler, the general counsel and legislative superintendent, this faction sought an emphasis on strict enforcement of the law. League resources should be focused on the political fight in the Congress and in the state legislatures to secure ample funding for police efforts. The Volstead Act had placed federal enforcement responsibilities in the Department of the Treasury, whose officials had experience enforcing liquor taxes. Unfortunately for the prohibitionists, however, this arrangement did not work well. Treasury officials were not especially sympathetic with Prohibition, and the Congress was reluctant to provide large resources for enforcement. Wheeler and his faction wanted to continue the political struggle so as to win better enforcement of Prohibition.

The disagreement between the league factions climaxed when Baker announced his retirement as general superintendent in 1924. Cherrington was a logical successor, but Wheeler and his faction successfully maneuvered to keep him from the post. Francis Scott McBride, the Illinois league's state superintendent since 1912 and a Wheeler supporter, succeeded Baker. The ASLA attempted to straddle the enforcement and education strategies. Cherrington remained in charge of education, about which he reported directly to the league's trustees, while on business and financial affairs he reported to McBride, who had no experience at the national level.

The choice of McBride and the disagreements within the league, however, seriously wounded it. The Federal Council of Churches, an ecumenical organization of large and important Protestant denominations, thought its members should em-

A 1924 photo of the board of directors of the Anti-Saloon League of America (Library of Congress)

phasize education, not law enforcement, and considered withdrawing its support from the ASLA altogether. Church support was waning in any case, as congregations, thinking the Prohibition victory won, lent support for other purposes. The league, in short, by the mid-1920s was a dying organization, losing its supporters and failing to recruit a new generation of leaders.

But it had not yet died. The ASLA orchestrated a mighty political effort in 1928 when the Democratic Party nominated Alfred Emanuel Smith, the governor of New York, for president. Smith was an open, defiant opponent of Prohibition who had supported New York's repeal of its enforcement statute. League leaders believed Smith had to be defeated at any cost. They campaigned across the South, winning five states for Hoover, the first Republican victories in the South since Reconstruction. In the North, the league also helped achieve a Republican landslide. The result was the election of the first prohibitionist president, Herbert Hoover, and the largest prohibition majorities in the Congress ever, along with large numbers of Prohibition supporters at state and local levels.

However, the victory and the preceding political machinations of the decade cost the ASLA its historic identification as a nonpartisan organization. In his fights in Washington to obtain better enforcement, Wheeler had identified closely with the Republican congressional majorities. Now in presidential politics, the league was identified with the Republican Party. The Republican identification may have served the league well in the short run, but in the long run it destroyed the organization as a potent force and helped lead to the repeal of Prohibition. When the Great Depression struck, voters turned on Republican officeholders and in 1932, elected as president the Democrat Franklin D. Roosevelt, along with Democratic, and antiprohibitionist, majorities in the Congress. They quickly arranged the repeal of the Eighteenth Amendment.

The ASLA's Death

The depression also seriously hurt the ASLA. Donations dried up, and the organization lost assets when its bank in Westerville failed. It was unable to mount any effective defense against the repeal movement, which steamrolled over Prohibition in even less time than the league had won its own amendment. After repeal, the league struggled on, with a significantly reduced staff and far fewer publications. For a brief time, it hoped to capitalize on the mobilization for World War II to advance its cause, but the country had turned on Prohibition. After 1945, the prohibition organizations were able to achieve nine separate hearings in the Congress on measures to control strictly the sales of alcoholic beverages, but no legislation resulted. Eventually the league reconstituted itself as the American Council on Alcohol Problems. At the start of the twenty-first century, that organization had thirty-six state affiliates and support from twenty-two Christian denominations. It sought to persuade legislative bodies to restrict sales of liquor in order to promote sobriety.

K. Austin Kerr

See also: Baker, Purley Albert; Cannon, James, Jr.; Cherrington, Ernest Hurst; Democratic Party (United States); Federal Regulation of Alcohol Before 1920 (United States); Hoover, Herbert Clark; McBride, Francis Scott; National Prohibition (United States); Prohibition Party (United States); Republican Party (United States); Russell, Howard Hyde; Smith, Alfred Emanuel; Wheeler, Wayne Bidwell

References

American Council on Alcohol Problems website. http://www.americancouncilonalcoholproblems.com/ [July 2002].

Anti-Saloon League Museum website. http://www.wpl.lib.oh.us/AntiSaloon/ [July 2002].

Blocker, Jack S., Jr. *Retreat from Reform: The Prohibition Movement in the United States, 1890–1913.* Westport, CT: Greenwood, 1976.

Hamm, Richard F. *Shaping the Eighteenth Amendment: Temperance Reform, Legal Culture, and the Polity, 1880–1920.* Chapel Hill: University of North Carolina Press, 1995.

Kerr, K. Austin. *Organized for Prohibition: A New History of the Anti-Saloon League.* New Haven, CT: Yale University Press, 1985.

Odegard, Peter H. *Pressure Politics: The Story of the Anti-Saloon League.* New York: Columbia University Press, 1928.

Pegram, Thomas R. *Battling Demon Rum: The Struggle for a Dry America, 1800–1933.* Chicago: Ivan R. Dee, 1998.

Temperance and Prohibition History website. http://www.prohibition.history.ohio-state.edu [June 2002].

Archaeological Approaches to Drinking and Temperance

Archaeology is the study of peoples and societies in the past through analysis of the material remains they left behind. It uses particularistic evidence from archaeological sites to reconstruct past human behavior and make generalizations about cultural processes. Its particularistic focus provides insights into the more ordinary activities of daily life that are often left out of written records. Moreover, the archaeological excavation of sites once occupied by subjugated social groups, such as slaves, women, and working classes, helps give voice to people who are frequently silent in the documentary record. In addition, archaeological evidence can test the accuracy of the written record and challenge dominant ideologies about race, class, and gender. The particularistic focus of archaeology and its ability to investigate critically the documentary record make it a valuable method for exploring the role of alcohol drinking in society, a common activity that is often couched in moralistic discourse.

Indeed, archaeologists have examined the production, distribution, and use of alcohol in the past. The material remains of these specialized activities are abundant and easily identifiable in the archaeological record. However, archaeological discussions about alcohol are typically fortuitous by-products of fieldwork that had other emphases, and few archaeologists have rigorously applied historical and anthropological theories to help them explain their alcohol-related discoveries. Yet, despite these shortcomings, archaeological evidence has added a new dimension to the holistic type of inquiry that the study of alcohol in society demands. The following survey examines some of the contributions archaeological methods have made to alcohol studies.

Identifying the Origins of Alcohol Use

Archaeologists have identified the origins of alcohol production in a number of historical and cross-cultural settings. One of the primary debates in archaeology involves the cause of the Neolithic revolution, the period 10,000 to 12,000 years ago when humans in the Near East shifted from a hunting and gathering style of subsistence to one based on the domestication and cultivation of plants. The shift was a major turning point in the evolution of world civilizations. A subsistence style based on the selective breeding and cultivation of cereals for the preparation of flour used for making bread fed and sustained larger populations than hunting and gathering and thus gave rise to more complex societies. According to many scholars, the overexploitation of wild food resources in the Near East and climate change forced hunter/gatherers to become sedentary grain cultivators. However, in 1953, anthropologist Robert J. Braidwood speculated that the domestication of cereals, especially barley and wheat, during the Neolithic period was spurred by the desire for beer rather than bread. Braidwood posed the question "Did man once live on beer alone?" to a symposium, and the responses were published in the journal *American Anthropologist* (Braidwood et al. 1953). Archaeological evidence included sickles and blades for reaping grain, mortars and pestles for grinding grains, ceramic jars for storing grain, and seeds, but as the respondents correctly pointed out, such evidence is ambiguous and can be used to support either the beer- or the bread-making hypothesis. Most of the symposium participants concluded that brewing was a serendipitous offshoot of bread making and the question was largely put to rest. However, in 1985, archaeologists Solomon Katz and Mary Voigt revived the debate. They argued that beer was highly nutritional and probably had social and religious value in hunting/gathering societies. According to Katz and Voigt, the selective cultivation of cereals for brewing provided surplus grain for bread making and thus led to the emergence of large complex societies during the Neolithic age.

Wine making requires distinct tools and materials that have allowed archaeologists to locate the origins of these operations in different regions. Archaeologists have used paleoethnobotanical evidence, including the seeds and stalks of wild and domesticated grapes, to identify viticulture and wine making at early sites in Europe, the Mediterranean, and the Near East. Wild grape seeds (*Vitis vinifera sylvestris*) have been recovered from human settlement sites in southern France as far back as 350,000 years ago, which hints at the possibility that Neanderthals and early modern humans fermented wine. Wine residues, including tannin and tartrate crystals, have been recovered from jars at ancient sites in the Near East. Archaeologists have recovered evidence of wine presses at Minoan-aged sites (3500 B.C.E.) in Greece and hieroglyphs show wine presses in Dynastic Egypt. Archaeological evidence has also been used to investigate the early origins of alcohol distillation. For example, while many scholars believe that alcohol distillation emerged in late medieval Europe, archaeologist F. R. Allchin (1979) conducted a critical reading of ancient Sanskrit texts to argue that ceramic pots recovered from 2,500-year-old village sites in Northern India and Pakistan may represent the earliest evidence of alcohol distillation.

Alcohol Making in the Modern Atlantic World

Although the major technological advances in alcohol production—brewing, fermenting, and distilling—developed long before the age of European exploration, the origins of alcohol making in the modern Atlantic world are no less interesting, and archaeological research has helped shed light on these endeavors. Brew houses have been unearthed at a number of early-seventeenth-century British and French colonial sites in North America. For example, at Jamestown, Virginia, the site of the first permanent English settlement in the New World, archaeologist John Cotter (1958: 102–109) identified and described an early-seventeenth-century brewery. According to Cotter, circular brick fireboxes, a portion of a copper kettle, lead fragments, and mortar analysis indicated a semi-industrial complex likely associated with brewing. Archaeological excavations have been conducted at a number of Spanish colonial wineries *(bodegas)* in the Moquegua Valley region of Peru, which have revealed insights into the material culture of winery operations. Archaeologists have identified and described rum distilleries at British colonial sites in New England and the Caribbean. Brandy distilleries have been excavated at urban Spanish colonial sites in Argentina and at Dutch colonial settlements in the Cape Coast region of South Africa. Archaeological excavations have also been conducted at a small eighteenth-century whiskey distillery at Mount Vernon, the home of George Washington.

Artifacts of Alcohol

Alcohol is a volatile fluid. If not consumed immediately after production, it must be stored in durable, airtight containers. Alcohol has also been a valuable commodity and a prominent item of trade. The volatile and valuable nature of alcohol has led to the production of a rich material culture for its storage and transport. Glass bottles, ceramic jars, and ironbound wooden casks not only served the immediate purpose of storage and transport, but these materials survive well in the archaeological record and have helped archaeologists identify patterns of trade. The most prolific research probably comes from archaeologists working at ancient and classical sites in Europe, the Near East, and the Mediterranean. These archaeologists have used *amphorae* jars to trace the early wine trades. In the Americas, handblown glass bottles are ubiquitous on colonial European sites, which attests to the magnitude of the Atlantic alcohol trade, especially from the Portuguese island of Madeira.

North America was one of the few culture areas that did not produce alcoholic beverages prior to European contact. Once Native North Americans were introduced to alcoholic beverages, however, the European alcohol trade became central to the economic success of many on the early colonial frontier. Archaeologists have recovered glass bottles and Spanish olive jars, often used for the storage and transport of wine, from Native American sites throughout North America. The presence of these materials on Native American sites highlights the commercial nature of European–Native American relations and reveals the extent to which the Native American fur and deerskin trades helped fuel the emerging Atlantic economy.

Alcohol Use and Foodway Studies

Historical archaeologists treat alcohol drinking, though not always explicitly, as part of the foodways subsystem. Foodway studies concentrate on the material culture of food and beverage consumption, especially within the context of formal dining. Foodway studies have been particularly popular at British colonial sites in North America. For example, in 1973, James Deetz examined ceramic assemblages from Plymouth, Massachusetts, between 1620 and 1835, in order to show changing foodway patterns. Deetz analyzed the relative proportion of ceramic eating and drinking vessels and distinguished three successive phases operating in Plymouth (1620–1660, 1660–1760, and 1760–1835). Deetz argued that the changes identified in each phase reflected an ideological shift in the American mind-set from a communal to a more individual pattern of eating and drinking. According to Deetz, individual ceramic plates and cups were rare in the early phase because colonists ate and drank from communal vessels. In the second phase, however, the increasing number of ceramic drinking vessels indicated a growing trend toward individualized foodways. By the third phase, residents of Plymouth ate and drank from matching sets of individual plates and cups. Although Deetz did not specifically examine alcohol use, he used ceramic drinking vessels to show how trends in beverage consumption might be viewed in the broader context of ideological change.

Structures and Dwellings

Archaeologists have identified and described the structures and dwellings used for alcohol consumption. Taverns, inns, ordinaries, saloons, cafés, brothels, fraternity houses, and other sites of social drinking provide archaeologists with many opportunities to explore alcohol use and its role in generating the appropriate atmosphere for sociability. Colonial American taverns have been particularly popular subjects of archaeological study. Tavern sites possess a distinct material culture, which makes them easily identifiable in the archaeological record. Unlike domestic dwelling sites, tavern sites usually have a high number of alcohol-related materials, including fragments of wine bottles, punch bowls, tankards, mugs, and wine glasses. Occasionally, archaeologists will recover complete wine bottles from archaeological sites (especially from underwater archaeological sites) that still contain remnants of their original alcoholic contents. Colonial tavern sites also tend to possess a high percentage of white kaolin clay tobacco pipes. As with alcohol drinking, tobacco smoking probably enhanced the sociable atmosphere of tavern life.

Archaeological evidence has been used to highlight other aspects of tavern life. The discovery of checkers and garter pins has helped reveal ancillary tavern activities, such as gaming and prostitution. A circular pit feature found in the backyard of an eighteenth-century tavern site in Williamsburg, Virginia, was probably used as a ring for cockfighting (Brown et al. 1990). Moreover, archaeologists are in an excellent position to identify decorations and special amenities, such as mirrors, lighting, and furnishings, that tavern owners, and the owners of other types of drinking establishments, used to entice patrons. The recovery of faunal remains from some saloon sites, for example, probably reflects the saloon owners' practice of offering free lunches to saloon patrons.

Evidence of Social and Economic Characteristics

Archaeologists have used the material culture evidence of alcohol use to determine the economic class of residents at particular sites. For example, the recovery of porcelain punch bowls and crystal wine decanters from eighteenth-century domestic sites in North America is usually a good indicator of wealth. Evidence of alcohol consumption has also helped archaeologists distinguish socioeconomic class within larger archaeological contexts. At late-nineteenth- and early-twentieth-century nitrate-mining camps in Northern Chile, archaeologists Bente Bittiviann and Gerde Alcaide (1984) used bottle-glass evidence to show that camp miners consumed cheap, locally made alcoholic beverages while camp employers consumed expensive alcoholic beverages imported from North America and Europe. However, the consumption of higher-quality alcoholic beverages is not always an indication of economic status. Historical anthropologist Peter Pope (1997) explored how the seventeenth-century fish trade between Newfoundland and Europe gave lowly fishermen at the margins of the Atlantic world access to expensive French wine and brandy.

Worker resistance is also evident in the archaeological evidence of alcohol consumption. For example, in the nineteenth century, the owners of the Boott Cotton Mill in Lowell, Massachusetts, instituted a policy that restricted alcohol use by mill workers. However, archaeologists recovered alcohol bottles from the boardinghouse sites of Boott Cotton Mill workers; this fact suggests that attempts to restrict drinking were unsuccessful. According to archaeologist Mary Beaudry (1989), alcohol use at the Boott Cotton Mill boardinghouses showed worker resistance to the dehumanizing effect of industrial labor and corporate attempts to control the workers' leisure time. Similarly, the presence of alcohol bottles at African slave sites in the American South might also be viewed as resistance to the paternalistic controls of slave owners.

The massive movement of people to new environmental and cultural settings is one of the defining features of the modern world. Historical archaeologists have explored the survival of Old World cultural traditions in new settings, including traditions involving the use of alcoholic beverages. For example, archaeologist Leland Ferguson (1992: 103) has hinted that large, locally made earthenware jars, otherwise known as *Colono Ware,* recovered from African slave sites in North America may have occasionally been used for brewing beer. According to Ferguson, similar jars were used for that purpose in West and West Central Africa and, therefore, the presence of Colono Ware jars at slave sites may reflect the survival of African brewing traditions in the Americas. At nineteenth-century urban domestic sites in New York City, archaeologists have attributed the discovery of whiskey-bottle fragments at Irish immigrant sites and wine-bottle fragments at Jewish immigrant sites to the survival of Old World drinking customs. Similarly, the discovery of a temperance cup, bearing the image of Irish temperance reformer Theobald Mathew, at a nineteenth-century Irish immigrant dwelling in the Five Points neighborhood of New York may reflect abstinence from alcohol, as well as the sense of Irish nationalism felt by the residents at that site (Reckner and Brighton 1999).

Alcohol and Health

Archaeologists have also identified links between alcohol and health. In the nineteenth and early twentieth centuries, high alcohol-content patent medicines became popular home remedies. The recovery of patent-medicine bottles from archaeological sites reveals the widespread belief about alcohol's salubrious qualities and the centrality of alcohol in home health care. Patent medicines also provided opportunities for people to consume alcoholic beverages and avoid the disdain of neighbors and local temperance reformers. The detrimental effects of alcohol are also evident in the archaeological record. Using bone chemical analysis, archaeologists Jerome Handler and others (1986) found evidence of lead toxicity in the skeletal remains of African slaves buried at the seventeenth-nineteenth century Newton plantation slave cemetery in Barbados. According to Handler, the consumption of rum, produced in lead-contaminated stills, was probably the primary source of lead toxicity in the slaves at Newton plantation.

The presence of alcohol-related materials at archaeological sites can no doubt provide insights into the ways people have used alcohol to cope with anxiety in different historical and cross-cultural settings. For example, the high percentage of alcohol-related material recovered from seventeenth-century British colonial sites in Bridgetown, Barbados, underscores the colonists' attempts to escape from the many anxieties they encountered on the Caribbean frontier, including loneliness, an unpredictable disease environment, and the constant threat of slave revolt. However, the presence of punch bowls, rather than individual bottles, highlights the Barbadians' special preoccupation with social drinking events and alcohol-based hospitality (Smith 2001). The presence of alcohol bottles at Native American sites may reflect the way Indians used alcohol to cope with the disintegration of traditional society and the rapid pace of culture change. The high percentage of alcohol bottles at military sites also suggests high levels of anxiety, as well as boredom and the need for alcoholic escape.

Frederick H. Smith

See also: Beer; Mathew, Father Theobald; Native Americans: Drinking Patterns and Temporance Reform; Patent Medicines; Rum; Wine

References

Allchin, F. R. "India: The Ancient Home of Distillation?" in *Man.* 14 (1979): 55–63.

Beaudry, Mary. "The Lowell Boott Mills Complex and Its Housing: Material Expressions of Corporate Ideology" in *Historical Archaeology.* 23, no. 1 (1989): 19–32.

Bittiviann, Bente, and Gerde Alcaide. "Historical Archaeology in Abandoned Nitrate 'Officinas' in Northern Chile: A Preliminary Report" in *Historical Archaeology.* 18, no. 1 (1984): 52–75.

Braidwood, Robert J., Jonathan D. Sauer, Hans Helbaek, Paul Mangelsdorf, Hugh C. Cutler, Carleton S. Coon, Ralph Linton, Julian Steward, and A. Leo Oppenheim. "Symposium: Did Man Once Live by Beer Alone?" in *American Anthropologist.* 55 (1953): 515–526.

Brown, Gregory, Thomas Higgins III, David Muraca, S. Kathleen Peper, and Roni Polk. "Archaeological Investigations of the Shields Tavern Site Williamsburg, Virginia." Colonial Williamsburg Foundation Research Report, Williamsburg, Virginia, 1990.

Cotter, John. *Archaeological Excavations at Jamestown, Virginia.* National Park Service Research Series, no. 4. Washington, DC: National Park Service, 1958.

Deetz, James. "Ceramics from Plymouth, 1635–1835: The Archaeological Evidence" in *Ceramics in America,* edited by I. Quimby, 15–40. Charlottesville: University Press of Virginia, 1973.

Ferguson, Leland. *Uncommon Ground: Archaeology and Early African America, 1650–1800.* Washington, DC: Smithsonian Institution Press, 1992.

Handler, Jerome, A. C. Aufderheide, R. Corruccini, E. Brandon, and L. Wittmers. "Lead Contact and Poisoning in Barbados Slaves: Historical, Chemical, and Biological Evidence" in *Journal of Social Science History.* 10, no. 4 (1986): 399–425.

Katz, Solomon, and Mary Voigt. "Bread and Beer: The Early Use of Cereals in the Human Diet" in *Expedition.* 28 (1985): 23–24.

Pope, Peter. "Fish into Wine: The Historical Anthropology of Demand for Alcohol in Seventeenth-Century Newfoundland" in *The Changing Face of Drink: Substance, Imagery, and Behaviour,* edited by Jack S. Blocker Jr. and Cheryl Krasnick Warsh, 43–64. Ottawa, Canada: Les Publications Histoire Sociale/Social History, 1997.

Reckner, Paul, and Stephen Brighton. "'Free from All Vicious Habits': Archaeological Perspectives on Class Conflict and the Rhetoric of Temperance" in *Historical Archaeology.* 33, no. 1 (1999): 63–86.

Smith, Frederick H. "Volatile Spirits: The Historical Archaeology of Alcohol and Drinking in the Caribbean" (Ph.D. dissertation, Department of Anthropology, University of Florida, Gainesville, 2001).

Army Temperance Association

The Army Temperance Association was organized in response to the problem of drinking by enlisted men in the British military. Heavy drinking was endemic to the early Victorian British army and navy. A culture of heavy drinking pervaded contemporary working-class life, and men enlisting as soldiers or sailors carried it into military life. In addition, the conditions of army life—especially garrison duty in Britain or the empire—conspired to encourage heavy drinking. Sailors were issued with a daily ration of "grog"—a pint of rum mixed with water—and infrequent "runs ashore" often ended in drunken binges. Until 1830, soldiers were also issued spirits. Despite often harassing duties, soldiers were generally left with little to do in their own time. At home, they were generally ostracized by the communities among which they were stationed. In India, boredom, isolation, and ready access to cheap and potent "country liquor" made drinking that was destructive to health and self-respect an inevitable part of cantonment life. Such a culture brought with it disciplinary consequences. Many military offenses, particularly disobedience and insubordination, were strongly associated with drunkenness. Offenders faced serious punishment, including (until the 1850s) flogging.

From about the 1830s, a new spirit of reform began to be evident in many individual regiments and ships. Mirroring movements for humanitarian reform in, say, children's employment, the antislavery movement, and parliamentary reform, military reformers, often inspired by the evangelical religion, identified heavy drinking as both a cause of and a response to the brutality of military life. Idealistic officers often implemented reforms within their regiments. The Baptist Lieutenant Henry Havelock—who was to die one of the heroes of the mutiny—formed a pioneering temperance society in the 13th Light Infantry in 1834. Havelock promoted the formation of other regimental societies in India, and thirty others had been established within two years. Over fifty were eventually formed, though many were short-lived, dependent upon the commitment of officers, and often lapsing on the regiments' departure from India. By founding savings banks, coffee shops, religious societies, and temperance societies, younger officers began a movement toward change that by the 1850s would result in permanent temperance organizations. "Habitual drunkenness," formerly offered as an excuse to crime, became instead an offense in itself.

Military temperance organizations in Britain itself waited until the mid-1850s, when "regimental" and "garrison" institutes were formed. Formed following the awakening of the liberal middle-class conscience regarding the military, and prompted by the revelations of the abuses and neglect at Scutari during the Crimean War, the institutes were the initiative of private benefactors in several garrison towns, such as Hythe, Portsmouth, and Chatham. Though often austere and uninviting, the institutes offered an alternative to the drinking shops and brothels clustering around barracks. Significantly, the more successful ones were established within barracks, dissuading soldiers likely to waver from passing more dubious places of recreation. Initially tolerated rather than supported by the authorities, the institutes' successes eventually led to them being encouraged. Developments in the navy paralleled those in the army and a naval temperance society was formed in 1868. By 1911, it had 25,000 members.

After the suppression of the 1857 mutiny, a much larger European force garrisoned India. The formation of supraregimental temperance institutes represented a more ambitious movement that supplanted individual regimental temperance societies. These supraregimental institutes were also promoted by influential figures. For instance, the earliest such institute was the Outram Institute, founded in Dum Dum at the instigation of another mutiny hero, Sir James Outram. Two years later, the Reverend John Gregson formed the Soldiers' Total Abstinence Association in Agra. By 1866, Gregson's association had 1,200 members in 29 branches. In

1877, with the help of official financial support, it had 10,000 members in 110 branches, and by 1885, it had 12,000 members in 144 branches. It awarded its members distinctive badges and medals to mark periods of abstinence from six months to twenty years. Worn on the right breast in uniform (but only at association functions), the medals bore the injunction "Watch and Be Sober," testifying to members' resolve in a culture in which "soaking" and "pegging" were tolerated and often expected.

In the 1880s, Gregson attracted the support of Sir Frederick (later Lord) Roberts, another mutiny hero, who, by 1885, was the commander in chief in India. Roberts, who had been a young officer in the 1850s and an advocate of reform, believed that "serious crime in the army is almost entirely due to the effects of drink." Roberts, however, considered that total abstinence was unreasonable and urged that the movement be recast as a nonteetotal temperance association. On Gregson's retirement in 1886, Roberts effected the amalgamation of the Outram Institute (never a very successful organization) and Gregson's Soldiers' Total Abstinence Association to create the Army Temperance Association in 1888. By Roberts's retirement in 1893, the association had 23,000 members.

Despite the establishment of institutes in garrison towns in Britain, formal organizations had never been popular at home. Roberts's standing, both within and beyond the army, helped him create an Army Temperance Association (Home Organization) that, by 1896, had 13,000 members. Changing to the Royal Army Temperance Association in 1902, it became a considerable influence within the professional British army. It was claimed that 25 percent of soldiers at home and 40 percent of soldiers in India were members of the association.

Temperance organizations declined when there were alternatives to wet canteens as places for soldiers and sailors to gather socially. The establishment of the Navy, Army and Air Force Institutes (NAAFI) in 1921 and long-term changes in the acceptability of heavy drinking led to the declining relevance and popularity of the Royal Army Temperance Association. It was disbanded in 1958. Though heavy drinking remains a notable part of service culture, during the first half of the twentieth century it became recognized as a welfare and medical issue and is far less prevalent than it had been in the early nineteenth century.

Peter Stanley

See also: National Temperance League (NTL); Robinson, Sarah; Weston, Agnes

References

Harris, David. *A Guide to Military Temperance Medals of the British Army and Royal Navy.* Markham, Ontario: self-published, 2001.

Skelley, Alan Ramsay. *The Victorian Army at Home.* London: Croom Helm, 1977.

Wood, Stephen. "Temperance and Its Rewards in the British Army" in *The Victorian Soldier.* 30 (1993): 86–96.

Arsenic-in-Beer Scare

The Manchester arsenic-in-beer crisis (1900–1901) was a major food poisoning epidemic caused by contaminated beer, affecting more than 6,000 people and claiming seventy lives. Arsenic entered the brewing process via contaminated sugar and passed undetected to beer drinkers for more than six months.

The crisis began in the autumn of 1900. Medical practitioners working in hospitals in the northwest of England noticed an exceptionally high incidence of "alcoholic neuritis," a type of paralysis attributed to chronic heavy drinking. This was initially blamed on celebrations associated with the Boer War and the recent general election. However, as the number of hospital admissions continued to increase, some practitioners questioned whether alcohol alone could explain the epidemic. They speculated that some other poison was causing the sickness, and, since beer drinking was the one common element in all cases, they reasoned that it must be contained in the beer. Beer samples were obtained, analyzed chemically, and found to contain substantial quantities of arsenic. The arsenic was traced to contaminated "invert sugar"—a type of sugar manufactured from vegetable starch using sulfuric acid and used primarily in cheap beer. The arsenic came from impure industrial-grade acid used by the sugar manufacturer. Contaminated sugar had been supplied to breweries for upward of six months. The greatest concentration of sickness was in Manchester, but arsenical beer was found across much of northern England.

News of arsenical beer prompted a major scare in the local and national press. Beer sales fell immediately and dramatically as drinkers withdrew their custom. The brewing industry responded to this potentially disastrous situation with a concerted attempt to win back customer confidence. Brewers worked closely with local health authorities to detect and remove all contaminated beer from the marketplace, while strict analytical safeguards were put in place to prevent the problem from recurring. At the same time, the industry mounted a major publicity campaign; newspaper advertisements, leaflets and posters, and analysts' certificates all reassured drinkers that beer was safe once again. By virtue of these actions and the eagerness of beer drinkers to return to the pub, customer confidence was successfully restored. Beer sales recovered to their former level within just one or two months.

Potentially more dangerous to the long-term future of the brewing industry was the resurrection of the pure beer movement. This was an agricultural pressure group interested in rejuvenating British barley growing by imposing a legislative ban on all brewing materials other than malt, hops, yeast, and water. New support resulted in a beer bill that was stopped only by the government's refusal to assist its further progress. Reluctant to become involved in the crisis, the government instead appointed a royal commission to investigate the crisis. Far more sympathetic to the brewing industry than to the pure beer movement, the commission agreed that the measures instituted by brewers after the crisis provided the public with an adequate safeguard against arsenic poisoning, and that further interference in the industry was unwarranted.

Matthew Copping

See also: Pure Beer Movement (United Kingdom)

References

Copping, Matthew C. "Death in the Beer-Glass: The Manchester Arsenic-in-Beer Epidemic" (M.A. thesis, University of Kent at Canterbury, 1999).

Phillips, Jim, and Michael French. "The Pure Beer Campaign and Arsenic Poisoning, 1896–1903" in *Rural History.* 9, no. 2 (1998): 195–209.

Art, Representations of Drinking in

Representations of alcohol consumption in Western art span the history of visual culture from at least 2000 B.C.E. to the present day, encompassing the ancient, medieval, Renaissance, baroque, and modern periods in art. Representations of drinking in art can be found in the traditional or high arts, such as painting and sculpture, and in the so-called popular arts, such as prints, posters, and folk art. As historian Susanna Barrows has suggested, representations of alcohol in art can function "as 'social facts' about alcohol use, as reconstructions of diverse 'social settings' for drinking, and as keys for unlocking 'cultural meanings'" of drinking in widely varied chronological and geographical settings (Barrows, Room, and Verhey 1987: 6). Representations of drinking in art possess disparate meanings, but many representations fall into one or more of the following broad categories: mythological or religious representations; genre scenes from everyday life; humorous anecdotes or moralistic tales; or even the warning sign of the potentially dangerous disease known as alcoholism.

In many cases, representations of drinking in art seem almost peripheral to the scene represented, a mere compositional detail in an overarching pictorial schema treating an entirely different theme. In other instances, the representation of drinking is central to the artwork's narrative, carrying much of the meaning of the scene itself, and may even be referenced in the title of the work. A crucial dichotomy exists in representations of drinking in art between those that seem to show merely the consumption of alcohol and those scenes that seem to depict drunkenness itself, the aftermath or consequences of inebriation, or even the modern disease concept of chronic alcoholism.

Ancient Art

The studied and elaborate preparations for the afterlife practiced by the ancient Egyptians demonstrate the multiple uses of alcohol in ancient Egyptian culture and provide some of the earliest representations of drinking. Wine jars dating from the Eighteenth Dynasty (1570–1450 B.C.E.) were found intact in the tomb of the pharaoh Tutankhamen when the burial chamber was excavated by the British archaeologist Howard Carter in 1922. It is possible that such vessels were intended to provide sustenance to the deceased or to function as a religious offering to the gods, in order to ensure one's place in the afterlife. Indeed, alcohol consumption is also represented in the paintings on Egyptian tomb walls in quotidian and ceremonial guises.

In the Eighteenth Dynasty tomb of the Vizier Rekhmiré, maidservants are represented pouring liquid into vessels held by women at a banquet. The women are likely drinking wine, a beverage largely reserved for upper-class Egyptians. In the Nineteenth Dynasty (1314–1085 B.C.E.) tomb of Queen Nefertari, alcohol is pictured as a religious offering (see Illustration 1). A tomb wall painting depicts the queen approaching and offering two pots of wine to the goddess Hathor. In the tomb of Senesem from the same dynasty, the deceased and his wife receive a libation as an offering from their son. The ancient Egyptians even painted detailed representations of alcohol production on tomb walls, though not of wine, but rather of beer, the alcoholic beverage of the lower classes in ancient Egypt (see Illustration 2).

Wine possessed great importance in ancient Greek culture, and was often consumed as part of communal activities. Wine was considered a gift of the gods, and its use was understood in a religious context, as in later theological traditions. Greek vase painting contains frequent representations of Dionysus, the Greek god of wine, and his retinue of male half-human, half-animal satyrs, and cavorting female maenads, often amidst grapevines. Representations of drinking occur in the context of the *symposion,* a community ritual in which adult men socialized and shared drink, song, and poetry together. Representations of symposion appear on wine storage containers and on the large vessels in which wine was mixed with water in preparation for consumption. Examples of Attic red-figure vases from around 500 B.C.E. depict men reclining on raised couches holding drinking cups to be filled with wine.

Representations on Greek vases of the potential aftermath of excessive drinking could be both ironic and humorous. The interiors of some Greek cups featured medallions circling the bottom of the vase, thus revealing the drinker's future as he drained the alcoholic contents from the cup. The internal medallion of a cup painted by the so-called Brygos Painter (ca. 480 B.C.E.) depicts a youth leaning heavily on a stick and being helped by a female companion, who steadies his head while he leans forward and vomits.

Dionysian subjects were also depicted on sarcophagi during the Roman period, an era that bridged the pagan and Christian worlds. In a sarcophagus (220–235 C.E.) now held in New York's Metropolitan Museum of Art, Dionysus, dispensing wine, is the central figure in a procession of satyrs and maenads, and is accompanied by allegorical figures representing the four seasons. Although to modern eyes the subject may seem curious for a coffin, art historian Anna McCann has noted that it was precisely through the "sacred wine of the god [that] the initiate was freed from the cares of his earthly life" (1978: 88–89).

Representations of the drunkenness of Noah, a biblical theme, can be found in the *Vienna Genesis*, an illuminated

Illustration 1: Painting of Nefertari sacrificing to the goddess Hathor, from Nineteenth Dynasty (1314–1085 B.C.E.) (Borromeo/Art Resource)

manuscript dating from the Christian period, around the fifth or sixth century. The theme emerges from the Old Testament, Book of Genesis, 9:20–27. Noah, having begun the cultivation of the vine, becomes drunk and lies naked in his tent. His son Ham witnesses his father's intoxication and informs his brothers. Shem and Japheth refuse to witness their father's shame and attempt to cover him by walking backwards into Noah's tent and throwing a cloak over him. Noah, aware of Ham's treachery, curses the descendants of Ham's son, Canaan. The illustration in the *Vienna Genesis* is continuously narrated, with characters appearing multiple times in the same scene. Noah appears twice, in an order that curiously reverses that of the original story. He is first shown cursing his grandson Canaan in the presence of the treacherous Ham, then shown again in the same scene lying drunken and naked in his tent while his loyal sons enter facing backwards carrying the cloak to cover their father.

The Middle Ages and Renaissance

Representations of drinking during the medieval period remained largely religious in nature and may associate excessive consumption of alcohol with vice. Such representations were hence opposed to virtue, and may be specifically associated with gluttony, one of the seven deadly sins. Representations of drunkenness as moralistic tales appeared on the bottom of medieval misericords, the hinged seats designed to support the clergy, who stood during church services. Such representations also appeared in the marginalia of medieval manuscript illumination. The treatment of the drunkenness of Noah theme continued during the medieval period, appearing even in sculptural form. Representations of the same theme extended into the Renaissance, culminating in Michelangelo's representation of *The Drunkenness of Noah* (1508–1512) in large scale on the ceiling of the Sistine Chapel in the Vatican (see Illustration 3).

Illustration 2: Monument of the Syrian soldier, Terrura, at the time of Amenophis IV, with his son and his Egyptian wife sipping beer through a cane. About 1350 B.C.E. (Bettman/Corbis)

Representations of alcohol consumption in liturgical contexts appear in the numerous scenes of the Last Supper. Though a relatively rare theme in northern art, Netherlandish artist Dirk Bouts painted a scene of the *Last Supper* as the central panel of the Holy Sacrament altarpiece for the Brotherhood of Leuven between 1464 and 1468. Bouts repositioned the historical scene of the Last Supper in a fifteenth-century Netherlandish interior. As Christ prepares to bless the bread and chalice of wine, the emphasis is on the drinking of wine and sharing of bread as an act of communion with Christ and within the family of Christians. The scene was perhaps most famously represented by the Renaissance master Leonardo da Vinci in the refectory of the church of Santa Maria delle Grazie in Milan (1494–1498), where the artist placed less emphasis on the sharing of bread and wine than on the apostles' varied reactions to Christ's announcement that he would be betrayed.

Renaissance art saw a return to representations of the mythological god of wine, now known under the Roman name Bacchus. Italian Renaissance artists including Titian and Michelangelo painted works of art inspired by bacchanalian themes.

Baroque and Seventeenth-Century Art

The appeal of bacchic subject matter continued throughout the Baroque period, inspiring artists such as Peter-Paul Rubens and

Illustration 3: The Drunkenness of Noah *(1508–1512) detail of the Sistine Chapel ceiling at the Vatican Palace (Scala/Art Resource)*

Caravaggio. Works such as the Spanish Baroque painter Diego Velázquez's *Bacchus* (ca. 1629; see Illustration 4) were largely devoid of their mythological and religious connotations. Instead, such representations were hybrids of mythological and contemporary scenes, as in Velázquez's juxtaposition of a figure in toga-like imitations of ancient dress with drinking mates in tattered contemporary attire.

Representations of drinking and of the consumption habits of the popular classes became increasingly commonplace with the rise of genre painting, or the painting of scenes of everyday life, which were conceived on a scale formerly reserved for historical or mythological subjects. The Netherlandish painter Pieter Brueghel the Elder painted the everyday life and locales of the sixteenth-century peasantry in works such as *Peasant Dance* (ca. 1568), in which men, women, and children are celebrating a local feast day. Alcohol consumption is part of the festivities. Genre painters of the sixteenth and seventeenth centuries represented alcohol consumption in the context of the kermis, village holidays, wedding feasts, and other occasions for drinking, celebration, and relaxed comportment.

Artists including Rembrandt, Frans Hals, Adriaen Brouwer, and Pieter Brueghel the Younger painted innumerable seventeenth-century Flemish and Dutch tavern and genre scenes depicting alcohol consumption by both groups and individuals. Like Bouts's *Last Supper,* Jan Steen's *Wine Is a Mocker* (1671–1674) weaves together a biblical text and a genre scene (see Illustration 5). The theme is taken from Proverbs 20:1, and the composition has been transposed into a seventeenth-century Dutch setting. Group drinking in a tavern setting has degenerated into violence, to the amusement of some in the scene. It is in seventeenth-century art that alcohol consumption became more closely associated with a host of illicit yet potentially semicomic vices as disparate as card playing, gambling, vagrancy, physical violence, and the potential for prostitution.

Illustration 4: The Drunkards *(1629) by Diego Rodriguez de Silva y Velázquez (Archivo Iconografico, S.A./Corbis)*

The English artist William Hogarth, who produced *Gin Lane* (1751) (see illustration, page 65) in response to the Gin Act of the same year took the negative associations surrounding alcohol consumption to an extreme. Hogarth's print associates gin drinking with vices as varied as neglectful parenting, gross immodesty, pauperism, and suicide (while in the companion print, *Beer Street* (see page 66), beer consumption is represented as nourishing and healthy). Gin was thus tied to a host of social ills that affected the entire populace. *Gin Lane* was a widely reproduced popular print. Despite its reproduction, the cost of the print would still have been outside the means of the very poor. Hogarth nonetheless intended the print to be a pedagogical tool—its pervasiveness and dire warnings designed to effect social change.

In representations of drinking during the modern period, the harmless drunk buffoon, who had heretofore existed on the margins of society for the amusement of those at its center, gradually metamorphosed into a potentially dangerous, even menacing presence that threatened the health and security of the entire society. These associations continued into and culminated in the art of the nineteenth century.

Modern Art: The Nineteenth and Twentieth Centuries

The rise of the temperance movement in the United States resulted in the incorporation of images of drinking in American folk art from an early period. Like Hogarth's work, folk artist Robert Peckham's *The Woes of Liquor* (ca. 1830) reveals the peril of alcoholism in the family interior, showing a dying mother, a father engrossed only in his drink, and deranged, violent children fighting or crawling along the floor. Alcohol or temperance-related imagery also appeared on a variety of household and commercial objects such as drinking jugs and tavern signs.

The modern period brought a new awareness of the potential perils of alcohol consumption in the form of the disease labeled alcoholism, a term coined by Swedish physician Magnus Huss in 1849 in his landmark work, *Alcoholismus Chronicus.* Huss's work was quickly translated throughout the world, and the disease concept of alcoholism began to hold sway. In the wake of this new concept, works featuring alcohol consumption often took on added significance.

Two works from nineteenth-century France illustrate this—Édouard Manet's *The Absinthe Drinker* (1859; see Illustration 6)

Illustration 5: Wine Is a Mocker *(1671–1674) by Jan Steen (Francis G. Mayer/Corbis)*

and Edgar Degas's *In a Café,* often also called *The Absinthe Drinker* (1876; see Illustration 7). The titles of both works refer specifically to the spirit absinthe, a potent opalescent green beverage that nineteenth-century medical authorities believed to be particularly addictive and dangerous. Such images demonstrate that the "new" alcoholism afflicted both men and women equally. The fact that the titles of the works reference the alcoholic beverage indicates that absinthe exists at the heart of the meaning of the image.

Both works place an emphasis on the solitude of the drinkers (despite the fact that in Degas's work, the woman is nominally seated with a man). Alcohol consumption replaces the expected camaraderie of a community of alcohol consumers with the utter solitude of the afflicted drinker. The melancholy of the figures is emphasized; they sit with slumping postures, their eyes fixed vaguely in the distance, with slack expressions crossing their faces. Such representations of alcohol consumption underlined the anomie and dehumanizing forces of modern urban life, and the perceived spiritual poverty that may result from excessive alcohol use and abuse. The gloom of Degas's painting *In a Café (The Absinthe Drinker)* contrasts with the folly, elegance, and pleasure promised by Belle Epoque advertising posters by Jules Chéret and others for alcoholic products (including absinthe) and the cafés in which such alcoholic beverages were served.

Representations of alcohol in twentieth-century art can be read through the lens of the popularization of the disease concept of alcoholism and the role of attendant self-help movements (such as Alcoholics Anonymous), which loom large in the modern cultural consciousness. Jasper Johns's sculpture *Painted Bronze* (1960) plays on the concept of the "found object" inspired directly by omnipresent contemporary mass cul-

Illustration 6: The Absinthe Drinker *(1859) by Edouard Manet (Erich Lessing/Art Resource)*

Illustration 7: In a Café [The Absinthe Drinker] *(1876) by Edgar Degas (Corel)*

ture. Johns constructed objects that mimic a pair of Ballantine ale cans, and the artist has cast the work in bronze. Although the work can be interpreted in many ways, *Painted Bronze* can be understood as a recognition and commentary on the everyday memorialization of alcohol in twentieth-century American culture.

Images of drinking traverse a long history of visual representation and offer proof of the important role of alcohol production and consumption throughout human history. Moreover, such images provide a window onto the attendant meanings of alcohol consumption, and often alcohol overconsumption, in varied cultural contexts and serve as visual commentaries and testimonies subject to widely varied interpretation.

Sara Harrington

See also: Absinthe; Alcoholism; Art as Temperance Activism; Beer; Cabaret (France); Drinking Establishments (France) Gin; Wine

References

Barrows, Susanna, Robin Room, and Jeffrey Verhey, eds. *The Social History of Alcohol: Drinking and Culture in Modern Society.* Berkeley: Alcohol Research Group, 1987.

Conrad, Barnaby, III. *Absinthe: History in a Bottle.* San Francisco: Chronicle Books, 1988.

Kern, Arthur, and Sybil Kern. "Alcoholism and the Temperance Movement in Early American Folk Art" in *Magazine Antiques.* 153 (February 1998): 292–299.

Lissarrague, François. *The Aesthetics of the Greek Banquet: Images of Wine and Ritual.* Translated by Andrew Szegedy-Maszak. Princeton: Princeton University Press, 1990.

McCann, Anna Marguerite. *Roman Sarcophagi in the Metropolitan Museum of Art.* New York: Metropolitan Museum of Art, 1978.

Sutton, Peter C., and Christopher Brown. *Masters of Seventeenth-Century Dutch Genre Painting.* Philadelphia: Philadelphia Museum of Art, 1984.

Westermann, Mariët. *The Amusements of Jan Steen: Comic Painting in the Seventeenth Century.* Studies in Netherlandish Art and Cultural History, edited by Reindert Falkenburg, Herman Roodenburg, and Frits Scholten, no. 1. Zwolle: Waanders Publishers, 1997.

Art as Temperance Activism

Art in the broadest sense as an expression of social meaning is an integral component of social movements, in which art and writing about art "stand as acts of critical resistance that actively introduce change" (hooks 1995: xvi) within existing politics. Art as temperance activism spans the visual arts, literary arts, and performing arts, and often interweaves these art forms. Antitemperance and antiprohibition activists use these same art forms. The multimedia of visual arts in contemporary alcohol education programs stand as a legacy of the temperance movement.

Visual Arts

The excessive consumption of gin in London between the 1720s and 1750s was the impetus behind the temperance pulpit of John Wesley, but it also provided the stimulus for William Hogarth's engravings, inspiring his companion prints of 1751 entitled *Gin Lane* and *Beer Street* (http://www.graphictype.co.uk/i_ginln.htm; http://www.graphictype.co.uk/i_beerst.htm; see Illustrations 1 and 2). Explicit in Hogarth's satirical prints is a morality tale pitched to the lower classes, in an affordable medium. Hogarth populates *Gin Lane* with working-class people suffering from the excesses of gin drinking, whereas *Beer Lane* depicts the "invigorating liquor" of beer that accompanies industry and prosperity. A list of these opposing ideas is offered on the website of Berkeley Art Museum Pacific Film Archive (http://www.bampfa.berkeley.edu/exhibits/hogarth/hogarth5b.html). The Gin Act, passed in 1751, increased taxation and banned distillers from selling spirits—a tribute to the force of art in arousing public opinion. *The Rake's Progress* (1735) is another series of eight prints in which Hogarth tells the story of a dissolute life that is the moral opposite of John Bunyan's (1678) *Pilgrim's Progress.*

Temperance lithographs appear a century later in New England echoing Hogarth's titles and moral themes. In 1826, J. W. Barber of New Haven, Connecticut, designed and published *The Drunkard's Progress, or the Direct Road to Poverty, Wretchedness & Ruin* (see Illustration 3). The four consecutive images depict the morning dram, the grog shop, the confirmed drunkard, and the concluding scene in which a sheriff's auction is posted on the family home, and mother and children are leaving for the poorhouse. Each panel is inscribed with a biblical passage at the top and a secular caption at the bottom (image available on the website of American Memory, Historical Collections for the National Digital Library: http://memory.loc.gov). Temperance prints were a significant line of production for Currier and Ives, a popular lithographic firm in New York City during the nineteenth century. A popular print was Nathaniel Currier's 1846 lithograph entitled *The Drunkard's Progress: From the First Glass to the Grave* (see Illustration 4), in which the nine steps of alcohol decay move through a scene taking place on each of nine stair steps—step nine is death by suicide (image available from LD "P" Alcoholics Anonymous History and Recovery Pages: http://www.aabibliography.com/aaphotonew/temper4.jpg; *see also* Rawls 1991; Rose 1996).

Nathaniel Currier and James Merritt Ives did not profess to be artists; although self-identifying as "Publishers of Cheap and Popular Pictures," they were known by their patrons as "The Printmakers to the American People." Nathaniel Currier's 1849 *The Tree of Intemperance* (see Illustration 5) is one among many etchings using tree symbolism and the one most commonly referred to in the speeches of the day and in historical research. Its companion print, *The Tree of Temperance,* a more decorative print targeted for American parlors, followed almost a quarter of a century later.

George Cruikshank, a British artist born in 1792 in Bloomsbury, England, used the media of etching, oil, pencil drawings, and political caricatures in his temperance polemic (see http://www.artcyclopedia.com/artists/cruikshank_george.html). He became a teetotaler toward the end of the 1840s and devoted most of his efforts to the British Temperance League, including his epic oil painting, *The Worship of Bacchus,* which is populated with hundreds of tableaux showing the ill effects of indulging in excessive drinking (see Illustration 6). This canvas, which was not fashionable enough to attract a single person to its opening in 1863, was stored in museum cellars for ninety-two years until newly restored and unveiled by the Tate Gallery in 2001. Cruikshank added moral tags to *The Worship of Bacchus* as well as to smaller works such as *The Bottle* and *The Drunkard's Children* as if to make sure that the temperance message was not overlooked (for example, see the captions that accompany the eight-slide sequence for the magic lantern show of *The Bottle:* http://hometown.aol.com/larrykench/WBottle1.html).

The temperance movement also provided enduring careers for illustrators and cartoonists in North America. Frank Beard was the principal illustrator for *The Ram's Horn: An Interdenominational Social Gospel Magazine,* published in Chicago during the 1890s and the early years of the twentieth century. Beard's "remarkable sketches" feature in Letitia Youmans's 1893 autobiography with reference to children's day at the Sunday School Assembly at Chautauqua in 1874 (also the organizing occasion for the Woman's Christian Temperance Union [WCTU]). Beard's sketches in *The Ram's Horn* support prohibition.

Many of the cartoons in *American Issue,* the magazine of the Anti-Saloon League, were drawn by Russell Henderson. Cartoons from *American Issue* of 1919—captions include *Liquor Octopus, Ratification Train, My Best Friend Poisoned—*

Illustration 1: Gin Lane *(1751) by William Hogarth (Burstein Collection/Corbis)*

Illustration 2: Beer Street *(1751) by William Hogarth*

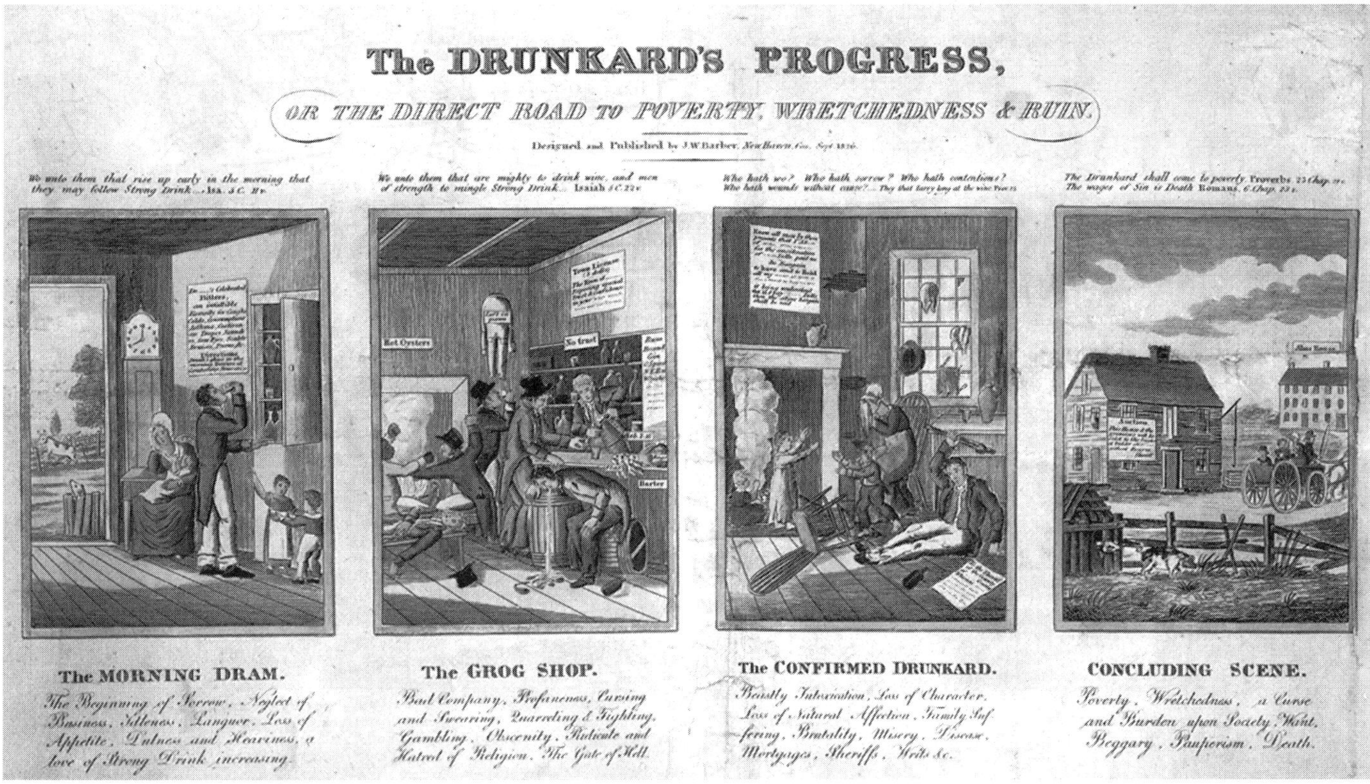

Illustration 3: The Drunkard's Progress *(ca. 1826) by J. W. Barber (Library of Congress)*

Illustration 4: The Drunkard's Progress: From the First Glass to the Grave *(1846) by Nathaniel Currier (Library of Congress)*

Illustration 5: The Tree of Intemperance *(1849) by Nathaniel Currier (Library of Congress)*

are available on the Anti-Saloon League website (http://www.wpl.lib.oh.us/AntiSaloon/print/cart.html).

Harper's Weekly featured cartoonist Thomas Nast; many of his illustrations supported the Women's Temperance Crusade. The illustration for 21 March 1874 entitled *The Bar of Destruction* depicts the bartender embodying the skull-and-crossbones symbol of poison. The visual and literary arts are used together in support of temperance in this same issue. Two weeks earlier, on 7 March 1874, Nast's illustration of the Women's Temperance Crusade in terms of Joan of Arc battling demon rum appeared on the cover of *Harper's.* The editor, George William Curtis, opposed prohibition but was sympathetic to the Women's Temperance Crusade.

Canadian cartoonist John Wilson Bengough attributed his interest in cartooning to the work of Thomas Nast in *Harper's Weekly.* Like Nast, Bengough was a prohibitionist, and the humor magazine *Grip,* which flourished for two decades after Bengough founded it in 1873, provided an outlet for his political cartoons. Bengough's illustrated lecture tours also followed Thomas Nast's example; *Bengough's Chalk Talks* (1922) is the book-length story of his lecturing tour of Canada, the United States, England, Australia, and New Zealand. The chapter "Anti-Barleycorn: A Chalk-Talk on Prohibition" is populated with caricatures of topers, brewers, and distillers, and includes the claim that "the only good liquor traffic dog is a dead one." Canada's WCTU leader, Letitia Youmans, features in a Bengough cartoon in *Grip;* she is seated in a big chair with Mr. George Foster (a cabinet minister in Prime Minister John A. MacDonald's government) across her lap, thrashing him with her slipper. This arose from an incident at an Ontario convention in Napanee, where she rose to speak in objection to Mr. Foster's speech, criticizing him so convincingly that the people stood and cheered. Len Norris (1913–1997), cartoonist and longtime contributor to the editorial pages of *The Vancouver Sun,* acknowledges John Bengough as the father of Canadian political cartooning. Included in the Editorial Cartoons Collection of the Simon Fraser University Library are 1,660 Len Norris original drawings, 44 of which address alcohol-related issues, particularly impaired driving (see http://mercury.lib.sfu.ca/cgi-bin/edocs/Cartoons).

Henrietta Briggs-Wall's now famous 1893 postcard-cartoon *American Woman and Her Political Peers,* features the photo-realism of Frances Willard in Victorian dress wearing the simple white ribbon emblem of the WCTU set against the stereotypical images of the outcasts of society—an idiot, a convict, a madman, and an "Indian."

Charts and diagrams, magic lantern slides, and stereopticon slides gave scientific cachet to the temperance movement (*see* Household and Smith, *To Catch a Sunbeam,* 1979). The website for the Seagram Collection at the University of Waterloo (Canada) includes an image of the tables and graphs that the Reverend William Burgess used in *Land, Labor and Liquor* (1887). The American Issue Publishing Company printed and disseminated the charts and diagrams employed by the Scientific Temperance Federation. This organization, initiated by Cora Frances Stoddard in 1906, presented a set of stereopticon slides on the effects of alcohol at the 1912 exhibit on Alcohol and Public Health at the Washington, D.C., International Congress in Hygiene and Demography. In Canada, the Dominion Scientific Temperance Committee and the Prohibition Federation of Canada produced a set of twelve posters, one of which juxtaposes an image of a biological specimen of a fish against a man in a Model T above the caption "Good for the engine, but not for the engineer; Good for commercial purposes but not as a beverage." Perhaps the most famous example of temperance visual imagery is Dr. Thomas Sewell's colored diagrams of the effects of alcohol on the stomach, which were published in 1842 in the midst of the early success of the Washingtonian movement.

Lantern slides were pressed into the service of the temperance movement in the UK as early as the 1870s. Most of the 3,000 temperance lantern slides in the Livesey Collection at the University of Central Lancashire are from the early decades of the twentieth century. The lantern slide shown here draws upon the scientific authority of a medical doctor and abstainer, Sir Wilfred Grenfell of Labrador.

Illustration 6: The Worship of Bacchus *(1863) by George Cruikshank (Courtesy of the author)*

Homespun visual media blossomed with women's public participation in the temperance movement, including flowers, ribbons, banners, quilts, and other forms of needle work. The quilt pattern The Drunkard's Path, often created in the blue and white symbolic colors of the WCTU, provided an educational centerpiece for WCTU fund-raisers. The Crusade Quilt, quilted by Ohio WCTU members in 1876 and presented as a tribute to Eliza Trimble "Mother" Thompson at the 1878 national WCTU convention, now resides in the WCTU collection in Evanston, Illinois. To make their opinions known, 3,000 women signed their names to the back of this quilt. The sheer size of the Polyglot Petition with its purported 7 million signatures sewn to rolls of muslin—sometimes referred to as the "monster"—provided a visual symbol of the size and strength of the women's protest movement. It also symbolized WCTU aspirations (and those of Frances Willard, who conceived of the idea in 1885) for worldwide prohibition. Willard's presentation of the Polyglot Petition to President Grover Cleveland in Washington in 1895 is memorialized in the stained-glass window of Marsh Chapel, at Boston University.

In 1984, archivist Wendy Harker discovered in the storehouses of Canadian WCTU headquarters twenty-one banners from WCTU chapters in Ontario for the period 1872 to 1932. These banners became the centerpiece of a traveling temperance exhibit that began at the Toronto Museum of Textiles in 1999. The story of the Canadian WCTU, complete with a picture gallery of these banners, is available from the radio archives of Tapestry, Canadian Broadcasting Corporation, aired in August 1999 (http://www.radio.cbc.ca/programs/Tapestry/temperance.html). The 1890 banner of the Hamilton WCTU served a century later as the message bearer for the exhibit and is featured on the front cover of the museum catalog.

The visual media employed by contemporary alcohol education programs are as diverse as those employed in the temperance era, and they continue to use art as activism. The message in the media has moved from sermonizing on total abstinence to harm-reduction and social-norms marketing, which aspires to correct the perception that "everybody's doing it."

Literary Arts

The temperance movement spawned a great mass of creative literature, including poems, short stories, novels, plays, biographies and autobiographies, mottoes, pledges, hymns, cookbooks, and primers. The literary arts and the visual arts appeared together in a collaborative connection between George Cruikshank and Charles Dickens, notably Cruikshank's illustrations for *Sketches by Boz* and *Oliver Twist.* In an article in *Household Words* (1853) under the heading "Frauds on Fairies," however, Dickens used parody to attack his friend Cruikshank for turning fairy tales into temperance propaganda, a manifestation of Dickens's conflicted attitude toward the temperance movement. Through the character of the Reverend Stiggins, otherwise known as the Reverend Gentleman with the Red Nose in *The Pickwick Papers,* Dickens used satire to convey the hypocrisy of temperance cast as religious devoutness.

Another great Victorian novelist, Robert Louis Stevenson, also felt ambivalent toward the temperance movement. No ambivalence, however, was evident in *Danesbury House,* written in 1860 by Ellen Wood under her trademark name of "Mrs. Henry Wood." *Danesbury House,* for which she won a prize of £100 offered by the Scottish Temperance League, was explicitly temperance fiction. The dangers of alcohol also feature in her first great success, *East Lynne* (1861), which also became a huge theatrical hit.

American Victorian novelists such as Louisa May Alcott, Harriet Beecher Stowe, and Timothy Shay Arthur also conveyed temperance messages in their fiction, often employing alcohol use to gauge the strength of their characters' moral fiber. Alcott served as president of the WCTU in Concord, Massachusetts, in 1883. Temperance themes figured even more strongly in children's literature, as in Ella Wilcox's (1872) collection of temperance verses entitled *Drops of Water*—her first of many books carrying the message of total abstinence to a children's audience.

Autobiography was a genre used across lines of gender, class, and race by American temperance activists. Examples include John Bartholomew Gough (*Platform Campaigns,* 1884); William Wells Brown, an African American who tells his story of lecturing on slavery and temperance reform (*Three Years in Europe,* 1852); John Cotton Mather (*Autobiography of a Reformed Drunkard,* 1845); and Carry Amelia Moore Nation (*The Use and Need of the Life of Carry A. Nation,* 1909). Frances Elizabeth Caroline Willard, president of the U.S. WCTU, wrote her autobiography, *Glimpses of Fifty Years* (1889), "by order of" the national WCTU. Letitia Youmans, first president of the Dominion WCTU, wrote her autobiography, *Campaign Echoes* (1893), "at the request of" the WCTU of Ontario. Eliza Stewart (Mother Stewart), a driving force in the Women's Temperance Crusade, wrote *Memories of the Crusade: A Thrilling Account of the Great Uprising of the Women of Ohio in 1873* (1889).

Twentieth-century Canadian novelist Nellie Letitia McClung was active in the WCTU in Manitoba, and the association between character and temperance underpins her fiction. An example is the Pearlie Watson trilogy (*Sowing Seeds in Danny,* 1908; *The Second Chance,* 1910; *Purple Springs,* 1921), in which art mirrors McClung's life of social activism. In *Purple Springs,* Pearl Watson lampoons "Premier Graham" in the Women's Parliament just as Nellie McClung lampooned Sir Rodmond Roblin, the Conservative premier of Manitoba from 1900 to 1915 and an opponent of women's suffrage and prohibition. The integral link between abolishing the bar and gaining women's suffrage dominated the mock debate of the Women's Parliament in both life and art. Cartoons in newspapers allied with the Conservative Party depicted McClung as "an angry mosquito, or as a raving battle-axe in trousers" (Warne 1993: 116). Stephen Leacock, a Canadian satirist, attacked Nellie McClung in *Maclean's* magazine (1915), although he does not name her explicitly as the "Awful Woman." His most famous and hilarious sketch of the hypocrisy of the temperance movement is "The Marine Excursion of the Knights of Pythias." Leacock's knights wear a blue ribbon and by their constitution are dedicated to temperance, but their ranks include the bank manager, Henry Mullins, who carries "a small flask of Pogram's Special in his hip pocket as a sort of amendment to the constitution."

Other literary efforts that do not stand out as great literature are the primers, temperance verse, and cookbooks. Russell Trall, author of the *Hydropathic Cook Book* (1854), Dio Lewis, author of *Our Digestion or My Jolly Friend's Secret* (1872), and Catherine Beecher, author of *A Treatise on Domestic Economy* (1841), interwove temperance and nutrition in their writings.

Performing Arts

English Methodism and the temperance pulpit of John Wesley are the provenance of temperance performances. This movement spread to North America, and in 1810, Congregationalist preacher Lyman Beecher delivered his famous series of six sermons against distilled liquor, later published as *Six Sermons on the Nature, Occasions, Signs, Evils and Remedy of Intemperance* (1826). W. H. Daniels's edited book, *The Temperance Reform and Its Great Reformers* (1877), bears witness to the primacy of platform oratory in the temperance movement, providing excerpts from addresses by Lyman Beecher, John B. Gough, Francis Murphy, Father Theobald Mathew, Frances E. Willard, Dwight L. Moody, the Reverend Theodore Cuyler, and the Reverend Charles Fuller. Scattered throughout Mark Lender's (1984) *Dictionary of American Temperance Biography* are profiles of platform orators, in which they tend to come down on the side of "moral suasion" (e.g., Theodore Cuyler, Dio Lewis, Dwight L. Moody, Hannah Whitall Smith, Annie Wittenmyer) or "prohibition" (e.g., Lyman Beecher, Amelia Jenks Bloomer, Harry Chalfant, William Ferguson, Clinton Howard, Mary Greenleaf Clement Leavitt, Mary Livermore, George Stuart, Frances Willard) as the way of eliminating the alcohol problem. John Gough, a drunkard who took the pledge during the Washingtonian revival in Massachusetts in 1842, went on to make a career as a temperance lecturer, drawing in audiences with lurid descriptions of his drunken binges. Other platform speakers who used the redemptive narratives of the reformed drinker include Lou Jenks Beauchamp, Frances Murphy, John Hawkins, John Sullivan, and David Isaac Kirwin Rine. Rine, an alcoholic and an ex-convict, after hearing Francis Murphy speak in 1876, signed the pledge and became a leading disciple of the Murphy movement of gospel temperance. He lectured in Erie County, Pennsylvania, and Canada, and in slavish imitation of Murphy, depicted the facts of his own struggle with alcohol, moving swiftly to secure signatures to the pledge.

Only a few temperance crusaders departed from these mainstream performances. Carry A. Nation, a WCTU activist in Kansas, performed her temperance sermons and hatchet-wielding attacks on multiple stages—in churches, civic centers, music halls, saloons, and vaudeville houses. The "hatchetations"—to use Nation's coined word—enacted the claim of Nation and her supporters that they were commanded by God to perform the smashing of "joints." Carry Nation evoked antiactivist sentiments, of which Thomas Edison's unfeminine caricature of her in the film *Why Mr. Nation Wants a Divorce* is representative (Grace 2001: 204). Phineas T. Barnum, American circus entrepreneur, featured an antiliquor message in his stage productions. In 1849, during the successful American tour of Jenny Lind, the Swedish singer, Barnum himself gave temperance lectures in the concert halls on the nights that Lind did not appear.

Edwin Excell wrote hymns and edited an *Anti-Saloon League Song-Book* but also took the solo part in "Down Among the Dead Men," which according to Lender (1984) was a favorite among the temperance faithful. Temperance songs were an integral part of popular culture during the late nineteenth and early twentieth centuries. The extensive temperance section in the Lester S. Levy sheet music collection (http://levysheetmusic.mse.jhu.edu) often makes reference to the performing artist as well as the composer, lyricist, and publisher (*see also* Music for the Nation: American Sheet Music, 1870–1885: http://memory.loc.gov). Several of the title sheets for songs such as "Girls, Wait for a Temperance Man" and "Sign the Pledge for Mother's Sake" written by Mrs. E. A. Parkhurst reference her daughter as the child performer: "As sung by Little Effie Parkhurst with great applause at the temperance meetings in New York and Brooklyn" (*see* Cohen-Stratyner 1991). The 1873 song entitled "A Cup of Cold Water" is dedicated to John B. Gough, Esq., and the title page depicts Gough with the temperance pledge in one hand and a glass of water in the other. The young members of the WCTU signed and sang their own version of the pledge in "Lips That Touch Liquor Will Never Touch Mine." Many temperance song sheets point to the melding of visual, literary, and performing arts.

The Elastic Millennium Choir, a contemporary choral group based in Nova Scotia, performs a number of these "songs of temperance and indulgence" on their compact disc *Touch It Not!* (2001).

A reference to the performance of George Cruikshank's tableaux, such as those in *The Worship of Bacchus,* appears in David Fahey's (2001) account of Jessie Forsyth's memoirs of her life in the Order of Good Templars fraternal temperance society in Australia. Jessie Forsyth moved to Australia from New England in 1912, but she was born in London. Her mother, Eliza Maria Kitteridge, was a favorite niece of George Cruikshank, and Andrew and Eliza Maria Forsythe sat in a private box at Sadler's Wells Theater to watch Cruikshank's temperance pictures dramatized as tableaux. T. P. Taylor wrote a temperance drama entitled *The Bottle* (1847) to accompany Cruikshank's engravings. A British Broadcasting Corporation television program, "1,000 Ways of Getting Drunk in England" (2 June 2001) hosted by Andrew Graham Dixon, is filmed in the streets, pubs, former gin palaces, churches, and galleries, illuminating the times in which George Cruikshank painted *The Worship of Bacchus* (*see* http://www.bbc.co.uk/factsheets/1000_ways_of_getting_drunk_in_england/) and reestablishing the importance of this artist and his masterpiece. One of the first temperance plays to appear on the London stage was Douglas Jerrold's *Fifteen Years of a Drunkard's Life* (1828).

Temperance plays were staged in U.S. locations from the 1830s and were closely allied with the prohibitionists' agenda in the early decades of the nineteenth century. The genre of melodrama—the pattern of drunkenness and ruination of the family, followed by rehabilitation and signing of the pledge in the presence of a temperance spokesman—inscribes two famous U.S. temperance plays: *Ten Nights in a Bar Room,* W. W. Pratt's (1858) adaptation of T. S. Arthur's novel; and W. H. Smith's (1844) *The Drunkard* or *The Fallen Saved.* Variations of the T. S. Arthur novel abounded in plays and lantern slide lectures throughout the latter half of the nineteenth century (*see* Cohen-Stratyner 1991 on starring performances of the child victim "Little Mary Morgan"). The temperance morality tale in William Hogarth's eighteenth-century satirical prints, *The Rake's Progress,* stood the test of time, reappearing as the title and story line for Igor Stravinsky's 1951 opera, which features W. H. Auden's libretto and David Hockney's sets and costumes.

Nellie McClung used her novels as the content for her speeches, often given in churches and church halls. She addressed over 400 public meetings between 1913 and 1921 (Bassett 1975: 137). McClung's first speaking engagement was reading from her novel *Sowing Seeds in Danny,* at the request of her mother-in-law, to help raise money for the WCTU's new home for friendless girls in Winnipeg. The mock Women's Parliament featured Nellie in the role of Premier Roblin, whom she burlesqued "so realistically that she left the packed Walker Theatre in Winnipeg rocking with laughter" (Bassett 1975: 139). In 1913, the *Telegram* in Winnipeg ran cartoons of McClung depicting her children as ragged and neglected. Randi Warne keeps the temperance tradition of dramatic performances alive into the twenty-first century, performing her dramatic monologues in the character of Nellie McClung throughout North America.

Dorothy A. Lander

See also: Art, Representations of Drinking in; Beecher, Lyman; Cruikshank, George; Drama, Representations of Temperance in; Gough, John Bartholomew; Leavitt, Mary Greenleaf Clement; Literature, Representations of Temperance in; Mathew, Father Theobald; McClung, Nellie Letitia; Murphy, Francis; Nation, Carry Amelia Moore; Scientific Temperance Federation; Stoddard, Cora Frances; Willard, Frances Elizabeth Caroline; Women's Temperance Crusade; World's Woman's Christian Temperance Union (WWCTU); Youmans, Letitia

References

Allingham, Philip. "Charles Dickens and Two Kinds of Punch." Paper available from The Victorian Web. http://www.victorianweb.org/dickens/pva/40.html/ [19 June 2002].

———. "Dickens's Aesthetic of the Short Story." Paper available from The Victorian Web. http://www.victorianweb.org/dickens/pva/4.html/ [19 June 2002].

Bassett, Isabel. *The Parlour Rebellion: Profiles in the Struggle for Women's Rights.* Toronto: McClelland and Stewart, 1975.

Birrell, A. J. "D. I. K. Rine and the Gospel Temperance Movement in Canada" in *The Canadian Historical Review.* 1: 23–42.

Cohen-Stratyner, Barbara. "Platform Pearls, or 19th Century American Temperance Performance Texts" in *Performing Arts Resources.* 15 (1991): 69–77.

Danahay, Martin. "Alcohol in 'Jekyll and Hyde'." [19 June 2002].

Daniels, W. H. *The Temperance Reform and Its Great Reformers.* New York: Nelson and Phillips, 1877.

Elastic Millennium Choir. *Touch It Not! Songs of Temperance and Indulgence* (compact disc). Halifax, Nova Scotia: Elastic Millennium Choir, 2001.

Fahey, David. "Jessie Forsyth, Good Templar: Family Records from Western Australia" in *The Social History of Alcohol Review* 2001. http://www.athg.org/forsyth.html [19 June 2002].

Grace, Fran. *Carry A. Nation: Retelling the Life.* Bloomington: Indiana University Press, 2001.

Harker, Wendy, and Max Allen. *Gather Beneath the Banner: Political and Religious Banners of the Woman's Christian Temperance Union 1877–1932.* Toronto: Museum for Textiles, 1999.

Hedges, Elaine, Pat Ferrero, and Julie Silber. *Hearts and Hands: Women, Quilts, and American Society.* Nashville: Rutledge Hill Press, 1987.

hooks, bell. *Art on My Mind: Visual Politics.* New York: The New Press, 1995.

Household, G. A., and L. M. H. Smith. *To Catch a Sunbeam: Victorian Reality through the Magic Lantern.* London: Michael Joseph, 1979.

Lander, Dorothy. "Re-membering and Re-picturing Activist Mothers in Civil Society: The Canadian Woman's Christian Temperance Union and the Audiovisual Rhetoric of 'Home Protection'." Proceedings of the 20th Annual Conference of the Canadian Association for the Study of Adult Education (CASAE), Laval University, Quebec City, 2001. http://www.oise.utoronto.ca/CASAE/cnf2001/lander.htm [24 June 2002].

Leacock, Stephen. "The Marine Excursion of the Knights of Pythias" in *Sunshine Sketches of a Little Town,* 64–96. Toronto: McClelland and Stewart, 1931.

———. "The Woman Question" in *Maclean's.* 28, no. 12 (October 1915): 7–9.

Lender, Mark. *Dictionary of American Temperance Biography.* Westport, CT: Greenwood, 1984.

Mattingly, Carol. *Water Drops from Women Writers: A Temperance Reader.* Carbondale: Southern Illinois Press, 2001.

Rawls, Walton H. *The Great Book of Currier and Ives' America.* New York: Abbeville Press, 1991.

Reynolds, David S., and Debra J. Rosenthal, eds. *The Serpent in the Cup: Temperance in American Literature.* Amherst: University of Massachusetts Press, 1997.

Romanovich, Robin. "The Role of Religion in Pickwick and Jane Eyre." Paper available from the Victorian Web. http://www.victorianweb.org/dickens/pickwick/rar4.html [19 June 2002].

Rose, Kenneth D. *American Women and the Repeal of Prohibition.* New York: New York University Press, 1996.

Seagram Museum website. http://www.lib.uwaterloo.ca/discipline/SpecColl/archives/seagram.html [June 2003].

Strand, Sharon. "Many a Drunkard Slept under a Drunkard's Path Quilt: The Use of Material Culture as Non-Verbal Rhetoric by the Woman's Christian Temperance Society." Paper available from author, English Department, Black Hills State University (SharonStrand@bhsu.edu).

Warne, Randi. *Literature as Pulpit: The Christian Social Activism of Nellie L. McClung.* Waterloo, Ontario: Wilfred Laurier University Press, 1993.

Youmans, Letitia. *Campaign Echoes: The Autobiography of Mrs. Letitia Youmans, the Pioneer of the White Ribbon Movement in Canada.* Toronto: William Briggs, 1893.

Zwick, Jim. Political Cartoons and Cartoonists. http://www.boondocksnet.com/cartoons/bengough22a.html [June 2002].

Association Against the Prohibition Amendment (AAPA)

The Association Against the Prohibition Amendment (AAPA) was a national organization prominent and influential in the successful campaign to repeal the Eighteenth Amendment to the United States Constitution. Founded by William H. Stayton immediately after the World War I armistice while the proposed National Prohibition amendment was in the final stages of ratification and incorporated in the District of Columbia in December 1920, the AAPA remained small and ineffectual until the mid-1920s. Then the Du Pont brothers of Delaware, former United States Senator James Wadsworth of New York, General Motors executive John Raskob, and various other corporate, political, and financial leaders joined its ranks. The AAPA reorganized in December 1927, employed an executive/spokesman and staff, expanded its public relations efforts, and began vigorously crusading for Prohibition repeal. Although its goal seemed at first unreachable because of the enormous difficulty of formal constitutional change, the AAPA persisted, forming political alliances that eventually proved fortuitous. Within six years, it both benefited from and shaped circumstances that allowed an overwhelming political expression of public opposition to Prohibition. On the evening of 5 December 1933, a few hours after three state ratifications completed the passage of the Twenty-First Amendment, 170 AAPA directors celebrated with a dinner at the Waldorf Astoria Hotel in New York City. Then, its goal achieved, the AAPA disbanded.

The AAPA opposition to the Eighteenth Amendment centered on its disapproval of expanded federal government authority under National Prohibition. Stayton initially argued that liquor control belonged in local hands. Giving federal authorities the power to control an individual's choice of what to drink placed too much power with a distant central government. As experience with Prohibition increased and the appearance of widespread violation spread, the AAPA gradually drew more members to its ranks by calling for an end to a law that it asserted was ineffective despite being enforced with a heavy hand. Supreme Court decisions expanding police powers of search and seizure to enforce the dry law (*Carroll v. U.S.* and *Olmstead v. U.S.* in particular) as well as confirming the power of both state and federal authorities to punish the same liquor offense (*Lanza v. U.S.*) increased the AAPA complaint. National Prohibition, the AAPA concluded, served to breed disrespect for government and the constitution.

The Eighteenth Amendment's ratification by state legislatures and the subsequent denial by the Supreme Court that such an action in Ohio could be made subject to referendum (*Hawke v. Smith*) led the AAPA to contend that Prohibition was improperly implemented against popular wishes. An AAPA-backed court challenge to the amendment's constitutional validity was upheld by a federal district court in New Jersey, but quickly rejected by the Supreme Court in 1931 (*U.S. v. Sprague*). Nevertheless, the AAPA continued to insist that any future constitutional action on Prohibition should be subject to popular vote.

With the onset of the Great Depression, economic hard times focused attention on the costs of Prohibition, which the AAPA claimed had totaled over $300 million in enforcement expenses and $11 billion in lost tax revenues by 1931. Not only did taxpayers bear Prohibition's considerable direct costs, the AAPA complained, but also the outlawing of the liquor industry eliminated many legitimate jobs in brewing and distilling, not to mention agriculture, bottle making, transportation and distribution, retail sales, and service. Ending Prohibition could ease the depression. Temperance advocates responded that wealthy AAPA members simply sought to avoid taxes.

In 1928 and 1932, AAPA leaders appealed to both the Republican and Democratic national conventions to endorse Prohibition repeal. Neither party was willing to do so in 1928, although the Democrats nominated a presidential candidate, New York governor Alfred Emanuel Smith, who was an outspoken critic of Prohibition. When Smith chose AAPA leader John Jakob Raskob as Democratic national chairman, the image of Democratic sympathy for repeal was enhanced. The landslide victory of Republican Herbert Hoover over Smith was widely read as a mandate for continued Prohibition. Four years later, however, the AAPA renewed its appeals. Republicans remained resistant, pledging continued enforcement of the law, but the Democrats, after a preconvention battle and a vigorous floor debate in which AAPA spokesmen were prominent, overwhelmingly embraced by a roll-call vote a platform plank favoring repeal. The party's subsequent presidential nominee, Franklin D. Roosevelt, who had avoided the issue throughout his career, grudgingly accepted the plank. The Democratic Party's identification with Prohibition repeal, which the AAPA helped establish, proved crucial. As in 1928, the clear-cut party victory, this time for the Democrats, was perceived as a popular mandate on Prohibition.

Congress, urged by the AAPA and allied organizations to respond to a popular demand for repeal, approved a Prohibition repeal amendment even before Roosevelt took office. A lame-duck session of the Seventy-Second Congress adopted by more than a two-thirds margin in each house a constitutional amendment overturning the Eighteenth Amendment. Congress heeded AAPA demands that the proposed amendment be sent for ratification to state conventions rather than the legislatures routinely employed for the purpose.

Most state legislatures quickly agreed to offer voters one slate of convention delegates pledged to support the new amendment and another committed to retaining the Eighteenth Amendment. AAPA members were prominent among the candidates favoring repeal. After generally low-key campaigning, the electorate left no doubt as to its preference. Between April and November, thirty-seven states held delegate elections, and nationwide, 73 percent of voters expressed a preference for Prohibition repeal. Only South Carolina, by a 52 percent margin, favored retaining the alcohol ban. When the final state conventions in Pennsylvania, Ohio, and Utah acted on 5 December 1933, the Twenty-First Amendment achieved ratification.

After repeal, some AAPA leaders helped establish and operate state alcoholic beverage control programs. A couple of thousand members, once claimed to number 560,000, and donors, who peaked at over 21,000, joined William Stayton's liquor policy watchdog organization, Repeal Associates. Convinced that it reflected popular opposition to expanded federal government, the core of the AAPA established the anti–New Deal American Liberty League in 1934. Roosevelt's triumphant reelection in 1936 vanquished the American Liberty League and made clear that the constitutional views of the AAPA were popular in the 1930s only when the issue was national alcoholic beverage prohibition.

David E. Kyvig

See also: Du Pont, Pierre Samuel; National Prohibition (United States); Raskob, John Jakob; Sabin, Pauline Morton; Stayton, William H.; Voluntary Committee of Lawyers; Women's Organization for National Prohibition Reform (WONPR)

References

Dobyns, Fletcher. *The Amazing Story of Repeal: An Exposé of the Power of Propaganda.* Chicago: Willet, Clark, 1940.

Kyvig, David E. *Repealing National Prohibition.* 2d ed. Kent, OH: Kent State University Press, 2000.

Association of Labor and Management Consultants and Administrators on Alcoholism

See Employee Assistance Programs (EAPs).

Astor, Lady Nancy Wicher Langhorne (1879–1964)

Nancy Wicher Langhorne Astor (1879–1964), the first woman to take a seat in the House of Commons, was also a tenacious advocate of temperance throughout her career. The daughter of an alcoholic Virginia railroad baron, two of her brothers drank themselves to death prematurely. Astor's first husband, Robert Gould Shaw, a wealthy playboy, was an abusive alcoholic, whom she divorced in 1903 for adultery. In 1905, on a trip to England, she met and married Waldorf Astor, the heir to the Astor newspaper fortune, and became a celebrated society hostess at their country estate, Cliveden, although insisting that no alcohol be served to guests (they had to bribe servants to get surreptitious drinks).

Waldorf Astor, a chronic invalid, stood for Parliament from Plymouth, and Nancy proved invaluable to his work, canvassing the working-class neighborhoods of the harbor city. Identifying the social ills she saw with alcohol—neglected children, poverty, and spousal abuse—she was even more convinced of her personal mission for temperance. When Waldorf Astor's father was elevated to a viscountcy, ending his son's chances of a career in the House of Commons, the Conservative Party nominated Nancy in his place in 1919. She would serve continuously until 1945, and although she would never commit to a British program of prohibition, she made her career pushing for pro-temperance legislation including one bill to retain World War I restrictions on licensing and strengths of alcohol, supporting the raising of the minimum drinking age in Britain, and sponsoring Ministry of Health activities like maternity centers.

Cliveden was a famous center of social activity, and Nancy entertained such varied guests as T. E. Lawrence, George Bernard Shaw, and Mahatma Gandhi, and hosted a landmark meeting between British Labour Party leaders and the royal family in 1923. Nancy's education was deficient, due to its having been undertaken at home, as with other daughters of the rich of the period, and her personal background led to beliefs that, even for the climate of the times, were tactless and virulently anti-Semitic, anti-Catholic, and racist. An enemy of Winston Churchill, Nancy Astor's circle contained a number of proappeasement leaders, an association that overshadowed her work in both World War I and World War II as a sponsor of evacuated children and a civil defense coordinator. In 1931, she was deeply embarrassed when her son by her first husband, Robert Shaw, was cashiered from the Horse Guards for being drunk on duty.

Increasingly out of touch with postwar Britain, Nancy Astor was asked by the Conservative Party to stand down in 1945, after which she continued to entertain, particularly on behalf of her two sons by Astor, both of whom entered Conservative politics. Anti-Soviet and thought by some to be senile, Nancy survived Waldorf Astor (d. 1952) by twelve years, abandoning teetotalism in her last years for spiked eggnog, which she insisted to her children was nonalcoholic. Dying on 2 May 1964, she was buried, at her insistence, under a Confederate flag.

Margaret Sankey

See also: Astor, Lord Waldorf; Churchill, Winston; Gandhi, Mohandas Karamchand

References

Halperin, John. *Eminent Georgians.* New York: St. Martin's, 1995.

Ravaler, Lucy. *The Astors: A Family Chronicle of Pomp and Power.* New York: Dodd, Mead, 1966.

Sykes, Christopher. *Nancy: The Life of Lady Astor.* London: Collins, 1972.

Astor, Lord Waldorf (1879–1952)

Waldorf Astor (second viscount) (1879–1952), British newspaper proprietor and politician, was the member of Parliament (M.P.) for Plymouth from 1910 to 1919. Astor was one of the few Conservative political figures in early-twentieth-century Britain who actively promoted temperance and licensing reform. Together with his formidable wife, Nancy Astor, he fervently believed that the drink trade was corrupting British public life. He saw public ownership and control of the liquor trade as providing a solution to this problem and to intemperance in general.

His father, William, a member of the wealthy New York business family, had settled in Britain, being naturalized as a British subject and ultimately raised to the peerage. Waldorf Astor developed an interest in a range of social questions, particularly that of health. His marriage to the intelligent Nancy, who held particularly strong views about the evils of drink, helped push him toward an interest in the drink issue, particularly its relationship to public health and industrial efficiency. Astor served as an enthusiastic member of the Central Control Board (Liquor Traffic), which was established in June 1915 and which imposed various restrictions throughout Britain, as well as taking direct control of the trade in intoxicants in Carlisle and some other

Portrait of Waldorf Astor, later Lord Astor (Library of Congress)

areas. Astor also served as a member of David Lloyd George's secretariat, known as the "garden suburb," at No. 10 Downing Street. Here, after first favoring prohibition for the duration of the war, he subsequently threw his weight behind Lord Milner in his drive to establish state purchase of the whole liquor trade in 1917 in the interests of national efficiency. He was a member of Lord Cave's committee, which drew up detailed proposals for purchase. The Cabinet did not adopt these proposals.

Subsequently, Astor served as a parliamentary secretary, first in the Ministry of Food (1918) and then in the new Ministry of Health (1919–1921). In 1919, when his father died and he was elevated to the House of Lords, Astor reluctantly resigned his seat in the House of Commons. Nancy (now Lady Astor) succeeded him as the M.P. for Plymouth, being the first elected female M.P. to take her seat. Between them, they helped pass legislation in 1923 to increase the age for drinking in licensed premises to eighteen. After the first world war, Lord Astor continued to show an interest in alcohol issues. He supported the Bishop of Oxford's attempts to legislate in favor of local option for both disinterested management and local veto. From 1925 through 1927, he devoted considerable time and expense in setting up his own "drink inquiry" to research the effects of alcohol both on individuals and on society and public life. He also campaigned against what he considered to be the baneful effects of the drink trade upon political life. These efforts, which continued many of the concerns and themes raised by the former Central Control Board, made little public or political impact. Astor's other chief interests were the League of Nations, agriculture, health policy, and racing. A rich collection of Lord Astor's papers is housed at the University of Reading.

John Greenaway

See also: Astor, Lady Nancy Wicher Langhorne; Carlisle System; Conservative Party (United Kingdom); Gothenburg Schemes/Disinterested Management

References

Astor, Waldorf. *Temperance and Politics.* New Way Series, no. 12. London: Daily News, 1925.

Greenaway, John R. *Drink and British Politics since 1830: A Study in Policy-Making.* Basingstoke, UK, and New York: Palgrave and Macmillan, 2003.

Turner, John. Chapter 8 in *Lloyd George's Secretariat.* Cambridge: Cambridge University Press, 1980.

———. "State Purchase of the Liquor Trade in the First World War" in *Historical Journal.* 23, no. 2 (1980): 589–615.

Australia

Alcohol has been an important part of Australia's economy and culture since colonial times. Australia, with a population of more than 19 million in 2002, began as six separate colonies of which the first, New South Wales, was founded in 1788. Each colony had its own alcohol laws and policies and also its own temperance groups. After Federation in 1901, when the colonies became states, they continued to largely control their own drinking regulations.

Until the 1860s, Australians drank considerably more alcohol than the British. This was particularly true of spirits. Spirit drinking was at its highest in New South Wales in the 1830s—four times as high as in Britain—mostly in the form of rum, brandy, and gin. The high proportion of single men in the population was no doubt one reason for such a high rate of alcohol consumption. In Australia's convict period, in the early nineteenth century, rum was used as currency. Coins were scarce and commerce was growing, so spirits were used as a substitute. Indeed, officers paid their convict workers with rum.

Australia may have been a country of high spirits consumption, but it was also a place where temperance organizations flourished. The first Australian temperance society is said to have been founded in Hobart in 1832 by two Quakers, James Backhouse and George Washington Walker. Within a few years, both men and women in large numbers were joining temperance groups in Sydney, Melbourne, and Launceston. As in the United States and Britain, the temperance societies of the early 1830s often confined their efforts to eliminating the drinking of spirits, but by the end of the decade total abstinence was the goal of most societies. The temperance societies organized public lectures (it is said that the first public lecture of any kind in Melbourne was a temperance lecture), issued their own magazines, and also urged their colonial governments to pass laws regulating the liquor trade. Tasmania banned local distillation of spirits in 1838, and in New South Wales, Governor George Gipps stopped issuing rum to imperial troops while at the same time imposing an increased excise on spirits. Legislation was also passed to prevent the selling of drink to Aborigines. The Australian Aborigines had traditionally produced no alcoholic drinks, but once the whites arrived they began to consume alcohol heavily whenever available. This was partly because much of their contact with whites was with pastoral workers who were intense binge drinkers. The dispossession and disease that Aborigines suffered upon the arrival of Europeans also no doubt contributed to alcoholism.

Overseas Influences

The main international temperance bodies formed branches in Australia throughout the nineteenth century. The Independent Order of Rechabites arrived in 1847, followed by the Sons of Temperance, and the Order of Good Templars set up their first branch in Queensland in 1872. Between them, these bodies had 63,000 Australian members by 1890. In addition to the international societies, Australian cities and towns had their own independent total abstinence societies. The temperance society in general received a huge boost from overseas missionaries, mostly evangelical. One of these was Matthew Burnett who traveled Australia during the 1860s conducting loud, flamboyant religious revival meetings. Believing that renunciation of alcohol was essential to salvation, he persuaded thousands to sign

A poster made by Australian Aborigines to warn of the dangers of alcohol, part of the federally sponsored National Drug Offensive of the 1980s. (Christine Osborne/Corbis)

the total abstinence pledge and numerous local temperance societies were launched as a result of his revival meetings. Burnett's missions were especially successful in recruiting the working classes both to the churches and to temperance organizations. The Blue Ribbon Movement, which swept through the United States and Britain, was brought to Australia by Richard Booth and William Noble in 1882. Like Burnett, these Evangelists stressed total abstinence as a necessary component of Christian faith, and they were most influential in forging a close relationship between the temperance movement and the nonconformist Protestant churches that by the late 1880s came to dominate the Australian temperance campaigns. Protestant churchgoers, especially the Wesleyan Methodists, flooded Parliament with petitions urging the Victorian Parliament to pass its first full local-option measures in 1885. The Roman Catholics and the Church of England had their own temperance societies also, but these were not very visible in the agitation for antiliquor laws. In fact, the Church of England tended toward moderation rather than total abstinence.

In the 1880s, the Australian temperance movement received a surge of support and activity from a number of sources. Mary Greenleaf Clement Leavitt, and later Jessie Ackermann, formed branches of the Woman's Christian Temperance Union (WCTU) throughout Australia, bringing thousands of women into temperance activity and leadership. Women had always made up a significant proportion of Australian temperance societies and of temperance sympathizers in general. In 1885, 45,000 Victorian women (almost a quarter of the adult female population) signed a petition asking the government to introduce local option to protect their sex from "ill usage," which often accompanied drinking.

Local Option

In the 1850s, shortly after the founding of the United Kingdom Alliance (UKA), Australian temperance organizations sought to secure local-option measures for the Australian colonies. Their goal was to give residents the right to veto licenses in their towns and suburbs rather than the more ambitious state prohibition, or "Maine Law," which had become the goal of the American temperance movement. In 1881, the local-option campaign became especially vigorous following an intercolonial convention at which temperance groups decided to join together to form "alliances" within their respective colonies for the purpose of lobbying their respective colonial governments for local-option policies.

Due to these organized efforts, by the 1890s, each colony had introduced Sunday closings of hotels, and except for Western Australia, each had introduced some form of local option. Queensland, in 1885, became the envy of temperance workers in other colonies when it enabled ratepayers to veto all licenses in their district. That same year, Victoria permitted all residents on the electoral roll to reduce the number of hotels in their locality to one for every 500 inhabitants. The other colonies at that time allowed for a veto on proposed new licenses but not for reduction of existing licenses. The temperance advocates continued to agitate. Their goal was for local-option laws in each colony that allowed for a veto of all licenses—which would include private clubs as well as public houses—and also a veto on all shops that sold liquor to take away. Furthermore, they wanted the local-option vote for all adult residents and not just ratepayers, and most particularly for women, whom they considered more likely to be on their side.

By 1911, each state had passed acts that allowed for some form of local option. New South Wales as well as Queensland allowed residents to veto all licenses in their district. By this time, every state except Tasmania had extended these voting rights to include every resident listed in the state electoral roll, and not just ratepayers. The electors included women, as Australian women in each state now had the vote on the same grounds as men.

Not every temperance advocate, however, favored local option. At the 1888 intercolonial convention, J. S. Shearston, secretary of the New South Wales Order of Good Templars, declared that the temperance alliances should demand nothing short of total prohibition for the colonies. He considered local option quite inadequate. Axel Gustafson, a Swede living in Victoria, shared that view, and soon afterward, he broke away from the Victorian Alliance to form his own prohibitionist society. Few followed him, however, and many temperance spokespeople saw such men as troublemakers, causing unnecessary conflict. The Victorian WCTU broke its association with Philip Moses, who founded a number of their branches, when he urged the members to stop wasting their time on local option. In the 1890s, further conflicts emerged when a number of local temperance advocates moved away from local option and favored the "Gothenburg system," which would place all sale of liquor under government control. This became the favored solution of many trade unionists as well as certain sectors of the Presbyterian and Methodist churches. However, the Gothenburg system was rather short-lived as a proposed plan, and by World War I, local option along with state prohibition became the most favored proposal of temperance advocates.

Temperance in the Twentieth Century

In 1916, the "alliances" of the various states formed a national body, the Australian Alliance Prohibition Council. By this time, the temperance movement was setting its sights on Australia-wide prohibition rather than confining itself to local option. The passing of the Volstead Act in the United States inspired hope that a similar Prohibition act might one day be introduced in Australia. The WCTU declared at its 1921 national convention that its aim would be for the whole of Australia to be dry by 1925. The hopes were by no means justified, however, for none of the state referenda held throughout the 1920s and 1930s produced a majority "yes" vote. The Victorian referendum of 1930 saw the largest prohibition vote, with 42 percent voting "yes." The legislation proposed was more modest than that of the Volstead Act, because it permitted the importation of alcohol from other states; it was only the sale and manufacture within Victoria that were to be prohibited. Queensland, New South Wales, and Western Australia held similar polls throughout the 1920s, but they each only produced a one-third "yes" vote. In Tasmania, such a small number turned out to vote that there were doubts as to the validity of the poll.

No state in Australia ever turned "dry." Indeed, local-option polls only rarely produced a dry suburb. The temperance advocates did, however, succeed in creating Australia's new capital city, Canberra, as a dry zone. Unfortunately for them, the measure was repealed by popular referendum in 1928. From the temperance point of view, local option was most successful in preventing new licenses. Polls held to determine whether residents consented to an increased number of licensed venues in their district frequently resulted in a refusal. The decreasing number of hotels between 1900 and 1930 was mostly due to the efforts of the state licensing boards. In Victoria, the number of publicans' licenses was halved during this period.

The most successful victory of the temperance movement in Australia was "six o'clock closing." In the early twentieth century, when early closing acts in the various Australian states required shops to be closed at six o'clock, temperance groups began to insist that the same law should apply to licensed hotels. At that time, hotels were normally open until eleven o'clock in the evening. They organized numerous petitions on the matter, causing the licensed victuallers' associations to organize their own petitions to keep existing hotel hours. The temperance side was given extra confidence when some state governments slightly reduced hotel hours as a temporary wartime measure. In March 1915, the state of South Australia held a referendum on the matter. The majority voted for the temperance movement proposal to shut hotels at six o'clock. Victoria and New South Wales and Tasmania held similar referenda that year, with similar results. By the end of 1916, only Queensland and Western Australia allowed hotels to remain open after six. Elsewhere, six o'clock closing remained—with Western Australia introducing nine o'clock closing and Queensland eight o'clock closing as a compromise.

Six o'clock closing may have been a less drastic antiliquor law than the Volstead Act of the United States, but it lasted for much longer. Tasmania extended its hotel closing hours to ten o'clock in 1932, and New South Wales followed in 1955, but Victorian and South Australian hotels were open not later than six until the 1960s.

Changing Drinking Patterns

After the 1830s, the rate of drinking gradually declined within the Australian population. Spirit drinking declined considerably. Beer was produced as early as 1796. Governor King encouraged beer in 1802 because it would be less intoxicating than the rum that prevailed. But beer did not overtake spirits in terms of amounts consumed until the late nineteenth century. By this time, the proportion of single men within the population had declined, and Australia had become a land of families. In fact, its people were moderate drinkers by international standards. The New South Wales inhabitants were spending a mere 9 percent of their wages on drink, while the British were spending 12 to 13 percent. Drinking rates did rise during mining booms, such as during the Victorian gold rush of the 1850s. The goldfields were notable for their high proportion of single men. In 1890, by far the highest drinking rate was in western Australia, which also had the highest number of single men. Socially, western Australia was more like the eastern Australia of the early days.

Although men were the heaviest drinkers, and women a significant force in temperance, the Australian pubs were not as male-dominated as the American saloons. In the 1890s, young women who were free of family responsibilities could be found in city pubs. In the middle part of the twentieth century, housewives would gather in the ladies' lounges of pubs, bringing their vegetables, which they would proceed to cut up for the evening meal. Moreover, heavy drinking at home or private functions seems to have been not uncommon among women. It seems to have been less common among women of the poorer classes, because when disposable income was scarce, it mostly went to the husband. But the frequency of drinking problems among more well-to-do women is evident from the WCTU's attempts to set up inebriate retreats for women of the "better class." In the 1880s, when American Mary Love, Victorian WCTU president, first visited Melbourne from the United States, she remarked on the regular drinking habits of Australian middle-class women, which contrasted with the more abstemious American women.

In the nineteenth century, the hotels themselves were often owned and run by women. Around three-fifths of self-employed women in Sydney in 1891 owned a public house. Many other hotels were family enterprises that the publican's wife would run on a day-to-day basis. And despite the efforts of the WCTU and other temperance groups, women were never prohibited from serving behind the bar. Indeed, the presence of women behind the bar was another feature of Australia that amazed temperance visitors from America.

After World War II, the alcohol consumption rate began to rise, despite the fact that six o'clock closing was still in force in the most populated states. Despite the temperance hopes, the restricted hotel hours did not lead to a reduction in alcohol consumption. The main effect of the early closing measure was to make public houses incredibly crowded and hectic in the short space between the end of the workday and closing time. Moreover, evening drinking still continued at home or in restaurants. The drinking rate continued to rise dramatically throughout the 1950s and 1960s also, and in the late 1960s, wine consumption rose most notably. Although wine had constituted a small proportion of the alcohol consumed throughout most of the nation's history, Australia was becoming a nation of wine drinkers.

Australia had a small wine industry in the nineteenth century, run by families such as the Lindemans in the Hunter Valley. Though wine grapes grow in all states, Victoria had the largest production until the 1890s, when *Phylloxera vastatrix* (also known as *Phylloxera vitifoliae)* devastated the vineyards. Then South Australia became the leading wine-producing state. The German immigrants of South Australia's Barossa Valley, such as the founders of what became B. Seppelt and Sons in 1851, were among the state's earliest vignerons.

Per capita wine consumption more than doubled from 8.9 liters (2.35 U.S. gallons) in 1969 to 19.7 liters (5.2 U.S. gallons) in 1999. Conversely, beer consumption declined from its highest level of 134.8 liters (35.6 U.S. gallons) per capita per annum in 1977 to 95 liters (25.1 U.S. gallons) in 1999. Migrants from European wine-drinking cultures contributed to this shift. Another factor, however, was the growth and improved quality of Australian wines. Not until the 1960s and 1970s did Australia develop a reputation as a producer of fine table wines. Then wine production grew rapidly. By the 1990s, wine was a major export industry, especially to Britain, but also to parts of the Asia-Pacific region, and many new vineyards were continually emerging.

The brewing industry had also changed dramatically. In the nineteenth century, beer production was in the hands of small family firms, but in the twentieth century these were taken over by a small number of large breweries. Victoria, for example, had 116 separate breweries in 1870, but only 6 by 1960. By the 1990s only one remained—Carlton United Breweries, makers of Foster's Lager. However, small boutique brewers appeared in the 1980s as a countervailing trend.

From the 1960s, licensing hours expanded, and new types of drinking venues emerged, competing with the public houses. Public drinking is now just as likely to occur in wine bars and clubs, some of which are permitted to sell liquor until 3 A.M. or later. Although these venues are popular with young people, the "over-fifties" crowd is most likely to drink in leagues clubs, which are often sponsored by sporting organizations and are most numerous in New South Wales. These leagues clubs, and an increasing number of public houses, obtain their revenue from gambling facilities such as poker machines rather than just from the sale of alcohol.

The old temperance societies have been dwindling in recent years, but antidrug organizations, both state and private, continue to campaign against alcohol abuse and particularly against drunk driving. Throughout the 1970s and 1980s, the Australian states introduced drunk driving laws that included random Breathalyzer testing and strict (0.05) blood-alcohol limits for drivers. These laws have helped to reduce excessive alcohol consumption. Some campaigners against alcohol abuse have attempted to procure prohibitions against alcohol advertising, similar to those against tobacco advertising, but so far they have been unsuccessful.

Anna Blainey

See also: Barmaids (Australia); Drinking Sites and Culture (Australia); Foster's; Liquor Licensing (Australia); Wine; Woman's Christian Temperance Union (WCTU) (Australia); Women Publicans (Australia)

References

Blainey, A. E. "The 'Fallen' Are Every Mother's Children: The Woman's Christian Temperance Union's Campaigns for Temperance, Women's Suffrage and Sexual Reform in Australia, 1885–1905" (Ph.D. dissertation, La Trobe University, 2000).

Bollen, J. D. *Protestantism and Social Reform in New South Wales, 1890–1910.* Melbourne: Melbourne University Press, 1972.

Dingle, A. E. "'The Truly Magnificent Thirst': An Historical Survey of Australian Drinking Habits" in *Historical Studies.* 19, no. 75 (October 1980): 227–249.

Kirkby, D. *Barmaids: A History of Women's Work in Pubs.* Melbourne: Cambridge University Press, 1997.

Phillips, W. "'Six O'clock Swill': The Introduction of Early Closing of Hotel Bars in Australia" in *Historical Studies.* 19, no. 75 (October 1980): 250–266.

Roe, M. *Quest for Authority in Eastern Australia, 1835–1851.* Melbourne: Melbourne University Press, 1965.

Austria

The history of alcohol consumption and temperance in Austria is underdeveloped for many reasons. One important reason is the changing geopolitical nature of the country. The small republic of Austria, with its 8 million inhabitants, is only a creation of World War I, and even since 1918, it has not always remained within the same borders. Between 1938 and 1945, it was part of the Third Reich. Before 1918, it belonged to the core land of a multinational monarchy, called the Austrian Empire before 1867 and the Austrian-Hungarian Monarchy afterward. The basic entity "Austria" thus changed several times during the last two centuries.

Different geopolitical settings correlate with populations of varying size and demographic composition and also with different systems of administration and different modes of registration. For example, production and consumption data collected in different phases of the monarchy and of the republic are hardly comparable.

A last reason for the limits to knowledge is the low public and private attention paid to alcohol-related problems in Middle Europe. Research on this issue was consequently established late in Austria, was only weakly developed, and remained concentrated within a special discipline.

Per Capita Consumption and Beverage Preferences

The first calculations of per capita consumption of pure alcohol in the western part of the Austrian-Hungarian Monarchy—including Austria today, but, besides others, also the Czech Republic, Galicia, Slovenia, and Dalmatia—allocate Austria a middle range in the international statistics. The maximum was about 11 liters (2.9 U.S. gallons) between 1881 and 1910. Spirits represented more than 40 percent of the alcohol consumed. This has not always been the case.

Wine was the beverage mostly commonly drunk in the Austrian Empire in the centuries before, and per capita consumption was much higher. Sandgruber reports an average annual consumption of about 250 liters (66 U.S. gallons) of wine per capita in Vienna (the capital of the Austrian Empire as well as of the Austrian republic) in the sixteenth century, and still about 160 liters (42 U.S. gallons) in 1730. By 1800, wine consumption seems to have dropped to 100 to 120 liters (26 to 32 U.S. gallons) per capita, as its favored position in Viennese drinking patterns was taken over by beer.

Outside Vienna, beer consumption increased more slowly, from about 20 liters (5 U.S. gallons) per capita in 1800 to about 70 liters (18 U.S. gallons) by 1900 in the western part of the monarchy. But the beverage rapidly conquering the market in the nineteenth century was spirits. Spirits consumption, having increased since the sixteenth century, reached a peak in the middle of the nineteenth century, when about 10 liters (2.6 U.S. gallons) per capita were consumed. By the end of the nineteenth century, however, spirits consumption had already dropped. Wine lost its favored position in part because it became relatively expensive compared to beer and spirits, which increasingly were industrially produced.

Consumption patterns after 1900 are better documented. Consumption slightly decreased before 1914, and dropped remarkably during World War I. It did not recover during the so-called First Republic, that is, between 1918 and 1934, or during the Austrofascist regime (between 1934 and 1938, the Parliament was dissolved and Austria was ruled by an authoritarian regime). Between the world wars, per capita consumption only rose to about 6 liters of pure alcohol (1.6 U.S. gallons), that is, to about half of the amount drunk at the turn of the century. The most important reason for this development is to be found in the difficult economic situation of the republic, only one small successor of the Austrian-Hungarian Monarchy, and in the severe impact upon Austria of the Great Depression at the end of the 1920s.

In the so-called Second Republic (1945 until today), the Austrian economy and per capita consumption of pure alcohol both recovered quickly. At the beginning of the 1970s, the level of per capita consumption already had reached that of 1900, and it has, roughly speaking, remained at that level since, decreasing only slightly in the 1990s. In 2000, per capita consumption of pure alcohol was about 10.5 liters (2.8 U.S. gallons).

The share of pure alcohol consumed as spirits continued to drop, from about one-half at the beginning of the twentieth century to about one-seventh at the onset of the twenty-first century. The share of wine consumption showed a less simple development. It dropped further, to one-fourth, during the First Republic, due to the geopolitical changes on one hand (important wine growing areas of the Austrian-Hungarian Monarchy no longer belonged to the republic) and due to long-term effects of the vine diseases of the nineteenth century on the other. After World War II, the percentage of pure alcohol consumed as wine increased again to one-third, but since the 1980s, the tendency of wine's share has been to decrease. Beer, without question, is the "winner": For several decades its share has been about one-half, and its popularity is increasing.

Drinking Patterns and Temperance

Drinking patterns seem to have started to change in the eighteenth century. Until this time, heavy drinking and intoxication were part of everyday life as far as it could be afforded. Consequently, alcohol consumption mirrored the social hierarchy: Noblemen drank more than the priests, the bourgeois, and the farmers, and men drank much more than women. Alcoholic beverages were considered to be nutritious and were generally consumed with meals.

Heavy drinking and intoxication were already becoming less acceptable within the upper classes during the nineteenth century, and beer consequently became more fashionable. For different reasons, spirits consumption grew. Spirits became cheaper, and thus the new working class could afford them and use them to illuminate their hard and long-lasting working days and their never-changing scanty diet. Spirits consumption became an indicator for areas of distress.

The social distribution of drinking patterns thus became reversed in the nineteenth century and thereby promoted the development of temperance sentiments. The first temperance movement developed in the first half of the nineteenth century in the state of Tyrol, where the consumption of spirits was especially high and where the movement was supported by the Catholic Church. A few decades later, temperance activities developed in another part of the periphery of the Austrian-Hungarian Monarchy, in the kingdom of Galicia and Lodomeria, inclusive of the Grand Duchy of Cracow and the Duchy of Bukovina. This movement was also linked to the Catholic Church. The culmination of the temperance activities in this part of the monarchy was a draft submitted to the Austrian Parliament concerning a law by which measures to prevent inebriety in the above-mentioned states could be taken. After a short and vivid discussion and with minor changes, the draft, which disclosed rather openly nationalistic and anti-Semitic sentiments on the one hand and conservative characteristics on the other (protection of the economic privileges of the local nobles), became law in 1877.

The temperance activities of the bourgeois classes with links to the Catholic Church finally were concentrated in an association called Österreichischer Verein gegen Trunksucht (Austrian Association against Inebriety) at the end of the nineteenth century. It did not ask for the personal temperance of its members, but rather aimed at state measures against the misuse of alcoholic beverages; it never became particularly influential. It was only at the beginning of the twentieth century that those most concerned—the workers—themselves became active in temperance. In 1905, regional abstainer clubs of workers united in the Arbeiter-Abstinentenbund, which in the following two decades became the strongest and most influential temperance organization in Austria until today. It was part of the Socialist Party. Both were prohibited in 1934, but reorganized after World War II.

The Arbeiter-Abstinentenbund demanded abstinence from its members and aimed at prohibition. In accordance with the principles of the Socialist Party, this goal was to be achieved by democratic means. As in Sweden, every community should have the right to regulate alcohol distribution and consumption within its borders. Also in accordance with the principles of the Socialist Party, the Arbeiter-Abstinentenbund considered drunkards as diseased and therefore in need of treatment instead of punishment. The organization requested the establishment of a special treatment system and of state-paid cures. The culminating point of the Arbeiter-Abstinentenbund, as of the other temperance organizations with whom it collaborated within an umbrella organization, was 1923. After this time, political conflicts became stronger and split the different temperance organizations.

Though small in the number of its members, the Arbeiter-Abstinentenbund was quite influential, especially in "Red Vienna," the Austrian state ruled uninterruptedly by the Socialist Party between 1922 and 1934. The younger generation of workers became quite sober, and a special treatment system was established. The workers' temperance movement was supported by the famous leaders of the Socialists. Dr. Viktor Adler and Dr. Otto Bauer both became members and repeatedly emphasized the value of abstinence, though both argued that renunciation of alcohol was for the sake of the party and of political discipline, rather than for personal health. The well-known slogan was: "A drinking worker does not think, a thinking worker does not drink."

The temperance movements and their umbrella organization were rebuilt after World War II, but never regained their earlier social or political influence. Along with other interest groups, such as delegates of the trade unions and the alcohol producers, the temperance organizations were integrated into the Beirat für Alkoholfragen (Advisory Board for Alcohol Problems), established at the Ministry of Social Affairs in 1955. After

1971, the mandate of the board was expanded to include "other addictive substances" (especially illegal drugs) until it was dissolved in the beginning of the 1990s. The state's activities since the first half of the 1990s have been directed toward establishing a preventive structure focusing on youth.

The Arbeiter-Abstinentenbund was reorganized in 1974, when it got a new name and new aims. It was now called Aktion 0,0 Promille (Action 0.0 BAC [blood-alcohol content]), and its activities were restricted to the reduction of alcohol-related problems, especially drunk driving.

The development of attitudes toward drinking and of drinking and abstention patterns after World War II corresponds to the direction taken by public and private temperance activities. Drinking again became an everyday practice, especially among men, but the awareness of special alcohol-related problems has increased, and drinking has become increasingly separated from other activities, for instance driving and working. Abstention again became a rare attitude except among children and youth, who increasingly became the target of prevention activities, and who since the 1920s in fact have remained abstainers.

Production and Retail

Austria always has been mostly self-sustaining concerning alcoholic beverages. The climate allows the cultivation of grapes for both red and white wine, as well as the production of most ingredients of beer and a variety of spirits. The production of alcoholic beverages therefore has been an important branch of the economy and a reliable source of state income or an object of state protection and promotion. Consequently, most alcohol-related state regulations have been aimed at the different branches of the alcohol economy rather than at drinking habits, and the two types of controls were and continue to be strictly separated.

Beer production is the most industrialized branch of alcohol production, and the degree of concentration was exceptionally high in the nineteenth century. The Austrian brewery Dreher was the biggest one on the European continent. World War I, the economic problems of the First Republic, and the depression of 1929 had disastrous effects, but beer production recovered during the *Anschluß* (industrial production was promoted by the Third Reich) and during the Second Republic, though it did not regain the concentration and the position in international production that it held in the nineteenth century.

Wine has traditionally been produced on small, diversified farms. In the nineteenth century, Austrian wine production was strongly hit by vine diseases and still suffered their long-term effects until after World War I. In World War II, vineyards were destroyed because they became battlefields. During the Second Republic, wine production recovered, and wine quality improved continuously, especially after the so-called wine scandal of 1985, when it was discovered that antifreeze had been added to wine in order to produce cheap dessert wines. Though much more professional today than 100 years ago, wine production remains small-scale agrarian production.

Spirits production is partly agrarian and partly industrial, and the small-scale agrarian sector was traditionally protected against the industrial one by measures resembling an incomplete monopoly. During the Anschluß, the German Branntweinmonopolgesetz (Spirits Monopoly Law) was put in force, which protected agrarian production even more effectively than the Austrian regulations. The Branntweinmonopolgesetz was kept after 1945, but it had to be abolished when Austria joined the European Union in the first half of the 1990s.

The retailing of alcoholic beverages has never been very different from that of other commodities. Alcoholic beverages are sold in all food stores and in a variety of other outlets such as gasoline stations. Alcoholic beverages are served in all restaurants and bars without a special license. Historical research suggests that the number and variety of outlets were even higher in earlier centuries, but efforts to reduce their number and thereby restrict drinking and drunkenness were also more common. Additionally, more regulations existed previously to limit retail sales and on-premises consumption.

Alcohol-Related Problems, Alcohol Policy, and Research

Before 1800, numerous regional regulations were directed at alcohol-related problems, and quite a few of these regulations directly targeted consumption. In the sixteenth century, it was forbidden to encourage one's drinking companion to drink, and a few years later, drunkenness was prohibited and punished by a fine, imprisonment, or public chastisement. Drinking also was prohibited in connection with other activities, for instance steering a ship or carrying fire. The regulations were elaborated in the following two centuries.

During the nineteenth century, however, almost no regulations on alcohol consumption existed, and the few concerning alcohol-related problems were very mild. A prominent example is the penal code's view of intoxication as a mitigating circumstance. In accordance with this norm, a crime committed under intoxication was punished as a minor offense, and a minor offense committed under intoxication was not punished at all. In the twentieth century, these regulations were tightened up and supplemented by regulations redefining intoxication as an aggravating circumstance. In 1961, for example, the blood-alcohol content of drivers was restricted to 0.08 percent, in 1998 to 0.05 percent, and the respective sanctions were significantly increased and diversified.

Besides drunken driving, alcoholism became the alcohol-related problem attracting most state attention. At the end of the nineteenth century, few private sanatoria for inebriates had been established. Between the wars, a special public treatment system with in- and outpatient facilities was established in Vienna, which was partly closed by the Austrofascist regime and closed completely by the Nazis. It was rebuilt about 1960 and has spread to other Austrian states since then. In the 1950s, alcoholism was acknowledged as a disease by health insurers, who since then have paid for cures. Today there are about 800 beds for alcoholics, that is, about 10 beds for 100,000 inhabitants.

The treatment of alcoholism is part of psychiatry, and alcohol-related problems are defined and explained predominantly by this discipline. Alcohol research was established within psychiatry as late as 1972, and from the beginning, it was considered to be a part of addiction research. There are two small research centers attached to clinics for addicts today. Due to this scientific location, the separation of research into consumption and into alcohol-related problems has remained strong, although the preventive activities established during the last decade have promoted the placing of consumption and problems on a continuum.

Irmgard Eisenbach-Stangl

References

Eisenbach-Stangl, Irmgard. "The Beginnings of Galician and Austrian Alcohol Policy: A Common Discourse on Dependence" in *Contemporary Drug Problems.* 20, no. 4 (1995): 705–718.

———. *Eine Gesellschaftsgeschichte des Alkohols. Produktion, Konsum und soziale Kontrolle alkoholischer Rausch- und Genussmittel in Österreich 1918–1984.* Frankfurt: Campus, 1991.

Gehmacher, Johanna. "Das Glück der Nüchternheit" in *Familie, Arbeitsplatz oder Ort des Glücks?,* edited by Monika Bernold et al., 51–79. Wien: Picus, 1990.

Lehner, Oskar. "Drogenpolitik in Österreich, dargestellt am Beispiel der Alkoholgesetzgebung," vom 15. bis ins frühe 19. Jahrhund, in *Gedächtnisschrift Herbert Hofmeister,* edited by Werner Ogris and Walter H. Rechberger, 347–368. Wien: Manzsche-Verlags-und Universitätsbuchhandlung, 1996.

Sandgruber, Roman. *Bittersüße Genüsse. Kulturgeschichte der Rauschmittel.* Wien: Böhlau, 1986.

Wlassak, Rudolf. *Grundriss der Alkoholfrage.* Leipzig: Verlag von S. Hirzel, 1929.

B

Bacon, Selden Daskam (1909–1992)

Selden Daskam Bacon (1909–1992) is widely regarded as the father of American alcohol sociology, with the influence of his work extending worldwide. He served multiple roles as administrator, theoretician, and researcher. His key work is a compelling 1943 essay on the range of applications of sociological concepts and methods to the study of drinking, drunkenness, and the micro and macro sequelae of these behaviors. This monograph remains useful in its outline of research and conceptual projects, many of which are yet to be addressed.

A native of Pleasantville, New York, Bacon completed all of his formal education at Yale University, including a Ph.D. in sociology. After a brief tenure at Pennsylvania State University, Bacon returned to Yale as a faculty member in sociology, where he remained until 1962, moving to Rutgers University until his retirement in 1975.

Perhaps his greatest achievement occurred when he was an assistant professor at Yale. This was his persuasion of the leadership of the Laboratory of Applied Physiology (LAP) of Yale University that sociological studies were a critical component of an interdisciplinary approach to understanding alcohol, alcohol abuse, and alcoholism. These biomedical researchers were impressed by Bacon's study (with F. L. Roth) that linked wartime manpower shortages in Connecticut to the jailing of employable persons for drunkenness. This early demonstration of the utility of sociological methods for informing social policy, which led to a position for Bacon in the newly emerging Yale Center of Alcohol Studies, created a niche for sociological work within alcohol studies that has endured for sixty years.

Bacon's contributions to theory and research in alcohol studies include a sociological specification of the changes in role relationships that accompany progression into addictive drinking, the critical notion of the disjunction between sociocultural concepts of "drinking" and the alcohol consumption behaviors of alcoholics, and the importance of cultural context in the discontinuity of drinking behavior between college-student status and later adulthood. He and Robert Straus contributed a 1951 study that first established the distribution of alcohol problems across the social spectrum, challenging the previous belief that alcohol problems were concentrated among homeless men. This conception eventually became the foundation for much of the programming and public-education efforts of the National Institute on Alcohol Abuse and Alcoholism (NIAAA).

Bacon became a role model for later academicians through his extensive involvement as an administrator and change agent. He was one of the authors of the Yale Plan Clinics for outpatient treatment of alcoholism. He helped conceptualize and promote industrial alcoholism programs. He was the first chair of the Connecticut Commission on Alcoholism, and worked extensively in supporting the development of the National Council on Alcoholism and Drug Dependence (NCADD). Bacon was director of the Center of Alcohol Studies at Yale from 1950 to 1962, and continued in this role until 1975, after the Center moved to Rutgers. The move to Rutgers, which assured the survival of the center after hostile relationships formed at Yale, was largely brokered by Bacon.

Under Bacon's quarter-century leadership, the Yale/Rutgers Center played a vital role in institutionalizing a scientific and interdisciplinary approach to alcohol studies. The center also houses the premier U.S. journal in alcohol studies, the *Journal of Studies on Alcohol.* The center also pioneered the international documentation of alcohol-related research, a function more recently assumed by the NIAAA.

Bacon's early leadership in legitimizing the involvement of sociology in alcohol studies is represented today by the numerous sociologists whose research is supported by the NIAAA, and by organized sections dedicated to alcohol and drug research in the American Sociological Association and the Society for the Study of Social Problems.

Paul M. Roman

See also: Alcoholism; *Journal of Studies on Alcohol;* National Council on Alcoholism and Drug Dependence (NCADD); National Institute on Alcohol Abuse and Alcoholism (NIAAA); Rutgers Center of Alcohol Studies; Sociological Theories of Drinking and Temperance; Yale Center of Alcohol Studies

References

Bacon, Selden. "Alcoholics Do Not Drink" in *Annals of the American Academy of Political and Social Science.* 315 (1958): 55–64.

———. "The Process of Addiction to Alcohol: Social Aspects" in *Quarterly Journal of Studies on Alcohol.* 34 (1973): 1–27.

———. "Sociology and the Problems of Alcohol: Foundations for a Sociologic Study of Drinking Behavior" in *Quarterly Journal of Studies on Alcohol.* 4 (1943): 402–445.

Henderson, R. M., and Selden Bacon. *Drinking in College.* New Haven, CT: Yale University Press, 1953.

Straus, Robert, and Selden Bacon. "Alcoholism and Social Stability: A Study of Occupational Integration in 2,023 Male

Alcoholism Clinic Patients" in *Quarterly Journal of Studies on Alcohol.* 12 (1951): 231–260.

Baker, Purley Albert (1858–1924)

Purley Albert Baker (1858–1924) served as general superintendent of the Anti-Saloon League of America (ASLA) from 1903 to 1924, when, in failing health, he resigned. An Ohioan, Baker left a successful career as a preacher in local Methodist churches in 1896 to join the full-time staff of the league, first as superintendent of the Cleveland (Ohio) district, and in 1897, as superintendent of the Ohio Anti-Saloon League. He became general superintendent of the national league in 1903. Baker was thus the "commander in chief" of the league's successful quest for National Prohibition, although in 1916, he turned over most of the work to his protégé, Ernest Hurst Cherrington. Baker's vision was simple: that upon prohibition rested the success of civilization itself.

Educated in local and normal schools in southern Ohio, Baker brought teaching experience and a record of popular preaching and determined temperance agitation to his new posts in the league. An inspiring public speaker, at least to sympathetic audiences, Baker was also effective working with small groups. In helping league leaders reach decisions and providing both political knowledge and a steady hand in seeking the league's goals, he proved himself a skilled tactician, strategist, and executive in the dry cause. Prohibitionists generally revered Baker, just as opponents reviled him.

As general superintendent, Baker exercised considerable authority over the Anti-Saloon League. He appointed each state superintendent; the state superintendents collectively comprised a significant portion (the ratio varied as the league amended its constitution) of the Board of Trustees, the league's governing body. After 1909, Baker also controlled the state leagues' political strategy, determining centrally the timing for important prohibition campaigns. In exercising his authority, however, Baker, while always in control, was not completely dictatorial, choosing to negotiate policy and personnel matters with subordinate bodies. Nonetheless, he always demanded a coordinated, united front in the campaign against the liquor interests. "Reformers must preach a shut-fist Gospel," Baker told the 1906 league convention, "which develops within them a spirit of fight-righteous warfare, and when engaging the enemy they are in danger of engaging each other." He used prayer to overcome disagreements, but did not hesitate to fire men who disobeyed him. Subordinate league leaders understood and, even though they might have disagreed with the general superintendent on a subject, granted him his wishes. Nevertheless, Baker sometimes understood his own limitations. As a Northerner, he recognized the need to defer to advice from Southerners in the dry campaigns in that region.

Baker also kept a steady eye on the need to enlarge public support for prohibition. He used league resources to try to enlist support from both rural Americans and urban industrial workers, including recent immigrants. Baker's vision included harnessing modern publishing and advertising techniques to the cause. He also reached out to other reform groups.

Baker was most successful in the campaign to achieve prohibition, and much less successful as a leader thereafter, when the purpose of the league was less clear. Other executives were bitterly divided over the balance between law enforcement and educational strategies, and Baker could not keep them together amicably. In the end, months before his death, Baker sided with the faction seeking an emphasis on law enforcement.

K. Austin Kerr

See also: Anti-Saloon League of America (ASLA); Cherrington, Ernest Hurst

References

Blocker, Jack S., Jr. *Retreat from Reform: The Prohibition Movement in the United States, 1890–1913.* Westport, CT: Greenwood, 1976.

Chalfant, Harry Malcolm. *These Agitators and Their Idea.* Nashville, TN: Cokesbury Press, 1931.

Kerr, K. Austin. *Organized for Prohibition: A New History of the Anti-Saloon League.* New Haven, CT: Yale University Press, 1985.

Banana Wine

In several parts of Africa, the fruit of various banana species (members of the widespread family *Musa*) are crushed to extract a juice, which is used to produce a fermented beverage. In some areas of interlacustrine East Africa (that is, parts of modern Uganda, Tanzania, Rwanda, and Burundi), this is the principal fermented beverage. The use of bananas to produce beverage alcohol is reported on a smaller scale in Nigeria, Benin, and the Democratic Republic of Congo, but not in areas of banana cultivation elsewhere in the world. The beverage product is not infrequently described as "banana beer," a term that is perhaps misleading as to the process of production, which usually involves no brewing; banana wine is a more accurate term, since fermentation involves fruit sugars only.

Production Techniques

Production techniques have remained largely unchanged for the last hundred years. Ripening fruit are picked, and a degree of overripening is encouraged by piling them, sometimes in a pit into which heat from a fire is directed. The juice is then extracted from the fruit, either by treading upon them in a pit or basket, or by hand-squeezing, although the latter technique now seems uncommon. Where the bananas are trodden upon, the skins are not removed beforehand, but the bananas are mixed with a grass (in Uganda, usually spear grass, *Imperata cylindrica*) to which the pulped flesh and skins adhere, allowing the juice to run free and be collected. The juice is subject to a further rough filtering through grass and poured into a large vessel—a wooden trough, or a large pot or gourd—in which it is left to ferment, having been covered over with banana leaves and grass. Around 20 percent of this juice may be composed of fermentable sugars. In some areas, a handful of grains of fried red sorghum are added to the juice, a procedure explained as one that encourages fermentation; in practice, it is presumably yeasts, which survive in the fermenting vessel, that are primarily responsible for fermentation. Banana wine is produced in relatively warm areas, and the juice is considered ready for drinking in two or three days and spoils in around five days. The liquor is cloudy and thick, but has fewer suspended particles than grain beer. It may be drunk either through a straw or directly from a vessel and is served without any kind of watering down, and usually without blending. The alcohol content varies according to a number of factors; it has been recorded as high as 11 percent by volume, but it is likely that it is usually consumed before attaining this strength, at 5 or 6 percent.

Social Practices and Rituals

Banana wine played a prominent role in the ritual and social events of the major interlacustrine kingdoms of East Africa. Large amounts were consumed at the court of the king of Buganda, for example, and presenting banana wine to the king or to his representatives was an important demonstration of loyalty. The most prominent drinking was done by elder men, but the court in particular saw a substantial amount of drinking by women, both members of the royal family and ritual specialists; there are colorful reports of such drinking in the accounts of nineteenth-century travelers.

A man scoops out the mash of a home-brewed banana beer. (Kennan Ward/Corbis)

Production was, and still seems to be, mostly small-scale, and is usually on a household basis, using the fruit of banana plants owned by the household; though in some cases, a woman producing liquor for sale may buy bananas for this purpose, in order to establish unequivocally her ownership of the resulting liquor. Treading is the task of men, generally—a restriction explained in terms of the possibility of menstrual blood entering the juice should women do the treading. There have been some recent attempts in Uganda to make a bottled, stable banana wine for the market through a partial industrialization of production. The output of these ventures remains small at present. There are some other modern variations in small-scale production. Banana wine is used extensively as a basis for distillation in interlacustrine East Africa, and wine produced for this purpose does not have sorghum added to it before fermentation. The use of dried baker's yeast to accelerate fermentation has also become more common.

In the region around Mount Kilimanjaro in Tanzania, a slightly different kind of banana-based liquor called *mbege* is made. This involves the use of considerable quantities of germinated millet as well as bananas and an extended period of "cooking"; sugars from the grain as well as from the fruit seem to be involved in the fermentation. There is no information on the potency of this beverage, although it may be that the "banana wine" tested by Mosha, Wangabo, and Mhinzi in Dar es Salaam was actually mbege; that beverage had an average alcohol content of 2.0–3.5 percent.

The popularity of banana wine has, since the colonial period, given rise to periodic official alarms over the extent to which people concentrate on growing bananas for this purpose rather than as a foodstuff; the identification of particular varieties as being "beer bananas" has encouraged this alarm. The concern is probably misplaced—a typical example of the ability of alcohol to serve as a focus for a wider debate, which in this case concerns official suspicions that the populace is thriftless. Banana wine is an important item of local commerce. Banana varieties used for producing beverage alcohol may also be eaten—though people prefer not to—and there seems in fact to be a considerable element of change and innovation in the selection of varieties for alcohol production, with both sweet and starchy varieties being used for the purpose. Overall, the growing of "beer bananas" suggests a willingness to adapt to changing market circumstances, rather than rural indolence.

Justin Willis

See also: Africa, Central; Wine

References

Ashe, Robert P. *Two Kings of Uganda, or Life by the Shores of Victoria Nyanza.* London: Frank Cass, 1970.

Carlson, Robert. "Banana Beer, Reciprocity and Ancestor Propitiation among the Haya of Bukoba, Tanzania" in *Ethnology.* 29 (1990): 297–311.

Masefield, G. "The Production of Native Beer in Uganda" in *East African Agricultural Journal.* 10 (1944): 12–17.

Mosha, Donnati, J. Wangabo, and G. Mhinzi. "African Traditional Brews: How Safe Are They?" in *Food Chemistry.* 57 (1996): 205–209.

Mwesigye, Patrick, and Tom Okurut. "A Survey of the Production and Consumption of Traditional Alcoholic Beverages in Uganda" in *Process Biochemistry.* 30 (1995): 497–501.

Okafor, Noluka. "Traditional Alcoholic Beverages of Tropical Africa: Strategies for Scale-up" in *Process Biochemistry.* 25 (1990): 213–220.

Simmonds, Norman. *Bananas.* London: Longmans, 1959.

Band of Hope

The Band of Hope was one of the great Victorian and Edwardian organizations. Many of those who attended Bands of Hope in Sunday school or chapel remember the experience with affection. They were taught the temperance way of life and encouraged to sign the teetotal pledge. Band of Hope became a generic term for children's temperance organizations, and the title was used by many Protestant denominations for their children's branches. Millions of children belonged to Bands of Hope in the United Kingdom, and the movement spread to other countries. Even in the twenty-first century, Bands of Hope can be found in Australia and South Africa, although they have disappeared in Britain.

Beginnings

Beginning in 1833, a number of small children's temperance organizations were formed. It was, however, the Band of Hope that caught the imagination of the temperance movement, perhaps because of its simple but inspiring title. Debates surround the naming of the organization, but the balance of evidence suggests that it was Ann Jane Carlile (1775–1864) who coined the name Band of Hope. In 1847, Carlile and the Reverend Jabez Tunnicliff (1809–1865), a Baptist minister, were joint founders of the movement. Helped by the women's section of the Leeds Temperance Society, Leeds became an early stronghold. The Bands of Hope rapidly spread along the Leeds-Manchester axis, becoming another example of the importance of the north of England in the early-nineteenth-century temperance movement. In 1849, the Leeds' band claimed to have received over 4,000 pledges from affiliated bands.

Expansion

Bands quickly became an integral part of the temperance movement as Nonconformists embraced the concept of educating young children in temperance. The Band of Hope strategy was to teach children to abstain from intoxicating liquors from an early age so that they would become adult abstainers. Unlike the Nonconformists, the Roman Catholic Church rejected the name Band of Hope but, without the name, organized similar temperance societies for children under the auspices of the women's guild.

In the nineteenth century, women's sphere was to care for the family and home, especially to ensure that the family was taught purity and the Christian way of life. It might appear that the bands would fall within this women's sphere, but although women were active in the movement, it was usually by assisting male teachers. Women typically taught only the youngest children, and they did not participate in decision making. When women submitted papers to annual conferences, men read the papers for them.

Clara Lucas Balfour (1808–1878) challenged men's role as teachers in bands. She argued that women should undertake this role. She believed that women were central to the battle against alcoholic beverages. They were indispensable in teaching children the temperance message as well as training them in a Christian way of life. Balfour contributed papers to Band of Hope conferences as early as 1857. She is best known for her popular temperance stories such as *Morning Dew-Drops* and *The Garland of Water Flowers.*

The Bands of Hope targeted the children of parents who had aspiration for education and a secure future. For instance, the teetotal pioneer Joseph Livesey (1794–1884) supported the Band of Hope movement, but not for the desperately poor. He wanted to develop self-reliant workingmen able to follow temperance as a route to self-improvement. He stressed that parents should lead their children to temperance rather than assuming that they would, unguided, become adult abstainers. Livesey disagreed with most Band of Hope activists in his opposition to any denominational affiliation for individual bands.

After the north led the way, other parts of the country quickly followed. After John H. Esterbrooke (1817–1897) held meetings in the lecture hall of the National Temperance Society, and later at the Pear Street Mission, he founded the first London Band of Hope in 1848. In the following year, Esterbrooke published a pamphlet on how to establish, run, and sustain branches so that others could emulate his work. When a national organization was formed in 1851, the first general secretary was a London printer, Stephen Shirley (1820–1897). In 1855, the London Band of Hope Union was established to promote Bands of Hope in the capital.

Throughout the nineteenth century, the movement flourished. In particular, branches were established in Nonconformist chapels. By 1889, there were over 16,000 societies in the United Kingdom that claimed over 2 million young members.

Retaining Members

There is no doubt that children and their parents were attracted to the movement. The annual outings were a great draw for membership, as were the tea meetings, newspapers, tracts, and the music that were provided. For instance, Bands of Hope opened many opportunities to children between the ages of six and sixteen who enjoyed music. They offered music lessons and a chance to play in one of the many orchestras and bands that were formed. Choirs and bands gave children a chance to travel locally and nationally. Festivals and competitions widened horizons, sometimes with a long journey, perhaps to the Free Trade Hall in Manchester, Saint George's in Liverpool, or the Crystal Palace, Sydenham, in London. There were also trips organized by local temperance societies to seaside resorts in the summer months.

The meetings of the Bands were ritual: They commenced with a temperance hymn, prayers, and the chairman's speech. Pledge signing might follow the music, readings, and recitations. The link between Bands of Hope and Sunday schools helped to maintain regular attendance, as did the appointment of women who visited homes, distributed tracts, recruited new members, and won back strays.

Onward, the first of many Band of Hope newspapers intended for children, began publication in 1865. The paper included music, moral tales, stories, and poetry aimed at reinforcing the temperance way of life. The paper emphasized the need to be on guard against temptations and keep on the straight and narrow. Well-known temperance luminaries such as Clara Lucas Balfour contributed to *Onward.*

Late Nineteenth Century and Early Twentieth Century

The radical changes in the teaching of children during the last three decades of the century did not bypass the children's temperance movement. The introduction of the Education Act in 1870, which laid the foundation for universal elementary education for all, changed the way in which those involved in teaching children could work. The act opened up another route to influence children. Seeing this as a challenge, the Scientific Temperance Instruction (STI) movement attempted to introduce temperance into the classroom. Initially, men were hired to teach STI, but this was expensive because school boards required trained teachers. By the end of the century, temperance societies were lobbying for the inclusion of STI in the curriculum. The National British Women's Temperance Association (NBWTA) and the Women's Total Abstinence Union drafted a curriculum based on STI by the American Mary Hunt. They believed that formalized STI was a way to reach a much larger audience. The disbanding of the school boards in 1903, which had included women members, meant that societies had to redirect their efforts. One method was to award temperance prizes to children for good results in Bands of Hope and Sunday schools. Most prizes were temperance or "moral" novels.

By the turn of the century, the Band of Hope movement claimed that they had access to 10 percent of the British population, and that there were over 10,000 bands that met weekly. A school "lecturer" service was available in many parts of the country, and Band of Hope organizations printed teaching materials for Sunday schools.

The movement started to decline following the first world war, but Sunday schools in Methodist denominations sustained the bands. The second world war saw a drastic decline in numbers, but for a time, some bands continued. For instance, Bradford in Yorkshire hosted the 1951 Band of Hope conference. Cynics suggested that children were sent to the meetings of bands to give parents time for themselves and not to learn about temperance.

The Band of Hope tradition continues in Hope UK, a Christian charity providing education and training for parents, churches, and voluntary youth organizations with focus on drugs and alcohol abuse. Hope UK estimates that in early-twenty-first-century Britain there might be a million people alive who had belonged to a Band of Hope, mostly in the interwar years.

Margaret Barrow

See also: Carlile, Ann Jane; Livesey, Joseph; National British Women's Temperance Association (NBWTA); Nonconformists (United Kingdom); Women's Total Abstinence Union (WTAU)

References

Doern, Kristin G. "Equal Questions: The 'Woman Question' and the 'Drink Question' in the Writings of Clara Lucas Balfour, 1808–1878" in *Women, Religion and Feminism in Britain, 1750–1900,* edited by Sue Morgan. Basingstoke, UK: Palgrave Macmillan, 2002.

Harrison, Brian. *Drink and the Victorians: The Temperance Question in England 1815–72.* 2d ed. Keele: Keele University Press, 1994.

Hope UK website. http://www.hopeuk.org.

Shiman, Lilian Lewis. "Band of Hope Movement: Respectable Recreation for Working Class Children" in *Victorian Studies.* 7 (1973): 49–74.

———. *Crusade against Drink in Victorian England.* London: Macmillan, 1988.

Winskill, Peter Turner. *The Temperance Movement and Its Workers. A Record of Social, Moral, Religious, and Political Progress.* 4 vols. London: Blackie, 1891–1892.

———. *Temperance Standard Bearers of the Nineteenth Century: A Biographical and Statistical Temperance Dictionary.* Liverpool: author, 1897–1898.

Barker, Thomas Halliday (1818–1889)

Thomas Halliday Barker (1818–1889) was a founding member and the influential secretary of the prohibitionist United Kingdom Alliance (UKA) from shortly after its organization in 1853 until his retirement in 1883. Born in Peterborough, the son of a cabinetmaker and upholsterer, Barker was first employed as a clerk for a wine and spirits merchant. As a young man, he suffered from poor health, and this probably encouraged his conversion to teetotalism, which occurred after listening to a lecture by John Cassell in 1837. In 1843, Barker caused a scandal at his Wesleyan chapel in Lincoln by his refusal to drink fermented wine in the sacrament. He appealed for support to Frederic Richard Lees, then editor of the *British Temperance Advocate.* Barker left Lincoln for Manchester in 1844 and eventually became an accountant and commission agent, with an office at Princess Street, Manchester.

Barker received the news of the Maine Law for statewide prohibition with enthusiasm and was a founding member of the UKA, formally established in June 1853 following private meetings at the home of Alderman William Harvey of Salford. It was Barker who drafted the constitution and declaration of principles for the new organization. His talent was for administration and written propaganda rather than the platform speaking. He was employed by the alliance as its salaried secretary, well paid at £500 a year. Tireless in this role, he was described by his contemporary W. E. Adams as "absolutely absorbed in his work." Another contemporary, F. R. Lees, emphasized his tenacity of purpose. Through his correspondence, he helped win the support of figures such as Sir W. C. Trevelyan (who bequeathed him £250 in 1879), Sir Wilfrid Lawson, and Lord Brougham. The personal friend of many temperance leaders in Britain, he also built friendships with leaders in the United States, such as Neal Dow (after whom he named one of his sons), E. C. Delavan, and Lloyd Garrison. He closely followed events in the United States and became a founder of the Union and Emancipation Society.

Barker was a vegetarian as well as a teetotaler. He served on the committee of the Manchester and Salford Vegetarian Association in the 1850s, and, as shown in letters published in the *Dietetic Reformer* (April 1868), was instrumental in the radical F. W. Newman's conversion to vegetarianism. Barker contributed to F. R. Lees's *Truth-Seeker* (1845–1846), as well as to the *Temperance Spectator* and other temperance journals, and published several prohibitionist pamphlets. He also published a vegetarian tract, *Thoughts, Facts and Hints on Human Dietetics* (4th ed., 1879). About 1844, he married Millicent Bates, the daughter of a Lincolnshire farmer, and they had four sons. His three surviving sons emigrated to California. Worn out by his work, Barker undertook a tour of the Middle East and a trip to the United States and Canada in the company of William Hoyle. These travels failed to restore Barker to good health, so in 1883, he resigned from his alliance position to become consulting secretary. Never well again, he died at his home near Manchester on 26 June 1889.

James Gregory

See also: Bible Wine; Dow, Neal; Hoyle, William; Lawson, Sir Wilfrid; Lees, Frederic Richard; Maine Law; United Kingdom Alliance (UKA); Vegetarianism and the Anti-Tobacco Movement (United Kingdom)

References

Adams, W. E. *Memoirs of a Social Atom.* New York: Augustus M. Kelley Publishers, 1968 [1903]: 387.

Alliance News. 5 July 1889: 530.

Dietetic Reformer. April 1868: 33–40.

Harrison, Brian. *Dictionary of British Temperance Biography.* Coventry: The Society for the Study of Labour History. Aids to Research, no. 1. *Bulletin Supplement,* 1973: 7.

Barmaids (Australia)

Women's involvement in brewing and selling beer (as alewives) was well known in England and Europe in the Middle Ages. As the science and trade of brewing grew in complexity, men gradually replaced women as brewers, but serving beer remained available as women's work in inns and alehouses. In the late eighteenth and early nineteenth centuries, this work became a distinct occupation: "barmaid." The social mores and labor practices that developed thereafter in Britain provided strong parallels with—and the cultural background of—the occupation in colonial Australia in the nineteenth century.

In an industry that has always been heavily regulated, changes in the licensing laws could affect the definition of the work and the conditions under which it was performed. When inns and alehouses in England were also the homes of the licensee, customers were guests, and refreshments were served by the host and the host's family at long, communal tables. Beer was carried from the cellar in large jugs and poured for the guests. This work was frequently done by women. The introduction of counters transformed this interior design of public houses. Now guests were separated from their host by a large barrier and, in turn, they ceased to be guests and became customers. However, while elements of this old relationship remained for the licensee/owner of a public house catering to travelers, the rise of wage labor in towns and cities altered the employment experience of staff serving behind the bar.

Being a barmaid was a highly gender-specific occupation in Britain. Although men also worked in public houses as barmen, the skills required of each were differentiated. Women found ready employment if they were attractive and well dressed, and by the middle of the nineteenth century, this physical attractiveness was becoming the prime attribute of the barmaid. Yet the work itself was a superior form of domestic service, and most of the women seeking work behind the bar were former domestic servants who saw the opportunity to improve their chances. Bar work offered better wages than either domestic service or any other similar work. Bar work was categorized as "unskilled"; it was not a trade but a service occupation, and the skills required were those associated with other service occupations such as shop assistant. It also had attributes similar to the work of acting because the space behind the counter (the bar) became like a stage where the bar staff "performed" their skills.

The theatricality of the bar was at its height at the close of the nineteenth and turn of the twentieth century, when bar fixtures were luxuriously designed to frame and reflect the fantasy world that had "the barmaid" at its center. Mirrors, glass, polished brass, wood paneling, and beautiful women tantalized and mimicked the world of the theater, but the reality of that world for the women working there was a different story. Long hours in stuffy, poorly ventilated, smoke-filled rooms meant fatigue and poor health. Publicans themselves had the highest mortality rate of any employer group. Furthermore, the work could be dangerous. Hazards included broken glass, slippery floors, and violent customers.

Fueled by temperance advocates and assisted by labor reformers, a sustained campaign began to get women removed from bars, but it only succeeded in some jurisdictions. These, notably, were in the Australasian colonies where the occupation of barmaid had grown along with its advance in England. As many of the colonists were themselves immigrants from English, Scottish, and Irish cities, the customs and practices of drinking and of serving alcohol in many ways followed traditional practices. But in the colonies, the demands of accommodating and refreshing travelers led to modifications to the English-style alehouse, and the absence of other forms of work made hotel keeping a very attractive option for colonial women. Pubs proliferated in country areas and cities alike, and by 1890, running a hotel was the major avenue of self-employment for women. This meant that young women working behind the bar could also expect to become licensees in their own right if they saved enough. Hotel keeping was a means to economic independence from wage labor, and it gave women working there a certain autonomy. Wages in the colonies were high and barmaids were paid well.

Increasing numbers of young women moved into the occupation, but from the mid-1880s, there were more strident calls to prevent them from so doing. Restrictions began to be imposed on the ages at which they could work, and in the early twentieth century, at least two states—Victoria and South Australia—following the example of New Zealand, legislated to ban any further employment and to require the registration of those already working. This ban remained in force until the late 1960s.

By then, Australian drinking customs, which had taken on their own peculiar pattern known as "the six o'clock swill," were being reviewed and reformed. Early closing, introduced at roughly the same time as the restrictions on barmaids, had led to a highly gender-segregated drinking culture where the work of women took on even greater symbolic meaning. Barmaids became like a national icon as beer drinking became identified with Australian masculinity. The skills required of barmaids were even more akin to running a house as they kept the premises clean and catered to the desires of their thirsty "boys." As this era came to an end, barmaids disappeared as a distinct occupational category. Equal pay, credentials obtained in hospitality training, and the increasing transience of the labor force brought new meaning to the relationship between customers and bar staff and introduced the gender-neutral language of "bar attendant."

Diane Kirkby

See also: Australia; Barmaids (England); Drinking Sites and Culture (Australia); Liquor Licensing (Australia); Woman's Christian Temperance Union (WCTU) (Australia); Women Publicans (Australia)

References

Bailey, Peter. "Parasexuality and Glamour: The Victorian Barmaid as Cultural Prototype" in *Gender and History.* 2 (Summer 1990): 148–169.

Bennett, Judith. "The Village Ale-Wife: Women and Brewing in Fourteenth-Century England" in *Women and Work in Pre-Industrial Europe,* edited by Barbara Hanawalt, 20–36. Bloomington: Indiana University Press, 1986.

Joint Committee on the Employment of Women as Barmaids. *The Employment of Women as Barmaids.* London: King and Son, 1905.

Kirkby, Diane. *Barmaids: A History of Women's Work in Pubs.* Cambridge: Cambridge University Press, 1997.

Barmaids (England)

Women have served drinks to the public in England for a long time. The wives, daughters, and other female relatives of the owners worked in alehouses, taverns, and inns. The modern English pub or public house and the barmaids that work there are a product of the Industrial Revolution and can first be recognized in the gin palaces of the early nineteenth century. The barmaids in these pubs were not necessarily family members of the publicans.

The Industrial Revolution decreased the costs of production and distribution of alcoholic drinks. At the same time, the increase in urbanization resulted in visits to pubs being the main recreational pastime for many men. With many rural men moving to cities, young women who might otherwise have married and settled down with these men also moved to the cities and took jobs as barmaids, seamstresses, nursery maids, laundresses, and shop girls.

The barmaid had a significant role in the literature and art of the nineteenth century. She was portrayed as an attractive and glamorous figure that created a jovial atmosphere in the pub, smiling at the customers and flirting with them. She was seen as ruling the pub from behind the bar. No doubt many men who went to bars did see barmaids as they were portrayed in fiction and frequented bars where they found barmaids to be attractive.

Barmaids were mostly young single women in their early twenties. The publicans for whom they worked usually provided them with board and lodging (living-in system). The hours of work were very long, ten or more hours per day and six or seven days per week. In addition to serving drinks, barmaids cleaned up the pub and helped with the chores in the publicans' household. The wages that barmaids received for this work were quite low, ranging from six to fifteen shillings per week—even lower than wages for barmen.

In the latter half of the nineteenth century, several movements for social reform relating to barmaids occurred. Many people thought that the proper role for women was at home—as wives and mothers—and believed at the very least women should not work at jobs perceived to put them in physical and moral danger. There were therefore attempts to prohibit women from working as acrobats, circus girls, florists, mine pit-brow workers, and barmaids.

Future Labour Party leader and Prime Minister J. Ramsay MacDonald and his wife Margaret MacDonald of the Women's Labour League were prominent leaders in the movement to "abolish barmaids." They believed that men were the natural breadwinners and that women working outside the home robbed men of job opportunities and reduced their wages. Temperance advocates sought to end the drink trade altogether and, in the interim, at least prevent women from working as barmaids. Encouraged by Glasgow, which in 1902 prohibited the employment as barmaids of women unrelated to publicans, a vigorous campaign was mounted by Margaret MacDonald; the National British Women's Temperance Association (NBWTA), led by Rosalind Howard, Countess of Carlisle; the Women's Total Abstinence Union, led by M. E. Docwra; the Church of England Temperance Society; the United Kingdom Alliance (UKA); the National Temperance Federation; and the Male Waiters Union. They published handbooks, pamphlets, and newspaper articles and petitioned legislators to remove barmaids from such work on moral and economic grounds. They argued that only 27,000 women worked as barmaids, and hence abolishing barmaids would not inconvenience too many women.

The drink trade had a vested interest in opposing the movement to abolish barmaids. The drink trade argued that the census figure of 27,000 barmaids was wrong and estimated that there were about 100,000 barmaids. The second group that countered the campaign to abolish barmaids included women trade unionists and "industrial suffragists" (Northern England Women's Suffrage Association) who believed that enfranchisement would strengthen working women's positions. Prominent among this group were Eva Gore-Booth, Esther Roper, and Sarah Dickenson. Forming the Barmaids Political Defence League, they galvanized barmaids into action. They held rallies and led barmaids in a deputation to the home secretary, Herbert Gladstone, asking him to withdraw Clause 20 of the licensing bill of 1908 that would have endangered barmaids' employment.

The opponents of barmaids were defeated, and the licensing bill that the House of Commons approved in 1908 had no provision to restrict women's employment as barmaids. The victory of the barmaids removed the one issue over which a large number of barmaids were successfully organized. From the late nineteenth century to the eve of the first world war, all attempts to unionize barmaids were failures. After World War I, the special attention given to barmaids ended, and the occupation became not very different from other women's occupations.

Padma Manian

See also: Barmaids (Australia); Carlisle, Countess of (Rosalind Howard); Church of England Temperance Society (CETS); Labour Party (United Kingdom); National British Women's Temperance Association (NBWTA); National Temperance Federation (NTF); Publicans (England); Pubs and Beerhouses (United Kingdom); United Kingdom Alliance (UKA); Women Publicans (Australia); Women's Total Abstinence Union (WTAU)

Reference

Padmavathy, V. [later Padma Manian]. "The English Barmaid, 1874–1914: A Case Study of Unskilled and Non-Unionized Women Workers" (Ph.D. dissertation, Miami University, 1989).

Bass

The success of its India Pale Ale made Bass, Ratcliff and Gretton the premier British brewer from the 1860s until well into the twentieth century. Complacent management then weakened the company, and by the 1950s it had faded badly. Successive mergers with Mitchells and Butlers in 1961 and Charrington United Breweries in 1967 created the biggest of the "Big Six" brewers that dominated the British industry for nearly thirty years. In the wake of government intervention, the firm sold its beer brands, breweries, and most of its pubs in the last decade of the twentieth century, while buying international hotel chains. The company took the name Six Continents in 2001, by which time it was solely a hotel and pub owner.

Founding his brewery in 1777, William Bass enjoyed early success as a mercantile brewer, trading through Hull and the Baltic ports. International fame came under William's grandson Michael Thomas Bass II, who was senior partner in Bass, Ratcliff and Gretton for half a century. In the mid-1870s, the company was briefly the largest brewer in the world, with an output close to 1.5 million hectoliters (39.6 million U.S. gallons) from three breweries in Burton on Trent, backed by a network of agencies and stores. A feature of the massive 140-acre Burton complex was the sixteen miles of private railway track for moving raw materials and beer around the town. Astute management ensured that growth continued to the end of the century (by which time the company was making nearly 2.4 million hectoliters [63.4 million U.S. gallons], 4 percent of Great Britain's beer) and brought stability in the difficult years for brewers leading up to World War I. In 1926, the company merged with neighbor Worthington, although independent operation of the two companies continued for many years thereafter. Conservative attitudes came to epitomize a company that was slow to adapt to commercial and technological change in the industry. An acerbic comment in the *Economist* (19 September 1964) was particularly apt in the case of Bass, Ratcliff and Gretton: "Traditionalist, paternalistic, inbred, secretive—Britain's brewing industry slumbered through the nineteen fifties . . . A picturesque dinosaur." A much needed shake-up of the company came through merger with the Birmingham brewer Mitchells and Butlers, which brought with it Alan Walker, a forceful reforming managing director untainted by long years in the brewing industry. Even more usefully, Mitchells and Butlers had a significant estate of tied pubs, making up for Bass's weakness in this important area.

Charrington

Charrington United Breweries was the creation of Edward Plunket Taylor, who had built up Canadian Breweries through acquisition in the 1930s and 1940s, and used the same tactic in Britain in the late 1950s, buying predominantly small northern breweries as potential vehicles for his lager brand, Carling Black Label. Attempts to merge with bigger regional brewers foundered on Taylor's status as an outsider in the eyes of the British industry's leaders, who instead took fright and merged with each other. Nonetheless, Taylor's company, United Breweries, had 2,800 pubs by the time it merged with the long-established London brewer Charrington in 1962 to place it third, in terms of numbers of pubs owned, among the country's brewers. Other acquisitions followed, notably J and R Tennent of Glasgow in 1963, before the formation of Bass Charrington in 1967 created a truly national company with 10,320 pubs. Strict control from the top and through the hierarchy was the defining characteristic of the company over the next thirty-five years. This approach may have been a factor in the failure of the new 4 million hectoliters (106 million U.S. gallons) per year brewery completed in 1975 at Runcorn in Cheshire and it closed in 1991 after years of industrial strife. But the hierarchical control also produced a company that performed better than its rivals. It was not that top management was any more sure-footed than the management of its competitors, but it was relatively consistent and focused. Bass (the shortened name was adopted from 1979) was among the most beer-oriented of the Big Six, with only minor diversions into ownership of wine merchants, bingo halls, and betting shops. The company's market share of beer in the United Kingdom increased steadily, reaching 23 percent by 1985, against the 13 percent of its nearest rival, Allied Breweries.

Goodbye to All That

The 1990s brought a complete change in the company. Following the Beer Orders of December 1989, which resulted in big brewers having to choose between being pub owners or brewers with reduced tied estates, Bass elected to keep its breweries and scaled down its pubs. The company also greatly increased its hotel ownership through the purchase of Holiday Inns for £1.25 billion in August 1989. In 1995, Bass ceased to be the biggest UK brewer when, in a surprise decision, the government allowed Scottish and Newcastle Breweries (S&N) to buy Courage, creating a company with an approximate 30 percent market share.

An attempt to regain the top spot through the takeover of ailing Carlsberg-Tetley was blocked by the government in June 1997, and Bass's enthusiasm for brewing waned thereafter. In February 1998, it bought Inter-Continental Hotels for £1.75 billion. In June 2000, the company's brewing interests were sold to Interbrew for £2.3 billion, a figure that reflected the strength of the major brands, Carling (Britain's best-selling beer), Bass (the biggest imported ale in the United States), Tennents, and Caffreys. Bass reduced its pub chain by one-third to just over 2,000 mainly branded houses in February 2001, purchased the Posthouse hotel group in April, and changed its name to Six Continents in June of that year. The Belgian company Interbrew, which had taken over Whitbread's breweries only a month before it acquired Bass's breweries, was subsequently required to reduce its stake in the United Kingdom beer market. After much wrangling and a legal challenge to the government's ruling, Interbrew eventually sold the former Bass breweries located in England (including the original brewery in Burton) and the Carling and Worthington brands to the U.S. brewer Coors for £1.2 billion in February 2002. Interbrew retained the Tennents brewery, a brewery in Northern Ireland, and the brand name Bass.

Raymond G. Anderson

See also: Allied Breweries; Beer; Beer Orders (United Kingdom); Carling Brewery; Carlsberg; Coors, Adolph, Brewing Company; Courage Brewery; Interbrew; Pubs and Beerhouses (United Kingdom); Scottish & Newcastle Breweries Limited

References

Avis, Anthony. *The Brewing Industry, 1950–1990.* Norwich: privately published, 1997.

Economist. 19 September 1964: 3.

Gourvish, Terry R., and Richard G. Wilson. *The British Brewing Industry, 1830–1980.* Cambridge: Cambridge University Press, 1994.

Hawkins, Kevin H. *A History of Bass Charrington.* Oxford: privately published, 1978.

Owen, Colin C. *The Greatest Brewery in the World: A History of Bass, Ratcliff & Gretton.* Chesterfield: Derbyshire Record Society, 1992.

Beecher, Lyman (1775–1863)

Lyman Beecher (1775–1863) was one of the best known and most controversial preachers in nineteenth-century United States. A vocal advocate in the temperance movement, he believed a civic morality was indispensable in the preservation of a republican form of government. Born 12 October 1775 in New Haven, Connecticut, Beecher was educated at Yale. It was there that he came under the influence of Timothy Dwight and was ordained a Presbyterian minister in 1799. He served churches in East Hampton, Long Island, and Litchfield, Connecticut (1810), before becoming pastor of Boston's Hanover Church in 1826. In 1833, Beecher became president of Lane Theological Seminary in Cincinnati, Ohio, where he trained future church leaders who held many of the same positions that he did on issues of temperance and abolition.

Lyman Beecher (1775–1863) (Dictionary of American Portraits)

In the early 1800s, Beecher believed that his country was in the midst of a crisis. Alcoholism, poverty, illiteracy, and other social ills seemed to be on the rise, while church attendance was slipping. He believed "[w]e may form free constitutions, but our vices will destroy them; we may enact laws, but they will not protect us." Only a virtuous citizenry could save the nation. By the second decade of the nineteenth century, he was actively preaching against excessive drinking and the vices it promoted. The six sermons that he preached in the fall of 1825 and published the next year had the most influence. Beecher believed that the next generation would accomplish the "banishment of ardent spirits from the list of lawful articles of commerce." Although not the first person to raise the possibility of outlawing the consumption of spirits and far from original, his voice was the most powerful and articulate on the subject. He proclaimed, "Almost the entire amount of national ignorance and crime is the offspring of intemperance. Throughout the land, the intemperate are hewing down the pillars, and undermining the foundations of our national edifice." He demanded that those listening to him engage in a new, vigorous attack on alcohol by voluntary organizations. People had to address the social problems in their neighborhoods by alleviating poverty and preventing alcohol abuse. He urged his listeners to increase the number of temperance societies and fashion them into a national organization. His sermons and tracts were partly responsible for the founding of the American Society for the Promotion of Temperance (American Temperance Society [ATS]) in February 1826. Although Beecher himself was not present, at least sixteen of his associates were present as delegates, and this new organization supported Beecher's position.

Lyman Beecher's importance to the temperance movement did not end with his public message but continued in the lives of his thirteen children, with Harriet, Catherine, Charles, Edward, Thomas, and Henry Ward being the most famous. Although better known in other areas of moral reform, they pursued their father's vision of a "benevolent empire" and were involved in the temperance movement. When Beecher died in Brooklyn on 10 January 1863, a common joke in the country was, "This country is inhabited by saints, sinners, and Beechers."

T. Jason Soderstrum

See also: American Temperance Society (ATS)

References

Beecher, Lyman. *Autobiography.* Cambridge: Belknap Press of Harvard University Press, 1961.
Harding, Vincent. *A Certain Magnificence: Lyman Beecher and the Transformation of American Protestantism, 1775–1863.* Brooklyn, NY: Carlson Publishing, 1991.
Snyder, Stephen H. *Lyman Beecher and His Children: The Transformation of a Religious Tradition.* Brooklyn, NY: Carlson Publishing, 1991.

Beer

"Brewing involves the warm aqueous extraction (mashing) of ground barley malt (often supplemented by other sources of carbohydrate) followed by separation of the soluble extract (wort), boiling with hops and fermentation by yeast to give a complex alcoholic solution which is clarified and sold as a sparkling beverage (beer) with an ethanol content of ca. 3–10 percent by volume." This recent definition by R. G. Anderson (2000) is meant to describe the brewing process in the twenty-first century, but it serves almost as well to describe the essentials of the brewing process in the eighteenth century (with the proviso that there would have been less emphasis on clarity and sparkle in the 1700s). However, this unchangeability in the brewing process masks massive changes in the spread, scale, organization, economic importance, technology, and scientific understanding of brewing, and in the social function and nature of beer. Three hundred years ago, brewing was a domestic or small-scale commercial activity, producing an essential element of diet for the agrarian population of Northern and Central Europe. Now, it is an industry dominated by large companies supplying branded recreational beverages worldwide.

In 1700, domestic brewing still accounted for well over half of the beer produced. Commercial brewing was confined to taverns and small breweries that produced a wide selection of beers for local consumption. The industrialization of brewing began in the eighteenth century in London, where increased urbanization and concentrated population growth provided a ready market for beer produced on a large scale. By 1800, the largest London breweries were producing over 300,000 hectoliters (7,930,000 U.S. gallons) a year of their specialist beer, porter. During the nineteenth century, other major brewing centers arose: notably, Burton on Trent, Munich, and Milwaukee. With burgeoning per capita consumption by the urban lower classes, economies of scale prevailed, and the number of small breweries declined. Beer became more consistent in quality through improved control and better technology. The industry made increasing contributions to government revenue through taxation and helped to fuel the economy through the increased employment of capital and labor.

The nineteenth century saw temperance campaigners turn their attentions to beer for the first time. In Britain, the United States, Scandinavia, Canada, Australia, and New Zealand, attacks on the industry gained momentum, but did not prevent the increasing consumption of beer. The predominant style of beer changed in the nineteenth century. Bottom-fermented, cold-produced "lager" beer was little known outside Bavaria until the 1840s, but this type of beer, particularly the straw-colored variant developed in Pilsen, had replaced heavier top-fermented, warm-produced beer in most of Europe and the United States within fifty years. The United Kingdom was largely impervious to lager but nonetheless underwent its own beer style change toward lighter beers, with porter decreasing in popularity concomitant with a rise in mild and pale ales and, in the last decades of the century, less heavily hopped, quickly matured beers. By the mid-1880s, Germany had overtaken the United Kingdom as the world's largest producer of beer.

The first world war had a profound effect on brewing in Europe. Raw material prices and duties rose steeply, and production volumes collapsed. After the war, following a brief spurt in growth, output remained flat as a result of high beer prices, unprecedented unemployment, economic calamities, and changes in public leisure spending patterns, which all influenced sales. The United States had become the leading brewing nation on the eve of war but faced thirteen years of National Prohibition from 1920. Stagnation continued in Europe until the late 1950s when, as prosperity returned, consumption started to rise consistently. Similar increases were seen in the United States and Australia, and the people of Southern Europe, South America, and Asia took to beer in significant numbers for the first time. After 1980, output declined in much of Western Europe, North America, and the antipodes, but worldwide sales continued to rise. Consolidation led to domination by a few large firms in many countries as regional breweries faded, while, paradoxically, tiny craft breweries sprung up to cater for a discerning minority market. The largest brewers sought to become international and then global suppliers, building huge breweries

A man drinks beer beneath a sign advertising "Pabst—Milwaukee," ca. 1900. (Library of Congress)

housing large stainless steel conversion vessels, giant fermentation tanks, centrifuges, sensors, filters, and control panels. Straw-colored, undemanding, heavily promoted lagers fought for supremacy as the distinction between branded chilled and filtered beers became blurred. During the twentieth century, estimated output of beer increased by 400 percent and per capita consumption by 30 percent. By the dawn of the twenty-first century, annual world production of beer approached 1.4 billion hectoliters (37 billion U.S. gallons), with nearly half coming from just ten companies.

Eighteenth-Century Brewing

During the eighteenth century, weak beers, 2–3 percent alcohol by volume (ABV), were everyday drinks consumed by all classes and ages, particularly at meals, in preference to unreliable water. Strong beers, 7–8 percent ABV, were particularly favored to celebrate church festivals and family celebrations and as a necessary solace in moments of leisure in a harsh world. Brewing was restricted to the period roughly between October and March, because attempts at summer brewing often led to spoilage. The typical brewing technique was cumbersome. The first extraction of the crushed malt (grist) yielded wort for strong beers; after drainage, subsequent mashing of the same grist produced weaker brews. The scale of brewing ranged from a few hectoliters (about 100 U.S. gallons) in the average home, to a few hundred hectoliters (about 10,000 U.S. gallons) in monasteries and taverns, to tens of thousands (over 500,000 U.S. gallons) in the biggest breweries in 1700.

By 1750, the output of London's top five brewers averaged 80,000 hectoliters (2,113,000 U.S. gallons); in 1799, it was 240,000 hectoliters (6,340,000 U.S. gallons). The breweries of Thrale/Barclay Perkins, Whitbread, Truman, Meux, and Calvert were wonders of the age. The major product of these mammoth breweries, which far outstripped in size any others elsewhere, was a bitter-tasting inexpensive brown beer that acquired the popular name of porter in the 1720s. Both the origin and name of this beer are unclear and controversial. The name is most commonly believed, without any convincing evidence, to have come from the drink's popularity among London's market porters, while stories of its origin are frequently drawn from embellishments on a single pseudonymous source published in 1760. What is clear is that freshly brewed porter must have been a rather coarse beer. It was made with cheap brown malt and a high level of cheap hops. Before release, its coarseness of flavor was mellowed by storage. Its dark brown color, typical of London-brewed beers, disguised its murky appearance, and its high hop rate protected it from developing excessive acidity through spoilage. This robustness and cheapness made it suitable for mass production.

The eighteenth century saw significant advances in the quantification of brewing operations. The first recorded use of a thermometer in a brewery was in 1758 by the London ale brewer Michael Combrune. John Richardson, a Hull brewer, linked the use of the thermometer with his saccharometer, introduced in 1784, for measuring the strength of worts. The two instruments allowed brewers to derive economic benefit from accurate measurement through the best and most efficient use of raw materials. By 1800, many of the larger brewers had adopted the instruments. Trade in beer everywhere remained predominantly local. What little national or regional trade there was went by canal and ship. International trade was exceptional and confined to the most enterprising merchant brewers.

Nineteenth-Century Brewing Industry

The leading European beer-drinking countries—the United Kingdom, Germany, and Belgium—all saw a two- to threefold increase in output between 1830 and 1900. The United States industry grew from negligible proportions to the world's third largest producer by 1900. Growth in population was a major factor, particularly the growth of population in cities. The coming of the railways from the 1830s opened up markets and favored the larger-scale producers who made their regional beers available nationally. The new breed of industrial workers, with the novelty of relative prosperity, drank heroic quantities of beer in the growing numbers of retail outlets, raising levels of per capita consumption by up to 50 percent. The rise of commercial brewing and the decline of domestic brewing accompanied this rise in consumption. With the growing scale and economic importance of brewing came increased government interest in the industry as a generator of revenue. Commercial expediency saw the eventual eradication of adulteration, both innocuous and harmful, which had been rife at the beginning of the century. As breweries grew bigger, the potential financial consequences of damage to reputation outweighed the immediate pecuniary advantage that had tempted the small producer. The last quarter of the nineteenth century saw a rush to incorporation by the leading European brewing firms, practically all of which became public companies between the 1870s and the 1890s. At first, this did not alter the management style of the companies, and control tended to remain in the same hands. But in the next century, the move toward incorporation would lead to the conversion of personally controlled individual enterprises into conglomerate companies run by a bureaucratic hierarchy of salaried managers.

The Rise of Lager in the Nineteenth Century

In 1830, most of the world's brewers used yeasts that floated up to the surface of the fermenting wort and were accommodated to high fermentation (15 to 25°C) and maturation (13°C) temperatures. Bottom-fermented beers had been brewed in Bavaria since at least the 1400s but were little known outside the state. Their defining characteristics included the utilization of yeasts that sank to the bottom of the vessel toward the end of fermentation and the use of low fermentation (4 to 10°C) and maturation (–2 to 4°C) temperatures. Lager (from the German verb *lagern,* to store) has been adopted as a generic term for bottom-fermented beer in anglophone countries. The proximity of the foothills of the Alps and cool caves provided the Bavarian brewer monks with a convenient place to store beer. The facility of this system in leading to stable, bright, sparkling beers was then pursued by commercial brewers who, using ice taken from frozen lakes and rivers to cool cellars constructed at their breweries, mimicked the natural caves. The lagers of Bavaria were brewed with malt that had been dried at relatively high temperatures, and the beer was consequently fairly dark in color. This malt also tended to be less highly processed than the malt used for top-fermented beers, and this led to the evolution of a more intensive mashing process in lager brewing in order to maximize the yield of extract from the malt.

North German brewers started to convert to bottom fermentation from the late 1830s, as did Austrian and Czech brewers. In October 1842, a Bavarian-born brewer produced a variant brew in Pilsen using lightly dried, low-color malt and soft water—the first example of a straw-colored lager. Over the next half century, both light-colored lager (pilsner) and dark lager based on the German muenchner spread throughout Europe and beyond. The pilsner style had proved the most popular by the end of the century. Carlsberg brewed their first lager in 1847, a dark variety, using yeast obtained from Munich. Tuborg introduced pilsner-style lager brewing to Denmark in 1880. Heineken, founded as an ale brewer in 1864 in Amsterdam, switched to lager within ten years. Bernard Stroh, Eberhard Anheuser, Adolphus Busch, Frederick Pabst, Frederick Miller, Joseph Schlitz, and Adolph Coors, all first-generation immigrants from Germany, came into brewing in the United States between the 1840s and 1870s and specialized in lager. The Midwest became the heartland of United States brewing, with Milwaukee (and its plentiful supplies of ice from Lake Michigan) as its capital. From the 1880s, these German American brewers developed their own style of lager utilizing readily available cereals, notably maize (corn) and rice, as diluents for the high-nitrogen six-rowed barleys grown in the United States. Unmalted adjuncts had been used in brewing elsewhere before this time (although forbidden in Bavaria), but the high level of use, sometimes exceeding the quantity of malt, became a particular feature of United States brewing technique. The result was very pale, stable, easy drinking beers of unrivaled blandness.

The increasing introduction of efficient artificial refrigeration from the 1870s freed lager brewers from the need for natural ice, allowed easier cold transport of beer, and permitted year-round brewing for lager and ale brewers alike. Initially, refrigeration was used to produce ice but was soon applied to direct cooling via expansion coils. Germany was producing more beer than any other nation by the 1880s, with bottom-fermented beer predominating across the country; specialty wheat beers were the only significant top-fermented beer still in production. Still a country of predominantly small brewers, Germany had its main brewing centers (with several large, modern breweries) in Munich, Dortmund, and Berlin. Brewing had also boomed in the United States, where the refrigerated railcars introduced by Anheuser-Busch in 1878 became a particular feature of expansion. By the 1890s, lager brewing had reached Asia, South America, and Australia. Of the major brewing nations, only the United Kingdom, with the exception of a few scattered attempts, stood aloof from the shift to lager.

Nineteenth-Century Porter, Stout, and Ale

Around 1800, the methodology for porter changed. The use of Richardson's saccharometer provided information on the relative amounts of extract achieved with different styles of malt. This led to the realization that the use of pale malt, with beer color derived from a small proportion of very dark malt, was more cost effective than the previous use of brown malt. In the 1810s, roasted barley was adopted following advances in technique, and porter became ever darker, ultimately becoming black. Up to the 1830s, the British beer market was characterized by the dominance of porter in London and the bigger cities, and numerous strong, regionally variant ales in the rest of the country. Over the next fifty years, this market characteristic changed with the rise of mild and pale ale.

Victorian mild was a well-hopped, but noticeably sweet, strong, dark brown beer, which grew in popularity with the laboring classes. A strong, heavily hopped version of pale ale was brewed for export to India by a London brewer, Mark Hodgson, from around 1815, before being made in Burton in 1822. The hard Burton water proved particularly suitable for this type of beer. Burton India Pale Ale (IPA) soon captured the export market and from the 1840s built up a considerable home trade. Although relatively expensive, the beer appealed to the aspirations of the growing band of lower-middle-class clerks and shopkeepers. The output of the major Burton brewers—Bass, Ratcliff and Gretton, and Samuel Allsopp and Sons—trebled each decade such that by the mid-1870s Bass was briefly the biggest brewer in the world, with an output of nearly 1.5 million hectoliters (40 million U.S. gallons), and Allsopps was not far behind. Burton's star faded in the last two decades of the century as their products became more difficult to sell. Rival brewers increasingly bought up or provided loans to pubs and so tied them to selling the brewery's own products to the exclusion of competitors' products. At least 75 percent of public houses in England were tied to a brewer by 1900. In Scotland, large brewing firms (for instance, McEwans and William Younger) had developed their own version of pale ale that, like the Burton brewers, they sold primarily through the wholesale market. They were heavily involved in exporting to England and suffered similarly to their Burton rivals, particularly from the turn of the century. The market for Burton beers was also eroded by a shift in public taste away from matured, complex, stock winter-brewed beers like India Pale Ale, to more easily produced, lighter "running ales" that required minimal maturation. Burton brewers could brew these beers as well as anyone, but the unique selling point of their prestigious products was lost. By the early 1900s, classic IPA had virtually disappeared.

Ireland remained loyal to porter throughout the nineteenth century. Arthur Guinness had started as an ale brewer in Dublin in 1759, but in response to the success of imported London porter in the Irish market, the company had switched entirely to porter by 1799. Guinness brewed two strengths of porter, and by 1840, the stronger version, known as stout, accounted for 80 percent of production. The brewer expanded massively after the 1860s, becoming the world's largest brewery in the 1880s. Guinness brewed 3.8 million hectoliters (100 million U.S. gallons) by 1900. This constituted 8.5 percent of United Kingdom beer and was nearly twice as much as was brewed in the whole of Scotland in that year. Guinness was unique among major brewers in the British Isles in remaining entirely a wholesaler and not a retailer of beer.

Nineteenth-Century Science and Technology

Scientific research in brewing was minimal until Louis Pasteur's work on wine and beer fermentations, carried out in the 1860s and 1870s, showed the importance of eliminating deleterious bacteria from fermentations. The heating of beer in order to preserve it (pasteurization) was introduced into German and United States breweries in the early 1870s. Emil Christian Hansen of Carlsberg extended Pasteur's work in 1883 when he introduced the concept of pure yeast culture and the technology for achieving it. In this, a single strain of brewer's yeast, free not only from contaminating bacteria but also from any yeast other than the strain required to give the most satisfactory fermentation, is isolated, propagated, and used for fermentation. Progressive brewers soon adopted his technique. Within ten years, Hansen's yeast propagation plants had been installed in 173 breweries in 23 different countries.

Wort production protocols had undergone an earlier transformation. Mashing rakes powered by horses and then steam were the norm by 1800 in large breweries. After 1800, the technique of "sparging" was used increasingly. This involved the continuous washing of the partially extracted malt in the mash tun with hot water during drainage, enabling all the wort to be collected in one operation and obviating the need for multiple extractions. This procedure, which seems to have originated in Scotland, was universal by the 1870s. In 1853, Steel's mashing machine was introduced. It provided efficient mixing of ground malt with water on entry to the mash tun.

During the century, increasing numbers of brewers started to utilize analytical data, particularly to evaluate water and malt quality. Usually, breweries relied upon external consultants for their analysis, but a few of the large companies employed chemists directly. German brewers' chemists led the industry in establishing professional journals from the 1860s, and from the 1880s there was a proliferation of scientific and technical journals in many countries. The teaching and research establishments founded in Weihenstephan (near Munich) in 1873 and in Berlin in 1883 epitomized the new techno-scientific approach to brewing. Similar institutions appeared at this time in Vienna and Zurich, and John Siebel, a German immigrant, founded a school for brewers in Chicago in 1882. In Britain, education was on a more ad hoc basis, with prospective brewers being taken on as pupils and receiving on-the-job training. There was no brewing school in England until 1900, when classes started at the newly formed University of Birmingham. Classes for brewing started in Edinburgh in 1903.

The bottling of beer was not of any real importance until the 1860s. Hand bottling was the only option until the 1880s. At that time, bottling machinery was introduced, prompting a surge of interest. Multiple-head filters appeared in 1899 and fully automatic rotary fillers in 1903. Increases in bottling activity went hand in hand with the lighter beers produced from the 1880s. Beers were specially produced for bottling using additions of sugar and unmalted cereals. These adjunct beers tended to stay bright longer than all-malt beers. Originally, beer was bottled with a proportion of yeast and fermentable matter still present and was "naturally conditioned" by continued limited fermentation that generated carbon dioxide and gave it sparkle. This technique remained the most usual in many countries until the 1920s and is still employed, but gradually lost ground to filtration and artificial carbonation introduced from the United States, where it was the norm by the 1890s.

Temperance and Prohibition

Beer was largely immune from temperance attacks when cheap spirits remained the reformers' target and beer was regarded as relatively harmless. The position changed from the mid-nineteenth century as teetotalism became the goal of some temperance reformers. In the fifty years after the mid-1880s, the brewers gradually won the struggle, more because of divisions among their opponents, weaker beer, and the demonstrated downside of Prohibition than because of their superior strength or unity. Growth of sentiment for prohibition in the United States in the late nineteenth and early twentieth centuries resulted in "local option," which led to many smaller towns and districts going dry, causing the closure of small local breweries even though beer consumption nationally was increasing. National Prohibition followed on 16 January 1920. Some breweries continued to produce legal "near beer." When Prohibition ended, 164 breweries were still employed in making this 0.5 percent ABV product, but as illegal alcohol proliferated, output had fallen from nearly 11 million hectoliters (290 million U.S. gallons) in 1920 to just 3 million hectoliters (79 million U.S. gallons) in 1932. Some brewers turned to alternative products (yeast, malted milk, ice cream, malt syrup, and so forth), but many did not survive Prohibition. In 1913, there were 1,462 breweries in the United States; on 1 May 1933, three weeks after the repeal of Prohibition, 191 were listed as authorized to brew, rising with perhaps surprising rapidity to 700 by June 1934. The United States was not the only country to "experiment" with Prohibition. Iceland (from 1915), Finland (from 1919), and Canada (with its own haphazard form from 1918) had abortive experiences similar to the experiment in the United States. Denmark, Norway, and Sweden had close escapes, and in the United Kingdom and Australia, there was considerable prohibitionist fervor. In New Zealand, votes for prohibition very nearly reached a majority in national referendums in the early 1920s. New Zealand's brewers came together for self-protection in 1923 when the ten principal companies amalgamated, ending up with 75 percent of the market. After 1925, the vote swung toward continuance of liquor licenses, and prohibition was defeated. Both Australia and New Zealand introduced 6 o'clock closing during the first world war, leading to the "6 o'clock swill" as drinkers downed as much as possible in the limited hours available. Early closing was not eased in Australia until the 1960s. In the United Kingdom, the restriction of opening hours introduced as a temporary measure in the first world war was only relaxed in 1988. Some Canadians still needed to buy drinking permits in the 1950s; drinkers in Utah still do.

Consumption, 1900–1950

In 1901, total world beer production was estimated at 262.7 million hectoliters (6,940 million U.S. gallons) from 36,472 breweries, with the top three brewing countries accounting for 68.5 percent of output: Germany 66.5 million hectoliters (1,757 million U.S. gallons) from 18,630 breweries, the United Kingdom 60.9 million hectoliters (1,609 million U.S. gallons) from 6,324 breweries, and the United States 52.6 million hectoliters (1,390 million U.S. gallons) from 1,714 breweries. By mid-decade, the United States had overtaken the United Kingdom, and by 1910, with production still rising, the United States was ahead of Germany with 72.2 million hectoliters (1,910 million U.S. gallons; 64.4 and 56.4 million hectoliters [1,700 and 1,490 million U.S. gallons] in Germany and the United Kingdom respectively). Having doubled output since the 1870s, German beer production peaked in 1909. Production in the United Kingdom also stalled in the first decade of the century. The first world war transformed a slowdown in output in these countries into a collapse. Shortages of brewing materials and increases in prices and taxes were largely responsible. In the years 1915 through 1919, output in the United Kingdom and Germany fell by 37 and 52 percent respectively compared with the previous five-year period. The strength of beer in the United Kingdom in 1919 was only 58 percent of what it had been in 1914, and it never returned to its former level. After 1914 and for the first time, duty became the main determinant of beer prices in the United Kingdom. By the mid-1920s, the output of beer had stagnated across Europe and was to remain flat as high taxes, the depression, and increasing alternatives for leisure spending took effect.

Beers from regional and local breweries continued to cater to the majority, with only the biggest and most adventurous producers engaging in national and very limited international distribution. By the 1930s, porter had disappeared from England (it was to continue in Ireland until 1973, and the name saw a revival among microbrewers in the 1980s). The most popular draft ale was mild, by then a very weak beer (about 3–3.5 percent ABV). The alternative was bitter, a lineal descendant of the running ales of the 1880s, but again much weaker at about 3.5–4.5 percent ABV. Scotland had its own distinctive reddish brown, rather sweet Scotch ales. Dark muenchner lagers still kept their popularity with the working classes in Bavaria until the 1950s, but light "helles" pilsner-style beers gained ground even there, as they had done everywhere except in Britain.

Consumption since 1950

Output remained flat or showed relatively modest growth until the mid- to late 1950s. Between 1960 and 1990, world production increased threefold. Within this overall increase, national differences are evident. After a fall during postwar austerity, between 1959 and 1979 the United Kingdom saw its only sustained increase in output of the century, with a rise of nearly 70 percent before volumes started to fall again. In Australia and New Zealand, with growing immigration (the population went up 50 percent between 1950 and 1970), output also peaked in the late 1970s after having nearly trebled in thirty years. Canada, with similar absolute consumption levels, showed similar growth before plateauing in the 1980s. In Germany, after near collapse at the end of the war, volumes had recovered to prewar levels by 1960 and continued to grow before leveling out in the mid-1970s and then declining. In the United States, after the sluggish 1950s, volume more than doubled in the thirty years to 1990. Increased demand in all these countries came primarily from prosperous young adults specifically targeted by marketing. Between 1960 and 1980, there were per capita increases of 17 percent in Belgium, 39 percent in the United Kingdom, 54 percent in West Germany, 61 percent in the United States, and 83 percent in Denmark. Consumption also took off in countries not previously noted for drinking beer. The effect was noticed in Spain, Portugal, and Italy in Southern Europe, but was particularly evident in South America, where, for example, Brazil showed a sixfold increase in output between 1970 and 1990, and in South Africa with a tenfold increase in output in the same period. Growth in Japan was also noteworthy and created a significant new force. Beer had been a luxury item in Japan before the war, with the country's total output in 1939 at only 3 million hectoliters (79 million U.S. gallons). Consumption boomed in the 1950s as the economy blossomed, reaching 40 million hectoliters (1,057 million U.S. gallons) by the mid-1970s, a per capita increase of around 300 percent. The rate of increase then slowed in what appeared to be a mature market. The introduction of a range of new products and packaging, particularly the heavily hyped "super dry" beer in 1987, gave a new boost to sales. Dry beer had 34 percent of the market within two years, and total beer consumption went up by 40 percent in five years, topping 70 million hectoliters (1,850 U.S. gallons, or 57 liters per capita [60 U.S. quarts]) by 1992, making Japan the world's fourth biggest producer of beer. During the 1990s, a quick succession of other expensive marketing initiatives followed but failed to boost overall sales in a declining economy. Even more spectacular growth came in China, which had become the primary target for international companies looking for new markets and showed an increase from 1 million hectoliters (26.4 million U.S. gallons) in 1970 to 196 million hectoliters (5,180 million U.S. gallons) in 1998. By then, although per capita consumption in China, at 15.6 liters (16.5 U.S. quarts), was only a fraction of that in the heaviest drinking nation (Czech Republic, 161 liters [170 U.S. quarts]), with its population of 1.26 billion, the country was second only to the United States in terms of output (236 million hectoliters [6,230 million U.S. gallons], 84 liters per capita [almost 89 U.S. quarts]) and was set to become the world's leading brewing country by 2003.

By the end of the century, pilsner-style lagers had completed their dominance of the world market. Visual appeal, refreshing qualities, consistency, and easy drinkability were important factors in this success. Often, however, beers called pilsner bore only a superficial resemblance to the original; they deceived the eye but not the palate. This was particularly true in Britain, where lager increasingly gained popularity from the 1960s to become the dominant beer in the 1990s. Despite the best efforts of the Campaign for Real Ale (CAMRA), which saved traditional British cask beer from extinction in the 1970s, cask beer suffered a severe downturn in the late 1990s, falling below 10 percent of total UK sales. Everywhere, there was a swing away from draft beer drunk in bars toward bottled and canned beer drunk at home. In the United States, draft beer sales were in the minority by 1941, and by the 1990s cans and nonreturnable glass bottles held around 85 percent of the market. Only in the United Kingdom and Ireland does draft beer and drinking in the pub still predominate, and even in the United Kingdom draft is losing ground, with nearly 40 percent sold in cans and nonreturnable bottles by 2000. In most of the rest of the world, the returnable bottle remained the most popular container at the end of the century.

With more attention to drunk driving, alcohol-free (less than 0.05 percent ABV) and low-alcohol (less than 1.2 percent ABV) beers were strongly marketed in the 1980s. The unsatisfactory taste of these products and uncertain market positioning limited their appeal, and by the end of the 1990s they held less than 1 percent of the world beer market. Retail outlets across Europe became eating and entertainment venues rather than drinking establishments. The move was particularly obvious in the pubs of the United Kingdom, where catering, for so long a secondary consideration, became *de rigueur* by the 1990s. In a trend that has gone on for forty years, the old beer-drinking countries saw an increasing move to wine consumption spreading down from their affluent middle classes. Among younger citizens, a more recent move has been away from beer toward flavored spirit-based mixer drinks. Brewers have joined in their manufacture.

Consolidation of the Brewing Industry since 1950

The trend toward reducing numbers and increasing size of breweries continued during the twentieth century. The drive by major companies toward an oligopoly was restrained in many countries by government regulation, resented by smaller brewers, and to an extent met with consumer resistance, but by the end of the century the big battalions had largely prevailed. In the United Kingdom, of the 362 companies active in 1950, 65 remained in 1990, with an eightfold increase in average output to 0.60 million hectoliters (15.9 million U.S. gallons) per annum. By the 1970s, six companies controlled over 80 percent of beer production and half of full-on licensed outlets. British brewing companies, already vertically integrated into material provision (malt and hops) and alcohol retailing, became horizontally integrated through takeover into spirit, wine, cider, soft drink, food, and leisure businesses. The United Kingdom industry went through further upheaval in the 1990s as the long-established tie between the brewer and the pub was severely weakened through government legislation. Partly in response to this, most parent companies of the major UK brewers disposed of their breweries and then their pubs, creating a new dichotomy of pub chains and wholesale brewers.

In the United States, by 1990 the 380 brewing companies active in 1950 had been reduced to 30, and the average output per company had increased twenty-eight-fold to 3.76 million hectoliters (99 million U.S. gallons) per annum. At the close of the twentieth century, three companies (Anheuser-Busch, Miller, and Coors) held 80 percent of the U.S. market. In Australia, after years of peaceful coexistence among the country's brewers, a shake-up of the market in the 1970s led to the industry being a virtual duopoly by the mid-1980s. Foster's and Lion Nathan held 97 percent of the market in the antipodes by 2000. Denmark and the Netherlands have been dominated by single companies for decades; South African Breweries holds 98 percent of its home market; there are only five brewing companies in Japan; two brewers make 95 percent of Canada's beer; and 80 percent of Belgium's beer comes from three brewers. Even in Germany, where the existence of conglomerates and interlocking shareholdings disguised the true level of concentration in the industry and consumer loyalty was strong, the number of breweries had decreased from about 2,100 in 1950 to about 1,150 in 1990, and the average output has gone up ninefold to 0.09 million hectoliters (2.38 million U.S. gallons) per annum.

In a contrasting trend, small producers (microbrewers) staged a resurgence in the 1970s in the United Kingdom, with a similar trend in the 1980s in the United States, Canada, Australia, and elsewhere. Output from these microbrewers remains quantitatively small (e.g., 2 percent of total United Kingdom sales in 2001) and qualitatively diverse. By the end of the century, three scales of brewing plant could be identified: (1) major national and international brewers with plants of capacities up to 10 million hectoliters (264 million U.S. gallons) per annum, occasionally exceeding that level in the United States (the largest plant, Coors in Colorado, brews 19 million hectoliters [500 million U.S. gallons] per annum); (2) regional brewers with 0.1–1.0 million hectoliter (2.6–26 million U.S. gallons) per annum plants; and (3) craft or microbrewers producing 1–10 thousand hectoliters 26 to 260 thousand U.S. gallons) per annum.

Despite this inexorable swing toward consolidation within countries, the move to international brewing is less evident, and globalization is only in its infancy. In 1999, the top three world brewers (Anheuser-Bush, Heineken, and Interbrew) accounted for 20 percent of the market, whereas the top three soft drink companies had 75 percent of global sales. In Europe, with the exception of Britain, France, Italy, and Greece, local brands have more than 75 percent of the market. International brands have made little impact in South America, North America, and Africa. In the Asia Pacific region, only in China have foreign brewers made an impact through massive investment, and even here their strategy of promoting expensive western brands has largely come unstuck. At the end of the century, only 6 percent of Anheuser-Busch's sales came from outside the United States, and 12 of its 14 breweries were located in the United States. Prior to the move of Coors into the United Kingdom in 2002 with the takeover of some of Bass's former breweries and brands, other American brewers have concentrated almost exclusively on their domestic market. The European groups Heineken, Carlsberg, and Guinness have spearheaded moves toward international and global brewing. These companies, long known as exporters of beer, sought to extend their markets by establishing breweries and trading partners worldwide from the 1960s onward. Heineken has been particularly successful in this strategy. In 2000, its beer was produced in more than 110 breweries in over 50 countries, with 90 percent of the company's sales coming from outside the Netherlands. Other aspirants to global brewing emerged at the end of the century, most notably the Belgian group Interbrew, which mopped up many old established brewers including Labatt's of Canada and a major portion of the United Kingdom industry. South African Breweries (SAB), enjoying new postapartheid respectability, specialized in emerging markets and became one of the few to make some success of its investment in China. SAB controlled 108 breweries in 24 countries even before its takeover of U.S. brewer Miller, in May 2002, made the new company, SAB-Miller, the world's second largest brewer.

Science and Technology in the Twentieth Century

Science only impinged on the periphery of the average brewer's activities in the years up to the second world war. Improved barley varieties became generally available in the 1920s. Attention was given to diseases of hops and the chemical nature of their antimicrobial and bittering properties (alpha acids). From the 1930s, chemical and microbiological analytical techniques were extended and improved. But these were largely ad hoc developments, and the brewing process itself was little investigated. Similarly, with the exception of the counter-current heat exchanger introduced in 1923, which allowed sterile wort cooling, technological change was only attempted by the most adventurous brewers, who experimented with mash filters, new designs of fermentors, and metal beer containers.

From the 1950s, new, if still relatively modest, investment in scientific research spread with the establishment or extension of laboratories and pilot brewing facilities both on a national scale and by individual brewers. New approaches, together with adoption of techniques that had their origin many years earlier but had been held back by prevailing attitudes and difficulties of construction and operation, transformed brewing technology. Large vessels began to be introduced into maltings and breweries in the 1950s. The use of stainless steel, advances in basic knowledge, better analytical control, greater availability of process aids (plant growth regulators, enzymes, coagulants, and so forth), and then automated computer-controlled plants provided brewers with new confidence. Whole leaf hops, originally the only method of bittering, were increasingly replaced by milled and later solvent-extracted preparations. From the 1960s, segregated mash converters (mash tuns) and wort separators (lauter tuns) became standard in large breweries, even for ale brewing. In the 1980s, improved mash filters arrived, offering benefits in terms of yield and ease of operation. The whirlpool separator, a device invented in Canada in 1960 for removing hop residues and other material after wort boiling, was adopted with alacrity to replace more cumbersome "hopbacks." Cylindro-conical fermentors, patented in 1910 and introduced to a limited extent by the 1930s in continental Europe and America, became the norm everywhere after the 1960s. Fermentors up to 6,000-hectoliter (158,500 U.S. gallons) capacity came to replace smaller (200–500 hectoliter [5,283–13,210 U.S. gallon]) box-shaped vessels. Until the mid-1970s, beers were sold at the strength at which they had been brewed. The introduction of "high gravity brewing," in which a strong wort is fermented and then diluted with deaerated water before packaging, became the norm by the mid-1980s, allowing better plant utilization. Beers received increasingly sophisticated postfermentation treatments to delay haze development, and improved techniques for excluding oxygen during packaging meant that flavor shelf life was also extended, often to a year or more. The can was introduced in the United States in 1935, and everywhere metal instead of wood became the favorite packaging material for draft beer by the end of the 1960s. Filling line speeds increased tenfold and more. Process times generally were shortened. Lagering of beer over a period of months by storage in the presence of yeast to stabilize, carbonate, and modify the flavor was increasingly replaced by the much more rapid process (originated in the United States at the end of the nineteenth century) of cold filtration and injection of carbon dioxide. The distinctions between the processing of ales and lagers became increasingly blurred as they merged as predominantly chilled and filtered cold-served beers from the 1960s. Multiplant brewing of the same brand of beer, pioneered by Anton Dreher in Central Europe in the nineteenth century, was adopted by Pabst Brewery in 1948 and soon taken up by other brewers both in the United States and elsewhere.

There were some false starts, most notably with continuous brewing, which was seen as the technology of the future in the 1950s but failed to fulfill these hopes. In the 1980s and 1990s, much activity went into the construction of genetically modified (GM) strains of yeast that gave a technological advantage, but no GM strains have been used in commercial brewing. Transgenic maize is ubiquitous in the United States, where it must necessarily be used in brewing. Elsewhere in the world, brewers are keen to reassure the public that their beers are free from genetically modified material. In the final decade of the twentieth century, sentiment in many large brewing companies in the United Kingdom and North America turned against further investment in process research.

Budgets were cut, and remaining funds directed in the main toward "near market" product and packaging innovations.

Raymond G. Anderson

See also: Allied Breweries; Allsopps; Anheuser-Busch; Bass; Beer Orders (United Kingdom); Campaign for Real Ale (CAMRA); Coors, Adolph, Brewing Company; Courage Brewery; Foster's; Guinness Brewery; Heileman, G., Brewing Company; Home Brewing; Interbrew; Labatt Brewing Company Limited; Microbreweries (United States, United Kingdom, and Canada); Miller Brewing Company; Molson Incorporated; O'Keefe Brewery; Olympia Brewing Company; Pabst Brewing Company; Schlitz, Joseph, Brewing Company; Scottish & Newcastle Breweries Limited; Shea's Winnipeg Brewery Limited; South African Breweries (SAB); Stroh Brewery Company; Whitbread; Working Men's Clubs Breweries (United Kingdom)

References

Anderson, Raymond G. "Current Practice in Malting, Brewing and Distilling" in *Cereal Biotechnology,* edited by Peter C. Morris and James H. Bryce, 183–215. Cambridge, UK: Woodhead; Boca Raton, FL: CRC Press, 2000.

———. "Highlights in the History of International Brewing Science" in *Ferment.* 6 (1993): 191–198.

Anderson, Will. *Beer, USA.* New York: Morgan and Morgan, 1986.

Arnold, J. P., and F. Penman. *History of the Brewing Industry and Brewing Science in America.* Chicago: J. E. Siebel, 1933.

Brewers and Licensed Retailers Association. *Statistical Handbook.* London: Brewing Publications Limited, 2000.

Corran, H. S. *A History of Brewing.* Newton Abbot, Devon: David and Charles, 1975.

Glamann, Kristof. "Founders and Successors: Managerial Changes during the Rise of the Modern Brewing Industry" in *Proceedings of the Eighteenth European Brewery Convention Congress, Copenhagen,* 1–10. London: IRL Press, 1981.

Gourvish, Terry R. "Economics of Brewing, Theory and Practice: Concentration and Technological Change in the USA, UK and West Germany since 1945" in *Business and Economic History.* 23 (1994): 253–261.

Gourvish, Terry R., and Richard G. Wilson. *The British Brewing Industry 1830–1980.* Cambridge, UK: Cambridge University Press, 1994.

Gutzke, David W. *Protecting the Pub: Brewers and Publicans against Temperance.* Woodbridge, Suffolk: Boydell and Brewer, 1989.

Jackson, Michael. *Michael Jackson's Beer Companion.* London: Mitchell Beazley, 1993.

Mathias, Peter. *The Brewing Industry in England, 1700–1830.* Cambridge, UK: Cambridge University Press, 1959.

Wilson, Richard G., and Terry R. Gourvish. "The Production and Consumption of Alcoholic Beverages in Western Europe" in *Alcoholic Beverages and European Society, Annex 1,* 1–34. Amsterdam: Elsevier, 1993.

Beer Institute

See United States Brewers' Association (USBA).

Beer Orders (United Kingdom)

The Beer Orders of 1989 provided the occasion, if not the reason, for a restructuring of the brewing trade in the United Kingdom that ultimately led to a new dichotomy of pub-owning companies and wholesale brewers. The Beer Orders were designed to weaken the tie between the big brewers and public houses by forcing the disposal of a proportion of outlets, thereby opening the retail market to smaller regional breweries and micro companies. But the outcome was much more far-reaching.

Within a little more than a decade, of the six vertically integrated national companies that had dominated the industry from the 1960s, only Scottish and Newcastle Breweries Limited (S&N) survived, trading as Scottish Courage after the takeover of Courage. The remnants of the other national brewers' production capacity often were in foreign hands, and their pubs had gone to newly formed independent retailing groups known as "pubcos." Consolidation of smaller companies continued unabated, with such historic companies as Brakspears, Morrells, Morland, and Vaux all soon taken over. The well-meaning aims of the Beer Orders, to lower retail prices and increase consumer choice, remained unfulfilled.

Decades of official concern over the tied-house system, coupled with disquiet at the increase in beer prices above the rate of inflation for much of the 1980s, culminated in the Monopolies and Mergers Commission report on the Supply of Beer in March 1989. In a weakened form, the major proposals in this report were given force through two statutory instruments, known as the Beer Orders, issued in December 1989. The prime requirement was that brewers owning more than 2,000 pubs dispose of half of the licenses in excess of this number or dispose of their breweries. The orders also required that tenants of national brewers be allowed to stock one "guest" cask-conditioned beer from another brewer. The industry was given three years to implement the orders, with a deadline of 31 October 1992.

The brewers responded to the orders in different ways. On the one hand, some major players who had recognized retailing rather than manufacturing as their prime activity some years before the Beer Orders quit brewing and retained their pubs. These included the national brewer Grand Metropolitan (who swapped breweries for pubs with Courage) and the major regional brewers Greenalls and Boddingtons. Similarly, Allied-Lyons prepared the way for its exit by merging its brewing interests with those of the Danish brewer Carlsberg in the United Kingdom to form Carlsberg-Tetley Brewing Limited.

On the other hand, Bass, Whitbread, and S&N complied with the orders by selling off the requisite number of pubs in large blocks to emerging pubcos and staying in the brewing business. In both cases, the deals were accompanied by long-term (five- to seven-year) supply agreements between pub chains and brewers. Thus, although by the end of 1992 some 12,000 pubs had new owners, almost invariably they remained effectively tied to a brewer. Also, although the guest beer provision was operating, the range of choice offered was often restricted to well-known brands from regional brewers. In effect, the letter but not the spirit of the Beer Orders had been observed.

In the decade following the implementation of the Beer Orders, the UK's national brewers continued to unravel, with parent companies withdrawing from brewing and then, as the pressure on profits continued, selling off their pub chains. In the spring of 2003, Scottish Courage, which had stood alone against the trend, announced that it would sell off its pubs and concentrate on brewing. The Beer Orders, by now irrelevant in a market dominated by their unforeseen legacy (the pubcos), were revoked in December 2002. Nothing had been done to perpetuate the survival of the smaller regional breweries.

The Beer Orders failed partly because consumers no longer demanded the distinctive "real ales" brewed by the small independent brewers who specialized in this prekeg (pasteurized) beer style. After 1994 and the widespread introduction of keg beer served with nitrogen, the "real ale" market collapsed, falling to about half its size (10 percent from 22 percent) in less than a decade.

Raymond G. Anderson and David W. Gutzke

See also: Allied Breweries; Bass; Beer; Brewers' Society (BS); Campaign for Real Ale (CAMRA); Courage Brewery; Scottish & Newcastle Breweries Limited; Watneys; Whitbread

References

Crompton, Gerald. "'Well-Intentioned Meddling.' The Beer Orders and the British Brewing Industry" in *The Dynamics of the International Brewing Industry since 1800,* edited by Richard G. Wilson and Terry R. Gourvish, 160–175. London and New York: Routledge, 1998.

Everitt, John C., and Ian R. Bowler. "Bitter-Sweet Conversions: Changing Times in the British Pub" in *Journal of Popular Culture.* 32 (Fall 1996): 101–122.

Presnell, Ian. "Structural Changes to British Brewing and the Pub Trade, 1989–94" in *BDI* (Brewing and Distilling International). March 1995: 14–17.

Bees

Alcohol has been an important component of reciprocal farm labor in many countries. Farmers in Haiti, South America, Mexico, Bulgaria, Japan, Central and West Africa, Norway, Ireland, Scotland, the United States, and elsewhere have long used mutual helpfulness to erect buildings, harvest produce, and create cloth. In nineteenth-century Ontario, Canada, reciprocal labor took place at a "bee," where settlers gathered to assist each other and work industriously like bees in a hive. In the early days of settlement, alcohol was used to entice workers to travel long distances to bees and was used as a form of payment, a measure of hospitality and masculinity. By midcentury, temperance advocates had attacked the central role of whiskey at Ontario bees and its use had become more restrained, even entirely replaced by more elaborate feasts and festivities.

Making a farm out of wild land required the combined strength and skills of more than one family. Bees were called to clear the land, raise barns, chop wood, harvest crops, butcher livestock, make rugs, sew quilts, and even spread manure. Everyone could find a role. At a logging bee, for example, young boys gathered up the branches, old men gave advice, newcomers learned, experienced men in their prime hoisted the heavy logs into piles to burn, and women prepared the feast—the grand finale to the day. The bee, therefore, had great practical value in an economy where hired labor and cash were in short supply. An accounting process, albeit subtle, was at work as guests clearly understood they would be paid for their effort with fitting hospitality and a day's labor in return.

Hospitality was an integral part of the labor exchange and neighborly behavior. In the early days of sparse settlement and rough ways, it took the form of simple food, games, dancing, and plenty of whiskey. Whiskey, in particular, was the measure of hospitality. In the 1820s, one simply could not raise a barn without it. Just how generous the "grog boss" should be with this refreshment was a matter of some concern. To him fell the difficult job of keeping workers satisfied but sober enough to do the job efficiently. Sometimes grog (whiskey mixed with water) was served before the work began and was the only drink during the entire affair. An inexperienced grog boss could inadvertently wreak havoc by being too generous too early in the day, making the men quarrelsome and the work more dangerous. Generally, it took sixteen men to raise a building, and five gallons of whiskey was the recommended store to have on hand, but at one bee, the men reputedly consumed eighty gallons over two days. Consumption was not its only use; alcohol had a symbolic value at these events. After a barn was raised, a whiskey bottle was often broken over, or flung from, the top rafter, symbolizing the completion of the task, good luck to the owners, and the beginning of the evening's festivities.

Whiskey and the drunkenness, shoddy work, expense of provisions, fighting, and accidents that sometimes resulted soon came under attack. Susanna Moodie, backwoods settler and writer who endured three logging bees, thought that they were "the most disgusting picture of bush life. They [were] noisy, riotous drunken meetings, often terminating in violent quarrels, sometimes even bloodshed" (Moodie 1962: 156). Evangelicals and temperance advocates attacked the custom of heavy drinking at bees as early as the 1830s, but met with considerable resistance in their attempt to redefine traditional patterns of hospitality as sinful. Whiskey supporters refused to attend bees where no alcohol was served and would even quit the job or refuse to finish it if no grog was forthcoming. At times, resistance could take a nasty turn. For example, when Thomas Brown, who had previously been part of a gang of young men who caroused at any bee within riding distance, took the pledge, he became a target of ridicule. When he next attended a bee and refused to

A barn-raising bee at the farmhouse of Mrs. William Grice of Minto Township, Ontario, June 1908. Alcohol was a frequent form of labor compensation at such events. (Wellington County Museum and Archives)

drink, whiskey was forcibly poured down his throat, and he was beaten and later ridiculed while the crowd sang about the terrible effects of cold water. By the 1870s, however, as the farming population became more established, older, and respectable, and Evangelicalism gained converts, strong drink was either not offered or was limited to moderate amounts after the job was done. Though hospitality continued to be a vital component of the exchange, the generous quantities of whiskey were replaced with more elaborate meals and entertainment.

How a man handled his grog affected his reputation. At a logging bee, which was substantively about men and the rituals of manliness, whiskey was often consumed throughout the entire day. The loggers formed gangs in different parts of the field and competed to see who would finish logging their section first. It was strenuous work shifting and heaping logs. In the hottest days of summer, the hours were long, the logs heavy, the work tiring, and the grog foul-tasting and plentiful. It took physical stamina to last the day and a great deal of self-control to keep a clear head. Contemporaries claimed that logging really tried a man's mettle. Though much alcohol was consumed, one had to be able to handle it. Lives were at stake. Save for the skill of a good axe man, a tree might fall on man or beast. Men gained and lost reputations at these events as the strongest, the fastest, or the most skillful. Such identities were created in the heat of work and then confirmed in the competitive sports and fighting that followed. The drunken often hurt themselves or others, performed inferior work, or made mistakes, and their reputations suffered. This rough, backcountryman style of manhood where alcohol was a component, however, gradually lost favor to the more morally upright male who was esteemed for his strength, skill, stamina—and his self-restraint.

Catharine Anne Wilson

References

Brown, Rev. Thomas Brush. *Autobiography of the Rev. Thomas Brush Brown.* Saint Mary's, Ontario: Saint Mary's Journal, 1899.

Erasmus, Charles J. "Culture Structure and Process: The Occurrence and Disappearance of Reciprocal Farm Labor" in *Southwestern Journal of Anthropology.* 12 (1956): 444–469.

Kimball, Solon T. "Rural Social Organization and Co-operative Labor" in *American Journal of Sociology.* 55 (1949): 38–49.
Moodie, Susanna. *Roughing It in the Bush.* 1852. Toronto: McClelland and Stewart, 1962.
Pederson, Jane Marie. *Between Memory and Reality: Family and Community in Rural Wisconsin 1870–1970.* Madison: University of Wisconsin Press, 1992.
Wilson, Catharine Anne. "Reciprocal Work Bees and the Meaning of Neighbourhood" in *Canadian Historical Review.* 82 (September 2001): 431–464.

Belgium

Belgium is one of the leading beer-drinking countries in the world. Belgium is also characterized by its multilingual federal structure that divides the country into three administrative and cultural regions: the Dutch Flanders, the French Wallonia, and the capital, Brussels. In addition to these, there is a small German province situated in the eastern part of Belgium.

At the end of the eighteenth century, there were several laws and decrees in force that condemned drunkenness in the society. For instance in 1799, while Belgium was under French rule, drunkenness was severely punished in the military code. This was also the case under Dutch rule at the beginning of the nineteenth century. Although the influence of the temperance movement was not as great in Belgium as in Northern Europe, several temperance societies were established in the bigger cities around the mid-1850s. In 1911, there were 4,626 temperance organizations in Belgium with almost 100,000 members (Cherrington et al.). The popularity of the temperance movement did, however, decline substantially since the beginning of the twentieth century.

Alcohol Consumption and Drinking Habits

Beer has been the preferred and dominant alcoholic beverage in Belgium all through modern history. There is little research-based information about how Belgian drinking habits have changed during the past centuries (Simpura and Karlsson). There have been some differences in drinking habits depending on the cultural region, and wine has been more popular in the French-speaking regions, whereas beer has been the clearly preferred beverage among the Flemish. At the beginning of the twentieth century, the consumption of distilled spirits was also high. In 1900, it was 4.7 liters of pure alcohol per capita (1.2 U.S. gallons). In the same year, the consumption of beer, counted in liters of the product, was 220 liters per capita (58.2 U.S. gallons). The total consumption of alcoholic beverages was 12.5 liters of pure alcohol per capita (3.3 U.S. gallons).

Due to strict government measures and sharp increases in excise duty rates for distilled spirits, the consumption of distilled spirits dropped to 0.6 liter of pure alcohol per capita (0.16 U.S. gallon) by the end of the 1930s (Österberg and Karlsson). At the beginning of the 1950s, the trend in total alcohol consumption turned, and the per capita rate of alcohol consumption doubled between 1950 and the mid-1980s. Alcohol consumption peaked in 1983 at 10.8 liters of pure alcohol per capita (2.9 U.S. gallons). Since then, alcohol consumption has again decreased, falling to 8.4 liters per capita (2.2 U.S. gallons) by 2000, which is the lowest level since the late 1960s (*World Drink Trends*).

Beer consumption increased in Belgium in the 1950s and 1960s, and reached a peak of 143 liters of the product per capita in 1973 (37.8 U.S. gallons). Since then, beer consumption has declined to 98 liters per capita (25.9 U.S. gallons) by 2000, which is the lowest level since the beginning of the twentieth century (Österberg and Karlsson).

The popularity of wine has been on the increase since the 1950s. In 1993, the level of wine consumption reached a level of 25.6 liters of the product per capita (6.8 U.S. gallons), which was almost a fivefold increase compared to the level at the beginning of the 1950s. In 2000, the per capita consumption of wine was 20 liters per capita (5.3 U.S. gallons) (*World Drink Trends*).

A Belgian waiter holding a tray of beers in Namur (Dave Bartruff/Corbis)

The consumption of distilled spirits peaked in 1980 at 2.4 liters of pure alcohol per capita (0.6 U.S. gallon). In the 1980s, the consumption of distilled spirits decreased, and in 2000 the consumption of distilled spirits was 1.2 liters of pure alcohol per capita (0.3 U.S. gallon) (*World Drink Trends*).

Beer's proportion of total alcohol consumption has decreased significantly since the late 1950s, going from 76 percent in 1959 to 54 percent in 1985. In 2000, the proportion of beer in total alcohol consumption was 53 percent. The proportion of distilled spirits peaked in 1978 at 23 percent. At the end of the 1990s, this proportion had declined to 12 percent. The proportion of wine in total alcohol consumption has increased from 13 percent in 1950 to 35 percent in 2000.

In 1997, the National Health Interview Survey reported that 21 percent of women and 10 percent of men had not drunk alcoholic beverages during the past twelve months. Abstinence rates were highest among the youngest respondents, and declined with increasing age. The heaviest drinking age group was found among men between 30 and 50 years of age, and among women between 40 and 50 years of age. In 1997, women drank about 26 percent of all alcohol consumed by the adult population (Simpura and Karlsson).

Beer is typically consumed every day and wine on weekends or on special occasions. Wine and distilled spirits are mostly consumed with meals at home, whereas beer is consumed more often on the premises where purchased (Hurst, Gregory, and Gussman). Drinking is unevenly distributed over the weekdays. Weekends account for more than half of weekly alcohol consumption. According to the National Health Interview Survey in 1997, some 30 percent of the respondents usually drank on working days and 57 percent during the weekend.

Alcohol Production and Trade

In 1850, there were 2,894 breweries operating in Belgium. During the next thirty years, their number decreased to 2,576. The number of breweries in Belgium increased rapidly, however, during the last few decades of the nineteenth century, and by 1900 their number had grown to over 3,200. In 1913, there were still over 3,300 breweries in Belgium (Cherrington et al.). By 1998, the number of breweries had decreased to 110. Despite the substantial decline in the number of small breweries, the methods of craftsman brewing are still practiced, and Belgium is famous nowadays for its unique and special beers. Pilsner is the most popular beer, accounting for over 65 percent of the beer market. In 1995, packaged beer accounted for 61 percent of total beer production. Nearly one-third of the beer produced in Belgium was exported, mainly to the neighboring countries. Imported beer accounted for 5 percent of the total beer consumption in Belgium (Hurst, Gregory, and Gussman).

Because of the climate, there has hardly been any viticulture in Belgium, and imported wines account for almost all of the wine consumed in Belgium. About 80 percent of the wine sales in Belgium are of French origin. Still, wines account for 90 percent of the wine market. Red wines are more popular than white wines and cover about 70 percent of the wine sales, although white wines increased in popularity in the 1990s (Hurst, Gregory, and Gussman).

The number of distilleries declined substantially in the nineteenth century. In 1850, there were 590 distilleries, whereas in 1900 the number of distilleries had decreased to 270. In 1912, there were only 125 distilleries left. Although the number of distilleries declined, their production increased from approximately 277,000 hectoliters in 1850 (7.3 million U.S. gallons) to 835,000 hectoliters in 1912 (22.1 million U.S. gallons) (Cherrington et al.). In the twentieth century, the production of distilled spirits in Belgium was very limited. Consequently, most of the distilled spirits consumed in Belgium are imported.

Administrative Structure for Preventive Alcohol Policies

Alcohol problem prevention in Belgium was a federal matter until the 1980s, and in the whole of Belgium there was only one coordinating agency, which was mainly focused on the primary prevention of alcohol problems. In 1982, the regions and linguistic communities were given larger responsibilities in the formation of preventive alcohol policies, and coordinating agencies were established in each linguistic community.

At present, each linguistic community, as well as Brussels, supports a coordinating agency that is responsible for the implementation of alcohol and drug abuse prevention. The coordinating agency for the Flemish Community is Vereniging voor Alcohol en andere Drugproblemen (VAD); for the French Community, Comité de Concertation sur l'Alcool et les autres Drogues (CCAD); for the German Community, Arbeitsgemeinschaft für Suchtvorbeugung und Lebensbewaltigung (ASL); and for Brussels, Overleg Drugs Brussel/Concentration Toxicomanie Bruxelles (ODB/CTB).

Although primary prevention of alcohol-related problems is mainly a matter for the linguistic communities, security problems such as public order and problems related to traffic such as drunk driving, as well as the financing of treatment, are within the competency of the federal government. Legislation, taxing, and licensing with regard to alcoholic beverages also fall within the competence of the federal government.

Alcohol Control Measures

In the nineteenth century, there were a lot of decrees and laws enacted in Belgium, especially concerning public drunkenness and nuisances associated with drunken behavior. For instance, in 1887 a law to prevent public drunkenness also made sale of intoxicants to minors punishable, and an 1896 report of a Royal Inquiry Commission suggested that a government monopoly for the manufacturing of spirits should be established and that temperance societies in schools should be a part of the school system. The government introduced two bills, in 1901 and 1908 respectively, that suggested stricter control of the alcohol retail trade, but these laws were never passed (Cherrington et al.).

A licensing system for retail sales of alcoholic beverages was adopted as early as 1849. The adoption of the license system was an attempt to fight illegal sales of alcoholic beverages and divided the retailers of alcoholic beverages into several classes. In 1912, the license system was abolished, which led to an increase in the number of spirits retailers (ibid.).

In 1918, a new piece of liquor legislation, known as the Vandervelde law, prohibited the sale of distilled spirits in Belgium for a brief period of time. This law was modified in 1919 to allow off-premises retail sale of distilled spirits from licensed premises, provided that the sale amounted to at least 2 liters (0.5 U.S. gallon). This rule was aimed at preventing the poor from buying distilled spirits, but it was never seriously enforced. The prohibition of retail sales of any alcoholic beverages of over 22 percent alcohol by volume in cafés or other on-premises public places was, however, continued. After a change in this law in 1983, it has been legal to buy all kinds of alcoholic beverages for both off- and on-premises consumption (Österberg and Karlsson).

Because granting licenses for trade in alcoholic beverages is a federal matter, the same kind of licensing policy is implemented in the whole country. Alcohol producers as well as alcohol importers and wholesalers need a license, which is granted to them by the federal Ministry of Finance. The license must be renewed annually. The overall regulations governing alcohol production, import, and wholesaling are linked to the general legislation on taxation and import in Belgium. The regulations are supervised and controlled at the local level.

On- and off-premises retailers of alcoholic beverages also need a license. The license is granted to them by the federal Ministry of Finance. The retail license, the fee for which depends on the type of establishment, must be renewed annually. An additional license is needed for on-premises retail sale of alcoholic beverages with an alcohol content over 22 percent by volume (Österberg and Karlsson).

Local authorities regulate hours of sale, and usually no special regulations for the retail sales of alcoholic beverages are prescribed (Hurst, Gregory, and Gussman). There are, however, special restrictions on serving distilled spirits along highways or with certain public leisure events. The usual business hours of ordinary shops are from 8 A.M. to 8 P.M. (9 P.M. on Fridays). Special night shops have the permission to remain open from 6 P.M. to 7 A.M. This means that in practice, alcohol is available all times of the day. The closing hours of cafés and bars depend on local rules, but they are usually open rather late. In cities, cafés and bars are usually open until 1 A.M. or 3 A.M., and they can exceed their time regulation by paying an extra tax per hour (Österberg and Karlsson).

A 1939 law concerning the control of drunkenness prohibited sales of alcoholic beverages on the premises to adolescents under sixteen years of age. The same law also prohibited serving alcoholic beverages to intoxicated persons. The 1983 law concerning licenses and the supply of distilled spirits prohibited the sale of distilled spirits to adolescents under eighteen years of age for on- and off-premises consumption. On the other hand, there are no legal age limits in Belgium for selling or buying beer or wine for off-premises consumption.

Alcohol advertising is regulated currently by the 1991 law on commercial practices and by voluntary guidelines. Since 1989, the Francophone National Broadcasting Company has not accepted advertising for products containing more than 10 percent alcohol by volume, and the Flemish National Broadcasting Company will only broadcast advertising for alcoholic beverages after 6 P.M. According to a decree from July 1991, radio stations that broadcast advertisements for medicines or medical treatment, as well as for alcoholic beverages, have to give free transmission time to the government. The free transmission time is used by the government for health-education campaigns.

In July 1995, the Flemish government imposed several restrictions on the advertising of alcoholic beverages. According to these regulations, alcohol advertising, among other kinds, may not be addressed to minors, may not connect alcohol consumption to improvement of physical performance, and may not imply that drinking alcohol leads to social or sexual success. Moreover, advertisements for alcoholic beverages may not give a negative picture of abstinence or of moderate alcohol consumption.

Blood testing for drivers was introduced as early as 1958, the maximum permissible blood-alcohol concentration (BAC) level being set at 0.15 percent. In 1968, the BAC level was reduced to 0.08 percent and Breathalyzer tests were introduced. In December 1994, the maximum BAC level while driving was decreased to 0.05 percent. At the same time, the fines increased and more offenses than before were followed up with suspension of the driving license.

Alcohol Taxation

During the nineteenth century, there were several attempts to amend alcohol taxation in order to receive more revenues and fight drunkenness. In 1838, for instance, a tax was imposed on all small dealers in distilled spirits. The purpose of the tax was both to raise revenues and to discourage the misuse of alcoholic beverages. Not only the sale but also the manufacture and import of alcoholic beverages were taxed. For most of the nineteenth century, the taxation structure favored rural distillation.

The current method of alcohol taxation varies depending on the beverage category. For beer, excise duties are levied on the basis of alcohol content in the finished product. For wine and intermediate products, the excise duties are applied on the basis of hectoliters of the product, and for distilled spirits, the excise duty is levied per hectoliter of pure alcohol in the finished product. The value-added tax (VAT) of 21 percent is the same for all alcoholic beverages.

The excise duty rates calculated per liter of pure alcohol are the same for beer and wine, and almost the same for intermediate products. The excise duty rate for distilled spirits is nearly four times the rate for beer and wine. In the late 1990s, some 31 percent of beer prices consisted of taxes. The corresponding figure for distilled spirits was 55 percent and for wine 28 percent. (Österberg and Karlsson).

Thomas Karlsson and Esa Österberg

References

Cherrington, Ernest Hurst, et al., eds. *Standard Encyclopedia of the Alcohol Problem,* 6 vols., vol. 1: 305–321. Westerville, OH: American Issue Publishing Company, 1924–1930.

Hurst, Wendy, Ed Gregory, and Thomas Gussman. *International Survey. Alcoholic Beverage Taxation and Control Policies.* 9th ed. Ottawa: Brewers Association of Canada, 1997.

Österberg, Esa, and Thomas Karlsson, eds. *Alcohol Policies in EU Member States and Norway. A Collection of Country Reports.* Helsinki: Stakes, 2002.

Simpura, Jussi, and Thomas Karlsson. *Trends in Drinking Patterns among Adult Population in 15 European Countries, 1950 to 2000. A Collection of Country Reports.* Helsinki: Stakes, 2001.

World Drink Trends 2002 Edition. Oxfordshire, UK: NTC Publications, 2002.

Bible Wine

During the nineteenth and early twentieth centuries, Protestants throughout the English-speaking world debated the use of fermented communion wine. In the sacrament of Holy Communion, the reenactment of the Last Supper, wine recalled Christ's blood. Traditionalists argued that the Bible called for fermented wine. Encouraged by the Blue Ribbon Army in the United States, teetotalers often demanded the substitution of grape juice.

During the early moderationist temperance movement in the late 1820s, wine was considered acceptable. In the 1830s, some teetotalers insisted on abstinence from all alcoholic beverages, including Communion wine. In Britain, local residents, especially working people, pressed Christian ministers of all denominations to endorse teetotalism or risk defections from their congregations. In 1837, the Manchester Nonconformist minister Francis Beardsall insisted on a nonintoxicating sacrament, and manufactured what he called unfermented wine. The controversy became intense after 1855. A grape juice manufacturer, Frank Wright, claimed that from 1868 to 1875, the number of British churches that used his product grew from 100 to 1,000.

The Communion wine question was part of a wider debate concerning the scriptural implications of abstinence. Traditionalists pointed to frequent biblical wine drinking. Teetotalers answered that: (1) both fermented and unfermented wines were described in the Bible; (2) Scripture praised teetotalers, such as the disciple Timothy; and (3) not all Christian reforms were specified in the Bible.

Unfermented Communion wine advocates denied the propriety of using a poison to represent Christ's blood. A "two wine theory," propounded in England by the Nonconformist Dr. Frederic Richard Lees and the Manchester Anglican priest William Caine held that the two biblical Hebrew words "Tirosh" and "Yayin" distinguished between fermented and nonalcoholic wines. Teetotalers argued that since Christ would have been unwilling to intoxicate guests who had already exhausted the wine reserves of their hosts, he offered celebrants grape juice when he turned water into wine at the Cana wedding feast. Teetotalers invoked Hebrew tradition to explain Christ's use of wine at the Last Supper, claiming that since Jewish law forbade fermented products during Passover, Christ used unfermented wine, thus justifying the nonalcoholic commemoration of Holy Thursday.

Anglicans cited the Bible, Thomas Aquinas, Thomas Hooker, and contemporary rabbis; and most, such as Canon William Hopkins, sometime chairman of the Convocation of Canterbury Intemperance Committee, insisted on the ancient Christian rubric of fermented Communion wine. Traditionalists counted on the Holy Spirit to prevent fermented-wine communicants from falling into temptation.

By the 1880s, most Nonconformist chapels used grape juice in Communion. Wesleyan Methodists reversed an earlier ban on unfermented Communion wine. Roman Catholic and Anglican officials, however, forbade the practice. Disappointing a militant Anglican teetotal minority, the 1883 Convocation of Canterbury and the 1888 worldwide Lambeth Conference insisted that only fermented wine be used for Communion.

The Bible wine controversy occurred in all English-speaking countries. For instance, by the late nineteenth century, most Protestant denominations in North America substituted grape juice for intoxicating wine. In 1869, a Methodist dentist named Welch pasteurized Concord grape juice in order to produce an unfermented communion wine for his church; his son founded the well-known grape juice company. In 1917, staunchly prohibitionist Oklahoma made the purchase or consumption of sacramental wine illegal.

Cynthia Belaskie

See also: Burns, (James) Dawson; Christian Socialism; Church of England Temperance Society (CETS); Close, Francis; Ellison, Henry; Evangelical Temperance (United Kingdom); Lees, Frederic Richard; Lewis, Elizabeth Ann; Wilberforce, Basil, and Wilberforce, Ernest

References

Miller, Doris I. "Unfermented Wine on the Lord's Table: Origins and Implementation in Nineteenth Century Canadian Methodism" in *Methodist History.* 29, no. 1 (1990): 3–13.

O'Brien, Betty A. "The Lord's Supper: Fruit of the Vine or Cup of Devils?" in *Methodist History.* 31, no. 4 (1993): 202–223.

Olsen G. W. *Drink and the British Establishment: The Church of England Temperance Society, 1873–1914.* Forthcoming.

———. *Pub and Parish: Drink and Temperance in the Church of England, 1829–1875.* Forthcoming.

Shiman, Lilian Lewis. *Crusade against Drink in Victorian England.* New York: St. Martin's, 1988.

Blaikie, Margaret Catherine (1823–1915)

Mrs. Margaret Catherine Blaikie (1823–1915), Scottish temperance reformer, was, for the twenty-seven years between 1878 and 1905, president of both the Scottish Christian Union (SCU) and of the SCU's Edinburgh central branch. Between 1906 and 1914, she had the title of honorary president. She was involved in several imperial projects, including the Foreign Missionary Society and the resettlement of orphan children.

Margaret Blaikie was born in Banff in 1823, the daughter of an Edinburgh gentleman, Walter Biggar, and Ann (born Duff), daughter of an old Banffshire family. Ann was an inspiring role model for her daughter. In the first half of the nineteenth century, Ann Biggar became a total abstainer in the hope that her example would influence Banff's poor. In 1841, Margaret's family moved to Edinburgh. Four years later, Margaret married William Gardener Blaikie, at various times the Free Church of Scotland minister at Pilrig, professor of divinity, moderator of the General Assembly of the Free Church, and the president of the Pan-Presbyterian Council. The Blaikies made their home first in Edinburgh and then in North Berwick on the Firth of Forth.

William Blaikie's clerical career influenced Margaret's interest in temperance reform and other public work. Between 1871 and 1873, the famous American Evangelist Dwight L. Moody was a guest of the Blaikies. Moody persuaded William and Margaret of the righteousness of total abstinence. Moody also encouraged Margaret to start a mothers' meeting in 1874; the meeting was still active in 1898. In 1870, William's work took the couple to Toronto, where they met Miss Annie Macpherson, a social reformer interested in the immigration of London's poor orphans to the white settler colonies. This meeting resulted in the Blaikies' decision to establish the Emigration Home in Lauriston Lane, Edinburgh. The home operated for twenty years, during which time about 700 children entered the home and approximately 300 children were sent to Canada.

Margaret Blaikie's experience with destitute children convinced her of the urgent need for temperance reform. She viewed total abstinence and prohibition as a matter of Christian duty. She became the center of the SCU, presiding over the work of the Edinburgh branch and of the SCU itself. She was keenly interested in the "rescue" work associated with temperance reform and devoted her attention to work among "inebriate" women and girls.

In the late nineteenth century, Margaret established a female auxiliary in cooperation with the Foreign Missionary Society in North Berwick. At least between the years 1898 and 1903, Margaret organized local women's "home work" on behalf of female foreign missionaries.

Some of her correspondence can be found in the (Scottish) Foreign Missionary Society letters at the National Library of Scotland, Edinburgh.

Megan Smitley

See also: Scotland; Scottish Christian Union (SCU)

References

Darling, Jane. "The Late Mrs. Blaikie" in *Scottish Women's Temperance News.* 19, no. 9 (September 1915): 107.

"Mrs. Margaret Blaikie. President of the Scottish Christian Union (British Women's Temperance Association)" in *Scottish Women's Temperance News.* 1, no. 2 (January 1898): 5–6.

Smitley, Megan. "'Inebriates,' 'Heathens,' Templars and Suffragists: Scotland and Imperial Feminism, c1870–1914" in *Women's History Review.* 11, no. 3 (2002): 455–480.

———. "'Woman's Mission': The Temperance and Women's Suffrage Movements in Scotland, c1870–1914" (Ph.D. dissertation, University of Glasgow, 2002).

Blue Ribbon Movement

The Blue Ribbon Movement was a leading force in the larger Gospel Temperance Movement and one of the most successful and wide-reaching branches of the broader late-nineteenth-century temperance movement in general. The Blue Ribbon Movement emerged in the northeastern United States during the early 1870s. It spread to Canada and Great Britain by the end of that decade. The movement got its name from the blue lapel ribbons that its members wore to announce that they had signed a pledge to abstain from alcohol. By the mid-1880s, millions had taken the temperance pledge and donned the blue ribbon.

Francis Murphy and the Evangelical Style

Francis Murphy led the Blue Ribbon Movement in the United States. An Irish Catholic immigrant, Murphy settled in the state of Maine and became a hard-drinking hotel keeper. In 1870, he found himself serving a prison sentence for liquor sales that violated the famous Maine Law. Murphy experienced Protestant conversion in the Portland jail where he was incarcerated, and he vowed never to drink again. Soon after his release, Murphy began giving temperance speeches throughout New England. Despite limited education, Murphy honed his talent for public speaking and developed a distinct style of evangelical temperance oratory.

The Blue Ribbon Movement grew out of the New England reform club movement, in which ex-drinkers and men who wanted to stop drinking formed local clubs to help each other achieve lasting sobriety. Murphy effectively took over New England's Reform Club and Blue Ribbon Association. He then proceeded to make evangelical Protestantism a central feature of the Blue Ribbon Movement's approach to temperance. Although many of his prominent evangelical contemporaries spoke to the issue of temperance, Murphy used evangelical techniques to focus specifically on drunkards. Murphy led the movement's initial spread by holding meetings in large public halls over a period of several days. In these carefully structured, revival-like meetings, collective song and personal testimonies by reformed drunkards set the stage for Murphy's rousing speeches, after which a mass of men typically came forward to sign the temperance pledge. Designed to evoke feelings of camaraderie, salvation, and common cause, the meetings also laid the basis for local Blue Ribbon clubs. Printed on its pledge certificates, the phrase "with malice toward none and charity for all" served as the movement's guiding motto. In keeping with this ideal, Murphy refused to condemn saloon owners, liquor sellers, or their customers. Murphy and his followers had little taste for the coercive approach of prohibitionists or for the rationalistic and often browbeating style of many temperance reformers. In contrast, Murphy structured his speeches around his own personal story to demonstrate the power of unprejudiced Christian love. Indeed, Murphy and his followers identified with drunkards and their suffering, confronting them not as social pariahs but as fellow men. They favored moral suasion over coercion, appealing to the drunkard's heart instead of his head, and sometimes giving him material aid.

The Blue Ribbon Movement in the United States

The Blue Ribbon Movement was attractive both to its members and to many middle-class reformers for a number of reasons. Like the earlier Washingtonian movement and modern-day Alcoholics Anonymous, Blue Ribbon clubs offered the reforming drunkard valuable moral support. Members also found that working to save other drunkards helped them maintain their own sobriety. Like the gatherings of the Washingtonians, Blue Ribbon meetings were entertaining. The clubs and meetings also fostered a sense of belonging. In so doing, they provided sociable alternatives to the culture of the saloon. Given the dominant belief that economic success required temperance, the Blue Ribbon Movement appealed to many working- and lower-middle-class men who sought a better standard of living for themselves and their families. The movement's charitable activities and its soothing message of Christian love also attracted people struggling amid the erratic economic conditions in America and Europe at that time. Although they often differed on the prohibition issue, middle-class temperance reformers supported the movement because it inspired men to take the pledge and left the saloons with fewer customers. Conversely, the Blue Ribbon Movement benefited from middle-class and well-to-do temperance activists who provided financial support and helped coordinate and publicize Blue Ribbon campaigns.

Indeed, it was the invitation and support of reformer Frances Elizabeth Caroline Willard, then president of Chicago's Woman's Christian Temperance Union (WCTU), that brought Murphy to the Midwest in 1874. The investment paid big dividends for the region's temperance reformers, and it expanded the Blue Ribbon Movement beyond New England. In Illinois, Murphy left eleven newly formed Chicago reform clubs in his wake, and within days of his arrival in Sterling, owners had voluntarily closed the town's fifteen saloons due to a lack of customers. The movement was especially successful among native-born populations in midsized towns and in the West, but it had a harder time convincing working-class immigrants in the larger cities to give up their drinking customs. Murphy's greatest urban success came when business leaders and prominent temperance reformers invited him to Pittsburgh, where he gave his first speech on 26 November 1876. Forty thousand Pittsburgh residents signed the pledge and wore the blue ribbon within ten weeks. In several of the city's respectable churches, conventional class boundaries temporarily collapsed as middle-class churchgoers mingled with rowdy laborers. In 1877, the WCTU supporter and retailing mogul John Wanamaker brought Murphy to Philadelphia, where he held meetings in Wanamaker's famous Sunday school. Murphy also traveled to Canada in 1877, and he later crossed the Atlantic for a tour of Great Britain, where he met with Queen Victoria. However, it was several of Murphy's followers who took the Blue Ribbon Movement beyond U.S. borders.

The Blue Ribbon Movement in Canada and Great Britain

Adopting Murphy's style and method, D. I. K. Rhine became the figurehead of the Canadian Blue Ribbon Movement. Rhine's disreputable past and his rise to prominence also recalled Murphy. After a long career of drunkenness, theft, and several failed attempts to become sober, Rhine became a Murphy follower during the 1876 Pittsburgh campaign. Rhine quickly became a full-time speaker and brought the movement to Erie County, Pennsylvania. By 1877, he had moved into Canada, where temperance activity was focused mainly in support of the Dunkin Act, a local-option law that prohibited liquor sales in quantities less than five gallons. The Canadian temperance movement was focusing on prohibition and doing little to help drunkards. Rhine reaped immediate success in Saint Catharines, and he was then promptly invited to Toronto. As he moved eastward, thousands took the pledge, joined the Rhine Total Abstinence Clubs, and enjoyed the movement's offer of free breakfasts. However, Rhine's reputation fell as fast as it rose. In March of 1878, he was arrested for sexually assaulting the daughter of his Stratford host. Although Rhine was acquitted, the incident turned much of the Canadian press against the movement. Conflict erupted between Rhine's supporters and detractors within the movement, and Rhine decided to rejoin Murphy in New York. Although it continued to bring in converts, the Canadian movement lost momentum and the nation's press lost interest in it.

The Blue Ribbon Movement's advance was more gradual in Great Britain. After visiting America and hearing Murphy speak, William Noble took the movement home to England in

1877. The wealthy temperance supporter W. J. Palmer purchased London's Huxton Hall, where Noble established a permanent Blue Ribbon mission to promote temperance among the working-class residents in the area. Noble's Blue Ribbon mission took its place among London's other Gospel Temperance missions, but the Blue Ribbon movement did not reach into the provinces until Richard T. Booth arrived from America in 1880. Like Murphy and Rhine, Booth was a reformed drunkard with a similar talent for temperance speeches. Booth launched a Blue Ribbon campaign that developed into a nationwide mass movement over the next five years. Reaching beyond London's poor, Booth's Blue Ribbon Gospel Army attracted increasing converts from the lower middle class. By the end of the decade, over a million British had taken the pledge and worn the blue ribbon. However, as it had elsewhere, the movement sparked controversy and brought criticism. Accusations of financial mismanagement and the substantial fees that Murphy and other speakers earned provoked consistent public skepticism. In England, conflict and competition flared up between Huxton Hall and the missions of the Blue Ribbon Gospel Army. At times, self-appointed speakers were exposed as unreformed opportunists. On both sides of the Atlantic, some longtime temperance reformers came to resent the Blue Ribbon newcomers, and some were put off by the movement's intense emotionalism.

The Blue Ribbon Movement lost momentum everywhere by the latter half of the 1880s. Perhaps what most plagued the movement was the accusation that after the initial enthusiasm wore off, most pledge takers fell off the wagon and resumed their drinking. Although the accusation probably bore some truth, the movement certainly helped establish lasting temperance activity in towns, provinces, and—in America—newly settled western regions, where temperance had made little or no headway before the movement's arrival. Perhaps the decline of the Blue Ribbon Movement was inevitable because so much of its appeal derived from an emotional intensity that proved easier to create than sustain. Neither gospel temperance nor the drunkard disappeared from the social landscape of Great Britain and North America, but more and more temperance reformers grew increasingly impatient with moral suasion. By the end of the 1880s, campaigns for prohibition once again dominated the temperance movement on both sides of the Atlantic.

Timothy Yates

See also: Alcoholic Mutual Aid Groups (United States); Alcoholics Anonymous (AA); Murphy, Francis; Washingtonians

References

Birrell, A. J. "D. I. K. Rhine and the Gospel Temperance Movement in Canada" in *The Canadian Historical Review.* 58, no. 1 (March 1977): 23–42.

Chavigny, Katherine Ann. "American Confessions: Reformed Drunkards and the Origins of Therapeutic Culture" (Ph.D. dissertation, University of Chicago, 1999).

Daniels, W. H. *The Temperance Reform and Its Great Reformers.* New York: Nelson and Phillips, 1877.

Murphy, Rebecca Johnstone. *Memories of Francis Murphy, the Great Apostle of Gospel Temperance, by His Wife.* Long Beach, CA: Graves and Hersey, ca. 1908.

Shiman, Lilian Lewis. *Crusade against Drink in Victorian England.* London: Macmillan, 1988.

Vandersloot, J. Samuel. *The True Path, or, Gospel Temperance Being the Life, Work and Speeches of Francis Murphy, Dr. Henry A. Reynolds, and Their Co-laborers: Embracing Also a History of the Woman's Christian Temperance Union.* Chicago: Palmer, 1877.

Boole, Ella Alexander (1858–1952)

Ella A. Boole (1858–1952) was president of the national Woman's Christian Temperance Union (WCTU) and ran unsuccessfully for the U.S. Senate from New York for the Prohibition Party in 1920. Born 26 July 1858 in Van Wert, Ohio, to prominent lawyer and Civil War hero Isaac N. and Rebecca (Alban) Alexander, Ella attended school at Wooster College. In 1883, two years after graduation with her M.A. degree, she married Methodist Episcopal pastor William H. Boole of New York. Always concerned about temperance issues, she was elected corresponding secretary of the New York State Woman's Christian Temperance Union (NYSWCTU) in 1885. Fourteen years later, she ascended to the presidency of this organization, a position she held until 1903. During this time, she received her Ph.D. from Wooster in 1895, and her husband died a year later. Boole left the leadership of the NYSWCTU for six years when she became secretary of the Woman's Board of Home Missions of the Presbyterian Church. In 1909, she returned to the presidency of the NYSWCTU. Five years later, she was elected vice president of the national WCTU, and in 1925, she became its national president. Although nominally a Republican, she ran as the Prohibition Party candidate for the United States Senate seat in New York in 1920, after losing the Republican primary. A gifted speaker, she ran on a platform that included support for women's suffrage and a modified League of Nations. During the campaign against the incumbent, James Wadsworth, Boole stressed that Prohibition and women's involvement in politics were necessary to protect the future of children. She was able to garner only 5.8 percent of the vote.

Upon passage of the Eighteenth Amendment, Boole was forceful in turning the WCTU's focus toward enforcement of the Volstead Act. Some of her statements regarding the violence and corruption surrounding enforcement of the law became a target for the national press. In April 1926, Boole testified before a Senate judiciary subcommittee hearing regarding the flagrant violations of Prohibition and calls for repealing the Eighteenth Amendment. Instead of retreating in the face of criticism, she urged that the law be strengthened and claimed that legal temperance had had a positive effect in America. She stated, "It has resulted in better national health, children are born under better conditions, homes are better, and the mother is delivered

Ella Alexander Boole (1858–1952) (Library of Congress)

from fear of a drunken husband." Many of her arguments in favor of strengthening the Prohibition laws can be found in her book *Give Prohibition Its Chance,* published in 1929.

In 1931, she was elected president of the World's WCTU, a position she held until 1946, four years before her death. She struggled to keep the organization moving forward after Prohibition laws were repealed in the United States, Finland, and Iceland. At the World's WCTU Stockholm convention in 1934, Boole told the gathering that these were "simply skirmishes lost" and that the women needed to renew their efforts "for world wide strengthening of the temperance movement." Yet in the last few years of her life, to many listening to her, these seemed like hollow words. She died in Brooklyn, New York.

T. Jason Soderstrum

See also: National Prohibition (United States); Prohibition Party (United States); Woman's Christian Temperance Union (WCTU) (United States); World's Woman's Christian Temperance Union (WWCTU)

References

Boole, Ella A. *The Reminiscences of Ella A. Boole.* New York: Columbia University Oral History Collection, 1950.

Graham, Frances W. *Four Decades, 1874–1914: A History of Forty Years' Work of the Woman's Christian Temperance Union of the State of New York.* New York: Salvation Army Press, 1910.

———. *Give Prohibition Its Chance.* Evanston, IL: National Woman's Christian Temperance Union Publication House, 1929.

Brewers' Association of Scotland (BAS)

Dating from 2002, the Scottish Beer and Pub Association (SBPA) succeeded the Brewers and Licensed Retailers Association of Scotland, itself briefly a successor in 1994 to the Brewers' Association of Scotland (BAS). The SBPA is a trade association made up of brewers and brewer-owned retailers and independent multiple-site retailers representing the beer industry in Scotland. The main aim of the association is to contribute to the economic and social well-being of Scotland through employment, investment, and training.

The BAS had its origins in the nineteenth-century Edinburgh Brewers' Association, a powerful amalgam of brewing interests in the major center of the Scottish industry. These bodies emerged because Scottish brewers felt that English associations had not adequately represented their interests. Indeed, just as the Brewers' Society had in 1904 assumed an all-England role, so the Edinburgh association was dissolved and converted in 1906 into the BAS, to act as the sole trade association for wholesale brewers throughout Scotland. The first general meeting was held in 1907, when there were forty-eight members.

Like those of its English counterpart, the corporate functions of the BAS were long overshadowed by temperance and prohibitionist activities, most threateningly in the early 1900s by the clamor for local veto polls and by parliamentary legislation threatening to curb alcohol consumption. This found expression in the Temperance (Scotland) Act (1913), which after World War I resulted in local prohibition orders in areas where the movement was politically active, a few such bans on alcohol taking place as late as the 1960s and 1970s.

According to the surviving BAS records, the main concerns of the association, apart from representing the interests of members nationally and locally, were industrial relations, in particular wage bargaining, brewing education and training, collecting production and other data, and, increasingly, public relations on behalf of the industry in Scotland. Scottish brewing companies funded the BAS, with contributions being in proportion to production.

Until the interwar period, union organization was limited, and labor relations were hardly a problem in the paternalistic setting of dominant family enterprises. In times of retrenchment, such as the 1920s and 1930s, and during the hectic mergers of the 1950 and 1960s, growing labor unrest and union recruitment forced brewers to bargain with unions. As an example, in what were evidently path-breaking negotiations with the Transport and General Workers Union, the BAS in 1937 and 1938 helped resolve the recognition issue and broker a wide-ranging agreement on pay and conditions.

Another significant interest since inception has been education and research, notably through the BAS's support of the only brewing school in Scotland at Heriot-Watt College (renamed Heriot-Watt University in 1966), where courses were taught from 1903. In 1920, the BAS supported a lectureship in biochemistry and fermentation in what grew into a substantial department. Now called the International Centre for Brewing and Distilling, it not only offers one of the few undergraduate courses in brewing, but is also a major research institute for malting, brewing, and distilling.

The BAS and its successors have been extensively involved in promotional activities as the voice of the industry in Scotland. This aspect of its work allied the BAS increasingly closely with the Scottish licensed retailers, leading ultimately to a merger of trade organizations in 1994. The current membership includes all the major Scottish companies and multinationals with brewing or retailing interests in the country. Records of the BAS and its successors are held in the Scottish Brewing Archive, University of Glasgow.

Ian Donnachie

See also: Scotland

References

Donnachie, Ian. *A History of the Brewing Industry in Scotland.* 2d ed. Edinburgh: John Donald, 1998.

Richmond, Lesley, and Alison Turton. *The Brewing Industry: A Guide to Historical Records.* Manchester and New York: Manchester University Press, 1990.

Brewers' Company

London brewers formed an association to protect their interests as early as the thirteenth century. At that period, the mayor and aldermen of the city of London regulated the prices and measures of ale for retail, but in 1406 the brewers successfully petitioned for the right to control the trade themselves subject to the overall authority of the city corporation. In 1437, Henry VI granted the Brewers' Company the first of its eight charters, confirming rights over the trade and its status as a corporate body.

Due to the prosperity of the industry in the rapidly expanding metropolis, many members of the society became rich, and beginning in the sixteenth century, the Brewers' Company was responsible for the administration of numerous charitable bequests, mainly supporting schools and almshouses.

By the eighteenth century, the company had lost much of its momentum, partly it seems because the major London brewers had grown so powerful that, independent of any cartel arrangements, they exercised control of the market in and beyond the metropolis. But after 1795, its authority revived through the Committee of Porter Brewers, which effectively fixed the price of porter during the Napoleonic War.

Only brewers brewing in the City of London district could be members of the Brewers' Company, so an overlapping London Brewers' Association was organized late in the nineteenth century to enroll brewers in greater London, such as Fullers and Youngs.

According to the historians Terry Gourvish and Richard Wilson, the Brewers' Company, through its brewing trade committee, at least until the 1880s was reasonably effective in maintaining collective action on prices, discounts, and practices in the metropolitan beer trade. As competition increased, the major brewers largely went their own way, and the company's authority in these traditional spheres disintegrated.

At this juncture, and facing increased action from the temperance movement, the company regained its momentum especially after 1880 by focusing its activities on trade defense in London. It worked closely with the National Trade Defence Fund (Association from 1900), the (Country) Brewers' Society, and the London Brewers' Association, and as historian David W. Gutzke notes, its wealthy members were among the largest contributors to the fund. The invigorated company also gained considerable influence over London publicans, effectively eliminating competition from provincial brewers and retailers.

During the twentieth century, the society, in common with the other brewing trade associations, concerned itself with a growing range of issues affecting the industry, for example, personnel management, wage rates, industrial disputes, licensing, beer pricing and, increasingly, public relations and promotional activities.

Several powers given to the company by its charters, such as rights to search all premises used for brewing to ensure the brew was sound, the materials wholesome and without adulterates, the vats and vessels clean, and measures accurate, have lapsed or been subsumed in state legislation. But this ancient body, through its influential members (still drawn from the major brewing companies), court, and committees, has significant residual influence in the brewing industry nationally and internationally.

There are extensive archives covering the administration and many interests of the society held at the Brewers' Hall, Aldermanbury Square, at the Guildhall Library, and at Westminster City Archives, all in London.

Ian Donnachie

See also: Brewers' Society (BS); Licensed Victuallers' Protection Society of London

References

Ball, Mia. *The Worshipful Company of Brewers: A Short History.* London: Hutchinson, 1977.

Gourvish, Terry R., and Richard G. Wilson. *The British Brewing Industry, 1830–1980.* Cambridge: Cambridge University Press, 1994.

Gutzke, David W. *Protecting the Pub: Brewers and Publicans against Temperance.* Woodbridge, Suffolk: Royal Historical Society; Wolfeboro, NH: Boydell and Brewer, 1989.

Richmond, Lesley, and Alison Turton, eds. *The Brewing Industry: A Guide to Historical Records.* Manchester and New York: Manchester University Press, 1990.

Brewers' Society (BS)

The Brewers' Society (BS) for ninety years was the most important trade association for the brewing industry in the United

Kingdom. It was established in 1904 as a federation of the Country Brewers' Society (CBS), the London Brewers' Association, and the Burton Brewers' Association. It also aimed at incorporating northern brewers, who often disagreed with other provincial brewers. Senior figures from the brewing industry, including members of the Bass, Charrington, Guinness, and Whitbread families, were early BS leaders.

The BS superseded the CBS, which had been founded in 1822 to oppose legislation designed to promote greater competition in the industry, notably, brewers supplying independent public houses. Throughout the nineteenth century, the CBS continued intermittently to represent the interests of provincial brewers. In growing cooperation with the more powerful London brewers and key licensed victuallers' organizations, it resisted the national temperance agitations that increased from the 1880s. This cooperation in the fight against the temperance reformers led to the formation of the National Trade Defence Fund in 1888 (renamed the Association in 1900) and ultimately to the merger that created the BS. Over the course of its history, the CBS (and later the BS) sponsored several official newspapers, successively the *Brewers' Guardian* (1871–1878), *Brewers' Gazette* (1878–1886), *Brewing Trade Review* (1886–1972), and, finally, the *Brewing Review*.

The activities of the BS have been so diverse that it is difficult to summarize them briefly, but among the major concerns historically have been licensing, industrial relations, and the support of education, training, and research. In cooperation with the National Trade Defence Association, the BS was prominently involved in parliamentary campaigns and legal battles in defense of the industry, answering the onslaught from the teetotal organizations.

The BS represented the brewing interest in many major issues affecting relations between the industry and Parliament, notably on licensing legislation, excise and other taxation, and, at different periods, items as diverse as wartime restrictions on raw materials and production, beer gravities, social problems of alcohol, and monopolies and mergers. According to historian David W. Gutzke, the society, as the most affluent trade organization in Britain, was "unrivalled in sustaining agitation against the government to protect the brewing industry."

One significant counter to temperance reform and to further national and local government intervention was public house improvement. The society published several pamphlets on behalf of the public house improvement between the world wars and promoted it during the period of post-1945 austerity and reconstruction and from the 1960s, when there was increasing competition from other sectors for leisure spending.

Although brewers in Scotland had collectively addressed labor relations in the 1930s, it was not until 1946 that the BS began to exercise a monitoring role in pay and conditions. Industrial relations subsequently became a significant area of activity, though as historians Terry Gourvish and Richard Wilson indicate, individual companies settled most problems.

The BS, along with the Institute of Brewing, played a major role in the 1951 establishment of the Brewing Industry Research Foundation. Working closely with other brewing organizations and with the universities, notably Birmingham and Heriot-Watt, the foundation became one of the most important international centers of research on every aspect of the industry, including malting, brewing, yeast culture, and hops.

The role of the BS as the industry's voice was significant and its public relations and promotional activities generally very successful. Its publications on many aspects of the industry were extensive, including, for example, pub safety, problem drinking, monopolies and mergers, and numerous statistical and other surveys of the drinks trade. The BS was the major trade association for the brewing industry in the United Kingdom and represented it in the European Union and internationally.

At the beginning of 1994, the BS joined with multiple-site drink retailers to become the Brewers and Licensed Retailers Association. This reflected the upheaval in the beer trade. Following the Watneys and Courage swap of breweries for tied houses, many big pub owners (notably Entrepreneur, formerly Watneys) no longer owned breweries. Having difficulty raising funds, the Brewers and Licensed Retailers Association played a diminishing role. In 2001, it changed its name to the British Beer and Pub Association, left the old Portman Square headquarters of the BS, and deposited the bulk of its archives at the Modern Records Centre, University of Warwick, and its extensive library at the National Brewing Library at Oxford Brookes University. The Warwick deposit included the minutes of the old CBS.

Ian Donnachie

See also: Beer; Brewers' Company; Licensed Victuallers' Protection Society of London; National Trade Defence Association (NTDA)

References

Gourvish, Terry R., and Richard G. Wilson. *The British Brewing Industry, 1830–1980.* Cambridge: Cambridge University Press, 1994.

Gutzke, David W. *Protecting the Pub: Brewers and Publicans against Temperance.* Woodbridge, Suffolk: Royal Historical Society; Wolfeboro, NH: Boydell and Brewer, 1989.

Richmond, Lesley, and Alison Turton, eds. *The Brewing Industry: A Guide to Historical Records.* Manchester and New York: Manchester University Press, 1990.

British Medical Temperance Association (BMTA)

The British Medical Temperance Association (BMTA) was organized in 1876 to promote total abstinence among members of the medical profession and to study the physiological and pathological effects of alcohol on the human body. The establishment of the BMTA grew out of the medical evidence that appeared in the second half of the nineteenth century concerning the harmful effects of drink, as well as a sentiment among some physicians that the medical community needed to play a leading role in disseminating this information.

Ten physicians attended the first meeting of the BMTA, held in London at the headquarters of the National Temperance League (NTL). The league had earlier sponsored the formation of other temperance organizations, including the Church of England Temperance Society. Beginning in 1869, the league published *The Medical Temperance Journal* to extend the temperance message to the medical profession. The league also sponsored temperance breakfasts at the annual meeting of the British Medical Association. To build upon these efforts, the league decided to help establish an organization explicitly for teetotaler doctors.

Convincing the British medical establishment of the need for such an organization would prove to be a difficult task. Despite growing medical evidence of the harmful effects of drink and the establishment of a temperance hospital in London in 1873, many physicians still viewed members of Victorian temperance organizations as eccentrics and fanatics. Beginning in the 1830s, alcohol had replaced bloodletting as a standard treatment for everything from pain relief to respiratory problems like asthma and bronchitis. Those physicians who refused to prescribe alcohol often found their medical practices declined and themselves ostracized by colleagues. In addition, the medical community resented any infringement of physicians' claims to professional expertise.

At the first meeting of the BMTA, a constitution was drawn up that asked members to affirm that at the present time they abstained from alcohol, but the constitution did not require a lifetime teetotal pledge. Besides this promise and the payment of an annual subscription of a half guinea, there were no other requirements. The BMTA did not mandate a ban on the use of alcohol in treatment and made it clear in its bylaws that "every member is free to form his own opinion as to the value of alcohol in disease" treatment. An annual general meeting was held in London in May, while at other times, an executive council managed the affairs of the organization. Dr. James Edmunds served as the first president. The BMTA chose as its second president a far more distinguished physician, Dr. Benjamin Ward Richardson (1828–1896), who retained that position until his death. Richardson was one of the most prominent doctors of his day, a pioneer in the use of anesthesia. A member of the Royal Society and knighted in 1893, Richardson was also a preeminent figure in the field of public health. It was as an investigator in that field that he first became involved with the temperance cause.

As its principal work, the BMTA compiled medical testimony in favor of total abstinence that could not be ignored by their more skeptical colleagues. After initially making use of the *Medical Temperance Journal,* the BMTA decided to launch its own journal, the *Medical Pioneer,* in 1892. Publishing the *Medical Pioneer* on a monthly basis became the work of Dr. James Ridge, a member of the Independent Order of Good Templars and the United Kingdom Alliance (UKA), who was known within the medical community for his work at the London Temperance Hospital. Since the BMTA did not sponsor its own research, every month Ridge faced the daunting task of filling the pages of the journal. Besides biographies of leading teetotaler doctors, the journal consisted of measured scientific articles as well as reports about foreign medical temperance organizations and meetings. Although there was a conscious attempt to avoid sensationalist stories, such items occasionally found a place within the journal, as with a report on a four-year-old boy who, after being pulled out of the sea, was given milk laced with so much brandy that he died. The *Medical Pioneer* was distributed without charge, and 10,000 copies were distributed over the first six months of its existence.

Besides publishing this journal, the BMTA attempted to influence the medical community by setting up an informational stall at the annual meeting of the British Medical Association. Disappointed in the response of British physicians, the BMTA directed much of its energy toward influencing the next generation of doctors in training. Medical students were allowed to join as associate members without paying a fee. Articles in the *Medical Pioneer* were often geared toward this younger audience. For instance, "A Medical Student's Life in London" revealed the devastating impact of drink on a young man's career. The BMTA awarded a five-pound prize at the annual examination on the subject of alcohol that it sponsored for third-year medical students. After several years, it became apparent that few students would show up on exam days and that those who did were poorly prepared. Eventually, the association substituted an essay for the in-house examination, and even then the results were considered so inadequate that often no prizes were awarded.

Following the death of Richardson in 1896, the BMTA selected another prominent physician, Sir Victor Horsley, to serve as president. Under Horsley, the association would hit its peak membership of 568, but it was clear that the message had not reached most of the 30,000 members of the British medical profession. Also, the problem of printing a monthly journal was beginning to weigh on the BMTA. Ridge pleaded in vain for someone to contribute articles other than himself. Growing financial problems led to a request for donations to keep the journal going. It became apparent that advertisements from cocoa manufacturers and companies such as the Abstainers and General Insurance Company (which claimed to be the first company that offered lower rates to abstainers) were not enough to pay the printing bills. The BMTA found it difficult to convince other British temperance societies to buy the journal in bulk and distribute it among local physicians. As a result of these problems, in January 1898 the *Medical Temperance Review* replaced the *Medical Pioneer.* The new publication too was a monthly, but printed on cheaper paper and without pictures.

By the second decade of the twentieth century, the decline of the BMTA was clear. Increasingly, those members of the medical community interested in the alcohol problem moved away from the teetotaler model provided by the BMTA. They preferred a new approach based on moderation as a result of research that revealed that alcohol consumed in moderate amounts had minimal impact on overall health. By 1912, the *Medical Temperance Review* ended its publication run. In 1921, the BMTA changed its name to the Medical Abstainers Association, at which point it disappeared from sight.

Kenneth Pearl

See also: Good Templars (IOGT); Horsley, Sir Victor; National Temperance League (NTL); United Kingdom Alliance (UKA)

References

Gourlay, William. "The League's Share in the Great Medical Movement," chap. 7 in *"National Temperance": A Jubilee Biograph of the National Temperance League.* London: Richard J. James, 1908.

Woiak, Joanne. "'A Medical Cromwell to Depose King Alcohol': Medical Scientists, Temperance Reformers, and the Alcohol Problem in Britain" in *The Changing Face of Drink: Substance, Imagery, and Behaviour,* edited by Jack S. Blocker Jr. and Cheryl Krasnick Warsh, 237–270. Ottawa: Social History, 1997.

British Temperance League (BTL)

The British Temperance League (BTL), a predominantly north of England teetotal and Christian society, was the new name in 1854 for the British Association for the Promotion of Temperance (BAPT); the BAPT had been organized in 1833 as the first national teetotal organization. In 1880, the BTL moved its headquarters from Bolton to Sheffield, where it has remained for more than a century. In the late nineteenth century, it cooperated with the United Kingdom Alliance (UKA) in organizing the National Temperance Federation in the hope of uniting temperance reformers on behalf of prohibition legislation.

A handful of names dominate the history of the BTL. For instance, Joseph Thorp (1803–1873), a Quaker minister, served as the BTL president from 1850 to 1873; his son Fielden Thorp (1832–1920) later served as president, too. The younger Thorp's successor for the years 1912 through 1921 was the prominent pathologist Sir German Sims Woodhead (1855–1921). Successive members of the Clegg family served as chairman of the executive committee: William Johnson Clegg (1826–1895), sometime alderman of Sheffield, and his son Sir (John) Charles Clegg, best known as an early football player. His brother Sir William Edwin Clegg, sometime mayor of Sheffield, was a BTL vice president. A Congregational minister, Hugh Joseph Boyd, held office as secretary from 1884 to 1903; his successor, Charles Smith, served at least until 1929; he also edited the *British Temperance Advocate.* In 1903, the agents working for the BTL received a salary of 130 pounds plus 10 percent of any new subscriptions that they had solicited; according to historian Lilian Lewis Shiman, the agents also received three weeks' paid vacation.

By the 1890s, the finances and the prestige of the BTL were in marked decline. As a result, in 1897 it negotiated with the London-based moral suasionist National Temperance League (NTL) for a merger. There were many other specialized antidrink societies, but the BTL and the NTL were England's only national temperance organizations that welcomed into membership all teetotalers. At this date, the NTL was considered the stronger society. The headquarters of the united organization was to have been in London, and its president was to have been the NTL president. The negotiations failed.

In 1952, the BTL belatedly united with the NTL. (The historian Norman Longmate cites 1949 as the date for union.) At this time, the northerners of the BTL dominated the amalgamated organization, called the British National Temperance League (BNTL). The new organization retained the BTL's Sheffield headquarters. In 1987, the BNTL transferred its historically valuable library from Livesey-Clegg House to the University of Central Lancashire. Now known as the Livesey Library (after the teetotal pioneer Joseph Livesey), it includes records of the annual conferences of the BAPT and the BTL for 1835 through 1940.

In the twenty-first century, the BNTL's Freeway Initiative focuses on children and young people. The BNTL publishes a newsletter, *BarTales,* and maintains a website.

David Fahey

See also: Hoyle, William; Lees, Frederic Richard; Livesey, Joseph; National Temperance Federation (NTF); National Temperance League (NTL); United Kingdom Alliance (UKA); Whittaker, Thomas

References

British National Temperance League's website: http://www.bntl.org/web/history.html

Harrison, Brian. *Drink and the Victorians: The Temperance Question in England 1815–1872.* 2d ed. Keele: Keele University Press, 1994.

Longmate, Norman. *The Waterdrinkers: A History of Temperance.* London: Hamish Hamilton, 1968.

Shiman, Lilian Lewis. *Crusade against Drink in Victorian England.* London: Macmillan, 1988.

British Women's Temperance Association (BWTA)

The British Women's Temperance Association (BWTA), later called the National British Women's Temperance Association (NBWTA), was the national association for temperance women in England and Wales. It still exists today as the White Ribbon Association.

Women had participated in the British temperance campaign from the earliest days, and many became household names in the movement. These women often worked alone or locally, such as Julia Bainbrigge Wightman, who is identified with Shrewsbury. Despite their efforts, there was no national organization to which local societies or individuals could subscribe. It was well into the nineteenth century before there was any kind of national organization for women other than the Church of England's women's section. As the BWTA organizers were generally Nonconformists, they were unlikely to join an Anglican society.

The impetus to form a national organization came as a result of the news from the United States of what was called the women's whiskey campaign or women's temperance crusade. The arrival in England of one of the leaders of the American women, Eliza Stewart, generally known as Mother Stewart, and her speech at the national convention of the Independent Order of Good Templars (IOGT) in Newcastle in 1876 laid the foundations of the BWTA. Women who attended the Good Templars annual meeting elected an executive committee and drafted a constitution for the BWTA. The founding members included Margaret Eleanor Parker, Margaret Bright Lucas, and Mrs. Scholfield of Newcastle.

The name British Women's Temperance Association deserves analysis. It implied the inclusion of Scottish women, but in fact, they developed their own organization. It also may be puzzling that the BWTA omitted the word "Christian" from its title, contrasting it with that of the Woman's Christian Temperance Union (WCTU) organized two years earlier in the United States. The lack of "Christian" in the BWTA name influenced the decision of the Scottish Christian Union (SCU) to become a separate organization. Possibly the Quaker and other Nonconformist women who organized the BWTA rejected a title that included "Christian" because they believed that it could be misinterpreted as implying that the new society was affiliated with the Church of England. A few BWTA affiliates did include "Christian" in their names.

Margaret Eleanor Parker became the first BWTA president. Shortly afterwards, she went to the United States to attend an international meeting of the IOGT. During Parker's absence, Clara Lucas Balfour became president. Balfour, a long-standing Christian temperance advocate, was well known throughout the temperance movement as an author of temperance books and tracts. In poor health when elected, she died in 1878.

After Balfour's death, Margaret Bright Lucas, a Quaker and member of the IOGT, was elected BWTA president. She began to change the association from a loose grouping of local societies to a more structured organization. Lucas also widened the scope of the BWTA by introducing a political agenda. She persuaded the executive committee to pass a resolution in favor of a permissive bill for local prohibition referendums. She believed that the BWTA should focus on issues relating to women, including the problem of licensed grocers who enabled women to have access to alcohol by ordering drink delivered to their homes and charged on their grocery bill. The BWTA campaigned against grocers' licenses. Lucas risked more controversy when she drew attention to the Representation of the People Act (1884), highlighting an amendment proposed for women's suffrage. Lucas, a longtime supporter of women's suffrage, believed that the parliamentary vote would enable women to be more effective and efficient in furthering their temperance aims. It was Lucas's political awareness that enabled her to understand that the politics of temperance were within the capabilities of women.

Under Lucas's presidency, the BWTA managed to avoid the differences of opinions and splits that were prevalent in so many of the male organizations. She gave the women's temperance organization a distinct voice. She took the BWTA from its early Christian temperance beginning to a political organization with a membership of more than 27,000 in 1890. Her death in that year was a great loss for the BWTA.

After Lucas's death, the executive committee decided to seek a titled lady to enhance its status. After a shortlist was compiled, Lady Henry Somerset was comfortably elected. Some members had reservations about the choice, believing that she might become more active than the executive committee wanted, and some doubted her abilities.

Shortly after her election, Somerset traveled to the United States to study the methods of the WCTU and meet Frances Willard, the leader of the women's temperance movement in America. On her return, Somerset sent out a call to temperance societies to organize Sunday temperance meetings. She hoped to ensure a place for temperance on the Liberal Party's manifesto. There is no doubt that her actions gave the BWTA a higher profile within the temperance movement. Despite this success, the executive committee became increasingly anxious about the changes in policy.

Greatly influenced by Willard, Somerset wanted to emulate her "do everything" policy. Somerset also proposed renaming the organization to symbolize the changes in it. Her critics objected to what they regarded as Somerset's policy of Americanization, broadening the program, changing a revered name, and affiliating with the American-based WCTU. The executive committee resented Somerset's high-handed manner. Under Margaret Bright Lucas, the association had prided itself on always allowing each branch to arrange its own methods of work, so Somerset's directives were anathema to many in the BWTA. The debate over suffrage became antagonistic; the majority in the executive committee wanted a single-issue anti-alcohol association.

The controversy came to a head during the 1893 annual meeting. The single-issue members believed a focused organization would be more effective. It was the politics of temperance and traditional methods against the "do everything" policy that included women's suffrage. After Somerset won the vote at the annual meeting, the majority of the executive members left and immediately formed the Women's Total Abstinence Union. The BWTA changed its name to National British Women's Temperance Association, a minor and redundant change that suggested both continuity and novelty. It was to be thirty years before the two societies reunited as the National British Women's Total Abstinence Union.

The annual reports and minutes of the BWTA for 1876 through 1893 reside in the custody of the White Ribbon Association.

Margaret Barrow

See also: Band of Hope; Burns, (James) Dawson; Good Templars (IOGT); Lucas, Margaret Bright; Parker, Margaret Eleanor; Scottish Christian Union (SCU); Somerset, Isabella Caroline (Lady Henry Somerset); Wightman, Julia Bainbrigge; Willard, Frances Elizabeth Caroline; Woman's Christian Temperance Union (WCTU) (United States); Woman's Total Abstinence Union (WTAU); World's Woman's Christian Temperance Union (WWCTU)

Reference

Barrow, Margaret. "Temperate Feminist: The British Women's Temperance Association" (Ph.D. thesis, University of Manchester, 1999).

Tyrrell, Ian R. *Woman's World/Woman's Empire: The Woman's Christian Temperance Union in International Perspective, 1880–1930.* Chapel Hill: University of North Carolina Press, 1991.

Bronfman Family

The Bronfman family consisted of Russian Jewish immigrants Ekiel (or Yechiel) and Mindel Bronfman (or Braufman), along with their eight children: Abe, Harry, Laura, Sam, Jean, Bessie, Allan, and Rose. The children of Ekiel and Mindel became involved in the hotel and liquor industry. Under the leadership of Ekiel and Mindel's son Sam, the Bronfmans acquired Seagram Distilleries, expanding it into a liquor, energy, and entertainment empire.

In 1903, Abe and Harry Bronfman bought a hotel in Emerson, Manitoba, a business that was partially backed by local liquor and brewing interests. From these beginnings, the Bronfmans began to purchase other hotels in Saskatchewan, Manitoba, and Ontario, placing various members of the family or friends of the family in charge of these enterprises. Faced with increased prohibition that challenged the highly lucrative bar business prior to and during World War I, the Bronfmans dabbled briefly in selling "medicated wine," but when further government prohibition damaged those prospects, new enterprises were necessary. Sam Bronfman went to Montreal to pursue the liquor business. He opened the Bonaventure Liquor Store Company in 1916, a storefront and mail-order operation made possible because federal law did not prohibit the interprovincial liquor trade. When the government closed the interprovincial loophole in 1918, the Bronfmans exploited a loophole that permitted wholesale druggists to sell liquor. Harry Bronfman established the Canada Drug Pure Company in Yorkton, Saskatchewan. When wartime prohibition controls ended in 1919, the Bronfmans expanded their operations across the country.

With the advent of Prohibition in the United States, the Bronfmans' mail-order business became involved in the liquor export business to the United States, an enterprise of questionable legality. Much of Canada was also under some form of provincial liquor prohibition, and while the manufacture and export of liquor was not illegal, sales within provinces had numerous controls.

In 1922, Canadian provincial governments began to end prohibition, but most placed the sale of liquor under provincial auspices, forcing the Bronfmans to look for other areas of the liquor industry to develop. Sam and Harry established a distillery in Montreal using equipment purchased from the Greenbriar Distillery of Louisville, Kentucky, in 1923, and incorporated the company as Distillers Corporation Limited in May 1924, with Sam as president. Production began in 1925. Sam aspired to follow Scottish distilling methods, and he traveled to Scotland to woo Distillers Company Limited (DCL), which controlled over half of the world's Scotch whiskey trade. After several years of discussion with DCL and visits to Canadian distilleries by DCL chairman William H. Ross, a distribution and manufacturing deal was signed in 1927. The new company would be jointly owned by the Bronfmans' "Brintcan Investments" and DCL.

In 1928, hoping to exploit the huge market in the province of Ontario, the Bronfmans purchased Seagram's Distilleries of Waterloo, Ontario. The company was incorporated as Distillers Corporation–Seagram Limited (DC-SL). The Bronfmans were now poised to challenge their main Canadian rival, Hiram Walker of Windsor, Ontario.

Prohibition remained in effect in the United States, and the Bronfmans took advantage of the situation. Through various enterprises and tactics, the Bronfmans ensured that DC-SL products were reaching the United States. This activity was not without its dangers. In 1922, during a botched trade with bootleggers in Saskatchewan, Paul Matoff, husband of Jean Bronfman, was murdered. This event created increased awareness of the dangers of the liquor trade, as well as intensified public and official scrutiny of the Bronfman enterprises. In 1929, Harry Bronfman was charged with bootlegging in Saskatchewan. He was acquitted.

The end of Prohibition in the United States created tremendous opportunities for DC-SL. The Bronfmans split amicably with Scottish DCL in 1933—such arrangements were not necessary once the American market reopened. Seagram launched its highly successful "Crown" brands, Five Crowns and Seven Crowns—which quickly became, by volume, the leaders of all brands in the U.S. market—and later, Crown Royal.

The Bronfmans also were active in the Canadian Jewish community. Allan became heavily involved in efforts to establish a Jewish hospital in the late 1920s. Sam became an officer of the businessman's council of the Federation of Jewish Philanthropies in 1929, cochaired the Jewish Immigrant Aid Society in 1931, was named honorary Dominion chairman of the

United Palestine Appeal in 1936, and was elected president of the Canadian Jewish Congress in 1939. Their descendants continue this legacy of active participation in the international Jewish organizations.

During the second world war, in a climate of restrictions on liquor and tight economic times, the Bronfmans expanded their holdings. They purchased Browne-Vintners in 1940; British Columbia Distillery in 1941; Bedford Distilling, Blair Distilling, Old Colonel Distillery, William Jameson, Dant and Dant, Majestic Distilling, and Kasko Distillers in 1942; and Frankfurt Distilleries in 1943. They expanded into West Indian rum production, purchasing Long Pond Estates in Jamaica, and entered the wine business in 1942, first helping friends purchase wineries, and in 1943, acquiring and expanding the Paul Masson Vineyard.

The postwar period saw continued expansion into diverse liquor interests with a global scope. Seagram expanded rum production in the Caribbean, establishing Captain Morgan and acquiring controlling interest in several other distillers. In 1948, Seagram purchased the Jordan Wine Company of Ontario, followed soon by the purchase of Toronto's Danforth Wines, extending wine operations to British Columbia and Manitoba. The company purchased Chivas Brothers in 1950, a Scottish grocer and liquor merchant with a distinguished name, and introduced Chivas Regal two years later. Seagram gained controlling interest in G. H. Mumm and Company, in Rheims, and in 1954, it secured part of Barton and Guestier. In 1956, Seagram established the Seagram Overseas Corporation and a decade later the Seagram Overseas Sales Company (1965).

Business continued to diversify in the last half of the twentieth century. Sam and Allan invested in an Alberta oil company, Royalite, then the Oklahoma-based Frankfort Oil company, and in 1963, they invested in Texas Pacific Coal and Oil Company, the fifth-largest U.S. independent oil producer. Sam's son Edgar became Seagram's president in 1957. He expanded product lines and was instrumental in placing the company's investments in businesses ranging from Texas oil to British clothing retailers. In the 1980s and 1990s, acquisitions continued: Du Pont in 1980, Tropicana in 1988, and Dole in 1993. The company brokered deals to market and distribute a number of beverages in the United States, including Absolut Vodka and Grolsch beer in the 1990s. The 1990s found the Bronfmans actively pursuing the entertainment business, with investment in Time Warner (1993) and an 80 percent controlling interest in MCA (1995), an acquisition that included Universal Studios and Polygram Records (1998).

In 2000, Seagram CEO Edgar Bronfman Jr. announced the sale of Seagram to Vivendi; Bronfman became a vice chairman of the new Vivendi Universal. On 19 December 2000, Vivendi Universal agreed to sell the spirits and wine business to Diageo and Pernod Ricard. This sale divided the many Seagram brands between the two companies and was completed on 21 December 2001. On the final details of the Seagram selloff, see the Pernod Ricard website, at www.seagram.com as of autumn 2003.

Daniel J. Malleck

See also: National Prohibition (United States); Provincial Prohibition (Canada); Seagram; Whiskies

References

Bianco, Anthony. "Deal Time at Seagram" in *Business Week International [on-line] Edition.* http://www.businessweek.com/2000/00_26/b3687039.htm [March 2002].

Marrus, Michael R. *Mr. Sam: The Life and Times of Samuel Bronfman.* Toronto: Penguin, 1991.

Newman, Peter C. *The Bronfman Dynasty: The Rothschilds of the New World.* Toronto: McClelland and Stewart, 1978.

Rannie, William F. *Canadian Whisky: The Product and the Industry.* Lincoln, Ontario: Rannie, 1976.

Seagram website. http://www.seagram.com/.

Stone, S. I. "Throwing Stones: The Elements That for Approximately 75 Years Defined the Beverage Alcohol Industry in the United States Are, Obviously, Disappearing." *Massachusetts Beverage Business* (on-line journal). http://www.beveragebusiness.com/art-arch/mmthrowingstone08a.html [March 2002].

Brookhart, Smith Wildman (1869–1944)

Smith Wildman Brookhart (1869–1944) served as Iowa's Republican senator from 1922 to 1926 and again from 1927 to 1933. He was always as an outspoken proponent of Prohibition as a legal and economic measure at both the local and national levels.

Brookhart's first political action as county attorney of Washington County, Iowa, in 1895 was to adamantly prosecute violators of local prohibition laws because county officials would not accept the state's new "mulct" law, and his last action in the Senate in January 1933 was to threaten a filibuster against a bill for prescription of medicinal liquors. Brookhart's biographer described him as a "fervent dry" (McDaniel 1995: 57), although Brookhart considered temperance not a moral issue but rather a necessity for health, productivity, and efficiency in personal and political life. Still, Brookhart once stated that "liquor is a poison and drinking is a crime" ("Senator Brookhart" 1930: 1).

Brookhart's Senate career was marked as a political outsider (one of the Republican insurgents, along with George Norris of Nebraska and William Borah of Idaho) who consistently expressed distrust of and disgust against vested interests, especially any "big business," whether the monopoly was in agriculture or liquor. Some politicians believed Brookhart's continual fight for prohibition seemed more foolish than principled, a sentiment reflected in the "poem" that Senator David Walsh of Massachusetts read to the Senate:

I come from way out in Iowa,
The home of corn and many an art,
Where bootleggin's so bad
It makes all of us sad
That everyone knows it but BROOKHART.

Even by 1930, Brookhart did not believe that National Prohibition was failing. Rather, he believed it was inadequately enforced, especially by Secretary of the Treasury Andrew Mellon. Brookhart often spoke about the prohibition cause on the Chautauqua circuit, but he gained national attention in January 1930 when he called for Secretary Mellon's removal for failure to enforce Prohibition laws and also when he charged the New York Century Club with elitist escape from national law with their "Fish House rum punch."

In February and March 1930, Brookhart debated Congressman Fiorello La Guardia in Cleveland and attorney Clarence Darrow in New York. Both audiences heckled "no" and "never" while booing and hissing Brookhart, but his opponents admired his patience and determination. In Cleveland, Brookhart told the angry crowd, "Prohibition can be enforced. I have enforced it . . . America is dry; there are a few wet cities, but a few wet cities cannot overthrow America" ("'I've Enforced Dry Law'" 1930: 1). Brookhart believed that if enough money were devoted to the cause ($2.00 per person in America or $240 million), Prohibition could be enforced. And in the New York debate, Brookhart accused Darrow of preaching anarchy because it was the "duty of every man to obey the will of the majority." Darrow later described Brookhart as "sincere but uncivilized" (McDaniel 1995: 251).

When Brookhart was honored with a dry dinner in March 1931 at the Panama Canal Zone, he again created a national controversy with his criticism of wet districts in Panama. Although other senators and newspapers often mocked Brookhart's devotion to Prohibition, he never wavered. Later, Brookhart would consistently oppose the proposed Twenty-First Amendment, believing the original law had never been adequately enforced. Brookhart did not win his party's Republican primary nomination in June 1932 and was also unsuccessful as an independent candidate that November. He served as foreign trade advisor in the Agricultural Adjustment Administration from 1933 to 1935 and later practiced law in Washington, D.C., until his death in 1944.

Lisa L. Ossian

References

Biographical Directory of the United States Congress, 1774–Present. http://www.bioguide.congress.gov [May 2002].

"'I've Enforced Dry Law,' Cries Brookhart" in *Des Moines Register.* 8 February 1930.

McDaniel, George William. *Smith Wildman Brookhart: Iowa's Renegade Republican.* Ames: Iowa State University Press, 1995.

"Senator Brookhart Proud of His Unique Reputation" in *Des Moines Tribune.* 27 January 1930.

Brussels Act and Conventions, 1890–1912

The grand conference that met in Brussels from 1889 to 1890 was largely concerned with the slave trade and its suppression. There was, however, a belief—particularly strong in Britain—that the importation of spirits to West Africa fueled the slave trade. The arguments of campaigners on this topic had a major effect, and alcohol control had become established in British rhetoric as part of a wider imperial mission. The British government therefore insisted that the Brussels negotiations should address this issue, and as a result of the conference, a concluding chapter of the Brussels Act imposed restrictions on the importation of spirits to parts of Africa. A series of subsequent agreements, in which the British government was the principal mover, introduced further restrictions, but the controls were never as strict as the British government—and British campaign groups—would have wished.

The Act of 1890

At the Berlin conference of 1884–1885—which was essentially concerned with European agreements on commercial access to Africa as the pace of the "scramble" quickened—the British delegation had called for new measures against the slave trade. These were not included in the final Act of Berlin of 1885, but the European powers agreed to a further meeting at Brussels, which would concentrate on the slave trade. The Brussels conference was a prolonged affair, involving several months of meetings, dinners, and social events. Throughout it, the British delegation pushed for restrictions on the supply of spirits to Africa as part of an overall anti–slave trade package. There was considerable resistance to this from the Portuguese delegation, and also from the French. In neither of those countries was there the sort of active temperance movement that existed in Britain and that consistently lobbied on the issue of the "liquor traffic," and there was a substantial liquor industry in Portuguese possessions in Africa. There was also opposition from the Dutch and German governments because of the role of their spirits industry in supplying the West African market—a consideration that apparently outweighed the influence of temperance campaigners in Germany.

The agreement finally reached reflected both the rhetoric of British temperance and the reality of wider opposition to restrictions. In Articles 90 through 95 of the act, "being justly anxious concerning the moral and material consequences to which the abuse of spirituous liquors subjects the native population," the signatory powers agreed that the import or manufacture of spirits for African consumption would be banned in any area of Africa between the latitudes of 20° north and 22° south, in which "the use of distilled liquors does not exist or has not been developed." A limited quantity might be imported for the use of the "non-native population." Crucially, the act left the definition of these areas to the discretion of the colonial power involved. In those areas in which spirits were already in use, distilled liquor could be imported or manufactured, but a minimum level of duty was imposed, at the rate of "fifteen francs per hectolitre [presumably absolute alcohol, though the text was not specific on this point in comparison with later treaties] at fifty degree centigrade," a figure much lower than the British delegation would have liked, but which was to be reviewed by subsequent conferences. The powers also agreed to share information "relating to the traffic in alcoholic liquors" through the office that the act established at Brussels.

The consequences of the act were somewhat varied: No prohibition zone was declared in Portuguese territories, and prohibition zones were declared only in one part of French Equatorial Africa. On the other hand, British and German colonies in East and Central Africa and much of the Congo Free State did become prohibition zones, as did parts of the West African territories held by Britain and Germany. The British went beyond the terms of the act and banned the supply to Africans of beer and wine, as well as spirits, in their East and Central African possessions. The British and German governments also routinely imposed duties that were higher than the agreed minimum.

The Conferences of 1899, 1906, and 1912

Disappointed by the effects of the 1890 act, the British government called another conference in Brussels in 1899. Less grand than the 1889–1890 meeting, this conference produced an agreement to raise the minimum duty in the nonprohibition zones to 70 francs per hectoliter. The 1899 convention provided for a review by a subsequent meeting; when the meeting was held in 1906, it raised the agreed duty to 100 francs per hectoliter. A further conference in 1912 failed to reach any agreement. A proposal by the British and German delegates to introduce by stages a duty that would reach 200 francs per hectoliter was considered unacceptable by the French, as was a proposal that prohibition zones should be constituted into solid blocks. The latter proposal would have taken the definition of "prohibition" zones out of the hands of particular colonial states, and the French government, which had recently rescinded the only prohibition zone that it had ever declared, refused to accept this.

Overall, the effects on spirits consumption of the duties agreed upon under the Brussels Act and the conventions of 1899 and 1906 were limited; during the period up to 1914, the importation of spirits into areas outside the "prohibition zones" continued to grow. In the prohibition zones, the act had considerable effect, despite a degree of smuggling and "leakage" from European consumers to Africans. The prohibition was zealously enforced in British and German territories, and this was particularly effective in those areas where there were no adjacent "nonprohibition" zones.

Justin Willis

See also: Africa, Central; Indigenous Peoples and the Liquor Traffic Controversy; St. Germain en Laye Convention, 1919

References

Miers, Suzanne. *Britain and the Ending of the Slave Trade.* London: Longman, 1975.

———. "The Brussels Conference of 1889–90: The Place of the Slave Trade in the Politics of Great Britain and Germany" in *Britain and Germany in Africa,* edited by P. Gifford and W. Roger Louis, 83–117. New Haven, CT: Yale University Press, 1967.

Pan, Lynn. *Alcohol in Colonial Africa.* Helsinki and Uppsala: Finnish Institute for Alcohol Studies, 1975.

Bryan, William Jennings (1860–1925)

William Jennings Bryan's (1860–1925) career as a politician, statesman, and reformer spanned four decades and found him engaged in every major issue in American political life. He led crusades against the gold standard, world war, and evolution. A champion of reform and democracy, once he took up the fight for national prohibition, he became a leader of the movement.

A lifelong abstainer, Bryan nevertheless did not endorse prohibition early in his political career. In his 1890 bid for a congressional seat, he ran on a statewide Democratic platform that called for high license and local option, but in his campaign, he emphasized other issues. His opponent likewise was not a prohibitionist, so Bryan was able to steer clear of the issue and managed to win the election. For two decades, as he emerged as the leader of the Democratic Party, Bryan remained in the orthodox antiprohibition camp, but his politics and his supporters were reformist, evangelical, and progressive. In 1910, he lent his support to a movement to give Nebraska voters access to the initiative and referendum and to "county option"—local option on alcohol sales at the county level instead of the local and town levels. He lost his bid to include these reforms in the state Democratic platform, but he began to move into the political prohibitionist camp. Two years later, he announced that he was personally a prohibitionist, but he did not yet endorse the movement to amend the federal constitution.

In 1912, President-elect Woodrow Wilson asked Bryan to serve as secretary of state. Bryan expressed concern that he might be unable to serve as the nation's chief diplomat because he was unwilling to serve alcohol at his table. After assurances from Wilson that he could use his own judgment, Bryan accepted the post.

Bryan did not endorse the national prohibition movement until 1914, but soon became a principal spokesman for the cause. In 1915, he preached prohibition to 20,000 at a Billy Sunday revival at Philadelphia, and 1,500 of his listeners came forward to sign a temperance pledge. He stumped extensively that year, giving 60 speeches in Ohio alone. Echoing his electrifying 1896 "Cross of Gold" speech, he proclaimed, "You shall not bury the Democratic Party in a drunkard's grave!" In 1916, he unsuccessfully pressed for the

William Jennings Bryan (1860–1925) (Library of Congress)

party to adopt the Prohibition amendment in its national platform.

After resigning as secretary of state, he increased his prohibition activity. He watched the House of Representatives debate the proposed Eighteenth Amendment from the gallery, and when it received the necessary two-thirds majority, he was called down to the House floor for congratulations. He took to the stump to lobby state legislatures to ratify the amendment, and was named the president of the National Dry Federation. Under pressure from Bryan, Nebraska became the thirty-sixth state to ratify the amendment, codifying National Prohibition. He was on hand when his successor, Acting Secretary of State Frank Polk, signed the proclamation amending the Constitution.

James D. Ivy

See also: Democratic Party (United States)

References

Cherny, Robert W. *A Righteous Cause: The Life of William Jennings Bryan.* Boston: Little, Brown, 1985.

Coletta, Paolo E. *William Jennings Bryan.* 3 vols. Lincoln: University of Nebraska Press, 1964, 1969.

Levine, Lawrence W. *Defender of the Faith: William Jennings Bryan: The Last Decade, 1915–1925.* New York: Oxford University Press, 1965.

Buckingham, James Silk (1787–1855)

James Silk Buckingham (1787–1855), an early British teetotaler, prohibitionist, and temperance historian, lived a varied life as sea captain, newspaper editor in both India and England, member of Parliament (M.P.) (1832–1837), and advocate of reforms that ranged from the abolition of slavery to the creation of a congress of nations for the promotion of world peace. He sadly contrasted the temperance of Muslim countries with the drinking habits of Christian countries. After 1826, he no longer drank wine or spirits. He persuaded the House of Commons to appoint a committee to investigate working-class drunkenness and propose legislative remedies. Buckingham chaired the committee that examined fifty witnesses. Contemporaries ridiculed the report of the "drunken committee." A great traveler, Buckingham toured the United States in the late 1830s, where he visited all but two states and delivered many temperance lectures. He also visited Canada. Buckingham served as one of the original vice presidents of the National Temperance Society, organized in 1842 and later reorganized as the National Temperance League (NTL). From 1851 until his death, he headed the London Temperance League. In 1854, the year after the founding of the United Kingdom Alliance (UKA), he published his *History and Progress of the Temperance Reformation in Great Britain and Other Countries of the Globe, with Statistical and Documentary Evidence of Its Beneficial Results, and a Plea for a Maine Law to Enforce the Suppression of All Traffic in Intoxicating Liquors.*

David M. Fahey

See also: Islam as Cultural Influence; National Temperance League (NTL); United Kingdom Alliance (UKA)

References

Harrison, Brian. *Dictionary of British Temperance Biography.* Coventry, England: Society for the Study of Labour History. Aids to Research, no. 1. *Bulletin Supplement,* 1973: 17.

Turner, Ralph E. *James Silk Buckingham, 1786–1855: A Social Biography.* New York: McGraw-Hill, 1934.

Buddhism

Buddhism is a religion common in China, Japan, Southeast Asia, and parts of South Asia. It is based on the teachings of the historical Buddha, Siddhartha Gautama, known as Shakyamuni after his enlightenment in the sixth century B.C.E.

Early History and Basic Teachings

The teachings of the Buddha prohibit the drinking of alcohol for both laity and clergy. Alcohol is detrimental to the goal of enlightenment, for it prevents the attainment of mental clarity necessary to gain enlightenment. Buddhism teaches a Middle Path between the extremes of self-indulgence and self-mortification to nourish the body so that it will have the strength and health necessary to undergo the practices to attain enlightenment; alcohol is unnecessary and often detrimental to physical health and mental well-being. Worse, when under the influence of alcohol, a person is more likely to commit immoral acts that create bad karma and increase one's bonds to samsara, the cycle of birth, death, and rebirth from which the Buddhist seeks escape. Buddhism spread to a variety of cultures throughout Asia in the premodern era; practices among laity and even clerics have varied. Some schools of Buddhism developed rationales for drinking alcohol, such as the Tantric tradition found today among Tibetans and Pure Land Buddhism.

The Five Precepts constitute the most basic ethical practices of Buddhism; they are followed by laypeople and constitute the basis for the elaborate code of conduct laid out for monastics. The Five Precepts prohibit murder, theft, improper sexual activity, false speech, and intoxicants. It is said that abstaining from alcohol, which destroys shame and the fear of hell (where one must suffer to account for bad karma in a future life), facilitates observing the first four. Laypeople are also advised to engage in an appropriate livelihood that does not add to their karmic burden. Thus, ideally, one would not brew or sell intoxicants, either. The Sigalaka Sutta, a sutra (teaching of the Buddha) for laypeople, describes the dangers of addiction to intoxicants: wasted money, increased quarreling, ill health, the loss of one's good name, and the weakening of the mind. Temperance is thus a means of controlling the six sense organs (the mind is considered the sixth sense), which is considered essential for spiritual progress. The rule for clergy is stricter. Prohibition of alcohol is one of the Ten Precepts for a novice. Monks are forbidden to drink alcohol, even the amount that would be held by a blade of grass. The code of monastic discipline, the Vinaya, states that a little alcohol is permitted as a medicine, but it is to be boiled with oil so that it will have neither the taste, color, nor smell of liquor.

Mahayana Teachings and the Use of Alcohol

Buddhist ontology underwent a significant change with the rise of the Mahayana schools, and with this shift came different teachings regarding alcohol. The earlier schools, including Theravada Buddhism (today the Buddhism of Sri Lanka, Thailand, Burma/Myanmar, Laos, and Cambodia), taught that our perceptions are clouded by ignorance. This is ignorance of the fundamental nature of our experience of reality: that all things are composite, conditional (that is, their existence depends on other things for their being), without a permanent self, and subject to change. The path to enlightenment is to perceive things as they really are through the practice of meditation and purification. The result of enlightenment is the end of karmic bonds and the attainment of nirvana, the only unconditioned state. The Perfection of Wisdom sutras of Mahayana Buddhism, which arose in the first centuries of the common era, take this teaching further. They insisted on the nonduality of reality, asserting that there was no ultimate difference between samsara, conditioned existence, and nirvana, the unconditioned. Another important Mahayana teaching was the use of upaya, or skillful means, referring to the timely use of circumstances to progress toward enlightenment or help others along that path. In one story, a prince asked permission from the Buddha to imbibe, as he had many friends who drank and when drinking, he himself never became drunk or forgot the precepts. In the story, Shakyamuni praises the prince for having wisdom and mastering skillful means.

In Tantric Buddhism, which originated in northeast India and is the core of Tibetan Buddhism, these teachings meant that previously prohibited activities and substances, rather than being a hindrance to spiritual progress, were regarded as tools to enlightenment when used by the properly initiated adept. The prohibited substances and activities are the *pañca-makara* ("five M's"), five ritual elements whose first letter is "m" in Sanskrit: alcohol, meat, fish, parched grain, and sexual intercourse. In Tantric practice, alcohol is used to achieve perfection through powerful—and dangerous—rituals that could result in thousands of years in hell for the uninitiated or the careless, but enlightenment in one lifetime for the initiated. Use of the five M's is performed by some groups ritually, in others symbolically or as an element of meditation.

Japanese Pure Land Buddhism, another Mahayana school and the most popular Buddhist school in Japan, also does not prohibit alcohol, but for a different reason. The Pure Land School taught that we have entered *mappo,* the degenerate period when Buddhist law has become so attenuated that people are no longer able to follow the precepts. Instead, they must throw themselves on the mercy of Amida Buddha. Amida rules over the Pure Land he created to provide salvation for those who call his name in earnest supplication. Pure Land theorists claimed that there was nothing that could be done to save oneself; those who were unable to follow the precepts would not suffer so long as they chanted the *nembutsu,* a set phrase of supplication to Amida. Pure Land's most famous abrogation of Buddhist law is in its married clergy, but the use of alcohol was also justified in this way.

In practice, consumption of alcohol among Buddhists differs according to regional customs, history, and personal considerations. In Meiji Japan, a period of westernization and nation building, the Japanese government made it legal for clergy to drink alcohol. Another example is Sri Lanka, which has a significant Buddhist population as well as a recent history of British colonization. There, strict adherence to the Buddhist precepts is seen as a mark of the unworldly and nonelite; drinking alcohol is a mark of higher social status.

Jennifer Oldstone-Moore

See also: India; Japan; Literature, Representations of Drinking in

References

de Silva, P. "The Buddhist Attitude to Alcoholism" in *Drug Use and Misuse: Cultural Perspectives,* edited by Griffith A. Edwards, Awni Arif, and Jerome Jaffe, 33–41. London: Croom Helm, 1983.

Harvey, Peter. *Introduction to Buddhist Ethics.* Cambridge: Cambridge University Press, 2000.
Keown, Damien. *The Nature of Buddhist Ethics.* Richmond: Curzon Press, 1992.

Bureau of Alcohol, Tobacco, and Firearms (BATF)

The United States Bureau of Alcohol, Tobacco, and Firearms (BATF) is part of the United States Treasury Department and was created in 1972. Prior to the establishment of the ATF, the Internal Revenue Service performed its duties. The authority for the agency's regulation of alcoholic beverages comes from the Federal Alcohol Administration Act of 1935 and subsequent revisions and amendments to that law.

The mission of the BATF is to reduce crime, collect revenue, and protect the public. The BATF is responsible for enforcing legislation regarding firearms and explosives and the production, taxation, and distribution of alcohol, tobacco, and firearms. In 1982, the BATF gained oversight of commercial arson under the Anti-Arson Act of 1982. Following passage of the Brady law in 1993, the bureau became responsible for the transfer of handguns. As of 20 December 1999, Bradley A. Buckles is the director.

In the aftermath of the terrorist attacks of 11 September 2001, the BATF has renewed its commitment to ensuring the safety of the American people and protecting the country from violent crime. Following the increased emphasis on combating terrorism, the BATF is participating in the Joint Terrorism Task Forces with other law enforcement agencies, including the Federal Bureau of Investigation (FBI). Further, given the agency's experience with alcohol and tobacco diversion and smuggling, the BATF expects to play a large role in pursuing terrorist financing.

In 2002, the agency was working on finalizing a system of electronic filing of label applications for the liquor industry. These labels are known as COLAs, which stands for Application for and Certification/Exemption Of Label/Bottle Approval. Any producer of an alcoholic beverage must obtain this approval prior to proceeding with bottling, packing, importing, or removing any beer, wine, or liquor from customs' custody or the point of production. Another e-government program is Pay.gov. A pilot program for paying fees on-line, Pay.gov received 13 percent of all revenue in 2001.

In 2001, the BATF collected $14.1 billion in taxes. Of this total, $13.8 billion came from alcohol and excise taxes; firearms and ammunition excise taxes generated $176 million; special occupational taxes another $103.6 million; and $6 million came from licensing and transfer fees. The BATF also collected $1.6 million in penalties, interest, and unpaid taxes, as well as fines for record-keeping violations, and conducted seventy-seven separate investigations of alcohol and tobacco diversion. These investigations resulted in seizures of property valued at over $1.8 million.

Waco

The BATF is responsible for the enforcement of federal firearm legislation. Acting under this authority, the BATF was the original law enforcement agency at Waco. On 28 February 1993, BATF agents attempted to search the Branch Davidian compound, resulting in the killing of four agents and the wounding of 116. This initial event quickly became the infamous fifty-one-day standoff in which law enforcement officers as well as the majority of Branch Davidians, including women and children, lost their lives.

The original investigation by the BATF of David Koresh and the Branch Davidians involved the illegal manufacture and possession of firearms and weapons. A 1995 FBI report stated that over 300 firearms were recovered from the compound. Texas Rangers recovered over 300 grenade components and hundreds of thousands of rounds of ammunition.

The Waco events were and remain highly controversial and political. Many people, particularly Republicans, criticized Janet Reno, the FBI, and the Clinton administration's handling of the affair. Many libertarians and gun advocates saw Waco as an assault on personal liberty and horrendous evidence of the overarching power of the federal government. On the other hand, gun-control proponents and many Democrats felt the administration had acted properly and that David Koresh was a dangerous and perhaps perverted individual who was defying the legal authority of the federal government.

On 14 July 2000, an advisory jury ruled that the BATF had not used excessive force at Waco in 1993. This finding concurred with the Treasury Department investigation, which concluded that the BATF agents had been ambushed. Surviving Branch Davidians continue to maintain that they did not fire until fired upon. Two BATF supervisors lost their jobs, but later returned to work at a lower rank. Nine Branch Davidians received varying prison sentences for their participation in the event.

Firearms

The BATF licenses 104,000 firearm owners after ensuring that they are in compliance with all federal regulations pertaining to guns. For most of its existence, the agency has focused on the use of guns in the commission of a crime and the criminals who use them. It has given less emphasis to the gun traffickers and the minority of licensed dealers who sell weapons to criminals and underage persons. The BATF's licensing authority over gun owners and dealers dates from the Gun Control Act of 1968, which Congress passed in the aftermath of the assassinations of Martin Luther King Jr. and Robert F. Kennedy. At that time, the BATF was in a previous incarnation as the Alcohol and Tobacco Tax Division of the Treasury Department. It was not yet an autonomous bureau, and its staff was primarily focused on moonshine and revenue fraud, which had been the historic mission of the various agencies formed to collect the alcohol and tobacco taxes first instituted in 1863 to finance the Civil War.

Since 1968, when the BATF became responsible for limited federal gun control, it has faced the formidable opposition of the National Rifle Association (NRA). The NRA was able to convince President Ronald Reagan to call for the dissolution of the BATF in 1981. This never happened, but during Reagan's administration, the Firearms Owners Protection Act of 1986 was passed. This legislation has made the BATF's goal of combating illegal gun trade more difficult.

Following the loss of BATF agents at Waco, the agency developed a "critical incident management plan." There are four national response teams as part of this system. Each team has thirty experts, including forensic chemists, canine handlers, and explosive-technology professionals. The teams are able to respond to an incident within twenty-four hours. In 1998, the teams were used thirty times.

Explosives and Arson

In 2001, the BATF was responsible for licensing and regulating over 9,000 explosives manufacturers. In the mid-1990s, the BATF led the National Church Arson Task Force and conducted over 1,000 investigations of bombings, attempted bombings, and arson at religious institutions. The agency was able to solve twice as many arson cases as usual. Following the Oklahoma City bombing of a federal building in 1995, the agency now devotes a considerable amount of time, as mandated by Congress, to explosives. The Oklahoma City bombing was directed at BATF offices as retaliation for its actions at Waco.

Tobacco

Under legislation that dates back to the Civil War, the BATF has the responsibility for collecting the excise taxes on tobacco products, licensing manufacturers and exports, and inspecting the facilities where production takes place. Diversion is a big problem for the agency. Until recently, high Canadian taxes on cigarettes made cross-border smuggling a major issue. Canadian officials claim that millions of dollars are lost in tobacco and alcohol diversion.

Alcohol

The BATF administers viticultural areas and establishes new ones. A viticultural area is a specific geographic area with boundaries recognized by the BATF. The area has to have distinctive geographical features to receive the designation. There are more than 140 such areas in the United States, in California, Arizona, Missouri, New York, Pennsylvania, Washington State, Oregon, Michigan, Ohio, Colorado, New Mexico, Texas, Connecticut, and Rhode Island. A viticultural area can cross state lines.

The newest viticultural area is in Sonoma County, California. The Rockpile viticultural area is 15,400 acres with 11 vineyards and 160 acres of planted wine grapes. In the 1850s, Rockpile was a cattle ranch and in the early twentieth century became a hunting and sheep-raising ranch. During the Great Depression, the area was subdivided. It is now being restored in its entirety and used for wine production.

The BATF operates in all fifty states, regulating and overseeing the production of alcohol. Some states, however, do not usually have any taxable removal of beer, while others, centers of production, have large amounts. In 2001, the states with the largest amount of taxable removals of bottles, cans, and thirty-one-gallon barrels were California, Texas, and Colorado.

Wine and distilled spirits labels list their containers' alcoholic content, while beer labels do not. In 1989, public-health advocates succeeded in placing health warnings on alcoholic beverages. The warnings inform consumers about the dangers of drinking and driving as well as the dangers of alcohol consumption while pregnant. The previous decade had witnessed a great deal of new information about fetal alcohol syndrome and heightened concern about drunk driving.

A decade later, in 1999, scientific claims about the healthful benefits of moderate drinking prompted the BATF to allow wine labels to direct consumers to places where they could get further information on these benefits. These labels did not last very long; the agency halted the practice in 2000. The seventeen wineries that had already placed the information on their bottles were allowed to keep the labels. Debate continues about placing health claims on alcoholic beverage labels as well as ingredient listing and alcoholic content for beer.

The agency inspects 74,000 labels a year to ensure that they are not misleading and that they contain the appropriate information required by the law. In 2001, there were twelve cases of alcoholic beverage mislabeling. The BATF collects alcohol beverage excise taxes and regulates the whole industry, covering distilleries, breweries, wineries, and importers and wholesalers. Some of the most frequently asked questions the BATF receives relate to the definition of taxable production and the ensuing paperwork, free home production of alcoholic beverages, sale of liquor on the Internet, and whether it is legal for school-age children to distill liquor for science projects.

Each branch of the alcoholic beverage industry faces different regulations and tax procedures, continuing the precedent first established in 1863. Home production of beer and wine is not always taxed, but distillation of spirits for home use is prohibited. Distilling spirits always requires payment of taxes and filing of paperwork prior to beginning production. Since the imposition of federal liquor taxes in 1863, the government has faced enforcement problems. Particularly in the Southeast, illicit distilling or moonshine remains a problem for the BATF. This ongoing struggle is reflected in the prohibition of home distillation. For the past several years, the BATF has been the lead agency in Operation Lightning Strike, formed in Virginia and North Carolina to fight the often big business of illicit distillation of alcohol. Operation Lightning Strike was the first time federal money-laundering legislation was used to combat moonshine.

The regulatory focus of the BATF is on revenue collection. Thus, the agency does not enforce laws concerning the consumer aspects of the alcoholic beverage industry. However, because of the agency's jurisdiction over labeling, it is responsible for evaluating industry advertising in regard to health claims or exaggerated quality claims as well as label fraud.

The Federal Trade Commission (FTC) also monitors the advertising of alcoholic beverages and tobacco products and has specific authority for television advertising. The Food and Drug Administration (FDA) has responsibility for diluted alcoholic beverages such as cooking wine and any other substances that have less than 7 percent alcohol by volume. The FDA is also responsible for ensuring that harmful or toxic substances are not present in alcoholic beverages.

The individual states are usually responsible for law enforcement pertaining to the sale or service of alcoholic beverages to the public; nor is the BATF responsible for consumption issues.

Amy Mittelman

See also: Moonshine; Taxation of Liquor (United States)

References

ATF Online. http://www.atf.treas.gov/.

Buckles, Bradley A. Statement before the Subcommittee on Treasury, Postal Service and General Government, House Appropriations. 28 February 2002. http://www.atf.treas.gov/press/speech/fy02/022802testimony.htm.

Butterfield, Fox. "Limits on Power and Zeal Hamper Firearms Agency" in *New York Times.* 22 July 1999, sec. A, 1, 19.

Food, Nutrition, and Cosmetics Questions and Answers. http://www.cfsan.fda.gov/~dms/qa-ind4a.html.

Hunter, Beatrice Trim. "More Informative Beer Labels" in *Consumer's Research Magazine.* 79, no. 10 (October 1996): 10–15. In InfoTrac, Expanded Academic ASAP, 1980–August 2002 (database on-line). Gale Group, 2002.

Kilborn, Peter T. "U.S. Cracks Down on Rise in Appalachia Moonshine" in *New York Times.* 23 March 2000, sec. A, 1, 18.

Krautheim, Adam. "New Microsoft Word Version of COLA Form" in *The Alcohol and Tobacco Newsletter.* 3, no. 2 (February 2002). http://www.atf.treas.gov/pub/alctob_pub/at_news/feb_2002/index.htm.

Magaw, John. Remarks before the American Society for Industrial Security. 25 February 1999. http://www.atf.treas.gov.

New York Times. 15 November 1989, sec. III, 1.

Sutton, Nancy. "Rockpile Viticultural Area Established" in *The Alcohol and Tobacco Newsletter.* 3, no. 3. http:// www.aft.treas.gov./pub/alctob_pub/at_news/mar_2002/index.htm.

"U.S. Puts Wine Health Label on Hold" in *Beverage Industry.* 91, no. 1 (January 2000): 9.

"Waco: The Inside Story." *Frontline.* http://www.pbs.org/wgbh/pages/frontline/waco/primary.html.

"Waco Verdict." *ATF News.* 14 July 2000. http://www.aft.treas.gov/press/fy00press/071400wacoverdict.htm.

"Weapons Possessed by the Branch Davidians." *The Department of Treasury.* 13 July 1995. http://www.pbs.org/wgbh/pages/frontline/waco/treasury.html.

Burns, (James) Dawson (1828–1909)

(James) Dawson Burns (1828–1909), Baptist minister, temperance organizer, and editor, was Victorian England's outstanding temperance historian. His major work was called *Temperance History: A Consecutive Narrative of the Rise, Development, and Extension of the Temperance Reform,* and it numbered nearly a thousand pages in two volumes, published in 1889–1891. Although factually accurate, it is a "dry and institutional record," according to historian Brian Harrison. Organized chronologically and heavily biographical, it is most detailed for the 1860s and 1870s. It is exhaustively indexed, with separate indices for persons, places, organizations, religious denominations, and publications, as well as a general index.

Burns was the son and the son-in-law of important temperance reformers (respectively, Jabez Burns and Clara Lucas Balfour). He became a pledged teetotaler in 1839. He served as secretary of the National Temperance Society from 1853 until 1856, when it was reorganized as the National Temperance League (NTL). He was one of the founders of the United Kingdom Alliance (UKA) and the salaried superintendent of its London auxiliary from 1856 to 1893. In 1859, he unsuccessfully recommended to the alliance that temperance reformers organize constituency organizations that would reward or punish parliamentary candidates with a bloc vote.

Burns was an active writer, speaker, and organizer. As an outspoken critic of the use of intoxicating wine in the eucharistic sacrament, he collaborated with Frederic Richard Lees in writing the *Temperance Bible Commentary* (1868). Burns wrote many other books in the cause of sobriety and edited several temperance newspapers. After the death of William Hoyle, he assumed the responsibility of writing annual letters to the *Times* that calculated the cost of alcoholic drink borne by British society. Beginning in 1875, he preached an annual temperance sermon at Church Street Chapel, a series begun by his father in 1839. Burns was one of the founders of the London Temperance Hospital. After he received an honorary doctorate in 1882, he called himself Dr. Dawson Burns.

The reputation of Burns was tarnished when a brother-in-law's devious financial speculations cost many temperance people their life savings. Unlike this brother-in-law, Burns was spared criminal prosecution. Fortunately for him, he had resigned from the board of directors of the Liberator Building Society prior to its collapse in 1892, but his reputation inevitably was tainted. The liberal journalist J. A. Spender pilloried Burns in a series of articles, "Philanthropic Finance: A Forgotten Chapter in the Temperance Movement," published in the *Westminster Gazette* in July and August 1893. Burns also had critics within the alliance who claimed that he was ineffective as superintendent of the London auxiliary. When he refused to resign, the position was abolished at the end of 1893. The Liberator affair continued to cast its shadow. Despite his encyclopedic knowledge of licensing law, the alliance failed to nominate Burns as a witness for the Royal Commission on Liquor Licensing Laws that met in 1896–1899.

David M. Fahey

See also: Band of Hope; Bible Wine; Hoyle, William; Lees, Frederic Richard; National Temperance League (NTL); United Kingdom Alliance (UKA); Winskill, Peter Turner

References

Cherrington, Ernest Hurst, ed. *Standard Encyclopedia of the Alcohol Problem.* 6 vols. Westerville, OH: American Issue, 1926–1930. 460–461.

Fell-Smith, Charlotte. *Dictionary of National Biography, Second Supplement.* 272–273. London: Oxford University Press, 1912.

Harrison, Brian. *Dictionary of British Temperance Biography.* Coventry, England: Society for the Study of Labour History. Aids to Research, no. 1. *Bulletin Supplement,* 1973: vi–vii, 17–18.

Busch Family

The Busch family are descendants of German immigrant Adolphus Busch, who built Anheuser-Busch to a position of dominance in the U.S. beer market; the family also became heavily involved in family entertainment and other enterprises.

Adolphus Busch was the youngest of twenty-one children born to Ulrich Busch and Barbara Pfeiffer at Mainz on the Rhine, Hesse (now part of Germany). His father was a wealthy landowner, vineyard owner, and merchant. Adolphus was fluent in German, English, and French. He followed several brothers to America, arriving in Saint Louis, Missouri, in 1857. In 1859, he opened a malt house with Ernst Wattenberg and a brewery supply business with his brother Ulrich. (Here he was following a family trend: His brothers George and John had become brewers in Saint Louis and nearby Washington, Missouri, respectively. John Busch's brewery remained in operation until after National Prohibition.) One of his customers was Eberhard Anheuser, who had purchased the Bavarian Brewery (established 1852) in 1860. Augustus and Ulrich began to court Anheuser's daughters, Lily and Anna, respectively. The two couples married in a double wedding in 1861. Augustus and Lily had fourteen children, nine of whom survived into adulthood.

Anheuser became in debt to Busch's supply company, and in 1865 he offered his son-in-law an interest in the brewery in lieu of payment. In 1873, Adolphus became a full partner in the brewery. Busch envisioned distribution far beyond the local market. In 1872, he began shipping beer to Texas by icing down shipments and building icehouses by the railroads. In 1873, Anheuser-Busch began pasteurizing bottles. Bottling was not the most predominant method of selling beer, and by developing a broader bottling market, Busch stimulated associated industries such as bottle, cork, and label manufacturing. Busch also pioneered the refrigerated railway car, which was introduced at the 1876 Centennial Exhibition in Philadelphia. These developments in distribution enabled Anheuser-Busch to sell well beyond the local market.

In 1876, Busch and friend Carl Conrad developed Budweiser. Conrad brought the recipe back from Bohemia after tasting the lager in a monastery there and acquiring the recipe. Anheuser-Busch brewed it, and it was bottled by Conrad's company. By some accounts, when Conrad found himself in debt to Busch in 1883, Adolphus took over the trademark and offered Conrad a position in the brewery.

The company was renamed the Anheuser-Busch Brewing Association in 1879. The following year, Anheuser died, and Busch became the sole leader of the company. The company continued to grow and expand its holdings. In 1898, Busch bought the U.S. rights to the diesel engine for $1 million. Adolphus Busch was known for his flamboyant style, which translated itself into ostentatious living for him and his family. He had a home in Saint Louis near the plant called No. 1 Busch Place; a country estate called Grant's Farm; two homes in Pasadena, California; a property and hop farm in Cooperstown, New York; two villas in Langenschwalbach, Germany; and a private railroad car named "Adolphus." He was a favorite son; during Augustus and Lily's fiftieth anniversary in 1911, Saint Louis held a huge celebration, though the couple was celebrating in California and receiving gifts from presidents and the Kaiser.

Busch's ostentation was accompanied by charitable largesse. In 1907, for example, after the San Francisco earthquake, Busch donated $100,000 for relief work. That year, he also prevented a run on the LaFayette South Side Bank in Saint Louis when he personally guaranteed every deposit. The following year, he gave $100,000 to victims of earthquakes in Italy and gave $150,000 to the Germanic Museum at Harvard.

After Adolphus's death in 1913, his son August A. Busch (1865–1934) took over the company. August guided the company through three major crises: world war, Prohibition, and depression. During Prohibition, Anheuser-Busch diversified into a number of new areas, including baker's yeast, ice cream, soft drinks, barley malt syrup, refrigerator cabinets, and dealcoholized beer. August A. Busch committed suicide in 1934 and his son Adolphus Busch III took over. National sales of Anheuser-Busch slipped during Adolphus III's leadership.

After Adolphus III's death in 1946, his brother August A. (Gussie) Busch Jr. (1899–1989) became president. In contrast to his brother, and more in keeping with his father's leadership, Gussie was determined to take Anheuser-Busch into new territory. He totally renovated the Saint Louis plant and built branches in four new cities. Revenues skyrocketed. He oversaw the purchase of the Saint Louis Cardinals baseball team in 1953 and attempted to rename the stadium "Budweiser Stadium" but was thwarted by the National League president and the Woman's Christian Temperance Union (WCTU), which did not want professional sports to encourage drinking. They settled on "Busch Stadium." Gussie was also notorious for his marriages, of which there were four, the first in 1918 and the last in 1981, with a total of eleven children. Under Gussie's presidency, Anheuser-Busch also created Busch Gardens in Tampa, Florida, in 1959, and became involved in real estate and transportation. When he retired as president of Anheuser-Busch, Gussie remained at the head of the Cardinals, who won six pennants and three World Series during his tenure. Busch's family had its share of tragedies. A nephew was kidnapped in 1930, a daughter was killed in a car accident in 1974, and Busch's son accidentally shot a friend in 1975.

August A. Busch III replaced his father as president of Anheuser-Busch in 1975. He continued his father's trend of diversification, acquiring Sea World in 1989, while overseeing the growth of the brewing interest from 24 percent market share in 1975 to 45 percent in 1995. He also relentlessly pursued the European and Asian markets, which are difficult for U.S. breweries to crack. To further reach the youth market, in 1994 August promoted his son, thirty-year-old August Busch IV, to vice president of brand management. "The Fourth," as he is known, approved a range of advertising campaigns that included croaking frogs, partying ants, and retro disco music.

Daniel J. Malleck

See also: Anheuser-Busch

References

Anheuser-Busch website. www.anheuser-busch.com/history [January 2003].

Hernon, Peter, and Terry Ganey. *Under the Influence: The Unauthorized Story of the Anheuser-Busch Dynasty.* New York: Simon and Schuster, 1991.

Holland, Gerald. "The King of Beers" in *American Mercury.* October 1929. http://www.beerhistory.com/library/holdings/kingofbeer1.shtml [January 2003].

Krebs, Roland, and Percy J. Orthwein. *Making Friends Is Our Business: 100 Years of Anheuser-Busch.* Saint Louis: Cuneo Press, 1953.

Lubove, Seth. "Get 'Em before They Get You" in *Forbes.* 156, no. 3 (31 July 1995): 88–93.

Miller, William J. "Busch, August Anheuser Jr." in *Dictionary of American Biography,* edited by Allen Johnson. 22 vols. 4: 71–72. New York: Scribner, 1918–1958.

Ronnenberg, Herman W. "Busch, Adolphus" in *Dictionary of American Biography,* edited by Allen Johnson. 22 vols. 4: 69–71. New York: Scribner, 1918–1958.

C

Cabaret (France)

In France during the nineteenth century, the café was mostly attended by the middle class, and the pub (*bistrot*) mainly by the working class; both were places where people would drink only. The cabaret allowed its patrons to eat and to drink, mainly wine, but sometimes also beer. Actually, the cabaret keeper was a wine merchant who also served meals *à la fourchette.* The word cabaret first appeared around the late thirteenth century. It started with *chambrette* (small room), a French expression that was transformed into the Dutch *cabret* and into *cambrette* in the Picardy, before taking its present form and meaning.

There are thousands of stories worth telling about the cabarets in France, and the social meaning of this kind of place deserves a full analysis. The French cabaret—as we know it today—appeared around the year 1880. The cabaret was dedicated to relaxing and entertaining the lower middle class living in towns, typically in Paris. The part of Paris called Montmartre was the birthplace of the cabaret. Authors, painters, writers, musicians, chansonniers, and poets—some famous, some unknown—and generally those who led a bohemian way of life would meet in the Paris cabarets. These were places for vice and all kinds of excesses, probably for madness, where drinking and smoking too much were principles. Absinthe, the main target of the antialcohol leagues, was the chief beverage. The cabaret was the place for social life. It was also a place for discussing politics and for transgressing all rules. The most important role of the cabaret would be missed if it were considered as a place for entertainment only. In fact, the social life in the cabaret involved not only the drinking at the bar, but also the mingling—the establishing of relationships among the Paris intelligentsia, young men from the country, impecunious artists, and politicians, who all discussed the world and set forth their ideals and expectations, from the most serious to the most crazy.

At this time, the external boulevards of the capital city concentrated heavy commercial activity. Many alcohol-selling places blossomed on these wide avenues and attracted a heterogeneous set of customers, mainly from the lower middle class and the Parisian bohemia. For the record, the number of all sorts of pubs in France was 241,847 in 1830 and 418,773 in 1920. As early as 1880, France contained one pub for every 103 persons.

The most famous among all cabarets in Paris was without doubt the Chat Noir, which was founded by Rodolphe Salis (1852–1897) on 18 November 1881 at the bottom of the Montmartre hill at number 84, boulevard de Rochechouart. Typical of the nineteenth-century cabarets, the Chat Noir was very successful until it closed down in 1897. Rodolphe Salis is a good example of a small-town, middle-class man who transformed his short career as a painter and a sketcher (started when he first arrived in Paris in 1875 at the age of twenty-three) into an alcohol-selling business, under the pressure of his family. His father, a rich distiller from Châtellerault, disapproved of his wild kind of life. The father eventually agreed to support his son financially, provided he married a rich bride and gave up painting.

Salis happened to be an outstanding businessman. The Chat Noir quickly became one of the very fashionable places for the Parisian bohemia. The cabaret, located in a working-class part of town, was a meeting place for literature lovers and aspiring artists. Emile Goudeau, a novelist and political satirist, a friend and a coworker of Salis, transferred his literary club (the Hydropathes), together with a large number of customers, to the Chat Noir. Contributing to the celebrity of the cabaret were the painter Willette, who created the cabaret's poster, the chansonniers Aristide Bruant and Jules Jouy, the humorist writer Alphonse Allais, and the poets Charles Cros, Albert Samain, and Jean Richepin. The jokes in the cabaret stigmatized the upper-middle-class way of life, politics, and business. The pun became a characteristic of the bohemian culture, and the Chat Noir became a symbol of the fin-de-siècle spirit, with the emerging new artistic and literary trends, like naturalism, symbolism, and neomysticism—trends that opposed the dominant establishment, represented by the Salons, which were attended by academic and established artists.

Salis became a wealthy man due to the success of the cabaret. The growing reputation of the Chat Noir reached well beyond the Montmartre poets and chansonniers. More and more celebrities from the upper middle class visited the cabaret. In fact, all the celebrities in Paris attended the Chat Noir for the singing, the text and poetry reading, and joking on any subjects; even a shadow theater was set up on the second floor and immediately became a huge success.

However, the success of the Chat Noir did not survive its creator, and the place closed down in 1897, due to several reasons. The competition between the cabaret owners increased during the 1880s and 1890s. Rodolphe Salis invented the artistic type of cabaret. The Elysée Montmartre, Le Moulin Rouge, and the Casino de Paris attracted a fine clientele where members of the high society mingled with painters and writers. This was the time of *café-concert,* when the naturalist and realist quadrille dancing and, later, the French cancan were invented. The vogue of ballroom dancing and the emerging movie theaters contributed to the end of the cabarets; the shows in Le Moulin Rouge ended in 1892. World War I and the antialcohol campaign, especially its success in the prohibition of absinthe, also contributed to the closing down of many places. Although some famous Paris cabarets are still producing shows, the audience is completely different: Instead of the Montmartre bohemians, the present audience is made up largely of tourists.

Bertrand Dargelos

See also: Absinthe; Drinking Establishments (France)

References

Bologne, J. C. *Histoire des cafés et des cafetiers.* Paris: Larousse, 1993.

Bourdieu, P. *Les règles de l'art. Genèse et structure du champ littéraire.* Paris: Seuil, 1998.

Prestwich, Patricia E. *Drink and the Politics of Social Reform: Anti-Alcoholism in France since 1870.* Palo Alto, CA: Society for the Promotion of Science and Scholarship, 1988.

Richard, L. *Cabaret, Cabarets. Origines et décadences.* Paris: Plon, 1991.

Caine, William Sproston (1842–1903)

William Sproston Caine (1842–1903), English temperance advocate, was a Liberal politician who championed temperance legislation. He was coauthor of *Local Option* (1885), a book that argued in favor of a local option for prohibition in the form of a referendum, sometimes called direct local veto. He was president of the National Temperance Federation—a coalition of temperance organizations that favored prohibition—from its founding in 1884 until his death. Although he always believed that prohibition was the best answer to the drink question, he showed more tactical flexibility than his colleague in the House of Commons, Sir Wilfrid Lawson.

Caine's career exemplified the growing identification between the Liberal Party and advanced temperance reformers. Initially opposed to William Gladstone's policy of home rule for Ireland, in 1886 Caine joined the breakaway Liberal Unionist faction that became allied with the Conservative Party. As a result, he frequently supported antiprohibition parliamentary candidates against Liberal prohibitionists. This made Caine unpopular at temperance meetings, where he sometimes was booed. In 1888, the Conservatives proposed that the proceeds of a special liquor tax be used to pay compensation for public houses denied renewal of their licenses, and in 1890, Conservatives revived the idea of financial compensation for pubs whose annual licenses were not continued. On both occasions, Caine led the opposition and in both cases forced the government to withdraw the compensation proposals. By the early 1890s, the licensing policies of the Conservative government drove Caine back into the ranks of Gladstone's Liberal Party.

Caine was not doctrinaire. In 1888 and 1890, he objected to specific proposals and not to the principle of compensation. He worked behind the scenes in 1888 with the Church of England Temperance Society (CETS) to persuade the Conservatives to set a time limit for compensation. He always was willing to compromise in order to get a sweeping licensing reform bill enacted into law. Consequently, he supported the so-called united temperance parliaments, organized by A. F. Hills in 1894 through 1896, to rally temperance reformers behind a common program. Caine served on the Royal Commission on Liquor Licensing Laws from 1896 to 1899. To get support for a large reduction in the number of pubs, he signed the minority report drafted by the chairman, Lord Peel, even though Lord Peel's report recommended postponing the veto and providing compensation to the owners of licensed premises who lost their businesses because of a change in government policy. Lord Peel's report divided the United Kingdom Alliance (UKA) and other prohibitionists, with a majority favoring the report and a diehard minority bitterly opposed.

Strongly religious, Caine founded a mission church, Wheatsheaf Hall, in a poor district of London, where he served as a lay preacher. He served successively as president of Baptist and Congregational temperance societies.

In contrast to his lack of enthusiasm for Irish home rule, he favored self-government for India and was a friend of the Indian National Congress. In 1888, he helped organize the Anglo-Indian Temperance Association.

David M. Fahey

See also: Church of England Temperance Society (CETS); Conservative Party (United Kingdom); Gladstone, William Ewart; Harcourt, Sir William; Hills, Arnold Frank; India; Lawson, Sir Wilfrid; Liberal Party (United Kingdom); National Temperance Federation (NTF); United Kingdom Alliance (UKA)

References

Fahey, David M. "William Sproston Caine (1842–1903)" in *Biographical Dictionary of Modern British Radicals,* vol. 3, edited by Joseph O. Baylen and Norbert J. Gossman, 171–173. Hemel Hempstead, Herefordshire, UK: Harvester Wheatsheaf, 1988.

Newton, John. *W. S. Caine, M.P.: A Biography.* London: James Nisbet, 1907.

Campaign for Real Ale (CAMRA)

The Campaign for Real Ale (CAMRA), a not-for-profit pressure group, was founded in 1971 as a reaction to the consolidation of the brewing industry in Britain, the loss of local breweries, and the promotion of national brewery-conditioned ("keg") brands at the expense of local brews. Following early success in its campaign against keg beers, the CAMRA widened its role to include all aspects of the brewing industry, the public house, and customer rights. It now has more than 64,000 members and has inspired similar campaigning groups throughout Europe.

The CAMRA was founded by four friends who were concerned about the increasing trend toward the replacement of locally brewed ales (most of which were "cask-conditioned," living beers that continued to mature in the barrel) by a handful of national "keg" brands, which were filtered, pasteurized, and artificially carbonated. Three of the founders were journalists, which helped the new campaign gain media attention. The term "real ale" was coined to describe cask-conditioned brews.

The new campaign struck a chord with the drinking public. Articles in national newspapers by writers such as Richard Boston supported its activities, while the publication from June 1972 of the monthly newsletter *What's Brewing* and from 1974 of the annual *Good Beer Guide* helped to direct drinkers to brewers who still produced real ale and to pubs that sold it. A beer festival (an exhibition of real ales) held in Cambridge in July 1974 proved successful and was followed in September 1975 by a national beer festival at Covent Garden in London. A limited company, CAMRA (Real Ale) Investments Limited was set up to purchase and run public houses as showcases for real ale. The CAMRA had 30,000 members by 1976.

For the first time in years, new breweries appeared to cater to the demand for real ale. The first of them, Selby Brewery, began brewing in 1972 (it was a revival of an old firm that had ceased brewing in 1954). Others soon followed. Former employees of national brewers who seized the opportunity to run their own businesses operated many of the new breweries. The CAMRA publicized the new brewers in its newsletter and showcased their products at its beer festivals.

Although the quality and availability of real ale were publicized, the national brands were subjected to ridicule. So effective was the campaign against Watneys Red Barrel (invariably referred to as "Grotney's" in CAMRA literature) that the beer, once one of the biggest selling brands in Britain, was withdrawn in June 1979.

The apparent success of the campaign to save real ale resulted in a loss of members (down to 15,000 by 1981) and a debate about the CAMRA's role. Some argued that it should continue to concentrate on supporting real ale and the brewers who supplied it; others insisted that it was essential for the CAMRA to become involved in wider issues of government policy and consumer rights.

Whose Pint Is It Anyway? (1981) was subtitled "a call from the consumer for radical change in the British brewing industry." It analyzed the development of the brewing industry and identified features that were said to act against consumers' interests. It recommended changes ranging from the breakup of the six large combines that dominated the industry and the placing of a maximum limit on the number of outlets a brewer could own, to the relaxation of the "tie" (under which a brewer limited sales in a public house to its own products) to allow a publican to sell his choice of another brewer's beer.

Some of the changes championed by the CAMRA, notably a partial relaxation of the tie, were incorporated into government regulations for the brewing industry, the Beer Orders of 1989. The Beer Orders, however, had unforeseen impacts upon the brewing industry, with many brewers disposing of their public houses to separate companies set up especially for this purpose. Because these companies did not brew, they were not subject to the regulations requiring brewery companies to relax the tie. This allowed them to sign profitable supply deals with the national brewers while denying a market to smaller brewers—the opposite effect to that intended by the Beer Orders.

The upheaval in the brewing industry restricted the market for real ale, which came under increasing pressure from mass-produced and heavily advertised lagers, as well as from a new form of keg beer, "smooth" beer. The national brewers aggressively marketed these beers, while real ale received little or no promotion. In 2001, to counter the heavy advertising of lager and smooth beers, the CAMRA launched the "Ask if it's cask" campaign, advertising the virtues of real ale in national newspapers and on billboards across the country.

In recent years, there has been an equal focus upon the public house, both as a social institution and as an important part of Britain's physical fabric. Changes in drinking habits, the consolidation of the brewing industry, and the upheaval in pub ownership caused by the Beer Orders has threatened the viability of many of the country's pubs, particularly in rural areas. The CAMRA has campaigned for measures intended to improve the viability of public houses—the relaxation of restrictions on opening hours, and reductions in rates (local community taxes) for rural pubs—as well as for measures to prevent their closure against the wishes of their customers. Increasingly, the CAMRA works in partnership with others to ensure the survival of the public house.

The publication in 1991 of *Trouble Brewing,* a report by conservation groups including the CAMRA, drew attention to the extent to which historic pubs, and particularly their interiors, had been damaged by poor-quality refurbishment and alterations since the second world war. Further research led to the publication of the *CAMRA National Inventory* (1999), listing pub interiors "of outstanding heritage interest"—less than 250 unaltered examples predating 1939 could be identified in the entire United Kingdom—and a campaign for official protection for the best surviving pub interiors.

The CAMRA has inspired similar campaigning groups throughout Europe and elsewhere. It is a founding member of the European Beer Consumers' Union, which includes a number of similar consumer groups that campaign in support of their country's beer heritage.

An unsuccessful precursor of the CAMRA was the Society for the Preservation of Beers from the Wood, organized in 1963.

Andrew P. Davison

See also: Beer; Beer Orders (United Kingdom); Pubs and Beerhouses (United Kingdom); Watneys

References

Boston, Richard. *Beer and Skittles.* Glasgow: Collins, 1976.

CAMRA. *The CAMRA National Inventory: Pub Interiors of Outstanding Heritage Interest.* Saint Albans: CAMRA, 1999.

———. *Whose Pint Is It Anyway?* Saint Albans: CAMRA, 1981.

Gamston, David, et al. *Trouble Brewing.* London: Georgian Group, 1991.

Protz, Roger, and Tony Millns, eds. *Called to the Bar: An Account of the First 21 Years of the Campaign for Real Ale.* Saint Albans: CAMRA, 1992.

Canada, Alcohol Consumption in

See Alcohol, Consumption of, per Capita (Canada)

Canada Temperance Act

The Canada Temperance Act was a federal law providing for local option, which was passed in 1878 and was quickly challenged under the division of powers established by the British North America Act (BNA Act) (1867). In *Russell v. The Queen* (1882), the Judicial Committee of the Privy Council (Privy Council) upheld the act under federal authority for the "peace, order and good government of Canada." This was an episode in the larger contest between the provinces (especially Ontario) and the Dominion government over the interpretation of the BNA Act in the early years of Confederation, in which cases on liquor legislation figured prominently. Cases after *Russell* interpreted federal powers more narrowly and provincial powers more expansively, largely to accommodate provincial autonomy. By 1946, this judicial doctrine made a constitutional anomaly of the Canada Temperance Act, which survived another challenge only out of respect for the longevity of *Russell v. The Queen.*

The Canada Temperance Act (also known as the Scott Act) prohibited retailing of "intoxicating liquor" in counties and municipalities that had adopted the act by majority vote. Purchases for medicinal, sacramental, and industrial purposes and of larger quantities for transportation beyond Scott Act territory were exempted. The act was similar to the Dunkin Act (1864), the local-option law of the province of pre-Confederation Canada (Ontario and Quebec). The jurisdictional premise was obvious: Confederation had transferred prohibition authority to the new federal government.

The act was adopted first in Fredericton, New Brunswick, and was immediately challenged. In *The Queen on the Prosecution of Thomas Barker v. The City of Fredericton* (1879), the provincial supreme court ruled that the act violated provincial jurisdictions over liquor licensing, property and civil rights, and local matters. The Supreme Court of Canada reversed in 1880, principally on the ground that the Scott Act regulated trade and commerce. At this juncture, Thomas Barker died, and his place in the litigation was taken by Charles Russell, another Fredericton tavern keeper. In 1882, the Privy Council denied Russell's appeal, finding the act to be legislation for the "peace, order and good government of Canada," while withholding judgment on whether it was also trade and commerce legislation. All transpired as a staged contest between larger forces. Barker and Russell were stand-ins for the "liquor interests" that funded and guided the litigation. Federal funding ensured the appeal to the Supreme Court and the representation of each side by prominent central Canadian lawyers. The Dominion Alliance for the Suppression of the Liquor Traffic, which had led the advocacy for passage of the act, funded Montreal counsel to defend it in the Supreme Court and Privy Council.

As was typical in constitutional cases in the 1870s, the Canadian judges explicitly related the constitutionality of the Scott Act to the objects of Confederation and to the nature of Canada as a federal state. In the provincial court, Charles Fisher, a Father of Confederation, derived a judicial mandate for strict protection of provincial power over property and civil rights partly from the fact that the power was made a condition of Confederation by one province (Quebec) and partly from the concern that a federal authority to affect such rights would cause their infringement and violation. Fisher denied the applicability of the trade and commerce power by arguing that it existed to facilitate uniform trade between and within provinces, not to authorize the federal imposition of moral reforms on local communities and individual households. This argument connected provincial and personal autonomy, and connected both with Fisher's denunciation of "sumptuary laws." A different understanding of Confederation and of Canada flowed through the judgments in the Supreme Court of Canada. The common theme was the importance of a comprehensive national power over trade and commerce that, unlike the United States equivalent, embraced trade within as well as between provinces (states). Ontario's John Wellington Gwynne went farthest. The Dominion Parliament was a "quasi-imperial power," not one limited to specific functions. Like the Imperial Parliament, it could legislate on whatever it determined to be necessary or beneficial for the nation under peace, order, and good government, including suppression of the scourge of intemperance. This approach raised a fundamental question: Were provinces autonomous societies or had they instead been reconstituted as subordinate administrative units?

The contrasting approach of the Privy Council was to treat *Russell v. The Queen* largely as an ordinary exercise in statutory interpretation—the analysis did not go much beyond the textual organization of the BNA Act and the ordinary meaning of the words of specific clauses. Prohibition was not within the property and civil rights power simply because it affected property and civil rights—all legislation did that. Prohibition was not within provincial power to raise revenue from licenses, since it would limit or reduce revenue. The Scott Act was not provincial simply because it was local option. Rather, the act was national, and what Parliament could do directly it could do conditionally, through local plebiscites. These discreet assertions about distinct heads of provincial power made the act valid by default, as all that was not provincial came under peace, order, and good government. But "peace, order and good government" also applied because the objectives of the act ("public order, safety or morals") had a "direct relation to criminal law" (a specified head of federal power) and therefore contributed to "peace, order and good government." The form of words of federal power determined constitutionality, not the general theories of the mandate of the two levels of Canadian government or whether intemperance affected Canadians as members of one national, or of separate provincial, societies.

The Scott Act was challenged again in 1946. By then, *Local Prohibition Reference* (1896) had placed prohibition outside the trade and commerce power, and a series of Privy Council decisions had (temporarily) reduced peace, order, and good government to an emergency power so exceptional that it did not apply to the depression of the 1930s. *Russell* therefore appeared vulnerable. But in *A. G. Ont. v. Canada Temperance Federation,* the Privy Council upheld the act simply because it had become an accepted part of Canadian law. The Canada Temperance Act was a constitutional anomaly, but one that lasted until its repeal in 1984.

William Lahey

See also: Provincial Prohibition (Canada); Provincial Regulation (Canada)

References

Hogg, Peter W. *Constitutional Law of Canada.* 4th ed. Toronto: Carswell, 1997. 103–139 and 443–470.

Lahey, William. "Constitutional Adjudication, Provincial Rights and the Structure of Legal Thought in Late Nineteenth-Century New Brunswick" in *University of New Brunswick Law Journal.* 39 (1990): 185–223.

Risk, R. C. B. "Canadian Courts under the Influence" in *University of Toronto Law Journal.* 40 (1990): 687–737.

Russell, Peter H. *Leading Constitutional Decisions.* Ottawa: Carleton University Press, 1987. 3–24 and 41–49.

Saywell, John T. *The Lawmakers: Judicial Power and the Shaping of the Canadian Constitution.* Toronto: University of Toronto Press for the Osgoode Society, 2002.

Cannon, James, Jr. (1864–1944)

James Cannon Jr. (1864–1944) was a Methodist bishop and temperance reformer. Intense, confrontational, and extraordinarily energetic, Cannon was a ruthless and resourceful political combatant. Leader of the Anti-Saloon League of Virginia, he led the prohibitionists to victory in a statewide prohibition referendum in 1914. He was also the chief Washington lobbyist for the national Anti-Saloon League and played a major role in securing the federal Prohibition legislation that culminated in the Eighteenth Amendment. In the presidential election of 1928, he led southern Democrats in revolt against Alfred Emanuel Smith, the antiprohibitionist, Roman Catholic governor of New York, breaking the "Solid South" for the first time since Reconstruction. Beginning in 1929, however, Cannon became embroiled in a series of scandals that generated sensational headlines and destroyed his political influence.

Cannon was born on the Eastern Shore in Salisbury, Maryland, the son of a prominent local merchant. He was educated at Randolph-Macon College (B.A. 1884), Princeton Theological Seminary (B.D. 1888), and the College of New Jersey, later Princeton University (M.A. 1890). On 1 August 1888, he married Lura Virginia Bennett, the daughter of the president of Randolph-Macon. They had six sons and two daughters. Admitted to the Virginia Conference of the Methodist Episcopal Church, South in November 1888, Cannon served pastorates in Charlotte County, Newport News, and Farmville. He achieved early prominence as principal of Blackstone Female Institute, a secondary school in Virginia; as editor of the *Baltimore and Richmond Christian Advocate,* the organ of the Virginia Conference; and as superintendent of the Southern Assembly, a Methodist conference and recreational center at Lake Junaluska, North Carolina. After being elected a bishop of his church in 1918, Cannon in 1925 assumed the southern leadership of the bitter and unsuccessful struggle for Methodist unification.

An indefatigable traveler, Cannon spent much of the 1920s abroad. He supervised southern Methodist missions in Mexico, the Belgian Congo, and Brazil; served as the chief agent in Europe of the World League Against Alcoholism (WLAA), the international arm of the Anti-Saloon League of America (ASLA); actively participated in the ecumenical movement; and served as a spokesman for Near East Relief, the American philanthropy that assisted victims of Turkish atrocities.

Cannon was hailed in 1928 as the champion of dry, Protestant America, but his moment of national triumph was brief. His wife died shortly after the presidential election, and in Virginia the anti-Smith Democrats were defeated in 1929. Cannon himself was then indicted in federal court for embezzlement and investigated by his church for stock-market gambling and adultery, the latter charge stemming from his courtship in New York of Helen Hawley McCallum, a widow whom he married on 15 July 1930. By 1934, he was acquitted of all charges, but the scandals undermined his moral authority, discredited Prohibition, and bitterly divided his church. After the repeal of Prohibition in 1933, he faded into obscurity and retired in 1938. He died of a heart attack in Chicago and was buried in Hollywood Cemetery, Richmond.

Robert A. Hohner

See also: Anti-Saloon League of America (ASLA); Democratic Party (United States); National Prohibition (United States); Smith, Alfred Emanuel

References

Cannon, James, Jr. *Bishop Cannon's Own Story: Life as I Have Seen It,* edited by Richard L. Watson Jr. Durham, NC: Duke University Press, 1955.

Dabney, Virginius. *Dry Messiah: The Life of Bishop Cannon.* New York: Alfred A. Knopf, 1949.

Hohner, Robert A. *Prohibition and Politics: The Life of Bishop James Cannon, Jr.* Columbia: University of South Carolina Press, 1999.

———. "'The Woes of a Holy Man': Bishop James Cannon, Jr. and H. L. Mencken" in *South Atlantic Quarterly.* 85 (Summer 1986): 228–238.

Caribbean

Although their total landmass and population are relatively small, the islands of the Caribbean are numerous and culturally varied, and beverage alcohol is often intimately linked with history and economics. More revealing than a listing by individual names or groups of islands is a description of certain aspects of alcohol and temperance history highlighting some of the more distinctive regional patterns and a few specific features.

Beverages

Probably the most famous beverage throughout the Caribbean is rum, distilled from molasses or from the juice that is squeezed from sugarcane and fermented. During the 1600s and 1700s, the Caribbean was the destination of a great involuntary diaspora as natives from western Africa, often captives of their black neighbors, were sold into slavery to do heavy agricultural work throughout much of tropical America. Although the reality is much more complex than usually described, the infamous "triangle trade" often saw blacks shipped to the Caribbean, where they were traded for molasses. In turn, the molasses was taken to northeastern North America (Newport and Boston, in New England) and converted to rum, which in turn was shipped to West Africa as a major commodity to be exchanged for enslaved human beings, often with the same ships and crews on each leg of such a voyage.

As the United States won independence from the British Empire, that regional division of labor was abandoned, and the distillation of rum became commonplace throughout the Caribbean, the rum often used in lieu of money for partial payment to workers.

Indigenous native peoples on the various Caribbean islands had, in many instances, been largely killed off in the early decades of European contact, but the continued presence of native home-brewed beers in a few places suggests that some enclaves of indigenes may have survived, or at least major social and cultural mixing occurred.

The combined advent of tourism and refrigeration in the 1800s made lager and pilsner beers available, although they continue to be more expensive than native spirits. Only in the Dominican Republic does beer seriously compete for popularity with rum. Wine has never been produced in the region and still has little popularity except among a few wealthy urban cosmopolites, who tend also to be the ones who drink most of the wide range of other spirits, most of which are imported.

Drinking Patterns

Although many of the writings that deal with the Caribbean make mention of drinking as a commonplace activity in everyday life, only a few historians and anthropologists have paid close attention to who drinks what, where, when, how, and why. Recent interest in drinking patterns as intermediators between sheer measures of consumption and various types of alcohol-related harm hold some promise of increasing our understanding. Paying additional attention to such qualitative data as context and attitudes can suggest meanings that have been lacking in the overwhelming attention that has been paid to exclusively quantitative data on quantity and frequency of drinking.

As in virtually every population that has been studied, males drink more—and more often—than do females throughout the Caribbean. Also nearly universal is that the difference is slowly narrowing in recent years, although a double standard persists by which male drinking is generally accepted, whereas female drinking is often construed as symptomatic of immorality.

The offer of a drink is often an important symbol of friendship or hospitality, to the point where one may cause offense by declining such an offer. Toasting is a common pattern. Sometimes it involves elaborate wordplay or teasing in informal settings, or elaborate speech making in more formal contexts. Games and competitions are often closely associated with recreational drinking, and few drinkers pay much attention to flavor, color, or other aesthetic aspects of beverages, preferring whatever delivers the most alcohol for the price.

Adolescence and young adulthood tend to be the periods of maximum drinking, with the quantity of consumption by most individuals tapering off rapidly once they marry or reach the age of thirty.

Males tend most often to drink with male friends away from home. On those occasions when women do drink, it tends to be in the company of other women or of family, and in the home. In general, there is a high correlation between level of schooling, prestige of occupation, and income as joint markers of socioeconomic class standing, and all such measures tend to be inversely correlated with levels of consumption of beverage alcohol. Drinking patterns vary little among groups descended from Africa, China, or Asian India.

Drunkenness tends to be viewed as exhilarating and as confirming of one's masculinity, especially among those who have little wealth, power, or social status. For those reasons, many drink primarily for the psychoactive effect; this probably also is connected to the fact that little official attention is paid to low levels of intoxication or blood-alcohol concentration.

One confounding factor with respect to alcohol consumption in most of the Caribbean is the presence of a disproportionate number of free ports, in which untaxed beverages are bought and sold in quantity. Another is the presence of large numbers of tourists, often exceeding the local population. At leisure and in warm sunny climates, such tourists tend to be unusually heavy drinkers, whose consumption distorts simple formulas that take into consideration only population and registered sales of alcohol. By special arrangement, some countries enjoy tax advantages with respect to sales of alcohol to U.S. citizens. During U.S. Prohibition, distilled beverages were often smuggled from the Caribbean region.

In general, there is a dearth of detailed information about alcohol use and its outcomes in every Caribbean country. Occasional articles that purport to provide statistical information about per capita consumption, psychiatric effects, traffic fatalities, or other alcohol-related issues tend to be local in scope, using samples and methods that instill little confidence among an international readership, and they are often frank and explicit about their limitations. Ethnographic or anthropological studies, where they occur, are often richly detailed about single communities but unrepresentative of the nation.

Attitudes and Images of Drinking and Temperance

There is often an attitude that hard-working men "have earned" or "deserve" to drink for relaxation, camaraderie, and enjoyment, or even to drink to intoxication. Depending on how they are paid, this often results in episodic heavy drinking on weekends, monthly, or at the end of a season's work, with little drinking between times. Holidays, both religious and secular, are usually marked by heavy drinking, as are weddings, birthdays, funerals, and various other special occasions.

The reasons or justifications that people give for drinking include pleasure, celebration, social interaction, relaxation, and change of mood, all positive from the perspectives of the people reporting. Apart from isolated instances in which excessive drinking results in major problems in terms of health, economics, or social relationships, most view drinking as a pleasant and rewarding activity, finding it difficult to comprehend the negative moral evaluation that Protestants give to it, or the occasional alarm with which it is portrayed by public-health authorities.

In recent decades, Protestantism (especially more fundamentalist or ascetic versions) is gaining ground in what had traditionally been overwhelmingly Roman Catholic populations. When abstention from alcohol is an article of faith, drinking (or not) can be an important boundary marker between social groups.

Dominicans often speak of drinking as an important part of their national character. A fashionable badge of modernity among young men is their prominent displaying of a "beeper" in a pouch on their belt; the beeper is not an electronic device but a distinctive 175 cc bottle of rum.

Patterns of Regulation

A small but highly vocal group of self-styled public-health advocates have, for the past three decades, promoted a variety of policies that they claim would reduce the availability of alcoholic beverages, thereby diminishing average per capita consumption and consequently reducing or preventing dependence and various kinds of alcohol-related damage, to the drinker or to others. Although both conceptual and empirical bases for those assumptions remain questionable, the World Health Organization (WHO) has vigorously promoted such policies, and the policies have been widely adopted, even in areas where there was little previous tradition of control. It remains to be seen whether the more recent General Agreement on Trade in Services will render all or most of such restrictions moot. Among the controversial efforts at control, some refer to sales, others to advertising, and others to labeling, as illustrated below.

Many who would restrict alcohol consumption presume that demand for alcoholic beverages is a function of advertising, and so a number of different types and degrees of regulation have been applied. The long panorama of history, including the Soviet experience through most of the twentieth century, reinforces findings that advertising has little effect on alcohol consumption. However, there has been no such research in the Caribbean, and a few countries have adopted a patchwork quilt of policies restrictive of advertising. The attitudes of former colonial powers are faintly reflected in policies that various Caribbean nations have adopted with respect to the advertising of alcoholic beverages.

Guadeloupe and Martinique reflect the recent strictness of France (of which they are "overseas provinces"). The use of television and of cinema is banned, as is that of radio (but only at certain times of day and with a mandatory reminder of the importance of moderation). Advertising in print is allowable, except in youth magazines, so long as a mandatory health warning is included. Outdoor advertising is subject to elaborate specifications (most about location).

In Barbados, it is permissible to use all of the media, but advertising is subject to "judgment of reason and good taste." Advertisements should "preferably" not appear on television before 7 P.M., "to protect the young." Similarly, Jamaica allows the use of all media, with some restrictions on content.

In other respects, restrictive policies about beverage alcohol appear to be minimal throughout the Caribbean. Only Trinidad and Tobago lists a "minimum drinking age"; it is sixteen. The idea of setting a specific blood-alcohol concentration as prima facie evidence of "driving while impaired" appears not to have been adopted anywhere in the region, and health warning labels on containers are not required, as is the case in many parts of the world. All in all, governments appear to be permissive about drinking generally, and to rank alcohol-related problems as relatively unimportant in relation to other issues of health and social welfare.

Research in Alcohol

Alcohol has rarely been viewed as problematic in the Caribbean, except inasmuch as a small minority of individuals, usually long-term, heavy drinkers, create problems for themselves and others. Rightly or wrongly, research has often been viewed as a luxury, especially in developing nations that have limited resources and many pressing health problems.

In the 1970s, Trinidad and Tobago did some pioneering work on links between drinking and traffic accidents, but it was not long sustained. Cuban political doctrine holds that alcohol-related problems are symptomatic of capitalism, and many Caribbean countries encourage consumption of the distilled beverages they produce.

Producers and Distributors

The beverage alcohol trade is one in which many companies deal with more than a single class of beverage, for example, producing wine or beer and simultaneously distributing distilled spirits that were produced elsewhere. It is also a business in which actors come and go with some frequency. Because of licensing agreements, mergers, and other arrangements, it is not always clear whether a company is indigenous to the country or acting as an agent for a larger international organization. With those caveats in mind, some of the major producers and distributors in the region at the end of 2001 are the following. In Aruba, Licore Aruba NV produces and distributes a large variety of beverages. In British Virgin Islands, John Morrel and Company Limited does also, as does Jaques Scott Group Limited in the Cayman Islands. Bacardi-Martini International takes pains to distance itself from the Bacardi label that was nationalized by Cuba, although several popular rums are produced in the Caribbean. Cervecería Dominicana produces a widely exported beer in the Dominican Republic, and international brands of distilled beverages are distributed throughout the islands.

Dwight B. Heath

See also: Rum; World Health Organization (WHO)

References

Acta Psiquiátrica y Psicológica de América latina (special issue on alcohol in Latin America). 20, no. 2 (1974).

Heath, Dwight B. *Drinking Occasions: Comparative Perspectives on Alcohol and Culture.* Philadelphia: Brunner/Mazell, 2000.

———, ed. *International Handbook on Alcohol and Culture.* Westport, CT: Greenwood, 1995.

Horwitz, José, Juan Marconi, and Gonzalo Adis Castro. *Bases para una epidemiología del alcoholismo en América latina.* (Monografía de Acta Psiquiátrica y Psicológica de América latina 1). Buenos Aires: Fondo para la Salud Mental, 1967.

Institute of Medicine. Legislative Approaches to Prevention of Alcohol-Related Problems: An Inter-American Workshop. Washington, DC: National Academy Press, 1982.

Marshall, Mac, ed. *Beliefs, Behaviors, and Alcoholic Beverages: A Cross-Cultural Survey.* Ann Arbor: University of Michigan Press, 1979.

Carlile, Ann Jane (1775–1864)

Ann Jane Carlile (1775–1864) was one of the first women to work for the temperance cause in the British Isles. When widowed in 1811 at the age of thirty-one, she set up in business as a flax buyer. After the business prospered, she moved from County Monaghan to Dublin in 1826. Her philanthropic work commenced when she began to visit women in prison, shortly before Elizabeth Fry came to Dublin. Carlile joined with Fry in fighting for the abolition of penal transportation, and she became a member of the female jail visitors committee.

Carlile's experience of visiting women in prison made her aware of the links between drink, poverty, and prostitution and why women turned to petty crime resulting in their imprisonment. It was around this time that she signed the pledge in order to be able to speak from experience on the benefits of temperance. In 1830, she founded an antispirits temperance society for sailors in Poolbeg Street, Dublin, but she quickly became aware that total abstinence was the only way forward to ensure temperance families.

Carlile had a long career as a temperance speaker from her earliest days when she lectured the workmen and servants on her brother's estates in Monaghan. Elsewhere, she at first would only speak to women and children, but as she gained confidence she began to speak to mixed audiences. In the 1840s, she was one of the first women to speak in public on temperance. As a result of the general hostility toward women's participation in public affairs, even though her subject was the respectable one of Christian temperance, her papers were frequently read for her at conferences while she sat silent in the halls.

Her work was organized around children, and she became committed to teaching them the temperance way of life, believing that they would remain temperate for the rest of their lives. During a visit to Leeds in 1847, she participated in the naming of a temperance organization for children, the Band of Hope. Although there has been debate over who devised this name, the historian R. H. Crofton concludes that Carlile helped choose it. The Band of Hope was to be one of the most popular temperance movements. Diverse religious dominations formed Bands of Hope throughout the United Kingdom and in other parts of the English-speaking world.

Carlile was, arguably, the first woman to travel for the temperance cause. Her travels took her throughout England, Scotland, and Wales, as well as Ireland. During a visit to Belfast, she founded the Victorian Temperance League in 1841. Despite her eminence in the temperance movement, she complained that she had experienced "coldness" from the clergy, particularly in Scotland, who objected to any woman speaking on the temperance platform. She believed that there was a greater acceptance of her work in England. She was a frequent guest of Dr. Dawson Burns during her travels to London. Carlile was also a writer of popular temperance tracts. Her publications stressed the value of the reformed drunkard.

Throughout her life, she tried to ignore religious differences in the fight against alcoholic drink. Although a Protestant, she worked with Father Theobald Mathew. She remained a teetotaler until her death.

Margaret Barrow

See also: Band of Hope; Burns, (James) Dawson; Ireland; Mathew, Father Theobald

References

Burns, Dawson. *Temperance History. A Consequential Narrative of the Rise, Development and Extension of the Temperance Reform,* vol. 2: 424–426. London: National Temperance Publication Depot, 1889–1891.

Crofton, R. H. *Anne* [sic] *Jane Carlile and Her Dependents.* Saint Leonard-on-Sea: King Bros. and Potts, 1950.

Englishwoman's Review. 15 February 1883: 62.

Sherlock, Frederick. *Ann Jane Carlile, a Temperance Pioneer.* London: F. Sherlock, 1897.

Carling, Sir John (1828–1911)

Sir John Carling was a brewer and politician. Born 23 January 1828 in London Township, Ontario, Canada, to Thomas Carling and Margaret Routledge, he died 6 November 1911 in London, Ontario, Canada. From 1849 until 1911, Sir John Carling, a strong believer in capitalism, oversaw one of Canada's largest brewing concerns, the Carling Brewing and Malting Company, Limited, of London, Ontario. He was also a politician, most notably sitting as a cabinet minister under Prime Minister Sir John A. Macdonald. In 1849, John Carling and his older brother, William, purchased their father's brewery in London, Ontario. The Carling brothers took advantage of Canada's expanding railway network to enhance their sales reach to the point where their brewery had become one of Canada's biggest by the 1870s. John Carling was the largest shareholder in the Carling Brewing and Malting Company, Limited, upon its incorporation in 1882. Political commitments, however, kept him from presiding over the company until 1894. He also was a shareholder in and a director of other enterprises, most notably the Great Western Railway, a company in which he exerted his influence to secure favorable shipping terms for his beer.

Although brewing stood as one pillar of Carling's national fame, politics was the other. He began public life as a school trustee and municipal councilor during the 1850s. This political apprenticeship taught Carling the value of lubricating the electorate with free beer of his own making. Nevertheless, he earned a reputation as an informed debater and honest dealer in office. A Conservative, he moved on to provincial politics in 1857 and continued as London's representative in the provincial assembly until 1872. In 1862, he became provincial receiver-general. Five years later, he became Ontario's commissioner of agriculture and public works. Carling shone brightest in federal politics and sat as London's member of Parliament (M.P.) from 1867 to 1874, 1878 to 1891, and 1892 to 1895. A loyal supporter of Sir John A. Macdonald, Carling entered the federal cabinet as postmaster general in 1882. Three years later, he was appointed minister of agriculture, an office that he occupied until 1892. The appointment was a fine match, especially considering Carling's rural upbringing and the brewing industry's links with agriculture. In this position, Carling oversaw the establishment and development of Canada's system of experimental farms, an important support structure in a country in which well over half the population derived a livelihood from farming. Carling became a senator in 1891, but resigned to return to the House of Commons. He was reappointed as a senator in 1896 and served as such until his death in 1911. Carling ensured that London benefited from his political influence. He secured for his home city a grand post office building, a provincial psychiatric hospital, a large military barracks and camp, railway car shops, and placement on the Canadian Pacific Railway's southern branch. In 1893, Carling received a knighthood for his public service. Ironically, despite his profession and the raucous nature of his electoral victory parties, Sir John Carling never drank a drop of beer. The beverage reputedly disagreed with him.

Glen C. Phillips

See also: Carling Brewery

References

Armstrong, Frederick H. *The Forest City: An Illustrated History of London, Canada.* Burlington, Ontario: Windsor, 1986.

Carling, Louisa. *Sketch of Sir John Carling.* London, Ontario: n.p., n.d.

Phillips, Glen C. *On Tap: The Odyssey of Beer and Brewing in Victorian London-Middlesex.* London, Ontario: Cheshire Cat Press, 2000.

Carling Brewery

Today, Carling is Britain's most prominent lager. Carling traces its origins to the brewery established in 1843 at London, Ontario, Canada, by Thomas Carling, a native of Yorkshire, England. Six years later, Carling sold the enterprise to his sons, William and John. Keen businessmen, the brothers enlarged their brewery in anticipation of the Great Western Railway's link to London. The railway, once completed, allowed William and John Carling access to a wider market, which they reached by developing agency and tavern accounts across the province. Having enjoyed success in London, the Carlings possessed sufficient capital strength and production economy to maintain a broadening sales network and to be price competitive in distant markets. By virtue of strong sales and through timely plant improvement, the Carlings' brewery grew into one of the most prominent in Ontario by 1870. Despite the economic depression of the 1870s, the need for greater production capacity pressed the brothers to construct a new brewery on Talbot Street in 1875. When it opened two years later, the four-story ale and porter facility, with a capacity of 2.5 million imperial gallons, was the single largest brewery building in Canada. The new brewery was conducted by a new partnership, Carling and Company, consisting of William Carling, John Carling, their brother-in-law Joshua Dalton, and John Carling's eldest son, Thomas Henry "Harry" Carling. In 1877 through 1878, the firm, responding to shifting popular taste, built a three-story lager plant onto their main brewery.

On 13 February 1879, a fire destroyed the entire Talbot Street works. The financial loss, though substantial, was eventually overcome; however, the fire claimed the life of senior partner William Carling, who died from pneumonia contracted while fighting the blaze. A year later, despite or perhaps because of the fire, Carling and Company bought a brewery in Cleveland, Ohio, a venture that remained in Carling hands for three years (afterwards, the Cleveland brewery brewed Carling brands under license). Nevertheless, the Carlings remained focused upon Canada. On 1 December 1882, the Carling Brewing and Malting Company of London Limited was incorporated. Over the rest of the century, Carling enlarged its sales agency network into a coast-to-coast operation. This geographic breadth allowed the brewer to survive the vagaries of local-option prohibition under the Canada Temperance Act. During the same period, Carling also adopted sophisticated branding and marketing techniques to distinguish its products in an increasingly integrated national beer market. For example, to bestow its lager with a more dynamic image, Carling changed its name from the generic-sounding Carling's Lager to the more exotic Carling's Bavarian Stock Lager. The brand was later rechristened Carling's Imperial Club Lager to find favor with Canadians who prized their country's ties to empire. Brand-driven advertising in major national journals supported Carling's brand development.

In the early twentieth century, Carling maintained its place as a major Canadian brewer by continuing its national promotional strategy. Marketing was augmented by the adoption of new technologies, such as mechanical refrigeration, plant electrification, automated crown-cap bottling lines, and motorized delivery vehicles. With John Carling's death in 1911, Harry Carling became company president. However, World War I restrictions on beer manufacture hit the brewery hard. After the war, an initial reluctance to circumvent Prohibition under the Ontario Temperance Act (1916–1927) imperiled the brewery. Brewing stopped at Carling in 1920. It was not recommenced until two years later, when J. Innes Carling, John Carling's grandson, assumed control of the brewery under the Carling Export Brewing and Malting Company Limited. The brewery's name reflected the younger Carling's intentions, and with a new sales manager who possessed the requisite underworld connections, Carling began smuggling huge volumes of beer into a dry United States. In 1927, the company was reincorporated as Carling Breweries Limited. That year, Carling's Black and White Lager was renamed Black Label Lager and joined the recently introduced Red Cap Ale as the brewery's principal brands. Supplying the U.S. market brought mixed blessings. Booming sales looked good on the books, but encouraged imprudent expansion, most notably a $400,000 bottling plant in Montreal. In 1930, E. P. Taylor bought the overextended Carling Breweries Limited and folded it into his recently formed conglomerate, Brewing Corporation of Canada Limited (later Canadian Breweries Limited). Six years later, he closed the London plant and merged its production with the Kuntz brewery in Waterloo, Ontario.

Under Taylor, Carling Black Label became the world's first beer brand to be brewed on a mass international scale. In Canada, he promoted Black Label as his flagship lager from the 1930s onward. The brand came into its own on the world stage beginning in the late 1950s and early 1960s, when Taylor licensed its production in the U.S. and Great Britain. Indeed, the rapid U.S. climb of Black Label, materially assisted by the catchy ad slogan "Hey Mabel, Black Label," catapulted Taylor's Brewing Corporation of America into the top echelon of U.S. beer producers. When Hope and Anchor began brewing Black Label in Britain in 1954, lager constituted a mere 2 percent of the British beer market. However, a combination of Taylor's worldly promotional experience, changing British tastes, and aggressive marketing by Hope and Anchor and later by Bass propelled Black Label's rise in Britain. By the mid-1970s, the Canadian lager was annually selling at around 1 million barrels. In 1988, it was the first brand in Britain to reach the 2-million-barrel milestone. In 2001, when Black Label's annual sales hit 4 million barrels, the brand was Britain's single best-selling brand. At the end of 2001, Belgium's Interbrew, which had bought Bass, was ordered by trade authorities to sell control of Carling. The Adolph Coors Company of Golden, Colorado, purchased the brand rights, along with those to a few other brands, for £1.2 billion sterling, instantly giving the American brewer an 18 percent stake in the British beer market. Meanwhile, Carling has faded from prominence in North America. Ironically, Black Label, presently owned by Molson in Canada, is now of minor significance in the country of its birth.

Glen C. Phillips

See also: Canada Temperance Act; Carling, Sir John; Interbrew; Labatt Brewing Company Limited; O'Keefe Brewery

References

Bowering, Ian. *The Art and Mystery of Brewing in Ontario.* Burnstown, Ontario: General Store Publishing, 1988.

Miller, Carl H. *Breweries of Cleveland.* Cleveland, Ohio: Schnitzelbank Press, 1998.

Phillips, Glen C. *On Tap: The Odyssey of Beer and Brewing in Victorian London-Middlesex.* London, Ontario: Cheshire Cat Press, 2000.

Report Concerning an Alleged Combine in the Manufacture, Distribution and Sale of Beer in Canada. Ottawa: Restrictive Trade Practices Commission of Canada, 1955.

Carlisle, Countess of (Rosalind Howard) (1845–1921)

Rosalind Howard, Countess of Carlisle (1845–1921), brought a new political dimension to the women's temperance movement in the United Kingdom. She was one of the most problematic women to espouse the temperance cause. Born into the Stanley family of Alderley, Rosalind Frances Stanley married George Howard in 1864 and became Rosalind Howard, Countess of Carlisle, on the death of her father-in-law.

An itinerant temperance evangelist converted both husband and wife to total abstinence in 1881. Brewing was discontinued at Castle Howard, and temperance became a condition of tenancy on the Howard estates. The expansion of the railways enabled the Carlisles to buy up coaching inns bypassed by the railways and close them down. Lady Carlisle's early temperance activities began with organizing local Bands of Hope and temperance societies. She went on to become the first woman to serve as president of a mixed temperance organization when she took the mainly honorific role in the North of England Temperance League in 1892.

Lady Carlisle became president of the National British Women's Temperance Association (NBWTA) in 1903, following the resignation of Lady Henry Somerset. In many ways, Lady Carlisle was an awkward choice. For instance, she was an atheist or agnostic, while most of her members were devout Quakers, Methodists, and other Nonconformists. It was only at this time that she belatedly stopped serving wine to her family and guests. An autocrat, she immediately began to impose her methods on the NBWTA. She saw it principally as a national political organization. She quickly discontinued all departments that were in her opinion unnecessary, including many inspired by Frances Willard. Lady Carlisle did favor one nonpolitical agitation. She believed that lobbying for Scientific Temperance Instruction (STI) should be an NBWTA priority. The schools had to teach children the dangers of alcohol. The membership of the association had been steadily increasing from 23,000 members in 1889–1890 to 92,000 in 1901–1902 on the eve of Carlisle's presidency. Some members objected to her tactics and resented the orders that she expected all to obey. Yet, most admired her. Significantly, when she died after nearly twenty years as president, the NBWTA selected one of her daughters, Lady Cecilia Roberts, to be the new president.

The World's Woman's Christian Temperance Union (WWCTU) offered Lady Carlisle the post of president in 1906. She accepted but was horrified to discover that its executive staff consisted of five dispersed officers and was, in her opinion, disorganized. She was generous in funding the union and its missionaries, but she believed that temperance women in the United Kingdom were indifferent to the WWCTU. Agnes Slack, an English stalwart of the WWCTU, clashed with Lady Carlisle over the value of the international organization, a controversy that rumbled on unresolved between these two determined women.

When she became president of the NBWTA, Lady Carlisle wanted her society and the smaller Women's Total Abstinence Union to cooperate with the London auxiliary of the United Kingdom Alliance (UKA) in organizing metropolitan demonstrations. Although she had softened Lady Henry Somerset's controversial "do-everything" program, this effort at reconciliation was not as successful as Lady Carlisle would have wished. Attempts to merge the two rival women's organizations failed. It was not until 1925, after her death, that they rejoined forces once more.

Lady Carlisle had long-established contacts within the UKA and the Liberal Party. Not the least of her allies was Sir Wilfrid Lawson, a Liberal member of Parliament (M.P.), whose estates were adjacent to Carlisle lands in Cumberland. Together with Lawson, she fought for the introduction of the direct veto. Like him, she considered the 1899 reports of the Royal Commission on Liquor Licensing Laws a disappointment and opposed proposals for disinterested management, as well as the call by some in the Labour Party for nationalization of the drink trade. It was ironic that, during the first world war, the Carlisle experiment should be based in Cumberland. When Lawson died, Lady Carlisle's former secretary, Leif Jones, became president of the UKA.

Lady Carlisle was unfortunate in her timing. At one time she could boast the presence in the House of Commons of a son, a son-in-law, and her former secretary, but it was in a rapidly shrinking world of prohibitionist diehards that she enjoyed prominence. When she became president of the NBWTA, the prohibitionist UKA was losing its influence in the Liberal Party and even within the temperance movement. Lady Carlisle fought to keep the UKA faithful to its prohibitionist heritage.

Although a keen Liberal partisan, Lady Carlisle at first refused to join the Women's Liberal Federation (WLF) under the presidency of Mrs. W. E. Gladstone because the organization would not press for women's suffrage. When she did join, in 1890, she lobbied for the inclusion of suffrage in concert with other temperance women such as Bertha Mason and Eva McLaren. From 1902, Lady Carlisle would not support the candidacies of antisuffrage Liberals.

She founded WLF local branches in Carlisle and Bampton, expecting members to follow her lead in supporting the campaign for women's franchise. Her political stance on the vote for women was that women's franchise should not be restricted to women owning property. Such a restriction, she believed, would benefit the Conservative Party. Her strong support of women's suffrage did not extend to suffragette militancy, which she believed damaged the relationship with the Liberal Party. When she became president of the WLF, she attempted to persuade the membership to support her on the direct local veto but failed.

Her advocacy of women's suffrage, her support for Irish home rule, and her opposition to the Boer War divided her family. In her later years, she was estranged from her husband and most of her children. Adding to her disappointments, Lady

Carlisle suffered the loss of several of her sons during her own lifetime. She was a vehement opponent of imperialism and militarism, so it is ironic that most of them died on the battlefield between 1896 and 1917.

A voluminous, well-indexed collection of her correspondence and papers is preserved at the Castle Howard archives in Yorkshire.

Margaret Barrow

See also: British Women's Temperance Association (BWTA); Carlisle System; Gothenburg Schemes/Disinterested Management; Jones, Leif; Lawson, Sir Wilfrid; Liberal Party (United Kingdom); Local Option; National British Women's Temperance Association (NBWTA); Slack, Agnes Elizabeth; Somerset, Isabella Caroline (Lady Henry Somerset); Women's Total Abstinence Union (WTAU); World's Woman's Christian Temperance Union (WWCTU)

References

Barrow, Margaret. "Temperate Feminists: The British Women's Temperance Association, 1870–1914" (Ph.D. dissertation, University of Manchester, 1999).

Henley, Lady Dorothy. *Rosalind Howard, Countess of Carlisle.* London: Hogarth Press, 1958.

Roberts, Charles. *The Radical Countess: The History of the Life of Rosalind Countess of Carlisle.* Carlisle: Steel Brothers, 1962.

Surtees, Virginia. *The Artist and the Aristocrat: George and Rosalind Howard, Earl and Countess of Carlisle.* Salisbury, Wiltshire: Michael Russell, 1988.

Carlisle System

In 1916, the British government took over the ownership and management of the entire drink industry in the Carlisle area, in the very northwest of England. Breweries, public houses, and off-licenses all came into state ownership, with their owners being paid some £900,000 in compensation. As an experiment in drink control, the Carlisle System was to be of considerable influence, but the system of state management in the United Kingdom was never expanded further.

The immediate context for this experiment was World War I. There was considerable concern that drunkenness would undermine the war effort, and King George V and others had made public declarations of abstinence. The political prominence of David Lloyd George—the architect of a general wartime increase in the state management of economy and society and an enthusiastic temperance supporter—further inspired a number of changes in drinking laws from 1914 to 1916. These were to play an important part—though how important a part is subject to some debate—in the general reduction in alcohol consumption in the United Kingdom in the next two decades. Restrictions on hours of sale were applied across the country, followed by a series of measures to increase the tax on beer and to reduce its alcoholic strength. Wartime legislation also created a Central Control Board (CCB) for the liquor trade, and gave this board the power to take complete control of the liquor trade where it was deemed necessary. This was first done on a relatively small scale early in 1916, at Enfield Lock, in London, where there was an armaments factory, and at Invergordon and Cromarty in Scotland, where there was particular concern over drinking because of the labor needs of arms factories and a naval base. Later the same year, control was extended south of Cromarty to the much larger area in and around the city of Carlisle, where a new armaments factory was under construction, and an influx of casual laborers had led to a rapid rise in conspicuous drunkenness. This took in some 500 square miles, with a population of 140,000; four breweries and a considerable number of licensed premises—119 in the city alone—were taken over in this area.

This form of control had been advocated for some time by some temperance campaigners, and was inspired by the idea of "disinterested ownership." Excessive drinking, it was argued, was the result of profit-seeking publicans plying customers with drink, and might be limited by establishing a drink industry that had no interest in increasing consumption. Managers of the state-owned premises in Carlisle received no commission on drink sales, and were therefore assumed to have no interest in promoting the sale of beverage alcohol. The efficacy of ventures in public control in Sweden and Norway and in parts of Russia had been debated at some length. At the turn of the century, the writings of Joseph Rowntree and Arthur Sherwell had identified this as the real "solution" to the "temperance problem." The way that the Carlisle System was managed also showed the influence of ideas about the "improvement" of drinking places. Public houses with larger spaces and better—and separate—facilities for women, and for games, were created to encourage more responsible drinking. The hope was that these would, under disinterested management, become increasingly places for the sale of food and nonintoxicating beverages rather than alcohol. Once state control was established in Carlisle, fifty licensed premises were shut down, three of the four breweries were closed, and a program of improvement was instituted for the remaining licensed premises.

Advocates of the scheme emphasized its success in reducing drinking, drunkenness, and forms of crime associated with drink. With the backing of Lloyd George, there were, in 1917, serious discussions about extending state control dramatically across the country; at this time, the uncertain profitability of the major brewing companies made them amenable to proposals that might offer them guaranteed profits or a buyout at good prices. But these talks came to nothing, partly because of a change of mind by Lloyd George, who apparently believed that too many concessions had been made to brewers' interests in the negotiations over the details of state control. New licensing legislation brought in after the war, in 1921, created a peacetime legal framework for public ownership, but no further extension of state ownership or management was pursued. The cost of compensation that would have been required to be paid to the industry in the event of a state takeover, initially estimated at around £250 million, was by 1920 being estimated at £1,000 million. The perceived problems of excessive drinking had also been curtailed considerably. The end of hostilities eased anxiety over the danger to national security posed by drunken workers, and there had been a general reduction in drinking—and in public drunkenness—that resulted from the other restrictions imposed during the war, by no means all of which were withdrawn at the end of hostilities. Additionally, "state management" had long had vociferous critics within the chronically faction-ridden temperance lobby, not only from "moral suasionists" who eschewed legislative compulsion of all kinds, but also from outright prohibitionists and those who believed that the state should not acquire any role in the trade lest it become "interested" for revenue reasons. The danger of the state's becoming financially interested had concerned Rowntree and Sherwell, and had been particularly emphasized by Joseph Malins, of the National Temperance Federation, a long-term opponent of schemes for public ownership. Prohibitionists associated with the United Kingdom Alliance (UKA) revived this criticism in the early 1920s. Such critics favored alternative schemes: "local option" to allow particular communities to ban the trade, tighter controls on Sunday drinking, or further restrictions on the number of licenses in an area and on off-license sale.

The Enfield Lock state monopoly was ended in 1924; the Carlisle System itself, however, remained in existence—under the Home Secretary, because the CCB was abolished. Some of the Carlisle System's ambitions were modified—by 1923, only nine "food taverns" serving full, hot meals were still in operation. There were also some problems with the quality of the beer supplied by the brewery. But the principles of improved drinking places and "disinterested management" were maintained, and as an experimental model, Carlisle continued to attract attention in the empire as well as in the United Kingdom itself. A form of municipal ownership of "beer halls" for Africans was introduced in Nairobi in 1921, and Carlisle was cited as a precedent in Tanganyika in the 1930s when a similar system with a municipally owned beer shop supplying grain beer (to Africans only) was created—briefly—in Dar es Salaam.

In Britain, the Southborough Committee, appointed specifically to consider the value of "disinterested management" schemes, produced a report in 1927 that suggested that the Carlisle System was financially sound, but that there was no evidence that this system had had any especial effect in reducing alcohol consumption. The 1931 royal commission on licensing was rather more favorable in its discussion of Carlisle—though evidence given there also suggested that the reduction in consumption in Carlisle was by no means exceptional—and again raised the possibility that it might be extended, but noted that "financial circumstances" made any wholesale extension of state control "out of the question at present." Wilson's *Alcohol and the Nation* made clear the continuing appeal of the scheme to one strand of temperance thought, but state management seems never to have been considered again as a realistic option, and it has been suggested that the most enduring influence of the Carlisle System was through the model that it provided for improved public houses, rather than state control in itself. By 1940, the Carlisle System covered 176 licensed premises, including a number of hotels and restaurants, as well as one brewery. State management continued in Carlisle until 1974.

Justin Willis

See also: Gothenburg Schemes/Disinterested Management; Lloyd George, David; Malins, Joseph; Rowntree, Joseph

References

Gourvish, Terry R., and Richard G. Wilson. *The British Brewing Industry, 1830–1980.* Cambridge: Cambridge University Press, 1994.

Rowntree, Joseph, and Arthur Sherwell. *The Temperance Problem and Social Reform.* London: Hodder and Stoughton, 1899.

Sherwell, Arthur. *Carlisle and Its Critics.* London: Temperance Legislation League, 1923.

Turner, John. "State Purchase of the Liquor Trade in the First World War" in *Historical Journal.* 23 (1980): 589–615.

Wilson, George B. *Alcohol and the Nation.* London: Nicholson and Watson, 1940.

Carlsberg

When Jacob Christian Jacobsen established his brewery on a hill overlooking Copenhagen in 1847 and named it after his son Carl, he created what was to become a focus for Danish national pride: the Carlsberg brewery. In later life, Jacobsen eschewed the purely commercial aspects of business and placed his brewery under the control of disinterested academics in perpetuity. Carl Jacobsen, who established his own brewery, also showed philanthropic tendencies and enhanced his father's legacy. In the twentieth century, Carlsberg and Tuborg, aided by a cartel agreement and the helpful attitude of the industry's trade body, dominated the Danish brewing industry. The two companies were early exporters of beer and in the second half of the twentieth century turned increasingly to foreign trade. They merged in 1970 and evolved into an international brewer by the end of the century, with over 90 percent of sales coming from abroad.

J. C. Jacobsen introduced bottom fermentation to Denmark in the mid-1840s and soon prospered as the new style of beer gained popularity. Long enthusiastic about science and keen to see it applied to brewing, Jacobsen established the Carlsberg Laboratory in 1875, and it was there in 1883 that Emil Christian Hansen devised "pure yeast culture." The new technique significantly reduced spoilage in brewing and was eagerly adopted by the industry. Although Hansen wished to exploit his invention commercially, Jacobsen would not allow it, forbidding patenting and even offering free delivery of pure yeast to his competitors. This move was typical of the altruistic Jacobsen's attitude to business by this time. He attempted to inculcate his son with this philosophy, but was not happy with the results. In 1870 and

1871, Jacob built a brewery adjacent to his original Gamle (old) Carlsberg brewery and leased it to the twenty-eight-year-old Carl. As trade grew, Carl pressed for the extension of this Ny (new) Carlsberg brewery, but Jacob objected to such naked commercialism, causing Carl to set up another Ny Carlsberg nearby in 1880 through 1883. Remaining unconvinced of Carl's strength of character, Jacob ensured that his own breweries were left in the hands of the Carlsberg Foundation when he died in 1887. The foundation, created in 1876, continues to hold a majority of shares in Carlsberg and operates under the control of a board of five academics from the Royal Danish Academy of Sciences and Letters. Carl, who proved a more rounded personality than his father appreciated, incorporated his own brewery into the foundation in 1902, extending its scope to cover the arts as well as the sciences.

In 1891, United Breweries was formed by the merger of eleven breweries and was joined three years later by the Tuborg brewery (founded in 1873). The company became generally known as Tuborg, its major brand. Carlsberg and Tuborg signed a cartel agreement in 1895 covering competition and profit sharing that was extended to other areas in 1903 and 1912. The effectiveness of this cartel was enhanced by the Danish Brewers Association, which encouraged fixed prices and restricted distribution and advertising. Restrictive practice legislation was not introduced in Denmark until 1937. High tariffs on imported beers also discouraged foreign competition prior to the formation of European trading areas in the 1960s. These factors led to a limited choice of beers in Denmark and, combined with the parochialism and patriotism of the Danish consumer, allowed Carlsberg and Tuborg to control 70 to 80 percent of their home market. In the 1960s, after the relationship between the two companies had become strained over export policy, they merged, taking on the name United Breweries (reverting to Carlsberg in 1987). The Danish brewing industry became more open in the 1970s but without significant effect on Carlsberg's domestic dominance. The Tuborg brewery was closed in 1997, and production concentrated at Carlsberg's Copenhagen and Fredericia plants.

Carlsberg exported limited quantities of bottled lager to Nordic markets from the 1850s, reaching Britain in the late 1860s and Asia and South America by the 1880s. Exports remained at a relatively low level until after World War II when both Carlsberg and Tuborg, secure at home, followed the lead of the Dutch brewer Heineken and stepped up activity. At the time of their merger, around 25 percent of combined output was exported, with the United Kingdom as the major recipient. As trade increased, it became economical to license production with local breweries or to open new breweries abroad. Carlsberg built a brewery in Malawi in 1968, and Tuborg built a plant in Turkey a year later. Investment in breweries in Brazil, Malaysia, Italy, and the United Kingdom followed in the 1970s. Particularly significant was the high profitability achieved in the United Kingdom where weak (3.2 percent alcohol by volume) beer was successfully marketed to the undiscerning British lager drinker under the slogan "Carlsberg—probably the best lager in the world." From 1974, Carlsberg's foreign production exceeded exports from Denmark, and by 1976 sales in the international market exceeded domestic sales. By 1990, around 75 percent of Carlsberg's beer was brewed outside Denmark. The company has had mixed experiences in the last decade. Merger of its British brewing interests with those of Allied Breweries in 1993 produced a floundering company, Carlsberg-Tetley, where Carlsberg's sacerdotal self-regard sat uneasily with Allied's worldly pragmatism. By the turn of the century, over one-third of United Kingdom market share and three out of five breweries had gone. In May 2000, Carlsberg merged its worldwide brewing and soft drinks activities with those of Orkla, a Norwegian conglomerate owning Pripps and Ringnes breweries. This move increased total volume by 50 percent at a stroke, making Carlsberg the world's fifth biggest brewer, producing 60 million hectoliters (1,585 million U.S. gallons) of beer in eighty-five breweries operating in forty-six countries. Investments in the crucial Chinese market, however, continued to be unprofitable, and following delays in establishing new operations in Asia, the chief executive was replaced in August 2001. The European Community Commission announced in March 2002 that they were investigating alleged "cartel-like" behavior of Carlsberg and Heineken in agreeing not to compete too strongly in each other's home markets.

Raymond G. Anderson

See also: Allied Breweries; Beer

References

"An Elephant Conquers the World: The International Activities of the Carlsberg Group" in *Brewing and Beverage Industry International.* 1, no. 2 (1993): 10–12.

Glamman, Kristof. "The Carlsberg Foundation" in *Brewers' Guardian.* 111 (May 1981): 52–53.

High, Richard. "A Brief History of Tuborg" in *Journal of the Brewery History Society.* 94 (1998): 11–16.

Holter, H., and K. Max Moller. *The Carlsberg Laboratory 1876/1976.* Copenhagen: Carlsberg Foundation, 1976.

Johansen, Hans Christian. "Marketing and Competition in Danish Brewing" in *Adding Value: Brands and Marketing in Food and Drink,* edited by Geoffery Jones and Nicholas J. Morgan, 126–138. London: Routledge, 1994.

Carter, Henry (1874–1951)

Henry Carter (1874–1951), Wesleyan Methodist minister, was an influential voice in temperance politics in Britain in the early twentieth century, serving as a member of both the Central Control Board (Liquor Traffic) (CCB) (1916–1921) and the Royal Commission on Liquor Licensing Laws (1929–1931). He also wrote on temperance history.

From his early years, Carter displayed an interest in social and economic questions and during his long public life helped to develop the Methodist tradition of pioneering inquiry and work on social issues. In 1905, Carter was appointed lay connectional temperance Evangelist for the Wesleyan Methodists and in 1911 general secretary of the Temperance and Social Welfare Department of the (Wesleyan) Methodist Church, a position he held for thirty-one years. In 1916, he was appointed a member of the CCB. The work of this body suited Carter's approach, which was to place the temperance and alcohol questions in a broader context of social problems. He supported the policy of combining general restrictions with positive initiatives, such as the provision of canteens in factories, as well as direct state control of the alcoholic drinks trade in Carlisle along the lines of disinterested management. In 1918, he published a detailed account of the first two years of the CCB's work. Although this book had a propagandist purpose, insofar as it argued for the continuation of the CCB and its alcohol policy after the war, it provides a useful and comprehensive account of drink control from 1915 to 1917.

To Carter's regret, the CCB was wound up in 1921. During the interwar period, Carter used his position as chair of the executive committee of the Temperance Council of the Christian Churches to argue for a "constructive" policy of temperance reform. In his dedication to this policy, he clashed with the prohibitionists of the United Kingdom Alliance (UKA). The royal commission on which he served, appointed by the Labour government, proposed a program of legislative reforms designed to reduce consumption. Its proposals were, however, ignored by the national government that took office in 1931.

On the eve of the repeal of National Prohibition in the United States, Carter embarked on a history of the English temperance movement. Once again, his purpose was in large part propagandist: to argue the case that the early temperance movement had enjoyed success when it stressed the educational approaches of temperance work. This education had to go in tandem with gradual advances in the legislative sphere. He argued that the primary purpose of the movement should be moral rather than legislative.

Only the first volume of this work, covering the period up to 1899, appeared. It had outraged prohibitionists, who discouraged him from publishing the projected second volume on the twentieth century. The temperance authorities Gwylmor Prys Williams and George Thompson Brake speculate that the merger of Carter's Wesleyan church with the UKA-friendly Primitive Methodists and United Methodists in 1932 persuaded him to mute his criticism of prohibition.

After 1933, Carter was at the forefront in fighting the moves by the drinks industry to use seductive advertising for their products, in the course of which campaign he did much to unite the various strands of the now weakened British temperance movement.

Carter was also active in the peace movement and, after the second world war, served on the Central Council for Refugees. A man never afraid to fight his corner, he attracted widespread respect for his sincerity and selfless dedication. He had a reputation as a quiet and thoughtful preacher.

John Greenaway

See also: Carlisle System; D'Abernon, Lord (Sir Edgar Vincent); Gothenburg Schemes/Disinterested Management; Labour Party (United Kingdom); Temperance Council of the Christian Churches; United Kingdom Alliance (UKA); Wilson Black, Robert

References

Carter, Henry. *The Control of the Drink Trade: A Contribution to National Efficiency.* London: Longmans, Green, 1918.

———. *The English Temperance Movement: A Study in Objectives,* vol. 1, *The Formative Period, 1830–99.* London: Epworth, 1933.

Greenaway, John. *Drink and British Politics since 1830: A Study in Policy-Making.* Basingstoke, England, and New York: Palgrave Macmillan, 2003.

Urwin, E. C. *Henry Carter, C. B. E.: A Memoir.* London: Epworth, 1955.

Williams, Gwylmor Prys, and George Thompson Brake. *Drink in Great Britain, 1900–1979.* London: Edsall, 1980.

Central America

Not clearly delineated in geographical or political terms, Central America in general usage refers to the predominantly mestizo and Spanish-speaking republics that lie between Mexico and Panama, namely, Costa Rica, El Salvador, Guatemala, Honduras, and Nicaragua. The history and demography of Belize (formerly British Honduras, peopled largely by English-speaking blacks) differ from those of its neighbors, but beliefs and behaviors concerning alcohol are remarkably similar. Although each country is characterized by ethnic and ecological variation, the important roles of beverage alcohol have been similar in broad outline.

Beverages

The Central American countries all still have populations who speak indigenous languages and retain important portions of their distinctive non-Western cultures—in Guatemala, a majority, and in Costa Rica, relatively few. Often called "Indians," these traditionally rural people often still produce home brews from various fruits, vegetables, or tubers and use these brews as important staples in their diet. Low in alcohol (about 4–6 percent by volume), such brews tend to be nutritious and are consumed by people of all ages.

Rum (of various grades and under various names) is manufactured locally and is extremely important as an intoxicant. Lager and pilsen beers were introduced 100 years ago and have continued to gain popularity as electricity and refrigeration are more widely available. A recent multinational study suggests that attitudes toward rum and beer are remarkably similar, with the same people drinking either or both on different occasions, and with overall consumption differing pretty much in proportion to their respective retail prices. Little wine was ever produced in this area, and it is still rare except among a few relatively affluent cosmopolites. In areas where taxes make legal rum too costly, illicit production is commonplace, and deaths from faulty moonshine sporadically occur. Spirits other than rum have some prestige value; imports are expensive and local counterfeits tend to be of poor quality.

Drinking Patterns

As throughout Latin America, men drink more, and more often, than do women, and there is a clear double standard whereby female drinkers are suspected of moral laxity. Episodic heavy drinking (to the point of intoxication on weekends and holidays) is common and generally accepted among adolescent and older males. The rare occasions when women drink are usually at home; most male drinking takes place in public at designated drinking places and without meals. Occasionally, small amounts are drunk for relaxation or sociability or while watching sports, but it is also commonplace for men to set out to become drunk. The reasons most often given are to forget one's troubles, or to assert masculinity and independence.

Although some indigenous home brews serve as daily food, others play special symbolic roles in connection with both religious and secular ceremonies. Specific details vary from one population to another, but it is normal to find native beer ritually consumed at marriages, harvest rites, and political events, and associated with religious practices.

The offer of a drink is an important gesture, and one can cause offense by declining. Drinking together implies trust and camaraderie among men, often with toasting, wordplay, games, or singing as accompaniments. Few drinkers pay attention to flavor, color, or other aspects of beverages, preferring whatever provides the most alcohol for the price.

Adolescence and young adulthood are the ages of heaviest drinking, the quantity of consumption by individuals usually tapering off after marriage. In general, there is a strong inverse correlation between alcohol consumption on the one hand and schooling, income, and prestige on the other. Small enclaves of Africans (descended from slaves), East Indians, and Chinese (descended from indentured laborers) or people of Near Eastern ancestry (from the early-twentieth-century diaspora) tend to have distinctive drinking patterns. Women and Protestants make up most of the abstainers.

Drunkenness tends to be viewed as exhilarating and as confirming one's masculinity, especially among those who have little wealth, power, or social status. Presumably for those reasons, many drink primarily for the psychoactive effect.

Attitudes and Images of Drinking and Temperance

There is often an attitude that hard-working men "deserve" to drink, first for sociability and later for intoxication (which has connotations of being liberating). Because of these men's marginal economic situation, this attitude often results in marked periodicity with heavy drinking on paydays and relatively dry periods intervening. Holidays, both religious and secular, are often marked by heavy drinking, as are weddings, funerals, and other special occasions.

The benefits that drinkers claim to seek are sociability, celebration, change of mood, and relaxation, all very positively valued. The most obvious costs to drinkers are economic, strain on family relations, and occasional accidents.

In recent decades, Protestantism (especially more fundamentalist versions) is gaining ground in what had traditionally been overwhelmingly Roman Catholic populations. When abstention from alcohol is an article of faith, drinking (or not) can be an important boundary marker between social groups.

An interesting anomaly is the fact that, in such small countries, one or two energetic and politically astute individuals can have a disproportionate impact. This occurred in Honduras, where a recent constitution makes specific mention that the state should defend its citizens against the ravages of alcohol. In Costa Rica, a cabinet-level agency briefly provided treatment and a little research on alcoholism. But no Central American nation has demonstrated meaningful or sustained effort toward understanding alcohol or its impact on people.

Patterns of Regulation

A small but highly vocal group of self-styled public-health advocates has, for the past three decades, promoted a variety of policies that they claim would reduce the availability of alcoholic beverages, thereby diminishing average per capita consumption and consequently reducing or preventing dependence and various kinds of alcohol-related damage, to the drinker and to others. Although both conceptual and empirical bases for those assumptions remain questionable, the World Health Organization (WHO) has vigorously promoted such policies, and they have been widely adopted, even in areas where there was little previous tradition of control. It remains to be seen whether the more recent General Agreement on Trade in Services will render all or most of such restrictions moot. Among the controversial efforts at control, some refer to sales, others to advertising, and others to labeling, as illustrated below.

Costa Rica has some restrictions on the content of advertising for alcohol, especially in print, and it requires that containers carry warning labels: "Drinking liquor is harmful to health" or "The abuse of liquor is harmful to health." Honduras has banned advertisements that are associated with sports, aimed at young people, or that denigrate women. El Salvador does not even license sellers.

Research on Alcohol

Alcohol has rarely been viewed as problematic in Central America, and, in general, there is little information available about alcohol use and its outcomes in any of the countries. Occasional articles are admittedly weak in terms of both samples and methods. Ethnographic or anthropological studies, where they occur, tend to be richly detailed but unrepresentative.

In Costa Rica, some epidemiological studies were made by the National Institute on Alcoholism (IMSA) during the 1960s and by its successor, Center for Studies on Alcoholism (CESA), in the 1970s and 1980s. A few psychiatrists occasionally deal with aspects of alcohol in Honduras, but little else has been done. This neglect is understandable because, as in developing countries around the world, resources are limited and demands are large with respect to the many pressing problems of health and social welfare.

Producers and Distributors

The beverage alcohol trade is one in which many companies deal with more than a single class of beverage, for example, producing wine or beer and simultaneously distributing distilled spirits that were produced elsewhere. It is also a business in which actors come and go with some frequency. Because of licensing agreements, mergers, and other arrangements, it is not always clear whether a company is indigenous to the country or acting as an agent for a larger international organization. With those caveats in mind, some of the major producers and distributors in the region in 2002 are the following. Beer and spirits are produced in Belize, El Salvador, Guatemala, and Nicaragua. Spirits and wine are imported to all countries, and beer is produced in Costa Rica (Cervecería Costa Rica and Cervecería Americana) and in Honduras (Cervecería Hondureña).

Dwight B. Heath

See also: Rum; World Health Organization (WHO)

References

Acta Psiquiátrica y Psicológica de América latina (special issue on alcohol in Latin America). 20, no. 2 (1974).

Heath, Dwight B. *Drinking Occasions: Comparative Perspectives on Alcohol and Culture.* Philadelphia: Brunner/Mazell, 2000.

———, ed. *International Handbook on Alcohol and Culture.* Westport, CT: Greenwood, 1995.

Horwitz, José, Juan Marconi, and Gonzalo Adis Castro. *Bases para una epidemiología del alcoholismo en América latina (Monografía de Acta Psiquiátrica y Psicológica de América latina 1).* Buenos Aires: Fondo para la Salud Mental, 1967.

Institute of Medicine. *Legislative Approaches to Prevention of Alcohol-Related Problems: An Inter American Workshop.* Washington, DC: National Academy Press, 1982.

Marshall, Mac, ed. *Beliefs, Behaviors, and Alcoholic Beverages: A Cross-Cultural Survey.* Ann Arbor: University of Michigan Press, 1979.

Central Policy Review Staff (CPRS) Report (United Kingdom)

The Central Policy Review Staff (CPRS), popularly known as the Think Tank, was established by Edward Heath's Conservative government in Britain in 1970 to provide strategic advice, to examine issues of long-term concern, and to address problems that fell across existing departmental lines. By 1977, alcohol policy lay in this last category, and the CPRS chose it as one of its topics of study. Its report in March 1979 came down firmly in favor of control policies. This caused great internal controversy, with stout resistance coming from those departments favoring liberalization of the existing licensing laws. The report was never published in Britain but was leaked and eventually published independently in Sweden. In 1983, Prime Minister Margaret Thatcher abolished the CPRS.

The CPRS recommended that the government adopt policies that sought to prevent an increase in alcohol consumption. These included maintaining the real price of drinks, avoiding liberalization of the licensing laws, and imposing controls on advertising. Such views chimed with those in the Department of Health and Social Security (DHSS) but ran against the interests of the departments responsible for employment, trade (including tourism), and the drinks industry. The CPRS also advocated the creation of an advisory council on alcohol policies to coordinate and monitor policies. The CPRS's draft report, started under a Labour government, appeared on the eve of the return to power of the Conservatives. The Conservatives were temperamentally inclined to support the drinks industry and were also ideologically strongly opposed to unnecessary state interference. Nevertheless, interdepartmental clashes were the main source of tension and delay, and the government had to admit continually that the "consultation document" produced by the CPRS was undergoing revision. The DHSS's policy document *Drinking Sensibly* (1981) emerged as a result of a long series of interdepartmental clashes and revisions. It was an equivocal document, which, though endorsing a health education program against alcohol abuse and urging responsible advertising, backed away from using taxation as a tool to discourage consumption.

After 1981, the dominant political ethos in Britain was strongly influenced by "New Right" ideas of market liberalism. Mrs. Thatcher's government wished to reduce the number of government agencies and bodies; moreover, in the health area, the emphasis was upon education and allowing people to take responsibility for their own lifestyles. The drinks business was rapidly becoming part and parcel of a broader leisure industry, and the popular mood swung in favor of liberalization of alcohol sales and even legalization of soft drugs. Occasional, but short-lived, moral panics on subjects such as alcohol-induced soccer hooliganism or loutish misbehavior in city centers did nothing to reverse this shift. Moreover, the impact of the European Union on taxation and retail policies further shifted policy away from restriction. The availability of alcohol increased, and its price declined. Both drinking patterns and attitudes in Britain have become more akin to those of continental Europe.

John Greenaway

See also: Conservative Party (United Kingdom)

References
Baggott, Rob. *Alcohol, Politics and Social Policy.* Aldershot: Gower, 1990.
Central Policy Review Staff. *Alcohol Policies in the UK.* Stockholm: Sociologiska Institutionen, 1982.
Department of Health and Social Security. *Drinking Sensibly.* London: HMSO, 1981.
Greenaway, John. *Drink and British Politics since 1830: A Study in Policy-Making.* Basingstoke, UK, and New York: Palgrave Macmillan, 2003.

Central Sunday Closing Association

The Central Association for Stopping the Sale of Intoxicating Liquors on Sunday (CASSILS) was organized in 1866 at Manchester, England. It received support from the British Temperance Association for the Promotion of Temperance (later called the British Temperance League), a society that had agitated for Sunday closing since 1844. In 1868, the CASSILS absorbed the Sunday Closing Association, based in Hull, which had been founded in 1861. From this time, the organization was generally known as the Central Sunday Closing Association. For many years, it maintained its headquarters in Manchester, later in London. It was relatively successful in raising funds. The historian Howard L. Malchow provides a list of members and officials from 1865 to 1886. For a long period, Joseph Woodford Causer served as secretary.

Although essentially a temperance organization, the CASSILS got support from Sabbatarians who were not otherwise active in the temperance movement. For instance, in the late 1860s, the Archbishops of Canterbury and of York were vice presidents. Among Nonconformists, Wesleyan Methodists showed much more keenness about Sabbatarianism than about temperance. Among temperance reformers, both prohibitionists and advocates of moral suasion supported Sunday closing.

The CASSILS created an elaborate organization: salaried agents, mostly Nonconformist ministers, answerable to Manchester; and relatively autonomous auxiliaries. The historian Lilian Lewis Shiman points out that Bradford, for example, had an active Sunday closing auxiliary.

Although Sunday closing enjoyed broad support, it had its critics. Secularists who resented Sabbatarianism occasionally disrupted Sunday closing meetings. A staunch prohibitionist, Sir Wilfrid Lawson considered Sunday closing a distraction. He said that he supported Sunday closing but that, if given a choice, he would prefer Saturday closing, since more alcohol was sold on that day.

The association wanted Sunday closing by parliamentary statute and not by local option. Although Parliament enacted Sunday closing laws for Scotland (1853), most of Ireland (1878), and Wales (1881), it never passed a law for Sunday closing for England.

David M. Fahey

See also: British Temperance League (BTL); Lawson, Sir Wilfrid

References
Harrison, Brian. *Drink and the Victorians: The Temperance Question in England 1815–1872.* 2d ed. Keele: Keele University Press, 1994.
Malchow, Howard LeRoy. *Agitators and Promoters in the Age of Gladstone and Disraeli: A Biographical Dictionary of the Leaders of British Pressure Groups Founded between 1865 and 1886.* New York: Garland, 1983.
Shiman, Lilian Lewis. *Crusade against Drink in Victorian England.* London: Macmillan, and New York: St. Martin's, 1988.

Chafetz, Morris Edward (1924–)

Born in Worcester, Massachusetts, Dr. Morris Edward Chafetz (1924–) is currently president of the Health Education Foundation, based in Washington, D.C. He graduated from Tufts Medical School in Boston, Massachusetts, in 1948 as a psychiatrist. A diplomat from the American Board of Psychiatry and Neurology, Chafetz has conducted many studies in the field of psychiatry and has dedicated his life to the study of alcoholism in society. His first article on alcoholism, published in 1959 and entitled "Practical and Theoretical Considerations in the Psychotherapy of Alcoholism," dealt with the clinical aspect of the alcoholic patient. Chafetz's interest in alcoholism started in 1952 while he was working as a clinical and research fellow in psychiatry at the Massachusetts General Hospital. He soon came to believe that the real problem of alcoholism is not the alcoholic beverage itself but rather the individual's capacity for self-destruction. He further developed his theory in articles such as "Alcoholism" in *Comprehensive Textbook of Psychiatry* and a "Foreword" in *Alcoholism: Modern Psychological Approach to Treatment.* Both articles appeared in 1967, setting forth Chafetz's theory that alcohol is an individual's problem and not a societal issue.

In Chafetz's view, the problem of alcoholism lies not in the bottle but rather within the individual involved in drinking. The individual is the first one responsible for his or her alcoholic behavior and remains the only one who can change it. It follows that laws written to regulate the use of alcohol are simply not capable of accomplishing that task. Underage drinking laws, for example, which are meant to keep young people away from alcohol, are doing exactly the opposite of what they are meant to do, according to Chafetz. In his worldwide study of alcoholism, Dr. Chafetz points out that U.S. children are not drinking more than other children worldwide; the problem is in the laws relating to underage drinking in the United States. Although the laws prohibit children under the age of twenty-one from drinking alcoholic beverages, children are allowed to drive at age sixteen, regardless of the dangers driving represents at that young age. Such problems stem from what Chafetz calls the "tyranny of experts," that is, the "diagnostic" attitude of experts studying alcoholism. To Chafetz, they all miss the point by focusing the problem of alcoholism on alcohol itself, thereby ignoring the opportunity to regard the drinker as the culprit.

Chafetz was the first director of the National Institute on Alcohol Abuse and Alcoholism (NIAAA), serving from 1971 to 1975. He has also served as member of the board of directors of the Presidential Commission on Drunk Driving in 1984, and as a presidential appointee for the White House Conference for a Drug-Free America in 1987. In these roles, he has defined the problem of drinking as actually a political matter. Chafetz attacks the "hypocrisy" encountered in regulating the advertising of alcoholic beverages. In an article published in 1997 entitled "Should the Government Restrict Advertising of Alcoholic Beverages," his answer is categorically "No." The first reason is that there is no scientific proof that advertising alcohol will boost drinking among children, as some experts claim. He writes: "The cult of expertise has made parents feel incapable of raising their children. But as a parent and psychiatrist, I trust the instincts of parents more than I do the hubris of child-protection experts." The idea that alcohol "advertising can lead anyone down the bottle-strewn garden path" is, to Chafetz, "pure hokum." The problem lies in how governments control alcohol drinking through a policy that aggravates the accidents or incidents related to alcohol. He recommends that parents teach their children about substance abuse and stop simply blaming alcohol as the sole source of the problem. In addition, Chafetz does not support the idea of restricting alcohol advertising because of what he calls a hypocritical double standard: Although it is acceptable to publicize alcohol in newspapers and magazines, it is still restricted on television because it is believed that children are most likely to be seduced by an advertisement on television rather than in a newspaper. To him, this is pure politics and bad policy.

Chafetz has served on many boards and taught at many universities throughout the world. He has written hundreds of articles on alcoholism and its effects in society. His contribution to human health and especially to the study of alcoholism has drawn both criticism and praise.

Sylvain B. Poosson

References

Chafetz, Morris E. *The Alcoholic Patient: Diagnosis and Management.* Oradell, NJ: Medical Economics Books, 1983.

———. *Liquor: The Servant of Man.* Boston: Little, Brown, 1965.

———. "Should the Government Restrict Advertising of Alcoholic Beverages?—No." 1997. http://www.acsh.org/publications/priorities/0903/govadno.html [February 2002].

Chafetz, Morris E., and Harold W. Demone. *Alcoholism and Society.* New York: Oxford University Press, 1962.

Chamberlain, Joseph (1836–1914)

Joseph Chamberlain (1836–1914), British politician, was prominent in the Liberal and Liberal Unionist Parties. Although he personally drank alcoholic beverages (except briefly in 1876), he joined the prohibitionist United Kingdom Alliance (UKA) in 1871. He endorsed direct local veto when he stood for Parliament at Sheffield in 1873 but deviated from alliance orthodoxy. He doubted that the working-class districts most in need of reform would vote for local prohibition, so he advocated that other restrictions supplement local veto. In addition, he argued that the owners of licensed property ought to receive financial compensation if the voters imposed prohibition for the district in which the public houses were located. Chamberlain lost the election, perhaps because nearly half of the public houses in Sheffield campaigned for his opponent.

His distinctive role in the Victorian temperance movement grew partly out of his Sheffield-inspired desire to drive the drink trade from electoral politics and partly out of his experiences as mayor of Birmingham. Most of all, Chamberlain was influenced by his belief that local prohibition would not work in the unlikely event that Parliament authorized it. The places that most needed reform would be the least likely to vote themselves dry. He became an advocate of municipal ownership and management of the retail sale of alcohol for on-premises consumption. This sometimes was called the Gothenburg scheme, after

Joseph Chamberlain (1836–1914) (Library of Congress)

the Swedish port that pioneered it, and sometimes disinterested management to contrast it with profit-motivated capitalism. He published an article in the *Fortnightly Review* in May 1876 and visited Gothenburg in October of that year to learn more about drink municipalization. He succeeded in getting support in Birmingham for a Gothenburg experiment in the city. In 1877, Chamberlain introduced a bill in the House of Commons to authorize such an experiment. Sir Wilfrid Lawson, then a vice president of the UKA, ridiculed the proposal, and no prominent politician supported Chamberlain. The Conservatives were hostile and the Liberals apathetic. After Chamberlain's bill failed, he testified before the House of Lords committee on intemperance. He got only half-hearted support for the Gothenburg scheme when the committee published its report.

In the mid-1890s, Chamberlain once again spoke out on behalf of the Gothenburg scheme, but the Conservative Party leader, Lord Salisbury, rejected it as a part of a Conservative-Liberal Unionist joint program. Despite this brief revival of his interest in the Gothenburg principle, Chamberlain essentially had abandoned temperance reform in 1877 on the grounds that it was not practical politics. He became bitterly opposed to prohibitionists such as Lawson. In 1894, Chamberlain said that "until wiser councils prevail among the temperance party, until the majority of the party is, at all events, willing to accept 1/2 a loaf rather than have no bread, I say that the history of temperance agitation will continue to be a dismal record of the wrecks and well-meant efforts and promising experiments."

Occasionally, Chamberlain pleased temperance reformers, as for instance, when as colonial secretary he opposed the sale of alcoholic drink to black Africans. In 1901, he also suggested the extension of magisterial discretion to include off-licenses, pre-1869 beer shops, and clubs. But when his brother Austen became the darling of temperance reformers in the early 1900s for presiding over a drastic reduction of Birmingham public houses as chairman of the licensing justices, Joseph Chamberlain took the side of the alcoholic drink trade.

David M. Fahey

See also: Conservative Party (United Kingdom); Gladstone, William Ewart; Gothenburg Schemes/Disinterested Management; Lawson, Sir Wilfrid; Liberal Party (United Kingdom)

References

Brown, James B. "The Temperance Career of Joseph Chamberlain, 1870–77: A Study in Political Frustration" in *Albion*. 4 (1972): 29–44.

Jay, Richard. *Joseph Chamberlain: A Political Study*. Oxford: Clarendon Press, 1981.

Chartism

Chartism, a mass movement for radical political reform in Britain from 1838 to 1858, contained strong temperance currents. Chartism took its name from the People's Charter, a document issued in May 1838 calling for universal male suffrage and other sweeping changes to parliamentary elections. A movement rather than an organization, the principal cohesive force for Chartism was the weekly paper the *Northern Star* (selling over 42,000 copies at its height in 1839) and its proprietor, Feargus O'Connor. He was a man of prodigious energies and oratorical gifts whose single-mindedness and egotism gained him enemies both inside and outside Chartism. At its peak in 1842, Chartism marshaled the signatures of more than 3.3 million workers in a petition to Parliament demanding the charter. Many of these workers already inhabited a culture of self-improvement and religious nonconformity, in which temperance was often an important constituent. In the early stages of the movement's history, and in the absence of any central organizing force, local Chartist organizations often emerged from or in tandem with temperance ones. On the other hand, the considerable hostility that Chartists encountered from the political establishment at the local level often impelled them to meet in public houses. Premises licensed for the sale of alcohol were often the only meeting places available to workers denied the use of town halls and market squares. Moreover, pubs had long been the traditional resort of both workers and their trade unions. Rent paid for pub meetings was usually "wet," taking the form of buying drinks. In any case, the poor condition of water in rapidly expanding urban centers frequently meant it was more prudent to drink alcohol than water. If the connections between Chartism and temperance were to be anything other than incidental and local, then a concerted effort would be needed to reform the nature of the whole movement and the culture of those who actively supported it.

The case for such a reform seemed strengthened by the setbacks endured by the movement in 1839, when Parliament peremptorily rejected Chartism's first monster petition, and a month-long general strike, planned in protest, dwindled to a few days of demonstrations. The suppression of an uprising by some Welsh Chartists in November that year reinforced a mood of critical self-examination among many in the movement. This was particularly so in the case of Henry Vincent, one of the prime movers of the original People's Charter. Vincent issued a personal temperance manifesto in December 1840. This in turn formed the basis of an "Address to the Working Men of England, Scotland, and Wales," signed by 135 key Chartist activists and published in the recently founded *English Chartist Circular and Temperance Record* in March 1841. "Believing that the ignorance and vices of the people are the chief impediments in the way of all political and social improvement," the signatories argued that alcohol was an enemy within the Chartist movement that debased the character and health of its supporters while depriving families of much needed income and boosting the revenues of the corrupt political system they were supposedly dedicated to overthrowing. It called for all Chartist leaders to take the teetotal pledge and for rank and file Chartists to give abstinence a fair trial. It also called for the formation of Chartist teetotal societies in every city, town, and village.

Feargus O'Connor was not among the signatories, though the editor of the *Northern Star* was, and both the paper and its proprietor were supportive of the temperance cause. O'Connor was highly suspicious of any disposition within the movement that might divide its supporters. Educational, religious, and teetotal tendencies were very prominent in 1841 and were lumped together by a doubtful O'Connor and his supporters under the heading of "the new move." O'Connor's central concern was to keep the movement unified around the basic demands of the People's Charter, to further which a National Charter Association had recently been formed. The new move drew from O'Connor biting sarcasm. Furthermore, teetotal Chartism undermined the essential principle of suffrage as a universal right, because it could be seen as conceding that excessive alcohol consumption rendered many among the working class unfit to exercise the vote. O'Connor did not quarrel with the principles of self-improvement embodied in the temperance movement. Indeed, in the very week of his most vituperative attack on teetotal Chartism, his newspaper announced the forthcoming gift to subscribers of "a splendid full-length portrait" of the great Irish temperance advocate Father Mathew, administering the pledge (*Northern Star* 3 April 1841).

O'Connor's personal authority within the movement was sufficient to nullify all moves for a distinct teetotal Chartist organization. Henry Vincent drifted to the periphery of the movement and into a career as an independent lecturer, one of the most notable in Victorian England. Yet, despite Chartism's frequent overlap at a local level with pub culture, a strong temperance strand persisted within Chartism, especially in Scotland. The *English Chartist Circular and Temperance Record* continued to publish until 1844, with O'Connor among its contributors. The *Northern Star* gave generous support to Father Mathew and attacked drunkenness among Chartist speakers. When he initiated the Chartist Land Plan, a "back to the land" scheme that held the movement together during its doldrums years of the mid-1840s, O'Connor forbade the sale of alcohol on the scheme's estates, claiming "if I was monarch for twenty-four hours, I'd level every gin palace with the dust" (*Northern Star* 10 October 1846). After the presentation of a further, and again rejected, petition in 1848, Chartism entered a protracted final phase of decline. O'Connor's sometime lieutenant, Ernest Jones, gave space to temperance in his Chartist weekly, the *People's Paper.* In 1855, Jones even indicated a readiness to campaign for prohibition, arguing "democracy must often be despotic, in order to save Liberty" (Harrison 1973).

Malcolm Chase

See also: Pubs and Beerhouses (United Kingdom)

References

English Chartist Circular and Temperance Record. 1, no. 9 (March 1841): 35.

Harrison, Brian. *Drink and the Victorians: The Temperance Question in England, 1815–1872.* 2d ed. Keele: Keele University Press, 1994.

———. "Teetotal Chartism" in *History.* 58 (June 1973): 193–217.

Northern Star. 3 April 1841; 10 October 1846.

Thompson, Dorothy. *The Chartists: Popular Politics in the Industrial Revolution.* New York: Pantheon, 1984.

Cherrington, Ernest Hurst (1877–1950)

Ernest Hurst Cherrington (1877–1950), temperance reformer and Methodist layman, was the youngest of the Ohio leaders who dominated the Anti-Saloon League of America (ASLA). As manager of the national league's huge publishing plant in Westerville, just north of Columbus, he produced in vast quantities the temperance propaganda so important to the success of the prohibition movement. Sometimes overshadowed publicly by more flamboyant colleagues, Cherrington was a resourceful organizer, an effective administrator, and a powerful influence within the league's inner circle. Under his leadership, the league in 1919 established an international arm, the World League Against Alcoholism (WLAA), which promoted U.S. Prohibition as a model for the world. The World League's European headquarters was in London, England, but its work was directed by Cherrington from Westerville.

Cherrington was born in Hamden, Ohio, the son of a Methodist clergyman. After attending the preparatory department of Ohio Wesleyan University, he taught school and edited a small-town newspaper. On 17 March 1903, he married Betty Clifford Denny of Greenville, Illinois. They had two children. In 1902, Cherrington became a district superintendent of the Ohio Anti-Saloon League, and he quickly rose to prominence within the state and national organizations. From 1905 to 1908, he served with striking success as superintendent of the Washington State league. When the national league moved its headquarters to Westerville in 1909, Cherrington returned to Ohio as general manager of the American Issue Publishing Company and editor of the league's national newspaper, the *American Issue.* Secretary of the league's national executive committee, he also directed its fund-raising, managed its finances, and organized its speakers' bureau. In addition, he was the league's statistician and historian, writing three books and numerous pamphlets and articles, compiling the *Anti-Saloon League Yearbook* (1908–1932), and editing a six-volume reference work, the *Standard Encyclopedia of the Alcohol Problem* (1924–1930).

The Anti-Saloon League's rapid success took its leaders by surprise, and they were unable to agree on an effective policy once National Prohibition became a reality in 1920. Underneath its formidable public image, the organization was rent by dissension and factional dispute, and it was increasingly unable to raise adequate funds. Unlike his chief rival, Wayne Bidwell Wheeler, the league's powerful attorney in Washington, Cherrington believed that the ultimate success of Prohibition depended not upon political coercion and law enforcement but on education. After Wheeler's sudden death in 1927, the league adopted Cherrington's strategy, but it was too late. Prohibition had been undermined by changes in American social and cultural values, and the Great Depression dealt it a fatal blow.

Cherrington was a prominent northern Methodist layman, and after the repeal of Prohibition, he moved to Washington in 1936 to become executive secretary of the board of temperance of the Methodist Episcopal Church and editor of its organ, the *Voice.* Upon retirement in 1948, he returned to Westerville and died of cancer in nearby Worthington two years later. He was buried in Otterbein Cemetery, Westerville.

Robert A. Hohner

See also: Anti-Saloon League of America (ASLA); *Standard Encyclopedia of the Alcohol Problem;* Wheeler, Wayne Bidwell; World League Against Alcoholism (WLAA)

References

"Cherrington, Ernest Hurst," in *Standard Encyclopedia of the Alcohol Problem,* vol. 2, edited by Ernest H. Cherrington et al., 565–566. Westerville, OH: American Issue Publishing, 1924.

Clark, Norman H. *The Dry Years: Prohibition and Social Change in Washington.* Seattle: University of Washington Press, 1965.

Hohner, Robert A. *Prohibition and Politics: The Life of Bishop James Cannon, Jr.* Columbia: University of South Carolina Press, 1999.

Kerr, K. Austin. *Organized for Prohibition: A New History of the Anti-Saloon League.* New Haven, CT: Yale University Press, 1985.

China

Alcohol has occupied an important place in Chinese culture throughout history (Xiao 1995). Since ancient times, wine and spirits were a medium of ceremonies, ranging from religious rituals practiced by the emperors to festive social gatherings of the people. The popularity of alcohol in everyday life was also facilitated by its link to medicinal effects. Alcohol was presented in the oldest traditional Chinese medicinal text as one of the most powerful medicines. Some medicinal alcoholic beverages could heal specific illnesses; others could provide tonic care and strengthen the body. Although alcohol was used in rituals, celebrations, social occasions, and artistic creativity, it was also consumed in association with hardship and miserable times.

Alcohol Consumption

If alcohol is an important part of Chinese culture, it is interesting to note that relatively low levels of alcohol consumption have consistently been found in China and other Chinese-speaking societies. In 1996, for example, China's per capita alcohol consumption (per adult fifteen years of age and over) was estimated as 5.4 liters (1.4 U.S. gallons), whereas those of many Western countries were much higher (e.g., 13.7 liters [3.6 U.S. gallons] for France, 11.7 liters [3.1 U.S. gallons] for Germany, 9.6 liters [2.5 U.S. gallons] for Italy, 9.5 liters [2.5 U.S. gallons] for Australia, 8.9 liters [2.3 U.S. gallons] for the United States, and 7.5 liters [2.0 U.S. gallons] for Canada) (WHO 1999). Among Asian countries, China's per capita alcohol consumption was lower than those of Thailand (8.6 liters [2.3 U.S. gallons]), Japan (7.8 liters [2.1 U.S. gallons]), and the Philippines (6.8 liters [1.8 U.S. gallons]), but higher than those of Singapore (2.1 liters [0.55 U.S. gallon]), Vietnam (1.2 liters [0.3 U.S. gallon]), India (1.0 liter [0.3 U.S. gallon]), Malaysia (0.9 liter [0.2 U.S. gallon]), Cambodia (0.3 liter [0.1 U.S. gallon]), and Indonesia (0.1 liter [0.03 U.S. gallon]).

Results of epidemiological studies have also revealed low prevalence rates of alcohol use among the Chinese. For example, a 1993–1994 survey of 23,513 residents fifteen to sixty-five years of age selected from six sites in five provinces of China showed that the proportion of "current drinkers" (one who reported alcohol use in the twelve months prior to the interview) in the total sample was 56.3 percent (Hao et al. 1999). A smaller study, conducted in 1993 in Hong Kong (under British rule for a century before reverting to China in 1997), reported that 49.9 percent of the 359 respondents in the sample were current drinkers (Cheung 1995). When compared with Western countries, the proportion of current drinkers in China was substantially smaller. Even for Canada, which has one of the lowest per capita consumption levels among "wet" countries, the percentage of current drinkers reported in 1993 was 74.4 percent (Single et al. 1995), roughly 30 to 50 percent larger than that of China.

Multicultural societies such as the United States and Canada offer good opportunities for testing the thesis of a low level of alcohol use in people of Chinese origin. With few exceptions, findings of self-report surveys that compared drinking patterns of Chinese immigrants or second-generation Chinese in North America with Caucasians and other non-Chinese ethnic groups have consistently found that the Chinese exhibited lower levels of alcohol use than other ethnic groups (Bennett and Ames 1985; Cheung 1993b).

Chinese drinkers tend to drink lightly to moderately, and a majority of them drink once or less a week. As in many countries, males, young adults, people with higher education and income, and unmarried people are more likely to be current drinkers according to the Institute for Marketing Information (IMI) (Hao et al. 1999; Cheung 1995; IMI 2002). A majority of alcohol use takes place during social occasions such as banquets, parties, or dinners (IMI 2002; Cheung 1995). The most common reasons for drinking are associated with the ability of alcohol to increase sociability, improve friendship, make celebration activities more enjoyable, and relieve stress and fatigue (Hao et al. 2001; Cheung 1995).

Findings regarding the most popular type of alcoholic beverage in China have not been consistent. The above-mentioned 1993–1994 six-site survey reported that 55.5 percent of the current drinkers in the total sample consumed spirits and only 29.3 percent drank beer (Hao et al. 1999). However, an annual consumer behavior and lifestyles survey of residents of twenty-one cities indicated that in 2002, beer was the most popular alcohol beverage (consumed by about half of the drinkers), followed by hard liquor (consumed by about one-third of the drinkers) and wine (consumed by about one-quarter of the drinkers) (IMI 2002). In Hong Kong, beer was consumed by most of the current drinkers (94.4 percent) in 1993. About half of the current drinkers consumed spirits, and about one-third drank wine (Cheung 1995).

Two major theories have been proposed to explain the relatively low level of alcohol use among the Chinese, namely, a physiological explanation and a cultural explanation (for a review, see Cheung 1993a). According to the physiological perspective, the Chinese, and some other Asian groups as well, tend to develop more quickly unpleasant physical experiences, such as flushing of the face and a faster heart rate, than non-Asian groups when they drink. This physiological reaction to alcohol is the result of the Chinese liver system not producing enough enzymes to break down the acetaldehyde produced in alcohol metabolism. The flushing response thus protects the Chinese from drinking as frequently and as heavily as non-Asian groups.

Results of numerous clinical studies have indeed confirmed the greater flushing tendencies of the Chinese, but the negative relationship between flushing and drinking has been assumed rather than empirically demonstrated. Also, this perspective cannot explain why Native Americans in North America, who flush even faster than the Chinese, have exhibited higher levels of alcohol use and misuse than the Chinese; nor can it explain the variations in the level of alcohol use between Chinese immigrants in North America and North American–born Chinese, who have the same physiological structure.

The cultural perspective focuses on how traditional Chinese values protect the Chinese from excessive drinking. Chinese cultural values, shaped by Confucian and Taoist ideologies, stress the importance of conformity, moderation, and harmony with the environment, thereby discouraging drinking to the point of drunkenness, especially in the presence of others. Moreover, as they believe that "drinking with an empty stomach" invites faster flushing and other physical discomfort, the Chinese tend to drink with food to slow down the rate of alcohol absorption and metabolism. Drinking at mealtimes also serves to restrict the frequency of drinking.

There is no shortage of findings of studies conducted in North America that support the cultural explanation. However, one of the major drawbacks of these studies is the lack of precise measurements of traditional Chinese cultural values. The degree of assimilation to mainstream North American society and whether or not study subjects were born in North America were inaccurately treated as indicators of possession of Chinese cultural values. Sometimes the very ethnic status of Chinese was equated with possession of Chinese cultural values in studies that compared North American–born Chinese with other ethnic groups in North America.

Alcohol-Related Problems

Since the level of alcohol consumption among the Chinese is low, it is no surprise that the levels of alcohol dependence and abuse among them are also low, compared with people in Western countries. But as in many other countries, men drink much more heavily than women in China and therefore suffer many more alcohol disorders than women. An earlier study of 3,108 residents of Shanghai in 1983 reported that the lifetime prevalence rate of alcohol abuse/dependence, measured with DSM-III (*Diagnostic and Statistical Manual of Mental Disorders,* third edition, published by the American Psychiatric Association), was as low as 0.45 percent (Wang et al. 1992). A 1993 study of psychoactive substance use of 14,000 residents in three provinces found that the prevalence of alcohol dependence/abuse, measured with DSM-III-R (revised third edition of the manual) for males ranged from 1.55 percent to 10.81 percent, whereas that for females ranged from 0.10 percent to 0.30 percent (Hao et al. 1995). The above-mentioned 1993–1994 six-site survey reported that the prevalence rate of alcohol dependence and abuse was 8.84 percent for males, 0.12 percent for females, and 4.56 percent for the total sample. In Hong Kong, a 1985–1986 mental-health survey of 7,229 residents in a district reported that the lifetime prevalence of alcohol abuse/dependence (DSM-III) was 8.6 percent for males and 0.62 percent for females (Chen et al. 1993).

The literature demonstrates that the prevalence rates of alcohol dependence and abuse are considerably lower than those of the United States. For example, the 1992 National Longitudinal Alcohol Epidemiological Survey reported a lifetime prevalence rate of 11.00 percent of alcohol abuse and dependence, measured with DSM-IV (fourth edition of the manual) in the male subsample, 4.08 percent in the female subsample, and 7.41 percent for the total sample (Grant et al. 1992).

Besides alcohol dependence/abuse and other alcohol-related disorders, heavy drinkers are also at risk of other individual and social consequences. In the absence of readily available self-report data on these kinds of alcohol-related problems facing Chinese drinkers, a comparison of findings of the 1993 Hong Kong study (Cheung 1995) and the 1989 National Alcohol and Other Drugs Survey of Canada (Health and Welfare Canada 1990) suggested that although Hong Kong drinkers do not drink as frequently and as heavily as Canadian drinkers, they somehow exhibit similar levels and types of alcohol-related problems. In the Hong Kong sample of current drinkers, 14 percent had suffered alcohol's harmful effect on physical health, compared with 12 percent of the Canadian drinkers. Other alcohol-related problems commonly faced by heavy drinkers of Hong Kong and Canada included financial difficulties, problems with career or studies, and deteriorating family and other social relationships (Cheung 1995).

Alcoholic Beverage Production in China

Although individually the Chinese do not drink as heavily as people in Western countries, the sheer size of China's population (1,290 million in 2000) guarantees an enormous demand for alcoholic beverages. Beer, liquor, and wine are the main types of

A woman hand-paints wine containers in a factory in Shaoxing, China (Alain Le Garsmeur/Corbis)

alcohol beverage industries in China. Although beer has the shortest history among the three industries, it has experienced the fastest development rate of all, which took place in the 1980s and early 1990s, before maintaining a steady growth thereafter. The output of beer has increased from 0.4 million ton in the early 1980s to 20 million tons in 2002. The liquor industry has the longest tradition in alcohol industries in China. It reached its peak of development in the 1990s, and its output in 2001 was 4.2 million tons. The wine industry has also developed at an accelerated rate in the mid-1990s, producing 0.23 million tons in 1998 (IMI 2000).

A distinguished feature of the alcoholic beverage market in China is the dominance of local industries in the market (IMI 2002). The beer market is segmented regionally, with almost each central city having its own popular local brand, such as Yanjing Beer in Beijing, Tsingtao Beer in Qindao, and Zhujiang Beer in Guangzhou. Yanjing and Tsingtao are among the several brands that also enjoy a national fame and a national market. The mixture of regional and national markets is also found in the liquor industry, and national giant corporations such as Wuliangye and Maotai have successfully established themselves as leading liquor vendors. Unlike beer and liquor, wine is a more centralized market, and the four major players are Changyu, Great Wall, Dynasty, and Tonghua.

Since the beginning of the economic reform in 1980, a number of foreign brands of alcoholic beverage have found their way into the Chinese market, and the joint venture has become an innovative modality of the industry. For example, Budweiser, Heineken, and Kirin are now able to capture a significant share of the high-grade beer market. Dynasty Winery, a Sino-French joint venture with over twenty years of history, has long enjoyed a prestigious niche in the China market. As China has now entered the World Trade Organization, future competition from foreign brands of alcoholic beverage is expected to be more severe, and joint ventures between national giants and renowned foreign enterprises will become stronger players in the market than before (IMI 2002).

Trends in Alcohol Consumption and Alcohol-Related Problems

The *Global Status Report on Alcohol* published by the World Health Organization (WHO) in 1999 documented the global trend that alcohol consumption is declining in most of the developed countries but rising in many of the developing countries, including China. China's per capita consumption of alcohol (adults fifteen years of age and over) was only 1.03 liters (0.3 U.S. gallon) in the period 1970 to 1972, but increased by 400 percent to 5.17 liters (1.4 U.S. gallons) in the period 1994 to 1996. The prevalence of alcohol-related disorders has also increased sharply in national or regional sample surveys, from 0.018 percent in 1982 to 2.363 percent (using the ICD-9 or ICD-10 [*International Classification of Diseases,* published by WHO, ninth edition, 1978; tenth edition, 1990]) in 1990, and to 6.504 percent (using the DSM-III-R) in 1993 (WHO 1999). A survey of seventeen psychiatric hospitals showed that the proportion of consecutively admitted patients with an alcohol-related disorder rose from 0.53 percent in 1980 to 2.26 percent in 1993 (Hao 1994).

In contrast, Canada and the United States had a decrease of 16.81 percent and 9.48 percent, respectively, in per capita alcohol consumption from the period 1970 to 1972 to the period 1994 to 1996 (WHO 1999). Findings of national surveys on health and related issues in Canada revealed that there has been a general decline in the percentages of current drinkers and heavy drinkers and in the rates of alcoholism and alcohol-related problems among Canadians since the 1980s (Cheung and Erickson 1995; Single et al. 1995).

A variety of factors may have contributed to the trend of rising levels of alcohol use and abuse in China in the past two decades, but since the trend coincides with the period of economic reform in China since 1980, economic development is likely to be the most salient factor (Hao et al. 2001). The implementation of the market economy and the opening up of the country for foreign investment and joint ventures have brought about remarkable economic success. When the purchasing power of the people increases, the demand for alcoholic beverages also grows. The upsurge in demand has stimulated alcoholic beverage production by leaps and bounds in the past two decades.

Economic growth has also ushered in a period of westernization and modernization since the 1980s. Although alcohol consumption in the general population has been increasing, special sectors of the population, such as young people and women, are catching up quickly with their counterparts in the West in alcohol consumption. China may be heading in the direction of convergence with Western countries in patterns of drinking and alcohol-related problems.

Alcohol Policy

Against the backdrop of increasing alcohol consumption and growing seriousness of the alcohol problem in society, the present alcohol policy in China does not seem to be able to face the challenge (Hao et al. 1999). Currently, there are no legislative controls directed at the licensing of outlets and their opening hours. There is no definition of a minimum legal drinking age. There is little legislative regulation of promotion of alcoholic beverages in the media. Taxation is imposed on the production, distribution, and sale of alcohol for the purpose of generating revenue rather than reducing alcohol consumption.

The improvement of China's alcohol policy will involve not only the implementation of stricter control measures to rectify existing weaknesses. It would also benefit from the adoption of a public-health framework that estimates the social and economic costs of alcohol abuse in society, emphasizes the need for preventive and education efforts, and provides facilities, ranging from detoxification to aftercare and self-help groups, for the treatment of alcoholism.

Yuet W. Cheung

See also: Buddhism; Confucianism; Daoism

References

Bennett, Linda A., and Genevieve M. Ames, eds. *The American Experience with Alcohol: Contrasting Cultural Perspectives.* New York: Plenum, 1985.

Chen, C. N., J. Wong, N. Lee, M. Chan-Ho, J. T. F. Lau, and M. Fung. "The Shatin Community Mental Health Survey in Hong Kong. II. Major Findings" in *Archives of General Psychiatry.* 50 (1993): 125–133.

Cheung, Y. Wah. "Alcohol Use: A General Profile" in *Indicators of Social Development: Hong Kong 1993,* edited by S. K. Lau, M. K. Lee, P. S. Wan, and S. L. Wong, 114–144. Hong Kong: Hong Kong Institute of Asia-Pacific Studies, Chinese University of Hong Kong, 1995.

———. "Beyond Liver and Culture: A Review of Theories and Research in Drinking among Chinese in North America" in *International Journal of the Addictions.* 28, no. 14 (1993a): 1497–1513.

———. "Ethnic Identification and Alcohol Use among Canadian-Born and Foreign-Born High School Students in Toronto" in *International Journal of the Addictions.* 28, no. 11 (1993b): 1095–1109.

Cheung, Y. Wah, and P. G. Erickson. "Canada" in *International Handbook on Alcohol and Culture,* edited by Dwight B. Heath, 20–30. Westport, CT: Greenwood, 1995.

Grant, B., T. C. Harford, D. A. Dawson, P. Chou, M. Dufour, and R. Pickering. "Prevalence of DSM-IV Alcohol Abuse and Dependence: United States 1992" in *Alcohol Health & Research World.* 18, no. 3 (1992): 243–248.

Hao, W. "Women and Substance Use in China" in *Women and Substance Abuse: 1993 Country Assessment Report.* Geneva: World Health Organization, 1994. 197–203.

Hao, W., D. Young, L. Li, S. Xiao, J. Tu, H. Shen, Z. Yu, X. Teng, and X. Wan. "Psychoactive Substance Use in Three Sites in China: Gender Differences and Related Factors" in *Addiction.* 90 (1995): 1503–1515.

Hao, W., D. Young, S. Xiao, and L. Li. "China" in *Surveys of Drinking Patterns and Problems in Seven Developing Countries,* edited by A. Demers, R. Room, and C. Bourgault, 115–129. Geneva: World Health Organization, 2001.

Hao, W., D. Young, S. Xiao, L. Li, and Y. Zhang. "Alcohol Consumption and Alcohol-Related Problems: Chinese Experience from Six Area Samples, 1994" in *Addiction.* 94, no. 10 (1999): 1467–1476.

Health and Welfare Canada. *National Alcohol and Other Drugs Survey: Highlights Report.* Ottawa: Ministry of Supply and Services of Canada, 1990.

Institute for Marketing Information. *2000 IMI Consumer Behaviour and Life Patterns Yearbook.* Beijing: Beijing Broadcasting Institute, 2000.

———. *2002–2003 IMI Consumer Behaviours and Life Styles Yearbook.* Beijing: Beijing Broadcasting Institute, 2002.

Single, E., J. M. Brewster, P. MacNeil, J. Hatcher, and C. Trainor. "Alcohol and Drug Use: Results from the 1993 General Social Survey" in *Report Prepared for the Studies Unit, Health Promotion Directorate, Health Canada.* Ottawa: Canadian Centre on Substance Abuse, 1995.

Wang, C. H., W. T. Liu, M. Y. Zhang, E. S. H. Yu, Z. Y. Xia, M. Fernandez, C. T. Lung, C. L. Xu, and G. Y. Qu. "Alcohol Use, Abuse, and Dependency in Shanghai" in *Alcoholism in North America, Europe, and Asia,* edited by John E. Helzer and Glorisa J. Canino, 264–286. New York: Oxford University Press, 1992.

World Health Organization. *Global Status Report on Alcohol.* Geneva: World Health Organization, 1999.

———. *International Classification of Diseases.* 9th ed. (1978); 10th ed. (1990). Geneva: World Health Organization.

Xiao, Jiacheng. "China" in *International Handbook on Alcohol and Culture,* edited by D. B. Heath, 42–50. Westport, CT: Greenwood, 1995.

Chiniquy, Father Charles Paschal Telesphore (1809–1899)

Father Charles Paschal Telesphore Chiniquy (1809–1899) was a charismatic Catholic temperance preacher active in French Canada in the 1840s. Known as the "Father Mathew of Canada," Father Chiniquy led a mass pledge campaign modeled on the work of the illustrious Irish preacher. With the assistance of other priests, the Chiniquy-led crusade of 1848 to 1851 elicited temperance pledges from 400,000 French Canadians, well over half the population of Canada East (Quebec). Chiniquy presented temperance as a patriotic crusade, a way his people could become more educated, industrious, and progressive, so that their culture could survive surging immigration from the British Isles. A controversial figure, Chiniquy was eventually banned from the Montreal diocese for sexual misdemeanors; converting to Presbyterianism, he became a virulent polemicist against Catholicism. He remained a figure of legend in French Canada. His enduring contributions there were to discredit excess drinking and to establish the tradition of clergy leading the response to pressing social problems in Quebec.

Ordained at Quebec City in 1829, Charles Chiniquy served several nearby parishes. As chaplain of the Marine and Emigrant Hospital, he came under the influence of temperance advocate Dr. James Douglas. Further encouraged by Father Theobald Mathew's crusade in Ireland, Chiniquy and several other priests began preaching temperance in the parishes around Quebec. Chiniquy enjoyed a great public triumph when 10,000 people gathered for a ceremony in 1841 to bless a column marking the new temperance convictions of his Beauport parish. Blessing the column was Charles Forbin-Janson, a revivalist from France invited by the Church to tour parishes of Canada East castigating drunkenness and other sins. The Canadian hierarchy now clearly endorsed a cause generally associated with Protestants. Chiniquy's 1844 *Manuel ou règlement de la Société de tempérance,* a compendium of temperance tales and testimonials, established him as the movement's spokesman.

At the invitation of the Bishop of Montreal, Chiniquy began his great campaign in 1848 through 1851. The Irish famine brought diseased and desperate immigrants to Canada, as well as new competition for scarce lands and jobs. Criticism of traditional farming techniques and the departure of youths to the United States made the French Canadian way of life seem moribund. A number of prominent jurists, journalists, and radical nationalists began to embrace Father Chiniquy's message. Sobriety, he promised, would alleviate all these problems, energizing French Canadians for the struggle to survive on a progressive, anglophone continent.

Alive to this message, thousands turned out during the dynamic preacher's four-year tour, which began in the Montreal diocese in early 1848. Parish after parish pledged never to drink again. They poured liquor into bonfires, closed taverns, and called for an end to licensing. By the end of 1850, Chiniquy and other priests had enrolled 400,000 pledge takers, nearly half the population of Canada East and a clear majority of its francophones. With most distilleries closed, a society known for its high spirits now seemed a bone-dry fortress. Particularly in rural areas, sobriety prevailed even after Chiniquy's sudden departure. Several attempts to seduce women led to the hero's expulsion from Montreal diocese, relocation to Illinois, excommunication, and subsequent international career as an anti-Catholic polemicist. A dynamic orator addressing the social problems of his day, Chiniquy was the first priest to become a Quebec hero, setting a pattern for priestly champions of colonization and national rights in decades to come.

Jan Noel

See also: Alcohol, Consumption of, per Capita (Canada); Mathew, Father Theobald

References

Chiniquy, Charles Paschal Telesphore. *Manuel ou règlements de la société de tempérance dédié à la jeunesse canadienne.* Quebec: S. Drapeau, 1844.

Noel, Jan. "Dry Patriotism: The Chiniquy Crusade" in *Canadian Historical Review.* 71, no. 2 (1995): 189–207.

Roby, Yves. "Chiniquy, Charles" in *Dictionary of Canadian Biography,* vol. 12. Toronto: University of Toronto Press, 1990. 189–193.

Christian Socialism

Christian Socialist involvement in the British temperance movement began in the early 1850s when Anglicans of various stripes—broad-church, Anglo-Catholic, and especially Evangelicals—expressed their growing social concern by embracing antidrink movements. Contrary to Evangelical teetotalers' stress on individualism, Christian Socialists emphasized collectivism in temperance reform. Seldom abstainers at first, they preferred legislative reform of the drink trade to teetotalism or prohibition. Seeking solid theological and pastoral foundations for their social reformism, Christian Socialists responded to the problems of industrial England with a communal emphasis building on broad-church and Anglo-Catholic traditions.

Early Initiatives

Modern Christian Socialism began in 1848. Motivated by Chartist demonstrations at Kennington Common, John Malcolm Forbes Ludlow (1821–1911) and Charles Kingsley (1819–1875) joined Frederick Denison Maurice (1805–1872) in launching the movement with a penny journal, *Politics for the People* (1848). Subsequent meetings attracted others, including Thomas Hughes (1822–1896), best known for his prescriptive novel *Tom Brown's School Days* (1857), and the wealthy Edward Vansittart Neale (1810–1892), who helped finance the movement. Christian Socialism's social conscience inspired the first issues of *Tracts on Christian Socialism* and *The Christian Socialist,* with Ludlow as coeditor of the first and editor of the second; Kingsley's sketches of village life in his novels *Yeast: A Problem* (1848) and *Alton Locke* (1850); and Maurice's first Working Men's Association.

Before the establishment of the Church of England Temperance Society (CETS) in 1873, both broad-church and Anglo-Catholic Christian Socialists were reluctant to embrace teetotalism. Ludlow revealed some respect for teetotalism while moderating a debate in *The Christian Socialist;* Kingsley was not himself an abstainer, but antidrink sentiment can be found in *Alton Locke;* nor was Hughes a teetotaler, but he was one of the few early Christian Socialists to embrace the political temperance movement publicly and to remain involved in it for the duration of his career.

Broad-church members and Anglo-Catholics were most active in the temperance movement in the generation between 1873 and 1914, when the Anglican temperance movement was expanding beyond Evangelicals. Broad-church traditions, particularly the emphasis on "muscular Christianity," gained particular currency in Evangelicalism's declining years, as did increasing efforts by Anglo-Catholics, heirs of the Oxford Movement and Tractarianism, to fuse liberal Catholic theology with advanced social concern. Charles Gore (1853–1932), Henry Scott Holland (1847–1918), Stewart Headlam (1847–1924), and Brooke Foss Westcott (1825–1901) overcame their own reservations about teetotalism and developed theoretical justifications for the cause, inspired by the experiences of Vicar Walter F. Hook (1798–1875) of Leeds and his followers, who were unusual as Anglo-Catholics in their early support of teetotalism. The Hegelian idealist T. H. Green (1836–1882), late Victorian Oxford's most influential philosopher, encouraged Christian Socialists to trust the state to remove impediments, such as intemperance, to individual moral reform.

Christian Socialist Theology and Activism

Anglo-Catholics and other Christian Socialists differed from Evangelicals in their approach to the drink issue and social improvement. Evangelicalism's theological and reformist individualism competed with Christian Socialism's corporate Christianity. To participate in social reformist initiatives such as the temperance movement, Anglo-Catholics and the Christian Socialists reconciled their incarnational theology—Christ's sanctification of earth by his birth as man—with more practical manifestations of their developing social concern. Led by Charles Gore, the most formative theologian of his time, the *Lux Mundi* (1889) school performed a major task in defining Christian Socialism and advancing appreciation of the temperance movement.

Gore, Scott Holland, Headlam, and Westcott developed a strong theological and practical basis for their Christian Socialism and a model for their later participation in the temperance movement. From 1877 to 1893, Headlam's Guild of Saint Matthew (GSM) represented the balanced Anglo-Catholic theology and social principles that marked Anglican Socialism until the first world war. The GSM gave way in the end to the Christian Social Union (CSU). Stimulated by both the GSM and *Lux Mundi* school, Gore and Scott Holland formed the CSU in 1889, to be joined later by Westcott.

The CSU collected information on drink and temperance, and hosted discussions and meetings. Mission houses such as Westcott's South-London Cambridge Settlement and E. S. Talbot's East-London Oxford House brought Anglo-Catholic temperance and social improvement to working-class centers, which in turn helped convert young priests to teetotalism.

Anglo-Catholic/Christian Socialists remained unconvinced, nonetheless, that temperance reform was more important than other basic improvements such as rational amusements, education, and housing. Christian Socialists were receptive to state intervention. Gore, with other Anglicans, supported the unsuccessful 1908 Liberal licensing bill. Christian Socialist participation in the temperance cause helped transform the late Victorian/Edwardian conflict between pub and parish into a national movement.

Anglo-Catholics and Evangelicals continued to disagree and to cooperate in the twentieth century, although the Anglo-Catholic temperance worldview had largely succeeded that of the Evangelicals. Anglo-Catholics and Christian Socialists helped steer the temperance movement away from an individualist stress on temperance as the cure for the evils of industrial society toward more collectivist answers to the problems of the exploited.

Matthew K. McKean and Gerald Wayne Olsen

See also: Church of England Temperance Society (CETS); Church of England Temperance Society (CETS) Inebriate Homes; Church of England Temperance Society (CETS) Police Court Mission; Davidson, Randall; Ellison, Henry; Evangelical Temperance (United Kindgom); Gore, Charles; Green, T. H.; Temple, Frederick; Wilberforce, Basil and Wilberforce, Ernest

References

Nicholson, Peter P. *The Political Philosophy of the British Idealists.* Cambridge: Cambridge University Press, 1990.

Norman, Edward. *Victorian Christian Socialists.* Cambridge: Cambridge University Press, 1987.

Olsen, Gerald Wayne. *Drink and the British Establishment—The Church of England Temperance Society, 1873–1914.* Unpublished book manuscript.

———. *Pub and Parish—Drink and Temperance in the Church of England, 1829–1875.* Unpublished book manuscript.

Christopher D. Smithers Foundation

The Christopher D. Smithers Foundation has for fifty years promoted the understanding, prevention, and treatment of alcoholism. The foundation funds alcoholism-related projects, disseminates alcoholism-related information through the print and electronic media, and participates in alcoholism-related public policy forums.

Christopher Duncan Smithers was one of the founders and major stockholders of IBM. His son, R. Brinkley Smithers, was born in 1907 in Glen Cove, New York. The young Smithers was painfully shy during his developmental years, but discovered the liberating effects of alcohol while studying medicine at Johns Hopkins University. When it was evident that Brinkley's love of alcohol far exceeded his devotion to his studies, his father withdrew him from the university. Brinkley then worked as an investment banker through the Wall Street crash of 1929 and went on to work as a salesman at IBM. His business success was accompanied by an escalation in drinking that led to Brinkley's decision to retire at the age of thirty. The retired life proved very conducive to his advancing alcoholism, which continued through his service in World War II. Following his discharge from military service, Brinkley operated a successful auto franchise, but was admitted more than fifty times for discreet detoxification at the Charles B. Towns Hospital in New York City.

In 1952, Brinkley created a philanthropic foundation to honor his father, who had died earlier that year. Originally chartered to support a wide variety of charitable activities, the mission of the Christopher D. Smithers Foundation was changed following R. Brinkley Smithers's recovery from alcoholism in 1954 and his attendance at the Yale School of Alcohol Studies in 1956. Ironically, it was through an employee he had once fired for drinking and who later found sobriety that Brinkley was linked to Yev Gardner and to the beginning of his own recovery from alcoholism. Gardner was a recovered alcoholic who, at the time he met Brinkley, was working as Marty Mann's assistant at the fledgling National Committee for Education on Alcoholism. It was an auspicious meeting for both Brinkley Smithers and the alcoholism field. The new mission of the foundation was to address alcoholism as a public-health problem. Over the next half century, the Smithers Foundation would provide more than $13 million to alcoholism-related projects, with more than double that amount contributed to such projects by members of the Smithers family.

The role of the Smithers family and the Smithers Foundation in the history of alcoholism treatment and recovery in the United States is difficult to measure precisely because of the length and breadth of its scope. This support included enhancing the development of nearly every area of the alcoholism field, from support in building its organizational infrastructure to the fostering of public and professional education, policy advocacy, research, treatment, and prevention.

The Smithers Foundation provided crucial financial support to the National Council on Alcoholism and Drug Dependence (NCADD), both in the operation of the national office and in providing seed grants to nurture the development of more than fifty local NCADD affiliates. It also provided financial support to such key institutions as the Center of Alcohol Studies (in its transition from Yale to Rutgers), the North American Association for Alcoholism Programs, the North Conway Institute, and the American Society of Addiction Medicine.

Smithers actively supported the spread of occupational alcoholism programs within business and industry and provided a $6.7 million gift to Cornell and Rutgers Universities to establish the R. Brinkley Smithers Institute for Alcoholism Prevention and Workplace Problems. The Smithers Foundation also supported the development of many prominent treatment institutions, including Hazelden Foundation and the Chit Chat Foundation. In the early 1970s, Brinkley Smithers provided a personal gift of $10 million to Roosevelt Hospital in New York City to open the Smithers Alcoholism Treatment and Training Center.

In addition to financially supporting journals (such as the *Quarterly Journal of Studies on Alcohol*) and seminal books in the field (such as E. M. Jellinek's *The Disease Concept of Alcoholism*), the Smithers Foundation published and distributed its public information and professional education materials on alcoholism. Particularly significant was its support in getting alcoholism books, pamphlets, and treatment resource guides into the nation's libraries. R. Brinkley Smithers's legacy transcends the financial resources that he infused into the alcoholism field at crucial points in its modern history. From the early days of his recovery from alcoholism, Smithers remained personally involved in leadership roles with NCADD and the larger alcoholism field. In addition to serving as chairman and president of the NCADD board, he founded the Long Island Council on Alcoholism and was cofounder of the Alcoholism Council of New York. He personally involved himself at critical times in the field's history. For example, when the most critical piece of legislation in the history of modern alcoholism treatment in the United States (the 1970 Hughes Act) had passed both houses of Congress, but was not supported by the president, it was Smithers who rallied the political forces that reached President Richard Nixon on 31 December 1970 and persuaded him to sign the act into law only hours before it would have died by pocket veto.

R. Brinkley Smithers died at the age of eighty-six in 1994. He dedicated his life and financial resources to the proposition that alcoholism was a treatable disease. That legacy continues today through the ongoing work of the Christopher D. Smithers Foundation under the leadership of Brinkley's widow, Adele C. Smithers-Fornaci, who at the time of this writing serves as president of the Smithers Foundation and the chair of the board of the NCADD.

William L. White

See also: Employee Assistance Programs (EAPs); Hazelden Foundation; *Journal of Studies on Alcohol;* Mann, Marty; National Council on Alcoholism and Drug Dependence (NCADD); Rutgers Center of Alcohol Studies; Yale Center of Alcohol Studies

References

"History of the Smithers Foundation." http://www.smithersfoundation.org. [January 2002].

Minetree, Harry. "Alcoholism's Sober Philanthropist" in *Town & Country.* (May 1986): 184–243.

Scott, Neil. "R. Brinkley Smithers: 35 Years of Leadership" in *Alcoholism and Addictions Magazine.* (October 1988): 15–17.

Smithers, R. Brinkley. *40th Anniversary Report.* Mill Neck, NY: Christopher D. Smithers Foundation, 1992.

Church of England Temperance Society (CETS)

The Church of England Temperance Society (CETS), founded at Lambeth Palace in 1873, was the most far-reaching, prestigious, and influential temperance society in Victorian and Edwardian Britain, and one of its most extensive voluntary agencies. The CETS grew from the unsuccessful efforts of clergymen in the "Church teetotal society," 1862–1873 (also known as the Church of England Total Abstinence Society and the Church of England and Ireland Temperance Reformation Society), to convert their superiors to teetotalism and, in some instances, to advocate prohibition.

Encouraged by Americans, Nonconformists, and parish working people, teetotal clergymen attacked the pub, traditionally regarded as a complementary community center but now seen as the parish's overly successful rival in attracting early industrial workers. As the parish appeared increasingly irrelevant to factory workers, the pub filled gaps, as a center for camaraderie and solace, benefit societies, employment, banking, and child minding. Clergymen blamed the pub for their parishioners' vice, poverty, and misery, and their social and ideological disorientation. At the time of the first Gladstone government (1868–1874), friendly to non-Anglicans and temperance zealots, leading Church people applauded antidrink movements, but beyond a tiny Evangelical minority, few quit drinking to join the "Church teetotal society."

The 1869 Canterbury Convocation Report on Intemperance encouraged the CETS compromise, a "dual basis"—teetotalism for the mainly working-class majority and reformative work for the "better-class," nonabstaining general section. To create the CETS, Henry Ellison, vicar of Windsor, and John Sandford, Convocation committee chairman, negotiated with the Archbishop of Canterbury, A. C. Tait, aided by Sandford's son, Tait's chaplain. In an era of debate over disestablishment, the establishment (that is, the established church) supported the CETS, partly to show Liberal governments and their non-Anglican supporters the continuing usefulness of the Church of England.

CETS Compromise

Chairman of the Church teetotal society since 1862, the Reverend Henry Ellison led the CETS until his 1891 retirement, bridging gaps between radicals—adamant teetotalers and prohibitionists, advocates of unfermented Communion wine and of complete drink disinvestment—and moderates who sought reform without abolishing drink's traditional roles.

A revolt (led by the slave emancipator's broad-church grandson, Basil Wilberforce) forced Ellison's 1891 resignation as chairman. He was succeeded by Bishop Frederick Temple of London, once a radical teetotaler and prohibitionist, who since had embraced more accommodating CETS principles. Later chairmen included Bishops Ernest Wilberforce of Chichester (Basil's moderate brother) and H. H. Pereira of Croydon (suffragan of Archbishop Randall Davidson of Canterbury).

With their monarchs as patrons, prominent Anglicans propagated CETS influence among the establishment, the previously resistant universities, and rural areas, greatly extending the battle between parish and pub. The Evangelical Earl of Shaftsbury banned drink on his own estates and supported the Missions to Cabmen. The first Duke of Westminster promoted the Native Races' Committee and also the CETS agricultural division's barely successful attempts to diminish rural drinking. Lord (A. W.) Peel chaired the CETS-dominated Royal Commission on Liquor Licensing Laws (1896–1899), the "Peel Commission," which set the licensing reform agenda for the early 1900s. The few early Evangelical teetotalers were joined by Bishop A. W. Thorold of Rochester, who helped introduce Anglican temperance to the United States, and by William Joynson-Hicks, a future cabinet minister, who advanced CETS legislative policy by collaborating with fellow Conservatives William Houldsworth and Ernest Tritton, and with moderate Liberals, especially Sir Stafford Howard, the Duke of Norfolk's cousin and eventually a Liberal Unionist. The broad-churchman F. W. Farrar and the celebrated Anglo-Catholics Charles Gore and Henry Scott Holland also supported Anglican temperance. T. H. Green, the Oxford liberal and idealist philosopher, afforded the CETS the support of

Christian Socialist theories, while Handley Moule, the Evangelical Bishop of Durham, justified it through laissez-faire principles.

CETS Accomplishments

Establishment support helped the CETS propagate temperance in the empire, the United States, and at home. By 1901, more than half the domestic bishops abstained; the CETS included 116,287 adult teetotalers, 35,460 in the "general section" and 442,040 juvenile abstainers. The CETS Women's Union attacked intemperance, especially among working-class women, whose drunkenness the union regarded as especially distressing. Children were approached through juvenile branches and educational programs. The CETS-sponsored "Child Messengers' Act" (1901) barred children under fourteen from fetching beer in unsealed containers.

A new sober industrial ethos was offered urban working people, cabmen, barmaids, soldiers, and sailors through specialized organizations, a benefit society, the *Temperance Chronicle* newspaper, and other publications that filled an eight-page list.

The CETS combination of radicals and moderates effected compromises between extremes (total abstinence when needed, otherwise moderate drinking); reduced, but not discontinued, medical usage of alcohol; retained the use of fermented Communion wine, perhaps watered down for teetotalers; and encouraged more limited and conscientious investment in the drinks industry. Politically, due largely to Lord Peel and Archbishop Davidson, CETS licensing restriction prevailed over United Kingdom Alliance (UKA) prohibitionism. The CETS-influenced 1902 Conservative licensing act helped set in motion a reduction in the numbers of British pubs and their reform. CETS medical programs and inebriate homes increased knowledge of alcoholism. In 1906, the Police Court Mission (1876) became the permanent state probation system.

A more mature industrial society provided improved infrastructure, with improved dining, employment, and banking facilities. Mass consumerism offered soft drinks and counterattractive rational recreation, and working people embraced more mature and disciplined attitudes. In addition to these broad social changes, the CETS moral suasionist and legislative efforts helped reduce drink's influence. Compared to a century before, by 1935, alcohol's role had been diminished by about 300 percent—in number of pubs, drink production and expenditure, drunkenness arrests, and alcohol mortality. These declines began before the first world war, when the CETS already suffered diminishing membership, enrollment, and influence.

The CETS, with other Anglican social agencies, helped prevent disestablishment, but only delayed the decline of the Anglican parish among more self-reliant working people. In 1967, the CETS was reorganized as the Church of England Council for Social Aid (CECSA), which also incorporated the Police Court Mission (PCM).

Gerald Wayne Olsen

See also: Church of England Temperance Society (CETS) Inebriate Homes; Church of England Temperance Society (CETS) Police Court Mission; Close, Francis; Davidson, Randall; Ellison, Henry; Gore, Charles; Green, T. H.; Kerr, Norman Shanks; Maguire, Robert; Moule, Handley Carr Glyn; Temple, Frederick; United Kingdom Alliance (UKA); Wilberforce, Basil and Wilberforce, Ernest

References

Fahey, David. "Temperance and the Liberal Party—Lord Peel's Report, 1899," in *Journal of British Studies.* 10, no. 2 (1971): 132–159.

Harrison, Brian. *Drink and the Victorians: The Temperance Question in England 1815–1872.* 2d ed. Keele: Keele University Press, 1994.

Olsen, G. W. *Drink and the British Establishment: The Church of England Temperance Society, 1873–1914.* Unpublished book manuscript.

———. *Drink and Temperance in the Church of England, 1829–1875.* Unpublished book manuscript.

———. "From Parish to Palace: Working-Class Influences on Anglican Temperance Movements, 1835–1914" in *Journal of Ecclesiastical History.* 40 (1989): 239–252.

———. "Physician Heal Thyself: Drink, Temperance and the Medical Question in the Victorian and Edwardian Church of England, 1830–1914" in *Addiction.* 79 (1964): 1167–1176.

Shiman, Lilian L. "The Church of England Temperance Society in the Nineteenth Century" in *Historical Magazine of the Protestant Episcopal Church.* 41 (1972): 179–195.

———. *Crusade against Drink in Victorian England.* New York: St. Martin's, and London: Macmillan, 1988.

Church of England Temperance Society (CETS) Inebriate Homes

Church of England Temperance Society (CETS) Inebriate Homes for Women developed early methods for treating chronic drunkards. The CETS Women's Union operated these institutions when alcoholism was first being treated as a disease, rather than as a specific form of insanity or immorality, encouraging the expectation that alcoholic women could be cured.

The Women's Union, initiated in 1876 amid an increasing concern with female intemperance, also worked among the general population. Although the Women's Union proclaimed that drunkenness defied class, and the CETS opposed grocers' drink licenses as tempting privileged ladies, most attention was given to more noticeably drunken working-class women. Exceptions permitted limited prescription of alcohol as medicine, and drink was never denied to "the more responsible classes," but the CETS advised teetotalism for reformers, working people, children, and inebriates.

The CETS sponsored numerous institutions for juveniles and the chronically alcoholic, such as work yards and homes for drunkards found by their Police Court Missionaries, and separate CETS Inebriate Homes for men and women, with sections for differing social classes.

THE

CHURCH OF ENGLAND

TEMPERANCE CHRONICLE.

No. 1.—Vol. I. JANUARY 1, 1873. PRICE ONE PENNY.

HIS GRACE THE ARCHBISHOP OF CANTERBURY.

The first issue of the Church of England Temperance Chronicle, *with a portrait of its first copresident, Archbishop A. C. Tait of Canterbury*

By 1907, the CETS Women's Union operated five residences for female alcoholics—Women's Temperance Home (Liverpool), Corngreaves Hall (Birmingham), Hammond Lodge (King's Lynn), Temple Lodge (Torquay), and Ellison Lodge (London). A CETS radical, Lady Henry Somerset, president of the National British Women's Temperance Association (BWTA), superintended another inebriate women's home at Duxhurst, Surrey, informed by the North American experiences of a frequent visitor, Frances Elizabeth Caroline Willard, World's Woman's Christian Temperance Union (WWCTU) president. The CETS also operated Abbotswood House (Gloucester) for alcoholic men. Government certification and supervision under the terms of habitual drunkards acts ensured that the homes operated according to standard.

Patients at the homes included women from all classes and both voluntary patients and, the least successful, those patients whose stays were legally enforced. Beyond a few "drawing-room" patients, most were "kitchen patients" and the even more modest "workroom inmates," who performed domestic duties.

In an era when volunteer activities were gradually becoming professionalized, women, often unmarried, ran CETS homes and practically, more than theoretically, developed curative regimes for alcoholics. Although occasionally new treatments involving drugs were reluctantly tested, CETS homes stressed abstinence, nutrition, industry, and discipline. Religion was much emphasized, sometimes in the nondenominational sense of the current Alcoholics Anonymous. The existential and practical knowledge that grew from the day-by-day treatment of alcoholic women helped dispel myths—especially about female drinkers, often called fallen angels—and allowed for increasingly expert care. In British homes for inebriates generally, 81 percent were female, though 82 percent of those convicted of drunkenness were men. Sounding much like Lady Henry Somerset, a 1902 CETS report would "not in any way confirm the belief that is commonly held that a female inebriate is incapable of cure."

CETS and Inebriate Home Reports are in the Lambeth Palace Library.

Stephanie Olsen and Gerald Wayne Olsen

See also: British Women's Temperance Association (BWTA); Christian Socialism; Church of England Temperance Society (CETS); Church of England Temperance Society (CETS) Police Court Mission; Conservative Party (United Kingdom); Davidson, Randall; Ellison, Henry; Evangelical Temperance (United Kingdom); Gore, Charles; Somerset, Isabella Caroline (Lady Henry Somerset); Temple, Frederick; Wilberforce, Basil and Wilberforce, Ernest; Willard, Frances Elizabeth Caroline; World's Woman's Christian Temperance Union (WWCTU)

References

Hunt, Geoffrey, Jenny Mellor, and Janet Turner. "Wretched, Hatless and Miserable Clad: Women and the Inebriate Reformatories from 1900–1913" in *British Journal of Sociology.* 40, no. 2 (1989): 244–270.

Olsen, G. W. *Drink and the British Establishment—The Church of England Temperance Society, 1873–1914.* Unpublished book manuscript.

Church of England Temperance Society (CETS) Police Court Mission

The Church of England Temperance Society's (CETS) Police Court Mission (PCM) illustrates a smooth transition in Britain from voluntary reform to state social welfare. Financed in part by five shillings from a Hertford journeyman printer, Frederick Rainer, the PCM was established in 1876, initially to rescue drunkards found in London courts. Thirty years later, the PCM provided the first government probation officers.

The House of Lords' Committee on Intemperance (1876–1879), which emphasized connections between drink and crime, as well as female drunkenness, advanced both the PCM and the CETS's Women's Union, also founded in 1876. George Nelson, veteran of both the prestigious Cold Stream Guards and of CETS chairman Henry Ellison's Windsor parish teetotal society, was employed by the PCM as its first missionary. He served until 1885. Beyond visiting drunkards in London police courts, Nelson organized temperance meetings at work sites. The PCM expanded numerically and functionally. The number of CETS Police Court Missionaries grew from 7 in 1881, in metropolitan London and the dioceses of Liverpool and Lichfield, to 153 across Britain in 1913, including 20 women. The mission distributed bibles, CETS journals, and tracts to 415 courts. Women's Union members helped Police Court Missionaries approach drunkards, prostitutes, and other female criminals. Chronic alcoholics were sent to CETS Inebriate Homes. Police Court Missionaries soon broadened their knowledge of intemperance and criminal behavior.

Patronized by the celebrated Evangelical, the earl of Shaftesbury, the Mission to Cabmen was founded in 1880 as a special PCM department. By 1890, the PCM worked regularly among 15,000 cabmen, a group thought to be especially intemperate. Cabmen invested in savings clubs, and several recovered licenses they had lost for drunkenness. CETS Women's Union members ran PCM libraries and sometimes conducted temperance meetings for cabmen in their own mansions.

When the Liberal government initiated a probation system in 1906, administrators agreed to a CETS request and employed the society's Police Court Missionaries as paid state agents, thus providing an instance when progress from voluntary philanthropy to the welfare state was easy and seamless. Annual remuneration by 1939 was £220 to £400 a year for male Police Court Missionaries and £220 to £320 for females.

Aided by the CETS veteran officer and Conservative home secretary (1924–1929) William Joynson-Hicks, Lord Bentford, the PCM continued to operate in the twentieth century. Yet the role of the CETS and other voluntary societies diminished as the welfare state grew. The state continued to employ CETS Police Court Missionaries, but, generally, social work was secularized and made professional, and by World War II, non-CETS probation officers began to assume more responsibilities.

Records of the CETS and PCM are in the Lambeth Palace Library.

Stephanie Olsen and Gerald Wayne Olsen

See also: Christian Socialism; Church of England Temperance Society (CETS); Church of England Temperance Society (CETS) Inebriate Homes; Conservative Party (United Kingdom); Davidson, Randall; Ellison, Henry; Evangelical Temperance (United Kingdom); Gore, Charles; Green, T. H.; Liberal Party (United Kingdom); Moule, Handley Carr Glyn; Temple, Frederick; Wilberforce, Basil and Wilberforce, Ernest

References

Dark, Sidney. *Inasmuch . . . Christianity and the Police Courts.* London: Student Christian Movement Press, 1939.

National Police Court Mission. *Annual Report.* London: The Mission, [1938?]–1966.

Olsen, G. W. *Drink and the British Establishment—The Church of England Temperance Society, 1873–1914.* Unpublished book manuscript.

———. "From Parish to Palace: Working-Class Influences on Anglican Temperance Movements, 1835–1914" in *Journal of Ecclesiastical History.* 40, no. 2 (April 1989): 239–252.

Winston Churchill, prime minister of Great Britain (Library of Congress)

Churchill, Winston (1874–1965)

Sir Winston Churchill (1874–1965), Liberal cabinet minister and Conservative prime minister, was in foreign eyes the archetypal Englishman, but he disliked the archetypal English beverage, tea. Toward the end of Churchill's career a young Conservative member of Parliament (M.P.) asked him in the smoking room of the House of Commons if he would like a cup of tea. According to the historian Robert Rhodes James, the young man was rebuked with a thunderous "Don't be a bloody fool. I want a *large* glass of whisky." Churchill explained in his book, *My Early Life,* that it was in India that he had acquired his taste for whiskey: he had no real choice when he joined the Malakand Field Force in 1897. The heat was unbearable, and the water was undrinkable unless used for tea, with lime juice or with whiskey: "Until this time I had never been able to drink whisky. I disliked the flavour intensely." Churchill also disliked teetotalers, whom he considered extremists (like Hitler, who never drank alcohol). Churchill had another reason for disliking teetotalers. In 1922, he lost his parliamentary seat to Edwin Scrymgeour, the only candidate of a party organized to promote prohibition to have ever been elected to the House of Commons. Churchill took for granted moderate drinking but condemned drunkenness (which he believed had precipitated the Liberal prime minister H. H. Asquith's fall). Churchill never said where he drew the dividing line between drinking and getting drunk, apart perhaps from the celebrated boast, quoted by the historian Michael Richards: "I have taken more out of alcohol than alcohol has taken out of me." The average person who reads about his daily schedule of drinking, with hock at breakfast; port, champagne, and brandy at lunch and dinner; and a continuous absorption of whiskey outside meals (often, admittedly, in the form of a nip of Scotch drowned in water), cannot believe that he was not drunk every night or even by lunchtime. That he was "alcohol-dependent" is in no doubt. According to the historian Robert Rhodes James, in 1948, Churchill said to Lord Boothby, "I find alcohol a great support in life." That he was an "alcohol abuser" by most medical definitions of the word is also in no doubt, but it seems that he had a superhuman capacity for absorbing hard liquor without getting intoxicated. Aides and foreign statesmen have remarked in their war memoirs on how he could conduct the most momentous discussions on complicated strategic decisions in perfect lucidity after imbibing a quantity of drink that would have made most mortals lose their consciousness.

Antoine Capet

See also: Conservative Party (United Kingdom); Liberal Party (United Kingdom); Scrymgeour, Edwin

References

Churchill, Winston. *My Early Life: A Roving Commission.* London: Collins Fontana, 1959 [1930]. 132–133.

James, Robert Rhodes. "Churchill the Parliamentarian, Orator and Statesman" in *Churchill: A Major New Assessment of His Life in*

Peace and War, edited by Robert Blake and William Roger Louis, 504, 516–517, 564. Oxford: Oxford University Press, 1993.

Kersaudy, François. "Churchill et l'alcool: Les coulisses de l'exploit" in *Historia.* 619 (1998): 76–81.

Richards, Michael. "Leading Churchill Myths. (1) 'Alcohol Abuser'" in *Finest Hour: Journal of the Churchill Center and Societies.* 111 (2001): 33.

Rintala, Marvin. "Family Portrait: Churchills at Drink" in *Biography.* 21 (Winter 1998): 1–23.

Cider

Easy and inexpensive to produce, cider once served as the drink of choice in England and North America. Usually a fizzy beverage made from fresh apples, it came in many styles, including draft, bottled, ciderkin, and scrumpy. By the first decades of the twentieth century, the difficulty of obtaining quality cider and the growing temperance movement caused most of the market for hard cider to disappear. Cider reemerged in the 1990s as a gourmet drink, and its popularity is on the rise.

Cider may well be among the oldest of alcoholic beverages. Drawings from the Paleolithic age depict apples, and the people of this era probably discovered that wild yeast would quickly act upon the fruit to ferment it. The Spanish were making *sidra* when the Romans invaded Britain in 55 B.C.E. and found the Celts fermenting the juice of native crab apples to make cider. By the second and third centuries, Roman authorities reported that various European peoples were making a number of cider-like drinks created from different types of fruit. But cider remained a drink of last resort that was consumed only in years when there was a shortage of beer or other drinks brewed from grains and herbs.

After the collapse of the Roman Empire, Christian monastic orders encouraged the large-scale planting of fruit trees, while the Muslim Moors of Spain developed new apple varieties. The Moors are probably responsible for developing the bitter, high-tannin apples that make the richest ciders. In France, the Normans developed a love for cider and apple brandy, *calvados.* In fourteenth-century France, cider became as popular as beer, and production gradually spread from Normandy to other temperate parts of the country. A Norman physician, Julien le Paulmier, aided this movement by authoring *De Vino et Pomaceo,* a guide to varieties of cider apples.

Interest in cider in Britain faded after the fall of Rome because many orchards were abandoned when invading Jutes and Danes attacked British settlements. The Norman Conquest in 1066 renewed cider interest among the British. The Normans had developed a number of apple varieties, which they then introduced to England. Cider soon became the most popular drink after ale, and it began to be widely used as a means of exchange to pay rents and tithes. Unlike ale, cider production did not require fuel for heat, a significant concern in England, where burnable wood was scarce. Any farmer with an apple tree could easily press the fruit and then ferment the juice. Once pressed into cider, the leftover apple pomace could be soaked with water and pressed again to make a weak ciderkin. The keen interest in identifying and improving cider apple varieties in the seventeenth century led to both technological advancements and a marked improvement in the quality of cider. An English noble, Lord Scudamore, is credited with having bottled cider as early as the 1640s, when almost all cider was stored in wooden barrels and drawn off "on draft" as needed. The slight fermentation that took place in the bottles released carbon dioxide gas that produced a sparkling drink and helped preserve the cider better than could half-emptied wooden barrels, in which aerobic organisms came into contact with the cider and often spoiled it.

By the eighteenth century, the English thirst for cider had become unquenchable, and this demand combined with industrialization to destroy the beverage's market. Homemade farm cider, unfiltered and unpasteurized, did not transport well, but city dwellers still sought it. Cider factories consequently sprang up, and the quality of cider began to drop. Many of these firms produced heavily adulterated or watered-down ciders that were barely recognizable as cider. Other companies sold unappetizing scrumpy, a beverage made from rotten fruit, vegetables, and sugar. Devonshire colic, a palsy-like sickness caused by lead leaching into cider from the pipes of manufacturing equipment, further scared off customers. Cider became associated with the lower classes and drinking to get drunk. Anyone who could afford to purchase a healthy drink chose ale. In the late nineteenth century, regional cider making gave way to a more centralized system, and the quality of cider improved. One of the factories that appeared at this time, H. P. Bulmer, founded in 1887 by Percy Bulmer, is now the largest cider maker in the world.

Colonists from Western Europe brought apples to America, but Native Americans had already been making a cider from crab apples. In 1623, William Blackstone of Plymouth planted the first cultivated tree. Other Americans followed suit and planted trees wherever they would grow. A nurseryman from Pennsylvania, John Chapman, became folk hero Johnny Appleseed for his habit of spreading seeds on his travels through the Midwest. Pressing and fermenting apple juice served as the easiest way for farmers to preserve the apple harvest, and farmers typically used cider as the basis for many other products, including cider vinegar, applejack (a strong, concentrated liquor made by freezing hard cider), and apple brandy. At a time when water quality was poor and milk unpasteurized, cider was an inexpensive, safe drink with an alcohol content of 6 percent. Readily available and a useful commodity, it became a common unit of exchange, especially in rural areas where currency was often scarce. The first blow to American cider came when insects such as the codling moth and diseases such as apple scab attacked the vast orchards in New York. Many of the trees were chopped down. The growing temperance movement threw the

Mr. William Bufton judges entrants in the cider making competition at the Royal Counties Agricultural Show in 1948. (Hulton/Archive)

next blow. Although some farmers cut down their trees, others simply stopped producing alcoholic beverages altogether in favor of apple juice or sweet cider. Manufacturers did not help their cause by increasing the alcohol content of cider, often by the addition of rum, and producing an inferior product from a variety of sources that occasionally had little or no apple flavor. By the advent of National Prohibition, the production of hard cider had dramatically fallen. A few farmers kept the old traditions alive, though, and in the 1990s, American demand for hard cider rose as part of an increased worldwide interest in traditional foods.

Caryn E. Neumann

References

Brown, John Hull. *Early American Beverages.* New York: Bonanza Books, 1966.

Orton, Vrest. *The American Cider Book.* New York: North Point Press, 1995.

Watson, Ben. *Cider Hard and Sweet: History, Traditions, and Making Your Own.* Woodstock, VT: Countryman Press, 1999.

Cirrhosis of the Liver

Cirrhosis is a liver disease that changes the shape of the liver, replacing normal tissue with constrictive connective tissue. Cirrhosis is an outcome of several chronic liver disease processes. It takes many years to develop and then presents with abdominal pain, swelling, edema, fever, nausea, vomiting, jaundice, gastrointestinal bleeding, and bruising of the skin. Advanced symptoms include portal hypertension, ascites, and hepatic coma.

Experts agree that alcoholism most often causes cirrhosis. Cirrhosis is the result of a cumulative process with damage to the liver occurring over time. Alcohol is metabolized in the liver. The breakdown of alcohol produces potentially dangerous byproducts. Both alcohol and its byproducts are capable of damaging the liver. Because the liver can repair itself, the assault on it must be chronic and longstanding before damage will be apparent. For men, daily drinking of 72 ounces of beer, 1 liter of wine, or 5 to 6 drinks of distilled spirits for twenty years constitutes a threshold dose of alcohol that will result in symptomatic liver disease. For women, the same damage will occur with one-quarter to one-half of the above consumption. However, no more than half of heavy drinkers actually develop cirrhosis.

Progression of the Disease

Scientists consider alcohol-induced liver disease to have three stages and classify it as a progressive disease. The first stage is fatty liver, in which fat deposits are found on the liver. This condition is reversible and does not lead, on its own, to further damage. If a heavy drinker ceases drinking at this point, he or she would not suffer any permanent liver damage.

The second stage is alcoholic hepatitis. Liver tissue undergoes inflammation and necrosis. Scar or fibrotic tissue replaces healthy tissue. A person may develop symptoms, including fever, abdominal pain, and jaundice. Alcoholic hepatitis can be fatal, sometimes before cirrhosis develops. Abstaining from alcohol sometimes reverses the process. As many as 50 percent of heavy drinkers develop alcoholic hepatitis.

Alcoholic cirrhosis is considered the final stage of liver disease. Among heavy drinkers, 15 to 30 percent receive a diagnosis of cirrhosis. In cirrhosis, the liver is riddled with fibrotic tissue that alters the organ's structure. The liver's inability to function normally impacts other organs, including the brain and the kidneys. Kidney failure and portal hypertension often cause death. Abstention may halt the progress of cirrhosis, but the damage is not reversible. Chronic viral hepatitis can also develop into cirrhosis. Although alcohol abuse is the major risk factor for cirrhosis, other factors include genetic differences, gender, diet, hepatitis C infection, and coffee and tobacco use. Because women proportionately have more fatty tissue than men, there is a greater potential for female tissue to be exposed to alcohol. Alcoholic liver disease affects women after less exposure to alcohol. Shorter duration and smaller doses lead to cirrhosis in women. Once women have alcohol-induced liver disease, the disease progresses differently. Even when abstaining, women remain more likely to die from cirrhosis than men do.

One-half of people infected with hepatitis C have a history of intravenous drug use. Among alcoholics, 18 to 25 percent have symptoms indicative of hepatitis C infection. Hepatitis C increases the risk of liver disease among alcoholics. Alcoholics who also smoke have three times greater risk of developing cirrhosis. However, coffee drinking seems to diminish the risk of cirrhosis for alcoholics.

Demographic Differences

Cirrhosis was the ninth leading cause of death in the United States in 1990. Officials estimate that alcohol-related cirrhosis deaths account for 41 to 95 percent of all cirrhosis deaths. Alcohol-related disease often goes unreported as a cause of death. Because there is not a perfect correlation between heavy chronic drinking and cirrhosis, different demographic groups within the United States have different rates of liver disease. There is also variation compared to the rates of other countries.

Chronic liver disease and cirrhosis are the fifth leading cause of death for Native Americans; within this ethnic group, for the population aged twenty-five to forty-four, it is second. The age-adjusted death rate for this group of all ages was over 4.4 times greater for liver disease than in the general population.

In the past, Africans Americans have had higher rates of cirrhosis, but new research shows that white Hispanics are dying from cirrhosis at a faster rate than African Americans. This is particularly true for people of Mexican and South American descent.

In Great Britain, cirrhosis rates have been rising, with women more often dying from this disease than from cervical cancer. The increase in cirrhosis rates is most pronounced among young British women. Both young men and women are dying from cirrhosis at four times the rate of the early 1970s. This increase in cirrhosis deaths in Britain is more significant in light of the fact that European rates have been declining.

There is no cure for cirrhosis, but people can stop progressive liver damage related to alcohol abuse by refraining from drinking. Liver transplantation is the only available treatment for people with terminal liver disease. People with cirrhotic liver damage should be on high-fiber, low-fat, and low-salt diets. A vaccination for hepatitis B is available. Safe sex is also part of prevention, since sexually transmitted diseases are a cause of liver damage.

Amy Mittelman

See also: Alcoholism

References

"Are Women More Susceptible than Men to Alcohol-Induced Cirrhosis" in *Alcohol Health and Research World.* (Part 7 of 25) 18 (1 January 1994). In Electronic Library, http://www.elibrary.com [March 2002].

"Britain Cirrhosis Deaths Up." AP online. 11 January 2001. In Electronic Library. http://www.elibrary.com. [March 2002].

"Cirrhosis." WebMD/Lycos. http:/wbmd.lycos.com/content/asset/miller_keane_7294 [March 2002].

Cole, Elaine, "Alcohol Abuse Is Now Biggest Killer among Women" in *Independent.* (Britain) 10 January 2001: 10. In Electronic Library, http://www.elibrary.com [March 2002].

Indian Health Service. *Trends in Indian Health—1997.* Washington, DC: United States Department of Health and Human Services, 1997. http://www.ihs.gov/publicinfo/publications/trends98/trends98.asp [March 2002].

Kubetin, Sally Koch, "Hispanics Top Cirrhosis Deaths" in *Internal Medicine News.* 34 (15 September 2001): 40. In Infotrac Web: Health Reference Center—Academic A788957142 (database on-line). Gale Group, 2002. [March 2002].

LaPook, Jonathan. "Cirrhosis" in *The Columbia University College of Physicians and Surgeons Complete Home Medical Guide.* New York: Crown Publishers, 1995. In Infotrac Health Reference Center, Article A19035982 (database on-line). Gale Group, 2002. [March 2002].

Maher, Jacquelyn. "Exploring Alcohol's Effects on Liver Function" in *Alcohol Health and Research World.* 21 (1 January 1997):

5–12. In Electronic Library, http://www.elibrary.com [March 2002].

National Center for Health Statistics. *Healthy People 2000 Review, 1992.* Hyattsville, MD: Public Health Service, 1993.

Civil Damage Laws

These state laws, sometimes known as Dramshop Laws, allowed those damaged by other people's drinking to sue alcohol purveyors for compensation. In the mid- and late nineteenth century, these laws were used primarily by wives and minor children of drinkers. These wives and children claimed their inebriate husbands and fathers had failed adequately to support their families, either because of their accidental death or injury while intoxicated, because they were jailed for crimes committed while intoxicated, or because their regular saloon-going interfered with their work habits or absorbed their earnings. Most state laws, however, also allowed other types of people to sue, such as parents who relied on their children's earnings for support, employers who lost worker productivity or sustained other damages, and other third parties who were assaulted or accidentally injured by intoxicated people.

Although a full study of the state legislative history of the civil damage laws never has been conducted, the first known civil damage law was passed in Pennsylvania (1846). This law provided damages only to those parties who had been injured by drinkers who had purchased alcohol illegally. Ohio (1854), New Hampshire (1855), Nebraska (1858), and Kansas (1859) passed versions of the law in the next decade. During the Civil War, Massachusetts (1861) and Iowa (1862) passed their laws. Between 1869 and 1890, Colorado (1870), Connecticut (1888), Dakota Territory (1873), Delaware (1881), Illinois (1872), Indiana (1873), Maine (1871), Michigan (1871), New Mexico Territory (1887), New York (1873), North Carolina (1874), Rhode Island (1889), Vermont (1869), West Virginia (1872), Wisconsin (1872), and some counties in Arkansas (1873) followed suit.

Under common law, those who sold alcohol had not been liable for damage caused by drinkers. Under the doctrine of "proximate cause," only the person who made the last voluntary choice in the chain of causation that caused an injury was liable for its consequences. That is, even though a saloon keeper may have contributed to the series of events that led to a plaintiff's injury, the drinker was solely liable because the drinker's act of consuming the liquor rather than the saloon keeper's act of selling it was the last voluntary act. As nineteenth-century legislators increasingly doubted that the habitual or intoxicated drinker possessed the strength of will to resist a drink offered to him, they came to consider the saloon keeper as exercising the last free choice that led to the injury, and thus as civilly responsible for it. This did not erase the drinker's own legal responsibility, however; in all states, he remained both criminally and civilly liable for the same acts.

Civil damage laws had no apparent British or European precedents. The closest thing to a precedent to these unusual laws in the United States was decisions in antebellum Southern courts that held those who sold liquor to slaves liable if those slaves were injured or killed while intoxicated. Like many civil damage decisions, these Southern decisions sometimes explicitly noted the slave's lack of volitional choice when explaining the vendor's responsibility for the damage to the intoxicated slave.

Civil damage laws varied significantly from state to state. In a few states, for instance, it was only possible for a plaintiff to recover under the law if she or he had previously given a written request to the defendant to stop serving the drinker in question and had been ignored. Some states allowed for exemplary damages, while others prohibited them. Other states exempted sales of certain kinds of alcoholic beverages, such as beer or locally produced wines or ciders, from the law. Some states held owners of buildings used as saloons jointly liable with saloon keepers, while others did not. North Carolina only allowed for recovery (by parents, guardians, or employers) when alcohol had been illegally sold to a minor.

Although many potential plaintiffs lacked the money to bring suits, they were sometimes aided either by lawyers working for a percentage of the award or by organizations like the Woman's Christian Temperance Union (WCTU) and Citizens' Law and Order Leagues, which encouraged and financially supported "drunkards' wives" who brought the suits. These suits were frequently successful in local courtrooms, perhaps because the impoverished families of drinkers often were more compelling to jurors than were saloon keepers. They were often, however, overturned as courts of appeal detected bias in the proceedings, the inclusion of improper testimony, or the awarding of improper sums.

These laws had an ambiguous impact on women's rights. Because they were primarily intended for use by women with inebriate husbands and because, when they were passed in many states, women lacked the right to bring lawsuits in their own name, the laws frequently specifically provided that women could bring this type of suit on their own behalf. On the other hand, because some legislatures passed them to placate women who were dissatisfied with the enforcement of liquor laws and because the suits were expensive, difficult to pursue, and often ultimately unsuccessful, the passage of civil damage laws may have further angered women concerned about the well-being of inebriates' families.

The impact of civil damage laws on saloon keepers is difficult to gauge. At the height of their popularity, from the late 1870s to the mid-1890s, the likelihood that a given saloon would be named in a suit was high. In 1884, according to Perry Duis, there were at least 2,042 suits brought against Chicago's 2,928 saloons.

These laws were used most heavily during the late nineteenth century. Most of them, however, remained on the books until National Prohibition. Some continue, in altered form, to the present, though they are now used almost exclusively by victims of intoxicated drivers.

Elaine Frantz Parsons

See also: Server Responsibility Laws (United States)

References

Blocker, Jack S., Jr. *"Give to the Winds Thy Fears": The Women's Temperance Crusade, 1873–1874.* Westport, CT: Greenwood, 1985.

"Civil Damage Acts" in *Standard Encyclopedia of the Alcohol Problem,* edited by Ernest Hurst Cherrington et al. 6 vols. 2: 617–618. Westerville, OH: American Issue Publishing, 1924–1930.

Duis, Perry. *The Saloon: Public Drinking in Chicago and Boston 1880–1920.* Urbana: University of Illinois Press, 1983.

Parsons, Elaine Frantz. "Risky Business: The Uncertain Boundaries of Manhood in the Midwestern Saloon" in *Journal of Social History.* 34, no. 2 (2000): 283–307.

———. "Slaves to the Bottle: Smith's Civil Damage Liquor Law" in *Annals of Iowa.* 59, no. 4 (2000): 347–373.

Clark, Norman Harold (1925–)

Norman Harold Clark (1925–) is one of the most original historians of modern American society. Although he specialized in the history of the Northwest, he always wrote at the same time about general U.S. history—what used to be called not local history, but localized history. In his most important work, he used local (state) history to challenge the received wisdom of what happened in the social history of alcoholic beverage use in the United States. In 1976, he extrapolated his insight into the classic *Deliver Us from Evil: An Interpretation of American Prohibition,* which decades later remained the best general account of Prohibition in the United States.

Clark was born in Mesa, Arizona, on 10 May 1925. He graduated from public school in El Paso, Texas, and served in the U.S. Marines from 1943 to 1946. He took a B.A. from Southern Methodist University in 1949, with some study in Stockholm, Sweden, in 1947 through 1948. He went on to take a master's degree at the University of Washington in 1950, and he started teaching American history at Everett Community College in 1959, just after that institution moved to a new, permanent campus. In 1964, working with Robert E. Burke, Clark took his Ph.D. at Washington and lectured there in American studies for two years, meantime holding an American Philosophical Society research grant. In 1966, he chose to take up his continuing appointment at Everett Community College. He later served as president of that institution, and he retired from the faculty in 1985. He was a National Endowment for the Humanities fellow in 1967.

In 1970, Clark published *Mill Town,* another localized history in which, through a compelling account of one community, he explored American social history in the turn-of-the-century years. It was only natural that he was chosen to write the history of his state in the bicentennial history series, a work that appeared in 1976. It was a thoughtful (and of course readable) and distinguished contribution.

In the early 1960s, when Clark began his work on the experience of people in Washington State with alcoholic beverages, a great deal of exciting sociocultural history was appearing. Yet, as Clark later commented, urbane liberals led by Richard Hofstadter continued to dominate historical interpretations of temperance and prohibition. Historians of that persuasion portrayed temperance advocates as quaint, backward-looking rural people and extremists, represented by Carry Amelia Moore Nation—the "hatchetry" school of historians, in Clark's words. Yet already, empirical scholars were producing histories that suggested that a new view was in the offing—in James H. Timberlake's *Prohibition and the Progressive Movement* (1963) and in Joseph R. Gusfield's sociological essay, *Symbolic Crusade: Status Politics and the American Temperance Movement* (1963). Above all, there was a scholarly book that, as Clark observed, extended the work of the Hofstadter school, but, it must be added, a book in which the author at the end questioned the extreme step of repealing Prohibition: Andrew Sinclair's *Prohibition: The Era of Excess* (1962).

In his dissertation, later published as *The Dry Years,* Clark did two things. First, he moved the history of temperance and Prohibition from a general and impressionistic level to an examination of specific factors operating with actual people in a concrete setting. On this level, glib generalizations and journalistic stereotypes gave way to complicated actuality with accidental factors in trends that were clearly national as well as local. Second, Clark was open to the idea that, on balance, National Prohibition was not an aberration in U.S. history. He accepted that the temperance crusade produced real, needed reform at the same time that it muddled laws and policy. As he observed, the old saloon never came back after National Prohibition. Scholars then and ever since recognized the fundamental nature of Clark's contribution, and a second edition of *The Dry Years* was published in 1988.

Clark's ability to write colorfully and empathetically showed dramatically well a decade later in *Deliver Us from Evil.* Temperance, Prohibition, and repeal were not, he insisted, separate acts. They were all part of a complex interaction of values—especially family values—with rapid social change. His successors, however excellent their research, have still not improved on his basic, albeit sophisticated, narrative line.

John C. Burnham

See also: Gusfield, Joseph R.

References

Clark, Norman H. *Deliver Us from Evil: An Interpretation of American Prohibition.* New York: W. W. Norton, 1976.

———. *The Dry Years: Prohibition and Social Change in Washington.* Rev. ed. Seattle: University of Washington Press, 1988 [1965].

Gusfield, Joseph R. *Symbolic Crusade: Status Politics and the American Temperance Movement.* Urbana: University of Illinois Press, 1996 [1963].
Sinclair, Andrew. *Prohibition: Era of Excess.* New York: Harper and Row, 1962.
Timberlake, James A. *Prohibition and the Progressive Movement, 1900–1920.* Cambridge: Harvard University Press, 1963.

Close, Francis (1797–1882)

Francis Close (1797–1882), dean of Carlisle and vicar of Cheltenham; controversialist; antitractarian Evangelical and reformer; and opponent of tobacco, horse racing, and the theater, was a founder and first president of the Church of England Total Abstinence Society (1862), later the Church of England and Ireland Temperance Reformation Society (1864), both teetotal organizations.

Confronting local Chartists, Close comprehensively addressed social problems in his highly proletarian northern region; but, although an evangelical Puritan, he at first resisted teetotalism. Close had to cope with strong sentiments of antipapism before supporting the temperance movement in which prominent Roman Catholics, including the Irish Capuchin Theobald Mathew, Father James Nugent of Liverpool, and, later, Cardinal Henry Edward Manning, Archbishop of Westminster, were active. Before 1855, when his physician ordered abstinence from drink because of his gout, Close had medical fears about eliminating alcohol. For another four years, he refused the pledge as a "carnal and superogatory method of doing that which ought to be done by the gospel alone."

He took the pledge and endorsed teetotal societies in 1859, when he submitted to the influence of local working people. Close later joined about fifty other teetotal clergymen in helping organize the May 1862 London Coffee House Conference, which led, by October, to the initiation of the Church teetotal society, much aided by two Nonconformist-supported groups, the prohibitionist United Kingdom Alliance (UKA) and the moral-suasionist National Temperance League (NTL), to which many teetotal clergymen belonged. A league member and alliance vice president, Close addressed an international, prohibitionist congress in the year the Church teetotal society was founded. Concerned with his obligations as dean of Carlisle, Close's presidency of the Church teetotal society was more honorary than active; he presided over only two of the society's annual meetings.

Teetotal priests were unsuccessful in converting the Church hierarchy to total abstinence or prohibition. They offended Church congresses by their sometimes fanatical opposition to drink and by their Evangelicalism. Close vowed never to attend another Church congress after his first at York in 1866. He frightened others by his prohibitionism and by exceeding medical researchers in attacking the widespread clinical use of alcohol and opposing even moderate prescriptions of the "poison," strong drink. He angered many, especially Anglo-Catholics, by considering unfermented Communion wine for Anglican services and later by openly espousing a nonalcoholic sacrament.

Having failed to convert the Anglican hierarchy to strict antidrink principles, the teetotal clergy settled for the Church of England Temperance Society (CETS), blessed in 1873 by the British establishment, who admired the ecumenical nature of the temperance movement in a disestablishment era and its "dual basis," with sections for largely proletarian abstainers and for "better-class" moderate drinkers, who addressed the deeper social, political, and cultural causes of intemperance.

Close's writings are in the British Library.

Stephanie Olsen and Gerald Wayne Olsen

See also: Chartism; Christian Socialism; Church of England Temperance Society (CETS); Cruikshank, George; Ellison, Henry; Evangelical Temperance (United Kingdom); Maguire, Robert; Manning, Henry Edward; Mathew, Theobald; Moule, Handley Carr Glyn; National Temperance League (NTL); Nugent, James; United Kingdom Alliance (UKA); Wightman, Julia Bainbrigge

References

Boase, George C. "Close, Francis" in *Dictionary of National Biography.* London: Oxford University Press, 1960: 4, 179.
Close, Francis. *Why I Have Taken the Pledge.* London: Hatchford, 1861.
Harrison, Brian. "Close, Dean Francis" in *Dictionary of British Temperance Biography,* 29. Coventry: Society for the Study of Labour History. Aids to Research, no. 1, *Bulletin Supplement,* 1973.
Olsen, G. W. *Pub and Parish—Drink and Temperance in the Church of England, 1829–1875.* Unpublished book manuscript.

Colonization, European, and Drinking Behavior among Indigenous Peoples (Portuguese America)

The Portuguese conquest and colonization of America from the South Atlantic coast gave birth to a society whose drinking habits and behavior were deeply affected by the culture of that European nation, by colonialist trading impositions, and by the survival of indigenous culture. Along with drinking patterns ranging from the comparative temperance practiced by the Portuguese elite of the colony to the excesses of the huge population of slaves in the New World, Portuguese America between the sixteenth and nineteenth centuries saw an increase in the number of new types of alcoholic beverages, from imported Portuguese wine to a sugarcane brandy produced in Brazil and a variety of fermented drinks learned from the experience of the African and indigenous populations. In spite of the wealth of historical information available, there are no recent studies on the subjects of alcohol and temperance in colonial Brazil. However, there are important medical studies developed in the nineteenth century in medical colleges and studies on folklore focusing on the popular culture surrounding the consumption of

Men drink cachaça *to celebrate the June 1986 festival of Bumba meu Boi in Alcantara, Brazil. (Barnabas Bosshart/Corbis)*

cachaça. More recently, although the focus of research has been on the history of *aguardente,* there has also been a new tendency to investigate its commerce and regional production structures.

In this sense, the history of alcoholic beverages in Portuguese America merges with the colonial condition of the region that, with its political emancipation in 1822, would give birth to the national state of Brazil. The arrival of the first Portuguese in Bahia in 1530 was followed by their efforts to cultivate vineyards for the production of wine to cater to the taste of Portuguese colonizers. This initiative proved a failure from the very beginning, not only because of climatic factors but particularly because it was crushed by the interests of tradesmen from the metropolis who made a profit from exporting wine to the colony. The implantation of a sugarcane-based economy, on the other hand, resulted in the production of a variety of beverages made from sugarcane, such as cachaça and aguardente.

The production of aguardente was further fostered because of the role it played in slave-trade exchange currency in central Africa. As the South Atlantic trade circuit became integrated, aguardente came to dominate the African market in distilled drinks, thus quickly defeating the competition of European distilled drinks as a barter currency, as was the case with wines with a higher alcohol content from the Canaries, Madeira, and Malaga. As a result of the increased African demand for the beverage produced in Brazil, which became the drink of choice of the *Sobas* (African tribal chiefs) and African tradesmen, sugarcane farms expanded their lines of products to cater to this profitable market. Like all the other types of brandy, aguardente, obtained from the juice extracted from sugarcane, was produced from fermentation and distillation and possessed an alcohol content not exceeding 65 percent. Either inside or outside the sugar mills and plantation complexes, the aguardente, also known as *jeribita,* was distilled in stills, where the alcohol was separated from the liquid. Byproducts included *garapa* (sugarcane juice) and cachaça, drinks of low alcohol content consumed by the slaves, who skimmed the foam produced by the boiled juice, or ate the molasses that trickled from the receptacles before it was transformed into sugar.

From *Cauim* to Aguardente

The variety of drinks produced in Portuguese America was outstanding. Records of the early years of colonization reveal that *tupi* tribes, living on the coast, drank *cauim* in their celebrations and religious ceremonies. Cauim was a fermented beverage produced from tubers, such as cassava, as well as cereals, such as corn, or even fruit, such as pineapple. Sometimes honey was added to it, which increased the alcohol content. Recent archaeological research has revealed the presence, in periods prior to the arrival of the Portuguese, of fragments of ceramic pots (in *tupi-guarani, Cambuchi* or *Camuci*), used by the Indians in the preparation of cauim, proving that their habit of consuming alcoholic beverages dates back to antiquity.

The innovations introduced by the Portuguese soon affected the consumption patterns of the aborigines. The ingestion of cauim was a collective practice regulated by a religious calendar. The colonizers introduced daily individual consumption. This new pattern led to the intensive ingestion of cauim. The dietary disturbances brought about by these changes enfeebled the indigenous groups, thus exposing them to the diseases brought in by the colonizers.

In the different regions of America where the Portuguese settled, local types of drinks were created. In São Paulo, the growth in the production of fermented and distilled wheat and corn beverages was accelerated. Besides being consumed in that region, these drinks became quite successful in neighboring markets. In the captaincy of Minas Gerais, a drink known as corn wine or *aluá* was the favorite among the Africans brought there from Costa da Mina. Its production process reveals the cultural exchanges that took place among the African populations in Minas Gerais. The grass-like American plant was soaked, placed on banana tree leaves, soaked again, and allowed to dry in the sun, then ground, sifted, and put into a pot with boiling water. After that, the mixture was strained and left to ferment in a cask. In the south region of colonial Brazil, there appeared a type of aguardente known as *beiju,* produced from the fermentation and distillation of the juice extracted from grated cassava.

The Brazilian beverages market, intent on meeting conspicuous consumption by the members of higher social classes, was still dependent on imports. Drinks such as wine and one made from grapes—known as *bagaceira*—were imported into Brazil in small quantities. Beer, in turn, would only gain popularity in the mid-nineteenth century, initially as an import from the United States, and was known as English beer.

It is important to point out that in those days, curative powers were ascribed to most of these drinks. Wine was often recommended by doctors as a base in the preparation of herbal medicines or to be used in cauterization or to rub onto the skin. Aguardente was used to relieve pains, heal festered spots and wounds, and treat eye disorders and deafness; in some regions, it was used in the treatment of smallpox and measles.

Between Temperance and Alcoholism

Records on the consumption of alcohol, collected from Europeans visiting Brazil from the time the Braganças (the Portuguese royal family) settled in the tropics in 1808, insist that it was rare to see public drunkenness, and some state that it was not very usual to find wines on the farms. Although these reports are not unanimous, the image still prevails of squires and urban upper classes drinking moderately and consuming only a few goblets of port and Madeira wines, orange wine, and liqueurs on special occasions.

Such temperance, however, did not thrive in more popular quarters. The consumption, especially of sugarcane aguardente, was widely spread among the large population of slaves and poor mixed-breed people. To a certain extent, this consumption was encouraged by slave masters, who believed that aguardente was a perfect substitute for the calories lacked by this poorly nourished segment of the population, who spent their days in backbreaking labor. This New World development proceeded parallel to the general lines that marked the expansion of distilled drinks in Europe from the eighteenth century on, when such beverages, besides the pleasure of intoxication they gave, represented an alternative to the calories unaffordable by the very poor. Civil governmental and religious officials in Brazil were greatly concerned about alcohol abuse by the poorer population, and some brotherhoods went as far as to deny admittance to heavy drinkers, although no specific legislation is known to have existed to regulate drinking. There used to be recipes, developed in the tropics, against alcohol addiction. For wine addicts, the remedy was learned from the indigenous population, and consisted of inhaling *petume* (*Nicotiana tabacum*) smoke. Against drunkenness, a medical treatise of the eighteenth century included curious recommendations, such as giving the person a little bit of wine left to rest for half an hour in the shoe of a drunken man, or wine mixed with human manure.

From the nineteenth century on, academic studies developed by the doctors in Brazilian medical colleges took the first step in the direction of investigating alcohol consumption among the lower classes. At that time, some studies confirmed that alcoholism, included in the group of toxic and infectious psychoses, was the cause of almost 12 percent of hospitalizations among black people, but only 7 percent of hospitalizations among white and mixed-breed patients. In the twentieth century, new studies on alcoholism in Brazil concluded that most of the cases of serious intoxication caused by the ingestion of alcohol resulted from the excessive consumption of the aguardente introduced in Brazil by the Portuguese during the colonial period.

Luciano R. A. Figueiredo and Renato P. Venâncio

See also: Native Americans: Drinking Patterns and Temperance Reform; South America

References

Curto, José C. "Luso-Brazilian Alcohol and the Legal Slave Trade at Benguela and Its Hinterland, c. 1617–1830" in *Négoce Blanc en Afrique Noire: L'évolution du commerce à longue distance en Afrique noire du 18e au 20e siècles,* edited by H. Bonin and M. Cahen, 351–369. Paris: Publications de la société française d'histoire d'outre-mer, 2001.

Freyre, Gilberto. *The Mansions and the Shanties (The Making of Modern Brazil).* New York: Alfred A. Knopf, 1963.

Schwartz, Stuart B. *Sugar Plantations in the Formation of Brazilian Society: Bahia, 1550–1835.* Cambridge: Cambridge University Press, 1985.

Comité Nacional de Lucha contra el Alcoholismo

The Comité Nacional de Lucha contra el Alcoholismo (National Committee for the Struggle against Alcoholism) was founded on 14 May 1929 by Interim President Emilio Portes Gil. It represents the institutional beginning of the official temperance campaign of the revolutionary government in Mexico. The Comité Nacional was short-lived and was replaced by the more centralized Dirección Anti-Alcohólica by 1933.

The 1930s marked the high point of activism, zeal, and idealism of the social revolution in Mexico. Revolutionary leaders ascribed meaning to the violent years of the armed struggle by asserting that the war had been necessary to wipe away the corrupt so-called feudal social structures that had dominated during the dictatorship of Porfirio Díaz. Once the old order had been swept away, a second, cultural or social revolution was required to mold a "new generation." According to the ideology of the social revolution, the new Mexico would be modern, industrial, secular, hygienic, and sober. Many of the leaders who espoused this ideology felt that, unfortunately, most of the Mexicans were in fact backward, superstitious, dirty, and intemperate peasants. The 1930s temperance movement was one of several government-led campaigns aimed at transfiguring Mexico into its leaders' vision of an ideal society.

The revolutionary government's temperance crusade was one of the most notable ideological thefts from the "feudal" Porfirian regime that the revolutionaries sought to erase. What was new in the 1930s, however, was the scale of popular mobilization, particularly of women, in a new national project to overcome what had been long considered a widespread vice of the Mexican lower, especially indigenous, classes.

Interim President Emilio Portes Gil founded the National Committee for the Struggle against Alcoholism in 1929 to stimulate popular mobilization against alcoholism. The Committee was not given a bureaucratic home within any single government department, but instead was formed of representatives from each federal ministry. The aim of the Comité Nacional was to reproduce, on a national scale, the antialcohol measures Portes Gil had undertaken while governor of Tamaulipas.

In Tamaulipas, Portes Gil had instituted policies to raise public awareness about the dangers of alcoholism, with the goal of catalyzing a popular temperance movement. The Comité Nacional was designed to avoid the mistakes of the United States prohibition effort by encouraging the emergence of a grassroots protemperance movement. As governor, Portes Gil had used government authority to combat alcoholism in three ways only: by disseminating propaganda decrying the evils of alcohol; by establishing opportunities for spending leisure time engaged in activities disassociated with drinking, such as sports; and by decreeing prohibition when it was requested by residents in particular localities. Portes Gil's 1929 creation of the Comité Nacional de Lucha contra el Alcoholismo was intended to replicate his Tamaulipas experiment throughout the Republic. The Comité Nacional set about gathering statistics regarding alcohol use and abuse, creating and disseminating antialcohol propaganda, and encouraging the development of a national grassroots temperance movement.

Portes Gil's strategy reflected assumptions held by contemporary Mexican sociologists, whose understanding of the causes of alcoholism had advanced little since the previous century. Factors thought to contribute to alcoholism included climate, economic status, and religious ideology, as well as race/ethnicity and culture. Alcoholism was usually defined as frequent consumption of alcohol, although the quality of alcohol was also thought to be important. Thus, considerable study was devoted to comparisons among (particularly indigenous) tastes for *pulque* as against *chicha, bacanora* as against *aguardiente de caña,* and *mezcal* as against *sotol.* The evils of alcoholism were often described in exaggerated terms. Alcohol was variously blamed as a leading cause of premature death, madness, poverty, and cultural isolation among the indigenous population, and of crime of all descriptions, industrial stagnation, the spread of disease, and social backwardness.

Mexican sociologists in the 1930s defined alcoholism as a social disease—a sickness that affected society as a whole as well as the individual. Social diseases were supposed to have social causes, and therefore demanded a social cure. Various remedies were thought to be effective, including the improvement of the economic conditions of the proletariat, the implementation of mass antialcohol campaigns, the construction of good community sports facilities, and the introduction of wholesome, alcohol-free, civic festivals. Education was the panacea. It was assumed that if people fully understood the deleterious effects of alcohol on individuals, families, and society as a whole, they would stop drinking.

By 1932, the Comité Nacional had disappeared. However, the national temperance campaign continued, particularly within the Departments of Industry, Agriculture, Hygiene, and Education. By 1933, a new official national antialcohol directorate had been formed. Luis G. Franco became the "head of activities" of the new Dirección Anti-Alcohólica. The functions of the Dirección Anti-Alcohólica were similar to those of the Comité Nacional, although its bureaucratic structure had changed. It was no longer a body composed of representatives from each of the executive departments. As in the past, the advocacy of temperance continued within the various executive departments in a quasi-autonomous fashion. The Dirección Anti-Alcohólica's motto was "*Temperancia: Por la Patria y Por la Raza*" (for the Fatherland and for the race). Primarily dedicated to propagandizing in favor of temperance, it sponsored activities such as a national contest for the best antialcoholism song. The national directorate also promoted parades and public ceremonies championing temperance.

Stephanie Mitchell

See also: Dirección Anti-Alcohólica; Franco, *Ing.* Luis G.; Mexico; Portes Gil, Emilio

References

Joseph, Gilbert M., and Daniel Nugent, eds. *Everyday Forms of State Formation: Revolution and the Negotiation of Rule in Modern Mexico.* Durham, NC: Duke University Press, 1994.

Vaughan, Mary Kay. *Cultural Politics in Revolution: Teachers, Peasants, and Schools in Mexico (1930–1940).* Tucson: University of Arizona Press, 1997.

Committee of Fifty

Organized for the purpose of investigating and publishing reports on various aspects of the "liquor problem," the Committee of Fifty (1893–1905) was made up of leaders from divergent fields. Members included university professors, clergy, and physicians, as well as figures prominent in politics, law, and industry. During the first decade of the twentieth century, the Committee of Fifty was one of the few voices advocating moderation in alcohol consumption. According to historical sociologist Harry Gene Levine, the Committee of Fifty's concept of "alcohol control" "represents the first substantial articulation of what would be the distinctive 20th century intellectual and political framework for viewing the place of alcohol in society" (Levine 1983: 97).

The committee was originally composed of about fifteen men who were active in religion and education. In 1889, they began to contribute a series of articles on social questions to the *Century Magazine.* The group met for discussion of papers and social problems twice a year and critiqued each other's papers. In 1893, members decided to enlarge their number to fifty and focus upon problems associated with alcohol in the United States. The committee was established in part as a reaction against the campaign of the Woman's Christian Temperance Union's (WCTU) Scientific Temperance Instruction (STI) program under the leadership of Mary Hunt. Members of this committee clashed with Hunt over what they regarded as inaccurate information about the physiological effects of alcohol taught in the schools. The Committee of Fifty was formally organized on 5 April 1893. New members were mostly selected from eastern cities so they would be able to easily attend the biannual meetings. Members included Professors Felix Adler, W. O. Atwater, John S. Billings, H. P. Bowditch, R. H. Chittenden, Richard T. Ely, Henry W. Farnham, Francis G. Peabody, William M. Sloane, Bishops Edward G. Andrews and Alexander Mackay-Smith, James C. Carter, William E. Dodge, the Reverend Father A. P. Doyle, Harvard president Charles W. Eliot, the Reverend Washington Gladden, Dr. Elgin R. L. Gould, the Reverend W. R. Huntington, Mayor Seth Low, and Dr. William H. Welch, among others.

The committee established four subcommittees to investigate "impartial facts" concerning the "physiological, legislative, ethical, and economic aspects of the drink question." The Committee of Fifty published information based upon the subcommittees' reports over a ten-year period. Other than for four members, the membership of the committee was stable for the twelve years of its existence. Members were unpaid, and the studies were supported by private individuals and committee members.

The legislation subcommittee, under the direction of Eliot, Low, and Carter, examined the social and political effects of liquor legislation in several states and cities with varying temperance reform laws. Political entities investigated included the state of Maine, where prohibitory legislation had existed since 1851, Boston under local option, Pennsylvania under a licensing system, and South Carolina with its innovative dispensary, a state monopoly retailer. The effects of the Missouri law in the city of Saint Louis, the operation of Iowa's and Indiana's legislation, and the Ohio law, in which a tax was levied on liquor sellers, were also studied. The first of the series of monographs emanating from the Committee of Fifty, *The Liquor Problem in Its Legislative Aspects* (1897), was based upon the laws of the eight states studied. A second edition was published in 1898, in which a chapter was added on the New York liquor laws and legislation of other states.

The economic subcommittee published *Economic Aspects of the Liquor Problem* (1899) under the direction of Farnham. This volume dealt with the relationship of the liquor traffic to poverty, pauperism, crime, child neglect, minority groups, and other topics. The committee concluded that "37 percent of paupers in almshouses were there because of their own or others' intemperance." It reported that 49 percent of criminal cases, 25 percent of poverty, and 45 percent of child neglect cases coming to the attention of charity organizations were attributed to intemperance. The report recognized the liquor traffic as a prevailing cause of many social problems.

The subcommittee on the physiological aspects of alcohol was under the direction of Atwater, Billings, Bowditch, Chittenden, and Welch. In 1894, it began a series of investigations concerning the effects of alcohol on animals. Reports from these studies began to be published in scientific journals in the late 1890s. The committee published *Physiological Aspects of the Liquor Problem* (1903) in two volumes. This report discussed public school instruction regarding the physiological action of alcohol, the influence of alcohol upon digestion, the use of alcoholic drinks among "brain workers," the relationship of drink habits to insanity, the influence of alcohol on growth and development, and the pharmacological action and nutritive value of alcohol. The report estimated that 20 percent of the population were abstainers, 50 percent occasional drinkers, and 25 percent regular but moderate drinkers. The committee concluded that alcohol was considered useless in preventing infectious or contagious diseases and was most likely harmful to young people, as they tended to drink to excess. It criticized STI in the public schools as based upon inaccurate information.

Under the direction of Peabody, Gould, and Sloane, the ethics committee published *Substitutes for the Saloon* (1901). This work acknowledged that the saloon was a workingman's "club." It satisfied a twofold thirst—"intoxicating liquor" and the need for fellowship and recreation. The saloon provided entertainment, job tips, newspapers, card tables, and a "free lunch." Saloons provided meeting space for labor unions and lodges and sometimes served as polling places. It was estimated that in Boston over 50 percent of male inhabitants daily visited a saloon. The report recommend that night schools, public lectures, physical activity, free public libraries, and education classes connected with the YMCA, churches, and other organizations be instituted as alternative "wholesome activities" to saloons.

In its summary report volume, *The Liquor Problem: A Summary of Investigations* (1905), the committee noted that among "those whose drinking is limited to one or two glasses of wine at dinner or of beer at the end of the day, no especial effect upon the health seems to be observed either by themselves or by their physicians" (Peabody et al. 1905: 20). The summary volume abstracted the most important findings from the other reports. The Committee of Fifty dissolved 6 June 1905, its work being completed. Although the committee had little impact at the time, after the repeal of National Prohibition, its policy recommendations played an influential part in the shaping of modern American alcohol control systems.

Ruth Clifford Engs

See also: Hunt, Mary Hannah Hanchett; Scientific Temperance Federation

References

Atwater, Wilbur D., et al. *Physiological Aspects of the Liquor Problem.* Boston: Houghton Mifflin, 1903.

Calkins, Raymond. *Substitutes for the Saloon.* Boston: Houghton Mifflin, 1901.

Cherrington, Ernest Hurst, et al., eds. *Standard Encyclopedia of the Alcohol Problem,* 6 vols. 2: 663–664. Westerville, OH: American Issue Publishing, 1924–1930.

Eliot, Charles W. "A Study of American Liquor Laws" in *Atlantic Monthly.* 79 (January–June 1897): 177–187.

Engs, Ruth Clifford. *Historical Dictionary of the Progressive Era's Health Reform Movement.* Westport, CT: Greenwood, 2002: xxx.

Koren, John. *Economic Aspects of the Liquor Problem.* Boston: Houghton Mifflin, 1899.

Levine, Harry Gene. "The Committee of Fifty and the Origins of Alcohol Control" in *Journal of Drug Issues.* 13 (Winter 1983): 95–116.

Peabody, Francis, et al., eds. *The Liquor Problem: A Summary of Investigations.* New York: Committee of Fifty, 1905.

Timberlake, James H. *Prohibition and the Progressive Movement, 1900–1920.* Cambridge: Harvard University Press, 1963.

Wines, Frederick H., and John Koren. *The Liquor Problem in Its Legislative Aspects.* Boston: Houghton Mifflin, 1897.

Confucianism

Confucianism is a system of ethical and moral beliefs and practices based on the teachings of the Chinese scholar Confucius (551–479 B.C.E.). It has maintained an important place for the use of alcohol beverages in its traditional rituals. The use of alcohol has been significant and widespread in both the institutional and diffuse forms of Confucianism in China, and continues to influence Chinese drinking customs today.

History and State Rites

Alcohol has been a key element in state ritual and sacrifice, a primary aspect of institutional Confucianism since the Shang dynasty (ca. 1500–1050 B.C.E.). It has also been an important element in the rites of passage and social gatherings and events, helping nurture the bonds between families, friends, and associates that mark Confucianism's more diffuse aspects. Although the Chinese word for alcohol, *jiu,* is usually translated as "wine," various forms of alcoholic beverages were developed and used for all manner of occasions.

Although known in the West by the name of its key interpreter, the Confucian tradition long predates the man Confucius, who drew from the legacy and records of exemplary figures from the golden age of antiquity. Confucius considered himself to be a transmitter of tradition rather than an innovator. The ancient texts revered by Confucius and his followers record the story of Yi Di, a servant in the legendary Xia dynasty (twenty-first century B.C.E.) who ate a dish of cooked grain that had fermented, finding it delicious and producing a delightful effect. It was then offered to the king who, becoming tipsy, remarked that there would be those who would lose the country on account of this substance, and banned it. Indeed, the cause attributed to the fall of the last Shang king included a forest of meat and lake of wine, where 3,000 could drink like cattle at one time.

These morality tales, however, were not interpreted so much as interdictions against alcohol as they were examples of wise and of wayward rulers. Wine was an important part of official sacrifices that were vital to the well-being of the state. The Shang is famous for the elaborate bronze vessels cast for such ceremonies. Alcohol was used as offerings to heaven, earth, and to denizens of the spirit world, especially gods and ancestors. Over time, these rituals were replaced by the emperor's sacrifices to heaven and earth. Wine continued to be a key element in these sacrifices that continued until the demise of imperial China in 1911.

Alcohol in Rites of Passage and Celebrations

Alcohol has also been a vital element in the rites of passage of ordinary Chinese. These rituals have remained relatively constant through the centuries and are still performed today in many places. Confucianism stresses the importance of filial piety, the obedient and dutiful service to one's parents for males, and parents and parents-in-law for females. The most significant rites demonstrating filial behavior were funerals and marriages. Funerals guarantee that the deceased spirit will be content and well cared for in the afterlife. Weddings ensure the continuation of the family line. Alcohol is used at funerals as an oblation to the earth as well as an offering to the deceased. After burial, alcohol is offered on the ancestral altar in the home, which holds the spirit tablets of those from recent generations, especially on important days such as death day anniversaries and holidays. Alcohol is also offered in the ancestral halls of the more distant dead of the clan. At weddings, alcohol is an important part of the wedding banquet. In a centuries-old practice, parents put wine in earthen jars at the birth of a daughter and open them only at her wedding. The wine is called *nuer hong* or "daughter's red," referring to the color of a traditional Chinese wedding gown. Traditionally, the couple shared a special joined nuptial cup to cement the pledge of the bride and groom, and the bride poured wine for her parents-in-law as part of the rite to be presented to them.

Confucianism stresses the importance of nurturing social bonds, which is frequently done in the context of food and drink. Toasting is important at banquets, although the actual amount of alcohol consumed may be small. Traditions from the past included reciting or composing poetry while drinking, a favorite pastime of the educated who learned and appreciated literature as a part of their Confucian training. Other drinking activities included telling jokes and riddles, singing, and other games, which were to contribute to an enjoyable and relaxed atmosphere of closeness and camaraderie.

Although not strictly speaking Confucian, the seasonal festivals of Chinese religion express the Confucian values that have become diffuse in Chinese culture. At Chinese New Year, the most important holiday of the year, there are toasts for the New Year, health, and prosperity, and notably for the longevity of family elders. Wine offerings are made to ancestors at this time. Special drinks are enjoyed at the Lantern festival, the last day of New Year festivities. Alcohol is used medicinally at the Double Five festival, which falls at midsummer and the season of epidemics; it is enjoyed at the Mid-Autumn festival during moonviewing parties that feature family reunions and storytelling. A festival more widely observed in the past, the Double Nine, includes drinking chrysanthemum wine and hikes in the hills. All of these festivals use alcohol as an element that brings happy, relaxed times to the gathering of family and friends.

In addition to ritual and social life, alcohol has played an important role as medicine in Chinese culture. It is considered a "yang" or heating element, and Chinese medical texts provide lists of the benefits to be enjoyed by specific types of alcohol, including relief of rheumatism, mental well-being, aid to digestion and appetite, and the increase of blood. A special drink made of wine and other ingredients is prepared for postpartum mothers to fortify them and help increase their blood supply after giving birth.

It is said in the *Analects* that while Confucius enjoyed wine, he never became bewildered by it. In the Confucian tradition, there is no prescribed limit to the quantity of alcohol one might consume. However, alcohol is typically consumed with others and while eating. Confucianism stresses the importance of maintaining respectability, thus drunkenness means a loss of social status. In drinking games, the winner is generally the one who keeps a clear head. Consumption of alcohol is to provide health benefits and pleasant socialization, one part of creating a harmonious group, a primary goal of the Confucianism.

Jennifer Oldstone-Moore

See also: China; Daoism

References

Chen, Tien Chi, Michael Tao, and Guangseng Cheng. "Perspectives on Alcoholic Beverages in China," in *Asian Foods: Science and Technology,* edited by Catharina Ang, KeShun Liu, and Yaowen Huang, 383–408. Lancaster, PA: Technomic Publishing, 1999.

Ebrey, Patricia B., ed. and trans. *Chu Hsi's Family Rituals: A Twelfth-Century Chinese Manual for the Performance of Cappings, Weddings, Funerals, and Ancestral Rites.* Translated, with annotations and introduction. Princeton, NJ: Princeton University Press, 1991.

Xiao, Jiacheng. "China" in *International Handbook on Alcohol and Culture,* edited by Dwight B. Heath, 42–50. Westport, CT: Greenwood, 1995.

Congressional Temperance Society (CTS)

The Congressional Temperance Society (CTS) was an unofficial body of the nineteenth-century United States Congress devoted to supporting temperance. The CTS's impact was largely symbolic, and its existence sporadic, over the course of fifty years. Its purposes included reforming the drinking behavior of members within Congress and serving as an example to other public bodies. The CTS's initial establishment, on 26 February 1833, coincided with the national day of meeting sponsored by the American Temperance Society (ATS) and was clearly tied to the latter group's efforts at making temperance reform a national priority. In early February, ATS corresponding-secretary Justin Edwards addressed both houses of Congress. Later in the month, he helped lead a public meeting in the House chamber during which elected and appointed officials spoke on behalf of the cause. The meeting "produced a highly salutary effect," according to the later report of the ATS, and many of the congressional speeches were reprinted in pamphlets distributed as temperance literature throughout the country.

On founding day, twenty-five public officials including senators and congressmen from Pennsylvania, Massachusetts, Tennessee, New Jersey, and Indiana pledged to abstain from "ardent spirits" (distilled alcohol) and issued resolutions setting forth, among other things, that "the manufacture of, and traffic in ardent spirit ought to be discountenanced and abandoned, as incompatible with the obligations of social and moral duty." Beyond the enumeration of principles, however, no specific legislative proposals were set forth. Secretary of War Lewis Cass, whose credentials included banning the issue of alcohol rations in the army, assumed the CTS presidency. The participation of members of Congress at this time—during the last days of the Twenty-second Congress and in the midst of the Nullification Crisis—certainly testified to the growing presence of temperance in American public debate. Conversely, establishment of the CTS provided temperance advocates with the imprimatur of official sanction. Other than speechifying and the establishment of an organizational framework, however, the only immediate result of the society's creation was the founding of a similar group by the Massachusetts legislature.

The 1834 annual meeting of the CTS was well attended, but thereafter, participation appears to have slackened. The society was rejuvenated in 1842, when it reorganized on the basis of total abstinence from all alcoholic beverages. Approximately eighty congressmen attended the second founding and elected Representative George N. Briggs (Massachusetts) president. In the words of Senator T. F. Marshall (Kentucky), who participated in the second inaugural public meeting, "Mr. President, the old Congressional Temperance Society has died of intemperance, holding the pledge in one hand and the champagne-bottle in the other." As was the case previously, the new CTS reflected ongoing temperance agitation. Marshall's statement expressed the prevailing sentiment among temperance advocates that abstaining from ardent spirits alone had failed to curb the vice of drinking, and in fact had caused many to fall into greater ruin. Total abstinence was the only answer. The guiding agencies this time were the short-lived, working-class Washingtonian movement and the Sons of Temperance.

After a prolonged hibernation, the CTS reappeared following the Civil War. The political forces influencing temperance agitation had changed significantly from those of the antebellum period. Taxation of alcoholic beverages, beginning with the Internal Revenue Act of 1862, affected the relationship between government and liquor interests. The creation of national lobby groups such as the United States Brewers' Association presented another serious challenge to temperance advocates. By 1868, organizations including the Order of Good Templars were abandoning their nonpartisan stance to advocate direct political action, leading to the founding of the Prohibition Party in 1869. These new political currents, and the growing partisan nature of the temperance cause, undermined whatever moral influence the prewar CTS may have exercised. Nonetheless, in the midst of congressional preparations to impeach President Andrew Johnson, Senator Henry Wilson (Massachusetts) established the CTS for a third time on 17 February 1867. Speaker of the House Schuyler Colfax assumed the presidency. Interest appears to have been short-lived. In 1876, following the Whiskey Ring scandal and the growing list of petitions presented to Congress calling for prohibitory legislation and a commission of inquiry into the effects of the "liquor traffic," the society was revived for a fourth time. In its last incarnation, the CTS continued on into the 1880s, with a membership drawn increasingly from the ranks of "dry" Republicans.

C. Wyatt Evans

See also: American Temperance Society (ATS); Edwards, Justin; Prohibition Party (United States); Washingtonians

References

"A Century of Lawmaking for a New Nation: U.S. Congressional Documents and Debates, 1774–1873." Library of Congress website containing facsimiles of congressional records for the period. http://memory.loc.gov/ammem/amlaw/lawhome.html [20 July 2002].

Cherrington, Ernest H. *The Evolution of Prohibition in the United States of America.* Westerville, OH: American Issue Press, 1920.

Fehlandt, August F. *A Century of Drink Reform in the United States.* Cincinnati: Jennings and Graham; New York: Eaton and Mains, 1904.

One Hundred Years of Temperance: A Memorial Volume of the Centennial Temperance Conference. New York: National Temperance Society & Publishing House, 1886.

Permanent Temperance Documents of the American Temperance Society, vol. 1. New York: Arno Press, 1972 [1835].

Sprunger, Keith L. "Cold Water Congressmen: The Congressional Temperance Society before the Civil War" in *Historian.* 27, no. 4 (1965): 498–515.

Conservative Party (United Kingdom)

In Britain, the Conservative Party and the alcohol drink trade became close allies for about thirty years, from the 1880s through the general elections of 1910. In part, this was the result of a general shift of commercial and industrial entrepreneurs out of the Liberal Party into the Conservative Party, a shift hurried by the Irish home rule controversy. Often the Liberal Unionist Party provided a transition between membership in the Liberal and Conservative Parties. In part, drink trade support for the Conservatives (called the Unionists during much of this period) was a defensive response to the growing identification of the Liberals with advanced temperance reformers who supported local referendums for prohibition and opposed financial compensation for the owners of licensed property who suffered because of a change in public policy. In 1888 and 1890, Conservative proposals in favor of compensation helped polarize temperance reform on partisan lines. There were many moderate temperance reformers in the Conservative and Liberal Unionist Parties, so the alliance between these parties and the drink trade always had its tensions and limits. Although some historians describe this alliance as having begun in the 1870s or even earlier, there were many Liberal brewers and distillers, as well as local publicans, well into the 1880s. By the eve of the first world war, the drink question was fading as a major division between the Conservative and Liberal Parties. Ironically, it was coalition government that helped make the war years and postwar reconstruction dangerous for the drink trade.

In a speech at Newport prior to the general election of 1885, the Conservative leader Lord Salisbury insisted that when a licensing authority refused to renew licenses for reasons other than misconduct, the license holders had a right to financial compensation. In 1888 and 1890, the Conservative government that he headed attempted to enact legislation that included a statutory right to compensation. The men behind the proposals, George Goschen, the Liberal Unionist chancellor of the exchequer, and C. T. Ritchie, the Conservative president of the local government board, wanted to reduce the number of licensed premises and considered compensation necessary as a prerequisite. Their proposals failed, largely because the projected reduction in licensed premises was not enough for temperance reformers to accept the creation of a statutory right to compensation.

In the 1890s, many Tories and Liberal Unionists favored a middle way between the advanced temperance reformers and the drink trade. Lord Randolph Churchill drafted the first of the several compromise schemes that abounded in the 1890s. The bills of the Manchester and Westminster licensing reform committees and of the Church of England Temperance Society (CETS) represent the approach to compromise most characteristic of the moderate reformers: statutory reduction in the number of licensed premises in proportion to the local population. In the mid-1890s, a wealthy Conservative shipbuilder, Arnold F. Hills, tried to unite advanced and moderate reformers behind a consensus bill. Under pressure from the Archbishop of Canterbury and other moderate reformers, the Salisbury ministry created a Royal Commission on Liquor Licensing Laws in 1896. The government ignored the majority and minority reports that the royal commission presented in 1899. Despite serious disagreements, both reports had agreed that there should be a substantial reduction in the number of licensed premises. In retrospect, it was the publication of the reports of the royal commission and the minutes of evidence that preceded them that created the climate of opinion that eventually forced a Unionist government to sponsor a major licensing bill.

In 1903, the prolonged stalemate over major licensing reform came to an end. The licensing justices enjoyed great discretionary powers, seldom exercised but repeatedly reaffirmed by the courts. When licensing committees began to refuse to renew large numbers of licenses in order to reduce the number of public houses, the old status quo broke down without any new legislation. The magisterial reduction movement threatened to do, in a few years, what the organized temperance movement had failed to achieve in several generations of agitation: close large numbers of licensed premises and cripple the trade financially. It was the drink trade rather than the temperance party that had to appeal for legislation. The trade was relatively isolated. In the battle against local veto, it could rally the support of working-class electors who considered prohibition as class legislation, an affront to their liberties as Englishmen. When the justices winnowed the numbers of licensed premises, the public answered the trade's cry of confiscation with a yawn. The justices embodied a tradition of responsible, conservative-minded paternalism unlike the faddist radicalism of the prohibitionists. In addition, A. J. Balfour's government was tottering, the Unionist Party torn by the emotional issue of tariff reform.

The licensing crisis of 1903 to 1904 illustrated the strengths and weaknesses of the trade alliance with the Unionist Party. It was easier to get the Unionist leadership to stop hostile legislation than to sponsor a friendly bill. Despite frantic trade appeals for help, the government initially did nothing. After much delay, Balfour offered a bill that he hoped both moderate reformers and the drink trade could accept. The trade preferred a bill that would limit the discretionary authority of the licensing magistrates, but Balfour decided that such a break with tradition would be too controversial. The bill that he proposed let licensing justices in England and Wales retain their traditional discretionary authority to refuse to renew licenses provided that compensation was paid. Quarter Sessions were given the discretionary power to impose a levy on the trade to provide the money. As the bill set a maximum limit to the levy, the pace of reduction was necessarily restrained. As part of the price the trade was to pay for its security, the bill eliminated the right that pre-1869 beerhouses previously had to renewal and required that any new public houses pay a large fee for the monopoly value acquired through licensed status. Although advanced temperance reformers and the Liberals bitterly opposed Balfour's bill, the Conservative victory was an expensive one for the drink trade.

In contrast to the reluctance of a Conservative government to legislate on behalf of the drink trade, the Conservative opposition had little hesitation in fighting a Liberal government's licensing bill in 1908. Instead of offering a compromise, the Conservative leadership killed the bill in the House of Lords. Although the Liberals retaliated in the budget of 1909 with higher drink taxes, the licensing bill of 1908 was the last instance of a partisan fight over the laws regulating the sale of alcoholic drink.

David M. Fahey

See also: Church of England Temperance Society (CETS); Hills, Arnold Frank; Liberal Party (United Kingdom); Pubs and Beerhouses (United Kingdom)

References

Fahey, David M. "Brewers, Publicans, and Working-Class Drinkers: Pressure Group Politics in Late Victorian and Edwardian England" in *Histoire sociale.* 3 (1980): 85–103.

Greenaway, John R. "Bishops, Brewers and the Liquor Question in England, 1880–1914" in *Historical Magazine of the Protestant Episcopal Church.* 53 (1984): 61–75.

———. *Drink and British Politics since 1830: A Study in Policy-Making.* Basingstoke, UK, and New York: Palgrave Macmillan, 2003.

Gutzke, David W. *Protecting the Pub: Brewers and Publicans against Temperance.* Woodbridge, Suffolk: Boydell for the Royal Historical Society; Wolfeboro, NH: Boydell & Brewer, 1989.

———. "Rhetoric and Reality: The Political Influence of British Brewers, 1832–1914" in *Parliamentary History.* 9 (1990): 71–115.

Mathias, Peter. "The Brewing Industry, Temperance and Politics" in *Historical Journal.* 1 (1958): 97–114.

Coors, Adolph, Brewing Company

The Adolph Coors Brewing Company, a regional brewery of modest size for most of its history, grew rapidly during the late twentieth century to international stature. The company was established in 1873 in Golden, Colorado, by Adolph Coors and Jacob Schuler. Adolph Coors was born in Barmen, Prussia (now Wuppertal, Germany), in 1847. At age fourteen, he became a brewer's apprentice in Dortmund. In 1868, he emigrated to Baltimore and soon thereafter to Chicago. After a year in Chicago, he worked with John Stenger at his brewery in Napierville, Illinois, until 1872. He moved to Denver, bought a partnership in a bottling plant, and was soon its sole owner. In 1873, Coors and Schuler opened the Golden Brewery in Golden, Colorado. Schuler put up most of the money, and Coors provided the brewing knowledge. The business thrived, and by 1880 Coors was able to buy out Schuler and become the sole proprietor of Adolph Coors Golden Brewery. During the next decade, Coors's production increased from 3,500 to 17,600 barrels annually, and the brewery continued to prosper until Colorado adopted prohibition in 1916.

Adolph Coors and his sons had already established a porcelain business in Golden, which did well during Prohibition with a broad range of scientific and consumer products. Coors Porcelain Products continues today as part of the Adolph Coors Company, the holding company for the family's business interests. The firm also produced several food products, including malted milk and a near beer, Mannah. The malted milk business continued until 1955. Adolph died in 1929 in a fall from a hotel window in Virginia Beach, Virginia, and was succeeded by his son Adolph Jr. The company returned to beer production after repeal and produced approximately 136,000 barrels the first year. The company also expanded its distribution into eleven western states. During World War II, half of the beer Coors produced went to the military. By 1945, the brewery in Golden produced 300,000 barrels.

During the decade after the war, production increased steadily, exceeding 1 million barrels in 1955. Leadership passed to a third generation, led by Adolph Coors III. After his murder by a kidnapper in 1960, his brothers William K. (Bill) and Joseph Coors took over the firm. In 1959, Coors pioneered the development of aluminum cans. Although increasing production and developing new packaging, Coors was very conservative about its brewing methods. Coors beer was not pasteurized, but cold filtered and shipped in specially insulated rail cars and trucks. The single label, Original Coors, its special handling, and limited availability led to a mystique attaching to Coors. When President Gerald Ford was reported to transport several cases back to the White House after visits to Colorado, the mystique grew. The middle-sized regional brewer attracted national attention.

Coors began to expand both its distribution area and its product line in the late 1970s. In 1978, Coors Light was introduced and is now the brewery's largest-selling label. In 1981, Coors products became available east of the Mississippi River for the first time, and by 1991 Coors products were available in all fifty states. As part of this expansion, Coors built a packaging plant in the Shenandoah Valley of Virginia in 1985 and acquired a brewery in Memphis in 1990. As other national brewers did, Coors responded to the rising interest in craft brewing by introducing a line of Blue Moon specialty beers along with Killian's Irish Red and Killian's Irish Honey beers to compete with imports. Keystone and Keystone Light were introduced for the lower-priced market, Coors NA for the nonalcoholic beer niche, and Zima for the new flavored-malt-beverage market. In 1990, Coors ranked third in the country in production, a position it has held since. In December 2001, Coors acquired the Carling group of beers from Belgian brewer Interbrew, making Coors the second largest brewer in Britain, and its products are available in more than thirty countries around the world.

During its expansion from regional to national and, ultimately, international brewer, Coors was involved in a great deal of controversy surrounding the politics of members of the family and its labor policies. Critics charged that the firm was antiunion and supported extreme conservative groups that opposed gay rights and civil rights for African Americans. Critics pointed to the family's role in founding and funding the Heritage Foundation. Several groups organized boycotts of Coors's products from the mid-1960s to the early 1980s. Under the leadership of Peter Coors, the fourth generation of the family to be involved in the business, the company has been recognized for its support of the environment and a broad array of cultural and community events. Peter Coors was named vice chairman and chief executive officer for Coors Brewing Company in 1993. In May 2000, he was named chairman of Coors Brewing Company and president and chief executive officer of Adolph Coors Company. In 2002, *Fortune* listed Coors as one of "America's Most Admired Corporations."

Although the Coors family still controls the voting stock in the company, and Peter Coors serves as chief executive officer, Leo Kiely has served as president and chief operating officer since 1993. Coors's brewing production has exceeded 20 million barrels in recent years. Its Golden, Colorado, brewery is the largest-capacity brewery in the world.

William H. Mulligan Jr.

See also: Carling Brewery

References

Banham, Russ. *Coors: A Rocky Mountain Legend.* Lyme, CT: Greenwich Publishing Group, 1998.

Baron, Stanley. *Brewed in America: The History of Beer and Ale in the United States.* Boston: Little, Brown, 1962.

Baum, Dan. *Citizen Coors: A Grand Family Saga of Business, Politics, and Beer.* New York: HarperCollins, 1999.

Greer, Douglas F. "The Causes and Consequences of Concentration in the US Brewing Industry" in *Quarterly Review of Economics and Business.* 21, no. 4 (1981): 87–106.

Kostka, William. *The Pre-Prohibition History of Adolph Coors Company 1873–1933.* Golden, CO: Adolph Coors, 1973.

McGahan, A. M. "The Emergence of the National Brewing Oligopoly: Competition in the American Market, 1933–58" in *Business History Review.* 65, no. 2 (1991): 229–284.

"Where Companies Rank in Their Industries" in *Fortune.* 4 March 2002: 77–80.

Corby Distilleries Limited

Corby Distilleries Limited is the largest combined distiller and distributor of imported spirits, wines, and brandies in Canada. Corby was founded by Henry Corby, a baker, who, at age twenty-six, emigrated from his native England to Belleville, Ontario, Canada, in 1832. Corby's early years in Canada were spent as a baker and a general storekeeper. In the late 1830s, he began shipping grain along the Lake Ontario–St. Lawrence River waterway. This pursuit schooled Corby in the economics of cereals agriculture. In 1855, he purchased a gristmill on the Moira River, four miles north of Belleville, to which he added a distillery four years later, in order to process coarse and waste grains into marketable product. Although ancillary to the mill, Corby's distillery earned a local reputation for quality whiskey. As the business grew, Corby's sons, Henry Jr., George, and Edward, joined the enterprise. The Corbys subsequently diversified into wine and liquor importing. Henry Corby died on 25 October 1881, but prior to his passing, he sold the entire business to his son, Henry Jr., for $10,000. In commemoration of the elder Corby, the workers' village that had developed around the distillery was officially named Corbyville.

Henry Corby Jr. carried the distillery in new directions. Crucially, he expanded the market for Corby whiskey throughout eastern Ontario, Montreal, western Quebec, and parts of New York State. Corby reached consumers in these targeted areas by cultivating a network of retail agents, and thanks to such regional expansion, he weathered the vagaries of local-option prohibition under the Canada Temperance Act during the 1880s. Corby's geographic sales strategy was informed by Corbyville's location in eastern Ontario and by the dominance that three other Ontario distilleries, Gooderham and Worts, Seagram, and Walker, held over the market in central and western Ontario. In an age when railway transport had become the industry standard, he abandoned heavy stoneware jugs, which added unnecessarily to freight charges, in favor of lighter glass bottles. Bottles also permitted greater branding opportunities through label lithography. Corby's overall business plan returned remarkable dividends. In the revenue year ending 30 June 1881, the Corby distillery produced 65,453 imperial gallons of proof whiskey, or around 2 percent of all spirits manufactured in Canada. Not quite twenty years later, Corby produced 251,821 imperial gallons of proof whiskey, an absolute increase of nearly 400 percent. This represented a fivefold jump to 10 percent of total Canadian spirits production. Shortly after the turn of the century, Corby incorporated as the H. Corby Distillery Limited.

In 1905, Henry Corby Jr. sold the H. Corby Distillery Limited to Mortimer Davis, a Montreal-based tobacco tycoon, for a reported $1 million. Apart from a fire interruption in 1907, Davis enjoyed good sales until the first world war, when wartime regulations forbade the use of grain for whiskey manufacture. Even so, Davis profited from producing industrial alcohol for the war effort. At war's end, the market for industrial alcohol shrank dramatically, and Davis, like other provincial distillers, was left to contend with province-wide prohibition under the Ontario Temperance Act of 1916. Although Quebec sales generated some cash flow, the closure of Ontario's bars and liquor stores threatened profitability. Sales plunged to around 500 gallons per month. Nevertheless, the opportunistic Davis, who enjoyed other sources of income, acquired the Wiser distillery in Prescott, Ontario, which, along with his Corby distillery, he operated through the Canadian Industrial Alcohol Company Limited, a holding company that he incorporated in 1918. Production was eventually consolidated at Corbyville. In 1921, Davis hired Harold C. "Harry" Hatch, a former liquor merchant, as his sales manager. The hiring was no accident, since Hatch had the requisite connections along the Lake Ontario–St. Lawrence River waterway to reach a Prohibition-locked United States. Unlike the Volstead Act, the Ontario Temperance Act only outlawed the sale of beverage alcohol and not its manufacture or possession, so the Corbyville distillery could remain legally open. Under Hatch and his web of rumrunners, and by virtue of transactions technically recorded outside provincial jurisdiction, sales of Davis's whiskey increased a hundredfold. Having become wealthy through a commission arrangement with Davis, Hatch left Corby in 1923 and, with others, acquired the venerable Ontario distillers Hiram Walker and Gooderham and Worts.

With the end of Prohibition in Ontario (1927) and the United States (1933), along with the effects of the Great Depression, the Corby distillery suffered a reversal in fortune. During the 1930s, Harry Hatch acquired a majority of shares in Davis's Canadian Industrial Alcohol Company and thus the rights to Corby and Wiser. The second world war saw a return to industrial alcohol production at Corbyville. After 1945, the distillery greatly benefited from Canada's postwar economic and population boom. Indeed, sales annually increased by as much as 10 percent in some years during the 1950s and 1960s. In 1969, the company was reincorporated under its current name, Corby Distilleries Limited. Eight years later, Corby acquired Meagher's distillery in Montreal. Growth continued until 1981, when Canada's distilling sector experienced a two-decade slide, owing to an older generation that reduced its alcohol consumption, a younger generation that was less likely to drink spirits, and rising taxation, which made spirits an expensive consumer alternative.

As sales dropped, Corby executed an acquisitions strategy to stem losses in market share. Notably, McGuinness Distillers was acquired in 1987. Corby Distillers also bought the Canadian rights to a number of foreign liqueurs, white spirits, wines, and wine coolers, and it flirted with ownership of Toronto's Upper Canada Brewing Company from 1991 to 1994. Much of this acquisitions program was facilitated by Allied Lyons PLC (now Allied Domecq), which acquired Corby by purchasing Corby's parent company, Hiram Walker–Gooderham and Worts Limited, in 1987. In 1991, the Corbyville plant was closed. Today, Corby Distillers Limited is headquartered in Toronto and directly owns a distillery in Montreal. Corby's production-distribution portfolio accounts for 27 percent of the Canadian spirits market and includes Corby's Royal Reserve Whisky, Wiser's De Luxe Whisky, Ballantine's Scotch, Polar Ice Vodka, Kahlúa, Tia Maria, Beefeater Dry Gin, Courvoisier Cognac, and several Allied Domecq brands.

Glen C. Phillips

See also: Gooderham and Worts Distillery; Hiram Walker; Provincial Prohibition (Canada); Whiskies; Wiser Distillery

References

Belleville, Ontario Public Library. Hastings County Historical Society Archives, Henry Corby Files.

Calnan, David M. "Henry Corby" in *Dictionary of Canadian Biography,* vol. 11: *1881–1890.* Toronto: University of Toronto Press, 1982.

Corby's Distilleries Limited. *Annual Report, 2001.*

Mote, Dave. "Corby Distilleries Limited" in *International Directory of Company Histories,* vol. 14. Chicago: St. James Press, 1996.

Rannie, W. F. *Canadian Whisky: The Product and the Industry.* Lincoln, Ontario: W. F. Rannie, 1976.

Courage Brewery

Barclay Perkins and Courage were neighboring brewers on the south bank of the Thames in London from the 1780s until they merged in 1955. For most of this period, Barclay Perkins was the bigger concern, but by the time of the merger, the companies were of similar size, both holding over 1,000 tied houses. Major acquisitions by the new company saw it spread out from London and southeast England over the next fifteen years to become one of the "big six" national brewers. The company became part of a conglomerate when taken over by Imperial Tobacco in 1972. It subsequently passed through other hands before, in some financial difficulty and having shed its pubs, it was sold by the Australian group Elders IXL to Scottish and Newcastle Breweries (S&N) in 1995. This move, first mooted over two decades earlier, supplanted Bass as the United Kingdom's biggest brewer and created a company with approaching 30 percent of the UK market.

John Courage, a native of Aberdeen, bought a small brewery in Horselydown, Southwark, in 1787. Primarily an ale brewery, it remained in the lower ranks of London's brewers until favored by the mid-nineteenth-century swing from porter to mild. Between 1830 and 1888, when the firm was incorporated, annual output increased from about 15,000 hectoliters (400,000 U.S. gallons) to nearly 500,000 hectoliters (13,000,000 U.S. gallons). Courage was unable to produce acceptable pale ale with soft London water and met the increasing demand for this beer by contracting out production to better-placed brewers from 1872, before buying a pale ale brewery in Alton, Hampshire, in 1903. Like other London brewers, the company suffered as property values fell and the burden of loans to publicans mounted in the early years of the last century. Unlike some less prudent concerns, Courage avoided writing down capital, but dividends dropped to 1 percent between 1910 and 1913. Courage acquired five brewing companies between 1923 and 1943, all in southern England.

The origins of the firm known as Barclay, Perkins and Company from 1785 go back to 1616 when a brew house was built adjacent to the Globe Theatre. The small, prosperous concern was purchased in 1729 by Ralph Thrale, brewery manager and nephew of the late owner. Thrales grew to equal Trumans as London's greatest porter brewers in 1750 but experienced financial problems thereafter as Ralph's son Henry overstretched the business. The death of Henry in 1781 and subsequent sale of the brewery by his widow, the talented Hester, led family friend and confidante Samuel Johnson to make his famous remark that purchase provided "the potentiality of growing rich beyond the dreams of avarice." The brewery came under the control of Robert Barclay, a banker, and John Perkins, its former manager, and it again began to outstrip its rivals. Every year between 1809 and 1853, it had the greatest output of any brewery in London. Production never dropped below 0.5 million hectoliters (13 million U.S. gallons) per year between 1830 and the start of the first world war, by which time the company, which was incorporated in 1896, had slipped down the rankings, but it still brewed close to 1 million hectoliters (26.4 million U.S. gallons). Even this impressive output could not save the company from liquidity problems, primarily due to publicans' bad debts. Profits plummeted, dividends were passed between 1909 and 1919, and capital severely written down in 1911. The company embraced the reformed pub movement in the interwar period. In 1930, it built the largest of all such establishments, the Downham Tavern, on a new housing estate. The massive pub initially had waiter service in lounges rather than bars and came complete with an entertainment hall that staged theatrical performances and seated some 800 people around tables. Since the time of Henry Thrale, the company had enjoyed some overseas trade, notably with Imperial Russian Stout. This developed in the twentieth century with production of lager from 1922, both for export to the empire and for the home market, and construction of a brewery in the Sudan in the early 1950s. But Barclay, Perkins and Company's primary market, like that of Courage, remained in London and the South East.

The formation of Courage and Barclay in 1955 created a company with some 2,500 tied houses. Acquisitions of H and G Simmonds of Reading in 1960, Bristol Brewery Georges and Company in 1961, and the Yorkshire brewers John Smiths in 1970 extended the company's base geographically and increased the tied estate to over 6,000 and the breweries to six. Courage, Barclay and Simmonds, as it was then known, was a founding member of the initially successful Harp Lager consortium in 1961 and, with Guinness, built a new lager brewery at Alton in 1963, the first totally new brewery in Britain since the 1930s. An ill-conceived brewing venture in Australia was begun in the late 1960s and humiliatingly abandoned in 1978. An attempted synergistic merger with S&N in 1972, which would have created a truly national company, fell through when directors of the two companies failed to agree on terms. In the same year, Courage and Company (the name since 1970) was taken over by Imperial Tobacco for £320 million. Brewing and packaging ceased in Southwark in 1981 as the company, now renamed Imperial Brewing and Leisure, diversified into roadside catering chains and followed the industry pattern of rationalization. Three other breweries were closed by 1984, and a new brewery built near Reading. By 1985, Courage's output was the lowest of the big six brewers. When Imperial was acquired by Hanson Trust in 1986, the brewing arm was promptly sold for £1.4 billion to Elders IXL, who had recently failed in a bid to take over Allied-Lyons. Elders attempted to take over S&N in 1988, but the move was blocked by the United Kingdom government as not in the public interest after strenuous opposition from the Scots. In 1991, following the Beer Orders, pubs were swapped for breweries; Grand Metropolitan and Courage became solely a brewing group. Amid liquidity problems, Elders IXL (by then called Foster's, after their major brand) negotiated to sell Courage to S&N in 1995. This time, the linkup met with regulatory approval, much to the surprise and chagrin of other UK brewers who had eagerly anticipated the collapse of the company, and the British industry had a new number one in Scottish Courage.

Raymond G. Anderson

See also: Allied Breweries; Bass; Beer; Beer Orders (United Kingdom); Courage Family; Guinness Brewery; Scottish & Newcastle Breweries Limited

References

Gourvish, Terry R., and Richard G. Wilson. *The British Brewing Industry 1830–1980.* Cambridge: Cambridge University Press, 1994.

Mathias, Peter. *The Brewing Industry in England 1730–1830.* Cambridge: Cambridge University Press, 1959.

Millns, Tony. "The British Brewing Industry, 1945–95" in *The Dynamics of the International Brewing Industry since 1800,* edited by Richard G. Wilson and Terry R. Gourvish, 142–159. London and New York: Routledge, 1998.

Pudney, John. *A Draught of Contentment. The Story of the Courage Group.* London: New English Library, 1971.

Courage Family

For 200 years, the family of Courage was an important constituent part of the British brewing industry. Originally of French Protestant origin, the family immigrated to Aberdeen, Scotland, after the revocation of the Edict of Nantes in 1685 and became variously engaged as clock makers, tailors, farmers, and opticians. In 1780, John Courage (known as the Founder) moved to London and acted as a shipping agent for Scottish traders before buying a brew house on the south bank of the Thames at Horselydown, Southwark, London, in 1787 for a little over £600. This became known as the Anchor brew house and was the base for the family's growing importance within the industry.

John Courage the Founder died in either 1793 or 1797 (there being some confusion in the legend) and left a widow, Harriet, a son also called John, and three daughters. At this point, the firm's chief clerk, John Donaldson, entered the business as a partner, and he ran what was known as Courage and Donaldson until John Courage Jr. became a full partner in 1811, at the age of twenty-one. By about 1851, the firm was once again wholly owned by the Courage family and, before his death in 1854, John Courage Jr. brought two of his sons, Robert and John III, into the partnership. In 1856, they were joined as managing partners by another brother, Edward, and on John Courage III's early death in 1861, by another brother, Henry. Yet another brother, Alfred, set up the malt business of Tompkins and Courage that became closely associated with the brewery. Robert, Edward, and Henry remained the owners of the Courage family firm until April 1888 when Courage and Company Limited was registered as a limited liability company.

The three former partners, Robert, Edward, and Henry, became the directors of the new public company, the output of which was by then over 300,000 barrels per annum. By 1914, Robert and Edward had died, and Courage and Company was led by Edward's son Raymond. He was joined on the board by Oswald Courage, Commander A. V. Courage, Maj. M. R. F. Courage, and Henry Courage. These family members were later joined by M. V. "Bay" Courage (a direct descendant of John the Founder), Lt. Col. J. H. Courage, and Lt. Comdr. A. D. Courage. Since incorporation, the original firm of Courage and Company had greatly expanded and had taken over a number of smaller brewers: G. E. Hall in Alton, Hampshire, in 1903; Camden Brewery in London, in 1923; Farnham United Breweries in Surrey, in

1927; Noakes and Company of Bermondsey and Windsor, in 1930; C. N. Kidd and Sons in Dartford, Kent, in 1937; and Hodgsons Kingston Brewery in Surrey, in 1943. In 1955, a merger with near Southwark neighbors Barclay, Perkins and Company led to the formation of the much larger company of Courage and Barclay Limited, and from this point, Courage family domination of the company was weakened.

However, Lt. Col. J. H. Courage was still the chairman, and he was succeeded by a rising star, Richard H. Courage, who was to guide the company through the turbulent 1960s. Under his leadership, the firm expanded further, taking over Refells Bexley Brewery, Kent, in 1956; Nicholsons of Maidenhead in 1959; H. and G. Simonds of Reading in 1960; Georges Bristol Brewery in 1961; Clinch and Company of Witney, Oxfordshire, in 1962; Harmans Uxbridge Brewery of Middlesex, also in 1962; Charles Beasley of Plumstead, Kent, in 1963; the Star Brewery of Eastbourne, Sussex, in 1965; James Hole of Newark-on-Trent, Nottinghamshire, in 1967; and Plymouth Breweries of Devon in 1969. In 1970, Richard Courage led the company through a major geographical expansion when it acquired John Smiths Tadcaster Brewery, Yorkshire, and cemented its membership of the so-called big six of the contemporary British brewing industry. Richard Courage, a direct descendant of John Courage the Founder, still chaired the company in 1972 when Courage Limited, as it was by then called, was itself acquired by the Imperial Tobacco Group.

Courage family members continued to play a part in both the company and the industry, notably Alexander "Sandy" Courage, a property executive, and Michael Courage, son of M. V. "Bay" Courage, who now runs Cockerel Inns, his own chain of public houses in the southeast of England.

Kenneth Thomas

See also: Courage Brewery

References

Hardinge, G. N. *The Development and Growth of Courage's Brewery.* London: Courage, 1932.

Pudney, John. *A Draught of Contentment.* London: New English Library, 1971.

Richmond, Lesley, and Alison Turton, eds. *The Brewing Industry: A Guide to Historical Records.* Manchester: Manchester University Press, 1990.

Crafts, Wilbur Fisk (1850–1922)

Wilbur Fisk Crafts (1850–1922) was an American clergyman, temperance supporter, and advocate of Sabbath legislation. The son of a Methodist minister and abolitionist, Crafts was born in Fryeburg, Maine, on 12 January 1850. He was educated at Wesleyan University, Middletown, Connecticut (A.B. 1869), and Boston University School of Theology (B.D. 1871). He served as the pastor of Methodist congregations in Haverhill, Massachusetts; Dover, New Hampshire; New Bedford, Massachusetts; and Chicago, Illinois (1870–1879). Following travel in Europe and Palestine, Crafts served as a pastor of Congregational and Presbyterian churches in Brooklyn, New York, and New York City (1880–1888). Crafts was noted for his successful promotion of Sunday schools, and he frequently lectured on that theme. His first book, *Through the Eye to the Heart* (1873), enhanced his reputation as an innovator in Christian education.

While in New York, he began to focus his reform efforts on questions of appropriate Sunday observance. Following the publication of a compendium of information on worldwide Sabbath observance, *The Sabbath for Man* (1884), Crafts left the pastoral ministry. He organized the American Sabbath Union in 1888 and served as its field secretary. He was a popular speaker, and his lectures at Marietta College and Princeton Theological Seminary formed the bases for his widely distributed *Practical Christian Sociology* (1895). Recognized as a pioneer social gospel text, *Practical Christian Sociology* went through four editions in the next twelve years.

In 1895, Crafts established the Washington-based International Reform Bureau (IRB), now the International Reform Federation Inc., as a clearinghouse for all "Christian" reform efforts. The IRB played a significant role in coordinating political action on a variety of issues besides temperance and Sabbath reform, including municipal reform, reform of immigration laws, restriction of divorce, women's suffrage, Mormonism, and arbitration of international disputes. He was instrumental in the passage of eight laws that were passed by the U.S. Congress dealing with limiting Sunday business; the sale of liquor on military posts and at immigration stations; and the sale of intoxicants, opium, and firearms on certain islands in the Pacific. In 1909, Crafts served as chair of the U.S. delegation to the Twelfth International Congress on Alcoholism in London. Besides writing for numerous religious, temperance, and reform periodicals, Crafts served as founding editor of the *Twentieth Century Quarterly,* now *Progress,* the IRB periodical.

Joining Crafts in all his reform efforts was his wife, Sara Jane Timanus Crafts (d. 1930), whom he married in 1874. A noted Sunday school proponent in her own right, she served as the superintendent of the Sunday School Department for the World's Woman's Christian Temperance Union (WWCTU) and lectured in the United States, Iceland, Norway, Holland, Switzerland, and Italy. Wilbur Crafts died in Washington, D.C., on 27 December 1922.

William C. Kostlevy

See also: International Congress on Alcoholism; International Reform Federation, Inc.; Pacific Islands; World's Woman's Christian Temperance Union (WWCTU)

References

Cook, Joseph. "Introduction" in *Practical Christian Sociology,* by Wilbur F. Crafts. New York: Funk and Wagnalls, 1895.

"Crafts, Wilbur Fisk" in *National Cyclopedia of American Biography,* vol. 14: 172–173. New York: James T. White, 1917.

"Crafts, Wilbur Fisk" in *Standard Encyclopedia of Alcohol Problem,* edited by Ernest Hurst Cherrington et al., vol. 2. Westerville, OH: American Issue Publishing, 1925.

Lender, Mark Edward. *Dictionary of American Temperance Biography.* Westport, CT: Greenwood, 1984. 112–113.

Crothers, Thomas Davison (1842–1918)

Thomas Davison Crothers (1842–1918) was an American physician, internationally renowned inebriety treatment specialist, writer, and editor of the *Quarterly Journal of Inebriety* for its entire publication history. He was born 21 September 1842 in West Charlton, New York, and died at Hartford, Connecticut, 12 January 1918.

Educated at the Fort Edward Seminary and then Albany Medical College, Crothers served as a medical cadet at the Ira Harris Military College during the Civil War. He was awarded an M.D. in 1865 and set up practice in West Galway, New York, in 1866. He became assistant professor of the practice of medicine at Albany Medical College in 1871. In the mid-1870s, he took a position in Binghamton, New York, home of the New York State Inebriate Asylum.

Crothers's formal involvement with the treatment of inebriety began in the early 1870s, and he quickly gained an international reputation as an expert on the topic. He joined the American Association for the Study and Cure of Inebriety (AASCI) in 1873 and edited its *Quarterly Journal of Inebriety* from the journal's creation in 1876 to its demise in 1914. In 1878, he established Walnut Hill Asylum (later Walnut Lodge Hospital), a private inebriate asylum in Hartford, Connecticut. Crothers was secretary to the American Medical Temperance Association (AMTA) from 1891 to 1904. He was a member of the British Society for the Study of Inebriety (SSI) from its inception in 1884, and was invited to deliver the first Norman Kerr Memorial Lecture to that society in 1905. He was a noted participant in the Colonial and International Congress on Inebriety in London (1886), the International Temperance Congress in London (1897), the International Congress against the Abuse of Alcoholic Drinks in Paris (1899), and the International Congress on Alcoholism in London (1909).

Crothers's work emphasized a medical view that inebriety was a disease and not a moral failing, and therefore physical, necessitating medical treatment rather than legal or moral condemnation. In 1888, he delivered the first course on the disease of inebriety in the United States to students at Albany and repeated these lectures to Vermont University medical students in 1889. Beginning in 1900, Crothers gave lectures on alcoholic and drug neurosis in his role as professor of nervous and mental diseases in the New York School of Clinical Medicine. His books include *Morphinism and Other Drug Diseases* (1892), *Inebriety* (1893), *Drug Habits and Their Treatment* (1901), *Morphinism and Its Treatment* (1902), and *Clinical Study of Inebriety* (1911).

Although concerned primarily with educating physicians, Crothers also authored articles and lectures for popular audiences. He also helped the national Woman's Christian Temperance Union (WCTU) to develop Scientific Temperance Instruction (STI) material for public schools.

Although many historians dismiss the work of Crothers and his colleagues as lacking in scientific rigor, recent reviews of his work suggest that it was more sophisticated than it may appear. He presented a nuanced understanding of the etiology of inebriety, and developed a classification scheme that mirrors the system developed by E. M. Jellinek years later. Near the end of his life, Crothers became preoccupied with organizing thousands of patient records and data that he had accumulated through his work at Walnut Lodge. He hoped that these data would form a basis for his Research Institute at Hartford, which he founded to pursue original research on alcohol.

Daniel J. Malleck

See also: Alcoholism; American Association for the Study and Cure of Inebriety (AASCI); International Congresses on Alcoholism; Jellinek, Elvin Morton; Society for the Study of Addiction

References

Berridge, Virginia. "The Society for the Study of Addiction. 2. The Origins and Early Years of the Society" in *British Journal of Addiction.* 85 (1990): 991–1003.

Blumberg, Leonard. "The American Association for the Study and Cure of Inebriety" in *Alcoholism: Clinical and Experimental Research.* 2 (July 1978): 235–240.

"Crothers, Thomas Davison" in *Standard Encyclopedia of the Alcohol Problem,* edited by Ernest Hurst Cherrington et al. 6 vols. 2: 735–736. Westerville, OH: American Issue Publishing, 1924–1930.

Jaffe, Arnold. "Reform in American Medical Science: The Inebriety Movement and the Origins of the Psychological Disease Theory of Addiction, 1870–1920" in *British Journal of Addiction.* 73 (1978): 139–147.

Lender, Mark. "Crothers, Thomas Davison" in *Dictionary of American Temperance Biography: From Temperance Reform to Alcohol Research, the 1600s to the 1980s,* 116–118. Westport, CT: Greenwood, 1984.

Tracy, Sarah W. "Crothers, Thomas Davison" in *American National Biography,* edited by John C. Garraty and Mark C. Carnes, 24 vols. 5: 798–799. New York: Oxford University Press, 1999.

Cruikshank, George (1792–1878)

George Cruikshank (1792–1878), the most celebrated teetotal caricaturist, depicted the transformation of the British temperance movement from moderation to abstinence. Influenced by three caricaturists, Thomas Rowlandson, James Gillray, and his father Isaac Cruikshank, George Cruikshank drew satires and illustrations for Charles Dickens and William Thackeray.

His early works occasionally ridiculed alcohol (which had hastened his father's death), but Cruikshank became an antidrink caricaturist with the publication of *The Bottle* (8 plates, 1847), chronicling a family's ruin, from a husband initiating his wife's tippling to his murdering her with "the bottle." In Cruikshank's

Caricature of George Cruikshank (1792–1878) from The Hornet *(1871).*

words, the *Drunkard's Children,* "neglected by their parents," are "led to the gin-shops," "which nourish . . . every species of crime" (8 plates, 1848). Staged in eight theaters, the *Drunkard's Children* inspired a Matthew Arnold sonnet.

In a temperance speech, Cruikshank described his monumental painting (over seven by thirteen feet), *The Worship of Bacchus or the Drinking Customs of Society* (1862), viewed by Queen Victoria, and restored in 2001 by the Tate Gallery, London. Bacchus signifies drinkers' decline, from innocent first indulgences to commemorating life events—birth, christening, coming of age, marriage, and death—to consequent calamities—railway crash, ship burning, flogging, and hanging. Midcanvas, "Mad Tom" illustrates alcohol's destruction, "dancing on the tomb of his relations, having sacrificed at the shrine of Bacchus" family, "property, friends, body, and mind." Two details mark Cruikshank's place in the temperance movement. The scene where a mother, drunk with wine, drops her infant to the ground recalls William Hogarth's *Gin Lane* (1751), where excessive maternal gin tippling causes the same result. Showing superior morality, on Cruikshank's tableau, "a Mahometan Turk" and a "Hindoo" refuse wine offered by Christian ministers.

Hogarth's and Cruikshank's works illustrate contrasts between the eighteenth-century antispirits movement and nineteenth-century teetotalism. Hogarth's *Gin Lane* depicts foreign gin's dangers to ordinary Britons, in contrast with *Beer Street,* which depicts wholesome English brew. The initial moderationist British temperance movement (introduced from 1826 to 1829) forbade spirits, but allowed other drink socially, sacramentally, and medically. Legislatively, the Duke of Wellington encouraged beer, and W. E. Gladstone, wine.

In Cruikshank's sphere, after 1832, the largely proletarian teetotalers sought total abstinence and, by 1853, some pursued prohibition. Before midcentury, few privileged people embraced teetotalism. Thus, *The Bottle*'s cheap edition sold well, its deluxe version poorly. Cruikshank abstained only from his mid-fifties, after a Quaker condemned the inconsistency of his drinking with his teetotal art. Cruikshank thereafter appeared frequently at abstainers' gatherings, arousing Dickens's hostility. *The Worship of Bacchus* appeared the year a teetotal minority of Anglican clergymen created the Church of England Total Abstinence Society; and Cruikshank attended the 1873 Lambeth Palace founding of the influential Church of England Temperance Society (CETS), with sections for largely working-class teetotalers and for "better-class" moderates. Cruikshank applauded establishment support for temperance, but continued to advocate teetotalism.

Gerald Wayne Olsen

See also: Church of England Temperance Society (CETS); Gladstone, William Ewart

References

Olsen, G. W. *Drink and Temperance in the Church of England, 1829–1875.* Unpublished book manuscript.

———. "George Cruikshank, *The Worship of Bacchus* (1862): On display at Tate Britain, Millbank, London," in *Social History of Alcohol Review.* 17, nos. 1–2 (Fall–Winter 2002): 91–96.

Patten, R. L. *George Cruikshank's Life, Time and Art,* 2 vols. New Brunswick, NJ: Rutgers, 1992–1996.

Upstone, Robert, and Christopher Hollis. *George Cruikshank's* The Worship of Bacchus *in Focus.* London: Tate Publishing, 2001.

Cumming, Sir Ronald Stuart (1900–1982)

Sir Ronald Stuart Cumming (1900–1982) served as chairman of the Distillers Company Limited (DCL) from 1963 to 1967. He helped expand the DCL's whiskey exports and sold the DCL's chemicals and plastics interests.

He was born at Aberlour, Banffshire, Scotland. The Cumming family had been in distilling since 1824, when his great-grandfather, John Cumming, took out a license and established Cardhu distillery. Ronald Cumming was educated at Uppingham School and commissioned at the end of the first world war into the Grenadier Guards. He studied agriculture at Aberdeen University before training as a chartered accountant in Glasgow. In 1921, he joined John Walker and Sons, Scotch whiskey blenders, who had acquired Cardhu in 1894. Cumming was made Walker's export manager in 1925 and export director in 1931.

Walker's had become part of the DCL group in 1925, and in March 1939 Cumming transferred to another of the DCL's blending subsidiaries, James Buchanan and Company Limited, as its joint managing director. As a Territorial army officer with the Seaforth Highlanders, he was called up on the outbreak of the second world war, returning to Buchanan's as sole managing director in August 1946. Due to the retirement of its senior directors, he was in a position to shape the firm's future development. He believed the firm needed new blood and established a management training program, selecting trainees from young officers who had been demobilized. With his first-hand knowledge of export markets, he began the task of reestablishing Buchanan's worldwide distribution network, but in September 1950 he was transferred to the DCL's head office and in April 1951 became a member of its management committee. He had been a director of the DCL since September 1946.

Cumming played a key role in the DCL's export drive. Responsible for export marketing, he made frequent visits to the main markets, especially the United States and Canada. Between 1951 and 1963, when Cumming became the chairman of the DCL, the group's export sales increased from 6.9 million proof gallons to 20.3 million proof gallons; by then, the group accounted for 53 percent of the Scotch whiskey industry's worldwide sales. In 1965, he received a knighthood for his services to exports.

During Cumming's chairmanship (1963–1967), the group faced increasingly competitive conditions in the home market. The long postwar shortage of whiskey had ended, new competitors had emerged, resale price maintenance was abolished, and access to public houses was restricted by concentration in the brewing industry. The group struggled to retain market share and resorted to discounting, which reduced profit margins and yielded little permanent gain in sales volume. Exports also became more competitive, particularly in North America, and the group began to export in bulk, reversing its long-standing opposition to this practice. The group was, however, successful in opening new export markets, particularly in Western Europe, to offset its competitive disadvantage in North America.

The issue of compensation for the victims of thalidomide, a legacy of the DCL's postwar diversification into pharmaceuticals and its marketing of "Distaval," remained unsettled and attracted increasing criticism. Treating the matter as *sub judice* and making no comment pending the settlement of legal proceedings fostered the suspicion that the group had something to hide. Cumming's largest decision was the sale of the DCL's chemical and plastics interests to British Petroleum in 1967. The DCL had concluded that its chemical and plastics interests were "just not large enough to compete effectively in the future with the great international chemical corporations on both sides of the Atlantic. In view of the increasing interdependence of the chemical and oil-refining industries, integration with a major oil company for further expansion was the obvious answer" (Cumming 1967).

Ronald Weir

See also: Distillers Company Limited (DCL)

References

Cumming, Ronald Stuart. Letter to employees transferred to British Petroleum. 30 March 1967. Reprinted in *DCL Gazette.* Spring (1967).

Spiller, Brian. *The Chameleon's Eye: James Buchanan & Co. Ltd., 1884–1994.* London: James Buchanan, 1984.

Cyclopædia of Temperance and Prohibition

The 1891 encyclopedia *Cyclopædia of Temperance and Prohibition* was published by Funk and Wagnalls. (A note on the spelling convention for *cyclopædia:* The editor acknowledges as a "chief source" the earlier 739-page *Temperance Cyclopædia* compiled by the Reverend William Reid and published by the Scottish Temperance League in 1882.) The influence of American prohibition interests in the nineteenth century dominates this 671-page volume, which is subtitled *A Reference Book of Facts, Statistics, and General Information on All Phases of the Drink Question, the Temperance Movement and the Prohibition Agitation.* The encyclopedia is organized alphabetically, with entries from "Absinthe" and "Adulteration" to "Woman Suffrage" and "Wyoming." The editor rigorously credits earlier reference books as well as autobiographical and historical writings on temperance; unfortunately, there is no bibliography to facilitate tracing these titles. Extensive passages focus on the temperance movement in the United States; for example, there is a state-by-state discussion in the entries on "Legislation" (89 pages), "Liquor Traffic" (19 pages), and "Benefits of Prohibition" (61 pages). The international sweep takes the form of relatively short entries on alcohol preferences and practices. "Spirituous Liquors" is a comprehensive entry on the origins and development of alcohol internationally; however, the history of beverages associated with a particular country—e.g., Jamaica rum, pulque and tequila (Mexico), sake (Japan), vodka (Russia)—receives more coverage in the country profiles. The comprehensive index and cross-referencing are of considerable value to the historical researcher. The editor explains the omission of "biographical sketches of eminent living representatives of the temperance cause" on the basis that it is "highly perplexing to all compilers of cyclopædias to make discriminating choices." This neglect is mitigated somewhat for today's reader, as the index leads readily to some aspects of these missing biographies. For example, Frances Willard of the Woman's Christian Temperance Union (WCTU) contributes the entry "Social Purity," in which she tells of her role in preparing a petition for the protection of women for circulation to the Local Assemblies of the Knights of Labor. Mary Clement Leavitt contributes the entry "Burmah," in which she records her 1887 visit there and the organizing of the first temperance society—a WCTU. The index reference to William Hoyle takes the reader to the entry "Great Britain," offering some examples of the work of this "eminent writer on the statistical aspects of drink" (p. 195). The index reference to Mary Hunt takes the reader to the entry "Scientific Temperance Laws," which applauds Mrs. Hunt's efforts as head of this specially created department of the WCTU.

The social and moral issues in the late nineteenth century may help today's reader to interpret some of the "facts" of the drink question in this reference book and to assess the political correctness of language practices in this historical context. "Colored people" is a repeated phrase in the entry "Negroes." The entry on "Foreigners" associates "the adopted citizens of this country" with antiprohibition sentiments. The contributing writer, John Sobieski (perhaps an adopted citizen?) makes this statement of fact: "It is an undeniable and very significant fact that the liquor traffic of the United States is almost exclusively in the hands of foreigners" (p. 182). The *Cyclopædia* includes entries for "Crime," "Divorce," "Illiteracy," "Lawlessness," and "Pauperism," all of which are linked causally to intemperance. Other facts are embedded in the historically and culturally situated moral discourses of scientific temperance and social purity prevalent in North America. The entry "Saloon" contains the assertion that it is common for the saloon "to make merchandise of prostitution, gambling and all forms of vice, crime and wrong" (p. 606). The entry "Epilepsy" includes the statement that the excessive drinker is subject to this fearful disease and that it appears most frequently among absinthe drinkers. The four-page entry "Phylloxera" provides details of the ravages of this insect (*Phylloxera vastatrix*) upon the roots of the grapevine and the disputed opinion of its American origin. This entry seems to warrant inclusion in order to demonstrate that "no one but an expert" can venture to drink the "decoctions labeled wine" with any assurance that the "article consumed is not highly and poisonously adulterated" (p. 481). The entry "Equal Suffrage," composed by three different writers—two men and one woman—exemplifies the editor's efforts to be objective; yet his bias in favor of the Prohibition Party pervades this encyclopedia. The values that enter into these three interpretations of the relationship of women's suffrage to prohibition are stunningly different.

Dorothy A. Lander

See also: Hoyle, William; Hunt, Mary Hannah Hanchett; Leavitt, Mary Greenleaf Clement; Prohibition Party (United States); *Standard Encyclopedia of the Alcohol Problem;* Willard, Frances Elizabeth Caroline

References

The Cyclopædia of Temperance and Prohibition. New York: Funk and Wagnalls, 1891.

Reid, William. *Temperance Cyclopædia.* Glasgow: Scottish Temperance League, 1882.

D

D'Abernon, Lord (Sir Edgar Vincent) (1857–1941)

Lord D'Abernon (1857–1941), formerly Sir Edgar Vincent, was chairman of the Central Control Board (Liquor Traffic) (CCB) in the United Kingdom from 1915 until 1920. He proactively set about not only enforcing restrictions but also pursuing constructive social policies. Under his leadership, the CCB established direct control of both the wholesale and retail drink trade in several areas, most prominently in Carlisle in northern England. D'Abernon argued the merits of both public control and state purchase during the war.

Before his elevation to the peerage in 1914, D'Abernon had been a banker and Conservative member of Parliament (M.P.) for Exeter from 1899 to 1906. In 1915, widespread hysteria arose about the supposed harmful effects that drinking was having upon the war effort in Britain, and the CCB was set up with wide-ranging powers. D'Abernon, who possessed considerable knowledge of industrial resources, thus came to the alcohol question as an outsider without preconceived ideas. The climate of the time favored extensive and unprecedented state control and regulation on industrial matters. D'Abernon by 1916 took advantage of this by moving beyond imposing mere restrictions on the sale and use of alcohol toward taking direct control of the drink trade where there were concentrations of troops or munitions workers. The idea of disinterested public management, which had been advocated by Joseph Rowntree and Arthur Sherwell since 1899, was adapted for the licensed outlets in Carlisle and elsewhere. The CCB also set about sanitizing and improving the public houses in the Carlisle area.

D'Abernon soon came to view the work of the CCB less in terms of the war emergency and more as a solution to the underlying problems of intemperance. The CCB widened its role and set up various committees, for example to promote industrial canteens and to consider the policy toward women drinking. D'Abernon was convinced of the importance of scientific research. Accordingly, the CCB set up an alcohol committee, chaired by D'Abernon himself, which actively pursued research into the physiological, social, and economic effects of alcohol. In 1916, D'Abernon pressed for the state purchase of the whole liquor industry—a proposal that was seriously considered by the Cabinet but not proceeded with. However, unlike some of his colleagues and associates, he was less concerned about wholesale government ownership than with the promotion of a proper regulation of alcohol and drinking. He urged the continuation of a proactive alcohol policy after the end of the war. When it became apparent that the CCB would not survive permanently into peacetime, he argued for the transfer of its powers to the new Ministry of Health and for the creation of a licensing commission. In 1920, he was appointed British ambassador to Germany. Although he took no further part in temperance politics, he continued on occasions to justify the work of the CCB. He argued the case for improved public houses and for the state to cooperate with progressive elements among the brewers. He contributed an introduction to a book by H. M. Vernon on the alcohol problem in 1928, which he commended as providing a good, scientific, and independent approach to the subject. A rich collection of D'Abernon's wartime papers are to be found in the records of the CCB in the (London) Public Record Office, class HO/185/263.

John Greenaway

See also: Carlisle System; Carter, Henry; Gothenburg Schemes/Disinterested Management; Lloyd George, David; Rowntree, Joseph

References

Aldcroft, Derek H. "Control of the Liquor Trade in Great Britain, 1914–21" in *Trade and Transport: Essays in Economic History in Honour of T. S. Willan,* edited by W. H. Chalnoner and Barrie M. Ratcliffe, 242–257. Manchester: Manchester University Press, 1977.

D'Abernon, Lord. Preface to *The Alcohol Problem,* by H. M. Vernon. London: Baillière, 1928.

Donnachie, Ian. "World War I and the Drink Question: State Control of the Drink Trade" in *Journal of the Scottish Labour History Society.* 17 (1982): 19–26.

Rose, Michael E. "The Success of Social Reform? The Central Control Board (Liquor Traffic) 1915–21" in *War and Society: Historical Essays in Honour and Memory of J. R. Western, 1928–1971,* edited by M. R. D. Foot, 71–84, 298–304. London: P. Eleck, 1973.

Daoism

Daoism (often rendered as Taoism) is a complex and multifaceted religion that is notoriously difficult to define; Daoist attitudes toward the use of alcohol are similarly diverse and complex. In general, alcohol (*jiu,* usually translated as "wine" but in fact including a variety of beverages) was cherished by Daoist poets and bon vivants who were inspired while drinking, conversing and composing with like-minded friends, or who had retired to the solitude of nature. These individuals are often identified with the "philosophical" strand of Daoism *(dao jia).* Philosophical Daoism, which coalesced in the fourth century B.C.E., is noteworthy for its mysticism, fascination with nature, and its writings that typically delight in paradox and wordplay, typified in the *Dao De Jing* (Tao te Ching). This strand of Daoism became integrated with the later development of organized schools and practices usually termed "religious Daoism" *(dao jiao)* beginning in the second century C.E. Religious Daoists appreciate alcohol not only for its use as a social lubricant, but also for its therapeutic qualities. However, alcohol is sometimes proscribed as a hindrance to the spiritual and physical perfection necessary to attaining the goal of immortality, the core of religious Daoist practices.

Daoism in Chinese Culture

Daoism is distinct from the popular religion of China, but there are many points of overlap. Daoist priests are hired by community temples and individuals to perform various rituals, and Daoism is integrated into the fabric of the popular religious practice followed by the majority of Chinese. In Chinese culture, alcohol has been important for ritual offerings from the earliest records as an integral part of communal and familial rituals, gatherings, and celebrations, all of which express the worldview of Daoism.

Philosophical Daoism and the enjoyment of alcohol and inebriation are closely linked in the Chinese imagination. Many poets, artists, eccentrics, and recluses were associated with Daoism and noted for their love of alcohol and inebriation, including the Seven Sages of the Bamboo Grove, who lived in the third century C.E. and the eighth-century poet Li Bo (Li Bai). A group of disaffected men during a time of political turmoil, the Seven Sages delighted in eccentricity, conversation, and drunkenness. One of the seven, Liu Ling, wrote a poem "In Praise of the Virtue of Wine," in which he portrays himself as happily detached from the troubles of the world, much to the disapproval of the more conventional courtiers who visit him. Li Bo, one of China's most famous poets, wrote several poems extolling the pleasures of nature, wine, and friends; legend has it that he met his demise after consuming much wine and leaning out of his boat to embrace the moon. For all these figures, alcohol and inebriation are symbols of the freedom from human convention and the spontaneous enjoyment of the moment—important themes of Daoism.

Alcohol in the Rituals of Daoism

The use of alcohol in the rituals of religious Daoism developed in the context of ancient Chinese practices, in which alcohol was included in offerings to gods and ancestors as gestures of hospitality and supplication. The first organized school of Daoism, the Celestial Masters, established a theocracy for a short time in the third century C.E. The state was administered in part by *jijiu* (libationers), which included both men and women. The title libationer was drawn from an earlier usage referring to respected local leaders who participated in communal rituals. The rituals performed by these officials were in effect healing rites, bringing blessings from the gods to individuals and to the state. The Celestial Masters' state did not survive, but many of their rituals and ideas did, altered and developed in later schools of Daoism. In these later schools, alcohol continued to be an important ritual offering. Daoists priests today of the Orthodox Unity school, which claims lineage with the original Celestial Masters, frequently officiate at funeral services, where alcohol is a standard offering. They also perform the *jiao* (offering) ritual, an elaborate, many-day event performed for the renewal of the community. In this ritual, the focus of worship and supplication is the Three Pure Ones, who are not the ordinary gods of the popular pantheon, but emanations of the Tao, the source and pattern of the universe. The Three Pure Ones receive only "pure" offerings, including wine. Although they abstain from sexual relations and certain foods, priests performing the jiao are not required to abstain from alcohol prior to the ceremony: Their partaking of wine is an indication of their rank equal to gods in receiving such offerings.

Enjoyment of alcohol and inebriation is a part of many stories of the lives of immortals, individuals who have realized the Dao and live in freedom from cares. There are also stories of immortals and lucky mortals sharing wine in a happy fellowship. The Chinese value alcohol for its medicinal qualities, and it is used in some Daoist recipes for transcendence. Reflecting Daoist concerns, although not exclusively Daoist in practice, many medicines are made by infusing alcohol with herbs and other ingredients; this reflects the yin/yang theory that underlies Daoist thinking and practice.

Temperance and Daoism

Alcohol was not universally considered a boon to achieving Daoist goals, however. Some Daoist scriptures prohibit alcohol. Other warnings do not completely prohibit alcoholic consumption, but warn against drinking with "reckless abandon" as detrimental to the quest for immortality. Alcohol was not permitted by the Complete Perfection school, a celibate monastic order still active today whose practices centered on "internal alchemy," a means to purify and refine the body through meditation and physical regimes to create a holy embryo leading to an immortal body. It is likely that these attitudes reflect the influence of Buddhism, which entered China at the beginning of the common era.

No single source sums up the relationship between Daoism and alcohol. There is, however, regular mention of Daoism and alcohol in sources on Chinese culture in general and Daoism in particular.

Jennifer Oldstone-Moore

See also: Buddhism; China; Confucianism; Literature, Representations of Drinking in

References
Kohn, Livia, ed. *Daoism Handbook.* Leiden: Brill, 2000.
———. *The Taoist Experience.* Albany: State University of New York Press, 1993.
Simoons, Frederick J. *Food in China: A Cultural and Historical Inquiry.* Boca Raton, FL: CRC Press, 1991.

Dashaway Association

Founded by a group of San Francisco volunteer firemen in January 1859, the Dashaway Association was a male fraternal society devoted to encouraging its members to "dash away the intoxicating bowl." Reminiscent of the defunct Washingtonian Total Abstinence Society, the Dashaways combined teetotalism with a democratic rhetoric that emphasized individual responsibility. The society provided an array of social activities for its white, largely lower-middle-class membership. By 1865, the height of the association's popularity, there were approximately 15,000 Dashaways in more than twenty chapters throughout northern California. The San Francisco chapter founded the San Francisco Home for the Care of the Inebriate (1859–1898), initially a boardinghouse for drunken men and women picked up by the local police department, but later transformed into an asylum. The Dashaways declined in the late 1860s, supplanted in California by local branches of national fraternal organizations such as the Freemasons and Odd Fellows.

The Dashaway Association began as a New Year's resolution. After a "grand celebration" on 1 January 1859, nineteen volunteer firefighters at San Francisco's Howard Engine Company formed an association devoted to promoting total abstinence "from *any* and *all* intoxicating drinks." The Dashaways' first president and guiding force was Franklin E. R. Whitney, a lifelong firefighter who had almost certainly been exposed to the tenets of Washingtonianism in his native Boston. Although the association's founders were for the most part upper class, the group attracted significant numbers of middle- and working-class Californians. Most Dashaways were Protestants, but about one-fifth of the San Francisco chapter was Irish Catholic, a traditional enemy of the temperance cause. Illustrious members included Mexican American war hero and former U.S. senator John C. Fremont, former California governor John McDougal, San Francisco mayor Ephraim Burr, and ex-Mormon entrepreneur Samuel Brannan. The Dashaways also won praise from such luminaries as Mark Twain and Horace Greeley.

The Dashaways blended aspects of Washingtonian doctrines with aspects of those of the Sons of Temperance (active in California after 1850) to forge a new ideology uniquely appealing to the bibulous men of northern California. From the Washingtonians, the group borrowed moral suasion, inclusiveness, and down-to-earth pragmatism; inebriated men were at times literally picked up from gutters and barroom floors, sobered up, and persuaded to take the Dashaway pledge of total abstinence. From the Sons of Temperance, the association took initiation ceremonies, fraternal rites, and homosociality. The Dashaways viewed themselves as the progressive embodiment of their new state. They had a utopian vision of society wherein each individual, supported by his brothers, would make the rational and moral decision to give up the bottle.

The Dashaway Association grew by providing a number of tangible day-to-day benefits for members. A relief committee helped out-of-work Dashaways find employment. Members could take advantage of an array of affiliated social societies, including debating groups, literary unions, theater companies, orchestras, and glee clubs. Dashaway Hall in San Francisco was busy with activities six nights a week, serving as a lyceum, theater, music hall, library, billiard parlor, and ballroom. An investigating committee encouraged sobriety through accountability and peer pressure. Women and nonwhite men were permitted to join, but extremely few did so, although a short-lived Ladies' Dashaway Association was founded in San Francisco in 1860.

Joshua Paddison

See also: Alcoholic Mutual Aid Groups (United States); Sons of Temperance; Treatment Institutions; Washingtonians

References
Baumohl, James Andrew. "Dashaways and Doctors: The Treatment of Habitual Drunkards in San Francisco from the Gold Rush to Prohibition" (Ph.D. dissertation, University of California, Berkeley, 1986).
Ostrander, Gilbert. *The Prohibition Movement in California, 1848–1933.* Berkeley: University of California Press, 1957.
Paddison, Joshua. "Temperance and Gender in Northern California, 1850–1900" (M.A. thesis, San Francisco State University, 2001).

Daughters of Temperance

The Daughters of Temperance originated as the sororal auxiliary of the Sons of Temperance, a fraternal and benevolent society formed in 1842. Claiming approximately 30,000 members by 1850, the Daughters of Temperance was the largest women's organization in the antebellum United States. Like the Sons, the Daughters of Temperance promoted alcohol reform, provided members with sickness and death benefits, and offered venues for respectable socializing and alcohol-free leisure. Both the Sons and Daughters employed secret passwords and the surveillance of their members to protect their ranks from being infiltrated by the unworthy or intemperate. The two organizations differed, however, in the extent and type of their public and private activities. Modeled on Freemasonry and other secret societies, the largely middle-class Sons relished ornate regalia and elaborate rituals at their private meetings. They also engaged in forceful public advocacy of temperance by marching in parades, organizing temperance celebrations for the Fourth of July and other holidays, and delivering addresses to civic and benevolent groups. Middle-class gender norms discouraged women's emulation of male fraternal organizations

A Currier and Ives lithograph, "The Daughters of Temperance." (Library of Congress)

in private, and prevailing social conventions prohibited an active role or public voice for respectable female reformers. The Daughters of Temperance supported the Sons, providing food and decorations for festivities, adding decorum to public temperance activities with their presence and refined behavior, presenting Bibles or other tokens to male speakers, or perhaps writing odes or poems that could be read by the Sons. Notions of middle-class female propriety shaped the evolution of the Daughters of Temperance, limiting its members to activities and roles subordinate to those of male temperance advocates.

Organization

Women banded together into Daughters of Temperance "unions," as their societies were called, to promote total abstinence, the general welfare of mankind, and the ennoblement of the female sex. Age requirements varied, but in general, females over the age of fifteen were eligible for membership; by 1851, a subordinate organization, the Juvenile Daughters of Temperance, had been created to accommodate girls and young women between ten and eighteen. For an initiation fee of approximately one dollar and weekly dues of a few cents, the Daughters became entitled to sick benefits if they were unable to work, and a funeral benefit in the event of their deaths. Taking "Virtue, Love, and Temperance" as their motto, the unions attempted to provide a support network for young women, especially those who had left home to find employment in the nation's burgeoning cities and towns. Without the solicitude, care, and advice of a mother, young women might experience undue distress in their unfamiliar and sometimes threatening new environments. The Daughters of Temperance unions hoped to serve as surrogate mothers or older sisters for these women, encouraging them in times of distress and helping them to avoid temptation, vice, and immorality. To this end, members promised to support each other in case of illness or adversity, and to promote temperance and morality. The Daughters of Temperance swore never to use, buy, or sell spirituous liquors and always to discountenance their use in the community.

The Daughters strove to maintain the decorum, respectability, and virtue of their organization. Their bylaws required that potential members possess a good moral character and be capable of earning a living. In addition, their constitutions stipulated that any woman who followed "wicked practices" or earned her living through any unlawful means would be expelled from the order. Despite their efforts to maintain high standards of morality and deportment, the Daughters of Temperance still drew fire from critics who considered the women's use of secret passwords and rituals, similar to those employed by the Sons of Temperance, at best unseemly and at worst immoral. Concerned about retaining their respectability, the Daughters explained that they were not a secret society and used passwords only to protect themselves from the imposition of the unworthy and immoral, and to recognize genuine members who might be visiting from other areas. Appealing to conventional notions of female virtue, a Cincinnati union asked its detractors in 1851, when, in the history of the world, were "wives, mothers, sisters daughters, ever combined for evil?"

Conflicts and Limitations

Though they effectively defended their respectability and morality against critics of female temperance activism, the Daughters' success did not protect them from organizational growing pains as their membership grew dramatically during the late 1840s. In late 1846 and early 1847, the Daughters split into two organizations: the Original Daughters of Temperance, and the Grand Union, Daughters of Temperance. At issue was who would control the burgeoning movement. The Original Daughters, based in New York City, wished to retain the prerogatives that the New York union had enjoyed since the founding of the movement in the early 1840s. Specifically, the Original Daughters claimed that only they could issue new charters for Daughters of Temperance unions. Newer members in other parts of the country, on the other hand, wanted to organize existing unions into a series of locally based Grand Unions, which would confer over matters of policy and be empowered to issue new charters. The schism appears to have been solely over questions of power and authority, for the two organizations retained nearly identical constitutions and goals. Though the schism did not impair the Daughters of Temperance overmuch, it did shift membership to the newer and more democratic Grand Union.

By the early 1850s, the Daughters of Temperance faced a more serious difficulty than the division in their ranks. Despite a decade of growth, the Daughters were unable to expand their subordinate role within the temperance movement. As Daughters interested in social activism found, they might be invited to male temperance meetings but were expected to listen and learn rather than participate. Susan B. Anthony, for instance, found to her frustration that her credentials as a delegate of the Daughters of Temperance to a male temperance convention did not gain her acceptance as a full participant. Indeed, the inability (and sometimes unwillingness) of the Daughters to participate fully in temperance reform drove its more radical members, like Anthony, out of the temperance movement and into the women's rights movement. This ineffectiveness, along with the waning of the Sons of Temperance by the late 1850s, spelled the demise of the Daughters of Temperance by the eve of the Civil War. Though largely ineffective as a vehicle for either women's rights or temperance reform, the Daughters did provide organizational and reform experience for many young women who would resume their antialcohol activism in the surge of women's temperance activism during the 1870s.

Scott C. Martin

See also: Sons of Temperance

References

Dannenbaum, Jed. "The Origins of Temperance Activism and Militancy among American Women" in *Journal of Social History.* 15 (Winter 1981): 235–252.

Francis, E., ed. *The Beauties of Temperance; or, The Principles and Organization of the Sons, Daughters, Cadets, and Juvenile Sisters of Temperance.* Philadelphia: W. A. Leary, 1851.

Tyrrell, Ian. "Women and Temperance in Antebellum America, 1830–1860" in *Civil War History.* 28 (June 1982): 128–152.

Davidson, Randall (1848–1930)

Randall Davidson (1848–1930) was archbishop of Canterbury and a life-long abstainer. More than any other prelate, he advanced the moral suasionist and legislative aims of the Church of England Temperance Society (CETS), founded in 1873. He collaborated with the CETS founder-chairman, Henry Ellison, through Ellison's son. Both John Ellison and Davidson were chaplains and sons-in-law of the archbishop of Canterbury, A. C. Tait.

Charles Booth's seventeen-volume *Life and Labour of the People in London* (1889–1903) influenced Davidson. Formerly dean of Windsor (1883–1891), a prestigious position, he chose as his first bishopric the proletarian Rochester diocese (1891–1895).

Later, as Bishop of Winchester (1895–1903) and as archbishop of Canterbury (1903–1928), Davidson advocated tem-

Randall Davidson (1848–1930) (Library of Congress)

perance, partly to protect Anglican institutions, especially schools, from disendowment. He consistently supported the policies of the CETS chairmen, first Ellison and later bishops Frederick Temple, Ernest Wilberforce (the emancipator's grandson), and H. H. Pereira of Croydon, his own suffragan as archbishop, who faithfully, if sometimes regretfully, represented him.

In the House of Lords, Davidson advanced the consensus recommendations of the so-called Peel Commission, the Royal Commission on Liquor Licensing Laws (1896–1899): a reduction in the number of licenses, drinking club registration, abolition of child drinking, and protection for drunkards' relatives. Davidson's three bills influenced the reluctant Salisbury government to approve the 1902 licensing act, which was so effective in stimulating pub reduction that the Conservatives, responding to drink investors, constrained the licensing justices with new legislation in 1904.

In 1908, Davidson masterfully balanced his two major interests as the Liberal government introduced far-reaching liquor licensing and education bills. He showed strategic goodwill by supporting the licensing bill, based largely on CETS recommendations in the minority Peel report that advanced temperance, while he also argued on behalf of church schools. Davidson was amazed at the controversy his temperance politics aroused within the church and the CETS. Most Conservatives, even those who strongly supported temperance reform, condemned equally both Liberal measures as robbery. Davidson received massive amounts of hostile mail on the bill from church people, who showed how much Anglicans had invested in the drink trade, even for such biblical unfortunates as spinsters, widows, and orphans.

When the Liberal-controlled House of Commons was debating the licensing bill, Davidson denied entreaties from Pereira and many of the CETS executives for permission to speak out in favor of the bill. Davidson wanted to conceal divisions among the bishops and in the CETS membership in order to enhance the prospect that the establishment could persuade the House of Lords to enact the bill. Most of the laity in the representative church council opposed the bill. When the bill reached the upper house, Davidson and slightly over half of the bishops supported the bill, as did lay members of the CETS executive board. The Lords defeated the bill quickly and by an overwhelming vote. Davidson was more successful on the education question. Anglican schools were better treated than he had feared in the Liberal legislative proposals that, in any event, were withdrawn.

Davidson could not compromise his ecclesiastical position with overzealous teetotalism. In 1907, he rejected the campaign for an alcohol-free London Lord Mayor's banquet, causing a much-resented postcard to be circulated, ridiculing bishops who helped drink seventy-four bottles of champagne. Davidson diplomatically advocated temperance and Anglican schools, but met privileged drinkers at the elite Athenaeum Club.

Gerald Wayne Olsen

See also: Church of England Temperance Society (CETS); Conservative Party (United Kingdom); Ellison, Henry; Gore, Charles; Green, T. H.; Liberal Party (United Kingdom); Moule, Handley Carr Glyn; Temple, Frederick; Wilberforce, Basil and Wilberforce, Ernest

References

Bell, G. K. A. *Randall Davidson, Archbishop of Canterbury.* London: Oxford University Press, 1952 [1938].

Fahey, David M. "The Politics of Drink: Pressure Groups and the British Liberal Party, 1883–1908" in *Social Science.* 54 (1979): 76–85.

Greenaway, John R. "Bishops, Brewers and the Licensing Question in England, 1890–1914" in *Historical Magazine of the Protestant Episcopal Church.* 53, no. 1 (1984): 61–75.

Gutzke, David W. *Protecting the Pub: Brewers and Publicans against Temperance.* Woodbridge, Suffolk: Boydell and Royal Historical Society, 1989.

Olsen, G. W. *Drink and the British Establishment: The Church of England Temperance Society, 1873–1914.* Unpublished book manuscript.

———. *Drink and Temperance in the Church of England, 1829–1875.* Unpublished book manuscript.

Davies, Arthur C. (1909–1992)

Arthur C. Davies (1909–1992), English temperance reformer, was born in Somerset, graduated from Bristol University with a first-class honors degree in modern history, and entered the Baptist ministry in 1932.

Though small in stature, he was a giant of a man, as testified by all those who had the privilege of hearing him speak from the pulpit or the courtroom floor. He had a deep hatred of war and of economic injustice, fostered by his ministry during the years of the depression. But the larger part of his life was given to the care of those who suffered from the use of alcohol and to the prevention of such suffering. In the 1950s, he worked in a voluntary capacity with the National United Temperance Council, a London organization that primarily worked in the licensing courts. He became the full-time secretary of the Temperance Council of the Christian Churches in 1961. He was responsible for its diamond jubilee celebrations in 1975, when the Anglican archbishop of Canterbury, the secretary of the Methodist Conference, and the cardinal archbishop of Westminster addressed the anniversary meetings. He retired as secretary in 1978.

Davies was a well-known figure in and around the licensing courts of London and had the deep respect both of the justices' clerks and of his legal opponents. Although neither a solicitor nor barrister, he knew his licensing law inside out. His first experience of liquor licensing opposition came in 1934, as secretary of the Wandsworth Free Church Council; he won his case.

In 1976, his commitment and tenacity were well tested in the House of Commons. He sat through long sessions (lasting until 2 A.M.) of the committee stages of a licensing bill that would have allowed unaccompanied children under fourteen to be in public houses. It had been proposed as a private member's bill by Kenneth Clarke, later to hold senior Cabinet posts in Conservative governments. Davies ably briefed Ron Lewis, the member of Parliament (M.P.) for Carlisle, in successfully opposing the bill.

One of Davies's favorite books was *Pilgrim's Progress,* and there could be no better example of Mr. Valiant for Truth than Arthur Davies himself. In his Ernest Winterton memorial lecture (1968), he emphasized the priority of legislation in reducing alcohol-related harm. In his final peroration, he declared: "We must seek amelioration of conditions, we must spread education, we must keep legislation. The word you must never omit is the last." He died on 16 April 1992.

Derek Rutherford

See also: Temperance Council of the Christian Churches

Reference

Davies, Arthur C. *The Vital Role of Legislation in the Promotion of National Sobriety.* [Ernest Winterton memorial lecture, 19] London: United Kingdom Temperance Alliance, 1972.

Degeneration Theories

Anxieties about the decline of "the West" and about the wasting of the biological and moral capital accumulated by generations of Victorians encouraged the dissemination of theories of physical and moral "degeneration" throughout Europe and North America from the 1880s onward. These theories did not always take a biological determinist form, sometimes relying on culturalist notions about degenerate artists. Further, degeneration theories were not all equally conservative: They were sometimes used by feminist thinkers to denounce male vice and by missionaries working against "the liquor traffic" to denounce white European alcoholism as an evil threatening innocent aboriginal cultures. But by the 1930s, the rich and complex edifice of degeneration thought had been supplanted by one particularly nasty project that claimed to be the successor to Darwinism: eugenics. Eugenics, popularized in the United States through family studies of "feeblemindedness" and congenital alcoholism, led to compulsory sterilization laws in some American states and Canadian provinces shortly before the project was adopted by the Nazis to lend scientific legitimacy to their "racial hygiene" project. After the misuse of science by the Nazis was revealed to the world, eugenics was quickly discredited, and with it degeneration theory generally. The degeneration paradigm, however, was a capacious one, and it is a mistake to take one part of it—Nazi eugenics—as the whole.

Degeneration discourse originated in the pessimistic suggestion that, because of unnatural reproductive patterns, the human race as a whole or particular groups were experiencing a negative form of evolution through the intergenerational amplification of unhealthy traits. Some writers on degeneration eschewed biology, focusing instead on moral and cultural degeneration, for example denouncing avant-garde artists and immoral symbolist poets. But whatever their particular target, discourses of degeneration saw the physical as irrevocably intertwined with the moral and cultural. Whereas in the twentieth century, it became possible to talk about "the alcoholic personality" or about neurosis among physically superior people, in the late nineteenth century, terms like "constitution" and "disposition" served to underline that physical and moral traits were always of a piece. This had a profound effect on perceptions of drinking and of alcoholism.

The history of alcohol—and particularly of alcoholism—is intimately connected to the rise and later decline of the degeneration paradigm. Indeed, the intellectual machinery of degeneration provided biomedical science with a powerful tool with which to draw (or redraw) the distinction between "drunkenness" and "alcoholism," a fundamental distinction in the cultural history of alcohol consumption. In years subsequent to the discrediting of eugenics, alcoholism was reconfigured as a purely psychological condition rooted in that key posteugenics scientific entity, "personality," with "the alcoholic personality" explained in terms of "maladjustment," deviant gender formation, and/or bad mothering. The commitment to reject biological explanations was so strong that in the 1950s even separated-twin studies and studies of maternal drinking claimed there was no biological effect on drinking patterns. The mid-twentieth century emphasis on psychology and personality in the etiology of alcoholism was thus grounded in the demise of the degeneration paradigm.

The Concept of Inebriety

The best way to begin outlining the important, shifting connection between "degeneration" and perceptions of drinking behavior is by discussing a term that, while in use before the late nineteenth century, acquired a new meaning in the same circles that promoted "degeneration" concepts and models. In the 1880s and 1890s, the term "inebriety" began to be used in scientific circles in a more precise sense than as a polite synonym for habitual drunkenness. Inebriety was not simply an inability to regulate and moderate one's alcohol consumption: Children and people of "savage" and "primitive" races were thought to be unable to regulate alcohol consumption and, thus, proper subjects of specific prohibitions; but they were not "inebriates." "Inebriety" was thought to be a chronic and difficult-to-treat condition, akin to neurasthenia, involving both the body and the mind and particularly affecting the faculty of volition, or willpower. The much discussed drunkenness of aboriginal and other "primitive" peoples was regarded as a side effect of an intellectual deficit—the lack of calculative rationality. Inebriates, by contrast, were those adult Europeans who, either through an inherited bad constitution or as the accumulated result of years of abuse, came to suffer from what was often called a "paralysis of the will." In the case of middle- and upper-class patients particularly, the problem was that they had the intellectual capacity to foresee the consequences of heavy drinking but were somehow unable to govern their consumption accordingly. This lack of fit between knowledge and volition in the case of upper-class inebriates was described with the same conceptual tools used to diagnose the paradigmatically modern conditions of neurosis, agoraphobia, hysteria, and neurasthenia.

Although the upper classes were thought to be susceptible to imbalances in the nervous constitution that indicated a tendency to "degeneration" in certain families or individuals, working-class inebriety was more often linked to feeblemindedness and other symptoms of biological degeneration, and was usually ascribed to the poor physiological and cultural capital of the working class as a whole (or particular racial groups, the Irish most notably). Thus, degeneration could affect all classes and ethnic groups—though not aboriginals or Africans, who were understood to be constructed similar to children, not as having degenerated—and both genders, but its etiology and treatment differed according to demographics. Upper-class inebriates tended to disappear into the capacious category of "neurosis" (and later, "maladjustment"), while working-class and Irish inebriates were lumped with the "feebleminded." The state asylums for inebriates built in the United Kingdom and populated mostly by neglectful mothers and prostitutes were, after 1914, smoothly converted into institutions for feebleminded women.

The inherited "degenerate" constitution that was thought to sometimes cause "inebriety" was not a specifically alcoholic condition. Degeneration, it was thought, took different forms, not only depending on class and gender but also across generations and among individuals of the same generation. Family studies claimed that degenerate person X might have an epileptic daughter or an alcoholic son, and that those children could in turn give birth to feebleminded offspring or lunatics. The emphasis in the highly popular family studies was on the wasting of physical and cultural stock, rather than on the differences distinguishing, for example, alcoholism from mental retardation. In discussing the various forms that degeneration took, scientists—as well as literary and journalistic popularizers—de-emphasized cultural practices, including drinking habits, focusing instead on the hidden inner "taint."

Variations in the Paradigm

Some proponents of degeneration rejected the biological determinism that is associated with eugenics. Evangelical Protestantism often led Anglo-American degeneration writers to stress that some people could avoid perpetuating their family curse. Dr. Norman Kerr, head of the British Society for the Scientific Study of Inebriety (SSI), invoked degeneration to explain congenital tendencies toward alcoholism, but in his influential work *Inebriety or Narcomania,* he stressed the ability of the "cursed" to struggle and to conquer their biological heritage: "The continuous and victorious struggle of such heroic souls with their hereditary enemy—an enemy the more powerful because ever leading its treacherous life within their breasts, presents to my mind such a glorious conflict, such an august spectacle, as should evoke the highest efforts of the painter and the sculptor" (17).

In France, by contrast, a stricter biological determinism pervaded both scientific and popular discussions of nervous and physiological defects like inebriety. The most memorable account of degeneration is French: the multivolume saga about the Rougon-Macquart family narrated by Émile Zola in full scientific detail to a large reading public. Different volumes of Zola's opus focus on different symptoms of degeneration. The alcoholic delusions and deathbed hallucinations of one volume's ill-fated protagonist are presented, in keeping with the degeneration paradigm, not as rooted in psychological quirks or social circumstances but as the inevitable culmination of a several-generation process that could only end in the extinction of that extended family.

Despite differences in views about inevitability, scientific as well as popular writers across Western Europe and North America believed that while drunkenness was primarily a matter of cultural training and habits, with working-class people and aboriginals regarded as the most likely to get drunk, inebriety was relatively independent of environment and upbringing. Indeed, insofar as inebriety was thought to be a condition affecting the more sophisticated nervous system of Europeans, some medical experts argued that inebriety was the unique curse of the more evolved. From the 1880s through the 1930s, some well-to-do families in the United Kingdom, the United States, and Canada sent their relatives for long stays in privately run "inebriate homes" that promised either drug-based or purely environmental cures for "inebriety." These homes often claimed also to cure "the morphia habit" and opiate addiction—the "narcomania" that experts invented by analogizing drugs to alcohol.

Impact of the Paradigm

The emergence of a diagnosis of inebriety or "alcoholism" (later, alcohol dependence) and its distinction from habitual drunkenness was thus made possible by the powerful intellectual machinery of the degeneration paradigm. Some medical and religious writers of earlier times had distinguished the inability to stop drinking as a behavior distinct from ordinary drunkenness. But inebriety—the immediate predecessor of twentieth-century "alcoholism"—was a historically specific condition rooted in the main scientific paradigm of the end of the nineteenth century. As the paradigm waned in the mid-twentieth century, alcoholism might well have disappeared, like neurasthenia and hysteria among the middle classes and feeblemindedness among the poor. But this did not happen. Alcoholism was detached from "degeneration" and reconfigured through the intellectual apparatus of 1950s psychological science: The alcoholic personality replaced the degenerate, in a key shift in the history of alcohol in the Western world.

Mariana Valverde

See also: Alcoholism; Forel, Auguste; France, Temperance in; Gin; Kerr, Norman Shanks; Psychological Theories of Drinking; Treatment Institutions

References

Kerr, Norman. *Inebriety or Narcomania: Its Etiology, Pathology, Treatment and Jurisprudence.* 3rd ed. London: H. K. Lewis, 1894.

Pick, Daniel. *Faces of Degeneration: A European Disorder 1848–1918.* Cambridge: Cambridge University Press, 1989.

Valverde, Mariana. *Diseases of the Will: Alcohol and the Dilemmas of Freedom.* Cambridge: Cambridge University Press, 1998.

———. "'Slavery from Within': The Invention of Alcoholism and the Question of Free Will" in *Social History/Histoire sociale.* 22, no. 3 (1997): 251–268.

Delavan, Edward Cornelius (1793–1871)

Edward Cornelius Delavan (1793–1871) was a New York temperance leader and propagandist who had a slander lawsuit brought against him by Albany brewers. Born in 1793 in Schenectady County, New York, Delavan made a fortune as a wine merchant. In his thirties, he converted to the temperance cause, discontinued his business, and destroyed his immense wine cellar. In 1829, he and the Reverend Dr. Eliphalet Nott founded the New York State Temperance Society (NYSTS). He also used his wealth to bankroll a range of temperance activities, missions, and speaking tours of other temperance advocates. In 1834, at his urging, Dr. Justin Edwards drew up a temperance declaration, which in time was signed by Presidents James Madison, John Quincy Adams, John Tyler, Millard Fillmore, Franklin Pierce, Andrew Jackson, Martin Van Buren, Zachary Taylor, James Polk, James Buchanan, Abraham Lincoln, and Andrew Johnson. This document declared that people, especially young men, would benefit, as would the nation, by discontinuing their drinking. It declared that alcohol "is not only needless, but hurtful, and that the entire disuse of it would tend to promote the health, the virtue and the happiness of the community."

Delavan's leadership of the state's temperance cause was solidified by his control of the widely circulated *American Temperance Intelligencer* and the *Temperance Recorder.* In 1835, he became chairman of the NYSTS and became more prominent among the reading public through his eloquent argument against the notion that the Bible sanctioned the drinking of wine and other spirits. He also found himself in the midst of controversy over an article he published in the *Albany Evening Journal* in which he charged that Albany brewers were using foul water in the making of their beer. Feeling that his charges had hurt their business, eight brewers brought suits against him, seeking damages totaling $300,000. It took five years for the first of the five cases to make its way before the court, and Delavan was acquitted in a widely publicized trial. As a result of the outcome, the other seven lawsuits were quietly dropped.

In 1836, Delavan was prominent in the establishment and founding of the American Temperance Union. He not only contributed $10,000 to its coffers but also was elected chairman of its executive committee. Three years later, he made a speaking tour of Europe to promote his cause, carrying with him a large amount of temperance literature, including 800 copies of Dr. Edwards's "Permanent Temperance Documents." Gaining access to King Louis Philippe, he persuaded the ruler to sign a declaration stating that the habitual use of intoxicating liquors was injurious and France would benefit from increased sobriety. Upon returning to America, he continued to support the New York movement financially. Through his offices in Albany and as chairman of the state's temperance movement, he oversaw the distribution of 13,000,000 pieces of material and pamphlets. Delavan continued to support the cause throughout the rest of his life. He died in Schenectady on 15 January 1871.

T. Jason Soderstrum

See also: American Temperance Society (ATS); Edwards, Justin

References

Damrell, William Shapleigh. *Lament of the Albany Brewers: After the Verdict in the Libel Case* Taylor vs. Delavan. Boston: Whipple and Damrell, 1840.

Smith, Gerrit, and Edward C. Delavan. *Edward C. Delavan, Esquire.* Peterboro, NY: n.p., 1855.

Democratic Party (United States)

Tracing its roots to Thomas Jefferson and Andrew Jackson, the Democratic Party was generally skeptical of prohibition and centralized liquor regulation. Celebrating the personal liberty of American citizens and drawing the support of many immigrants and most American Catholics, Democratic leaders throughout the nineteenth century viewed temperance as a matter of personal choice and tended to characterize liquor regulation emanating from the federal or state level as an untoward and unhealthy intrusion of government into the individual lives of citizens. Nevertheless, a significant minority of antiliquor Democrats, especially in the western and southern states, made prohibition a divisive issue among Democrats and prevented the national party from adopting clear positions on the matter after 1884. The accumulation of state prohibition laws and the drive toward national prohibition in the early twentieth century split the party between a faction of rural, western or southern native, Protestant prohibitionists, on the one hand, and a body of antiprohibitionist, urban, ethnic or Catholic northeasterners, on the other. The imposition of National Prohibition and the nomination of the antiprohibitionist New Yorker Alfred Emanuel Smith in 1928 tilted the party toward a position favoring repeal. That viewpoint was formalized in 1932 and acted upon after the election of Franklin D. Roosevelt.

Democrats and Temperance

Jeffersonian suspicion of centralized government authority and Jacksonian devotion to the interests of free, white, male citizens as the cornerstone of democracy shaped the Democratic Party's position on liquor regulation, beginning in the 1830s. Some Democrats, especially Methodists and Baptists who stressed the moral dimensions of temperance reform, supported popular referenda to deny licenses to sell liquor and, in a few cases, legislation that prevented the purchase of liquor by the drink. Overall, however, Democratic beliefs in localism and the freedom of citizens to control their own behavior and amusements led most Democrats to resist temperance legislation and emphasize instead the voluntary cultivation of temperate habits for those so inclined. The party's identification with the slogan of personal liberty increased with the influx of Irish and Catholic German immigrants into the United States in the 1840s. These immigrants, whose cultural traditions valued the moderate use of alcoholic beverages, were welcomed into the Democratic Party as equal citizens. Still, the push for state prohibition statutes during the Maine Law agitation of the early 1850s caused some division among Democrats and contributed, along with the great sectional issue and the rise of nativism, to the reshuffling of partisan identification in the years leading to the Civil War. Losing some members to the Republican Party and the Know-Nothings, Democratic leaders, as they did with other divisive issues, attempted to confine the prohibition question to local affairs and keep it out of national party politics.

Democrats and the Prohibition Movement

As the drive for state and, later, national prohibition laws intensified after the Civil War, the Democratic Party presented a double image on the liquor issue. On the one hand, the most zealous antiliquor crusaders considered the Democratic Party the unswerving ally of the "Rumocracy," a coalition made up of the drink industry, imbibers, immigrant Catholics, and limited-government ideologues who resisted any attempts to regulate or restrain the traffic in alcohol. On the other hand, the diverse constituency of the Democratic Party included both supporters and opponents of prohibition, which influenced the party to largely refrain from clear national positions on prohibition while retaining enough flexibility for local Democratic organizations to resist or pursue prohibition initiatives. Home to most committed opponents of prohibition, the Democratic Party nevertheless defined its positions on liquor regulation warily.

Surges in Republican-backed temperance legislation prompted strong Democratic responses and Democratic electoral victories in the North and particularly in the Midwest during the 1870s and 1880s. State Democratic organizations handled the antiprohibition campaigns in the 1870s. But after the successful passage of prohibition amendments in several states following the takeover of state Republican organizations by dry activists in the early 1880s, the national Democratic Party, wooing disaffected German Republicans, placed statements opposing sumptuary legislation in the 1880 and 1884 Democratic national platforms. After that, the party became more cautious on the matter of liquor regulation. White Protestants in the Democratic stronghold of the South began to push for local option, bans on liquor sales near schools and churches, and other formal restrictions on the drink trade. By 1900, the nonpartisan political agitation of the Anti-Saloon League of America (ASLA) and the Woman's Christian Temperance Union (WCTU) had built sentiment for prohibition laws among some Democrats, especially in the rural West and South. Meanwhile, the great wave of immigration between 1880 and World War I brought millions of southern and central Europeans to America and into the Democratic Party, reinforcing the antiprohibitionist sentiments among urban and eastern Democrats.

From 1896 until the onset of National Prohibition in 1920, the Democratic Party was hamstrung between its prohibitionist, rural and antiprohibitionist, urban wings. William Jennings Bryan, three-time Democratic presidential nominee and the hero of rural Democrats, was personally a teetotaler, yet he did not advocate county-level local option as a party question until 1910 and refused to support National Prohibition until 1916, but then lent his prestige to the reform. Urban Democrats kept the Northeast free from prohibition laws until 1920. Fearing schism (including religious and ethnic conflict), the national party tried to downplay prohibition. But the inadequate enforcement of National Prohibition and the resistance to the measure in urban centers forced the party into a cultural struggle. The boisterous 1924 Democratic convention in New York City revealed the gulf between Bryan's Democracy and the party of New York governor Alfred Emanuel Smith—an antiprohibitionist, a Catholic, and the son of immigrants. In 1928, Smith received the Democratic nomination and moved beyond the party platform by calling for fundamental changes in National Prohibition. Smith was defeated, but the failure of Herbert Hoover's attempt to enforce Prohibition, the weight of the depression, and the surprising strength of the repeal movement allowed antiprohibitionist Democrats to commit the party to repeal in 1932. Candidate Franklin Roosevelt, who had previously avoided taking a position on Prohibition, endorsed the plank and benefited from the rapid success of the repeal process.

Thomas R. Pegram

See also: Bryan, William Jennings; Local Option; Maine Law; National Prohibition (United States); Republican Party (United States); Smith, Alfred Emanuel; State Prohibition (United States)

References

Craig, Douglas B. *After Wilson: The Struggle for the Democratic Party, 1920–1924.* Chapel Hill: University of North Carolina Press, 1992.

Kleppner, Paul. *The Third Electoral System, 1853–1892: Parties, Voters, and Political Cultures.* Chapel Hill: University of North Carolina Press, 1979.

Levine, Lawrence W. *Defender of the Faith: William Jennings Bryan: The Last Decade 1915–1925.* New York: Oxford University Press, 1965.

Pegram, Thomas R. *Battling Demon Rum: The Struggle for a Dry America, 1800–1933.* Chicago: Ivan R. Dee, 1998.

Denmark

Denmark is one of a number of small but socially innovative Scandinavian countries. But unlike the other Scandinavian countries (Sweden, Norway, Finland, and Iceland), the Danes did not adopt prohibition or other heavy alcohol control measures apart from a few decades between World War I and World War II. An important factor historically was the role of the official Lutheran church and its connections with the state. Lutheranism did not encourage a separate total-abstinence movement, unlike the role of the leading Protestant churches in the United States.

Danish society has in general accepted a rather high average alcohol consumption, mostly based on a high consumption of beer, and it is therefore considered a "wet" alcohol culture compared to the Scandinavian "dry" alcohol cultures. At the same time, Danish alcohol culture has been thought historically to have been happy, relaxed, and tolerant, and Denmark is therefore often considered a country that has realized "the impossible dream": combining a high alcohol consumption with few problems. In reality, the key to understanding Danish alcohol culture is not only a heavy taxation policy on alcohol, but also the fact that the possible effects of high alcohol consumption are widely tolerated—or neglected.

Traditional Drinking Cultures

There are no indications of significant differences across the drinking cultures of the various Scandinavian countries in the nineteenth century. A Danish happy beer-drinking country is normally dated back to the traditional peasant society. Danes drank mostly top-fermented beer, which could be strong, but for daily use was not strong. Distilled liqueur (schnapps) had been the main source of intoxication combined with home-brewed beer, which sometimes had a high alcohol content. As in the other Fenno Scandinavian countries, Danish alcohol consumption had been rather high in the middle of the nineteenth century. Privileged distillers located mainly in the provincial towns and the capital, Copenhagen, produced most of the spirits, but illicit home distilling was widely spread among the peasants throughout the countryside.

First Measures to Control Alcohol Consumption

In order to gain the maximum tax revenue from alcohol produced and consumed in Denmark, the government initiated a campaign in 1843 against home distillation of spirits (illicit production of distilled liquor). Government officials shut down home distilleries and confiscated peasants' copper "tools," and thereby made it rather difficult for them to make their own schnapps. Since then, Denmark has had a relatively reliable registration of domestic liquor production.

Yet, more than a government drive for revenue lay behind this first great campaign in 1843. Also important was the public discussion initiated by the formation of the *Totalafholdsselskabet* (Teetotal Society) and a *Maadeholdsforeningen* (Moderation Society) for moderate (wine and beer) drinkers. These two societies soon had the reputation that they were organized for people without personal willpower. Their activities were actively suppressed by Copenhagen's dominating elite (influenced by Søren Kirkegaard and the Lutheran priesthood), who did not approve of mystic and moral societies outside the church and thereby made the movements an easy target for ridicule. In the countryside, *Grundtvigianism* (the dominating political and revivalist movement in the Danish countryside) and its maintenance of pure Lutheranism turned the Danish revivalist movement in a Lutheran direction, where the individual's salvation was not something that could be obtained through temperance activities. The principle that temperance had nothing to do with salvation also dominated the more fundamentalist Inner Mission, the second biggest lay Lutheran revivalist movement in Denmark. Anglo-American nonconformist religious movements such as Baptism and Methodism, which were the traditional supporters of temperance, never became influential movements within the Danish religious scene.

The Liberal Policy of the Mid-Nineteenth Century

A Liberal alcohol policy dominated Danish society in the 1860s and 1870s, and in 1873 Denmark instituted a new law that made it easier to get a license as a saloon keeper. The period from 1873 through the 1880s was characterized by the spread of beer consumption through an increase in the number of public pubs and alehouses. The establishment and development of two new breweries encouraged this development. Carlsberg was founded in 1847 by the enterprising brewer I. C. Jacobsen, who introduced a new and stronger bottom-fermented beer, which fundamentally changed the Danish beer-drinking tradition from weak beer at meals to stronger beer at leisure time. And following brewer Jacobsen's success, the Tuborg brewery was established in 1873. Taxation and the industrial production of beer in 1892, along with a more precise tax (by volume) on distilled spirits in 1887, made consumption statistics more reliable. It has been widely discussed whether the introduction of the new bottom-fermented Carlsberg and Tuborg beer was a substitute for distilled liquor (schnapps), and therefore a healthy product (as pointed out by the brewers), or a dangerous supplement for distilled liquor (as argued by the temperance people). There is no doubt, however, that in the last part of the nineteenth century, Danish alcohol consumption grew to a rather high level.

A New Temperance Movement

A second wave of the temperance movement emerged in the 1880s. Once more, the temperance message was unappealing to the dominating Lutheran revivalist groups in the countryside, which of course meant that temperance organizations recruited their members from the less influential strata in society. Even so, the Danish temperance movement grew to a rather remarkable size of 180,000 members (10–15 percent of the adult population), mostly in Jylland (Jutland) in the western (and more agriculturally based) part of the country. Unlike the Anglo-American world, the World's Woman's Christian Temperance Union (WWCTU) did not take deep root, and the Danish feminists never engaged seriously in this resurgence of temperance reform. The temperance movement never dominated the elite culture in society, and it therefore never became part of the Danish (elite) urban culture and Danish identity. In spite of this lack of sympathy from the rest of the Danish population (both drinkers and nondrinkers), temperance activities among a small group of responsible intellectuals and professionals in the emerging welfare state (teachers, physicians, lawyers) put heavy pressure on the government to impose a very restrictive alcohol legislation after the turn of the century as a means to solve social problems.

Impact of World War I

The period of grain shortage caused by World War I made it possible—and necessary—to restrict to food production the uses to which the available grain could be put. Production, transportation, and sale of distilled spirit were simply forbidden in a three-month period in the spring of 1917. When the sale restrictions were abandoned, the production of spirits was still kept at a very low level, which made the shortage of distilled spirits obvious (and created great potential profits for the distillers) during the rest of the war. In order to ration the remaining amount of spirits, the state imposed a very high tax on spirits, which overnight greatly increased the price. In alcohol literature since then, it has often been said that Denmark got its taxation-based alcohol policy by coincidence or by chance—thereby denying the efforts and influence of temperance circles, whose ideas were still considered unfamiliar in Danish culture. But the coincidence or chance explanation overlooks two causes of high taxes. First, taxation on distilled spirits has a long tradition in Denmark, as explored previously. Second, and perhaps more important, temperate physicians were very active to prove the positive health consequences of the three-month prohibition period, and therefore their health statistics played an important part in the scientific background used as justification for the continuation of high alcohol taxation.

Changes in Consumption Patterns

The heavy tax imposed on distilled spirits (schnapps) in 1917 swiftly and dramatically changed the Danish alcohol culture from a liquor-drinking culture to a beer-drinking one. Although beer was also taxed in the 1920s, the brewing industry (including the Carlsberg and Tuborg breweries and the workers' new cooperative brewery, Stjernen [the Star]) benefited from the abolition of distilled spirits. In contrast with Sweden, temperance never became part of the workers' self-help program adopted in order to save the workers' income for more rational and necessary purposes. The cooperative Star brewery was established in 1902 by the workers' movement in order to retain the revenue generated by what was assumed to be the workers' natural habit of beer consumption and to use the profits for the workers' own benefit.

Beer—and especially branded beer—became a form of "conspicuous" product consumption in which Danes identified themselves with particular brands that had symbolic and social significance. Drinking the Star beer, owned and produced by the workers' cooperative, became a symbol of solidarity with the working-class culture. But many workers preferred the "capitalistic" Carlsberg and Tuborg beers, which were considered to be better, stronger, and tastier. Tuborg and especially Carlsberg beer developed the reputation of first-class beers in accordance with an active policy whereby the breweries used their surplus (through the Tuborgfondet, Clarsbergfondet, and New Carlsberg foundations) to fund cultural and especially scientific activities. For instance, the Carlsberg foundation funds a huge amount of the Danish humanistic research as a supplement to state finance. The branding of the breweries systematically managed to identify Carlsberg and Tuborg with the intellectual and the economic elite in society, and the drinking of their products was interpreted as expressing identification with the "quality" of Danish culture.

Due to the shift from distilled spirits to beer and to the high tax regime, Danish alcohol consumption measured in terms of pure alcohol per capita reached a rather low level during the 1920s and the 1930s—far lower even than consumption in traditionally "dry" Sweden. The heavy tax came to define "the solution" to the Danish alcohol question and was called the "Danish System," under which a national referendum and an alcohol monopoly—existing in Norway, Finland, Sweden, and Iceland—seemed to be unnecessary. That did not mean that Denmark did not have some alcohol restrictions comparable to Sweden's. From about 1905 to World War II, a local-option system for the granting of licenses to sell alcohol was one of the very big issues within Danish domestic politics. The leading figure in the Danish prohibition movement was journalist Lars Larsen-Leddet, a drinkers' son, who organized in the Independent Order of Good Templars (IOGT). Under Larsen-Leddet's guidance, the countryside was divided into "wet" and "dry" parishes, and many parishes went dry as a result of temperance lobbying in this period. The possibility of restricting the availability of alcohol was introduced by the *Bevaerterloven* (a law on the publican's license), passed in 1912, and made even more easy by the revision of the law in 1924. Denmark never instituted a law directed toward the drinkers, but the alcohol question became part of the laws on marriage, punishment, mental illness, and sterilization, which made it difficult or impossible for many heavy drinkers to continue drinking.

Contemporary Developments

The general opinion in Danish society in the post–World War II period has been that Danes do not have any alcohol problems. Taxation on alcohol has been relatively high, but there have been relatively few restrictions and very little research on alcohol problems, even though consumption slowly grew to a relatively high rate in the 1980s (12 liters [3.17 gallons] of pure alcohol annually per inhabitant over fourteen years of age). This level has not fluctuated much since then. The statistics do not, however, take into account private border purchasing of cheap alcohol (beer, wine, and spirits) from Germany.

A remarkable and decisive change came with Denmark's entrance into the Faellesmarkede (the European Union [EU]) in 1973. Thereafter, it became difficult for Denmark to maintain the traditional Danish alcohol policy based on high taxation. The tax on imported distilled spirits was reduced to the same level as Danish schnapps, and the value of the tax no longer followed the trend of prices. At the same time, inexpensive, Southern European wine entered the Danish market and converted Danes into wine drinkers. In 1992, the Danish beer tax was reduced to a remarkably low level also in order to equalize the taxes within the EU and to reduce border purchasing. The result of the lower price was not, however, a rise in recorded consumption rates, possibly because legal purchase replaced cross-border, unregistered purchase. Additionally, the increase has been explained as an indication that the Danes' alcohol "need" is now fully covered—independently of the actual price level. Demand remains fairly static or inelastic and does not vary much with the level of taxation of intoxicating beverages.

Within the last decade, Danes have been much more concerned about the combined health and social problems associated with alcohol consumption. Research budgets and research in alcohol have increased, and the Danish government has imposed a more restricted alcohol policy. In 2000, the legal blood-alcohol limit to drive a car has fallen from 0.08 to 0.05 parts per thousand. At the same time, the age for purchasing alcohol in normal retail stores (and drinking alcohol at bars) has risen from fifteen to eighteen years (but still, the shopkeepers and bar owners are not willing to comply with the law, and they continue to serve underage drinkers).

The effect of the drug Antabuse (disulfiram) was discovered in Denmark in 1947, and since then Antabuse has been a cornerstone in Danish alcohol treatment. Since the beginning of the 1990s, the so-called Minnesota cure (twelve-step treatment) and Alcoholics Anonymous have been much more accepted as part of an official treatment policy and among people in general.

Sidsel Eriksen

See also: Beer; Carlsberg; Finland; Good Templars (IOGT); Norway; Sweden

References

Elmeland, Karen. *Dansk Alkoholkultur. Rus, ritual og regulering.* Holte: Koebenhavn, 1996.

Eriksen, Sidsel. "Alcohol as a Gender Symbol. Women and the Alcohol Question in Turn-of-the Century Denmark" in *Scandinavian Journal of History.* 24 (1999): 45–73.

———. "Drunken Danes and Sober Swedes? Religious Revivalism and the Temperance Movements as Keys to Danish and Swedish Folk Cultures," in *Language and the Construction of Class Identities. The Struggle for Discursive Power in Social Organisation: Scandinavia and Germany after 1800,* edited by Bo Straath, 55–94. Gothenburg: Department of History, Gothenburg University, 1990.

———. "The Making of the Danish Liberal Drinking Style. The Construction of a 'Wet' Alcohol Discourse in Denmark." Paper presented at the Kettil Bruun Society Conference in Toronto, 31 May–5 June 1992, in *Contemporary Drug Problems.* 19, no. 4 (1992): 1–31.

———. *Neither Wet nor Dry. A Study in Danish Alcohol Culture 1850–1950.* Part I: Asceticism (temperance movement), Part II: Expertism (intellectuals), Part III: Consumerism (politics of brewers and distillers). Forthcoming, 2004.

———. "Something Rotten in Grindsted." Afholdsproblemer i en stationsby, i: *Nyt fra stationsbyen,* no. 8 (Viborg 1985): 3–35.

Thorsen, Thorkil. *Dansk alkoholpolitik efter 1950.* Holte: Forlaget Socpol, 1993.

———. *Hundrede aars alkoholmisbrug.* Koebenhavn: Alkohol- og Narkotikarådet, 1990.

Dirección Anti-Alcohólica

The Dirección Anti-Alcohólica was the national directorate of the postrevolutionary Mexican government's official temperance campaign after 1933. Representatives from federal bureaus joined with delegates from nongovernmental, yet prorevolutionary-regime elements of civil society to encourage the growth of a popular, grassroots temperance movement.

The Mexican government that emerged from the revolutionary violence of 1910 through 1917 put forth an extensive program of cultural and social change. The cultural program of this social revolution sought to transfigure Mexico and Mexicans. The revolutionary elite felt that in order for their country to establish itself as a leading modern, industrialized nation, great programs of cultural transformation were necessary. The revolutionary temperance campaign was one of a number of government initiatives aimed at achieving this goal. Other similar efforts attempted to promote sanitation and hygiene in the countryside and to limit the influence of priests in order to secularize society. Although the Porfirian regime, which revolutionaries had overthrown, had made repeated, unsuccessful attempts to promote sobriety through various legislative reforms, the new government viewed alcoholism as one of the social ills the revolution had come to correct.

The postrevolutionary national temperance crusade began as an official government program during the period known as the Maximato (about 1928 to 1934). Three presidents served during this period, during which ex-President Plutarcho Elías Calles actually exercised power. Interim President Emilio Portes Gil officially launched the antialcohol campaign with the establishment of the Comité Nacional de Lucha Contra el Alcoholismo on 14 May 1929. Although Calles doubtless endorsed the project, it appears that the design of the temperance effort was Portes Gil's own creation. The Comité was intended to replicate a program Portes Gil had implemented while he was governor of the state of Tamaulipas. Portes Gil felt that the reason National Prohibition had been unsuccessful in the United States was that alcohol had been made illegal before the population was duly prepared for it. In order for temperance legislation to be successful, he argued, it must not be imposed from above, but rather proposed by the people themselves. Thus, Portes Gil's temperance program aimed primarily at propaganda efforts intended to convince people of the evils of alcohol use, so that they would demand prohibitory laws. Grassroots organizations were promoted, particularly among women, to campaign locally in favor of temperance.

The Comité Nacional was formed from representatives of each federal ministry; however, it disappeared within three years of its foundation and was replaced a year later by the slightly different Dirección Anti-Alcohólica. The Dirección included delegates from the federal dependencies, as before, but added representatives from civil society as well. Its motto was "*Por la Patria y Por la Raza!*" (For the Fatherland and for the race!). The leader of the new organization was Luis G. Franco, who had been the representative to the Comité Nacional from the Ministry of Industry. Franco continued the strategies used previously by the Comité Nacional, issuing propaganda throughout the country and encouraging the formation of grassroots temperance organizations, again, particularly among women. He often resorted to personal appeals to individuals at the local and municipal levels, exhorting them to mobilize groups in their community behind the temperance effort.

Franco, Portes Gil, and most contemporaries viewed alcoholism as a social disease. In other words, alcoholism was caused by social factors and affected not just individuals, but society as a whole. Alcohol was blamed as a leading cause of premature death, madness, poverty and cultural isolation among Natives, crime, industrial stagnation, the spread of disease, and social backwardness. Since the disease affected all of society, the cure was thought to involve the wider community as well. Most temperance advocates assumed that, once the people were convinced of the deleterious effects of alcohol on the individual and the broader community, alcohol would cease to be a problem.

As had been assumed during the previous century, most contemporary scientists felt that a variety of factors including climate, race, economic status, and religion were relevant. Alcoholism was considered primarily a problem associated with poor, particularly indigenous people, who lived in hot climates and held superstitious religious beliefs. Thus, other, related government programs such as the anticlerical campaign and programs to benefit poor peasants and workers were felt to be linked to solving the alcohol problem. In addition, the kind of alcohol consumed was thought to be important. Thus, studies emerged comparing various varieties of indigenous brews including *pulque, chicha, bacanora, aguardiente de caña, mezcal,* and *sotol.*

Because alcohol was blamed for a variety of social ills, its eradication was thought to promise numerous positive changes. The custom known as "*San Lunes,*" wherein workers remained at home on Mondays to recover from their weekend hangovers, would disappear. Once the Mexican worker was sober, many felt that little could stand in the way of Mexico's ascendance to a prominent position among the most important nations in the world.

By 1935, the Dirección Anti-Alcohólica had undergone another structural change. Luis Franco moved from the Department of Industry to the Department of Public Health and Hygiene, where he continued to serve as the director of the antialcoholic campaign. At this point, the national temperance effort became nominally centralized under the Department of Health and Hygiene. The program still bore the title Dirección Anti-Alcohólica, and Franco remained in charge. In practice, however, the Departments of Education, Agriculture, and Industry continued with their own temperance efforts.

The temperance campaign was never as successful as its founders had hoped. A complicated system of prohibitory laws emerged, at both the federal and state level. In most communities, however, alcohol vendors were able to circumvent the law through bribes with complicit local authorities. Grassroots activists were frustrated in their attempts to enforce what laws existed, and a blanket prohibition was never imposed.

Stephanie Mitchell

See also: Comité Nacional de Lucha contra el Alcoholismo; Franco, *Ing.* Luis G.; Mexico; Portes Gil, Emilio

References

Joseph, Gilbert M., and Daniel Nugent, eds. *Everyday Forms of State Formation: Revolution and the Negotiation of Rule in Modern Mexico.* Durham, NC: Duke University Press, 1994.

Vaughan, Mary Kay. *Cultural Politics in Revolution: Teachers, Peasants, and Schools in Mexico (1930–1940).* Tucson: University of Arizona Press, 1997.

Distillers Company Limited (DCL)

The Distillers Company Limited (DCL) was a dominant force in the Scotch whiskey industry during the period of its existence, 1877 to 1986.

The invention in 1830 of the continuous Coffey still divided the Scotch whiskey industry into two groups of producers. On the one hand, there were the numerous pot-still malt distillers, mainly in the Highlands, and, on the other, there were grain distillers with much larger plants, located in the Lowlands. Grain spirit had two markets. It was sold as whiskey, either on its own or blended with malt whiskey, and it was sold as spirit to be rectified into gin in England.

Origins of the Distillers Company Limited

Fierce competition in the grain spirit market reduced margins and brought about the formation of the Scotch Distillers' Association (SDA) in 1865 with the aim of regulating price and production. However, new grain distilleries continued to be built, and competition from cheap German spirit in the 1870s caused the SDA members to seek a more effective solution by amalgamation. Partners exchanged ownership of distilleries for shares in the new company, DCL, which would benefit from its greater scale of production and trade. DCL was registered in 1877 with six participating firms bringing together the grain distilleries of Port Dundas, Carsebridge, Cameronbridge, Glenochil, Cambus, and Kirkliston. Together with Caledonian Distillery, which worked closely with DCL before joining the company in 1885, it accounted for three-quarters of grain spirit production in Scotland.

Despite its size, DCL continued to support trade organizations and was a key player in the United Kingdom Distillers Association, often referred to as the "Whisky Parliament," during the period 1878 to 1888. For the first twenty years of its history, DCL remained in the hands of members drawn from the families of the original six distillery owners. However, in 1897 W. H. Ross, the first salaried official from outside these families, was appointed general manager, and he was to become the dominant figure in the industry until his retirement in 1935. Ross played a leading role in steering the industry through the period of declining consumption and confidence following the Pattison scandal in 1898 (a mixture of recklessness and criminality), the prosecutions over the definition of whiskey, and the royal commission on whiskey, 1907–1909. He also dealt with the government during the first world war when the impact of consumption on munitions production became an issue, and the industry had to respond to a demand for industrial alcohol.

In 1885, DCL began manufacturing baker's yeast using the Vienna process, and a ban on imported yeast during the war helped to boost this diversification. The production of acetone in 1916, for use in nitroglycerine, was the first small step into chemical manufacturing.

Diversification

The company gradually changed shape. A malt distillery was built at Knockdhu in 1894, and other malt distilleries were acquired, as well as a share in Dailuaine-Talisker distilleries. Grain distilleries were acquired in Scotland, England, and Ireland; two export houses were bought in 1916; and blends were produced for the home market where the position was strengthened by the purchase of the blending houses of Haig, Usher, Gray, and Thomson.

But the industry awaited the big amalgamation. The three largest blenders, Dewar, Walker, and Buchanan, began to discuss a merger in 1909, and DCL was soon involved, but progress was slow, and the first step was the merging of Buchanan and Dewar in 1915. In 1925, the amalgamation returned to the limelight, and the deal was put together involving Walker, Buchanan-Dewars, and DCL, with DCL as the holding company and Ross as the chairman and managing director. DCL was now a vertically integrated distilling and blending firm. Acquisitions continued, including White Horse Distillers in 1927, and by 1935 DCL owned fifty-one malt distilleries, had more than 60 percent of the whiskey market, and held a prime position in the gin market.

DCL was not just a drinks company; it was a diverse business covering yeast, industrial alcohol, solvents, carbon dioxide, and a range of chemicals. This growing diversification was a feature of the period 1918 to 1925 when there was uncertainty about the future of the potable spirits market. By then, DCL dominated the production of industrial alcohol from molasses, pursuing a similar strategy of merger and acquisition to that employed with whiskey. It succeeded in marketing Discol, an alcohol fuel, in 1921. Collaborative ventures with such companies as Union Carbide and Imperial Chemicals Industries followed.

During the second world war, DCL was asked by the government to undertake the manufacture of penicillin. In 1957, it began manufacturing thalidomide under license, with disastrous consequences and compensation payments.

The 1960s was a period of rapid growth with spectacular increases in sales in the United States, and by 1970 Japan had become a significant market. Many distilleries were expanded or refurbished. But the recession in the world economy following the oil crisis of 1975 to 1976 brought about a slump in fortunes. By 1980, DCL's share of the home market, which had been about 50 percent in 1971, had fallen to about 20 percent, and between 1983 and 1985, twenty-one malt distilleries and one grain distillery were closed. Throughout its existence, the company had continued to operate with a brand structure, a policy that meant that in some markets DCL brands competed with one another, and this attracted criticism.

In 1985, the Argyll Group, a food retailing chain, made a bid for DCL. Argyll had no significant spirits involvement, and DCL rejected the bid. Guinness, the brewing company, which had recently moved into the spirits market with the acquisition of Arthur Bell, was more acceptable and launched a rival bid with the backing of DCL. The final bid of £2,447 billion was referred to the Monopolies and Mergers Commission, but by April 1986, Guinness was the new owner. It disposed of almost all of the diversification activities to concentrate on the core business of spirits. The takeover was later the subject of legal action over a share support system, which resulted in jail sentences for several participants including Ernest Saunders, the chairman and chief executive of Guinness.

Frank O. Robson

See also: Cumming, Sir Ronald Stuart; Guinness Brewery; Hayman, Sir (Cecil George) Graham; Ross, Sir Henry (James); Scotland; Whiskies

References

Craig, H. Charles. *The Scotch Whisky Industry Record.* Dunbarton: Index Publishing, 1994.

Moss, Michael S., and John R. Hume. *The Making of Scotch Whisky.* Edinburgh: James and James, 1981.

Weir, Ronald B. *The History of the Distillers Company, 1877–1939.* Oxford: Oxford University Press, 1995.

Wilson, Ross. *Scotch: The Formative Years.* London: Constable, 1970.

Dominion Alliance for the Total Suppression of the Liquor Traffic

The Dominion Alliance for the Total Suppression of the Liquor Traffic, incorporated in 1887, was a national lobby group for temperance legislation in late-nineteenth-century Canada. Paralleling the efforts of the Woman's Christian Temperance Union (WCTU), the Dominion Alliance produced countless pamphlets, books, and flyers; presented lectures and displays; and supported protemperance national, provincial, and municipal political candidates and legislative initiatives. The Dominion Alliance had branches throughout Canada, yet its Protestant, anglophone leadership and outlook (overtly racist, anti-Catholic, and anti-Semitic at times) limited the appeal of its message to the larger community. Its greatest success was pushing the federal Conservative government into setting up a Royal

Commission on the Liquor Traffic in 1892, and forcing the new Liberal prime minister, Wilfrid Laurier, into holding a plebiscite on prohibition in 1898. The Dominion Alliance was instrumental in the enactment and enforcement of the various provincial and local liquor laws.

Much of the Dominion Alliance's administrative strength was due to the energies of Francis Spence, the organization's secretary and only full-time worker, who guided the alliance's policies until 1907. Spence, a Liberal, supported the temperance measures of Ontario's Mowat government, even though they were extremely tentative. This frustrated the more radical wing of the alliance, the Advanced Prohibitionists, who distrusted Mowat's commitment to temperance and Spence's allegiances. When the Ontario government held a plebiscite on prohibition in 1894, the radicals' distrust was confirmed, as the premier claimed uncertainty about constitutional jurisdictions to avoid passing prohibitory legislation.

The Dominion Alliance also participated in the Royal Commission on the Liquor Traffic, a national road show formed by the Conservative government in 1892 to deflect calls for prohibition. The final report reflected the perspective of the commissioners, who favored liquor-licensing laws over prohibition. Undeterred by this setback, Spence responded with publication of *The Facts of the Case,* a compilation of the detailed, statistics-based arguments presented by the alliance to the commission, and through the alliance's persistent lobbying, forced the newly elected prime minister, Wilfrid Laurier, to hold a plebiscite in 1898. Laurier, a French Canadian and a staunch advocate of the British imperial connection, was loath to threaten his fragile coalition of French and English support over the liquor issue. The Dominion Alliance's avowal of national support was belied by its membership, which included WCTU and YMCA branches, Sons of Temperance lodges, Salvation Army Corps, Societies of Christian Endeavour, and the Baptist Young People's Unions, but few Catholics, Jews, or immigrants. The results of the plebiscite were, as Laurier feared, a split between an anglophone/rural protemperance vote and a francophone/immigrant/urban antitemperance vote. Laurier used the small voter turnout to refuse to enact prohibition, and the alliance responded to their bitter disappointment with invective toward Quebec and non-Protestants.

The Dominion Alliance's provincial fortunes apparently turned when one of their members, George William Ross, became Ontario premier in 1899 and passed prohibitory legislation in 1902. Since it was also an election year, Ross added the proviso that a large majority had to support the legislation in a referendum. The Advanced Prohibitionists revolted at this tactic and ran six candidates (unsuccessfully) against the Liberals. Their suspicions once again were confirmed when the protemperance vote won the referendum but did not meet the majority required, and Ross deferred the final enactment of the legislation. The alliance at least had the vindictive satisfaction of throwing Ross out of the association in 1903.

Spence again turned his considerable talents to directing Dominion Alliance initiatives at the local government level, since local option (i.e., that each county could outlaw alcohol sales within its boundaries) remained a legal avenue. Alliance members spoke in Ontario churches and raised funds for the campaigns; more importantly, they galvanized rural support for the proliquor law policies of Ross's successor, Conservative James P. Whitney. In 1907, Spence was succeeded as secretary of the Ontario branch by his brother, the Reverend Ben Spence. In 1915, the alliance leadership joined the efforts of the Ontario Conservative government and federal Conservative/Unionist government to include prohibition in the war effort, and in 1917 National Prohibition was enacted as part of the War Measures Act. When World War I did not bring about the new social millennium in Canada, the alliance soon sputtered out as an artifact of Victorian ideals.

Cheryl Krasnick Warsh

See also: Federal Prohibition (Canada); Laurier, Sir Wilfrid; Provincial Prohibition (Canada); Provincial Regulation (Canada); Royal Commission on the Liquor Traffic (Canada); Spence, Francis Stephens

References

Decarie, Graeme. "Spence, Francis Stephens" in *Dictionary of Canadian Biography,* vol. XIV (1911–1920). Toronto: University of Toronto Press, 1998.

Spence, Francis. *The Facts of the Case: A Summary of the Most Important Evidence and Argument Presented in the Report of the Royal Commission on the Liquor Traffic Compiled under the Direction of the Dominion Alliance for the Total Suppression of the Liquor Traffic.* Toronto: Newton and Treloar, 1896. [Facsimile reprint, Toronto: Cole's, 1973.]

Spence, Ruth Elizabeth. *Prohibition in Canada: A Memorial to Francis Stephens Spence.* Toronto: Ontario Branch of the Dominion Alliance, 1919.

Dougall, John (1808–1886)

For more than twenty years the most prominent temperance leader in English Canada, John Dougall (1808–1886) was a proselytizer, editor, and organizer for the cause. After emigrating from Scotland to Montreal, this businessman had a conversion experience that focused his considerable talents on social reform. As managing editor of two important newspapers, the *Canada Temperance Advocate* and the *Montreal Witness,* he espoused public schooling, abolitionism, sailors' homes, and other causes. He was a long-standing officer of the Montreal Temperance Society, serving as president during the 1840s when the society resolved to establish temperance societies in every English-speaking community from Gaspé to Lake Huron.

Dougall edited the widely circulated *Canada Temperance Advocate* for some two decades beginning in 1835, and in 1846 he initiated the *Montreal Witness.* In these evangelical papers and also in journeys through Canada West and Canada East (latter-day Ontario and Quebec), Dougall preached to all classes of people the need to rise above sectarian and political divisions, to unite in raising humanity to its full potential through the mighty temperance reformation. This broad-based crusade met a warm reception after years of rancor, which culminated in Canadian political rebellions in 1837 and 1838. It also coincided with Canada West's emergence from the pioneer era, when it had been cheaper to distill local whiskey than to transport grain to distant markets. Not only agriculturalists and tradespeople but also influential editors and pastors who had dismissed temperance as political or religious radicalism now came to support the cause.

The Montreal Temperance Society's decade of spectacular outreach opened in 1840. Its Ladies' Committee raised funds to send a traveling agent to carry the message to rural districts. When he reported remarkable receptivity to the temperance gospel in far-flung hamlets he visited, the prosperous businessmen of the Montreal society sprang into action. They sent six agents into the field and hundreds of free copies of the *Canada Temperance Advocate* to politicians, teachers, and preachers.

Under Dougall's editorship, the *Canada Temperance Advocate*'s circulation soared to 8,000 in 1841, and publication continued until 1854. It was an intelligent repository of international temperance polemics, agricultural news, moralistic verse, and fiction. The paper served to coordinate the Canadian movement by printing agents' schedules, overseeing the general switch to total abstinence in the early 1840s, and printing news of local societies. By 1844, the *Advocate* boasted 120,000 teetotalers in the province of Canada and a sharp drop in workplace drinking. By the late 1840s, temperance halls supplied dry venues for public events, liquor taxes had risen, taverns faced growing restrictions, and drunkenness was increasingly seen as disreputable.

In 1848, when the Sons of Temperance organization appeared in Canada West, the more secular attractions of insurance benefits, comic speeches, and alternate forms of leisure began to replace the Montreal society's Evangelism. John Dougall supported but did not lead the nearly successful prohibition campaign in the province in 1854 and 1855. Dougall was fundamentally a moral suasionist, a veritable prophet to his devoted readers. Moving to New York City in 1871, he won an even larger following for the *American Weekly Witness* he founded there.

John Dougall's millennial vision of temperance as a transcendent force riveted a population weary of strife and eager for development, which they saw in moral as well as material terms. Dougall made the realistic promise that curbing widespread drunkenness would do wonders for both.

Jan Noel

See also: Provincial Prohibition (Canada); Sons of Temperance

References

Noel, Jan. *Canada Dry: Temperance Crusades before Confederation.* Toronto: University of Toronto Press, 1995. 77–88.

Snell, J. G. "Dougall, John" in *Dictionary of Canadian Biography,* vol XI: 270–271. Toronto: University of Toronto Press, 1982.

Dow, Neal (1804–1897)

Neal Dow (1804–1897) was the mayor of Portland, Maine; a candidate for president in 1880 for the Prohibition Party; and a Civil War hero, who is often referred to as the "Father of Prohibition." Born on 20 March 1804 in Portland, Maine, to Quaker parents, Dow worked in his father's tannery after graduating from high school. At the time, Portland was the center of the rum-running trade with the West Indies, and the young man became outraged at the social chaos he saw around him. As a result, he became involved in the temperance movement and sought to destroy the city's liquor trade. In 1838, he formed the Maine Temperance Union, and began a campaign to pressure the state legislature for passage of a prohibition law. He pressured the state legislature to pass a statewide prohibition law in 1846. Yet, the law had a number of loopholes that allowed some alcohol sales to continue. Five years later, his efforts were rewarded with the passage of the "Maine Law," which was the first state law prohibiting the manufacturing or sale of alcohol except for medical or mechanical purposes. This law would stand until 1933, and other states and nations used it as a model for their own legislation. As a result, Dow became a national figure.

Dow's popularity led him to become mayor of Portland, and from that position Dow tried to smash the rum industry. He soon became unpopular among various segments of Portland's population, particularly among the Irish. In June 1855, a riot broke out in the city in which a sailor named John Robins was killed by a gunshot wound. There is a great amount of debate among historians as to what caused the riot and whether Dow was responsible in part for Robins's death. A few months later, the Republican Party was defeated in the statewide elections. Many in his party blamed Dow for the loss, and his influence in state politics disappeared. Yet, his image among prohibitionists in the rest of the nation remained bright.

During the Civil War, he was made a colonel in the 13th Maine Volunteer Infantry. His regiment became known as the "Temperance Regiment" because he made his men "take the pledge." Given his reputation, many mothers pushed for their sons to soldier under him. He was promoted to the rank of brigadier general in April 1862. Commanding forts below New Orleans and in Florida, he saw action at Port Hudson. Dow was wounded in combat and taken prisoner. Confined at the Libby prison in Richmond, Virginia, for nine months, his stay there was filled with controversy. Accused of hoarding food and blankets, he was exchanged in March 1864. He later resigned from the army due to ill health.

After the war, Dow continued to speak out for the prohibition cause. Traveling widely, he also campaigned and lobbied on issues such as crime prevention, prison reform, and women's rights. He was named the Prohibition Party's candidate for president in 1880 and, while he did not garner many votes, he remained personally popular. His son, Fred N. Dow, a prominent political figure in his own right, continued to press his father's temperance cause after the general's death on 2 October 1897.

His home was willed to the Maine Woman's Christian Temperance Union (WCTU) and became their headquarters. It has been restored and is now a popular tourist site for many visiting Portland.

T. Jason Soderstrum

See also: Maine Law; Prohibition Party (United States); State Prohibition (United States)

References

Byrne, Frank Loyola. *Prophet of Prohibition: Neal Dow and His Crusade.* Magnolia, MA: Peter Smith, 1969.

Clubb, Henry S. *The Maine Liquor Law: Its Origin, History & Results, Including a Life of Hon. Neal Dow.* New York: Fowler and Wells, 1856.

Dow, Neal. *The Reminiscences of Neal Dow: Recollections of Eighty Years.* Portland, ME: Evening Express, 1898.

Drama, Representations of Temperance in

The representation of temperance in drama in England and the United States, the two countries where it was principally written and produced, is nearly as old as temperance activism itself. Whether written and produced by activists working from within the various temperance movements or by "independent" reformers who often were more interested in the sensational aspects of drunkenness than they were in eradicating intemperance, the temperance drama mirrored the dominant temperance ideology of the time and played a significant role in shaping public attitudes toward drinking. Before the demise of temperance dramaturgy following Prohibition, more than 200 such plays had been written.

During its century-long life, the temperance drama covered practically every aspect of the reform. It represented British teetotalism of the 1830s, Washingtonian experiences and assimilative reform, the efficacy of moral suasion, the prohibitionist sentiments and coercive tactics of Neal Dow and Maine Law proponents, the influence of women and the Woman's Christian Temperance Union (WCTU), the Anti-Saloon League of America's (ASLA) method-oriented approach to reform, the politicization of temperance reform, and ultimately National Prohibition in the United States. In a minor key, the temperance drama also represented the dangers of family and social drinking, total abstinence versus moderation, the value of temperance societies, the negative influence of "bad company" and the "bachelor culture" of the barroom upon American working men, the physical abuse of women and children by the drunken heads of households, the economic destruction of the drunkard's family, and even the dangers of drinking cider.

In addition to preaching against the evils and dangers of drink, the temperance drama was an integral part of rational recreation movements in both England and the United States and attempts to provide alternative, substitutive social environments and activities for drinkers and potential drinkers. The goal of activities such as temperance dances, lectures, poetry readings, musical concerts, and dramatic presentations in specially constructed "communities of enjoyment" that would substitute for the "degrading"' working-class recreations presented in sites like the pub, gaming hall, and the street was to satisfy the need for "regulated" amusement. Presented in nineteenth-century temperance halls, opera houses, town halls, and mechanics' institutes, the temperance drama became a prominent component in the alternative culture for working- and middle-class males.

The British Temperance Drama

The temperance drama had its origins in England early in the nineteenth century. In 1828, Douglas Jerrold, a noted journal editor, reformer, and dramatist, wrote *Fifteen Years of a Drunkard's Life,* the play that is now considered the prototype of the temperance drama. An American play, *The Forgers* (1825), a "dramatic poem" written in blank verse by John Blake White, utilized drinking as a plot device (i.e., the means for destroying a character) three years earlier, but *Fifteen Years of a Drunkard's Life* was the first to outline the identifying characteristics of the stage drunkard and came quite close to espousing teetotalism before that policy gained popularity. In his native England, Jerrold's drama was highly successful at working-class theaters like the Coburg (where it debuted), the Britannia, and the Surrey; but when it was exported to the United States, it was judged too harsh for the more optimistic American audiences, and it failed both critically and financially. Unlike the majority of American temperance melodramas that end happily with the drunkard being reclaimed and restored to his family and social position, both drunkards in *Fifteen Years of a Drunkard's Life* meet an unhappy fate. In his drunken stupor, Vernon, the middle-class protagonist, murders his wife and, in his turn, dies; Copsewood, the working-class drunkard, is arrested for his many crimes committed while intoxicated, is publicly disgraced, and is led off to prison at the end of the play. The lesson that audiences at theaters in both England and the United States were meant to take home with them was unmistakable: If you are intemperate, you will be severely punished and may even perish.

As harsh as the penalties for intemperance were in *Fifteen Years of a Drunkard's Life,* few temperance dramas could match the draconian punishments meted out in two plays staged in the 1840s that were based upon the protemperance drawings of graphic artist and political commentator George Cruikshank. *The Bottle* (1847) and its sequel, *The Drunkard's Children* (1848), were adapted from Cruikshank's serial graphic illustrations into no less than ten separate dramas by playwrights T. P. Taylor, George Dibdin Pitt, C. Z. Barnett, J. B. Johnstone, J. Courtney, and T. H. Reynoldson and mounted at a series of London's "minor" theaters. In these plays, an entire family, the Thornleys, suffer the humiliations that result from living with a drunkard and experience horrible deaths because of the bottle. Accurately conforming to the eight plates of Cruikshank's seriographic drawings, the first play, *The Bottle,* begins with the mechanic and his family enjoying prosperity and sobriety until, as the stage directions for the first scene indicate, "The bottle is brought out for the first time—The husband induces his wife to take a drop." Subsequent scenes depict the mechanic's being discharged from his job; the family's pawning their furniture and clothes to buy liquor; the drunkard's wife and children being forced to beg in the streets; the starvation death of the youngest child; violent quarrels and brutal beatings; and the drunkard's eventual murder of his wife with an empty liquor bottle, the natural consequences of intemperance. By the final scene, "the bottle has done its work! It has destroyed the infant and the mother—it has brought the son and daughter to vice and the streets, and has left the father a hopeless maniac" awaiting certain death in a prison cell.

The Drunkard's Children chronicles the plight of the Thornley children following their parents' deaths, graphically representing their suffering, degradation, and violent deaths. Robert, the son, dies in prison during a fit of delirium tremens while his sister, left alone by her brother's death and believing herself unfit to live in respectable society, commits "self-murder" by jumping from London Bridge. Although it utilized some of the most effective dramatic devices of the era, including the river suicide and the image of a woman visiting a loved one in prison (a recurrent feature of the iconography of the age), when compared to its more famous predecessor, because the Thornley children are doomed from the outset, *The Drunkard's Children* lacked the tension generated by the anticipation and uncertainty of the outcome of *The Bottle;* hence, the sequel was inherently less dramatic. Its structural deficiencies notwithstanding, *The Drunkard's Children* was popular with British working-class audiences, and its utility as propaganda was indisputable.

A minority strain of the British temperance drama (including plays like *The Drunkard's Doom* by George Dibdin Pitt [1832] and Thomas Morton's *Another Glass* [1848]) closely resembled American temperance dramaturgy by allowing the drunkard to repent and be reclaimed, to be restored to moral and societal health, and to be reunited with his family. However, the dominant plot pattern of the British temperance drama was more like that of *The Bottle* and *The Drunkard's Children:* a tightly woven causal chain that began with the first, fatal glass and saw the unrepentant drinker and his family destroyed by alcohol. This catastrophic plot pattern, in addition to serving as the base for the two Cruikshank-derived plays, was also featured in two later-nineteenth-century temperance dramas: *The Village Bane; or, Two High Roads of Life* and *Danesbury House: A Temperance Entertainment* (1862), both written by Arthur Moulds.

Three American "Classics"

Unlike the more pessimistic and deterministic British temperance drama in which the drunkard followed a linear path to destruction, the United States temperance drama assumed the pattern of an inverted arc that, like the Washingtonian experience speech before it, represented the drinker's falling into despair and degradation because of his habit and then being reclaimed through his signing the abstinence pledge and swearing off liquor. Thus, although U.S. temperance dramas retained many of the same "stock" dramatic devices employed in their British counterparts—battered wives, abused and/or neglected children, the decline of an entire family from prosperity to poverty and degradation, and the drunkard's social and physical deterioration to a point of crisis—they espoused a more assimilative brand of reform that allowed for the reclamation of drunkards and the salvation of families. As a consequence, they were considerably more optimistic in their outlook and prognosis for both drinker and his family and more reflective of a young country in which social mobility and a bright cultural and economic future were guaranteed to the sober and the "good at heart."

This structural pattern and optimistic outlook were clearly illustrated in the classic American temperance drama, *The Drunkard,* written by W. H. Smith and "a Gentleman." First produced at the Boston Museum in 1844 and a prominent feature in Massachusetts temperance rallies during the 1840s, *The Drunkard* was written while Washingtonianism was still influential. The play shows a middle-class, well-educated young husband, Edward Middleton, succumbing to the temptations of the bottle, assisted by a villainous lawyer who was motivated by both revenge against Middleton's family and his covetous desire for Middleton's wife. Progressing downward, both socially and physically, due to the progressive nature of his intemperance, Middleton reaches his nadir in Boston's Dock Square and "a well-known barroom on School Street," both decayed and degraded environments in Boston at the time. In the New York production, his moral decline leads him to the infamous Five Points slum on the city's Lower East Side. Regardless of the locus of the play, the degree of Middleton's alcohol-induced deterioration is materially represented by his physical condition, the shabbiness of his clothes, and the neighborhoods he frequents. In the final act of the play, Middleton is saved through the auspices of a Washingtonian representative and reunited with his family while the townspeople sing "Home, Sweet Home" outside the Middleton house. Thus, the inverted arc pattern was enabled by the Washingtonian spokesman, and *The Drunkard* reinforced Washingtonian ideology and practices.

With Smith, who was both coauthor and the theater's stage manager, in the role of Edward Middleton, George E. "Yankee" Locke as the original landlord, and Adelaide Phillips (later renowned as an opera star) as Julia Middleton, *The Drunkard* opened at the Boston Museum on 12 February 1844 and during the 1844–1845 season was presented a record 140 times. Five years later, in 1850, the legendary show-business impresario P. T. Barnum chose the play to open the newly renovated "moral lecture room" at his American Museum in New York. Barnum, a teetotaler himself and a "podium star" on the temperance lecture circuit, was so vehemently opposed to intemperance that not only did he sponsor temperance dramas like *The Drunkard* and *The Bottle* and horrific displays like a tableau titled *The Drunken Family,* which was a wax replication of a drunkard's family looking down upon the face of a small boy who has starved to death, but he also permanently banished liquor from his establishment and refused readmission to those who sneaked out to a nearby pub at intermission.

The second American temperance classic, *Ten Nights in a Bar-room and What I Saw There,* was published as a novel a decade after the decline of Washingtonianism but before *The Drunkard* disappeared from New York's first-class theaters. Written by journalist/novelist/reformer Timothy Shay Arthur, *Ten Nights in a Bar-room* achieved immediate success upon its publication in novel form and a long and prosperous life when converted to the stage by William W. Pratt, a New York playwright, actor, temperance lecturer, and preacher. Although it never matched *The Drunkard* in total attendance in America's major cities, it far surpassed its rival in both popularity and longevity once it began to tour to the country's small towns and even challenged *Uncle Tom's Cabin,* the most successful moral reform drama of all time, in number of road companies and total attendance.

Written shortly after Arthur had rejected Washingtonianism and moral suasion as the means to national temperance, *Ten Nights in a Bar-room* is an unveiled call for prohibition. Initially attracted to the Washingtonians because of their advocacy of Emersonian notions of self-reliance and individualism as a means to temperance, Arthur became disenchanted with the group's approach after witnessing the backsliding of many of their members in the mid-1840s. Subsequently, he lost faith in the efficacy of moral suasion and became convinced that collective action was the only solution to intemperance. By the time he wrote *Ten Nights in a Bar-room,* Arthur had become a staunch advocate of the coercive reform advocated by Neal Dow through his Maine Law. The degree of his conversion is evident in the final scene of his play, which contains an impassioned plea for legalized prohibition, uttered in the novel by Joe Morgan (the reformed drunkard) himself, but declaimed from the stage by the play's temperance spokesman, Romaine. *Ten Nights in a Bar-room* has also been immortalized because it contains what is arguably one of the most poignant scenes in all temperance literature: the death of the drunkard's daughter, Mary, after she is hit in the forehead with a shot glass thrown in anger by the local tavern keeper.

The third major American temperance drama, *Little Katy, or the Hot Corn Girl,* opened in New York in 1854 at three theaters simultaneously: the Bowery, Purdy's National Theatre, and Barnum's Museum. Published as a series of "editorials" by Solon Robinson in the *New York Tribune* and as a novel before being adapted for the stage, *Hot Corn* narrates the story of a pathetic twelve-year-old corn seller on New York's streets who is forced to return home without selling her corn and is subsequently beaten to death by her drunken mother who needs the proceeds of her daughter's enterprise to finance her drinking. All versions of the story graphically depicted the hideous conditions on New York's streets and in its tenements, focused public attention upon the plight of children of drunkards, and, in the process, demonstrated that not only was intemperance a significant problem among recent immigrants from Ireland, but that the Irish American community was acutely aware of the severity of the problem. In their efforts to disseminate the temperance message and demonstrate the impact of intemperance upon immigrant populations, temperance proponents were greatly aided by the popularity of *Hot Corn,* which was said to be the second most popular play in New York in the 1850s—second only to *Uncle Tom's Cabin.* One of the productions of *Hot Corn* was staged in the same theater and by the same company as *Uncle Tom's Cabin,* and the role of Little Katy was played by the same actress, Cordelia Howard, who played Little Eva in the abolitionist classic. As a consequence, on an average day, Howard was required to perform two different ascension scenes: one as Little Eva; another as Little Katy, who ascends to heaven after forgiving her mother for killing her.

Temperance Drama Outside of the "Big City"

The golden age of the temperance drama ended with the Civil War. After their popularity in the cities of the Northeast waned, *The Drunkard* and *Ten Nights in a Bar-room* joined other popular nineteenth-century stage favorites on the road to the secondary cities and small towns in the United States. These plays were brought to the rural United States by family touring troups or "mom and pop" companies like The Thorne Comedy Company, The Grace George Dramatic Company, The Switzer Comedy Company, and the Old Reliable Company that followed the country's small opera house circuits.

Probably of more importance to the spread of temperance imperatives than sporadic visits by touring companies, however, were the myriad amateur productions mounted in rural temperance halls, opera houses, and town halls. Written by nonprofessionals like Nellie Bradley, a Woman's Christian Temperance Union (WCTU) activist from Washington D.C., and disseminated as inexpensive scripts by publishers like A. D. Ames of Clyde, Ohio, Z. Pope Vose of Rockland, Maine, or The National Temperance Society and Publications Association, these simple plays proliferated during the final decades of the nineteenth century and served as the basis of recreations designed to supplant those found in barrooms. Although temperance dramas could be staged anywhere there was adequate space, and many were presented in local town halls and opera houses, from roughly the mid-nineteenth century onward the venue of choice was the center of local activism, the temperance hall. Not only did temperance halls afford adequate spaces for staging entertainments, but they also ensured that all activities sponsored and all beverages served could be regulated, whereas activities at commercial theaters or neighborhood bars were often beyond social control.

A French Temperance Drama

While, for the most part, temperance dramas were not written in countries where there were strong cultural traditions supporting drinking or where temperance reform developed after the late nineteenth century, one of the most famous plays exposing the dangers of drinking originated in France. First written in 1877 as a set of serialized episodes in the newspaper and then as a novel, Emile Zola's *L'Assommoir* (The Drinking Den) was created, not as a temperance tract, but rather as a naturalistic narrative designed to expose the squalor of slum life. When adapted to the stage in 1878 by William Busnach, Octave Gastineau, and Zola himself, however, the original story became a melodrama, and a temperance theme was written into it. Onstage, the character of the machinist Goujet, who in the novel professed no particular ideology or social interest, was transformed into the temperance spokesman, and the delirium tremens scene, minor in the novel, became one of the play's high points and served to frighten audience members to sign the pledge, often available at the theater's box office, and to abstain from drink.

L'Assommoir didn't remain solely French for long. The year after its Paris debut, *L'Assommoir* was translated and adapted to the English stage by British novelist/reformer Charles Reade. Renamed *Drink*, Reade's drama ran for more than 5,000 nights and elevated the lead actor, Charles Warner, to star status. Subsequently, Zola's original story was brought to American stages by Dion Boucicault and by Augustin Daly, who claimed a translation by Olive Logan as his own and copyrighted the play under his own name. The story was also prominently displayed as a play-within-a-play device in D. W. Griffith's *A Drunkard's Reformation* (1909), which depicted a drunkard father teaching his child about the horrors of alcoholism by taking him to a temperance drama: *Drink*.

The Demise of Temperance Dramaturgy

By the beginning of the twentieth century, even though antidrink plays were written by major dramatists like James A. Herne, temperance dramaturgy had virtually disappeared in Great Britain and was declining precipitously in the United States. The handful of temperance dramas written around the turn of the century also began to depart from temperance orthodoxy, sometimes significantly. Some, like Herne's *Drifting Apart* (1888) and Elliot McBride's *As by Fire* (1895), maintained at least a surface fidelity to established temperance imperatives; others, like Charles Hoyt's *A Temperance Town* (1892) and J. W. Todd's *Arthur Eustace; or A Mother's Love* (1891), betrayed doubts about temperance philosophy and tactics, especially those of the ASLA; while still others, like Edward Locke's *The Drunkard's Daughter* (ca. 1905), overtly attacked, lampooned, and/or dismissed reform efforts. At first, the void left by the decline in temperance dramaturgy was filled by a spate of reformist movies like *In the Grip of Alcohol* (1912), *John Barleycorn* (1914), and *Prohibition* (1915), each representing the horrors of drink as faithfully as had *The Drunkard;* but the depiction of intemperance on film was ostensibly killed by the passage of Prohibition. Thereafter, with the exception of *I'll Cry Tomorrow, The Days of Wine and Roses,* and other cinematic anomalies, temperance ceased to be an issue in film, while dramas like *The Time of Your Life* (1939) and *Harvey* (1944) started to represent the drunkard as a "lovable old sot," a depiction that perhaps crystallized in W. C. Fields's characterizations in the films *Poppy* and *The Fatal Glass of Beer.* In these representations, the drunkard had traveled a tortuous route, from either helpless victim or demonic villain to harmless "old soak," and in each era, such representations permeated the host culture and influenced public opinion toward alcohol consumption.

John W. Frick

See also: Anti-Saloon League of America (ASLA); Cruikshank, George; Dow, Neal; Film, Representations of Drinking and Temperance in; Literature, Representations of Drinking in; Literature, Representations of Temperance in; Washingtonians; Woman's Christian Temperance Union (WCTU) (United States)

References

Booth, Michael R. "The Drunkard's Progress: Nineteenth-Century Temperance Drama" in *Dalhousie Review.* 44 (1964–1965): 205–212.

Frick, John W. "He Drank from the Poisoned Cup: Theatre, Culture and Temperance in Antebellum America" in *Journal of American Drama and Theatre.* 4 (Spring 1992): 21–41.

———. *Theatre, Culture and Temperance Reform in Nineteenth-Century America.* Cambridge: Cambridge University Press, 2003.

———. "Victims of the Bottle, from Printed Page to Gilded Stage: T. P. Taylor's Dramatization of George Cruikshank's Serial Illustrations, *The Bottle*" in *Performing Arts Resources.* 16 (1992): 1–7.

Mason, Jeffrey D. *Melodrama and the Myth of America.* Bloomington: Indiana University Press, 1993.

McArthur, Judith N. "Demon Rum on the Boards: Melodrama and the Tradition of Antebellum Reform" in *Journal of the Early Republic.* 9 (Winter 1989): 517–540.

Drinking Establishments (France)

The writings of François Villon, François Rabelais, Charles Baudelaire, Jean-Paul Sartre, Simone de Beauvoir, and others attest to the pervasive influence of drinking establishments on French literature and history. Although the number of drinking establishments waxed during the nineteenth and early twentieth centuries and waned after World War II, these spaces remain vital. Today, virtually all the diverse subcultures of immigrant and postmodern France have their own types of drinking establishment.

Tavern, Cabaret, and Café

The original term for drinking establishments was "taverns" (from the Latin *taberne*). We glimpse the odium surrounding their existence in Nicolas Delamare's eighteenth-century treatise on the Paris police. Taberne, he asserted, originally signified the person who led animals to pagan altars for slaughter, and he felt that tavern owners continued such a sacrificial rite with their customers. Such sentiments echoed the attitude of generations of prelates, as well as the 1256 law that banned residents from drinking on a tavern's premises, although they could buy beverage alcohol for home consumption. Only travelers had permission to consume on the premises.

By the fourteenth century, the term "cabaret" became applied to drinking establishments. Again according to Delamare, the word derived from the traditional custom of putting leaves or cork stoppers (Latin *cobretum*) on tavern doors. Unlike taverns, cabarets sold not only wine but also food to be consumed on the premises, thus attracting a wealthier clientele.

By the late seventeenth century, a new drink, coffee, and a new type of establishment, the café, emerged. Spreading from the Islamic world, cafés arrived in Paris in 1686 when a Sicilian, Francesco Procopio Cotilli, opened his successful Café Procope in Paris, where it became a center of fashionable sociability. Its chandeliers, marble-topped tables, Turkish rugs, mirrors, and robed waiters were soon copied by other cafés, and cabarets declined markedly in social status.

How many of these various types of establishment flourished in early modern France? Numbers are extremely unreliable until the time of Louis XIV. At the end of the Sun King's reign, the great fortification builder and pioneer social statistician Sébastien Vaubin, in his *Projet d'une dîme royale* (1707), estimated the number at 40,000, excluding Paris—roughly one for each village or parish in France.

At the same time, a new medium of expression and information was emerging: the newspaper. Until well into the nineteenth century, newspapers had remained too expensive for mass circulation, and consequently cafés became sites where a large number of newspapers could be read on a regular basis. The intellectual cachet of the café also rose across the eighteenth century as Enlightenment thinkers such as Voltaire, Diderot, and Rousseau gathered and socialized therein. German philosopher Jürgen Habermas argues that cafés, along with reading rooms and learned societies, became significant breeding grounds for the modern democratic culture emerging in the eighteenth century.

At this point, however, the world of the upper-class café and the lower-class tavern were largely two different worlds. Thomas Brennan's detailed study of tavern popular culture in Paris between 1690 and 1770 reveals these spaces as vital for working-class life, but not for politics.

The French Revolution and After

The French Revolution of 1789 transformed not only the functions but also the numbers of Parisian (and French) drinking establishments. The distinctions separating wine and coffee merchants were obliterated with the proclamation of freedom of commerce and industry set forth in the laws of 2 through 17 March 1791. Now any drinking establishment owner could serve any drink he or she wished. In addition, the explosion of newspapers during revolutionary ferment resulted in more reading and political discussion in lower-class taverns as well as in upper-class cafés. This change marks the birth of the working-class café: an institution that integrated coffee drinking and newspaper reading into the milieu of the French working classes.

The most dramatic impact of the Revolution on drinking-establishment life emerged during the succeeding thirty years. By 1830, the number of drinking establishments in France had soared to 280,000 (seven times Vaubin's 1707 figure of 40,000), far outpacing the population increase from 20 to 35 million. (Interestingly, the rise of alcohol consumption paralleled only the rate of population increase.) Between the revolutions of 1830 and 1848, the political role of these proliferating public establishments became obvious. As political agitation rose, so too did the number of cafés outside Paris—totaling over 350,000 in 1848. Conservatives correctly accused radicals of using cafés for revolutionary politics. To stem this "red threat," Louis Napoleon Bonaparte, first as president and then as emperor, instituted a draconian decree in December 1851 and had various police and military forces close 50,000 drinking establishments between 1848 and 1855.

Nevertheless, under this same Napoleon III the rate of wine and spirit consumption in France soared. With the completion of a national railroad network, the great wine-producing regions of the south supplied northern cities with unprecedented amounts of wine. Between 1840 and 1870, French wine production and consumption rose by 50 percent. The urban renewal of Paris between 1852 and 1870, including the creation of broad, spacious boulevards, swelled the number of the capital's cafés from fewer than 4,000 in 1848 to over 22,000 by 1870. In Napoleon III's more "liberal" phase during the 1860s, the number of drinking establishments outside Paris climbed to 370,000.

After 1870, France became less concerned about the threat of café politics and far more worried about alcoholism. Conservatives attributed the Paris Commune of 1871 to heavy drinking in the cafés as well as to the Marxian Communism discussed there. The monarchist "moral order" Parliament promptly passed the first modern law in France repressing public drunkenness, a law that quickly fell into disuse. Once republicans gained control of the French Parliament (late 1870s), they abrogated the 1851 decree and restored freedom of commerce for cafés. Between 1880 and 1914, the number of shops climbed to over 480,000. During this same era, due partly to a vine disease that ravaged the vineyards in the 1860s and 1890s, consumers turned to spirits. In the decade before World War I, consumption of absinthe and other distilled spirits rose by 51 and 16 percent respectively.

Janet Flanner and Ernest Hemingway, both in uniform, read papers at a table in Les Deux Magots literary café in Paris, ca. 1945. (Library of Congress)

A frustrated French temperance movement finally found a ready audience within the Parliament during the horrors of 1914 through 18, but only temporarily. From across the political spectrum arose a groundswell and then a law to limit the number of drinking establishments. Many legislators hoped that the France emerging from the war—thanks to zoning ordinances and urban renewal—would eventually contain more hospitals than cafés! Their hopes were quickly dashed after the war as the rate of alcohol consumption and the number of cafés returned to, even exceeded, prewar levels by the late 1930s. Moreover, the artistic and literary life of Paris cafés shone with particular intensity through such figures as Proust, Picasso, and Hemingway, and the term *bistrot* became a common appellation for neighborhood establishments.

Finally, the effects of World War II and the subsequent national modernization permanently diminished the café culture of France. The devastations of war, occupation, and a collaborationist government (Vichy) plunged the number of shops to a mere 314,000 by 1946. Although the Resistance had heavily patronized cafés, succeeding governments modeled on national regeneration were no more sympathetic to the café than Vichy had been. Restrictive legislation remained in effect and was complemented by rigorous zoning ordinances in the new towns and city districts constructed during the 1960s and 1970s. Consequently, the number of cafés fell from 262,525 (1959) to 228,759 (1973) to 66,000 (1986) to about 50,000 (2001). Concomitantly, the French rate of alcohol consumption also dropped dramatically, by more than half. The new consumer culture—cars, TV, stereos, vacations, and the Internet—has given the French an entirely new set of leisure options.

Despite these dramatic changes, cafés remain a vital institution in France. Since the late 1970s, a new fascination with the "world we have lost" has led to new types of establishments. Philosophical, music, and cyber cafés complement the traditional literary and artistic cafés. Immigrants have also re-created café life in their own image, so that one now finds Algerian, Turkish, Chinese, Vietnamese, Senegalese, and Caribbean cafés. Thus, from sites of anticlericalism to republicanism to multiculturalism, cafés have remained a vital space in France.

W. Scott Haine

See also: Absinthe; Cabaret (France); France, Production and Consumption of Alcohol in; France, Temperance in

References

Barrows, Susanna. "After the Commune: Alcoholism, Temperance, and Literature in the Early Third Republic" in *Consciousness and Class Experience in Nineteenth-Century Europe,* edited by John M. Merriman, 205–218. New York: Holmes and Meier, 1979.

Bihl-Willette, Luc. *Des taverns aux bistrots: Une histoire des cafés.* Lausanne: L'Age d'Homme, 1997.

Brennan, Thomas. *Public Drinking and Popular Culture in Eighteenth-Century Paris.* Princeton: Princeton University Press, 1988.

Cafés, bistrots et compagnie. Expositions itinerantes CCI, no. 4. Centre de Création Industrielle. Paris: Centre national d'art et de culture Georges Pompidou, 1977.

Dion, Roger. *Histoire de la vigne et du vin en France des origins au XIXe siècle.* Paris: Flammarion, 1977 [1959].

Haine, W. Scott. *The World of the Paris Café: Sociability among the French Working Class, 1789–1914.* Baltimore: Johns Hopkins University Press, 1996.

Nourrisson, Didier. *Le buveur du XIXe siècle.* Paris: Albin Michel, 1990.

Prestwich, Patricia. *Drink and the Politics of Social Reform: Antialcoholism in France since 1870.* Palo Alto, CA: Society for the Promotion of Science and Scholarship, 1988.

Drinking Sites and Culture (Australia)

Australian drinking sites and culture were shaped in the colonial era, giving rise to a tradition of heavy and largely masculine drinking, especially in pubs. Since World War II, sites and patterns of drinking have changed markedly as Australia has become a modern and more multicultural society.

Colonial/Early Twentieth-Century Drinking Culture

The origins of Australian settlement in 1788 as a British penal colony greatly influenced drinking patterns and drinking cultures. The harsh, hot climate of New South Wales (NSW), combined with the population's Anglo-Celtic histories of drinking, suggests an early pattern of heavy consumption by convicts, soldiers, and the relatively few free settlers. Historians have emphasized the role of alcohol in the formation of the Australian character, particularly in the tradition of male "mateship" and mythical notions of the practical, sports-loving bushman (Ward 1981). Indeed, the use of rum as wages in the building of the colony's early infrastructure has entered into local myth as indicative of the central importance of alcohol (Hughes 1987), although consumption was probably no greater than in the United States or Britain through most of the nineteenth century (Dingle 1978; Powell 1988).

Hotels were often the first public buildings to be constructed, along with churches and government offices. Brandy, whiskey, and rum were popular choices until the late 1800s, when beer consumption increased significantly prior to World War I. Pubs and taverns were modeled upon British designs, with some important architectural modifications: longer bar counter areas to accommodate a greater number of drinkers, the relegation of women to saloon bars, and the ubiquitous tiled walls and floors to ensure ease of cleaning (Kirkby 1997). These features encouraged a rough-and-ready male drinking culture at odds with British attempts to ensure a more refined drinking environment. This was particularly evident in the tradition of the "six o'clock swill," a cattle-call rush to consume in the hour after work, until the pubs closed at 6 P.M. The early closing law that existed between 1916 and 1955 in NSW, and endured even later in other states, encouraged home drinking and a thriving illegal nightclub culture of consumption.

Changes in Drinking Culture since the 1950s

From the 1950s, the distinctly male pub culture was challenged by the rapid growth in registered clubs, fuelled by (with the exception of Victoria) poker (slot) machine revenue. The assortment of lawn bowls, sport and recreation, football clubs, and Returned Services League (RSL) clubs have remained popular with older communities and women as welcome alternatives to the pub culture (Caldwell 1972). Drinking in these contexts reaffirmed the alliance of alcohol with (mostly male) sporting activity and earlier notions of mateship. Women were not the only ones to be excluded from public drinking sites; indigenous Aboriginal populations were regulated, with some exceptions, out of the local hotel and club (Lewis 1992; Bourbon, Saggers, and Gray 1999). The eventual extension of hotel trading hours to 10 P.M. enabled pubs to offer "variety" entertainment to compete with the clubs' practice of subsidizing meals, entertainment, and alcohol through poker machine profits.

The influx of (mainly) southern Europeans, the result of successive federal governments' abolition of the "White Australia" policy, challenged the Australian preference for the pub and club after World War II. Since 1945, Australian per capita consumption of alcohol had risen steadily, peaking in the late 1970s. The new arrivals introduced café culture and wine consumption as an alternative to beer. This shift in drinking patterns and culture is clear in comparisons of national per capita consumption. Beer peaked at 134.8 liters (35.6 U.S. gallons) per capita in 1977, declining to 95 liters (25.1 U.S. gallons) in 1999. Conversely, per capita wine consumption over a longer period had more than doubled, from 8.9 liters in 1969 to 19.7 liters in 1999 (Australian Institute of Criminology). Migrants were also crucial, along with an increasing tourist population, in calls for more sophisticated drinking environments. However, the height of beer-drinking culture was evident in 1970s conversions of the local hotel into the nightly rock pub, with alcohol and loud rock-and-roll a perfect marriage of masculine leisure pursuits. By the early 1980s, Sydney hotels with the highest alcohol revenues were suburban rock pubs (NSW Liquor Administration Board 1983).

Ettamogah Pub near Albury, New South Wales, Australia. The building was inspired by a cartoon. (John Slater/Corbis)

The gradual, persistent liberalization of liquor laws since the early 1990s has changed the type and scope of public drinking. First, pub/club trading hours have expanded and, where appropriate, twenty-four-hour trading has emerged. Second, the states of Victoria and NSW have led the expansion of drinking sites, encompassing the serving of alcohol in cafés, restaurants, and nightclubs without the older regulatory requirement that it be accompanied by a meal. These changes have enabled cities to further their claims to a "cosmopolitan" ambience and attitude, of particular importance in Sydney's desire to compare favorably with international cultures during the 2000 Olympic Games. This has ended the historic partitioning of drinking from other social activity and leisure experiences.

Third, and perhaps paradoxically, liquor law liberalization has broadly coincided with pubs' and clubs' inability to survive on alcohol consumption alone. Hotels have invested heavily in responding to demands for more sophisticated dining and other leisure experiences; "pub grub" has now improved to the extent that restaurant chefs are often employed in inner city hotels. This is also reflected in the increasing popularity of imported beers at the expense of local brews. The steady decline in beer consumption, accompanied by Australians' increasing desire for wine as outlined earlier, has complemented shifts to more refined settings. Those wishing to attract a more traditional clientele have expanded the range of available gaming—poker machines, horse-race betting—and advertised the viewing of sporting fixtures exclusively offered through pay (cable) television. Not surprisingly, given the long history of Irish immigration, an increasing number of Australian hotels have converted to Irish theme pubs, popular with locals and tourists seeking an (in)authentic Gaelic drinking experience. The increased diversity of pub drinking contexts, also incorporating jukebox, Trivial Pursuit, and pool competitions, has revived women's interest.

The higher rates of heavy drinkers in Australia highlight that, for all of the "civilizing" influences upon Australian drinking sites in the past decade, concern with social and public-health problems related to alcohol persists. This is particularly the case with young drinkers, where social pressures to drink remain tied to the ritualistic transition from adolescence to adulthood (Shanahan and Hewitt 1999). The cultural pervasiveness of this ritual is reinforced in the continuing rights of alcohol manufacturers to advertise their products, something that is denied to cigarette companies. It remains the case that "the right to drink has a place in Australian history analogous to the right to carry a gun in America as one of our national symbols of full social maturity and acceptance" (Johnson 1992: 132).

Shane Homan

See also: Australia; Barmaids (Australia); Liquor Licensing (Australia); Women Publicans (Australia); Woman's Christian Temperance Union (WCTU) (Australia)

References

Australian Institute of Criminology. Consumption of Alcohol, Australia, 1961–2000. Australian Institute of Criminology website. http:www.aic.gov.au/research/drugconsumption/alcoholconsumption.html.

Bourbon, Deidre, Sherry Saggers, and Dennis Gray. *Indigenous Australians and Liquor Licensing Legislation.* Bentley: National Centre for Research into the Prevention of Drug Abuse, 1999.

Caldwell, Geoff. "Leisure Co-Operatives: 'The Institutionalisation of Gambling and the Growth of Large Leisure Organisations in New South Wales.'" (Ph.D. thesis, Australian National University, 1972).

Dingle, A. E. *Drink and Drinking in Nineteenth Century Australia: A Statistical Commentary.* Monash Papers in Economic History, no. 6. Melbourne: Monash University, 1978.

Freeland, John. *The Australian Pub.* Carlton: Melbourne University Press, 1966.

Hughes, Robert. *The Fatal Shore: A History of the Transportation of Convicts to Australia 1787–1868.* London: Pan Books, 1987.

Johnson, Vivien. "Be My Woman Rock and Roll" in *From Pop to Punk to Postmodernism: Popular Music and Australian Culture from the 1960s to the 1990s,* edited by Philip Hayward. Sydney: Allen and Unwin, 1992.

Kirkby, Diane. *Barmaids: A History of Women's Work in Pubs.* Cambridge and New York: Cambridge University Press, 1997.

Lewis, Milton. *A Rum State: Alcohol and State Policy in Australia 1788–1988.* Canberra: Australian Government Publishing Service, 1992.

NSW Liquor Administration Board. *Annual Report.* Sydney: NSW Government Printing Service, 1983.

Powell, K. C. *Drinking and Alcohol in Colonial Australia 1788–1901 for the Eastern Colonies.* Canberra: Australian Government Publishing Service, 1988.

Shanahan, Patrick, and Nicole Hewitt. *Developmental Research for a National Alcohol Campaign, Summary Report.* Canberra: Commonwealth Department of Health and Aged Care, 1999.

Ward, Russell. *The Australian Legend.* Melbourne: Oxford University Press, 1981.

Drinking Songs (United States)

American drinking songs are a form of folk music: The tunes are borrowed or by unknown composers, and the lyrics may vary from person to person and from bar to bar. In general, drinking songs fall into two main categories: songs about drinking or drunkenness ("It's beer, beer, beer that makes me wanna cheer. . . ."), and songs unrelated to alcohol but frequently sung when drinking or drunk.

Drinking songs are almost always loud, boisterous, and long ("Ninety-Nine Bottles of Beer on the Wall" is seldom sung from start to finish—an earlier version had only forty-nine bottles); they are often sentimental, profane, racist, sexist, or homophobic. These are songs that are usually sung slightly out of tune in large groups—the idea being that sober people are too repressed to sing them, but people (usually men, sometimes women) fortified with alcohol can drape arms around one another's shoulders, let go of all inhibitions, and sing from the heart.

Many of the earliest U.S. drinking songs were imported from England (Robert Burns's "Auld Lang Syne" is still sung in the twenty-first century by American New Year's revelers), Ireland ("Danny Boy"), and Germany; others were quintessential American folk songs: "Clementine," "I've Been Working on the Railroad," "The Erie Canal," "Shenandoah," "On Top of Old Smokey," and "The Yellow Rose of Texas," among others. Two drinking songs that appear regularly in published collections of drinking songs are "Little Brown Jug" ("My wife and I live all alone / In a little brown hut we call our own, / She loves gin and I love rum, / Tell you what, don't we have fun?") and "Frankie and Johnnie" ("He was her man, but he done her wrong"). Dean Henry Aldrich's early British verse on drink is also well-known to Americans:

> If on my theme I rightly think,
> There are five reasons why I drink,—
> Good wine, a friend, because I'm dry,
> Or lest I should be by and by,
> Or any other reason why.

Drinking songs are part of popular culture, and as such they are not static but exist in several versions, each more ribald than the last. Published drinking songs tend to be toned down, with "dirty" words removed; others deliberately play with the idea of obscenity, like "The Crayfish in the Chamber-Pot," which repeatedly begins a rhyme for a particularly strong piece of profanity and then backs off:

> In the middle of the night, I thought I'd have a fit,
> When my old lady got up to . . . wash her face,
> By the wayside aye diddlie-i-do.
> Children, children, hear your mother grunt,
> The crayfish in the chamber pot has got your mother's . . .
>   nose,
> By the wayside aye diddlie-i-do.

At their most innocent, drinking songs are bawdy and fun; at the other end of the spectrum, they can be obnoxious and disgusting. "Oral Sex Is Good for You" (to the tune of "Camptown Races"), for example, contains the lines "Cum between her eyes, cum between her thighs / Cuz anal sex bugs my ass, all the doo dah day." They often incorporate vernacular language—bad grammar, slang, and racial epithets ("Way Down Yonder in the Cornfield" begins "Some folks say that a nigger won't steal," for example). A great many drinking songs, especially military ones, are homophobic ("Fighter Pilots" begins "Oh there ain't no fighter pilots down in Hell / The place is full of queers, navigators, bombardiers"). After a while, some of the titles of these songs start to sound similar: "Drunkard John," "Whisky Bill," "Champagne Charlie," "Cocaine Bill [or Lil] and Morphine Sue," "Willy the Weeper," "An Ode to Charlie Mopps—The Man Who Invented Beer."

Drinking songs are often familiar tunes with new lyrics, like "I Want a Beer, Just Like the Beer that Pickled Dear Old Dad" (to the tune of "I Want a Girl"), "Alcoholic Baby" (to the tune of "Melancholy Baby"), and "Merrily We Roll the Keg" (to the tune of "Merrily We Roll Along"). Other drinking songs have become so well known that children sing them on the playground or at summer camp: "Be Kind to Your Web-Footed Friends" (to the tune of John Philip Sousa's "The Stars and Stripes Forever") or "Great Green Gobs of Greasy Grimy Gopher Guts" (to the tune of "The Old Gray Mare").

The most famous example of this sort of tune borrowing is, of course, "The Star Spangled Banner," the national anthem of the United States, which is based on a drinking song: "The Anacreontic Song" or "Anacreon in Heaven," lyrics by Ralph Tomlinson, president of the Anacreontic Society in London. The sheet music to the song was first published in England about 1780 and in the United States as early as 1798, with several versions of lyrics. In 1806, Francis Scott Key published a version with lyrics based on his poem "When the Warrior Returns"; later, in 1814, he published the version that Americans sing at baseball games.

In the late nineteenth century, the American temperance movement countered popular drinking songs with songs of its own, often borrowing drinking-song tunes. Three of these are "Father, Come Home," from the temperance play *Ten Nights in a Bar-Room,* "Touch Not the Cup" (to the tune of "Long Long Ago"), and "'Twas the Last, Last Rumseller" to the tune of "Last Rose of Summer." Lord Charles Neaves responded to songs like these with "I'm Very Fond of Water: A New Temperance Song":

I'm very fond of water,
I drink it noon and night [. . .]
But I forgot to mention—
Tis best to be sincere—
I use an old invention
That makes it into Beer.

Also during this period, from the Civil War until the end of the Victorian era, drinking songs were performed on the vaudeville stage, often by women dressed as men. Their songs suggested that drunken men preferred alcohol to the companionship of women or families, and their cross-dressing may be a not-so-subtle suggestion that drunken men lack virility.

Many drinking songs, from all periods, are about women, some praising the goodness of young girls and mothers, others complaining of shrewish wives. The anonymous seventeenth-century tidbit "A Farewell to Wives" includes these typical lines:

Once in our lives
Let us drink to our Wives!
Though the number of them is but small.
God take the best;
And the devil take the rest!
And so we shall be rid of them all.

Other titles of this ilk might include "The Bad Girl's Lament," "The Girl with the Golden Hair," "My Scolding Wife," "Little Maggie," "Old Grandma," "Drink on, Little Girl," and "Mother's Prayers."

Another subgenre is the culture-specific drinking song, with references to particular geographic locations, college, military, or club rivalries, and perceived social differences. "The Engineers' Drinking Song" from M.I.T., for example, which has over thirty verses, includes these lines:

Princeton's run by Wellesley, and Wellesley's run by Yale
And Yale is run by Vassar, and Vassar's run by tail
Harvard's run by stiff pricks, the kind you raise by hand
But M.I.T. is run by engineers, the finest in the land.
M.I.T. was M.I.T. when Harvard was a pup
And M.I.T. will be M.I.T. when Harvard's time is up
And any Harvard son of a bitch who thinks he's in our class
Can pucker up his rosy lips and kiss the beaver's ass
A friend in ol' New Haven called me up the other day.
He said he was depressed because he hadn't got an A.
I said to him, "You idiot! Why did you go to Yale?
If you had come to M.I.T. you'd still be on Pass/Fail!"

The chorus, sung between each verse, begins with the braggadocio common to drinking songs: "We are, we are, we are, we are, we are the Engineers / We can, we can, we can, we can, demolish forty beers."

Lesbian bars have their own songs, too, like "I Spent My Last $10 on Birth Control and Beer" ("My life was so much simpler when I was sober and queer / But the love of a strong hairy man has turned my head I fear").

Fraternity brothers can egg each other on with a drinking song to the tune of "Have You Ever Seen a Lassie":

Here's to brother Jason, brother Jason, brother Jason,
Here's to brother Jason, who's with us tonight.
He's happy, he's jolly,

He's horny, by golly.
Here's to brother Jason, who's with us tonight.
So drink, motherfucker, drink, motherfucker, drink,
motherfucker, drink . . .
[until the named fraternity member has chugged his drink]

Science fiction and fantasy aficionados might sing "What Do We Do with a Drunken Alien" (to the tune of "What Shall We Do with a Drunken Sailor") or "Star Trekking across the Universe" (partial lyrics below) around the campfire at pagan festivals or at science-fiction convention parties. These are examples of "filk" songs—a term that began as a typographical misspelling of "folk" in the 1970s science-fiction/fantasy world and came to describe a mixture of song parodies and original music, usually humorous, about science fiction, fantasy, computers, *Star Trek*, and other topics.

Star Trekking, across the universe,
On the Starship Enterprise, under Captain Kirk.
Star Trekking, across the universe,
Only going forward, 'cause we can't find reverse.
Analysis, Mister Spock!
It's life, Jim, but not as we know it, not as we know it, not as we
know it.
It's life, Jim, but not as we know it, not as we know it, Captain.

Some drinking songs do have known composers, of course. In the first half of the twentieth century, Cole Porter wrote several songs about drinking: "Make It Another Old-Fashioned, Please," "Say It with Gin," "Absinthe Drip," "Cocktail Time," and "Drink Drink Drink," to name a few. Bing Crosby's "Learn to Croon" in the 1931 film *College Humor* contained the first instance of what became his trademark drunken "boo boo boo boo," and Sam Coslow wrote a classic post-Prohibition drinking song, "Cocktails for Two," which appears in the 1934 film *Murder at the Vanities.* Crooners like Frank Sinatra, Tony Bennett, and Dean Martin ushered in the era of cocktail lounge singing, later parodied by Bill Murray on *Saturday Night Live.*

Several comic drinking songs entered public consciousness in the twentieth century: Benjamin Hapgood Burt's "The Pig Got Up and Slowly Walked Away," Tom Lehrer's "Irish Ballad," Eric Idle's "Philosopher's Song," David Diamond's "Folksinger's Lament," and "Have Some Madeira, M'Dear" by Michael Flanders and Donald Swan. And in the 1960s and 1970s, catchy drinking songs found great popularity on the radio—Neil Diamond's "Red Red Wine," Jimmy Buffett's "Margaritaville" and Rupert Holmes's "Escape (The Piña Colada Song)."

Some might contend that many American country-and-western songs are cry-in-your-beer-style drinking songs bemoaning lost love and loneliness, like "I Think I'll Drink Myself into the Past," "How Can a Whiskey Six Years Old Whip a Man That's Thirty-Two?" and "He's Been Drunk since His Wife's Gone Punk." The lyrics of these songs usually suggest that alcohol is a poor substitute for love, but better than nothing. Rap and rock music also incorporate drinking themes, usually promoting drinking as exciting or wild.

In the late 1980s and early 1990s, U.S. bars began purchasing karaoke machines, which allowed patrons to sing along to recorded music. Karaoke originated in Japan and was particularly popular with Asian Americans, but spilled over into mainstream culture too. Performing popular songs solo, and watching your friends do the same, became one more form of entertainment to accompany drinking; American films (*The Cable Guy* [1996], *My Best Friend's Wedding* [1997], *Duets* [2000]) and TV shows (*Mad about You, Ally McBeal* [1998]) have incorporated karaoke scenes.

Jessy Randall

See also: English Songs, Representations of Drinking in (1600–1900)

References

Connors, Gerald J., and Victor S. Alpher. "Alcohol Themes within Country-Western Songs" in *The International Journal of the Addictions.* (May 1989): 445–451.

Lynn, Frank. *The Beer Bust Songbook, or, Pictures to Look at While Others Are Singing.* San Francisco: Fearon, 1963.

McClure, John, ed. *The Stag's Hornbook.* New York: Alfred A. Knopf, 1943.

Parsons, Elaine Frantz. "Risky Business: The Uncertain Boundaries of Manhood in the Midwestern Saloon" in *Journal of Social History.* 34, no. 2 (2000): 283–307.

Rice, Wallace, and Frances Rice, comps. *Toasts & Tipple: A Book of Conviviality.* Chicago: M. A. Donohue, 1914.

Shay, Frank, comp. *Barroom Ballads.* New York: Dover, 1961. Reprinting of *My Pious Friends and Drunken Companions* and *More Pious Friends and Drunken Companions,* first published by Macaulay: 1927–1928.

Drunk Driving Laws (United Kingdom)

Laws against driving while under the influence of alcohol (or, as it is known in the United Kingdom, "drink driving") were introduced in the United Kingdom as a result of a campaign from the late 1950s directed against the large accident-casualty figures. Campaigners drew their inspiration from Scandinavian countries where there was a strict legal blood-alcohol limit for drivers. However, moves in Britain were cautious: Legislation in 1962, 1967, and 1981 progressively tightened the law. Opposition came from libertarians and from motorist organizations. The highest-profile change came with the introduction of the "Breathalyzer" by Barbara Castle, the Transport minister, in 1965. The movement toward tighter restriction in this area contrasts strikingly with the movement toward liberalization in other alcohol matters in the United Kingdom during this period.

Before 1962, it was an offense to drive a motor vehicle if drunk and "incapable." Few motorists were convicted on these grounds, and the Pedestrians' Association and the British Medical Association began to press for tighter restrictions, including a legal limit on the amount of alcohol in the bloodstream of drivers. By 1959, there was a mounting press campaign against the "slaughter on the roads," especially at the Christmas period. By this date, officials in the Ministry of Transport had also been persuaded by research in the United States, Scandinavia, and by Professor G. C. Drew in England that drivers' reaction times became significantly impaired after even comparatively modest intakes of alcohol. However, both the Home Office and the police were cautious, and the technology for testing alcohol in blood levels was somewhat uncertain. The 1962 Road Traffic Act made it an offense to drive if "impaired" by alcohol and allowed a chemical test to be used in evidence. It was not until after the election of a Labour government in 1964 that a statutory legal limit (of 80 milligrams of alcohol per 100 milliliters of blood) was introduced in the Road Safety Act of 1967. By now, the focus of controversy was about random breath testing, and once again ministers took a cautious view.

A feature of the post-1970 period was the large expenditure on anti–drunk driving publicity that by 1987 ran at five times the amount the Health Education Authority was able to spend on alcohol education in general. Partly as a result, the climate of opinion had shifted further, with even the motoring organizations supporting "discretionary" tests. The departmental Blennerhasset Committee of 1975 supported the tightening up of the law that was achieved under the Conservative's Transport Act of 1981.

From 1960 to 1962 and 1964 to 1967, British politicians regarded drunk driving legislation as politically sensitive, and the issue was discussed at the highest political level in the Cabinet. Legislation in this area was helped by drunk driving being seen as primarily a road safety rather than a temperance issue, and it went hand in hand with the tightening up of laws on vehicle safety and the like. The drinks industry was neutral rather than antagonistic on the subject and firmly supported anti–drunk driving advertising campaigns.

John Greenaway

References

Baggott, Rob. *Alcohol, Politics and Social Policy.* Aldershot: Gower, 1990.

Greenaway, John. *Drink and British Politics since 1830: A Study in Policy-Making.* Basingstoke, UK, and New York: Palgrave Macmillan, 2003.

Drunk Driving Laws (United States)

Every year in the United States, motor vehicle accidents involving alcohol have claimed lives, caused injuries, and damaged property. As a result, the laws related to drunk driving have become more stringent to meet the demands of the public as well as the advocacy of groups such as Mothers Against Drunk Driving (MADD), Students Against Destructive Decisions (SADD), and Remove Intoxicated Drivers (RID).

Drunk driving occurs when a person operates a motor vehicle after drinking alcohol in excess of the legal limit. Terms such as Operating While Intoxicated (OWI), Driving Under the Influence (DUI) or Driving While Intoxicated (DWI) are used interchangeably with drunk driving, and they all have the same definition, that is, an offense committed by consuming more alcohol than the legal limit and operating a motor vehicle, or "drunk driving." Currently, twenty-nine states across the United States, the District of Columbia, and Puerto Rico have adopted a legal limit for alcohol that is 0.08 BAC or Blood-Alcohol Concentration. The remaining states have adopted the legal limit of 0.10. Since drunk driving laws are state laws, the federal government can set standards, make recommendations, or provide incentives for states to encourage them to lower their legal limit to meet the 0.08 BAC standards, but cannot legislate directly. In 2000, the Congress of the United States passed 0.08 BAC as the national standard for drunk driving as part of the appropriations of the Department of Transportation for the fiscal year 2001. In order to make all of the states comply with this standard, the federal government will withhold highway construction funds from those states that retain the higher level. In addition to the criminal statutes, civil statutes have been enacted that allow injured parties to gain compensation from the offending drunk driver or his or her estate.

In 2000, 16,653 people were killed in crashes that involved alcohol. This number represents 40 percent of the total number of people killed in automobile crashes, up from 38 percent in 1999. Research conducted by the National Highway Traffic Safety Administration (NHTSA) has proven that reducing the legal limit to 0.08 BAC has reduced the number of drunk driving fatalities. This study also found that there were no significant problems encountered by local law enforcement officials or the court systems in enforcing the standard. A 1988 research study conducted by the NHTSA resulted in findings that virtually all drinkers at 0.08 BAC, even experienced ones, are impaired, which includes important driving tasks such changing lanes, judging reaction time, steering, and focusing. Many countries have set their BAC limits at 0.08 or lower and have done so for many years. Sweden's BAC limit is 0.02, while Norway, France, and Australia have a 0.05 limit, and Canada, Switzerland, Austria, and Great Britain have set their limits at 0.08. The NHTSA surveys also show that the public endorses the lower BAC limit of 0.08 because of the perceived heightening of safety. The average 170-pound male would have to drink more than four twelve-ounce beers on an empty stomach to reach that limit. In addition to the gender and size of the person, medical conditions may affect the body's ability to metabolize alcohol, which will affect the BAC level.

Due to the fact that every thirty-two minutes across the United States someone is killed in an alcohol-related crash, states have adopted other legislation in addition to the BAC limits in an effort to reduce the effects of drunk driving. These include but are not limited to mandatory sentencing, defined as

An anti–drunk driving poster (Library of Congress)

minimum imprisonment and/or community service for first time as well as repeat offenders; assessment, defined as being seen by a specialist to determine the severity of the problem and determine appropriate treatment; licensing sanctions, defined as revocation of driving privileges, progressively more stringent from first time offenders through repeat offenders; and vehicle sanctions, defined as impounding or immobilizing the drunk driver's vehicle. Some states also require an ignition interlock system, which requires the driver to pass a Breathalyzer test before the car will start. A Breathalyzer is a mechanical device that requires the person suspected of being intoxicated to breathe into it through a small straw. The device measures the alcohol on the person's breath and produces an approximate BAC level. In order for the reading to be accurate, a blood sample does need to be drawn. Since one-third of all drivers arrested or convicted of drunk driving are repeat offenders, states have increased the penalties in their drunk driver laws to match the number of offenses. The laws governing drunk driving require coordinated effort by the judicial system, addiction specialists, and law enforcement officials. Research has been conducted that proves the effectiveness of this coordination in reducing the number of drunk driving fatalities and crashes each year.

Drunk driving laws mandate field sobriety tests that allow law enforcement officers to assess the driver's ability to operate a motor vehicle if he or she is stopped for suspicion of drunk driving. These tests include but are not limited to walking heel to toe in a straight line, reciting the alphabet backwards, and closing the eyes while trying to touch the end of the nose with the fingertip. These tests would be simple for a person who is not intoxicated, however, they are difficult for a person who is. These tests, when recorded and combined with the BAC or Breathalyzer results, have allowed law enforcement officers to enforce drunk driving laws by detaining and removing drunk drivers from the roads.

Janice E. Jones

See also: Drunk Driving Laws (United Kingdom); Mothers Against Drunk Driving (MADD); Students Against Destructive Decisions (SADD)

References

State Legislative Fact Sheet. http://www.nhtsa.com 2002. [15 July 2002].

U.S. Department of Transportation Fact Sheet. http://www.nhtsa.dot.gov/people/injury/alcohol/limit.08/merits/merits08.html. 2002. [15 July 2002].

Du Pont, Pierre Samuel (1870–1954)

Pierre Samuel du Pont (1870–1954), a leading corporate innovator, played an active role in efforts to repeal National Prohibition in the United States through the Association Against the Prohibition Amendment (AAPA). Pierre Samuel du Pont was born in 1870 at Nemours, a family estate near Wilmington, Delaware, the oldest child of Lammot and Mary Belin du Pont. His father died in an explosion at a dynamite plant in Repauno, New Jersey, in 1884. Pierre graduated from the Massachusetts Institute of Technology in 1890, majoring in chemistry, and joined the Du Pont Company the same year. He left the firm in 1899 to go into business with a cousin, T. Coleman du Pont. In 1902, he, Coleman, and a third cousin, Alfred I. du Pont, bought the company from the rest of the family and began its transformation. In 1914, Pierre and his brothers Lammot and Irenée bought out Coleman's share of the firm. A bitter feud followed that split the family into warring camps, but Pierre emerged with complete control of the firm when the lawsuits were settled. In 1915, Pierre became chairman of General Motors (GM) and in 1920 replaced William C. Durant as its president. He reorganized General Motors according to the same principles by which he had organized Du Pont, and GM soon passed Ford as the largest auto manufacturer in the United States. More than any other person, Pierre S. du Pont created the modern corporate structure. Among his key allies in building both firms were his brothers and John J. Raskob.

Raskob had joined the AAPA in 1922. He soon persuaded Lammot and Irenée du Pont to join. Pierre, however, did not become active in the AAPA until late in 1925. Prohibition was an important issue for du Pont at several levels. Practically, he believed that it had failed. Rather than promote abstinence from alcohol, it had promoted abuse. Further, the government had given up a source of revenue in the excise taxes on alcohol and provided an opportunity for organized crime. Philosophically, he saw federal prohibition as an infringement of the rights of the states and had concerns about using constitutional amendments to legislate. Although slower than his brothers to become involved in the organization, Pierre quickly emerged as a leader. He and his brothers led efforts to recruit corporate support and increased their own financial support. Pierre also reorganized AAPA, using the same principles he had used with Du Pont and GM.

Because of the Republican Party's continuing support for National Prohibition, du Pont broke with the party in 1928 and supported Alfred Emanuel Smith for president. He urged the Democratic Party to adopt an anti-Prohibition plank in its 1932 party platform and supported Roosevelt largely because of the Prohibition issue. Never an enthusiastic New Dealer, however, du Pont and his brothers were soon at odds with Roosevelt. They were among the founders of the American Liberty League, a leading critic of the New Deal from an antistatist perspective.

Pierre spent most of the last two decades of his life as a power behind the scenes at Du Pont, in philanthropy, and pursuing interests in family history and gardening. He died on 5 April 1954.

William H. Mulligan Jr.

See also: Association Against the Prohibition Amendment (AAPA); Democratic Party (United States); National Prohibition (United States); Raskob, John Jakob; Smith, Alfred Emanuel

References

Burk, Robert F. *The Corporate State and the Broker State: The Du Ponts and American National Politics, 1925–1940.* Cambridge: Harvard University Press, 1990.

Chandler, Alfred D., and Stephen Salsbury. *Pierre S. du Pont and the Making of the Modern Corporation.* New York: Harper and Row, 1971.

Kyvig, David E. *Repealing National Prohibition.* 2d ed. Kent, OH: Kent State University Press, 2000.

Mosley, Leonard. *Blood Relations: The Rise and Fall of the du Ponts of Delaware.* New York: Atheneum, 1980.

Mulligan, William H., Jr. "Du Pont, Pierre S." in *Encyclopedia USA.* 23 (1996): 167–170.

Dunlop, John (1789–1868)

John Dunlop (1789–1868) was a pioneer of the organized temperance movement in the United Kingdom and a prolific and influential writer on the subject of drinking customs and usages.

Born in the port town of Greenock, Renfrewshire, in western Scotland, in 1789, he became a campaigner for temperance reform in 1828, in the belief that associational activity at the community level provided the most effective and motivational means of eradicating drunkenness. The following year, Dunlop was instrumental in the formation of temperance societies in Greenock, Gairbraid, and Maryhill, near Glasgow—an innovation that encouraged the rapid expansion of similar societies throughout the west of Scotland and created the popular image of Dunlop as the "father" or "founder" of the British temperance movement.

The eldest child of Alexander Dunlop, a banker, and Janet Graham, Dunlop was descended on his father's side from a distinguished line of Glasgow academics, while his mother's family derived considerable income from the landed estate of Gairbraid, Dunbartonshire. Although he inherited the estate in 1836, Dunlop had embarked on a law career in 1804, after attending Glasgow University for three years. He lived in the city up to 1809 and then briefly moved to Edinburgh, where he studied law. However, his marriage in 1813 to the wealthy Janet Napier Dunsmore gave Dunlop the financial security to devote his energies to philanthropic and business activities in Greenock. From 1833, he worked full time for temperance.

Dunlop's commitment was shaped by his religious convictions. He identified with the evangelical wing of the Church of Scotland, and although temperance did not initially feature in the evangelical call to missionary action, from 1828 Dunlop adapted evangelical rhetoric to promote the cause. He was a passionate writer—a talent evident in his 1829 pamphlet, *On the Extent and Remedy of National Intemperance,* published in Glasgow by William Collins, a fellow Evangelical and temperance campaigner. Dunlop argued that Scotland was losing its moral standing compared with continental countries because of the corrupting influence of alcohol. His remedy, based on North American examples, was to create an organized, interlinking community of temperance societies, which would serve as a powerful collective vehicle for reform.

Dunlop and Collins were the driving forces behind the Scottish Temperance Society, which originated in 1830 under a different name. Although Dunlop did not share Collins's rousing platform style, his writing made a public impact, especially his best-selling study of drink usages, which ran through several editions from 1833. Yet by the mid-1830s Dunlop's views were changing. He lost faith in the antispirits movement, favored by Collins, and espoused total abstinence. Contact with temperance radicals also helped to politicize Dunlop, and he became a forthright Liberal. In 1838, he moved permanently to London to secure a metropolitan base for the promotion of his ideas. The relocation was less successful than he hoped, largely because Dunlop could not identify wholeheartedly with prohibition or what he saw as the British temperance leadership's predominantly middle-class profile. Nevertheless, he remained active as a campaigner until 1859, when he retired from public life. Dunlop died in London in 1868.

Irene Maver

See also: Scotland

References

Dunlop, John. *Autobiography of John Dunlop.* London: privately printed by Spottiswoode, Ballantyne, and Co., 1932.

Greenock Total Abstinence Society, the Temperance Reformation in Scotland, with Special Reference to John Dunlop and Greenock: A Century of Work and Progress, 1829–1929. Greenock: Greenock Total Abstinence Society, 1929.

Harrison, Brian. *Dictionary of British Temperance Biography.* Coventry, England: Society for the Study of Labour History. Aids to Research, no. 1. *Bulletin Supplement,* 1973: 40–41.

———. *Drink and the Victorians: The Temperance Question in England, 1815–1872.* 2d ed. Keele: Keele University Press, 1994.

Thomson, Alexander. *Random Notes and Rambling Recollections of the Drydock, the Dock, or Kelvin Dock, All Now Known by the More Modern Name of Maryhill, 1750–1894.* Glasgow: Kerr and Richardson, 1895.

E

Edwards, Justin (1787–1853)

Justin Edwards (1787–1853), pioneer American temperance reformer, once wrote: "A Society is formed, not for the suppression of intemperance, but for the promotion of temperance." These words, from an 1826 letter, accurately define the reform impulse of Edwards, a minister and founder of the American Temperance Society (ATS). Born 25 April 1787 in Westhampton, Massachusetts, Justin Edwards became one of the leading early figures of the temperance movement. Since his father was unable financially to support his education, Edwards had to support himself, so he joined the staff of the Andover Theological Seminary in 1811. His ideals were well liked, and on 2 December 1812 he became an ordained minister and became pastor of the "South" Andover parish. In 1817, he became a member of the executive committee of the New England Tract Society, and by 1821 he had become the corresponding secretary, ultimately responsible for the supervision of the press.

In autumn 1824, Edwards joined with the Reverend Woods and fourteen other members in Boston in the process that led to the creation of the American Society for the Promotion of Temperance, the creation of which was formally announced in 1826. Edwards argued that if all temperate men could be induced to continue temperate, all drunkards would soon die, and the land be eased of an overwhelming burden. In order to pursue this endeavor, he resigned from his position in Andover in October 1827, and he accepted a request to become pastor of a new church in Boston, where his health soon began to fail. He was forced to resign the following summer. This resignation left him with much free time to continue his temperance work, allowing him to travel and alert the public to the importance of reform movements, particularly temperance. He believed that alcohol, or "intoxicating drinks," were an obstacle to the spread and advent of the gospel, and he felt that alcohol consumption only created an endless cycle that would eventually end in death. Only total abstinence from alcohol could ensure the salvation of the soul, a concept he included in his *Permanent Documents,* as well as his numerous tracts issued by the American Tract Society. In Tract 125, "The Immortality of the Traffic in Ardent Spirit," Edwards argued that temperance was more than a secular concern, but rather, intemperance affected the spiritual and emotional, as well as the physical, condition of men. He argued that those who sold the "ardent spirits," such as barkeepers, were just as guilty in the perpetuation of the use of alcohol as the drunkard himself. Those who were temperate, he thought, could urge others to join in the quest for temperance and, at the same time, promote the Christian cause.

Promoting both temperance and Christianity was his lifelong quest, a platform that he pushed through his speeches and during his presidency of Andover Theological Seminary from 1836 to April 1842. From 1842 to 1849, he continued to publish tracts for the American Tract Society, and he spent the last four years of his life, until his death on 23 July 1853, preparing a condensed commentary on the Scriptures at the request of the American Tract Society. At his death, he had completed his commentary on the New Testament, and on a portion of the Old Testament, leaving this work unfinished, just as his death left temperance an unfinished movement.

Jennifer Harrison

See also: American Temperance Society (ATS)

References

Edwards, Justin. *Permanent Temperance Documents of the American Temperence Society.* Boston: Seth Bless, 1935.

Hallock, William A. *A Sketch of the Life and Labors of the Rev. Justin Edwards, D.D. The Evangelical Pastor, the Advocate of Temperance, the Sabbath, and the Bible.* New York: American Tract Society, 1855.

Rohrer, James R. "The Origins of the Temperance Movement: A Reinterpretation" in *Journal of American Studies.* 24, no. 2 (1990): 228–236.

Ellison, Henry (1813–1899)

Henry Ellison (1813–1899) was chairman of successive Anglican temperance organizations from 1862 to 1891. Although insufficiently recognized by historians as a major activist in a voluntary era, Ellison helped transform sectarian teetotal and prohibitionist movements into the establishment-sanctioned moral suasionist, legislative, and restrictionist Church of England Temperance Society (CETS). Ellison saw Anglican temperance as important to Church defense at a time when Liberals and non-Anglicans sought to reduce establishment influence.

His *Times* obituary asserted that the well-connected Ellison qualified for high church preferment, but in an age when teetotal zealots were denied promotion, he chose temperance. He had been the duke of Devonshire's chaplain, vicar of Windsor, and the Queen's reader; and was later connected to Archbishops of Canterbury A. C. Tait and Randall Davidson by his son's and Davidson's marriages to Tait's daughters. Instead of receiving a

*Henry Ellison (1813–1899) (*Church of England Temperance Chronicle I, *May 1873)*

more prestigious position, Ellison became vicar of Great Hazeley, Oxfordshire (1875), to accommodate temperance work.

Before his 1860 teetotal conversion, Ellison had encountered drunkenness among farmers, working people, and sailors in Suffolk, Brighton, and Derbyshire, but had resisted the teetotal pledge for medical, social, and religious reasons. As vicar of Windsor, despite successful ameliorative ventures, in 1859 Ellison only patronized a temperance society for both abstainers and nonabstainers, with night classes for teetotalers. A drunken father's murder of his daughter pressed Ellison to accept a reformed drunkard carpenter's suggestion that he lead a teetotal society. By 1862, it had 120 members. He kept his pledge despite health complaints. Although he insisted on clerical control in his parish teetotal society, he relied on a lay committee and district visitors. Windsor teetotalers later administered the CETS agricultural division and Police Court Mission.

Ellison's guidelines transformed the "sectarian" church teetotal society, which he helped found (1862), into the "established" CETS (1873), characterized by: (1) cooperation with Nonconformists, but Anglican principles and control; (2) accommodation of nonabstaining clergymen in parish teetotal societies; and (3) restrictive licensing, rather than the United Kingdom Alliance's (UKA) program of prohibition.

Negotiating compromises between strict clerical abstainers and the establishment, Ellison helped initiate the CETS, Britain's most prestigious and influential temperance society and one of its most extensive voluntary organizations. The CETS grew in numbers and effectiveness. Ellison encouraged its compromises: teetotalism and moderate drinking; continuation of fermented Communion wine; licensing reform, rather than prohibition; and reduced alcohol usage, socially, medically, and financially. Ellison's CETS could take some credit for the later reduction in the number of pubs (and their effects) by about 300 percent from 1835 to 1935. Pushed by a radical revolt, Ellison retired as CETS chairman in 1891 for "health reasons," but his successors, Bishops Frederick Temple, Ernest Wilberforce, and H. H. Pereira (representing Randall Davidson, the archbishop of Canterbury), consciously pursued Ellison's program.

Gerald Wayne Olsen

See also: Church of England Temperance Society (CETS); Davidson, Randall; Temple, Frederick; United Kingdom Alliance (UKA)

References

Ellison, Henry. *The Temperance Reformation in the Church of England.* London: Wells, Gardner, 1894.

Harrison, Brian. "Ellison, Henry John" in *Dictionary of British Temperance Biography.* Coventry, England: Society for the Study of Labour History. Aids to Research, no. 1. *Bulletin Supplement,* 1973: 45.

Olsen, Gerald Wayne. *Drink and the British Establishment: The Church of England Temperance Society, 1873–1914.* Unpublished book manuscript.

———. *Drink and the Temperance in the Church of England, 1829–1875.* Unpublished book manuscript.

———. "From Parish to Palace: Working-Class Influences on Anglican Temperance Movements, 1835–1914" in *Journal of Ecclesiastical History.* 40 (1989): 239–252.

Sherlock, Frederick. *Henry John Ellison. Founder of the Church of England Temperance Society.* London: Wells, Gardner, 1910.

The Times. 26 December 1899: 7.

Employee Assistance Programs (EAPs)

Employee assistance programs (EAPs) are the primary mechanisms for identifying employees with alcohol problems and referring them for treatment. Workplaces provide structural opportunities for both early identification of drinking problems and effective motivational intervention to encourage behavioral change. EAP effectiveness is founded upon the visibility of work and leverage that are built into the employer-employee relationship. Further, the workplace provides an excellent setting to guide employees to appropriate sources of assistance and to ensure that referral advice is followed. Finally, because of their access to program clients, workplace programs are singular in their ability to sustain long-term posttreatment follow-up with employees with alcohol problems.

EAPs were first developed in the United States in the early 1970s. EAPs have diffused worldwide, are widely prevalent in Canada, the United Kingdom, Australia, New Zealand, and South Africa, and are identifiable in some form elsewhere around the world. EAPs stem from industrial alcoholism programs that developed in several major U.S. companies beginning in the early 1940s. Research in the 1960s confirmed the effectiveness of these strategies. Their narrow focus, however, restricted their adoption to workplaces where executives were personally committed to deal with alcohol problems.

The broadly focused EAP model was developed to avoid the problems associated with this narrow focus. The EAP model assumes that concern with the entire range of behavioral health problems that affect an employee's performance will include appropriate attention to alcohol problems.

Although such "mainstreaming" is attractive, it has had its costs. In North America and elsewhere in the world, most EAPs have come to deal primarily with problems other than employee alcohol dependence. Thus, while the majority of U.S. employees report the presence of EAPs in their workplaces, this does not mean that these programs address a substantial portion of extant alcohol problems or that alcohol problems are even addressed in an effective way. Descriptions of EAPs in nations such as South Africa and Australia indicate that attention to alcohol problems is often not even considered among the reasons for EAP adoption.

A historical overview suggests how a mechanism designed to address employee alcohol problems was widely adopted but shifted its emphasis away from alcohol problems. In 1970, the U.S. federal government established the National Institute on Alcohol Abuse and Alcoholism (NIAAA) as its first major initiative to deal with alcohol issues since the repeal of National Prohibition in 1933. Leadership of this new organization needed a cultural definition of alcohol problems that attracted broad constituency support. Replacing the "skid-row bum," this new agency targeted employed people as constituting the majority of the alcoholic population, who were considered to be largely "hidden" due to their social status. New forms of treatment, as well as mechanisms to get them into treatment, were needed for this population.

In 1971, the NIAAA provided grants to each state for diffusion agents to develop workplace alcoholism programs. The EAP model was articulated with NIAAA support and was widely endorsed by the agency. In 1971, workers who were engaged in diffusion of these programs formed the Association of Labor and Management Consultants and Administrators on Alcoholism (ALMACA). As this organization became viable, the NIAAA created a funding mechanism to ensure its further growth and development.

The NIAAA provided grant funding for a considerable number of "demonstration projects" to explore how EAP mechanisms could be most effectively implemented in a range of settings. Substantial support was also provided to a number of labor unions to demonstrate the viability of union-based programming. A very large grant went to the National Council on Alcoholism (NCA) for the development of joint labor-management EAPs. Employees of these multiple projects became members of the ALMACA and assured its rapid growth as an organization supporting EAP development, albeit with an emphasis on employee alcohol problems.

These efforts contributed substantially to the nationwide diffusion of EAPs and their association with an alcohol problem emphasis. In 1981, however, the authority of the NIAAA and many other federal agencies to provide support for service delivery at the community level was terminated. This ended the majority of the funding that had been used to support the development and maintenance of a strong employee alcohol problem emphasis within EAPs. EAPs themselves have flourished, but the absence of external support for an alcohol emphasis coupled with the widespread stigma associated with alcohol problems has led EAPs to focus their interests in the directions favored by management, such as work-family conflicts, downsizing, workplace conflict, and organizational development. In recognition of these trends and its changed identity, the ALMACA changed its name in 1990 to the Employee Assistance Professionals Association, a pattern earlier adopted by the parallel professional organization, the Employee Assistance Society of North America.

Despite these changes, an EAP offers the potential for addressing employee alcohol problems. Based on earlier research, a number of ingredients are essential for an EAP to effectively address alcohol problems:

- Policy design, including top management and union commitment to addressing alcohol problems in the context of medical disorders, supervisory training, and distinction of EAP services from alcohol-related rules of conduct;
- Program personnel readily accessible to supervisors and employees who can provide consultative assistance to supervisors on how to deal appropriately with employees with alcohol problems and who are fully trained to be able to recognize alcohol problems or readily access a diagnostic resource; and
- Treatment and follow-up, linking the alcohol-troubled employee with the most appropriate treatment resource, monitoring treatment compliance, orchestrating and supporting reentry to work, and follow-up to assure the maintenance of treatment gains.

As industrialization, broad-based service delivery, and employment by large organizations become the global norms of work, the potential value of EAPs in addressing the accompanying alcohol problems of employees cannot be exaggerated. Maintaining people in work roles as they attempt to deal with problematic behavior disorders is an obvious source of cost saving. Using workplaces as conduits to support alcohol problem counseling and treatment programs in the community demonstrates another important benefit.

Introducing and sustaining these components of an EAP requires continuing attention to the extent to which they address employee alcohol problems and other employee substance abuse issues. In order for EAPs to achieve their potential in addressing employee alcohol problems, managers and decision makers in workplaces, including union leaders, need to be convinced of the importance of this use of EAPs, based upon their received knowledge of the significance of employee alcohol problems, the effectiveness of EAPs in addressing these problems, and the resultant value that is received from such a use of EAP mechanisms.

Paul M. Roman

See also: Alcoholism; National Council on Alcoholism and Drug Dependence (NCADD); National Institute on Alcohol Abuse and Alcoholism (NIAAA)

References

Blum, Terry, and Paul Roman. *Cost Effectiveness and Preventive Impact of Employee Assistance Programs* (Center for Substance Abuse Prevention Monograph 5). Washington, DC: Department of Health and Human Services, 1995.

———. "Employee Assistance and Human Resources Management" in *Research in Personnel and Human Resources Management.* 7 (1989): 258–312.

Hartwell, Tyler, et al. "Aiding Troubled Employees: The Prevalence, Cost and Characteristics of Employee Assistance Programs in the United States" in *American Journal of Public Health.* 86, no. 6 (1996): 804–808.

Roman, Paul. "From Employee Alcoholism to Employee Assistance: An Analysis of the De-Emphasis on Prevention and on Alcoholism Problems in Work-Based Programs" in *Journal of Studies on Alcohol.* 42, no. 3 (1981): 244–272.

———. "Missing Work: The Decline in Infrastructure and Support for Workplace Alcohol Intervention in the United States, with Implications for Developments in Other Nations" in *Changing Substance Abuse through Health and Social Systems,* edited by W. Miller and C. Weisner, 197–210. New York: Kluwer/Plenum, 2002.

Roman, Paul, and Terry Blum. "Notes on the New Epidemiology of Alcoholism in the USA" in *Journal of Drug Issues.* 11, no. 3 (1987): 321–332.

Trice, Harrison, and Janice Beyer. "Work-Related Outcomes of Constructive Confrontation Strategies in a Job-Based Alcoholism Program" in *Journal of Studies on Alcohol.* 45, no. 3 (1984): 393–404.

Trice, Harrison, and Paul Roman. *Spirits and Demons at Work: Alcohol and Other Drugs on the Job.* New York: Publications Division of the New York State School of Industrial and Labor Relations at Cornell University, 1972. 393–404.

Trice, Harrison, and Mona Schonbrunn. "A History of Job-Based Alcoholism Programs, 1900–1995" in *Journal of Drug Issues.* 11, no. 1 (1981): 171–198.

Wrich, James. *The Employee Assistance Program.* Minnesota: Hazelden Foundation, 1973.

English Songs, Representations of Drinking in (1600–1900)

This entry focuses on the themes of 477 popular English songs, originating between 1600 and 1900, about the effects of alcoholic drinks. These are divided almost evenly between songs from gentlemen's taverns and street ballads written for common folks. Because these songs often convey the outlooks and values of ordinary drinkers with a directness and vividness unmatched by other historians' sources, they provide useful windows on the social history of drinking at both levels of society. Songs from the nineteenth century (from both sources) are compared with earlier songs, in order to determine which themes increased or decreased in popularity after 1800. The songs indicate which benefits or penalties of drinking are more often associated with ale, wine, or hard liquors. They also reveal attitudes on the elusive topic of women as drinkers.

This entry expands an earlier study (Ingle 2000) comparing themes of songs about drink from Ireland, Scotland, and England. Although this entry examines twice the number of English songs previously surveyed, the national differences revealed in that report are still valid. Because there is no published list of drink-related songs, Appendix C lists all English songs found, together with their sources and their main themes, along with tables referred to in this entry. Thus, others can use this database for further analyses. Although concentrating on songs that depict effects of drinking, toasts and wassail songs have generally been excluded. However, the latter genre is well reviewed, with many examples, by Marchant (1888). His volume is the most useful companion to this review for cultural historians of drink in England.

The Bacchanalian Tradition

About half of all English drink-related songs reflect a bacchanalian tradition among educated tavern habitués, who learned in school of the mythological and poeticized Bacchus/Dionysus from Renaissance translations of Greek poets, philosophers, and playwrights. (An introduction to this tradition may be found in Ingle 2001.) The classical Greek symposium was a world to itself where gentlemen could ignore distractions of the workaday world in order to focus on both pleasurable and cultural activities while drinking wine. They were to avoid altogether talking of money, war, or death. It is this Greek inwardness that is reflected in the intense male bonding and antiworldliness found in many later bacchanalian songs. These lyrics explicitly reject wealth, politics, or even security as worthy goals. The association of wine with an antiworldly sentiment is much more common than for other drinks (*see* Appendix C, Table 1). An example is the song "Pleasant and divertive":

> Let us drink and be merry, dance, joke and rejoice,
> With claret and sherry, the orbo and voice.
> The changeable world to our joy is unjust;
> All treasure's uncertain, then down with your dust.

In frolicks dispose your pounds, shillings and pence,
For we shall be nothing one hundred years hence.

In "Tosse the pot," the topers have no worries about spending their savings on ale:

We take no thought, we have no care, for still we spend and never spare,
Till of all our money our purse is bare—and ever tosse the pot.
And when our money is all spent, then sell our goods and spend the rent
Or drinke it up with one consent—and ever tosse the pot.

Wine Enhances the Imagination

Wit was a central concern to writers and intellectuals of the English Renaissance (Ingle 2001). Although wit is a term originally derived from "wisdom," in seventeenth-century England it took on a meaning akin to "rhetoric" and implies verbal fluency in debate. Shakespeare's comic spokesman, Sir John Falstaff, praises "sack" (sherry) as a liquor that increases mental nimbleness, as well as enhancing courage. From *Henry IV*, part 2:

> A good sherris-sack hath a twofold operation in it. It ascends me to the brain, dries me there all the foolish & dull & crudy vapors which environ it, makes it apprehensive, quick, forgetive, full of firey & delectable shapes, which delivered o'er to the voice—the tongue—becomes excellent wit.

The song references are typically terse, as if the listener knows well their meanings. Thus ale "quickens the poet's wit and pen" ("In praise of ale"), while wine "heightens the fancy, the wit doth refine."

Occasionally a song waxes poetic:

Canary it's thou that doth inspire and actuate the soul with heavenly fire
That thou sublimest the genius making wit. ("Canary crowned")

"The generous toper" agrees that wine helps us transcend conventional thinking:

Give me the choice guest, whose ideas refine,
Whose native good humor is strengthened by wine.
Who, in spite of a rigid, grave censuring world
With rapture beholds fancy's streamers unfurled.

"The tippling philosophers" marches comically down a list of ancient Greek and Renaissance greats inspired by Bacchus. For example:

Copernicus, like to the rest, believed there was wisdom in wine,
And fancied a cup of the best made reason the brighter to shine.
With wine he replenished his veins, and made his philosophy reel,
Then fancied the world, like his brains, ran round like a chariot wheel.
By wine we are generous made, it furnishes fancy with wings;
Without it we ne'er should have had philosophers, poets or kings.

The Bacchanalian Worldview in the Alehouse

Bacchanalian songs reflect the values of (mostly) men seeking pleasure and fellowship in taverns or alehouses (and later in pubs). Such songs place greatest emphasis upon the benefits of drink, although some of them mention "bad ends" almost as an afterthought (*see* Appendix C, Table 1). (Songs that do not stress positive outcomes are referred to in this entry as "nonbacchanalian.") The benefits classically attributed to wine are also found in songs about quaffers of ale. In fact, one benefit, health, is more common among ale-related songs than in those about wine. "High and mighty commendation of the virtue of a pot of good ale" adds imagination to other benefits:

When heaviness the mind doth oppress and sorry and grief the heart doth assail,
No remedy quicker than take up your liquor and wash away care with a pot of good ale.
The poet divine that cannot reach wine because that his memory doth often times fail,
Will hit on the veine and reach the high strain, if he be but inspired with a pot of good ale.
The wooer that feareth his suite to begin and blushes and simpers and often looks pale,
Though he miss in his speech and his heart were at his breech,
If he liquor his tongue with a pot of good ale.
The widow that buried her husband of late will soon have forgotten to weep and to wail,
And think each day twain till she marry again, if she take the contents of a pint of good ale.

"The Little Barleycorn" adds some lyrical verses on the benefits of ale consumption:

It lends more years into old age than 'ere was lent by nature,
It makes the poet's fancy rage more than castil and water.
'Twill make a weeping widow laugh and soon incline to pleasure,
'Twill make an old man leave his staff and dance a youthful measure.
Thus Barley Corne hath power even for to change our nature,
And make a shrew within an hour prove a kind-hearted creature.

Drink and Health

A widespread intuitive idea is that alcoholic beverages must be healthful because they induce a warm feeling (dilation of vessels in skin and muscles), a state of arousal, and a sense of well-being. In this energized state, we may feel invulnerable. A well-known song with this theme is "Back and side go bare," in which ale insulates against cold and hunger.

A more dramatic belief is that ale can cure serious disabilities, as in "The churn supper":

> This ale is a gallant thing—it cheers the spirits of a king.
> It makes the dumb man strive to sing; aye and a beggar play.
> A cripple that is lame and halt, and scarce a mile a day can walk,
> When he feels the juice of malt, will throw his crutch away.

The lyrics of "Nottingham Ale," one of several songs praising a regional brew, has a witty take on doctors' warnings about alcoholic beverages:

> Ye doctors who more executions have done, with powder and potion and bolus and pill.
> Than hangman with halter and soldier with gun, miser with famine and lawyer with quill.
> To kill us the quicker ye ban our malt liquor tho our bodies consume and our faces grow pale
> What liquor both pleases and cures all diseases? A comforting glass of old Nottingham ale.

That drink "loosens the tongue" is a truism, and several songs also propose that drink (here, ale) enhances oratory in the pulpit, as in "Nottingham Ale":

> You curates and bishops, priests, deacons and vicars, once you have tasted,
> You'll own it is true that Nottingham ale is the best of all liquors . . .
> Twill open your vapours, save pen, ink and papers, for you who inclined in the pulpit to rail
> Twill open your throats, you may preach without notes, inspired by a bumper of . . .

Ale versus Stronger Drinks

A number of songs reflect social-class values by praising affordable English-brewed ale over the gentleman's predilection for imported wines and brandies. The playwright and songster John Gay writes in "A ballad on ale":

> Rum, brandy, gin with choicest smack, from Holland bouthe, Batavia sack,
> All these will not avail to cheer a truely British heart like gen'rous nappy ale.

The criticism of unhealthy effects of other drinks can become quite graphic, as in the nineteenth-century favorite, "I likes a drop of good beer":

> Brandy and gin blows out the skin and makes one feel very queer;
> But I always find both colic and wind are driven away by beer.
> Whenever I puts them into my stomach, I always wishes 'twas beer.
> From drinking rum the maggots come, and bowel pains appear. . . .

Most songs of this genre inveigh specifically against wine. From "Good ale for my money":

> Canary . . . cures no pain but breaks the brain and raps out oaths and curses;
> And makes men part with heavy heart, but light it makes their purses.

Drink and Foolishness

Although the enthusiasm engendered by a cheerful alcohol-induced state enlivens a dull mind, at the same time it may impair caution and common sense. The theme of drink-induced foolishness, as told in "A cup of old Stingo" (a strong beer), is usually treated as a benign human failing, even a source of humor:

> Twill make a man indentures make, twill make a fool seem wise;
> Twill make a Puritan sociable, and leave to be precise,
> Twill make him dance about a cross, and eke to run the ring too,
> Or anything he once thought gross, such virtue has Old Stingo.
> Twill make a constable oversee, sometimes to serve a warrant;
> Twill make a bailiff lose his fee, though he be a knave-errant.
> Twill make a lawyer, though that he to ruin oft' men bring to,
> Sometimes forget to take his fee, if his head be lin'd with Stingo.

Wine and Women in Synergy

The association of wine, women, and song is at the core of the bacchanalian tradition and indeed the nineteenth-century compilation *The Universal Songster* includes over 100 lyrical tributes to the union of Bacchus and Venus. For example, "When Bacchus, jolly god, invites":

> When Bacchus, jolly god, invites to revel in his evening rites,
> In vain his alters I surround, tho' with Burgundian incense crowned.
> No charm has wine without the lass; 'tis love gives relish to the glass.
> Whilst all around, with jocund glee, in brimmers toast their favorite she;
> Tho' every nymph my lips proclaim, my heart still whispers Chloe's name
> And thus with me, by am'rous stealth, drink every glass to Chloe's health.

The association of romance with wine is stronger than with ale in songs prior to the nineteenth century (*see* Appendix C, Table

1). Yet these earlier songs are frequently more down-to-earth in stressing the release of lustful behavior. One line of "A cup of old Stingo" reminds us that another symptom of foolishness in the drinker is his sexual impropriety:

> Twill make a parson not to flinch, though he be wond'rous holy,
> And for to kiss a pretty wench, and think it is no folly.

A related theme is the enhancement of male potency, as in "Since Tom's in the chair":

> Have any got wives that lead' em sad lives, for you know what pouting and storming,
> Then drink of this wine and it will incline the weakest to vig'rous performing.

Ned Ward (1720) sums up the power of wine in canto 1 of his "Delights of the bottle":

> What am'rous Youth, to love inclin'd, can press dear Phyllis to be kind,
> In words that will at once inspire the blushing nymph with like desire,
> Till noble wine has wash'd away those fears that do their joys delay,
> And banish'd from their trembling youth, the native bashfulness of both;
> Then, mutually inclin'd to bless each other with a soft embrace,
> Their struggling souls with vigour meet, and kindly taste the short and sweet.
> Thus love can only with his darts perplex and terrify our hearts,
> But gen'rous Bacchus pity takes, and heals the wounds that Cupid makes.

Even the aging toper can hope for rejuvenation from wine, as in "In praise of sack":

> And am grown young again; my phsysick now hath left me, and my judge's graver brow
> Is smooth'd, and I turn'd amorous as May, when she invites young lovers forth to play
> Upon her flowry bosom I could win a vestal now or tempt a Queen to sin.

The effects of drink on sexual behaviors are often embellished with humor. In "A blessing on brandy and beer," one's perception of beauty becomes less discriminating:

> When one's drunk, not a girl but looks pretty, the country's as gay as the city;
> And all one that says is so witty—a blessing on brandy and beer.

"The joys of dear women and wine" offers the joke that wine can enhance lust without making a toper completely indiscriminate. He still prefers other women to his own wife:

> Give me the gay fellow in life, who seldom a dull thought has known,
> That would rather kiss any man's wife by the one half, than he'd kiss his own;
> Then fill up the glasses, dear boys and make the best use of your time,
> For, believe me, here's nothing surpasses the joys of dear women and wine.

Despite the frequent equation of "bacchanalian" with romance (*see* Appendix C, Table 1), there are many songs that portray women as threats to men's wine-enriched fellowship. A comical song of this genre is "The jolly toper," in which a good fellow jokingly justifies to his cronies his leaving his mistress (Chloe) in favor of his bumper (glass). In the third verse, he reflects the bacchanalian view that jealousies over women are the real threat to his peace.

> My Chloe had dimples and smiles, I must own;
> But—though she could smile—yet in truth she could frown!
> But tell me, ye lovers of liquor divine,
> Did you e'er see a frown in a bumper of wine?
> Her lilies and roses were just in their prime;
> Yet lilies and roses are conquered by time.
> But in wine, from its age, such a benefit flows,
> That we like it the better the older it grows.
> Let murders and battles and history prove
> The mischiefs that wait upon rivals in love;
> But in drinking—thank Heaven—no rival contends,
> For the more we love liquor, the more we are friends!

Topers in seventeenth- and eighteenth-century songs tend to view their domestic conflicts as jokes, which their drinking companions can enjoy, as in "The toper":

> Had she taxed me with gaming and bade me forbear,
> 'Tis a thousand to one I had lent her my ear;
> Had she found out my Chloris up three pairs of stairs,
> I had baulk'd her and gone to St. James to pray'rs'
> But at night to deny me my flask of dear red,
> Let her go to the devil, there's no more to be said.

Another seventeenth-century Chloris inspired these antiromantic sentiments:

> Your coyness, Chloris, pray give o'er and turn your tempting eyes away;
> From ladies I'll withdraw my heart and fix it only on the quart.
> 'Tis wine alone that cheers the soul but love and ladies make us sad;

I'm merry when I court the bowl, while he who courts the
madam's mad.

Nonbacchanalian Song Themes

By definition, themes that define bacchanalian songs (hedonism, health, fellowship, romance) are much less frequent in the list of nonbacchanalian songs (*see* Appendix C). Yet the number of nonbacchanalian songs that mention hedonism and romance is quite high. Although another theme common among bacchanalian songs—women drinking—often appears among nonbacchanalian songs, the two kinds of songs feature different drinking scenarios for women, as discussed below in the section "Women Drinkers in Street Ballads." Of course the major difference between bacchanalian and nonbacchanalian songs is the large number of bad ends in the latter (*see* Appendix C, Table 2); bacchanalian songs stress benefits (not penalties) of drinking. Bad ends are more commonly associated with indulging in hard liquor than with drinking ale or beer. Thus, the fact that songs about hard liquor became more common in the nineteenth century keeps the total frequency of bad ends the same as among the seventeenth- and eighteenth-century songs collected for this entry. Gin was the most common hard liquor leading to bad ends long after the "gin craze" of the eighteenth century had abated. (Frequencies of each kind of bad end are given in Appendix C, Table 3.) In songs from both before and after 1800, poverty and fighting are the most common bad ends.

Poverty and Bad Husbands

Among both earlier and later songs, the most common curse of drinking was poverty (as Appendix C, Table 3 shows). The need to pawn one's clothes is often used as the indicator of poverty. Indeed "drinking one's clothes" is a synonym for "pawning" in seventeenth-century parlance. Among the most common scenes is that of an unmarried young "rake" losing his fortune (and parental loyalty) by reckless carousing. In the collection *Merrie Drolleries,* "A catch" presents a stark image:

Sack, sack is a thing that makes the brain rumble.
It fools the wise and makes the gallant stumble.
Sack hath the power the sense of man depriving—oh, take
heed then—
Sack keeps the wealthy man from thriving.

In a second common situation, a man living more in the alehouse than at home leads his family to poverty and even to starvation. In the dark tale, "The bad husband turned thrifty":

Thus I frequented an ale-bench, so long as my money would
hold;
Whilst my wife and children at home would pinch with
hunger and cold
My wife would often me persuade and mildly to me say,
"Good loving husband, follow your trade and do not go
astray."
But with foul words I'd her abuse, and call her "bitch" and
"whore,"
But now my counsel, I will choose and keep my money in
store.

"The good fellowe's resolution" ends with these lines: "Then learn for to lay up your money in store / resolve to play the bad husband no more." This song is the origin of a still-popular Irish ballad in which a prodigal son declares: "I never shall play the wild rover no more." It still contains the verses about his rejection by an alewife when he appears to be out of money. There is a family of ballads in which a mercenary alewife is vilified along with the errant husband.

One subgenre of the bad-husband ballad anticipates the temperance movement by stressing the inherent disorder and corruption of tavern and alehouse cultures. The wife of "The poor miller" urges him to invest in an alehouse to secure their fortune. The raucous life overwhelms him with confusion and corruption, including unruly drinkers and his wife sitting on the knee of her customers to keep them drinking:

Men ran up the score and little they paid, which made the
poor smith be greatly dismayed.
And bonny Bess tho' she were not slack to welcome her guests
yet things went to whack,
For she would exchange a pot for a kiss, which any fellow
should seldom times miss.
He came home again and then did he see his wife kindly
sitting on a man's knee . . .
A sort of sailors were drinking one night and when they were
drunk began for to fight;
The smith came to part them, as some do report—for his
good will was beat in such sort.

There are groupings of such songs in *The Roxburghe Ballads* (from the seventeenth century) with tales about "good fellows" or "bad husbands" in which self-realization, repentance, and rehabilitation occur in part two of the ballad. These early songs provide a model followed by temperance tales of the nineteenth century, in which a wife's loyalty finally brings her drunkard husband back to responsible support of the family. "The bad husband turned thrifty" depicts stark degradation:

To see men when they are full of drink, what a beastly
condition we may think.
They hardly know one from another, abuse their friend if it be
their own brother.
They' tumble in dirt and stagger in street, affront every man
and woman they meet.

Women Drinkers in Street Ballads

Women also drink in these folk songs, sometimes with their husbands. Seventeenth-century wives may even compete with their husbands in base behavior, a source of both comedy and disaster. In the song "John and Joan," the wife strives to keep up, even in foolishness:

> John would have sold his doublet, his cloak or anything,
> And Joan would pawn her coife of lawn, her bodkin or her ring.
> If John had called his host "knave," Joan called her hostess "whore."
> For such like crimes they often times were both thrust out of doors.

After sharing rejection and ruin together, they jointly resolve to repent and start over.

There are several mentions of women who run amok on drink. In "The praise and dispraise of women" they are labeled as both seductresses and viragos:

> Women are witches when they may, so is wine—so is wine;
> Which causeth men from their wives to stray—so twill wine, so will wine.
> Women they will fight and brawl—fill'd with wine, fill'd with wine;
> Their husbands they will cuckold all—fill'd with wine, fill'd with wine.

In the nine volumes of *The Roxburghe Ballads* there are thirty songs about bad wives, but few about bad husbands. Their usual vice is cuckoldry, and sometimes this is attributed to the "disinhibiting" effects of drink, as in "Cuckolds' haven":

> Nay you would little think how they will friendly link,
> And how they'll sit and drink till they begin to wink;
> And they if Vulcan will but ride, some cuckold shall be hornified.
> A woman that will be drunk will easily play the punk;
> For when her wits are sunk, all keys will fit her trunk;
> Then by experience oft' is tried, poor men that way are hornified.

Yet, while the loose morality of the bad husbands in the Roxburghe collection is attributed to drinking, the majority of bad wives are motivated to steal and to insult and even beat their husbands without an explicit mention of drink. These songs seem to reflect a recurrent anxiety about unruly wives by "the patriarchy," which was not simply derived from puritanical concerns about effects of drinking. The bad behavior of wives was regarded by topers, it seems, as a threat to the husband rather than an insult to God. Such depiction of women's drinking in seventeenth-century street ballads appears to be a special subtype of the "unruly woman" caricature (Wiltenburg 1992). Of course, among bacchanalian songs, women's drinking is a plus for topers.

Multiple Scenarios of Women's Drinking

Among 225 bacchanalian songs, only 12 featured women as drinkers. Of these, 5 concerned romantic connections between the sexes, and wine was the facilitative agent in all 5 songs. Cheerful females who imbibed ale are featured in 5 other songs. Two of these—"Back and side go bare" and "High and mighty commendation of a pot of ale"—are prime examples of bacchanalian revelry in alehouses. None of these 12 female topers came to a bad end.

Among nonbacchanalian songs, romance themes appeared rarely among songs about women drinkers. However, thirteen nonbacchanalian songs were about cheerful females, enjoying mostly ale. In contrast, most of their nineteenth-century equivalents were cheered by gin (nearly always the hard liquor of female topers). There was often a touch of humor in these songs. For example, in "Booze is there," the image of gin in granny's tea has a comic resonance. And again, in "The thirsty family," the idea that a fellow has inherited his overpowering thirst from a family where mom swills gin has the listener smirking rather than sensing tragedy. In "Fuddling day" and in "How 5 and 20 shillings were spent," the dramas end with the beleaguered wives taking comfort from their drop of gin.

As with the fates of male drinkers, nonbacchanalian songs about women are dominated by bad ends. Of those originating in the seventeenth and eighteenth centuries, nine of eighteen of such negative songs witnessed misfortune to the woman herself, while in three others the woman robbed a man seduced under the influence of drink (the tavern-con genre). Of twenty-four songs on drinking women in the nineteenth century, bad fortune visited thirteen women, while three songs described tavern cons on intoxicated men. In one tale—reactivated by pop singers in our time—the guilty lass is sent to a penal colony in Australia:

> Oh, Maggie, Maggie May, ye robbed me of me pay
> When I slep't with you last night ashore.
> But guilty the jury found 'er, for robbin' an 'omeward bounder,
> Now she'll never cruise 'round Liverpool any more.

In the worst of scenarios (e.g., "The taylor's lamentation"), the conned man is not only robbed but is physically attacked by his seducer.

Songs about female drinkers' bad ends in the seventeenth and eighteenth centuries were divided among three themes. Three songs witness injury or bad health (even death) as a consequence of hard drinking, while in four songs poverty (having to pawn one's clothes) is the penalty of the drinking habit. The other three songs depict a release of sexual passion (or bad judgment) by intoxication. In two cases, women are accused of being sluttish seducers of men, while in the final case the wine-drunk girl is herself seduced and becomes pregnant out of wedlock. These stories anticipate the dark plots of temperance songs without their repetitive stereotypes.

The thirteen female bad-end songs from the nineteenth century also include poverty and loss of health as wages of sin, with even more songs featuring fights or physical attacks by women, a theme not seen in earlier songs. Irish street ballads about drink reveal the same surprisingly large number of songs about drinking women's aggression toward men (both husbands and lovers). These songs about unruly or subversive women are seldom humorous, although they inspired nineteenth-century songs of the English music hall and on the Irish American stage, where battering wives were standard comic fare.

Fighting

In English songs of the nineteenth century, fighting assumes less prominence than in contemporary Irish drinking songs (Ingle 2000). Only 16 English songs of this period contain fight-related themes, and 7 songs from the seventeenth and eighteenth centuries have been identified. In contrast, over 70 of 200 Irish drink-related songs of the same era concerned fighting. Of those, half were concerned with a peculiar Irish institution, "faction fighting," which is foreign to British tradition (Conley 2000). Only 2 English songs have been found with comparable themes. "Pleasures of the fair" (in which a mob at a rural carnival "drinks and fights uproariously") depicts a brawl that apparently arises from high spirits. And "Pace egging song" also depicts a spontaneous group fight among a reveling throng at an Easter festival.

Other English group fight-theme songs include "Dramatic morality," in which drinking at a theater leads to disorder wherein men cuff and spar with each other, with no mention of anger as a motive. In a playful scene at "The Manchester races," a throng eats and drinks with abandon, while others fight. Three songs depict group fights, growing out of arguments at sporting events. "Wednesbury cocking" describes a bloody affair, to be long remembered (and thus atypical), while in "Wedgfield wake" (a seasonal fair) another cockfight debate triggers a fight. Finally, in "Humors of Eccles wake," an unspecified sporting dispute also leads to a brawl. In reviewing "recreational fighting," it appears that the group fights depicted in these English songs are neither as organized nor as damaging as Irish faction fights.

The other main category of drink-enhanced fighting involves gender antagonisms. In three nineteenth-century songs ("Bunch of grapes," "Gin shop" number 2, and "John Strong"), drunken wives attack their husbands and, in the last case, one bites off his nose. In "Billy Yarn," a sailor and a girl, discovered drinking together by her boyfriend, attack the interloper. In "The bold cockney," an honorable man fights his rival over a woman. Five songs prior to 1800 involve drink, fights, and women. In "The taylor's lamentation," a man is beaten in a tavern after being conned by a woman—a genre in which the insult is seldom fatal.

Concluding Remarks

Much remains to be discovered about correlations of the most common song themes and actual beliefs of different social groups in England. Does the emphasis on bad ends in street ballads, but not in gentlemen's tavern songs, mean that working-class and lower-middle-class citizens stressed the dangers of excessive drinking more strongly than did men of the educated classes? Did women really suffer from gin drinking more than from other beverages, as the song-theme frequencies suggest?

The contrasts between song themes from Scotland, Ireland, and England are also intriguing and suggest topics for social historians to pursue. The balance between perceived benefits and dangers of drinking is significantly different between Irish and British songs, for one thing—and the Irish reverence for fighting as a recreation in their street ballads (Ingle 2000) could not be discovered in English street ballads or in rural folk songs. Are the British really so different in their attitudes toward drink-enhanced fighting, or are they simply disinclined to sing about them? Similar analyses of songs and poetry of other nations (and cultures within a given nation) may reveal distinctive values and premises about drinking, which may persist into the present day.

The bacchanalian tradition proposes several benefits of social drinking. In recent years, strong biomedical evidence has emerged for the proposition that moderate drinking is healthy. What of the other claims? Bacchanalian folklore nourishes the belief that drink not only increases the frequency of speech and laughter but also the levels of eloquence, imagination, and wit. It may now be timely to test critically the idea that moderate intoxication does facilitate, in certain situations, a freer flow of mental associations and occasionally novel ideas. A prominent psychiatrist has summarized the high frequency of alcoholism among the best American twentieth-century writers (Goodwin 1991). For those whose brain is habituated to frequent lubrication by alcohol, heavy drinking may produce a "state of arousal" equivalent to that caused by moderate intake in most others. Methods are now available (e.g., fast-MRI scans, used for localizing brain activity during short events such as responses to music) to determine whether parts of the brain active during imagination (e.g., the temporal lobe) are more metabolically active after a suitable priming with drink. Viewed from a biopsychological perspective, song themes may lead to new understanding of behavior.

David Ingle

See also: Art, Representations of Drinking in; Drinking Songs (United States); Film, Representations of Drinking and Temperance in; Gin Craze; Literature, Representations of Drinking in; Music, Popular, Representations of Drinking in; Psychological Theories of Drinking; Toasts

References

Conley, Carolyn. "The Agreeable Recreation of Fighting" in *Journal of Social History.* 33 (2000): 57–72.

Goodwin, Donald W. *Alcohol and the Writer.* New York: Viking/Penguin, 1991.

Ingle, David. "Drink, Drama, Poetry and Song: A Conference Report" in *Social History of Alcohol Review.* 15 (2001): 33–41.

———. "Drink-Related Songs in the British Isles" in *Social History of Alcohol Review.* 15 (2000): 20–27.

Marchant, W. T. *In Praise of Ale; or Songs, Ballads, Epigrams and Anecdotes Relating to Beer, Malt and Hops, with Some Curious Particulars Concerning Ale-Wives and Brewers, Drinking Clubs and Customs.* London: G. Redway, 1888.

Wiltenburg, Joy. *Disorderly Women and Female Power in the Street Literature of Early Modern England and Germany.* Charlottesville: University Press of Virginia, 1992.

Erroll and Clayson Committees (United Kingdom)

The Erroll and Clayson committees were departmental committees set up during the Conservative government of 1970–1974 to consider the liberalization of the licensing laws in England and Wales and in Scotland, respectively. Both recommended extension of permitted hours of sale, including the abolition of the "afternoon gap" introduced during the first world war, along with various other reforms such as allowing children under fourteen to sit in licensed premises subject to certain conditions. Their reports had contrasting fates: The Scottish Clayson report recommendations were accepted, while the Erroll report was ignored. However, Erroll set the tone for the liberalization of attitudes toward alcohol in England and Wales during the last quarter of the twentieth century.

By the 1970s, the steam had long gone out of the old temperance/drink controversies in Britain. Although there was little popular feeling on the issue, a lobby emerged—based around the tourist industry—which sought the liberalization of the restrictive licensing laws that regulated the "on" sale of alcohol, that is, for consumption at licensed premises. Visitors from continental Europe were said to find the British laws archaic and incomprehensible. The Monopolies Commission in 1969 had recommended liberalization of the law, and this was endorsed by the Department of Trade and Industry. The Scottish Clayson report received a broader range of support because it justified its findings on medical grounds—liberalization was seen as a means of reducing "binge drinking" before closing time—and because the Scottish licensed victuallers wanted liberalization. This left the temperance lobby isolated. In contrast, in England and Wales strong opposition emerged both from the publicans, who did not want to face increased competition or to work longer hours, and from the medical lobby. As a result, after the Scottish Licensing Act of 1976, the law in Scotland went from being more restrictive to more liberal than that in England and Wales.

The government remained officially neutral on the issue for a while. Some departments, such as those responsible for trade, food, and employment, favored liberalization. Those in charge of health and public order (especially regarding soccer violence) were hostile or more cautious. By the late 1980s, the prevailing ideology in Margaret Thatcher's Britain strongly favored general liberalization of trade, and all the evidence was that the public favored liberalization of drink sales. Scottish experience suggested that liberalization had not led to major health problems, and in 1988 Mrs. Thatcher's Conservative government passed a measure that effectively allowed public houses flexible hours of opening between 11 A.M. and 11 P.M.

John Greenaway

See also: Licensing Hours (United Kingdom); Pubs and Beerhouses (United Kingdom)

References

Baggott, Rob. *Alcohol, Politics and Social Policy.* Aldershot: Gower, 1990.

Greenaway, John R. *Drink and British Politics since 1830: A Study in Policy-Making.* Basingstoke, UK, and New York: Palgrave Macmillan, 2003.

Home Office. *Report of the Departmental Committee on Liquor Licensing in England and Wales.* [The Erroll Report]. Cmnd. 5154. London: HMSO, 1972.

Scottish Home and Health Department. *Report of the Departmental Committee on Scottish Licensing Laws.* [The Clayson Report]. Cmnd. 5354. London: HMSO, 1973.

Evangelical Temperance (United Kingdom)

The growth of the British temperance movement and its acceptance by the 1860s in the Anglican Church owed much to the growing social concern of Evangelicals. Evangelicals spearheaded the debate over teetotalism and religion, and helped Christianize antidrink movements by 1873, permitting the establishment of Britain's most extensive and prestigious temperance organization, the Church of England Temperance Society (CETS), and the kindred groups that clergymen helped organize in the United States and the empire. Evangelical teetotalers viewed temperance as the key to almost all social and moral improvement. Despite their traditional disbelief in earthly amelioration, they embraced a "root-branch" explanation of social distress, insisting that society's vices would be virtually wiped out if drink were eliminated. Many blamed the poor themselves for their hardship and insisted that individuals, not society, were responsible for their own betterment. Contrary to the growing collectivism of Anglo-Catholic and Christian Socialist temperance advocates, Evangelical antidrink reformers stressed individualism. They trusted moral suasion and governmental restrictionist or prohibitionist intervention against drink, the root of social distress, to obviate the need for greater state action.

Evangelicalism helped shape the religious, intellectual, cultural, and social character of the Victorian age. It developed with the mid-eighteenth-century revival inspired by the Methodist John Wesley (1703–1791), during which traveling preachers undertook to convert the masses by assuring the forgiveness of sins and personal salvation. Evangelicals, whether

Methodist, other Nonconformist, or Anglican, stressed an individualistic relationship with God and faith over good works as the keys to salvation through the grace of Christ's atonement. By insisting that personal redemption was the means to individual improvement, Evangelicals advocated spiritual perfectionism in a society caught up in intellectual and social conflict.

England's early Evangelicals exerted their greatest influence from the London suburb of Clapham, under William Wilberforce (1759–1833) and Hannah More (1745–1833), and from Cambridge, led by Charles Simeon (1759–1836). Evangelicals considered it their moral duty to act as role models for the "lower orders." Believing that they could expect to influence the poor only after reforming the upper class, they worked to curb society's vices and to improve public morality from the top down. Yet, in their own circles, including Oxford and Cambridge, early Evangelicals met for evening wine tasting.

Before initiation of the moderationist temperance movement in the late 1820s, Evangelicals had considered drink an ordinary pleasure. Some prominent Anglicans embraced the moderationist movement that forbade drinking spirits, but permitted investment in the drink industry and the use of beer and wine, socially, sacramentally, and medicinally. From about 1835 to 1855, Anglican clergymen, except for a handful, resisted teetotalism for religious, social, cultural, medical, and economic reasons. They were disinclined to follow working people's lead, and they condemned teetotalers as followers of a "false religion" who advocated the still un-Christianized pledge as a secular solution for drunkenness, promising the earthly perfection that could be achieved only by faith, grace, and the Bible. Nonconformist Evangelicals often embraced teetotalism more easily than Anglican Evangelicals.

Early Anglican Evangelicals did not share the melioristic assumptions of teetotal and prohibitionist advocates. Prohibition, many believed, was an ineffective attempt to "cure" intemperance by state-led coercion. Concern for the deteriorating condition of Britain's poor and crises in proletarian attendance at local services forced Evangelicals to realize teetotalism's immediate significance, as well as their own spiritual and social responsibilities to promote it. Evangelicals endorsed teetotalism when necessary, but feared financial loss, violating basic Church and medical tenets, and reversing their traditional top-down approach to social reform.

Evangelical Teetotalers

Five Evangelicals played a leading role in introducing teetotalism to Anglican parishes in the 1850s and in the 1862 founding of the Church of England Total Abstinence Society—Julia Bainbrigge Wightman (1817–1898) and the Anglican priests Stopford Ram

Crusading members of the Evangelical Church Army profess love of God and temperance, ca. 1900 (Hulton/Archive)

(d. 1881), Robert Maguire (1826–1890), Francis Close (1797–1882), and Henry Ellison (1813–1899). Their relations with parish working people convinced them that the benefits of teetotalism outweighed the cultural, social, medical, and theological obstacles that previously kept them from the movement.

By accepting and leading the teetotal movement, Evangelicals overcame their reservations after 1855. They adopted the previously working-class total abstinence movement and insisted that their own social example and leadership were consistent with Evangelicalism. They challenged the prevailing medical opinion by arguing that abstinence improved rather than hurt health and advocated teetotalism's unique role in eradicating social distress. Although some also supported other reforms, including improved housing, education, and working conditions, and the female franchise, most, unlike the Christian Socialists, saw teetotalism as the primary reform. A generation of Christianized teetotalism enabled some Anglican Evangelicals, in close relations with Nonconformists, to reject drinking as sinful, to take the pledge, and to sanction unfermented Communion wine.

Cambridge's Evangelical tradition was embodied in life abstainer Handley Carr Glynn Moule (1841–1920), who, as principal of the Evangelical Ridley Hall, and later as bishop of Durham, promoted temperance as an individualistic response to Anglo-Catholic collectivism. Charles Simeon's wine-drinking soirées were often replaced by socials with nonalcoholic drinks. The earl of Shaftesbury (1801–1885) expressed his biblical responsibility to provide an example to the "lower orders" and banned drink on his own estates, and the duke of Westminster (1825–1899) supported CETS moral suasionist and political initiatives. Increasingly, Evangelical teetotal Conservative politicians, such as C. E. Tritton (1845–1918) and William Joynson-Hicks (1865–1932), advocated voluntary reform and limited restrictionist temperance legislation, but not the prohibitionism sometimes advanced by Liberals. Cooperation between the CETS and Conservatives helped bring about the 1904 licensing act that helped greatly to reduce the number of pubs.

In a period that began with the Enlightenment and ended with the liberal idealism of T. H. Green (1836–1882), Evangelicalism emerged as a formidable contrary intellectual and social force in England. Following the period of its greatest influence, between 1800 and 1860, Evangelicalism largely gave way to Anglo-Catholic Christian Socialism. Evangelicals' individualist stress on temperance as the cure for all of society's evils was surpassed by a more collectivist understanding of temperance reform as secondary to deeper and broader state action.

Matthew K. McKean and Gerald Wayne Olsen

See also: Bible Wine; Christian Socialism; Church of England Temperance Society (CETS); Church of England Temperance Society (CETS) Inebriate Homes; Church of England Temperance Society (CETS) Police Court Mission; Close, Francis; Conservative Party (United Kingdom); Dunlop, John; Ellison, Henry; Maguire, Robert; Moule, Handley Carr Glyn; Nonconformists (United Kingdom); Wightman, Julia Bainbrigge; Wilberforce, Basil and Wilberforce, Ernest

References

Brown, Callum G. *The Death of Christian Britain.* London: Routledge, 2001.

Hilton, Boyd. *The Age of Atonement: The Influence of Evangelicalism on Social and Economic Thought, 1795–1865.* Oxford: Clarendon Press, 1988.

Olsen, Gerald Wayne. *Drink and the British Establishment—The Church of England Temperance Society, 1873–1914.* Unpublished book manuscript.

———. *Pub and Parish—Drink and Temperance in the Church of England, 1829–1875.* Unpublished book manuscript.

Shiman, Lilian Lewis. *Crusade against Drink in Victorian England.* London: Macmillan, 1988.

F

Federal Council of Churches

See Temperance Commission of the Federal Council of Churches

Federal Prohibition (Canada)

Federal Prohibition in Canada was a temporary war measure enacted in 1918 to prevent the importation, manufacture, distribution, or sale of liquor for the duration of the war, and for one year after.

During the first world war, the federal government of Sir Robert Borden began to explore the need for liquor prohibition, primarily as an efficiency measure. A few provinces had prohibition legislation before the war, and the remaining English-speaking provinces passed prohibition legislation between 1915 and 1917. In 1916, Borden's government passed legislation aimed at outlawing the export of liquor into provinces where prohibition was in force. This legislation, commonly known as the Doherty Act, after Attorney General Charles Doherty, was adjusted and tightened over the next two years. At the beginning of 1918, the government announced Prohibition by Order-in-Council, made possible by powers under the War Measures Act. Recognizing that Quebec would not pass its prohibition law until 1 May 1918, the federal government made its legislation fully effective on that date.

The federal measure reinforced provincial prohibition legislation. It prohibited the use of foodstuffs for alcohol production and strengthened restrictions on interprovincial liquor trade and on importation of liquor into the country. The law defined intoxicating liquor as any liquor containing more than 2.5 percent proof spirit, in keeping with the definitions at the provincial level. It did permit the manufacture, use, and sale of alcohol for sacramental, medicinal, scientific, and manufacturing purposes, as long as the product being manufactured was not beverage alcohol. Borden argued that the measure would prevent waste, promote thrift and economy, and conserve financial resources. The legislation was to take effect until one year after the cessation of the war, and therefore ceased effect at the end of 1919.

When Prohibition ended, the federal government required each province that wanted to continue its prohibitory legislation to put the question to a plebiscite. All but Quebec approved continuing provincial prohibition. In 1919, Quebec voters permitted the sale of beer, wine, and cider. However, enthusiasm for provincial prohibition waned in the early 1920s. Beginning with British Columbia in 1921, provinces began to replace prohibition laws with government control of distribution. The last province to repeal prohibition was Prince Edward Island (where prohibition began in 1907) in 1948. Government control has characterized liquor distribution in most of English Canada ever since.

Daniel J. Malleck

See also: Provincial Liquor Boards (Canada); Provincial Prohibition (Canada); Provincial Regulation (Canada); Provincial Stores (Canada)

References

Canada. *Debates of the House of Commons of Canada* (1916–1919).

———. *Journals of the House of Commons of Canada* (1916–1919).

———. *Sessional Papers of the Dominion of Canada* (1916–1919).

———. *Statutes of the Dominion of Canada* (1916–1919).

Gray, James. *Bacchanalia Revisited: Western Canada's Boozy Skid to Social Disaster.* Saskatoon, Saskatchewan: Western Producer Prairie Books, 1982.

———. *Booze: The Impact of Whisky on the Prairie West.* Toronto: Macmillan, 1972.

Hallowell, Gerald A. *Prohibition in Ontario.* Ottawa: Ontario Historical Society, 1972.

Hose, Reginald. *Prohibition or Control?: Canada's Experience with the Liquor Problem, 1921–1927.* Toronto: Longmans, Green, 1928.

Smart, Reginald G., and Alan C. Ogborne. *Northern Spirits: A Social History of Alcohol in Canada.* Toronto: Addiction Research Foundation, 1996.

Federal Regulation of Alcohol before 1920 (United States)

The United States government's regulation of alcohol before National Prohibition reflected both the powers and scope of the federal government and the developing views of liquor held in American society. At the founding of the republic, liquor was usually held to be a benign product regulated as any other commodity. It quickly became recognized as one of the best sources of government revenue. With the emergence of the temperance and prohibition movements, the government's regulation of liquor became more complex and contradictory. But, as the prohibitionists gained political power, the trend was toward increasing the federal government's restriction of liquor production and use.

Before 1920, the federal government operated within a limited sphere through the exercise of its enumerated powers. Thus, through the treaty, territorial, tax, postal, commerce, and war powers, the government regulated liquor. The overall history of the development of federal government regulation can be seen in the use of the treaty power, especially as it related to the Native American nations. At first, the government entered into treaties to supply liquor to various nations as part of their annuities. Later, it used treaties to stipulate that Native American reservations be liquor-free, and in the early twentieth century the government attempted to use the treaty power to enforce "Indian prohibition" on reservations that had been overrun with Anglos.

The trend in the area of taxation shows a similar, though more significant, pattern. The 1796 whiskey tax established a precedent of reliance on a liquor tax to fund the government, especially in times of fiscal stress such as war. Thus, during the Civil War, the federal government constructed an extensive system of taxing liquor production and licensing retail sellers. From the Whiskey Ring frauds (1869–1875) to the period of World War I, liquor taxes generated between 20 and 40 percent of federal revenue annually. The liquor-tax system required daily contact between federal employees and liquor producers, resulting in a favorable view of the industry (and of liquor) within the government and extensive ties between the federal government and the liquor industry. Liquor lobbyists remained powerful in Washington until World War I. From the first federal tax on liquor until National Prohibition, the federal government expended much effort on suppressing tax-evading liquor producers. Compared to the efforts to suppress liquor under National Prohibition, these efforts against moonshiners were successful. But strict enforcement of the tax laws did not change the government's attitude toward liquor. The accustomed perception of liquor as a legitimate source of government revenue died hard. Indeed, on the day the thirty-sixth state ratified the Prohibition amendment, a congressional conference committee was considering raising liquor tax rates. But this tendency to define liquor only as a revenue source conflicted with the rising moral and social condemnation of liquor.

As a consequence of the federalist nature of the American government, it was the states and localities that first responded to the rising temperance and prohibition movements. The regulation of public morals and public health was a state responsibility. The federal courts recognized that states had broad powers over liquor, including the power to ban its production and sale. At the same time, the federal government refused to condemn liquor as a moral or health threat. Indeed, Congress rebuffed temperance advocates' demand for an inquiry into the effects of alcohol on society.

As prohibitionists began to win victories in the states, federal policy clashed with the new antidrink policies. The conflicts became particularly acute in the 1880s and lasted at least until National Prohibition. Federal interstate commerce doctrines, as enunciated by the courts (most notably the ideas of freedom of commerce and the original package doctrine), and the federal postal power were used by liquor producers in nonprohibition areas to send their products into dry territories. Federalism meant that states could not interfere with liquor until it passed out of federal commerce or postal control—that is, until it was in the hands of the final consumer. Similarly, the federal government continued to tax liquor producers who operated contrary to state or local prohibition laws, supplying revenue stamps to retailers in dry territories. Moreover, the tax officials routinely auctioned liquor seized for taxes in dry areas and protected the privacy of liquor-tax payers from state investigators. The upshot was that federal policies significantly hampered state liquor regulation and prohibition. These frictions prompted prohibitionists to seek to turn federal powers against liquor.

Every federal power was eventually turned into a prohibitionist tool. Through a series of laws, including the Wilson Act (1890), the C. O. D. Act (1909), and the Webb-Kenyon Act (1913), Congress limited the commerce power over liquor. These three laws allowed dry territories to intercept, regulate, and ban liquor shipments originating in other states. At the same time, dry states used the federal tax lists to find liquor sellers in their jurisdictions, a process made easier by a 1907 federal law that facilitated access to the tax records. In the Reed Amendment to the Postal Act of 1917, prohibitionists pressured the Congress into using the commerce and postal powers to ban the transportation of liquor into any dry state or region.

The war powers completed the transformation of the federal government's regulation of liquor from ordinary regulations to prohibitory enactments. Under the guise of food conservation, the Lever Act (1917) banned the use of foodstuffs in the production of distilled liquor until the end of the war. The act also allowed the government to set the alcoholic content of beer and to prescribe how much grain could be made into beer. And, even though the fighting was over, on 21 November 1918 Congress passed a Wartime Prohibition Act, thus making the nation dry before the Prohibition amendment went into effect.

Richard F. Hamm

See also: Native Americans: Drinking Patterns and Temperance Reform; State Prohibition (United States); Taxation of Liquor (United States)

References

Hamm, Richard F. *Shaping the Eighteenth Amendment: Temperance Reform, Legal Culture, and the Polity, 1880–1920.* Chapel Hill: University of North Carolina Press, 1995.

Hu, Tun-Yuan. *The Liquor Tax in the United States, 1791–1947.* New York: Graduate School of Business, Columbia University Monographs in Public Finance and National Income, 1951.

Miller, Wilbur R. *Revenuers and Moonshiners: Enforcing Federal Liquor Law in the Mountain South, 1865–1900.* Chapel Hill: University of North Carolina Press, 1991.

Mittelman, Amy. "The Politics of Alcohol Production: The Liquor Industry and the Federal Government, 1862–1900." (Ph.D. dissertation, Columbia University, 1986).

Unrau, William E. *White Man's Wicked Water: The Alcohol Trade and Prohibition in Indian Country, 1802–1892.* Lawrence: University Press of Kansas, 1996.

Fetal Alcohol Syndrome (FAS)

Fetal alcohol syndrome (FAS) is a pattern of abnormalities occurring in children born to alcoholic women. The abnormalities include: prenatal growth retardation below the tenth percentile (corrected for gestational age); intellectual/behavioral anomalies such as mental retardation; and unusual facial features such as small head size (microcephaly), absence or decreased prominence of the philtrum (the vertical groove between the nose and mouth), and a thin upper lip lacking the "cupid's bow."

Soon after FAS was identified as a distinct clinical entity in 1973, it became evident that there were other individuals affected by alcohol who had some but not all of the features of the syndrome. "Fetal alcohol effects" (FAEs) and "alcohol-related birth defects" (ARBDs) were two of the most common terms that were subsequently coined to describe these conditions. However, in contrast to FAS, which had distinctive criteria, the individual components of the syndrome are associated with many different problems. The often haphazard application of the term FAEs to effects associated with alcohol led to the creation of an ever-growing catalog of effects and related skepticism as to linkage, and considerable misunderstanding about the distinction between FAS and FAEs even among clinicians and medical researchers. Subsequent clarity with respect to terminology and causality was introduced in 1996 by the Institute of Medicine (IOM) in its lengthy review of many of these and other related concerns about alcohol's effects on gestational development. The IOM's recommended that the previous criteria for making an FAS diagnosis remain in place but that a distinction be made between FAS cases in which maternal drinking was confirmed and cases where it was not. The institute defined risky drinking as substantial, regular, or heavy episodic, as indicated by several signs of dependence such as withdrawal and by social or legal difficulties relating to drinking. The IOM also recommended the creation of three new categories that did not meet the FAS criteria but included indications associated with the syndrome. However, the institute stressed that each of these categories should only be used if maternal drinking could be substantiated, since none of them was unique to drinking. The newly created categories were: partial FAS with confirmed maternal alcohol exposure; ARBDs; and "alcohol-related neurodevelopmental disorder" (ARND). Inclusion in the category of partial FAS required some but not all of the typical facial anomalies and either growth retardation or neurodevelopmental difficulties similar to those associated with FAS. ARBDs subsumed various anomalies affecting the heart, kidneys, and other organs. ARND encompassed cases with neurodevelopmental problems but no facial anomalies.

Incidence

The overall incidence of FAS in the industrialized world is 0.97 births per 1,000. When only women identified as problem drinkers or alcohol abusers are considered, the incidence is a much higher 43 births per 1,000. Overall rates, however, obscure important differences between populations that reveal how factors interact with alcohol to produce FAS. For instance, incidence rates for FAS are highest in the United States (1.95 births per 1,000) compared to Europe (0.08 births per 1,000). Since per capital alcohol consumption is considerably lower in the United States than in many European countries, the higher incidence of FAS in the United States has been dubbed the "American paradox." One of the possible explanations for this paradox is better ascertainment in the United States.

Risk Factors

Among the risk factors contributing to FAS and associated anomalies are drinking behavior, socioeconomic status, smoking, and genetic susceptibility. All substances capable of producing birth defects, including alcohol, do not always produce damage. This is because there are levels of exposure ("thresholds") below which no damage is induced. If the threshold level is exceeded, however, damage may occur, and the extent of damage is often related to the extent of exposure. At very high levels, the damage to the embryo/fetus may be so extensive that death occurs, thereby providing an upper limit to the number of children born with defects due to a particular agent. In nonhuman primates, abortions related to alcohol occur at blood-alcohol levels of 200 milligrams per 100 milliliters, which is twice the legal level of intoxication in most states in the United States, and corresponds to consumption of about 8.5 drinks within a four-hour period for a 55-kilogram (120-pound) woman.

One of the perennial questions associated with prenatal alcohol exposure is whether there is a safe level of alcohol consumption during pregnancy. In the United States, about 60 percent of all women drink to some degree. This means that most Americans have been exposed to alcohol prior to birth. If any amount of exposure were harmful, the impact would be staggering (e.g., two of every three readers of this book would have some defect due to prenatal alcohol exposure). Although drinking behavior is commonly described in terms of the average number of drinks per week or month, the critical factor creating a risk for prenatal damage is the blood-alcohol level associated with the number of drinks consumed per drinking occasion. The minimum number of drinks per day during pregnancy found to cause prenatal damage is five drinks per drinking occasion. Damage to the embryo/fetus is much more closely associated with consumption during pregnancy of five drinks on one night during a week than one drink on five different nights within a week. About 2 to 3 percent of pregnant women drink above this threshold, but even when the threshold is exceeded, relatively few women give birth to children with FAS. This selectivity implies that alcohol consumption is a necessary but not sufficient cause of FAS and related disorders.

Poverty is another major risk factor associated with prenatal damage from drinking. The overwhelming majority of FAS cases in the United States have been diagnosed in inner-city hospitals, which generally serve a lower socioeconomic patient population than hospitals in the suburbs. For example, the rate for FAS is considerably higher (2.29 births per 1,000) where the patient population is primarily African American/low socioeconomic status compared to populations that are predominantly Caucasian/middle socioeconomic status (0.26 per 1,000). The reason why poverty is such a major contributing factor to FAS is that poverty is associated with poor nutrition, smoking, high parity, stress, and other conditions known to affect prenatal development adversely. These conditions contribute to the occurrence of FAS because they influence the mechanisms by which alcohol causes prenatal damage.

Although different kinds of alcoholic beverages are consumed in different countries, beverage type is not itself a risk factor, nor does it account for the American paradox. Although different alcoholic beverages contain various flavoring agents and ingredients that are potentially harmful, it is alcohol and not any of these other substances that causes the prenatal damage associated with FAS and related disorders. Although beer has been linked to a higher rate of FAEs than other beverages, it is not beer but rather its association with low socioeconomic status that is critical. The conclusion from most studies that have taken socioeconomic distinctions in beverage use into account is that it is the alcohol and not the form in which it is taken that is the major determinant affecting prenatal development.

Drinking only during a particular time in pregnancy is also not a risk factor. There is no "safe" time during pregnancy when drinking has no effect, although one reason for the occurrence of partial FAS, rather than the full-blown syndrome, is timing of exposure.

Knowing when exposure to a possible damaging substance during pregnancy occurs is important in understanding and predicting outcomes, because there are critical periods in development when the embryo/fetus is especially vulnerable to insults. Organ damage and facial anomalies, for instance, are most likely to occur if a fetus is exposed to alcohol or some other damaging substance during the first trimester of pregnancy, when these areas of the body are forming. On the other hand, decreased birth weight is more likely to occur if exposure occurs during the third trimester of pregnancy. Because the brain develops throughout pregnancy, brain damage is not as closely related to timing of exposure. Since FAS includes facial anomalies, growth retardation, and brain damage, it requires a drinking pattern that exceeds the threshold for damage and one that is sustained throughout pregnancy. Since partial FAS includes only some of the tripartite pattern, drinking above a threshold level is more likely to be associated with consumption during a particular trimester of development than with consumption throughout pregnancy.

Paternal drinking prior to conception is similarly not a major contributing risk factor. Although studies in animals indicate that paternal drinking prior to conception can result in some of the same kinds of prenatal damage that occurs in FAS/FAEs, the probability of damage is far less than that associated with maternal drinking.

Mechanisms

There is no single mechanism by which alcohol causes prenatal injury. Among the possible mechanisms causing damage are interference with the way cells transport glucose into their interiors—without glucose, they lack the fuel to function optimally.

Other mechanisms include disruption of cell adhesion—the way cells form contacts with one another during development; interference with gene expression and cellular growth factors that direct cellular growth and development; and interference with the activity of neurotransmitters—the chemicals that mediate signal transmission between nerves and in some cases, regulate early nerve-cell development. Another mechanism that has received considerable attention with respect to alcohol's effects is oxygenated free radical formation. Oxygenated free radicals are highly reactive chemical molecules that are formed during a cell's many biochemical reactions involving oxygen. Oxygenated free radicals attack a cell's chromosomes, receptors, membranes, proteins, and so forth, causing cellular injury and death.

Free radicals are normally prevented from causing cell damage by scavenger molecules within the cell called antioxidants. One reason why poverty is a major risk factor for alcohol-related prenatal damage is that many of these antioxidants are supplied through diet. Since poverty often prevents adequate diet, levels of antioxidants from food may be insufficient to deal with free radicals. Smoking, which is also associated with poverty, is likewise a contributor to alcohol-related damage because it introduces free radicals into the body, and these free radicals place demands on the cell for inactivation, thereby rendering the cell vulnerable to radicals produced by alcohol.

Prevention

From a prevention standpoint, the most conservative strategy is to refrain from drinking alcohol at any time during pregnancy. The advice to abstain has been widely disseminated in the media and through professional education efforts. In the United States, every bottle or can containing beverage alcohol is required by law to warn consumers that alcohol can cause birth defects. Although these efforts have raised public awareness of the potential harm associated with drinking during pregnancy, several surveys have found that this awareness has had little impact in actually modifying drinking behavior. Women who engage in the kind of heavy drinking that leads to FAS have been found to be especially resistant to such public-health messages. This dilute impact has prompted proposals for different strategies, among which is to focus prevention efforts in the clinic on those women who are most at risk for FAS/FAEs. Although most of these proposals relate to voluntary screening, proposals for mandatory screening for alcohol abuse during pregnancy have also been suggested. In Michigan, about half the physicians responding to a survey assessing attitudes toward involvement of the criminal justice system in preventing alcohol abuse during pregnancy were in favor of enacting a statute that included alcohol use during pregnancy as "child abuse" for purposes of removing a child from maternal custody, and more than 75 percent were in favor of compulsory treatment for alcohol abuse for women already in the criminal justice system.

Ernest L. Abel

References

Abel, Ernest L. "An Update on Incidence of FAS: FAS Is Not an Equal Opportunity Birth Defect" in *Neurotoxicology and Teratology.* 17 (1995): 437–443.

———. *Fetal Alcohol Abuse Syndrome.* New York: Plenum Press, 1998.

———. "Fetal Alcohol Syndrome: The American Paradox" in *Alcohol and Alcoholism.* 33 (1998): 195–201.

Abel, Ernest L., and J. Hannigan. "Maternal Risk Factors in Fetal Alcohol Syndrome: Provocative and Permissive Influences" in *Neurotoxicology and Teratology.* 17 (1995): 445–462.

Abel, Ernest L., and M. Kruger. "Physician Attitudes Concerning Legal Coercion of Pregnant Alcohol/Drug Abusers" in *American Journal of Obstetrics and Gynecology.* 186 (2002): 168–172.

Goodlett, C. R., and K. H. Horn. "Mechanisms of Alcohol-Induced Damage to the Developing Nervous System" in *Alcohol Research and Health.* 25 (2001): 175–184.

Stratton, K., C. Howe, and F. Battaglia, eds. *Fetal Alcohol Syndrome: Diagnosis, Epidemiology, Prevention, and Treatment.* Washington, DC: National Academy Press, 1996.

Fifteen Gallon Law

The Fifteen Gallon Law was a Massachusetts law designed to restrict access to alcoholic spirits by requiring purchase in quantities of fifteen gallons or more. In April 1838, the Massachusetts legislature restricted the sale of spirits more severely than any state had ever done. Apart from licensed physicians and apothecaries, no licensed inn keeper, retailer, or grocer could sell distilled liquor in quantities under fifteen gallons ("and that delivered and carried away all at one time"). The controversial law dominated state politics for two years, and it was repealed in April 1840.

Neighborhood taverns and "grog shops" alarmed temperance reformers. There the poor squandered time, money, health, and virtue. If they lacked the cash to buy fifteen gallons, then their meager funds could be better spent. In response, opponents charged discrimination. The well-off could easily make bulk purchases, and they could still buy wine, supposedly the drink of choice in their social class.

Ideals of egalitarianism and respect for the common man were cherished by the Democrats, who ridiculed the law and capitalized on its unpopularity, although a faction of temperance Democrats occasionally forced the party to hedge its opposition. The Fifteen Gallon Law arguments resonated with the Whigs' conviction that an activist state should promote the public welfare through the vigorous use of its powers. But this form of activism split the Whigs more deeply than it divided the Democrats. Often the local and county Whig parties tried to avoid or straddle liquor issues, to the irritation of both prohibitionist and antiprohibitionist Whigs. In legislative elections in 1838 and 1839, "liberal" slates pledged to vote for repeal battled the Whig and Democrat nominees in several counties, siphoning more Whig than Democratic votes. In 1839, the Democrats elected their gubernatorial candidate for the first time and nearly captured the legislature. With the Whig legislators split and the Democrats quite cohesive, the Fifteen Gallon Law was repealed by a margin of 295 to 172, leaving an 1832 license law in force.

The Fifteen Gallon Law was as difficult to enforce as it was politically volatile. Police departments were small and weak, so temperance men often filed the complaints and also gathered the evidence of illicit sales. When vigilantes bought liquor at suspect shops, they were usually vilified as dishonorable. Critics and defense attorneys claimed that some informers were drunks hired to spy. If temperance men, they compromised their abstinence by drinking the liquor and risked prosecution as a party to the alleged crime. Outside the courtrooms, some complainants and informers were assaulted and others were heckled by angry crowds.

Despite the enforcement difficulties, the Fifteen Gallon Law filled the courts with cases. From 1834 to 1838, license violation cases averaged around 400 annually. The number of license cases exceeded 600 in 1839. However, the ratio of convictions to acquittals fell sharply in 1839, and the number of pending license cases soared (because no court had established the constitutionality of the law, many defendants sought postponement in the hope of favorable judicial rulings or legislative repeal).

After repeal, the prohibitionists fared well at the local and county levels. In the 1840s, many of the counties in the middle and western sections of the state—the areas where political disarray flared in 1838 and 1839—withheld licenses. The eastern and southeastern counties that had always been the heart of no-license policy remained so. But the detection and prosecution of offenders remained onerous throughout the decade.

That ongoing frustration with law enforcement explains why, in Massachusetts, part of the appeal of the Maine Law of 1852 was its provision that simple possession of liquor, tumblers, and other "tools" associated with the liquor trade was considered evidence of illicit sale.

Robert L. Hampel

See also: Maine Law; State Prohibition (United States)

References

Dodd, Jill S. "The Working Classes and the Temperance Movement in Ante-Bellum Boston" in *Labor History.* 19 (Fall 1978): 510–531.

Hampel, Robert L. *Temperance and Prohibition in Massachusetts, 1813–1852.* Ann Arbor, MI: UMI Research Press, 1982.

Investigation into the 15 Gallon Law of Massachusetts, before a Joint Committee of the Legislature, January 29–February 20, 1839. Boston: Buckingham, 1839.

Film, Representations of Drinking and Temperance in

Feature films have conveyed various representations of drinking, alcoholism, and temperance since the invention of cinema in 1895. From a sociological perspective, these references to alcohol reflect what is or was considered suitable or not suitable to be shown on screen according to cultures, countries, epochs, and local censorship. Documentaries have also presented alcoholism in various and often informative ways. A study of the many ways in which drinking and alcoholism have been presented and prevented in many documentaries, newsreels, educational, and scientific films could be valuable from a historical, anthropological, or sociological point of view. But feature films are also possible windows to observe selected visions and controlled representations of alcoholism. Actors and actresses usually have to be sober to play the role of a drunken man or woman, but they also have to render the situation with realism and credibility. Therefore, they try to act according to their perception of real persons in the same situation. Of course, feature films are not reality, especially in cases where drinking is socially controlled by rules (politeness, forbidding the use of alcohol for minors); for instance, it was not suitable throughout most of film history to show someone drinking from a bottle of liquor without using a glass, although we know some people did drink this way in real life.

It is also interesting to compare how, why, and when people drank, got drunk, or decided to be sober in many different occasions in movies from the 1930s until today. For a scriptwriter, a simple action such as offering a drink when two characters meet at the beginning of a scene was often a natural way to begin a scene, a logical gesture that was related to hospitality. These proffered drinks were never a Coke, a juice, or even a beer, but mostly gin, whiskey, scotch, or some exotic mix.

Alcoholism in Films from the United States: The Silent Era

During the silent era (before 1930), the alcoholic character often was a comic, sometimes even a clownish man who behaved oddly, in a funny way, to make the audience laugh at him. Two famous masterpieces by Charlie Chaplin perfectly illustrate this trend. In a short film titled *One A. M.* (1916), a rich drunk man (played by Chaplin himself) gets back home late at night. In the burlesque tradition, he walks with difficulty: Even climbing the stairs demands many efforts and hesitation. He realizes he doesn't have his key. He tries to find it and then, after many tries, gets in through the window. When he is in, he finally finds his key, goes again through the window and opens the door from the outside! As the film goes on, the character faces other problems caused by his dizziness and his troubled vision of the familiar objects that seem to attack him (the clock, the door, the bed). Because his bed moves all the time, he falls asleep in the bathtub. This is the classic example of comedy about the drunken man going home and living a nightmare.

Another Chaplin movie partly dealing with alcoholism is *City Lights* (1931) (see illustration on p. 236). Here, the alcoholic is not played by Chaplin, by rather by Harry Myers. A handsome millionaire is saved from suicide by the tramp (Chaplin). While the millionaire is drunk, bumbling and stumbling, he considers the tramp as his savior and best friend; the millionaire brings him home and shares everything he owns with him. But a day later, when the alcoholic is sober, he has forgotten everything he did while he was drunk! He doesn't even recognize the tramp and expels him. But when he gets drunk again, the millionaire discovers his old pal, and they become friends as before. His attitude changes every day. Here, humor and surprises appear because the millionaire is unpredictable and full of contradiction: a simple, prodigal man when he is drunk; a grumpy and nasty bourgeois when he is sober. The film implies that alcohol makes a man better or can reveal one's truest qualities and authentic personality.

U.S. Films: The Talkies

In John Ford's *The Informer* (1935), one of his great non-Western movies, a poor Irishman (played by Victor McLaglen) betrays a friend, a wanted man, to the English police for £20. Full of guilt, he goes to a bar and gets drunk when he learns that his friend has been arrested; therefore, he wastes all the money he earned. His betrayal has been useless; he is killed when his mates learn about his betrayal. The film's strength is found in the hallucinated images of the drunken man, who seems to see his betrayed friend's face anywhere he looks. All the words he hears remind him of his unfair attitude. Even though the informer is obsessed by his crime, alcohol can't help him escape or make him forget what he has done; the money he got for his gesture does not help him to get out of his poverty. The film won four Academy Awards. A remake of that movie (also from a novel written by L. O'Flaherty) was made in 1968 by director

Jules Dassin, titled *Up Tight,* with African American characters. The leading role of the alcoholic traitor is played by Julian Mayfield. The film is set in the United States during the post–Martin Luther King era, and the Irish dissidents are replaced by followers of Black Power. It is interesting to compare these two films based on the same story and made at a thirty-three-year distance, but Dassin's film eschews most of the visual effects and hallucinations of Ford's.

John Ford's inventive images created to depict the subjective point of view of the drunken man were inspired by a German film made by a director he admired, Friedrich Wilhelm Murnau, who made a silent masterpiece, *The Last Laugh* (*Der Letze Mann,* 1924). A lonely man loses his job and therefore his social esteem. One night, he gets drunk and sees strange visions. While he is drunk, he dreams he is young, strong, and at work again. Fantasy images turn into moving visual effects. But his reality is not like his dreams of youth and strength. He has to accept the plain fact of his own destitution. The film was not a comedy but rather a tragic story. The German producers, however, imposed a new ending on the director, who had to add a new scene to his film: After finding another miserable job in a hotel's washrooms, the sad man becomes a millionaire and escapes his bitter situation. He doesn't depend on alcohol anymore. The film was nonetheless a huge success in Germany; in the United States, critics especially appreciated the happy ending.

Before John Ford's *The Informer* introduced a negative view of the drunken man, famous actor W. C. Fields starred in a light comedy, *The Fatal Glass of Beer* (1933), made by Arthur Ripley. This was the period when many films dealt with temperance and prohibition, such as Edward Sedwick's funny *What! No Beer?* (1933), starring Buster Keaton and Jimmy Durante. This MGM film tells the story of two men who are in the beer business, but have to face the law and the mafia during National Prohibition. A brilliant actor and creative director, Buster Keaton lost his own career to alcoholism, although he underwent many detoxification cures (*The Buster Keaton Story,* 1957, directed by Sidney Shelton). Many films and series have been made about National Prohibition, such as *Al Capone* (1959), by Richard Wilson, and *Capone* (1975), directed by Steve Carver.

Strangely, some alcoholic actors succeeded at playing alcoholic characters. In George Cukor's *Dinner at Eight* (1933), taken from a play by George S. Kaufman and Edna Ferber, actor John Barrymore (1882–1942) took on his (often played) role of an alcoholic; here he is Larry Renault, an alcoholic actor on the run. Barrymore's career was broken because his alcoholism made him lose his memory; he needed cue cards when playing from 1936 on. Nevertheless, audiences loved to see him play the sympathetic alcoholic, a role he could do more and more easily from the mid-1930s. Two almost autobiographical films with John Barrymore also showed a decadent man who falls into heavy alcohol abuse: *The Great Profile* (1940), by Walter Lang, and *Playmates* (1941), by David Butler.

George Cukor's *A Star Is Born* (1954) features the same kind of drunken-man character, whose alcoholism stops him in his artistic career, although he is an excellent *faire-valoir* for the young lady he transforms into a star. In fact, Cukor did the third version of that story (with Judy Garland as Esther Blodgett and James Mason as Marion Maine). William Wellman directed the second version of *A Star Is Born* in 1937; it is usually considered the best one ever. Oddly, the most famous version is also the worst, directed in 1976 by Franck Pierson, with Barbra Streisand and Kris Kristofferson. In all these versions, Marion Maine is a generous character the audience cannot hate or reject; he is played by a charismatic actor and is shown as a victim of alcoholism, despite the fact that he does not really try to become sober.

U.S. Films: The Classic Examples

Those who are not aware of the films mentioned previously often consider Billy Wilder's *The Lost Weekend* as the first serious movie about alcoholism, perhaps because the drinking problem is the center of the plot. Adapted from a novel by Charles R. Jackson, it was probably the most unusual Hollywood film of 1945, and it won four Academy Awards: Best Director (Billy Wilder), Best Picture, Best Actor (Ray Milland), and Best Screenplay (Charles Brackett and Billy Wilder). The story is about an unrecognized writer, Don Birman, who became an alcoholic because of his lack of professional success. When a holiday arrives, his worried brother and his charming girlfriend (Jane Wyman) offer to join him (to take a trip, to go to an opera), but the novelist prefers to stay on his own, going from bar to bar, drinking, borrowing money, stealing, lying, promising things he can't deliver. This well-respected man becomes a slave in front of our eyes. He has hallucinations, and he thinks about suicide. Set in Manhattan, the entire film is a description of the alcoholic's self-destructive behavior, without any melodramatic effects. Some scenes were shot on location at the New York City Bellevue Hospital. It is a fact that a whiskey company offered to the producers (Paramount Pictures) $5 million to have this antialcoholic film destroyed before its release.

After the huge success of *The Lost Weekend,* Hollywood made a few other films that were more or less copies of that story. In Stuart Heisler's *Smash-Up, the Story of a Woman* (1947), Susan Hayward is Angie Evans, an alcoholic nightclub singer, who tries to help the man she loves break through in his own career. She goes deep into alcoholism, but there is a happy ending. In a way, the story suggests a reversed version of *A Star Is Born.* The same actress also played an alcoholic woman (the Broadway star Lillian Roth) who recovered, in *I'll Cry Tomorrow* (1955); Susan Hayward won a prize at the Cannes Film Festival in 1955 for her performance. That film was based on Lillian Roth's autobiography.

Another Hollywood thriller, Gordon Douglas's *Come Fill the Cup* (1951), with James Cagney, tells the story of an alcoholic who goes successfully through a detoxification cure. Then, he

In this scene from City Lights, *a humble man (played by Charlie Chaplin) restrains a rich alcoholic (played by Harry Myers) from suicide. (Association Chaplin, Paris)*

finds a better job as a reporter and later finds an even better-paid position in the same newspaper. But he now has to work with a younger colleague (played by Gig Young) who is a real alcoholic. The film was a huge success, because of its artistic qualities and because of the topic. The next year, *Something to Live For* (1952), with Ray Milland, was also a success.

Daniel Mann directed a popular melodrama, *Come Back, Little Sheba* (1952) from a play by William Inge. A man who failed to become a doctor, Doc Delaney (Burt Lancaster) agrees with his wife (Shirley Booth) to take in a young woman (Terry Moore) as a boarder. The Doc and his wife wanted to have a baby but couldn't; they had a beloved dog, and they lost it. Now, Doc is torn between three temptations: the two women and the bottle. After hitting bottom, the man has to go through the many steps of recovering through a patient detoxification, with the help of his forgiving wife.

Crooner Bing Crosby and elegant Grace Kelly starred in George Seaton's *The Country Girl* (1954), an adaptation of a play by Clifford Odets. It is the story of an actor who has a big chance to play an important role in the theater. He used to be a star. But he needs the help of his wife to avoid his finding support in the bottle. The film shows how much strength one needs to escape from the temptation.

Henry Hattaway's *Bottom of the Bottle* (1956), with Joseph Cotten and Van Johnson, was adapted from a novel by Belgian author Georges Simenon. This color movie tells the story of a wanted man—an alcoholic—who tries to hide at his brother's place. But the latter is an attorney. The police knock. . . . It is one of those films that ask the questions (to the audience): Should we help an alcoholic? Can we believe him?

Blake Edwards's *Days of Wine and Roses* (1962) was a very good film about alcoholism and temperance. An alcoholic man (Joe Clay, played by Jack Lemmon) marries his secretary, Kristen (Lee Remick), who then becomes alcoholic too. After a year of drinking madness, Joe goes to the detoxification hospital, attends Alcoholics Anonymous (AA) meetings, and finally becomes sober. The couple splits up. One year later, Kristen wants to begin a new life with recovered Joe, but he refuses, because she has not recovered yet. This film contains many interesting aspects: the contagious side of alcoholism (the woman who learns to drink because of the man she loves), the detoxification, the AA meetings, the many accidents that can happen in a house because of alcoholism. The central question is: Can two alcoholic persons help each other by living together, or will they destroy themselves by doing so? The film was adapted from a TV series (of the same title) from 1958 that was directed by John Frankenheimer, starring Cliff Robertson and Piper Laurie. The film *Days of Wine and Roses* (1962) was the end of a period, one of Hollywood's last theatrical releases to deal as a whole with the subject of alcoholism.

Alcoholic characters remained present in Hollywood films during the 1960s, but alcoholism was not the central element of the action. In *The Night of the Iguana* (1964), directed by John Huston from a play by Tennessee Williams, the alcoholic who used to be a priest has a new job as a tourist guide, but he doesn't try to quit or change; alcoholism is just the cause of his present situation. How he became enmeshed in the situation is not dramatized.

One of the last Hollywood movies presenting heavy drinking in the 1960s was *Who's Afraid of Virginia Woolf?* (Mike Nichols, 1966), adapted from a famous play by Edward Albee. After a reception, a young couple is invited to assist in a fight between an older husband and wife. Alcohol helps some hidden truths to come out. The film was popular because of the presence of the couple Elizabeth Taylor and Richard Burton, who knew well about fights and drinking.

During the 1970s, Hollywood movies concentrated on other problems, such as drugs and substance abuse, as seen in Otto Preminger's movie *The Man with the Golden Arm* (1955), adapted from Nelson Algren's novel (published in 1949), and Dennis Hopper's *Easy Rider* (1969).

U.S. Films: The Recent Decades

Hollywood has produced many easy-to-find minor movies about drinking and alcoholism during the last two decades, but few of them can be compared to the earlier examples mentioned previously, either from an artistic or sociological perspective. They are just standard products with predictable plots.

Although it did not have a theatrical release, the made-for-television movie *MADD: Mothers Against Drunk Drivers* (1983) is the true story of a woman, Candy Lightner (played by Mariette Hartley), whose daughter was killed by a drunk driver. Lightner founded an association named Mothers Against Drunk Drivers to advocate this cause. Produced and written by Michael Braverman, it shows important issues related to the social effects of drinking and alcoholism. It is one of the strongest stories ever filmed about the effects of alcoholism.

The model of the drinking couple was used in many different films about alcoholism through the years. In *Barfly* (1987), Mickey Rourke and Faye Dunaway play two lovers who share their common taste for bars and fondness for liquor. An unknown writer (Rourke) has a marginal life until he meets a publisher who believes in him. This could be the start of a brilliant career. But the drinker prefers his bottle! The film's script (by alcoholic author Charles Bukowski) is almost an apology for heavy drinking and alcoholism. The huge success of this mediocre film can only be explained by the presence of the two stars.

Glenn Gordon Caron's *Clean and Sober* (1988) is about a young man (Michael Keaton) who goes into a drug rehabilitation program and also finds help from AA. But his rude counselor is very hard on him.

In a lighter tone, *My Name Is Bill W.* (1989), directed by Daniel Petrie, is more flamboyant. During the 1920s, a businessman goes to AA meetings, but when the Wall Street crash happens, it just expands his problems. The film tries to show the perception of alcoholism at a time when drinking was supposed to be fun.

Some films, such as *When a Man Loves a Woman* (1994), directed by Luis Mandoki and written by Al Franken and Ron Bass, were quite popular, and this one featured a double-sided woman as the alcoholic character. The story is about Alice Green (Meg Ryan), a school counselor who is adorable most of the time, but often gets drunk and then changes her personality. She even forgets about her children while drunk. She decides to undergo a cure, and when she is back home, her loving husband has to readjust himself to his "new" wife, who is now really temperate and completely in control. He used to see his wife as someone fragile who needed help, but now she is full of energy and so sure of herself. He will need a marriage counselor to adapt to this new life.

Mike Figgis's *Leaving Las Vegas* (1995) is a dark drama about Ben, an alcoholic screenwriter who has lost his family. He goes to Las Vegas with a plan to drink himself to death. Even though Ben falls in love with Sera (Elisabeth Shue), he recognizes he prefers drinking above everything else. She fully accepts the situation and lovingly assists him toward his lethal goal. Here, helping the alcoholic means—in the logic depicted in the film—giving the drinker everything he needs, plus love and comfort, to make him drink more and more. Rehabilitation and recovery are not on the agenda in this case. This film is based on a novel by John O'Neil, who himself died of alcoholism.

Drunks (1997) was Peter Cohn's first movie, adapted from Gary Lennon's play *Blackout*. It depicts the dynamics of some AA meetings in the basement of a Times Square church. Even after months of temperance, a few still hunger for a bottle. Some of them deny their addiction, some admit they are having a drinking problem, and others, just passing by, realize they are in the same situation.

Made by a woman, *28 Days* (2000) was a popular film about an alcoholic woman who realizes (too late?) her drinking problem after a long period of denial. Directed by Betty Thomas, it shows the inside of the rehabilitation program, day-to-day. Gwen (Sandra Bullock) is surrounded by masculine friends, providing either good or bad examples. The scene when she drives a car into the pool while drunk is unforgettable.

U.S. Films: The Barman as a Character

The barman can be an important character in the universe created by films. In many thrillers, such as Robert Siodmak's film noir, *Phantom Lady* (1944, from a novel by William Irish) or Fritz Lang's *The Big Heat* (1953), the sympathetic barman is part of the action, sometimes serving as an informer. In Barbet Schroeder's *Barfly* (1987), a drinker (Mickey Rourke) is having a fight with the bartender (Frank Stallone). But the most spectacular fight scene in a bar was made by Charlton Heston, who just hits anyone he sees in Orson Welles's masterpiece, *Touch of Evil* (1958), a film in which the policeman Quinland (played by Orson Welles) is an old, fat alcoholic whom no one respects.

U.S. Films: The Drunken Man as a Character

It is interesting to study how some scriptwriters have used the feeble drunken man as a character in movies because he cannot achieve credibility even though he is right in some situations. For instance, in Alfred Hitchcock's *North by Northwest* (1959), Cary Grant is kidnapped and sequestered by two spies; he is released after being forced to drink too many whiskies. When he goes to the police, nobody believes him. The same problem appears in many other films, for instance in a German movie, *Veronika Voss* (by Rainer Werner Fassbinder, 1982), when the drunken reporter calls the police to show a sequestered woman he has found in a private clinic. But when the police arrive and see how drunk the reporter is, they just bring him in without asking any more questions; they understand a drunken man can't be right.

Alcoholism in Films from Other Countries: Canada

The movie considered as the best Canadian film ever is *Mon Oncle Antoine* (1971), directed by Claude Jutra. It is sometimes known in English as *Silent Night.* In a Quebec village during the 1940s, Benoît, a teenager, discovers love, life, and death at his uncle's general store, where he works. He and his uncle also deliver coffins. One day, while driving the body of a dead teenager, Benoît discovers his uncle's deepest secret when the old man says: "I have been alcoholic for twenty-five years because I hate this job, I am afraid of the death. I hate to serve as the undertaker's man." This is the most touching film about alcoholism because it is humanistic, and also because the teenager now feels disgust toward the uncle he once respected.

Alcohol is also an important part of the films directed by André Forcier, such as the dark *Bar Salon* (1973), a miserable movie where most of the characters are gentle alcoholics. It is the story of a bartender who becomes manager of another bar. Here, men and women get drunk together, at the same bar. The same director made many fantasy movies, including *Au Clair de la Lune* (1982), a poetic story of two hobos who become friends during a long, cold winter. They sometimes get drunk and sing a song about temperance, echoing the leagues of virtues' slogans that were popular in Canada in the early twentieth century. The lyrics are sung in French and sound like a beer-drinking song: *"Tempérance, tempérance, vertu des Canadiens-Français"* (Temperance, virtue of the French Canadians).

A fascinating moment of cinema verité is shown in another Canadian film, a strong documentary made by Pierre Perrault, titled *La Bête lumineuse* (1983). Here, a group of friends in their forties go for a moose-hunting weekend. One night, after taking several drinks each, one of the men (Stéphane-Albert, who is a literary teacher) reads a poem of friendship to his mate Bernard. The latter gets angry and insults the poet. There is a big argument, a violent fight between both men. Alcohol made them show what they wouldn't have expressed in any other circumstance: their true feelings of friendship. There was of course no homosexual intention here, just a pure and sincere friendship. But it is easier for these men to show anger, even toward a friend.

The first feature film directed by Thom Fitzgerald, *The Hanging Garden* (1997), was the winner of two prizes in Canada. Set in Nova Scotia, we see a man going back to his father's house after many years of absence. He realizes his father is an alcoholic. Memories come back. The film is valuable in the way it presents the slow evolution of alcoholism and its effects on other members of the family.

Alcoholism in French Films

The first film ever to mention alcoholism was made in France more than a hundred years ago and directed by Ferdinand Zecca; the title was *Les victimes de l'alcoolisme* (1902). It was a short, silent movie (about six minutes) with a strong melodramatic atmosphere in a proletarian milieu, freely adapted from *L'Assommoir,* a novel by Émile Zola.

As we know, drinking is part of French culture: Wine is an everyday accompaniment to meals, and examples of drinking in French movies would be too numerous to list. Many characters drink, but very few are drunk; alcoholics are rare exceptions in French movies. In the first French adaptation of Dostoyevsky's *Crime and Punishment* (by Pierre Chenal, 1935), we see the poor family with the alcoholic father who takes the money his daughter earns to eat and uses it to drink. This situation is less clear in Georges Lampin's remake, *Crime et châtiment* (1956), with Jean Gabin, although the main story remains the same, being set in the middle of the twentieth century. Joseph von Sternberg made in Hollywood a tedious version of *Crime and Punishment* (1935) with actor Peter Lorre, in the same year as Pierre Chenal, who created the best adaptation of the Russian novel.

French master Jean Renoir adapted Émile Zola's novel, *La Bête humaine* (1938), about an alcoholic man who falls in love with a married woman whose husband is a murderer. In this context, alcoholism meant a tragic destiny the man can't escape. In Hollywood, Fritz Lang did a remake of Renoir's adaptation, *Human Desire* (1954).

In a beautiful film, again adapted from Émile Zola, *Gervaise* (directed by René Clément, 1955), a woman abandoned by her lover meets Coupeau, who can't work anymore. He becomes an alcoholic, and his new wife does the same. The film offers a description of alcoholism in the poor parts of Paris during the nineteenth century.

In Claude Zidi's comedy titled *Le Grand Bazar* (1973), Émile is a bartender in a little French bistro; when he gets too many bills and too much bad news, he asks his friends to read his mail for him. For every piece of bad news he hears, he drinks a bigger glass; for the last one, when he realizes he is going bankrupt, he takes a giant jug of many gallons! But amazingly, Émile is never drunk!

A very popular French film, *La Femme de ma vie* (1986), had a brilliant cast: Christophe Malavoy, Jane Birkin, Jean-Louis Trintignant, and Dominique Blanc. In this first film directed by Régis Wargnier, we see a talented violin player who becomes an alcoholic even though he is handsome, happy, and successful, and has a wonderful wife and very good friends. Something new in his life will change his reason to live. This original movie doesn't show a man who becomes an alcoholic because he has "lost" something; there is no apparent reason for his behavior, and therefore the treatment seems to be more complex. The ending is debatable: Can a talented artist who is an alcoholic lose his inspiration if he stops drinking? In other words, is alcohol a necessary element for some artists? Answers in feature films are just opinions and subjective points of view.

A very provocative French film made by singer Serge Gainsbourg (*Charlotte for Ever,* 1986) shows the ambiguous relationship between an alcoholic father (Gainsbourg himself) and his teenager daughter (Charlotte Gainsbourg, his real child). The father is an artist—a bad scriptwriter—and tries to seduce his daughter's young friends, an attitude that raises moral problems. The film was one of the worst French films ever, but was a huge success because of the scandal it caused in Europe with the song sung by the daughter, "Lemon Incest." Most people considered this portrait of the alcoholic as worse than reality; perversity and incest are seen as exceptions in the alcoholic behavior.

In another French film, *Nord* (*North,* 1991), directed by Xavier Beauvois (who also wrote the script and stars in it), we see how an alcoholic father can influence his whole family. During the day, he is the respected owner of a drugstore in northern France, but at night, he is dependent on the bottle. This is one of the very few films dealing with the effects of alcoholism on the rest of the family.

Alcoholism in German Films

Many German movies have been made about drinking; this section will just present a few that are available on video. In 1959, Rolf Thiele made *Labyrinth,* a story about a woman novelist (the very sexy Nadja Tiller) who is about to touch the bottom, but she finds the strength to go for a cure, and she meets two handsome men in the facility. This optimistic film about female alcoholism featured an actress who often played such characters.

Another populist film, *The Merchant of the Four Seasons* (1971), by Rainer Werner Fassbinder, tells how a merchant in the streets of a small city becomes more and more frustrated and alienated by his work. He becomes a violent alcoholic, and he beats his wife. He finally dies of an overdose of alcohol. This brutal film links alcoholism with poverty and shows specific social functions that make the local bar the only place where frustrations can be forgotten.

In West Berlin, a woman named Ulrike Ottinger made an almost avant-garde film about an alcoholic woman. The film, *Ticket of No Return* (*Bildnis einer Trinkerin,* 1979), is also known by its French title, *Aller Jamais Retour.* This is a strange story of a glamorous woman (the actress and cultural icon Tabea Blumschein), who drinks in many weird Berlin bars, and meets someone very different from her: a poor, alcoholic woman. Narrated in a complex way, this underground film tries to show a fascinating Berlinese nightlife with eccentric characters such as singer Nina Hagen and actor Eddie Constantine.

Examples of Alcoholism in Movies from Various Countries

British filmmaker Ken Loach directed *My Name Is Joe* (1998) with actor Peter Mullan. Set in Glasgow around 1930, it shows how optimism can help the alcoholic who wants to change his bad habits. It also shows the role (good or bad) of former friends with whom the alcoholic used to drink. The film has a strong social commentary; it is probably the best film on this matter in the last twenty years.

Alcoholism is not frequently dramatized in Japanese films; only a few movies have dared to present this matter. One of the earliest films by Akira Kurosawa, *Drunken Angel* (1948), is the story of an injured gangster who needs a doctor, but the latter is alcoholic and choleric. Nonetheless, the shaking doctor is the only one who agrees to help the young gangster. *An Autumn Afternoon* (1962), the last film directed by Japanese master Yasujiro Ozu, is about an old man who finds himself alone after his children have all married. He begins to drink sake, a traditional Japanese drink. This becomes his new habit, to help him get over his solitude. This color movie shows the man gently drinking at his favorite bar, in a very humanistic way.

A Mexican film about the singer Lucha Reyes, a cultural icon of the 1930s, *La Reina de la Noche* (1994), presents many characters addicted to alcohol. Directed by Arturo Ripstein, it portrays the nightlife of Mexico City in a very flamboyant atmosphere.

Few Russian films are comedies, but *Irony of Fate, or Have a Good Sauna* (1975), directed by Eldar Ryazanov, is a very funny example. A drunken man from Moscow gets back into what he thinks is his apartment. But he is not in the same town (he is mistakenly in Leningrad), although the buildings and furniture are so alike that he doesn't notice the difference. Here, drunkenness is an easy way to show a character who doesn't see small changes in strange situations.

The Danish film *Heart of Light* (*Qaamarngup Uummataa*, 1998) is also known under its Danish title, *Lysets Hjerte*. Directed by Jacob Grønlykke, it is the first feature film shot entirely in Greenland. It tells the story of an Innu, an alcoholic who has a difficult relationship with one of his adult sons who commits a violent crime. The father quits the village and goes north, trying to find the meaning of life. When he is sober again, he goes back to the village. Thanks to the redemption of recovery, he is like a new man. This inventive movie presents the problem of alcoholism in the Arctic region from the Innu point of view. As a matter of fact, it was written by an Innu poet.

Yves Laberge

See also: Alcoholics Anonymous (AA); Drama, Representations of Temperance in

References

Cartwright, Lisa. *Screening the Body: Tracing Medicine's Visual Culture.* Minneapolis: University of Minnesota Press, 1995.

Laberge, Yves. "Portée idéologique du cinéma: propagande et désinformation dans l'imaginaire" in *Communication information.* 17, no. 1 (June 1996): 184–224.

Leach, Jim. "Double Vision: *Mon Oncle Antoine* and the Cinema of Fable" in *Canada's Best Features: Critical Essays on 15 Canadian Films,* edited by Eugene P. Walz. Cross/Cultures: Readings in Post/Colonial Literatures in English, no. 56. Amsterdam: Editions Rodopi, 2002. 25–49.

Legrand, Jacques, ed. *Chronique du cinema.* Bassillac: Éditions Chronique et Jacques Legrand, 1996.

Passek, Jean-Loup, ed. *Dictionnaire du cinéma.* Paris: Larousse, 1998.

Permick, Martin S. "Film: Medical Films" in *Censorship: A World Encyclopedia,* edited by Derek Jones. 815–816. Chicago: Fitzroy Dearborn, 2001.

Rapp, Bernard, and Jean-Claude Lamy, eds. *Dictionnaire des films.* Paris: Larousse, 1999.

Shortland, Michael. *Medicine and Film: A Checklist, Survey, and Research Resource.* Oxford: Wellcome Unit for the History of Medicine, 1989.

Tinkcom, Matthew, and Amy Villarejo, eds. *Keyframes: Popular Cinema and Cultural Studies.* London: Routledge, 2001.

Tulard, Jean, ed. *Guide des films.* Paris: Robert Laffont, 1991.

Finland

In Finland, beer was an everyday food item and almost the sole alcoholic beverage until the latter half of the seventeenth century, when distilling spirits from grain spread very quickly throughout the country. By the eighteenth century, home-distilled spirits had displaced beer as the dominant alcoholic beverage in Finland (Österberg 1985). The first temperance societies were formed in Finland in the 1840s, and during the second half of the nineteenth century the temperance movement made vociferous efforts to modify Finnish alcohol legislation, with nationwide total prohibition as the ultimate goal. These efforts led to very restricted alcohol availability in the countryside and to the spread of the Gothenburg system in towns. The hallmarks of the Gothenburg system were guaranteeing the quality and orderliness of licensed premises and using the profits from alcohol sales to further the common good. The Prohibition Act became effective in Finland in June 1919 and banned all beverages containing more than 2 percent alcohol by volume. In the 1920s, despite harsher penalties and more effective policing, it proved impossible to put an end to the newly emerged smuggling and bootlegging, which led to growth in alcohol consumption and drunkenness. In 1932, the Finnish Parliament enacted alcohol legislation that abolished the Prohibition Act and gave the country a system of alcohol control based on a comprehensive state alcohol monopoly on production, import, export, wholesale, and retail sale of alcoholic beverages. This system was the cornerstone of Finnish alcohol control until 1995.

Alcohol Consumption

It is difficult to determine how high total alcohol consumption really was in the nineteenth century before the banning of home distillation in 1866. It was clearly higher than at the beginning of the 1870s, when total annual alcohol consumption was estimated at 3 liters of pure alcohol per capita (0.8 U.S. gallon). Total alcohol consumption decreased during the following decades. In the mid-1910s, before the Prohibition Act came into force, total alcohol consumption was less than 0.5 liter per capita (0.2 U.S. gallon), which meant that Finland at that time was one of the driest countries in Europe. In the mid-1930s, after Prohibition ended, the yearly alcohol consumption was a little over one liter of pure alcohol per capita (0.4 U.S. gallon). There are, of course, no statistics detailing alcohol consumption during the Prohibition period, but it has been estimated that alcohol consumption during the last years of Prohibition was clearly higher than in the mid-1910s and probably also higher than in the mid-1930s.

At the beginning of the 1950s, recorded alcohol consumption was just below 2 liters per capita (0.5 U.S. gallon). When the 1968 Alcohol Act and the Medium Beer Act came into force in 1969, total alcohol consumption increased almost 50 percent in one year and continued to grow very fast in the first half of the 1970s. In the mid-1970s, total alcohol consumption leveled off, and during the next decade it was about 6.5 liters per capita (1.7 U.S. gallons). The rapid economic growth in the second half of the 1980s was accompanied by a strong growth in alcohol consumption. In the same manner, the economic recession in the first half of the 1990s led to a clear decrease in recorded alcohol consumption. Since the mid-1990s, total alcohol consumption has been growing slightly.

At the beginning of the 1950s, Finland was still a spirits-drinking country with nearly 70 percent of all alcohol consumed in the form of distilled spirits. This percentage was down to 47 percent in the mid-1980s. However, it was only in the first half of the 1990s that the consumption of distilled spirits did clearly decrease, and currently distilled spirits account for less than one-third of total alcohol consumption.

The consumption of wine has increased quite slowly but steadily during the period from 1950 to 2000. Wine now accounts for about 16 percent of total alcohol consumption. Within the wine category, table wines have increased their market share, and the share of fortified wines has gone down. During recent years, the consumption of red wines has increased especially quickly, and white and red wines are now consumed equally in Finland. In the second half of the 1990s, the consumption of cider has increased very rapidly.

Beer consumption increased in the 1950 to 1990 period, but has decreased somewhat in the 1990s. The consumption of medium beer—beer under 4.7 percent alcohol by volume—jumped in 1969 from 0.5 liter to 1.6 liters of pure alcohol per capita (0.1 to 0.4 U.S. gallon). During the recent past, Finland has definitively changed back to a country that prefers beer.

Because of high alcohol prices and restrictions on alcohol availability, unrecorded alcohol consumption has always played a part in Finnish consumption. With the exception of the mid-1990s, unrecorded alcohol consumption has, however, not changed the picture of trends in total alcohol consumption given by the figures for recorded alcohol consumption. In 1995, recorded alcohol consumption showed only a slight increase, whereas in reality total alcohol consumption increased by some 10 percent because of the huge increase in travelers' alcohol imports as a consequence of Finnish membership in the European Union (EU) (Österberg and Pehkonen 1996). It has been estimated that in the second half of the 1990s, some 20 percent of the total alcohol consumption came from unrecorded sources.

Drinking Habits

After the second world war, Finnish drinking habits were still characterized by very high abstinence rates, particularly among women and in the countryside, and, at the same time, by a cultural appreciation for drinking to intoxication. During the last half century, abstinence rates among women have fallen from 40 percent to around 10 percent. At the same time, women's proportion of alcohol consumption has risen from about 10 percent to almost 25 percent. Also, drinking by adolescents has become much more common. Traditional qualitative features of Finnish drinking patterns, that is, a high prevalence of binge drinking, have not, however, shown any clear weakening. On the contrary, binge drinking has become more prevalent among women (Simpura and Karlsson 2001).

Daily drinking has been quite rare in Finland, because alcoholic beverages have seldom been consumed with food and because alcohol does not have any important everyday social function. Water and milk are the most important beverages at meals, and coffee is the dominant drink in social situations. Also, on-the-job drinking and drinking and driving have been very uncommon in Finland. The most common times to consume alcohol in Finland are Friday and Saturday evenings.

Finland has one peculiar feature of drinking patterns that is not found elsewhere in the world. This is the importance of drinking in the context of taking sauna baths. In the 1990s, as many as one out of six drinking occasions was related to sauna baths. Typically, this kind of drinking consists of one or two beers after the sauna bath. This pattern became more popular after the 1969 alcohol policy reform, which brought medium beer into ordinary grocery stores.

Finnish Alcohol Control

In the first half of the eighteenth century, home distillation grew in importance, with a consequent rise in the use of distilled spirits and in drunkenness. By the nineteenth century, distilled spirits had become almost the sole alcoholic beverage used in Finland. The ban on home distillation in 1866 aimed, on the one hand, to concentrate distilling in large-scale commercial factories in order to gain control over the level of production and to bring more tax income to the state, and on the other hand to combat drunkenness. This latter goal also led to more and more restricted alcohol availability, especially in the countryside, and with the exception of beer, retail sales of alcoholic beverages had become a thing of the past in the countryside by the end of the nineteenth century.

Since the repeal of the Prohibition Act in 1932, the cornerstones of Finnish alcohol control have been restricted physical availability of alcoholic beverages and high alcohol taxes. The Finnish state alcohol monopoly, Alko, was a crucial part of the alcohol control machinery until 1 January 1995, when Finland joined the EU. Until that date, Alko had a monopoly on the production, import, export, wholesale, and retail sale of alcoholic beverages, defined as all beverages containing more than 2.8 percent alcohol by volume. Alko also set both off- and on-premises prices for alcoholic beverages (Karlsson and Österberg 2002).

According to the 1932 Alcohol Act, Alko could entrust the serving of alcoholic beverages as well as the production of beer and wine to private enterprises. As a consequence, all beer production and a part of the production of fruit and fortified wines, as well as most of the on-premises retail sales of alcoholic beverages, have been taken care of by the private sector since 1932. On the other hand, Alko controlled very tightly private activities in the alcohol field, and legally, all licensed private alcohol producers and retailers were Alko's agents.

In 1968, Finland enacted new alcohol legislation that increased alcohol availability in many ways. The Medium Beer Act gave Alko the right to grant ordinary grocery stores and cafés licenses to sell beer containing less than 4.7 percent alcohol by volume. Alko still retained, however, the power to set retail prices for medium beer as well as the profit margins for medium-beer retailers. Under the 1932 Alcohol Act, Alko was not allowed to open liquor stores in rural municipalities, and the few licensed restaurants in rural areas were meant to serve travelers. The 1968 Alcohol Act repealed this rural prohibition and also lowered age limits for buying alcoholic beverages off the premises (Karlsson and Österberg 2002).

There were some amendments to alcohol legislation between 1969 and 1995. The most important concerned the introduction of a total ban on alcohol advertising in 1977. Alcohol availability became also stricter, as Alko began in 1979 to keep its stores closed on Saturdays during the summer months. This policy was, however, discontinued in 1991, and the late 1980s and early 1990s also saw other kinds of increases in alcohol availability. Among others, Alko stores were changed from counter to self-service stores, and the opening hours were lengthened both in Alko stores and in licensed restaurants.

A Competitive Alcohol Market

Liberalizing of the Finnish alcohol markets in 1995 was for the most part a reaction to the European Economic Area agreement and Finnish membership in the EU. The 1994 Alcohol Act repealed alcohol monopolies on production, import, export, and wholesale, but left the monopoly on off-premises retail sale of alcoholic beverages almost intact (Holder et al. 1998).

One outcome of the opening of alcohol markets was that the number of alcohol producers, importers, and wholesalers increased dramatically. At the same time, the concentration of the alcohol industry went further. After the second world war, Finland had nearly twenty brewing companies. Their number had decreased considerably by the 1970s, but until the twenty-first century the industry was still mostly owned by Finns. During the last decade, Finnish breweries have expanded their activities to Russia and to the Baltic countries, and in recent years the two biggest Finnish breweries, which between them control 90 percent of the domestic market, have been sold to foreign brewing companies.

The 1994 Alcohol Act also includes changes that were related to domestic interests only. For instance, from the beginning of 1995, ordinary grocery stores, kiosks, gasoline stations, and medium-beer cafés could, for the first time, sell all alcoholic beverages produced by fermentation that were under 4.7 percent alcohol by volume. From the same day, the advertising of alcoholic beverages with alcohol content between 1.2 and 22 percent alcohol by volume was legalized (Alavaikko and Österberg 2000).

Finnish EU membership also affected alcohol taxation. Since 1994, alcohol excise duties have basically been in relation to alcohol content. The restructuring of the excise duty system in 1994 was designed to keep the average alcohol duty rates and alcohol prices constant. In 2001, the alcohol prices in Finland were in real terms nearly the same as in 1951, and in fact clearly higher than they had been in the mid-1930s.

Increases in travelers' allowances for importing alcoholic beverages without paying duties on them was another effect of EU membership. Here, Finland received a derogation for two years, and the derogation was later prolonged to the year 2004. Travelers' allowances for alcohol import and travelers' alcohol imports have increased since 1994 and put some pressure on alcohol excise duty levels (Österberg and Pehkonen 1996). Thus far, only the excise duty rates on wine and intermediate products have been lowered, by 17 percent since the beginning of 1998.

Drunk Driving and Drunkenness

The first known traffic accident in Finland involving a motor car occurred in 1907 when a drunken driver in Helsinki ran into a lamppost in the Railway Station Square. This, however, did not involve a criminal offense, because drunk driving was not criminalized in Finland until 1926. At that time, the punishment for driving a motor vehicle when intoxicated was a fine or a maximum of one year's imprisonment. In 1937, the maximum term of imprisonment was raised to two years, and in 1950 to four years. Furthermore, in 1950, the maximum punishment for drunk driving resulting in another's death was seven years' imprisonment. In 1957, this maximum was raised to eight years.

It was not until 1959 that blood-alcohol tests and clinical examinations became mandatory in Finland. Before 1977, there was no statutory limit for blood-alcohol concentration (BAC). In March 1977, two BAC limits were introduced. The lower was set at 0.05 percent and the upper at 0.15 percent. In autumn 1994, the upper limit, or the limit for aggravated drunk driving, was lowered from 0.15 percent to 0.12 percent. At the same time, the BAC limit for those in charge of a boat was set at 0.1 percent.

Until 1969, appearing drunk in public was a criminal offense in Finland. In 1969, it was decriminalized, but still police could take drunken people to a shelter for sobering up. Until 1995, it was illegal to drink in public. This law was changed in 1995, but there is still much discussion about whether public drinking should be allowed, and several local municipalities have in fact forbidden it.

Esa Österberg

References

Alavaikko, M., and E. Österberg. "The Influence of Economic Interests on Alcohol Control Policy: A Case Study from Finland" in *Addiction.* 95, supplement 4 (2000): S565–S579.

Holder, H. D., E. Kühlhorn, S. Nordlund, E. Österberg, A. Romelsjö, and T. Ugland. *European Integration and Nordic Alcohol Policies. Changes in Alcohol Controls and Consequences in Finland, Norway and Sweden, 1980–1997.* Ashgate: Aldershot, 1998.

Karlsson, T., and E. Österberg. "Finland" in *Alcohol Policies in EU Member States and Norway. A Collection of Country Reports,* edited by E. Österberg and T. Karlsson. Helsinki: Stakes, 2002.

Österberg, E. "From Home Distillation to the State Alcohol Monopoly" in *Contemporary Drug Problems.* 12 (1985): 31–51.

Österberg, E., and J. Pehkonen. "Travellers' Imports of Alcoholic Beverages into Finland before and after EU" in *Nordisk Alkoholtidskrift, Nordic Alcohol Studies.* 13 (English Supplement, 1996): 22–32.

Simpura, J., and T. Karlsson. *Trends in Drinking Patterns among Adult Population in 15 European Countries, 1950 to 2000. A Collection of Country Reports.* Helsinki: Stakes, 2001.

Sulkunen, Irma. *History of the Finnish Temperance Movement: Temperance as a Civic Religion.* Lewiston, ME: Edwin Mellen Press, 1990.

First Nations, the Indian Act, and Prohibition (Canada)

Although indigenous cultures in the Americas had varied experience and traditions surrounding alcohol-containing beverages, it was not until the introduction of alcohol as a trade item by European colonists that many aboriginal peoples in northern North America were consistently exposed to the product. In what would later become Canada, alcohol was a trade item used by both the British and the French in the fur trade until colonial governments began to legislate bans on the selling of alcohol to Native Canadian populations. As early as 1775, Governor Guy Carleton issued instructions including the directive: "That no Trader shall sell or otherwise supply the Indians with Rum, or other spirit[u]ous liquors." From the colonial period through the modern era in Canada, controlling access to liquor by First Nations has been a consistent governmental preoccupation. This fact is perhaps best reflected in Canada's most important federal statute related to First Nations, the Indian Act.

From a Euro-Canadian perspective, the consumption of alcohol by First Nations peoples was frequently viewed as an activity hindering First Nations' "civilization" and thus constituting an activity that required strict control. Canada's Indian Act (1876), a federal statute representing the first large-scale consolidation of colonial law pertaining to First Nations or Indian people, contained sections regulating "Status Indian" alcohol consumption (a "Status Indian" under the act is a person recognized as a native person by the federal government). From the 1876 act through its 1970 version, the law continued to impose a form of prohibition for Indian reserve communities across Canada. From its inception, the law reflected Canadian government preoccupation with what Canadian society, rightly or wrongly, viewed as a moral stance it had a right and obligation to enforce among its First Nations populations. As historian John Tobias points out, the Canadian government believed its duty was to "protect" and "civilize" Native American peoples, and inhibiting Native American consumption of alcohol became part of that burden.

Despite its regular modification, the Indian Act changed little over the century in its sections relating to alcohol consumption by registered Indians. Beginning in 1876, sections 79 and 80 of the act made the sale of intoxicants to Native Canadians illegal across the Dominion. In 1884, the law was amended to extend penalties for those found guilty of supplying a Native Canadian person with intoxicants and, in a rewording, linked drinking alcohol directly to the vice of gambling. Subsequent amendments to the law in 1894 allowed constables to arrest and detain without a warrant Native Canadian people found "drunk" or "with intoxicants in [their] possession." By 1927, the Indian Act contained several references to intoxicants and their control in sections 126 through 137, which outlined conditions under which Native Canadian peoples or those associated with Native Americans could be arrested for possession of alcohol. In 1936, the law was extended to include First Nations people both on and off reserves.

First Nations leaders made clear their dissatisfaction with many parts of the Indian Act at the Special Committee hearings held between 1946 and 1948, and into the early 1950s. At these meetings, leaders voiced their perspectives on prohibition in their communities. Their opinions proved to be divided, as some leaders supported prohibition while others favored the application of provincial alcohol consumption laws to First Nations peoples. The Indian Association of Alberta commented on the debate in 1949: "Give our people BREAD not BEER." After 1956, following a major revision of the Indian Act, the sections pertaining to intoxicants were greatly reduced in the statute. Registered Indian peoples were given the right to possess and drink alcohol in public places off the reserve in accordance with provincial law, as per sections 94 through 96. The government's regulatory influence had thus been diminished somewhat. At this time, bands were also given the opportunity to determine, by referendum, whether these new rules applied to their communities.

In 1970, the prohibition sections of the Indian Act came under scrutiny by the Supreme Court of Canada, and a significant ruling was made. In the *R. v. Drybones* case, the Court ruled that section 94 of the Indian Act violated the Canadian Bill of Rights, thereby rendering it inoperable. By 1971, section 94 was removed from the act, signaling the initial death knell to continued government control over registered Indian use of intoxicants in Canada. Today, bands are self-governing on this front: since 1985, band councils have been able to regulate intoxicants on reservations through their own by-laws.

Laurie Meijer Drees

See also: Native Americans: Drinking Patterns and Temperance Reform

References

Leslie, John F., and Ron Maguire. *The Historical Development of the Indian Act.* Ottawa: Indian and Northern Affairs, Treaties and Historical Research Centre, 1978.

Tobias, John L. "Protection, Civilization, Assimilation: An Outline History of Canada's Indian Policy" in *Sweet Promises,* edited by J. R. Miller, 127–144. Toronto: University of Toronto Press, 1991.

Treaties and Historical Research Centre. *Contemporary Indian Legislation, 1951–1978,* vol. II. Ottawa: Department of Indian Affairs and Northern Development, 1981.

———. *Indian Acts and Amendments, 1868–1950,* vol. I. Ottawa: Department of Indian Affairs and Northern Development, 1981.

Fisher, Irving (1867–1947)

An economics professor, Irving Fisher (1867–1947) was a pivotal reformer in many Progressive Era health-reform crusades. Through his leadership positions and his publications, he influenced campaigns embracing diet and nutrition, eugenics, physical exercise, public health, tuberculosis, and temperance. He was a staunch supporter of National Prohibition and wrote several books purporting to show its effectiveness in terms of economics.

Fisher, the third of four children, was born in Saugerties, New York, the son of a Congregational minister. Soon after his birth, his family moved several times, finally settling in Saint Louis. He graduated from Smith Academy in Saint Louis (1884) and received a B.A. from Yale University, where he was class valedictorian. Under full scholarship, he immediately began working on a doctorate in mathematics. Fisher joined the Yale faculty in 1890 as an instructor and completed his Ph.D. (1891). He then studied in Berlin and Paris (1893–1894). Upon returning to Yale, he switched from the mathematics department to the department of political economy, where he remained for the rest of his career. Over his lifetime, Fisher became one of the nation's leading economists. In 1898, he was stricken with tuberculosis, from which he took three years to recover. This experience awoke a life-long interest in hygiene, public health, and temperance.

Irving Fisher (1867–1947) (Library of Congress)

Over a period of twenty years, Fisher gravitated from tolerance of moderate alcohol consumption to a position in favor of total abstinence and national prohibition. He wrote more than a hundred publications discussing the subject and increasingly saw the liquor traffic as an enemy of public health. In 1916, Fisher volunteered to serve on the Council of National Defense. In that capacity, he organized a conference to address the effects of alcohol and venereal disease on military efficiency. This conference, which met in April 1917 in Washington, D.C., recommended the establishing of a dry zone around military camps and wartime prohibition. Both of these suggestions were eventually adopted. Fisher in 1920 became honorary president of the Scientific Temperance Federation, led by Cora Stoddard. He retained this position for a number of years and wrote for its publication, the *Scientific Temperance Journal.*

Fisher stoutly defended National Prohibition in numerous articles and two popular books, *Prohibition at Its Worst* (1927) and *The Noble Experiment* (1930), coauthored with H. Bruce Brougham. The books purported to show a decrease in social problems associated with alcohol. In 1935, Fisher retired from Yale. Over his lifetime, he published more than 2,000 works and received many awards. Fisher was among the last of a once numerous and influential but now vanishing breed, the academic supporter of prohibition.

Ruth Clifford Engs

See also: National Prohibition (United States); Scientific Temperance Federation; Stoddard, Cora Frances

References

Cherrington, Ernest Hurst, et al., eds. *Standard Encyclopedia of the Alcohol Problem.* 6 vols. 3: 996. Westerville, OH: American Issue Publishing, 1924–1930.

Fisher, Irving Norton. *My Father, Irving Fisher.* New York: Comet Press, 1956.

Hirshbein, Laura Davidow. "Irving Fisher and the Life Extension Institute, 1914–1931" in *Canadian Bulletin of Medical History.* 16 (January 1999): 89–124.

Kerr, K. Austin. *Organized for Prohibition: A New History of the Anti-Saloon League.* New Haven: Yale University Press, 1985.

Miller, John Perry. "Fisher, Irving" in *Dictionary of American Biography, 1946–1950,* edited by John A. Garraty, supplement 4, 272–276. New York: Scribners, 1974.

Porter, Theodore M. "Fisher, Irving" in *American National Biography,* edited by John A. Garraty and Marc C. Carnes. 24 vols. 8: 12–15. New York: Oxford University Press, 1999.

Forel, Auguste (1848–1931)

Auguste H. Forel (1848–1931) was a Swiss psychiatrist, entomologist, anatomist, and one of the founding fathers of alcohol research. Around 1900, he was the most influential expert in Europe, pursuing his ideas with organizational vigor and crusading fervor. Although the Anglo-American historiography takes little notice of him, his role in the formation of a scientifically based alcohol discourse can hardly be overestimated. In Central Europe, with its pioneering psychiatry, and also in France and Scandinavia, his works met with a lively—although divided—resonance. Forel transferred the ideal of abstinence from the disreputable sphere of the religiously oriented self-help organizations into the sphere of science and reason. Since his struggle for sobriety was based on eugenic theories, Forel also helped eugenics penetrate the public-health policies during the interwar period.

Forel was a talented man of many interests who made a brilliant career. Born 1 September 1848 near Morges, he grew up in the French-speaking Canton of Waadt (Vaud) in a strictly Calvinist family. After medical studies and a doctorate in Zurich and Vienna, he habilitated himself in Munich in 1877. Simultaneously, Forel worked on such different topics such as the anatomy of the brain (neuron theory and so forth), insects (where his main work was *Social World of the Ants Compared with That of Man,* 1921–1923), and hypnosis and sexual behavior (where his main work was *Sexual Question,* 1905). In 1879, he became director of the Burghölzli insane asylum and professor of psychiatry in Zurich; in 1888, he founded the drinker asylum Ellikon (today known as Forel-Klinik). At the age of fifty, he began to shed his official posts, and from 1907 he lived as a private scholar.

Forel was engaged in politics as well. As a follower of monism, Ernst Haeckel's atheistic doctrine, Forel regarded socialism as the only rational political force. To him, it was more a broad reform movement than a political party (which he did not join until 1916). He struggled for women's rights, sexual reform (contraception and so forth), Esperanto, and particularly for pacifism. He outlined a plan for the "United States of the World," broke with Haeckel for his support of German imperialism, and rejected the Versailles Treaty as immoral and dangerous. In his late years, however, Forel converted to the teetotal Bahai religion, which he then called the "real socialism."

Forel was exposed to the concept of alcoholism—around 1880 still a contentious theory in medicine—in Burghölzli. According to his memoirs, a member of the Blue Cross convinced him to make abstinence mandatory in therapy and also, in 1886, to abstain from alcohol himself. His "pledge" was probably also influenced by his colleague Gustav von Bunge, who in the same year had published a manifesto that engendered the split of the European temperance movement into a "temperate" and an "abstinent" wing. Attacking the German League against the Abuse of Alcoholic Beverages (DVMG) that praised beer as a substitute for liquor, Bunge for the first time gave a scientific explanation of "total prohibition" as an "act of self-defense." To the DVMG, the "alcohol question" was part of the "social question"; now it turned it into a "racial question."

To Forel, alcohol became a key issue, and he published unflaggingly on it; his first book on *Drinking Habits* (1891) made him a famous fighter for sobriety. Switzerland became the hub of Continental alcohol research. Based on assumptions about the hereditary nature of mental illness and deviance—as developed by Benedict Morel, Valentine Magnan, and Francis Galton—the circle of reformers and researchers linked the "alcohol question" to the degeneration theory, that is, to the emerging eugenics or racial hygiene, as named by Alfred Ploetz, the leading German eugenicist who had been converted to abstinence by Forel. Leftist politicians and naturalist writers, like Gerhart Hauptmann, were also close to this circle. To them, abstinence meant much more than a means of therapy. Rather, it was a remedy against the evils of civilization. Modern society, Forel taught, suffered from the "incurable disease of emasculation, wimpishness, and degeneration through voluptuousness" and functioned in a "counter-selective" or contradictory way (Spode 1993: 137). On one hand, it granted costly medical care for degenerates, who otherwise would die out; on the other hand, it produced "artificial poisons" that in the long run would doom the race to extinction. Among these poisons, alcohol was particularly dangerous. Rather than killing immediately, it spoiled the "germ-plasm" so that "trained" drinkers fathered "born" drinkers, criminals, and other social deviants who again would father degenerates. Forel named his—more Lamarckian than Darwinist—notion of alcohol-induced genetic defects "blastophtoric degeneration" (*Blastophtorie*). On this basis, he called for birth control for drinkers and other "plague boils on the social body": "Those who are bright, efficient and strong should reproduce vigorously; those who are weak, miserable, bad and stupid should not reproduce at all." Consequently, Forel in 1886 castrated a handful of mentally ill people and was the first to undertake such sterilization in Europe. This was a medical experiment, but the plans were far-reaching. As early as 1884, Forel spoke of killing "dreadful specimens" of human beings, and in 1903, at the Ninth International Congress against Alcoholism, Ploetz demanded that drinkers be "eliminated" by "extermination or expulsion."

Forel headed and influenced numerous organizations. In 1892, he founded the first Swiss lodge of the Good Templars (this was part of the International Order of Good Templars [IOGT]). But in 1906, he formed a rival, religiously "neutral" order, the International Order of Good Templars (Neutral), or IOGTN, which in Switzerland and Hungary took over the majority of the old order, and in Germany and other countries captured some 10 percent of adherents of the IOGT. In many countries, he helped to establish teetotal organizations such as the socialist German Abstinent Worker's Union in Berlin, and he played a prominent role at the antialcohol congresses (today known as the International Council on Alcohol and Addictions). However, Forel failed to make prohibition popular in Continental Europe. But although the "water apostles" remained culturally isolated, the notions of racial hygiene, largely based on alcohol research, found their way into legislation, first in the United States, and then, with help from Forel, in Europe. In 1928, the Canton of Waadt introduced a sterilization law; other states, above all the Nordic countries and Germany, followed suit. (In the Third Reich alone, 30,000 alcoholics had been sterilized; in Scandinavia, forced sterilization was common up to the 1970s.)

Forel died 27 July 1931, and though forgotten outside Switzerland, in his homeland, he is held in great esteem (the 1,000-franc bill bore his image). But in recent times, a critical assessment has also gained ground, and Forel remains a controversial figure to this day. Decades before Elvin Morton Jellinek, Forel promoted a disease model of alcoholism and introduced abstinence into professional therapy. His struggle for "truth" and "sobriety"—deeply rooted both in Calvinism and scientism—serves as a warning example of the "dialectics of enlightenment."

Hasso Spode, translated by Jennifer Hosek

See also: Alcoholism; Degeneration Theories; Good Templars (IOGT); International Congresses on Alcoholism; Jellinek, Elvin Norton; World Health Organization (WHO)

References

Bynum, William F. "Alcoholism and Degeneration in 19th Century European Medicine and Psychiatry" in *British Journal of Addiction.* 79 (1984): 59–70.

Forel, Auguste. *Out of My Life and Work.* London: Allen and Unwin, 1937 (cited acc. *Rückblick auf mein Leben.* Prague: Büchergilde Gutenberg, 1935).

Spode, Hasso. *Die Macht der Trunkenheit. Kultur- und Sozialgeschichte des Alkohols.* rev. ed. Opladen: Leske and Budrich, 2003.

———. *Die Macht der Trunkenheit. Kultur- und Sozialgeschichte des Alkohols in Deutschland.* Opladen: Leske & Budrich, 1993.

———. "From the 'Brandy Plague' to the 'Alcohol Question'" in *Comparative Alcohol Research. Reading Material,* edited by the Nordic Council for Alcohol and Drug Research et al., 1–15. Hornbaek: NAD 1997 (abbr. also as KBS-Congress-Paper, Porto 1995).

Foster, Judith Ellen Horton (1840–1910)

Judith Ellen Horton Foster (1840–1910), temperance activist, lawyer, and Republican Party leader, was active in the Woman's Christian Temperance Union (WCTU) on the local, state, and national level. Drawing on her training as a lawyer, she advocated legal and legislative actions to promote prohibition. A staunch Republican, her political beliefs brought her into conflict with the national WCTU when the organization moved to form an alliance with the Prohibition Party.

Foster was born 3 November 1840 in Lowell, Massachusetts, to a Methodist minister and his wife. Her parents died when she was young, and she moved to Boston to live with her older married sister. After graduating from Genesee Wesleyan Seminary,

A 1908 portrait of Judith Ellen Foster (1840–1910) (Library of Congress)

she taught school until she married Addison Avery in 1860. They had two children before they divorced in about 1866. Foster taught music in a mission school in Chicago until 1869, when she married Elijah Caleb Foster, a recent law school graduate. They moved to Clinton, Iowa, and had two children.

Foster studied law under her husband's tutelage, and in 1872 she became one of the first women admitted to the Iowa bar. The couple practiced law together in Clinton and became involved in Iowa temperance politics. In 1873, Foster founded the Woman's Temperance Society of Clinton. A year later, she attended the founding convention of the national WCTU and soon became an important figure in that organization. Foster not only held the position of superintendent of the Office of Legislation and Petitions from 1874 through 1888, she also helped write the first constitution of the WCTU. A polished and effective speaker, Foster made nationwide lecture tours advocating prohibition and women's suffrage. In 1878, she began organizing a campaign to add a prohibition amendment to the Iowa constitution. Although the amendment passed in 1882, it was declared void on technical grounds by the Iowa Supreme Court.

In 1881, Foster came into conflict with national WCTU president Frances Elizabeth Caroline Willard, who wished to affiliate the organization with the Prohibition Party. Foster, a loyal Republican, believed that the WCTU should be nonpartisan, allowing individual members to make their own political decisions. When her private protests to Willard failed, Foster openly rebelled. With the backing of the Iowa WCTU, Foster entered official protests at the annual conventions of the national WCTU from 1885 until 1888, but to no avail. The Iowa union left the national organization, and Foster formed the Non-Partisan Woman's Christian Temperance Union, which held national conventions and published the *Temperance Tribune* and sixteen pamphlets. Foster then sought to win international support for her nonpartisan position when she attended the British Women's Total Abstinence Union meeting in 1890. Nevertheless, her organization never became particularly strong or effective, even in its U.S. base, although it had branches in seven states.

In addition to the Non-Partisan WCTU, Foster formed the Woman's Republican Association of the United States (later known as the Woman's National Republican Association). Its purpose was to promote the Republican Party through the educational work and social influence of women. When it was recognized by the National Republican Committee, she became its president. Foster's work for the Republican Party resulted in her relocation with her husband to Washington, D.C., where she died 11 August 1910 at age sixty-nine.

Jana Brubaker

See also: Non-Partisan Woman's Christian Temperance Union; Republican Party (United States); Willard, Frances Elizabeth Caroline; Woman's Christian Temperance Union (WCTU) (United States)

References

Byrne, Frank L. "Foster, Judith Ellen Horton," in *Notable American Women 1607–1950: A Biographical Dictionary,* edited by Edward T. James, vol. 1: 651–652. Cambridge, MA: Belknap Press of Harvard University Press, 1971.

Gustafson, Melanie. "Partisan and Nonpartisan: The Political Career of Judith Ellen Foster, 1881–1910" in *We Have Come to Stay: American Political Parties 1880–1960,* edited by Melanie S. Gustafson, Kristi Miller, and Elisabeth I. Perry, 1–12. Albuquerque: University of New Mexico Press, 1999.

Mott, David C. "Judith Ellen Foster" in *Annals of Iowa: A Historical Quarterly.* 19 (October 1933): 126–138.

Tyrrell, Ian. *Woman's World, Woman's Empire: The Woman's Christian Temperance Union in International Perspective, 1880–1930.* Chapel Hill: University of North Carolina Press, 1991.

Foster's

Foster's is a multinational corporation headquartered in Australia that produces and distributes beer and wine to consumers around the world. The company makes and markets Foster's Lager, as well as the Australian brands Victoria Bitter, Crown Lager, Carlton Draught, and Cascade Premium Lager. As a result of purchases in the 1990s, Foster's also produces wines such as Wolf Blass, Beringer, Matua, and Chateau St. Jean. According to company annual reports, at the beginning of the twenty-first century it generated $5 billion (in Australian dollars) in sales and had breweries in Australia, Fiji, Vietnam, India, and China. Foster's also had wine operations in Australia, Italy, Chile, the United States, the Netherlands, France, and Germany.

Origins and Expansion

The multinational corporation began in 1887 when two brothers from New York, William Manning Foster and Ralph Rose Foster, started the Foster Brewing Company in Melbourne. The new brewery was the first commercial lager brewery established in Australia. Although their beer won a first prize at the Centennial Exhibition in 1888, their brewery was not profitable. Part of the problem was that the beer had to be kept cold, so the brewery provided a free supply of ice to every hotel that sold the beer. Foster's also became the target of importers who reduced the prices of German and American lagers in order to drive the Fosters out of business. About eighteen months after arriving in Australia, the brothers sold their company and returned to the United States.

Late in 1889, Foster's was chartered as a private company. An economic recession hit Australia in the 1890s, and the brewing industry was particularly affected. To cut costs, Foster's merged with five other Melbourne breweries to form Carlton and United Breweries (CUB). The merger was officially completed on 8 May 1907. Representatives from each of the six breweries comprised the board of directors of the new company. In 1909, CUB expanded by purchasing the Yorkshire Brewery to serve as a replacement plant should fire strike one of the other brewing facilities.

Prior to World War I, CUB found success in the Australian and export markets, selling beer in Australia and on surrounding islands. The company adopted the new crown-seal bottle caps in 1911 to replace corks. In 1913, CUB was formed into a public company.

The company experienced a dip in profits during World War I because of wartime rationing. After the war, Australians wanted beer, and by 1919, demand was exceeding CUB's capacity to produce lager. In the 1920s, the company expanded its trade to markets in India and China. It also purchased more breweries including Hodges Brothers, Fitzgerald's Brewing and Malting Company, and the Cohn Brothers Victoria Brewing Company. In 1925, CUB purchased its strongest competitor in Melbourne, the Melbourne Co-operative Brewing Company. The Great Depression of the 1930s reduced profits, but the company continued growing by acquiring the Northern Australian Breweries in 1931. This was the company's first acquisition outside the Australian state of Victoria.

World War II posed more challenges for CUB. Rationing created shortages of raw materials, and shipping difficulties reduced the export trade, except for beer shipped to Australian forces serving overseas. Brewing was reduced by one-third during the war. Despite the lifting of rationing in 1946, shortages of raw materials such as barley still slowed production even as the demand for beer increased.

The 1950s was another period of expansion for CUB. Company scientists developed a new variety of hops that became the standard used by all Australian brewers. In 1957, a state-of-the-art brewery was built in Darwin. This facility remained in operation until 1989. A second brewery was constructed in Fiji. CUB purchased Ballarat Brewing Company in 1958; the Queensland Brewery of Brisbane and Toowoomba, and Thomas McLaughlin and Company of Rockhampton in 1961; and the Richmond Brewery in 1962.

In the 1970s and early 1980s, Foster's Lager became the leading brand of beer sold in Australia. Exports also increased as CUB looked to enter new foreign markets. By 1980, a consumer could purchase a CUB beer in 65 countries. Foster's Lager began to make an impact in the U.S. and British markets during this decade. CUB reached a milestone in 1983 when it acquired the assets of Tooth and Company in New South Wales, expanding into Sydney. The company became a national brewer, producing about half of the beer in Australia.

The Internationalization of Foster's Lager

Elders IXL, Australia's largest farm service conglomerate, launched a takeover bid for CUB in 1983. This was the largest corporate takeover in Australian history and marked Elders IXL's first venture in the alcoholic beverage industry. Peter Bartels, the new managing director, developed a strategy to make Foster's a truly international beer. Part of this strategy involved the purchase of breweries in other countries. In September 1986, Elders IXL acquired Courage Breweries, the sixth largest brewer in the United Kingdom. Carling O'Keefe, one of Canada's top brewers, was purchased in early 1987. Elders IXL's brewing concerns now had a foothold in the North American market.

Elders IXL's brewing concern changed its name to the Foster's Brewing Group in 1990, with Peter Bartels remaining as chief executive officer. The new company became a single-purpose international brewing company. In 1992, Bartels stepped down as CEO and was replaced by Ted Kunkel. Kunkel launched a reorganization of the company and purchased several large Australian brewing companies to solidify Foster's hold as Australia's beer. Foster's entered the Chinese market with the opening of Shanghai Foster's Brewery Limited as a joint venture with Huaguang Brewery in 1993.

Foster's Brewing Group diversified during the 1990s. In addition to purchasing a number of Australian brewing companies, the company established Australian Leisure and Hospitality Group (ALH) in 1995. The ALH group included a portfolio of more than 150 hotels and 90 other liquor outlets across Australia. In 1996, Foster's Brewing Group entered the wine industry with the purchase of Mildara Blass, a leading premium wine producer in Australia. Recognizing the company's diversification, the board of directors voted to change the name to Foster's Group in 2001.

John David Rausch Jr.

See also: Australia; Carling Brewery; Courage Brewery; O'Keefe Brewery

References

Dunstan, Keith. *The Amber Nectar: A Celebration of Beer and Brewing in Australia.* Victoria: Viking O'Neil, 1987.

Foster's Group corporate website. West Texas A & M University. http://www.fostersgroup.com [August 2002].

Hewat, Tim. *The Elders Explosion: One Hundred and Fifty Years of Progress from Elder to Elliott.* Sydney: Bay Books, 1988.

France, Production and Consumption of Alcohol in

The French have long been and remain among the chief producers and consumers of alcohol in the world. Their history demonstrates the importance of viticulture to an economy and a society. Viticulture offered small landowners the opportunity for participation in the market and economic self-sufficiency. Viticulture also tended to encourage democratic social structures at the local level, as well as mutual aid societies and often radical politics. French consumption of alcohol also demonstrates the complexity of its social role. Both cherished and condemned as a mainstay of popular culture, wine was mostly drunk in sociable and commensal settings. Consumption rates rose sharply in the nineteenth century but mostly due to changes in rural patterns as peasants introduced alcohol into their diet. The rapid rise in the consumption of spirits provoked considerably more concern, though this use tended to be more limited regionally.

Wine Production

At least since the Middle Ages, France had produced wine throughout most of the country. The principal viticultural regions grouped themselves along the major rivers and coasts that gave them access to long-distance markets. Yet every town needed vineyards in its hinterland, and much of the wine was aimed at local consumption. As late as the Revolution, every region of the country produced some wine, except for the Channel coast where people made beer or cider instead, and fifty of eighty-six departments had at least 10,000 hectares (4,050 acres) of vines. The largest amounts of wine came from the Atlantic coast, from which it was exported, but considerable amounts were still produced in the region immediately to the east and south of Paris.

Since viticulture offered the possibility of economic self-sufficiency on microproperties (as little as half an acre), it was attractive to the smallest landowners. Royal government before the Revolution fought, with only moderate success, to restrict the growth of vineyards. In the century following the Revolution, vineyards expanded overall by some 50 percent, and wine production nearly doubled. Viticulture also shifted from coexisting in a polyculture, with the production of grain and other fruits, to being increasingly a monoculture. Expansion was par-

French tapestry, ca. 1500, depicts members of the aristocracy treading and pressing grapes to make wine. (Hulton/Archive)

ticularly evident in the south, where growers planted high-yielding vines of low quality.

A few regions also developed low-yielding, high-quality viticulture—the *grands crus.* Already in the old regime, the viticulture in a few areas had turned to the production of expensive wines using expensive techniques. Many of the now famous wines of Bordeaux owe their fame to this period, when growers began to select their grapes more carefully and vinify to make a wine that aged well. The winegrowers of upper Burgundy, south of Dijon, began in the late eighteenth century to harvest grapes later in the season for greater sugar and to vinify longer for more intense color and alcohol. Bottling in both regions aided the creation of wines that gained value with age. Similarly, the region of Champagne had sent appreciable quantities of wines to Paris and to the neighboring states of Northern Europe, but most of this was barrels of still wine. Only during the eighteenth century did negotiants and growers turn to a trade in expensive sparkling wine in bottles.

The viticultural economy was thus increasingly bifurcated between the mass of low-quality production by small landowners and the capital-intensive production of luxury wines. The disruptions of the late nineteenth century made these disparities even sharper. The last half of the nineteenth century brought disease and devastation to French vineyards. Oidium and mildew arrived in the middle of the century and required expensive applications of chemicals to be defeated. *Phylloxera vastatrix,* arriving in the 1870s, eventually forced practically all vineyards to be replanted with American rootstock. Although the diseases fell like a plague on winegrowers of every social and economic level, their successful treatment burdened the small growers far more than the large ones. The yearly treatments against mildew, black rot, or oidium, and the prohibitive expense of replanting with American rootstock required substantial capital outlays. Such costs and the comparative efficiency of wine production in the south, particularly for cheap wine, slowly persuaded northern regions to abandon the mass market and in some cases to give up wine production entirely.

The 1870s were the high-water mark of vine growing, and the area under cultivation had declined to eighteenth-century levels by World War I, from which it has continued to decline steadily to the present. By the 1980s, only twenty-three departments had as much as 10,000 hectares (4,050 acres) of vines, and 40 percent of the vines were concentrated in only four southern departments. Yet production of wine had recovered by the early twentieth century and has continued to grow, somewhat sporadically, since. Twentieth-century viticulture is the product of mechanized and scientific agriculture that has pushed yields steadily higher.

Yet success has posed problems just as devastating as disease. The viticultural economy has wrestled with overproduction for centuries, but with the unification of the French market and the introduction of scientific techniques, increased productivity of vines has challenged growers considerably. Through the nineteenth century, the Mediterranean coast became increasingly productive, concentrating more and more of the country's vineyards and tripling the yield per hectare. By early in the twentieth century, this one small region had roughly one-third of the country's vines but was producing nearly half of its wine. At the same time, a growing number of Algerian vineyards, now within French borders, added to the surfeit of wine. The result was a social and political crisis at the beginning of the twentieth century, as growers in the south and north went on strike to protest the disastrous decline in wine prices. Although their problems had roots in overproduction, their movements attacked the fraudulent production and sale of wines that were unnatural and even unhealthy or were dishonestly identified. The state's initial response was ruthless repression of the disorders, but it also began to offer various legislation against fraud. Poor growers in the south also began to organize cooperatives intended to help them buy equipment and market their wines. When conditions of overproduction returned in the 1930s, made much worse by the world depression, the state finally developed the system of Appelations d'Origine Controlée (AOC). This system offered strict definitions of viticultural regions and the vines they grew. Initially, it included only the best vineyards and left the vast majority undefined. Since the 1950s, however, the AOC has incorporated more of the country and now covers almost half of the vineyards and one-third of the wine.

Consumption

French consumption of alcohol rose dramatically during the nineteenth century, encouraged by the growth in production, improvements in transportation, and the rapid spread of drink sellers. National rates of wine consumption climbed steadily through the nineteenth century, from roughly 80 liters (20 U.S. gallons) per capita in the 1830s to 110 liters (nearly 30 U.S. gallons) at the end of the century and 160 liters (42 U.S. gallons) early in the twentieth. The consumption of beer and cider, which had been localized in the regions that did not produce wine, also increased and spread throughout the country. The growing array of spirits offered to the public led to more than a tripling of consumption through the century, from 1.2 liters (0.36 U.S. gallon) of pure alcohol to 4.3 liters (1.3 U.S. gallons) in the 1890s. The rapid growth in the alcohol ingested from various sources shocked contemporaries and later historians alike. France saw a temperance movement of its own in the last years of the nineteenth century, presumably provoked by such excess.

These aggregate figures misrepresent the social reality, however. Premodern wine consumption was overwhelmingly urban, particularly if we focus on taxed, and therefore recorded, wine. And the common people in towns had long drunk wine regularly in taverns. The rate of wine consumption in many premodern towns and cities was nearly 200 liters (53 U.S. gallons) per capita in the seventeenth and eighteenth centuries. But urban consumption would change relatively little through the nineteenth century and so does little to explain the growth in national trends. Instead, the evolution of national drinking patterns resulted chiefly from the slow process of turning peasants into wine drinkers, either by moving them into the cities as the country became more urbanized or by developing a wine trade throughout the country. There is little evidence that premodern peasants drank wine, although winegrowers had probably always imbibed their unmarketable wine and a coarse *piquette* made from pressed grapes, most of which escaped the attention of old-regime record keepers. The nineteenth century recorded increased rural consumption both because more peasants began to drink and because more of their drinking was taxed and recorded. The spread of rural cafés made drinking a fundamental part of peasant sociability. But rural wine consumption remained quite modest compared to urban consumption rates.

Urban consumers did increase their consumption of spirits, however. Despite the large quantities of brandy produced along the Atlantic coast since the sixteenth century, most of the brandy was exported and the French drank little distilled alcohol before the Revolution. Consumption in town and country alike rose dramatically in the nineteenth century, though the rate of consumption in cities was more than double that of the countryside. Nationally, the consumption of spirits tripled in the nineteenth century, but most of it was localized in the departments of the north and northwest, which grew no grapes. Through the first half of the century, some 90 percent of distilled spirits had been made from "natural" (that is, fermented fruit) sources. With the viticultural crises of the 1880s, however, distillers turned to "industrial" spirits made from sugar beets. One effect of this switch was to produce an industrial spirit for a small fraction of the cost of natural spirits, making it cheaper even than wine and available to the poorest consumer. Consumption rates would nearly double in the next twenty years. The other effect was to shut out the distilling industry as an outlet for excess wine, once viticulture had recovered. By the end of the nineteenth century, only some 10 percent of spirits would be distilled from fermented fruits.

The affordability of industrial spirits was only a part of their success in France. Distillers created a market through creative advertising that emphasized the healthful and sociable qualities of spirits. Their products promoted the "appetite" before a meal and the "digestion" afterwards. Packaging their alcohol into hundreds of different distinct drinks and brands, distillers offered variety and social cachet. The most notorious of these spirits, absinthe or the "green fairy," boasted exotic ingredients and a high alcohol level. It was originally a drink of bohemian writers, who made it famous among the middle class. Its phenomenal success owed as much to its elaborate rituals of consumption as to any mysterious ingredients. As its popularity slowly spread, and workers sought to emulate high society, absinthe increased its sales 3,500 percent in the last quarter of the nineteenth century. The government responded by banning absinthe in the crisis of World War I. They need not have bothered. The consumption of spirits was already declining and would continue to decline through the first half of the twentieth century, though the consumption of wine rose to take part of its place. Since the 1950s, however, the per capita consumption of wine has declined by roughly a half, while the consumption of spirits has remained fairly stable. Through the century, then, the French have been drinking less, though they have been drinking better. They are gradually turning from table wines to AOC wines.

The trends in the twentieth century have remained more or less unchanged. Areas under viticultural cultivation declined steadily, to barely two-thirds of their old-regime extent, and are now concentrated overwhelmingly in the south. Total production, however, has remained largely unchanged or even increased due to greater yields. Domestic consumption has declined steadily, leaving a growing surplus. Fortunately, much of that surplus has found an expanding export market. Both foreign and French consumers are also turning to higher-quality wine, which seems to be sending a message to the low-quality, high-yield producers of the south, who are slowly planting better vines. Wine continues to be central to France's economy and culture.

Thomas Brennan

See also: Absinthe; France, Temperance in; Wine

References

Brennan, Thomas. *Burgundy to Champagne: The Wine Trade in Early Modern France.* Baltimore, MD: Johns Hopkins University Press, 1997.

———. "Towards the Cultural History of Alcohol in France" in *Journal of Social History.* 23, no. 1 (1989): 71–92.

Lachiver, Marcel. *Vins, vignes et vignerons: Histoire du vignoble français.* Paris: Fayard, 1988.

Nourrisson, Didier. *Le buveur du XIXe siècle.* Paris: Albin Michel, 1990.

Prestwich, Patricia. *Drink and the Politics of Social Reform: Antialcoholism in France since 1870.* Palo Alto, CA: Society for Promotion of Science and Scholarship, 1988.

France, Temperance in

Since the 1870s, the modern French temperance movement has been characterized by a policy of advocating the moderate consumption of alcohol. This has been a prudent approach in a country where, until recently, abstinence or "teetotalism" was considered a foreign concept and where the consumption of wine continues to be associated with a certain Gallic charm. Nevertheless, temperance organizations attracted little public or political support except in periods of crisis, when France's high rates of consumption and of alcoholic-related disorders became associated with fears of national decline. Only after World War II, with rapid modernization and the establishment of a national system of health care, did the temperance message become part of long-term official policies to deal with the health and economic consequences of France's continuing overproduction of alcohol.

Beginnings

The first modern French temperance association was founded as the new Third Republic struggled to establish itself after France's crushing military defeat by the Prussians in 1870. Although there had been complaints about widespread drunkenness in the 1860s, a period of bumper wine harvests, it was concern about national survival that prompted a group of eminent scientists, politicians, educators, and physicians to found the Société française de tempérance (SFT) in 1872. Its policies were shaped by French scientific beliefs that alcoholism was caused by the excessive consumption of cheap, industrially produced, distilled alcohols, such as brandies, or by adulterated wine. The SFT therefore directed its efforts to lobbying politicians for legislation to reduce the production of distilled alcohols and to promote the consumption of "pure," that is, unadulterated, wine. It made only a modest effort to reach a wider public, particularly working-class men, who were judged to be the largest consumers of these unhealthy wines and brandies. Women, it was assumed, were by nature abstinent.

By the late 1880s, the SFT was almost moribund. By 1900, it had been reinvigorated by an influx of new leaders, new organizations, and a wider membership. In part, this was the result of an increasing awareness by French scientists that the so-called healthy alcohols—wine, beer, and cider—were potentially as dangerous to health as distilled alcohols and that the issue was the quantity of alcohol consumed, not its quality. This change in scientific doctrine coincided with dramatic evidence of increased consumption of all types of alcohol. By 1900, the annual rate of consumption of taxed alcohol in France was 15.9 liters (4.2 U.S. gallons) of pure alcohol per inhabitant, a level that far surpassed that of other nations. (The comparable rates for Britain, the United States, and Russia were, respectively, 8.2, 5.8, and 5.2 liters [or 2. 17, 1.5, and 1.37 U.S. gallons] per inhabitant.) By 1900, France had 435,000 cafés or retail outlets for alcohol, and by 1914 there was one retail outlet for every 82 inhabitants, a higher concentration than in any other western nation. Consumption of alcohol was increasing in rural areas as a result of the growth in legal home distilling. Since the time of Napoleon, French farmers had enjoyed the right to distil their surplus fruit, without taxation, for home consumption. By 1890, the number of legal home distillers or *bouilleurs de cru* had reached half a million; by 1900, their numbers had doubled.

Although such statistics were a concern to advocates of public health, they became alarming to politicians and to the general public because of widespread fears in the 1890s about France's declining population and the growing military and economic might of Germany. Writers, artists, scientists, and politicians began to speak of a biological degeneration of the French nation, and alcoholism became a convenient symbol of this seemingly inevitable decline. Dr. Valentin Magnan, France's most eminent psychiatrist and an expert on alcoholism, maintained that alcoholism was both a cause of degeneration and a sign that degeneration had already begun. As the admitting physician for all the psychiatric hospitals of Paris, Magnan could provide statistical evidence to support his claim that alcoholism was the leading cause of psychiatric disorders among men. Since public hospitals admitted mostly working-class patients, such statistics reinforced the assumption that alcoholism was primarily a problem for the working classes. Indeed, in 1877, the novelist Émile Zola had drawn on psychiatric theories of degeneration for his popular novel *L'Assommoir,* which portrayed the inevitable decline from alcoholism to madness of a Parisian worker.

Renewal in the 1890s: The Union française antialcoolique

The result of these developments was the emergence of a renewed and more popular temperance movement in the 1890s. In 1895, Paul-Maurice Legrain, a psychiatrist and student of Magnan, established the Union française antialcoolique (UFA). Believing that desperate situations required desperate measures, Legrain preached abstinence from all alcohol, including wine. He sought to create a mass movement by appealing both to women, whom he considered to be the victims of alcoholic husbands, and to France's radical labor union movement, which sought to better the lives of workers. In 1896, the UFA had 200 members; by 1905, membership had reached 50,000. In 1896, the psychiatrist Jacques Roubinovitch, a pioneer in the treatment of mentally handicapped children, founded a temperance group for schoolchildren, the Association de la jeunesse française tempérante, which was subsidized by the Ministry of Education. Most of the new groups maintained a religious and political neutrality, but in the 1890s several religious groups were established, particularly the Protestant Croix bleue and a very small Catholic movement supported by French bishops, the Croix blanche. By 1914, there was also a lively working-class temperance movement that was linked with the radical labor union movement.

By 1903, under the impetus of the SFT, these diverse temperance groups had united into one large federation, the Ligue nationale contre l'alcoolisme, with a broad program of prevention that ranged from alleviating the poverty of the working classes to supporting women's suffrage. It was, however, not interested in the treatment of alcoholics, an attitude that reflected the medical and popular opinion that alcoholics could not be cured. The Ligue nationale adopted the policy of counseling the moderate use of wine, beer, and cider, a decision that led to a bitter rupture with Legrain, who left to found the French section of the Order of Good Templars, an international movement that advocated total abstinence. By 1914, the new Ligue nationale had grown from 50,000 members in 1906 to 125,000 members and, with support from the ministries of war and education, had introduced temperance programs in the army and public schools. It also launched campaigns for legislation to limit the number of cafés and to ban the production of absinthe, a popular aperitif, on the grounds that it contained an ingredient, thujone, that caused hallucinations and, eventually, madness. Both these prewar legislative campaigns produced excellent propaganda and much debate, but no results.

The Impact of Wars, American Prohibition, and the Great Depression

With the outbreak of World War I, action against alcoholism became a symbol of national determination. On 16 August 1914, as French troops marched to the front, the government banned the production and consumption of absinthe. By 1915, armed with emergency powers, the government attempted, with modest success, to restrict the consumption of distilled alcohol and to impose harsher penalties for drunkenness. Temperance organizations prospered under wartime conditions and adopted a suitably bellicose slogan that labeled alcohol "the enemy within." Alcohol producers protested the wartime restrictions and countered temperance propaganda by offering gifts of wine to the army and by linking the valor of French troops to their daily wine ration, the *pinard.* Although the army provided rations of wine and distilled alcohol to the troops, after the army mutinies of 1917, it began to restrict the consumption of alcohol in the war zones.

After the end of the war, the fortunes of the Ligue nationale declined until the eve of World War II. Both the public and politicians assumed, wrongly, that wartime restrictions had solved the problem of excessive consumption. The French temperance movement also suffered from the success of Prohibition in the United States and in parts of Canada. French public opinion and the popular press, adroitly aided by the propaganda of wine producers, associated Prohibition with gangsters and what they termed an "Anglo-Saxon Puritanism." The Ligue nationale received discreet funding from American prohibitionist organizations and did try to point out that in areas where prohibition was strictly enforced, the health of the population improved, but such propaganda had little effect. Wartime legislation was gradually dismantled, and the production and consumption of alcohol returned to prewar levels. The Great Depression of the 1930s was marked by a severe crisis of overproduction of alcohol, particularly wine. Governments tried to solve the problem by purchasing the surplus alcohol and by promoting consumption. In 1931, the minister of education, Mario Roustan, ordered that health classes in the public schools should emphasize the benefits of wine for children.

As a new war with Germany loomed in the late 1930s, France's high rate of consumption and of alcoholic disorders again became a matter of political and public concern. In 1939, as part of an effort to increase the birth rate, the government passed a series of measures to restrict the number of cafés and to limit home distilling. After the defeat of France by Germany in June 1940, the new authoritarian and collaborationist government of Vichy, led by Marshal Pétain, instituted a policy of national regeneration that included strict measures to reduce alcoholism by restricting the production and consumption of distilled alcohols, but not of wine. The Ligue nationale, hampered by wartime hardships and its association with the now discredited Third Republic, played only a limited role in the regime's temperance campaigns. Wartime rationing, labor shortages, and the demands of the occupying German forces restricted the supply of all alcohols, including wine, and by 1944, one result was a noticeable improvement in the health of French men.

Post-1945 Developments

After 1945, there was a familiar shift from crisis to complacency. In the public's mind, campaigns against alcoholism were associated with the now repudiated wartime regime. The postwar governments of the new Fourth Republic did not repeal Vichy's restrictive legislation, but as the production of alcohol returned to prewar levels and cafés reopened, the rates of consumption rose. By 1954, alcoholism was considered the third most important cause of death for men and the fourth for women. However, the establishment of universal health care in postwar France made the costs of alcoholic disorders and of alcohol-related accidents more evident. As well, in the 1940s and 1950s, as France began to modernize rapidly through state planning, policy makers became concerned about the high cost of subsidizing the overproduction of alcohol and about the amount of disposable income being diverted from the purchase of consumer goods to the consumption of alcohol. In 1954, the government of Premier Pierre Mendès-France acted. In a dramatic gesture, Mendès-France raised a glass of milk as he announced a series of measures to restrict the production and consumption of alcohol. He also created a permanent official organization, the Haut Comité d'étude et d'information sur l'alcoolisme, to promote research and to develop new policies in collaboration with private organizations, such as the Ligue nationale. In 1958, under the new Fifth Republic, the government began to confront the problem of rural alcoholism by decreeing that the right of farmers to distill their fruit without being taxed would no longer be hereditary.

The postwar period was also marked by renewed scientific interest in alcoholism and by new efforts to treat drink-related disorders. French researchers and physicians were stimulated by the research of E. M. Jellinek and the Yale Center of Alcohol Studies and by the development of new methods of treatment such as the drug disulfiram. A young psychiatrist, Dr. Pierre Fouquet was both a pioneer in the treatment of alcoholics and the originator of the concept of *alcoologie* (alcohology), a comprehensive discipline that seeks to understand alcoholism as a social as well as medical phenomenon. These new efforts, both official and private, stimulated the renewal of the temperance movement. The heir of the SFT and the Ligue nationale, now entitled the Association nationale de la prévention de l'alcoolisme, continues to support research on alcoholism and to educate the public about the benefits of moderate consumption.

Since the 1970s, the consumption of alcohol in France has declined dramatically, from 15.67 liters (4.14 U.S. gallons) of pure alcohol per inhabitant in 1970 to 10.7 liters (2.83 U.S. gallons) in 1999. The current level of consumption remains high in comparison with that of Britain (8.1 liters [2.4 U.S. gallons] in 1999) or the United States (6.7 liters [1.77 U.S. gallons]), and French authorities continue to warn of the serious health problems caused by this excessive consumption. Nevertheless, France is the only country in the European Union where consumption has continued to decline. As well, the popularity of nonalcoholic drinks continues to grow, as does the number of people who consume no alcohol at all. Although the French temperance movement that emerged in the latter decades of the nineteenth century was never as popular or as powerful as its counterparts in North America or Northern Europe, its policy of advocating moderation rather than abstinence has, in the long run, proved effective.

Patricia E. Prestwich

See also: Absinthe; Degeneration Theories; Drinking Establishments (France); France, Production and Consumption of Alcohol in; Good Templars (IOGT); Wine

References

Haine, W. Scott. *The World of the Paris Café: Sociability among the French Working Class, 1789–1914.* Baltimore, MD: Johns Hopkins University Press, 1996.

Marrus, Michael R. "Social Drinking in the *Belle Epoque*" in *Journal of Social History.* 7 (1973–1974): 115–141.

Prestwich, Patricia E. *Drink and the Politics of Social Reform: Antialcoholism in France since 1870.* Palo Alto, CA: Society for the Promotion of Science and Scholarship, 1988.

———. "Female Alcoholism in Paris, 1870–1920: Psychiatric Theory and the Asylum Experience" in *History of Psychiatry.* June 2003.

———. "Paul-Maurice Legrain (1860–1939)" in *Addiction.* 92, no. 10 (1997): 1255–1263.

Franco, *Ing.* Luis G. (fl. 1930s)

Ingeniero Luis G. Franco was the leading temperance advocate of the postrevolutionary national temperance campaign in Mexico. He became involved in the campaign from its inception as the delegate from the Ministry of Industry to President Emilio Portes Gil's National Committee for the Struggle against Alcoholism in 1929, and later went on to head up the national Anti-Alcohol Directorate.

From his position as Ministry of Industry delegate to the Comité Nacional de Lucha contra el Alcoholismo, Luis Franco emerged as the most visible crusader in the national temperance campaign. Franco, like many of his contemporaries, viewed alcoholism as a social disease in the sense of a pathology that affected not just individuals, but society as a whole. He felt that alcoholism constituted an impediment to Mexico's industrial progress. Sobriety was, in his perception, a prerequisite for Mexico if it was to take its place among the modern, industrial nations of the world.

Franco gave public lectures and recorded radio programs in order to raise public awareness about the problem of alcoholism. He also authored printed propaganda, which he sent to state and municipal authorities, along with instructions to use it in the promotion of grassroots temperance organization. He often resorted to personal appeals to individuals at the local level in order to aid in the struggle and mobilize their communities in support of temperance.

Luis Franco referred to alcoholism as "the most tenacious enemy the woman has ever had." He appealed to women and children to use their indirect influence to persuade their husbands and fathers not to drink. He believed that women must help men fight against alcoholism because men, though stronger than women, were not strong enough to fight the temperance battle alone. Franco encouraged children to join the struggle as well and told them that they were like "Archimedes' lever," with which one could move the entire world.

Despite his praise of Mexican women, Franco chose to look to the United States for an ideal paradigm of womanhood. First Lady Lucy Webb Hayes, wife of United States president Rutherford B. Hayes, had refused to permit alcohol in the White House during her husband's presidency, from 1877 to 1881. Franco contrasted this example with a sordid image of a Mexican mother who offered her children the mildly alcoholic traditional Indian beverage *pulque.* He admonished Mexican mothers who drank while their children were small. He informed them that such a practice would pass on "alcoholic germs" to their young.

By 1933, Franco became the head of activities of the new Dirección Anti-Alcohólica. By 1935, Franco had moved from the Department of Industry to the Department of Public Health and Hygiene, where he continued to serve as the director of the antialcoholic campaign. At this point, the national temperance effort underwent another structural change, as it became nominally centralized under the Department of Health and Hygiene. The program still bore the title Dirección Anti-Alcohólica, and Franco remained in charge. In practice, however, the Departments of Education, Agriculture, and Industry continued with their own temperance efforts.

Stephanie Mitchell

See also: Comité Nacional de Lucha contra el Alcoholismo; Dirección Anti-Alcohólica; Mexico; Portes Gil, Emilio

References

Joseph, Gilbert M., and Daniel Nugent, eds. *Everyday Forms of State Formation: Revolution and the Negotiation of Rule in Modern Mexico.* Durham, NC: Duke University Press, 1994.

Vaughan, Mary Kay. *Cultural Politics in Revolution: Teachers, Peasants, and Schools in Mexico (1930–1940).* Tucson: University of Arizona Press, 1997.

G

Gallo

The Ernest and Julio Gallo Winery is the world's single largest wine producer. Its 2001 production was in excess of 950 million bottles, and it makes one bottle of every three or four consumed in the United States. (Compare this with the 35 million bottles produced under the various labels of the other California wine giant, Mondavi.)

Gallo is a family-owned enterprise that was founded by two brothers, Ernest and Julio Gallo, in 1933, soon after the end of Prohibition. Starting with a modest wine-making facility in Modesto, California, the Gallos (then in their early twenties) began by making bulk red wine and soon expanded their portfolio to include whites and fortified wines. Within two years of the repeal of Prohibition, the Gallo brothers were producing 350,000 gallons of wine a year, and in 1936 they constructed a winery with a production capacity of 1.5 million gallons. At this time, most of the wine was sold in bulk and bottled by merchants, but in 1937 the company began to bottle its own wine under the Gallo label.

Gallo soon became the first large-scale wine producer to own or control every aspect of the production and marketing process. Gallo either owned its own vineyards or established long-term contracts with independent grape growers, and during the 1950s and 1960s Gallo was responsible for 40 to 50 percent of all the wine produced in Napa and Sonoma counties. From the early 1950s to the mid-1980s, the company purchased the entire production of the Napa Cooperative Winery, which made up to 40 percent of the wine made in the Napa Valley. Gallo even owned a glass factory where bottles were made, a print shop for labels, and a transport company for shipping wine to merchants.

By 1950, the Gallo wineries collectively possessed greater production capacity than any other in the United States, and by the late 1960s the company was the national sales leader (a position it has maintained since). In this period, Gallo built a massive bottling and storage facility (with space for 12 million cases of wine) in Modesto, but actual production was and is distributed among wineries in other parts of California, notably Fresno, Livingston, and Dry Creek Valley.

One of the reasons for the success of the company has been its ability to stay abreast of changing consumer tastes and to target specific markets. During the 1950s, Gallo produced semi-sweet carbonated wines called Thunderbird and Ripple, which attracted a following among beer-drinking consumers and those whose nonalcoholic preferences were carbonated soda pop. A famous radio jingle for Thunderbird ran:

> What's the word?
> Thunderbird.
> How's it sold?
> Good and cold.
> What's the jive?
> Bird's alive.
> What's the price?
> Thirty twice!

In the 1960s, when table wines gathered popularity, Gallo provided a range of reds and whites carrying quasi-French names like Hearty Burgundy and Chablis Blanc (names that are now reserved for wines from those regions in France). There was little attention to grape varieties: The Burgundy was made of Barbera (rather than Pinot Noir) and the Chablis was Colombard (rather than Chardonnay).

For many years, the Gallo name was associated primarily with bulk-produced jug wines that were blends of unspecified grapes and of vintages. Vintage-dated wines were introduced to the Gallo portfolio as recently as 1978. In the 1970s, Gallo began to establish a line of higher-quality wines that were labeled by variety and vintage. It purchased quality vineyard land and some existing vineyards like the Frei Ranch (bought in 1977), which is now central to Gallo's Sonoma operations and produces vineyard-designated wines.

Diversification of Marketing Strategies

In the 1990s, the company began to target the high-price end of the wine market by producing premium-level wines under the Gallo of Sonoma label. Most of these wines are varietals (made from a single grape variety) such as Cabernet Sauvignon and Zinfandel. More attention is being paid to the geographical location of the vineyards as Gallo and other California producers increasingly embrace the European notion of *terroir* (the theory that wines express the environment in which they are grown). Not only has this led Gallo to label wines from specific designated wine regions (American Viticultural Areas such as Dry Creek Valley and Alexander Valley), but Gallo also has a range of premium vineyard-designated wines.

Key to the drive to make premium wines is a new production facility in Sonoma's Dry Creek Valley, not far from the Frei Ranch. Although much smaller than the huge Modesto winery, this five-acre operation is a mass of stainless steel tanks and presses, and a massive underground barrel room that houses 50,000 barrels. Gallo can make 7 million gallons of wine a year here.

But although the winery looks like a factory, it was designed to produce anything but bulk wine, and many of the methods in operation are more common in small-scale premium wineries rather than large-scale production facilities. Grapes from different vineyards are crushed and fermented separately, and much of the wine is barrel fermented. For the rest, rotary fermentors are widely used, and Gallo's wine makers often use indigenous, rather than industrial yeasts. The pipes through which wine is pumped at various stages of production have smooth, gradual curves so that the wine is treated as gently as possible. Fining and filtration are used sparingly. Not all the wine made at this facility is premium quality, and about half is sold under the successful Turning Leaf brand of inexpensive midrange wines.

Gallo also makes sparkling wines under several labels (including Totts and André). In addition to its wine production, Gallo also makes coolers (blends of wine and fruit juice) under the Bartles & James label. Gallo Brandy is one of America's biggest-selling brands.

Gallo produces a wide range of wines in terms of style and price under a sometimes bewildering range of brands and labels. The Sonoma winery produces wines under more than fifty different names, some as straightforward as Turning Leaf, others as unusual as Anapamu and Zabaco. It caters to the lower price ranges with brands like Carlo Rossi, to middle price ranges with Turning Leaf, and to the higher end of the market with Gallo of Sonoma. Other brands are produced specifically for export markets. Overall, however, there is a general tendency to reserve the Gallo name for higher-end products.

Despite its massive growth since the 1930s, Gallo remains a family-owned company and its marketing stresses the generational continuity. Many third-generation Gallos (G3s, as they are known) work for the company in various aspects of viticulture, wine making, and management. In the first years of the twenty-first century, many of the company's promotional campaigns centered on Gina Gallo, granddaughter of Julio Gallo and carefully described as a "third-generation winemaker." In this respect, Gallo follows the wine industry's hallowed practice of stressing tradition and lineage. But Gallo is also highlighting the leading role of a woman in wine production, a sphere in which women are still a small minority in California and elsewhere.

Rod Phillips

See also: Labor in the U.S. Liquor Industry; Wine

References

Brook, Stephen. *The Wines of California.* London: Faber and Faber, 1999.

Gallo, Ernest and Julio. *Our Story.* New York: Random House, 1994.

Robinson, Jancis. *Oxford Companion to Wine.* 2nd ed. Oxford: Oxford University Press, 1999.

Sullivan, Charles L. *A Companion to California Wine.* Berkeley: University of California Press, 1998.

Gandhi, Mohandas Karamchand (1869–1947)

Mohandas Karamchand Gandhi (1869–1947), the father of the Indian nation and more popularly known as the "Bapu" or "Mahatma," was one of the pioneers of the temperance movement in modern India. He was born in a small town of the modern state of Gujarat in India at Porbandar, then popularly known as Sudamapuri, on 2 October 1869. Gandhi's mass movement against British colonial rule included temperance as one of the important social and moral positions working to support his views.

Although the Indian National Congress Party under Gandhi's leadership had other constructive programs (such as popularization of *Khadi*—a homespun cloth championed by Gandhi to symbolize resistance to British imported cloth—and promotion of the Hindi language), its temperance program was one of the most important ingredients in garnering mass support against British imperialism. The taxing of alcohol by the British for revenue purposes made prohibition an important moral symbol of renunciation of corrupt Western ways and imperial rule. Moreover, for Gandhi, temperance was not only relevant for the health and hygiene of citizens but also important to the successful practice of principles of "nonviolence." After 1920, the Congress Party under Gandhi's leadership started an all-out campaign against drinking. Gandhi used to say that, if the people of India were to reach their goal through nonviolent effort, they should not leave to the future government the fate of millions of men and women who were laboring under the curse of intoxicants and narcotics.

To raise awareness on this issue, Gandhi even called upon medical professionals, women, and students to come forward to help him in eradicating the habit. According to him, medical men could make a most effective contribution in discovering ways of weaning the drunkard and the opium addict from their habits. For women and students, temperance presented a special opportunity that, by many acts of loving service, they could acquire a hold on addicts, which would compel them to listen to temperance appeals. An avid observer of Indian society, he knew that this habit disproportionately affected poor Indians, since this underprivileged class suffered from harsh and busy working conditions that encouraged drinking. So Gandhi encouraged and directed the Congress Party to open recreation booths where the tired laborers could rest, get healthy and cheap refreshment, and find suitable games for enjoyment.

Following this ideology, during the "Quit India Movement" or "Bharat Choro" movement in August, 1942, thousands of liquor-selling shops were picketed by Indian people and congress workers as part of the congress programs or as a result of Gandhi's calls. He used to say that the phrase *"Mens Sana in corpore sano"* (a healthy mind in a healthy body is a self-evident

Mohandas Karamchand Gandhi (1869–1947) (Library of Congress)

truth) is perhaps the first law of humanity. His conviction of truth was that if a man was in possession of a healthy mind, he would naturally shed all violence. By naturally obeying the laws of health, men could have healthy bodies without extra effort. According to Gandhi, wine destroyed the soul of human beings and was followed by insanity, adultery, and gambling. For him, it was universally acknowledged that drinking was not necessary for man, and it was axiomatic that a drunken man was incapable of self-control.

Gandhi not only popularized the cause of prohibition in India but also in other countries like Burma as well. During his trip to Burma in March 1929, in one of his public meetings at Moulmein, he said: "I was intensely pained to learn yesterday that the drink evil was on the increase in Burma and more pained to learn that drink revenue amounted to one-third of the land revenue. History records that empires have been destroyed through this habit. We have it in India that the great community to which Shri Krishna belonged was ruined by that habit and this monstrous evil was undoubtedly one of the contributing factors in the fall of Rome." At another public meeting in Burma, he cautioned the Burmese women by saying that visitors from India were painfully surprised to see the beautiful Burmese women disfigure their mouths by "Cheroots" and "Cigars" (Rajshekhar 2000).

Gandhi's ideological conviction on temperance issues and his strong moral authority gave his message a certain force of "truth" in the campaigns against the drinking habit and the British colonial regime. Quoting history, health and hygiene, family, and the well-being of the nation, Gandhi built and waged a persuasive and influential campaign against drinking. As one of the greatest men in modern India, he not only influenced the Indian people with his commitment and sacrifice to the causes of temperance and nationalism, but his movement had an effect on other Asian countries such as Burma as well.

Dr. Rajshekhar

See also: India; Johnson, William Eugene "Pussyfoot"; World League Against Alcoholism (WLAA)

References

Chandra, Bipan. *India's Struggle for Independence (1857–1947).* New Delhi: Penguin Books, 1989.

The Collected Works of Mahatma Gandhi, vol. XVIII (July–November 1920). New Delhi: Publication Division, Ministry of Information and Broadcasting, Government of India, 1965.

The Collected Works of Mahatma Gandhi, vol. LXXV (11 October 1941–31 March 1942). New Delhi: Publication Division, Ministry of Information and Broadcasting, Government of India, 1979.

Gandhi, M. K. *An Autobiography, or The Story of My Experiments with Truth.* Ahmedabad: Navajivan Press, 1927.

Rajshekhar, Dr. *Burma's (Myanmar's) Nationalist Movement (1906–1948) and India.* (Ph.D. thesis. Jawaharlal Nehru University, New Delhi, 2000).

Germany

The history of alcohol in Germany has been shaped principally by two factors: its central position in Europe both geographically and culturally, and the marked independence of its constituent regions. Only in the twentieth century can we speak of a more or less unified drinking culture, which can be characterized as "permissive-ambivalent." Meanwhile, both its southern and northern neighbors have moved toward this Central European pattern of consumption. Previously, German drinking culture consisted of regional, partial cultures that were, at most, united by the consensus that occasional intoxication was the natural right of a (male) German. Although Germany was the birthplace of Protestantism and, with it, the first temperance movement, later stimuli for addressing the alcohol question consistently came from outside. And although they were highly successful in mobilizing the population, modern champions of temperance came up against the proud defense of "personal freedom" among the majority of German citizens. Nevertheless, temperance advocates did manage to influence both public opinion and politics in a lasting manner. Alcohol was viewed thereafter as a potentially dangerous substance: One recognized that the consumption was to be controlled but not however suppressed.

The Early Modern Roots

Germans since the sixteenth century were reckoned to be the most enthusiastic drinkers of any nation. Two accidents account for this stereotype. First, the fact that the Reformation arose here: Martin Luther and other Reformation leaders unleashed the first temperance campaign in history. It was all in vain, for the "boozing devil," in Martin Luther's words, remained "an all-powerful idol among us Germans" (Spode 1994: 498 n.) The campaign was not so much directed against the high, day-to-day nutritive consumption of alcohol (and also not against strong spirits), but rather against the excessive drinking bouts on special occasions. Both sermons and outright bans were directed against the compulsion to drink, as in toasting (*Zutrinken*)—that is, intoxication following strict rules, often to the point of unconsciousness. The aristocracy set an especially bad example, complained Emperor Charles V, with its toasts and drinking contests, and made itself a laughing stock abroad. Admittedly, old-style drinking bouts were common in many countries, and even the high average consumption of 300 to 1,000 liters (80 to 270 U.S. gallons) of wine or beer per year was no exception. But this could simply not be reconciled with the new Protestant ethic. The second source of the stereotype of German booziness derived from the almost coterminous rediscovery of the essay "Germania," written by the Roman historian Tacitus. In this essay, the ancient Germanic tribes were presented as a model of virtue and of the love of freedom. Only their love of drink was reprehensible: "They count it as no shame to carouse for days and nights on end." Now the Germanic peoples were simply equated with the contemporary Germans without further ado. A tradition was invented that was to define for centuries the way Germans viewed themselves and others viewed them.

One result was that criticism of the "boozing devil" became transformed into the pride of intellectuals in the "German national tendency to drink" as a sign of natural openness and a love of freedom (F. W. Petersen 1782, quoted in Spode 1993: 260 n.). Yet by the late eighteenth century, the compulsion to drink had virtually disappeared in the upper and middle classes. It is true that opposition to this sobering process grew in the ritualized drinking excesses of students (the *Kommers* ritual). This indeed became a particular German custom that flourished into the early twentieth century (and finds isolated expression up to the present day). These ceremonies always restricted themselves to the allegedly quintessential German beverage: beer. In truth, the brewer's art—which flourished in medieval monasteries and towns—experienced a long decline following the Thirty Years War. The vineyards that once stretched to the Baltic Sea also receded. Brandy and (Ersatz) malt-based coffee became everyday drinks alongside beer. Bavaria, however, experienced a special development: In 1516, the Purity Law (*Reinheitsgebot,* the oldest still-valid food law) was promulgated here, permitting the use only of barley (later also wheat), hops, and water in the brewing process. On top of this the new, bottom-fermenting style of brewing, the more durable lager (i.e., storable) beer took hold, guaranteeing a high quality. So three regional drinking cultures stood alongside one another: Along the Rhine and its tributaries, wine dominated, while in the south, it was beer; and in the other areas, spirits were popular in towns, while thin beer was drunk in the countryside, where brandy or schnapps only appeared on the table on holidays.

Early Industrialization

In the early nineteenth century, a rapid industrialization of spirits took place. Freedom of trade, the planting of potatoes, and new distillation techniques made production possible under factory conditions. The hitherto prestigious drink became cheaper, coming within reach of even the rural underclass. In Prussia, the per capita consumption of spirits around 1840 rose to almost 30 liters (8 U.S. gallons), while the consumption of beer fell to 20 liters (a little more than 5 U.S. gallons). Adult men drank an average of approximately 60 liters per year. The advance of spirits was by no means restricted to the Protestant North and Northeast, but extended also to the Catholic West and East; at the same time, however, consumption remained significantly lower in the southern beer and wine regions. This development cannot therefore be explained in denominational terms, but rather must be explained by the drinking culture, along with socioeconomic factors and a zeitgeist that transcended regions and countries. The concentrated alcoholic beverage collided with a premodern drinking culture among social classes that had been impoverished by early capitalism and were uprooted and undernourished ("pauperism"). Spirits destroyed that culture, as Friedrich Engels observed: "The character of intoxication had totally changed."

Following the examples of Ireland and the United States, pastors and a few rulers initiated a "crusade against spirits." The leading figure was the clergyman Johann H. Böttcher from the kingdom of Hanover. He was convinced that poverty, criminality, godlessness, and immorality were all dramatically on the rise, the cause being an "artificial poison": spirituous liquors. Throughout the 1840s, apostles of sobriety crisscrossed the country, taking the pledge from hundreds of thousands who promised never again to drink spirits (beer and wine were still permitted). By 1847, there were a good 1,200 local temperance leagues. Counting whole families, they comprised between 1 and 2 million members, the majority of whom resided in the rural areas of northern and eastern Germany, as well as in Prussia's Polish districts. Overall per capita consumption sank slightly, though heavily in some areas. At the same time, this very emotionally fought "crusade" met with rejection and scorn on the part of the medical profession and the urban bourgeoisie, especially in the big cities of Berlin and Hamburg. It was claimed that this reactionary missionary work would merely result in an ineffective "curing of symptoms," while the true causes of pauperism lay in the political-economic system. When that system began to wobble in the March Revolution of 1848, the movement collapsed and became a tiny sect. On the one hand, the champions of temperance had lastingly undermined the image of spirits as a medicine and tonic; on the other hand, they created a negative image of temperance activists as sanctimonious zealots, out to destroy pleasure and freedom.

High Industrialism

For three decades, one heard very little about alcohol, in spite of a renewed rise in consumption. Spirits emerged again as a topic only after Germany's rise, in the wake of its proclamation of the empire in 1871, from a predominantly agrarian collection of states to a leading industrial nation. At the initiative of the Berlin physician Abraham Baer, the German League against the Abuse of Alcoholic Beverages (Deutscher Verein gegen den Mißbrauch geistiger Getränke [DVMG]) was formed in 1883 under the presidency of the professor of psychiatry, Werner Nasse. At the same time, the Blue Cross and the International Order of Good Templars (IOGT) set up self-help groups. Initially, the debate was dominated by the DVMG, in which the educated and propertied bourgeoisie of a national-liberal slant set the tone. Turning its back on the religious overtones of the earlier "crusade" and the self-help societies, the DVMG functioned as a modern interest group. At first, it demanded the banishment of schnapps from factories and the substitution of beer for spirits in general. Yet, soon a complex program emerged for solving the "alcohol question" (*Alkoholfrage*), which was defined as part of the "social question" (i.e., the integration of the working class into the emerging industrial society): scientifically based education, legal limitations such as tax hikes and sales restrictions, development of treatment centers for alcoholics, tavern reform on the Swedish model, promotion of nonalcoholic beverages and drinking fountains, and so forth. Initially, the working class, the primary target of the program, reacted dismissively. The activities of the Social Democratic Party had been severely restricted by Bismarck's antisocialist legislation (1878–1890), so that above all else, taverns functioned as the party's main sociocultural and political space ("the bulwark of the proletarian's political freedom," as a leading socialist politician put it [Spode 1993: 237]). Nonetheless, the workers' movement, too, took up many of the demands of the DVMG after 1900.

At the same time, the DVMG lost much of its scientific credibility. Alcohol research—represented by psychiatrists like Emil Kraepelin and eugenicists like Ernst Rüdin—turned against the "moderate standpoint" of the league. It was proclaimed as proven that alcohol in any form or quantity not only led to horrendous medical, social, and economic damage, but above all caused genetic harm and thus acted as a creeping "racial poison." The antialcohol movement split into "moderates" and "abstainers," who no longer viewed the "alcohol question" as a social problem, but as a "racial question" (such as Auguste Forel, the leading abstinence campaigner in the German-speaking area). Scientists flocked to the IOGT, which transformed itself into a propaganda organization. Together with a good seventy other abstinence associations, the IOGT demanded tougher laws, such as the local option, and compulsory sterilization. Its long-term goal was prohibition. The abstainers provoked a heated debate through lectures, exhibitions, leaflets, and so forth. At the close of the empire they had overtaken, with their 400,000 members, the DVMG tenfold. In the context of "life reform," an alcohol-free subculture had arisen, albeit one that remained socially and politically isolated. To the vast majority, the abstainers were viewed as sectarian cranks ("American water apostles"), while the "moderate standpoint" began to find increasing acceptance.

During the empire (1871–1918), a radical modernization of the drinking culture occurred. The per capita consumption of pure alcohol sank from 10 to 7 liters (2.6 to 1.8 U.S. gallons) between 1872 and 1913, but more importantly, the proportion of spirits dropped from two-thirds to one-third (beer consumption grew until 1900, then it stagnated). The DVMG was largely responsible for this decline, although there were other, no less important factors as well. The decline of spirits consumption had been set in motion by Bismarck's tax increases of 1887. Above all, growing prosperity spurred the working class to take the "comfortable enjoyment of life" as its model. This was symbolized not by schnapps, but by beer. Hand in hand with this shift to beer came changes in the beer market: Beer production had been transformed from an artisanal craft into a major industry. Half the beer in Germany was now provided by big, joint-stock breweries. Advertisers successfully propagated the image of the respectable beer drinker, rooted in the alleged traditions of the old Germanic tribes. The Purity Law was applied nationwide. Although consumption in Bavaria remained way above the national average (in 1900, 246 liters [65 U.S. gallons] in comparison with 114 liters [30 U.S. gallons] nationally), the upmarket bottom-fermented beer (known as Bavarian beer or Pilsner) did conquer the urban markets, just as bottled beer made consumption possible beyond the tavern. The brewing industry soared with higher productivity than the mighty coal-mining sector. Distilleries, on the other hand, were subject to a subsidized quota system and shifted increasingly to the export market and to the manufacture of industrial alcohol.

The second empire was the decisive phase in the modern history of alcohol in Germany. During this period, the structures of drinking culture and alcohol knowledge that by and large still obtain today were established. Alcohol was domesticated and marginalized, its consumption restricted as far as possible to enclaves of leisure time. Within this context, occasional intoxication was admissible. On the other hand, "alcoholism" (as addictive drinking was called since the turn of the century) was finally viewed as a disease and remained an unsolved problem. Germans changed from schnapps drinkers to beer drinkers; boozing became less common and less visible; and despite the multitude of taverns, bars, and beer palaces, consumption, excessive or not, shifted more toward the domestic arena.

The Interwar Years

With the first world war, the peak of the antialcohol movement had passed, even though its ultimate decline was delayed until the second world war. The crisis-ridden Weimar Republic (1919–1933) saw per capita consumption plummet to historical lows of 3 to 4 liters (around 1 U.S. gallon) of pure alcohol per capita. The brewing industry experienced a consolidation process, in which the leading beverage giant was the Berlin Schultheiss company. The plunge in consumption was not simply a result of low purchasing power, but also of a changed climate of opinion in the wake of the debates prior to 1914 and of the success of prohibition abroad. Even the church-supported welfare organizations for alcoholics now made themselves heard in alcohol policy debates. Yet the disputes over the "alcohol question," of which most people had heard quite enough before 1914, met with little sympathy. The "opponents of alcohol," in spite of considerable funding from the spirits monopoly created in 1918, rapidly lost support. Paradoxically, the influence of alcohol opponents grew in government health and welfare circles, particularly through the National Center against Alcoholism (Reichshauptstelle gegen den Alkoholismus), in which from 1921, like it or not, the temperance and abstinence forces sat down at the same table. The mass movement became professionalized. Ignoring low consumption, the experts proclaimed a "growing alcohol emergency," and the committal of alcoholics to medical institutions multiplied. When, however, the world economic crisis dictated more stringent savings measures, the abstainers' notions of racial hygiene experienced a renaissance: The "preservation of the race" was deemed to take precedence over therapy (thus the "conference of opponents of alcohol" in 1930).

In 1933, the country gained in Adolf Hitler a chancellor who was an abstainer (in public at least). The abstinence organizations believed their hour had come, and the Good Templars, for example, trumpeted: "The solution of the Jewish question must be followed by the solution of the alcohol question—Germany from alcohol free!" (quoted in Spode 1997: 51). Yet the "Führer" had no intention of splitting the "people's community" by means of a renewed conflict over alcohol, especially since Prohibition had failed in America and the Nazi Party held numerous drinkers in its own ranks. Rather, the regime put a stop to abstinence propaganda, disbanded the smaller associations, and placed reliable National Socialists in charge of the larger ones. In these measures, they experienced the least success with the churches and the most with the IOGT. Under its secretary-general, Theo Gläß, the IOGT admittedly had to dissolve its youth section and abandon its masonic ritual and its name (which it reinterpreted after 1945 as a "ban"), but at the same time it struggled successfully into a leading position in therapy and prevention.

The top organization, after several reincarnations, was the National Office against the Dangers of Alcohol and Tobacco (Reichsstelle gegen die Alkohol- und Tabakgefahren [RAT]). Nazi alcohol policies did not in the first instance strike out along any fundamentally distinctive path. According to the dominant German theory of the "addictive personality" (*Süchtigkeit*), whereby only those with prior congenital or psychic damage developed an addiction (to alcohol, drugs, or a certain behavior), a strict alcohol control policy along Scandinavian lines was regarded as pointless (consumption rose slightly up to the war but remained at the levels of the late 1920s). Instead, a mixture of measures still familiar today was employed, such as reduction of accessibility, educational campaigns, protective measures for youths, restrictions on advertising, and introduction of alcohol tests to curb drunken driving (a law especially fostered by SS chief Heinrich Himmler). These were expanded by some repressive measures on alcoholics, such as registration, bans on marriage, interdiction, and in some cases compulsory (rather than voluntary) committal to institutions.

The "alcohol emergency" would be conquered, as the Good Templars put it, "when everything biologically inferior is eradicated by the state, and everything fundamentally healthy is freed from addiction by the cooperation of the party, the asylums and the organizations of alcohol opponents" (quoted in Spode 1996: 166). The 1934 Law for the Prevention of Hereditarily Sick Offspring *(Gesetz zur Verhütung erbkranken Nachwuchses)* formed the centerpiece of this "eradication." It provided for forced sterilization in the event of eight hereditary diseases (epilepsy, blindness, deafness, and so forth), and in addition *could* be used in cases of "severe alcoholism." The law was largely drafted by Rüdin and was altogether a reflection of the contemporary state of research; it was known that an unequivocal diagnosis of alcoholism—whether genetic or acquired—is scarcely feasible. Therefore, the number of cases ordered to be sterilized by the "hereditary health courts" lagged behind the expectations of the antialcohol organizations. Around one-tenth of the estimated total number of 300,000 alcoholics (mostly male, in a population of 68 million) were compulsorily sterilized. The "reformable" were increasingly placed in institutions, in part even in concentration camps, where they were meant to be liberated from their addiction through hard labor. During the war, it is likely that some alcoholics fell victim to the euthanasia program, while others were assigned to "punishment battalions" on suicidal missions at the front line. The total number of victims of Nazi alcohol policies is not known.

The Postwar Period

In Germany, too, after the war a "wet" phase set in, in line with the global zeitgeist—a consequence of the double disaster of alcohol policy: prohibition and eugenics. Alcohol was considered to be harmless and chic. The antialcohol organizations became welfare and self-help agencies again after the foundation in the west of the Federal Republic of Germany in 1949. Alcoholics Anonymous (AA) arrived as a newcomer in 1953 (though only attracting significant membership a couple of decades later). Previously, pioneering alcohol research dwindled to a state of international marginalization (the hereditary-biological viewpoint and the theory of Süchtigkeit held sway into the 1970s). Altogether, the per capita consumption of pure alcohol tripled.

A woman lifts a large German beer mug (stein) *at the Oktoberfest beer festival in Munich (1952). (Hulton/Archive)*

A high of around 12 liters (3.2 U.S. gallons) was reached at the beginning of the 1980s, which reflected the record level of 1875. Yet, this concealed certain differences: First, the increase was greater with women than with men (who were therefore now drinking less than under the empire); second, wine, the hitherto exclusive beverage, penetrated into the urban middle classes in the 1950s and 1960s (reaching a per capita consumption level of 25 liters [6.6 U.S. gallons] by the 1980s). In the beginning, sweet wines of German origin predominated. Likewise, the beer market remained entirely the province of national products (approximately 145 liters [38 U.S. gallons] per capita), the largest manufacturer being Brau und Brunnen, which absorbed the Schultheiss company among others. In the first postwar decades, the "economic miracle" allowed strong growth in both purchasing power and leisure time, both of which encouraged consumption. Political intervention was cautious, however, and confined itself to the introduction of a blood-alcohol limit for car drivers in 1953, as well as moderate tax hikes and the distribution of educational materials. The discourse on prevention since the 1960s was fixated on the "new" drugs (hash, heroin, and so on), thus ignoring the growing number of alcohol-related deaths.

In the German Democratic Republic (GDR), too, per capita alcohol consumption tripled, reaching over 13 liters (3.4 U.S. gallons) of pure alcohol by 1989. One peculiarity was the enormous consumption of spirits (rising in the 1980s to 15 liters [nearly 4 U.S. gallons] per capita), despite heavy taxation. There were three decisive reasons for this: the schnapps tradition in the northeast, the surplus of purchasing power, and the shortage of wine. There were few vineyards to be found in East Germany, which therefore had to import inferior wines from southeastern Europe (some 11 liters [3.3 U.S. gallons] per capita in the 1980s). By 1980, the GDR drew level with the Federal Republic in beer consumption (around 140 liters [42 U.S. gallons]). The state breweries produced just two premium beers (which were usually difficult to obtain) and were not bound by the Purity Law.

In its battle against alcohol abuse, the GDR virtually returned to the eighteenth century. Alcoholism was viewed not as a disease, but as a kind of insubordination, as "a behavior foreign and damaging to socialist society" (quoted in Spode 1999: 55). Widespread abuse was officially ignored. Sovietization after 1945 under Walter Ulbricht destroyed existing structures and spaces infinitely more radically than had the Nazis in 1933. Thus, there were no longer any temperance or self-help organizations (the Protestant Church alone ran a substitute for the Blue Cross after 1957). Prevention and therapy were defined rather as a "pre-eminent task for the prevention of criminality" (quoted in Spode 1999: 55). On the Soviet model the zero blood-alcohol limit prevailed for drivers. And yet drunken driving was by no means uncommon. In the many "niches" of GDR society, an excessive drinking culture blossomed: in the family, circle of friends, workplace, or weekend cottage. Consumption occurred by preference in private: In the first place one did not then have to fear spies, and on the other hand the number of bars and restaurants had been drastically reduced, and began a gradual, renewed expansion only in the late 1970s. At the same time, in the Honecker era, alcoholism came to be seen officially as a disease and could be discussed in the media. Modern therapeutic institutions were set up, self-help groups allowed to form, and educational campaigns launched. By the time the Berlin Wall fell in 1989, both East and West Germany looked very similar in respect to the prevention of alcoholism.

The Present-Day Drinking Culture

Today, the division into wine, beer, and spirits regions cannot be delineated so sharply as before. Since the unification, there has occurred a sweeping assimilation of the new states in the east to the consumption levels and patterns of the old. Some regional characteristics have not of course altogether died out. In the northern coastal areas and in part also in the east, the consumption of schnapps remains the highest; in the south (Bavaria, Württemberg), it is beer that is the most consumed beverage; while in the wine-growing areas (the Rhine and Moselle valleys, Baden, Franconia, and so forth), wine predominates. And different beverage preferences conform to different consumption patterns. In the south and the southwest, moderate daily consumption at mealtimes and in the evening remains the rule: a half or a whole "measure" (*Maß*) of beer (1 liter or approximately 1 U.S. quart), or one or two *Schoppen* of wine (one-fourth liter or a little over one-half of a U.S. pint). In other regions and in the big cities, alcohol consumption is tied more strongly to social occasions or the weekend; alcohol is consumed less frequently, but in greater quantities on those occasions.

In many places, regional preferences in spirits prevail. The most important are clear brandies and cognacs, and with imports, rum and whiskey. The wine market in the wine-growing areas is dominated completely by the local product. Apart from this, wines from all over the world are consumed (primarily dry wines), with a preference for wines from Germany itself, France, Italy, and Spain. Germany is the world's largest importer and the fourth largest exporter of wine. With a per capita consumption of up to 5 liters (1.3 U.S. gallons), the Germans consume a great deal of sparkling wine; the preference here is for the (in part, very good) native champagnes (*Sekt*). In Hesse, cider maintains its position against beer. Germany is the fourth largest beer producer in the world; barely one-tenth of that beer is exported. The domestic market remains firmly in German hands, despite the fact that the Purity Law has been rescinded by the European Union and functions purely for identification purposes now. There exist some 5,000 kinds of beer, among them countless regional specialties (*Rauchbier, Kölsch, Weisse,* and so on). Although the beer market is dominated increasingly on the one hand by premium beers marketed nationwide and on the other by cheap brands, almost 1,300 independent breweries have managed to survive, most of them small concerns in northern Bavaria.

Overall alcohol consumption remains at a high, albeit slowly sinking, level of around 10 liters (2.6 U.S. gallons) of pure alcohol per capita. At least half of this is beer (120 liters [31.5 U.S. gallons]), with wine and Sekt (together around 23 liters [6 U.S. gallons]) and spirits (around 6 liters [1.5 U.S. gallons]) each accounting for one-quarter. Income from tax stands at 3.5 billion Euros; spirits and Sekt are taxed the most heavily, and wine not at all since 1925. As usual, consumption is distributed unevenly. Men drink almost twice as much as women. About one-tenth of the population are (almost) total abstainers, while at the other end of the scale, one-tenth are heavy consumers, imbibing nearly one-half of the entire amount of alcohol.

Given the large number and variety of drinking establishments, it may come as a surprise to learn that most alcohol is drunk at home with the family. A frequent occasion for this is the visit of acquaintances or relatives. The shared meal without beer or wine is scarcely imaginable. And here a toast (*Prost!* or *Zum Wohl!*) is obligatory before the first sip, at which the glasses are often clinked together. The typical drink for special occasions is Sekt, though occasionally a punch bowl is prepared. And yet, the home is also a location of unsociable drinking. On the one hand, drinking excesses can be kept hidden there, and on the other, the increase in single households and the decline of the pub lead to solitary consumption.

In public, drinking is strictly limited to certain times and locations. The person who climbs on board the tram with an open beer can, for example, risks disapproving stares. Eastern European immigrants who do not know this rule are therefore regarded as drunkards. The most important space for public consumption is the tavern, which is merely a juridical umbrella term, encompassing everything from an expensive restaurant to a beer garden to a discotheque. The most common type of tavern is the traditional bar or pub (*Kneipe*): It consists of a serving area with the bar and some tables, usually with a couple of additional rooms. The beer is drawn from the tap, the food consists of mostly just simple dishes, and the air is heavy with smoke. The pub serves primarily as a neighborhood communication center, though outsiders, too, can make contact quickly here. Originally a male domain, the pub has become frequented by women as well, even though they are still in the minority. Drinking times in the pub are generally the late evening and Sunday morning, though in the big cities it is only the elderly who still go for a Sunday morning drink. In general, the significance of the pub is in decline, for it is being preempted increasingly by restaurants, cafés, and bars or nightclubs, respectively.

Alcohol consumption on the streets is at best a sign of youthful exuberance rather than depravity. At the same time, however, there are special occasions on which public drunkenness is positively expected, such as Ascension Day or village marksmen's festivals. At Mardi Gras (*Karneval*) in the south and west, scarcely anyone remains sober, while in the Protestant big cities, especially Berlin, street festivals are increasingly assuming this function. In the pub and the domestic sphere, too, it is permissible to "drink one more than thirst demands," though not in the face of emotional problems: Alcohol is a drug of sociability, bound by norms and rules that limit its abuse. In this vein, drunken driving is not merely regarded as a legal problem (the blood-alcohol limit is 0.05), but usually also as a moral one. Children are not meant to drink any alcohol, while youths may do so from the age of fourteen to sixteen (the Youth Protection Law permits the purchase of wine and beer from age sixteen, and of spirits from age eighteen). Admittedly, the boundaries of what is permitted are often trampled on, and they are also hotly disputed in various social settings and interest groups. It comes as no surprise that estimates of the numbers of alcoholics are also contradictory, reaching from 1 percent to 5 percent of the population. Since 1947, the prevention of alcohol abuse has been the domain above all of the German Central Office against the Dangers of Addiction (Deutsche Hauptstelle gegen die Suchtgefahren [DHS]). As the successor organization to the

RAT, the DHS was and is connected with the Good Templars (Theo Gläß held the presidency, with gaps, from 1951 to 1965). Its principal aim is the reduction of average consumption, according to the "total consumption model" (as explained in the World Health Organization entry in this volume). The Federal Agency for Health Education (Bundeszentrale für gesundheitliche Aufklärung) devotes itself primarily to youth, often in cooperation with the DHS. On top of this, the forum associated with the German Initiative for the Promotion of a Responsible Usage of Alcoholic Beverages (DIFA) is financed by the alcohol industry to promote "responsible drinking," especially in high-risk groups.

Hasso Spode, translated by Geoffrey Giles

See also: Alcoholics Anonymous (AA); Austria; Beer; Forel, Auguste; Good Templars (IOGT); Toasts; Wine; World Health Organization (WHO)

References

Fahrenkrug, Hermann. "Alcohol and the State in Nazi Germany, 1933–1945" in *Drinking, Behavior and Belief in Modern History,* edited by Susanna Barrows and Robin Room, 315–334. Berkeley: University of California Press, 1991.

Giles, Geoffrey J. "Classroom Temperance in Early Twentieth Century Germany" in *The Social Role and Evolution of the Teaching Profession in Historical Context,* edited by Simo Seppo, 4: 77–86. 6 vols. Joensuu: University of Joensuu Faculty of Education, 1988.

———. "Die Alkoholfrage im Dritten Reich" in *Drogalkohol.* 10, no. 3 (1986): 257–265.

———. "Student Drinking in the Third Reich: Academic Tradition and the Nazi Revolution" in *Drinking, Behavior and Belief in Modern History,* edited by Susanna Barrows and Robin Room, 132–143. Berkeley: University of California Press, 1991.

Jahrbuch Sucht. Geesthacht: Neuland-Verlag; annual journal of the Deutsche Hauptstelle gegen die Suchtgefahren.

Roberts, James S. *Drink, Temperance and the Working Class in Nineteenth-Century Germany.* Boston: Allen and Unwin, 1984.

———. "The Tavern and Politics in the German Labor Movement, c. 1870–1914" in *Drinking, Behavior and Belief in Modern History,* edited by Susanna Barrows and Robin Room, 98–111. Berkeley: University of California Press, 1991.

Spode, Hasso. "Alkoholismusprävention in Deutschland. Vom 'Kreuzug wider den Branntwein' zum 'Aktionsplan Alkohol'" in *Suchtwirtschaft,* edited by Aldo Legnaro and Arnold Schmieder, 41–69. Münster: Lit-Verlag, 1999.

———. "The First Step Toward Sobriety: The 'Boozing Devil' in Sixteenth-Century Germany" in *Contemporary Drug Problems.* 21, no. 3 (1994): 453–484.

———. *Die Macht der Trunkenheit. Kultur- und Sozialgeschichte des Alkohols in Deutschland.* Opladen: Leske & Budrich, 1993.

———. "Thematisierungskonjunkturen des Problems Alkohol" in *Psychomed.* 8, no. 3 (1996): 163–172.

Tappe, Heinrich. *Auf dem Weg zur modernen Alkoholkultur. Alkoholproduktion . . . vom frühen 19. Jahrhundert bis zum Ersten Weltkrieg.* Stuttgart: Steiner, 1994.

Tlusty, B. Ann. *Bacchus and Civic Order: The Culture of Drink in Early Modern Germany.* Charlottesville: University Press of Virginia, 2001.

Gin

Gin is a distilled alcoholic beverage that can be made from a variety of cereals and draws its signature flavor from the juniper berries that also give it its name. Originally known as *eau de genièvre* (juniper water), it was later contracted to *geneva,* which in turn was shortened and anglicized to "gin" when the drink became popular in England. The historical importance of gin lies largely in a supposed "gin craze" in England in the first half of the eighteenth century, when gin consumption was blamed for widespread immorality and social disruption.

Origins and Development of the Trade

Gin was originally developed in the Netherlands in the sixteenth century. It seems to have been very popular among English soldiers who served in Europe during the religious wars, and was very likely brought to England by them. But its real popularity in England dated from 1688, when William of Orange, a Dutch noble, replaced James II as king of England in the "Glorious Revolution."

The presence of a popular king of Dutch origin, together with a series of wars between England and France, gave gin a potential advantage over French wine and brandy on the English market. French wine and brandy were in erratic supply because of the wars, and from 1690 until the 1720s, the English Parliament began to favor gin, which was increasingly portrayed as a patriotic drink. Parliament broke the Distillers Company's monopoly over distilling and allowed virtually anyone to make spirits commercially as long as they paid the required duties. At two pence a gallon, the duty on spirits was low, while those that applied to beer were increased by up to 100 percent.

Deregulation led to the establishment of many distilleries, such that there were an estimated 1,500 in and around London by 1736. Most (perhaps 1,200) were small-scale operations using equipment worth less than £100, and only perhaps one in six owned stills and other equipment valued at more than £1,000.

Parliament also made it easier to sell spirits. Retailers did not have to buy licenses and, because they did not sell food or offer accommodation, they needed more modest premises than alehouse keepers. In 1720, legislation exempted distillers and spirits retailers from the detested obligation of billeting troops—a burden that remained on innkeepers, stable keepers, and others.

Under these favorable commercial conditions, a buoyant market, and growing demand, the number of "dramshops" (as small retailers of spirits were known) flourished. According to contemporary reports, there were more than 6,000 in London by 1725, and they accounted for one in every four houses in districts like Westminster and Saint Giles.

The output from London's stills fed what appeared to be insatiable appetites for spirits. Taxed production rose fivefold between 1688 and 1720 (from half a million to 2.5 million gallons) and to that must be added an unknown volume of spirits produced illicitly and not recorded in the official figures. But the duty on spirits was low enough that, even when it was applied, spirits remained an attractive alternative to ale and beer in the all-important terms of cost in relation to alcoholic strength.

The character and quality of the spirits were very varied. Most were made from corn, but they were often flavored—sometimes with juniper berries, sometimes by such additives as coriander, sulfuric acid, and oil of turpentine—and often sweetened with sugar. The sweetness is thought to have contributed to its appeal to women in particular, although European tastes were tending toward sweetness in a more general sense.

The "Gin Panic"

Everything supported the English spirits industry in the early 1700s, and by the 1720s alarm was being expressed about levels of spirits consumption and the implications for health and social order. The 2.5 million gallons legally produced in 1720 were enough to provide every Londoner each year with three gallons of spirits, the equivalent of 15 standard modern bottles, or an ounce a day for every man, woman, and child in the metropolis.

The formula "man, woman, and child" is generally a pointless abstraction when expressing the per capita consumption of alcohol, for children historically drank far less than adults, and women less than men. But it has resonance in the context of the eighteenth-century English "gin panic" because much of the anxiety rested on the belief that gin was being abused not only by men, but also by women and children.

The spirits in question were dubbed "Mother Gin," a name that clearly linked it to women and children, and it was claimed that women fed gin to their older children directly and to their infants via maternal milk. Front and center in the most famous representation of the gin craze, William Hogarth's *Gin Alley* (etched in 1751 as the gin panic drew to a close) depicts a nursing woman, her breasts exposed. She is sprawled on a flight of steps and so insensibly drunk that she is unaware that her infant has fallen from her arms and is toppling head-first to the street below.

Hogarth was inspired by the many works of the period that vividly described the effects of gin drinking on women and their families. One wrote that if "child-bearing Women are habituated to strong inflaming Liquors, the little Embrios [sic] must and will have a share" that would cause them to develop "a Love of Strong Liquors before they can call for them, or even see them" (*Distilled Spirituous Liquors the Bane* 1736: 35–36). It was one thing to drink while pregnant, he noted, but many mothers and nurses fed their children gin, and the result was a decline in the demand for milk.

Another described the progeny of the gin-drinking mother in these words: "one is bandy-legg'd, another hump-back'd, another goggle-ey'd, another with a Monkey's Face, and all of them wearing some visible Mark of their Mother's Folly" (*Dissertation on Mr. Hogarth's Six Prints* 1751: 14). ("Mother" here might refer both to the mother of the children and to "Mother Gin.") One commentator noted that the demand for milk had declined, and he attributed it to mothers and nurses feeding their children gin.

As monstrous as were the children described here, they were at least the survivors of their mothers' alcoholic habits. Many antispirits writers pointed out that these deadly beverages led to a declining birth rate and rising death rate.

The special attention to the effects of alcohol on children reflected an eighteenth-century interest in and concern for fertility and population growth. This was not confined to England, for all European states had an interest in fostering robust demographic growth for political, economic, and military purposes. The stress on the particular evils of women's drinking also echoed a contemporary reassertion of the belief that women were destined by nature to be mothers and that they bore particular responsibilities toward their families. From this perspective, excessive drinking by women was unnatural.

An array of other arguments was ranged against spirits. One was that drinking gin led to a dramatic loss of appetite for nourishing food. But scenarios of an undernourished underclass were not as alarming as the prospect of declining profits for producers and merchants of meat and other produce. Some works told of butchers throwing meat away, or feeding it to the dogs, because no one was buying it. Others reported dairy farmers pouring unsold milk into the sewers.

Finally, there was the argument that the gin craze was socially disruptive in the most banal sense. Not only did it interfere with family stability and the prosperity and health of the population, but it also led to crime and immorality. Men and women were driven to theft, murder, and prostitution in order to support their drinking.

Against the arguments for prohibiting or restricting distilling and the sale of spirits were more modest proposals based on the assumption that the scenarios of social collapse were exaggerated. Some writers in this vein insisted that ale drinkers were as unruly as gin drinkers and that, as far as immorality went, dramshops paled against the excesses to be found in alehouses. They argued that the distilling industry contributed to the prosperity of grain growers and that others benefited in turn, among them implement makers, carters, and the seamen who manned the coastal vessels that carried the grain to London.

Legal Restrictions on the Gin Trade

The debate on the scale of the gin craze and its social effects continued from the 1720s until the 1750s and resulted in a series of laws that attempted to deal with the problems. The first Gin Act, passed in 1729, raised the duty on spirits thirtyfold, from two pence to five shillings, and imposed a licensing fee of £20 a year. The act remained in force only four years, however, before being repealed as ineffective. The volume of spirits produced legally continued to rise, from 2.5 million gallons in 1720 to 3.8 million in 1730. And once the 1729 law was repealed, the volume shot up to 6.4 million gallons in 1735. To these taxed totals, we must add an unknown quantity of illicitly made spirits.

Soon after the repeal of the 1729 Gin Act, another campaign, led by judges and bishops, argued that gin was causing lawlessness to spread. Parliament responded by passing a law in 1736 that imposed a licensing fee of £50 a year. At this point, the defenders of gin reacted, and there were threats of riots in the streets of London.

As unworkable as the 1729 act, this new law was abandoned after only three years, and the manufacture, sale, and consumption of spirits was effectively unrestrained. Consumption seems to have peaked in 1743, when 8.2 million gallons were taxed. That represented more than a gallon per head of the English population, but if we take into account illicit production, variations in consumption by gender and age, and the fact that the drinking of spirits was concentrated in London and a few other ports and industrial centers, adult men must have had easy access to up to ten gallons of spirits a year, about a modern bottle per week. Clearly, there was enough in circulation for a substantial minority of adults to drink large quantities on a regular basis.

From the mid-1740s, however, spirits production declined, and when another act was passed in 1751 the "craze" was already ebbing. The 1751 regulations forbade distillers to sell their own product, and imposed a modest licensing fee of £2 on retailers. It is easier to understand why spirits became so attractive in the first place than why they lost their appeal. Perhaps the series of laws, as ineffective as they were, dislocated production and made supplies unreliable. Perhaps consumer tastes shifted back to beer, and to the new, stronger porter variety in preference.

In the later 1750s, too, the thirty-year series of good corn harvests came to an end. The 1757, 1759, and 1760 harvests were so poor that distilling was banned in order to protect food supplies. By then, spirits production was already in decline, and the bans simply intensified an existing trend.

The Discourse over Gin's Social Roots: Class and Gender Perspectives

The gin panic brought into the open a number of attitudes toward the relationship of alcohol to society. The war waged against gin was also class war. The opponents of unregulated spirits selling portrayed the industry as one largely maintained by and for the indigent, unruly, and dangerous popular classes. Gin shops were described as squalid hangouts for the dregs of society, and dram sellers as poor and shiftless. The link between spirits and crime was carefully drawn in class terms: Better-off citizens were portrayed as able to enjoy their brandy and cordials (flavored spirits) responsibly, but the lower classes were shown as able neither to afford their coarse liquor without condemning their families to destitution at best and death at worst, nor to consume it without sinking into immorality and crime.

In fact, the bulk of spirits retailers appear to have been drawn from the same social groups as other food and drink retailers, and their premises were little different from those of other small-scale traders. But in some respects, the gin trade was somewhat different from others, and again there was a link to women. It seems likely, first, that women were more highly represented as gin sellers. About a quarter of licensed sellers and perhaps a third of unlicensed traders were women, while three-quarters of sellers jailed between 1738 and 1739 because they could not pay the £10 fine were women.

These figures suggest that women were more highly represented in the gin trade than among, say, food sellers (where they made up 10 to 15 percent of the total), and were especially common at the poorer levels, probably among street sellers who offered gin from stalls or barrows. This would have reinforced the feminization of the gin panic.

It is possible, too, that women patronized dramshops more frequently than they did alehouses. Women rarely visited alehouses without their men, but they might well have gone to drink spirits. Gin was often identified as a woman's drink, especially when it was sweetened, and the fact that many dram sellers were women might have made dramshops new centers of female sociability. The recurrent association of gin and women in the antispirits campaigns raises the possibility that it reflected, at least in part, anxiety about women as well as about the social implications of lower-class drinking.

Although gin has a longer history as one of the spectrum of distilled alcoholic beverages widely available since the seventeenth century, it is one of only two (the other is absinthe) to have given rise to such concern that attempts were made to ban it or limit its availability specifically.

Rod Phillips

See also: Absinthe; Art, Representations of Drinking in; Gin Craze

References

A Dissertation on Mr. Hogarth's Six Prints Lately Publish'd. London: 1751.

Distilled Spirituous Liquors the Bane of the Nation. London: 1736.

Warner, Jessica. *Craze: Gin and Debauchery in an Age of Reason.* London: Profile, 2003.

Watney, John. *Mother's Ruin: The Story of Gin.* London: Owen, 1976.

Gin Craze

The "gin craze" refers to several decades of strife involving consumption of gin in eighteenth-century London. From 1721 to 1751, excessive drinking of *geneva,* as gin was called in Holland, was blamed for escalating crime rates, increasing mortality, and a host of issues relating to a stable society. The impetus for this

The Drunkard's Children *(1848) by George Cruikshank depicts children neglected by their parents and drunkards having a drink at a gin palace. (Hulton/Archive)*

prodigious consumption is found in protectionist laws, taxing and licensing policies, a surplus of grain, and political influence of those benefiting from the "craze."

In 1690, the Dutch-born King William III prohibited the importing of foreign wines and spirits, a decision related to hostilities with France. The king broke the monopoly of the London distillers' guild and encouraged entrepreneurs to enter the liquor business by utilizing English grain. Before this, English consumption of gin was a little over a half a million gallons annually; it would grow to 11 million gallons by 1750.

In 1720, an act of Parliament excused any distiller from quartering soldiers, an expensive requirement for alehouse keepers, innkeepers, and the like. Over the next several decades, Parliament waffled as it attempted to meet complaints about too much gin consumption and the interests of landowners who profited from excellent harvests of grain and a strong distillery market. In 1726, author Daniel Defoe submitted a lengthy document to Parliament stressing the benefits of the industry for the English economy. Despite this support, Parliament attempted on several occasions to regulate the selling of spirits but without much success. For instance, a gin-specific licensing bill led to the selling of "parliament brandy" on the streets, a new name for the same old gin. The 1736 Gin Act created an informer system in an attempt to arrest violators of distillery laws. Informers often had to be rescued from mobs that would throw them in the Thames River or attempt to burn down their quarters. Troops had to be called out several times to quell street disturbances provoked by political efforts to control gin drinking.

During the "craze" decades, availability of geneva was remarkable. Street vendors offered a ladle of gin at a half pence, from a kettle being pushed in a wheelbarrow-like vehicle. Shops of all sorts sold gin. Signs appeared advertising "drunk for a penny, dead drunk for two pence and straw for nothing," the last being a generous offer of bedding. At one time, surveys indicated there were 7,000 gin shops in London. In a notorious area, where 2,000 houses existed, 506 were gin shops. Newspapers reported geneva-drinking contests in which a winner consumed three quarts of gin and then died or was drinking his eleventh half pint of gin when he died. Horror stories of children's deaths as a result of gin-drinking mothers or nannies further aroused public concern.

Such reports stimulated public consciousness, and intensive lobbying efforts culminated in legislation in 1751 that raised the price of licenses and prohibited distillers from selling liquor directly to the public or to unlicensed retailers. Defoe recanted his earlier support for favorable distilling laws, and as the "craze" era was winding down, William Hogarth's prints of *Gin Lane* and *Beer Street* articulated the antigin position. Strong opposition, combined with economic changes, brought geneva under control.

James R. McIntosh

See also: Gin

References

Austin, Gregory A. *Alcohol in Western Society from Antiquity to 1800.* Santa Barbara, CA: ABC-CLIO, 1985.

Clark, Peter. "The 'Mother Gin' Controversy in the Early Eighteenth Century" in *Transactions of the Royal Historical Society.* 38 (1988): 63–84.

Coffey, T. G. "Beer Street: Gin Lane: Some Views of 18th-Century Drinking" in *Quarterly Journal of Studies on Alcohol.* 27 (1966): 669–692.

Dillon, Patrick. *The Much-Lamented Death of Madam Geneva: The Eighteenth-Century Gin Craze.* London: Review, 2002 [also published as *Gin: The Much-Lamented Death of Madam Geneva.* Boston: Justin, Charles, 2003].

Warner, Jessica. *Craze: Gin and Debauchery in an Age of Reason.* New York: Four Walls Eight Windows, 2002.

Warner, Jessica, and Frank Ives. "'Damn You, You Informing Bitch': Vox Populi and the Unmaking of the Gin Act of 1736" in *Journal of Social History.* 33, no. 2 (1999): 299–330.

"Girl" Drinks

"Girl" drinks are sugary, syrupy, sweet alcoholic drinks, often in bright colors and with cutesy names. Both men and women may enjoy girl drinks, which are also known as after-dinner drinks, fruity drinks, beach drinks, boat drinks, coronary cocktails, prom cocktails, nickname drinks, and umbrella drinks. They may seem more like milkshakes or desserts than alcoholic drinks, but they can pack a punch in large quantities.

Some of the more notorious girl drinks include the Brandy Alexander (brandy, crème de cacao, cream), Pink Lady (gin, grenadine syrup, cream), Pink Squirrel (crème de cacao, crème de noyau, grenadine syrup, cream, maraschino cherry), Grasshopper (crème de menthe, crème de cacao, cream), Kamikaze (vodka, triple sec, lime juice), Piña Colada (rum, coconut milk, pineapple juice), Sex on the Beach (black raspberry liqueur, melon liqueur, pineapple and/or cranberry juice, vodka), Fuzzy Navel (orange juice, peach schnapps, vodka), Cuba Libre (rum, cola), Sidecar (brandy, lemon, cointreau), Singapore Sling (gin, cherry brandy, sugar, lemon juice, bitters, soda), Angel's Tit (maraschino liqueur with whipped cream on top and a maraschino cherry nipple), Screaming Orgasm (Grand Marnier, Kahlua, Bailey's Irish Cream), Teeny Weeny Woo Woo (peach schnapps, vodka, cranberry juice), Slippery Nipple (peppermint schnapps, Bailey's Irish Cream), Silk Panties (peach schnapps, vodka), and the Snickertini (sweet liqueurs, vanilla ice cream, pieces of Snickers candy bars). Recipes, of course, vary from bartender to bartender.

Questionable drinks, halfway between girl drinks and something respectable, might include the Cosmopolitan, Margarita, Daiquiri, White Russian, and Mai Tai.

Early forms of the girl drink existed as early as the 1890s in the Ladies' Delight (brandy, rum, cold coffee, ice cream, and sugar) and the Ladies' Great Favorite (sherry, port wine, brandy, seltzer, ice cream, sugar). Sweet, often fruity cocktails, precursors to girl drinks, were popular during the Prohibition era, when fruit juice was used to mask poor-quality liquor. The girl drink's heyday was the 1970s and 1980s, but even in the early part of the twenty-first century, chain restaurants like TGI Fridays boast glossy menus of dessert drinks.

The idea of the girl drink has become a part of popular culture, often as a way for men to question each other's masculinity. The Canadian comedy troupe the Kids in the Hall, for example, performed a television sketch called "Girl Drink Drunk" in which one character abstains from drinking since he doesn't like the taste of alcohol; the other convinces him to try a "Chocolate Choo Choo," a girl drink that he promises will taste like candy. Soon, the would-be abstainer turns into a Girl Drink Drunk, hiding paper umbrellas and coconuts and straws in his office, drinking beverages like the "Squash Strawberry Alley Cat." And the 9 October 2002 issue of the on-line humor magazine *The Onion* contained an article titled "Newly Out Gay Man Overdoing It," in which a character who used to drink single-malt scotch—a perfectly masculine choice—now prefers Cosmos and Mai Tais.

Jessy Randall

References

Federman, Rachel. *Girl Drinks: 101 Cocktails for Every Occasion.* London: Carlton, 2002.

Lanza, Joseph. *The Cocktail: The Influence of Spirits on the American Psyche.* New York: St. Martin's, 1995.

Gladstone, William Ewart (1809–1898)

William Ewart Gladstone (1809–1898), Liberal prime minister in Britain, irritated and frustrated temperance reformers, most of whom were his enthusiastic supporters on other questions. Regarding alcoholic drink, Gladstone and the temperance reformers often disagreed. In 1860, to promote light wines as a less intoxicating alternative to beer, he helped create a new "grocers' license" for the sale of wine for off-premises consumption. This extended the alcoholic drink sales to a new and respectable site that middle-class women frequented. In gratitude, the proprietors of Gilbeys, a wine distribution company, remained staunch Liberals when most other leaders in the alcoholic drink trade became Unionists. For many years, Gladstone resisted the pressure of advanced temperance reformers to endorse what they called direct local veto—referendums for local prohibition. Nor did he think that the program of moderate reformers,

William Ewart Gladstone (1809–1898) (Perry-Castaneda Library)

the reduction in the number of licensed premises, would bring about sobriety. He appeared willing to consider financial compensation of licensed holders who lost their property because of a change in public policy. It was for tactical political reasons that Gladstone in 1891 included direct local veto in the Newcastle program.

Toward the end of his life, in 1895, Gladstone declared his sympathy for free trade in drink sales—the issue of an unlimited number of licenses for the sale of alcoholic drink. Both temperance reformers and those who had invested in licensed premises made valuable by their monopoly value were hostile to this policy. At the same time, Gladstone expressed sympathy for the Scandinavian experiments, called the Gothenburg scheme, for quasi-public management of the retail sale of alcoholic drink in order to eliminate the profit motive for increasing sales. Halfheartedly, he acknowledged that he did "not doubt that Local Option is in principle sound" but questioned whether it offered a practical solution to the drink problem.

David M. Fahey

See also: Gothenburg Schemes/Disinterested Management; Liberal Party (United Kingdom)

Reference

Cherrington, Ernest Hurst, et al., eds. *Standard Encyclopedia of the Alcohol Problem.* 6 vols. Westerville, OH: American Issue Publishing, 1925–1930. 1111–1112.

Good Templars (IOGT)

The Good Templars, a fraternal temperance society, comprised the world's largest and most militant teetotal organization in the late nineteenth and early twentieth centuries. For many years an English-speaking organization, the core of its membership today is in Sweden, with many affiliated organizations in Asia and Africa.

Origins

In 1851, young men and boys who previously had belonged to the Knights of Jericho founded the original Order of Good Templars in west-central New York State. It disappeared after a breakaway group in the city of Syracuse organized the Independent Order of Good Templars (IOGT) in 1852. A few days after the IOGT came into existence, a new recruit named Nathaniel Curtis, a poorly educated reformed drinker, was elected to be its leader. He established two of its distinctive principles: acceptance of women as members on a basis of nominal equality and avoidance of mutual insurance schemes that might exclude the very poor and the unwell. During the few months that he headed the IOGT, he recruited a cadre of leaders who, like him, lived in Ithaca, New York. A Methodist minister drafted a new, more religious ritual that borrowed heavily from that of the Odd Fellows. After Curtis stepped aside, middle-class, life-long abstainers dominated the IOGT leadership. In its first years, the IOGT grew rapidly in upstate New York, adjacent Ontario and Pennsylvania, and beyond.

In 1855, a convention held at Cleveland, Ohio, restructured the central organization. State and provincial grand lodges sent representatives to annual meetings of the Right Worthy Grand Lodge (RWGL), the supreme authority in the IOGT. The chief officer was called the Right Worthy Grand Templar. At first, the reorganized IOGT stumbled. Its first secretary, a woman, was ineffective and resigned. In one year, the head of the IOGT did not even bother to attend the annual meeting of the RWGL. A quarrel over a revised ritual led to a schism. Some Canadian members broke away to organize the British-American Templar Order. More important, membership fell drastically during the early years of the U.S. Civil War.

Revival and Decline in North America

The IOGT survived, recovered, and by the last years of the war, began to grow rapidly. In the mid-1850s, when many teetotalers abandoned the Maine Law as politically impracticable, the IOGT had boldly committed itself to prohibition. In the mid-1860s, the temperance movement made prohibition its objective, and the IOGT stood in the front lines of the battle. In addi-

The Independent Order of Good Templars, the world's largest and most militant fraternal temperance society (Library of Congress)

tion, the IOGT benefited from able leaders: Simeon B. Chase of Pennsylvania and Samuel D. Hastings of Wisconsin. In 1863, the Good Templars of the United States and Canada numbered about 57,000. By the end of 1868, the IOGT claimed more than a half million members.

For the rest of the nineteenth century, the IOGT in North America remained successful at recruiting large numbers of new members. Unfortunately, it had difficulty retaining them, so, although the total membership fluctuated, it drifted downwards. New strategies competed with the fraternal lodges for the time and energy of committed teetotalers. Ironically, Good Templars dominated the National Prohibition Party, founded in 1869, in its early years. Female Good Templars played a large role in the direct action women's temperance crusade of 1873 through 1874. When a single-sex organization, the Woman's Christian Temperance Union (WCTU), was created later in 1874, women such as Amanda M. Way and Martha McClellan, who had headed Midwestern grand lodges in the late 1860s and mid-1870s, could sidestep male sexism and fight drink in their own national organization.

In North America, after the late 1860s, many grand lodges declined, but a few flourished. For instance, the order had virtually died out during the late 1850s in its native New York State, but after the Civil War it reconstituted its grand lodge there. New York State became a durable stronghold that published a succession of Good Templar newspapers such as the *New York Templar.* More important, after the war, the IOGT attracted numerous recruits from the white population in Kentucky and other former slave states and also in England and Scotland.

Joseph Malins and England

In 1868, a young working-class English immigrant named Joseph Malins was initiated as a member of the Good Templar order in Philadelphia. Soon he returned to England, where in the same year in his home city of Birmingham he organized the first Good Templar lodge outside North America. It was named

Columbia Lodge in recognition of the American origins of Good Templary. Completely inexperienced, Malins had to develop his skills as an organizer and presiding officer, speaker, and writer. From the start, he demonstrated complete commitment to Good Templary.

After a difficult beginning, Malins made England's the most important grand lodge in the IOGT. In 1873, the Grand Lodge of England played host to the first meeting of the RWGL held outside North America. In 1874, the Grand Lodge of England attained its largest membership, over 210,000. Although the membership subsequently declined, the Grand Lodge of England retained a substantial membership well into the twentieth century. Few Good Templars headed a grand lodge for more than a few years, but Malins headed England's from its institution in 1870 until his retirement in 1914. The Grand Lodge of England for many years sponsored a weekly newspaper, first the *Templar* and later the *Good Templars' Watchword.*

The Good Templars also established themselves elsewhere in the British Isles, notably in Scotland. Good Templary often flourished among evangelical Protestants in proximity to hard drinking. Sometimes this meant that drinkers, even alcoholics, sought fraternal support in breaking the drink habit by becoming Good Templars but, in the end, lacked perseverance in maintaining their new obligation to total abstinence. Probably this helps explain why Scotland exhibited a dramatic membership turnover. During the late nineteenth century, this small country initiated over a million members in a little over thirty years, but at any particular time had only a few tens of thousands of members in good standing. The Scottish Grand Lodge published a monthly newspaper, the *Good Templar.*

Conflict over African American Membership

At the same time that the British grand lodges sprang into existence, Good Templary grew rapidly in the American South. The Grand Lodge of Kentucky, the largest of the southern grand lodges, often claimed to speak for the entire South. In recognition of the new prominence in the order of the southerners, J. J. Hickman of Kentucky headed the RWGL from 1874 to 1877 and again from 1879 to 1881. A kind of alliance developed between the southern grand lodges and the Grand Lodge of Ontario, with a Canadian serving as international secretary during much of the 1870s.

A crisis developed in the IOGT over the rights of prospective African American members in jurisdictions that did not want them. From its earliest days, the IOGT had taught a kind of universalism that welcomed men and women, prosperous and poor, life-long abstainers and reformed drinkers. Unlike the situation in other fraternal temperance societies, the IOGT never adopted a general rule against African American membership, and there were a few blacks in the order prior to the Civil War. Individual grand lodges decided whether to admit blacks or not. In practice, admitting blacks often meant segregated local lodges that had a right to representation at grand lodge meetings. The question of African American membership became important after the Civil War when ex-slaves could ask to join. A few black lodges were organized in North Carolina before a white grand lodge was organized and acquired a monopoly over chartering lodges within its jurisdiction.

The IOGT was on the road to schism. The newly important Grand Lodges of England and Scotland fought for the principle of universal membership without regard to race. Some North Americans accused Malins of wanting to dominate the international organization and also of fearing that the RWGL might break up the English Grand Lodge into smaller provincial grand lodges. The grand lodges of white southerners tried to conciliate the grand lodges in the Midwest, in New England, and in Canada by sponsoring a fraternal temperance society for blacks only, called the True Reformers. In 1876, unable to get support for a policy that would welcome blacks into the IOGT, Malins and the other British delegates and a few North American allies walked out of a RWGL meeting in Louisville, Kentucky, and formed their own RWGL of the World. The white southerners offered a further concession, the creation of dual grand lodges, black organizations to parallel the white grand lodges.

From 1876 to 1887, two different international Good Templar organizations claimed to be the true IOGT. Often they were called the Malinites and the Hickmanites, after the English and Kentucky leaders. In some cases, there were bitter and long-lasting local splits, as for instance, in England where F. R. Lees rallied a minority of Good Templars against Malins in his own jurisdiction. For the most part, the schism was geographical, with North America, except for Nova Scotia, on one side and most of the British Isles, except for Ireland, on the other side. During the years of the schism, the IOGT spread beyond the English-speaking world. In particular, Sweden became the site of a powerful Good Templar movement, with two rival grand lodges affiliated with the different RWGLs.

Angry with Malins, nearly all the Good Templars in North America accepted the compromise of segregated grand lodges. Recent immigrants from England and black teetotalers, some of them from the British Empire, took a leading role in the small pro-Malins organizations. For instance, London-born Jessie Forsyth edited *Temperance Brotherhood* in Boston, while Nassau-born W. M. Artrell helped lead Florida's black grand lodge. William Wells Brown, best known as the first African American novelist, tried to organize blacks in Virginia, West Virginia, and Tennessee. In contrast, veteran abolitionists in the IOGT supported the Hickmanites. One of the most vehement opponents of Malins was a Canadian Indian known as Oronhyatekha, who did not see the conflict as being about white supremacy.

The practical reasons for the schism began to disintegrate. Although the British-dominated RWGL of the World tried to organize African American lodges, most of these lodges had only short lives. At the same time, the white grand lodges in the American South faded away. After the American-dominated RWGL elected a Midwestern leader, John B. Finch, who was

Jessie Forsyth (1847–1937) ca. 1887

committed to reunion, delegates from the two factions met in 1886 at Boston to negotiate an end to the schism. A key provision of the Boston basis for reunion declared segregated Good Templary a temporary expedient but did not give it any time limit. In the same geographical jurisdiction, there could be senior and subsequently chartered junior grand lodges. Meeting in 1887, at Saratoga Springs, New York, the rival RWGLs ratified the Boston agreement. In some grand lodges, the quarrel continued. Catherine Impey, a strong advocate of the rights of black people, eventually quit the Grand Lodge of England. Unexpectedly, Scandinavian immigrants made the most use of the option of parallel junior grand lodges. Language, not race, became the practical basis for separation in North America.

Internationalism

In the decades immediately following the 1887 reunion, the IOGT changed in various ways. Most obviously, it emphasized its internationalism. As a symbol of this, at the turn of the century the meaning of the initials IOGT was changed to International Order of Good Templars. The international organization tolerated controversial local policies in order to avoid schism. There still were splits, but they almost always were within national jurisdictions and often as much about personalities as about principles. The IOGT increasingly recruited the children of teetotal families and less often targeted adult drinkers. By the early twentieth century, the IOGT had collapsed in most of North America and had become essentially a northern European organization. When the British grand lodges also faded, the Grand Lodge of Sweden became dominant; there also was a large grand lodge in Germany. Edvard Wavrinsky was the first Scandinavian to head the Good Templar international organization. There was a brief international split in 1906 through 1923 when a few Europeans who disliked the religious character of the Good Templar ritual formed a small Neutral Order that substituted an ethical, nonreligious ritual. In the heyday of the Good Templar order, women in the northern grand lodges of the United States occasionally headed a grand lodge, often were elected to the important office of secretary, and usually were in charge of the work for children. Women seldom office held high office in England and still less frequently in Scotland and Scandinavia.

IOGT in the Twentieth Century and Beyond

In the 1950s, the initials IOGT acquired a new meaning, the International Organization of Good Templars. By that time, the notion of a fraternal order, with ritual lodges and ceremonial regalia, had lost appeal. Germany was virtually the only country where many Good Templars were recovering alcoholics.

Current IOGT membership figures are hard to find. In 1992, the IOGT claimed that with its youth organization it had 3.5 million members in more than fifty countries. In practice, most of these members belonged to organizations affiliated with the IOGT and did not necessarily identify themselves principally with the Good Templar society. Many of these men and women live in Asia and Africa.

Today, the IOGT maintains its world headquarters in England (known since 1990 as the IOGT International), where it publishes a magazine called the *Globe*. Strongly committed to internationalism, it emphasizes coalition with like-minded organizations around the globe and worries less about obtaining total abstinence pledges from a few than reducing the use of alcoholic beverages and drugs by the many. At the beginning of the twenty-first century, the *Globe* became the organ of the Global Alcohol Policy Alliance.

David M. Fahey

See also: British Medical Temperance Association (BMTA); British Women's Temperance Association (BWTA); Forel, Auguste; Germany; Hayler, Guy; Hoyle, William; Impey, Catherine; International Congresses on Alcoholism; IOGT International; Lees, Frederic Richard; Lucas, Margaret Bright; Malins, Joseph; Parker, Margaret Eleanor; Rechabite Friendly Society; Rutherford, Derek; Sons of Temperance; Winskill, Peter Turner; World Prohibition Federation

References

Fahey, David M., ed. *The Collected Writings of Jessie Forsyth, 1847–1937: The Good Templars and Temperance Reform on Three Continents.* Lewiston, NY: Edwin Mellen Press, 1988.

———. "How the Good Templars Began: Fraternal Temperance in New York State" in *Social History of Alcohol Review.* 38/39 (1999): 17–27.

———. "Joseph Malins" in *Oxford Dictionary of National Biography,* edited by H. C. G. Mathew and Brian Harrison. Oxford: Oxford University Press, forthcoming 2004.

———. *Temperance and Racism: John Bull, Johnny Reb, and the Good Templars.* Lexington: University Press of Kentucky, 1996.

Gooderham and Worts Distillery

Toronto's Gooderham and Worts distillery, once one of North America's largest nineteenth-century distilleries, is presently a whiskey brand name held by Hiram Walker and Sons Limited, a Canadian subsidiary of Allied Domecq. Gooderham and Worts traces its origins to a gristmill that English emigrant James Worts established at the mouth of Toronto's Don River in 1832. Upon Worts's death in 1834, the mill passed to his brother-in-law, William Gooderham, another emigrant Englishman. Three years later, Gooderham added a distillery to his mill for processing coarse grain into saleable whiskey. In 1845, he took his nephew, James Gooderham Worts, into a partnership styled Gooderham and Worts (G&W). From its earliest years, the G&W distillery benefited from a large and growing market in Toronto. The partners used this local advantage to finance the development of a sales agency network throughout Ontario and Quebec during the 1840s and 1850s. Such commercial links gave the Toronto distillers a decided advantage over most competitors when the completion of Canada's trunk-line railway system sped up the pace of consumer goods distribution. Timely plant improvement further enhanced G&W's competitive edge and afforded the firm the requisite scales of economy and capital strength to be price competitive in distant markets.

In 1856, James Gooderham Worts Jr. and William Gooderham's third and most commercially minded son, George Gooderham, were admitted to the firm. At the younger Gooderham's behest, the firm, anticipating the promise of interprovincial rail links, constructed a fully automated, five-story, brick and stone distillery of "mammoth proportions" in 1859 through 1861. Costing $200,000, the new distillery was the country's biggest and ranked among the continent's largest. In its first full year, 1862, the facility turned out over 700,000 imperial gallons (840,700 U.S. gallons) of proof spirits, a figure representing a quarter of Canadian production. Before construction, G&W accounted for only 6 percent of the national total. Most G&W whiskey was rye bottled under the brand names Toddy and Old Rye, sales of which ranged over the whole of central Canada and parts of the northern United States. The firm also exported to England. Despite a serious fire in 1869, G&W continued to grow as the frontrunner in a remarkably competitive race that saw the number of Canadian distilleries plunge from several dozen in 1860 to twelve by 1880. In the 1870s, the G&W distillery stood as Toronto's single largest industrial enterprise. By then, G&W had diversified into grain shipping and brokering, hog and cattle fattening (a sizeable business in its own right), and dairying. The firm also invested in railways, most especially in lines that radiated northward into Toronto's agricultural hinterland. Thus, G&W gained better control over their grain inputs. The partners also invested in financial institutions and real estate.

Distilling, however, remained the firm's core business. At the Paris world fair of 1878, G&W won a gold medal for its aged rye whiskey, the first of many such accolades. In the 1870s, the firm branched into supplying industrial alcohol for Canada's drug, chemical, and perfume sectors. In 1881 and 1882 respectively, William Gooderham and James Gooderham Worts died. George Gooderham took over the firm and incorporated it as Gooderham and Worts Limited in 1882. Under his first year of full control, the distillery attained a production milestone of 2 million imperial gallons (2,402,000 U.S. gallons), nearly half of the total Canadian output. Although Gooderham capably navigated the business through prohibition under the Canada Temperance Act during the 1880s, the distillery's output trailed off during the next decade, owing to competition from Hiram Walker (Canada's other major distiller), the rising popularity of beer and wine, a tariff-protected U.S. market, and a general economic depression. Nonetheless, G&W remained quite viable and even built a grand headquarters building in 1892. George Gooderham died in 1905 and willed the distillery to his four sons and T. G. Blackstock. New company President William G. Gooderham expanded sales in a western Canada swelling with millions of immigrants. He also seized upon new technologies, electrifying the distillery in the early 1900s and replacing horse-drawn wagons with gasoline-powered trucks. Moreover, he answered the automobile age's demand for alcohol-based antifreeze. Fortuitously, G&W's experience in industrial alcohol served the company well when whiskey distilling was forbidden under World War I restrictions.

After the war, G&W, as Canada's preeminent distiller, stood much to lose when confronted with various provincial statutes of prohibition. The Ontario Temperance Act of 1916, which only outlawed the provincial sale of beverage alcohol and not its manufacture, was cleverly circumvented by registering liquor sales outside the province. In the early 1920s, this was handled through an arrangement with Labatt, the London, Ontario, brewer, who maintained a nominal sales office in Buffalo, New York. A federal Order-in-Council soon closed such a loophole, and the Gooderhams, who were reluctant to involve themselves in rumrunning, but who had considerable means of income through nondistillery investments, sold their distillery to Harry Hatch's syndicate in 1923. Hatch merged it with Windsor's Hiram Walker to form Hiram Walker-Gooderham and Worts Limited. Under Hatch's management, smuggled G&W whiskey found ready reception with Americans thirsting under the Volstead Act. The Toronto distillery suffered somewhat under the Great Depression and the second world war, but the postwar boom was kind to G&W and saw the distillery diversify to meet the burgeoning markets for premium whiskey and gin. Industrial alcohol production also continued in importance.

Domestic fortunes reversed beginning in the 1980s, when the Canadian public turned away from spirits because of increasing abstinence, a growing preference for beer and wine, and the rising price of liquor resulting from higher taxation. Allied Lyons (now Allied Domecq) acquired Hiram Walker-Gooderham and Worts Limited in 1987. Three years later, Allied closed the G&W plant in Toronto, thus concluding 153 years of whiskey distilling on the site. Today, the G&W name lives on as an Allied Domecq brand name distilled by Hiram Walker and distributed by Corby Distilleries Limited, another of Allied's Canadian subsidiaries. Some of the G&W distillery buildings have been architecturally conserved to commemorate their prominent role in Canada's industrial heritage.

Glen C. Phillips

See also: Canada Temperance Act; Hiram Walker; Labatt Brewing Company Limited; Whiskies

References

Beeby, Dean. "George Gooderham" in *Dictionary of Canadian Biography,* vol. XIII: 1901–1910. Toronto: University of Toronto Press, 1994.

Canadian Illustrated News, 25 April 1863.

Newell, Dianne. "James Gooderham Worts" in *Dictionary of Canadian Biography,* vol. XI: 1881–1890. Toronto: University of Toronto Press, 1982.

———. "William Gooderham" in *Dictionary of Canadian Biography,* vol. XI: 1881–1890. Toronto: University of Toronto Press, 1982.

Rannie, W. F. *Canadian Whisky: The Product and the Industry.* Lincoln, Ontario: W. F. Rannie, 1976.

Gordon, Anna Adams (1853–1931)

Anna Adams Gordon (1853–1931) was personal secretary to Frances Elizabeth Caroline Willard and the national president of the Woman's Christian Temperance Union (WCTU) when the United States adopted the Eighteenth Amendment. Born 7 July 1853 in Boston, Massachusetts, Gordon attended Mount Holyoke College and then spent a year studying music under her sister, Alice Gordon Gulick, at the College for Girls in San Sebastian, Spain. This talent would help her write a number of marching songs and hymnals for the movement over the rest of her life, including *White Ribbon Hymnal* (1911), *Young People's Temperance Chorus Book* (1911), *Marching Songs for Young Crusaders* (1916), *Jubilee Songs* (1923), and *Everybody Sing* (1924). In 1877, the twenty-four-year-old Gordon came to meet Frances E. Willard at a Dwight Moody revival at the Tabernacle in Boston, where Willard was holding temperance meetings. Soon after, Gordon began to play organ for Willard's meetings, and this led to her becoming Willard's live-in private secretary and companion, a position she held until Willard's death in 1898. This relationship was so close that other activists in the WCTU talked about having their own "little Anna Gordon." Willard called Anna her "loved and last." The young woman's devotion to the older temperance leader can be seen in her book *The Beautiful Life of Frances E. Willard,* published in 1905.

Upon Willard's death, Gordon was elected national vice president of the WCTU and worked tirelessly for the temperance cause, not only in the United States but throughout the world, for the rest of her life. She stated, "It would be criminally selfish in us as Christian temperance women to content ourselves with ridding our own lands of the greatest enemy of the home and childhood" (Tyrrell 1991, 256) Gordon was president of the World League Against Alcoholism (WLAA), vice president of the National Temperance Council, and vice chairman of the Commission of Nineteen on the National Constitutional Prohibition Amendment. She was also involved in temperance work with the National Council of Women, the International Sunday-School Association, the World's Woman's Christian Temperance Union (WWCTU), the National Legislative Council, and various other organizations. In 1914, she ascended to the WCTU presidency when Lillian M. N. Stevens died. In the same year, she assumed the position of editor in chief of the *Union Signal,* the WCTU's national organ. During World War I, she helped to persuade U.S. President Woodrow Wilson to toughen the federal government's stance against alcohol manufacturing to include such steps as prohibiting the use of foodstuffs for the making of alcoholic beverages. In January 1919, she celebrated the ratification of the Eighteenth Amendment. After this monumental event, under her direction the WCTU began to refocus its efforts on Prohibition enforcement, the Americanization of immigrants, the conditions of women in the workplace, and child welfare. In November 1922, she was elected president of the WWCTU and resigned her presidency of the national WCTU. Gordon died on 15 June 1931 in Castile, New York, believing her life-long efforts had nearly come to fruition.

T. Jason Soderstrum

See also: Willard, Frances Elizabeth Caroline; Woman's Christian Temperance Union (WCTU) (United States); World's Woman's Christian Temperance Union (WWCTU)

References

Deane, Julia Freeman. *Anna Adams Gordon: A Story of Her Life.* Evanston, IL: Woman's Christian Temperance Union, 1928.

Tyrrell, Ian R. *Woman's World/Woman's Empire: The World's Woman's Christian Temperance Union in International Perspective, 1880–1930.* Chapel Hill: University of North Carolina Press, 1991.

Gore, Charles (1853–1932)

Charles Gore (1853–1932), an Anglo-Catholic and socialist, was his era's most influential theologian. As principal librarian at Pusey House, Oxford University (1884–1893), as canon of Westminster (1894–1902), as bishop of Worcester (1902–1905), bishop of Birmingham (1905–1911), and bishop of Oxford (1911–1919), he selectively patronized the Church of England Temperance Society (CETS), founded in 1873. Anglo-Catholic/socialists overcame earlier reluctance to join the temperance movement partly because of their incarnational theology that saw the world as sanctified by Christ's birth, leading them to seek new practical expressions for their heightened social conscience.

At Pusey House, Gore combined Anglo-Catholic/socialist principles with judicious temperance activity, deeply influenced by the idealist Oxford Hegelian philosopher T. H. Green, whose antidrink commitments reinforced his interventionist left-liberalism. The Christian Social Union, which Gore founded in 1886 with B. F. Westcott and Henry Scott Holland, fused liberal Catholic pastoral theology with advanced social concern. In an Anglo-Catholic/socialist sense, Gore's *Lux Mundi* (1889), reconciled Anglican tradition with current thought. Gore and his fellow Anglo-Catholic/socialists supported temperance for reasons that contrasted with those of evangelical teetotal priests, like Bishop Handley Carr Glyn Moule of Durham, who were often laissez-faire individualists. Anglo-Catholic/socialists avoided exaggerating the role of teetotalism and prohibition in lessening state action in other sectors; and their incarnational theology suggested broader solutions for intemperance and its effects. As canon of Westminster, Gore preached temperance in the slums around Parliament; as bishop of Worcester and as first bishop of Birmingham, both proletarian centers, Gore inherited a generation's existential experiences of parish teetotalism.

Insistent on principle over property, Gore joined Anglican teetotal radicals in protesting the 1890 Conservative license purchase scheme, which was considered too friendly to the drink trade, and he was adamantly committed to the Liberal government's radical 1908 Licensing Bill, attacked by the drink interests. Gore supported the bill, together with a slight majority of Anglican bishops, but they could not prevent its defeat by drink supporters in the House of Lords.

Although practical abstainers, some Anglo-Catholic bishops, like Gore, defended fermented Communion wine and opposed the teetotal pledge as denying the sufficiency of baptismal vows. As bishop of Oxford, Gore took the pledge only for the period of World War I, together with King George V and Randall Davidson, archbishop of Canterbury, as a practical example to Britain, but Gore never endorsed questionable teetotal doctrine.

Gore recognized that the temperance movement highlighted and encouraged broader and deeper organic transformations. He angered church temperance militants by attributing greater British sobriety not to the efforts of the church or of temperance reformers but to more comprehensive tidal improvements—social, cultural, humanitarian, educational, scientific, and moral. Applauding positive state action, Anglo-Catholic/socialists like Gore were content when wider, more collectivist responses to the plight of the oppressed surpassed the temperance movement.

The Lambeth Palace Library holds Gore's temperance correspondence.

Stephanie Olsen and Gerald Wayne Olsen

See also: Christian Socialism; Church of England Temperance Society (CETS); Conservative Party (United Kingdom); Davidson, Randall; Ellison, Henry; Evangelical Temperance (United Kingdom); Green, T. H.; Liberal Party (United Kingdom); Moule, Handley Carr Glyn; Temple, Frederick; Wilberforce, Basil and Wilberforce, Ernest

References

Carpenter, James. *Gore: A Study in Liberal Catholic Thought.* London: Faith Press, 1960.

Gore, Charles. *The Incarnation of the Son of God, Being the Bampton Lectures for the Year 1891.* London: John Murray, 1916.

Olsen, G. W. *Drink and the British Establishment—The Church of England Temperance Society, 1873–1914.* Unpublished book manuscript.

Williams, A. T. P. "Gore, Charles" in *Dictionary of National Biography. Supplement, 1931–1940,* 349–353. London: Oxford University Press, 1949.

Gothenburg Schemes/ Disinterested Management

Pioneered in Sweden and Norway between 1865 and 1877, the Gothenburg system proposed to eliminate the profit incentive from liquor retailing. Some British temperance reformers viewed the method of dispensing alcohol, not alcohol itself, as the source of the evil. With this reform, they expected far-reaching benefits: Alcohol would not be foisted upon customers; only unadulterated alcohol would be sold; and managers would encourage food sales and nonintoxicants. It acquired the name "disinterested" because liquor retailers, as salaried employees of the company running drink shops, would lack what temperance reformers saw as the corrosive profit motive of commercial retailers to sell as much alcohol as possible, thereby making drunkenness more likely.

Throughout the 1870s to 1890s, disinterested management became a credible alternative to prohibition. As Birmingham's mayor early in the 1870s, Joseph Chamberlain championed the system as part of his "gas and water" socialism, but met defeat after provoking prohibitionist hostility. More sustained effort to promote the concept came in 1896, when the bishop of Chester (Francis John Jayne) and Maj. H. J. Craufurd cofounded the People's Refreshment House Association. It assumed control of pubs, installed disinterested managers who cultivated a food trade, guaranteed investors 5 percent annual profits, and, going beyond what Scandinavians had envisaged, sought to instill middle-class values into patrons by setting limits on both alcohol consumption and obscene language. Temperance critics disliked the association's fostering of recreation on liquor premises because it contravened the traditional temperance philosophy of initiating counterattractions to keep people out of pubs. Earl Grey soon secured the success of the fledgling movement with the Central Public House Trust Association: a coalition of landowners, Anglican officials, and businessmen organized nationally in county trust-house companies pledged to rewarding investors with 5 percent annual dividends. Established in 1901, it had a much bigger base of supporters with a much larger share of capital than the earlier association, and accounted for nearly three-fifths of the 250 trust houses by 1914. By the early 1920s, the total numbers had soared to some 420, the pinnacle of the movement's influence. Fragmentation impeded further growth: The most successful trust company based in Hertfordshire and surrounding counties separated from the Central Trust, and adopted a new name, Trust Houses Limited, the forerunner of the hotel chain Trust House Forte. Competition heightened too. Brewers began promoting an "improved public house," with food sales, respectability, and family recreation integral to the concept. Disinterested management attracted extremely prominent supporters, especially Liberals such as Chamberlain and later William Gladstone. Leading prohibitionists recanted outlawing liquor sales as a solution to the drink question around the turn of the century. In the most formidable critique of prohibition, *The Temperance Problem and Social Reform,* published in 1899 and an immediate best seller, Joseph Rowntree and Arthur Sherwell denounced prohibition with the same ardor and academic rigor as they endorsed disinterested management. Another damaging defector was Sir Thomas P. Whittaker, an influential United Kingdom Alliance (UKA) vice president. He helped establish the Temperance Legislation League in 1905, which was committed to disinterested management as its official policy. Its newsletter, the *Monthly Bulletin,* and pamphlets appeared throughout the interwar era. The concept's appeal transcended party lines. Sir Edgar Vincent (later first Baron D'Abernon) served as an official of an Edwardian trust company. Here, the subsequent impact of the trust-house philosophy was most apparent. As chairman of the Central Control Board (CCB) that oversaw the areas where the government nationalized the liquor industry in the first world war, D'Abernon instituted disinterested management, and offered catering facilities, recreation, and nonintoxicants.

David W. Gutzke

See also: Astor, Lord Waldorf; Carlisle System; Chamberlain, Joseph; D'Abernon, Lord (Sir Edgar Vincent); Gladstone, William Ewart; Rowntree, Joseph; United Kingdom Alliance (UKA); Whittaker, Sir Thomas Palmer

References

Anderson, Alasdair. *The Dean Tavern: A Gothenburg Experiment.* Newtongrange: Dean Tavern Trust, 1986.

Brown, James B. "The Temperance Career of Joseph Chamberlain, 1870–77: A Study in Political Frustration" in *Albion.* 4 (1972): 29–44.

Fahey, David M. "Sir Thomas Palmer Whittaker, Kt" in *Biographical Dictionary of Modern British Radicals,* edited by Joseph O. Baylen and Norbert J. Gossman, 3: 866–868. 3 vols. Hassocks: Harvester, 1984.

Gutzke, David W. "Gentrifying the British Public House, 1896–1914" in *International Labor and Working-Class History* 45 (1994): 29–43.

———. *Progressivism in Britain: The Public House Reform Movement, 1890–1939.* Unpublished book manuscript.

Rose, Michael E. "The Success of Social Reform? The Central Control Board Liquor Traffic, 1915–21" in *War and Society: Historical Essays in Honour and Memory of J.R. Western, 1928–1971,* edited by M. R. D. Foot, 71–84. New York: Barnes & Noble, 1973.

Rowntree, Joseph, and Arthur Sherwell. *British "Gothenburg" Experiments and Public-House Trusts.* London: Hodder and Stoughton, 1901.

Smith, J. H. *Grayshott: The Story of a Hampshire Village.* Petersfield: Frank Westwood, 1978.

Gough, John Bartholomew (1817–1886)

John Bartholomew Gough (1817–1886), temperance orator, was one of the most popular platform speakers of his day, both in the United States and in his native England. Audiences thrilled to his emotional testimony about his dissolute youth before his redemption, at age twenty-five, by the Washingtonians. During his subsequent four-decade-long career on the lecture circuit, he traveled, by his own estimate, 450,000 miles to deliver some 8,600 addresses to as many as 9 million men and women.

Born on 22 August 1817, in Sandgate, County Kent, Gough was the son of a career soldier and a schoolteacher. Although a good student, he left school at age ten because his family could not afford to continue his education. Two years later, his father decided that England held no promise for his son, so he arranged in 1829 to have the boy taken to the United States, where he could learn a trade. Gough eked out a meager living in New York City by working as an errand boy and as an apprentice in a bookbinding business.

In an autobiography first published in 1845 and frequently updated, Gough recounted many of the details of the "unfortunate habits of dissipation" and the "almost unlimited indulgence" of his youth and early adulthood. While working variously as a binder and as a fisherman in Rhode Island, he became interested in singing and performing, and eventually moved to Boston to pursue an acting career. In 1841, the deaths of his wife and son from what he termed his "neglect" exacerbated his drinking. "Frequently was I tempted to take my life," he admitted. He considered himself "apparently beyond the hope of redemption."

In October 1842, a stranger approached Gough, who was intoxicated and staggering along the streets of Worcester, Massachusetts. The man persuaded Gough to accompany him to a meeting of the Washingtonian Total Abstinence Society, where a skeptical Gough signed the total abstinence pledge. He soon began to give his testimony throughout the country. As he later wrote, his "career as an intemperate man having been notorious, a little curiosity concerning my addresses was excited."

Gough was modest. He quickly became one of the most sought-after speakers on the temperance circuit, becoming a full-time temperance speaker in 1843. During his first year, he delivered 383 addresses. At first concentrating on the New England states, he gradually extended his engagements southward. By 1850, he was accepting invitations to speak as far west as Quebec, Montreal, and Detroit. Although he earned his living as a lecturer, he often spoke "gratuitously" at prisons, reform schools, and eleemosynary institutions. To him, one of his most memorable appearances occurred in 1846, when he spoke before 2,500 African Americans, apparently slaves, at a Richmond, Virginia, church. The experience made him "more strongly antislavery than ever before."

By his reckoning, Gough had led 215,179 individuals to sign the abstinence pledge by 1853. That same year, he embarked on an extensive speaking tour of Britain, where he was credited with reviving the prohibitionist crusade. He spent twenty-four months in England and Scotland, including five days in his home village in Kent, before arriving in the United States in August 1855. British admirers persuaded him to return for another tour, which lasted three years (1857–1860) and included appearances in Ireland. Gough calculated that, all told, he spoke on 1,043 occasions during five years in the British Isles.

Although Gough had devoted himself on the lecture circuit strictly to the temperance cause, he saw "the necessity of some change," for he feared "losing the elasticity of mind" that invariably accompanied speaking so often and solely on one theme, "with so little possible variety." Beginning in November 1860, he cut back on his schedule and expanded his repertoire to include such titles as "Curiosity," "Eloquence and Orators," and "Here and There in Britain." When some longtime friends accused him of deserting the prohibition cause, he replied that in all of his appearances he managed to introduce the subject of temperance "prominently."

The public retained their fascination with Gough, whose popularity on the circuit remained strong. His early experiences in the theater served him well. Audiences delighted in his unscripted performances, which featured elaborate gesturing and posturing as well as comedic elements. A talented mimic, he could speak in a variety of dialects, including an Irish brogue. He captivated his listeners by the content of his message and the passion of his convictions. Regrettably, his widely published lectures, when read today, scarcely convey the drama inherent in one of his performances.

Invariably accompanied by his second wife, the former Mary Whitcomb, whom he married in 1843, Gough maintained a rigorous speaking schedule for more than four decades. On 15 July 1886, he collapsed during a talk in Philadelphia and died three days later. He was sixty-nine.

Thomas H. Appleton Jr.

See also: Washingtonians

References

Gough, John B. *Autobiography and Personal Recollections.* Springfield, MA: Bill, Nichols, 1869.

———. *Platform Echoes.* Hartford, CT: A. D. Worthington, 1886.

Martyn, Carlos. *John B. Gough: The Apostle of Cold Water.* New York: Funk and Wagnalls, 1894.

Greece

Alcohol consumption and production have been interwoven with Greek social life and economy for a very long time. Wine especially has been closely associated with the basic Mediterranean diet for centuries, and even today wine is considered a foodstuff in wine-producing rural areas of the country. Generally, drinking alcohol is perceived in Greece as a positive feature of social life (Gefou-Madianou 1992). However, no detailed information is available on the consumption of alcoholic beverages in Greece in the eighteenth and nineteenth centuries, and exact consumption figures for all alcoholic beverage categories are not available until 1976 (Gefou-Madianou, Karlsson, and Österberg 2002).

Greece has not had any temperance movements. Instead, a long history of alcohol production and use has enabled Greek society to develop effective ways of dealing with the regulation and control of alcohol consumption. These are often hidden regulations, constituting a part of everyday life and being thus linked with informal social and cultural structures and very seldom with official legal regulations and written laws. This pattern of unofficial regulation is partly reflected in the relatively stable total alcohol consumption during the last decades (*World Drink Trends* 2002). There is a strong belief in Greece that there are no serious alcohol-related problems in the country. This belief is shared by both the state officials and the general public (Fahrenkrug 1990).

Alcohol Production and Consumption

The production of beer and distilled spirits in Greece has increased substantially since the beginning of the 1950s, while the production of the dominant beverage, wine, has been more or less stable. In the early 1950s, about 4 million hectoliters of wine (1.1 million U.S. gallons) were produced annually. In the second half of the 1960s and in the 1970s, wine production was on the increase, reaching the amount of 5.6 million hectoliters in 1984 (1.5 million U.S. gallons). Since then, the amount of wine produced has decreased to 3.7 million hectoliters in 2000 (979,000 U.S. gallons). Industrial companies and cooperatives produce about two-thirds of Greek wine. One-third is produced in small farms and households (Gefou-Madianou, Karlsson and Österberg 2002).

Total alcohol consumption showed a slight increase in Greece both in the 1960s and in the 1970s, reaching a level of 10 liters of pure alcohol per capita (2.6 U.S. gallons) in 1980. Since then it has slightly decreased and reached the level of 8 liters of

Wineskins being loaded onto the backs of donkeys in Greece, 1925. (Hulton/Archive)

pure alcohol per capita (2.1 U.S. gallons) in 2000 (*World Drink Trends* 2002).

Beer consumption has clearly increased, from 5.3 liters of the product per capita in 1961 (1.4 U.S. gallons) to 40 liters in 2000 (10.6 U.S. gallons). The consumption of distilled spirits seems to have been quite stable from the beginning of the 1960s until the mid-1990s. In the 1994 to 2000 period, the consumption of distilled spirits is estimated to have decreased from 2.8 to 1.9 liters of pure alcohol per capita (0.7 to 0.5 U.S. gallon) (*World Drink Trends* 2002).

The consumption of wine has been quite stable during the last two decades. In 2000, consumption stood at 34 liters of the product per capita (9 U.S. gallons), which in fact is very low when taking into account that wine is a common beverage at meals. Even at its highest, the recorded consumption of wine was only 45 liters per capita at the beginning of the 1980s (11.9 U.S. gallons) (*World Drink Trends* 2002).

Despite the growth in beer consumption, wine still accounts for the greatest proportion of total alcohol consumption. In 2000, half of all alcohol consumed in Greece was in the form of wine. The corresponding figure both for distilled spirits and beer was about one-fourth.

There are reasons to question the official alcohol consumption figures. Officially, about one-third of all wine is produced by domestic means, and the excise duty rate for wine is set at zero. These facts mean that the official quantity of wine produced and consumed may be underestimated. Also, the figures for the consumption of distilled spirits have been for many years crude estimates only (*World Drink Trends* 2002).

Drinking Habits

Especially in rural areas, alcoholic beverages are consumed at meals every day and identified with a traditional way of life. Not only is alcohol legally available, but people are also more or less culturally forced to drink on certain social occasions. This does not, however, mean that alcohol consumption, and especially wine consumption, reinforces or is related to social problems. On the contrary, wine may be associated with spiritual qualities, since drinking in Greek society is still integrated into social and religious structures, and under certain circumstances drinking alcohol functions as a sign of social integration and socialization (Gefou-Madianou 1992). Traditional drinking patterns, like the association of drinking with meals, family rituals, community or religious ceremonies, and recreational activities, have also merged with the urban lifestyles during the transitional postwar modern Greek society (Gefou-Madianou 1996).

In Greece, drinking alcohol is a traditional way of socializing among men and more recently also among women and youth. With regard to youth, drinking is considered a rite of passage from adolescence to adulthood. In some rural areas, it is also thought that red wine is good for the blood and can cure anemia, and it is therefore given to young children as a medicament. Hot red wine with sugar and bread was provided to young children for breakfast in some areas until the 1960s.

Traditional distilled aromatic beverages, like ouzo, *raki, tsikoudia,* and *tsipouro,* are very popular in Greece. However, an increase in the consumption of imported distilled alcoholic beverages, such as whiskey, vodka, gin, tequila, and rum, can be noticed especially among younger generations. Greeks also seem to prefer domestic wine, as the market share of imported wine has been very low (Yfantopoulos 1985).

In 1994, the proportion of abstainers, defined as not having drunk alcoholic beverages during the previous twelve months, was 6.5 percent for men between twelve and sixty-four years of age and 18.3 percent for women. Higher than average abstinence rates were found among the elderly, those with lower education, single and widowed men, and widowed women. Divorced women, on the other hand, had lower than average abstinence rates. Abstinence was more common outside the capital region than in Athens (Simpura and Karlsson 2001).

Women drank about one-third of all alcohol. The highest prevalence and highest estimated weekly alcohol consumption were found among males between 25 and 44 years of age. Results from 1994 show that the difference between this group and the older age groups was very small. Adolescents below eighteen years of age drank much less than adults (Simpura and Karlsson 2001).

Administrative Structure of Preventive Alcohol Policies

Social and religious structures provide controls against excessive drinking, as do close family and neighborhood ties in rural areas. Family and community control, in the form of negative and nonpermissive attitudes toward excessive drinking behavior, also play a preventive role in the case of individuals susceptible to alcohol abuse and dependence. These unwritten control mechanisms, together with the fact that the wine industry has contributed significantly to the country's economy, have led to the absence of coordinated preventive alcohol policies.

However, despite the absence of a comprehensive state preventive alcohol policy, the individual ministries and organizations have developed since the 1950s a number of policy measures also affecting the alcohol field. These measures mainly deal with the production, distillation, and sale of alcoholic beverages, with taxation controls, and more recently with drunk driving.

Awareness of the issue of preventing alcohol problems has, however, grown during the 1990s. The current administrative structure of preventive alcohol policies in Greece involves several ministries and organizations. One of these is the Organization against Drugs (OKANA), which was established in 1994. It mainly offers its services to illicit-drug addicts. However, in its plan of activities for the years 2000 through 2004, the range of activities has also included alcohol and tobacco. In recent years, OKANA has organized and financially supported preventive programs in local communities and, lately, in workplaces in collaboration with the Ministry of Labor and Health Promotion Agency in Working Places.

Greece's participation in the Collaborative Study on Community Response to Alcohol-Related Problems (initiated by the World Health Organization through its Regional Office for Europe [WHO-EURO]) and its acceptance of the European Alcohol Charter (initiated by the WHO-EURO in December 1995) have resulted in the Greek Ministry of Health taking some action on preventive alcohol policy issues. The National Council on Alcohol, consisting of alcohol experts and representatives from several ministries, has worked toward action in this area. During the last couple of years, some progress has been made, including the implementation of health-education programs in schools. Measures have also been taken to ban alcohol sale in places like school canteens and at sport games, and to institute more systematic law enforcement of traffic-safety regulations, including the implementation of breath tests to determine a driver's blood-alcohol concentration (BAC). Some television spots and radio messages against drinking and driving have also been introduced.

Public television channels have recently initiated a policy to reduce alcohol advertisements. A very positive development has been the inclusion of alcohol in the range of activities of OKANA. All the previously mentioned activities seem to have had an influence on the general public's awareness of and attitudes toward drinking—a shift that is reflected in public debates and in the mass media.

Alcohol Control Measures

Alcohol producers in Greece need licenses to operate. The license to produce alcoholic beverages is granted by the Ministry of Commerce and the State General Chemical Laboratory. The license includes specific rules and regulations that have been in force since the mid-1940s concerning pure alcohol production, labeling of the contents, and sales and restrictions of use by persons other than alcohol producers and pharmacists. The license is permanent (Gefou-Madianou, Karlsson, and Österberg 2002).

The importers and wholesalers of alcoholic beverages also need licenses to operate. The license, which has to be renewed periodically, is granted to the licensee by the Ministry of Economics, Department of Trade, and the Chamber of Commerce. Also, off-premises retailers of alcoholic beverages need licenses.

The license is permanent and it is granted by the local municipalities and the prefecture authorities at the Department of Health. Some on-premises establishments are required to have licences as well. This concerns mostly bars that are restricted to certain rules by the police and the prefecture authorities. Ordinary restaurants are not required to have licenses.

Since 1971, the legal age limit for off-premises purchases of distilled spirits has been eighteen years (Yfantopoulos 1985). For off-premises retail sale of beer and wine, there are no legal age limits, and these beverages can also be purchased in a variety of places other than special liquor stores, such as food markets, kiosks, gas stations, open-air canteens, bus or train stations, and airports. For on-premises sale of alcoholic beverages, including all cafeterias, bars, and discotheques, there is an age limit of eighteen years for all alcoholic beverages, wine and beer included. This age limit was introduced in 1989, but has not been strictly enforced until recent years (Gefou-Madianou, Karlsson, and Österberg 2002).

Alcoholic beverages are available in food markets and in specialized liquor stores. The business hours for off- and on-premises sale of alcoholic beverages depend on the type of premise. For on-premises sale, the business hours extend until midnight or 1 A.M. for restaurants. For bars and discotheques, they used to extend until 3 A.M. or all night long. Presently, the business hours for bars and discotheques should officially extend until 2:30 A.M. The law, however, is not at all strictly enforced, and in practice, this time limit is frequently violated. Especially in summertime on the islands, bars and discotheques are open all night.

There are currently no restrictions concerning alcohol advertising, sales promotion, and sponsorship. At the beginning of the 1990s, however, an effort was made to decrease the number of alcohol advertisements on television, and some regulations designed to further this goal, including provisions for public-service announcements against drunk driving, were introduced by the Ministry of Social Security.

At the beginning of the 1990s, a driver's BAC level could not exceed 0.08 percent. Currently, the driver is considered to be driving under the influence of alcohol if his or her BAC level is over 0.05 percent. The punishment for drunk driving is usually a fine. In general, the punishments are not severe unless the driver in question has been involved in a car accident. If the BAC level is higher than 0.1 percent, the driver's driving license may be suspended temporarily. From 1999 onward, there has been more systematic traffic-safety law enforcement, with the implementation of Breathalyzer tests.

Alcohol Taxation

The current method of alcohol taxation varies depending on the beverage category. For beer, excise duties are levied on the basis of alcohol content in the finished product. For wine and intermediate products, the excise duties are applied on the basis of hectoliters of the product, but the excise duty rate for wine has been set at zero. For distilled spirits, the excise duty is levied per hectoliter of pure alcohol in the finished product. The value-added tax (VAT) of 18 percent is the same for all alcoholic beverages.

In Greece, the excise duty rates calculated per liter of pure alcohol are almost the same for intermediate products and beer. The excise duty rate for distilled spirits is over three times the rate for beer. For beer and distilled spirits, the excise duty rate in Greece is nearly twice the minimum rate set by the European Union (Österberg and Karlsson 2002). In the 1990s, the real burden of excise duty on distilled spirits has clearly increased, and the real value of the excise duty on beer has also increased slightly. The tax burden on wine has increased in the 1990s as the VAT rose from 8 to 18 percent in the late 1990s.

Thomas Karlsson and Esa Österberg

References

Fahrenkrug, Herman. "Alcohol Control Policy in the EC Member States" in *Contemporary Drug Problems.* 17 (1990): 525–544.

Gefou-Madianou, Dimitra, ed. *Alcohol Gender and Culture.* London and New York: Routledge, 1992.

———. "Community Response to Alcohol-Related Problems. Case Study: Greece" in *Alcohol and the Community—Case Studies. Report on an International Study on Community Response to Alcohol-Related Problems.* unpaginated. Copenhagen: WHO Regional Office for Europe, 1996.

Gefou-Madianou, Dimitra, Thomas Karlsson, and Esa Österberg. "Greece" in *Alcohol Policies in EU Member States and Norway. A Collection of Country Reports,* edited by Esa Österberg and Thomas Karlsson, 217–232. Helsinki: Stakes, 2002.

Madianos, M., Dimitra Gefou-Madianou, and C. Stefanis. "Adolescent Drinking and Related Problems in Greece" in *International Journal of Addictions.* 29 (1994): 1581–1599.

Österberg, Esa, and Thomas Karlsson, eds. *Alcohol Policies in EU Member States and Norway. A Collection of Country Reports.* Helsinki: Stakes, 2002.

Simpura, Jussi, and Thomas Karlsson. *Trends in Drinking Patterns among Adult Population in 15 European Countries, 1950 to 2000. A Collection of Country Reports.* Helsinki: Stakes, 2001.

World Drink Trends. 2002 Edition. Oxfordshire, United Kingdom: NTC Publications, 2002.

Yfantopoulos, J. N. "Four Country Profiles, Greece" in *Alcohol Policies,* edited by Marcus Grant, 92–109. WHO Regional Publications, European Series No. 18. Copenhagen: WHO Regional Office for Europe, 1985.

Green, T. H. (1836–1882)

Thomas Hill Green (1836–1882), the Hegelian idealist who was late-Victorian Oxford's most formative philosopher, effectively reshaped British liberalism from laissez-faire individualism to a more interventionist political movement. The transformation moved from the mistrust of the state of Herbert Spencer and John Stuart Mill (particularly regarding its temperance legislation), to Green's own trust in progressive governmental action.

Green supported the prohibitionist United Kingdom Alliance (UKA), but preferred the restrictionist Church of England Temperance Society (CETS).

Green was remembered as the only abstainer among 400 Rugby senior students. His later temperance activities helped advance his influential idealistic leftist liberalism. Nationally, Green joined the UKA in 1872. Although an alliance supporter and local-option advocate, Green was more comfortable with the CETS's goal of gradually reducing the number of pubs through licensing restriction, which he saw as more attainable than prohibition. He criticized Liberal politician Sir William Harcourt for insufficiently attacking drink. Unlike some temperance reformers, Green understood the ameliorative value of governmental intervention in promoting temperance and other cultural and social reforms. In allowing the state the moral right to remove impediments to individual progress, Green saw temperance, together with educational and improving agencies, as justifying greater governmental activity.

Locally, Green sponsored a coffee stall at Saint Hilda's College and served as an officer of the Oxford Temperance Society, the Oxfordshire Band of Hope and Temperance Union, and the Oxford Diocesan CETS, which he helped inaugurate at the Oxford Town Hall in 1875, in the presence of the national chairman, Henry Ellison, and Queen Victoria's son, Prince Leopold. Exemplifying the complex relationships that marked the CETS, he shared incarnational theology with the Anglo-Catholic/socialists he mentored, and he also collaborated in temperance activities with Nonconformists.

Temperance reform afforded Green a paradigm for governmental activities. For him, a three-stage formula justified governmental interference with personal freedom. Intemperance was "an obstacle to the moral life"—an obstacle that the state could diminish "by legally controlling the sale of alcohol" (Nicholson 1990). State action was necessary because the problem could not be solved personally or by voluntary groups. Stressing more comprehensive and significant reformist movements, in opposition to other, often single-minded, antidrink movements, Green advocated governmental reforms of factories, mines, housing, food, sanitation, primary schooling, and higher education. In the CETS, by 1914, the brand of temperance Green propagated among broad-church and Anglo-Catholic Christian socialists largely surpassed the individualistic, laissez-faire variety favored by Evangelicals. Green's greater posthumous influences were in making the Liberal Party more interventionist and encouraging Fabian Socialism and the Labour Party. Intemperance and social distress were thereby addressed in broader, deeper, and more effective ways.

T. H. Green's temperance activities are described in CETS reports, minutes, and journals at Lambeth Palace Library.

Stephanie Olsen and Gerald Wayne Olsen

See also: Band of Hope; Christian Socialism; Church of England Temperance Society (CETS); Church of England Temperance Society (CETS) Inebriate Homes; Conservative Party (United Kingdom); Davidson, Randall; Ellison, Henry; Evangelical Temperance (United Kingdom); Gore, Charles; Harcourt, Sir William; Liberal Party (United Kingdom); Moule, Handley Carr Glyn; Temple, Frederick; United Kingdom Alliance (UKA); Wilberforce, Basil and Wilberforce, Ernest

References

Green, T. H. *Collected Works,* edited by Peter Nicholson, 5 vols. Bristol: Thoemmes, 1997.

Nicholson, Peter. *The Political Philosophy of the British Idealists, Selected Studies.* Cambridge: Cambridge University Press, 1990.

———. "T. H. Green and State Liquor Legislation" in *History of Political Thought.* 6, no. 3 (Winter 1985): 17–50.

Olsen, G. W. *Drink and the British Establishment—The Church of England Temperance Society, 1873–1914.* Unpublished book manuscript.

Greene, Edward (1815–1891)

Edward Greene (1815–1891), of Bury Saint Edmunds, Suffolk, was the archetypal successful Victorian country brewer. His father, Benjamin, the son of a South Midlands draper, had served an apprenticeship in the 1790s with Whitbreads, the great London brewers, before becoming a partner in a long-established Bury brewery in 1806. He was not particularly successful but inherited from a neighbor a West Indies sugar estate in Saint Kitts. The interests of the family then diversified. Benjamin founded a firm of sugar merchants in London after 1836, and Edward's elder brother managed sugar estates in the West Indies and Mauritius before becoming a director of the Bank of England in 1850.

Edward started work in the brewery at the age of thirteen; on his coming of age in 1836, his father sold the brewery to him. He later maintained that it then produced no more than 2,000 barrels a year. A British imperial barrel equals 43.2 U.S. gallons. By dint of hard work, Edward transformed the fortunes of the Westgate brewery, reorganizing it and building malt houses in 1846, 1856 through 1858, 1865 through 1866, and 1880. Westgate was never a model affair like the state-of-the-art, architect-designed breweries that began to be described in the brewers' journals after the 1870s and in the four volumes of Alfred Barnard's *Noted Breweries of Great Britain and Ireland* (1888–1891). But by 1875, Westgate was producing 40,000 barrels of beer a year. Success was achieved entirely in the free trade before 1865. From the mid-1840s, the railways allowed Greene to build up, with a network of travelers, agents, and stores scattered across East Anglia, one of the most noted breweries in the region. Although the small town of Bury Saint Edmunds was an unlikely base, the brewery competed and advanced because Greene produced a fine bitter that he sold at a keen price. On his death in 1891, the *London Star* put the secret of his success in a nutshell: "He was one of the first country brewers to discover that beer need not be vile, black, turgid stuff, but brewed a bright amber-coloured liquid of Burton type, which he sold at a shilling per gallon, and made a fortune" (quoted in the *Bury and Norwich Post* 21 April 1891).

After 1868, driven by rivalry with an aggressive competitor, F. W. King, from a brewery erected literally next door, Greene began to acquire a protective umbrella of public houses. In the next twenty years, he acquired ninety-one public houses. He therefore had reversed his free trade stance and was an early entrant in the field of public house purchase by brewers. In 1887, the company merged with F. W. King. With almost 150 pubs and a nominal capital of £550,000, Greene King was among the leading country brewers in England.

Edward Greene's career was typical of the most successful Victorian brewers. He made a considerable fortune (he left £356,945 gross on his death); he acquired a landed estate of 1,200 acres near Bury; he farmed progressively on a large scale; a Conservative, he was a member of Parliament (M.P.) almost continuously from 1865 to 1891. As a result, he became well known across Suffolk, speaking on many platforms about his views on the rewards of hard work, labor relations (more accurately paternalism), rural housing, and Protestantism. When he died in 1891, the Bury newspaper issued a twenty-four-page booklet reviewing his life. He achieved no official recognition of his public standing in the county, but his son, Walter, was created a baronet in 1900, largely as a mark of his father's achievements.

Richard G. Wilson

See also: Beer; Whitbread

References

The Bury and Norwich Post. 21 April 1891.

Gourvish, Terry R., and Richard G. Wilson. *The British Brewing Industry, 1830–1980.* Cambridge: Cambridge University Press, 1994.

Wilson, Richard G. *Greene King: A Business and Family History.* London: Bodley Head and Jonathan Cape, 1983.

Guinness, Edward Cecil, First Earl of Iveagh (1847–1927)

Edward Cecil Guinness, first earl of Iveagh (1847–1927), the youngest of the three sons of Sir Benjamin Lee Guinness, was the most famous brewer of his day. Few men have enjoyed greater success in business; even fewer enjoyed great affluence so soon. When his father died in 1867, he inherited a private fortune of at least £250,000 and a half share in Arthur Guinness and Son, founded in 1757. Already, the brewery produced 350,000 barrels a year and profits of £120,000. And in the next decade, as the consumption of beer in Britain and Ireland leaped ahead, Guinness fully enjoyed the general surge. By 1876, its sales had soared to 779,000 barrels and profits had grown to a massive £302,000. Growth came from porter or single stout sales in Ireland and double or extra stout in Britain. The brewery owned no public houses; independent agencies and bottlers set their own prices and operated under exclusive dealing clauses—an unusual practice for the trade.

In 1879, Edward Guinness, his father's choice for managing the brewery, bought out his eldest brother, Arthur (1840–1915, later first Lord Ardilaun), for £680,000. Edward was now sole proprietor of the second largest brewery in the world. Under his astute management, the brewery went from strength to strength. When in October 1886 it became a public company, the measure of his success was revealed to all. Sales had averaged 1,138,000 barrels and net profits £452,000 over each of the previous four years. Floated for £6 million, shares were oversubscribed twenty times. Edward Guinness retained one-third of the equity and continued to buy further shares in the late 1880s. He remained chairman and managing director until 1890. Then, between 1890 and 1897, he officially removed himself from the brewery's affairs, although as principal shareholder he was consulted on every matter. Indeed, throughout his life, he received almost daily reports from the brewery. In 1902, he resumed chairmanship of Guinness, the post he retained until his death. Sales grew by some 3 percent per annum between 1886 and 1914. Without the cost of buying public houses at inflated prices and with low raw material prices, Guinness profits soared in contrast with those of other breweries. After 1903, they were never less than £1 million each year; in 1910 Guinness, now Lord Iveagh, reckoned his income to be an incredible £650,000. By 1914, the brewery produced 2,652,000 barrels a year (more than twice its nearest rival, Bass), to supply over 10 percent of the United Kingdom beer market.

What did Edward Guinness do with his great fortune? He and his wife, a distant cousin and great socialite, lived the lives of the superrich. In addition to two great houses in Dublin, one in London, and one in Cowes, he bought a 17,000-acre shooting estate in West Suffolk in 1894. He vastly extended the house and transformed the shoot into the most famed in the annals of Edwardian shooting parties. Edward VII and George V were constantly entertained. In 1914, the estate was run with an incredible staff of almost 400 people, seventy-six in the game department alone. But Edward Guinness was also well known for his philanthropy. His largesse in Dublin was legendary. The firm's own welfare schemes for its 5,000 employees were innovative and generous. There were liberally funded housing trusts in Dublin and London; £250,000 was given to the Lister Institute of Preventative Medicine, besides generous benefactions to Trinity College Dublin, Saint Patrick's Cathedral, and the Dublin hospitals. In 1925, he bought Kenwood House, Hampstead, and filled it with the pictures he had bought (principally between 1887 and 1891, when he spent £530,000 on 200 pictures). He lived in it for a mere five nights. He then set up a trust to maintain the house and open its wonderful collection (the Iveagh Bequest) to the public. Edward Guinness was rewarded for his benefactions and his quiet but firm pro-union (of Ireland with Britain) stance by obtaining four titles—baronet in 1885, baron in 1891, viscount in 1905, and earl in 1919. When he died in 1927, survived by his sons to share his great riches, he left a fortune of £14 million, the second largest then recorded in Britain.

Richard G. Wilson

See also: Bass; Beer; Guinness Brewery; Ireland

References

Dennison, S. R., and Oliver MacDonagh. *Guinness, 1886–1939: From Incorporation to the Second World War.* Cork: Cork University Press, 1998.

Gourvish, Terry R., and Richard G. Wilson. *The British Brewing Industry, 1830–1980.* Cambridge: Cambridge University Press, 1994.

Lynch, Patrick, and John Vaizey. *Guinness's Brewery in the Irish Economy 1759–1876.* Cambridge: Cambridge University Press, 1960.

Guinness Brewery

Guinness was a Dublin brewing company established in 1742 by Arthur Guinness (1725–1803). By the 1770s, Guinness's brewery was known for its roasted barley-based porters, and by 1833 it was the largest brewery in Ireland, specializing in a distinctively dark "extra stout." Over the course of the nineteenth century, Guinness succeeded in obtaining a dominant share of the Irish beer market and developed a profitable niche in the highly competitive English market. The remarkable success over time of Guinness's brewery, despite the traditional preference for whiskey among most Irish drinkers and in the face of stiff competition from large English brewers and a host of Irish rivals, must be attributed to the considerable capital resources and sound business sense of the Guinness family, as well as a consistent emphasis on processes and ingredients that secured a reputation for a high-quality product. The brewery became a public concern in 1886, when 49 percent of the company's equity was floated on the London Stock Exchange. By 1914, the company's brewery at Saint James Gate was the largest in the world, although today it no longer holds that distinction. Expanding into spirits, Guinness acquired the Scottish-based Distillers Company Limited (DCL) in 1986. Owned by British-based Diageo Limited since 1997, Guinness remains one of the world's largest brewing concerns. Guinness stout is sold in over 150 countries.

The Guinness brewing tradition began when Arthur Price, archbishop of Cashel in the Church of Ireland, died in 1752, leaving a legacy of £100 pounds to his agent Richard Guinness's son, Arthur. After initially establishing a brewery at Leixlip outside Dublin in 1755, in the following year Arthur took out a 9,000-year lease on a failed brewery located at Saint James Gate in Dublin. Initially, Guinness brewed ale, but from 1799, Guinness brewed porter or stout exclusively. Arthur Guinness became master of the Corporation of Brewers in Dublin in 1767 and occupied a prominent position in civic life from the 1760s until his death in 1803 at the age of seventy-eight. His thriving brewery was passed on to his second surviving son, Arthur, and Arthur's younger brothers, Benjamin and William. Arthur Guinness II carried on the family tradition of combining brewing with a wide range of civic, charitable, and political activity, most notably when he became governor of the recently established Bank of Ireland in 1820. Guinness combined brewing with an evangelical ethos and the advocacy of reforming political causes. He was a prominent supporter of Daniel O'Connell's campaign for Catholic emancipation, although he opposed O'Connell's subsequent attempts to secure repeal of the Act of Union between Britain and Ireland. Arthur Guinness II also endorsed parliamentary reform. Arthur's access to capital and his influential place in the Dublin business community (he was for many years president of the Dublin Chamber of Commerce) left his brewery well positioned to take advantage of the expansion and consolidation of the Irish brewing industry that occurred in the first half of the nineteenth century.

The growth of Guinness brewery began in earnest in the first decades of the nineteenth century. From 1800 until 1850, Guinness's production increased tenfold, from 6,704 hogsheads (435,760 U.S. gallons) in 1801 to over 65,541 hogsheads (4,260,165 U.S. gallons) in 1850. Nearly two-thirds of that production was exported to England. After 1850, beer consumption in Ireland, previously largely confined to Dublin and a handful of other large towns, began to rise steadily. Beer became cheaper to produce, improved transportation dramatically lowered distribution costs, and Ireland's agricultural economy stabilized and became more cash-based after the famine years of the 1840s. Guinness was a significant beneficiary of these trends. The firm's reliable product, access to capital, decentralized distribution network, and careful system of cost controls produced a rapid expansion in sales, almost 600 percent between 1840 and 1870, all across Ireland. To keep up with growing demand, an enormous physical expansion of the Saint James Gate brewery occurred between 1860 and 1870 under the direction of Arthur Guinness's son Benjamin Lee Guinness (lord mayor of Dublin and Conservative member of Parliament [M.P.] for Dublin, 1865–1868) and grandsons Arthur Edward Guinness and Edward Cecil Guinness. During the same period, production became increasingly mechanized and standardized. The brewery became one of the largest industrial employers in Dublin and was admired for its progressive provision of health care, sick pay, and death benefits to workers eager to compete for available jobs.

Ten years after Arthur Edward bought out his brother Edward in 1867, shares of Guinness stock were offered for sale on the London Stock Exchange, raising £6 million. Arthur Guinness and Sons thus became the first large British brewery to become a public company, setting off a wave of public offerings by British brewers. By 1905, Guinness was the tenth largest company in Britain. Members of the Guinness family remained actively involved in the management and direction of the firm into the twentieth century. The family's civic-minded philanthropy continued and preserved the popularity in Ireland of the "Protestant Porter" amid the political turmoil of late-nineteenth- and early-twentieth-century Irish politics despite the increasingly Conservative and unionist politics of the Guinness family.

Workers at the Guinness brewery at Saint James's Gate, Dublin, hose down barrels (1925). (Hulton/Archive)

The Irish diaspora of the second half of the nineteenth century spread not only Irish men and women, but also a taste for Guinness. By the early thirties, increasing global consumption, now exceeding 3 million barrels a year, spurred by the firm's enormously successful first advertising campaign with its slogan "Guinness Is Good for You" (see illustration on page 5), was outpacing the Dublin brewery's productive capacity. New tariff duties between England and the newly independent Ireland also contributed to the firm's decision to open a second brewery in London in 1936.

Expansion, technical innovations, careful diversification, and innovative marketing have characterized Guinness from the twentieth century on. The firm reentered the ale trade in the 1950s. Draft Guinness was first brewed and offered for sale in 1961. The Saint James Gate Brewery was extensively modernized in the middle years of the 1980s. In 1989, the company pioneered the "widget," a device that releases nitrogen into a beer can when opened. Today, Guinness has an increasingly international profile and brews or licenses the brewing of a variety of beers in fifty countries all over the world, producing over 11 million cases of beer in 2001.

Paul Townend

See also: Beer; Distillers Company Limited (DCL); Guinness, Edward Cecil, First Earl of Iveagh; Ireland

References

Dennison, S. R., and Oliver MacDonagh. *Guinness, 1886–1939: From Incorporation to the Second World War.* Cork: Cork University Press, 1998.

Diageo plc. *2001 Annual Report.*

Guinness corporate website. http://www.Guinness.com. [27 February 2002].

Lee, J. J. "Money and Beer in Ireland, 1790–1870" in *Economic History Review.* New Series 19 (1966): 183–194.

Lynch, Patrick, and John Vaizey. *Guinness's Brewery in the Irish Economy 1759–1876.* Cambridge: Cambridge University Press, 1960.

Walsh, Peter. *Guinness.* Dublin: Easons and Sons, 1980.

Gusfield, Joseph R. (1923–)

Joseph R. Gusfield (1923–) is considered by many to be the most creative and farsighted sociologist of alcohol's ambiguous place in American society. Having combated sociologists' insufficient attention to alcohol use in modern life, Gusfield, retired from the University of California at San Diego, leaves a substantial legacy to future scholars of alcohol and drugs.

Gusfield was a student of Herbert Blumer at the University of Chicago. There, Gusfield's 1954 Ph.D. dissertation was "Organizational Change: A Study of the Women's Christian Temperance Union." Gusfield later revised this into the book *Symbolic Crusade: Status Politics and the American Temperance Movement,* first published in 1963. *Symbolic Crusade,* influential in both alcohol studies and the sociological analysis of social movements, was released in a second edition in 1986.

Gusfield's sociology of alcohol rests on the proposition that alcohol drinking in the United States has been immersed in political conflicts between "status" groups, and has had relatively little to do with social class. In Gusfield's view, the sheer wealth of the United States has dampened class conflict within its borders. Consequently, for Gusfield, class analysis is less salient to U.S. society generally, and to alcohol politics specifically, than it may be elsewhere.

Starting from this axiom, Gusfield treats alcohol use in the United States as a running political struggle between pro- and antitemperance forces that are only lightly touched by class relations and processes. For Gusfield, U.S. alcohol usage is best framed and studied as a moral issue "divorced from any direct economic interests in abstinence or indulgence" (Gusfield 1986, 2)

From within this framework, Gusfield has published not only *Symbolic Crusade,* but also a host of important essays on historical trends in alcohol politics. Among these is a handful of influential studies of drinkers' and drunk drivers' self-interpretations. Based on the author's daring to sit on barstools and talk to alcohol drinkers of varying kinds, Gusfield's ethnological papers suggest a multitude of fruitful methods for further investigation of the close-up meanings of alcohol usage to alcohol users themselves.

Those who would advance Gusfield's pioneering work may eventually best do so by relaxing some of his core axioms and theoretical commitments. Inclusion of class analysis seems a likely modification. In jettisoning class, Gusfield ignores his subjects' often conflictual interactions with big businesses. In particular, major alcohol-selling corporations and their increasingly ubiquitous marketing campaigns are conspicuously absent from Gusfield's writings. What power might a Gusfieldian analysis of alcohol's meanings assume if such class-based institutions and processes are included in the frame of analysis? Second, Gusfield's social constructionism could be seen as diminishing the power of his research. Dwelling on symbolic crusades and resistances, Gusfield never correlates his findings about drinkers' activities and perceptions with any serious accounting of ethanol's biochemical effects on the human individual. As a result, Gusfield often implies that alcohol addiction is a mere social construct, and alcohol politics a mere ideological game. What should and will happen to such social constructionist interpretations as we continue to learn more about both addiction and the human brain? What place might Gusfield's valuable techniques for discovering hidden psycho-social meanings have in enriching such learning?

Michael Dawson

See also: Clark, Norman Harold; Harrison, Brian; Sociological Theories of Drinking and Temperance

References

Gusfield, Joseph R. *Contested Meanings: The Construction of Alcohol Problems.* Madison: University of Wisconsin Press, 1996.

———. *Symbolic Crusade: Status Politics and the American Temperance Movement.* Rev. ed. Urbana: University of Illinois Press, 1986 [1963].

H

Haggard, Howard Wilcox (1891–1959)

Howard Wilcox Haggard (1891–1959), physician, author, and lecturer, served as director of the Laboratory of Applied Physiology (LAP) at Yale University from 1926 until his retirement in 1956. Under his direction, the LAP and the Center of Alcohol Studies, which he cofounded at Yale in the late 1930s, were in the forefront of the movement to recognize alcoholism as a major public-health concern and to have the medical community accept alcoholism as a treatable illness. The Yale Plan Clinics, which he launched in 1944, are considered the first-ever outpatient facilities for the treatment of alcoholism.

Born in La Porte, Indiana, on 19 July 1891, Haggard graduated from Phillips Exeter Academy before enrolling at Yale, where he received his baccalaureate degree in 1914 and his medical degree three years later. During World War I, he served as a captain in the Chemical Warfare Service of the U.S. army. In his early career at Yale, where he joined the faculty in 1919, he took particular interest in cardiorespiratory physiology. With his colleague Yandell Henderson, he invented the H and H inhalator, which rescue crews used extensively to revive victims of carbon monoxide poisoning. Engineers credited Haggard's research on oxygen in their design of ventilation for such structures as the Holland Tunnel in New York City.

Haggard wrote and lectured widely, not only for fellow scholars but also for a popular audience. His books, written in a nontechnical style and often lavishly illustrated, went through numerous editions and translations. Among his most influential were *Devils, Drugs, and Doctors: The Story of the Science of Healing from Medicine-Man to Doctor* (1929), *Mystery, Magic, and Medicine: The Rise of Medicine from Superstition to Science* (1933), and *The Lame, the Halt, and the Blind: Staying Young Beyond Your Years* (1937). In the early 1930s, he offered "practical health information" on a Sunday-evening radio show broadcast weekly from New York City.

That same decade, Haggard and his Yale colleagues undertook pioneering explorations into the causes and treatment of alcoholism. In 1943, the Center of Alcohol Studies offered a summer school that attracted 80 students to New Haven; the next year 147 attended. Haggard worked closely with E. M. Jellinek, with whom he published *Alcohol Explored* (1942), which argued that alcoholism had multiple causes and should be treated as a disease. Contemporary reviewers generally praised the monograph as a model of scientific objectivity.

Following his retirement from Yale in 1956, Haggard continued to edit the *Quarterly Journal of Studies on Alcohol* (today the *Journal of Studies on Alcohol*), as he had done from the appearance of the first issue in June 1940. He died in Fort Lauderdale, Florida, on 22 April 1959.

Thomas H. Appleton Jr.

See also: Alcoholism; Jellinek, Elvin Morton; *Journal of Studies on Alcohol;* Yale Center of Alcohol Studies

References

Greenberg, Leon A. "Howard Wilcox Haggard, 1891–1959" in *Quarterly Journal of Studies of Alcohol.* 20, no. 2 (June 1959): 211–212.

Haggard, Howard Wilcox, and E. M. Jellinek. *Alcohol Explored.* Garden City: NY: Doubleday, Doran, 1942.

Roizen, Ron. "Paradigm Sidetracked: Explaining Early Resistance to the Alcoholism Paradigm at Yale's Laboratory of Applied Physiology, 1940–1944." http://www.roizen.com/ron/sidetracked.htm [14 September 2002].

Hall, W. Glenvil (1887–1962)

W. Glenvil Hall (1887–1962) was a Labour Party member of Parliament (M.P.) and, briefly, president of the United Kingdom Alliance (UKA). Hall's life mixed temperance and party politics. Born in Herefordshire, he was associated in his younger days with Hoxton Hall, where the Blue Ribbon Movement had its headquarters. He became a barrister and was active in the Labour Party. He first entered Parliament in 1929 for Central Portsmouth. He lost the seat in 1931 when the Labour Party was routed but won Colne Valley in a by-election in 1939. After the formation of the postwar Labour government in 1945, Hall was appointed financial secretary to the Treasury, serving under Hugh Dalton and Sir Stafford Cripps. In 1950, when Hall was in his mid-sixties, he became chairman of the parliamentary Labour Party and held this office for two years.

Hall was a delegate to the United Nations Assembly in 1945, 1946, and 1948; to the Paris Peace Conference in 1946; and to the Consultative Assembly at Strasbourg in 1950 and 1952. In 1952, he became a member of the British Broadcasting Company's General Advisory Council. He was made a privy counsellor in 1947.

In 1959, at the time of accepting the presidency of the UKA, he was the M.P. for Colne Valley, a constituency that for many years had been represented by Philip (later Viscount) Snowden who also had been a supporter of the alliance. Since Nathaniel Card, a founder of the UKA, had been a Quaker, Glenvil Hall was especially proud of the fact that he was the first Quaker to become an alliance president.

Hall worked for temperance in the House of Commons. In 1961, R. A. Butler, home secretary in the Conservative government, introduced a licensing bill that set out to liberalize regulations on the sale of alcohol by extending the kinds of establishments that could sell alcohol, increasing the hours of sale, and curtailing some of the powers of magistrates. Despite the odds against any attempt to improve the bill from a temperance point of view, Hall kept up a consistent attack against the legislation. In July 1962, he made his last speech in Parliament urging the minister of transport to set a blood-alcohol concentration for motorists that would be accepted by the courts as a level above which it was unfit to drive. Although his amendment to the bill failed, he was pleased by the fact that the government majority, which was usually over 100, dropped to 40. Five years later, after his death, Barbara Castle, the Labour minister of transport, passed her Road Safety Act that brought in a drunk driving limit of 80 milligrams of alcohol in 100 milliliters of blood.

A month before his death, Glenvil Hall represented the UKA at the International Alcohol and Traffic conference and presided over the annual meeting of Ansvar Insurance Company, a temperance insurance company of which he was a director. When he died in October 1962, Hugh Gaitskell, the leader of the Labour Party, paid the following tribute: "He was a man without guile or vanity, whose kindliness, wisdom and modesty endeared him to us all."

Derek Rutherford

See also: Labour Party (United Kingdom); United Kingdom Alliance (UKA)

Reference

Hayler, Mark H. C. *The Vision of a Century, 1853–1953: The United Kingdom Alliance in Historical Retrospect.* London: United Kingdom Alliance, 1953.

Handsome Lake (Ga-nya-di-yoh) (ca. 1735–1815)

Handsome Lake (ca. 1735–1815) was a prophet of the Seneca tribe of the Iroquois Confederacy who advocated temperance. In the aftermath of the American Revolution, the Iroquois Confederacy of upper New York State was in many ways devastated. From a precontact population high of between 20,000 and 30,000, by 1800 the Iroquois numbered only about 4,000. One scholar has described the Iroquois communities of this era as "slums in the wilderness" (Wallace 1970: 184). Women continued to plant and harvest as they had done traditionally, but the hunting territory for men was severely constricted. Some men had begun to work as day laborers, guides, or boatmen, but for many others there was nothing to do. For a society whose traditions were based on a division of responsibilities between the sexes and whose spiritual ethos was grounded in that division, combining agrarian and hunting traditions, the collapse of traditional male roles was disastrous. At the same time, New York had been opened for settlement by Euro-Americans. For the Iroquois, it was a time of extreme hardship. Endemic alcoholism was symptomatic of the cultural dislocation felt by the Iroquois people in the 1790s.

Some Seneca leaders advocated adopting Euro-American models of farming, religion, social organization, and gender divisions. Others argued that it was impossible for the Seneca to give up the most basic aspects of their culture without ceasing to be Indians. Into this potentially harmful division stepped Handsome Lake, who offered a middle way for the Iroquois.

Born about 1735, Handsome Lake had distinguished himself in the wars of the latter eighteenth century, but in the aftermath of the American Revolution he became a drunk. After a drinking binge in 1799, Handsome Lake fell into a coma, and his family thought he was dead. But slowly he returned to consciousness and told of wondrous visions. Four guides communicated to him something he called the Good Message. The Iroquois ghosts told him that there were "four words that tell a great story of wrong"—alcohol, witchcraft, love magic, and abortion (Parker 1968: 27)

In his extended preaching on these four evil words, Handsome Lake made it clear that the words had symbolic as well as literal significance. Alcohol impoverished Iroquois peoples—thus, Handsome Lake emphasized the importance of frugality. Violence associated with drinking disrupted Iroquois lives, so not only did the Iroquois have to give up drinking but also quarrelling among themselves. Handsome Lake's message had many elements in common with Christianity—temperance, nonviolence, frugality, and an emphasis on good and evil, with judgment in the afterlife. He advocated that Iroquois men become farmers and that families live in American-style homes. Yet his message was presented as a return to Iroquois tradition. He stressed the importance of traditional agrarian rituals, and his followers met in longhouses. Handsome Lake's followers mobilized in the early nineteenth century to enforce a regimen of sobriety. Most village and tribal councils had at least some warnings about the harmful effects of alcohol. Although the Longhouse religion did not solve the problem of being a colonized people, it did help restore the Iroquois's self-respect and sense of control, allowing them to adapt to rather than assimilate into the Euro-American system.

Kathryn A. Abbott

See also: Native Americans: Drinking Patterns and Temperance Reform; Tenskwatawa

References

Parker, Arthur C. "The Code of Handsome Lake" in *Parker on the Iroquois,* edited by William N. Fenton, part 2, 1–117. Syracuse: Syracuse University Press, 1968.

Wallace, Anthony F. C. *The Death and Rebirth of the Seneca.* New York: Alfred A. Knopf, 1970.

Harcourt, Sir William (1827–1904)

Sir William Harcourt, baronet (1827–1904) and British politician, was the principal supporter of local-option prohibition in the Liberal Party leadership during the late nineteenth century. In 1872, Harcourt had scorned temperance legislation as interfering with personal liberties: "grand-maternal Government which ties nightcaps on a grown-up nation by Act of Parliament." Some contemporaries explained his later change of mind as the result of his anger at losing a parliamentary seat to a Conservative brewer. Harcourt himself said that his experience with the consequences of drunkenness while home secretary convinced him of the importance of temperance legislation. Most likely, he regarded Liberal commitment to direct local veto as the best strategy for rallying support among nonconformist voters. In 1888, he told a colleague: "Temperance is the backbone of the Liberal Party *vice* [the religious disabilities of] Nonconformity retired." In 1893 and 1895, Harcourt introduced the only government bills for local veto in England that the House of Commons ever considered. Prohibitionists were unenthusiastic because the proposed legislation affected only public houses and beerhouses and not other drink sellers. Moreover, the bill postponed local prohibition for several years to make it more acceptable. Most damaging of all, the government did not make the bills a priority, so the House of Commons never had the opportunity to send either of the bills to the House of Lords. From his perspective, Harcourt grumbled to Sir Wilfrid Lawson that the advocates of direct local veto had given him only half-hearted support. He particularly resented those prohibitionists (such as W. S. Caine) who had participated in the conferences organized by A. F. Hills to draft alternative legislation. Harcourt ridiculed the antiprohibition Church of England Temperance Society (CETS) as "very much Church and very little Temperance."

David M. Fahey

See also: Caine, William Sproston; Church of England Temperance Society (CETS); Gladstone, William Ewart; Hills, Arnold Frank; Lawson, Sir Wilfrid; Liberal Party (United Kingdom)

Reference

"Harcourt, Sir William" in *Standard Encyclopedia of the Alcohol Problem,* edited by Ernest Hurst Cherrington et al. 6 vols. Westerville, OH: American Issue Publishing, 1925–1930. 1177.

Harrison, Brian (1937–)

Brian Harrison (1937–), fellow of Corpus Christi College, University of Oxford, ranks as the leading modern historian of the temperance movement and the drink question in mid-nineteenth-century England. In the 1960s and 1970s, he published a major book and a large number of scholarly articles on these subjects, as well as a comprehensive bibliography, before moving on to research other aspects of Victorian Britain, notably the women's suffrage movement.

Before Harrison began his researches as a Ph.D. student at Oxford in the 1960s, the temperance history in Britain had been strangely neglected. The little work that existed either was popular and superficial or else was written by uncritical partisans of ancient controversies. Although academic historians had begun to pay more attention to social history, most had concentrated on labor history. Harrison's major work, *Drink and the Victorians: The Temperance Question in England, 1815–1872,* was published to critical acclaim in 1971. It was immediately recognized as a major contribution to our understanding of Victorian England. It demonstrated many strengths. First, it was a fully dispassionate account, written by a professional, academic historian with no axe to grind. Second, it was based on exhaustive scholarly research into a massive range of primary sources, including the temperance press, provincial newspapers, drink trade records, parliamentary papers, and private papers. Third, the breadth of Harrison's intellectual outlook meant that the book spanned the realms of political, social, and economic history. Finally, the book related the drink and temperance questions to more general issues of concern to historians, such as the standard-of-living debate, the nature of Chartism and early English socialism, the role of religion in liberalism, and the characteristics of Victorian pressure-group politics. The book contained sensitive analysis of the role played by alcoholic drink in society both in the 1820s and the 1870s and, hence, an evaluation of the changes that had occurred during the intervening period. It also offered a full and analytical account of the various stages of the temperance movement during this period: the antispirits movement, the teetotal pioneers, the prohibitionists, and more moderate restrictionist reformers. Harrison also discussed the response of political leaders and other elite groups.

In addition to his main book, Harrison took the opportunity to elaborate many of his findings in a range of scholarly articles in academic journals covering such topics as the temperance press, the relationship of temperance to Chartism, drink and sexuality, and a number of political episodes. He also published an extensive bibliography on the subject and a dictionary of British temperance biography. Having delivered this massive output of publications, Harrison decided to leave the drink and temperance field in order to research other areas. He did publish a slightly revised second edition of *Drink and the Victorians* in 1994. His recent publications include a wide-ranging and challenging book on the changing nature of the British political system from 1860 to 1975. He currently is editing the *Oxford Dictionary of National Biography.*

John Greenaway

References

Harrison, Brian. *Dictionary of British Temperance Biography.* Coventry, England: Society for the Study of Labour History. Aids to Research, no. 1. *Bulletin Supplement,* 1973.

———. "Drink and Sobriety in England, 1815–1872. A Critical Bibliography" in *International Review of Social History.* 12, part 2 (1967): 204–272.

———. *Drink and the Victorians: The Temperance Question in England, 1815–1872.* London: Faber and Faber, 1971 [2d ed., Keele: Keele University Press, 1994].

Haughton, James (1795–1873)

James Haughton (1795–1873), Irish temperance reformer, was a social and political activist and propagandist. He was an associate of Father Theobald Mathew and Daniel O'Connell. Born into a Quaker family in Carlow, Ireland, Haughton as a young man moved to Dublin, where he became a successful corn and flour merchant.

Remarkably active and public spirited, Haughton dedicated much of his time to a wide range of philanthropic and political activities, including the movements against alcohol, slavery, capital punishment, and war. Critics dubbed Haughton and his fellow Dublin reform activists Richard Allen and Richard Webb the "anti-everything-arians." Haughton was associated with other reformers in the Atlantic world. He corresponded regularly with William Lloyd Garrison, James Silk Buckingham, Matthew Sturge, and Charles Gilpin. Also a supporter of parliamentary reform and free trade, Haughton became an ally of Daniel O'Connell during his efforts to reform or repeal the political union between England and Ireland. Haughton's activities on behalf of these causes included organizing and serving on local committees, giving public lectures and platform appearances, and, most notably, authoring a steady stream of eloquent reform-minded letters published in Irish newspapers.

Temperance reform was Haughton's particular passion. From that movement's earliest beginnings in Ireland in 1829, he labored tirelessly on behalf of a steady succession of Irish temperance organizations, including the Hibernian Temperance Society and Father Mathew's Cork Total Abstinence Association. It was typical of Haughton's ecumenical temperament that he ignored sectarian differences in this work, and also typical of his impatience with halfway measures that by the late 1830s, he came to advocate total abstinence. Haughton, like many early temperance reformers, saw the movement as a panacea. He believed that the poverty of Ireland was directly related to the widespread abuse of alcohol and that the British government was implicated in what amounted to a national tragedy by its reliance on revenue derived from alcohol taxation. He regularly and publicly denounced the indifference of the Irish upper classes to the plight of the Irish poor, and in particular their lukewarm support of temperance efforts.

Haughton became a close friend and regular correspondent of temperance reformer Father Theobald Mathew during the early 1840s. Eventually, differences arose as Mathew came to resent what he saw as the politicization of his crusade by Haughton and O'Connell. Haughton's position as the secretary of the Mathew Relief Committee, inaugurated in 1843 to relieve Mathew of the debts acquired in his promotion of temperance, led to a public and private rift between the two. Haughton's insistence on controlling the distribution of funds and inspecting Mathew's expenditures offended the friar.

Haughton continued his advocacy of temperance long after the collapse of Mathew's crusade in the mid-1940s. Haughton served as a vice president of the English-based United Kingdom Alliance for the Total Suppression of the Liquor Traffic from its foundation in 1853 and published several pamphlets endorsing prohibition and the Maine Law. Haughton died in Dublin on 20 February 1873 at the age of seventy-eight.

Paul Townend

See also: Buckingham, James Silk; Ireland; Mathew, Father Theobald; United Kingdom Alliance (UKA)

Reference

Haughton, Samuel. *A Memoir of James Haughton.* London: Longmans, Green, 1877.

Hayler, Guy (1850–1943)

Guy Hayler (1850–1943), dedicated reformer in Britain's temperance crusade and advocate for worldwide prohibition, was born on 5 November 1850 in Battle, Sussex, to a working-class family. Reared as a child in sobriety, he eventually became involved in the temperance and international prohibition movements while living in London and northern England. For most of his career, Hayler was a household name in the fight against intemperance, and he became widely recognized later in life as a propagandist for the movement to advance prohibition in all lands.

Hayler was active in a number of formidable temperance organizations. He joined the Good Templar order in London in 1870. After his marriage to Ann Elizabeth Harris (1848–1941), he moved in 1874 to Hull where he served as agent and later as secretary for a local branch of the United Kingdom Alliance (UKA) until 1889. He next served until 1908 as general secretary for the North of England Temperance League in Newcastle upon Tyne, during which time he also wrote a number of temperance tracts and edited the league's newspaper, the *Temperance Witness.*

Hayler was honorary secretary for the National Prohibition Convention in 1897 and founded the Temperance Institute in Newcastle in 1899. He served as press commissioner for the American liquor inquiry in 1901, honorary secretary for the National Temperance Federation from 1895 to 1919, and international electoral superintendent for the Good Templars in the early 1900s. Upon his return to London in 1909, he served for the next thirty years as founding, honorary president of the International Prohibition Confederation, which became the World Prohibition Federation in 1919. Hayler edited the organization's quarterly journal, the *International Record,* from its first issue in 1917 until his death.

In practice, Hayler favored meetings, demonstrations, processions, and every form of modern agitation to advance prohibition. In theory, he believed that moral suasion was only partially effective and that the continuation of the liquor traffic was a problem that only national prohibition could solve. He eventually came to believe that prohibition also was the remedy for the world's drink problem and devoted the last thirty years of his life to advocating international prohibition. He traveled widely in his efforts to advance prohibition the world over.

Hayler was well versed in the history of drink and the liquor traffic in Britain and abroad. His reports, pamphlets, and books were generally considered to be unmatched in scope and research. Hayler's most important publications included *Famous Fanatics* (1910), *Prohibition Advance in all Lands* (1913), and *The New Europe and Prohibition: A Post-War Survey* (1923). His novel, *George Proctor, the Teetotaler* (1895), reached a second printing. Many of his lectures and temperance stories were published as widely circulated penny pamphlets.

Hayler was a great collector of temperance paraphernalia and, in a lifetime of cutting and pasting, assembled one of the most extensive libraries of temperance and prohibition. Although German bombs destroyed Hayler's home shortly after his death, most of his library survived. The Memorial Library at the University of Wisconsin, Madison, purchased part of it. The collection, which deals chiefly with the temperance question in Britain, includes a few manuscripts, many books, and hundreds of shorter publications. Thirty-five bound volumes of tracts collected by Hayler, and an additional index volume prepared by the librarians at the University of Wisconsin, have been microfilmed on eight reels with the title *Temperance Tracts: Collection of Pamphlets.*

Matthew K. McKean

See also: Good Templars (IOGT); Hayler, Mark; National Temperance Federation (NTF); United Kingdom Alliance (UKA); World Prohibition Federation

References

Fahey, David M. "Guy Hayler," in *Oxford Dictionary of National Biography,* ed. H. C. G. Mathew and Brian Harrison. Oxford: Oxford University Press, forthcoming 2004.

Hayler, M. H. C. *The Man from Battle: Being a Centenary Reinterpretation of the Life and Work of Guy Hayler, Social Reformer, 1850–1943.* Birmingham: International Order of Good Templars, 1950.

Temperance Tracts: Collection of Pamphlets. microfilm. La Crosse, WI: Brookhaven Press, 1982.

Hayler, Mark (1887–1986)

Mark Hayler (1887–1986) from the time of his birth in Hull was associated with the temperance movement. Guy Hayler, his father, was a prominent Good Templar and a full-time temperance official with the United Kingdom Alliance (UKA). Mark was a devoted son and loyal supporter of his father. From 1904 to 1909, he worked in the estate office of the earl of Carlisle at Brampton in Cumberland and Palace Green, London, and assisted Rosalind, Countess of Carlisle, the leader of the women's temperance movement. On leaving this position, he studied at Trevecca Theological College in Wales.

In 1909, his father established what became known as the World Prohibition Federation, and in 1925 Mark Hayler became its executive secretary. Two years later, Lawson House was opened as the federation's headquarters. In 1917, the *International Record* was first published to make "more generally known and better understood" the merits of prohibition and its advance throughout the world. Mark helped in the editing of the journal and, after his father's death in 1943, continued as editor until its final edition in January 1968.

He joined his father as a member of the executive committee of the UKA in 1938. For forty-nine years, the younger Hayler had a continuous service with the UKA and United Kingdom Temperance Association (UKTA). He was the author of the official history of the UKA, called the *Vision of a Century,* published in its centennial year.

In addition to his temperance work, Mark Hayler was a peace activist. During the first world war, he was imprisoned on several occasions for his beliefs and served his final imprisonment in Dartmoor from March 1918 to January 1919. During the last months of his imprisonment, he worked in the hospital. He was fond of telling the story of how, on returning to prison from work in the quarry, he came across a road accident and set about assisting an injured person. When he arrived back at the prison he found the doors closed. There followed a rare sight to see a prisoner banging on the gates to get back in.

Born into a Congregationalist family, his life experiences led him to the Religious Society of Friends in 1924. In 1938, he became a director of the Chelsea Building Society and served until 1973. He died at the age of ninety-nine in 1986. To the end, he was loyal to his principles, even though for him, like so many, the "vision" had become illusory. In 1969, his *International Record* valedictory editorial referred to John G. Woolley's remark that those who banded themselves together to do something about the drink habit were like a fire bell: They could ring the bell or put out the fire. Hayler concluded: "If this paper is no longer to ring the bell, it has played its part in endeavouring to put out the fire. It has shared in every campaign, at home and abroad, in favour of prohibitory legislation, nor has it wavered in that advocacy at any time."

This entry is based in part on personal information from Mark Hayler's son Wilfrid.

Derek Rutherford

See also: Carlisle, Countess of (Rosalind Howard); Good Templars (IOGT); Hayler, Guy; United Kingdom Alliance (UKA); United Kingdom Temperance Alliance (UKTA); World Prohibition Federation

Reference

Hayler, Mark H. C. *The Vision of a Century, 1853–1953: The United Kingdom Alliance in Historical Retrospect.* London: United Kingdom Alliance, 1953.

Hayman, Sir (Cecil George) Graham (1893–1966)

Sir (Cecil George) Graham Hayman (1893–1966) was chairman of the Distillers Company Limited (DCL) from 1958 to 1963. In response to a decline in the market for whiskey, he helped diversify DCL so that it became as much a chemicals, petroleum, and pharmaceuticals company as a whiskey-making one.

Graham Hayman was born at Poplar in London, the son of Charles Hayman, engine fitter, and Clara Anne Cuthbert. He was educated at state school, leaving at fifteen to work in a manufacturing chemist's office. After two years in a solicitor's office and two in a city finance house, he enlisted in 1914 in the 7th London Regiment, transferring in 1916 to the Royal Engineers. Demobilized with the rank of sergeant, he joined F. A. Hughes and Company Limited of London, a chemical manufacturing and merchandising firm. It had spotted the potential market in the United Kingdom for thermo-setting resin-based products that could be molded into consumer goods. A Hughes director recruited Hayman in 1922 to be secretary of Herbert Green and Company Limited, which was constructing an industrial alcohol distillery at Salt End, Hull. The industrial alcohol trade was undergoing rapid expansion; alcohol, distilled from molasses, had become a key raw material for new science-based industries. DCL dominated the trade and in 1925 acquired the Hull distillery. Hayman and D. H. Owen Edmunds, Green's former chairman, formed an independent company called Solvent Products Limited and constructed another distillery at Dagenham, Essex. Solvent Products established such a strong competitive position that DCL acquired a 50 percent holding of its rival in 1930. In 1935, DCL gained complete control and in the following year appointed Hayman to its board.

With the collapse of the potable spirit trade, DCL was diversifying into chemicals and allied products. Hayman's experience made him an ideal recruit. He quickly came to play a prominent part in DCL's industrial activities, including the negotiation of an agreement with Imperial Chemical Industries (ICI) in 1938 that divided much of the British chemical trade between the two firms. That agreement lessened the risk of diversification for DCL, but it was the opportunities afforded by the second world war that enabled DCL to push ahead with its chemical developments. Hayman chaired the industrial products committee from 1942, establishing close contacts with government departments that put DCL in a favorable position to purchase modern plants in the postwar disposal of government factories. By 1945, he was the senior director on DCL's industrial side and faced with important strategic decisions about the future of the company's chemical activities. When government support for molasses-based industrial alcohol was removed in 1945, it became vital for DCL to find a partner either in the chemical industry or the oil industry. ICI, DCL's obvious partner, refused DCL full participation and also announced its intention to end the 1938 agreement. Hayman had the demanding task of unravelling the agreement while finding a new partner for hydrocarbons. Success came in September 1947 when DCL and the Anglo-Iranian Oil Company (British Petroleum after 1955) announced a £5-million plan for the manufacture of chemicals in the United Kingdom through a jointly owned subsidiary, British Petroleum Chemicals (after 1956, the British Hydrocarbon Company). A massive plant at Grangemouth, Scotland, and another at Barry, South Wales, became the basis for a series of major investments in chemicals and plastics, frequently in conjunction with major U.S. firms. These were truly joint partnerships because Hayman had developed a highly successful research and development department under Dr. Frank Roffey and Dr. Herbert Stanley.

Hayman was appointed chairman of DCL's management committee in 1953 and succeeded Sir Henry Ross as board chairman in April 1958, the first such nonwhiskey appointment. Hayman made DCL into a dynamic force in the chemical and plastics industries, but before he retired, in March 1963, he had begun to question whether DCL's force was sufficiently large to compete internationally. In 1967, his successors concluded that it was not and sold the chemical and plastics interests to British Petroleum.

Ronald Weir

See also: Distillers Company Limited (DCL)

References

Ashford, G. G. Obituary of Sir Graham Hayman, in *Chemistry & Industry.* 16 April 1966: 646.

Weir, R. B. *The History of the Distillers Company, 1877–1939: Diversification and Growth In Whisky and Chemicals.* Oxford: Clarendon Press, 1995.

Hazelden Foundation

The Hazelden Foundation is a Minnesota-based, nonprofit organization with a mission to "help build recovery in the lives of individuals, families and communities affected by alcoholism, drug dependency and related diseases." For more than fifty years, Hazelden has been one of the best-known providers of addiction treatment services in the United States, as well as the largest publisher and distributor of addiction- and recovery-related publications. Since its opening in 1949, Hazelden has treated more than 200,000 chemically dependent individuals and their families from all fifty states and every continent, and has distributed more than 50 million pieces of addiction/recovery-related literature.

Hazelden was conceived during a period in which alcoholics languished in the "drunk tanks" of city and county jails, and in the "snake pits" of aging state psychiatric hospitals. Few resources existed for any alcoholic, either rich or poor. The first Hazelden treatment facility opened in Center City, Minnesota, following extended discussions about the need for an alcoholism treatment facility for priests and other professionals. Initial financial support came from the local Catholic diocese and contributions from local businesses. The expectations placed on its first residents were exceedingly simple: Make your bed, conduct yourself as a gentleman, attend the daily lectures on the Twelve Steps of Alcoholics Anonymous (AA), and talk with one another. Hazelden's treatment philosophy was able to expand and evolve, due in great part to the financial resources of Emmet, Patrick, and Lawrence Butler, whose combined largesse sustained Hazelden through its early years. During the 1950s, the collaboration between Hazelden and two other Minnesota alcoholism treatment facilities, Pioneer House and Willmar State Hospital, created a unique approach (the "Minnesota Model") that exerted an enormous influence on the evolution of addiction treatment in the second half of the twentieth century. This model—as articulated by its early proponents, Dr. Nelson Bradley, Dr. Dan Anderson, the Reverend John Keller, and the Reverend Gordon Grimm—defined alcoholism as a primary, progressive disease whose resolution required life-long abstinence; extolled the importance of treating the alcoholic and addict with dignity and respect; emphasized the importance of a mutually supportive treatment milieu; utilized a multidisciplinary treatment team and a full continuum of services; and integrated the steps and social support of AA during and following treatment.

Over the years, Hazelden grew beyond its humble beginnings as a small, obscure treatment facility by adding an array of programs and services. These expansions began with the opening of a halfway house for men (Fellowship Club) in 1953 and a treatment facility for women (Dia Linn) in 1956. Under the leadership of Dr. Dan Anderson, services available on the Center City campus continued to expand, both in residential treatment capacity and in the variety of new services offered, including a formal family program and outpatient services. Hazelden later expanded beyond Minnesota by opening treatment centers in Florida, New York, Texas, and Illinois.

In 1954, Hazelden entered the world of publishing when it bought the rights to *Twenty-Four Hours a Day,* a recovery meditation book that would go on to sell more than 7 million copies. Hazelden went on to publish materials ranging from scholarly texts such as *Not-God: A History of Alcoholics Anonymous* by Ernest Kurtz, to popular self-help books such as Melanie Beattie's *Codependent No More.* Hazelden publishing grew from this single title to a division that today distributes more than 3.5 million books, pamphlets, videos, and recovery celebration items per year.

Hazelden's commitment to provide public and professional education on addiction and related disorders has also led it into the arenas of training and consultation. Hazelden offers a chemical dependency counselor certificate training program as well as a master's degree and postgraduate certificate in addiction counseling. The Counselor Training Program in Center City has graduated more than 500 individuals from 32 countries, and more than 100 individuals have graduated from Hazelden's Counselor Training Program in Europe. Hazelden's Pastoral Training Program and its Professional-in-Residence and Physician-in-Residence programs have also trained more than 2,500 addiction treatment providers from all over the United States and more than 50 other countries.

Hazelden was the primary instrument through which the Minnesota Model of chemical dependency treatment spread throughout the United States and abroad. This model was spread by persons who had been treated at Hazelden, by graduates from Hazelden's training programs, by the thousands of addiction professionals from more than fifty countries who have visited Hazelden, and by the large body of professional literature and treatment aids published and distributed by the Hazelden Publishing and Educational Services Division. Hazelden staff also served as consultants on the development of alcoholism treatment programs in other countries.

Another Hazelden service milestone was the 1993 opening of the Hazelden-Pittman Archives, a repository of books, manuscripts, and artifacts related to the history of addiction treatment and recovery in America.

Today (2002), Hazelden's 400 clinical staff treat more than 9,000 individuals and their families each year within its treatment centers. The philosophy undergirding these services has shifted from one focused on providing treatment services to a mission of providing recovery services. Where the former focused on initiating release from addiction, the latter offers a wide range of services that can support individuals and families through the long-term developmental stages of recovery. Symbolizing this broadened vision was the opening of Hazelden's Renewal Center. This center provides relapse prevention training, as well as a wide variety of retreats aimed at strengthening sobriety and enhancing the emotional, relational, and spiritual growth of individuals and families in recovery from alcoholism and other addictions. Hazelden has also expanded its mission to address recovery support services for other chronic and related diseases. To that end, Hazelden provides mental-health services for recovering people who experience such cooccurring disorders as depression, anxiety, posttraumatic stress disorder, gambling, and eating disorders.

William L. White

See also: Alcoholics Anonymous (AA); Alcoholism; Treatment Institutions

References

McElrath, Damian. *Further Reflections on Hazelden's Spiritual Odyssey.* Center City, MN: Hazelden Information and Educational Services, 1999.

———. *Hazelden: A Spiritual Odyssey.* Center City, MN: Hazelden Foundation, 1987.

Spicer, Jerry. *The Minnesota Model: The Evolution of the Interdisciplinary Approach to Addiction Recovery.* Center City, MN: Hazelden Educational Materials, 1993.

Heath, H. Cecil (1898–1972)

H. Cecil Heath (1898–1972) served as general secretary and president of the United Kingdom Alliance (UKA) and as managing director of the United Kingdom Temperance Alliance

(UKTA). Heath and his predecessor, George B. Wilson, are regarded as the most important twentieth-century UKA officials.

Heath was born of Methodist parents and educated at Adams Grammar School, Wellington, Shropshire. Only sixteen years old at the outbreak of the first world war, he became a lieutenant in the Cheshire regiment serving in France. At the end of the war, Heath read English at Pembroke College, Oxford. Leaving Oxford, he was recruited by Lewis's (a department store chain) as a personnel officer at their factory in Liverpool.

In 1926, at the age of twenty-eight, Heath became general secretary of the UKA. In order to provide the alliance with effective leadership, he studied to become a barrister and was called to the bar. Had he practiced at the bar or stayed in the commercial world, he would have had a brilliant career and commanded a far greater income than as a temperance official. Cecil Heath possessed the ability to quickly master a brief and cogently argue its points. From 1962 until 1970, he served the UKA as president. In 1963, he was made managing director of the UKTA, a post he held until just before his death in 1972.

Heath was a prolific writer. As well as writing many pamphlets, he edited the *Alliance News* for over thirty years. It was in the field of liquor licensing that he was an expert. His book *Control of a Dangerous Trade* was, for many temperance advocates, the textbook on licensing law.

Heath served the UKA when national sobriety was at its zenith and when the temperance movement was in decline. In the 1930s, Britain experienced its lowest per capita consumption of alcohol, and it is estimated that 40 percent of the population were abstainers. In contrast, by the 1950s and 1960s, the influence of the temperance movement was fading. Heath recognized the need for new ways to focus the nation's attention on the alcohol problem and to revitalize the movement. He cooperated with the new Christian Economic Research Council; assisted Ansvar, the Swedish abstaining-motorists insurance company, to establish its work in Britain; and fully supported the formation of the Teachers Advisory Council on Alcohol and Drug Education.

He led many deputations to government ministers on drunk driving, school alcohol education, liquor advertising, and licensing.

Heath not only established a national reputation but also an international one. He worked closely with the International Temperance Union and the International Research Bureau in Lausanne, which later became the International Council on Alcohol and Other Addictions.

He was an elder of the Religious Society of Friends and served as president of the National Brotherhood Movement, chairman of the British Ansvar Insurance Company, and chairman of the Good Templar Children's Home. Although a single-minded advocate of temperance, he had a fun-loving character typified in his membership in the Magic Circle (a magicians' organization).

Heath's first wife died early in their marriage, leaving him with two young daughters. His second wife, Muriel, also a committed temperance worker, was president of the National British Women's Total Abstinence Union and secretary and later president of the World's Woman's Christian Temperance Union (WWCTU).

Derek Rutherford

See also: Good Templars (IOGT); National British Women's Temperance Association (NBWTA); United Kingdom Alliance (UKA); United Kingdom Temperance Alliance (UKTA); Wilson, George Bailey; World's Woman's Christian Temperance Union (WWCTU)

Reference

Hayler, Mark H. C. *The Vision of a Century, 1853–1953: The United Kingdom Alliance in Historical Retrospect.* London: United Kingdom Alliance, 1953.

Heileman, G., Brewing Company

In 1858, Gottlieb Heileman and John Gund founded the City Brewery in La Crosse, Wisconsin. Soon after Gund's departure in 1872, the City Brewery was renamed the G. Heileman Brewing Company. In 1902, the brewery introduced Old Style beer, the brand that would become its flagship product.

With the passing of the Twenty-First Amendment in 1933, Heileman regained its position as one of scores of regional-sized breweries. By 1941, total sales had reached $5.4 million. Nine years later, the Wisconsin brewery distinguished itself with annual sales of $17.7 million. In 1952, Heileman introduced the Special Export brand, a super-premium-priced product.

In 1957, when Roy E. Kumm was promoted to the role of president of Heileman, the brewery was ranked thirty-ninth among the dwindling number of small U.S. brewing operations. Impressed by the far-reaching and methodical business vision of his son-in-law, Russell G. Cleary, Kumm asked Cleary to join Heileman in 1960 as in-house counsel. In the next few years, the family team began the purchase of several failing smaller-sized breweries. Its first major acquisition was in 1967 when Heileman purchased the Weidemann Brewing Company in Newport, Kentucky, for $5 million.

In 1976, with a nationwide bottlers' strike at Anheuser-Busch Brewing Company and growing customer dissatisfaction with the troubled Schlitz beer brand, Heileman began an aggressive campaign to control the lucrative Chicago beer market. Cleary, who succeeded Kumm after his death in 1971, used price discounting to gain new retail accounts in Chicago. By 1978, the Old Style brand achieved a commanding 26 percent of the Chicago market. The brewery's continued success was reflected in total sales for 1979 at the $500 million mark.

In early 1981, chief executive officer Cleary attempted to acquire the Milwaukee-based Pabst Brewing Company, a business with the national stature and distribution that Heileman lacked.

During the negotiations for Pabst, Heileman abruptly lowered its initial offer of $45.00 per share for approximately 8.2 million shares of outstanding common stock to $24.00 a share after a management shake-up at Pabst. Pabst immediately pulled out of negotiations with Heileman.

Heileman next turned its attention to the ailing Joseph Schlitz Brewing Company. In July 1981, the Heileman brewery announced that it had made a proposal to buy Schlitz for $494 million, about $17.00 per share. Schlitz officials quickly agreed to accept the proposal.

The U.S. Justice Department, however, stopped the merger with Schlitz from continuing, claiming that it would be an antitrust violation. At the time, Anheuser-Busch controlled 28 percent of the national beer market, with the Miller Brewing Company at 21 percent. Heileman countered that a merger with Schlitz would only give it a combined market share of 16 percent, but the federal government stood firm.

Determined to gain access to a national market, Heileman turned its attention once again to the ailing Pabst Brewing Company. This time, Pabst officials were ready to deal. On 23 December 1982, the two breweries announced that a partial merger was proceeding. In the deal, Heileman acquired the Pabst plants at Perry, Georgia; Portland, Oregon; and San Antonio, Texas, for $30 million. With this acquisition, Heileman now had an expanded brewing capacity of 25 million barrels, a larger presence in the South, and a network of over 2,400 distributors.

However, by 1985, Heileman's plan of further growth by acquisition was stymied by falling sales, especially in the all-important Chicago market. From a 1982 high of 44 percent of the local market, Chicago sales of Old Style fell as growth in the light beer and import segment increased. Two years later, CEO Russell Cleary signed an agreement worth $1.26 billion for Heileman to be acquired by Bond Corporation Holdings Limited, owned by Australian millionaire Alan Bond.

Despite Heileman's 1986 sales of $1.33 billion, the highly leveraged buyout bogged down operations at Heileman, especially after a number of Australian banks claimed that Bond Holdings had breached several covenants in an unrelated loan agreement. This move by the banks forced the sale by Bond Holdings of its assets including real estate, media, and natural assets. In mid-1990, Alan Bond resigned as chairman of Bond Corporation Holdings, beginning the first step in the restructuring of thc parent company, and triggered the filing by the G. Heileman Brewing Company for reorganization under federal bankruptcy laws in January of 1991.

Now led by court-appointed CEO Thomas Rattigan, the financially stabilized Heileman was purchased on 1 November 1993 for $390 million by Hicks, Muse and Company, a Dallas-based investment firm that had a background in leveraged acquisitions in the beverage industry. In early 1996, however, Heileman once again went into bankruptcy proceedings as sales at Heileman continued to fall.

The Stroh Brewing Company of Detroit, Michigan, took control of Heileman in 1996 for $300 million and assumed Heileman's debt and absorbed the brewery as it had done the Joseph Schlitz Brewing Company fourteen years earlier. Faced with an overlapping of distributors picked up in the merger and a bloated portfolio of regional beer brands, Stroh began dropping wholesalers and curtailed a number of its most unprofitable brands.

A national price war, instigated by the Miller Brewing Company in 1997 to prop up falling sales of its Lite and Miller Genuine Draft brands, was joined by Anheuser-Busch, the Coors Brewing Company, and a reluctant Stroh. The price discounting, combined with debt load increased by the purchase of Heileman and the ending of an arrangement with Pabst to brew a number of their brands in Stroh-owned plants, forced the voluntary ending of the Stroh Brewing Company in 1999. At the time, the Pabst contract accounted for about 15 percent of Stroh's total production.

On 6 August 1999, brewing operations ceased at the old Heileman brewery in La Crosse. The Old Style brand is now owned by the S and P Corporation–controlled Pabst Brewing Company but brewed under contract by the Miller Brewing Company of Milwaukee, Wisconsin.

Bob Skilnik

See also: Anheuser-Busch; Beer; Coors, Adolph, Brewing Company; Miller Brewing Company; Pabst Brewing Company; Schlitz, Joseph, Brewing Company; Stroh Brewing Company

References

Federal Reserve Bank of Minneapolis. "'Beer Town' Holds on to Brewing Legacy" in *Fedgazette.* http://www.minneapolisfed.org/pubs/fedgaz/01-03/brewing.html. [15 January 2002].

"Heileman Holds Own with Army of Many Brands," *Chicago Tribune,* 15 November 1978, sec. 4.

"News Briefs" in *Brewers Digest.* 54, no. 11 (November 1979): 56; 55, no. 3 (March 1980): 42; 56, no. 9 (September 1981): 61; 57, no. 7 (July 1982): 37; 57, no. 8 (August 1982): 41; 58, no. 1 (January 1983): 30; 60, no. 2 (February 1985): 13; 61, no. 8 (August 1986): 10; 62, no. 9 (September 1987): 14; 74, no. 1 (January 1999): 7–8.

Skilnik, Bob. *The History of Beer and Brewing in Chicago,* vol. II. Haverford, PA: Infinity Publishing, 2002.

Hills, Arnold Frank (1857–1927)

Arnold Frank Hills (1857–1927), a wealthy shipbuilder, was a leading figure in late Victorian temperance. With the help of his personal fortune, Hills promoted unity among temperance organizations. He originated the United Temperance Association and drafted the first United Temperance bill. He also played a major role in the late Victorian vegetarian movement.

Born at Redleaf in Kent, Hills was the youngest of three sons of a distinguished manufacturing chemist, Frank Clarke Hills, who had become a millionaire and acquired a large interest in the Thames Ironworks and Shipbuilding Company. Educated at Harrow and Oxford, A. F. Hills excelled as an athlete. He joined the directorate of the Ironworks, one of the most important shipyards in Britain. This company struggled to compete with cheaper and more modern shipbuilders on the Merseyside. Hills succeeded in the short term in extending the business and improving technology.

A humanitarian, his interests encompassed his workers' welfare, wider problems of unemployment and poverty, and animal cruelty. Concern with the problems of modern industrial and urban life took practical form early in his career, in 1880 through 1885, with philanthropic work in Canning Town, near the Ironworks. A vegetarian as well as a teetotaler, in the 1880s and 1890s he linked his interest in food reform and teetotalism with a range of social measures combining public charity, local authorities, and the state.

Hills worked for a united temperance movement in which the various organizations surmounted their differences to reach agreement in support of a politically realistic program. The first United Temperance Council was formed in Chelmsford in January 1895. By early 1896, there were twenty councils in Britain. A national council was established with Hills as the first president. He sponsored national conferences, called the United Temperance Parliaments, in the mid-1890s and published the *United Temperance Gazette.* The first United Temperance bill focused on a reduction in the number of existing licenses. Courted for funds by the United Kingdom Alliance (UKA), he offered £1,000 and, in the future, a £250 yearly subscription on the condition that there be a dialogue between the UKA and the Church of England Temperance Society (CETS). Eventually, Hills's hope for temperance unity failed. The alliance would not abandon its policy of prohibition by local-option referendum. Hills also led a Sunday closing campaign and served as treasurer of the United Kingdom Railway Temperance Union.

Hills was president of the Vegetarian Federal Union, the London Vegetarian Society, and several local vegetarian societies. His mansion and estate were frequently used for vegetarian celebrations. As an athlete, he promoted a muscular image for vegetarianism. His *Essays,* promoting vegetarianism as a necessary component of the ideal, first appeared in the *Vegetarian,* a journal that he funded, and were republished in two volumes in 1895. In 1893, his financial support enabled the creation of the Ideal Publishing Union for publication of temperance and vegetarian literature.

His many schemes for improving the lives of his workforce and the residents of the Canning Town area included building a gymnasium and providing facilities for boxing, fencing, football (establishing what became West Ham Football Club), as well as lectures, debates, and music. A Conservative in politics and opposed to trade unions, he was involved in a long conflict leading to a strike at the Ironworks. Subsequently, he introduced profit sharing and supported an eight-hour working day. Overworked as a philanthropist and in his efforts to save his shipyard (which closed in 1911), Hills eventually fell victim to a paralysis from which he never recovered, but he maintained a close interest in social reform until his death.

James Gregory

See also: Church of England Temperance Society (CETS); Harcourt, Sir William; United Kingdom Alliance (UKA); Vegetarianism and the Anti-Tobacco Movement (United Kingdom)

References

Cameron, A. "A. F. Hills" in *Dictionary of National Biography. Twentieth Century. Persons who Died 1922–1930,* edited by J. R. H. Weaver, 418–420. London, Oxford University Press, 1937.

Dingle, A. E. *The Campaign for Prohibition in Victorian England. The United Kingdom Alliance, 1872–1895.* London: Croom Helm, 1980.

United Temperance Gazette. London. 1896–1897.

Vegetarian. London. 1888–1921.

Vegetarian News. London. 1922–1923.

Hiram Walker

Hiram Walker and Sons, Limited is a Canadian firm that is best known as the manufacturer of Canadian Club, the world's leading premium Canadian-style whiskey. The company became the first in the liquor industry to brand its product and sell it in bottles. Founded in 1858 by its American-born namesake, Hiram Walker today owns distilleries throughout the world and sells whiskey, cordials, and liquors in 150 countries.

Hiram Walker (1816–1899) worked as a merchant in Massachusetts before an economic downturn prompted him to try his luck in Detroit in 1838. He quickly found employment as a grocer, selling wines and liquors as well as food. Walker's experience as a cider-vinegar maker and grain buyer probably led him to consider starting a whiskey distillery. Michigan's temperance laws, as well as the availability of cheaper real estate, labor, and materials in Canada, led Walker to open his new business in East Sandwich, Ontario, in 1858.

Since the Canadian market was small, Walker immediately sought to establish his products in the much larger American market. His first brand of whiskey, Magnolia, a light-bodied liquor, met little success during its 1858 to 1900 lifespan. By 1892, the distillery offered twenty-seven different whiskey products, including Walker's Old Rye, Toddy, Superior, and Imperial. Although these liquors met with moderate success, none achieved the dominance that Walker sought, and the company decided to market a premium whiskey.

Canadian Club Whisky first appeared in 1881 under the name Three Star Club, but Walker quickly changed that in 1882 to Club Whisky. Like other typically Canadian whiskies, it was a blend that had been distilled at different proofs but aged together before going to market. Walker trademarked the Club name and proceeded to promote the brand as a liquor known for its smoothness and the length of time it was aged in oak barrels. In contrast to Club, most whiskey in this era was sold in barrels and aged briefly. Walker maintained lightness through the years by maturing a portion of its whiskey in charred new casks and a portion of it in charred used casks. With an abundance of private labels, quality was often spotty, and Walker believed that discerning consumers would flock to a reliable national brand. He was the first in the industry to brand whiskey and the first distiller to put whiskey into individually sealed bottles—a step beyond the usual practice of selling it in bulk from wooden barrels. With new methods of packaging and marketing whiskey available, distillers typically designated their best brands for bottling. The first of Walker's brands to be bottled were Old Rye and Club. Walker charged much more than the competition but slowly found a market for Club Whisky.

The success of Walker's whiskey in the United States alarmed American distillers and, in the belief that American drinkers would choose American whiskies, they persuaded the government to require Canadian products to be clearly labeled as such. Accordingly, Club whiskey became "Canada Club" in 1890. The brand was bottled in a distinctive pumpkinseed flask for a short time before returning to its familiar bottle. In 1893, another label change created the "Canadian Club" brand. Having successfully established Canadian Club in the United States, Walker fought to protect the integrity of the brand. As few marketplace regulations existed, bottlers frequently tried to sell their own inferior whiskies under Walker's trademarked label. In response, the company placed newspaper advertisements and put up billboards in numerous cities naming the fraudulent dealers and daring them to sue for libel. None accepted the offer.

The subsequent decades brought enormous challenges for the distillery. In 1890, the Canadian government passed the Two Year Maturing Law, requiring distillers to hold product in casks for two years before distribution. This law forced Walker to increase its storage capacity to 5 million gallons. As the distillery grew through the years, the Walker sons entered the business and, by 1895, they were fully in charge. In 1915, the distilling of grain in Canada was prohibited for two years since it was felt that grain should be used for wartime food supplies. The company had just begun to recover from the war when the advent of National Prohibition in the United States struck. Unlike many other distilleries, Walker managed to keep operating, though at reduced output. In 1926, the firm was sold to H. Clifford Hatch. Faced with a lack of American demand, Hatch sought to keep the firm afloat by expanding into Europe and Latin America. Incorporated in Scotland in 1937, the Dumbarton plant made grain whiskey for the blend and became the largest distillery in Europe. In 1943, Walker expanded to the south by purchasing the Mattaldi-Simon distillery in Argentina, the most important grain distillery in that region.

With the repeal of Prohibition in 1933, Walker struggled to increase production to meet the pent-up demand among Americans for quality liquor. Prior to repeal, there had been no Hiram Walker distillery in the United States, but the success of its liquors on the world market encouraged the company to design a new plant to produce a light-bodied whiskey as well as a premium gin. In 1934, Walker opened its Peoria, Illinois, distillery.

In the first few years after repeal, Walker offered two whiskies, Walker's DeLuxe Straight Rye and Walker's DeLuxe Straight Bourbon at 100 proof for sale in the United States. The company discontinued these two items in 1940 when stocks had matured at its Peoria plant, but it offered lower-proof whiskey under the same brand names. One of Walker's most successful products after resuming full operations was Imperial, a blend of four whiskies married to neutral spirits that was made both in Canada and the United States.

In the latter half of the twentieth century, Walker has continued to expand by purchasing distilleries. At Bardstown, Kentucky, the Ten High distillery produces Ten High Sourmash Bourbon, while Double-V Blended is made at the Destilerias Y Crianza del Whisky in Cadiz, Spain. The company has also moved into the cordial and liqueur market, achieving considerable success with its Kahlua.

Caryn E. Neumann

See also: Whiskies

References

Fraser, Wendy Carol. *Hiram Walker Remembered: Publication on the Occasion of the Windsor Centennial 1892–1992.* Windsor, Ontario, Canada: Forest Press, 1992.

Hiram Walker, Inc. *The Hiram Walker Outline of the Distilled Spirits Business.* Detroit: Hiram Walker, 1946.

Hobson, Richmond Pearson (1870–1937)

Richmond Pearson Hobson (1870–1937) was an admiral in the United States navy and a congressman who introduced a national prohibition bill. Born on 17 August 1870 in Greensboro, Alabama, Hobson attended Southern University and the United States Naval Academy. Graduating in 1889, he took advanced studies in Paris, France, at l'École National Supérieur des Mines and l'École d'Application du Génie Maritime until 1893. Returning to America, he became an assistant constructor in the Navy Department's Bureau of Construction and Repair in Washington, D.C. He then served on the USS *New York* and in various naval yards across the Northeast. In 1897, he became an instructor in naval construction at Annapolis. The next year, during the Spanish-American War, while on the USS *New York,* he was given the assignment of sinking the *Merrimac* to block Santiago Harbor. His attempt failed and he was taken prisoner. Freed on 6 July 1898, he became a national hero for his efforts. After the war, he was appointed inspector of Spanish wrecks and given the task of trying to raise any of the sunken Spanish vessels in Cuba, succeeding with the *Reina Mercedes* and the *Infanta Maria Teresa.* He retired from the navy in 1903 due to ill health and in 1933 was rewarded with the Medal of Honor and a retroactive promotion to admiral for his wartime service.

After conducting a speaking tour of the nation in which he frequently spoke on the evils of alcohol, Hobson was elected to Congress from an Alabama district in 1906, serving four terms. He gained national attention two years later when he claimed while speaking before the Democratic National Convention that Theodore Roosevelt had stated that war with Japan was close at hand, a claim the president denied. Serving on the Naval Affairs Committee from 1907 to 1914, he was at the forefront of many national issues.

During his time in Congress, Hobson spoke often about the dangers of alcohol for the nation's well-being. In 1911, he introduced a national prohibition bill to ban alcohol, and in succeeding years he proposed more than twenty similar constitutional amendments. He toured the country for the Anti-Saloon League and presented an hour-long lecture entitled "The Great Destroyer." Hobson was one of the leading prohibition figures of his day. Although stressing the traditional message of the destructive nature of alcohol, he also gave it a scientific rationale. Arguing that alcohol was a "protoplasmic poison," he claimed that it tears down the tissue of the top part of the brain, which was the most recently evolved area. He stated, "every time a man drinks, will power declines. In destroying the seat of the will power, alcohol destroys the seat of the moral senses, and the spiritual nature, the recognition of right and wrong, the consciousness of God and of duty and brotherly love and of self-sacrifice" (quoted in Hobson 1911) His message that 5 million Americans were slaves of the "Great Liquor Trust" was not a popular message with some of his constituents, and he was voted out of office in 1914.

When National Prohibition became law in 1920, Hobson turned his attention to heroin. Claiming to have recruited 21,000 major clubs and organizations to educate the nation against this new menace, he coined the term "living dead" and claimed that narcotics led to harder drugs. Hobson died in New York City on 16 March 1937, having lived four years past the repeal of the alcohol prohibition law he had worked so hard to enact.

T. Jason Soderstrum

References

Hobson, Richmond P. *Great Destroyer: The Speech of Hon. Richmond P. Hobson of Alabama in the House of Representatives, February 2, 1911.* Washington, DC: United States Government Printing Office, 1911.

Rosenfeld, Harvey. *Richmond Pearson Hobson: The Legendary Naval Hero of Magnolia Grove.* Las Cruces, NM: Yucca Tree Press, 2001.

Home, as Drinking Site

Americans have been drinking in their homes since the first colonists arrived with a thirst for ale. Today, more than two-thirds of all alcohol consumed in the United States is drunk at home or at private parties. It hasn't always been that way. In fact, throughout much of U.S. history, most alcohol was consumed in public venues. The current trend started after World War II. At that time, only 10 percent of alcohol was consumed away from taverns and restaurants.

What changed? A number of things, but among the most important was a significant decline in the number of taverns as the United States suburbanized, with the new suburbs finding little room for taverns. Coupled with a growing enforcement of laws dealing with driving under the influence of alcohol, this loss of the "neighborhood tavern" has had a major impact on home consumption of alcohol. Another key factor was a change in taverns themselves. Taverns became home to women and younger people in growing numbers after World War II and changed to accommodate their new customers. When more and more women and younger people started frequenting taverns, male patrons—long the mainstay of the tavern business—began to stay home to drink.

These changes are only the latest for home drinking, a practice that has long been directly influenced by matters of gender, age, social approval, and class. In early colonial America, virtually everyone drank alcohol since colonists felt water was unsafe, and drinking almost always took place in private homes. Americans brewed their ales and distilled their spirits and cider because it was cheaper, and there were few commercial establishments selling drink. This slowly changed as a colonial tavern system developed and the cost of public drinking injected class issues into the subject. The well-off could afford to drink in public, while others could only afford their home products.

Drinking in public became more popular and more available to the working class during the middle of the nineteenth century when the tavern system changed, becoming more affordable; development of the commercial alcohol industry lowered the price of drinks; and real wages grew. This growth in public drinking was brought about for the most part by male Americans. Women found themselves unwelcome at taverns during what is called the "Saloon Era," from the mid-nineteenth century until Prohibition in 1920. Women continued to drink during this period, but it was at home or in other women's kitchens. Some women, in fact, followed the Irish custom of shebeens, selling beer and spirits from their kitchens. Others went to taverns and groceries to purchase alcohol to take home. An emphasis on thrift and family by the middle class during this period led many men to join their women in drinking at home.

Prohibition changed America's drinking patterns in many ways, including fostering illegal production of liquor at home and temporarily increasing the share in American alcohol consumption of distilled liquors, often consumed as mixed drinks—"cocktails." In the period from 1933 until after World War II, the trend was toward drinking in public, in the nightclubs and cocktail lounges that replaced the old-time saloon. This trend, too, turned out to be short lived. Rooted in changing demographics and disapproval of public drunkenness, coupled with growing home consumption of beers and wines, the shift away from the tavern has resulted in the United States becoming the world's leading nation of home drinkers.

Stephen R. Byers

See also: Alcohol, Consumption of, by Indices (United States); Alcohol, Consumption of, per Capita (United States); Saloons and Taverns (United States)

References

Barr, Andrew. *Drink: A Social History of America.* New York: Carroll and Graf, 1999.

Jersild, Devon. *Happy Hours: Alcohol in a Woman's Life.* New York: Cliff Street Books, 2001.

Lender, Mark Edward, and James Kirby Martin. *Drinking in America: A History,* 2d ed. New York: Free Press, 1986.

Murdock, Catherine Gilbert. *Domesticating Drink: Women, Men, and Alcohol in America, 1870–1940.* Baltimore: Johns Hopkins University Press, 1998.

Oldenburg, Ray. *The Great Good Place.* New York: Paragon House, 1989.

Home Brewing

Home brewing of beer and ale has been a part of U.S. history since the arrival of Europeans. However, the interest has waxed and waned, with three distinct periods when home brewing was popular. They are: the colonial period, Prohibition, and the modern era. Although each was a time of great interest in home brewing, the reasons for that interest and for the popularity of brewing were different.

The colonial period, ranging from the first recorded instance of beer in 1630 through the middle of the nineteenth century, saw the widest home brewing. Virtually all New England and Middle Atlantic colonists brewed malt beverages at home. They were mostly English-style ales and porters (the favorite of George Washington, whose recipe for home brew exists today). Ale was assumed to be healthy. Not only did immigrants from overcrowded Europe, where the water was often polluted, distrust the healthfulness of all water, but they ascribed enough healthy qualities to ale that they seldom went a day without their brew.

Mrs. Vernon skims off the barm from the beer before pouring the brew into a barrel (1931). (Hulton-Deutsch Collection/Corbis)

Many historians explain the landing of the Pilgrims at Plymouth Rock by the ships' running out of beer and colonists' desire to replenish their supplies. Home brewing was vital to early settlers because commercial brewing was not established. Almost every home included brewing facilities. In many New England households, there was a small brew room attached to the living quarters, isolating heat generated during brewing and protecting dwellings from possible fires. These additions are still visible on the oldest American homes as a lower roofline jutting out from the main buildings. Like other household chores, home brewing was seen as women's work.

Three factors ended this era in the 1850s: urbanization and crowding in cities, reducing space for brewing; industrialization, providing more money for buying beer and reducing leisure time; and, most important, the popularity of inexpensive German-style lagers, which were more difficult to brew than Americans' traditional ales.

Passage of the Eighteenth Amendment banned the sale or manufacture of intoxicating beverages after 1920, putting commercial brewers out of business. Home brewing quickly revived, with sales of malt compounds and brewer's yeast indicating that millions of barrels were being produced in American homes. When National Prohibition was repealed in 1933, the amount of home brewing dropped dramatically because, even as commercial breweries resumed pumping out inexpensive beers, a clerical error in transcribing the new federal alcohol control legislation left home brewing illegal.

Thus it remained until the late 1970s. Industry consolidation had led to a uniformity of brewery products to the point that many beer drinkers felt commercial offerings, almost all light lagers, were nearly indistinguishable. During the 1970s, some American consumers revolted against uniform products such as breads, bakery products in general, and beer. An illegal home-brewing industry arose, and consumers pressured lawmakers to allow home brewing. In 1979, Congress passed the Cranston Act, allowing adults to brew up to 100 gallons a year for their own use (with a limit of 200 gallons per household). Most states followed suit, although home brewing remains illegal in some. Brewing kits, ingredients, and equipment are now widely available. Today, according to the American Home Brewers' Association, more than 1.5 million Americans have tried home brewing. Dark beers and ales are the most popular types brewed.

Stephen R. Byers

See also: Beer; Saloons and Taverns (United States)

References

Papazian, Charles. *The Home Brewer's Companion.* New York: Avon Books, 1994.

———. *The New Complete Joy of Home Brewing.* New York: Avon Books, 1991.

Smith, Gregg. *Beer in America: The Early Years: 1587–1840.* New York: Siris Books, 1998.

Snyder, Stephen. *The Brewmaster's Bible: The Gold Standard for Home Brewers.* New York: HarperCollins, 1997.

Home Protection

The rallying cry "Home Protection" justified the Woman's Christian Temperance Union's (WCTU) feminist reform work in terms of women's maternal role. It was initially used in the United States in the 1870s to persuade conservative members to support women's suffrage. Under the home protection banner, temperance women could demand the vote, not as a right, but to secure temperance legislation and thus protect women's traditional sphere. As the focus of WCTU reform widened in the 1880s and 1890s, home protection encompassed a broader range of feminist campaigns. It became an international slogan adopted by WCTUs throughout the world.

Frances Elizabeth Caroline Willard, national secretary and later president of the U.S. WCTU, coined the term in her speech entitled "Home Protection" at the 1876 Women's Congress in Philadelphia. She promoted women's suffrage as an effective way to close the saloons that wreaked havoc on family life. By 1881, the "home protection ballot" had won unanimous support from the WCTU National Convention.

Willard then sought an alliance between the Prohibition Party and the WCTU. To overcome reservations from the largely Republican WCTU membership, Willard organized "home protection clubs" for union members and their male relatives. In 1882, the Prohibition Party responded by changing its name to the Prohibition Home Protection Party. However, the WCTU never formally endorsed the party and the new name was dropped.

During the 1880s and 1890s, home protection expanded far beyond temperance votes. WCTU members interpreted their mission as large-scale social reform and the "home" as the wider urban environment. Equal pay, dress reform, free kindergartens, children's courts, raising the age of consent, prison reform, and even the nationalization of public utilities were advocated as home protection. As it diversified, the WCTU relied upon the concept of home protection less to justify the vote. By 1894, the union endorsed women's suffrage in terms of natural rights rather than home protection.

The WCTUs established in New Zealand and Australia in 1885 embraced this larger vision of home protection. The union's banner, "For God, Home and Humanity," clearly linked their platform of feminist reforms, similar in scope to the union's platforms in the United States, with the protection of home and family. However, support for women's suffrage relied less upon this argument. The New Zealand WCTU led the most successful national suffrage campaign in the world, achieving the vote in 1893, but Kate Sheppard, leader of the union's Franchise Department and the preeminent national spokeswoman for women's suffrage, argued "we do not wish to plead for a vote on Temperance . . . for we feel that it is wrong to exclude women from citizenship on account of her sex" (Lovell-Smith 1992: 67). Willard had used home protection to persuade a conservative hierarchy to support women's suffrage in the 1870s. In New Zealand and Australia in the 1880s, the WCTU attracted women already well versed in feminist thinking, happy to embrace women's suffrage and interpret home protection in the broadest terms.

The British Women's Temperance Association (BWTA) proved less receptive to home protection arguments. In the early 1890s, the BWTA split over support for women's suffrage and whether the organization should retain its single-issue focus on total abstinence or embrace wider social reform in line with the United States union. Arguments also erupted over who precisely threatened the home. Willard's original "Home Protection" speech drew a graphic picture of wives and children facing violence and destitution at the hands of drunken husbands. Lady Henry Somerset, president of the BWTA and promoter of broad reforms including women's suffrage, placed a similar emphasis on drink-induced domestic violence in her journal the *Woman's Signal.* In contrast, the *British Women's Temperance Journal* and its successor, *Wings,* representing the single-issue side, presented increasing intemperance among women as the major threat to the home. The *Woman's Signal* protested that there was no evidence for this and that drinking among men was more prevalent and harmful. The protest had little effect: *Wings* continued to print articles entitled "Drink in Married Life" or "Home Versus the Public House" that exposed drunken wives and mothers as the greatest threat to home life.

The *White Ribbon Signal,* the Australian WCTU journal, showed similar concern over drunken mothers, but also emphasized the economic and moral dangers that male drunkenness posed to the home. Sons and daughters, rather than wives, were most often the pitied victims of "King Alcohol" in the Australian women's temperance movement, particularly by World War I. Thus, home protection was a flexible concept, revolving around different threats and victims in different national contexts, from male violence, to negligent mothers, to soldier sons tempted by wet canteens.

Jo Aitken

See also: British Women's Temperance Association (BWTA); Prohibition Party (United States); Sheppard, Catherine ("Kate") Wilson; Willard, Frances Elizabeth Caroline; Woman's Christian Temperance Union (WCTU) (Australia); Woman's Christian Temperance Union (WCTU) (United States)

References

Bordin, Ruth. *Francis Willard: A Biography.* Chapel Hill: University of North Carolina Press, 1986.

Grimshaw, Patricia. *Women's Suffrage in New Zealand.* Auckland: Auckland University Press, 1987.

Hyslop, Anthea. "Christian Temperance and Social Reform: The Woman's Christian Temperance Union of Victoria, 1887–1912" in *Women, Faith and Fetes: Essays in the History of Women and the Church in Australia,* edited by Sabine Willis, 43–62. Melbourne: Dove Communications, 1977.

Lovell-Smith, Margaret. *The Woman Question: Writings by the Women Who Won the Vote.* Auckland: New Women's Press, 1992.

Homewood Retreat

The Homewood Retreat of Guelph, Ontario, established in 1883, was Canada's first large private asylum for nervous and mental disorders. It was an early leader in the treatment of alcoholism by necessity, if not by choice; in its first decade, the asylum's survival depended on income from an alcoholic population who comprised one-third of its male inmates. Founding medical superintendent Dr. Stephen Lett gained a reputation as a specialist in gradual-withdrawal therapy. Yet alcoholics were notorious for short-term stays, relapses, and generally disruptive behavior. Homewood remains a private center for the treatment of addictions.

When Homewood opened its doors, it was not advertised as a treatment center for alcoholism. Despite attempts by physicians to classify inebriety as a medical disorder, the retreat's middle-class target clientele in the 1880s considered alcoholism a moral failing requiring prohibitory legislation, not a disease. Nevertheless, by the 1890s, Lett's insistence that the hereditary disease of inebriety be differentiated from the vice of drunkenness and Homewood's protection of patient privacy attracted a substantial number of alcoholics. Yet alcoholics used the asylum primarily to dry out between long debauches rather than to effect a lasting cure. Lett believed inebriety could not be cured in less than several months. Administrators attempted to refuse to admit inebriates for less than six months, a policy they were financially unable to maintain. Subsequently, they demanded a month's payment in advance. During the Keeley Gold Cure craze, Lett developed his own version of the cure (based on atropine and strychnine). This attempt to follow a trend backfired when alcoholics insisted that all inebriate treatments, like Keeley's, required only a few weeks' confinement.

A large alcoholic population affected the retreat's internal dynamics. Patients escaped for short-term sprees, returning thoroughly drunk to the safety of the asylum. The asylum's model of paternalism had the unforeseen consequence of facilitating such "adolescent" patient behavior. Patients were admitted up to a dozen times over the course of years, so that the asylum was used as a companion to the home. Institutionalized when their behavior was no longer tolerable at home, these alcoholics often were ejected from the asylum when their behavior was too disruptive there. Patients replicated domestic patterns of rebellion, secretiveness, and irresponsibility in the institution—behavior that doomed successful treatment.

Alcoholic patients also were disruptive and damaging to the asylum's reputation since they wrote complaining letters to families and authorities and interfered with the institution's routines. This was not limited to male inebriates. Although alcoholics only comprised 6 percent of the female patient population, the women also broke rules, acted antagonistically, and started disturbances when they became intoxicated. By the late 1890s, Lett's replacement, Alfred Hobbs, was gratified as the numbers of "alcoholic degenerates" dissipated, since these patients would "heap abuse upon the institution at every opportunity" for failing "to pander to their depraved appetites" (Warsh 1989: 153). Unlike Lett but consistent with his medical colleagues, Hobbs had little sympathy or optimism for inebriates.

Cheryl Krasnick Warsh

See also: Keeley, Leslie Enraught; Keeley Institutes; Lett, Stephen; Treatment Institutions

References

Levine, Harry G. "The Discovery of Addiction: Changing Conceptions of Habitual Drunkenness in America" in *Journal of Studies on Alcohol.* 39, no. 1 (1978): 143–174.

Warsh, Cheryl Krasnick. *Moments of Unreason: The Practice of Canadian Psychiatry and the Homewood Retreat, 1883–1923.* Montreal: McGill-Queen's University Press, 1989.

Wilkerson, A. E. "A History of the Concept of Alcoholism as a Disease" (Ph.D. dissertation, University of Pennsylvania, 1966).

Honeyman, Tom (1858–1934)

Tom Honeyman (1858–1934) was a leading light of the temperance movement in Scotland. Honeyman was especially associated with temperance work in Glasgow and with the International Order of Good Templars (IOGT). He was a prolific writer and was responsible for a variety of temperance books, tracts, and periodicals. Honeyman's family, too, was devoted to the temperance cause.

For Tom Honeyman, the temperance movement also acted as a means of personal advancement. Born in Dunfermline, Fife, Honeyman began his working life as an apprentice engine fitter. Later, he was conductor of locomotives with the North British Railway Company. He joined the IOGT in 1875. Within seven years of joining, he became a full-time temperance agent. He attained the ranks of district deputy (1878–1883) and of grand secretary (1883–1891). He was also a member of the executive committee of the National Citizens' Council (NCC). The NCC was established in September 1919 at a convention organized by the National Temperance Council of Scotland at Saint Andrew's Hall, Glasgow. The NCC was formed with the view to unite all of Scotland's temperance societies working for no-license under the 1913 Temperance (Scotland) Act, which provided for prohibition legislation based on local option.

Although based in Glasgow, Honeyman was an international temperance figure who served as the IOGT international secretary (1909–1934). Moreover, Honeyman was the editor and writer of several national and international temperance publications such as the IOGT's *Scottish Temperance Annual* and the IOGT quarterly magazine that served five continents for twenty years. He also published two editions of a history of the Grand Lodge of Scotland.

His family echoed Tom Honeyman's temperance reforming zeal. Honeyman's own intense interest in the physiological effects of alcohol encouraged his son Tom J. Honeyman to train as a medical doctor. Tom J. Honeyman was a distinguished Glasgow man who pursued a variety of interests as a medical lecturer for the Band of Hope, artist, director of the Glasgow Art Gallery, and rector of the University of Glasgow. Furthermore, Tom Honeyman's wife was an active member of the Glasgow branch of a women's single-sex temperance society, the Scottish Christian Union.

Megan Smitley

See also: Band of Hope; Good Templars (IOGT); Scotland; Scottish Christian Union (SCU); World Prohibition Federation

References

Honeyman, Tom. *Good Templary in Scotland: Its Work and Workers, 1869–94.* Glasgow: Grand Lodge of Scotland, 1894 [Revised as *Good Templary in Scotland from its Inception to its Diamond Jubilee, 1869–1929.* Glasgow: Grand Lodge of Scotland, 1929].

———. *No Licence! The New Campaign: The Handbook of the National Citizens' Council Temperance (Scotland) Act.* Glasgow: National Citizens' Council, 1921.

King, Elspeth. *Scotland Sober and Free: The Temperance Movement, 1829–1979.* Glasgow: Glasgow Museum and Art Galleries, 1979.

Logan [later Denny], Norma Davies. "Drink and Society: Scotland 1870–1914" (Ph.D. thesis, University of Glasgow, 1983).

Hoover, Herbert Clark (1874–1964)

Herbert Hoover (1874–1964), United States president from 1929 to 1933, overcame his ambivalence concerning Prohibition to become the most eminent American public official committed to enforcement of the Eighteenth Amendment. Hoover also became associated with the deep flaws of Prohibition detailed by the 1931 report of his own National Commission on Law Observance and Enforcement. Overwhelmed by the Great Depression and denounced for his fidelity to constitutional Prohibition, Hoover was repudiated in the 1932 election and his public career of celebrated achievement became a sour legacy of failure.

As a small child in an Iowa Quaker family, Hoover was exposed to the temperance activism of his mother, and despite his parents' early deaths, he grew up in Oregon with an appreciation of the "ordered liberty" prized by the Religious Society of Friends. Devotion to individualism restrained by law shaped Hoover's outlook long after his formal religious practice waned. Trained as an engineer at Stanford University, Hoover conducted mining projects on five continents and by 1914 gained wealth and a reputation for technical skill and organizational brilliance. World War I brought Hoover international acclaim as a food relief expert and praise in Washington for efficient public service as food administrator, followed by two notable terms as commerce secretary in the 1920s.

During this period, Hoover occupied a middle ground on Prohibition. As food administrator, Hoover temporized on Prohibition, cutting grain supplies to breweries but opposing a shutdown of the industry. Later, Hoover offered the mixed judgment that National Prohibition was an economic success but a moral failure. He enjoyed wine and cocktails (in Prohibition Washington, he regularly drank legal cocktails at the Belgian Embassy) and smoked heavily. His wife, Lou Henry Hoover, however, was an abstainer, and Hoover sympathized with the prohibitionist commitment to order.

The presidential campaign of 1928 and the glaring antiprohibitionist convictions of Democratic candidate Alfred Emanuel Smith gradually transformed the Republican candidate Hoover into a defender of National Prohibition. His depiction of Prohibition as "a great social and economic experiment, noble in motive and far-reaching in purpose" reflected Hoover's initial centrist convictions (Burner 1979: 218). Ardent prohibitionists resented his characterization of Prohibition as an experiment, and antiprohibitionists refused to consider its motives noble. Corruption of the statement into an endorsement of a "noble experiment" irritated Hoover. Nevertheless, as President Hoover tried to enforce Prohibition; to slacken enforcement or endorse modification or repeal would be, in his view, to nullify the Constitution. He built prisons and moved the venal and ineffective Prohibition Bureau from the Treasury Department to the Justice Department. With considerable fanfare, Hoover authorized a review of Prohibition enforcement by a blue-ribbon commission headed by former attorney general George Wickersham. Despite startling evidence of enforcement failures compiled by the commission and revisionist sentiment from most commissioners, Hoover accepted a summary report in 1931 that opposed repeal. Amid blistering criticism, Hoover confirmed his intention to continue Prohibition enforcement. In the gloom of 1932, Hoover defeated Republican repeal proposals, won nomination again, and lost the presidency to Franklin D. Roosevelt. A long, productive, yet bitter retirement awaited him.

Thomas R. Pegram

See also: National Prohibition (United States); Smith, Alfred Emanuel

References

Burner, David. *Herbert Hoover: A Public Life.* New York: Alfred A. Knopf, 1979.

Fausold, Martin L. *The Presidency of Herbert C. Hoover.* Lawrence: University Press of Kansas, 1985.

Nash, George H. *The Life of Herbert Hoover: Master of Emergencies, 1917–1918.* New York: W. W. Norton, 1996.

Wilson, Joan Hoff. *Herbert Hoover: Forgotten Progressive.* Boston: Little, Brown, 1975.

Horsley, Sir Victor (1857–1916)

Sir Victor Horsley (1857–1916) was a celebrated British physician and medical researcher who brought the prestige of his scientific reputation as a pioneer neurologist to the agitation against alcohol. He was knighted in 1902.

Horsley adopted total abstinence in his student days. By his mid-twenties, he gave public lectures attacking alcoholic drink. In 1892, he became a vice president of the National Temperance League (NTL) and four years later president of the British Medical Temperance Association (BMTA). In his 1900 Lees and Raper memorial lecture, "The Effect of Alcohol on the Human Brain," he argued that even moderate consumption of alcoholic drink was harmful. An active and effective lecturer and a participant in many deputations to government officials, Horsley was noted for his energy and commitment. His biographer, Stephen Paget, described how he prepared a petition addressed at medical practitioners to obtain their support for the teaching of temperance and hygiene in the schools. Horsley "took the papers to the dining-room, corrected a proof with his left hand, fed himself with his right, and joined in the talk." His major temperance book was *Alcohol and the Human Body* (1907), written with Mary Sturge. Dr. Sturge explained that the first edition was written on Sundays "in [Horsley's] drawing-room, while family music went on as an enjoyable undercurrent—interrupted of course by the telephone," as well as by inquiries from Horsley's wife on how to answer his correspondence. In 1909, Horsley became the president of the International Association of Abstaining Physicians. Horsley was responsible for the changes and additions in the revised editions of *Alcohol and the Human Body.* By 1915, 20,000 copies had been sold.

Horsley's position on alcoholic drink became increasingly radical. In 1913, he was elected president of the National Temperance Federation, an umbrella organization that united advanced temperance societies. He was an opponent of financial compensation for owners of licensed premises who lost their investment because of a change in public policy. He rejected disinterested management on the Gothenburg model, a method of controlling the retail sale of drink by eliminating the profit motive. He condemned the trade in so-called medicated wines. When the first world war broke out, he proposed ending the rum ration for solders and sailors. In the later years of his life, he depicted the drink trade as a conspiracy of wealthy brewers and distillers who poisoned the poor. According to Dr. A. Salusbury MacNalty, Horsley "hated compromise." He described anybody who drank even moderately as an alcoholic.

Horsley died in Iraq while serving as a surgeon in the British army.

David M. Fahey

See also: British Medical Temperance Association (BMTA); Gothenburg Schemes/Disinterested Management; National Temperance Federation (NTF); National Temperance League (NTL)

Reference

Paget, Stephen. *Sir Victor Horsley: A Study of His Life and Work.* London: Constable, 1919.

Hoyle, William (1832–1886)

William Hoyle (1832–1886) was the acknowledged statistician of the British temperance movement in the Victorian era. The statistics that he assembled established the economic cost of alcoholic drink for the United Kingdom. He was also a prominent vegetarian and antismoker.

Hoyle was born in Summerseat near Bury, Lancashire, the fourth child of poor Methodist parents. Working half time at a mill from the age of eight, he was fully employed as a mill worker at thirteen. Three years later, he was a full operative, supervising several looms. He was also an earnest autodidact, building on Sunday school and dame school education by private reading and the study of arithmetic. At seventeen, through reading about foreign countries, he embarked on a dietetic experiment that left him a convinced vegetarian on economic and hygienic grounds. The mill owner at Brooksbottom (near Bury), where Hoyle then lived, had banned public houses from the locality, and Hoyle became a teetotaler about 1846. In 1851, he set up as a cotton manufacturer at Brooksbottom with his father. At Tottington in 1859, he established what became by 1877 a middling-size mill, employing 500 men.

Hoyle identified statistics as a neglected propagandist field for the temperance cause. He based his concise and characteristically plain-speaking pamphlets and letters to the press on his painstaking study of blue books on trade and other official documents. A pamphlet entitled *An Inquiry into the Long-Continued Depression in the Cotton Trade* (1869) was revised and expanded as *Our National Resources and How They Are Wasted* (1871, with three subsequent editions). In this pamphlet, he argued that it was a fall in home trade rather than foreign trade that led to the current depression. Unproductive and improvident labor and expenditure, that is, the drink trade, explained the sorry state of domestic trade. This publication brought him recognition within and outside the temperance movement. He followed it by *Crime in England and Wales in the Nineteenth Century* (1876) and some thirteen other tracts, including papers read at the Social Science Congress and the British Association for the Advancement of Science. A letter to the (London) *Times* on the "national drink bill" became an annual event. He was elected a Fellow of the Statistical Society.

As a vice president and executive member of the prohibitionist United Kingdom Alliance (UKA), Hoyle gave much financial support to the organization, preferring (so he said in 1876) to leave no inheritance to his children if the liquor trade still existed in Britain at his death. He was treasurer of the British Temperance League (BTL) and held posts in several local temperance societies. A former treasurer in the English Grand Lodge of the Good Templars, Hoyle refused to join Joseph Malins in breaking away from the North American organization and published several tracts on the subject of the "Negro exclusion."

Hoyle promoted evening and day schools, cooperative stores and cottages for the advancement of Tottington's working population. He remained a devout Wesleyan. Active in local politics, and a member of the local Liberal association, he unsuccessfully contested the Dewsbury parliamentary seat in 1880 as a Liberal candidate. He was secretary of a local vegetarian society at Crawshawbooth in the 1850s. In 1864, an article (his first published writing) in the vegetarian *Dietetic Reformer* was republished as a tract. He credited his commercial success in part to diet and plain living. Marrying in 1859, he, his wife (Alice, born Fenton), a son, and a daughter lived on £100 a year despite his wealth.

He died in Southport in February 1886, with overwork hastening his death. The *Alliance News* obituary (6 March 1886) described him as "greedy of almost incessant work." F. R. Lees edited and published Hoyle's final work, *Wealth and Social Progress.* It includes a substantial biographical essay written by Lees. Hoyle's temperance library may be consulted at Stanford University in California.

James Gregory

See also: British Temperance League (BTL); Burns, (James) Dawson; Good Templars (IOGT); Lees, Frederic Richard; Malins, Joseph; United Kingdom Alliance (UKA); Vegetarianism and the Anti-Tobacco Movement (United Kingdom)

References

Bayne, Ronald. "William Hoyle" in *Dictionary of National Biography,* 10: 135. reprinted ed. in 22 vols. London: Oxford University Press, 1921–1922.

Dietetic Reformer. January 1869, p. 7.

Lees, F. R. "The Biography of William Hoyle" in *Wealth and Social Progress in Relation to Thrift, Temperance, and Trade,* by William Hoyle, 241–312. Manchester: United Kingdom Alliance, 1887.

Obituaries of William Hoyle in *Alliance News.* 6 March 1886, 147–152; 13 March 1886, 164–165.

Hudson, James H. (1881–1962)

James Hudson (1881–1962) epitomized the strong influence that the temperance party exerted over the Labour Party for many years. He was a Labour member of Parliament (M.P.) who was active in various British temperance organizations. For instance, he served the United Kingdom Alliance (UKA) as parliamentary agent.

Born in Flixton, Lancashire, he graduated from Manchester University, where he studied political and economic science, and won the Cobden prize. From 1907 to 1916, he taught at a Salford boys' secondary school. During the first world war, he could easily have escaped being conscripted into the army by virtue of being a schoolteacher, but he preferred to register his conscientious objection to war. He was sent to prison for his beliefs on several occasions. In 1923, he was elected to Parliament as a Labour Party candidate and, shortly afterwards, was appointed parliamentary private secretary to Philip Snowden, chancellor of the exchequer. Hudson encountered vehement opposition from drinking clubs when he introduced parliamentary bills to control them.

He lost his seat in 1931 when the Labour Party was routed in a landslide. Hudson then devoted himself to the temperance cause. He became secretary to the Religious Society of Friends Temperance Union. The Workers' Temperance League, which had been founded by the Labour Party pioneer Keir Hardie, had become defunct. In 1933, Hudson reorganized it, with the help of George Lansbury (who at the time was leader of the Labour Party), Arthur Henderson, and Dr. Alfred Salter.

Temperance had had a great influence on the early leaders of the Labour Party. Prior to his political career, Keir Hardie, generally regarded as the founder of the Labour Party, was an active member of the Good Templars, as was Arthur Henderson, the first Labour foreign secretary and Nobel Peace Prize winner, and Philip Snowden, the first Labour chancellor of the exchequer. Half the parliamentary members of the Labour Party in 1935 were total abstainers.

In 1945, Hudson returned to Parliament for West Ealing, and from 1950 to 1955 he represented North Ealing. He was not reelected to Parliament in 1955, but this did not prevent him continuing his work for temperance at Westminster.

Hudson was appointed the UKA's parliamentary agent, and he already was secretary of the National Temperance Federation. After the 1955 general election, over 100 M.P.s joined the Parliamentary Temperance Group and, although Hudson was not an M.P., he continued as secretary to the group. In the Conservative government's edition of a new handbook for health education, the section on alcohol had been reduced to one page. On behalf of the Parliamentary Temperance Group, Hudson and Dr. Somerville Hastings, M.P., produced a supplementary handbook concentrating solely on alcohol.

Evidence of the esteem in which James Hudson was held is seen in the attendance of Clement Attlee, the postwar Labour prime minister, at a luncheon given by the UKA in Hudson's honor. Attlee described him "as a man who has rendered great service to his generation and who has endeared himself to all." H. Cecil Heath, Hudson's friend of thirty years, paid this tribute: "his passionate adherence to the causes in which he believed and his fearless advocacy of the truth as he saw it, never obscured his intense warmth of heart and mind."

Derek Rutherford

See also: Good Templars (IOGT); Heath, H. Cecil; Labour Party (United Kingdom); National Temperance Federation (NTF); United Kingdom Alliance (UKA)

Reference

Hayler, Mark H. C. *The Vision of a Century, 1853–1953: The United Kingdom Alliance in Historical Retrospect.* London: United Kingdom Alliance, 1953.

Hughes, Harold Everett (1922–1996)

Harold E. Hughes (1922–1996), following his own recovery from alcoholism, went on to serve as Iowa's governor and United States senator, and to become one of the nation's most effective advocates for federal and state support of alcoholism treatment. Hughes was born in 1922 in Ida Grove, Iowa. It was during his high school years that he discovered alcohol's ability to dissolve shyness and instill confidence. From his first contact with alcohol, he had little ability to control his drinking. He briefly attended the University of Iowa, but dropped out after his marriage to Eva Mercer.

After returning to Ida Grove following service in Italy during World War II, Hughes's drinking increased, forcing his wife to file papers with the Ida County Sanity Commission to have Hughes legally committed for hospitalization as an inebriate. Hughes escaped hospitalization, but his drinking problems continued. On a day when he was contemplating suicide, Hughes underwent a profound religious conversion that initiated his recovery from alcoholism and altered the course of his life. It was during this transition to sobriety (achieved in 1954) that Hughes, a truck driver by trade, accepted a position as an organizer for the Iowa Better Trucking Bureau. Switching his political affiliation from Republican to Democratic in a state dominated by Republicans, Hughes successfully served with the Iowa Commerce Commission from 1958 to 1962.

In a series of stunning upsets, Hughes was elected and served as Iowa's first three-term governor from 1962 to 1968. When his gubernatorial opponent, Evan Hultman, sought to use an old drunk driving arrest against him during the 1964 campaign, Hughes made public the story of his alcoholism and recovery. The result was a landslide victory for Hughes. As governor, Hughes pushed through funding to establish local alcoholism treatment resources, making Iowa a model for such services at that time.

Hughes went on to serve in the United States Senate from 1969 to 1975. In 1969, he was appointed to chair the first Senate Subcommittee on Alcoholism and Narcotics within the Labor and Public Welfare Committee. It was from this platform that Senator Hughes supported funding for alcoholism treatment programs through the Office of Economic Opportunity and authored and championed passage of the 1970 Comprehensive Alcoholism Treatment and Prevention Act (frequently referred to as the "Hughes Act").

Hughes served in other key positions, including Chairman of the Armed Services Subcommittee on Alcoholism and Drug

Abuse, and was a member of the National Commission on Marijuana and Drug Abuse. He also served on the board of directors of the National Council on Alcoholism (NCA) and as president of the World Council on Alcoholism.

In 1975, Hughes announced that he would not run for another term in the Senate, but would instead pursue his religious interests through the Fellowship Foundation in Washington, D.C. He remained involved in alcoholism-related causes, most significantly in his role as founder and executive director of the Society Of Americans for Recovery (SOAR). SOAR was never able to achieve its vision of mobilizing recovering people into a national political force. It collapsed as an organization in 1995, in part because of Hughes's declining health. Harold E. Hughes died 23 October 1996.

William L. White

See also: National Institute on Alcohol Abuse and Alcoholism (NIAAA)

Reference

Hughes, Harold, with Dick Schneider. *Harold E. Hughes: The Honorable Alcoholic.* Minneapolis, MN: Jeremy Books, 1979.

Hunt, Mary Hannah Hanchett (1830–1906)

Mary Hannah Hanchett Hunt (1830–1906) pioneered a widely adopted and significant American temperance and prohibition propaganda campaign, which she dubbed "Scientific Temperance Instruction (STI)." In pushing her movement forward, she also pioneered a nonpartisan lobbying approach that the Anti-Saloon League of America (ASLA) later adopted as a central strategy in the successful campaign for National Prohibition. Despite her success in securing adoption of favorable legislation, however, her ability to control the delivery of her message was limited.

Hunt was born in Canaan, Connecticut, in 1830 and died in Boston, Massachusetts, in 1906. She was educated in the Amenia Seminary in New York and the Patapsco Institute in Maryland, teaching at the latter until her marriage to Leander B. Hunt in 1852.

In 1878, Hunt and Julia Colman persuaded Massachusetts school boards to make Scientific Temperance a regular subject in classroom education. She argued that classroom education was an excellent strategy for shaping a generation of alcohol-free citizens. Soon after, she began to promote the idea of Scientific Temperance nationwide.

An active member of the Woman's Christian Temperance Union (WCTU), Hunt was invited to the 1879 national convention by Frances Elizabeth Caroline Willard. There, Hunt argued that temperance books should be brought into classrooms and that Scientific Temperance—the use of physiology and hygiene lessons to teach how alcohol and other narcotics destroyed the body—should be treated as a regular academic discipline. The convention formally adopted the strategy, and Hunt was named chairperson of the Committee on Temperance Textbooks in Schools and Colleges. In 1880, the WCTU created the Department of Scientific Temperance in Schools and Colleges, and Hunt was appointed superintendent. She held the position until her death.

Somewhat surprised by the resistance of many teachers and administrators to the new discipline, the Department of Scientific Temperance initiated a state-by-state campaign to mandate such instruction. In 1882, Vermont was the first state to comply with the WCTU's request for legislation. By 1887, twenty other state legislatures similarly mandated Scientific Temperance. In almost every case, Hunt personally spearheaded the lobbying campaign. The success of Hunt's campaign can be attributed both to her personal capacities as an organizer and to politicians' own enthusiasm. Some legislators saw temperance education as a potential alternative to absolute prohibition; others saw it as a first step toward prohibition.

Despite political support for STI laws, compliance with these laws varied greatly by city, state, and region. In some areas, there were not enough textbooks or dedicated teachers. Requirements could be, and often were, fulfilled with a simple annual lecture. In other cases, the required "education" about alcohol presented arguments favorable to consumption. Hunt was particularly appalled that many teachers and administrators were reluctant to instruct students in what she perceived to be the key tenets of Scientific Temperance: that alcohol was a poison, that complete abstinence was necessary, and that medicinal use should be avoided. Hunt's department encouraged WCTU members to make regular classroom visitations to prevent misinterpretations of teachers' responsibilities and disciplinary content.

To facilitate the education of teachers of the new discipline, Hunt created and edited *Science Temperance Monthly Advices,* later *School Physiology Journal.* Her other writings included *A History of the First Decade of the Department of Scientific Temperance Instruction in Schools and Colleges of the Woman's Christian Temperance Union* (1891), *An Epoch of the Nineteenth Century* (1897), *An Appeal to Truth* (1900), and a tersely written *Reply to the Physiological Sub-Committee of the Committee of Fifty* (1903).

To respond to the problem of finding appropriate educational materials, Hunt also edited and endorsed several textbooks including the Pathfinder Series. After her death, it became open knowledge that some royalties from the sale of these textbooks went to Hunt via the Scientific Temperance Association. The Scientific Temperance Association had been formed in 1886 to collect the money from textbook sales and use it to defray the costs of Hunt's department. The ensuing scandal was one of the factors that began to discredit Scientific Temperance.

The WCTU gradually transformed the Department of Scientific Temperance Instruction into a clearinghouse for alcohol information, eliminating this department's previous responsibilities as an educational lobbying group. The department's work was continued, however, by the Scientific Temperance Federation, under the leadership of Hunt's former colleague, Cora Frances Stoddard.

Lisa Andersen

See also: Committee of Fifty; Scientific Temperance Federation; Stoddard, Cora Frances; Woman's Christian Temperance Union (WCTU) (United States)

References

Mezvinsky, Norton. "Scientific Temperance Education in the Schools" in *History of Education Quarterly.* 1 (March 1961): 48–56.

Zimmerman, Jonathan. *Distilling Democracy: Alcohol Education in America's Public Schools, 1880–1925.* Lawrence: University Press of Kansas, 1999.

I

Impey, Catherine (1847–1923)

Catherine Impey (1847–1923) was a tireless worker for social reform in her native England and around the world. Some of Impey's causes have a distinctly modern familiarity: environmentalism, antimilitarism, vegetarianism, and humane treatment of animals. She is best known for her advocacy of the equality of races and her promotion of the complete abolition of alcohol consumption. Few of her papers and diaries have survived, so Impey's work is known mainly through her publications, especially the monthly *Anti-Caste* (meaning antiracism) and through the writings of contemporaries. Except for temperance, Impey's causes are still active reform movements.

Catherine Impey was born into a family that belonged to the Religious Society of Friends, and her strongly held humanitarian principles were firmly based in her Christianity. She frequently used the Bible to illustrate her points. Her Quaker background provided Impey with a vision of human brotherhood that transcended political, social, or racial boundaries. In 1886, when Impey traveled to the United States to attend a national convention of the Woman's Christian Temperance Union (WCTU), she openly opposed the segregation policy in force in the organization. She argued that persons of color were human beings equal in all ways, and she fought to end racial discrimination in the temperance movement. A few years later, she quit the Order of Good Templars when the Grand Lodge of England agreed to reunite with the North American lodges on a basis that accepted racial segregation. Impey also worked against exploitation and unfair practices in the British Empire, especially in India.

Early in her life, Impey chose to remain independent of the usual middle-class feminine route of devotion to husband and family. She consciously determined to devote herself to her political and social causes. Her mother and sister supported her in pursuing this goal. When her father died, Impey was offered the opportunity to run the family business, but her sister stepped into this role in order to free Impey to conduct her busy campaigns.

Although Catherine Impey lived a life of true independence in a time in which women were most often offered no alternative to subservience, and although Impey lived in a household of self-sufficient and busy women, she was not known to advocate women's rights or female suffrage. We do not know the cause of this startling omission in the philosophy of such a committed reformer. She served as a Poor Law Guardian at the end of her life, so Impey did involve herself in governmental

Catherine Impey (1847–1923)

policy. Perhaps she felt her other causes were more important and did not wish to alienate potential supporters.

Cynthia Curran

See also: Good Templars (IOGT); Lucas, Margaret Bright; Vegetarianism and the Anti-Tobacco Movement (United Kingdom); Woman's Christian Temperance Union (WCTU) (United States)

References

Fahey, David M. "Catherine Impey" in *Oxford Dictionary of National Biography,* edited by H. C. G. Matthew and Brian Harrison. Oxford University Press, forthcoming 2004.

———. *Temperance and Racism: John Bull, Johnny Reb, and the Good Templars.* Lexington: University Press of Kentucky, 1996.

Impey, Catherine, ed. "The W.C.T.U. and the Colour Question" in *Anti-Caste.* (March 1895): 4 [reprinted in microfilm edition of

Temperance and Prohibition Papers (1977), section III, reel 32, scrapbook 13, frame 215].

Ware, Vron. *Beyond the Pale: White Women, Racism and History.* London: Verso, 1992.

Independent Order of Good Templars

See Good Templars (IOGT)

Independent Order of Rechabites

See Rechabite Friendly Society

India

India, a country of over 1 billion people in 2002, has had a long association with both alcohol and alcohol control policies. Under the charge of the British East India Company (EIC) as a crown monopoly, British rule was gradually extended from the 1760s to the 1810s to cover most of India. The EIC was by this time really an arm of the state. Only after the Indian Rebellion (commonly known in British imperial history as the Indian Mutiny) of 1857, however, did the British government assume direct imperial control in 1858. The "Raj" as it was called also included the princely states, what is now Myanmar (Burma), and the present-day countries of Bangladesh and Pakistan. Ceylon (now Sri Lanka) was administered separately but followed similar patterns. In the mid-1920s, twenty British provinces contained 247 million people and covered over 1.8 million square miles, while the Indian states and agencies covered 711,000 square miles and contained 71.9 million people. After a protracted struggle, India gained its independence in 1947, but at the cost of partition with the state of Pakistan, and the separate nations of Ceylon and Burma were also created around this time.

In pre-European and early colonial times, Indians produced and used alcoholic beverages. In the south, a toddy palm wine was fermented from palm sap; in other areas, for example Bihar and Orissa, rice beer was brewed. Elsewhere, spirits were produced from ground rice, sugar (molasses), and a honey tree (*Bassia latifolia*), and from cashew and other flowers. Though toddies and beers fermented from the juice of various plants were the most common beverages, Sanskrit writers described thirteen spirituous liquors known to the population in ancient times. Liquor was leisurely consumed and closely woven into religious rituals and caste customs, both in terms of production and consumption. Alcohol was produced everywhere by specialized low-caste groups; thus in Madras (now Tamil Nadu), the Nadars made their living from toddy production, and the Sundi in Orissa distilled spirits and were known in British records as the distillers' caste.

All of India's major religions had made pronouncements on alcohol. Within the predominant Hindu faith, drinking was set down under Hindu scripture as a mortal sin, but over time this prohibition only came to apply to the highest Brahmin caste, and the use of alcohol spread widely among lower-caste people, and among aboriginal tribes beyond the reach of Hinduism. Moreover, in the Middle Ages and later, the cult offshoot from Hinduism called Tantra associated drinking with religious exercises.

Muslims in theory prohibited the use of alcohol under the Qur'an, though in practice some Muslims did partake of alcoholic beverages, and Sufi mysticism's ecstatic devotional practices became associated with ritual drinking. Buddhism, which spread especially in Ceylon, included among the Five Precepts of Buddha the goal of abstinence from all intoxicating and spirituous liquors because they caused weakness in the discharge of personal duties. But the arrival of Portuguese traders in the sixteenth century and Dutch traders in the seventeenth led to the adoption of European drinking practices among a few Buddhists in Ceylon, and among other groups along the coasts of India where European countries, including the French and British, set up trading posts in the seventeenth and eighteenth

A Lepcha bomthing, *or priest, uses millet beer to capture spirits. (Earl and Nazima Kowall/Corbis)*

centuries. Other more minor religions such as Sikhism banned the use of alcohol (but the prohibition was routinely transgressed, especially among males). Jains were especially important in opposing alcohol because they dominated the industrial bourgeoisie who financed the nationalist movement that later came out against alcohol. Parsis, too, often abjured alcohol, especially for women, but their traders took part in the liquor business from the eighteenth century onwards; as the most Westernized group, they often mimicked the British.

When the British took undisputed European dominion of the subcontinent after the Seven Years War in 1764, the EIC extended its administrative control. Most of India was taken by 1818, except the Northwest Sikh state. Among the administrative controls was the excise on alcohol introduced in 1790 through 1791. Supposedly to suppress illegal distilleries and restrict consumption, this policy bore heavily upon poor, low-caste, and tribal communities who had hitherto distilled their own alcohol. Over the course of the next hundred years, the liquor excise became a growing source of revenue for the company and then the British government after 1858. However, the revenue did not come close to the financial windfall brought by the licensing of opium production for export to China until the turn of the twentieth century.

Though the methods of administration differed from one province to another and within provinces too, licensing was generally based on the "farming-out system." In this system, licenses to operate distilleries and to open liquor shops were granted on the basis of auctions. In some provinces, the liquor was manufactured by the government and only the liquor shop licenses were farmed out. Liquor was, at least in theory, under imperial policy, taxed to the point that it would not drive manufacturers to illicit distillation. But under the licensing system, from the 1860s onward, the number of shops had been greatly extended. One key problem was that the licensing system was not separate from the excise system, thus encouraging more licenses.

Land tax remained the staple of government finances, but liquor excise grew from 2 percent of government revenues in 1874 to 7 percent in the 1890s, then rose to 10 percent in 1905 and 27 percent by the mid-1920s. It had exceeded the politically sensitive opium excise by 1900. Total revenues had grown 430 percent from 1874 to 1908. The number of liquor shops had increased greatly in line with this output.

Opposition came from both British and indigenous sources. The Anglo-Indian Temperance Association was founded in 1888 by a prominent British member of Parliament (M.P.), William S. Caine. Though based in London and with the support of leading British reformers, the Anglo-Indian Temperance Association had, by the 1920s, 195 affiliates in India with a membership mainly of Indians. The association published in London an informative journal, *Abkari* (or "Excise"), that documented the links of the government to liquor production and sale as well as opium problems.

The new movement to attack alcohol garnered some indigenous supporters. Mahant K. R. Roy, for example, was called the "Father Mathew of India" for his work in getting pledges. He worked from Benares (now Varanasi) and persuaded whole communities to enforce caste rules against the use of drink. This method was effective in India in view of the strength of the caste system. Indigenous reformers such as the leader of the Brahmo Samaj reformed-Hindu movement also attacked alcohol, but focused on it as Western imposed and urged revitalization of traditional taboos.

However, these indigenous Indian reformers were matched by Christian missionary activity. These aided the founding of the Woman's Christian Temperance Union (WCTU), which was brought to India by the American Mary Greenleaf Clement Leavitt in the mid-1880s. By 1920, the WCTU was organized throughout India, often through American leadership. Other groups attracted to the WCTU were some Anglo-Indian Eurasian women and high-caste Hindu widows. Pandita Ramabai campaigned against the confinement of widows and child brides, and became affiliated in the late 1880s with the World's WCTU (WWCTU) as an official lecturer and missionary. The WCTU and other European-imported groups developed critiques of the imperial government, and some, such as the WCTU, questioned the need for continued British rule.

The reform agitation by Caine, the Anglo-Indian Association, and indigenous groups led only to a ponderous inquiry by the government of India under the direction of the secretary of state for India in 1889. This led to instructions to raise taxes as a way of reducing consumption, and actions limiting the number of liquor outlets as well as the encouragement of police operations against illegal distilling and sale.

However, the British Parliament then appointed an Excise Committee in 1905 that reported in 1906. This committee made stronger recommendations, including the complete abolition of the out-still system, prohibition of the employment of women on licensed premises, and prohibition of sale to children and drunken persons. Adoption of the Madras system, giving monopolies to distillers and holding auctions for the liquor ships, came as a result of the Excise Committee deliberations.

But, the British administration moved very slowly. In 1912, a deputation led by G. K. Gokale, then a leader of the majority tendency in the Indian National Congress, asked the government of India for local option. This meeting led to the establishment of licensing boards in the capitals of the various presidencies such as Bengal. These boards included members of the local temperance societies, and in Calcutta the local board was given the authority to determine licenses. Prohibition was instituted within the wards of the cities where colleges were located. The results in other presidencies such as Madras were more disappointing. By the 1920s, the fixed fee system rather than the auction system was introduced in some provinces, to the approval of some temperance groups.

Temperance and nationalism became closely associated in the early twentieth century. Men like Sir Bhalchandra Kishna, president of the Bombay Temperance Council, had declared as early as 1907 that temperance was the only common platform for the diverse castes and religions to unite behind. This connection reflected the fact that modern nationalism emerged first among the Western-educated professionals and the business classes who were traditionally associated with the strains of Hinduism, for example Jainism, that were condemnatory of stimulants. However, these moderate reformers often prevaricated over the role of imperial authorities and British imperialism, believing that the British rule brought benefits.

By the late 1910s, Indian nationalists had taken up part of the temperance movement's anti-imperialist critique to criticize the British Empire and as a means to revitalize traditional culture. An Indian nationalist named Taraknath Das wrote on the "Progress of Prohibition in India" in 1921. He stated that "the Prohibition movement is known in India as the National Purification movement and is designed to make the people more capable of carrying on their struggle for independence." The controversial nature of the material in the colonial setting was quickly emphasized when Das was arrested amid a government crackdown on seditious literature in 1922.

American temperance reformers also stirred up trouble. In 1921, W. E. "Pussyfoot" Johnson toured India for the Anglo-Indian Temperance Society and the World League against Alcoholism. He lectured and gave stirring speeches to vast crowds, but discomforted the British government by suggesting that Indians should have more self-government.

Of much greater significance was the work of M. K. Gandhi. For him, drink was a problem of Western origins. In America, he argued, it was the people who impeded prohibition in the 1920s, but in India it was a foreign government. As part of his moral resistance to British rule known as the *satyagraha* program, begun after his return from South Africa in 1914, drink shops were picketed by groups of noncooperators to hit British revenue and reduce alcohol consumption. These protests grew in the early 1920s. They were mainly carried out along peaceful lines, as Gandhi instructed, but in some cases zealous followers removed customers from liquor shops by force and violators of caste rules against drinking had their heads shaven and were publicly humiliated. In July 1921, the Indian National Congress endorsed Gandhi's campaign of picketing liquor shops. As the main influence in the Indian National Congress from World War I onward and president at various times, Gandhi had great power to pursue his anti-alcohol strategy.

After the Government of India Act of 1919 gave some powers at the provincial level to India, the Punjab legislative council passed a resolution in favor of local option in 1921. But the central government then forbade legislation where it affected the sale of foreign spirits. The Bombay government introduced a lower rationing system, reducing the quantity of "country" spirits—produced in small distilleries and popular with poorer Indians—sent to shops in Bombay by 10 percent, and in the United Provinces, licensing boards were authorized to reduce the number of shops to not less than one-third of their number when the boards came into effect. Central interference in the implementation of these and other policies merely highlighted the failure of the British to give Indians a say in the running of their own lives, and added to the demands for and illustrated the need for independence.

Upon independence in 1947, prohibition was included in the Constitution of India and the government of several states such as Gujarat introduced it. Andhra Pradesh and other states witnessed grassroots movements against *arrack,* a popular local liquor among peasants that was charged with causing domestic violence and impoverishing families. Also Tamil Nadu introduced prohibition measures, of which vestiges still survived at the end of the twentieth century; however, the other states making up the old Madras Presidency (Andhra Pradesh, Mysore, and Kerala) had long since abandoned it. Prohibition was considered by most state governments as having been ineffective. "Country" liquor produced in local distilleries illegally, including the production of wood alcohol, led often to tragedies when dozens of Indian drinkers were poisoned. Most recently, the modern Indian state of Haryana imposed prohibition, forcing government-run rural liquor stores and privately owned outlets to close in 1996, but then the state abandoned its attempts in 1998.

The abandonment of prohibition in several states was linked with the fiscal need of the state governments, while a lesser motive was to combat the law-and-order problem produced by bootlegging. The only out-and-out prohibitionist state remaining is Gujarat, significantly the state where the "puritan" high-caste Hindu Jainist elites remain strongest. Thus there survives, as in the time of British rule, a conflict in India between alcohol as a revenue raiser and the vestiges of Gandhism that still receive copious lip service coming from such influential members of the political elite as Morarji Desai. As a strict antialcohol man, this Indian Prime Minister introduced and supported during his political career prohibition legislation in his home state of Gujarat.

Meanwhile, Indian use of alcohol has soared. Beer production has risen, especially in the prosperous north, which has experienced since the 1980s much economic development and further urbanization. Advertising of Western-style beverages has increased, and the habits of the young have changed, embracing these beverages. Both beer and spirits consumption in India have been rising, and even wine has begun to win market share. Multinational companies such as Anheuser-Busch have attempted to build a strong market for Western-style alcohol beverages, taking advantage of India's increasing economically liberal market orientation. Foreign brewers have entered into joint ventures with Indian companies such as the Bombay-based Shaw Wallace and Company Limited (with Anheuser-

Busch), the third largest brewer in India, while Guinness has entered a joint venture with United Breweries of India.

The class basis of drinking has now replaced caste-based patterns to a considerable degree. Beer remains relatively expensive, as are most Western-type drinks, but toddy in its various forms is much cheaper, and sometimes lethal. Hence, there is a strong class element in consumption patterns, with the elite drinking Western-style beverages, and sometimes even Western imports—Black Label whiskey, for example—while peasants continue drinking local concoctions. There is now a serious alcoholism problem in many regions as a result of these changes over the last twenty years. But there has been no real pressure for a return to prohibition. Instead, ameliorative measures like low alcohol beers are being advocated.

India has never fulfilled the hopes of Western-style temperance reformers who saw the emerging nation as an ally in the struggle for world prohibition. But alcohol has been and is likely to continue to be the subject of much controversy and debate due to the wide range of usages; the changing social mores; the conflict between older rituals and newer, Western-style capitalist marketing practice; and the modernization of India and its discontents.

Ian Tyrrell

See also: Anheuser-Busch; Buddhism; Caine, William Sproston; Gandhi, Mohandas Karamchand; Islam as Cultural Influence; Islamic World; Johnson, William Eugene "Pussyfoot"; Leavitt, Mary Greenleaf Clement; Rum; World League Against Alcoholism (WLAA); World's Woman's Christian Temperance Union (WWCTU)

References

Abkari. The Quarterly Organ of the Anglo-Indian Temperance Association. New series. nos. 1–168 April 1890–April 1932.

Arora, Monica. "Alcohol in India" in *The Globe Magazine.* http://www.ias.org.uk/theglobe/2001gapabangkok/india.htm.

Assunta, Mary. "Impact of Alcohol Consumption on Asia." http://www.ias.org.uk/theglobe/2001gapabangkok/asia.htm.

Das, Taraknath. "Progress of Prohibition in India." in *Union Signal.* 29 September 1921: 6.

Hardgrave, Robert L. *The Nadars of Tamilnad: The Political Culture of a Community in Change.* Berkeley: University of California Press, 1969.

Hardiman, David. *The Coming of the Devi: Adivasi Assertion in Western India.* Delhi and New York: Oxford University Press, 1987.

"India." *Standard Encyclopaedia of the Alcohol Problem,* vol. 3, 1295–1305. Westerville, Ohio: American Issue Publishing, 1925.

"India's Alcohol Nightmare" in *The Globe Magazine.* http://www.ias.org.uk/theglobe/jun98/india.htm.

Rao, Sarveswara, and B. G. Parthasarathy. *Anti-arrack Movement of Women in Andhra Pradesh and Prohibition Policy.* New Delhi: Har-Anand Publications, 1997.

Tyrrell, Ian. "Prohibition, American Cultural Expansion, and the New Hegemony in the 1920s: An Interpretation," *Histoire Sociale/Social History.* 27 (November 1994): 413–445.

———. *Woman's World/Woman's Empire: The Woman's Christian Temperance Union in International Perspective, 1880–1930.* Chapel Hill: University of North Carolina Press, 1991.

Indigenous Peoples and the Liquor Traffic Controversy

The later nineteenth century saw an impassioned debate over the supply of "European" liquors—and particularly distilled spirits—to the non-European world, and to Africa in particular. The issue raised major moral and economic issues, and while the debate was at its most fierce in Britain, it was also evident in the United States and Germany, and to a lesser extent in other European colonial nations. The debate led to a series of international agreements, including the various Brussels agreements signed between 1890 and 1912 and the Convention of St. Germain en Laye in 1919. The issue rapidly declined in political significance after the end of the 1930s.

Drink and the Slave Trade

The intensity of the debate can only be understood in terms of the perceived link between the import of European spirits and the export of African slaves. Anti–slave trade campaigners in Britain consistently argued that "trade spirits," like imported firearms, fueled the violence that produced slaves for export. As Thomas Fowell Buxton famously put it, this was a trade that exchanged "arms, ammunition and ardent spirits" for men, women and children (Buxton 1840: 280).There was in Britain an extensive crossover in the political constituency of the antislavery and temperance movements. The high tide of temperance agitation produced, by 1887, the United Committee for the Prevention of the Demoralization of the Native Races by the Liquor Traffic. Under the patronage of the Duke of Westminster, the committee called, in effect, for an end to the supply of spirits to Africa. Supporters of the committee included a number of bishops and many missionaries, and a notable recruit to its cause in the 1890s was Frederick Lugard, who already had considerable colonial experience in East Africa and was to achieve even greater prominence as a colonial administrator in Nigeria and Hong Kong.

The arguments of the committee centered on the idea that the moral well-being of Africans was profoundly threatened by spirits, particularly in West Africa, the principal region of both the slave trade and the legitimate commerce in oil products that succeeded it. Distillates were largely unknown in sub-Saharan Africa until European traders brought them; because they were much more potent than the various local fermented beverages they were identified as more likely to "demoralize" Africans. This explanation was, it has been argued, part of a wider rhetoric that "infantilized" Africans, presenting them as children who were unable to cope with the powerful forces of the modern world, and who must therefore be protected by Europeans; a pervading sense of disquiet about the "demoralizing" effects of all forms of commerce and change is evident in much of the British discussion about Africans and drink. This was very much a debate that was carried on in the metropolitan countries; the opinion of Africans might be cited by one side or another, but Africans took little direct part, though the rhetoric of this metropolitan controversy was in itself to become significant in debates over temperance within African societies. The controversy over the supply of spirits to Africa was at its height during the years in which the continent was divided up into new colonial territories, and there seems little doubt that the rhetoric about protecting Africans from the effects of drink played a part in generating the sense of imperial mission that helped drive British colonial expansion, though it is by no means so clear that the same could be argued of French expansion in the same period.

Critics and the Decline of the Controversy

In Britain, the Committee for the Prevention of the Demoralization of the Native Races by the Liquor Traffic had many critics, some of them evidently inspired by immediate material concerns. Trading companies relying upon spirits as a means of exchange for palm oil and other products objected to any proposals for a ban on spirit imports, though some British companies saw that there might be advantages in the banning of a trade that was largely supplied by German and Dutch gin factories. Some administrators and travelers questioned the vision of African "demoralization," insisting that drunkenness in Africa was probably less serious than it was in Europe. The ability of the committee and its partisans to achieve real controls was anyway limited by the need for agreement on these among European powers, and other European governments faced much less domestic popular pressure on this issue, though debates in Germany also pitted imperial reformers against major trade interests. The diffidence of some British colonial administrators was to be increased by financial realities. In West Africa, the preferred means of financing administration was through taxes on imports and exports. Spirit imports contributed substantially to revenue, and there was some reluctance to lose this revenue by ending imports, although Lugard demonstrated in Nigeria that the revenue could be made up in other ways.

The peak of metropolitan agitation on this issue had passed in Britain by the end of the nineteenth century, declining along with the temperance movement as a whole after its electoral failures in the 1890s. But the agitation had established, particularly in Britain, the principle that protecting Africans—and some other non-Europeans—from strong drink was an imperial duty. International agreements made after World War I, and the structure of the League of Nations Mandate system, maintained this principle; although what British officials called the "dry Africa" lobby was much shrunken by the 1930s, it still had some influence. The committee, which had changed its name to the Native Races and the Liquor Traffic United Committee almost immediately on its inception, remained active into the late 1920s, but its activities declined soon after. In the 1930s, the Anti-Slavery and Aborigines Protection Society took up some of the United Committee's former role as protector of Africans against the dangers of spirits. By 1945, however, the whole rhetoric of imperial rule had changed and the paternalism of the liquor traffic debate seemed entirely anachronistic: Official concern was rather with the need to encourage Africans to drink the same kinds of beverages as Europeans.

Justin Willis

See also: Brussels Act and Conventions, 1890–1912; St. Germain en Laye Convention, 1919

References

Buxton, Thomas. *The African Slave Trade and Its Remedy.* London: John Morray, 1840.

Lugard, Frederick. "The Liquor Traffic in Africa" in *The Nineteenth Century.* 52 (July-December 1897): 766–784.

Olokoju, Ayedeji. "Prohibition and Paternalism: The State and the Clandestine Liquor Traffic in Northern Nigeria, c. 1889–1918" in *International Journal of African Historical Studies.* 24 (1991): 349–368.

Olorunfemi, A. "The Liquor Traffic in British West Africa: The Southern Nigerian Example, 1895–1918" in *International Journal of African Historical Studies.* 17 (1984): 220–242.

Pan, Lyn. *Alcohol in Colonial Africa.* Helsinki/Uppsala: Finnish Institute for Alcohol Studies, 1975.

Willis, Justin. "Demoralised Natives, Black-Coated Consumers and Clean Spirit: European Liquor in East Africa, 1890–1955" in *Journal of Imperial and Commonwealth History.* 29 (2001): 55–74.

Inebriate Institutions (Australia)

In the later nineteenth century in Australia, as in other parts of the Western world, inebriety came to be seen as a disease to be cured, not a crime to be punished. A plethora of specialist institutions for the treatment of inebriates was established. In many institutions, middle-class patients paid for treatment, but government subsidies enabled some inebriates unable to afford fees to receive care. The first institutions came into being because of philanthropic efforts and lobbying of government by middle-class reformers concerned about what they saw as a rising tide of intemperance. Indeed, the annual arrest rate for drunkenness in the two largest colonies, Victoria and New South Wales, was rising. It peaked in the 1880s, and while it declined in the 1890s, it remained substantial until World War I.

Victoria Leads the Way

An Irish immigrant doctor, Charles McCarthy, who had read about inebriate asylums in the United States, raised the matter of treating inebriates in special institutions in a letter to the Melbourne *Argus* in June 1859. Over the next twelve years, he wrote a number of letters on the subject to the Melbourne press.

In September 1871, a public meeting appointed a deputation to see Sir Charles Gavan Duffy, the chief secretary. Duffy promised government support for an inebriates retreat if a moderate amount was subscribed by the public.

When no government funds were forthcoming, the management committee that had grown out of the public meeting purchased a property at Northcote in 1872. Successive governments subsequently provided funds. But Sir James McCulloch refused to do so in 1875. When there was no hope of further government aid, McCarthy purchased the property. After litigation, he was forced to surrender ownership but was allowed to stand as a candidate for the superintendent's position. Alcoholics had been housed in Yarra Bend, Melbourne's lunatic asylum, since its inception in 1848. Criticism by the inspector of lunatic asylums, Edward Paley, and the arguments of McCarthy led to abandonment of the practice and to enactment of inebriates legislation in 1872. McCarthy claimed that he could achieve an 80 percent cure rate.

The Royal Commission on Asylums for the Insane and Inebriate, 1884–1886, proposed that a government institution replace McCarthy's retreat. The resulting Inebriate Asylums Act (1888) provided for mandatory treatment. By 1890, the Victorian government had acquired control of the Northcote retreat and had established an institution at Beaconsfield. But the financial stringency resulting from the economic depression of the early 1890s together with low numbers of admissions forced closure of both institutions in 1892.

The Other Colonies Follow

The opening of the Northcote retreat inspired South Australian legislation in 1874. The private member's bill had not been opposed by the government, although the treasurer warned that government financial aid was unlikely. A second inebriates act was passed in 1881. But governments steadfastly refused to create a public institution, preferring to subsidize the work of philanthropic bodies. A medical critic of the private retreat claimed in 1910 that the legislation had become a dead letter. Tasmania also passed legislation in the 1870s, although little resulted immediately from it. The Royal Commission on the State of Lunatic Asylums in Tasmania of the early 1880s recommended less costly treatment than that provided at the private retreat. An Inebriate Act was passed in 1885 and an Inebriates Hospitals Act in 1892. In Queensland, as elsewhere, doctors called for treatment of inebriety in special facilities. In 1888, the Queensland Medical Association urged that an asylum for inebriates be immediately established. Finally, in 1896, the inebriate institutions bill was enacted. The grim and isolated Dunwich Benevolent Asylum was announced as a retreat and became operative as such from 1898.

In New South Wales, the idea of an inebriate institution was considered in an 1868 report on lunacy administration by Frederic Norton Manning, the distinguished psychiatrist. He supported the American practice of providing treatment in institutions separate from lunatic asylums. However, not until 1882 was the New South Wales Lunacy Act amended so that magistrates could send inebriates to the Darlinghurst reception house for treatment of acute alcoholism. In 1893, the New South Wales director of charities, Sidney Maxted, suggested that when government finances recovered from the economic depression, a public institution should be established. Provision was to exist for paying, voluntary patients as well as inebriates committed by the courts. In 1897, J. M. Creed, a senior member of the medical profession, introduced into Parliament an inebriates bill. Both the prisons department and the lunacy department supported Creed's initiative.

In the early 1900s, various states passed legislation concerning inebriates. The Victorian Act of 1904 was modeled on the New South Wales Act of 1900. Sir Samuel Gillot, the minister in charge of the Victorian legislation, had said that while the government intended to provide public institutions, it wanted to see private retreats established to cater for the well-to-do. The South Australian Inebriates Act of 1908 and the Western Australian Inebriates Act of 1912 closely followed the earlier legislation in Victoria and New South Wales. In 1913, the hospital for the insane at Claremont was listed as an inebriates institution under the Western Australian Inebriates Act.

Governments relied heavily on philanthropic organizations to provide specialist treatment facilities. Even where public facilities were established, they were commonly grim, poorly resourced places of harsh discipline rather than centers of skilled treatment. In New South Wales, for example, from 1915 to its closure in 1929, Shaftesbury, a forbidding institution run by the prisons department, "treated" voluntary and committed inebriate cases. From 1929 until well into the postwar era, long-term inebriate patients were housed in state psychiatric hospitals, often in conditions that were less than ideal.

From Optimism to Pessimism to Optimism

In Australia, the era of optimism about specialist inebriate institutions ended in the 1920s. Aware of the doubtful therapeutic capacity of such facilities, magistrates often refused to proceed under the inebriate legislation. Not until the 1950s and 1960s did a new wave of medical and official optimism about special services to treat alcoholics resurface, at a time of high and growing national consumption of alcoholic beverages. A spate of new legislation and new treatment facilities resulted. But from the 1970s, the strong focus on treatment as an answer to the growth of alcohol-related problems was challenged by proposals for collective political and economic measures to reduce general alcohol consumption and so to reduce the prevalence of inebriety and other harmful consequences of alcohol abuse.

Milton James Lewis

See also: Australia; Physicians and Alcohol (Australia)

References

Brothers, C. R. D. *Early Victorian Psychiatry, 1835–1905.* Melbourne: Government Printer, 1962.

Dax, E. C. *Asylum to Community: The Development of the Mental Hygiene Service in Victoria, Australia.* Melbourne: F. W. Cheshire, 1961.

"A Drink Cure" in *Australian Medical Journal.* 15 (1910): 683.
Garton, S. "'Once a Drunkard Always a Drunkard': Social Reform and the Problem of 'Habitual Drunkenness' in Australia, 1880–1914" in *Historical Studies.* 53 (1987): 38–53.
"An Inebriate Act for New South Wales" in *Australasian Medical Gazette.* 16 (1897): 564.
"Inebriate Asylums" in *Australasian Medical Gazette.* 12 (1893): 279–280.
Lewis, M. *A Rum State. Alcohol and State Policy in Australia.* Canberra: AGPS Press, 1992.
McCarthy, C. *Inebriate Retreats: Their Origin, Utility, Necessity, and Management.* Melbourne: Stillwell, 1888.
"Presidential Address" in *Australasian Medical Gazette.* 10 (1891): 205.
Royal Commission on Asylums for Insane and Inebriate Report. *Victoria Parliamentary Papers.* 2 (1886).

Institute and Guild of Brewing

The Institute and Guild of Brewing, a British-based member's organization, resulted from the merger in 2001 of the Institute of Brewing and the International Brewers' Guild. These two bodies evolved during the twentieth century to cater for the industry's technical personnel but developed along different lines. The guild was aimed at the practicing brewer, while the institute embraced brewers' chemists and allied traders as well as brewers. The institute became the industry's examining body in the United Kingdom and was responsible for standardization of brewing analysis and coordination of research, while the guild concentrated on the work and welfare of brewers. Decline in British membership during the 1990s in a shrinking industry, coupled with the unwillingness of United Kingdom companies to continue support of two similar organizations, forced a merger. The new body has some 4,000 members, with around half residing outside the United Kingdom, principally in British Commonwealth countries.

The Laboratory Club was founded in London in 1886 as a forum for discussion among pupil brewers, that is, those training to become operative brewers. The club had expanded to around 250 members by 1890 when it took the name Institute of Brewing. Three similar organizations grew up in the north and the midlands in the early 1890s, and in 1895 the four institutes began joint publication of a journal containing transactions of their meetings. These organizations merged in 1904 to form a single institute with regional sections, a Scottish section being added in the same year. Growing dissatisfaction among a group of Yorkshire brewers, who regarded the institute as insufficiently selective in its entry criteria and resented the relative power of the chemists, led to the formation of the Operative Brewers' Guild in 1908 (changing its name to the Incorporated Brewers' Guild in 1929 and the International Brewers' Guild in 1996). One of the guild's first moves was to set up a benevolent scheme to assist brewers who had fallen on hard times. The guild had 508 members to the institute's 1,005 by January 1914 and produced its own journal.

In 1920, the United Kingdom brewing industry began a modest investment in scientific research with five isolated workers at different sites. Funding was through subscription by companies to the institute, which administered the scheme. Subsequently, an industry research establishment, founded in Surrey in 1951, enjoyed central funding through the Brewers' Society (BS), with administration delegated to the institute.

The first institute examinations were held in 1922, giving admission to associate and diploma grades of membership, which continue to this day. Recommended methods of malt analysis were first issued by the institute in 1906 and regularly updated, although it was 1971 before comprehensive methods for the analysis of beer and brewing materials were published. The institute and the guild both expanded internationally after the second world war, beginning with the institute creating an Australian section in 1953 and the guild an East African section in 1956. The institute became an educational charity in 1975, and training is now the central concern of the merged body, although the main involvement of the majority of members remains attendance at the annual section dinners. The Institute and Guild of Brewing publishes both a glossy monthly magazine and a quarterly journal containing original research. In 2002, the new National Brewing Library at Oxford Brookes University received the Institute of Brewing Technical and History Library on permanent loan.

Raymond G. Anderson

See also: Beer; Brewers' Society (BS)

References

Bird, W. H. *A History of the Institute of Brewing.* London: Institute of Brewing, 1955.
Brookes, P. A. "The Institute of Brewing: Options and Opportunities" in *Proceedings of the Institute of Brewing Africa Section, 7th Convention, Nairobi,* xiii–xvi. Hout Bay, South Africa: Institute of Brewing, Africa Section, 1999.
"End of the Line." Editorial in *The Brewer.* 96 (2000): 430.
The Institute of Brewing Centenary. London: Institute of Brewing, 1986.

Institute of Alcohol Studies (IAS)

The Institute of Alcohol Studies was organized in the early 1980s in response to the alcohol problem in the United Kingdom and the widespread indifference to the traditional temperance policy that called for total abstinence.

In Britain, after the end of the second world war, there was no interest in alcohol policy among the general public. The birth of the "disease model" of alcoholism had placed prevention policies in the doldrums. The establishment in 1962 of the UK's National Council on Alcoholism (NCA), essentially an initiative of the Church of England Temperance Society (CETS), witnessed a revival of concern. The 1967 Road Traffic Act made it an offense to drive on British roads with a blood-alcohol level above 80 milligrams per 100 milliliters; on conviction, a drinking driver faced a statutory period of disqualification for a period of twelve months. But highway safety, not a broader concern about alcohol, was the framework for this legislation.

It was not until 1972 that the British government undertook initiatives relating to the drinking of alcoholic beverages. At that time, the Department of Health began funding alcohol problem-drinking services. By 1975, due to the growing awareness of alcohol-related harm, the Department of Health set up an Advisory Committee on Alcoholism, which, during its four-year existence, issued three reports on service provision, training, and prevention. Apart from the Salvation Army, no temperance organization was represented on the committee.

Decision makers saw the contribution of temperance organizations as irrelevant to modern needs—allegedly, they had become too "hung up" on total abstinence. Much earlier, in the 1930s, temperance supporters had warned about the emergence of this negative attitude. Henry Townsend, biographer of Robert Wilson Black, quotes a 1932 letter to Wilson Black by Sir Angus Watson: "We are reaching a very critical period in Temperance reform, and if we are to succeed in the future, it is essential that we should secure the sympathy of the 'moderate' man" (quoted in Townsend 1954).

Dr. Stuart Horner faced this reality when, in 1981, he became chairman of the United Kingdom Temperance Alliance (UKTA), a charitable trust. For most people, the temperance message of abstinence appeared irrelevant. From his vantage point as chairman of the Community Medicine Committee of the British Medical Association, he realized the need to overhaul the work of the trust. In 1982, he appointed Derek Rutherford as UKTA's chief executive. Rutherford brought with him, from the National Council on Alcoholism (NCA), Andrew McNeill, who was responsible for the council's workplace project.

As a consequence of this change in leadership, in 1983 the UKTA established the Institute of Alcohol Studies (IAS). The UKTA gave most of its funds to the new institute. Its basic aims were: (1) increasing knowledge of alcohol and of the social and health consequences of its misuse and (2) encouraging and supporting the adoption of effective measures for the management and prevention of alcohol-related problems. The IAS worked in accord with the 1980 recommendations of the World Health Organization (WHO). Since 1990, through its work in Eurocare, the IAS has been an important promoter of the WHO European Alcohol Action Plan.

During the twenty years of its existence, IAS has come to be recognized as an independent source of information; an advocate of effective drunk driving laws; a sponsor of university research on a range of subjects including alcohol and the heart, violence, economics, and licensing reform; a publisher of a wide range of papers and fact sheets; an organizer of conferences and workshops; the provider of a website (http://www.ias.org.uk); and the publisher of two quarterly journals, a UK publication called *Alcohol Alert* and an international publication called the *Globe*.

IAS provides the secretariat and an office in Brussels for Eurocare (which comprises 44 member organizations throughout the European Union). In 2000, the IAS, together with the Robert Wood Johnson Foundation, funded an international conference at Syracuse, in New York State, to seek to establish a Global Alcohol Policy Alliance with the aims of monitoring the activities of the international drinks industry and their "social aspect" organizations.

Derek Rutherford

See also: Rutherford, Derek; United Kingdom Temperance Alliance (UKTA)

References

Institute of Alcohol Studies website. http://www.ias.org.uk.
Townsend, Henry. *Robert Wilson Black.* London: Carey Kingsgate Press, 1954.

Interbrew

Interbrew, a Belgian-based brewing conglomerate, has very quickly grown into one of the world's largest brewing firms. It was formed in 1987 through a merger of Brasseries Artois and Brasseries Piedboeuf, at the time the second and third largest breweries in Belgium. Both of these firms brought rich brewing traditions to Interbrew. Artois was founded in the Flemish city of Leuven, where brewing has been an important part of the local culture for centuries. Artois traces its beginnings to a pub named Den Horen (the Horn) that began operations in 1366. In 1717, Sebastien Artois, a master brewer at Den Horen, bought the operation and renamed it Artois. One of his grandsons helped expand the brewery and bought two local rivals, offering a hint of the business dealings for which Interbrew has lately become famous. During the nineteenth and twentieth centuries, Artois incorporated many of the latest technical advances in brewing, becoming in the process one of Europe's premier breweries. In 1926, it began brewing what is today Interbrew's flagship brand, Stella Artois, a highly regarded pilsner-style beer, the production and flavor of which reflect a combination of new technology and traditional brewing and malting techniques. Initially, it was intended as a seasonal Christmas beer: "Stella" means star in Latin, and early on the beer was depicted against a background of the Christmas star. However, its great popularity convinced the brewery to begin year-round production.

In 1853, the Piedboeuf family founded a brewery in Jupille sur Meuse, near Liege in the French-speaking part of Belgium. Its most famous product has been the Jupiler brand, which, like Stella Artois, is a Belgian-style pilsner. Though introduced relatively recently in 1966, Jupiler soon became a national favorite, and it is currently Belgium's best-selling beer.

During the twentieth century, the Belgian brewing industry, like that in many other countries, underwent a great deal of consolidation, as many local firms went out of business or were bought up by larger competitors. In the decades following the second world war, both Artois and Piedboeuf acquired other breweries, including some outside of Belgium. For example, after buying Leffe, a popular domestic brand in 1952, Artois turned its attention abroad, acquiring breweries in Holland (Dommelsch in 1968) and in France (Brasseries Motte Cordonier in 1970). In 1984, three years before the creation of Interbrew, Piedboeuf bought Lamont, a rival Belgian brewery.

The merger of Artois and Piedboeuf into Interbrew gave birth to a new company that decided to pursue growth through acquisition much more deliberately than had the two companies by themselves. In 1989 and 1990, Interbrew acquired two famous Belgian specialty breweries, the very highly regarded Hoegaarden and Belle-Vue. Yet, it was not until the 1990s that Interbrew grew from a national into an international brewery. In 1995, it made its most significant acquisition to date, buying 100 percent of the shares of John Labatt Limited, Canada's second largest brewery. Labatt was not a stranger to corporate takeovers, having acquired Latrobe Brewing Company, the brewers of Rolling Rock, a popular brand in the east of the United States, in 1987. Interbrew's purchase of Labatt signaled its entry into the potentially lucrative but very competitive North American beer market.

Since its acquisition of Labatt, Interbrew has acquired a number of other breweries in a wide range of countries. Its next significant purchase came in 2000, when it bought Bass Breweries, one of the oldest and largest breweries in England. That same year, Interbrew, a privately held company, decided to go public, a decision driven in part by its need to attract capital for further acquisitions. In 2001, it acquired Becks, one of the leading beer brands in Germany. Becks has a much stronger presence than Stella Artois in the United States, where it outsells Artois thirty to one.

Interbrew's acquisition of Bass in 2000 made it the world's second largest brewery, with sales of over 80 million hectoliters (29 million U.S. gallons), putting it slightly ahead of its Dutch rival Heineken (74 million hectoliters [27 million U.S. gallons]), but leaving it well behind the world's largest brewery, Anheuser-Busch of the United States (155 million hectoliters [56 million U.S. gallons]).

Interestingly, its path to international brewery contrasts quite sharply with the strategy taken by Anheuser-Busch, Heineken, Carlsberg, and Guinness. These four firms are all trying to develop global beer brands, and each of them made Interbrand's 2001 survey of the world's 100 most valuable brands: Budweiser (# 26), Heineken (# 82), Guinness (# 94), and Carlsberg (# 97) ("The Best Global Brands" 2001). Yet, the degree to which these brands are truly global is debatable. Domestic consumers account for 90 percent of Budweiser's sales, while 61 percent of Heineken's sales and 68 percent of Carlsberg's sales are in the European Union.

Interbrew's strategy is considerably more complicated. Rather than trying to build sales around one marquee brand, it has chosen to buy or partner with existing breweries in many of the countries in which it operates. The company has based this approach on the belief that the vast majority of beer consumers will continue to prefer local over global beer brands, a pattern that has certainly held throughout the twentieth century. Interbrew is seeking to become the "world's local brewer," a phrase intended to convey its commitment to producing local beers in many of the markets in which it operates.

This is not to suggest, however, that Interbrew is uninterested in promoting the sales of its marquee brands as well. Rather, Interbrew envisions a complementary approach in which the company uses local breweries abroad to help distribute and market their flagship brands such as Stella Artois, Bass, and Becks, along with some of their more expensive specialty beers such as Hoegaarden and Belle-Vue. The challenge for Interbrew is to see if it can successfully manage over 200 brands in the more than 100 countries in which it operates. So far, it has achieved a relatively balanced geographical distribution of its sales, with 22 percent in North America, 46 percent in Western Europe, and 32 percent in emerging markets (primarily Eastern Europe and East Asia). It remains to be seen if it will be able to continue its rapid growth through additional acquisitions, or if it will have to generate increased sales from the host of breweries it currently operates.

Martin Stack

See also: Anheuser-Busch; Bass; Labatt Brewing Company Limited

References

"The Best Global Brands" in *Business Week.* 6 August 2001: 50–64.

"The Big Pitcher" in *Economist.* 18 January 2001: 63–64.

Bilefsky, Dan. "Interbrew Aims to Boost Its Profits by Elevating Stella to the Top Shelf" in *Wall Street Journal.* 12 April 2002.

Foote, Andrea. "The World's Local Brewer" in *Beverage World.* November 2000.

Interbrew corporate website. http://www.interbrew.com [October 2002].

Jackson, Michael. *The Great Beers of Belgium.* 3d ed. London: Duncan Baird, 1995.

Marinov, Marin, and Svelta Marinova. "Investor Strategy Development and Adaptation: The Case of Interbrew" in *European Management Journal.* 16 (1998): 400–410.

Protz, Roger. *The Ultimate Encyclopedia of Beer.* New York: Smithmark, 1995.

Thornhill, John. "Interbrew Still Thirsting for Fresh Acquisitions in Its Quest to Consolidate the World's Beers" in *Financial Times.* 27 September 2000: 19.

Intercollegiate Prohibition Association (IPA)

The Intercollegiate Prohibition Association (IPA) coordinated the activities of prohibition clubs on college campuses. The formal goal of the organization was to improve alcohol education for university students, but its activities ranged more widely, revealing the prohibition movement's determination to enlist youth in its campaign for an alcohol-free United States.

With the support of the Prohibition Party, college students founded the IPA at a multistate convention held in Cincinnati, Ohio, in 1892. By 1893, there were student organizations at 146 universities. It was widely hoped that the IPA would create a new generation of youth leadership for its sponsoring organization, but only about a dozen additional campuses were organized by 1899, and many of the previously established clubs became defunct. However, the Prohibition Party's National Committee revitalized the IPA in 1899–1900 to bring together support during an emerging rivalry with the Anti-Saloon League of America (ASLA) for national temperance leadership. D. Leigh Colvin, Harry S. Warner, and Virgil Hinshaw were among the most active supporters of the IPA during this second phase; in 1900, the IPA established itself as a permanent political organization. In the first decade of the century, the IPA was second only to the Young Men's and Young Women's Christian Association in total membership among American college students.

In 1910, the IPA eliminated its formal affiliation with the Prohibition Party and gradually came under the ASLA's influence. This influence would be consolidated in 1924, when the ASLA assumed financial responsibility for the IPA. At this time, the organization also became the World League Against Alcoholism's (WLAA) student department.

The IPA incorporated college temperance organizations in the West, Midwest, East, and South. From its origin, the organization included both men and women members who primarily engaged in local, state, and national oratorical contests on temperance topics. In addition, members volunteered for speaking and song tours, particularly during the summer, and petitioned universities for coursework on temperance topics while simultaneously creating independent temperance study groups. Affiliated clubs also participated in a broad range of local programs. They petitioned to eliminate references to alcohol consumption in the lyrics of alma maters, removed the liquor licenses of local saloons, placed liquor-problem books in college libraries, and lobbied to eliminate university banquets where alcohol was served. Volunteers often engaged in explicitly political activities by lending their support to Prohibition Party candidates in local elections.

The College Patriot, founded in 1903, was the main publication of the IPA. The name of this publication changed to *Intercollegiate Statesman* in 1904 and, upon joining the WLAA, the name again changed to *International Student.* The publication regularly included addresses from prominent national temperance leaders, notes on the activities of local affiliates throughout the country, and a concluding section with suggested oratorical topics.

Lisa Andersen

See also: Anti-Saloon League of America (ASLA); Prohibition Party (United States); World League Against Alcoholism (WLAA); Young Women's Christian Association (YWCA)

References

Colvin, D. Leigh. *Prohibition in the United States: A History of the Prohibition Party, and the Prohibition Movement.* New York: George H. Doran, 1926.

Higley, Mary S. "Intercollegiate Prohibition Association, 1892–1963" in *Guide to the Microfilm Edition of Temperance and Prohibition Papers,* edited by Randall C. Jimerson, Francis X. Blouin, and Charles A. Isetts, 101–103. Ann Arbor: University of Michigan, 1977.

Warner, Harry S. *An Evolution in Understanding of the Problem of Alcohol: A History of College Idealism.* Boston: Christopher Publishing House, 1966.

Interdiction and Curatorship

Interdiction and curatorship are two complementary measures of civil law that, in the province of Quebec (Canada), permitted the removal of the legal capacity (interdiction) of a person deemed to be a "habitual drunkard" and the transfer of the administration of his or her property to another person (the curator). The procedure eventually resulted in the forced confinement of the alcoholic so interdicted. The passing, in 1870, of the Act to Provide for the Interdiction and Cure of Habitual Drunkards, the bill that inaugurated this procedure, is a clear symptom of the more prohibitionist and legislation-oriented reactions against alcohol and alcohol abuse of the second half of the nineteenth century. This wave of antialcoholism completed a change from the more voluntary and conversion-like methods of the temperance societies of the first decades of the nineteenth century.

Obtaining the interdiction of an individual under this legislation was relatively simple, although families resorted to it, seemingly, only after having endured a number of years of problematic conduct related to alcohol. Presented as a means of protecting families against ruin, the procedure was similar to the interdiction of mentally disordered people and of prodigals, measures already available before 1870. First, a relation, by blood or affinity, or a friend submitted a request to a judge. Then, a family council met. Members of this council gave their opinion on the drunken habits of the individual, on the necessity of the interdiction, and on the choice of the curator to be named. Finally, the judge rendered his decision, pronouncing, in most of the cases, the interdiction asked for. An interesting aspect of the law was that the habitual drunkard was defined as a person who had such a reputation in his or her neighborhood.

The legislation specifically applied to alcoholics proved to be quite harsh. No appeal of the decision of the magistrate could be lodged. But, above all, the interdicted alcoholic could be sent to an establishment authorized to receive habitual drunkards. From 1870 to 1884, the confinement and its duration depended only on the named curator, usually a near family member. Sir Antoine-Aimé Dorion, chief justice of the Court of Queen's Bench (the higher civil court of the province of Quebec legal system at that time), labeled the act as "a pretty crude piece of legislation, lacking in several particulars of the means of protection which ought to be available to those who might be harshly or improperly dealt with" (Ex parte Walsh: 366). In 1884, confinement was placed under the supervision of the judicial system. In the years following 1884, most interdicted drunkards of Montreal (Quebec) subjected to an order of confinement would have to go to the Saint-Benoît-Joseph Asylum, a small private institution near the city and directed by a religious community, the Brothers of Charity.

From 1870 to 1895 inclusively, over 140 inhabitants of the city of Montreal went through an interdiction owing to their drinking habits. Many were men of the middle class (professionals, white-collar workers) and of the business sector. Despite its harshness, the measure allowed a number of families to withstand, at least partially, the sometimes dramatic consequences that a heavy consumption of alcohol had for them and their financial health in an industrializing society.

Thierry Nootens

See also: Treatment Institutions

References

An Act to Amend the Act 33 Victoria, Chapter 26, entitled: "An Act to Provide for the Interdiction and Cure of Habitual Drunkards." *Statutes of the Province of Quebec.* 47 Victoria (1884): chap. 21.

An Act to Provide for the Interdiction and Cure of Habitual Drunkards. *Statutes of the Province of Quebec.* 33 Victoria (1870): chap. 26.

Ex parte Walsh. *Queen's Bench Reports,* vol. 3: 365–368. 26 February 1884.

Sirois, L. P. *Tutelles et curatelles.* Québec: Imprimerie de l'Action Sociale, 1911.

International Congresses on Alcoholism

The international temperance congresses were pre–World War I forums for individuals, societies, and governments to discuss and disseminate ideas about restricting alcohol use and for furthering the understanding of alcohol problems. The first congress was the Antwerp Meeting against the Abuse of Alcoholic Beverages, in 1885. By 1923, seventeen such congresses had been held, fourteen of them before 1914. Each congress was held in a different European capital city, approximately one every two years. The meetings therefore tended to stress the host country's problems and approaches to the issues of alcoholic beverages and their abuse. At the same time, the country's organizers attempted to establish broad, general guidelines that would obviate heated confrontations. The statement included in the proceedings of the Tenth International Congress held in Budapest, Hungary, in 1905 expresses a commitment "not to be bound down to one special line" and to "unite everybody and everything which aims at combating alcoholism, whether it be on the lines of moderation or abstinence." The last pre–World War I congress was held in London in 1913. Other sites included Christiania [Oslo], Stockholm, Basel, Vienna, The Hague, Brussels, Paris, Hamburg, Budapest, Milan, and Zurich.

Structure and Representation

From the very beginning, the congresses consisted of a Standing Committee that included temperance advocates of the host country in which the congress was held and an honorary president representing the same country. Indeed, except for the congress held in Basel, Switzerland, in 1895 and in Paris in 1899, this honorary personage was either a relatively minor member of the ruling family or a member of the high nobility distinguished for their past championship of temperance. Including, then, a large number of members drawn from cultural, scientific, humanitarian, and other walks of life, each congress was backed up by a standing Organizational Committee. This latter body not only planned the location of the ensuing congress, but also established broad guidelines for the issues to be raised in the oral presentations that characterized the sessions of the congresses. Usually numbering around a dozen luminaries of the various national temperance movements, the Organizational Committee's membership was remarkably consistent. For example, the noted Swiss physician and temperance activist Auguste Forel as well as Charlotte Gray of England (a Good Templar and Woman's Christian Temperance Union [WCTU] worker) were on this body right up to the final prewar congress in 1913.

The international congresses also made distinctions between representatives to their sessions. There were "official" delegates—individuals who were the official representatives of governments in their respective countries; delegates representing scientific and temperance organizations that were not connected to government agencies; and a large number of delegates who represented no official temperance organization or cause. The nations generally represented by the first kind of organization varied in number from congress to congress, but, generally speaking, France, Great Britain, Germany, and Russia were consistently represented. The initial congresses were overwhelmingly Eurocentric in both their composition and their focus, but several of the later congresses saw the appearance on a more consistent basis of non-European and nonwestern delegates.

It was in the second and third kinds of delegate that the great bulk of congress participants were represented. The first usually numbered at least a dozen delegates (and, in the later congresses, even more) from institutions and organizations that ranged from the international branches of large-scale temperance behemoths such as the International Order of Good Templars (IOGT), the Blue Cross, and the World's Woman's Christian Temperance Union (WWCTU), to the miniscule or internationally insignificant—for example, the Russian temperance newspaper *Vestnik trezvosti* (*The Temperance Courier*), the Moscow Temperance Society, and the Anti-Saloon League of America (ASLA). Some delegates, such as Dr. Norman Kerr of Britain (1834–1899), author of the influential *On Inebriety*, was noteworthy enough that he simply represented himself at several of these early congresses before his death. No explanation was ever offered as to why such a luminary of European temperance circles was never made a member of the Organizational Committee.

The nonvoting, nonreporting delegates from various countries constituted the largest group by far, the overwhelming majority of which, generally speaking, were natives of the country hosting the congress. Thus, to cite but one example, at the 1899 congress held in Paris, of the over 1,000 people in attendance, over 500 were French, while only 21 were from Germany, 94 from Switzerland, and 78 from England. These proportions changed from congress to congress, naturally. But one ratio did not. The number of women at these congresses was always significantly smaller than the number of male delegates despite continued insistence that the question was a vital one for women and women's rights. Not surprisingly, those countries that consistently had large numbers of female participants were the United Kingdom, Germany, and the United States. Switzerland also showed high percentages of women among its delegates. Those with the consistently lowest number of women in their respective delegations were Russia, Rumania, and Italy.

Geographic Focus of the Congresses

The congresses were part of a late-nineteenth-century flowering of "internationalism," in which scientists, bureaucrats, intellectuals, politicians, reformers, and others could exchange information and enhance international cooperation on a variety of subjects. Yet the view of these proceedings, in the case of the alcohol congresses, as truly "international" also requires closer scrutiny. The initial congresses were, as noted, Eurocentric in both their composition and perspectives. It was not until the 1895 Congress in Paris, for example, that any western hemisphere nation other than the United States and Canada—Chile—sent "official" delegates. Moreover, much further progess would not come until the 1909 London Congress, where Mexico provided a governmental representative and the British colonies provided delegates from Australia, the Bahamas, Ceylon, West and East Africa, Hong Kong, and Jamaica. However, delegates from these colonial possessions were all British officials and professionals, *not* members of the indigenous populations themselves. Indeed, the only contrast to this unrelieved sea of white was the Honorary Vice President Ogawa of Japan at the Tenth Congress held in Budapest in 1905.

Moreover, the distinction between "official" and "unofficial" delegates was frequently (and deliberately) blurred. Louis Skarzynski, for example, appeared at one congress (the fourth, held at the Hague in 1894) as one of the third category of delegates, representing Poland. But in subsequent congresses, he served as an "official delegate," representing the imperial Russian government (and more particularly, the Ministry of Finance, since he had been an official of this department since the early 1890s). The Russian Finance Ministry was one of the leading voices for "moderate consumption" of alcohol as opposed to "abstinence." Skarzynski's report to the Russian finance minister, claiming the existence of a "pro-abstinence bloc" at the congresses, an observation that should come as no surprise.

Issues

Generally held in the late summer or early autumn, the congresses addressed many problems of vital concern to temperance advocates. Among these were the effects of alcohol abuse on industrial workers, their living conditions, their material well-being, and their work efficiency; the etiology of alcoholism (including not only the chemical, but also its biological and hereditary causes); women and alcoholism; and the associated problems of alcoholism in schools and how to combat it. Other subjects addressed at one congress or another were the relationship between poverty and alcoholism and—especially at the 1909 congress in London—alcoholism among the colonial peoples and methods for preventing or reducing the incidence. A number of the congresses further devoted sessions to the activities and purported triumphs of the IOGT, the Blue Cross, and other such bodies. Some few purely national campaigns by various countries also received attention—from private temperance crusades to such governmental efforts as the vodka monopoly in imperial Russia. Finally, whole sections were devoted to various efforts at the treatment of alcoholism undertaken by private individuals and the issue of alcohol consumption in the military.

After World War I, U.S. National Prohibition and the campaign of the World League Against Alcoholism introduced even more disagreement over how to handle the alcohol question into the European debate. U.S.-inspired or allied prohibitionist and other restrictionist groups held their own international congresses, and the few held under the banner of the International Congresses on Alcoholism were influenced by this American debate.

The prewar international temperance congresses were among the most noteworthy efforts of European civil society to transcend national borders in the quest for a greater public awareness of and concern about the dangers lurking behind widespread alcohol abuse.

George Snow

See also: Forel, Auguste; Kerr, Norman Shank; Russia, Imperial, Temperance in; World League Against Alcoholism (WLAA); World's Woman's Christian Temperance Union (WWCTU)

Reference

"International Temperance Congresses" in *Standard Encyclopedia of the Alcohol Problem,* vol. 3: 1343–1345. Westerville, OH: American Issue Publishing, 1926.

International Order of Good Templars

See Good Templars (IOGT)

International Organization of Good Templars

See Good Templars (IOGT); IOGT International

International Organization of Good Templars International

See IOGT International

International Prohibition Confederation

See World Prohibition Federation

International Reform Federation, Inc.

The International Reform Federation, Inc. was founded initially as the International Reform Bureau (IRB) in Washington, D.C., in 1895. The initial impetus for the organization was a series of lectures by noted Sabbath and temperance advocate Wilbur Fisk Crafts at Princeton Theological Seminary. In 1896, the IRB was incorporated with headquarters at 206 Pennsylvania Avenue S.E., Washington, D.C. Since 1924, it has been known as the International Reform Federation, Inc. Its current motto, "to support those moral and social reforms on which the churches generally agree," succinctly summarizes the organization's purpose.

Taking its direction from its founder, the organization was committed to civic education, good government, and exposure of such vices as liquor, narcotics, prostitution, and gambling, and faithful administration of the law. By the time of Crafts's death, the organization claimed 18,000 supporting members. By the 1920s, it supported an office in China to coordinate efforts to fight the opium traffic. By the mid-1920s, the body had taken credit for instigating 2,700 criminal prosecutions, with convictions and confiscation of liquor, drugs, gambling devices, and obscene literature.

Fittingly for its origins in the Progressive Era, the IRB served as the legislative reference library for religious moral reformers. It drafted the following congressional acts: the Bowersock Act, prohibiting liquor sales at immigrant stations; the Gallinger Amendment, forbidding liquor sales in old soldiers' homes; and the Gillet-Lodge Act, prohibiting U.S. traders from selling liquor on certain Pacific islands. In 1918, in an act that drew near universal approval, Crafts had a bronze tablet with the Ten Commandments erected in the Allegheny County Courthouse in Pittsburgh, Pennsylvania.

Among the most important second-generation leaders were Presbyterian minister Robert Watson (1865–1936), president of the federation from 1923 to 1936, and Clinton Norman Howard (1868–1955), who assumed the editorship of the IRB's publication *Twentieth Century Progress,* now *Progress.* Howard continued the moral agenda of his predecessor while strengthening the organization's efforts to promote disarmament and the arbitration of international disputes. Veteran temperance advocate D. Leigh Colvin served as president from 1937 to 1959. One of the group's most important leaders was Methodist Bishop Wilbur E. Hammaker, who served as treasurer from the 1940s to 1960s. Baptist minister and editor John W. Bradbury served as president from 1960 to 1982. During Bradbury's tenure, the organization sold its headquarters on Capitol Hill and began to move it in a more decidedly evangelical direction. Baptist minister Samuel A. Jeanes, who headed the group from 1982 to 1998, accelerated the evangelical orientation imitated during the Bradbury administration. Since 1998, Methodist minister Lawrence L. Dunn has served as president. Although still fighting a rear-guard action against liquor, in recent years the federation has focused more attention on drugs and the spread of legalized gambling. Today, the organization continues to support a "Christian" presence in the nation's capital while giving financial aid to a variety of evangelical causes.

William C. Kostlevy

See also: Crafts, Wilbur Fisk

References

"International Reform Federation, Inc." in *Standard Encyclopedia of the Alcohol Problem,* edited by Ernest Cherrington et al., vol. 3: 1342–1343. Westerville, OH: American Issue Publishing, 1925.

International Reform Federation, Inc. Records. Bentley Historical Library, University of Michigan.

Twentieth Century Progress (now *Progress*), vols. 47–104 (1946–2003).

IOGT International

Beginning in 1990, the IOGT International was used as the name for the international structure and work of the Good Templar temperance society. It had originated in the United States in the early 1850s. In August 2000, the IOGT International returned to its roots at a conference in Syracuse, New York. Its celebration of 150 years of active service culminated in its world congress in Eastbourne, England, in October 2002.

Over the years, the initials IOGT have represented slightly different organizational names—Independent Order of Good Templars, International Order of Good Templars, and International Organization of Good Templars—as the society came to emphasize its international character and later to de-emphasize its early fraternal society identity. The name IOGT International continued this evolution.

At the world congress in 1962, an important change took place in relation to membership. Organizations that included in their membership nonabstainers could become associates but without voting power.

For an organization arising out of societal concern for the epidemic of alcohol abuse in the mid-nineteenth century to be alive at the beginning of the twenty-first century says much for its preparedness to adapt its methods to new situations.

The present platform of the organization, adopted in 1990, is as follows:

> IOGT is a worldwide community. The aim of IOGT, founded in 1851, is the liberation of peoples of the world leading to a richer, freer and more rewarding life. As a means of attaining this aim, IOGT will promote a lifestyle free of alcohol and other drugs. The work of IOGT and its member organisations is built on the principles of universal fellowship and basic human democratic rights. The Good Templar movement believes that each individual is unique and has an infinite value. Everyone is entitled to personal freedom and is obliged to work for the improvement of the quality of life for all people. IOGT seeks to promote democracy on all levels of society, which means that all citizens must have the opportunity to actively participate in decision-making processes and freely express their opinions. IOGT works for peace by promoting human development and dignity, democracy, tolerance, equality and justice. Furthermore, IOGT advocates the peaceful settlement of conflicts between individuals and groups. Member organisations are encouraged to work towards peace between nations. IOGT recognises that alcohol and other drugs constitute a serious threat to the dignity and freedom of many people and their societies. As a part of the solution to alcohol and drug problems, members of IOGT organisations choose to live free from such substances. IOGT develops comprehensive programmes including prevention, reduction of consumption, education and the rehabilitation of users and those they affect.

At the same 1990 world congress, the name IOGT International was used for the first time. Although never authorized by a formal resolution, it became the standard usage.

In 2002, the IOGT International had 115 affiliates in 53 countries. Although it is extremely weak in the United States, the country of its origin, it has remained a significant force in Scandinavia and is growing in the developing world. Over the past twenty years, Good Templar growth internationally has been largely undertaken by its development agencies: the International Institute of the IOGT-NTO (a union of the IOGT with the breakaway National Temperance Order) movement in Sweden and FORUT, the Norwegian IOGT campaign for world development and solidarity.

The range of IOGT International activities is broad: street-children projects; support for victims of war and asylum seekers; sustainable development projects; savings schemes; children's rights; rehabilitation of dependent drinkers and their families; alcohol and drug information centers; and the advocacy of alcohol policies. Special projects are financed in the following continents and countries: in Africa, Gambia, Guinea Bissau, Sierre Leone, Senegal, Kenya, Tanzania, and Uganda; in Asia, India, Nepal, Sri Lanka, Thailand, and Vietnam; as well as in the Baltic States and Eastern Europe. The International Institute IOGT-NTO sponsored the WHO *Manual on Street Children.* Concerned about the targeting of developing countries by the drinks industry for new markets, the IOGT International funded the Marin Institute to produce the report *Thirsting for Markets* and has supported the formation of the new Global Alcohol Policy Alliance.

Derek Rutherford

See also: Good Templars (IOGT); Rutherford, Derek

Reference

IOGT International website. http://www.iogt-international.org.

Ireland

In popular culture, the Irish have an almost unequalled reputation as heavy and problem drinkers, yet during the nineteenth and twentieth centuries Ireland experienced some of the most successful temperance campaigns seen anywhere.

The Drink Industry

Brewing and distilling have long been major Irish industries, while the Irish pub as a drinking venue became so renowned during the late twentieth century that it was imitated in countries around the world.

Outside of Belfast, Ireland did not undergo an industrial revolution, and alcohol production was a major manufacturing industry from the late eighteenth century onward. Due to heavy taxation, much distilling was carried on illegally. The production of "poteen" (illicit spirits) and its sale in "shebeens" (unlicensed pubs) were important enterprises in a poor and overwhelmingly agricultural society. The spread of illicit distillation between the 1780s and the 1840s helped popularize whiskey as a drink. Improved policing from the 1830s onward slowly curbed the illegal industry and allowed large, commercial distilleries to satisfy the growing Irish taste for whiskey. However, as the Irish population was in serious decline for more than a century after the Great Famine of 1845 through 1849, Irish distillers were obliged to export if they wished to expand.

Governments in Ireland favored brewing over distilling because the country's English rulers regarded ale and beer as healthier drinks than spirits and also less likely to inflame rebels. Beer was mainly an urban drink until the mid-nineteenth century, when Guinness brewery, established in Dublin in 1759, led the way in promoting beer consumption in rural areas. But Guinness, like the distillers, was driven into large-scale exporting due to the small, and after 1845 declining, Irish home market.

Drinking Patterns

Drinking patterns in Ireland varied between cities and the countryside. Until the nineteenth century, rural drinking mainly occurred on festive occasions: at weddings and wakes, fairs and markets, religious and agricultural celebrations. Public houses were few, primitive, and often unlicensed. Licensed pubs spread from the cities during the nineteenth century, yet Irish pubs remained distinctly different from English ones.

A ca. 1900 photograph of Irish children watching the poteen still in Connemara, County Galway. Poteen is alcohol made illicitly from potatoes. (Hulton/Archive)

There were no tied houses in Ireland, and so the publican usually owned his or her premises. Indeed, the premises were often the publican's home. Only in the cities were purpose-built "gin palaces" found. Therefore, Irish pubs tended to be called by the name of the owner: Murphy's, O'Donoghue's, and so forth. The ambience was domestic and communal rather than commercial. But during the late nineteenth and early twentieth centuries, it was a domestic setting from which women were largely excluded. Public drinking was most common among men: in urban areas, among the unskilled and semiskilled working class, and in rural areas, among small farmers and agricultural laborers.

The role of drink in Irish culture, and especially the question of whether drinking in Ireland was excessive, has generated much debate. The statistics available, though far from reliable before 1900, suggest high levels of consumption by international standards, but at the same time, these levels were by no means the highest to be found. Also, heavy drinking was characteristic of certain defined groups, while other large sections of the population drank little or nothing at all.

Sociologists, anthropologists, and psychologists studied rural Ireland throughout the twentieth century, and a number of these studies identified problematical drinking practices. Some groups were prone to heavy drinking because, it was suggested, of their dysfunctional lifestyles. Drink cushioned the stresses of poverty, isolation, and celibacy that were endemic among the small farming communities in the west of Ireland. American researchers in particular were looking for explanations of apparently high levels of alcoholism and alcohol-related mental illness among Irish immigrants and their descendants in the United States. Rural life in the west provided the explanations they sought. In 1976, Richard Stivers argued that heavy drinking had been a prominent feature of male group identity in rural Ireland from at least the 1870s until the 1940s. The camaraderie of such groups was a compensation for the paucity of opportunities to marry and own land; and it was from such groups that most male emigrants to America had come.

The Temperance Movement

Yet, while Ireland has long supported an internationally important drinks industry, and heavy drinking has been an accepted feature of Irish culture, at the same time, the country has produced major antidrink campaigns that have captured the allegiance of large sections of the population, as well as exerting significant influence abroad.

The first organized temperance societies appeared in Ireland in 1829, mainly inspired by the U.S. antispirits movement. These societies reflected, in part, alarm at the increasing consumption of whiskey that had been evident since the end of the eighteenth century. These first groups, based largely in Dublin and Belfast, were organized by Protestant clergy, merchants, and professional men. They appealed to the upper classes to set an example to their inferiors by giving up spirits. In the wake of serious economic dislocation after the end of the Napoleonic Wars in 1815 and a massive popular campaign during the 1820s for greater Catholic involvement in the political life of the country, the antispirits movement was an attempt by the Protestant elite to bolster its ascendancy through a reassertion of its moral authority.

Although having some success among Anglicans, Quakers, and Presbyterians, especially in the north of Ireland, the antispirits societies made little headway among Catholics. They were feared—justifiably in some cases—as masking attempts at proselytization.

The total abstinence movement, with its more direct and emotional appeal to the working classes, was introduced to Ireland from England in 1835. It too had little success at first among the Catholic majority of the population. Then in 1838, an obscure Cork priest, Father Theobald Mathew (1790–1856), joined the Cork Total Abstinence Society and within months had launched an extraordinary crusade that by 1841 had won over perhaps half of the Irish population to teetotalism. As quickly as the crusade rose, it declined, leaving many of its supporters—not least Mathew himself—disillusioned. Nevertheless, he had demonstrated that teetotalism could have a powerful appeal in Ireland, and the Irish churches especially did not forget this lesson. Moreover, Mathew took his Catholic antidrink message to Britain and the United States and showed that total abstinence was by no means exclusively a Protestant cause.

The decline of Mathew's crusade also taught lessons. During the latter part of the nineteenth century, the Irish Catholic Church was reluctant to promote total abstinence vigorously, preaching instead the doctrine of moderation in the form of temperance. The drinks industry was a large and powerful one in Ireland, and the church was unwilling to offend it or the many drinkers among its flock. Irish Protestants, on the other hand, became increasingly committed to total abstinence. But they rejected the moral suasionist tactics of the 1830s and 1840s and instead looked to legislative coercion. Various secular antidrink societies flourished in late-nineteenth-century Ireland, mostly led by Protestants. These Irish organizations worked with English societies to win prohibition from the British Parliament. When this was not forthcoming, they campaigned for local option, Sunday closing, and more restrictive licensing laws. They had some limited successes, but the issue of home rule, or self-government increasingly dominated Irish politics from the 1870s, and thus the temperance issue failed to attract substantial political support.

The Irish Catholic Church underwent a religious revival during the nineteenth century. This revival, called by historians the "Devotional Revolution," entailed among other things the imposition of stricter discipline on clergy and laity, the introduction of new and more elaborate devotions, and an increasingly puritanical stance on social and moral issues. Although the church as a whole remained committed to temperance (as moderation in drinking), clergy influenced by the "Devotional Revolution" began to stress the importance of total abstinence as an essential ingredient of Catholic piety. The church was thus obliged to mediate between temperance and teetotalism. All Catholics were encouraged to practice temperance in their drinking, although the church was aware that many in its Irish flock did not do so. Total abstinence, on the other hand, was not obligatory, but it attracted clerical approval when practiced as a form of penance by the most devout.

A Jesuit, Father James Cullen (1841–1921), influenced by the "Devotional Revolution," established the Pioneer Total Abstinence Association of the Sacred Heart in Dublin in 1898. The Pioneers quickly became the most influential antidrink organization in the country and remained so throughout the twentieth century.

Although not on the same scale of Father Mathew's crusade, Pioneer numbers were still extremely impressive. By 1925, the Pioneer Association was claiming to have 250,000 members in Ireland; by 1945, close to 350,000 members; and by 1960, a peak of 500,000 members. This was at a time when the population of the Irish republic hovered around the 3 million mark. The Pioneers also spread abroad and won thousands of adherents in Britain, the United States, South America, Australia, and various parts of Africa. By the middle of the twentieth century, the Pioneer Association was probably one of the largest total abstinence organizations in the world.

In structuring the Pioneers, Cullen was explicitly reacting against Mathew's crusade, which had been poorly organized, interdenominational, and short lived. The Pioneers were a Catholic devotional society, not a secular welfare campaign trying to ameliorate social conditions. Their aim was not so much to reclaim drunkards as to strengthen the faith of Catholics through the practice of abstinence. They were pioneering a new, more rigorous form of Catholicism that Cullen believed would eventually reshape all of Irish society.

The essentially religious nature of the Pioneers, however, made it difficult for them to engage in politics and to influence drinking practices. Thus, despite their impressive growth in numbers during the early and mid-twentieth century, they had little impact on government policy regarding the sale of drink, which slowly became more permissive. Similarly, after 1945 alcohol consumption increased substantially in Ireland, despite the fact that a large minority of the population were total abstainers.

New attitudes and new approaches to problem drinking, especially the increasing influence of the disease model of alcoholism, made the Pioneers appear by the 1960s rather out of date. By the 1970s scholars, like Stivers, were even arguing that the authoritarian and puritanical nature of Irish Catholicism had produced an emotionally impoverished lifestyle and thus had helped promote heavy drinking rather than curbing it.

Alcohol consumption surged in Ireland during the 1970s and again during the 1990s. In the latter decade, licensing laws were liberalized, and more young people, and also far more women, were drinking. At the same time, the power and influence of the Catholic Church, beset by scandals and declining vocations, waned noticeably. At the end of the twentieth century, the Pioneers' crusade to promote both total abstinence from alcohol and Catholic devotion was in serious decline on all fronts.

Elizabeth Malcolm

See also: Carlile, Ann Jane; Guinness Brewery; Haughton, James; Loyal Orange Institution (Ireland and Britain); Mathew, Father Theobald; Nugent, James; Pioneer Total Abstinence Association of the Sacred Heart; Shebeens; St. Patrick's Day

References

Dennison, S. R., and Oliver MacDonagh. *Guinness, 1886–1939: from Incorporation to the Second World War.* Cork: Cork University Press, 1998.

Ferriter, Diarmaid. *A Nation of Extremes: the Pioneers in Twentieth-Century Ireland.* Dublin: Irish Academic Press, 1999.

Kerrigan, Colm. *Father Mathew and the Irish Temperance Movement, 1838–49.* Cork: Cork University Press, 1992.

Lynch, Patrick, and John Vaizey. *Guinness's Brewery in the Irish Economy, 1759–1876.* Cambridge: Cambridge University Press, 1960.

Malcolm, Elizabeth. *"Ireland Sober, Ireland Free": Drink and Temperance in Nineteenth-Century Ireland.* Dublin: Gill and Macmillan; Syracuse: Syracuse University Press, 1986.

———. "The Rise of the Pub: A Study in the Disciplining of Popular Culture" in *Irish Popular Culture, 1650–1850,* edited by J. S. Donnelly Jr. and Kerby Miller, 50–77. Dublin: Irish Academic Press, 1998.

McGuire, E. B. *Irish Whiskey: a History of Distilling in Ireland.* Dublin and New York: Gill and Macmillan/Barnes & Noble, 1973.

Quinn, J. F. *Father Mathew's Crusade: Temperance in Nineteenth-Century Ireland and Irish America.* Amherst: University of Massachusetts Press, 2002.

Stivers, Richard. *A Hair of the Dog: Irish Drinking and American Stereotype.* University Park and London: Pennsylvania State University Press, 1976.

Townend, Paul A. *Father Mathew, Temperance and Irish Identity.* Dublin: Irish Academic Press, 2002.

Irish Whiskey

See Whiskies

Islam as Cultural Influence

Most Muslims regard alcohol drinking as forbidden by their religion. They understand the ban on alcohol to be revealed in stages in the Qur'an, the holy book of the Muslims. The extent to which alcohol is deemed taboo is dependent upon the source of religious authority, which has a bearing on how drinking is interpreted. As such, historically there have been circumstances in which not only was alcohol drunk, but its consumption was actually encouraged. In the Islamic communities around the world today, the dominant trend is for alcohol to be avoided, especially among strict Muslims. In keeping with this rule of prohibiting alcohol in its original form, foods containing alcohol as an ingredient are also avoided.

Interpretations of the Qur'anic Teachings on Alcohol Drinking

The word alcohol has its roots in the Arabic *alkohl,* which refers to grains, fruits, or sugars that when fermented form an intoxicating beverage. Yet the Qur'an, which was written in Arabic, does not use this term but rather *khamr,* a derivative of the word *khamara* meaning "cover" or "veil," since alcohol has the potential of "covering" or "veiling" the normal functioning of the mind. However, what was meant by the term khamr at the time of the Prophet has induced much debate among Muslim scholars. Although some have taken the view that it was only date wine, which excluded alcoholic substances (such as qat), coffee, and a range of drugs, others have adopted a maximalist approach, claiming that khamr covered all alcoholic drinks with the inclusion of all mind-altering substances.

According to some interpretations of the Qur'an, the taboo on alcohol was never part of the Islamic faith's founder Prophet Muhammad's intent at the beginning, as there are verses that laud alcohol, describing it as one of God's bounties to humankind:

> And from the fruit
> Of the date-palm and the vine,
> Ye get out wholesome drink
> And food: behold, in this
> Also is a Sign
> For those who are wise. (Qur'an 16:67)

A favorable impression of alcohol is reiterated in the Qur'anic idea that it will be available to humanity in paradise in the afterlife, although this may have been allegorical rather than literal.

The Arabs before the time of the Prophet (also known as the *Jahiliyah* period or the period of "ignorance") were fond of bacchanalian parties. Generous servings of wine and food demonstrated the magnanimity of the host. The Arab love of wine may be deduced from the vast range of words that existed to describe this beverage. Arabic poems also sang the praises of wine. According to tradition, the drinking of wine was accompanied by a series of rituals. First, blessings had to be uttered before and after the wine was imbibed. The wine cup was always held in the right hand, although it is not clear if it was drunk standing up or sitting down. When drinking among friends, the cup was always passed to the right. The finer details of drinking wine included the forbiddance of drinking it out of the mouth of a water skin, drinking in seemingly uncouth ways, and consuming it all at once.

Before the rise of Islam in the seventh century, drinking was habitual among Arab men, as it was a means of demonstrating masculinity. Also at that time, "the sale of alcohol was so customary that the Arabic word, *tajir,* which literally means merchant, had become a synonym for the salesman of *khamr*" (Badri 1976: 16). Moreover, shops that sold alcohol were not only open all day and night, but were specially marked out with flags.

Some Muslim scholars emphasize the adverse effects drinking had on religious cultivation to have brought about its eventual ban. Primarily because of its intoxicating qualities, alcohol's disruptive consequence on prayer had a dramatic impact on how it came to be interpreted:

> O, ye who believe!
> Approach not prayers
> With a mind befogged,
> Until ye can understand
> All that ye say. (Qur'an 4:43)

That the harm accrued from drinking alcohol (treated together with the game of chance) was regarded to be greater than its profit has been interpreted by some Muslim scholars to be a later Qur'anic revelation:

> They will ask thee
> About intoxicants and games of chance.
> Say! "In both there is great evil
> As well as some benefit for man;
> But the evil that they cause
> Is greater than the benefit which they bring." (Qur'an 2:219)

It was interpreted by some scholars that while initially the Qur'an disapproves of rather than places an outright ban on alcohol, eventually the habit of drinking was condemned as the work of the devil:

> O ye who believe!
> Intoxicants and gambling,
> (Dedication of) stones,
> And (divination by) arrows,
> Are an abomination,—
> Of Satan's handiwork:
> Eschew such (abomination),
> That ye may prosper. (Qur'an 5:93)

Some scholars also assert that alcohol caused dissension among believers and fostered negligence to prayer:

> Satan's plan is (but)
> To excite enmity and hatred
> Between you, with intoxicants
> And gambling, and hinder you
> From the remembrance
> Of God, and from prayer: will ye not then abstain?
> (Qur'an 5:93)

It was recorded that Muhammad refused a gift of wine presented to him after the conquest of Mecca. He was said to have ordered the wine poured away instead.

That the Prophet's prohibition of alcohol became a historical fact was recorded in the traditions or sayings of the Prophet, collectively known as the Hadith. Khwaja Kamal-ud-Din notes that when the prohibition of wine was proclaimed, "the streets of Medina were overflowing with the detestable contents of the wine-barrels, which were emptied at the one magic word of the prophet" (cited in Altaf Ahmad Kherie 1994: 390), while the big clay pots holding the fermented drinks were instantly broken.

The Ban on Alcohol and Its Implications in Everyday Life

Diversity marks the interpretation and practice of Islamic tenets in Muslim communities around the world; as such, there exist a variety of Muslim juristic views and interpretations on the consumption and use of alcohol. In particular, the extent to which alcohol is treated as taboo depends on the source of authority.

Some Muslim scholars stress the moral principle and the preventive and precautionary value underlying the ban on alcohol. Hammudah Abdalati remarks that the negative sanction on alcohol is "to protect man from insanity and degeneration, from weakness and indulgence, from indecency and temptation" (1978: 46). It has also been surmised that alcohol addiction leads to the destruction of families. Furthermore, that alcohol destroys health, depresses the mind, and dulls the soul justifies its ban. Hence, among strict Muslims, alcohol drinking is considered *haram.*

The religious injunction against the drinking of alcohol held among some Muslims is reinforced further by how it has become viewed in other contexts aside from drinking. The Prophet was said to have proclaimed the following Hadith:

> God's curse falls on a group of people who deal with alcohol. The one who distils it, the one for whom it has been distilled, the one who drinks it, the one who transports it, the one to whom it has been brought, the one who serves it, the one who sells it, the one who utilizes money from it, the one who buys it and the one who buys it for someone else.

When paying *zakat* (an annual alms tax of 2.5 percent levied on wealth), which is required of every Muslim, the amount must come from honest means and not from selling goods and services prohibited in Islam (such as liquor and prostitution).

Some sources of authority on Islam take the ban on alcohol one step further. Although some Muslims maintain that the

Qur'anic ban on alcohol pertains to its consumption rather than application, there are Muslims who avoid medicines that contain alcohol; among them, nonalcoholic alternatives instead are used. Other Muslims may also refrain from using commercially produced perfumes, as alcohol would have been added as fillers to the distilled original oils.

Drinking in the History of the Muslim World

Although the Muslim majority followed the religious law of alcohol abstinence, sects within Islam had varying opinions on drinking. Thirteenth-century Sufi poetry and preaching gave prominence to worldly pleasures. A Sufi movement led by Ibn al-Arabi made the claim for the divine presence in creations such as wine, which was seen as a contact point between God and humankind.

The *A-in-i Akbari,* which chronicles Indian social and political life during the reign of the Moghul King Akbar, documents liquor production. After pounding *babul* bark and mixing ten parts of it with one part sugarcane, the mixture was left to ferment over seven to ten days. And if a stronger portion was required, "they again put to the mixture some brown sugar and sometimes even drugs" (Abu L-Fazl Allami 1989: 74). The fermented mixture was then distilled to produce *arrack.* Sometimes, the arrack was distilled twice to produce stronger liquor known as *duatasha.*

Drinking in the Muslim World Today

By and large, the dominant view across the Muslim world today, as it was in the past, is to shun alcohol, especially among strict Muslims. If alcohol is drunk, it is tempered by the laws of the state, public attitudes toward drinking, and even the extent to which this activity is viewed to be common practice.

The laws of some countries are based on the Shari'ah or law of Islam (derived from the Prophet Muhammad's pronouncements and practices and from the traditions of Islam's first adherents). Interpretations, however, vary among Muslim jurists as to the punishment for drinking. Some scholars regard the *hadd* for drinking to be fixed at forty lashes, based on the actions of the first Khalifa Abu Bakr, while others deem it at eighty lashes, as it was under the leadership of Khalifa Umar. In contrast, jurists such as Shawkani maintain that the offense is a *tazir* for which neither the Qur'an nor the Prophet had laid down a fixed punishment.

Although drinking is illegal in Saudi Arabia and punishable by the state given that the laws of the country are based on the Shari'ah law, the Register of Addiction Specialists has listed alcohol abuse centers for Muslims. Although alcohol is not available to local Arabs, addiction is a problem as it may be prepared at home from dates, grapes, and other fruit.

In Persia, a Sufi achieved oneness with God through intoxication with wine. At a later time in a very different context, the meaning imbued to wine was derogatory, as it became associated with the corrupt Pahlavi regime of the Shah, while abstinence was a metaphor for the revolutionary forces of Khomeini who were thought to be pure. Tapper describes the way in which alcohol became viewed at the time of the revolution in this country, which now adheres to the Shari'ah: "intoxication with 'wine' creates cowards, incapable of fighting or working, destroys inhibitions on sexual and other passions, and leads to hell, or an illusory 'heaven' on this earth. It stands in opposition to the 'intoxication' of the hero-martyr whose religious zeal and patriotism remove his inhibition on self-sacrifice, and bring him to the real heaven" (1994: 228).

A Muslim may order alcohol at restaurants and bars in Malaysia, although Islam has been declared the state religion. State law, however, demands abstinence in the month of Ramadan, during which a Muslim may be punished if caught drinking.

In a vast number of countries considered secular states with a Muslim majority, alcohol is not only widely drunk but may also be produced. In Egypt, where strict Muslims do not touch alcohol but are tolerant of others drinking, a fairly weak lager called Stella is brewed. Morocco also produces beer and wine. However, about a week before Ramadan, most stores take their liquor off the shelves, while a few others sell it only to foreigners and non-Muslim Moroccans. Although Algeria produces a few good wines, very few of them are sold in the country, possibly since the sale of alcohol is not encouraged.

When Azerbaijan fell to the Bolsheviks in 1920, religion was outlawed under Stalin's command. As time passed, succeeding generations of Azerbaijanis forgot Islamic dietary rules (especially when *halal* foods were hard to come by), and eventually took to non-Islamic habits such as drinking. When Azerbaijan became a republic in 1995, religion saw a revival, especially among the younger generation. Although many avoid pork, alcohol consumption is still prevalent; but among the very strict, both pork and alcohol are avoided.

Among the Uighurs of Zinjiang province in Communist China, drinking alcoholic beverages is common practice, especially in villages. Only recently have the *mullas* (local religious leaders) objected to this habit, refusing an Islamic burial to those who indulge in drinking.

Theresa W. Devasahayam

See also: Islamic World

References

Abdullah Yusuf Ali. *The Holy Qu-ran (Text, Translation and Commentary),* vols. 1 and 2. Lahore: M. Ashraf, 1938.

Abu L-Fazl Allami. *The A-in-I Akbari,* vol. 1. Translated by H. Blochmann. Delhi: Low Price, 1989.

Altaf Ahmad Kherie. *A Comprehensive Guide-Book of Islam.* Delhi: Adam Publishers, 1994.

Badri, M. B. *Islam and Alcoholism.* Plainfield, IN: American Trust Publications, 1976.

Ben-Adam, Justin. "China" in *Islam outside the Arab World,* edited by David Westerlund and Ingvar Svanberg, 190–211. London: Curzon, 1999.

Cederroth, Sven. "Indonesia and Malaysia" in *Islam outside the Arab World,* edited by David Westerlund and Ingvar Svanberg, 253–277. London: Curzon, 1999.
Hammudah Abdalati. *Islam in Focus.* Kuwait: International Islamic Federation of Student Organizations, 1978.
Ishtiaq Ahmed. "South Asia" in *Islam outside the Arab World,* edited by David Westerlund and Ingvar Svanberg, 212–252. London: Curzon, 1999.
Nakhooda, Rosy. "Attar or Eastern Perfume—An Enticing Fragrant Genie Wafting from a Bottle." Unpublished paper, 2002.
Roberts, D. S. *Islam: A Concise Introduction.* New York: Harper and Row, 1981.
Stork, Mokhtar. *A–Z Guide to the Qu'ran: A Must-Have Reference to Understanding the Contents of the Islamic Holy Book.* Singapore: Times Books International, 1999.
Tapper, Richard. "Blood, Wine and Water: Social and Symbolic Aspects of Drinks and Drinking in the Islamic Middle East" in *Culinary Cultures of the Middle East,* edited by Sami Zubaida and Richard Tapper, 215–231. London: I. B. Tauris, 1994.

Islamic World

The Islamic world prohibits the consumption of alcohol, although not every Muslim abstains. Although alcohol is not strictly forbidden in the Qur'an, later legal scholars, after much debate, found its drinking intolerable because of its intoxicating effects. Throughout their 1,500-year history, Muslims have embraced or flouted this strict law. The early *caliphs,* or leaders of the Islamic empire, were well known for their drunken debaucheries. Ironically, despite the prohibition, fourteenth-century Islamic alchemists perfected the art of distillation (*alcohol* is an Arabic word meaning antimony). The use of wine and other intoxicating drinks has also served as a poignant metaphor for many on the margins of the orthodox tradition, in particular, the mystics. In modern times, while observing the prohibition, some Islamic nations have tolerated to varying degrees the production and sale of alcoholic beverages to non-Muslims within their borders, while others have condemned such practices.

The history of the prohibition of alcohol in Islam must begin with a discussion about wine and its uses prior to the birth of Muhammad. Arabia does not contain the land or climate appropriate to the cultivation of the vine, although there were a few exceptions to this rule. Parts of Yemen were known for their ability to produce wine, and wine of some quality was associated with a handful of Arabian cities, including Medina and al-Ta'if. Whatever consumption took place in the region relied on imports from Syria and Iraq. Early Arabic poetry also links the selling of wine with Jewish and Christian merchants, who would set up their tents and distribute their products among the Bedouin. As poetic evidence suggests, wine drinking was quite prevalent in pre-Islamic times. Poets describe drinking parties where drunkenness and debauchery were embraced in wild abandon. Although these references suggest wine reveling and drunkenness played a prominent role in Bedouin life, they are often countered by strict moral indictments against any behaviors that divert anyone from tribal and communal obligations.

The Qur'an itself contains a number of contradictory statements about the position of alcohol in God's creation. Qur'anic commentators have organized these statements chronologically, and have linked them to questionable behaviors displayed by members within the burgeoning Islamic community. In one Qur'anic passage, wine is praised as one of God's gifts to humankind. However, as traditional commentators have noted, people began to abuse this sign from God and found themselves in states of compromising drunkenness. God sent another revelation to Muhammad, which states that both wine and gambling should be considered great sins and sources of usefulness for humankind, although their sinfulness in general is greater than their potential benefits. This revelation was not considered a flat prohibition of alcohol, but rather served as a divine warning and guidepost for human action. Because people's bad habits did not change after this proclamation was given, and certain vital rituals (like prayer) were often disturbed by drunken behavior, God sent another revelation to Muhammad. This revelation strictly condemned praying under the influence of alcohol. The drinking continued until God sent down a fourth revelation, which is considered by Muslims to be a strict and uncompromising prohibition of wine. This revelation states clearly that wine, gambling, idol worship, and divination are all abominations of Satan that must be avoided.

Legal Positions on Alcohol

The legal prohibition of wine is accepted by all the schools of law, both Sunni and Shia. However, within Islamic legal discourse, there is much discussion and debate about the extent and scope of the prohibition. The Qur'an prohibits the consumption of wine, but how does one define wine? There is discussion among legalists to determine what "wine" is actually made of; three out of the four legal Sunni schools in Islam (Shafi'ites, Malikites, Hanbalites) conclude that it can be produced from any substance, including grapes, dates, wheat, barley, honey, and milk, among others. These three schools determine by analogy that any fermented beverage falls under the heading of wine, and must be condemned in small or large quantities. The most liberal school on this issue, the Hanafites, suggests that wine comes solely from grapes or uncooked concoctions made from dates or raisins. This fourth school, which became the official school of the Ottoman state, allows infusions of dates and raisins if they have been cooked, even if they then ferment and become intoxicants. Other fermented drinks made from honey, wheat, barley figs, or millet, are all considered legal; the Hanafites believe fermented beverages made from these substances must be drunk in small amounts so that one does not become intoxicated. The Hanafites even allow the consumption of grape (uncooked), date, or (uncooked) raisin wine to be consumed under extreme conditions if, for example, it keeps one from dying of thirst. All four schools agree that wine should not be sold by or to Muslims, and that the destruction or theft of wine does not result in punishment, since its possession and consumption are illegal. All four also forbid the use of wine for medicinal, cosmetic, or economic purposes.

What these legal positions suggest is that wine itself is prohibited not simply for its value as a substance, but because of its intoxicating effects, which are believed to be destructive and corrosive to the Muslim community. In Islamic thought, intoxication stands at the root of all evil and should be avoided in any amount. God did not prohibit alcohol, one of his gifts or signs to humanity, because the drink itself is impure or faulty. He prohibited it because humans blindly and negligently consumed it to the point of intoxication, which led them to commit ritual and moral atrocities. The perils of drunkenness may serve as the reason why the Qur'an allows for endless amounts of wine—of a noninebriating vintage—to be consumed in Paradise as a reward for the righteous. Wine itself is fine as long as it is stripped of its potential to intoxicate.

Protests against the Prohibition

The prohibition of wine and other alcoholic beverages in the past as well as the present stands as one of the distinguishing marks of the Islamic world. The condemnation of alcohol does not suggest that every Muslim abstains. In the early centuries of Islam, a band of Muslim poets protested the prohibition by creating elaborate poems that sang the praises of wine and drunkenness, and called for a return to the liberal pre-Islamic position on alcohol. The Umayyad Caliphs, referred to as the "deputies of God" were well known for their drinking parties; they were later criticized by their more pious Abbasid successors for their consumption of pork, alcohol, and association with dancing girls. Judging from the early legal sources, the prophet Muhammad faced much resistance among the common people as he attempted to impose the newly stated prohibition on those accustomed to consuming their locally produced fermented beverages. Despite Muhammad's efforts, the quaffing of alcohol continued, though under the fear of punishment. Early sources point to a range of disciplinary actions for repeated drinking, from lashings to death, the latter being served in a minority of cases.

Wine plays an important role in the literary works of the mystics. In mystical thought, wine becomes a symbol of the divine love that permeates the creation. In many mystical works, wine imagery is used to portray God himself, or the source of divine knowledge all mystics must consume to remember their true origins and the divine reality. Intoxication and sobriety become the metaphors mystics employ to talk about their ineffable experiences of that divine love. To be "intoxicated" with love is to forget all that is not God; to be "sober" is to realize one's separation from that divine love. An intoxicated life is lived when all else passes away and only the divine exists; a sober life is lived in the world, where much clouds the mind and separates the self from the divine reality. According to the mystics, spiritual intoxication is not to be confused with earthly drunkenness. Only the ignorant would believe the Islamic mystic is referring to the forgetfulness that accompanies a state of human inebriation. The mystics use this play on the prohibition of alcohol to ridicule the orthodox tradition, which clings to its texts and laws and prohibitions. For the mystics, intoxication is the path through which one directly experiences divine love. They hold that those orthodox Muslims who assert the prohibition of intoxicating beverages are destined to wallow in ignorance of their impiety.

Despite its legal prohibition, Islam had much to do with the introduction of spirits. Although they did not create the science itself, medieval Muslim alchemists greatly improved the art of distillation as they sought to extract oils and perfumes from plants for aromatic, cosmetic, or medicinal purposes. In fact, the Arabic word *al-kuhul* (the powdered antimony; the distillate) comes from the root that refers to the blackening of the eyes with kohl for cosmetic purposes. Through their processes of extraction, these alchemists created an intensified form of alcoholic beverage, which gained much popularity among non-Muslim communities. Credit for refining the practice of distillation is given to Ibn Sina, known in the West as Avicenna (980 C.E.–1037 C.E.), the Arab alchemist, astronomer, philosopher, mathematician, and physician, who used essential plant oils in his medicinal practices.

Views on Alcohol in the Modern Muslim World

In the modern world, Muslims have continued to observe the ban on alcohol placed upon them since medieval times. The modern justification for the prohibition still rests on the Qur'anic passages noted previously, along with the strict rulings of Islamic law according to the four legal schools. In addition to upholding these traditional sources, many pious Muslims also point to modern maladies brought on by alcoholic consumption, including cirrhosis, divorce, cancer, diseases of the heart, fetal alcohol syndrome, and abuse. By using elaborate processes of analogy, Muslims have likened the effects of recreational drugs to alcohol, and have condemned their use as well. Many Muslims argue that the Qur'anic injunction condemned alcohol out of divine foresight for these biological diseases and social maladies brought forth by alcoholic abuse. Muslims see this material evidence of alcohol's devastation as justification for God's creation of and their adherence to the prohibition.

Despite the prohibition, Islamic countries today take a variety of stances with regard to the consumption, production, and sale of alcoholic products. Many of these countries face the problem of what to do about non-Muslim citizens or workers within their borders. The question many predominantly Muslim countries face is whether or not non-Muslims and foreigners living within their borders should be governed by Islamic law with regard to the consumption of alcoholic beverages. These countries have dealt with this question in a variety of ways. Libya, Saudi Arabia, and Kuwait permit the sale and consumption of alcohol by non-Muslims, but confine the sale and consumption to international hotels. Saudi Arabia condemns the import of any alcoholic beverage by Muslims and employs public lashings to serve as punishment for any Muslim caught drinking alcoholic beverages. Despite the public condemnation, alcohol clandestinely enters Saudi Arabia through smuggling from Jordan and Bahrain; there are also crude homemade beverages that people consume in private.

Kuwait has equally strict laws with regard to the consumption, production, and sale of alcohol; as a result, Kuwaitis found great pleasure in nonalcoholic beers, which were sold in great quantities until a small trace of alcohol was detected even in these versions. Now Kuwait condemns the consumption of such nonalcoholic beverages, suggesting that the mere taste of the nonalcoholic version can incite feelings similar to those of intoxication, which impairs both health and faith. Kuwait bases its position on Islamic law, which condemns the quaffing of even a small amount of alcohol, such as that found in nonalcoholic beers. The question as to whether any product that contains a trace of alcohol can be consumed or sold has also been raised in many Muslim countries. Kuwait, Libya, and Saudi Arabia have determined that the consumption and sale of items like perfumes and rubbing alcohol is acceptable.

In the sultanate of Brunei, alcoholic beverages are categorized as restricted imported goods. Only non-Muslims over the age of eighteen can buy alcohol for consumption, and then only up to ten cans of beer and two bottles of liquor. Bahrain allows for the import of alcoholic beverages for consumption by non-Muslims, but imposes a 125 percent duty on those imports. Iraq is well known for using foreign aid to finance its heavy imports of Scotch whiskey, although this practice is not publicly condoned. Pakistan has formally banned alcohol from its borders since 1977, but intoxicating beverages are still smuggled in with great regularity, and several home-brewed products are distributed on the sly. There is a liquor producer in Pakistan that began

A liquor store owner looks out of his shop window in Baghdad on 20 May 2003. Six breweries have recently been destroyed allegedly by Shi'ia Muslims who regard drinking alcohol as a violation of religious law. Under the previous secular government of Saddam Hussein, Iraqis could consume alcohol. (Reuters NewMedia Inc./Corbis)

136 years ago, that produces beer, vodka, gin, rum, brandy, and whiskey for foreigners and non-Muslim Pakistanis. Although this business has experienced much pressure from the government to shut down, its doors are still open to those not confined by Islamic law. In many predominantly Muslim countries, alcohol is produced illegally on the black market. As many Muslim women and children have been displaced from southern Sudan to refugee camps in the north, women living in these camps have exploited the only economic opportunities available to them to support their families: prostitution and the illegal brewing of alcohol. If prosecuted, these women are placed in prison for their crimes.

Many Islamic countries have taken a much more lenient approach to the production and sale of alcoholic beverages. Morocco and Egypt produce two brands of beer and a half-dozen brands of wine, and import a large number of spirits for their non-Muslim and foreign populations. Although non-Muslim minorities (Jews and Christians) are confined to consuming such products within the privacy of their own homes, foreigners are allowed to consume and purchase in public areas. Azerbaijan, now free of Soviet control, only loosely observes the prohibition of alcohol. Many Azerbaijani Muslims drink vodka, the beverage of choice, with little concern for the prohibition. In addition to many of these rules and restrictions, many Muslims will consume alcoholic beverages outside their own countries, where they feel the span of Islamic law does not reach. As with anything, the discrepancies between law and practice, the real and the ideal, vary greatly from place to place, from person to person.

Kathryn Kueny

See also: Islam as Cultural Influence; Wine

References

Harb, F. "Wine Poetry (Khamriyyat)" in *Abbasid Belles-Lettres.* vol. 2 of *Cambridge History of Arabic Literature,* edited by Julia Ashtiany, T. M. Johnstone, J. D. Latham, R. B. Serjeant, and G. Rex Smith, 219–234. Cambridge: Cambridge University Press, 1990.

Hattox, Ralph S. *Coffee and Coffeehouses.* Seattle: University of Washington Press, 1985.

Johnson, Hugh. *Vintage: The Story of Wine.* London: Michael Beazley, 1989.

Kueny, Kathryn. *The Rhetoric of Sobriety: Wine in Early Islam.* Albany: State University of New York Press, 2001.

Unwin, Tim. *Wine and the Vine: An Historical Geography of Viticulture and the Wine Trade.* London: Routledge and Kegan Paul, 1991.

Wensinck, A. J. "Khamr" in *The Encyclopedia of Islam,* edited by H. A. R. Gibb, et al., 2d ed., 9 vols. (to date). Leiden: E. J. Brill, 1954–.

Italy

Italy is a country in which wine is the predominant alcoholic beverage, and over a long period of time, it—with other Southern European countries—has developed a specificity in the way of drinking. In most Western cultures, alcohol is used as a psychotropic agent and is instrumental to achieve some goal or prove one's courage; however, in Italy, as well as in some other parts of Mediterranean Europe, the alcoholic beverage most used among adults, wine, is drunk for its positive taste and smell, and is part of meals and family and social life. Wine is not infrequently tasted during childhood on special occasions, and it is affordable for the greater part of the population. Beer and spirits are consumed in smaller proportions. Italians equate alcohol to spirits and perhaps beer to soft drinks, but certainly not alcohol to wine.

Italy is one of the top wine-producing countries in the world. Production and trade of alcohol beverages contribute substantially to the nation's gross national product. Places selling wine and other alcoholic drinks during the normal business hours, even at night or in the early hours of the morning, are largely diffused.

According to recent figures, 80 percent of the population drinks alcohol, women showing a slightly increasing share of about one-quarter of the whole alcohol intake. Italians between thirty-five and sixty years have the highest consumption, and they typically drink moderate amounts at meals daily. Wine's share of the total alcohol consumption is approximately 70 percent. Beer, which accounts for 20 percent of total alcohol consumption, is more and more popular among young people, who prefer to drink in such public places as bars and restaurants. The declining consumption of spirits, which account for 7 percent of the total alcohol consumed, is relatively more common in the north of the country. Drunkenness and binge drinking are infrequent, even if an increasing worry concerns the outrageous behavior of some immigrants and youngsters in the cities, considered as those who "do not know how to drink."

A remarkable phenomenon was the dramatic decrease in the intake of alcohol, mainly due to the decline of wine consumption, in the last thirty years. In fact, at the beginning of the 1970s the Italian average annual consumption per person of all types of alcoholic beverage, expressed in pure (100 percent) alcohol, was 13.9 liters (3.7 U.S. gallons), among the top consumption in the world; while at the end of the 1990s, this amount dropped by almost 50 percent, that is to 7.7 liters (2.03 U.S. gallons), a little higher than in the United States and the Nordic European countries and just lower than in Eastern Europe and elsewhere in Mediterranean Europe. The contemporary transformation from a predominantly rural to a postindustrial society, a certain influence of North European and American lifestyles (at least in the younger and more educated social strata), and modifications in the marketing factors have been invoked to explain such an impressive change.

Figures on alcohol-related harm, both acute or behavioral (for example, accidents) and especially chronic or biological (for example, liver cirrhosis) are noteworthy. During the 1990s, annual deaths from all the alcohol-related causes varied from

Transporting wine by mule cart from Frascati vineyards to Rome, 1904. (Library of Congress)

18,000 to 44,000 (in a total population of nearly 60,000,000), according to different sources. Nevertheless, problems have been overlooked by researchers, health professionals, politicians, and the general public.

Some special initiatives sometimes were able to reach a countrywide consensus. For example, a few temperance organizations formed at the end of the nineteenth century. Since the 1970s, Alcoholics Anonymous (AA) and voluntary clubs for treating alcoholics have emerged and blossomed. Further, a number of uncoordinated health and social service programs for alcoholics have flourished since the 1980s, and these programs provided support to the National Alcohol Law in 2001.

All in all, even if formal policy measures have increased since the late 1980s, they are seldom enforced. Although preventive initiatives occurred in the country during the 1990s, they were scattered and local. Up to the present time in Italy (2003), the state has mainly maintained a passive attitude toward alcohol control policies and prevention of alcohol-related problems.

National Beverages

In Italy, wine is one ingredient of the daily diet in keeping with a deep-rooted Mediterranean pattern. Also, people are able to perceive a deep connection between wine and nature, since wine is produced from the vineyard anybody can observe in the countryside and sometimes is cultivated within one's garden. Even if in the postwar period there was a remarkable decrease in both the number of residents and the size of the workforce in the rural areas, it is now fashionable for citizens to go to the countryside to purchase their wine from peasants or wineries, thus recalling the old values inherent to nature. The seasonal cycles of the grape harvest and fermentation are related to traditional local wine festivals, still attended by people in many places during the early autumn. A further meaning attributed to wine is its potential sacredness: During the Holy Mass, it is considered the Divine Blood, therefore connecting the limitation of the ego to the blessed experience of the Grace of God.

The reduction in the overall consumption of common wine during the last three decades paralleled an increase of more expensive high-quality wines and, to a minor extent, of sparkling wines, drunk mainly on special occasions (for example, meeting friends or enjoying a special dinner, and even outside mealtimes). Moreover, drinking wine at lunchtime is a decreasing practice since workers and employees in the cities no longer return home for lunch.

Beer consumption traditionally occurred especially during the warm season to quench thirst. Beer consumption has increased during the last thirty years among young people, who drink it in their peer groups but also in the family, while eating a pizza at a restaurant, and also outside mealtimes.

Spirits are drunk occasionally at home or in bars for company with friends after a meal among the upper classes of urban areas. Sweet liquors and digestive alcoholic drinks are more frequently drunk in the lower social classes and among women.

National Alcohol Production and the Retail System

At the end of the 1990s, alcoholic beverages played an important role in the Italian national economy. The production and trade of alcoholic beverages was estimated at 12,000 million Euros, contributing 1.5 percent to the gross national product. Italy produces about 22 percent of the world's wine; at the end of the 1990s, its production level was 53 million hectoliters (1,400 million U.S. gallons), and the overall vineyard-cultivated land was 0.8 million hectares (324,000 acres). At the same time, about half of Italy's wines were produced by 650 local wine cooperatives, while 18 percent of the vineyards were allocated for quality wines produced by major wine companies. Unlike beer and spirits, there is no tax on wine at the production level (excise tax). This indicates the inclination of the Italian state to support wine production.

The increasing production of beer in Italy reached 12 million hectoliters (317 million U.S. gallons) a year by the end of the 1990s. There are five brewing companies operating sixteen breweries; furthermore, a number of foreign beers were produced under license. One-fifth of the beer consumption in Italy consisted of imported beer. Spirits production has dropped since the 1970s.

Since the postwar period, there has been a licensing system for the production, import, wholesale, and retail sale of alcoholic beverages. The Ministry of Finance grants licenses for the production of beer, wine, and spirits, and the licenses are paid annually and reconfirmed. Off- and on-premises retailers are licensed by municipalities. Places selling alcoholic beverages on the premises are widely dispersed in Italy. You can purchase an alcoholic drink in nearly 200,000 outlets—restaurants, pizzerias, "trattorias," hotels *(pensioni),* fast food shops, bars, and coffeehouses, pubs, and discotheques.

Cultural Representations of Use and Abuse and Major Temperance Organizations

As already indicated, wine tends to be considered by Italians as a food item. A good wine is perceived with the same attitude as a bottle of good olive oil or another quality food. It is traditionally drunk at daily meals, with the family or in other social occasions. Also, a relatively novel alcoholic drink, beer, has partly acquired some of these meal-linked characteristics. In fact, even in the postindustrial culture, Italian eating still retains its old convivial properties as an occasion to interact with family members or friends. In this context, people do not drink because they want to be intoxicated or more sociable through the chemical effects of alcohol; on the contrary, wine just adds or integrates sociability to the already sociable aspects of dining.

Usually, consumption of wine, and to some extent beer, is not associated with a perceived need for external public control and does not elicit any image of either achievement or performance. By and large, in the past the strong extended families and the close community ties served as informal control measures over excessive drinking. Such ties have weakened since the 1970s, corresponding to increased urbanization, industrialization, migration, and tourism. Together with new attitudes, new types of alcohol beverages came in from abroad, especially beer and spirits. However, informal control on alcohol abuse is still the common custom. Thus, in many parts of Italy avoiding drinking in the morning and between the meals is regarded as correct behavior and is the subject of social approval, while the opposite behavior is frowned upon.

In Italy, the tolerance toward excessive drinking and alcoholism is low. This attitude parallels the low number of public drunkards that can be seen in the streets. Accordingly, alcohol-related problems and alcoholism have been considered by the general population a problem just for the individual person and not a social problem, in the same manner as has been the case with illicit drug use, or even with smoking.

Nevertheless, the question of alcohol abuse became somewhat important in the nineteenth century, at the time of the Industrial Revolution. The first temperance organization in Italy, the Società di Temperanza, was formed by Dr. Luigi Chierici in 1863 in Turin, an area of early industrial growth. The Italian Temperance League (Lega Italiana di Temperanza) was founded in 1892 by Giovanni Rochat. The league included both total abstainers and those who abstained only from spirits. These groups were particularly concerned with drinking among the urban proletariat, but they made little headway. The debates between the political parties changed the definition of alcohol problems into an issue of law and order, and in 1889 the government passed the first penal code resolution against public drunkenness, also punishing those who caused such a state of intoxication in another. The 1931 penal code, known as Code Rocco, enacted during the Fascist period of Benito Mussolini and still in force today, fixed the minimum legal age for alcohol purchase at sixteen years.

Modern attempts to deal with alcohol problems began in the 1970s and were modeled on imported programs. AA in Italy was established in Rome in 1972, thirty-seven years after its birth in the United States. Its beginning was rather inauspicious, but in the 1980s AA began to expand, and by the year 2000 there were about 500 Italian groups with at least 10,000 participants. The first AlAnon group (family members of alcoholics) was opened in Rome in 1976, and by 2000 there were 400 groups. As in the United States, both associations have their program based on an individual change in the context of a loving and nonjudgmental group; the program includes Twelve Steps, Twelve Traditions, and twelve concepts.

The other major nongovernmental alcohol association, the Clubs for Alcoholics in Treatment, imported from Croatia in 1979, is based on a multifamily group program invented by the late psychiatrist Vladimir Hudolin. The program involves a local support network within the community. About 40,000 people, approximately 0.1 percent of adult Italians, were estimated to attend either a twelve-step group or a club for alcoholics.

The media began to report on alcohol issues and alcohol-related problems in the late 1980s. The main issue concerned road-traffic accidents involving young people and alcohol dependence. More recently, articles have appeared in Italian (as well as international) newspapers focusing on the benefits of alcohol in the prevention of coronary heart disease, reinforcing the idea of moderate drinking as the best practice among the general public.

The opinion of health professionals has generally been in favor of "responsible" drinking, taking into account both the Mediterranean wine tradition and the risky behavior when alcohol is abused or the drinking pattern disrupts the traditional practices. However, a notable number of groups in the health sector favor more restrictive policies.

The Italian Society of Alcohology (SIA) was established in the late 1970s. SIA has sometimes taken the place of the university, which for a long time was not interested in or able to promote alcohol research and scientific meetings. The SIA is the only scientific society quoted in the new alcohol law. In 1996, the World Health Organization (WHO) identified a few university or National Health Service units as centers of excellence for research in Italy; nevertheless, their structure and visibility within the country are generally weak.

Patterns of Regulation

A liberal attitude toward alcohol regulation prevails in Italian society. Furthermore, a division between different public functions, for example the agricultural and the health sectors, made it difficult to work out and to enforce a coordinated alcohol control policy. However, some laws or acts have been approved in the last twenty-five years. In 1978, alcoholism was recognized as a disorder by the National Health Insurance. In 1988, a ministerial decree established the blood-alcohol concentration (BAC) of 0.8 grams per liter as the threshold above which a driving license was suspended. This threshold was set at 0.5 grams according to the 2001 alcohol law. In 1988, another ministry decree imposed the indication of alcohol content on the labels of alcoholic beverages. In 1993, the twenty Italian regions were delegated by the central government to provide prevention and treatment programs for alcohol addicts based on a multiprofessional approach. The role of self-help and voluntary groups was officially acknowledged.

In the 1990s, the directives of the European Union partly affected the advertising of alcohol products and some measures of control—prohibiting the sale of alcohol beverages with more than 21 percent of alcohol by volume at public concerts and sporting events. Yet, the most influential outside action has been taken by the European bureau of the WHO, which has positively affected health professionals' and governors' perceptions of alcohol-related problems and risks through both a European Alcohol Action Plan (1992) and a European Charter on Alcohol (1995).

In March 2001, the vast majority of the two chambers of the Italian Parliament finally approved a general policy law concerning alcohol and alcohol-related problems after nearly ten years of political debate. It established the maximum BAC permitted when driving at 0.5 grams per liter; prohibits drinking of alcoholic beverages in certain risky work settings; regulates the advertising of alcoholic beverages; prohibits the sale of beverages more than 21 percent alcohol by volume from 10 P.M. to 6 A.M. on premises along highways; and gave treatment guidelines to university and National Health services.

Despite the fact that Italy has a licensing system for production, import, and sale of alcoholic beverages, a BAC limit for traffic, and restrictions in advertising and selling, it would be a mistake to claim that Italy has a comprehensive alcohol control system. In fact, many of the aforementioned directives were infrequently enforced, and the real price of all the alcoholic beverages has indeed decreased since the late 1970s. Several educational school initiatives on alcohol and a few community alcohol prevention projects have been (unevenly) implemented since the 1980s. However, the sharp decrease of wine and spirit consumption since the 1970s can be attributed neither to nationwide policies nor to a number of patchy initiatives; it must be attributed to factors external to alcohol prevention policy or programs.

Allaman Allamani

See also: Wine; World Health Organization (WHO)

References

Allamani, Allaman, et al. "Drinking Cultures and the Position of Women in Nine European Countries" in *Substance Abuse.* 4 (2000): 231–247.

———. "Italy" in *Alcohol Policies in EU Member States,* edited by E. Örsterberg and T. Karlsson. Helsinki: Stakes, 2002, 258–284.

———, eds. *Il Libro Italiano di Alcologia.* vol. 2. Firenze: SEE, 2002.

Cottino, A. and P. Morgan. "Four Country Profiles: Italy" in *Alcohol Policies,* edited by M. Grant. WHO Regional Publications, European Studies. 18 (1985): 83–92.

Forni, E. "Alcohol and Youth" in *Alcologia.* 9 (1997): 65–68.

Mosher, J. "Italy" in *Alcohol Problems: Policies and Programmes in Europe,* 1175–1840. Copenhagen: WHO, 1992.

Osservatorio Permanente sui Giovani e l'Alcool. *Italians and Alcohol. Consumption, Trend and Attitudes in Italy and in the Regions,* vol. 12. Rome: Ed. Risa, 2000.

Productschap voor Gedistilleerde Dranken. *World Drink Trends,* Oxfordshire: NTC Publications, 2000.

Simpura, J., and T. Karlsson. "Italy" in *Trends in Drinking Patterns in Fifteen European Countries, 1950 to 2000,* 122–129. Helsinki: Stakes, 2001.

World Health Organization, Regional Office for Europe. *The Alcohol Charter.* Copenhagen: WHO, 1995.

———. *The European Alcohol Action Plan.* Copenhagen: WHO, 1992.

J

Japan

Japan is a world economic power and a center of international trade; as such, it is possible to find in the major cities virtually all the alcoholic beverages that circulate in the international marketplace. However, about 90 percent of the alcohol sold in Japan is limited to four beverages (Kokuzeicho 1997: 16). Two of these beverages—sake and *shōchū*—are traditional, while two others—beer and whiskey—were introduced from the West in the late nineteenth century.

Alcoholic Beverage Preferences

Sake (pronounced "sah-keh") is internationally identified as *the* Japanese alcoholic beverage, but it constitutes only about 12 percent of the volume of alcoholic beverages sold (Kokuzeicho 1997: 16). The common translation of sake as "rice wine" probably derives from its appearance, which is rather like white wine: clear, colorless or pale amber, and noneffervescent. The standard alcohol content of sake, at about 16 percent, is also closer to the 12 percent of wine than it is to the 5 percent of beer. In terms of production, however, sake is closer to being a "rice beer." Unlike wine, which is made from fruits that are naturally rich in the sugar necessary for yeast to produce alcohol, beer and sake are both made from grains, which are high in starches. The starches in grains must be processed into sugars for fermentation to proceed. Like beer, sake is fermented and aged a short time at low temperatures and considered to be best when consumed relatively soon after production. Sake is frequently drunk hot, but it is also drunk at room temperature or chilled.

Shōchū is the traditional distilled "vodka" of Japan and has an alcohol content in the range of 25 to 35 percent, making it less alcoholic than most of its Western counterparts. By beverage volume, shōchū makes up about 7 percent of alcohol sold in Japan (Kokuzeicho 1997: 16). It can be distilled from a rice mash, but also from buckwheat, millet, or sweet potatoes. Traditionally, shōchū was drunk hot or mixed with hot water. A lower tax rate on the beverage makes it possible to sell poor-quality shōchū very cheaply, hence it once carried a taint of being associated with the lower class. However, shōchū gained new cachet among young Japanese in the 1980s when it was added to soft drinks to produce sweet, inexpensive mixed drinks.

Despite the cultural preeminence of sake, the most popular alcoholic beverage in Japan is beer, making up more than two-thirds of the volume of beverage alcohol sold (Kokuzeicho 1997: 16). The market was long controlled by only five breweries—Asahi, Kirin, Orion, Sapporo, Suntory—because licensing required a production capacity of 2,000 kiloliters per year (528,400 U.S. gallons). However, a 1994 change in the law, lowering the minimum requirements to 60 kiloliters (15,852 U.S. gallons) per year, has led to the development of many pub brewers and microbrewers producing local beers. Aggressive marketing of beer in Japan has led to the availability of a seemingly endless variety of brews and packages, yet the preferred taste is for dry lager, full flavored, but not dark.

Although whiskey makes up less than 2 percent of the volume of alcoholic beverages sold in Japan (Kokuzeicho 1997: 16), it is the most prestigious of the four main alcoholic beverages. Suntory and Nikka are the biggest distillers, with both producing a variety of blended whiskeys. Imported whiskeys are available but heavily taxed, making them quite exclusive and assuring their desirability. The standard way of consuming whiskey is with water over ice, although serving it like shōchū—with hot water—is not unknown.

Drinking Etiquette

There are several rules that govern polite drinking behavior in Japan. First, no one starts to consume the initial drink until everyone has been served. When all glasses are filled, they are raised and a toast of *kanpai* ("bottoms up" or, literally, "empty glass") is said in unison. A swallow is taken by everyone, and the drinking then proceeds at a personal pace.

Second, one does not fill one's own cup, certainly not to start with. You should show concern for others by making sure that everyone else's cup is filled, but you humbly wait for someone else to pour for you. You may, as the drinking progresses, relieve others of the burden of pouring for you by saying "I'll pour for myself" (*tejaku shimsu*), but it is perfectly appropriate to continue to make sure that others' glasses are full.

Third, when someone makes motions toward pouring for you by holding out a bottle in your direction, you should always pick up your glass, swallow off some of your drink to make room for what is being offered, and then hold your cup out to receive the liquor. It is interesting to note that, while the proffering of a drink is ordinarily a small act of kindness that functions to bind pourer and recipient together, it can be used as an act of aggression. A hostile drinking partner can invoke the etiquette that one must receive (and consume) a proffered drink, using the social pressure and repeated offers to make you drink more than you wish.

Fourth, the etiquette of pouring and receiving reflects the social relationship between the pourer and the recipient, as in employer/employee, older/younger, or male/female relations. Social subordinates should be more solicitous. When offering the bottle or holding the cup, the subordinate should use two hands while the superior uses one.

Fifth, when someone has poured for you, you should repay the gesture by offering to pour a glass in return. The obligation to repay can be used to your advantage. If your cup is empty the sure way to get it filled is to pour for someone else and wait for them to repay the favor.

The rules of etiquette make it clear that in Japan drinking is understood to be a social and interactive practice. There is an underlying principle of pour-receive-repay that is more powerful than Americans are used to and can potentially produce heavy drinking. It is possible to drink alone, but that is awkward or inappropriate in ways that go beyond fear of being seen as alcohol dependent. Japanese bartenders are not only permitted to drink on the job, they are expected to interact with patrons, pouring drinks for them and sometimes receiving drinks in return. Thus, not surprisingly, people in Japan's "water trades" are at high risk for alcohol-related problems. There is also a cliché of family alcohol problems when men want a nightcap at home and insist that their wives drink with them.

Etiquette also requires that drinks should always be accompanied by food. Of course, alcoholic beverages may accompany meals. There is also a genre of appetizer-like foods, known as *sakana,* that are intended to be eaten with, and enhance the enjoyment of, alcoholic beverages. It is said that eating while drinking is also imperative for good health, but, in practice, the sakana may be no more than a few green soybeans, a couple of chocolate-covered pretzels or, for the poor, nothing but a pinch of salt to stimulate thirst.

Attitudes toward Alcohol and Alcoholism

Generally speaking, the Japanese are favorably disposed toward the drinking of alcohol, considering it to be one of life's pleasures. Men who are strong drinkers are admired, and those who abstain are socially problematic. Sake and drunkenness have a sacramental place in Shinto, the indigenous Japanese religion. Formal religious rites include offerings of food and sake to the spirits (*kami*) and end with feasting upon the offerings. Such feasting may appropriately result in inebriation, for such a state produces a transcendence that takes one closer to the spirits. Sake is a must at sacred and celebratory events such as weddings.

In secular settings, tolerance for drinking and drunkenness derives from a clear-cut separation of work and leisure. In the late premodern Tokugawa period (1603–1868), alcohol consumption for the great majority of Japanese was limited to special events and holidays. These occasions were often accompanied by great revelry and abandonment of the usual rules of decorum and social hierarchy. It was held that any inappropriate words or behaviors were a product of the liquor and should be excused. A similar pattern continues in contemporary Japan as a necessity in the business world. Drinking during normal working hours, as in the case of liquor with lunch, is severely frowned upon. However, much Japanese business is conducted after hours and over drinks. Japanese white-collar business organizations are hierarchical and follow clear chains of command that may inhibit the free flow of information. The trading of information that may be inappropriate in sober sunlight is granted indulgence in a bar. Likewise, business deals are often finalized with drinking because it permits relaxed and emotionally warmer relations between partners. The result is that it is widely held that drinking is a social necessity and that no teetotaler can be a success. Drinking is also widely held to be a reasonable release from the stresses of the workaday world. Wives often view their husbands' nights out drinking as the lesser of two evils; better that he should leave his tensions in a bar rather than bring them home.

Japanese women are generally expected to eschew alcohol. Men, on the other hand, may indulge in heavy drinking and frequent drunkenness as long as they fulfill their social roles and responsibilities. Despite the wide latitude given to heavy consumption of alcohol, or perhaps because of it, the label of alcoholic (*arukoru chūdokusha*) is seriously stigmatizing. Unlike the medical model of alcoholism as a disease found in America, the popular view in Japan is that alcoholism is a moral failing and a manifestation of a personal character that is too weak to delay the pleasures of drinking until an appropriate time. Hand tremors, drinking on the job, and drinking without eating are popularly held to be signs of alcoholism; frequency and quantity of consumption are not.

Although there is growing popular concern over drinking by teenagers and by housewives, alcoholism is not perceived as a high priority public-health issue in political or medical circles. Doctors get little training in diagnosing alcohol dependence, so they tend to treat specific symptoms rather than identifying a pattern. Since a large percentage of the Japanese population manifests physical responses to alcohol that include reddening of the skin, tachycardia, and discomfort, it is widely argued that this "flushing syndrome" naturally inhibits many people from becoming chronic alcoholics. However, there has been recent concern in the medical community that when people who flush do drink, they may be vulnerable to acute alcohol poisoning.

Temperance and Sobriety Movements

Through most of Japan's history, it has been held that there is nothing inherently immoral or shameful about drinking and drunkenness. It is no surprise then that there was not much of a movement for prohibition. There have been brief periods when authorities called for the cessation of sake production, but the reason was to conserve rice as food rather than to prevent drinking. Buddhism has injunctions against consuming alcohol, but these have no daily impact on the laity. Monks abstain while in the monastery, yet may drink when outside.

The miko *(shrine maiden) offers sacred sake to the bride and groom during a wedding ceremony at the Meiji shrine memorial hall in Tokyo, ca. 1955. (Hulton/Archive)*

The impetus for Japan's temperance and sobriety movements came from the West. Japan ended isolation and feudalism and committed itself to modernization in 1868. In 1873, the law forbidding the teaching of Christianity was rescinded, and there followed an influx of evangelical Protestant missionaries teaching abstinence in addition to the Gospel. The first temperance group in Japan was established in that same year for foreign seamen. Two years later, a group of Japanese created the Yokohama Japanese Temperance Society for themselves. The teachings of the Woman's Christian Temperance Union (WCTU) were carried to Japan in 1886 by Mary Greenleaf Clement Leavitt. The WCTU's original objective of prevention of drinking had, at that point, evolved beyond a call for total abstinence from alcohol, and beyond a demand for legal prohibition of selling alcohol, to a broad-based platform of moral reform. A moral reform movement began in Japan in 1886, but the abstemiousness called for by the Japan Christian Temperance Union seemed puritanical and alien in Japan, where the pleasures of the flesh were considered normal and acceptable when pursued in their socially appropriate context. The Tokyo Temperance

Union (later the Japan Temperance Union), with a narrow focus on alcohol, was not founded until 1900. Over the next half century—with the exception of spearheading the creation of the unenforced 1922 law establishing twenty as the age when one could buy alcoholic beverages—the temperance movement had very little impact on Japanese drinking culture.

Alcoholics Anonymous (AA) and *Danshukai* (Sobriety Groups)

Whatever the limitations of the temperance movement in general, the Japan Temperance Union (JTU) deserves credit for planting the seeds of successful lay alcoholism therapy in the forms of Alcoholics Anonymous (AA) and Danshukai. In 1952, JTU members traveling overseas returned to report enthusiastically on what they had learned about AA. AA groups were created by doctors, but they did not survive. Several independent sobriety groups were formed that took their inspiration from AA, but feeling that many of the principles were un-Japanese, they made a number of changes. In 1963, an umbrella organization was formed for all non-AA sobriety groups and was called the All Nippon Sobriety Association or ANSA (*Zennippon Danshu Renmei*). Ordinarily, member groups and the association are referred to simply as Danshukai. In the year 2000, there were 652 Danshukai groups with a combined membership of about 60,000.

Danshukai has taken on the basic format of AA. It is a voluntary organization run by alcoholics for alcoholics to help each other not drink. Groups meet weekly to tell, and listen to, stories of the problems caused by compulsive drinking. Many of the ideas and practices of AA have been altered, however, to make it more culturally appropriate. For example, there is no anonymity in Danshukai. When people arrive at meetings, they sign an attendance roster, and each is called upon by full name to say at least a few words. Where AA holds that it must avoid entanglement with any other organization, Danshukai feels that it can best achieve its goals by accepting financial aid from hospitals and government agencies, and the organization works closely with bureaucrats and medical personnel to coordinate policy and assist alcoholics. Where AA is openly spiritual in its invocation of a "higher power," Danshukai explicitly rejects all religious or philosophical affiliation. AA strives to maintain an essentially egalitarian organization; Danshukai, on the other hand, is hierarchically organized with local, regional, and national officers. Membership in AA is limited to alcoholics, and some meetings are closed to anyone who is not an alcoholic. There are no closed meetings of Danshukai. Furthermore, not only are alcoholics members of Danshukai, but it is assumed that family members—most often this means a wife—will join as auxiliary members who will give support and attend meetings even when the alcoholic does not.

Although initial attempts to establish AA groups in Japan foundered, AA ultimately found a foothold. An American priest in Japan, who was a recovering alcoholic and was familiar with the benefits of AA, took a Japanese alcoholic priest to Danshukai meetings in 1974. In time, the priests held their own meetings, in Japanese, that became AA. With only slight modifications, AA in Japan has maintained the original program and avoided the changes wrought by Danshukai. AA in Japan initially focused its efforts in helping derelicts, but the organization has since expanded to most major cities and few of the meetings are found in skid-row districts. Because of the principles of anonymity, AA in Japan does not take attendance or keep membership records; however, the number of places that hold AA meetings once a week approaches 400, while the number of regular attendees is estimated at less than 4,000.

Stephen R. Smith

See also: Alcoholics Anonymous (AA); Buddhism; Leavitt, Mary Greenleaf Clement; Microbreweries (Japan); Sake; Woman's Christian Temperance Union (WCTU) (Japan)

References

Gauntner, John. *The Saké Handbook.* North Clarendon, VT, and Tokyo: Yenbooks, Charles E. Tuttle, 1997.

Kokuzeicho. *Dai 123 kai Kokuzeicho Tōkei Nenpōsho* (The 123rd National Tax Office Statistical Report). Tokyo: Kokuzeicho Kanzeibu Shuzeika (National Tax Office, Indirect Tax Bureau, Alcohol Tax Section), 1997.

Kondō, Hiroshi. *Sake: A Drinker's Guide.* Tokyo, New York, and San Francisco: Kodansha International, 1984.

Smith, Stephen R. "Drinking Etiquette in a Changing Beverage Market" in *Remade in Japan,* edited by Joseph J. Tobin, 143–158. New Haven and London: Yale University Press, 1992.

———. "Good Old Boy into Alcoholic: Danshukai and Learning a New Drinking Role in Japan" in *Learning in Likely Places,* edited by John Singleton, 286–303. Cambridge: Cambridge University Press, 1998.

———. "Temperance and the Origins of Lay Alcoholism Therapy in Japan" in *Social History of Alcohol Review.* 34/35 (spring/fall 1997): 37–43.

Jellinek, Elvin Morton (1890–1963)

Elvin Morton Jellinek (1890–1963) was one of the most influential figures in alcohol research in the mid-twentieth century. From the late 1930s until his death, Jellinek helped to shape research priorities, public attitudes, and alcohol policies, advocating a scientific approach to alcohol problems that guided the way from prohibition to a new emphasis on research and treatment. He made notable contributions to the research literature in the areas of epidemiology and typology of alcohol problems. He was the first director of the Section of Studies on Alcohol at Yale University and helped establish its Summer School of Alcohol Studies—the first professional education program on alcohol issues. He directed a major literature review project for the Research Council on Problems of Alcohol (RCPA) and served as an associate editor for the *Quarterly Journal of Studies on Alcohol* for many years. He created the Yale Plan Clinics—the first American outpatient clinics for treating alcoholics. He also worked with Marty Mann, founder of the National Committee for Education on Alcoholism, to promote acceptance of alcoholism as a disease. In the early 1950s, he moved to the international arena, serving as consultant on alcohol problems to the World Health Organization (WHO). He returned to North America several years later as a consultant to the Addiction Research Foundation (ARF) of Ontario and the Alcoholism Foundation of Alberta. In 1962, he joined the staff of the Cooperative Commission on the Study of Alcoholism at Stanford University in California. He died in 1963 leaving unfinished his final project, an *Encyclopedia of Problems of Alcohol.*

Jellinek's educational credentials and early career are hazy. Born in New York City, he was raised in Hungary and studied at the Universities of Berlin, Grenoble, Leipzig, and possibly Tegucigalpa (Honduras). His studies included philosophy, anthropology, theology, languages, and linguistics. Although he claimed a master's degree in education and a doctorate of science (listed on an early publication as honorary) from Leipzig, the university has no records of these degrees. He left Hungary in the 1920s after a Communist rebellion, spent several years in Sierra Leone, then worked for the United Fruit Company in Honduras. In 1931, he joined the Memorial Foundation for Neuroendocrine Research at Worcester State Hospital in Massachusetts as director of the Biometric Laboratory. His introduction to alcohol issues came in 1939 when he accepted an offer from the RCPA to direct a review of the scientific literature on the effects of alcohol on the individual. In 1941, he joined a new alcohol research group at the Laboratory of Applied Physiology (LAP) at Yale and became associate editor of the newly created *Quarterly Journal of Studies on Alcohol.* In 1943, Howard Haggard, head of the laboratory, created a Section of Studies on Alcohol and named Jellinek director.

Jellinek spent nearly a decade at Yale, developing a range of alcohol research, professional education, and treatment programs. In 1942 at the request of the RCPA, he published an outline for an alcohol research program, which gave priority to alcohol addiction and its treatment. In 1943, he helped create the Yale School of Alcohol Studies to train professionals dealing with alcohol issues, and he served as its first director. That same year, Jellinek established two Yale Plan Clinics to provide outpatient treatment services for alcoholics, training for social service workers, and a research base for clinical studies. In 1944, he supported Marty Mann's founding of the National Committee for Education on Alcoholism, which focused on gaining public acceptance of alcoholism as a disease. He also worked with Alcoholics Anonymous (AA), analyzing results of their 1945 survey on the drinking history of alcoholics. From this, he developed a series of phases that showed a progression of alcohol-use behaviors leading to physical addiction and loss of control over drinking.

Jellinek left Yale in 1948 to establish the Yale Institute of Alcohol Studies in the Southwest at Texas Christian University. The new program included a small research staff and a Yale Plan Clinic on the TCU campus. Although a joint Yale/Southwest Institute summer program was held at TCU in 1949, Jellinek was unable to raise sufficient funding from Texas sponsors or other sources, and the institute closed in 1951. By that time, Jellinek had already accepted a position as a consultant on alcoholism to the World Health Organization (WHO) in Geneva.

At the WHO, Jellinek worked with a new Alcoholism Subcommittee of the Expert Committee on Mental Health to survey the nature and extent of alcohol problems in Europe and Latin America. Building on his earlier epidemiological work at Yale, he developed a formula for estimating the rate of alcoholism within specific populations. He also convinced the WHO to fund the duplication of the Classified Abstract Archive of the Alcohol Literature, an ongoing Yale collection of several thousand abstracts, for deposit at selected agencies and research centers around the world. In 1955, Jellinek retired from the WHO and became secretary general of the International Institute for Research on Problems of Alcohol. The WHO Alcoholism Subcommittee sponsored the establishment of this institute in Geneva as an umbrella for international societies and experts in the alcoholism field, but it failed to draw additional support and closed after Jellinek returned to the United States in 1957. He accepted a grant from the Christopher D. Smithers Foundation to prepare a manuscript for *The Disease Concept of Alcoholism,* published in 1960, in which he identified five "species" (types) of alcoholics. He designated only two of these types—gamma and delta—as actual diseases characterized by physiological addiction and loss of control (gamma) or inability to abstain (delta).

While working on *The Disease Concept,* Jellinek also served as a consultant for two Canadian agencies—the ARF of Ontario and the Alcoholism Foundation of Alberta. In 1961, he left Canada to become a full-time staff member for the Cooperative Commission on the Study of Alcoholism, a new program at Stanford University. The National Institute on Mental Health (NIMH) funded the commission for five years to make alcohol policy recommendations. As part of this project, Jellinek proposed to compile an *Encyclopedia of Problems of Alcohol* to serve as a reference on all aspects of alcohol for researchers and the knowledgeable public. When he died suddenly of a heart attack in 1963, NIMH discontinued the encyclopedia.

Penny B. Page

See also: Addiction Research Foundation of Ontario (ARF); Alcoholism; Christopher D. Smithers Foundation; Haggard, Howard Wilcox; *Journal of Studies on Alcohol;* Mann, Marty; National Council on Alcoholism and Drug Dependence (NCADD); Research Council on Problems of Alcohol (RCPA); Treatment Institutions; World Health Organization (WHO)

References

Jellinek, E. M. *The Disease Concept of Alcoholism.* New Haven, CT: College and University Press with Hillhouse Press, 1960.

Lender, Mark Edward. "Jellinek, Elvin Morton" in *Dictionary of American Temperance Biography: From Temperance Reform to Alcohol Research, the 1600s to the 1980s,* 257–259. Westport, CT: Greenwood, 1984:

Page, Penny Booth. "E. M. Jellinek and the Evolution of Alcohol Studies: A Critical Essay" in *Addiction.* vol. 92, no. 12 (1997): 1619–1637.

———. "The Origins of Alcohol Studies: E. M. Jellinek and the Documentation of the Alcohol Research Literature" in *British Journal of Addiction.* vol. 83 no. 9 (1988): 1095–1103.

Johnson, William Eugene "Pussyfoot" (1862–1945)

William Eugene "Pussyfoot" Johnson (1862–1945) was a controversial and colorful law enforcement official and journalist in the early twentieth century who became a martyr for the prohibitionist cause when he lost an eye during a speaking engagement in England. Born in Coventry, New York, on 25 March 1862, William Johnson attended the Western Reserve Normal School in Milan, Ohio, and the University of Nebraska. After a short period as a school teacher, he served as a reporter for the *Lincoln* [Nebraska] *Daily News* and manager of the Nebraska News Bureau. In the debate over the 1890 prohibition amendment to the Nebraska state constitution, Johnson, posing as the owner of "Johnson's Pale Ale," wrote a number of those who opposed prohibition asking how to best defeat it. He then published their incriminating letters. He caused further controversy in Nebraska by uncovering voting fraud among the antiprohibitionists in Omaha while working as correspondent for the *New York Voice* and *Lincoln Daily Call.*

In his zeal for the prohibition cause, Johnson took reporting jobs with several papers across the United States. His passionate journalism led to his being sued for libel, assaulted, and thrown in jail in Dallas, Texas, due to his coverage of a corrupt band of county officials known as the "Court House Ring." In 1896 in New York, he attacked the Raines Law, which had been designed to curb drinking, but which Johnson alleged promoted the vice. The law stipulated that restaurants could not serve alcohol with meals on Sunday. However, hotels were exempt from the law, and a number of restaurants began "masquerading" as hotels in order to sell alcohol. He then visited army bases in the South and started a campaign to close post canteens and wrote pamphlets charging alcohol abuse on college campuses. After writing and testifying in court against the dispensary system in South Carolina in 1899, he traveled to Europe and Far Eastern countries to detail their liquor systems, focusing his attacks against the Gothenburg system in Sweden, a system in which cities established a licensing company to operate public houses in the hope of eliminating private interests.

Returning to the United States in 1902, he became managing editor of the *New Voice* in New York, and again found himself in the midst of conflict over his exposés. A year later, he was the Prohibition Party candidate in two separate elections in Maryland. In 1906, because of his reputation, President Theodore Roosevelt appointed him as special officer in the Indian Territory of Oklahoma and later in Minnesota to suppress the liquor trade. Appointing his own assistants, Johnson made several seizures, arrested 5,473 individuals, and shut down 400 illegal establishments. In Tulsa, Oklahoma, he raided two warehouses and dumped 25,000 bottles of liquor into the Arkansas River. He claimed that his swift and stealthy nighttime activities led the president to give him his nickname of "Pussyfoot."

Resigning on 30 September 1911, Johnson worked for the Committee of Temperance of the Presbyterian Church, then for the Anti-Saloon League of America (ASLA), and was editor of the temperance journal *New Republic.* He also continued his international travels and crusading. In 1919, during a debate in London between Mitchell Banks, a barrister, and himself over temperance, a riot broke out, in which he lost an eye from the impact of a thrown stone. During the last decade of his public life, he traveled for the World League Against Alcoholism (WLAA). He was also associate editor of *Standard Encyclopedia of the Alcohol Problem* during this time. Never one to miss an opportunity for self-dramatization, in 1926 he published a popular magazine article in *Hearst's International-Cosmopolitan* entitled "I Had to Lie, Bribe and Drink to Put over Prohibition in America." Retiring in 1930, he returned to New York and died there in 1945. Johnson's self-publicized adventures and investigations made him a hero for the prohibitionist movement and one of the most controversial figures of the early twentieth century.

T. Jason Soderstrum

See also: Gothenburg Schemes/Disinterested Management; *Standard Encyclopedia of the Alcohol Problem;* World League Against Alcoholism (WLAA)

References

Burdick, Kim Rogers. *Pussyfoot Johnson.* Smithville, NY: Smithville Historical Society, 1978.

McKenzie, Fred A. *"Pussyfoot" Johnson: Crusader—Reformer—A Man among Men.* New York: Revell, 1920.

Sinha, Tarini Prasad. *"Pussyfoot" Johnson and His Campaign in Hindustan.* Madras: Ganesh, 1922.

Jones, Leif (1862–1939)

Leif Jones (1862–1939), created Baron Rhayader, was president of the United Kingdom Alliance (UKA), the leading British prohibitionist body, for twenty-six years beginning in 1906. He pursued the policy of local veto and prohibition in an uncompromising manner. He was a Liberal member of Parliament (M.P.) who remained faithful to Asquith when the party divided.

Leif Jones was the son of Thomas Jones, a prominent figure in Welsh Nonconformist circles. He was christened Leifchild Stratten Jones, but early in life simplified his name. Among fellow M.P.s he was nicknamed "Tea Leaf Jones" because of his persistent advocacy of the teetotal and prohibitionist causes. In 1889, he became the secretary and protégé of Rosalind Howard,

Countess of Carlisle, a political radical and ardent prohibitionist, who fought bitter battles with advocates of disinterested management and other compromise schemes for licensing reform. In 1895, Jones was elected to the executive committee of the UKA. He stood unsuccessfully for election to Parliament for the Liberal/Labour cause in 1892, but was M.P. for Appleby from 1905 until his defeat in January 1910. He subsequently served as M.P. for Rushcliffe from December 1910 to 1918 and for Camborne, Cornwall, a strong temperance area, from 1923 to 1924 and 1929 to 1931.

Like Lady Carlisle, Jones had no interest in seeking cooperation with those who sought to reform the licensing laws. Under his influence and leadership, after 1906 the UKA remained relatively aloof even from the Liberal licensing bill of 1908 that allowed opportunity for the local veto at the end of a seven-year time limit. Jones and his allies bitterly attacked the supporters of disinterested management who at this period were rallying around Thomas Palmer Whittaker and his Temperance Legislation League. After 1915, the scheme put in place in Carlisle for direct state control of the drink trade represented a new target, and Leif Jones and the UKA devoted a great deal of energy in attempting to discredit its workings both during the war and afterwards. Leif Jones urged Lloyd George to support prohibition rather than state purchase in the first world war and subsequently drew inspiration from the advance of the prohibitionist cause in the United States. In 1931, the UKA refused to endorse the restrictive reforms proposed by the royal commission, and in June 1932 Leif Jones concluded his presidency "by issuing a ringing commendation of prohibition and stressing the importance of work at the popular rather than the governmental level" (Haylor 1953: 139).

George B. Wilson's biography of Jones is hard to find. Never copyrighted, it cannot be found at major British libraries. It is available at the London headquarters of the United Kingdom Temperance Alliance (UKTA).

John Greenaway

See also: Carlisle, Countess of (Rosalind Howard); Carlisle System; Gothenburg Schemes/Disinterested Management; Liberal Party (United Kingdom); Lloyd George, David; United Kingdom Alliance (UKA); Whittaker, Sir Thomas Palmer

References

Fahey, David M. "Leif Jones" in *Biographical Dictionary of Modern British Radicals,* edited by Joseph O. Baylen and Norbert J. Gossman, vol. 3 (*1870–1974*), 490–493. Hemel Hempstead: Harvester Wheatsheaf, 1988.

Haylor, Mark H. C. *The Vision of a Century, 1853–1953: The United Kingdom Alliance in Historical Perspective.* London: United Kingdom Alliance, 1953.

Roberts, Charles H. *The Radical Countess: The History of the Life of Rosalind, Countess of Carlisle.* Carlisle: Steele Brothers, 1962.

Wilson, George B. *Leif Jones, Lord Rhayader, Temperance Reformer and Statesman 1862–1939.* London: United Kingdom Alliance, 1948.

Jones, Wesley Livsey (1863–1932)

Wesley L. Jones (1863–1932) was an influential prohibitionist U. S. senator who served from 1909 until his death in November 1932. His most significant act during these crucial years for the prohibition cause was his authorship in 1929 of the Jones Bill, which dramatically increased penalties under the Volstead Act, the Eighteenth Amendment's federal enforcement legislation.

Wesley L. Jones was born in Bethany, Illinois on 9 October 1863. He graduated from Southern Illinois College at Enfield in 1885 and later studied law and was admitted to the bar in 1886. He moved to Washington Territory in 1889, and after Washington gained statehood he was elected to the U.S. House of Representatives in 1898. He served in the House for four terms as a Republican until March 1909. Jones then served in the Senate and was reelected in 1914, 1920, and 1926, acting as Republican whip from 1924 through 1929, but was an unsuccessful candidate for reelection in 1932 and died 19 November that year.

During Senate debate over the proposed Eighteenth Amendment, several restrictions were suggested. Senator Harding of Ohio suggested a six-year time limit for state ratification. Senator Jones argued effectively to other prohibitionist senators that this was a necessary compromise, since without a time limit the whole proposal might be voted down. He stated, "A very careful investigation has convinced some of us that a two thirds vote is uncertain unless this limitation is put on" (Merz 1970: 31). The move turned out to be an astute one, because once the proposed amendment cleared Congress only thirteen months was needed for ratification by the required thirty-six states.

In early 1921, Senator Jones introduced a bill that would have extended the scope of the Volstead Act to the Philippines and another to extend it to consular districts of China. On 22 February 1922, Jones even introduced a resolution to express Senate reaction to Spanish-Icelandic relations after he read a newspaper account of a proposed Spanish boycott in opposition to Iceland's prohibition stance.

Early in 1929, Senator Jones introduced a bill that proposed a dramatic increase in the maximum penalties for first-time violation of the Volstead Act, an increase from six months' to five years' imprisonment and a jump in the fine from $1,000 to $10,000. The Jones Bill was technically an amendment to the Volstead Act and was nicknamed "The Five-and-Ten Bill." The debate was quite heated and direct. Senator James A. Reed of Missouri, a leader of the antiprohibitionist forces, ended his speech to the Senate with the following charge to the prohibitionists: "You did not exterminate the brewery [with the Volstead Act]. You made millions of little breweries and installed them in the homes of the people" (Cashman 1981: 201). This forceful speech convinced Jones to amend his bill to give courts discretion to distinguish between smaller violations by amateurs and more serious infractions by professionals. The Senate vote on 19 February 1929 was 65 votes for Jones's bill against 18 opposed. The House also approved the bill, 284 to 90.

President Coolidge signed the Jones Bill on 3 March 1929, the day before Herbert Hoover succeeded him as president. On that same day, Congress rejected a dramatic proposal to add $256 million to the appropriation for the Prohibition Bureau, instead adding only 1 percent of that sum. The Jones Bill seemed a victory, yet enforcement by the Prohibition Bureau did not increase. National Prohibition's effectiveness did not improve, and the Jones Bill added to its reputation as a harsh and unreasonable measure. In part as a result, in the 1932 election over 100 congressmen and senators failed at reelection—including the three most influential prohibitionist senators: Reed Smoot of Utah, James E. Watson of Indiana, and Wesley L. Jones of Washington.

Lisa L. Ossian

See also: National Prohibition (United States); Prohibition Bureau

References

Biographical Directory of the United States Congress, 1774–Present. http://www.bioguide.congress.gov [May 2002].

Cashman, Sean Dennis. *Prohibition: The Lie of the Land.* New York: Free Press, 1981.

Forth, Stuart. "Wesley L. Jones: A Political Biography" (Ph.D. dissertation, University of Washington, 1962).

Kyvig, David E. *Repealing National Prohibition.* 2d ed. Kent, OH: Kent State University Press, 2000.

Merz, Charles. *The Dry Decade.* Seattle: University of Washington Press, 1970.

Journal of Studies on Alcohol

The *Journal of Studies on Alcohol* was the first research journal in the United States following the repeal of National Prohibition to focus on alcohol use and alcohol problems. It was founded as the *Quarterly Journal of Studies on Alcohol* in 1940 by Dr. Howard W. Haggard, a noted physiologist and director of the Laboratory of Applied Physiology (LAP) at Yale University. The *Quarterly Journal* published original research on the biomedical, psychological, and social aspects of alcohol use, including the etiology and treatment of alcoholism. In addition, it provided abstracts of other published documents from around the world, serving as the major current-awareness resource for alcohol research in the mid-twentieth century. After expanding to a monthly publication in 1975, the journal was forced to discontinue its abstracts section in 1983 due to changes in funding and increased costs. It continued as a bimonthly publication, broadening its scope to include research on other substances of abuse.

When Haggard created the *Quarterly Journal,* he designated it as the official organ of the Research Council on Problems of Alcohol (RCPA). Founded in 1938, the RCPA was an association of scientists, doctors, and educators who were interested in fostering research and treatment for alcohol problems. Haggard published regular reports of their activities, as well as an extensive review of the research on alcohol's effects on the body, which was funded by a grant to the RCPA from the Carnegie Corporation. When the grant ended in 1941, some 3,000 research documents had been reviewed and abstracted, and Haggard invited E. M. Jellinek, executive director of the project, to join his laboratory at Yale. Under Haggard's editorship, Jellinek became managing editor of the *Quarterly Journal,* which continued to publish abstracts of the alcohol research literature. The abstracts were also printed on McBee cards, which were coded and punched for subject retrieval, and the full collection was formally designated the Classified Abstract Archive of the Alcohol Literature.

In its first decade, the *Quarterly Journal* published some of the most important alcohol research in the postrepeal era. This included a detailed alcohol research agenda (commissioned by the RCPA), as well as articles dealing with rates of alcohol consumption and problems, and with the disease nature of alcoholism. The *Quarterly Journal* was published by the Journal of Studies on Alcohol, Inc., a nonprofit corporation established at Yale as a project of the LAP. The editorial staff became part of the Section of Studies on Alcohol created within the laboratory in 1943 (renamed the Center of Alcohol Studies in 1950). Haggard remained as editor until 1959, when he was succeeded by Mark Keller, an original member of the RCPA literature review project. The publication moved to Rutgers University when the Center of Alcohol Studies relocated there in 1962.

In 1975, the *Quarterly Journal* became a monthly publication to accommodate the significant growth of the alcohol research literature. The *Journal of Studies on Alcohol* offered alternating monthly issues of original research articles and abstracts of published research. The editorial staff grew to include a team of subject analysts and language experts who created in-depth evaluative abstracts. Subscriptions alone could not support this activity, and from 1968 through 1972 additional support was provided by grants from the National Institute of Mental Health (NIMH). With the establishment of the National Institute on Alcohol Abuse and Alcoholism (NIAAA), support for the documentation activities of the Center of Alcohol Studies (including the journal) was transferred to that agency. The NIAAA provided grant and then contract support until 1983, when most federal funds for alcohol research were redirected through block grants to the states. Funding for the abstracting service was offered on a competitive bid, and the center lost its federal support for this activity. Unable to secure other funding, the journal discontinued its abstract issues, and it became a bimonthly publication in 1983. At that time, the Journal of Studies on Alcohol, Inc., reorganized as Alcohol Research Documentation, a nonprofit organization affiliated with Rutgers University.

Mark Keller served as editor for nearly twenty years; he was succeeded in 1977 by Timothy Coffey. In 1984, after the loss of the abstract issues, Alcohol Research Documentation selected the first editors of the *Journal of Studies on Alcohol* not affiliated with the Center of Alcohol Studies, Drs. Jack H. Mendelson and Nancy K. Mello from the Alcohol and Drug Abuse Research Center of the Harvard Medical School. They were succeeded in 1995 by Dr. Mark Schuckit of the Veterans Affairs Medical Center in San Diego, who broadened the scope of the journal to include research on other psychoactive substances of abuse.

Penny B. Page

See also: Haggard, Howard Wilcox; Jellinek, Elvin Morton; Keller, Mark; National Institute on Alcohol Abuse and Alcoholism (NIAAA); Research Council on Problems of Alcohol (RCPA); Rutgers Center of Alcohol Studies; Yale Center of Alcohol Studies

References

Keller, Mark. "Editor's Foreword" in *CAAAL Manual: A Guide to the Use of the Classified Abstract Archive of the Alcohol Literature,* edited by Mark Keller, Vera Efron, and E. M. Jellinek, xi-xvii. New Brunswick, NJ: Rutgers Center of Alcohol Studies, 1965.

Page, Penny Booth. "The Origins of Alcohol Studies: E. M. Jellinek and the Documentation of the Alcohol Research Literature" in *British Journal of Addiction.* 83 no. 9 (1988): 1095–1103.

Juke Joints

A descriptive term much romanticized, and weighty with cultural meaning in the heritage of American music and African American studies, juke joints refer essentially to the drinking establishments where the blues began. Juke joints are most identified with the rich cotton farmland of the Mississippi Delta from the 1920s to the 1950s, where, in small sharecropper houses or abandoned buildings, a local bootlegger would run gambling, present live music for dancing, and sell his liquor. Drinking was the primary purpose of juke joints.

The etymology of the word "juke" is unclear, but it is generally believed to be of West African origin, and it has various meanings of *wicked, disorderly,* or *to dance or act wildly.* It came into usage in the United States South by way of the Gullah speakers in the islands off the coast of South Carolina. Also spelled "jook" or "jouk," its indication as a drinking and party place in the Delta in the 1920s and its appearance in literature and journalism in the 1930s demonstrate that the word's journey began before the Civil War, eventually extending as far west as Texas. An associated term is "juke house," which in addition to drinking, gambling, and music, also included prostitution.

Much of the knowledge of juke joints comes by way of oral tradition. Given that these establishments operated on the fringes of the law, and were in effect closed societies to individuals outside of Southern rural African American culture, there has been little chance for ethnographic or sociological research. Even in the 1940s when ethnomusicologist Alan Lomax visited the Delta to make field recordings of the blues, he seldom strayed beyond the front porches of the singers. He was accompanied on some of his trips by John Work, a black musicologist from Fisk University, who also had little inclination or opportunity to visit juke joints.

Blues music, moving into its own as a form of entertainment in the 1920s, was the impetus to bringing in customers to the juke joints. Bootleggers would hear of a local singer or musician and hire them to play, knowing the music would entice patrons to drink and dance. In several interviews over the course of his career, bluesman Muddy Waters often described his start in the juke joints near the Stovall plantation in Mississippi. The bootleggers would string lights in the trees surrounding the house; the lights were a beacon to the locals. The owner of the juke joint sold whiskey and beer, the latter dispensed in cups and the whiskey drunk from the bottle to minimize the use of mugs or several bottles as weapons when the drinking got heavy. Dice games and other gambling went on outside.

Drunken violence was an acknowledged facet of a Saturday night in a juke joint. David "Honeyboy" Edwards, who, like Waters, had his start in blues on a Mississippi plantation, recalled in his memoirs how his father sold whiskey and played guitar. In one typical example, Edwards told about a drunken dance at which his father fought with a man and then ran for his life when the man flourished a gun. There was usually little interference from local law officers, who sometimes were paid off, or from the landowner in response to the illegal liquor and the violence. For these authority figures, the juke joints were a form of social control, acting as outlets for aggression and pent-up emotions. As long as farm workers and laborers were available to work when needed, and valuable workers were not victims of violence, rarely was the legal system involved.

As the farms became more mechanized in the years following World War II and the traditional workers found employment in neighboring towns or in cities in the Northeast and Midwest, juke joints became roadhouses and bars, the live music often replaced by "jukeboxes." Liquor became more accessible, and cheaper, than it was with the bootlegger. In popular usage now, the meaning of juke joint is synonymous with any bar featuring alcohol, dancing, and music.

Kevin Grace

References

Charters, Sam. *The Country Blues.* New York: Da Capo Press, 1975.

Davis, Francis. *The History of the Blues: The Roots, the Music, the People from Charley Patton to Robert Cray.* New York: Hyperion, 1995.

Edwards, David. "Honeyboy." *The World Don't Owe Me Nothing: The Life and Times of Delta Bluesman Honeyboy Edwards.* Chicago: Chicago Review Press, 1997.

Gordon, Robert. *Can't Be Satisfied: The Life and Times of Muddy Waters.* Boston: Little, Brown, 2002.

K

Kava

Kava is a nonalcoholic beverage made from the pounded, ground, or chewed root of a pepper plant (*Piper methysticum*) and mixed with water. From early on, it was vociferously opposed by many Christian missionaries to the Pacific Islands, and it continues to be prohibited by some churches today. The kava plant, a small shrub, is native to the southwest Pacific Islands and was probably domesticated from a wild relative in Vanuatu or elsewhere in eastern Melanesia. The plant contains several potent alkaloids that are pharmacologically active, and consumption of the drink typically produces a peaceful state of quiet relaxation. Those who drink kava rarely become quarrelsome and, unlike beverage alcohol, kava does not cause mental dullness after several draughts.

At the time of Western contact, kava use was found throughout most of Polynesia, in much of Vanuatu, in scattered locations in New Guinea and adjacent islands, and on two islands in eastern Micronesia (Pohnpei and Kosrae). Most islanders treated kava as a sacred or ritually potent substance, and its consumption usually was restricted to adult men or people of high rank. Elaborate kava ceremonies were developed, particularly in Samoa, Tonga, and Fiji. Kava was used medicinally, to communicate with the spirit world, and as a sign of hospitality and respect.

Today, kava has become secularized such that there are few restrictions on who can drink it, and it has entered the market economy. Kava is a significant export commodity from Fiji and Vanuatu; it is sold in special "kava bars" in much of the southwest Pacific, on Pohnpei, and in Hawaii, and Western firms have patented kava extracts for a variety of pills and potions sold throughout Europe and North America. Kava has received attention from anthropologists and other scholars for over a century, but during the past thirteen years, three major works have synthesized and summarized much of what is known about this substance (Brunton 1989; Lebot, Merlin, and Lindstrom 1992; Pollock 1995).

A man makes up a narcotic drink from the roots of the kava plant at a kava ceremony in Fiji. (Charles and Josette Lenars/Corbis)

Kava, Christianity, and Prohibition

Beginning in the 1850s, American Congregationalist missionaries on Kosrae and Pohnpei and British Presbyterian missionaries in Vanuatu sought to wean their converts from kava drinking (Brunton 1989: 114–128; Marshall and Marshall 1976; Young 1995). These efforts were only partially successful. Kosraens abandoned kava when they accepted Christianity, and this avoidance has endured to the present. However, Pohnpeians and the people of Vanuatu never completely gave up kava drinking, and now it is more widespread and commonplace than ever on those islands (Petersen 1995; Young 1995). Even so, some faiths like the Seventh Day Adventists require their adherents to eschew kava (along with alcohol), and in 1984 *Pacific Island Monthly* reported that the Methodist Church of Fiji passed a motion at its annual conference to discourage its members from "excessive" drinking of kava on the grounds that those who imbibed failed to carry out their responsibilities and were lazy.

The Saga of Kava among Australian Aborigines

One of the more interesting chapters concerning the recent spread of kava drinking beyond the places where it was used at contact with the West is its introduction to Aboriginal communities in northeastern Arnhem Land (Northern Territory), Australia. Those who initially brought kava from Fiji hoped that kava drinking would substitute for heavy alcohol consumption and its associated fighting, social disturbance, and damage to health. Despite its resolute antidrug stance, the Uniting Church—the dominant Christian mission in the area—strongly endorsed kava's introduction on grounds that it would provide a peaceful alternative to alcoholic beverages. However, as Peter d'Abbs (1995) has chronicled, kava drinking did not end up as a substitute for alcohol, but rather was added to it.

Kava was first imported to Arnhem Land in the early 1980s. Its consumption became controversial by the end of that decade, especially because Aboriginal kava drinkers came to consume this new substance in much greater quantities than any of their Pacific Islander counterparts, and because it did not eliminate the problems surrounding excessive alcohol use, as originally had been hoped. In May 1990, the Northern Territory government prohibited the sale and supply of kava except under special conditions. The goals of this intervention were to regulate this new drug; eliminate profiteering; reduce a host of kava-related economic, social, and health problems that had arisen very quickly; and diminish per capita levels of its consumption (d'Abbs 1993: 1). As seems generally true with efforts to legislate prohibition or strong controls over psychoactive substances, this law resulted in a short-term decline in sales but was soon followed by a continued increase in the number of kava drinkers (including more women) and in the typical quantities quaffed at a sitting. Much of this was consequent of a failure "to establish an orderly, regulated retail system under the control of community councils" (d'Abbs 1993: 3), and illegal trading and black markets in kava arose within months of passage of restrictive legislation. In concluding his account of kava in Arnhem Land, d'Abbs notes that government kava bans make little sense when the government allows alcohol use, which does much more harm, and that the right to drink kava—just like the right to drink liquor—is likely to be interpreted by many Aboriginal people "as symbolic of citizenship and equality" (d'Abbs 1995: 180).

Mac Marshall

See also: Anthropological Theories of Drinking and Temperance; Pacific Islands

References

Brunton, Ron. *The Abandoned Narcotic. Kava and Cultural Instability in Melanesia.* Cambridge: Cambridge University Press, 1989.

d'Abbs, Peter. "The Power of Kava or the Power of Ideas? Kava Use and Policy in the Northern Territory, Australia" in *Canberra Anthropology.* Special Issue, 18 (1995): 166–183.

———. *A Review of Kava Control Measures in the Northern Territory.* Casuarina, Northern Territory: Menzies School of Health Research, 1993.

Lebot, Vincent, Mark Merlin, and Lamont Lindstrom. *Kava: The Pacific Drug.* New Haven: Yale University Press, 1992.

Marshall, Mac, and Leslie B. Marshall. "Holy and Unholy Spirits: The Effects of Missionization on Alcohol Use in Eastern Micronesia" in *Journal of Pacific History.* 11, no. 3 (1976): 135–166.

Pollock, Nancy, ed. "The Power of Kava." *Canberra Anthropology.* Special Issue, 18, nos. 1 and 2 (1995): 1–182.

Young, Michael W. "Kava and Christianity in Central Vanuatu: With an Appendix on the Ethnography of Kava Drinking in Nikowia, Epi" in *Canberra Anthropology.* Special Issue, 18 (1995): 61–96.

Keeley, Leslie Enraught (1832–1900)

Leslie E. Keeley, M.D., of Dwight, Illinois, devised a popular patent medicine for the treatment of inebriety, the "Bi-chloride of Gold Cure," which was administered to tens of thousands of patients in Keeley Institute inebriate homes in North America and elsewhere during the 1880s and 1890s. A former Union army surgeon, Keeley developed a formula that he claimed effectively treated alcoholism. First hawking the cure as a patent medicine, Keeley found success in the late 1880s when he established in Dwight the Keeley Institute, a home for inebriates, which by 1893 had ninety-two franchised counterparts. In his writings, Keeley denied that inebriety was an inherited, incurable disease. His institutes were patronized by tens of thousands of alcoholics. Mounting rates of relapse and the unrelenting opposition of the medical establishment ended the Gold Cure craze, although Keeley died a millionaire in 1900. His treatment was a precursor to Alcoholics Anonymous (AA) and aversion therapy.

Born in Kings County, Ireland, Keeley immigrated with his parents to the United States at a young age. He graduated from the Rush Medical College of Chicago in 1864 and served as assistant surgeon for the Union army, where he first observed alcoholism. In 1866, he settled in Dwight, becoming surgeon for the Chicago and Alton Railroad, and experimenting with treatments for alcoholism. With his young chemist associate, John Oughton, Keeley devised a formula of chloride of gold and sodium in pill form, which nearly killed its first test patient. Incorporating themselves as Leslie E. Keeley, M.D., Keeley and Oughton combined atropine, strychnine, and arsenic into a more efficacious formula, which they called the Bi-chloride of Gold Cure. During the 1880s, the company followed standard patent-medicine practice: blanket advertising, fake (succeeded by real) testimonials, and mail-order "personalized treatments," which encouraged repurchase at $9.00 per two bottles. Cures for the opium and tobacco habits and neurasthenia followed, and Keeley opened a small sanitarium in Dwight. Following positive newspaper reports and the publication of several books and articles, such as "Drunkenness. A Curable Disease" in 1892, the institute became a success.

Keeley's philosophy, as written in "The Non-Heredity of Inebriety" (1890), emphasized the curability of the disease and avoided condemnation of the alcoholic. He only required a three- to four-week stay at the institute, and patients were free to leave, and even drink whiskey, so long as they took their injections four times daily. Keeley appealed to manly dignity, offering an alternative to imprisonment in the asylum and drunk tank. "What can be so unfortunate," he wrote, "as to deprive an inebriate of his liberty [and make him feel] that he is a lower animal?" (Keeley 1897).

By 1893, there were 118 franchised institutes in the United States, Canada, and Mexico, and Keeley enjoyed the patronage of the U.S. surgeon general, who authorized the employment of the Gold Cure in government homes for disabled soldiers. Keeley faced unrelenting opposition from the established medical profession, particularly from specialists in addictions. T. D. Crothers termed gold a "therapeutic nihility" and the treatment "chemical restraint," and challenged Keeley to reveal the formula, only to meet the opposition of Keeley's loyal ex-patients.

Keeley's biggest setback occurred when he attempted to set up an institute in Great Britain. Norman Kerr, Britain's leading inebriate expert, reported that the medicine contained alcohol and sugar but no gold, and successfully obstructed the cure's endorsement by the Church of England Temperance Society (CETS) in 1892. The London Keeley Institute nevertheless opened that year and enjoyed a distinguished clientele, but continual negative press propelled Keeley to sue the *Lancet* and *Medical Press and Circular* for libel, resulting in more adverse publicity. Keeley dropped the case and attempts to expand in Britain, and retired to California. Dying in 1900, he left a $1 million estate. Despite the elements of quackery inherent in a secret nostrum, Leslie E. Keeley's lasting contribution was his nonjudgmental attitude toward alcoholism, his aversion therapy (precursor to Antabuse), and especially the therapeutic benefits of mutual support, which anticipated AA.

Cheryl Krasnick Warsh

See also: Alcoholics Anonymous (AA); Alcoholism; Crothers, Thomas Davison; Keeley Institutes; Kerr, Norman Shanks; Treatment Institutions

References

Barclay, George A. "The Keeley League" in *Journal of the Illinois State Historical Society.* 57 (Winter 1964): 364–379.

Crellin, John K. "Alcoholism and Drug Addiction in the Nineties: An American in London" in *British Journal of Addiction.* 75 (1980): 156–159.

Keeley, Leslie E. *Opium: Its Use, Abuse and Cure: or From Bondage to Freedom.* Chicago: Banner of Gold, 1897; reprinted New York: Arno Press, 1981.

Warsh, Cheryl Krasnick. "Adventures in Maritime Quackery: The Leslie E. Keeley Gold Cure Institute of Fredericton, N.B." in *Acadiensis.* 17, no. 2 (Spring 1988): 109–130.

Keeley Institutes

The Keeley Institutes, established by Dr. Leslie Enraught Keeley, were franchised treatment centers for inebriates and drug addicts. At the height of their popularity in 1893, there were 118 facilities in 5 countries. The craze would run its course by the 1920s, although the last institute, the original at Dwight, Illinois, would remain open until 1966. The Keeley Institutes employed a combination of therapeutic environment, behavior modification techniques, and the Gold Cure, a secret remedy composed of atropine, strychnine, and arsenic, with traces of gold. A substantial part of its success was its patients' independent organization of the Bi-chloride of Gold Club, a mutual support society portending the success of Alcoholics Anonymous (AA). The Keeley Cure, with its nonjudgmental attitude toward alcohol abuse, attracted an affluent and professional clientele.

Dr Leslie Keeley established the first Keeley Institute in the town of Dwight, Illinois, in 1879, and it soon became the major industry for the community. Drawing its first patients from the Chicago area, it received favorable press reports, and a Keeley Day was an official part of the Chicago World's Fair of 1893. By then, there were 118 franchised institutes in the United States, England, Finland, Denmark, Sweden, and Canada. Between 1892 and 1900, the Keeley Company enjoyed a profit of $1.6 million, half of which was generated between 1892 and 1894.

The Keeley program appealed to alcoholics on many levels. Through his writings and interviews, Leslie Keeley emphasized that inebriety was a curable disease, not vicious conduct, as the temperance movement had characterized it. The institutes offered private residential care without the hardships of a lengthy stay. They employed licensed physicians (usually ex-patients), but also used the merchandising techniques of the patent-medicine trade.

A less tangible attraction was the Keeley program's appeal to manly dignity and its re-creation of the male saloon subculture that, in many instances, had contributed to the alcoholism. The Keeley remedies, although mysterious in content, were concrete and logical in application. Patients stayed for a three- or four-week period, during which time they were free to have as much whiskey as they craved and to wander the grounds and the town—so long as they lined up four times daily at the main building ("the shot tower") to receive a hypodermic injection ("the shot"). Every two hours, the patient also took a dram of tonic ("the dope"), which purportedly was composed of gold and sodium chloride, strychnine, atropine, cinchona, and glycerine. Strychnine and arsenic were medically accepted nerve tonics during the 1890s, while atropine was a highly effective counterirritant to alcohol. More recalcitrant patients were given whiskey, then a shot of strychnine and apomorphine (a strong emetic), which was an early form of aversion therapy. The "shot tower," the "dope," and the heroic aspect of apomorphine reaction were all masculine facets of Keeley care. Even the concept of injecting gold (symbol of the materialist, profit-oriented,

A group of temperance activists poses in front of the entrances of the Leslie E. Keeley Institute, an institute for the treatment of inebriety, in Dwight, Illinois, 1893. (Library of Congress)

nineteenth-century man) ensured that Keeleyism stripped a man of alcohol without stripping him of dignity.

Although there were some women treated at a separate Ladies Home at the Dwight Institute, they were secluded from the male inebriates and the community, reflecting the intense embarrassment associated with female alcoholism at this time. The male inebriates were free to leave the grounds, but there were numerous regulations, such as attending lectures and refraining from smoking, gambling, drinking sodas, or traveling in cars. The citizens of Dwight actively supported the institute, taking in lodgers, encouraging new arrivals, and reporting attempts to purchase alcohol. Many ex-patients remained in Dwight to sustain their sobriety.

Other patients received distinctly modern instructions for maintaining their sobriety. The pamphlet "To the Keeley Graduate" promised a permanent cure if the patient never drank again, established regular patterns of sleep and nutritional meals, exercised, and avoided tobacco, caffeine, and inappropriate acquaintances. They were also encouraged to correspond with the institute and fellow patients. The Bi-chloride of Gold Clubs, spontaneously organized by the Dwight patients in 1891, met every morning, greeted each new trainload of alcoholics, heard speeches from members, and read encouraging letters from graduates. By the following year, fifty branches of the club were holding services, concerts, and fundraisers for impoverished alcoholics. The members also petitioned state governments for the passage of Keeley Laws to provide public funding for the treatment of indigents at the institutes, and they were successful in getting the laws passed in six states.

The institutes and the Keeley craze did not survive the concerted opposition of the medical establishment and, more damaging, the mounting relapses of ex-patients. Many of the institutes, such as that established in Fredericton, New Brunswick, Canada, in 1894, suffered from the mismanagement of its ex-patient administrators and physicians.

After Keeley's death in 1900, the institutes were taken over by his partner, John Oughton, and his son, Dr. James H. Oughton. By then, more than 400,000 men and women had been treated. By the 1940s, the Dwight institute was holding AA meetings and affiliating with that organization, until the institute closed in 1966.

Cheryl Krasnick Warsh

See also: Alcoholics Anonymous (AA); Keeley, Leslie Enraught; Treatment Institutions

References

Clark, C. S. *The Perfect Keeley Cure.* Milwaukee: n.p., 1892.

Morgan, H. "No, Thank You, I've been to Dwight: Reflections on the Keeley Cure for Alcoholism" in *Illinois Historical Journal.* 82, no. 3 (1989): 147–166.

Warsh, Cheryl Krasnick. "Adventures in Maritime Quackery: The Leslie E. Keeley Gold Cure Institute of Fredericton, N.B." in *Acadiensis.* 17, no. 2 (Spring 1988): 109–130.

White, William L. *Slaying the Dragon: The History of Addiction Treatment and Recovery in America.* Bloomington, IL: Chestnut Health Systems, 1998.

Keller, Mark (1907–1995)

Mark Keller (1907–1995) rose from an editorial assistant to become editor of the prestigious *Quarterly Journal of Studies on Alcohol* in the mid-twentieth century. Over the course of a 40-year career, he authored over 100 publications including journal articles, books, and chapters on various aspects of alcohol use, alcoholism, and documentation of the alcohol literature. He served as editor for the multivolume *International Bibliography of Studies on Alcohol* and helped develop one of the world's foremost libraries of alcohol research literature at the Rutgers Center of Alcohol Studies. He was also a visiting scientist in the 1970s at the newly created National Institute on Alcohol Abuse and Alcoholism (NIAAA) and was a contributor to NIAAA's first three *Alcohol and Health* special reports to the U.S. Congress. On his retirement from the Center of Alcohol Studies in 1977, Rutgers named him editor emeritus of the *Journal of Studies on Alcohol,* and the journal created the annual Mark Keller Award to honor the best article published in the journal.

Keller was born in Austria in 1907 and moved with his family to the United States in 1913. He was a self-educated man who dropped out of high school and never attended college. In the mid-1930s he worked as an editorial assistant for Dr. Norman Jolliffe, who was head of the medical service of the psychiatric division at Bellevue Hospital in New York City. Jolliffe was interested in studying the nutritional diseases exhibited by alcoholics, and Keller became involved in collecting and organizing information and editing papers on these diseases. Jolliffe's work ultimately led to his involvement with the Research Council on Problems of Alcohol (RCPA), an association of scientists and physicians whose purpose was to raise money for alcohol-related research. When the RCPA received a grant to review the literature on the effects of alcohol on the individual, they appointed Jolliffe as medical director of the project. He took offices at the New York Academy of Medicine in 1939 and brought Keller along as an assistant. There Keller met E. M. Jellinek, who was hired by Jolliffe to serve as executive director of the project, and it was Keller who initiated Jellinek into the alcohol literature. When the project ended in 1941, Jellinek and Keller joined the Laboratory of Applied Physiology (LAP) at Yale University, home of the newly created *Quarterly Journal of Studies on Alcohol.* In 1942, Keller became editorial secretary of the *Quarterly Journal.* He quickly moved up to assistant editor in 1943 and managing editor in 1950. In 1959, he was named editor, a post that he held until his retirement in 1977. During that time, the *Quarterly Journal* moved with the Center of Alcohol Studies from Yale to Rutgers University (1962), and the publication expanded into the monthly *Journal of Studies on Alcohol* in 1975.

Keller's career included more than his editorial work. He authored numerous articles and chapters on such topics as alcohol consumption, alcoholism, and cultural aspects of drinking. From 1952 until 1976, he compiled and published an annual compendium, *Statistics on Consumption of Alcohol and on Alcoholism* (title varies), first with coauthor Vera Efron and later with Carol Gurioli. He lectured frequently at the annual Summer School of Alcohol Studies (at Yale and then Rutgers). Keller was also concerned with the documentation of the alcohol research literature. He worked with Jellinek to develop a system for organizing and retrieving research documents, which became known as the Classified Abstract Archive of the Alcohol Literature. He also directed and edited a project to identify the world's alcohol research literature from 1901 through 1960, which resulted in a three-volume series entitled *The International Bibliography of Studies on Alcohol.* As an editor of a multidisciplinary journal, Keller was aware of the disparities in the language used to describe alcohol use and alcohol problems. In *A Dictionary of Words about Alcohol* he provided definitions for over 1,700 terms. Under Keller's direction, the documentation activities at the Center of Alcohol Studies expanded into the world's foremost library on alcohol research as well as the major service for abstracting and indexing the alcohol literature.

When the federal government established the NIAAA, Keller was appointed as a visiting scientist (1974–1975). He edited the first two NIAAA *Alcohol and Health* special reports to Congress, and he also contributed to the third report. President Jimmy Carter appointed him to the Presidential Commission on Mental Health's Task Force on Alcoholism, for which he wrote the report in 1977. He also served on committees for the World Health Organization (WHO) and the National Council on Alcoholism (NCA), and he received an award for medical journalism in 1976. He retired as editor of the *Journal of Studies on Alcohol* and research specialist at the Center of Alcohol Studies in 1977, although he returned briefly as acting editor of the journal from 1981 through 1983. He also served as an adjunct professor at Brandeis University from 1980 to 1981. He was working on a third edition of his alcohol dictionary before his death in 1995.

Penny B. Page

See also: Jellinek, Elvin Morton; *Journal of Studies on Alcohol;* National Institute on Alcohol Abuse and Alcoholism (NIAAA); Research Council on Problems of Alcohol (RCPA); Rutgers Center of Alcohol Studies; Yale Center of Alcohol Studies

References

Carpenter, Marilyn Z. "In Memoriam: Mark Keller" in *Journal of Studies on Alcohol.* 57 no. 1 (1996): 5–6.

"Keller, Mark" in *Dictionary of American Temperance Biography: From Temperance Reform to Alcohol Research, the 1600s to the 1980s,* edited by Mark Edward Lender, 273–275. Westport, CT: Greenwood, 1984.

Keller, Mark, Mairi McCormick, and Vera Efron. *A Dictionary of Words about Alcohol.* 2d ed. New Brunswick, NJ: Rutgers Center of Alcohol Studies, 1982.

Kerr, Norman Shanks (1834–1899)

Norman Shanks Kerr (1834–1899) was a physician, medical officer of health, the founder and president of the Society for the Study and Cure of Inebriety (SSI), and a key British temperance advocate in the last quarter of the nineteenth century. Born 17 May 1834, in Glasgow, Scotland, he died 30 May 1899, in Hastings, Sussex, England.

Kerr worked at the *Glasgow Mail* and later the *North British Daily Mail,* work he continued sporadically until he graduated from Glasgow Medical School in 1861. As a student in 1857, he organized the first Total Abstinence Society among Glasgow students and became a director of the Coffee Tavern Company of Glasgow, a temperance organization. Kerr served as ship's surgeon in the Allan Canadian mail steamers after graduating from medical school. In 1871, he began practicing medicine in Bedford, England. He moved to London in 1874, where he was elected medical officer of health for Saint Marylebone, a post that he retained until the end of his life.

In London, Kerr became a notable temperance advocate and strict teetotaller. One story says that his dedication to total abstinence came after an encounter with a drunken patient, whom Kerr implored to stop drinking. Kerr and the patient agreed to sign the temperance pledge together. His reputation as an able and ready speaker on temperance brought many requests to talk on the cause in all parts of the country. He was a key member of the Society for Promoting Legislation for the Control and Cure of Habitual Drunkards. This was the precursor to the SSI, which Kerr founded in 1884. He was also corresponding secretary of the American Association for the Cure of Inebriates and physician to the Dalrymple Home for Inebriates at Rickmansworth. He was chair of the British Medical Association's Inebriates Legislation Committee, which in 1888 saw its draft bill extending the 1879 Habitual Drunkards Act become passed as the Inebriates Act (1888).

Kerr embraced a medical and scientific approach to temperance and the disease theory of addiction. He advocated legislative action based upon the idea that alcoholics suffered from a disease and were not simply morally bereft. This theme underlay his major works: *The Action of Alcoholic Liquors in Health* (1876); *Mortality from Intemperance* (1879); *Inebriety, its Etiology, Pathology, Treatment and Jurisprudence* (1888, 1889, 1894); and *Alcoholism and Drug Habits* (1895). He eschewed what he viewed as medical quackery in inebriety treatment, including hypnotism and the "Gold Cure" for inebriety. In 1890, he produced *Hypnotism not a Safe and Reliable Remedy.*

Along with his work in scientific temperance, Kerr was a member of the Obstetrical, the Medical, and the Harveian Societies of London, a Fellow of the Linnean society, and vice president of the International Congress of Medical Jurisprudence.

Kerr married in 1871, to Eleanor Georgina Gibson, Ballinderry, Ireland, who died in 1892 and with whom he had a son. In 1894, he married Edith Jane Henderson of Newry, County Down, with whom he had four daughters.

Daniel J. Malleck

See also: Society for the Study of Addiction

References

Berridge, Virginia. "Society for the Study of Addiction" in *British Journal of Addiction.* 85 (1990): 987–1077.

"Kerr, Norman (Shanks)" in *Standard Encyclopedia of the Alcohol Problem,* edited by Ernest Hurst Cherrington, et al., vol 4: 1457–1458. 6 vols. Westerville, OH: American Issue Publishing, 1925–1930.

"Kerr, Norman Shanks" in *Modern English Biography, Containing Many Thousand Concise Memoirs of Persons who Have Died between the Years 1851–1900,* edited by Frederic Boase, 817–818. London: F. Cass, 1965.

"Norman Kerr" (obituary) in *British Medical Journal.* 1 (10 June 1899): 1442.

Knights of Father Mathew

The Knights of Father Mathew was an Irish Catholic fraternal society that promoted total abstinence. It was organized in 1881 in Saint Louis, Missouri. Its predecessor, the Catholic Young Men's Total Abstinence Society, had been established in Saint Louis in 1872. The Knights of Father Mathew gained members in cities throughout the state of Missouri and three other Midwestern states. The knights promoted total abstinence from alcohol on the basis of individual decision, as new members took a pledge to abstain from all intoxicants. In addition to promoting temperance for its members, the Knights of Father Mathew served as an ethnic aid society, providing insurance programs as well as social and cultural activities. In 1895, the Knights of Father Mathew was affiliated with the Catholic Total Abstinence Union of America, a national organization based in Hartford, Connecticut. The Knights of Father Mathew eventually included Catholics who were not Irish as members, and also women and boys. The Knights of Father Mathew was named in honor of the celebrated Irish temperance leader, Father Theobald Mathew (1790–1856).

Membership in the Knights of Father Mathew grew steadily. In 1898, the organization had 3,000 members. By 1904, the knights claimed 6,000 members in thirty-seven parish councils in Missouri and three other Midwestern states—Illinois, Iowa, and Kansas. The knights, generally composed of young Irish men, began to widen their membership beginning in the early 1900s. Non-Irish Catholics were encouraged to join, especially second-generation German immigrants who spoke English. Women were allowed to form ladies auxiliaries beginning in 1902. In 1915, the male organization changed to the Knights and Ladies of Father Mathew, as women were admitted with full privileges and membership. Membership declined in the 1920s and the organization was disbanded in 1931.

Within the context of an ethnic aid society, the Knights of Father Mathew promoted total abstinence, frugality, and morality. As part of the induction ceremony, each new member had a pledge administered, promising, with divine assistance, to abstain from all alcohol and to prevent as much as possible, by advice and example, intemperance in others. The organization promoted abstinence through voluntary efforts and moral suasion. It did not endorse legal prohibition as a method of promoting temperance. It did not join the cause of the prohibitionists of the era, who sought to have legislation passed against alcohol sale and use.

The Knights of Father Mathew provided a variety of economic and social programs for its members. Insurance policies for both death and sick expenses were available at a bargain price. The organization sponsored celebrations, rallies, athletic events, and numerous social events for members and their guests. Most of the councils had access to their own building for meetings and activities. Knights marched in public parades in quasi-military uniforms and ranks. A junior organization for sons of members, the Junior Knights of Father Mathew, was established in 1901.

Katherine H. Nelson

See also: Ireland; Mathew, Father Theobald

References

Maguire, John Francis. *Father Mathew: A Biography.* London: Longman, Green, 1865.

Mathew, Frank J. *Father Mathew, His Life and Times.* London: Cassell, 1890.

New Advent website. http://www.newadvent.org/cathen/14482a.htm [April 2002].

Rogers, Patrick. *Father Theobald Mathew: Apostle of Temperance.* Dublin: Browne and Nolan, 1943.

Towey, Martin G., and Margaret Lopiccolo Sullivan. "The Knights of Father Mathew: Parallel Ethnic Reform," in *Missouri Historical Review.* 75 (January 1981): 168–183.

An 1886 sketch by Joseph Becker depicts the tenth annual convention of the Knights of Labor at Richmond, Virginia. (Library of Congress)

Knights of Labor

The first mass organization of the United States working class, the Knights of Labor advocated temperance as part of an effort to improve the quality of life for workers and their families. Headed during its heyday in the late 1870s and 1880s by the teetotaling Terence Powderly, the Knights of Labor feared that alcohol would enslave workers and endanger the well-being of their families. Though officially hostile to saloon keepers and distillers, most knights preferred persuasion rather than prohibition as a solution to the alcohol problem.

The Noble and Holy Order of the Knights of Labor originated in 1869 as a craft union of Philadelphia garment cutters; the order copied the rituals and secrecy of the then popular fraternal societies. Uriah Stephens, its first leader, called for an organization that would unite all workers, regardless of race, nationality, occupation, or skill level. In 1879, Powderly, a machinist from Pennsylvania, became the grand master workman of the organization, and he initiated a number of changes designed to increase membership. Under Powderly, the knights dropped all secrecy and opened their doors to all "producers," excluding from membership only bankers, lawyers, liquor dealers, speculators, and stockbrokers. When the Knights of Labor won victories against wage cuts for the workers of the largest railroads in the United States, membership soared. By 1886, the organization counted 15,000 local assemblies, representing about 1 million members. Unlike other labor unions of the day, the Knights of Labor welcomed women and African Americans, but most of those enrolled were unskilled, white, nonagricultural workers in the Northeast and Midwest.

Under Powderly, the Knights of Labor connected the struggle for labor reform with a broader vision that included opposition to liquor. As a young movement, labor needed the self-discipline of sober men to achieve both organization and power. In the eyes of many knights, alcohol hindered intellectual development and harmed the family since men who drank became enslaved by liquor. Additionally, growing capitalization of saloons, together with the expansion of saloon-linked variety theater, directly threatened a family-based producers' community. Although most unionists stopped short of prohibition, exhortations on behalf of temperance were commonplace. Abstinence never became a condition of membership, but the knights did develop an oath of temperance that became known as "the Powderly pledge."

The Knights of Labor took a number of steps to indicate their official support of temperance. Votes for women became a major goal of the union because it believed that suffrage would reduce the power of the liquor business. Prominent female knights, some of whom also belonged to the Woman's Christian Temperance Union (WCTU), often were sent by Powderly to speak before WCTU rallies. Frances Elizabeth Caroline Willard, leader of the WCTU, joined the knights in 1887, wrote frequently for its journal, and supported the union long after it had slipped in public esteem. The two organizations helped each other in securing signatures for petitions on issues of the workweek and temperance legislation.

The Knights of Labor began to collapse following Chicago's 1886 Haymarket Square riot because of a backlash against labor triggered by the violence of that day. By 1896, the Knights no longer identified themselves as a labor organization.

Caryn E. Neumann

See also: Willard, Frances Elizabeth Caroline; Woman's Christian Temperance Union (WCTU) (United States)

References

Bordin, Ruth. *Frances Willard: A Biography.* Chapel Hill: University of North Carolina Press, 1986.

Brundage, David. *The Making of Western Labor Radicalism: Denver's Organized Workers, 1878–1905.* Urbana: University of Illinois Press, 1991.

Fink, Leon. *Workingmen's Democracy: The Knights of Labor and American Politics.* Urbana: University of Illinois Press, 1983.

Gusfield, Joseph R. *Symbolic Crusade: Status Politics and the American Temperance Movement.* Urbana: University of Illinois Press, 1986.

Kolb, Lawrence (1881–1972)

Lawrence Kolb (1881–1972) was the addiction specialist of the United States Public Health Service (USPHS) from the end of World War I to the end of World War II. During that time, he handled the problems of iatrogenic addicts after passage of the Harrison Act, countered the cries of alarmists claiming the existence of millions of addicts, and became the first director of the Lexington Narcotics Farm (later the USPHS Hospital at Lexington). By the 1940s, Kolb counted alcoholism as a drug addiction and advocated building public hospitals for its treatment. Once retired from government, Kolb's opposition to the nation's draconian drug policy became more open, and he publicly called for a British-style program of drug maintenance to replace the present punitive system.

Born in 1881, Kolb graduated from the University of Maryland Medical School in 1908. Like many ambitious young physicians, especially from the rural South, Kolb was attracted to the USPHS by its professionalism, service, and paramilitary mystique. After working at a number of the least desirable stations, Kolb recognized the career advantage in becoming one of the agency's first psychiatrists.

After the end of the war, the USPHS wished to retreat from its wartime activism. Between the USPHS and this goal stood a number of propagandists, most notably the former Anti-Saloon League speaker Richmond Pearson Hobson, who asserted the existence of millions of addicts, thousands of them school children, and demanded a government solution. Lacking figures from the sale of narcotics or even numbers from the earlier maintenance clinics, Kolb and a coworker were still able to reach a remarkably accurate estimate of between 100,000 to 150,000 active addicts, which hardly constituted an epidemic.

From this start, Kolb began to study and write about addiction. Reflecting his Freudian-influenced psychiatric training, Kolb denied the prior conception of addiction as a physiological disease with hereditary components and perceived it as stemming either from careless treatment by a physician or psychological weakness rooted in one's social environment. In an investigation of 230 addicts, Kolb placed them into five psychiatric classifications: 1) mentally healthy persons who had become addicted accidentally; 2) hedonists; 3) psychoneurotics with various phobias; 4) criminal psychopaths; and 5) addictive personalities. Hedonists were by far the most common, with addictive personalities coming in second. At one point, Kolb denied the possibility of "normal" people enjoying the drug experience and becoming addicted.

For one showing such apparent lack of sympathy, Kolb ironically was tremendously empathetic toward individual addicts and bemoaned the shift from sympathy to rejection in public opinion. Kolb arranged morphine maintenance for those previously addicted. He perceived Lexington as a place for patients, not for prisoners, and blasted one of his successors for adopting the government's punitive policy. On numerous occasions, he noted that opiate addicts could work and be model citizens, while alcoholics were useless socially. The British system of opiate maintenance by physicians appealed to Kolb. The neurotic long-term addict would obtain from a doctor specializing in addiction treatment the minimum dosage needed for psychological survival; hedonists and addictive personalities would be denied access; and criminal addicts would be put in jail.

Mark C. Smith

See also: Alcoholism; Hobson, Richmond Pearson; Treatment Institutions

References

Jaffe, Arnold. *Addiction Reform in the Progressive Era: Scientific and Social Responses to Drug Dependence in the United States 1870–1930.* New York: Arno Press, 1976.

Kolb. Lawrence C. *Drug Addiction: A Medical Problem.* Springfield, IL: Charles C. Thomas, 1962.

Musto, David. *The American Disease: Origins of Narcotics Control.* New York: Oxford, 1973.

L

Labatt Brewing Company Limited

The Labatt Brewing Company Limited, rival to Molson Inc. as Canada's biggest brewer, is the chief North American arm of Belgian brewing giant Interbrew S.A. In 1828, John Balkwill established a brewery on the banks of the Thames River at London, Ontario. For the next two decades, he either personally operated his brewery or rented it to others. Burdened by debts incurred after a fire, Balkwill sold the brewery in 1847 to Samuel Eccles, an English brewmaster, and John Kinder Labatt, a farmer and native of Ireland. Eccles and Labatt put the brewery on solid financial ground and, like crosstown rivals W. and J. Carling, used the railway to develop a network of retail agencies across southwestern Ontario. By 1855, when Labatt bought out his senior partner, the brewery was a major regional player. Labatt continued to broaden the brewery's sales reach, a strategy that precipitated major plant additions in 1858 and 1863.

Upon his death in 1866, the brewery passed to his wife, Elizabeth, who operated it in partnership with their third oldest son, John Labatt. The younger Labatt bought out his mother six years later. In early 1874, a devastating fire nearly ended his venture. Shortly after rebuilding, John Labatt exercised his flair for promotion. In 1876, his India Pale Ale (the brewery's flagship brand until the 1950s) captured a gold medal at Philadelphia's Centennial Exhibition, the first of many such international prizes he would claim. The Londoner trumpeted his winning record in newspaper advertisements, promotional circulars and posters, and on his bottle labels. In the mid-1880s, the innovative Labatt began to feature label facsimiles in his advertising. Significantly, he was the first Canadian brewer to adopt this nontextual product recognition technique. He was also the first Canadian brewer to advertise consistently in demographically targeted national periodicals, ranging from highbrow current affairs monthlies to farm magazines and labor and ethnic journals.

Labatt's late-nineteenth-century national advertising campaign, together with coast-to-coast agency development and timely plant improvement, propelled his brewery to greater heights, despite the temporary spread of local-option prohibition under the Canada Temperance Act during the 1880s. By 1900, he owned one of Canada's largest brewing enterprises. Further growth and technical advancement, such as electrification and mechanical refrigeration, came early in the new century. In 1902, Labatt attained the annual production milestone of 1 million imperial gallons (1.2 million U.S. gallons). In 1911, Labatt incorporated as John Labatt Limited, a private entity. When he died four years later, his sons, John S. and Hugh F., assumed direction of the company. The brewery weathered World War I restrictions on beer making, and by routing domestic beer sales through extra-jurisdictional branch offices, the Labatt brothers cleverly steered themselves around prohibition under the Ontario Temperance Act. They also benefited from hiring a sales manager who knew how to penetrate a Prohibition-locked U.S. market. Indeed, profits from the 1920s allowed Labatt to meet the challenges of the 1930s posed by the Great Depression and the rise of E. P. Taylor's brewing conglomerate, the Brewing Corporation of Canada (later Canadian Breweries Limited). Remarkably, Labatt was one of the few Canadian brewers to survive Prohibition and the depression with its ownership and management intact. However, perhaps because of such success, John S. Labatt was kidnapped and held for ransom for a week in 1934. Although released physically unharmed, the crime diminished his trust in others, and he eventually withdrew from business affairs. In 1950, his brother, Hugh, assumed the company presidency.

In the early 1940s, Labatt management recognized that production had to move beyond London for survival in a market increasingly dominated by Canadian Breweries Limited. In 1945, John Labatt Limited went public and successfully raised capital for growth. The next year, Labatt acquired Toronto's Copland Brewery. Over the next decade and a half, the London company bought several other breweries across Canada and built a new brewery in the Montreal suburbs. A few other plants were acquired or built in the 1960s and 1970s, making for a peak total of fifteen breweries. Much of this physical expansion was carried out by a team of professional managers hired by the Labatt brothers. Reacting to changing consumer preference, this management group, led by president John H. "Jake" Moore, also committed Labatt to full-time lager brewing in the early 1950s with the development of Labatt Blue, a brand that became Canada's best-selling lager in the late 1960s and Canada's best-selling beer a decade later. During this era of expansion, Labatt turned to new forms of promotion, including television advertising and sports sponsorship. After a brief term under the ownership of Milwaukee's Joseph Schlitz Brewing Company during the mid-1960s, Labatt diversified into, among other things, chemicals, flour milling, candy retailing, wine and juice making, dairy products, and, through a part interest in the Toronto Blue Jays (named to promote Labatt Blue), major league baseball.

In the 1980s and 1990s, Labatt sold off its nonbrewing assets and faced shrinking domestic demand for beer by boosting the promotion of flagship brands, sharpening focus on niche segments within the beer market, acquiring the Canadian rights to brew Anheuser-Busch's world-famous Budweiser lager (which quickly rose to become a major selling brand in Canada), and enhancing manufacturing efficiency through plant consolidation and renovation. These changes were timely and allowed Labatt to regain market share lost to chief competitor Molson after the latter merged with Carling-O'Keefe in 1989. Indeed, since the mid-1990s, Labatt and Molson have each accounted for around 45 percent, more or less, of Canada's beer sales. The Belgium-based Interbrew S.A. bought Labatt in 1996–1997. The Belgian brewer subsequently reorganized its new acquisition as the Labatt Brewing Company Limited and placed Labatt in charge of Interbrew's affairs in North America. Now headquartered in Toronto, the Labatt Brewing Company currently operates eight breweries in Canada, including one on the original site of John Balkwill's London, Ontario, brewery. Through a subsidiary, Labatt U.S.A., Labatt controls Pennsylvania's Latrobe Brewing Company and distributes Labatt and Interbrew brands in the U.S. market.

Glen C. Phillips

See also: Canada Temperance Act; Carling Brewery; Interbrew; Molson Incorporated; Schlitz, Joseph, Brewing Company

References

Bowering, Ian. *The Art and Mystery of Brewing in Ontario.* Burnstown, Ontario: General Store Publishing, 1988.

London Free Press, 1849–2002 (select issues).

Phillips, Glen C. *On Tap: The Odyssey of Beer and Brewing in Victorian London-Middlesex.* London, Ontario: Cheshire Cat Press, 2000.

Tucker, Albert. "John Labatt" in *Dictionary of Canadian Biography,* vol. 14, *1911–1920.* Toronto: University of Toronto Press, 1998.

Labor and the Brewing Industry (United Kingdom)

Only a very small proportion of brewing historiography concerns the experiences of laborers. In most cases, little evidence has survived. Additionally, few company records convey much about the working conditions of the ordinary laborer. Some business records, however, provide valuable information about brewery workforces. Wage books, for example, give an idea of the size of a particular workforce, the length of time workers remained with firms, and rates of pay. Some newspaper material describes the paternalistic nature of labor relations, usually describing a firm's annual outing or an anniversary celebration of its owners. Not surprisingly, such optimistic sources were often created by company managers themselves, if not by a member of the clerical staff. Far more rare and neglected sources, such as punishment books, provide an interesting balance to such glowing accounts of brewery life and have made historians more skeptical of the actual workings of paternalistic managerial schemes in the industry.

In general, labor costs were low at breweries. At most firms, workers were drawn from agricultural trades, and wages were a little more than those offered by agricultural employers, but less than could be earned in most urban trades. This standard remained the case into the modern period. Averaging 24 shillings 3 pence in 1886 and only 26 shillings 3 pence in 1906, brewery wages increased more slowly than those of other industrial operatives. Wages were highest among draymen and coopers, as well as among those employed in London. In the early nineteenth century, many breweries were modest affairs, sometimes consisting only of an extension to a public house. These small operations were run by a single brewer with the assistance of a few laborers, who were employed for the extent of the brewing season, usually limited to the coldest months of the year. At the largest Burton breweries, wage ledgers in the mid-nineteenth century already listed more than 1,000 employees, though the average firm in England employed only a few dozen laborers. The entire industry in the 1870s employed more than 800,000 workers but provided employment for many more indirectly. Furthermore, these workers were not evenly distributed throughout the country but tended to concentrate in noted brewing centers, such as Burton-on-Trent and Tadcaster in England and Wrexham and Alloa in Wales and Scotland, respectively, and, in this way, greatly influenced the social and cultural life of particular regions. Despite a progressive growth in workforces over the past century, most brewers spent far greater sums on duties, raw materials, and the public houses from which their beer was sold than they did on the labor required to manufacture their product. Though the expenses associated with labor were not exorbitant at most breweries, that associated with cleaning did rise noticeably in the second half of the nineteenth century with developments in the science of fermentation.

Labor relations in the industry were in most cases very personal, breweries having been described as the most paternalistic of work environments. Most workers were known by name and encountered their employers face-to-face on a day-to-day basis, as employers, if not operative brewers themselves, often managed from the brewery floor. Even when breweries outgrew a size that permitted such intimate labor relations, paternalism remained the main method of labor management at firms well into the twentieth century. Wages were supplemented by generous benefits, including ale allowances, Christmas meat, annual outings, and even cottages, though the latter were usually reserved for a few core workers, namely, managers and the most senior employees. Although Guinness opened a brewery dispensary at the turn of the century to provide health care to its 3,500 employees and their dependents, most other breweries subscribed to local hospitals, distributing hospital admissions tickets to members of staff, or encouraged the formation of "sick clubs," which were administered by workers themselves. Not surprisingly, periods of tenure were longest among those enjoying the full range of such benefits, whereas labor turnover was at times very high among a less senior segment of brewery workforces.

Links between breweries and the countryside were very close. The same applies to distilleries. Materials and methods at firms were similar to those found on most farms. Generally, brewery laborers were recruited from rural districts and performed tasks that were familiar to most farm laborers, whether employed in malt houses or tending the horses that delivered much of the beer. As on farms, labor was very seasonal at most breweries until the late nineteenth and early twentieth centuries. The brewing season usually commenced in October and finished in the late spring with the arrival of warmer weather, which threatened to spoil entire brews. On such occasions, a large proportion of the workforce returned to their former rural occupations. With an increase in the size of breweries and, more important, the introduction of refrigeration technology, many more jobs at breweries became permanent year-round employment. As a result, flexibility, long associated with brewery work, also began to disappear.

Work was generally heavy and was carried out in the hot and dry environment of the malt house, on the one hand, or in the brewery, made warm and humid by its boiling vats, on the other. Strength was more important than skill, as raw material arrived in heavy sacks and beer was stored and delivered in heavy wooden casks. The nature of the work was often used to justify brewing as men's work, though women began to be employed in greater numbers in the late nineteenth century with the establishment of bottling plants. Hours were longest in the days before refrigeration, as it took much longer to get through an average brewing when beer was left to cool naturally through exposure to the open air. Accidents were also noticeably higher during this period, not necessarily because of the machinery but because of the long hours.

The skill associated with most brewing tasks may easily be underestimated as most laborers acquired their knowledge elsewhere, usually on farms. As a result, few laborers received any systematic training in breweries. Most entered employment with transferable skills and learned tasks by carrying them out repeatedly. Formal apprenticeships were limited to those undertaken by individuals who intended to become operative and managing brewers, though often pupils simply joined clerical staffs and never actually brewed. Such training cost between £100 and £400 at most provincial firms and lasted between two and seven years, shorter periods of instruction becoming more common in the late nineteenth century. Indentures survive for

Workers at Young's brewery in England unbung barrels for filling with beer, 1969. (Hulton/Archive)

an earlier period, but many apprenticeships in these years were informal contracts and evidence concerning agreements survives only in company letter books. Other workers who undertook formal apprenticeships at breweries included certain ancillary workers, such as coopers, painters, and carpenters. Terms and conditions of such indentures varied by region and depended on levels of unionization.

Most brewery workers remained nonunionized until the interwar period. The first workers to organize were coopers. Organization among ordinary brewery laborers commenced in the late nineteenth century and in the Burton-on-Trent region. In 1913 to 1914, approximately 3,700 Burton workers had unionized and strikes occurred at a number of firms for increased pay. In February 1914, the National Union of Brewery Workers was founded in London. Besides sending recruitment officers throughout the country, its leader, Ed Pratt, declared class war against "brewer kings." Despite such threats, unions remained weak after the war, presumably because disruption often resulted in the immediate loss of workers' numerous benefits, if not their actual jobs. In general, North American and German brewery workers organized far earlier and more effectively than their English counterparts.

Paternalism remained the main labor management strategy at breweries well into the twentieth century. Owners continued to deal with workers' demands on an individual basis, and many welfare schemes commenced by benevolent owner-employers were continued after incorporation. Regarded as out of place in an era of industrial capitalism, such schemes have been described by historians as little more than an antidote to unionization in the industry. In any case, welfare continued to expand at many breweries throughout the 1920s, and pensions and week-long paid holidays were provided at even the smallest provincial firms in these years. During the 1930s, modern cafeterias replaced many canteens, and sporting facilities became usual at most breweries. Profit-sharing schemes also were introduced in these years, occasionally in direct response to strike threats. With consolidation in the industry, numbers of employees at individual plants increased, averaging 150 in the early 1960s and more than 300 in the early 1970s. Nevertheless, compared with the other costs of production, labor still made up only 7.2 percent of brewery expenses in 1965.

Jonathan Reinarz

See also: Beer; Brewers' Society (BS)

References

Donnachie, Ian. *A History of the Brewing Industry in Scotland.* 2d ed. Edinburgh: John Donald Publishers, 1998.

Fitzgerald, Robert. *British Labour Management and Industrial Welfare, 1846–1939.* London: Croom Helm, 1988.

Freeman, Mark. "Employment in the Islay Distilleries, 1841–1914" in *Scottish Labour History.* 35 (2000): 55–67.

Gourvish, Terry R., and Richard G. Wilson. *The British Brewing Industry, 1830–1980.* Cambridge: Cambridge University Press, 1994.

Mathias, Peter. *The Brewing Industry in England, 1700–1830.* Cambridge: Cambridge University Press, 1959.

Reinarz, Jonathan. "An Easy Transition: Brewery Life and Labour in the Midlands, 1850–1914" in *Midland History.* 28 (2003): 88–89.

———. "Fit for Management: Apprenticeship and the English Brewing Industry, 1870–1914" in *Business History.* 43 (2001): 33–53.

———. "A Social History of a Midland Business: Flower & Sons Brewery, 1870–1914" (Ph.D. dissertation, University of Warwick, 1998).

Labor in the U.S. Liquor Industry

The U.S. liquor industry existed before the American Revolution and survived National Prohibition. The workers have undergone historic struggles and change as unions developed and labor standards improved.

Statistics

In 1997, there were 529 breweries in the United States, with 34,251 employees and a payroll of $1,598,573,000. Of this total, 24,205 employees were involved in production, working 43,800,000 hours with wages of $1,083,121,000, or, on average, 34 hours a week for $24 an hour. These workers were involved in all aspects of production below the rank of line supervisor, including assembly, fabrication, warehousing, and shipping, but not delivery (U.S. Census Bureau 2001a).

Most of these operations were small: In that same year, there were only 156 breweries with 20 or more employees. California, with the largest industry share, had 66 breweries and 3,642 employees, and Wisconsin, with the smallest, had 22 with 1,849 workers. The relatively large number of breweries in the United States reflects the expansion of microbreweries in the past twenty years (U.S. Census Bureau 2001a).

There were 60 distilleries, with 6,545 employees and a payroll of $252,392,000. Production workers made up over two-thirds of the workforce, 4,674, and worked 9,737,000 hours for $158,370,000. They made $16 an hour and worked a 40-hour week. Kentucky alone had 16 distilleries (U.S. Census Bureau 2001b).

The manufacture of beer and distilling have many similarities. By distilling a fermented mash, or "beer," producers create whiskey. Both industrial processes require the stages of grain handling, mashing, fermentation, storage, and delivery. They also require similar workforces.

There were 687 wineries in the United States, with 18,193 employees and a payroll of $668,051,000. There were 8,572 production workers, who worked 15,784,000 hours for wages of $238,543,000. Thus, they worked an average of 35 hours a week for $15 an hour. California had over half the wineries in the United States (U.S. Census Bureau 2001c).

In 2000, in New York State wineries 32 percent of the 2,700 workers made the wine. This group made up the largest part of

Women label bottles of wine at a winery in Sonoma County, California, 1942. (Library of Congress)

the workforce for this segment of the liquor industry. Another 30 percent worked in the tasting rooms, a retail offshoot of wine production (Blackson 2002).

In addition, approximately 379,990 people in the United States worked as bartenders. The mean hourly wage was $7.77 and their mean annual wage was $16,150. Bartenders, along with tasting room employees, are categorized in the retail end of the liquor industry, which also includes owners and employees of package and liquor stores. Other aspects of the liquor industry that fall outside of production or manufacturing include importers and wholesalers.

Unions

Many of the workers in the U.S. liquor industry belong to unions. Several of the unions have long histories. In 1884, New York brewery workers founded Brewer's Union No. 1 as part of the Knights of Labor Local Assembly 1672. Following a successful boycott in 1885, this group expanded to become an industry-wide union of all brewery workers in the New York City metropolitan area. This was the Brewer's, Beer Driver's and Maltsters Union.

In 1886, representatives from unions in New York City, Newark, Philadelphia, Detroit, and Baltimore met to organize a national brewery workers union, becoming the National Union of United Brewery Workmen. The United Brewery Workmen (UBW) was one of the nation's first industrial unions and included all brewery workers. Distillery workers remained unorganized until the 1930s, and the coopers had their own union, affiliated with the American Federation of Labor (AF of L). In an era of craft unionism, the UBW stood out for its dual commitment to socialism and industrial unionism. In 1887, it received an AF of L charter, eventually leading to the dissolution of the preexisting Knights of Labor locals. Over time, the UBW had become increasingly disenchanted with the prohibitionist stance of the Knights.

New York brewers locked out the union in 1888, and AF of L president Samuel Gompers acted as its counsel. Gompers seems to have been of two minds regarding the UBW and its industrial unionism, first proposing that the UBW join with two craft unions and essentially become a craft union itself. However, in 1906 he fought expulsion of the UBW from the AF of L. In 1900, the UBW faced competition from a newly formed Teamsters Union of midwestern deliverymen. The Teamsters sought jurisdiction over beer truck drivers, engineers, and firemen. In both 1901 and 1906, the AF of L voted against the UBW and granted jurisdiction to the Teamsters. The UBW was expelled from the

AF of L in 1907 because it would not abandon its industrial union structure. It was reinstated the following year. During Prohibition, the AF of L granted the UBW jurisdiction over flour, cereal, and soft-drink workers in an effort to increase membership.

Jurisdictional conflicts persisted through and beyond Prohibition, resulting in revocation of the UBW's charter again in 1941. In 1946, the UBW joined the Congress of Industrial Organizations (CIO), becoming the International Union of United Brewery, Flour, Cereal, Soft Drink and Distillery Workers of America. The current union is affiliated with the Teamsters and is called the Brewery and Soft Drink Workers Conference–U.S.A. and Canada. In 1998, it had 75,000 members.

The distilled spirits industry did not participate in the labor movement until the Great Depression, when workers formed the CIO's Distillery Workers' Organizing Committee. The Distillery, Wine and Allied Workers International Union was chartered in 1940. In 1995, it merged with the United Food and Commercial Workers International Union, or UFCW, which had been established in 1979. The organization today has approximately 1.4 million members in the United States, including distillery workers, liquor salesmen, and wholesale wine salesmen, and is part of the AFL-CIO.

The Hotel Employees and Restaurant Employees (HERE) International Union represents bartenders. Founded in 1891, the union was formerly called Hotel and Restaurant Employees and Bartenders Union. It has 265,000 members who are involved in various aspects of the hospitality industry. The union was originally craft-based, with the bartenders having a separate union, but in 1973 the union reorganized along industrial lines. It, too, is affiliated with the AFL-CIO.

To make wine you need someone to pick the grapes. Thus, many of the workers in the wine business are farm workers. There are 11,043 grape vineyards in the United States. The United Farm Workers (UFW) represents some of them.

Labor Disputes

Cesar Chavez and the United Farm Workers first gained national attention in 1965 over their involvement in a Filipino farm workers' strike at vineyards in Delano, California. A consumer boycott of grapes was one of the tactics the UFW successfully used to achieve victory in the 1970s.

In 1994, workers at an E&J Gallo vineyard in Sonoma County, California, voted to join the UFW. Gallo, the world's largest wine company, resisted, leading to a six-year battle. In 2000, the union and Gallo signed a contract, the first between the two sides since 1973. According to its terms, workers at Gallo Sonoma would make from $8.60 to $13.40 an hour and all direct-hire workers would continue to receive medical, vacation, and pension benefits. At the time, the vineyard employed 450 workers. The UFW also represents two other vineyards in Sonoma, as well as 350 workers at three vineyards in Napa Valley.

In 1998, Sonoma County vineyards employed 3,800 farm workers, primarily men. The average yearly salary was $18,500. Vineyards also contract with farm management and vineyard services companies for labor. These contract workers, about 500, make less than direct-hire workers. Neither group of workers makes a living wage. In 1977, Local 366 of the UBW in Colorado initiated a strike against the Adolph Coors Brewing Company, at that time the fifth largest brewer in the country. Coors had a history of supporting conservative causes and sought changes in the seniority system and a diminished role for the local union, particularly in disciplinary areas. The union saw these actions as attempts at union busting. After two weeks of striking, over half the workers returned to work. The company hired new workers to replace those who remained on strike. Coors was seeking an open shop, although it had been a union shop for forty-two years. In 1978, employees decertified the union.

In response, the union charged Coors with discriminatory hiring. Hispanics, feminists, and homosexual activists began a national boycott. The boycott was a tactic the UBW and other unions had used very successfully in the nineteenth century. This new boycott was very effective, cutting sales in California by 15 percent. California accounted for over 45 percent of Coors's market. Coors was attempting to expand its market base beyond the western states, and the boycott thwarted these efforts. The dispute between the union and Coors lasted ten years, ending in 1987. In the settlement, Coors pledged noninterference with union organizing and agreed to use union contractors for a proposed building project. In response, the union halted the boycott. Coors changed its hiring practices and advertising focus. By 2003, sixteen years after the strike ended, Coors had a national market and ranked as the nation's third largest brewer.

In 2000, the UFCW supported a strike of 118 workers against the Wild Turkey Distillery in Lawrenceburg, Kentucky. The strike, which lasted four weeks, involved wages, pension coverage, health insurance, and hiring of temporary workers. The union achieved all its demands except for the ones involving Workers' Compensation.

Amy Mittelman

See also: Coors, Adolph, Brewing Company; Gallo; Knights of Labor

References

Appalachian Focus Labor News website. http://www.appalachianfocus.org/_labor/00000054.htm.

Blackson, William. "New York Wineries Employ 2,700." U.S. Department of Agriculture, 8 March 2002 press release. http://www.nass.usda.gov/ny/03mar/win203038.htm.

Craft, Donna, and Terrance W. Peck, eds. *Profiles of American Labor Unions.* Detroit: Gale, 1998.

Downard, William L. *Dictionary of the History of the American Brewing and Distilling Industries.* Westport, CT: Greenwood, 1980.

Filippelli, Ronald, ed. *Labor Conflict in the United States: An Encyclopedia.* New York: Garland, 1990.

Fink, Gary M., ed. *Biographical Dictionary of American Labor.* Westport, CT: Greenwood, 1984.

Hotel Employees and Restaurant Employers (HERE) International Union website. http://www.hereunion.org/about/default.asp.

Mittelman, Amy H. "The Politics of Alcohol Production: The Liquor Industry and the Federal Government, 1862–1900" (Ph.D. dissertation, Columbia University, 1986).

Tesconi, Tim. "Historic Gallo-UFW Contract: Sonoma County Agreement Ends Bitter Dispute" in *The Press Democrat,* Santa Rosa, California. 1 September 2000.

———. "Spreading Vines: Farmworkers Not Prospering" in *The Press Democrat,* Santa Rosa, California. 1 November 1999.

U.S. Census Bureau. *Breweries: 1997 Economic Census, Manufacturing.* Washington, DC: GPO, 2001a. http://www.census.gov.

———. *Distilleries: 1997 Economic Census, Manufacturing.* Washington, DC: GPO, 2001b. http://www.census.gov.

———. *Wineries: 1997 Economic Census, Manufacturing.* Washington, DC: GPO, 2001c. http://www.census.gov.

Wall, J. K. "Strike Ends at Wild Turkey: Union Accepts 4-Year Deal" in *Herald-Leader.* 11 April 2000.

Labour Party (United Kingdom)

When investigating the relationship between the British Labour Party and the temperance movement, it is essential to distinguish between the views of nineteenth-century socialists and that of the Labour Party of the first three decades of the twentieth century. There was sympathy and support for drastic restriction of the drink trade or even for its abolition among the majority of Victorian socialists. With the growing political power of the Labour Party in the next century, other issues began to take precedence over the regulation of alcohol consumption.

For much of the nineteenth century, beer was cheaper than tea. When cost was added to the widespread belief in the physically strengthening and pain-killing properties of beer, there is little wonder that consumption of alcohol, mainly in the form of beer, was high. Public houses often served as meeting places for social and political organizations of the working population, and this reinforced the centrality of alcohol in working-class culture.

The Beginnings

Starting with the Chartist political reform movement in the mid-nineteenth century, there grew an easy alliance between those who worked for political change as a means of bettering the state of the workers and those who advocated restriction or abolition of drink as a means of improving the lives of the masses. Both groups were suspicious of the established Church of England and the aristocratic wielders of political power. In addition, the emphasis on individual effort provided common ground. The Chartists were also eager to attract middle-class support, which provided the backbone of the temperance movement.

A small schism in this coalition began to appear, however, with the growing numbers and influence of socialists. The aims of the two movements were the same: to end poverty and lift the standard of living of the average working person. But socialists blamed industrialization and urbanization for the degraded conditions of workers' lives. Instead of indicting the whole economic system, temperance advocates stressed the moral aspects of overindulgence. Temperance supporters argued that the individual was responsible for his poverty by spending his money on drink. If people would adhere to sobriety and the thrift ethic, then their savings would increase along with the well-being of their families.

This contrast between individual reform and economic revolution did not immediately cause widespread friction. By the 1880s, when politically active workingmen began standing for election, the most prominent among them, such as James Keir Hardie and Arthur Henderson, had been temperance activists. The temperance movement held a wide support and possessed a moral authority. Working-class advocates were reluctant to criticize it publicly.

With the two voting reform acts in the last third of the nineteenth century, labor leaders began to acquire a political base from which they could espouse their socialist philosophy. The solution to poverty and unemployment, they felt, was collective ownership and management of the means of production. In 1893, weary of relying on the promises of the Liberal and Conservative parties, workingmen formed the Independent Labour Party (ILP) to advance the socialist philosophy. Later, the ILP joined with other socialist societies and trade unions in the Labour Representation Committee, committed to electing workingmen to Parliament. By 1906, when there were twenty-nine Labor members of Parliament, the name of the committee was changed to the Labour Party.

The Labour Party and Temperance

It is in the early twentieth century that the sympathetic alliance among the Labour Party, socialists, and temperance advocates began to splinter badly. The aim of bettering the life of the working citizen remained foremost for all, but the means of doing so diverged. Temperance supporters still attributed the degraded living conditions to an individual weakness of will. Socialists argued that universal abstinence combined with the traditional Victorian value of thrift would convince employers that wages could be lowered and not produce a higher standard of living. Moreover, the official policy of the Labour Party urged public control of drinking establishments with the profits to be used for the benefit of the working class. This approach was anathema to most temperance reformers.

By the time that Ramsay MacDonald became the first Labour prime minister in 1924, there were three schools of thought in his party. One urged the transfer of the drink trade to public control. Another held that alcohol and drinking establishments were an integral part of working-class social life. And a small but vocal faction still argued for total abstinence. This internal dispute as to what the Labour Party policy should be is reflected in the 1923 Labour Party report on drink, which concluded that there was no single remedy that would cure social ills.

The drink problem gradually lost prominence in the debate over unemployment and poverty. In the early 1920s, the Labour Party dropped its committee on temperance. By the 1930s, with the failed U.S. experiment, prohibition seemed irrelevant. Instead, socialism was the answer to society's ills.

In 2003, a Labour government introduced a bill to end restrictions on hours when pubs could sell alcoholic beverages and to transfer authority over licensing from the justices of the peace to local councils. Any identification between Labour and temperance had disappeared many years earlier.

Cynthia Curran

See also: Chartism; Gothenburg Schemes/Disinterested Management; Scrymgeour, Edwin

References

Catterall, Peter. "Morality and Politics: The Free Churches and the Labour Party between the Wars" in *Historical Journal.* 36 (1993): 667–685.

Harrison, Brian. *Drink and the Victorians: The Temperance Question in England, 1815–1872.* London: Faber & Faber, 1971; 2d ed., Keele: Keele University Press, 1994.

Jones, Stephen G. "Labour, Society and the Drink Question in Britain, 1918–1939" in *Historical Journal.* 30 (March 1987): 105–122.

McKibbin, Ross. *The Evolution of the Labour Party, 1910–1924.* London: Oxford University Press, 1974.

Shiman, Lilian Lewis. *Crusade against Drink in Victorian England.* New York: St. Martin's, 1988.

Lane, William (1861–1917)

William Lane (1861–1917) was an influential Australian labor journalist, a utopian socialist, and a stern advocate of temperance. As editor of the union paper *The Worker,* Lane emerged as a prominent labor movement leader during the "great strikes" of 1890–1891 and played a key role in the foundation of the Australian Labor Party. Throughout this period, he was renowned for his uncompromising views on teetotalism. For Lane, drink was the worker's curse; it led to ill-disciplined behavior, personal weakness, domestic violence, and the betrayal of fellow workers. In his journalism and throughout his novel *The Workingman's Paradise,* first published in 1892, Lane portrayed temperance as a defining element of a new, industrially organized, respectable union movement. In contrast to most Christian temperance organizations, which linked intemperance with working-class poverty, Lane's position emphasized solidarity and self-respect. He wrote, for example, "Drink is the worker's greatest enemy; not because it costs so much, for if we all lived on rice we should not always have enough, but because it makes us as brutes who have not understanding, because it shears off the long hair of the Samson of labour" (*Worker,* 1 July 1890: 2)

For Lane, the temperance issue was ultimately one of the trustworthiness and reliability of political and industrial representatives. To this end, he argued that intemperate men should be blocked "from all prominence in the organization of labour" (*Worker,* 7 August 1890: 3). The wider influence of Lane's views on temperance was evident in the 1892 Labor electoral platform, which aimed to "secure sober men for election to parliament."

In 1893, disillusioned with the slow pace of reform, Lane led 400 Australians to Paraguay to found the "New Australia" colony—a cooperative land settlement hailed as an "experiment in practical communism." One of the articles in the constitution of the New Australia Cooperative Settlement Association required that "members shall pledge themselves to teetotalism until the initial difficulties of settlement have passed and the constitution has been established." For Lane, temperance was essential to ensure the colonists lived a "straight, honest and manly" life of "mateship" (*Worker* 6 February 1892: 1). This pledge was so scrupulously enforced that a keg of molasses, purchased for the colony children, was thrown overboard en route to the settlement. In the harsh conditions of the new colony, with few single women and much backbreaking labor, the temperance pledge proved too much for many of the colony's single men. Three members broke the pledge within weeks; they were expelled soon afterward. Opposition to the expulsion led to a major split in the New Australia colony and ultimately precipitated its downfall. In May 1894, Lane and sixty supporters split to form a separate colony, called Cosme, further south in Paraguay. Potential members of the new colony were advised that "Cosme is for English-speaking whites, who accept the life marriage, the colour line, and teetotalism among their principles, and who realise in their hearts that communism is right" (Whitehead 1997: 224). Cosme operated on communal and temperance principles until the remaining members dissolved the association in 1907. Lane left Cosme in 1899; after a brief stint as editor of the Sydney *Worker,* he moved to New Zealand, ultimately becoming a well-known conservative columnist for the *New Zealand Herald.*

Michael Leach

See also: Australia; Woman's Christian Temperance Union (WCTU) (Australia)

References

Lane, W. ("John Miller"). *The Workingman's Paradise: An Australian Labour Novel.* Sydney: Sydney University Press, 1980 [1892].

Souter, G. *A Peculiar People: The Australian in Paraguay.* Sydney: Sydney University Press, 1968.

Whitehead, A. *Paradise Mislaid: In Search of the Australian Tribe of Paraguay.* St. Lucia: University of Queensland Press, 1997.

The Worker. Brisbane, Queensland. 1890–1892.

Lauer, Frederick (1810–1883)

Frederick Lauer (1810–1883), one of the nineteenth century's most prominent brewers, was born in Germany, but his family, wealthy Bavarian landowners, left for political reasons and immigrated to Reading, Pennsylvania, in 1822. In 1826, George Lauer, Frederick's father, built a brewery on the site of an Indian cabin in Reading. Frederick eventually became the owner of this brewery, one of Reading's prominent citizens, and a well-known lobbyist for the United States Brewers' Association (USBA) in Washington. Lauer actively participated in the USBA from the first national convention in 1862 until his death in 1883.

German American brewers founded the USBA in response to the initiation of federal taxes on alcohol to help finance the Civil War. The first national meeting was in New York on 12 November 1862, where Frederick Lauer was elected president of the new organization. In 1863, the USBA appointed Lauer chair of a committee charged with oversight of the industry's Washington affairs.

The most pressing concern of the brewers was a refund of taxes paid on beer brewed before the tax law took effect. Lauer, along with other brewers, paid taxes on his stock on hand on 1 September 1862. The brewers' argument for a refund was based on the specific fermentation and storage involved in producing lager beer. Lauer worked diligently pursuing this matter with Congress, and ultimately the brewers won the issue by suing and winning in the Court of Claims. Lauer achieved both a personal and industry victory.

In 1865, Secretary of the Treasury Hugh McCulloch established a commission to study the U.S. revenue system. The USBA and the Association of Ale, Porter and Lager Beer Brewers, a sister organization of ale-brewers, successfully requested that a panel be authorized to investigate the excise laws of Europe as they pertained to malt beverages. Ale brewers Frederick Collins of New York and Mathew Read of Philadelphia visited Great Britain for two weeks. Frederick Lauer joined them in visiting Belgium, France, the German states, and Switzerland.

David Wells, the chair of the Revenue Commission, used the brewers' report, published under the auspices of the USBA, verbatim. Lauer and the USBA were very successful in establishing an amicable working relationship with government officials. The work they did with David Wells and the Revenue Commission in establishing the method of tax collection for beer was long-lasting. The stamp attached to the spigot of every barrel removed from a brewery remained the technique through which the federal government collected the excise until National Prohibition.

Building on their success with refunds and collections, the USBA established an Agitation Committee, which Frederick Lauer chaired. This committee met regularly with officials and legislators, particularly when legislation was pending that was relevant to the industry. Its greatest triumph came in holding the line on tax increases for thirty-four years. During the same period, 1864 to 1898, taxes on distilled spirits increased three times.

The Frederick Lauer Monument in Reading, Pennsylvania (Historical Society of Berks County)

Frederick Lauer was more prominent through his work as a brewing advocate than he was as a brewer. The Lauer brewery was never a national leader, although it was the third largest in Pennsylvania at one time. Lauer turned brewery management over to his sons, Frank and George, in 1882. He died on 12 September 1883. In 1885, the USBA erected a statue in his honor in City Park, Reading, Pennsylvania. It still exists and is maintained by the Historical Society of Berks County, Pennsylvania.

Amy Mittelman

See also: Taxation of Liquor (United States); United States Brewers' Association (USBA)

References

Downward, William L. *Dictionary of the History of the American Brewing and Distilling Industries.* Westport, CT: Greenwood, 1980.

Mittelman, Amy H. "The Politics of Alcohol Production: The Liquor Industry and the Federal Government, 1862–1900" (Ph.D. dissertation, Columbia University, 1986).

Smith, Gregg. "The Fredrick Lauer Story." The Real Beer Page. http://www.realbeer.com/.

Laurier, Sir Wilfrid (1841–1919)

Sir Wilfrid Laurier (1841–1919), Canadian statesman, prime minister, and leader of the Liberal Party, oversaw a prohibition plebiscite in 1898 but did not proceed with prohibition legislation. Born 20 November 1841 in St. Lin, Canada East (later Quebec), Laurier attended a local elementary school before going to New Glasgow to learn English. He studied at a Roman Catholic college for seven years, then entered the law school at McGill University, from which he graduated in 1864. He joined the provincial legislature in 1871 as the Liberal Party member for

Drummond-Athabaska and resigned in 1874 to become Liberal member to the federal parliament in Ottawa. In 1887, he succeeded Edward Blake as the leader of the federal Liberal Party.

Laurier was an admirer of British liberalism, and he believed that all Canadians of all ancestries could live together in one nation. This belief helped him to reconcile his earlier opposition to Confederation and colored much of his political career, including his relations to the prohibition movement.

In 1893, in spite of Laurier's misgivings, the Liberal Party resolved that when elected it would hold a national prohibition plebiscite and enact a prohibition law if the plebiscite should demonstrate support of the issue. In 1896, when the Liberal Party came to power, Laurier—who rarely drank but did not believe in prohibition—was faced with the task of honoring this pledge. The plebiscite was held in 1898. Although the national numbers showed that a majority favored prohibition, some provinces gave marginal support, and in Quebec 60,553 of 74,259 ballots were cast against prohibition. Quebec voters had apparently listened to Liberals in the province who had said that a vote for prohibition would cause the fall of Laurier, the first French Canadian prime minister.

In March 1899, after being urged by the Dominion Alliance for the Total Suppression of the Liquor Trade to enact the promised prohibitory legislation, Laurier refused to comply. He argued that the small voter turnout (only 44 percent of the electorate) meant that only 23 percent of the electors had voted for prohibition. The plebiscite, he argued, did not represent the will of the people. Cynics observed that much of his party's support was in Quebec, and that he could not afford to oppose the wishes of that province's voters. Yet there were other factors affecting Laurier's decision not to act. Although liquor brought in about $8 million (Canadian) in taxes, enforcing a prohibition law would have cost nearly $22 million (Canadian). Moreover, the outcome of the plebiscite must be considered in relation to Laurier's efforts to unify the country and promote equality among all the provinces. Legislation that was overwhelmingly opposed by French Canadians would have undermined Laurier's efforts at forging a united nation.

Laurier was strongly condemned for what prohibition forces saw as breaking the promise the party had made in 1893, though his decision does not appear to have affected his political future. He remained prime minister until 1911 and continued as Liberal leader until his death in 1919.

Daniel J. Malleck

See also: Dominion Alliance for the Total Suppression of the Liquor Traffic; Royal Commission on the Liquor Traffic (Canada)

References

Lapierre, Laurier L. *Sir Wilfrid Laurier and the Romance of Canada.* Toronto: Stoddart, 1996.

Smart, Reginald, and Alan Ogborne. *Northern Spirits: A Social History of Alcohol in Canada.* 2d ed. Toronto: Addiction Research Foundation of Ontario, 1996.

Spence, Ruth. *Prohibition in Canada: A Memorial to Francis Stephens Spence.* Toronto: Ontario Branch of the Dominion Alliance, 1919.

Lawson, Sir Wilfrid (1829–1906)

Sir Wilfrid Lawson, Bt. (1829–1906), was the chief parliamentary spokesman for the prohibitionists in the United Kingdom during the latter half of the nineteenth century. He was member of Parliament for most of the period from 1859 to 1906 (with three short gaps) and stood on the radical wing of the Gladstonian Liberal Party. He was president of the United Kingdom Alliance (UKA) from 1879 until his death and tirelessly promoted the cause of local veto.

The nephew of the statesman Sir James Graham, Lawson was an unlikely leader of the prohibitionists, coming as he did from a long-established landed family and enjoying country pursuits, such as fox-hunting. However, his father, also Sir Wilfrid Lawson, was a strong temperance supporter and had supported various radical and religious causes. In 1864, the younger Lawson agreed to take up the UKA's Permissive Bill, which was designed to allow prohibition by local veto on a plebiscitory vote by ratepayers. This he regularly introduced as a "hardy annual" until 1879, when he and the UKA changed tack and introduced a more general resolution for "local option," which received the support of a majority in the House of Commons in 1883.

Lawson was an extremely witty speaker who did much to popularize the cause of temperance reform both in Parliament and throughout the country. However, his somewhat unworldly approach to political life and his single-minded interest in local veto as the answer to the drink question left him open to the charge of obstruction. Compromise was alien to his political mentality, and he would have no truck with licensing reform schemes. Hence, he firmly opposed efforts by governments in 1871, 1888, and 1890 to introduce schemes to reduce the numbers of liquor licenses in the United Kingdom. He was equally intolerant of efforts by fellow reformers to combine local veto with other forms of local control of the liquor traffic, especially after the reports of the royal commission in 1899. Even when Sir William Harcourt, the chancellor of the exchequer, introduced local-veto bills in 1893 and 1895, Lawson was strangely aloof and did little to mobilize effective support. Indeed, throughout his career Lawson maintained a somewhat detached attitude to the UKA, regarding himself as its parliamentary spokesman rather than its leader.

Lawson was the archetypal backbencher who placed conscience above party considerations. He saw himself as an agitator, not a legislator. Temperance was only one of the causes he championed; among the others were extension of the franchise, anti-imperialism, reduced expenditure on armaments, disestablishment of the Church, and Irish home rule. He had a profound suspicion of all in authority and combined exaggerated rationality with great humor. In his view of the political process, progress came from below, being generated by the people. Stupid, timid, and corrupt politicians among the governing class, he believed, needed to be coerced by the force of public opinion.

John Greenaway

See also: Gothenburg Schemes/Disinterested Management; Harcourt, Sir William; Liberal Party (United Kingdom); Local Option; United Kingdom Alliance (UKA)

References

Dingle, A. E. *The Campaign for Prohibition in Victorian England: The United Kingdom Alliance, 1872–1895.* London: Croom Helm, 1980.

Hamer, D. A. *The Politics of Electoral Pressure: A Study in the History of Victorian Reform Agitations.* Hassocks: Harvester Press, 1977.

Harrison, Brian. *Drink and the Victorians: The Temperance Question in England, 1815–1872.* London: Faber & Faber, 1971; 2d ed., Keele: Keele University Press, 1994.

Russell, George W. E., ed. *Sir Wilfrid Lawson: A Memoir.* London: Smith Elder & Co., 1909.

League of Nations Health Organisation (LNHO)

The League of Nations Health Organisation (LNHO) was the first global institution to deal with a wide spectrum of health-related topics, above all infectious and social diseases. Among these alcoholism played a limited part, but one that suggested the difficulties of dealing with such a politically sensitive issue in an international forum.

Alcoholism was clearly of some concern to a number of countries, as became evident through its inclusion in the International Health Yearbook, published by the LNHO from 1924 to 1930. However, the organization was reluctant to take up the issue directly.

After a failed attempt in 1927, it was not until 1928 that a resolution was successfully submitted to the League of Nations Assembly by the Finnish, Swedish, and Polish delegations. This document advocated research on the effects of alcohol, particularly alcohol of bad quality, excluding wine, beer, and cider. Several nongovernmental organizations from various European countries expressed approval or disapproval based on the perceived danger of growing alcoholism and the perceived threat of liberty-curtailing tendencies in the temperance movement. Discussions in the Health Committee, a group of medical experts who formed the decision-making body of the LNHO, also proved controversial. It was questioned whether a collection of data would serve any useful purpose, given the abundance of already-existing material. In addition, the exclusion of soft alcohol and the lack of definition of terms such as "abuse of alcohol" and "alcoholism" were criticized. The issue, therefore, was referred back to the original governments so that they could define more precisely the lines of international inquiry to be undertaken and the type of international information that would address their needs. Eventually, the governments focused on possible connections between alcoholism and several illnesses (tuberculosis, mental illness, and venereal diseases) and accidents. Once more, the members of the Health Committee, particularly Medical Director Ludwik Rajchman, doubted the usefulness of amassing data that were already known and would in all probability result in no coherent picture. However, the scientific ambiguity was only part of the problem. There were explicit concerns that published results might alienate some groups and be misused by others. Finally, the LNHO merely prepared a bibliographic report on accidents and alcohol, collected data on the control of the consumption of spirits in selected countries, and provided the three interested governments with literature on tuberculosis and delirium tremens in Scandinavian countries.

The topic was taken up again in an article in the *Health Organisation Bulletin* in 1941, written by Dr. G. Szulc, the Polish member of the Health Committee. Szulc had taken part in the large XXIst International Congress on Alcoholism in Warsaw in 1937. He subsequently urged more active involvement of the League of Nations, which he considered particularly well placed to reconcile medical and economic interests in various countries. His lengthy report delineated the impact of alcohol on rural life in terms that were both positive (as a source of income to farmers growing grapes, grain, or potatoes and to people working in distilleries and pubs) and negative (as a factor contributing to crime, road accidents, illness, and other accidental deaths). World War II, however, prevented further involvement of the LNHO in issues surrounding alcoholism.

Iris Borowy

See also: World Health Organization (WHO)

References

Dubin, Martin. "The League of Nations Health Organisation" in *International Health Organisations and Movements, 1918–1939,* edited by Paul Weindling, 56–80. Cambridge: Cambridge University Press, 1995.

Goodman, Neville. *International Health Organizations and Their Work.* Edinburgh and London: Churchill Livingstone, 1971.

Leavitt, Mary Greenleaf Clement (1830–1912)

Peripatetic temperance crusader, protégée of Frances Willard, and "ambassador at large" for the Woman's Christian Temperance Union (WCTU), Mary Greenleaf Clement Leavitt (1830–1912) traveled the world spreading the call for temperance and establishing chapters of the WCTU. At Willard's encouragement, Leavitt spent nearly ten years organizing eighty-six international WCTU chapters and twenty-one men's temperance societies in more than forty countries.

Born on 22 September 1830 in Hopkinton, New Hampshire, Mary Clement was educated at the State Normal School in West

Newton, Massachusetts, graduating in 1851. She spent the next six years in various teaching positions before marrying Thomas H. Leavitt in 1857. The two had three daughters before Thomas Leavitt's death, at which time Leavitt returned to teaching. In 1867, she established her own private school for girls in Boston. In all, she spent twenty-five years teaching.

At around this same time, Leavitt became active in temperance work and was shortly appointed to the Massachusetts State Executive Board of the WCTU, quickly rising to prominence as a national speaker. Her speaking style was ministerial and evangelistic, and she emphasized the effects of alcohol abuse on the wives and children of drinkers. Her speeches often contained both Christian ideology and personal anecdotes bearing witness to the redemptive powers of prayer for problem drinkers. Her focus tended toward individual responsibility and social change rather than direct political action.

It is unclear when she first came to the attention of national WCTU leader Frances Willard (president from 1879 to 1898), but at the National Convention of 1883 the two women discussed the desire to create international chapters. Initially hesitant, Leavitt, her daughters now grown, was eventually persuaded by Willard to accept the role of ambassador and organizer. In late 1884, she departed San Francisco bound for Honolulu and began what would be nearly a decade of continuous travel proselytizing for the WCTU and its message.

Her journeys took her to every continent and to nearly fifty countries (accounts vary), alternating summers in Europe and Asia with winters in Central and South America. Often she carried with her the Willard-penned "Polyglot Petition," a document addressed "to all the nations of the world" urging world leaders to endorse temperance. The petition would eventually claim 7 million signatures gathered from more than fifty nations. By the end of her travels, Leavitt was an internationally known and celebrated figure in the temperance movement. At the first World WCTU Convention held in 1891 in Boston, she was hailed as "ambassador at large" to the world and elected "Honorary Life President of the World WCTU." Representatives of fourteen nations whose chapters had been organized by Leavitt attended the convention.

Leavitt spent her final years writing tracts and booklets on temperance and Christian topics. These works were distributed throughout the world and translated into forty-seven languages. She died in Boston on 6 February 1912.

John P. Hundley

See also: Willard, Frances Elizabeth Caroline; World's Woman's Christian Temperance Union (WWCTU)

References

Cherrington, Ernest Hurst, et al., eds. *Standard Encyclopedia of the Alcohol Problem,* 6 vols. Westerville, OH: American Issue Publishing Co., 1925–1930, vol. 4: 1525.

Leavitt, Mary Clement, "World Trip of a Pioneer: A Ten Years' White Ribbon Missionary Journey in Fifty Foreign Countries" in *The New Voice.* 4 February 1904.

"Leavitt, Mary Greenleaf Clement" in *Dictionary of American Temperance Biography: From Temperance Reform to Alcohol Research, the 1600s to the 1980s,* edited by Mark Edward Lender, 290–291. Westport, CT: Greenwood Press, 1984.

Munns, Margaret C. *First in the Field.* Evanston, IL: National WCTU Publishing House, n.d.

Tyrrell, Ian. *Woman's World/Woman's Empire: The Woman's Christian Temperance Union in International Perspective.* Chapel Hill: University of North Carolina Press, 1991.

Woloch, Nancy. *Early American Women: A Documentary History, 1600–1900.* New York: McGraw-Hill, 2002.

Lees, Frederic Richard (1815–1897)

Frederic Richard Lees (1815–1897) was a leading British prohibition propagandist in the Victorian era. Born in Meanwood, Leeds, he was the son of a wool-comber turned schoolmaster. Joseph Lees was a radical who opposed the payment of church rates and the corruptions of the corporation; in 1832, he became a founding member of the Leeds Political Union. His son Frederic was articled to a radical solicitor in 1828 but did not pursue a legal career. He signed the antispirits pledge in 1832 and became a teetotaler in 1835. A legacy from his maternal grandfather, although consumed largely in legal costs, enabled him to become a public advocate of teetotalism. He was editor of the *Leeds Temperance Herald* in 1837, the same year that he became secretary of the British Association for the Promotion of Temperance (which later became the British Temperance League). In 1840, he acquired its journal, which he successfully edited until 1844. From 1844 to 1850, he edited a review, *Truth-Seeker,* and in 1845–1846 he edited the *Truth-Tester: Temperance Advocate and Mona Journal of the Water Cure.* He edited the *Teetotal Topic* in 1847 and the *Temperance Spectator* in 1859. He was a founding member of the prohibitionist United Kingdom Alliance, established in 1853, and his *Prize Essay* expounding the alliance's doctrines was published in 1856.

Lees often figured in controversies that divided temperance reformers. He was involved in a lawsuit against the American temperance lecturer John B. Gough in 1857–1859, after Gough and several British supporters attacked prohibition and Lees, in turn, accused Gough of drinking. The Court of Exchequer ruled against Lees, but admirers collected a sum of 1,000 guineas with which he bought what became his home, Meanwood Lodge. In 1846, Lees had considered immigrating to the United States. He visited America in 1869–1870 as a temperance lecturer. In Chicago, he joined the Independent Order of Good Templars. He visited the United States again in 1875. In a schism in the Good Templar organization over the rights of African Americans, Lees opposed Joseph Malins and the majority of English Good Templars who had seceded from the international organization, which was dominated by North Americans. Lees headed a small new English Grand Lodge organized in opposition to Malins.

Lees was active on the platform and in print and was acknowledged as an expert on medical and scriptural aspects of temperance. In order to equip himself for polemics on the biblical attitude toward alcohol, he taught himself Hebrew. A thirty-volume collection of his works was published from 1884 to 1887.

Like many contemporary temperance activists, he was interested in other reforms. He won a Vegetarian Society essay competition in 1857 (republished in 1884), occasionally lectured on vegetarianism, and became an associate member of the Vegetarian Society in 1874. He supported reform of factory hours, opposed slavery, and advocated the abolition of taxes on knowledge. He favored Irish home rule. He received an honorary doctorate from Geissen University in Germany for his writings against Owenite socialism (and thereafter styled himself Dr. Lees). He was a Chartist town councillor in 1850, and he made several unsuccessful efforts to be elected a radical member of Parliament in 1860, 1868, and 1874. Although sometimes assumed to be theologically unorthodox, in later life Lees joined the Church of England. He was married twice: first in 1838 to Mary Jowett, and then in 1878 to Sarah Barnesley, widow of a Manchester merchant. He had two children by his first wife.

James Gregory

See also: British Temperance League (BTL); Good Templars (IOGT); Gough, John Bartholomew; Malins, Joseph; United Kingdom Alliance (UKA); Vegetarianism and the Anti-Tobacco Movement (United Kingdom)

References

Fahey, David M. Entry for F. R. Lees in *Biographical Dictionary of Modern British Radicals,* vol. 3, *1870–1914, L-Z,* edited by J. O. Baylen and N. J. Gossman, 519–523. Hemel Hempstead, UK: Harvester Wheatsheaf, 1988.

Harrison, Brian. *Dictionary of British Temperance Biography.* Coventry: Society for the Study of Labour History, 1973.

Lees, (George) Frederic (William). *Dr. Frederic Richard Lees.* London: H. J. Osborn, 1904.

Lett, Stephen (1847–1905)

Stephen Lett (1847–1905) was the superintendent of the Homewood Retreat of Guelph, Ontario (1883–1905), and an early specialist in the medical treatment of alcoholism and drug addictions. Born in Callan, Ireland, Lett served at the Ontario asylums in Malden, London, Toronto, and Hamilton before becoming a founding partner and medical superintendent of the Homewood Retreat. His gradual withdrawal therapy for "opium neurosis" proved popular with his upper- and middle-class clientele; however, his late-blooming success was cut short by illness.

The son of an Anglo-Irish minister, Stephen Lett graduated from Upper Canada College and served in the Canadian militia during the Fenian raids of 1866, where he met his lifelong mentor, J. W. Langmuir, head of Ontario's social welfare network. Lett married Annie MacLeod, the daughter of a former Liberal member of Parliament, and became a member of the College of Physicians and Surgeons of Ontario in 1870 without formal medical training. His connections assured him an appointment as assistant physician at the small Malden Asylum and then later in the same year at the larger London Asylum, where he received training under Dr. Henry Landor, the facility's first superintendent. When Landor died in 1877, Lett lost the superintendency to Richard M. Bucke, a physician of superior professional qualifications (and political connections). A lasting antipathy developed between the two imperious men and resulted in Lett's transfer to a post at the Toronto Asylum. While at Toronto he took his Bachelor (1878) and Doctor of Medicine (1879) degrees from Toronto University. After a brief, discouraging stint as head of the rowdy Hamilton Asylum, Lett joined Langmuir in 1883 as one-third owners of a new corporation, the Homewood Retreat.

Lett's anomalous position as both director and medical superintendent of Homewood created additional difficulties. Despite early optimism, by 1887 the financial picture was so bleak that Lett took a pay cut and the institution's sale was considered. By 1896, the situation had brightened with the increased admissions of male alcoholics.

Apprenticed in traditional moral treatment and influenced by late Victorian hereditarianism, Lett had little expectation of curing insanity. He maintained that controlled surroundings, good diet, and moderate exercise would alleviate symptoms. With a growing alcoholic patient base, however, Lett became more proactive to attract and maintain this clientele and carved his niche as a specialist in the medical treatment of alcoholism and drug addiction. He published widely in Ontario newspapers and in the *Quarterly Journal of Inebriety* on the treatment of alcoholics. A career highlight was his speech before the British Society for the Study and Cure of Inebriety, which elected him a member. The society printed 4,000 copies of Lett's paper for the society and distributed them to North American physicians.

Lett's therapeutic philosophy was that substance dependency was a hereditary disease and not a vice. His views did not, however, contradict the tenets of the powerful Victorian temperance movement because he differentiated between the vice of drunkenness, the product of a weak moral fiber, and the disease of inebriety, the consequence of chronic drunkenness. Where "vice and sin are the factors," he concluded, "we may safely leave the treatment to the care of the clergy and other well meaning people." When disease was present, however, "it rests with medical men and the state to take action." Lett argued that men drink because "there is pain," a "feeling of disturbance" produced by a hereditary predisposition, which "makes the victims an easy prey to the ravages of such stimulants" (Warsh 1989: 147).

The result of his increasing reputation as an alcoholism specialist was the Homewood's dependence upon a patient population notorious for short, revolving visits, as wealthy patients used the institution to dry out from alcoholic sprees. Lett was forced to demand a four-week advance payment from inebriates. Although his recommended treatment was a course of gradual withdrawal, Lett was required by patient demand to devise a gold cure during the Keeley Gold Cure craze, despite the treatment's condemnation as quackery by the medical establishment. By 1905, Lett's institution was finally achieving a solid financial footing, but his career and his life were cut short by a neurological disorder contracted in youth.

Cheryl Krasnick Warsh

See also: Alcoholism; Homewood Retreat; Keeley, Leslie Enraught; Keeley Institutes; Society for the Study of Addiction; Treatment Institutions

References

Lett, Stephen. "The Treatment of Drunkards" in *Monetary Times.* 9 May 1890.

———. "Why Do Men Drink?" in *Quarterly Journal of Inebriety.* 19, no. 3 (1897): 249–264.

Warsh, Cheryl Krasnick. *Moments of Unreason: The Practice of Canadian Psychiatry and the Homewood Retreat, 1883–1923.* Montreal: McGill-Queen's University Press, 1989.

Lewis, Elizabeth Ann (1849–1924)

Elizabeth Ann Lewis (1849–1924), known as the "Temperance Queen" and the "Drunkard's Friend," was an English temperance advocate. Beginning in 1872, she earned a reputation as a total abstinence activist. In 1882 and 1883, she helped introduce the controversial Blue Ribbon Army to Blackburn, England. Featuring reformed drunkards as speakers, the Blue Ribbon Army combined evangelical Protestantism with teetotalism. Critics complained about its emotionalism, its rejection of fermented Communion wine, and its loose ways with money. The term "blue ribbon" was derived from the Old Testament (Numbers 15:37–38). The Blue Ribbon Army, also called "gospel temperance," started in the United States. Lewis conducted a local teetotal mission and lectured throughout Britain. She also supported various other temperance organizations and institutions, such as the London Temperance Hospital, founded in 1873 to attack medical reliance on alcohol, and was a vice president of the British Temperance League.

Her father converted her mother, a well-educated church worker, to teetotalism. Both parents were social reformers. Elizabeth, their first-born child, debuted as a temperance worker at about age seven when she sang a temperance song at an outdoor rally. At school in Newcastle-under-Lyme, Staffordshire, she encouraged fellow students to sign the teetotal pledge. After leaving Newcastle, she studied music for two years, becoming an accomplished pianist. Shortly afterward, in 1867, she married her cousin, Thomas Lewis. (Her birth and marriage surnames were the same.) In the next year the couple moved to Blackburn in Lancashire. It was an early proletarian teetotal center. He founded a coach-manufacturing business, and she urged the pledge on his workers.

Elizabeth and Thomas Lewis entertained teetotalers at home, and they sang and provided music at concerts of the local Band of Hope, a children's teetotal organization that she helped conduct. He became an officer in the fraternal Independent Order of Good Templars, which established a lodge at Blackburn in 1872. In 1882, Elizabeth and her mother helped form the Blackburn branch of the British Women's Temperance Association (BWTA). Although Elizabeth Lewis favored women's suffrage, when the BWTA split over Lady Henry Somerset's "Do Everything" policy, she joined the breakaway Women's Total Abstinence Union.

At first too timid to be a public speaker, she began "Mrs. Lewis' Teetotal Mission," visiting the homes of nonabstainers, teetotalers, and "backsliders." To help her, she hired Richard Kilshaw, who had been a missionary for the revivalist Blue Ribbon Army. The two encouraged pledge-takers with temperance meetings and with entertainment, as counter attractions to pubs. Over the years, the mission collected between 1,000 and 2,000 pledges. Lewis organized temperance parades for Blackburn, and she delighted in persuading reformed drunkards to march in them.

Mission activities helped Lewis overcome her public shyness: She became a wedding officiator and nationally known inspirational public speaker, and the first woman to address the prisoners at Lancaster Castle. Cofounder of Blackburn's Lees Temperance Hall, Lewis exemplified the nondenominational, nonpartisan attitude of many nineteenth-century temperance militants. She believed that temperance reform, as the basis for all social improvement, especially among laborers, transcended religious and political differences.

Often bedridden with palsy, she continued temperance work until her death at age seventy-five. Eventually, she had to forgo the long and powerful speeches for which she had once been celebrated. Edward E. Moss, who had succeeded Kilshaw as her second missionary assistant, sustained the "Teetotal Mission" and wrote her biography.

Denied professional employment, Elizabeth Ann Lewis and other female temperance reformers, along with their male associates, reformed British society to suit new industrial realities. They also prepared for the fuller enfranchisement of women that some of them advocated.

Cynthia Belaskie

See also: Blue Ribbon Movement; British Temperance League (BTL); British Women's Temperance Association (BWTA); Good Templars (IOGT); Lees, Frederic Richard; Somerset, Isabella Caroline (Lady Henry Somerset); Wightman, Julia Bainbrigge

References

Moss, Edward E. *The Life of Mrs. Lewis, The "Drunkard's Friend."* London: Epworth, 1926.

Shiman, Lilian Lewis. *Crusade against Drink in Victorian England.* New York: St. Martin's, 1988; London: Macmillan, 1988.

———. *Women and Leadership in Nineteenth-Century England.* New York: St. Martin's, 1992; London: Macmillan, 1992.

Liberal Party (United Kingdom)

The Liberal Party in Britain became identified during the 1880s and 1890s with advanced temperance reformers who advocated local referendums for prohibition and rejected financial compensation for owners of licensed premises who lost their property because of a change in public policy. Pressure from Nonconformist supporters brought about the Liberal commitment to direct local veto. Virtually no Liberals who received Cabinet appointments were teetotalers. Most of the Liberal leadership distrusted the advanced temperance program and questioned whether, on balance, it gained or lost votes. As a result, the Liberal leadership offered the advanced temperance reformers symbolic commitments without making local veto a legislative priority.

Sir William Harcourt argued that to get Nonconformist support the Liberals had to support local veto. In 1883, William Gladstone and Harcourt supported a local-veto resolution, although with the reservation that elected local councils and not a direct vote of the people decide on prohibition. Two years later, Harcourt pressed Gladstone for a local-veto bill. "We have given [the temperance reformers] good words but nothing else and it is not unreasonable that they should expect some better butter for their parsnips," he wrote (Harcourt to Gladstone 1885). The schism over Irish home rule strengthened the need of the Liberals for temperance support. The Liberals took a hard line against the Conservative compensation proposals in 1888 and again in 1890. In 1889, the National Liberal Federation adopted a resolution in favor of direct local veto. Gladstone reluctantly included direct local veto in his Newcastle program of 1891.

After the Liberals formed a government in 1892, Harcourt introduced two veto bills for England and Wales. These bills constituted a symbolic triumph for the prohibitionists but offered them little of substance. The 1893 bill required a virtually unobtainable two-thirds majority in a local referendum and excluded the places where the middle classes got their drink, such as hotels and restaurants. The bill also provided for a referendum on Sunday closing. Most temperance reformers wanted mandatory Sunday closing legislation. The 1895 bill added a referendum for a reduction in the number of public houses, something that prohibitionists resented as a rival to their own local-veto referendum. The Liberal government did not press either bill to a final vote.

When the Liberals lost the general election of 1895, many voices called for the party to drop local veto from its program. In 1897, Herbert Gladstone, the former prime minister's son, joined this revolt. When politicians like the younger Gladstone complained that local veto was a burden, temperance reformers answered that the Liberals could not win without them. In practice, many issues, not just local veto, influenced the votes of temperance-minded electors. When an agent of the United Kingdom Alliance tried to organize abstentions to punish Herbert Gladstone in the general election of 1900, he discovered that "pious Wesleyans want to drown me, others prefer shooting me, and the parsons have deserted me" (Pearson to UKA 1900). Herbert Gladstone hoped to steer a middle course that might retain for his party the support of traditionally Liberal families in the drink trade, such as the Buxtons, who were London brewers.

Events at the turn of the century helped the Liberals to present themselves as the party of temperance reform while putting into the background local veto and opposition to compensation. When the Royal Commission on Liquor Licensing Laws reported in 1899, many prohibitionists rallied behind the minority report written by Lord Peel, who had chaired the commission. Lord Peel's report favored delaying local-veto legislation for Wales and Scotland for a few years, and for England indefinitely. It also advocated allowing license holders financial compensation, although limited in amount and duration, and emphasized substantial statutory reduction in the number of licensed premises. Herbert Gladstone, by this time Liberal chief whip, regarded Lord Peel's report as too extreme. It attacked grocers' licenses, and the few remaining drink traders active in the Liberal Party included members of the Gilbey firm that supplied this part of the trade in alcoholic beverages.

Already weakened by the general election of 1895 and by Lord Peel's report, the advanced temperance reformers suffered another blow when the Conservatives enacted the Licensing Act of 1904, which made compensation a statutory right. The most that the Liberals could be expected to do when they returned to power was to reduce the amount of compensation. The 1904 act also reinforced the tendency to regard reduction in numbers as central to temperance reform. Moreover, the turn-of-the-century agitation for a Gothenburg scheme or disinterested management provided another rival to divert attention from local veto.

After the Liberals returned to power, they introduced a Licensing Bill in 1908. This bill included local veto, but the bill's central provision was a sharper reduction in the number of licensed premises in proportion to population. After the Liberal-dominated House of Commons passed the bill, the Unionist-dominated House of Lords promptly rejected it. Although the Liberals punished the drink trade with increased taxes in the budget of 1909, they never again proposed a major licensing bill.

The World War I debate over alcoholic drink policies was not a partisan one, and by the time the Licensing Act of 1921 became law, the Liberals had fewer members of Parliament than Labour and were on their way to political irrelevance.

David M. Fahey

See also: Conservative Party (United Kingdom); Gladstone, William Ewart; Gothenburg Schemes/Disinterested Management; Harcourt, Sir William; Local Option; Nonconformists (United Kingdom); United Kingdom Alliance (UKA)

References

Fahey, David M. "The Politics of Drink: Pressure Groups and the British Liberal Party, 1882–1908" in *Social Science.* 54 (1979): 76–85.

———. "The Politics of Drink in Britain: Anglo-American Perspectives" in *Proceedings of the Ohio Academy of History.* Marion: Ohio Academy of History, 2000. Also available at Alcohol and Temperance History Group website, http://www.athg.org.

———. "Temperance and the Liberal Party: Lord Peel's Report, 1899" in *Journal of British Studies.* 10 (1971): 132–159.

Gutzke, David W. "Rhetoric and Reality: The Political Influence of British Brewers, 1832–1914" in *Parliamentary History.* 9 (1990): 71–115.

Harcourt to Gladstone, 18 January 1885. Bodleian, Harcourt MS 9, F., 118–119.

Harrison, Brian. *Drink and the Victorians: The Temperance Question in England, 1815–1872.* London: Faber & Faber, 1971; 2d ed., Keele: Keele University Press, 1994.

Pearson, William, to UKA, n.d., in Alliance minute books, 13 October 1900.

Rintala, Marvin. "Taking the Pledge: H. H. Asquith and Drink" in *Biography.* 16 (1993): 103–135.

Licensed Victuallers' National Defence League (LVNDL)

The Licensed Victuallers' National Defence League constituted the largest organization of English and Welsh licensed victuallers throughout the late nineteenth and twentieth centuries. Formed in late 1872, the league aimed to provide the provincial licensed trade with a national voice. Prominent in opposing temperance groups and restrictive legislation, the league continued to promote the interest of its members until its merger with a London organization in 1976.

Initially located in Birmingham, the league was formed by the merger of the Manchester-based United Towns Association and the Birmingham-centered Provincial Licensed Victuallers' Defence League. Both groups felt aggrieved at the passage of the 1872 Licensing Act and the perceived failure of existing trade groups to oppose the new legislation. By the end of the 1870s, the new league had more than 7,000 members.

Through a donation by the wholesale trade of £1,300 in 1882 and the purchase of the *Licensed Victuallers' Guardian* in 1883, the league reached the peak of its power in the early 1880s. This early success was short lived. The *Guardian* was sold in 1887, and despite relocating to London, the league failed to gain a level of national influence that reflected its membership base.

From its foundation, the power of the league was compromised by its failure to secure significant levels of long term-funding. Low membership fees presented the league with limited funds. Moreover, a desire to remain independent, and an air of mutual mistrust, left the league unable to obtain sustained financial support from the breweries. From the high point of 1882 their annual contributions to the league fell steadily, falling below £100 in the 1890s.

These financial difficulties were compounded by the existence of competing organizations—most notably the Licensed Victuallers' Protection Society of London (later reorganized as the Licensed Victuallers' Central Protection Society of London, also known as the London Central Board) and an organization that the Londoners dominated, the London and Home Counties League (later named the London and Provincial Licensed Victuallers' League). A number of attempts to formally combine the national league and the London society were made during the 1870s and 1880s, but all failed. A more limited merger between them was achieved in 1890, but differences over policy and capitation fees led the groups to split just two years later. A degree of cooperation between the national league and the London society was gained by their setting up of the United Parliamentary Council of the Retail Trade in 1896. In 1896, Samuel Hyslop, a former president of the league, was appointed to the Royal Commission on Liquor Licensing Laws, as was Charles Walker, chairman of the Licensed Victuallers' Central Protection Society of London.

The influence of the league continued to wane throughout the early twentieth century. However, it experienced a revival in popularity from the 1930s onward. Membership numbers increased dramatically from fewer than 14,000 members in 1931 to more than 37,000 in 1956. A new journal, the *Quarterly Review,* was published from 1933. In addition, from 1942 on, the league was again successful in securing annual funding from the wholesale trade.

From the late 1940s the league actively fostered closer ties with other trade bodies, particularly the Licensed Vituallers' Central Protection Society of London, commonly called the Central Board. The two groups increasingly cooperated on issues of mutual concern, and in 1961 the league allowed previously debarred licensed victuallers' associations from the metropolitan area to affiliate. Moves toward any formal union between the league and the board were slow, with formal discussions on the issue only taking place in May 1974. However, after this initial meeting both sides worked rapidly toward merger. On 1 January 1976, the league combined with the board and with the Amalgamated Licensed Retailers Society to form the National Union of Licensed Victuallers. It later became the National Licensed Victuallers' Association.

Perhaps responding to the 1990 Landlord and Tenant (Licensed Premises) Act, brewers and pub chains began in the 1990s to require tenants to sign lengthy and costly leases, arrangements that resulted in many licensees leaving the trade. As a result, in 1992 the National Licensed Victuallers' Association was dissolved. Later that year the Federation of Licensed Victuallers' Associations was organized to serve free traders, leaseholders, and tenants. The other national retail organization is the British Institute of Innkeeping, formed in 1981.

Kieran Foley

See also: Licensed Victuallers' Protection Society of London; Pubs and Beerhouses (United Kingdom)

References

Fahey, David M. "Brewers, Publicans and Working-Class Drinkers: Pressure Group Politics in Late Victorian and Edwardian England" in *Histoire Sociale/Social History.* No. 13 (1980): 85–103.

Gutzke, David W. *Protecting the Pub: Brewers and Publicans against Temperance.* Woodbridge, Suffolk: Boydell Press, 1989.

Licensed Victuallers' Protection Society of London

The Licensed Victuallers' Protection Society of London was the most effective British licensed retail trade organization of the nineteenth and twentieth centuries. Founded in October 1833 to protect the interests of metropolitan publicans, the society reached the peak of its power during the late Victorian era. Professionally organized and well funded, it constituted a potent adversary to temperance campaigners of the time. The society remained an independent organization until being subsumed into the newly created National Union of Licensed Victuallers on 1 January 1976.

Established in part out of concern over increased competition caused by passage of the 1830 Beer Act, the society sought to protect its members on a variety of levels. It provided legal advice, acted as an employment agency, and, most prominently, campaigned against legislation viewed as detrimental to the interests of the capital's publicans. Although active in lobbying from its foundation, it was with the growth in support for temperance in the last third of the nineteenth century that the society came to the fore within the political arena. Through a variety of techniques including mass meetings, petitions, and endorsements for sympathetic parliamentary candidates, the society attempted to combat the threat posed by antidrink campaigners.

Initially the society's responses to those who sought to limit the licensed trade were relatively limited. Its reaction to the 1872 Licensing Act, which allowed metropolitan publicans to trade for more hours than could their provincial counterparts, was muted in comparison to that of other retail trade organizations. This difference in approach created tensions, particularly between the society and the newly formed Licensed Victuallers' National Defence League. Consequently, the two organizations expended considerable energy vying with each other. A number of attempts to unite them were made, but the league's desire to dominate any new organization prevented the two groups from reaching any agreement during the 1870s and early 1880s.

A particular point of contention was the existence of the London and Home Counties League. Ostensibly an independent organization, it was little more than an instrument of the society. Not only did the Londoners supply funds for the organization, they also provided many of its main officials. Established in 1872, some months before the national league, the London and Home Counties League was perceived by many in the former as a preemptive measure to limit the power of their organization. In 1875, the Liverpool Licensed Victuallers' Society left the national league and affiliated with its society-backed rival. Five years later, the London and Home Counties League provocatively changed its name to the London and Provincial Licensed Victuallers' League. Both actions added to the tensions between the league and the society, but a degree of reconciliation was achieved during the later 1880s and 1890s. The two leagues briefly merged between 1890 and 1892, and the society and the national league created a platform for cooperation in 1896 with their establishment of a United Parliamentary Council of the Retail Trade.

The improvement in relations between the society and the league was paralleled by an increase in the society's influence. Throughout the 1880s, the society had been able to secure substantial donations from the wholesale trade. London brewers provided more than £2,500 annually. These funds allowed the society to increase and diversify its activities. In 1887, a quarrel with the Brewers' Company over the adulteration of beer led to a temporary dip in society fortunes. However, by the early 1890s they were once more resurgent. Not only was the society able to attract increased funding but it also underwent expansion and reorganization. In 1891, the society began to publish the *Licensed Victuallers' Official Annual,* and in 1892, it gained its own newspaper, the *Licensing World.* More important, the latter year also witnessed the restructuring and renaming of the society in response to complaints, both from within and outside of the organization, that it was no longer representing the interests of all of its members. Adopting the title of the Licensed Victuallers' Central Protection Society of London, more often known as the London Central Board, the remodeled society went on to incorporate in 1893.

This reorganization, coupled with continued donations from the wholesale trade, allowed the board to reach the height of its power in the early twentieth century. This was in sharp contrast to the fortunes of other trade organizations, whose influence had started to wane. With a membership of approximately 7,000 in 1902 and an average annual budget of £11,000 between 1899 and 1908, the board was able to mount a number of powerful campaigns during the Edwardian period and was particularly active in opposing the 1908 Licensing Bill. The influence enjoyed by the board should not, however, be overstated. Even at the pinnacle of its power, its executive recognized the value of accepting more moderate licensing measures, such as the 1904 Licensing Act. Moreover, a decline in membership and funds, combined with working-class voters increasingly concentrating on the issue of welfare reform, meant that by 1914 the board's political power had begun to decline.

In the post–World War I era the influence of the board continued to fade as both temperance challenge and the importance of public houses diminished. Although less active in the political arena, it continued to be run in a professional and stable manner. Between 1892 and 1975, the board had just eight chairmen and four secretaries. In addition, continued funding from the wholesale trade, although at a lower level than previously, allowed the board to continue to defend the interests of its members when necessary.

The society maintained its independent status until 1 January 1976, when it combined with the national league and the Amalgamated Licensed Retailers Society to establish the National Union of Licensed Victuallers. Formal negotiations on the creation of a single national organization of the retail trade had commenced less than two years previously. However, the creation of the union was the culmination of a much longer process of convergence. From the 1940s onward, the board actively collaborated with the league on a variety of issues. Changes to the nature of the wholesale trade, particularly consolidation, necessitated greater unity of purpose between retail trade organizations, and both groups adopted an increasingly friendly stance toward one another. By the mid-1970s, it was apparent that if the interests of London's publicans were to be represented adequately it would have to be through a national rather than solely metropolitan organization.

The National Union of Licensed Victuallers later was reorganized as the National Licensed Victuallers' Association. It was dissolved in 1992. The records of the Licensed Victuallers' Central Protection Society of London have been placed in The Guildhall Library, London.

Kieran Foley

See also: Brewers' Company; Licensed Victuallers' National Defence League (LVNDL); Publicans (England)

References

Fahey, David M. "Brewers, Publicans and Working-Class Drinkers: Pressure Group Politics in Late Victorian and Edwardian England" in *Histoire Sociale/Social History.* No. 13 (1980): 85–103.

Gutzke, David W. *Protecting the Pub: Brewers and Publicans against Temperance.* Woodbridge, Suffolk: Boydell Press, 1989.

Licensing (Canada)

The history of liquor licensing in Canada reflects changing patterns of Canadian liquor control. At first unregulated, liquor sales gradually became subject to increasingly tight control, culminating in Prohibition. Since the end of Prohibition, a closely managed system of government sales and regulation has been liberalized.

Early Years

During Canada's early history the liquor trade was virtually wide open; for the most part, both on-premise and off-premise establishments were unregulated. Prior to 1759, liquor regulations were directed primarily against those engaged in the fur trade in an attempt to stem the tide of alcohol to the First Nations people. After the British conquest of Canada in 1760, liquor was seen mainly from the point of view of profit, and authorities were loath to regulate an industry upon which government depended so heavily for customs revenue. Nevertheless, by 1774, all alcohol regulations imposed by the French had been repealed and replaced with a licensing system. Licenses to sell alcoholic beverages were easily obtained in the early 1800s. Originally, they were granted by the governor of the colony, but by 1794 they were given by local magistrates, who were to ensure that publicans kept a "decent and orderly" establishment. Most regulations dealt with license fees and their collection, not with drunkenness or other controls on consumption. Moreover, it was not that uncommon for a magistrate and tavern-owner to be the same person.

Anecdotal evidence from the period suggests that few regulations were enforced, and obtaining a license for an inn or tavern was an easy matter. Virtually anyone could open a tavern, and all that was required was a desire to do so. The licensing system, like drinking, was not at all restrictive, and abuse of the system was not uncommon. One settler reported that London, Ontario, in the 1830s had seven taverns for 1,300 people, as well as a number of grocery stores that were "grog shops," or drinking houses. In addition to taverns, many stores sold alcoholic beverages and allowed drinking by customers. Others gave it away, since whiskey was readily available and cheap—half a penny per gallon. A clergyman observed that most stores in Ontario kept a pail of whiskey and a cup at the back door where customers could help themselves. It was not until the advent of temperance societies and responsible government in the 1840s that regulation of the liquor trade began in earnest.

Increasing Regulation

Authorities were reluctant to impose strict regulations because governments relied on liquor imports for an estimated 25 to 50 percent of their revenue. In addition, taxes on liquor sales added to both municipal and provincial coffers. Furthermore, the licenses themselves were used as a form of political patronage. Nevertheless, officials were coming under increasing pressure to regulate the number of premises. One such measure taken to regulate the proliferation of drinking establishments was to double the license fee, which had the effect of cutting the number of establishments in half in many cities and towns. That said, license applications that were rejected by one magistrate could be granted by another who was more sympathetic to the applicant, or by provincial officials who had license-granting authority. Other measures included imposing a quota system that limited the number of establishments in each county, township, and settlement. As temperance reformers gained control of local town councils across the country, they moved to impose even stricter regulations. By 1851, for example, magistrates and grand juries in ten of Nova Scotia's seventeen counties refused to grant any licenses whatsoever, thereby creating "dry" counties. Not surprisingly, these counties spawned a number of illegal establishments, or people simply traveled to bordering counties where the sale and drinking of liquor was permitted. Local option was another effective licensing tool. In Nova Scotia, for example, in the early 1860s a law allowed a majority of ratepayers in any polling district to prohibit retail licenses. By 1870, licenses became that much more difficult to obtain when applicants were required to collect supporting signatures from two-thirds of ratepayers. Local measures, however, tended to be short-lived.

In the 1870s, the pendulum swung away from local control to provincial control. In 1875, Ontario passed the Crooks Act, named after Adam Crooks, treasurer and minister of education, which immediately reduced the number of establishments in the province by 35 percent. The legislation limited the number of licenses to be granted in every municipality, required that all taverns be well-appointed eating houses, and imposed a minimum fee for each of the three types of license—wholesale, tavern, and shop. Three years later, in 1878, the federal government passed the Canada Temperance Act (also known as the Scott Act), which placed control of licensing back into the hands of the municipalities. This was challenged in the courts and the Judicial Committee of the Privy Council eventually ruled that the legislation was unconstitutional and that the federal government did not have the right to encroach upon provincial jurisdiction (as outlined in Section 92, Subsections 9 and 13, of the British North America Act). Competition between Ontario and the federal government to regulate the consumption and sale of alcohol was a major source of constitutional litigation in the last two decades of the nineteenth century. In 1896, the matter was finally settled in favor of the provinces.

During World War I, pressure from the temperance societies forced both levels of government to impose prohibition. Provincial governments moved to close the bars, saloons, and privately run liquor stores. In Saskatchewan, for example, the government closed 406 bars, 38 liquor dealers, and 12 clubs and replaced them with 23 government dispensaries. To fill the void left by private enterprise, licensed druggists, doctors, dentists, and veterinarians purchased liquor from government vendors and dispensed alcohol to their patients and clients. Provincial prohibition outlawing retail sales had no effect on the manufacture or interprovincial trade of liquor, since this was a federal matter. Moreover, since no statute outlawed personal possession or consumption of alcohol, distillers and brewers could still ship their products to other provinces. Finally, prohibition did not ban saloons outright. Many survived by selling "near beer," which contained less than 2.5 percent proof spirits and was not liquor according to the law. To make matters worse from a regulation perspective, since near beer was not considered liquor, no restrictions existed as to who could sell it, and unlicensed bars sprang up across the country. This led to cries of unfair competition and calls for reform.

By the early 1920s the provinces moved toward state control of the liquor trade with the creation of Liquor Control Boards, thereby replacing private enterprise completely. All aspects of the trade, including licensing for both on-premise and off-premise establishments, would be controlled by the state. Gone were the days of private retailers.

Liberalization

By the 1960s, Canadians held more liberal views toward alcohol, and government policies mirrored those views. Liquor permit cards were discontinued altogether and motels and summer resorts were allowed to apply for liquor licenses. Public houses were no longer required to close over the dinner hour, and hours of operation were extended for on-premise establishments, which could now stay open up to twelve hours per day. Also, self-service government liquor stores were introduced. Previously, liquor stores were clerk-run and customers could not see, nor touch, the product—everything was kept out of view. As recently as the early 1990s, liquor outlets in Ontario were clerk-run operations. The liberalization of licensing continued unabated in the 1970s. For the first time, sex-segregated seating in licensed establishments was abolished: Single women and men were no longer seated in separate sections of the bar, and the practice whereby a man could only enter licensed premises that served women if he was accompanied by a woman was overturned. Other changes were equally significant. Drinking was allowed with meals on Sunday in licensed restaurants, and regulations that required patrons of dining-lounges to order a meal in order to have a drink were dropped. Finally, liquor licenses could be issued to new restaurants without the customary six-month waiting period.

In the 1980s, governments moved toward privatization when wine kiosks were permitted in grocery stores. During the following decade, brew pubs, shops selling kits for home brewing, and neighborhood pubs were springing up all across the country. Some provincial governments, such as British Columbia, permitted the sale of beer and wine in a select few nongovernment retail stores. And, although governments still oversee all facets of the liquor trade, regulations, including licensing of establishments, have been loosened significantly. The trend toward liberalization continues to this day—harking back to an earlier time in Canadian history.

Shawn Cafferky

See also: Canada Temperance Act; Federal Prohibition (Canada); Provincial Liquor Boards (Canada); Provincial Prohibition (Canada); Provincial Stores (Canada)

References

Campbell, Robert A. *Demon Rum or Easy Money: Government Control of Liquor in British Columbia from Prohibition to Privatization.* Ottawa: Carleton University Press, 1991.

———. *Sit Down and Drink Your Beer: Regulating Vancouver's Beer Parlours, 1925–1954.* Toronto: University of Toronto Press, 2001.

Smart, Reginald G., and Alan C. Ogborne. *Northern Spirits: A Social History of Alcohol in Canada.* Toronto: Addiction Research Foundation, 1996.

Spence, Ruth E. *Prohibition in Canada.* Toronto: Dominion Alliance, 1919.
Warsh, Cheryl Krasnick, ed. *Drink in Canada: Historical Essays.* Montreal and Kingston: McGill-Queen's University Press, 1993.

Licensing Hours (United Kingdom)

Licensing hours are the hours during which public houses (pubs) have been permitted to open in the United Kingdom since the nineteenth century. At first, they were expressed as closing hours, but after the Licensing Act of 1921 they have been stated in terms of permitted hours.

Restrictive opening hours were imposed during World War I as an alternative to prohibition. Pubs were permitted to open for only two and a half hours at lunchtime and three hours in the evening, with a latest closing time of 9 P.M. This restriction, together with an increase in the price and a reduction in the strength of alcoholic drinks, produced a marked decrease in public drunkenness. Ever since, opening hours for pubs have been restricted to an extent that continues to surprise visitors from continental Europe.

The first statutory controls on public houses' hours were imposed in London in 1839, where pubs were closed from midnight Saturday until 1 P.M. on Sunday. This measure proved so effective in reducing drunkenness that it was extended to some other towns in England and Wales in the 1840s. The Liberal government in 1872 extended restrictions to the rest of the week, setting the closing time at midnight in London, at 11 P.M. in most other cities (population over 2,500), and at 10 P.M. in small towns (population under 2,500). This restriction applied to the pubs that were frequented by the working classes but not to the clubs patronized by the middle and upper classes, leading to rioting in some cities by mobs who declared that there was "one law for the rich and another for the poor." The historian Brian Harrison (1994) has provided detailed charts of changes in beerhouse opening hours, 1830–1874, and public-house opening hours, 1828–1874.

The Conservative opposition exploited popular disaffection toward the new licensing legislation and won a general election in 1874 by a large majority. William Ewart Gladstone, who had been the Liberal prime minister, wrote to his brother that "we have been borne down in a torrent of gin and beer." The new Conservative government extended opening hours in London by half an hour at night.

No further change was made to licensing hours until World War I. In March 1915, the minister of munitions, later prime minister, David Lloyd George, received a deputation of shipbuilding employers who urged him to introduce prohibition because (they said) heavy drinking by their employees was affecting production. He supported their suggestion by declaring: "We are fighting Germany, Austria and the drink; and, as far as I can see, the greatest of these three deadly foes is drink" (Williams and Brake 1980: 47). Having inquired further, however, Lloyd George discovered that the imposition of prohibition would probably lead to public disorder. Instead, the government created the Central Control Board (Liquor Traffic) to regulate the supply of alcoholic drinks. This board severely limited the opening hours of pubs for a variety of reasons, including production limits later in the war, as food production took priority and the absence overseas of soldiers who ordinarily would have been pub drinkers reduced demand.

The restrictive hours so effectively controlled drinking by workers that they were not changed significantly after the war ended. Even pub owners were reluctant to agitate for liberalization; some commentators suggested that the shorter working hours suited them very well. Although it was widely considered from the 1960s onward that the restrictions on licensing hours were outdated and were hampering the tourist trade, not until 1987 did the government pass legislation to permit pubs in England and Wales to remain open through the afternoon on weekdays and Saturdays. (Different legislation in Scotland had led to afternoon opening in some areas from 1976 onward.)

Furthermore, despite repeated promises by successive governments, both Conservative and Labour, that legislation would be introduced to allow pubs to stay open later in the evening, the closing time remains fixed at 11 P.M. In 2003, the Labour government introduced legislation to end restrictions on hours for selling alcoholic drinks at pubs.

Opening hours on Sundays have generally been even more restrictive. A growth in Sabbatarianism led to the imposition of total Sunday closing in Scotland in 1853 and in Wales in 1881. This prohibition was not lifted in Scotland until 1976; in Wales "local option" was introduced in 1961, enabling voters in each locality to vote on whether to permit the sale of drink on Sundays. The last area of Wales to remain "dry" on Sundays was Dwyfor in Gwynedd, which introduced Sunday opening in 1996. Local option in Wales was abolished in 2003. In England, Sunday opening hours were further restricted in 1854 to between 12:30 and 2:30 and 6 and 10 P.M. This restriction having led to rioting in London, another act was passed the next year to extend opening times by thirty minutes at lunchtime and two hours in the evening. During World War I, pubs were allowed to open for a total of only five hours on Sundays. With minor changes, these restrictions remained in force for another eighty years. In 1995, legislation was passed to allow pubs in England to stay open through Sunday afternoon.

It should be pointed out that legislation does not necessarily coincide with practice. In the second half of the nineteenth century, "bona fide travellers" were exempt from the restrictive Sunday opening hours. This led to individual train tickets being passed around pubs to enable people to buy drinks out of hours. In the first half of the twentieth century, the majority of Welsh men belonged to private clubs that were permitted to sell drinks on Sundays, and it was possible to drink late at night in London if one attended a "private bottle party": a speciously private event at which the "guests" paid the "host" a contribution toward the cost of entertaining them. Even today, many pubs sell drinks illegally to regular customers after the official closing time, locking the doors to prevent new customers from entering. Provided this is done discreetly, and there is no disorder, the police have tended to turn a blind eye to these "lock-ins."

Andrew Barr

See also: Gladstone, William Ewart; Lloyd George, David; Pubs and Beerhouses (United Kingdom)

References

Carter, Henry. *The Control of the Drink Trade: A Contribution to National Efficiency, 1915–1917.* London: Longmans, 1918.

Harrison, Brian. *Drink and the Victorians: The Temperance Question in England, 1815–1872.* London: Faber and Faber, 1971; Keele: Keele University Press, 1994.

Shadwell, Arthur. *Drink in 1914–1922: A Lesson in Control.* London: Longmans, 1923.

Williams, Gwylmor Prys, and George Thompson Brake. *Drink in Great Britain, 1900–1979.* London: Edsall, 1980.

Wilson, George B. *Alcohol and the Nation.* London: Nicolson and Watson, 1940.

Ligue Nationale contre l'Alcoolisme

Alcoholism has long been a social and political issue in France. As early as the middle of the nineteenth century, some politicians, leading citizens, and doctors tried to understand the causes of alcoholism. Temperance concerns led in particular to scrutiny of the intemperate habits of the emerging proletariat. Alcoholism was considered to be both a moral and a public health issue. The leading classes of the society believed that leaving the workers and the poor to get drunk regularly was dangerous for the cohesion of the social order.

An association emerged to fight this social problem, with doctors as the initial leaders. The first antialcoholism organization, Société française contre l'abus des boissons alcooliques, was founded in 1871 at a meeting in Paris of the Académie de médecine. Two years later, this association was renamed Société française de tempérance. During the nineteenth and the first half of the twentieth century, the fight against alcoholism was mainly seen as a struggle against race degeneration and national depopulation. Well-known persons, such as Louis Pasteur, Hippolyte Taine, Victor Duruy, the Duke de Broglie, and the Duke of Noailles were founding members of the Société française de tempérance, which included as well important members of the Institut de France and the Académie de médecine. A strong competition arose from the Union française antialcoolique (UFA), created by the alienist Paul-Maurice Legrain. The UFA, with up to 40,000 members at the beginning of the twentieth century, promoted abstinence from all beverages containing alcohol and extended the link with degeneration to the entire alcoholic pathology.

At a founding congress held in 1903, the Société française de tempérance and the Union française antialcoolique, as well as a number of smaller organizations, merged into a new Ligue Nationale contre l'Alcoolisme, which had a real influence on politics and government. From 1906 to 1914, the number of members increased from 50,000 to 125,000. The budget was 4,000 francs around 1890 and reached 300,000 francs in 1914. Medical works, and especially popular tracts, reached a very large audience, which extended the influence of antialcoholism ideology far beyond the ranks of specialists. The hygienist ideology expanded into a new social ethos. The militant actions of the Ligue Nationale symbolized perfectly this new attitude. It was not enough to condemn the drunkard; rather, it was seen as necessary to change the habits and the way of life of the working class so as better to integrate its members into society. The hygienist discourse was shared and spread by various social agents, such as lawyers, doctors, politicians, writers, and members of the aristocracy. These persons, who belonged to the influential classes, sought to create better living conditions for the working class. The Ligue Nationale contre l'Alcoolisme included, besides famous doctors from the Académie de médecine, outstanding men such as Jules Siegfried and Emile Cheysson; Cheysson eventually served as chairman of the Ligue Nationale.

The French Parliament came to include a large number of antialcoholism supporters. The Ligue Nationale contre l'Alcoolisme, particularly active during the 1906 elections, demanded the suppression of the distillers' privileges, the prohibition of absinthe, and a limitation on the number of alcohol outlets. About 150 members of the Chamber of Deputies and 86 senators gathered into a group to promote the aims of the Ligue Nationale. This parliamentary group was not representative of any traditional political picture, as it included deputies from the socialist, radical, and center-right parties. At last, the antialcoholism militants met some success during World War I, when the virtues of patriotism were emphasized and alcohol was seen as the "enemy within." A general consensus prevailed at the governmental level on the necessity of taking drastic measures regarding the production and consumption of alcohol. This consensus was consistent with the views of the Ligue Nationale, although other factors contributed to the government's willingness to act. The best evidence of this mobilization was the prohibition of absinthe in 1915.

The lobbying effectiveness of the Ligue Nationale quickly decreased after the war, when fighting alcoholism lost priority among the leading classes to the urgent need of rebuilding the country's economy. The situation between the world wars, as well as the crisis in the 1930s, did not help the Ligue Nationale contre l'Alcoolisme to gain any real attention at the institutional level. A powerful and coherent fight against alcoholism would reemerge only after World War II. Alcoholism as the symbol of degeneration and working-class misery, which galvanized the elites of the Third Republic, faded away progressively during the 1950s and was replaced by a different medical model, one focusing on alcoholic pathology, based on the work in the United States of the alcoholism researcher E. M. Jellinek. Under a new name, Association nationale de la prévention de l'alcoolisme, the organization still plays a role in educating the French public about alcoholism.

Bertrand Dargelos

See also: Absinthe; France, Temperance in; Jellinek, Elvin Morton

References

Gusfield, Joseph R. *Symbolic Crusade: Status Politics and the American Temperance Movement.* 2d ed. Urbana: University of Illinois Press, 1990.

Nourrisson, D. *Le buveur du 19ème siècle.* Paris: Albin Michel, 1990.

Prestwich, Patricia E. *Drink and the Politics of Social Reform: Anti-Alcoholism in France Since 1870.* Palo Alto, CA: Society for the Promotion of Science and Scholarship, 1988.

Sournia, Jean-Charles. *Histoire de l'alcoolisme.* Paris: Flammarion, 1986.

Liquor Licensing (Australia)

From Australia's earliest days as a British penal settlement, liquor law has been an important consideration in the regulation of Australian life. The history of the debate in many respects has replicated British discussions about the place and frequency of drinking in everyday life and competing discourses of the home and the workplace. From the outset, home duties, family life, sobriety, and a strong work ethic were powerful goals of state management, with drinking presented as the "Other" of home and industry. Similarly, regulators have been historically incapable of reconciling the obvious fiscal and employment benefits of alcohol and its related industries with government's traditional emphases on health, social welfare, and public order policies (Lewis 1992). The cruder forms of regulation attest to the fears of churches, governments, and temperance movements of uncontrolled consumption.

These groups have had valid cause for their concerns: By 1870, for example, New South Wales (NSW) had 2,400 licensed hotels for a population of 540,000 (Australian Hotels Association 1988). Local temperance groups were formed, modeled upon British and U.S. organizations (Hyslop 1976). Their most spectacular success can be found in the "patriotic" decision in 1916 to close hotels at 6 P.M. in NSW, Victoria, South Australia, and Tasmania. In 1919, the creation of the NSW Licence Reduction Board lived up to its name, removing 1,000 hotel licenses within a decade (Australian Hotels Association 1988). Between 1860 and 1945, Australian consumption per capita levels had declined, in keeping with the economic downturns of the 1840s, 1890s and 1930s (Dingle 1980).

Early hotel closing nonetheless produced vivid effects in the peak-hour rush from five to six o'clock, accelerating public drunkenness. The 1952 NSW Liquor Royal Commission found the early closing law encouraged widespread illicit consumption, most evident in a thriving nightclub industry and other illegal retail sources, and police corruption. The commission's report, along with studies conducted in other states, noted that reduced trading hours had not reduced overall consumption, and that home drinking had increased. NSW hotels won the right to trade until 10 P.M. in late 1954; other states eventually followed.

A 1930 photograph of the innkeeper of the only hotel in Alice Springs, Australia (E. O. Hoppe/Corbis)

With the exception of Victoria, states found that laws allowing registered clubs the right to operate poker (slot) machines were significant in ensuring viable alternatives to pubs. Clubs also had a significant advantage in being exempted from the laws against Sunday trading, which derived from a still-powerful churches lobby. For Aboriginal populations, comprehensive bans on alcohol purchases had existed in all states, beginning in 1838 with the New South Wales Licensed Publicans Act. These bans were gradually repealed: in Victoria in 1957; NSW, 1963; the Northern Territory, 1964; Queensland, 1971; South Australia, 1971; and Western Australia, 1972 (Hunter 1993). Liquor law in relation to indigenous Australians was, and remains, a contentious issue, encompassing a complex variety of issues about full citizenship rights, welfare reliance, crime rates, community cohesiveness, and racism (Bourbon, Saggers, and Gray 1999).

From the late 1970s, various governments granted Sunday trading to hotels, beginning with NSW in 1979. This state was also the first to enact legislative sanction for women encountering the continued refusal of publicans to serve them in hotel public bars, through the 1977 NSW Anti-Discrimination Act. The financial benefits of the gradual increases in trading hours were partially offset by the increasing effectiveness of random breath testing, designed to discourage drinking and driving (Homel 1983).

By the late 1980s, the older argument that an increase in trading hours and sites led to increased consumption had effectively been discounted. In 1987, Victoria ended the national fixation with "seated consumption" laws that required liquor sales to be accompanied by a meal. The ability to purchase a general "on-licence" has resulted in a rapid expansion of wine bars, restaurant drinking without dining, and "bar cafes." NSW introduced similar laws in 1998, allowing restaurants and nightclubs to devote up to 30 percent of their floor space to drinking without dining. This marked the end of the "swill mentality" discourses and the legislative anxiety to protect drinkers from themselves. Hoteliers' complaints about the potential for loss of business were countered with the end of the clubs' monopoly on poker (slot) machines: In April 1997, poker machines were introduced in NSW hotels.

Against a steady liberalization of liquor laws can also be discerned a perverse trend in ensuring the proper behavior of both drinker and proprietor. Lower federal taxes on light alcohol beer since 1988; mandatory training for pub/club security personnel; proof-of-age identity cards for youth; local council zoning of no-alcohol areas—all signify the shift to controlling drinking behavior rather than the times and places of drinking. These changes, combined with the lapse in semi-prohibition policies, represent a move toward harm minimization strategies designed to reduce binge drinking and disorderly behavior. NSW regulations providing useful examples include the Alcohol and Anti-Social Behaviour Strategic Plan (1993); the Code of Practice for the Responsible Serving of Liquor (1994); and the "No More It's The Law" campaign (1996). "Public benefit" tests, requiring new licensees to show adequate demand and reasons for new hotels or clubs, have also become popular with state governments in reconciling financial and social concerns.

Shane Homan

See also: Australia; Drinking Sites and Culture (Australia); Woman's Christian Temperance Union (WCTU) (Australia)

References

Australian Hotels Association. *A History of the Australian Hotels Association in New South Wales, 1873–1988.* Sydney: Australian Hotels Association, 1988.

Bourbon, Deidre, Sherry Saggers, and Dennis Gray. *Indigenous Australians and Liquor Licensing Legislation.* Bentley: National Centre for Research into the Prevention of Drug Abuse, 1999.

Dingle, A. E. "'The Truly Magnificent Thirst': An Historical Survey of Australian Drinking Habits" in *Historical Studies.* 19, no.75 (1980): 227–249.

Homel, Ross. *The Impact of Random Breath Testing.* Sydney: NSW Drug and Alcohol Research Centre, 1983.

Hunter, Ernest. *Aboriginal Health and History: Power and Prejudice in Remote Australia.* London: Cambridge University Press, 1993.

Hyslop, Anthea. "Temperance, Christianity and Feminism: The Woman's Christian Temperance Union of Victoria, 1887–1897" in *Historical Studies.* 17, no. 66 (1976): 27–49.

Lewis, Milton. *A Rum State: Alcohol and State Policy in Australia, 1788–1988.* Canberra: Australian Government Publishing Service, 1992.

NSW Government. *Liquor Act (Restaurants and Nightclubs) Bill.* Sydney: NSW Government Printer, 1998.

Stockwell, Tim, ed. *An Examination of the Appropriateness and Efficacy of Liquor Licensing Laws across Australia.* Report 5, National Symposium on Alcohol Misuse and Violence. Canberra: Australian Government Publishing Service, 1994.

Literature, Representations of Drinking in

Just as alcoholic and intoxicating beverages have been ubiquitous throughout recorded history, so does drinking figure in the literary history of almost all cultures. Drinking alcoholic beverages is a basic human behavior. Most people have a wide range of experience with drinking. If most episodes of drinking are trivial and mundane, still they are rituals of the commonplace. Other episodes of drinking are life-altering and eminently memorable. As one of the few most basic human behaviors, drinking intoxicating liquor has profound and intimate connections to all things quotidian and remarkable. Not surprisingly, then, when creative writers examine the meaning of life, death, love, friendship, or any other subject of fundamental importance, they often work with representations of drinking just as they work with representations of eating, sleeping, or dreaming.

Ambiguity and Contradictions in Meaning

In literature, drink has no inevitable meaning. The meanings of drink are many, ambiguous, and contradictory. Since there can be no comprehensive summary of the representations of drinking in all of world literature, this article will survey this subject across many cultures from ancient to modern times, selecting representative texts for illustrative purposes.

Drink figures in world literature both as an object and as an agent. As a passive object, drink can be a luxury, like gold, or a necessity, like food. Many literary works make no allusion to the mood-altering properties of drink. For example, in the ancient Egyptian poem "The Tale of the Eloquent Peasant" (which dates to about the nineteenth century B.C.E.), an unusually articulate peasant learns about the fragile interdependence between the high and the low in his society. He has been robbed, and he demands justice from his superiors. A leader compensates his material loss without repairing the broader social conditions that make such robberies commonplace. At the climax, the peasant swears, "Shall I live on your bread, and drink your beer for ever?" He wants, but cannot receive, a broader justice. Here beer, with bread, figures only as a staple, as the representation of all drink. Similar examples abound. William Bradford's *Of Plymouth Plantation,* written in the early Puritan era and first published in 1856, famously describes the misery of the pilgrims denied beer by the sailors who brought them to North America in 1620: They behave as though they are incapable of drinking anything else. The denial of beer is figured as a cruel sentence to death by dehydration. Of course, the pilgrims learned to drink water.

As an agent, drink changes a character in literature much as it changes a person in real life. The mood- and health-altering properties of alcoholic and intoxicating beverages account for the considerable versatility of drinking as a subject in creative literature. Again, however, there is no inevitable meaning to the alteration of drink beyond the fact that drink should produce some change, be it slight or great. Drinking produces a good mood in many works of literature, and it produces a bad mood in many others. Sometimes, however, the drinker is unchanged by the drinking. In some of these cases, this is remarkable.

The ambiguities range further. In literature drinking may promote health or disease. It strengthens and enfeebles; brings focus or escape; and may be divine or devilish. Every representation has an opposite. Historians and literary critics must resist the impulse to summarize representations of drinking with sweeping generalizations. For example, in what may be the oldest extant work of creative literature, the Assyro-Babylonian *Epic of Gilgamesh* (which may date to the twenty-fifth century B.C.E.), Enkidu is created as a companion for Gilgamesh. He is born among wild animals and learns humanity later, first from his experience with a prostitute, and second from his experience of bread and beer. The second tablet describes how the prostitute must urge Enkidu to try the bread and beer because they are customs of the land. He becomes expansive and joyous after consuming his first seven jugs of beer. His face glows. For the first time, he feels human.

Drink may make Enkidu human, but in the literary history of drink it also at times dehumanizes. To cite just one example, drink gradually brutalizes the main character in Frank Norris's novel, *Vandover and the Brute* (1914). Vandover learns to drink. Then he drinks and drinks and leads a dissipate, fin-de-siècle bachelorhood. At the end of the novel, he crawls on all fours and behaves like a wild animal. Other naturalist works of this time, such as those by Emile Zola and Thomas Hardy, present essentially the same dehumanizing view of drink. This representation of drinking may be most common in the late nineteenth century, when many creative writers were fascinated with scientific theories of degeneration. Nevertheless, there is no steady trend in representations of drinking from *Gilgamesh* to *Vandover.* Attempts to find progress in the collected literary knowledge of drink will inevitably falter under the tremendous weight of the too-abundant evidence that must be considered.

Yet this fact should not dissuade historians and literary critics from the study of representations of drink. Representations of drink play an important part in the creation of later representations of drink, and all representations of drink influence the formation of drinking habits.

The Reflexivity of Representations of Drinking

Drinking figures in creative literature because it is an important and basic part of human life; it also figures in creative literature because literature, like all forms of art, often indulges in self-reflexivity. Art imitates life, but art also imitates art. In other words, some writers learn to represent drink by reading about drink and are inspired to write about it because they have read about it. When Robert Herrick covets the power of Bacchus in his short poem "The Vine" (1648), he is writing about his reading of Ovid and its effect on his sleep. No doubt, writers learn to describe drinking from their own experience with drink. But there is a circularity to literary evidence. Not all representations of drink arise from direct experience. Many accounts of drink come mainly from other literary representations of it.

And further, life imitates art. As literary representations are borrowed from other times and places, so they are endorsed for their new time and place. And so they influence new readers. For example, the ancient Hebrew texts of the Old Testament continue to influence the drinking habits of modern-day readers. And, in the future, we can be sure that some literary representations of drink will be drawn primarily from biblical—and not from experiential—models. Despite the disappearance of the particular historical context that made the ancient Hebrew representations vital in the first place, the story of Noah's drunkenness will be retold. A writer will read it, and make it new and appropriate for his or her time and place.

Historians often wonder how literary critics can interpret the representation of alcoholic beverages in texts from times and places with mysterious or unknown drinking practices. For certain, literary critics of drinking representations should consult the relevant historical scholarship. But when it does not exist, there should be no prohibition on the study of drinking in a given literature. After all, there is no guarantee that all drinking practices are shaped only by historically specific conditions. And, to some extent, all literary representations of drink are as timeless as they are the result of literary study.

Some representations of drinking will continue to circulate, despite their age or obsoleteness, and some people will learn to drink by reading, despite the inappropriateness of the reading materials for the drinker's time and place. That much is clear. It is not clear how representations of drinking interact with historically specific conditions to shape actual drinking practices. This interaction probably varies a great deal from person to person.

The Literature of the Ancient (Western) World

Drinking figures in the ancient literature that has most profoundly influenced the literary history of the Western world. The ancient Hebrew texts that make up the Old Testament record a wide range of drinking scenes that have been cited and reimagined for thousands of years. Alcoholic beverages also figure throughout the literature of ancient Greece. Drink plays many roles in the epic poetry of Homer (ninth century B.C.E.). Just fragments of his poetry survive, but Anacreon (sixth century B.C.E.) has been widely esteemed and imitated for his formal, graceful tributes to love and wine. The literary traditions of tragedy and comedy were born in festivals honoring Bacchus, the god of wine. In the *Oresteia* (fifth century B.C.E.), Aeschylus represents libations as having a power of reincarnation and regeneration. Euripides, in *The Bacchae* (also fifth century B.C.E.), examines the nature of religious intoxication. The wine bowl moves about the room in Plato's study of love, *Symposium* (fourth century B.C.E.). And it should, considering that "symposium" is Greek for "a drinking together." The teachings of Epicurus (fourth and third centuries B.C.E.) were eventually interpreted to mean that good drinking, with good eating, should be a primary aim of life (hence "epicurean"). In *The Metamorphoses* (about 1 C.E.), the Roman poet Ovid retells the story of Bacchus in a manner that has also been widely imitated.

World Literature: Drinking Representations in Folk Cultures and Myths

The classics of Western literature have no special claim on representations of intoxicating drink. The ninth book of the sacred Hindu *Rgveda,* which dates to about 900 B.C.E., contains 114 hymns honoring the ritual use of soma, a narcotic beverage made with an unknown plant, perhaps a mushroom. Drunkenness also figures in the *Mahabharata,* the great Indian epic compiled around 400 C.E.

Scenes of drinking enliven *The Arabian Nights' Entertainment* (compiled and revised from the eighth through the sixteenth centuries C.E.). This compilation of highly popular and influential fairy tales, legends, fables, and other genres of popular literature was culled from a wide area that roughly corresponds to what is now India, Iran, Iraq, Egypt, and Turkey. Many parts play with the meaning of drunkenness. In the tale of the Barmecide feast, for example, an impoverished, starving man is treated to empty plates, empty glasses, and the taunts of a princely host who pretends the plates and glasses are full. The poor man feigns drunkenness as an excuse for declining the illusory wine and thus wins the respect and sympathy of the prince. In another story, Sinbad can only free himself of the Old Man of the Sea, who clings to his shoulders for many days, by making him drunk. Another tale describes a classic trick, often imitated: A man awakens from a drunken sleep and is fooled by the servants of another man pretending he is someone else.

The folk literature of Northern Europe also contains many representations of drink. In one of the Norse myths, Thor nearly drinks the entire sea, unaware that his drinking horn has been magically connected to it. Drink figures as the source of all poetic inspiration in a Norse myth recorded in the early thirteenth century by the Icelandic poet and historian Snorri Sturluson, in his handbook on poetics, the *Prose Edda.* Here Odin steals the mead of poetry from a giant who took it, by force, from selfish dwarves. The dwarves made this mead with the blood of Kvasir, a tremendous sage the gods made with their collected spittle. (Spittle causes fermentation, like yeast; *kvas* is a Viking word for strong beer.) Thus drink, wisdom, and poetry are strongly associated.

A similar association between drink, wisdom, and poetry can be found in Chinese literature. The importation of Ch'an Buddhism from India inspired innovations in the Chinese representation of drink. For example, two major poets of the T'ang Dynasty, Tu Fu and Li Po (both eighth century C.E.), wrote often of wine and drunkenness. They belonged to a hard-drinking circle, "The Eight Immortals of Drinking," which Tu Fu immortalized in the famous poem of the same title. In the ninth century, Po Chu-i also wrote often of wine. For these Chinese poets, alcoholic intoxication catalyzes a religious ecstasy, the serene clarity of Ch'an Buddhism. As Po Chu-i writes in "Facing Wine," "insisting on clever or stupid, sage or fool, yes *this* and no *that:* it's nothing like wine. Drunk, you forget clean back to the very origin of things, fathom the expanse of all heaven and earth, a phoenix or eagle lofting itself out into flight and soaring free" (Po Chu-i 1999: 127).

Representations of drinking are also central in the literary history of the Islamic world. Perhaps the greatest lyric poet of Persia and of Islam, Hafez (fourteenth century C.E.) perfected the *ghazal* (pronounced "guzzle"), an ancient poetic form that traditionally addressed love and wine. His multilayered poems present the intoxication of wine as a taste or symbol of divine love. Not surprisingly, given the Islamic view of alcoholic beverages, there is debate today over the extent to which his poems can be read literally.

The pre-Hispanic poetry of Mesoamerica also records a literary interest in the interpretation of intoxicated states of mind. In the fifteenth-century Nahua poem, "I Shall Never Disappear," by Nezahualcoyotl, intoxication provides an intimation of immortality:

> I shall never disappear.
> I am intoxicated,
> I weep, I grieve,
> I think, I speak,
> within myself I discover this:
> I shall never die,
> never disappear.
>
> Let me go to the place
> where there is no death,

where death is overcome:
I shall never disappear.
(Leon-Portilla and Shorris 2001: 127)

This is much like another pre-Hispanic Nahua poem, "The Mushroom Drink":

I have taken the mushroom drink,
my heart weeps,
I am but a pauper;
on this earth I grieve.
(Leon-Portilla and Shorris 2001: 102)

In Nahua literature, as in the literatures of most cultures, the meaning of drink is ambiguous, many-sided, and contradictory. In these two examples, intoxication seems to be a legitimate or at least common avenue of religious insight. A third and more significant example portrays intoxication as inappropriate for religious leadership. As described in "Song of Tlaltecatzin of Quauhchinanco" (sixteenth century), the downfall of the great priest and culture hero, Quetzalcoatl, is wrought by three owl sorcerers with a supply of fresh, strong pulque. The owl sorcerers want human sacrifice adopted as a religious sacrament. When Quetzalcoatl resists, they tempt him with the pulque, make him drunk, and thus corrupt him. Corrupted, he abandons his people and the owl sorcerers prevail.

Drinking in English and American Literature

Representations of drinking appear throughout the classics of early English literature. The drinking scenes and characters in the works of Shakespeare are especially well documented and so well known as to require little comment. Some of the most important can be found in Part 1 of *Henry IV* (1597–1598). Another example deserving mention is the "Pardoner's Tale" from Chaucer's fourteenth-century *Canterbury Tales.* Here three rioters leave a tavern to find and kill Death. They ask directions of an old man, who points them to a tree. There they find not Death but treasure. They want to celebrate, so the youngest runs to town for food and drink. When he returns, the others murder him, planning to split his share. But they drink the wine, which the youngest had poisoned to murder them. Thus all three find death beneath the tree. Drink also has a dark representation in John Milton's *Paradise Lost* (1667). While in paradise, Eve presses grapes to make beverages for an angelic guest. We can presume this beverage is not alcoholic since she makes it at the last minute. After eating the apple, however, she is, at length, "satiate" and "h[e]ightened as with wine, jocund and boon."

As in William Bradford's observations cited above, early American literature very often describes drinking. Some of these representations are religious. In the late-seventeenth-century poetry of Edward Taylor, for example, the Communion wine stands for God's grace. The famous Quaker Elizabeth Ashbridge, in her 1754 autobiography, describes her feminist religious conversion as a rebellion against her alcoholic husband and the social pressures of the tavern. Just as often as not, however, early American representations of drinking have little to do with religion. Throughout his writings, for example, Benjamin Franklin's varied treatment of drink focuses on its relationship to one's economic and physical health. In the early nineteenth century, Washington Irving rewrote the old German legend of Peter Klaus as "Rip Van Winkle," another famous story of a twenty-year drunken sleep.

Alcohol abounds in the work of late-eighteenth- and nineteenth-century Romanticism. In the prototypical bildungsroman, Goethe's *Wilhelm Meister* (1795–1796), the main character indulges and then rejects hard-drinking company. John Keats's "Ode to a Nightingale" (1820) reworks Bacchic themes and imagery. Hafez was one of many influences on Ralph Waldo Emerson's transcendental view of intoxication.

The literary experimentation of the nineteenth and twentieth centuries was often alcoholic. Emily Dickinson figures herself as an "inebriate" in poems such as "I taste a liquor never brewed" (1860). Arthur Rimbaud, the young French symbolist, cultivated all varieties of delirium, not just those states induced by alcoholic beverages. In *Three Lives* (1909), Gertrude Stein figures drinking as a form of "wandering widely." Drinking is an important part of the climactic chapters of James Joyce's *Ulysses* (1922), which reworks Homer to describe life in Ireland.

American writers who came of age during the Prohibition era very often wrote much about drinking. The works of F. Scott Fitzgerald, Ernest Hemingway, Dorothy Parker, William Faulkner, and John O'Hara all contain a great deal of thought and self-consciousness on the subject. In the American literary world, the "wets" decidedly outnumbered the "drys." H. L. Mencken often spoke for the wets in his important Prohibition-era literary periodical, *The American Mercury.* Upton Sinclair—as in *The Jungle* (1905)—was one of the very few writers of consequence during the period that wrote often of drink from a dry perspective.

Drink figures in relation to the Americanization of everything in many novels by or about American minorities. In both John Okada's *No-No Boy* (1957) and Sherman Alexie's *The Lone Ranger and Tonto Fistfight in Heaven* (1993), painfully marginalized characters (Asian Americans and Native Americans, respectively) ironically turn to drink for escape and anesthesia. Given the role of alcoholic beverages in the conquest of Native Americans, it is not surprising that drink figures throughout their literatures.

A great many writers have drawn on their personal struggles with alcoholism to produce highly regarded literature that addresses the subject. The "Big Book" of Alcoholics Anonymous has been through many editions since 1934, and it has had a tremendous influence on perceptions of drink and problem drinking throughout the world. Raymond Carver's work, exemplified by collections such as *Cathedral* (1983), has also been highly regarded for the value of its representation of drinking.

Literary Criticism

Finally, much good literary criticism appeared in English at the end of the twentieth century on representations of drinking in literature. These studies have mainly focused on British and American literature. As the above survey suggests, however, they could be just the beginning of what might become a much broader and much more international field of study. A short list of books would include Thomas B. Gilmore's *Equivocal Spirits: Alcoholism and Drinking in Twentieth-Century Literature* (Chapel Hill: University of North Carolina Press, 1987); John Crowley's *The White Logic: Alcoholism and Gender in American Modernist Fiction* (Amherst: University of Massachusetts Press, 1994); Edmund B. O'Reilly's *Sobering Tales: Narratives of Alcoholism and Recovery* (Amherst: University of Massachusetts Press, 1997); Nicolas Warner's *Spirits of America: Intoxication in Nineteenth-Century American Literature* (Norman: University of Oklahoma Press, 1997); Anya Taylor's *Bacchus in Romantic England: Writers and Drink, 1780–1830* (New York: St. Martin's Press, 1999); Jane Lilienfeld's *Reading Alcoholisms: Theorizing Character and Narrative in Selected Novels of Thomas Hardy, James Joyce, and Virginia Woolf* (New York: St. Martin's Press, 1999); and Jane Lilienfeld and Jeffrey Oxford, eds., *The Languages of Addiction* (New York: St. Martin's Press, 1999). The American scholarly journal *Dionysos,* devoted to the study of drinking in literature, ran from 1989 to 2001, when it was suspended indefinitely.

Jon Miller

See also: Alcoholics Anonymous; Art, Representations of Drinking in; Buddhism; Degeneration Theories; India; Islam as Cultural Influence; Islamic World; Literature, Representations of Temperance in; National Prohibition (United States)

References

Leon-Portilla, Miguel, and Earl Shorris. *In the Language of Kings: An Anthology of Mesoamerican Literature—Pre-Columbian to the Present.* New York: W. W. Norton, 2001.

Po Chu-i. *Selected Poems,* translated by David Hinton. New York: New Directions, 1999.

"The Tale of the Eloquent Peasant" in *The Tale of Sinuhe and Other Ancient Egyptian Poems, 1940–1640 B.C.,* translated by R. B. Parkinson, 75. New York: Oxford University, 1999.

Literature, Representations of Temperance in

By "temperance," creative writers have generally meant one of two things: either moderation, and the avoidance of excess in all things, in the use of alcoholic beverages especially, or total abstinence from the consumption of alcoholic beverages. The former idea is common and has dawned, independently, on many different writers from many different cultures. Although the latter idea is strongly associated with nineteenth- and twentieth-century temperance movements, it should be noted that the former conception also appealed strongly to nineteenth- and twentieth-century temperance advocates. A history of moderation in world literature could have no end; there are far too many representations of moderation to present a comprehensive view in a few pages. It is possible, however, to touch on some highlights.

Ancient Philosophy

Temperance figures in the writing of many ancient and influential philosophers. From ancient Greece, the writings of Xenophon (roughly 444–357 B.C.E.) describe Socrates lecturing on the education of leaders. In his *Memorabilia,* he advises self-control in eating and drinking, sex, sleeping, and the endurance of cold, heat, and labor. Aristotle (384–322 B.C.E.) more famously develops the concept of virtue as the "golden mean." Mencius (372–289 B.C.E.), an important Confucian philosopher, warns of the danger of drunkenness. From ancient Rome, the writings of the Stoic philosophers Cicero (106–43 B.C.E.) and Seneca (d. 65 C.E.) counsel moderation.

Christian Religious Influences

Although such writings were valuable to nineteenth- and twentieth-century temperance reformers collecting historical validation of their principles, the Bible was more important and more widely read. Phrases such as "Wine is a Mocker" (Proverbs 20) became common invocations in the rhetoric of early temperance reformers. In the Middle Ages, Christian authors developed temperance as a virtue, contrasting it with gluttony, one of the seven deadly sins. It was often described in morality plays and is the main subject of an unusually secular morality play, Nicolas de la Chesnaye's *La Condamnation de Banquet* (1508).

John Bunyan's *Pilgrim's Progress* (second edition, 1678) was often cited, in the nineteenth century, as presenting the view that there were a few benefits in moderate drinking. The teetotal audience, like most readers in the Christian world, adored the work despite the occasional spirit-lifting cup. They could quote a speech by "Discretion" counseling moderation in eating and drinking lest one risk "intoxicating the brain, heating the blood, disordering the spirits," and cultivating an unhealthy "vice" or "passion."

Early Anglo-American Temperance Literature

By the eighteenth century, temperance was a major theme in American literature. Benjamin Franklin's *Autobiography* (1790) features a scheme for cultivating virtuous behavior that Franklin invented and employed by 1733; Franklin puts "Temperance" at the top of his list of thirteen virtues, defining it as "eating not to fullness and drinking not to elevation." Hector St. John de Crevecoeur's *Letters from an American Farmer* (1782), like many works of its time, stresses the unlimited potential for Americans who are sober, honest, and industrious.

A range of works celebrated temperance in the first quarter of the nineteenth century, when temperance organizations were in their infancy. In America, Samuel Woodworth (1784–1842) did much to elevate the practice of water-drinking with his work, "The Old Oaken Bucket" (1818), which was immensely popular for several decades as a poem and, when set to music, as a song. Meanwhile, in Scotland, Robert Tannahill (1774–1810) composed his "Epistle to Alexander Borland" by 1807. The editors of the *Standard Encyclopedia of the Alcohol Problem* (Cherrington et al. 1925–1930) heartily approved of these lines:

> Hail, Temperance! thou 'rt wisdom's first, best lore,
> The sage in ev'ry age does thee adore;
> Within thy pale we taste of ev'ry joy,
> O'erstepping that, our highest pleasures cloy:
> The heart-enliv'ning, friendly, social bowl
> To rapt'rous ecstasy exalts the soul;
> But when to midnight hour we keep it up,
> Next morning feels the poison of the cup.

Popular Temperance Literature as a Genre

The origins of a more narrowly conceived temperance literature can be found in antebellum temperance periodicals, where poems and tales were often presented on the front page alongside more traditional news items. Generally regarded as the first temperance periodical, Boston's *National Philanthropist* went through many titles—including *National Philanthropist and Investigator and Genius of Temperance*—in its short existence (1826–1830). Temperance poems and tales can be found on the front pages of a wide variety of American newspapers in the 1820s.

In 1831, George B. Cheever published his landmark anthology of early American poetry, *The American Common-Place Book of Poetry,* in Boston. It includes Nathaniel Parker Willis's poem "Look not upon the Wine when it is Red," which was widely hailed and cherished by the growing temperance audience in the 1830s. Hardly a temperance man, but rather a poet who changed with the times, Willis did whatever would make him popular; for a significant period in the 1830s, he was an editor of the *New York Mirror,* one of the nation's most influential literary periodicals. Cheever became a temperance celebrity with the publication of "Deacon Giles' Distillery," a short, fantastic story designed to expose the hypocrisy of Christian liquor sellers, in 1835. He was prosecuted for libel, and the story of his trial was reported in reform papers throughout the country. Nathaniel Hawthorne respected Cheever as an older man of letters, but he expressed his less-than-respectful estimate of his political passions in his short story "A Rill from the Town Pump" (1835), which was, arguably, the best-loved work of Hawthorne in his own day.

Lucius Manlius Sargent published *My Mother's Gold Ring* in 1833. This was the first of the original "temperance tales." Sargent's tales were printed in enormous editions—as tracts and as bound volumes—and circulated throughout the world. At this time, advances in printing technology aided massive editions of tracts. The American Tract Society (1825–) claimed to have issued 5 million temperance tracts and 150,000 bound volumes of temperance tracts by 1851. The British moral writer Hannah More (1745–1833) was clearly an inspiration to writers of antebellum temperance tracts. Her "Parley the Porter" (1796) deserves a place at the front of any shelf of temperance literature.

In 1841, John N. Stearns realized the dream of every aspiring writer and came before the public with his own magazine. Generally remembered now as *Merry's Museum,* it ran from 1841 to 1872, enjoying a large and loyal following of juvenile readers along with many changes in title—at one point it was known as *Merry's Museum and Parley's Magazine*—and sounded a temperance theme throughout its successful existence.

The Variety of Antebellum Temperance Literature

In antebellum America, temperance literature includes a wide range of political viewpoints. Scholars should be wary of literary criticism that speaks of temperance literature as a homogeneous category; the "wet" critics who wrote such things in the mid-twentieth century had not studied long in the temperance library. Outside of New England, Augustus Baldwin Longstreet (1790–1870) wrote temperance literature for his Georgia periodicals. To some extent, his *Georgia Scenes* (1835) can be read as a temperance work. In Baltimore, T. S. Arthur documents the rise of the Washingtonian movement in his *Six Nights with the Washingtonians* (1842). (In 1971, it was republished in a library edition with the title *Temperance Tales.*) In New York City, Walt Whitman hopped on the Washingtonian bandwagon long enough to write and promote his only novel, *Franklin Evans; or, The Inebriate* (1842).

Temperance remade the reputation of American theaters. In William Henry Smith's *The Drunkard* (1844), the evil lawyer Cribbs conspires to make an alcoholic of a dissipated collegian, William Dowton, before a mildly Christianized, family-friendly Washingtonianism saves the day.

Not all temperance authors were members of temperance societies, and many were skeptical of organizational trends just as they profited from the growth of the movement. For example, in her preface to *Water-drops* (1848), a collection with a temperance theme, Lydia Sigourney questions the temperance of the new breed of partisan reformers. Sigourney is a mainstay in the antebellum gift book genre—the expensive, lavishly bound, flowery-titled anthologies that are still collected as binding specimens. Many gift books were produced with the temperance audience specifically in mind. For example, Samuel Fenton Cary (1814–1900) edited *The National Temperance Offering* (1850), a gift book produced for the Sons of Temperance market.

In the decade before the Civil War, American temperance literature was epitomized by T. S. Arthur's *Ten Nights in a Bar-Room* (1854), which was adapted for the stage in 1858 by

William Pratt and enjoyed long runs in theaters across the country well into the moving-picture era. Such temperance drama produced temperance songs that were popular and well known across the country. Advocates such as Phineas Stowe (1812–1868) also contributed volumes of temperance songs such as *Melodies for the Temperance Ship* (1854).

Temperance is thoroughly promoted throughout the most successful work of the decade, *Uncle Tom's Cabin* (1852). This novel was translated into more than twenty languages and thus presented a model of the partisan social novel for the rest of the world. Abolitionism also figured powerfully in the temperance writings of David Ross Locke (1833–1888), the author of the Nasby letters, political satires linking patriotism with temperance during the Civil War. Locke edited the *Toledo Blade,* a temperance periodical described thus by the *Standard Encyclopedia of the Alcohol Problem:* "It is safe to say that no other temperance paper in the United States was so widely circulated or carried conviction to so many minds during the troubled period when temperance organizations were largely disrupted by the [Civil] War and its bitter controversies" (Cherrington et al. 1925–1930: 1588). Temperance also plays a strong role in the writings of the African American poet Frances Ellen Watkins Harper (1825–1911), a member of the Woman's Christian Temperance Union (WCTU) from the 1880s. She published her first book of verse, *Poems on Miscellaneous Subjects,* in 1854. Her novel, *Sowing and Reaping* (1876–1877), presents alcoholism as another form of slavery.

Temperance Themes in Other European Languages

Although American authors led the world in the production of temperance literature, it should be emphasized that temperance poems, tales, novels, and dramas were published wherever there were temperance papers. From its earliest models, the temperance paper always featured works of creative literature. Since temperance papers often advised readers on the management of temperance meetings, they often contained songs and poems that could be sung to known tunes at these meetings. These songs were important for recruiting and retention purposes. During his long career as a temperance advocate and editor, for example, Dawson Burns (1828–1909) composed many temperance hymns, songs, and ballads for the British periodicals that he tended. When the temperance movement appeared in India, Lala Nand Lal (b. 1871) aided its growth by publishing *Sangeet* (1891), a collection of temperance songs that achieved great popularity throughout the Punjab into the early twentieth century. Works of creative literature can also be found in Sweden's late-nineteenth-century *Study Circle,* which was edited by Mauritz Sterner (b. 1869), who translated Frances Willard's *Glimpses of Fifty Years* (1889) into Swedish and later edited the journal of Sweden's Independent Order of Good Templars (IOGT).

A partisan spirit also characterized British temperance writing in the middle of the century. For example, Henry Anderton (1808–1855), a saddler and harness-maker, was driven out of business by angry publicans after he did his best against their public houses. His works were collected and published posthumously as *The Temperance, and Other Poems* (1863). In Ireland, Alexander Martin Sullivan, a vice president of the United Kingdom Alliance, edited the *Nation,* a Dublin weekly journal of politics, literature, and the arts that was founded by three members of the Young Ireland Party, from 1865 to 1876. It was remembered for the "fire and spirit" of its political poetry.

One early European temperance author of note is Estonia's Friedrich Reinhold Kreutzwald (1803–1882). He was the author of that nation's *Kalevipoeg* (1861), a series of epic poems of peasant life based on ancient Estonian sagas about a giant who, at one point in his tale, gets drunk, commits a murder, and is cursed. Kreutzwald was also the author of numerous other works that we could reasonably expect to demonstrate temperance convictions, given that he turned temperance advocate in 1842. His work has been translated into German, Russian, English (partly), Hungarian, Latvian, French, Italian, Finnish, Czech, and Lithuanian.

Temperance readers hardly confined themselves to the consumption of works strictly or "officially" on temperance. The editors of the *Standard Encyclopedia of the Alcohol Problem,* in scattered articles, suggest that the English writers William Wordsworth (1770–1850), Percy Bysshe Shelley (1792–1822), and Rudyard Kipling (1865–1936) were read as temperance authors by the temperance-minded. Russia's Leo Tolstoy (1828–1910) also rewarded their attention to drinking scenes.

Post–Civil War Developments

After the Civil War, Americans continued to produce a tremendous quantity of temperance literature. John N. Stearns eventually left *Merry's Museum* to serve as the organizer, corresponding secretary, and publishing agent of the National Temperance Society and Publication House, which published a range of works, including books of temperance songs such as "The Temperance Chimes" (1867), "Bugle Notes" (1871), "Ripples of Song" (1875), "The Prohibition Songster" (1884), and "New Ripples of Song" (1887). Stearns also edited and published the *National Temperance Advocate* (1866–1897) and the *Youth's Temperance Banner* (1866–c. 1897). Between 1868 and 1895, the National Temperance Society and Publication House published well over 100 works of temperance fiction. Most volumes are at least 300 pages long. Authors included T. S. Arthur, Julia P. Ballard (1828–1894), Mary Dwinell Chellis, John Jay Dana (1811–1899), Frances Dana Gage (1808–1884), Mary J. Hedges, Sarepta Myrenda Henry (1839–1900), Annette Lucile Noble (1844–1932), Mary Anna Paull (b. 1878); Euphemia Johnson Richmond (b. 1825), Harriet Beecher Stowe (1811–1896), Margaret E. Wilmer, and Julia McNair Wright (1840–1903). Popular and interesting titles include Arthur's *Tom Blinn's Temperance Society* (1870); Chellis's *The Temperance Doctor* (1868), *Aunt Dinah's Pledge* (1869), *The Old Tavern*

(1886), and *The Attic Tenant* (1890); Dana's *Humpy Dumpy, or, The Corner Grocery* (1874); Noble's *The Queer Home in Rugby Court* (1878); Paull's *The Bird Angel* (1886); Stowe's *Betty's Bright Idea* (1875); and Wright's *Jug-or-Not* (1870).

The emergence of the Woman's Christian Temperance Union in 1874 and its subsequent spread in the 1880s to many countries provided an important vehicle for the dissemination of temperance themes in literature. The WCTU produced a host of papers for its mostly female readership—a readership with a thirst for creative literature embodying the moral themes of the WCTU. Thus, for example, after joining the WCTU in Vermont in 1876, Alice Matilda Smith contributed poems and short stories for the national WCTU journal, *Union Signal*, as "Alicia" and "August Noon." Isabella MacDonald Alden (1841–1930) filled a long shelf under her pseudonym, "Pansy." She joined the WCTU in its early years and wrote many temperance novels, including *Three People* (1871), which remained in print as a classic of Christian fiction in 2003, and *One Commonplace Day* (1893). Her fiction has been translated into Swedish, French, Japanese, Armenian, and other languages. Another prolific writer of this period, Ella Wheeler Wilcox, contributed her first volume of poems, *Drops of Water* (1872), to the movement. It was published when she was eighteen, living in rural Wisconsin, and attending meetings of the Good Templars. Frances Willard herself made significant contributions through her autobiography, the aforementioned *Glimpses of Fifty Years*, and *Woman and Temperance* (1884). *Glimpses of Fifty Years* is an exceptionally literary document insofar as it presents a thorough record of Willard's extensive reading.

In Norway, Bjørnstjerne Bjørnson (1832–1910) studied drunkenness and temperance throughout his work. In *The Heritage of the Kurts* (1892), he projects the degeneration of a hard-drinking family that ends on a slightly more encouraging note than that found at the end of *Jude the Obscure* (1895), an English novel of alcoholic degeneration by Thomas Hardy (1840–1928).

The Era of National Prohibition in the United States

Temperance literature flourished in the early twentieth century. A prohibitionist and member of the WCTU, Julia "Bernie" Babcock (1868–1962), wrote dozens of political works, a popular biography of Frances Willard (*The Uncrowned Queen* [1902]), and several dramas. England's Sir Harry Hamilton Johnston (1858–1927) wrote *The Gay-Dombeys*, a novel set, befitting the temperance movement's spread, in a wide range of nations. Narrated through various genres (fictional diaries, letters, and newspaper clippings), it demonstrates the literary ability of total abstinence men around the world. H. G. Wells contributed the preface. In Spain, Vicente Blasco Ibáñez (1867–1928) brought forth his *La Bodega* in 1919. It was immediately translated into English as *The Fruit of the Vine;* its teetotal hero moves in the depressed world of wine makers, growers, sellers, and drinkers. In Denmark, Lars Larsen-Ledet (b. 1881), a physician, became editor and publisher of *Afholdsdagbladet*, the official paper of the early-twentieth-century Danish temperance movement, in 1906. With poet Harald Alfred Bergstedt (b. 1877), Larsen-Ledet wrote *Galskabens land: nutids-roman* (1925), a novel that attacks the liquor business. It was immediately translated into German and Swedish. In the 1920s, Finland's temperance papers featured the fiction of Huldi Maria Torckell (b. 1871), and Vihtori Karpio (b. 1885) published *Herran vanki, Helsinkiläis romaani* (1923).

The last American temperance author may have been Upton Sinclair (1878–1968). Temperance themes can be found throughout his work, originally as part of the social reform advocated by *The Jungle* (1905), and eventually in the culmination that is his more traditional, nonfictional work of temperance literature, *The Cup of Fury* (1956). The swan song of American temperance fiction, however, might be his *The Wet Parade* (1931), which treats the repeal of Prohibition as inevitable. Although it is difficult to generalize about temperance literature with any effectiveness, American temperance literature typically emphasizes a model of steady, constant, cultivated character that is out of step with the passionate, protean, improvised personalities of twentieth-century consumer culture.

Scholarly Treatment of the Issue

After suffering as a whipping-boy for a generation or two of wet literary critics, temperance literature has finally begun to receive serious and productive attention from scholars. Highly recommended is Michael Warner's essay "Whitman Drunk," published in Betsy Erkkila and Jay Grossman, eds., *Breaking Bounds: Whitman and American Cultural Studies* (New York: Oxford University Press, 1996), 30–43. David S. Reynolds wrote two of the best available works on the subject: *Beneath the American Renaissance: The Subversive Imagination in the Age of Emerson and Melville* (New York: Knopf, 1988), and *The Serpent in the Cup: Temperance in American Literature* (Amherst: University of Massachusetts Press, 1997), a collection of essays edited with Debra J. Rosenthal. Another development has been the publication of long-lost or long-neglected temperance works. John W. Crowley prepared an edition of material associated with the Washingtonian movement, *Drunkard's Progress: Narratives of Addiction, Despair, and Recovery* (Baltimore: Johns Hopkins University Press, 1999). Carol Mattingly has edited a modern collection of temperance literature by women now available as *Water Drops from Woman Writers: A Temperance Reader* (Carbondale: Southern Illinois University Press, 2001). Finally, Jon Miller prepared a scholarly edition of T. S. Arthur's *Ten Nights in a Bar-Room* (Acton, MA: Copley Publishing, 2002) that reproduces two temperance tracts and a number of short excerpts to suggest the original literary context of the novel.

Jon Miller

See also: China; Confucianism; Daoism; Drama, Representations of Temperance in; Literature, Representations of Drinking in;

Sons of Temperance; Washingtonians; Willard, Frances Elizabeth Caroline; Wine; Woman's Christian Temperance Union (WCTU)

References

Cherrington, Ernest Hurst, et al., eds. *Standard Encyclopedia of the Alcohol Problem.* 6 vols. Westerville, OH: American Issue Publishing, 1925–1930.

Mattingly, Carol. *Well-Tempered Women: Nineteenth-Century Temperance Rhetoric.* Carbondale and Edwardsville: Southern Illinois University Press, 1998.

Reynolds, David S., and Debra J. Rosenthal, eds. *The Serpent in the Cup: Temperance in American Literature.* Amherst: University of Massachusetts Press, 1997.

Tannahill, Robert. *The Songs and Poems of Robert Tannahill: With Biography, Illustrations, and Music.* Edinburgh: John Menzies and Co., 1911. Retrieved by Chadwyck-Healey's English Poetry Full-Text Database (1992).

Livesey, Joseph (1794–1884)

Joseph Livesey (1794–1884) was a leading English temperance advocate, social reformer, journalist, and philanthropist. He was born on 5 March 1794 in Walton-le-Dale, near Preston. His parents, John and Janet, died in 1801, and he was brought up as a weaver by his grandparents. In 1815, at age twenty-one, he married Jane Williams and moved to Preston where he became a successful cheese-factor. His early years of poverty and his Nonconformist primitive Christianity—he was baptized in 1811—influenced his advocacy of individual reform. In the *Moral Reformer,* in 1831, he declared: "Every man ought, in the first instance, to reform himself." In 1815, he established an adult Sunday school. On 7 October 1828, he organized the inaugural meeting of the Preston Institution for the Diffusion of Knowledge, the direct antecedent of the University of Central Lancashire, where the Livesey library collection is located.

The 1830 Beer Act stimulated the opening of many beerhouses and an increase in drunkenness. Although temperance societies were established in many towns, the Preston Temperance Society was the first to pledge total abstinence, at a meeting on 1 September 1832. The "Seven Men of Preston," including Livesey, pledged "to abstain from all liquors of an intoxicating quality, whether ale, porter, wine or ardent spirits, except as medicine." By 1834 1,000 people had signed the pledge, and the movement began to spread across Britain. Livesey called Preston "the Jerusalem of the teetotalism" (Livesey 1885: 66).

Livesey was a skilled propagandist and journalist. He published the *Moral Reformer* (1831–1833), *Preston Temperance Advocate* (1834–1837), *Livesey's Moral Reformer* (1838–1839), *The Struggle* (1842–1846)—which campaigned for the repeal of the Corn Laws and the encouragement of free trade—*Livesey's Progressionist* (1852–1853), and *The Staunch Teetotaler* (1867–1868)—which was critical of the temperance establishment. In 1844, he founded the weekly *Preston Guardian.* He sold this newspaper on his retirement in 1859. He also was a prolific author of pamphlets, tracts, and handbills. His *Malt Liquor Lecture* (1836) was often reprinted and in 1870 was revised. Livesey was a popular and humorous speaker.

Livesey was antipathetic to the established Church of England and the landlord elite. He campaigned against Easter duties—taxes payable to the church, and in 1842 he was a member of a delegation of anti–Corn Law petitioners that met Sir Robert Peel, the prime minister, in London. During cotton textile industry depressions he organized soup kitchens for the unemployed. Campaigning against the harsh Poor Law, he blocked the construction of a new workhouse for thirty years.

Livesey had a keen interest in hydropathy and he invested in the hydro at Bowness-on-Windermere. He also was an enthusiast of phrenology and, after an experimental meatless year in 1867, vegetarianism. He died at age ninety on 2 September 1884 at 13, Bank Parade, Preston. He is buried, with his wife, in Preston cemetery.

Aidan Turner-Bishop

See also: Band of Hope; Nonconformists (United Kingdom); Preston Teetotal Monument; Vegetarianism and the Anti-Tobacco Movement (United Kingdom)

References

Levitt, Ian, ed. *Joseph Livesey of Preston: Business, Temperance and Moral Reform.* Preston: University of Central Lancashire, 1996.

Livesey, Joseph. *The Life and Teachings of Joseph Livesey, Comprising His Autobiography with an Introductory Review . . . by John Pearce.* London: National Temperance League, 1885.

University of Central Lancashire, "Livesey Collection." http://www.uclan.ac.uk/library/libspar1.htm.

Lloyd George, David (1863–1945)

David Lloyd George (1863–1945), Liberal prime minister of Great Britain from 1916 to 1922, played a significant part in promoting temperance in Britain during World War I. Entering Parliament in 1890, he championed the Old Liberalism, that is, church disestablishment, educational and land reform, recognition of Welsh nationhood, and temperance. He declared himself to be a total abstainer. He denounced "the unholy Trinity" of the bishop, the brewer, and the squire. He acclaimed the Welsh Sunday Closing Act of 1881 that closed public houses entirely on Sundays in Wales (excluding Monmouthshire). This legislation for the first time recognized that an act of Parliament could apply to Wales alone. In his maiden speech in the Commons (13 June 1890), he applauded a new tax on spirits, designed to compensate publicans for the loss of their licenses, but called for far more license reductions and far less compensation. For the next twenty-five years, however, temperance was only a marginal preoccupation. He denounced the House of Lords for destroying the Liberal government's 1908 Licensing Bill. His "People's Budget" of 1909 included the liquor trade as well as the landowners among his targets. Publicans would have to pay more for their licenses,

David Lloyd George (1863–1945) (Illustrated London News Group)

while the duties on spirits would go up (which led to criticism from the Irish Nationalist members).

His main attack on liquor, however, came during World War I. As chancellor of the exchequer, he declared that drink undermined armaments production by the workers. A major speech at Bangor (28 February 1915) included drink in a grand scheme to redirect the war effort. Drink, he declared, was doing more damage than all the German submarines. Prime Minister Herbert Asquith opposed total prohibition. Lloyd George pressed on with plans to nationalize the entire liquor trade, through state purchase of licenses, together with far higher taxes on alcoholic beverages. In May 1915, just after he went to the ministry of munitions, the Defense of the Realm Act (No. 111) set up a Central Control Board (Liquor Traffic), with wide powers to impose restrictions on licenses and licensing hours, and even to run its own breweries and pubs. By 1916, licensing hours had been significantly reduced. Meanwhile, the "Carlisle experiment" in Cumberland and Dumfriesshire opened state-run public houses that survived for decades. Music hall comedians derided the diluted quality of "Lloyd George's Beer." Less effectively, he later persuaded King George V to take the so-called "King's Pledge" to abstain from alcohol for the course of the war—which the unfortunate king seems to have been almost alone in observing. After considering state purchase of the drink trade in 1916 and 1917, Lloyd George abandoned the idea as impractical. Even so, there is no doubt that his measures significantly improved both the workers' productivity and their health.

Thereafter, temperance was only an occasional theme. His postwar coalition passed the 1921 Licensing Act that extended the Welsh Sunday closing to Monmouthshire and made many wartime experiments permanent. But drink was now very much on the margins of politics. Lloyd George ignored it in his last bids for power in 1929 and 1935. In private, he took the occasional tumbler of whiskey. Nevertheless, not the least of his achievements was to transform the nation's drinking habits.

Kenneth O. (Lord) Morgan

See also: Carlisle System; Gothenburg Schemes/Disinterested Management; Liberal Party (United Kingdom); Wales

References

Gilbert, Bentley. *David Lloyd George: A Political Life,* vol. 2, *Organizer of Victory, 1912–1916.* Columbus: Ohio State University Press, 1992.

Gourvish, Terence R. "The Business of Alcohol in the US and the UK: UK Regulation and Drinking Habits, 1914–39" in *Business and Economic History.* 26, no. 2 (1997): 609–616.

Morgan, Kenneth O. *Lloyd George.* London: Weidenfeld and Nicolson, 1974.

Turner, John. "State Purchase of the Liquor Trade in the First World War" in *Historical Journal.* 23 (1980): 589–615.

Local Option

Local option refers to state statutory or constitutional provision for local elections in which citizens choose to allow or prohibit the sale of beverage alcohol within a certain local political unit. Varying from state to state, local option may apply to areas as large as counties or as small as individual precincts. Although frequently criticized by staunch prohibitionists as an ineffective halfway measure, local-option elections in the United States set the groundwork for National Prohibition and remain an effective tool in recent temperance efforts.

In the early nineteenth century, local-option struggles generally took the form of campaigns for local officers pledged to a "no-license" position. In the 1830s, a number of counties, particularly in New England, were effectively dried up in local elections that put into office county officials who refused to grant licenses to alcohol retailers. Later, a few states adopted genuine local-option laws that allowed voters to cast ballots on the issue of alcohol sale directly, without endorsing a particular candidate. Following Reconstruction, a number of southern states adopted local-option clauses in their new constitutions. By the end of the nineteenth century, thirty-six states allowed for local elections on the issue of alcohol sale.

Local option became the centerpiece of prohibition strategy with the rise of the Anti-Saloon League of America (ASLA).

Howard Hyde Russell, founder of the league, embraced the strategy and quickly demonstrated its effectiveness. The ASLA could organize first where it would have the best chance of success, and the localized structure of the organization gave considerable freedom to local temperance activists to initiate campaigns. Criticized at first by such bastions of temperance reform as the Prohibition Party and the Woman's Christian Temperance Union as being "too local" and "too optional," local option began effectively curtailing the sale of liquor in large areas of the country. By 1906, 40 percent of Americans lived in "dry" territory, principally due to local-option elections. In New England and in the Midwest, where temperance sentiment had a long history, a large proportion of the population voted against liquor. In the South the changes were even more startling. By 1907, two-thirds of southern counties were dry. Local option was not only successful in rural areas and small towns, however. In 1908, Worcester, Massachusetts, voted dry. And occasionally, urban drinkers could vote "wet" and still lose their saloons in a county-wide election when rural residents overwhelmed them with dry votes.

Significantly, local option did not affect the private ownership or consumption of alcohol. It was offered by its proponents as a means to attack the saloon, which was viewed by many Americans, even those who drank, as a dangerous institution. A vote for local option did not require abstinence. And though coercive, it was clearly a democratic reform. As such it set the stage for popular acceptance of the Eighteenth Amendment. Even after repeal, local option continued to generate considerable political heat in communities debating the desirability of retail alcohol establishments.

James D. Ivy

See also: Anti-Saloon League of America (ASLA); Canada Temperance Act; Provincial Regulation (Canada)

References

Hamm, Richard F. *Shaping the Eighteenth Amendment: Temperance Reform, Legal Culture, and the Polity, 1880–1920.* Chapel Hill: University of North Carolina Press, 1995.

Kerr, K. Austin. *Organized for Prohibition: A New History of the Anti-Saloon League.* New Haven: Yale University Press, 1985.

Timberlake, James H. *Prohibition and the Progressive Movement, 1900–1920.* Cambridge: Harvard University Press, 1963.

Loyal Orange Institution (Ireland and Britain)

The Orange Order takes its name from the Dutch prince, William of Orange, who claimed the thrones of England, Scotland, and Ireland for the Protestants after defeating the Catholic king, James II, at the famous Battle of the Boyne in Ireland in 1690. However, the Orange Order did not emerge until 1795 in the wake of sectarian clashes at the Battle of the Diamond in County Armagh. Orangeism was intended to protect the Protestant ascendancy in Ireland; it was thus avowedly anti–Roman Catholic, but at this early stage not noticeably evangelical. Indeed, the "founding fathers" of the Orange Order, Dan Winter and James Sloan, were both publicans.

Winter's public house was destroyed in the Battle of the Diamond, but the site still proved significant because, among the debris, surviving militants gathered together, pledging to form a new organization to safeguard the Protestant dominance. These men then retired to Sloan's public house in the nearby village of Loughgall, where plans for a loyalist lodge were mooted. Thereafter, many Orange meetings were held in public houses around Ulster; some of them even housed weapons in case of violent threats to Protestant interests. Similarly, in England, the British Grand Lodge was formed at the Star Hotel, Manchester, in 1808. Subsequently, Orange Lodge meetings around England were commonly held at licensed premises, with the encouragement of publicans eager to cash in on thirsty patrons. This trend was also apparent in the north of Ireland, with some publicans attaching a picture of King William to their doors as an enticement to Orange clientele.

Although British governments at moments of crisis in Ireland made use of the Orange Order, up to the 1830s it was generally seen as a militant group lacking discipline. Twelfth of July parades that celebrated William's victory at the Boyne were provocative and sometimes violent toward Catholics. It was also not uncommon for groups of Catholics to attack Orange parades. Parades, like fairs and market days that ostensibly brought communities "together," became sites for sectarian clashes, whether planned or spontaneous. It seems no coincidence that at such events alcohol was liberally available. The "drink," it seems, emboldened those who enjoyed confrontation, and Orangemen were noticeable among them. Authorities in Ireland were so concerned that the Party Processions Act (1832) banned Orange marches, and a select committee of inquiry, formed to investigate the conduct of the Orange Order, had the effect of dissolving the organization in 1835.

Although institutional Orangeism was in abeyance, many local parades continued. In 1844, the movement was revived under a new body, the Grand Orange Lodge of Ulster, only to be frustrated again in 1850 by a further Party Processions Act, applying specifically to Orange marches. By the 1870s, though, the Twelfth of July had assumed newfound significance as an occasion on which to debate topical "Irish questions," such as land reform and home rule, both of which were opposed by Orange interests. The repeal of marching restrictions after 1872 provided Orangemen with a legitimate public forum by which to air their political views. To preserve this opportunity, Orange parade organizers faced the challenge of making the movement appear more "respectable" than it had been in the past. This goal was more likely to be achieved if Orangemen behaved in an orderly and sober manner while on public display. Thus, rules about alcohol consumption were now given more weight in Orange circles. In particular, Orangemen were not allowed to march while under the influence of alcohol, nor were they to drink in public houses while adorned in Orange regalia.

Concurrently, there were greater efforts to align Orange Lodges with temperance principles. This was largely a response to the increased influence of evangelicals within Orangeism. As the noted Presbyterian temperance advocate and Orange hero William Johnstone of Ballykilbeg concluded, brethren "would not be worse Orangemen on account of total abstinence from intoxicating drinks" (McClelland 1990: 82). It became quite common for the word "temperance" to become part of lodge nomenclature in Britain and Ireland. Alternatively, Orangemen were encouraged to align themselves with antidrink organizations such as the Blue Ribbon temperance movement in Scotland. Of course, the most famous temperance campaigner of the time was Catholic—Ireland's Father Theobald Mathew, a priest who endeavored to reach all faiths and denominations. But Irish nationalists, who used temperance rallies to spread their political message, thwarted his ecumenical appeal. Just as significantly, there were concerns within Protestant circles about a Catholic-led antidrink crusade. Ulster's Orange community did not make Father Theobald Mathew welcome. "At Loughall, a number of Orange Farmers entered into a resolution that they would not employ any labourer who had taken the temperance pledge" of Father Mathew (O'Niell Daunt 1886: 16).

Protestant temperance campaigners actively sought to modify drinking behavior among Orangemen. There were initiatives to ban alcohol from the parade fields on the Twelfth of July, and the induction of members to the Orange Order now tended to proceed without celebratory toasts. Unequivocal support for temperance among Orange Lodges was, however, unlikely. As the leading Presbyterian orator W. P. Nicholson complained during a sermon in Ulster in 1929, "Most of them [lodges] are booze-hoisting joints. If I am a member of such a lodge I am a partaker with them in their evil deeds. If they sell whisky or booze in their lodge, then I am in the booze business, and the curse of God is on every drop of liquor and every man who has anything to do with them" (Nicholson 1982: 160). The weakness of the antidrink message has, if anything, been more pronounced in Scottish Orangeism than in the Irish orders. There have been fewer "temperance" lodges there, and licensed bars now feature in many Scottish Orange Lodges. Even the temperance lodges in Scotland are not necessarily full of teetotalers; their concern is about members getting drunk, not drinking itself. In Ulster, in contrast, Orange Halls have generally not approved serving alcohol on the premises. Indeed, many of the Belfast Orange Lodges were built during the second half of the nineteenth century with the money of Protestant factory owners eager to keep their workers out of public houses. This can be seen as part of the drive for "respectability" among workingmen.

A constant element within Orange parades has been the attempt by senior Orangemen to forge respectability in events that are viewed by many participants and spectators as festive. There are rules in place to prevent Orangemen from parading while under the influence, and the Worshipful Master is "enjoined to exert authority to maintain sobriety and good conduct." Among the laws and ordinances of the Orange Institution is the following edict for Orangemen: "Wisdom and prudence should guide his actions; temperance and sobriety, honesty and integrity, direct his conduct." Yet contemporary Orange parades remain something of a contradiction. They are, in part, religious events, often include religious services, and still involve temperance and abstinence lodges. But they are also carnivalesque, and toward the end of the "Twelfth day" numerous Orangemen, bandsmen, and young supporters will be under the influence of alcohol. According to the Parades Commission, which was set up in 1997 in an attempt to manage disputes over the right to march, alcohol consumption has been a factor in the likelihood of aggressive behavior. Current legislation that restricts both the consumption of alcohol on buses going to parades and on the streets hosting the parades is frequently ignored.

Daryl Adair, Dominic Bryan, and Mike Cronin

See also: Ireland

References

Bryan, Dominic. *Orange Parades: The Politics of Ritual, Tradition and Control.* London: Pluto Press, 2000.

Cleary, Henry William. *The Orange Society.* 6th ed. Melbourne: Bernard King and Sons, 1897.

Edwards, Ruth Dudley. *The Faithful Tribe: An Intimate Portrayal of the Loyal Institutions.* London: HarperCollins, 2000.

Fraser, Thomas G., ed. *The Irish Parading Tradition: Following the Drum.* London: Macmillan, 2000.

Haddick-Flynn, Kevin. *Orangeism: The Making of a Tradition.* Dublin: Wolfhound Press, 1999.

Loftus, Belinda. *Mirrors: William III and Mother Ireland.* Dundrum: Picture Press, 1990.

Malcolm, Elizabeth. *"Ireland Sober, Ireland Free": Drink and Temperance in Nineteenth-Century Ireland.* Dublin: Gill and Macmillan, 1986; Syracuse: Syracuse University Press, 1986.

———. "The Rise of the Pub: A Study in the Disciplining of Popular Culture" in *Irish Popular Culture 1650–1850,* edited by J. S. Donnelly and K. A. Miller. Dublin: Irish Academic Press, 1998.

Marshall, William J. *"The Billy Boys": A Concise History of Orangeism in Scotland.* Edinburgh: Mercat, 1996.

McClelland, Aiken. *William Johnston of Ballykilbeg.* Lugan: Ulster Society, 1990.

McFarland, Elaine W. *Protestants First: Orangeism in Nineteenth-Century Scotland.* Edinburgh: Edinburgh University Press, 1990.

Nicholson, William Patteson. *Sermons by W. P. Nicholson: Tornado of the Pulpit.* Edited by Ian Paisley. Belfast: Martyrs Memorial Productions, 1982.

O'Neill Daunt, W. J. *Eighty-Five Years of Irish History.* Vol. 2. London: Ward and Downey, 1886.

Rushe, Denis Carolan. *History of Monaghan for Two Hundred Years.* Dundalk: Tempest, 1921.

Senior, Hereward. *Orangeism in Ireland and Britain, 1795–1836.* London: Routledge and Kegan Paul, 1966.

Sibbett, Robert M. *Orangeism in Ireland and throughout the Empire,* vol. 2. London: Thynne, 1939.

Loyal Temperance Legion (LTL)

The Loyal Temperance Legion (LTL) is a national and worldwide children's organization sponsored by the Woman's Christian Temperance Union (WCTU). The legion focuses on teaching temperance to children ages six through twelve. Although it is still in existence today, membership was largest in the late nineteenth and early twentieth centuries.

At its founding in 1874, WCTU members involved in "Juvenile Work" organized and led existing children's temperance organizations such as Bands of Hope, Cold Water Armies, Temperance Wide Awakes, and Home Guards, among others. Early Juvenile Work Committees (including later WCTU president Frances Willard and Eliza or "Mother" Stewart of Women's Temperance Crusade fame) successfully convinced Sunday school associations to provide quarterly lessons in temperance, believing this to be the most efficient way to reach the greatest number of children. However, not all Sunday school teachers were sympathetic to the temperance cause, and others complained that there were not enough biblical references for temperance to sustain quarterly lessons. In 1880, the Juvenile Work Committee endorsed *The Juvenile Temperance Manual,* written by Julia Colman, a Methodist medical writer. Moving toward establishing the WCTU's own children's organization, Anna Gordon, who would be associated with the LTL for over fifty years, published *Juvenile Work Questions Answered* for the WCTU exclusively in 1887. Building on the work of previous temperance organizations, the manual provided a constitution, an official badge, music, meeting plans, marches, and songs. Juvenile officers were appointed and encouraged to attend WCTU meetings as delegates. In 1890, the union formally established the Loyal Temperance Legion as a separate organization, and 1895, the LTL became an official branch of the WCTU, with Helen G. Rice of Massachusetts as general secretary. Legions were divided into junior and senior LTLs. The legion began publication of *The Young Crusader* in 1887, which continued until 1995.

The Loyal Temperance Legion's main purpose was and is to promote abstinence from alcohol, tobacco, and narcotics among children between the ages of six and twelve. The early organization endeavored to influence future voters, legislators, and government officials as a way to accomplish prohibition ("Tremble, King Alcohol, We Shall Grow Up!" was the first slogan of the LTL). As such, the LTL focused particularly on recruiting young boys to the temperance cause. This concern led to the controversial adoption of the military drill. Borrowing from military schools and militia companies, LTL leaders instructed boys in saluting, marching, posture, and rifle positions (with dummy guns).

Eager not to exclude young women, the WCTU created drills with domestic themes for girls. Rather than guns, the girls practiced routines with brooms and fans. Frances Willard and Anna Gordon promoted these militaristic techniques as a guaranteed method of attracting boys, particularly, because of a supposed natural love of martial music. Peace proponents within the WCTU, however, complained that the military drills trained future killers. Critics also ridiculed the girls' broom and fan drills and deemed them inappropriate for modest young ladies. Although the drills were popular from the beginning of WCTU Juvenile Work and Anna Gordon's *Marching Songs for Young Crusaders* (1885) sold more than 130,000 copies, the critics won out and the national WCTU requested that the drills be discontinued in 1890.

Loyal Temperance Legion activities included parades, picnics, playlets, recitations, socials, debates, and essay, poster, and coloring contests, all designed to encourage temperance, moral character, social purity, and good citizenship. Legionaires also funded a wide range of humanitarian projects, including relief for European orphans during World War I, milk goats for Japanese children after World War II, and shoes for Korean children during the early 1960s. Local LTLs installed water fountains, planted trees and gardens, and placed benches in parks. LTL leaders offered classes in sewing, knitting, woodcarving, and map drawing. Choral singing was another popular LTL activity. Leaders nourished children's enthusiasm for animals by promoting bird watching and membership in the Band of Mercy, an early humane society for children. They kept older children interested by offering them positions of leadership within the legion.

LTL members were not just the children of the WCTU or middle-class white Protestants. WCTU members organized Loyal Temperance Legions among immigrant groups, and both white and black WCTU members organized African American children. Working children such as messengers, newsboys, bootblacks, and cigar girls were organized into legions. Low membership dues encouraged wide participation (yearly dues in 1887 were only five cents).

The Young Crusader, the official Loyal Temperance Legion's magazine for children, fulfilled the WCTU's desire to provide "pure" and wholesome literature for children. Typical articles included stories written by WCTU members or sympathizers that advocated temperance, as well as the entire range of the WCTU reform agenda. Most of the magazine's pages were filled with fiction and poetry in order to increase readership. Stories honored political figures such as George Washington and Abraham Lincoln or applauded temperance teachers. The magazine employed the metaphor of youthful Christian "crusaders" growing up to literally vanquish alcohol. *The Young Crusader* encouraged boys to remain pure and avoid the temptations of the city, and urged girls to stride forth confidently to conquer the world with the domestic ideals of the WCTU.

The peak of the Loyal Temperance Legion's membership occurred around 1890, with an estimated membership of 240,000. By 1929, the national LTL reported 56,945 members.

By 2002, estimates place the U.S. national membership at only 400. Reasons for the decline of the LTL include the success and proliferation of other Protestant youth organizations around the turn of the last century, especially the Young People's Society for Christian Endeavor, which allowed its membership much more autonomy. The legion's narrow focus on temperance also hindered its growth, especially with the WCTU's success in making "Scientific Temperance Instruction" mandatory in all states by 1901.

Nancy G. Garner

See also: Gordon, Anna Adams; Willard, Frances Elizabeth Caroline; Woman's Christian Temperance Union (WCTU) (United States)

References

Cook, Sharon Anne. "Educating for Temperance: The Woman's Christian Temperance Union and Ontario Children, 1880–1916" in *Historical Studies in Education.* 5, no. 2 (1993): 251–277.

Erickson, Judith B. "Making King Alcohol Tremble: The Juvenile Work of the Woman's Christian Temperance Union, 1874–1900" in *Journal of Drug Education.* 18, no. 4 (1988): 333–352.

Garner, Nancy G. "Women's Mighty Moral Power: The Kansas WCTU's Political Strategy, 1878–1930" in *The Changing Face of Drink: Substance, Imagery, and Behaviour,* edited by Jack S. Blocker Jr. and Cheryl Krasnick Warsh, 271–290. Ottawa, Canada: Social History, 1997.

Gordon, Anna Adams. *Marching Songs for Young Crusaders: Temperance Songs for the Cold Water Army.* Chicago: Woman's Temperance Publishing Association, 1885.

"Loyal Temperance Legion" in *Standard Encyclopedia of the Alcohol Problem,* vol. 4, edited by Ernest Hurst Cherrington et al., 1611–1612. Westerville, OH: American Issue Publishing, 1928.

Parker, Alison M. "The Production of 'Pure' Children's Literature: The WCTU's Young Crusader" in *Purifying America: Women, Cultural Reform, and Pro-Censorship Activism, 1873–1933,* 158–194. Urbana: University of Illinois Press, 1997.

Lucas, Margaret Bright (1818–1890)

Margaret Bright Lucas (1818–1890) was the president of the British Women's Temperance Association (BWTA) from 1878 until her death. During this tenure she became the leader of the women's temperance movement in Britain. She had a wide range of political interests. As the third daughter of Jacob and Martha Bright, she came from a radical Quaker and Liberal family. At twenty, she married her cousin Samuel Lucas, who became the owner and editor of a radical newspaper, the *Morning Star.* Her brothers John and Jacob were members of Parliament during the mid- to late nineteenth century, representing radical-minded constituencies, and her sister Priscilla Bright McLaren was an early supporter of women's suffrage. With such a background it was not surprising that Lucas, after the death of her husband, should devote much of her life fighting for temperance and women's rights.

She began her political career working with her sister Priscilla for the Anti–Corn Law League and the antislavery movement. It was not until she was widowed, in 1865, that she began fully to enter the political sphere, becoming part of an expanding network around the Bright women and their connections. An eighteen-month visit to the United States inspired her to develop her own political agenda, with temperance and women's suffrage her priorities. For the rest of her life she was to keep in touch with the politics of the United States as well as with those of the United Kingdom.

In 1872, she joined the Independent Order of Good Templars (IOGT) on the condition that James Hayes Raper, the United Kingdom Alliance activist, join at the same time. By 1875, she had become a grand worthy vice templar, the highest Good Templar honor conferred on a woman in Europe. Despite finding the regalia somewhat strange to her Quaker eyes, she relished the chance to participate in the mixed-sex IOGT and took advantage of every opportunity to speak in public. She also used the IOGT as a channel for her campaign for women's suffrage.

In 1876 the National Temperance League invited Eliza D. Stewart (called "Mother Stewart") to visit the United Kingdom. Stewart was well known in Britain as a leader in the Women's Temperance Crusade in Ohio. Her visit served as a catalyst for the organization of the British Women's Temperance Association. Despite its name, it was predominantly an English organization. For instance, Scottish women preferred a more explicitly Christian society. Margaret E. Parker, an Englishwoman who resided in Scotland, was elected the first BWTA president. Clara Lucas Balfour succeeded her, and upon Balfour's death in 1878, Margaret Bright Lucas served as president until her own death in 1890.

Under her stewardship, the association grew and developed. By 1885, it had 365 branches in England. Some Scottish branches also paid affiliation dues to the BWTA. Under Lucas, the BWTA headquarters was moved from northeastern England to London in order to be near Parliament. Originally the BWTA's work was essentially religious, but under her guidance the organization entered into the politics of temperance. With Lucas at the helm, the BWTA expanded not only in numbers but also in scope. The "British Women," as the members styled themselves, became aware that without political power they were restricted in what they could achieve for the temperance cause. Lucas strongly believed that the prejudices of society had held women back from more active temperance reform and that the church had silenced women's voices.

It is to Lucas's credit that she not only united the fragmented women's temperance movement in England but was able to avoid the schisms and dissent that characterized the male societies. Her liberal connections and her early political agitation against slavery and for free trade helped give her the experience to expand into politics of temperance. She began by organizing appeals from the BWTA to the railway companies to promote temperance among porters and other railway servants. The major work of the British Women was to campaign continuously against grocers' licenses and for Sunday closing.

Lucas not only worked through the BWTA but also in other temperance organizations. She became a vice president of the National Temperance Federation and was the first woman to be a vice president of the United Kingdom Alliance. Traveling widely in the cause of temperance, she is credited with the foundation of the Ladies Temperance Society in Antwerp through a lecture that she gave there at the Belgian Patriotic League against the Abuse of Alcohol.

She crossed the Atlantic a number of times on temperance business. In 1885, she traveled to Minneapolis with Catherine Impey, Hannah Whitall Smith, Mrs. Pearson, and Mrs. Blakey, all members of the BWTA, to attend the World's Woman's Christian Temperance Union (WWCTU) convention. Despite illness, Lucas was determined to attend as she went as the first WWCTU president.

Lucas had other reform interests. She believed that the vote would enable temperance women to become more effective. Her support of the women's suffrage began when she signed the first women's suffrage petition. As a member of the Ladies National Association for the Repeal of the Contagious Diseases Acts, Lucas traveled with Josephine Butler to the Geneva International Congress on the Contagious Diseases Acts. She had an interest in women's prisons and suggested to the home office that it establish a separate department for women's prisons headed by a lady secretary. A long-standing supporter of the women's peace movement, she was president of the Women's Peace and Arbitration Association and a vice president of the Peace Society. She was a member of the executive committee of the Women's Liberal Federation and, like other radical women, supported home rule for Ireland.

Margaret Bright Lucas had a political career that embraced many causes, but she has been overlooked by history. There is no modern biography.

Margaret Barrow

See also: British Women's Temperance Association (BWTA); Good Templars (IOGT); Impey, Catherine; Liberal Party (United Kingdom); Raper, James Hayes; United Kingdom Alliance (UKA); World's Woman's Christian Temperance Union (WWCTU)

References

Heath, H. J. *Margaret Bright Lucas: The Life of a "British Woman," Being the Memoir of the Sister of the Rt. Hon. John Bright and the Leader of the British Women in their Warfare against the Drink Traffic.* London: the author, 1890.

Lucas, Margaret Bright. *Memoir of Margaret Bright Lucas.* Edited by Louisa Stewart and Jessie A. Fowler. London: British Women's Temperance Association, 1890.